"Invaluable . . ."

—*The New York Times*

"The best budget guidebooks for the independent budget traveler."

—*Chicago Tribune*

LET'S GO:

BRITAIN & IRELAND

is the best book for anyone traveling on a budget. Here's why:

No other guidebook has as many budget listings.

In Edinburgh we found dozens of bed and breakfasts for less than $15 a night. In the countryside we found hundreds more. We tell you how to get there the cheapest way, whether by bus, plane, or thumb, and where to get an inexpensive and satisfying meal once you've arrived. There are hundreds of money-saving tips for everyone plus lots of information on student discounts.

LET'S GO researchers have to make it on their own.

Our Harvard-Radcliffe researchers travel on budgets as tight as your own—no expense accounts, no free hotel rooms.

LET'S GO is completely revised every year.

We don't just update the prices, we go back to the places. If a charming restaurant has become an overpriced tourist trap, we'll replace the listing with a new and better one.

No other budget guidebook includes all this:

Coverage of both the cities and the countryside; directions, addresses, phone numbers, and hours to get you there and back; in-depth information on culture, history, and the people; listings on transportation between and within regions and cities; tips on work, study, sights, nightlife, and special splurges; city and regional maps; and much, much more.

LET'S GO is for anyone who wants to see Britain and Ireland on a budget.

Books by Harvard Student Agencies, Inc.

Let's Go: London
Let's Go: New York City
Let's Go: Washington, D.C.

Let's Go: Europe
Let's Go: Britain & Ireland
Let's Go: France
Let's Go: Germany, Austria & Switzerland
Let's Go: Greece & Turkey
Let's Go: Italy
Let's Go: Spain & Portugal
Let's Go: Israel & Egypt

Let's Go: USA
Let's Go: California & Hawaii
Let's Go: The Pacific Northwest, Western Canada & Alaska
Let's Go: Mexico

LET'S GO:

The Budget Guide to

BRITAIN & IRELAND

1992

Marlies Morsink
Editor

Lisa Woznica
Assistant Editor

Written by Harvard Student Agencies, Inc.

ST. MARTIN'S PRESS
NEW YORK

Helping Let's Go

If you have suggestions or corrections, or just want to share your discoveries, drop us a line. We read every piece of correspondence, whether a 10-page letter, a tacky Elvis postcard, or, as in one case, a collage. All suggestions are passed along to our researcher/writers. Please note that mail received after May 5, 1992 will probably be too late for the 1993 book, but will be retained for the following edition. **Address mail to:** ***Let's Go: Britain & Ireland;*** **Harvard Student Agencies, Inc.; Thayer Hall-B; Harvard University; Cambridge, MA 02138; USA.**

In addition to the invaluable travel advice our readers share with us, many are kind enough to offer their services as researchers or editors. Unfortunately, the charter of Harvard Student Agencies, Inc. enables us to employ only currently enrolled Harvard students.

Distributed outside the U.S. and Canada by Pan Books Ltd.

ISBN: 0-312-06389-X

First Edition
10 9 8 7 6 5 4 3 2 1

Let's Go: Britain & Ireland is written by Harvard Student Agencies, Inc., Harvard University, Thayer Hall-B, Cambridge, Mass. 02138.

ACKNOWLEDGMENTS

Let's Go B&I is nothing if not a cooperative effort. This is not a guide where researcher, writer and editor collapse into one; rather, it represents the tireless toiling of tens of dedicated spirits. Foremost among these are the travelers who crisscrossed Britain and Ireland, culling the fruits of change and weeding perennial *Let's Go* blossoms: my thanks to Zach, for steadfastly wringing out wool socks in the middle of an urban June to brave England's drenched cuisine and capture the land's essence in beguiling prose; to Abby, for loving Wales and West Country and finding abbeys so cool. . .she's right either way; to Maura, for looping London, filling in the gaps and satisfying the exigencies of no less than three editors; to Courtney, for gracing four lands with her delicate wit and sophistication, titillating the home guard with her subtle enigma; to Seth, seafarer and adventurer, for comforting the lonely albatross and fluidly enhancing the language of the north; and finally, to Woden, for wrapping the Emerald Land into a heartfelt bundel corded with humor, organization, and insight.

On the Cambridge front, I cannot say how much I've appreciated working with my colleagues: Lisa, who contributed her flawless competence at the most trying of times; taskmaster Pete, the Deemer Butcher of B&I, who sculpted the book with his blood-red cuts; Chris, who periodically pounded my keyboard with unruffled calm; Jane Yeh, whose good-natured alacrity and precision speeded the book to perfection; and Mike, whose flexible schedule and close reading added a unique charm to the final days. Alec, I wouldn't have survived without flying discs by sunset or your unshakable faith and understanding; Huub and Marybeth, your love has bridged oceans; Jim and Natalie, blessed be your food for thought; and Paul and Stephanie, I'll pop the champagne at the end of this passage.

Lastly, I acknowledge the discourse of tourism for providing this guide with a comfortable niche on bookstore shelves, and extend my gratitude to the local officials and brochure artists who so generously dispersed their talents.

—MFM

CONTENTS

LET'S GO: BRITAIN AND IRELAND ... 1
General Introduction ... 1
Before You Go ... 1
When to Go ... 1
Documents and Formalities ... 4
Money ... 6
Health ... 11
Safety and Security ... 12
Weather ... 14
Packing ... 14
Special Concerns ... 17
Useful Addresses ... 22
Alternatives to Tourism ... 25
Getting There ... 31
From North America ... 31
From Continental Europe ... 35
Once There ... 37
Getting Around ... 37
Accommodations ... 46
Staying in Touch ... 51

ENGLAND ... 55
History ... 55
The Media ... 57
Music ... 58
Food ... 59
Pubs and Beer ... 60
Sports ... 61
Language ... 61
London ... 64
Orientation ... 64
Practical Information ... 72
Accommodations ... 76
Food ... 84
Pubs ... 90
Tea ... 93
Sights ... 94
Museums ... 126
Entertainment ... 133
South and Southeast England ... 147
Getting Around ... 147
Canterbury ... 147
Deal ... 152
Dover ... 154
Rye ... 157
South Downs Way ... 160
Brighton ... 161
Arundel ... 165
Chichester ... 167
Portsmouth ... 170
Winchester ... 172
Salisbury ... 176
Southwest England ... 181
Getting There and Getting Around ... 182
Dorchester ... 183
Weymouth ... 186
Exeter ... 187
Lyme Regis ... 190
Exmoor National Park ... 192
Dartmoor National Park ... 195
Plymouth ... 199
Bodmin Moor ... 202
Falmouth ... 204
Lizard Peninsula (Landewednack) ... 206
Penwith and The North Cornish Coast ... 207
Penzance ... 208
Land's End to St. Ives ... 210
St. Ives ... 211
Newquay ... 212
Heart of England ... 215
Oxford ... 215
Cotswolds ... 226
Cheltenham ... 229
Worcester ... 232
Stratford-upon-Avon ... 235
Bath ... 239
Wells ... 245
Glastonbury ... 248
Stonehenge ... 251
East Anglia ... 252
Cambridge ... 253
Ely ... 264
Suffolk ... 265
Norwich ... 268
Norfolk Broads ... 273
King's Lynn ... 273
Peterborough ... 276
Central England ... 279
Birmingham ... 279
Lincoln ... 283
Nottingham ... 286
Liverpool ... 288
Chester ... 293
Manchester ... 297

Sheffield ... 301
Peak District National Park ... 304
North England ... 312
Getting Around ... 313
Pennine Way ... 313
Leeds ... 315
South Pennines ... 316
Yorkshire Dales National Park ... 318
York ... 323
North York Moors National Park ... 329
Durham ... 334
Northern (or High) Pennines ... 338
Newcastle-upon-Tyne ... 340
Northumbrian Coast ... 344
Northumberland National Park ... 346
Hadrian's Wall ... 348
Carlisle ... 350
Lake District National Park ... 351

WALES ... 364
South Wales ... 366
Cardiff (Caerdydd) ... 368
Wye Valley ... 372
Abergavenny (Y-Fenni) ... 375
Brecon Beacons National Park (Bannau Brycheiniog) ... 378
Brecon (Aberhonddu) ... 381
Swansea (Abertawe) ... 384
Gower Peninsula ... 385
Pembrokeshire Coast National Park ... 386
Tenby (Dinbych y Pysgod) ... 389
Pembroke (Penfro) and Pembroke Dock ... 391
St. David's (Tyddewi) ... 393
St. David's to Cardigan ... 394
Aberystwyth ... 395
North Wales ... 398
Machynlleth ... 399
Machynlleth to Harlech ... 400
Harlech ... 401
Llyn Peninsula ... 401
Caernarfon ... 403
Bangor ... 405
Isle of Anglesey (Ynys Môn) ... 407
Snowdonia Forest and National Park ... 409
Conwy ... 414
Vale of Conwy ... 416
Betws-y-Coed ... 417
Llangollen ... 417
Shrewsbury ... 419

SCOTLAND ... 421
Getting There ... 421
Getting Around ... 423
Accommodations ... 425
History ... 425
Literature ... 426
Food and Drink ... 427
Central Scotland ... 427
Edinburgh ... 427
St. Andrews ... 440
Glasgow ... 445
Loch Lomond, Loch Long, and the Trossachs ... 452
Southern Scotland ... 453
Ayr ... 453
Stranraer ... 454
The Borders ... 454
Northeast Scotland ... 458
Perth ... 458
Cairngorm Mountains ... 461
Aberdeen ... 463
Grampian ... 466
Inverness ... 468
Highlands and Islands ... 471
Arran ... 472
Mid Argyll and Kintyre Peninsula, Islay and Jura Islands ... 475
Oban ... 476
Mull ... 478
Glencoe ... 481
Fort William and Ben Nevis ... 482
Fort William to Mallaig ... 485
The Small Isles ... 486
Skye ... 486
Outer Hebrides ... 491
The Uists ... 491
Barra (Barraigh) ... 492
Northeast Coast, Inverness to Wick ... 492
Northeastern Ferry Ports ... 493
Orkney Islands ... 495
Shetland Islands ... 495

NORTHERN IRELAND ... 496
Belfast ... 500
Larne ... 506
Mourne Mountains ... 506
Armagh ... 508
Glens of Antrim ... 509
Causeway Coast ... 511
Fermanagh Lake District ... 514

IRELAND 517
Getting There 518
Getting Around 519
Accommodations 520
History 521
Literature 522
Music 523
Pubs and Food 524
East Coast 525
Dublin 525
North of Dublin 540
South of Dublin 543
Southeast Ireland 546
Enniscorthy 547
Wexford Town 548
Rosslare Harbour 550
Waterford Town 551
Kilkenny Town 552
Cashel 555
Cahir 556
Southwest Ireland 557
Cork Town 557
Youghal 561
Kinsale 561
Kinsale to Skibbereen and Bantry 562
Skibbereen 563
Baltimore, Sherkin Island, and Cape Clear Island 564
Bantry 566
Beara Peninsula 566
Iveragh Peninsula 568
Dingle Peninsula 574
Western Ireland 577
Limerick Town 577
Ennis 579
Clare Coast 580
Northwest Clare: The Burren 581
Galway Town 582
Aran Islands (Oileáin Árann) 586
Lough Corrib and Lough Mask 588
Connemara 589
Westport 593
Achill Island 594
Northwest Ireland 595
Sligo Town 596
Sligo to Donegal 599
Donegal Town 600
Southern Donegal Peninsula: From Donegal to Ardara 601
Northwest Donegal: Dungloe to Dunfanaghy 603
Northern Donegal Peninsulas 604
Letterkenny 604
Fanad Peninsula 605
Rosguill Peninsula and Horn Head 605
Inishowen Peninsula 606

INDEX 608

LIST OF MAPS

Great Britain
  Points of Interest 2-3
  Transport Map 38-39
  Regional Map 56
London 66-67
Around London 69
Southeast England 148
Southwest England 181
Heart of England 215
Oxford 216
Bath 240
East Anglia 252
Cambridge 254
Central England 279
North England 312
Wales 365
Scotland 422
Edinburgh 428
Northern Ireland 496
Ireland 517
Dublin 526

About Let's Go

A generation ago, Harvard Student Agencies, a three-year-old nonprofit corporation dedicated to providing employment to students, was doing a booming business booking charter flights to Europe. One of the extras offered to passengers on these flights was a 20-page mimeographed pahmplet entitled *1960 European Guide,* a collection of tips on continental travel compiled by the HSA staff. The following year, students traveling to Europe researched the first full-fledged edition of *Let's Go: Europe,* a pocket-sized book with tips on budget accommodations, irreverent write-ups of sights, and a decidedly youthful slant.

Throughout the 60s, the series reflected its era: a section of the 1968 *Let's Go: Europe* was entitled "Street Singing in Europe on No Dollars a Day." During the 70s *Let's Go* gradually became a large-scale operation, adding regional European guides and expanding coverage into North Africa and Asia. Now in its 31st year, *Let's Go* publishes 15 titles covering more than 40 countries. This year *Let's Go* proudly introduces two new guides: *Let's Go: Germany, Austria, and Switzerland* and *Let's Go: Washington, D.C.*

Each spring 80 Harvard-Radcliffe students are hired as researcher/writers for the summer months. They train intensively during April and May for their summer tour of duty. Each researcher/writer then hits the road on a shoestring budget for seven weeks, researching six days per week, and overcoming countless obstacles in a glorious quest for better bargains.

Back in a basement deep below Harvard yard, an editorial staff of 30, a management team of six, and countless typists and proofreaders—all students—spend four months poring over more than 70,000 pages of manuscript as they push the copy through a rigorous editing process. High tech has recently landed in the dungeon: some of the guides are now typeset in-house using sleek black desktop workstations.

And even before the books hit the stands, next year's editions are well underway.

At Harvard Student Agencies, CEO Michele Ponti and President Robert Frost graciously presided over the whole affair.

Did we mention that the Portland Trail Blazers are going all the way this year?

A Note to our Readers

The information for this book is gathered by Harvard Student Agencies' researchers during the late spring and summer months. Each listing is derived from the assigned researcher's opinion based upon his or her visit at a particular time. The opinions are expressed in a candid and forthright manner. Other travelers might disagree. Those traveling at a different time may have different experiences since prices, dates, hours, and conditions are always subject to change. You are urged to check beforehand to avoid inconvenience and surprises. Travel always involves a certain degree of risk, especially in low-cost areas. When traveling, especially on a budget, you should always take particular care to ensure your safety.

LET'S GO: BRITAIN AND IRELAND

General Introduction

As recently as fifty-five years ago, Great Britain was the center of the world's mental geography. Power and glory radiated from London, and politics, finance and much of culture found their source in the Mother Country. That era of British history has, of course, ended with a whimper. The future of the United Kingdom—even the extent to which it will remain "united"—is an open question.

Originally "England" meant a group of Anglo-Saxon principalities that were united in the 9th century. Over the years it came to mean that part of the British Isles which had managed to subdue the other parts. Ireland, Wales and Scotland were all under effective English control by 1603, but "The United Kingdom of Great Britain and Ireland" was not officially proclaimed until 1801. By the early 20th century, though, this union had already begun to disintegrate. Most of Ireland won its independence in 1921. Scotland and Wales were promised regional autonomy in 1975. English hegemony in the British Isles, more than half a millenium old, seems to be coming to an end.

The term "Britain" encompasses the three distinct regions of the largest British Isle: England, Scotland, and Wales. The dominance that the British Isles once held in world politics belies their small size: Britain is just under 600 miles long from the south coast to the extreme north in Scotland and just under 300 miles across at its widest. "Ireland" can include both the southern Republic of Ireland and Northern Ireland. Politically, the name "United Kingdom" (U.K.) includes Britain and Northern Ireland. The Republic of Ireland has been a separate state since 1921. *Let's Go* uses the term "Britain" to mean England, Scotland, Wales, and Northern Ireland; "Ireland" always refers to the Republic of Ireland.

Even within these separate regions, landscapes and cultures vary. This guide divides England into the coastal resorts and downs of the Southeast, the moors and rocky coastline of the Southwest (known as "West Country"), the traditionally cloistered calm of the Heartland, the industrial urban megalopoli of Central England, and the national parks of North England; Wales into the relatively untouched North and the more accessible but mine-gouged South; Scotland into the lovely urban swath of the Central region, the rolling hills of the South, the mountains and lonely fishing villages of the Northeast, and the stark beauty of the Highlands and Islands; Ireland into the East—within easy reach of Dublin, the sunny Southeast where the Vikings choose to rest awhile, the peninsulas of the Southwest, the lunar landscapes of the West, the rugged Northwest and the lake-bejewelled Midlands.

Before You Go

When to Go

Traveling during the low or off-season (October-May) is a great way to reduce the damage to your bank account. Airfares are considerably lower, and domestic travel is less congested. You won't have to compete with squadrons of fellow tourists crowding hotels, sights, and train stations, taking pictures of themselves, driving

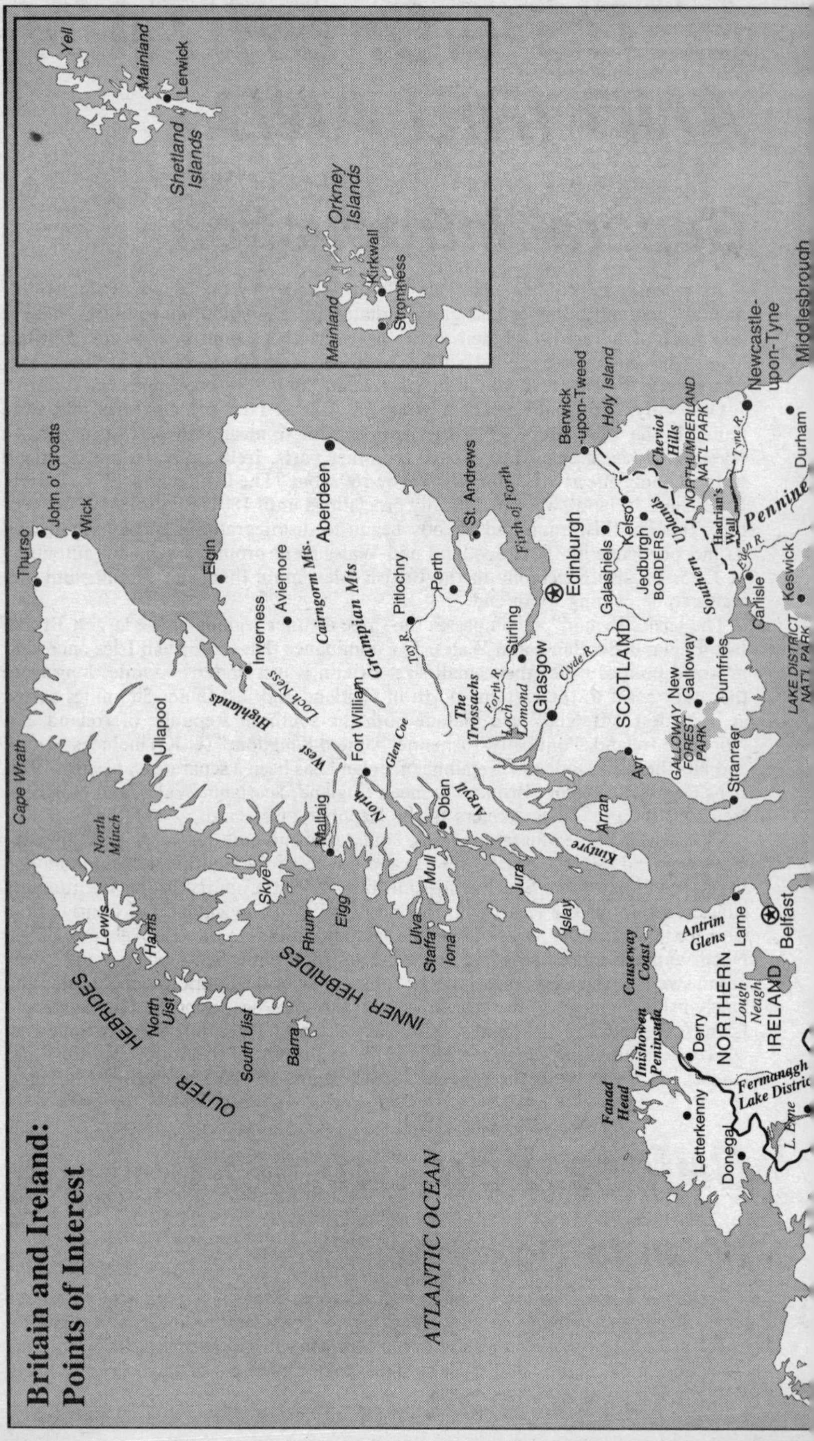

Britain and Ireland: Points of Interest

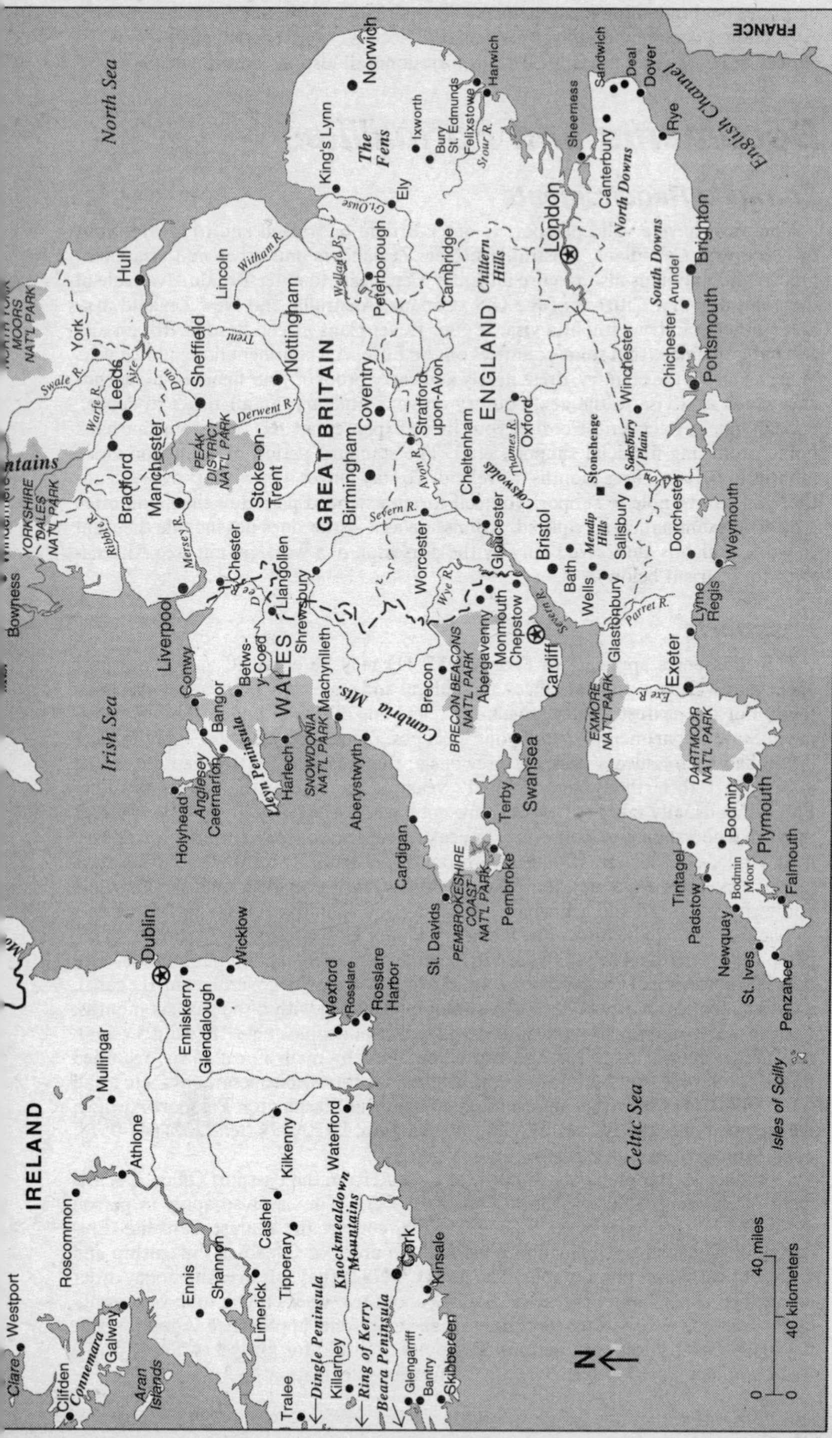

IRELAND
GREAT BRITAIN
ENGLAND
WALES
FRANCE
North Sea
Irish Sea
Celtic Sea
English Channel
Westport
Roscommon
Athlone
Mullingar
Clare
Clifden
Connemara
Galway
Aran Islands
Ennis
Shannon
Limerick
Tipperary
Cashel
Kilkenny
Waterford
Tralee
Dingle Peninsula
Killarney
Ring of Kerry
Beara Peninsula
Glengarriff
Bantry
Skibbereen
Knockmealdown Mountains
Cork
Kinsale
Dublin
Enniskerry
Glendalough
Wicklow
Wexford
Rosslare
Rosslare Harbor
Holyhead
Anglesey
Caernarfon
Bangor
Conwy
Lleyn Peninsula
Harlech
SNOWDONIA NAT'L PARK
Betws-y-Coed
Llangollen
Liverpool
Chester
Shrewsbury
Machynlleth
Aberystwyth
Cambria Mts.
Cardigan
St. Davids
PEMBROKESHIRE COAST NAT'L PARK
Pembroke
Terby
Swansea
Brecon
BRECON BEACONS NAT'L PARK
Abergavenny
Monmouth
Chepstow
Cardiff
Wye R.
Bowness
YORKSHIRE DALES NAT'L PARK
NORTH YORK MOORS NAT'L PARK
Ribble R.
Mersey R.
Dee R.
Bradford
Manchester
Leeds
Swale R.
Warfe R.
Aire
York
Hull
Sheffield
Don
PEAK DISTRICT NAT'L PARK
Stoke-on-Trent
Derwent R.
Nottingham
Trent
Lincoln
Witham R.
Birmingham
Coventry
Severn R.
Worcester
Gloucester
Cheltenham
Stratford-upon-Avon
Avon R.
Peterborough
Welland R.
Cambridge
Ely
Gt. Ouse
King's Lynn
The Fens
Norwich
Ixworth
Bury St. Edmunds
Felixstowe
Stour R.
Harwich
Chiltern Hills
Oxford
Thames R.
Cotswolds
Bristol
Bath
Mendip Hills
Wells
Glastonbury
Stonehenge
Salisbury
Salisbury Plain
Winchester
London
Sheerness
Canterbury
Sandwich
Deal
Dover
Rye
North Downs
South Downs
Arundel
Chichester
Brighton
Portsmouth
Dorchester
Weymouth
Lyme Regis
Parret R.
Exeter
Exe R.
EXMOORE NAT'L PARK
DARTMOOR NAT'L PARK
Plymouth
Bodmin
Bodmin Moor
Tintagel
Padstow
Newquay
Falmouth
St. Ives
Penzance
Isles of Scilly
N
0 40 miles
0 40 kilometers

up prices, and inflaming local tempers. There are, of course, disadvantages as well. Attractions, accommodations (particularly hostels), and tourist offices may be closed; in some rural areas local transportation will also be shut down.

Documents and Formalities

Entrance Requirements

You must have a valid passport to enter Britain or Ireland and to reenter your own country. Canadians, Australians, New Zealanders and other non-visa Commonwealth nationals also require an Entry Certificate to enter Britain, available at the point of entry. Citizens of the U.S., Canada, Australia, and New Zealand may enter either country without a visa. If your travel plans extend beyond Britain and Ireland, remember that some countries on the European continent do require a visa. When entering the country, dress neatly and carry proof of your financial independence (such as a visa to the next country on your itinerary, an air ticket to depart, enough money to cover the cost of your living expenses, a letter from someone back home promising financial support, etc.). The standard period of admission is six months in Britain, three months in Ireland. To stay longer, you must show evidence that you will be able to support yourself for an extended period of time, and often a medical examination is required. Admission as a visitor does not include the right to work, which is authorized only by the possesson of a work permit (see Alternatives to Tourism below).

Passports

U.S. Passports applications (Form DSP-11) may be obtained at any passport agency, as well as most post offices and federal and state courthouses will also issue them. For the nearest agency, check the telephone directory under "U.S. Government, State Department," or call your local post office. You may also apply by mail if you had been issued a passport previously; that passport must have been issued after your 16th birthday and within 12 years of the date of the new application. Processing usually takes two weeks through a passport agency, three to four weeks through a courthouse or post office; in peak travel season (March through August), it may take even longer. If you have proof of departure within five working days (an air ticket, for example), the Passport Agency will provide a rush service while you wait; call ahead and ask what time of day you should arrive for fastest service.

The passport application must include: proof of U.S. citizenship (a previous U.S. passport or a certified copy of your birth certificate), an unexpired photo or descrip-tion ID (a previous U.S. passport, a valid driver's license, a governement ID card), and two identical passport (2"×2") photographs taken within the past six months. Passports are valid for 10 years and cost $42, $27 for people under 18 (valid 5 years). A 10-year renewal costs $35 and can be obtained by mail. For a 24-hr. recorded message offering general information, agency locations, business hours, etc., call (202) 647-0518; for further information contact the Washington Passport Agency, Department of State, 1425 K St. NW, Washington, DC 20524 (tel. (202) 647-0518; open Mon.-Fri. 8am-4:15pm).

Canadian passports may be applied for by mail from the Passport Office, Department of External Affairs, Ottawa, Ont. K1A 0G3. You can also apply in person at any of 21 regional offices; outside Canada, contact the nearest Canadian Embasssy or Consulate. Application must include proof of Canadian citizenship and two identical signed photographs. The fee is CDN$25 (payable in cash, money order or certified check), and processing requires about two weeks if you mail your application, three to five working days if you make a personal appearance. Again, service is usually faster in off-peak periods. Passports are valid for five years. Send for the free pamphlet *Bon Voyage, But . . .* for further information.

Australian passports may be obtained at a Passport Office (usually in the provincial capital) or at any post office; if at all possible, every applicant must show up in person. The fee is AUS$76 for those over 18 (valid 10 years), otherwise AUS$37 (valid five years). For more information, consult your local post office or call toll free (in Australia: tel. (008) 026 022; open Mon.-Fri. during working hr.). Australian citizens age 12 and over must pay a Departure Tax of AUS$10 before leaving the country.

New Zealand passports may be obtained at a local passport office or consulate. The application must be accompanied by evidence of citizenship; the fee is NZ$50. The passport is valid for 10 years (5 years for those under 10). Allow three weeks for your passport to be processed. For more information, visit or write to the Department of Internal Affairs in Wellington.

Before you leave, record your passport number and keep it apart from the passport. If you lose your passport while traveling, notify the local police and the nearest consulate of your home government immediately. Carry an expired passport or a copy of your birth certificate in a separate part of your baggage; at the very least, carry a photocopy of the page of your passport that has your photograph and identifying information on it. Your consulate will be able to issue you temporary traveling papers or replace your passport.

Customs

Persons entering Britain and Ireland must declare at the point of entry the three great aromatic luxuries: alcohol, tobacco, and perfume. A duty is placed on excessive quantities of these substances. Travelers from the EC can bring in or take out of the U.K. 200 cigarettes, 50 cigars, or 250 grams of tobacco; 1 liter of over-40 proof liquor or 2 liters of under-40 proof liquor (sparkling or table wine); 50 grams of perfume; and £32 worth of other goods. Travelers from outside continental Europe can carry 400 cigarettes, 100 cigars, or 400g tobacco; 1.5 liters of over-40 proof or 3 liters of under-40 proof liquor; 75g perfume; and £265 worth of other goods. Britain also has very strict restrictions on imports: among those goods prohibited are controlled drugs, horror comics, fireworks, meat and poultry, fruits and vegetables, plants and plant material, and wood with bark attached. All animals brought into the country are subject to a six-month quarantine at the owner's expenses, as good a reason as any to leave Rover at home. Neither country limits the amount of currency you may bring in, though Ireland places restrictions on the amount taken out of the country—no more than IR£150 in Irish currency, plus no more than the value of IR£1200 in foreign currency. Britain has no such limits.

Upon returning home, you must declare all articles acquired abroad. It is wise to make a list (including serial numbers) of any valuables that you take with you from home; if you register this list with customs at the airport before departing, you'll avoid being charged import duties upon your return. **U.S. citizens** may bring home a maximum of $400 worth of goods duty-free; the next $1000 is subject to a 10% tax. Duty-free goods must be for personal or household use and cannot include more than 100 cigars, 200 cigarettes (1 carton), or one liter of wine or liquor (you must be 21 or older to bring liquor into the U.S.). All items included in your duty-free allowance must accompany you; you cannot ship them separately. You may mail unsolicited gifts back to the U.S. from abroad duty-free if they are worth less than $50, but you may not mail liquor, tobacco, or perfume. Mark the accurate price and nature of the gift on the package; as the customs service will continually remind you, "honesty is the best policy." If you mail home personal goods of U.S. origin, mark the package "American Goods Returned." For more information, consult *Know Before You Go,* available from the U.S. Customs Service, 1301 Constitution Ave., Washington, DC 20229 (tel. (202) 566-8195).

Regulations are similar for **Canadian citizens.** After you have been abroad at for least two days, you may bring in up to CDN$100 worth of goods duty-free. Once every calendar year, after you have been abroad at least seven days, you may bring in up to CDN$300 worth of goods duty-free. Duty-free goods can include no more than 200 cigarettes, one kg of tobacco, and 50 cigars (if you are 16 or older). You may not bring in more than 1.1 liters of alcohol. Anything above the duty-free allowance is taxed: 20% for goods that accompany you, more for shipped items. You can send unsolicited gifts worth up to CDN$40 duty-free, but, again, you cannot mail alcohol or tobacco. Before you leave, list any valuables that you are bringing out of the country (by serial number) on a Y-38 form, available at most customs offices. This will ensure that you can bring them back without paying duty. For more information, write or call the Revenue Canada Customs and Excise Department, Communications Branch, Mackenzie Ave., Ottawa, Ont. K1A 0L5 (tel. (613) 957-0275), for the pamphlet *I Declare,* which provides an outline of customs restrictions and addresses of regional customs offices.

Australian citizens aged 18 or older may bring in up to AUS$400 worth of duty-free goods; for those under 18, the limit is AUS$200. Duty-free allowances include no more than 1 liter of alcohol (for those over 18), and 250 cigarettes. Export of more than AUS$5000 without permission from the Reserve Bank of Australia is prohibited. These and other restrictions may be found in *Customs Information for All Travelers,* available from local customs offices. For more information, contact the Australian Customs Service, P.O. Box 874, Launceston 7250, Tasmania, Australia. **New Zealand citizens** can bring in NZ$500 of duty-free goods. Those 16 or older are allowed 250 grams of tobacco in any of its forms; 4.5 liters of beer and wine; and one 1125ml bottle of liquor. However, according to customs regulations, you will have to leave behind your birds' nests, dead bees, raw eggs, azaleas, and homemade noodles. *New Zealand Customs Guide for Travelers,* and *If You're Not Sure About It, DECLARE IT,* both available from any Customs Office, make fascinating reading.

The U.S. Customs Service has proclaimed that "a vital part of Customs' role is screening out items injurious to the well-being of our nation." The U.S., Canada, Australia, and New Zealand, like the U.K. all prohibit or restrict the import of firearms, explosives, ammunition, fireworks, plants, animals (including monkeys, humans, and other primates), lottery tickets, obscene literature and film, and controlled drugs. To avoid problems when carrying prescription drugs, make sure bottles are clearly marked, and have a copy of the prescription ready to show the customs officer.

Money

Currency and Exchange

US$1 = 0.60 British pounds	**£1 = US$1.67**
CDN$1 = £0.52	**£1 = CDN$1.92**
AUS$1 = £0.47	**£1 = AUS$2.13**
NZ$1 = £0.34	**£1 = NZ$2.94**
UK£1 = 1.09 Irish pounds	**IR£1 = UK£0.92**
US$1 = IR£0.65	**IR£1 = US$1.54**
CDN$1 = IR£0.57	**IR£1 = CDN$1.75**
AUS$1 = IR£0.51	**IR£1 = AUS$1.96**
NZ$1 = IR£0.37	**IR£1 = NZ$2.70**

Money tends to cause continual anxiety, even if you have enough of it—and a surplus of money is not ususally the problem for the budget traveler. To avoid some stress, follow the fluctuation of rates for several weeks while planning your trip. The exchange rates valid at press time are listed at the beginning of this section. If the trend is toward a stronger pound, you may want to exchange a significant amount of money at the beginning of your trip. Remember that it is usually more expensive to buy foreign currency than domestic; pounds will be less costly in Britain and Ireland than at home. Converting a small amount of money before you go, however, will allow you to breeze through the airport while others languish in exchange counter lines. Observe commission rates closely when abroad. Bank rates are always preferable to those of travel agencies, tourist offices, restaurants, hotels, and the dubious *bureaux de change.* Never change money at a post office; their rates are the worst of all. Since you lose money with every exchange transaction, it's wise to convert in large sums (provided the exchange rate is either staying constant or deteriorating), but not more than you will need. Planning a travel budget with a daily allowance can take some of the confusion out of this process.

The pound sterling (£) is the main unit of currency in Great Britain. It is divided into 100 pence (100p), issued in standard denominations of 1p, 2p, 5p, 10p, 20p, 50p, and £1 in coin, and £1, £5, £10, £20, and £50 in notes (observe, however, that the £1 note has been replaced by a heavy gold coin in all regions except Scotland). Currently, the old 5p coin is being replaced by a new smaller coin (about the size of the U.S. dime) that coin vending machine contraptions and telephones haven't yet been adjusted to accept. You may come across coins held over from Britain's previous monetary system, such as the shilling (5p) and the two-shilling "florin" (10p). These are still legal tender. The terminology used in the old system still lingers in street markets. "Half-a-crown" is approximately 12½p; a "quid" or "nicker" is £1; and a "guinea" is £1.05. The separate currencies issued in the Channel Islands, the Isle of Man, Scotland, and Northern Ireland can be used interchangeably with standard English currency. However, you may have difficulty using Scottish £1 notes outside Scotland.

The monetary unit of Irish currency is the punt, or "Irish pound." Irish and British currencies are issued in the same denominations, but the two are not of equal value; the Irish pound now buys about nine percent less than its British counterpart. Unless otherwise specified, prices quoted in the Ireland chapter of this book are in Irish pounds, while prices elsewhere are in British pounds.

Most banks are closed on Saturday, Sunday, and all public holidays; Britain and Ireland enjoy "bank holidays" several times a year (New Year's, Good Friday, Easter Monday, first Mon. in May, last Mon. in May, last Mon. in Aug., Christmas, and Boxing Day; also St. Patrick's Day in Ireland and Northern Ireland). Usual weekday bank hours in Britain are Monday through Friday 9:30am to 3:30pm, although more and more banks are finding Saturday a lucrative day to do business as well. These apply in Scotland and Northern Ireland as well, although some banks close for an hour around 12:30pm, and some banks in Scotland are open later one evening per week (usually Thurs.). Banks in Ireland are open from 10am to 12:30pm and 1:30pm to 3pm, closing later on Wednesday or Thursday.

Traveler's Checks

Traveler's checks are the safest way to carry money. The major brands can be exchanged at virtually every bank in Britain and Ireland, sometimes without a commission. Traveler's checks are also accepted at the great majority of B&Bs, shops and restaurants, though many smaller establishments, especially in remote towns, only take cash. Furthermore, if lost or stolen, traveler's checks can be replaced, often within a matter of hours.

The seven or eight major brands are sold at agencies and banks everywhere. Of these, American Express traveler's checks are perhaps the most widely accepted worldwide and the easiest to replace. However, in Britain, Barclay's and Thomas Cook's are just as widely recognized. If you will be visiting other countries in addition to Britain and Ireland, you should buy your checks in U.S. dollars. Few currencies are as easily exchanged worldwide, and you will save yourself the cost of repeatedly converting currency. However, if you are visiting only Britain and Ireland, you may be better off buying in pounds; you'll avoid losing money if the pound strengthens while you're in Britain. In addition, sterling travelers cheques are easier to cash (Barclay's will cash any sterling cheque for free, regardless of the issuer), and few establishments will take checks issued in foreign currency without taking a hefty

bite for themselves. The following companies offer checks in U.S. dollars or British pounds—often in both:

American Express, Traveler's Check Operations Center, Salt Lake City, UT 84184. Call (800) 221-7282 in the U.S. or (0273) 571 600 (Brighton, England) with questions or to report lost or stolen checks. Variable commission on purchase depending on bank—usually 1-3%. Official American Express Travel Service Offices will cash their own checks free. The **American Automobile Association (AAA)** and the **American Association of Retired Persons (AARP)** offer free American Express traveler's checks to their members.

Bank of America Traveler's Office: P.O. Box 37010, San Francisco, CA 94137. Call (800) 227-3333 in the U.S.; from Canada and abroad, call collect (415) 624-5400 (Canada). Checks in US$ only. Commission normally 1%. Checkholders may use **Travel Assistance Hotline,** offering, among other services, free legal assistance and urgent message relay (tel. (800) 368-7878 in the U.S.; from abroad, call collect (202) 347-7113).

Barclay's: Sells Visa traveler's checks. For lost or stolen checks, call Visa (listed below); for Barclay's information specifically, call (800) 221-2426 in the U.S. and Canada; in England call collect (202) 671 212. Commission on purchase varies from customer to customer and from branch to branch (usually 1-3%). Barclay's branches cash Barclay's-Visa and other Visa traveler's checks for free.

Citicorp: Call (800) 645-6556 in the U.S. and Canada; from abroad, call collect (813) 623-1709 or (071) 982 4040 (London). Usually 1% commission on purchase. Checkholders automatically enrolled in **Travel Assist Hotline** (tel. (800) 523-1199). Citicorp also has a World Courier Service which guarantees hand-delivery of traveler's checks anywhere in the world.

Mastercard International: Sells Thomas Cook traveler's checks. Call (800) 223-7373; from abroad call collect (609) 987-7300. Commission varies from 1 to 2% with issuing bank.

Thomas Cook: Call (800) 223-4030 for orders, (800) 223-7373 for refunds in the U.S.; from Canada, call collect (609) 987-7300; from England, call (733) 502 995 (Peterborough). 1% commission on purchase; an additional commission may be levied by the bank. You can buy Thomas Cook-Mastercard traveler's checks at any bank displaying a Mastercard sign, and cash them free at Thomas Cook locations.

Visa: Call (800) 227-6811 in the U.S.; from abroad, call collect (415) 574-7111 or (071) 937 80 91 (London). Visa doesn't charge a commission, but the bank that sells the checks usually levies a 1% commission on purchases. Cash them free at any Barclay's branch.

Traveler's cheque refunds should not be a painful process; issuing companies often include with your checks a slip of paper supplying your check serial numbers, toll-free telephone numbers for refunds from anywhere in the world, and explicit instructions to keep the slip of paper in a separate place from your checks. Follow their advice. You may also want to take the extra precaution of recording the serial numbers of checks as you use them. Refunds should be available within 24 hr.; you can pick up your money at the nearest office of your issuing company, or it can be hand-delivered to you. Nevertheless, you should always keep some cash on hand for those times when you are unable to use checks.

Credit Cards

Credit cards are not always useful to the budget traveler—many smaller establishments will not accept them, and many larger establishments accept them all too willingly—but they can be invaluable in a financial emergency. You can often reduce conversion fees by charging instead of changing traveler's checks. With credit cards such as **American Express, Visa,** and **Mastercard,** associated banks will give you an instant cash advance in local currency as large as your remaining credit line. The terms of this arrangement follow the policy of the bank that issued the card. Unfortunately, in most cases you will pay near-usurious rates of interest.

American Express offers several exciting services to their cardholders. Before you travel, you may want to enroll in "Express Cash," a free service that links your American Express account to your checking account and supplies you with a Personal Identification Number (PIN), with which you may access your account from Automatic Teller Machines (ATM) anywhere with the American Express trademark. (Each transaction costs about $1-2 plus conversion fees and interest.) To locate ATMs in Britain and Ireland where you can use your card, call American Express at 800-CASH-NOW (227-4669); they will send you a booklet of participating machines wherever you are going. Both gold and green cardholders may also cash personal checks for limited amounts. Cardholders may employ the services of **Global Assist,** a 24-hr. helpline offering emergency medical and legal assistance and other services (in the U.S. call (800) 554-2639; from abroad call collect to the U.S. (202) 783-7474). In dire emergencies, the operators at Global Assist can authorize cash advances. Finally, upon request American Express will send you their *American Express Traveler's Companion,* which summarizes all the above information in chic booklet form. For customer service and general card information, call (800) 528-4800 for green cards, (800) 327-2177 for Gold Cards. **Mastercard** offers cash advances up to the cardholder's daily limit, decided by the issuing bank (in the U.S. call (800) 826-2181). **Visa** also has a 24-hr. hotline to ask questions or report lost or stolen cards (tel. (800) 336-8472 or (415) 574-7700, (800) 847-2911 for Visa Gold); Visa cards can also access ATM networks (usually Cirrus, but it varies with the issuing bank).

ATMs in Britain and Ireland are not quite as prevalent as they are in North America, but you will find that most banks in the larger cities are connected to an international money network, usually PLUS (tel. (800) THE-PLUS (843-7587) or Cirrus (tel. (800) 4CI-RRUS (424-7787). Depending on the system that your bank at home uses, you will probably be able to access your own personal bank account whenever you're in need of funds. Don't make it a habit, however—exchange rates can play tricks on you and wreak havoc on your account balance.

Sending Money

Sending money overseas is a complicated, expensive, and often extremely frustrating adventure. Do your best to avoid it; carry a credit card or a separate stash of emergency traveler's checks. The simplest way to have money sent to you is to have someone **cable** money through a large commercial bank network. The sender should find a local bank big enough to have an international department and bring the address of the receiving bank and the destination account number. Both sender and receiver must usually have accoutns at the respective institutions. Transfers of this kind normally take up to a few days; the fee is a flat $20-30. In order to pick up the money, the recipient must always present some sort of positive identification. **Bank of America's Global Sellers Network** (tel. (800) 227-3460) has a Worldwide Delivery system that delivers to any Seller location in three to five working days. It operates through an affiliated bank and charges a 1% fee plus $15 telex charge ($12 buys you $100, $25 buys you $1000). Anyone can send the money by bringing cash, a credit card, or a cashier's check to a branch of Bank of America. The receiver must possess proper ID, such as a passport or driver's license. For $35, **Barclay's** (tel. (212) 233-4200) will deliver up to $1000 in one to three working days. The sender must have a Barclay's account. **Citibank** (tel. (212) 657-5161) will also transfer money in one to five days. The flat fee applies to all amounts sent. In addition, the receiving bank will probably charge a commission of 1%.

Western Union (tel. (800) 325-6000) offers a somewhat more convenient international money transfer system. Using a major credit card, the folks at home can send up to $2000; a sender without a credit card can go to one of Western Union's offices with cash or a cashier's check (no money orders accepted). The money should arrive at the Western Union Agency, the central telegram or post office of the city the sender designates within 24 hr., even quicker in a larger city. You will need suitable identification to pick it up (fees $25 to send $250, $70 to send $1000).

You can also turn to **American Express's** new Moneygram Money Transfer Service (tel. (800) 543-4080, 24 hr.; from abroad call collect (303) 980-3340). Money can be sent from any American Express Travel Office or affliated organization; the money transfer can take place in a matter of minutes. The recipient needs to fill out a "Receive Form" and supply valid identification or answer a skill-testing question pre-determined by the sender. Money must be sent in $50 increments; rates begin at $25 for $50-100 sent. American Express is slightly cheaper and serve more countries than Western Union.

Finally, if you are really struggling for survival, you can usually have money sent through your government's diplomatic mission in Britain or Ireland. American citizens who are very desperate should turn to a U.S. Consular Office, which will assist by contacting friends or family in the U.S. and arranging for them to send money. Senders at home should contact the State Department's Citizens Emergency Center, Department of State, #4811, 2201 C St. NW, Washington, DC 20520 (tel. (202) 647-5225). The Bureau can help those faced with only the most pressing problems—destitution, hospitalization, or probable death.

VAT (Value-Added Tax)

Both Britain and Ireland charge value-added tax (VAT), a national sales tax on most goods and some services. The British rate is 17.5% on many services (such as hairdressers, hotels, restaurants, and car rental agencies) and on all goods (except books, medicine, and food). In Ireland, VAT ranges from 8% on clothing to 35% on such luxury items as watches, jewelry, and cameras. The prices stated in *Let's Go* include VAT unless otherwise specified. Visitors to the United Kingdom can get a VAT refund through the Retail Export Scheme. Ask the shopkeeper from whom you buy your goods for the appropriate form, which customs officials will sign and stamp when you take your purchases through customs in your carry-on baggage. Once home, send the form and a self-addressed, British-stamped envelope to the shopkeeper, who will then send your refund. In order to use this scheme, you must export the goods within three months of purchase. Ireland has an identical scheme.

A Note on Prices

The information in this book was researched during the summer of 1991. Inflation may raise the prices we list by 10-20%. In the chapters on England, Wales, Scotland, and Northern Ireland, the symbol £ denotes British pounds. In the chapter on Ireland, it denotes Irish pounds (punts).

Health

In the event of sudden illness or an accident, dial **999,** the general emergency number for Britain and Ireland; it's a free call from any pay phone.

A self-assembled kit should suffice for minor health problems. You might include mild, antiseptic soap, vitamins, aspirin, antacid tablets, bandages, a protected thermometer, antibiotic ointment, burn ointment, tweezers, a Swiss Army knife (with as many attachments as it will hold—scissors are invaluable), sunscreen, a decongestent for flying, and an antihistamine.

If you're nervous about coming down with something particularly serious, ask your doctor for a general antibiotic. You will definitely want to take along medication for motion sickness and diarrhea. Contraception is of course available in the British Isles, but you may want to purchase it at home where you have a greater knowledge of the reliability of the manufacturer. Women taking the pill and diabetics taking insulin should remember to take time zone changes into account and to make the necessary adjustments in their medication schedules. All travelers on prescription drugs should be sure to bring extra medication (it will be difficult to match presciptions) and have a clearly legible explanatory note from a physician ready to show customs officials, particularly if you will be carrying syringes, insulin, or narcotic drugs. If you wear glasses or contact lenses, take an extra pair along. As an additional precaution, leave a copy of your prescription with someone at home and arrange to have a new pair sent if yours should be lost or smashed to smithereens. Most common brands of contact lens accoutrements may be purchased at chemists (drugstores) throughout Britain and Ireland. A final word of caution: know your blood type.

Any traveler with a medical condition that cannot be easily recognized (i.e. diabetes, allegies to penicillin) should seeriously consider obtaining a **Medic Alert Identification Tag.** In an emergency, this internationally recognized tag indicates the nature of the bearer's problem and provides the number of Medic Alert's 24-hr. hotline, though which attending medical personnel can obtain informaiton about the member's medical history. Lifetime membership and the tag cost $25; contact Medic Alert Foundation International, P.O. Box 1009, Turlock, CA 95831-1009 (tel. (800) IDA-LERT (432-5378). Also, the **American Diabetes Association** will supply free documents idnetifying the carrier as diabietic; write to 1660 Duke St., Alexandria, VA 22314 (tel. (800) 232-3472).

Try not to let your eating and sleeping habits get too disturbed while you're traveling. While it is rather difficult to lead a normal life while living out of a backpack, using common sense will keep you happy and healthy while you're roaming. If you're going to be doing a lot of walking, take along some quick-energy foods to keep your strength up. Resist the temptation of madcap tourism—don't press for that last obscure castle or cloister when you are too tired to enjoy it. And most importantly, don't go without proper nutrition just to save money. We at *Let's Go* understand the pressures on the budget traveler better than most, and we know that living on a diet of bread and cheese is simply not the way to spend your dream vacation in Britain and Ireland. Remember to splurge on occasion, both for your physical and your mental well-being.

The **International Association for Medical Assistance to Travellers (IAMAT)** publishes several helpful pamphlets on different health issues, as well as world-famous climate charts for various regions of the world. Write to them at 417 Center St., Lewiston, NY 14092 (tel. (716) 754-4883); in Canada at 40 Regal Rd., Guelph, Ontario N1K 1B5 (tel. (519) 836-0102) to apply for a free membership (donations are welcomed). The **Superintendent of Documents** (see Useful Addresses below) offers the pamphlet *Health Information on International Travel* for $5.

Britons obtain mainly free health care from the National Health Service (NHS). Foreign visitors do not, of course, get such favorable terms, but are nevertheless eligible for some free treatment, including: outpatient treatment in the Accident and Emergency ward of an NHS hospital; treatment of communicable diseases (such as V.D., typhoid or anthrax); and "compulsory" mental treatment.

Safety and Security

Some reasonable precautions and a general degree of street smarts will ward off most bad fortune. Sleepless vigilance and twitching paranoia accomplish little. Britain and Ireland are safer for the traveler than many other European countries, but you should still exercise caution, particularly in the larger cities. Keep all valuables on your person, preferably stowed away in a money belt or one of the newfangled necklace pouches that hides your money from prying eyes. Be wary on trains: sleeping tourists are a prize target for thieves. *Let's Go* lists locker availablility in hostels and stations, but you'll need your own padlock to feel secure; regardless, never store anything that you wouldn't hate to lose. Leave nothing unattended, even for a few minutes. Bicyclists and other wheeled travelers should be particularly watchful of their vehicles. Few valuables are more tempting to the thief than those that provide a built-in getaway. Another good idea is to make copies of all your important documents (passport, IDs, credit cards, etc.) and leave them at home; you won't have to rely only on your memory to reconstruct your entire life.

Drugs

Every year, hundreds of travelers are arrested in foreign countries for illegal possession of drugs. If you are caught with any quantity of illegal or controlled drugs in Britain or Ireland, one of two things may happen: you may be arrested and tried under British or Irish law; or you may be immediately expelled from the country. Your home government is powerless to shield you from the judicial system of a foreign country. If you are imprisoned, consular officers can visit you, provide you with a list of local attorneys, and inform your family and friends, but that is all. The London-based organization **Release** (tel. (071) 377 5905 or 603 8654) advises people who have been arrested on drug charges, but that's about all they can doFor more information on the subject of drugs overseas, send for the brochure *Travel Warning on Drugs Abroad* (Publication 9558) to the Bureau of Consular Affairs, U.S. Department of State, Washington, DC 20520 (tel. (202) 647-1488).

Insurance

The firms listed below offer insurance against theft, loss of luggage, or injury. You may buy a policy from them, or, in some cases, directly from a travel agent. Additionally, some traveler's check and credit card companies offer free insurance to their checkholders. **American Express** cardholders, for example, receive automatic rental-car and flight insurance on purchases made with the card. Check with your bank or issuing company. Remember two basic points when buying insurance. First, beware of unnecessary coverage. Check whether your homeowner's insurance (or your family's coverage) provides against theft during travel. Most homeowner's plans will provide against loss of travel documents up to $500. University term-time medical plans often include insurance for summer travel. Canadian citizens may be covered by their home province's health insurance plan up to 90 days after leaving the country. Second, insurance companies generally require that you submit documents relevant to the loss (and only upon returning home) before they will honor your claim. Keep all appropriate receipts, doctor's statements, police reports, or anything else that might be of use, and check the time limit on filing to make sure you will be returning home in time to secure reimbursement.

Access America, 6600 West Broad St., Richmond, VA 23230 (tel. (800) 424-3391; sales & marketing: 600 Third Ave., New York, NY 10016 (tel. (212) 949-5960). A subsidiary of Blue Cross/Blue Shield. Covers trip cancellation/interruption, on-the-spot hospital admittance costs, emergency medical evacuation, and maintains a 24-hr. hotline.

ARM Coverage, Inc., P.O. Box 310, Mineola, NY 11501 (tel. (800) 323-3149).

Carefree Travel Insurance, 120 Mineola Blvd., P.O. Box 310, Mineola, NY 11501 (tel. (800) 323-3149 or (516) 294-0220). Travel package includes accident and sickness coverage, 24-hr. emergency assistance service, baggage insurance, trip cancellation/interruption insurance.

Edmund A. Cocco Agency/GlobalCare Travel Insurance, 220 Broadway, #201, Lynnfield, MA 01940 (tel. (800) 821-2488). Covers travel, accident, sickness, and baggage loss, as well as on-the-spot payment for medical expenses. Trip cancellation/interruption insurance.

Wallach and Co., HealthCare Abroad, 243 Church St. NW, #1000, Vienna, VA 22180 (tel. (800) 237-6615, fax (703) 281-9504). 24-hr. medical assistance for ensured travelers. Policies cover hospitalization, doctor's office visits, prescriptions, medical evacuation to U.S.A. $100 deductible.

WorldCare Travel Assistance, 1150 South Olive St., Suite T-233, Los Angeles, CA 90015 (tel. (800) 253-1877). Annual membership ($162) covers an unlimited number of trips under 90 days. Shorter-term policies also available. **ScholarCare** program tailored to students and faculty spending a semester or year abroad.

If you have no medical insurance, or if your policy does not extend overseas (Medicare, for example, does not cover European travel), you may want to purchase a short-term policy for your trip. The **International Student Identification Card (ISIC), International Teacher Identity Card (ITIC),** or the **International Youth Card,** all offered by **CIEE** and *Let's Go Travel* (see Student and Youth Travelers below), provide accident/sickness coverage if purchased in the U.S. ID cards also provide a 24-hr. Traveler's Assistance Service for legal, medical, and financial emergencies. In addition, CIEE sells a moderately inexpensive plan called "Trip Safe," which doubles cardholders' insurance and can provide coverage for travelers ineligible for their ID cards. Trip Safe insures with options that cover medical treatment and hospitalization, accidents, lost baggage, and even charter flights missed due to illness. Trip Safe covers the individual outside of his country of domicile. As well, both **Travel Assistance International,** 1133 15th St. NW, Washington, DC 20005 (tel. (800) 821-2828 or (202) 331-1609) and **Traveler's Aid International,** 918 16th St. NW, Washington, DC 20006 (tel. (202) 659-9468) provide medical and legal assistance and various other services: Travel Assistance International has a 24-hr. hotline and also offers cash advances and medical transport information (membership fees depend on length of trip; $40 for 8 days); Traveler's Aid offers help for theft, car failure, illness, etc. (no fee; donations accepted).

Weather

The weather in Britain and Ireland is subject to frequent changes but few extremes, with an average temperature in the low to mid 60s in the summer and in the low 40s in the winter. Throughout the islands, you should expect unstable weather patterns; a bright and cloudless morning sky is often followed by intermittent drizzle throughout the afternoon. May and June have the best weather; days can be cloudless with temperatures in the 70s, even in the north.

Scotland is generally soggy; you should be prepared with warm, waterproof clothing at all times of year. Early August through September is heather time, when whole mountains erupt in purple; unnfortunately, the warm weather also brings midges (gnats). Though Scotland gets the most publicity for its wet weather, Wales also enjoys a great deal of moisture, averaging 200 rainy days a year. April is the driest month in Ireland, especially on the east coast near Dublin. May and June are the sunniest months, particularly in the south and southeast, and July and August are the warmest. December and January have the worst weather of the year—wet, cold, and cloudy.

The following provides a more specific idea of the British and Irish climate:

Dublin, Ireland:		
Jan.	**maximum temp. 8°C, 47°F**	**minimum temp. 1°C, 34°F**
July	**maximum temp. 20°C, 68°F**	**minimum temp. 11°C, 52°F**
Edinburgh, Scotland		
Jan.	**maximum temp. 6°C, 43°F**	**minimum temp. 1°C, 34°F**
July	**maximum temp. 18°C, 65°F**	**minimum temp. 11°C, 52°F**
London, England		
Jan.	**maximum temp. 7°C, 45°F**	**minimum temp. 2°C, 36°F**
July	**maximum temp. 22°C, 72°F**	**minimum temp. 13°C, 56°F**
Swansea, Wales		
Jan.	**maximum temp. 8°C, 47°F**	**minimum temp. 3°C, 38°F**
July	**maximum temp. 22°C, 72°F**	**minimum temp. 13°C, 56°F**

Packing

We cannot stress enough the importance of packing light: you will quickly find that the convenience of having less to carry far outweighs the inconvenience of having a small wardrobe. In the realm of luggage, the best piece to have is a good **backpack** with several compartments. Those planning to stay in one place for a long time might want to bring a small suitcase—preferably one with wheels—or shoulder bag. Packs come with either an external or an internal frame; internal-frame packs are less cumbersome and resist the ruthless treatment of baggage checkers more stoutly. Moreover, many can be converted quickly to shoulder or suitcase-style luggage. Packs with internal frames conform better to one's back and have a lower center of gravity than external frames, making hiking over uneven terrain easier. On the other hand, external frames may offer additional support and ventilation by lifting the pack off the back. Also keep in mind the arrangement of the pack's openings: outside pockets are convenient but offer little security against pick-pockets; a pack that loads from the front rather than from the top saves digging to the bottom to grope for buried, crumpled items. A good pack will cost you $110-150, with internal-frame packs running as high as $300. Beware of cheap packs; their straps are likely to fray under the strain of hard traveling or eat through your shoulders until the bone is exposed.

No matter what kind of luggage you choose, a small daypack is indispensable for carrying lunch, a camera, some valuables, *Let's Go: Britain and Ireland,* and other masterpieces of world literature. Some of the swankier backpacks come with a zip-off daypack. Guard your money, passport, and other valuables in a purse, pouch, or money belt that you keep with you at all times; a necklace money pouch that goes under your shirt is the best solution. Label every article of baggage both inside and outside with your name and address. For added security, you might want to purchase a combination lock for your main bag.

Warm clothing (wool is best), a windbreaker, and a waterproof poncho are essential. If you plan to do any camping, pay a little more for a lightweight poncho that unbuttons to form a groundcloth. Make sure the poncho will cover both you and your pack. Bicyclists should devote money and energy towards finding a *truly* waterproof jacket or poncho. Ordinary "rainproof" materials will not suffice in the eternal drizzle of the British Isles. Gore-Tex, or one of the other specialized materials, will make your life infinitely more comfortable. (A good rain poncho usually runs about $16-30.)

Footwear is perhaps the most crucial item on any packing list. Don't try to cut costs here. In the city or the country, walking shoes are preferable to running shoes or sandals. A number of hiking shoes that cost less than $50 will dry overnight. In any case, sturdy rubber-soled shoes are recommended. Always break in your boots before you go; stiff boots and tender feet are a painful combination. A double pair of socks—light, absorbent cotton inside, and rag wool outside—will cushion your feet and keep them dry.

One or two pockets of your luggage should be devoted to such sundry items as:

pocket knife
needle and thread
cord and/or clothesline
waterproof matches
clothes pins
rubber bands
earplugs
travel alarm clock
whistle
flashlight
plastic bags (for damp clothes)
padlock
soap
plastic water bottle
bath towel
insect repellent (particularly in Scotland)
safety pins
compass

Add a single-sheet sleeping sack: they're useful and required for many hostels. You'll have a hard time washing out your gamey clothes without a drainage plug, sometimes lacking in hotel basins (a well-placed rubber squash ball can also serve this purpose).

Finally, those North Americans who are unable to live without a beloved electrical appliance (including contact lens disinfection systems) will need an adapter and a converter. The voltage in most of Europe is 220 volts AC, which is enough to thoroughly fry any North American appliance (110 volts AC). Converters and adapters are available worldwide in department and hardware stores. (Because of the incompatability of a complex system of cycles, some appliances cannot be adapted to European voltage.) **Franzus Company** sells electrical convertors and adaptors (adaptor $3.50, 1600-watt convertor kit $27.50). Write to them at Murtha Industrial Park, P.O. Box 142, Railroad Ave., Beacon Falls, CT 06403 (tel. (203) 723-6664, fax (203) 723-6666); ask for their free pamphlet *Foreign Electricity is No Dark Secret.*

Special Concerns

Student and Youth Travelers

Student and/or youth status often facilities budget traveling; you will find that many expenditures, particularly transportation and sights admissions, can be substantially reduced if you flash your student ID. There are two main forms of student and youth identification that are accepted worldwide. The **International Student Identity Card (ISIC),** the most widely recognized proof of student status throughout the world, offers access to discounts on bus, train, ferry, and airfares, museum admission, theater tickets, and even accommodations. Present the card wherever you go; ask about discounts even when none are advertised. The annual *International Student Travel Guide,* distributed to card purchasers, lists some of the bargains available. It is available through CIEE and in Council Travel offices nationwide; pick it up when you apply for the ISIC, or write for a copy. If purchased in the U.S., the card also provides basic accident and health insurance. You must provide current, unambiguous proof of degree-seeking student status (e.g. a letter on school stationery signed and sealed by the registrar, photocopied transcript, grade report or bursar's receipt); a 1½×2-in. photo with your name printed on the back; date of birth (applicants must be 12 or over); name and address of beneficiary (for insurance purposes); and, in the U.S., a fee of $14.00. The 1992 card is valid from September 1991 to December 1992.

The **Federation of International Youth Travel Organizations (FIYTO)** card gives anyone under 26 discounts on North Sea Ferries, at the Vienna Group of Hotels in London, for USIT services to and from Ireland, and with many other member organizations. The card costs $14; you must provide your passport number, proof of your age (a photocopy of your birth certificate or a valid driver's license will suffice), and a 1½×2-inch photograph with your name printed on the back.

Both of these cards can be extremely useful, especially for the insurance packages that accompany them, but organizations overseas will often give you discounts if you show them your standard university ID card. Without a student card, your chances of obtaining discounts are somewhat reduced; passports are the best means of verifying your age. For more information contact CIEE in New York (see below), or write to FIYTO at: Islands Bryyge 81, DK-2300, Copenhagen S, Denmark (tel. (31) 546 080). The following is a short list of budget travel organizations that sell the ISIC and FIYTO cards and offer other services to student and youth travelers:

Council on International Educational Exchange (CIEE), 205 E. 42nd St., New York, NY 10017 (tel. (212) 661-1414). Information on academic, work, voluntary service, and professional opportunities abroad. Administers ISIC, FIYTO, and ITIC cards. Write for the free *Student Travel Catalog, updated annually, and other publications.* **Council Travel** and **Council Charter** are two budget subsidiaries of CIEE. **Council Travel** sells Eurail and individual country passes, guidebooks, travel gear, discounted flights, ISIC, FIYTO, ITIC cards, and IYHF memberships. Publishes *Council Travel's Budget Traveller* newsletter. Offices include 205 E. 42nd St., New York, NY 10017 (tel. (212) 661-1450); 729 Boylston St., Boston, MA 02116 (tel. (617) 266-1926); 1093 Broxton Ave., Los Angeles, CA 90024 (tel. (213) 208-3551); 1153 N. Dearborn St., Chicago, IL 60610 (tel. (312) 951-0585); 919 Irving St., San Francisco, CA 94122 (tel. (415) 566-9222); and 2000 Guadelupe St., Austin, TX 78705 (tel. 512) 472-4931); also in London at 28A Poland St., London W1V 3DB.

Education Travel Center (ETC), 438 North Frances St., Madison, WI 53703 (tel. (608) 256-5551). Flight information, IYHF/AYH cards, Eurail and British Rail passes. Write for their free pamphlet *Taking Off.*

International Student Exchange Flights (ISE), 5010 East Shea Blvd., #A104, Scottsdale, AZ 85254 (tel. (602) 951-1177). Budget student flights, IYHF/ISIC cards, coach and Eurail passes, traveler's checks, and travel guides, including the *Let's Go* series.

International Student Travel Confederation (ISTC), Gothersgade 30, 1123 Copenhagen K, Denmark (tel. (45) 3393 9303). Affiliates: in USA, CIEE (address above); in Canada, Travel CUTS (address below); in Britain, London Student Travel, 52 Grosvenor Gardens, London WC1 (tel. (071) 730 3402); in Ireland, USIT Ltd., Aston Quay, O'Connell Bridge, Dublin

2 (tel. (01) 778 117, fax (01) 778 843); in Australia, SSA/STA SWAP Program, P.O. Box 399, 220 Faraday St., Carlton South, Melbourne, Victoria 3053 (tel. (03) 348 1777); in New Zealand, Student Travel, 10 High ST., Auckland New Zealand (tel. (09) 309 9995).

Let's Go Travel Services, Harvard Student Agencies, Inc., Thayer Hall-B, Harvard University, Cambridge, MA 02138 (tel. (617) 495-9649). Sells Eurail and British Rail passes, AYH memberships (valid at all IYHF youth hostels), ISIC/ITIC/FIYTO cards, travel guides and maps (including the *Let's Go* series), discount airfares and a complete line of budget travel gear. All items are available by mail. Call or write for a catalogue.

STA Travel, over 100 offices worldwide. In the U.S., 17 East 45th St., New York, NY 10017 (tel. (800) 777-0112 or (212) 986-9470). In Britain, 74 and 86 Old Brompton Rd., London SW7 3LQ (tel. (071) 937 9921 for European travel; 937 9971 for North American; 937 9962 for the rest of the world). Offers bargain flights, accommodations, tours, Eurailpasses, insurance and ISIC cards to those under 26 and full-time students under 32.

Travel CUTS, (Canadian Universities Travel Service), 187 College St., Toronto, Ont. M5T 1P7 (tel. (416) 979-2406). In Britain, 295-A Regent St., London W1R 7YA (tel. (071) 255 1944). Other offices throughout Canada. Issues the ISIC, IYHF, and FIYTO cards to Canadian citizens. Discount transatlantic flights from Canadian cities. Runs the Canadian Student *Work Abroad* Programme. Prints a free newspaper, *The Canadian Student Traveler,* available at their offices and at campuses across Canada.

Senior Travelers

The following is a list of places and publications where senior citizens can obtain information about the discounts and special services available to them. Check with the British Tourist Authority and the Irish Tourist Board if you have questions. Your local travel agent might also have some helpful tips.

American Association of Retired Persons (AARP) Travel Service, P.O. Box 92964, Los Angeles, CA 90009 (tel. (800) 227-7737, membership information (800) 441-7575); or AARP, Special Services Department, 1909 K St. NW, Washington, DC 20049 (tel. (202) 662-4850). Plans and operates holidays, tours, and cruises for AARP members. Offers its members a tremendous range of services and discounts, including car and RV rentals, lodging, air travel, and sightseeing. Any person over 50 and their spouse can join for a $5 annual membership fee.

Superintendent of Documents, U.S. Government Printing Office, Washington, DC 20402 (tel. (202) 783-3238). Send for their free *Travel Tips for Senior Citizens,* which provides information on passports, visas, health, and currency, or for *Travel Tips for Older Americans,* which costs $1. Allow 4 wks. for delivery.

Elderhostel, 75 Federal St., 3rd Floor, Boston, MA 02110 (tel. (617) 426-7788). Participants spend a week studying subjects ranging from beekeeping to music appreciation. Weekly fee of $245-270 covers room, board, tuition, and extracurricular activities. You must be 60 or over to enroll, but you may bring a spouse or companion who is over 50. Scholarships are available. Also publishes a newsletter, *Between Classes.* Write for a free catalog.

John Muir Publications, P.O. Box 613, Santa Fe, NM 87504 (tel. (800) 888-7504). Distributes Mildred Hyman's *Elderhostels: The Student's Choice,* a guide to the 100 most popular hostels (2nd edition, $15.95).

Gateway Books, 13 Bedford Cove, San Rafael, CA 94901 (tel. (415) 454-5215) Offers *Get Up & Go: A Guide for the Mature Traveler* ($10.95, postage $1.75) by Gene and Adele Malott. General hints for seniors.

National Council of Senior Citizens, 1331 F St. NW, Washington, DC 20004 (tel. (202) 347-8800). For $12 per individual ($16 per couple) a year or $150 for a lifetime anyone can receive hotel and auto rental discounts, a senior citizen newspaper, and use of a discount travel agency, in addition to supplementary medical insurance for people over 65.

Pilot Books, 103 Cooper St., Babylon, NY 11702 (tel. (516) 422-2225). Distributes *The International Health Guide for Senior Travelers* and the *Senior Citizen's Guide to Budget Travel in Europe* ($4.95 each).

Gay and Lesbian Travelers

Attitudes towards gay and lesbian people in Britain and Ireland are comparatively liberal. Be aware that people in rural areas may not be as tolerant as those in big cities. In all of Britain, sex by consent between women is legal, as is sex by consent and in private between men aged 21 and over. The attitude of the police varies from resignedly tolerant to aggressively hostile. In Ireland, homosexual intercourse is technically illegal, but the government tolerates the gay and lesbian community. Listed below are several resources intended specifically for the gay or lesbian traveler.

Gay's the Word, 66 Marchmont St., London WCIN 1AB (tel. (071) 278 7654). Widest stock of gay and lesbian literature in England. Publishes guides for gay and lesbian travelers. Mail order service available. Open Mon.-Fri. 11am-7pm, Sat. 10am-6pm, Sun. and holidays 2-6pm.

Ferrari Publications, P.O. Box 37887, Phoenix, AZ 85069 (tel. (602) 863-2408). Write or call for *Places of Interest* ($12.50), *Places for Men* ($12.50), *Places of Interest to Women* ($10), or *Inn Places: USA and Worldwide Gay Accommodations* ($14.95). All publications also available from Giovanni's Room (see below).

Giovanni's Room, 345 S. 12th St., Philadelphia, PA 19107 (tel. (800) 222-6996). The best source for gay and lesbian travel books; also distributes feminist literature. $3.50 postage/book. The following publications are available at Giovanni's Room or the address listed:

Gaia's Guide, $12.50. Annually revised "international guide for traveling women" that lists local lesbian, feminist, and gay information numbers, publications, bookstores, cultural centers and resources, restaurants, accommodations. Also available at **9-11 Kensington High St.,** London W8, and **Open Leaves,** 71 Cardigan St., Carlton, Victoria 3053, Australia.

Spartacus International Gay Guide, $27.95. Lists bars, restaurants, hotels, bookstores, and hotlines throughout the world. Very specifically for men. Also available from **Bruno Gmünder Publishing,** 100 E. Biddle St., Baltimore, MD 21202 (tel. (301) 727 5677, fax (301) 727-5998) and from **Renaissance House,** P.O. Box 292, Village Station, New York, NY 10014-0292 (tel. (212) 674-0120).

Disabled Travelers

Transportation companies in Britain and Ireland are remarkably conscientious about providing facilities and services to meet the special needs of disabled travelers. Bus and coach companies and British Rail are very helpful to their special-needs passengers. Advance booking is strongly recommemded; if you notify the bus or coach company of your plans ahead of time, and they will have staff ready to assist you. British Rail (for address, see Once There: Getting Around, below) offers a railcard for disabled travelers (£12, valid for 1 year) that provides 1/3 off on most tickets, ½ off on day returns. If you do not have a railcard and are traveling in your own wheelchair or are blind and traveling with a companion you are eligible for the same discounts. If you let British Rail know ahead of time, they will assure a convenient spot for your wheelchair. Guide dogs accompanying blind people are always conveyed free of charge. Not all stations are accessible; write for the pamphlet, "British Rail and Disabled Travellers," which explains what services are available. National Express (coach travel) offers a similar discount. Both countries both impose a six-month quarantine on all animals entering the country, including seeing-eye dogs, and they require that the owner obtain an import license (consult your nearest British or Irish Consulate for details). You can write to the British Tourist Authority or the Irish Tourist Board for free handbooks and access guides. Other helpful sources of information are:

Access to the World: A travel guide for the disabled, by Louise Weiss ($16.95). Provides information on tours and organizations. Available from Facts on File, Inc., 460 Park Ave. S., New York, NY 10016 (tel. (212) 683-2244).

American Foundation for the Blind, 15 West 16th St., New York, NY 10011 (tel. (800) 232-5463 or (212) 620-2159). $6 ID cards, discount information, products and publications for the legally blind. Write for an application.

Directions Unlimited, 720 N. Bedford Rd., Bedford Hills, NY 10507 (tel. (800) 533-5343 or (914) 241-1700). Individual vacations as well as group tours and cruises for disabled travelers.

Evergreen Travel Service, 4114 198th Ave. SW, Suite #13, Lynnwood, WA 98036-6742 (tel. (800) 435-2288 or (206) 776-1184). Its "Wings on Wheels" tours provide charter buses with on-board, wheelchair accessible facilities. Other services include White Cane Tours for the Blind (1 guide for 3 travelers), tours for the deaf, and tours for "slow walkers."

Federation for the Handicapped, 211 14th St., New York, NY 10011 (tel. (212) 727-4268). Leads tours for physically disabled members; daytrips and longer excursions.

Flying Wheels Travel, 143 West Bridge St., P.O. Box 382, Owatonna, MN 55060 (tel. (800) 535-6790 or (507) 451-5005, fax (507) 451-1685). Arranges domestic and international trips and cruises for groups and individuals.

The Guided Tour, Inc., 613 West Cheltenham Ave., Suite 200, Melrose Park, PA 19126-2414 (tel. (215) 782-1370, fax (215) 635-2637). Year-round travel programs for developmentally handicapped and learning disabled adults; call or write for free brochure.

Pauline Hephaistos Survey Projects Group, 39 Bradley Gardens, West Ealing, London W13 8HE (tel. (081) 997 70 55). Distributes access guides to London (£4) detailing ease of access to accommodations and points of interest.

Mobility International, P.O. Box 3551, Eugene, OR 97403 (tel. (503) 343-1284; voice and TDD). International headquarters in Britain, Columbo St., London 5E1 8DP, England. Contacts in 25 countries and provides information on travel programs, study abroad, community service, access guides, and organized tours. Membership $20 per year. Publishes *A World of Options for the 1990s: A Guide to International Educational Exchange, Community Service, and Travel for Persons With Disabilities* (members $14, nonmembers $16). Referral network.

Moss Rehabilitation Hospital Travel Information Service, 1200 W. Tabor Rd., Philadelphia, PA 19141 (tel. (215) 456-9600). Information on international travel accessibililty: send nominal fee for packet of information on tourist sights, accommodations, and transportation.

Royal Association for Disability and Rehabilitation (RADAR), 25 Mortimer St., London W1N 8AB (tel. (071) 637 5400). Information on various aspects of traveling in Britain; publishes the annual handbook *Holidays in the British Isles—A Guide for Disabled People* (£4 postpaid).

Society for the Advancement of Travel for the Handicapped, 347 Fifth Ave., Suite 610, New York, NY 10016 (tel. (212) 447-SATH (447-7284), fax (212) 725-8253). Publishes quarterly travel newsletter *SATH News* and information booklets (free for members, $2 for nonmembers). Advice on trip planning for the disabled. Annual membership is $45, students and seniors $25.

Twin Peaks Press, P.O. Box 129, Vancouver, WA 98666 (tel. (800) 637-2256 or (206) 694-2462). Operates a worldwide traveling nurse network and publishes 3 books: *Directory of Travel Agencies for the Disabled* ($19.95); *Travel for the Disabled* (14.95); and *Wheelchair Vagabond* ($9.95). Postage $2 on all books. Travel hints and information on accommodations and literature geared to disabled travelers.

Whole Persons Tours, P.O. Box 1084, Bayonne, NJ 07002-1084 (tel. (201) 858-3400). Organizes international tours and publishes *The Itinerary,* a magazine for disabled travelers. Subscription one year (6 issues) $10.

Women Travelers

Women traveling in Britain and Ireland should exercise caution, particularly when traveling alone. Try to keep in shouting range of large mixed groups and/or police officers. If you feel particularly uncomfortable, you may want to carry mace; wearing a wedding ring or walking arm in arm with another woman are less violent ways of discouraging potential suitors. As well, try to dress in a subdued manner; though many people understand the distinction between dressing for comfort and dressing to be sexy, the subtlety is apparently lost on many others. For more safety tips, look to Maggie and Gemma Ross's *Handbook for Women Travellers* (£4.95) from Piatkus Books, 5 Windmill St., London W1P IHF (tel. (071) 631 0710).

Travelers With Children

Those traveling with young children might benefit from the following books: *Sharing Nature With Children* ($6.95) and *Backpacking With Babies and Small Children* ($8.95), both published by Wilderness Press, 2440 Bancroft Way, Berkeley, CA 94704 (tel. (800) 443-7227 or (415) 843-8080). *Travel With Children*

($10.95, postage $1.50), by Maureen Wheeler, is packed with user-friendly tips and anecdotes. In the U.S., order from Lonely Planet Publications (see Useful Addresses below); elsewhere, write P.O. Box 617, Hawthorn, Victoria 3122, Australia. The *Kidding Around* series of illustrated books *for* children includes one about London that might be educational and distracting on long trips ($9.95, postage $2.75 for the first book, 50¢ thereafter). Write to John Muir Publications, P.O. Box 613, Santa Fe, NM 87504 (tel. (800) 888-7504).

Special Diets

The following organizations can offer advice on how to meet your specific dietary needs while traveling.

North American Vegetarian Society, P.O. Box 72, Dolgeville, NY 13329 (tel. (518) 568-7970). Distributes the annual *Vegetarian Travel Guide* ($15.95, postage $2) and the *Vegetarian Handbook,* published by the Vegetarian Society of the United Kingdom, Parkdale, Dunham Rd., Altrincham, Cheshire, England WA14 4QG (tel. (061) 928 0793, fax (061) 926 9182). About two-thirds of the book deals with Britain and Ireland, listing restaurants, hotels, guesthouses, etc.

Sepher-Hermon Press, 1265 46th St., Brooklyn, NY 11219 (tel. (718) 972-9010). Distributes the *Jewish Travel Guide* ($11.50), edited by Danny Koffman and published by the London *Jewish Chronicle.* Updated annually, the guide lists synagogues, kosher restaurants, and other Jewish institutions in cities and towns throughout the world. In England order from Jewish Chronicle Publications, 25 Furnival St., London EC4A 1JT.

Alcoholics Anonymous and Narcotics Anonymous also have chapters in many areas abroad; check local phone directories for locations of meetings.

Useful Addresses

Much as we at *Let's Go* would like to think that the preceding information is sufficient preparation for the traveler to the British Isles, there is probably much more that you want to know. The amount of information available to potential travelers to Britain and Ireland from the organizations listed below is astounding, a kaleidoscopic sea of enticing pamphlets and brochures. Make your inquiries as specific as possible, and assess the information they give you with a skeptical eye. Remember the job of a tourist office is to lure you to a particular region, not to objectively present its virtues and flaws.

Tourist Offices

British Tourist Authority (BTA), 40 W. 57th St., 3rd Floor, New York, NY 10019 (tel. (212) 581-4700). In Canada, 94 Cumberland St., #600, Toronto, Ont. M5R 3N3 (tel. (416) 925-6326). Other U.S. branches in Chicago and Los Angeles. In Sydney: Midland House, 4th Floor, 171 Clarence St., Sydney, New South Wales 2000 (tel. (02) 298 627). Also in Wellington, New Zealand. Publishes helpful accommodations guides, including *Stay on a Farm, Stay With a British Family,* and detailed hotel, guesthouse, and B&B guides. Other useful publications include *Young Britain, Walking in Britain,* and the ever-popular *Call at a Pub.* The **British Travel Bookshop,** on the 3rd floor of the New York office, will send you their mail-order catalogue upon request.

Irish Tourist Board (Bord Fáilte), 757 Third Ave., 19th floor, New York, NY 10017 (tel. (800) 223-6470 or (212) 418-0800, fax (212) 371-9052); in Canada, 160 Bloor St. East, Suite 934, Toronto, Ont. M4W 1B9 (tel. (416) 929-2777, fax (416) 929-6783); in Britain, 150 New Bond St., London W1Y 0AQ (tel. (071) 493 3201); in Australia, Level 5, 36 Carrington Street, Sydney NSW 2000 (tel. (02) 299 6177, fax (02) 299 6323). Ask for general information on Ireland, including the four-color *Ireland* brochure, the *Hotels and Guesthouses* annual guide, and pamphlets on a variety of pastimes, including *Walking in Ireland, Cycling in Ireland,* and *Angling in Ireland.*

Northern Ireland Tourist Board, 276 Fifth Ave., Suite 500, New York, NY 10001-4509 (tel. (212) 686-6250). Head Office: 48 High St., River House, Belfast BT1 2DS Northern Ireland (tel. (0232) 231 221 or 246 609, fax (0232) 240 960); in Britain, 11 Berkeley St., London W1X

5AD (tel. (071) 493 0601, fax (071) 499 3731). Also in Dublin and Frankfurt. You can also contact any BTA for Northern Ireland info.

Consulates and High Commissions

British Consulates: In **U.S.,** British Embassy, 3100 Massachusetts Ave., Washington, DC 20008 (tel. (202) 462-1340); 845 Third Ave., New York, NY 10022 (tel. (212) 745-0200); Marquis One Tower, #2700, 245 Peachtree Center Ave., Atlanta, Georgia 30303 (tel. (404) 524-5856); 33 North Dearborn St., Chicago, IL 60602 (tel. (312) 346-1810); 1100 Milam Building, Suite 2260, 1100 Milam Rd., Houston, TX 77002 (tel. (713) 659-6270); and 3701 Wilshire Blvd., Los Angeles, CA 90010 (tel. (213) 385-7381). In **Canada,** British High Commission, 80 Elgin St., Ottawa, Ont. KIP 5K7 (tel. (613) 237-1530). In **Australia,** British High Commission, Commonwealth Ave., Canberra, ACT 2600 (tel. outside ACT 706 666; inside ACT 270 666). In **New Zealand,** British High Commission, Reserve Bank of New Zealand Building, 9th Floor, 2 The Terrace, Wellington 1 (tel. 726 049).

Irish Consulates: In U.S., Irsih Embassy, 2234 Massachusetts Ave. NW, Washington, DC 20008 (tel. (202) 462-3939); 515 Madison Ave., New York, NY 10022 (tel. (212) 319-2555); Wrigley Building, 400 N. Michigan Ave., Chicago, IL 60611 (tel. (312) 337-1868); 655 Montgomery St., #930, San Francisco, CA 94111 (tel. (415) 392-4214); 535 Boylston St., Boston, MA 02116 (tel. (617) 267-9330). In **Canada,** contact the Embassy at 170 Metcalfe St., Ottawa, Ont. K2P 1P3 (tel. (613) 233-6281); in **Australia** and **New Zealand,** write to the Embassy at 20 Arkana St., Yarralumla, Canberra City, A.C.T. 2600 (tel. 273 3022, fax 273 3741).

Hostel Associations

Main Office: International Youth Hostel Federation (IYHF), 9 Guessens Rd., Welwyn Garden City, Herts, England AL8 6QW (tel. (0707) 332 487). Contact for IYHF cards, information on budget travel, and summer positions as group leaders. Distributes the *International Youth Hostel Handbook,* Volume I and II ($10.95).

U.S.: American Youth Hostels (AYH), P.O. Box 37613, Washington, DC 20013-7613 (tel. (202) 783-6161); 425 Divisadero St., Suite 300, San Franscisco, CA 94117 (tel. (415) 863-9939). IYHF and ISIC cards, hostel handbooks, student and charter flights, travel equipment, and literature on budget travel. Membership for 1 year: 17 and under/55 and over $10, 18-54 $25, families $35.

Canada: Canadian Hostelling Association (CHA), National Office, 1600 James Naismith Dr., #608, Gloucester, Ontario, Canada K1B 5N4 (tel. (613) 748-5638). IYHF cards and hostel handboooks.

Australia: Australian Youth Hostels Association (AYHA), Level 3, 10 Mallett St., Camperdown, New South Wales 2050 Australia (tel. (02) 565 1699)

New Zealand: Youth Hostels Association of New Zealand, P.O. Box 436, Christchurch 1 (tel. (03) 799 970, fax (03) 654 476).

England and Wales: Youth Hostels Association of England and Wales (YHA), Trevalyn House, 8 St. Stephen's Hill, St. Albans, Hertfordshire AL1 2DY (tel. (0727) 552 15, fax (0727) 441 26).

Scotland: Scottish Youth Hostels Association, 7 Glebe Crescent, Stirling FK8 2JA (tel. (0786) 511 81), fax (0786) 501 98).

Northern Ireland: Youth Hostel Association, 56 Bradbury Place, Belfast BT7 1RU (tel. (0232) 324 733, fax (0232) 439 699).

Ireland: An Óige, 39 Mountjoy Sq., Dublin 1 (tel. (01) 363 111, fax (01) 365 807).

Books

Ford's Travel Guides, 19448 Londelius St., Northridge, CA 91324 (tel. (818) 701-7414). Hawks *Ford's Freighter Travel Guide & Waterways of the World* ($8.95, $15 for a semi-annual subscription), a listing of freighter companies that will take passengers for trans-Atlantic crossings.

Forsyth Travel Library, 9154 W. 57th St., P.O. Box 2975, Shawnee Mission, KS 66201 (tel. (800) FOR-SYTH (367-7984) or (913) 384-3440). Well-stocked mail-order service with a wide range of European city, area, and country maps, as well as rail and boat travel guides. Sells the *Thomas Cook's European Timetable* ($23.95, postage $4), and Thomas Cook's *Rail Map of Europe* ($9.95).

Hippocrene Books, Inc., 171 Madison Ave., New York NY 10016 (tel. (212) 685-4371; orders (718) 454-2360, fax (718) 454-1391). Publishes travel reference books, travel guides, maps and foreign language dictionaries.

Lonely Planet Publications, 112 Linden St., Oakland, CA 94607 (tel. (800) 229-0122 or (415) 893-8555). An exhaustive selection of travel guides and informative books; offers a free quarterly newsletter full of advice and anecdotes.

Michelin Maps and Guides, Davy House, Lyon Rd., Harrow, Middlesex, England, HA1 2DQ (tel. (18) 612 121). Guides for most regions of Western Europe. Available in most bookstores; in the U.S., write or call Michelin Maps and Guides, P.O. Box 3305, Spartanburg, SC 29304 (tel. (803) 599-0850).

Superintendent of Documents, U.S. Government Printing Office, Washington, DC 20402 (tel. (202) 783-3238, fax (202) 275-0019 for orders, (202) 275-2529 for publications). Publishes *Your Trip Abroad* ($1) and *Safe Trip Abroad* ($1), as well as more specific documents.

Travelling Books, P.O. Box 77114, Seattle, WA 98117 (tel. (206) 367-5848). Sells travel books, language aids and accessories for the independent traveler; offers general tips and helpful information. Mail order only. Write for their free catalogue.

Alternatives to Tourism

Work

There is no better way to immerse yourself in a foreign culture than to become part of its economy. You may not earn as much as you would at home, but you should generally be able to cover your living expenses, if not airfare. A range of short-term opportunities are available, from temporary positions like typist or bartender to skilled positions in training programs.

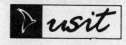

Unfortunately, if you are not a citizen of a Common Market or a British Commonwealth nation, you will have difficulty finding a paying job that you are legally entitled to take. Visitors between the ages of 17 and 27 who are citizens of British Commonwealth nations (including Canada, Australia, and New Zealand) may work in Britain during their visit without work permits if the employment they take is "incidental to their holiday." Other Commonwealth citizens with a parent or grandparent born in the United Kingdom may apply for a patriality certificate, which entitles them to live and work in Britain without any other formalities. If you do not fit into any of these categories, you must apply for a work permit to be considered for paid employment in Britain; contact your British Consulate (or High Commission, in Commonwealth countries) for details before you go, and the Department of Employment when you arrive. Regulations in Ireland are even stricter; contact the Irish Consulate before your departure. In both cases you would be allowed to accept paid employment only if no native-born person was found to be suitable; needless to say, the chances are somewhat slim.

Permits

In cooperation with the British government and the British Universities North America Club (BUNAC), CIEE (see Student and Youth Travelers above), under the **Student Exchange Employment Program (SEEP),** can issue American students a work permit (a "Blue Card") valid for six months in Britain. To qualify, you must be at least 18 years old, a full-time matriculated student at an American university or college, and a U.S. citizen. Students may participate in the program a seconf time provided that their total aggregate stay (not just work time) in the U.K. does not exceed six months. CIEE's similar program for Ireland (student permit valid for only 4 months; permanent residents of the U.S. are also eligible), administered in conjunction with USIT, the Irish student travel association, allows you to work tax-free. The charge for participating in the Work Abroad Program in $125; the actual work permit is free.

Canadian students between 18 and 25 should investigate the Student Work Abroad Program of Travel CUTS (see Student and Youth Travelers above). *Au pair* jobs, temporary volunteer positions, and jobs at work camps and farm camps do not require a work permit, although you will need an entrance card or letter of invitation from the organization concerned. This letter does not permit you to undertake any other kind of paid employment during your stay.

Finding A Job

Students should start their job hunt at their local university's work-abroad resource center. These organizations will supply further information:

CIEE (see Student and Youth Travelers above). Publishes *Work, Study, Travel Abroad: The Whole World Handbook* ($12.95, postage $1; available from CIEE and at many bookstores). For individual job listings, consult *Summer Jobs in Britain* ($13.95, postage $1). *The Teenager's Guide to Study, Travel, and Adventure Abroad* ($11.95, postage $1) describes over 150 travel and study programs abroad. *The Student Travel Catalog* (free from CIEE or any Council Travel office nationwide) contains a "Work Abroad" permit application.

Central Bureau for Educational Visits and Exchanges, Seymour Mews House, Seymour Mews, London W1H 9PE (tel. (071) 486 5101, fax (071) 935-5741). Offers information and advice to job-seekers in Britain; publishes *Working Holidays* (£15.85 worldwide postage), *Study Holidays* (£10.75), and *Volunteer Work* (£7.25), as well as a range of guides for European countries (£6.20).

Peterson's Guides, 202 Carnegie Center, P.O. Box 2123, Princeton, NJ 08543-2123 (tel. (800) EDU-DATA (338-3282)). Distributes the same books as **Vacation Work Publications,** 9 Park End St., Oxford OX1 1HJ (tel. (0865) 241 978, fax (0865) 790 885). *1991 Directory of Summer Jobs in Britain* ($16.95) lists 30,000 jobs in Scotland, Wales, and England, including openings for office help, farm laborers, chambermaids, and lorry drivers. *Work Your Way Around the World* is a useful compendium of information and tips ($18.95), and *The 1991 Directory of Summer Jobs Abroad* ($16.95) is a valuable resource.

World Trade Academy Press, 50 East 42nd St., New York, NY 10017 (tel. (212) 697-4999). Publishes the *Directory of American Firms Operating in Foreign Countries* (3 vol., $195); also offers directories of specific countries ($10-15/country).

Other Work Programs

American Youth Hostels (AYH) (see Useful Addresses above) hires tour group leaders for trips abroad. You must be 21 years of age and undergo a nine-day training course to partake of this adventure. You must lead a group in the U.S. before going abroad; leaders receive expenses and a small stipend. **The Experiment in International Living** offers similar employment opportunities, but their requirements are stiffer; you must be 24 and have established leadership abilities, language fluency, and in-depth overseas experience in the country in question. Group leaders have all their expenses paid and receive a $200 honorarium. Contact the organization at P.O. Box 676, Kipling Rd., Brattleboro, VT 05302 (tel. (802) 257-7751 or (800) 451-4465).

The **International Association for the Exchange of Students for Technical Experience (IAESTE),** under the auspices of the Association of International Practical Training, provides assistance to technical students who have secured internships with employers in Britain and Ireland (and other countries overseas). For a $75 fee, IAESTE will sponsor incoming students and offer assistance in many areas of potential confusion, such as insurance and housing. Write to them at 10400 Little Patuxent Parkay, Suite 250, Columbia, MD 21044-3510 (tel. (301) 997-3069).

Au pair positions are officially reserved for unmarried female nationals of Western European countries whose primary aim is to improve their English. However, it is sometimes possible for native English speakers to get these jobs. In Britain, *au pair* agencies are not allowed to charge a fee for finding you a post. The **Federation of Recruitment and Employment Services,** 36-38 Mortimer St., London W1N 7RB, is a trade association for private employment agencies and can offer advice to prospective *au pairs;* write to them and enclose an International Reply Coupon for receipt. You can also check the help-wanted columns of the *International Herald Tribune* for possible positions. You will be expected to help your host family care for children and do light housework for about five hours per day (1 day off per week); in return you will receive room, board, and a small monthly stipend. Always determine the details of pay and obligation *before* settling in with your family. The permitted length of stay in Britain and Ireland as an *au pair* is 2 years.

Volunteering

Opportunities may range from working on an archaeological dig to arranging a community play group for children. You can join a local community volunteer group—look in the local telephone directory under Voluntary Work Information Services, Volunteer Bureau, or Citizens Advice Bureau.

The 2000 **Work Camps** across Europe, established after World War I as a means of promoting peace and understanding, involve two to four weeks of labor. Projects generally involve one of the following types of work: social, construction/renovation, environmental/nature conservation, archaeology, or work with children, the disabled, or the elderly. You should expect to pay a registration fee (ranging from $25-$70), arrange your own travel, and sometimes contribute to your food and accommodation costs. Generally, no special skills are necessary. For information, write **Voluntary Service International,** Rte. 2, P.O. Box 506, Innisfree Village, Crozet, VA 22932 (tel. (804) 823-1826), or CIEE (see Student and Youth Travelers above). **International Farm Camps,** Hall Rd., Tiptree, Colchester, Essex C05 OQ5 (tel. (0621) 815 496), provides summer work camp opportunities for 18-25 year old students specifically in England. For information on work at archaeological digs, write to the **Council for British Archaeology,** 112 Kennington Rd., London SE11 6RE (tel. (071) 582 0494, fax (071) 587 5152). They publish *British Archaeological News* (send self-addressed envelope for details). In addition, **The Archaeological Institute of America,** 675 Commonwealth Ave., Boston, MA 02215 (tel. (617) 353-9361), publishes the *Archaeological Fieldwork Opportunities Bulletin,* listing 210 field sites throughout the world. **Volunteers for Peace** publishes a directory of 800 work camps in over 34 countries ($10). For more information and their free newsletter, write to 43 Tiffany Rd., Belmont, VT 05730 (tel. (802) 259-2759). Finally, the student traveler's friend **CIEE** will send you their *Volunteer! The Comprehensive Guide to Voluntary Service in The U.S. and Abroad* ($8.95, postage $1), and Vacation Work Publications (see Student and Youth Travelers above) also offers the *International Directory of Voluntary Work* (£6.95).

Study

It's not difficult to spend a summer, a term, or a year studying in Britain or Ireland under the auspices of a well-established program. Enrolling as a full-time student, however, is somewhat more difficult; the requirements for admission can be hard to meet unless you attended a British secondary school, and often only a limited number of foreign students are accepted each year. For initial information on studying in Britain, contact the British Council office in your home country. You could also turn to CIEE's publications *Work, Study, Travel Aboard: The Whole World Handbook* (see Work above) or *The Teenager's Guide to Study, Travel, And Adventure* ($9.95, postage $1), which lists 150 programs abroad that teenagers can take advantage of. As well, ACU (see list below) publishes the invaluable resource *Higher Education in the United Kingdom 1991-92: A Handbook for Students and their Advisers* ($32.95), available in most college libraries or from Oryx Press, 4041 N. Central Ave., #700, Phoenix, AZ 85012 (tel. (800) 279-6796 or (602) 265-2651). The following organizations and programs can also deluge you with information:

American Institute for Foreign Study (AIFS), 102 Greenwich Ave., Greenwich, CT 06830 (tel. (800) 727-2437 or (203) 869-9090; Boston office (617) 421-9575). Helps arrange study programs, transportation, room and board for both term-time and summer courses in Britain and Ireland. Participants must make arrangements for credit at their home institutions. Rolling admissions. Academic programs generally for high school graduates.

Association of Commonwealth Universities (ACU), John Foster House, 36 Gordon Sq., London WC1H 0PF (tel. (071) 387 8572, fax (071) 387 2655). 365 member institutions in 30 countries. Administers Marshall Scholarships for study anywhere in the U.K. Also an information center with 15,000-vol. reference library and publishing house; publishes *British Universities' Guide to Graduate Study* (£29) and *Commonwealth Universities Handbook* ($199), also available from Stockton Press, 15 East 26th St., New York, NY 10010.

Beaver College Center for Education Abroad, Glenside, PA 19038-3295 (tel. (800) 767-0029 or (215) 572-2901, fax (215) 572-2174). Operates semester- or year-long programs at 7 universities in Ireland and 21 institutions in Britain (including the London School of Economics); facilitates transfer credit for American students. Applicants must have completed 4 full semesters at an accredited university. $35 application fee.

British Information Services, 845 3rd Ave., 9th Floor, New York, NY 10022 (tel. (212) 745-0222). Gives information on study in Britain. Write for their imaginatively-named free pamphlet *Study in Britain.*

Experiment in International Living, School for International Training, College Semester Abroad Admissions Office, P.O. Box 676, Kipling Rd., Brattleboro, VT 05302 (tel. (800) 451-4465 or (802) 257-7751 ext. 2010). Offers 15-wk. programs to college sophomores, juniors and seniors. Most U.S. colleges will transfer credit from SIT. Some financial aid available; home institutions may also provide aid.

Institute of International Education (IIE), 809 United Nations Plaza, New York, NY 10017-3580 (tel. (212) 883-8200). Publishes several annual reference books on study abroad. The hefty *Academic Year Abroad* ($31.95, postage $3) and *Vacation Study Abroad* ($26.95, postage $3) detail over 3400 study programs offered by U.S. colleges and universities overseas. Also offers the less ambitious free pamphlet *Basic Facts on Study Abroad.*

Institute of Irish Studies, 6 Holyrood Park, Dublin 4, Ireland (tel. (01) 269 2491). On the campus of Trinity College Dublin; offers a 2-wk. course in both July and August that covers Irish history, literature, and archaeology.

Inter-Study Programmes, 42 Milson St., Bath BA1 1DN (tel. (0225) 464 769/464 096, fax (0225) 444 104). Organization will act as mediator between British academic your home university. They handle the details.

U.K. Council for Overseas Student Affairs, 60 Westbourne Grove, London W2 5SH (tel. (071) 229 9268). Advises those already enrolled in British programs on a wide range of student welfare topics.

Unipub, 4611-F Assembly Dr., Langam, MD 20706-4391 (tel. (800) 274-4888). Distributes International Agency Publications including UNESCO's *Study Abroad* ($24, $2.50 postage) and *Higher Education in the EC: A Student Handbook* ($24.95).

Universities Central Council on Admission, P.O. Box 28, Cheltenham, Glos. GL50 3SA (tel. (0242) 222 444). Provides information and handles applications for admission to all fulltime undergraduate courses in universities and their affiliated colleges in the U.K. Write to them for and application and the extremely informative *How to Apply for Admission to a University* handbook.

University College Dublin, Newman House, 86 St. Stephen's Green, Dublin 2, Ireland (tel. (01) 752 004/754 704). Offers the **Semester in Irish Studies** every fall semester for college juniors and seniors of all majors with solid academic records. Courses in Irish history, literature, politics, and folk culture. Applications are due in April. The affliated **International Summer School** also offers a 2½-week course in July on Irish tradition and contemporary culture for students 18 years and older. (Write for information at same address.)

University College Galway Summer School, Galway, Ireland (tel. (091) 244 11, fax (091) 257 00). Offers several 4-5-wk. courses in June-August on a variety of subjects, including Gaelic.

University of Dublin, Trinity College, Dublin 2, Ireland (tel. (01) 772 941, fax (01) 772 694). Offers a 1-yr. program for students who have completed one year of college study. rite to the Admissions Office, West Theatre.

Getting There

From North America

Flexibility is the best strategy. Regularly scheduled direct flights are often out of the budget traveler's range. If possible, leave from a travel hub; certain cities—such as New York, Atlanta, Dallas, Chicago, Los Angeles, San Francisco, Seattle, Montreal, Toronto, and Vancouver—are more competitive for flights than others. Off-season travelers will enjoy lower fares and face much less competition for inexpensive seats, but you don't have to travel in the dead of winter to save. Peak season rates begin on either May 15 or June 1 and run until about September 15. If you arrange travel dates carefully, you can travel in the summer and still save with shoulder-season or even low-season fares.

Shop around for a knowledgeable travel agent to guide you through the labyrinth of travel options. Unfortunately, some travel agents won't be eager to help you find the cheapest option, since commissions are smaller on budget flights. Fare brokers advertise incredibly cheap but erratic fares in the Sunday travel sections of the *New York Times* and other major newpapers. Student travel organizations such as CIEE or Travel CUTS (see Student and Youth Travelers above) offer special deals for students not available to regular travel agents.

Charter flights are the most consistently economical option. You can book charters up until the last minute, but most flights during the summer fill up months in advance. Later in the season, companies have trouble filling their planes and either cancel flights or offer special fares. In some cases, you will not be allowed to book charters until a month before your flight. Charters are more of a bargain during high than off season, when APEX fares (see below) on commercial carriers are comparable. Fares advertised in newspapers are usually the lowest possible; *always* read the fine print and ask lots of questions to be sure of the details. Charter flights

allow you to stay abroad for as long as you like and also often allow you to mix and match arrivals and departures from different cities. Once you've made your reservations with a charter company, though, you are committed to particular departure and return dates and generally threatened with harsh penalties for cancellation.

While charter flights are less expensive, you must figure in the intangible costs of overcrowding, waiting, and delays. The airport will more often than not become the first major sightseeing event of your trip. Ask a travel agent about your charter company's reliability. Charter companies reserve the right to cancel flights up to 48 hours before departure; they'll do their best to find you another flight, but your delay could take days rather than hours. To avoid eleventh-hour problems with your reservation, pick up your ticket well in advance of the departure date and get to the airport several hours before your flight is scheduled to leave.

CIEE offers flights from the U.S. to destinations all over the world through their subsidiary, **Council Charter** (205 E. 42nd St., New York, NY 10017 (tel. (800) 800-8222), which operates charters and scheduled flights to most major European cities. Tickets can be purchased at the given New York address or any Council Travel office in the U.S. These flights are extremely popular; reserve early. Other major charter companies include **DER Tours** (tel. (800) 782-2424 or (708) 635-5614), **Let's Go Travel Services** (tel. (617) 495-9649), and **TRAVAC** (tel. (800) TRAV-800 (872-8800) or (212) 563-3303). In Canada, try **Travel CUTS** (see Student and Youth Travelers above).

Even if you plan to spend most of your trip in Ireland or Scotland, flying into London is probably the most economical option. Most of the cheap transatlantic flights to Britain and Ireland arrive in London; from there you can easily find an inexpensive flight, train, coach, and/or ferry to Dublin, Edinburgh, Belfast, and other destinations (see London section for addresses of student and budget travel agencies).

Major airlines offer two options for the budget traveler. The first, offered by most airlines, is to fly **standby** (that is, without a reservation). The advantage of a standby fare is its flexibility; you can come and go as you please. However, flying standby can be very uncertain, especially during peak season. You may be able to purchase an open ticket that, depending on availability, is confirmed only on the day of departure. The number of available seats is determined moments before departure, though some airlines will issue predictions (sometimes more dire than necessary) of your chances on a given day. You will have to do most of the research yourself; travel agents can be both ill-informed and reluctant to help you. London is one of the more readily available standby destinations.

Advanced Purchase Excursion (APEX) fares provide the luxury of confirmed reservations and permit you to arrive and depart from different cities. Reservations must be made 21 days in advance with 7- to 14-day minimum and 90-day maximum excursions. **Super APEX** fares, which are even cheaper, apply only to flights between 7 and 21 days apart and booked at least 30 days in advance. For summer travel, book APEX fares early—by June, you may have difficulty getting the departure date you want. **British Airways** is probably the best-known carrier to Britain; their lowest APEX direct (New York-London) flight in the summer of 1991 was $366. The best choice For direct flights to Ireland, the most logical choice is **Aer Lingus** (tel. (800) 223-6537), the national airline of Ireland; you can fly into Shannon, on the west coast, or Dublin. In the summer of 1991, an APEX direct flight from New York to Dublin cost $729, and from New York to Shannon $699. Aer Lingus also offers a "Londonfare," with a triangular route from New York or Boston to Shannon or Dublin, to London, and back (summer 1991 midweek, $849, weekend $899). This arrangement allows you to stay up to six months in Britain and/or Ireland.

Yet another option is to try airlines that undercut the major carriers by offering bargain fares on regularly scheduled flights. **Virgin Atlantic's** (tel. (800) 862-8621) Late Saver fare in the high season of 1991 was as low as $359 one-way for those booking three or fewer days before departure. **Youth fares** are round-trip discounts available to those age 12 to 24 who purchase their tickets 72 hours before departure. Ask a travel agent or contact the airline directly for information about such fares.

Last-minute **discount clubs** and **fare brokers** offer members savings on European travel, including charter flights and tour packages. Organizations that are clearing houses for unsold airline, charter, and cruise tickets include **Airhitch** (tel. (212) 864-2000), Bargain Air (tel. (800) 347-2345 or (213) 377-2919), **Discount Travel International** (tel. (800) 324-9294 or (215) 668-7184), **Last Minute Travel** (tel. (800) LAST-MIN (527-8646) or (617) 267-9800), **Moment's Notice** (tel. (212) 486-0503), **Travelers Advantage** (tel. (800) 548-1116), **Unitravel** (tel. (800) 325-2222 or (314) 569-0900) and **Worldwide Discount Travel Club** (tel. (305) 534-2082). Clubs generally have a yearly subscription fee of $30-50, although fare brokers place no such obstacles. Both sell empty seats on commercial carriers and charters from three weeks to a few days before departure. The clubs also offer last-minute space on cruises and tours throughout Europe. The often labrynthine contracts bear close study—you may prefer not to stop over in Luxembourg for eleven hours. London's **bucket shops** offer similar deals; these are travel agencies which sell leftover tickets on commercial flights at unofficially discounted prices. (They are unable to sell tickets to Ireland, however.)

Enterprising people who can travel light might consider flying to Britain as a **courier.** A company hiring you as a courier will use your checked luggage space for freight, leaving you with only the carry-on allowance; usually you vacation is limited to one or two weeks. Fares vary widely, depending on proximity to departure date; they tend to be standby level or lower—sometimes dramatically lower. **Now Voyager** (tel. (212) 431-1616) couriers fly to London from New York (they may offer flights from other U.S. cities this year). **Halbert Express** (tel. (718) 656-8189) and **TNT Skypack** (tel. (516) 745-9000) advertise similar opportunities. Check the travel section of a major newspaper or the *Courier Air Travel Handbook* ($8.95, available from Thunderbird Press, 5930-10 West Greenway Blvd., #112H, Glendale, AZ 85306) for other courier companies.

From Continental Europe

As a rule, air travel is prohibitively expensive across much of Europe. In high season, however, budget fares make flights between England and the Continent quite affordable. Look for student discounts and holiday charters available through budget travel agents and local newspapers and magazines. **STA Travel** and **CIEE** offices throughout Europe are good contacts for inexpensive flights throughout Europe. If you're coming from southern Europe, you might want to look into the **Italy Sky Shuttle** (formerly Pilgrim Air), 227 Shepherds Bush Rd., London W6 2AS (tel. (081) 748 1333), which runs low-cost flights on various ailrines from 21 Italian cities to 8 airports in the U.K.

Sealink Stena Line and **P&O European Ferries** offer extensive ferry service across the channel between France (Calais or Boulogne) and England (Dover or Folkestone). Sealink ferries are the most frequent and take 1½-¾ hours (26 trips/day; about $36 one way). Other routes between the Continent and England include Bergen, Norway to Newcastle (on DFDS Ferries); Cherbourg to Weymouth or Southampton (Sealink); Dieppe to Newhaven (Sealink); Esbjerg, Denmark to Harwich or Newcastle (DFDS); Gotherburg, Sweden to Harwich or Newcastle (DFDS); Hamburg to Harwich (DFDS); Hook of Holland, Belgium to Harwich (Sealink); Le Havre to Southampton (Sealink); Oostende, Belgium to Dover (P&O); Rotterdam to Hull; and Zeebrugge, Belgium to Dover (P&O) or Hull or Felixstowe (North Sea Ferries). **Brittany Ferries** has service between Plymouth and Roscoff or Portsmouth and St. Malo. **Irish Ferries** offers ferry service from Cherbourg or Le Havre to Rosslare in Ireland, **B&I Line** has ferries between Cork and Le Havre; and **Belfast Car Ferries** runs from Roscoff to Cork. Ferry service between Britain and Ireland is quick and frequent as well. Sealink goes from Holyhead to Dun Láoghaire, Fishguard to Rosslare, and Stranraer, Scotland to Larne, Northern Ireland; B&I runs between Dublin and Holyhead and Pembroke and Rosslare; and Belfast Car Ferries offers service from Liverpool to Belfast. These ferries are relatively inexpensive; Sealink offers a 25% discount for IHYF members.

The hovercraft is more rapid (40 min.), but it must be booked in advance. **Hoverspeed** services depart from Boulogne for Dover, with extra craft operating to Ramsgate from Dunkerque during the summer. The service is suspended in rough weather, so you might have to wait for the ferry. Contact **Travelloyd,** 8 Berkeley Sq., London SW1 for information on Transalpino's reduced rates on hovercraft services, or the British Rail Travel Centre, 4-12 Regent St., London SW1Y 4PQ. For more extensive information on both ferries and hovercrafts, see individual listings on port towns.

The cross-Channel services await with dread the completion of **Chunnel,** the undersea road-and-rail connection which has been dreamed and planned since the 19th century. The 1987 Channel Link Treaty between Britain and France lay the groundwork for the realization of the Chunnel project. Twin rail tunnels (operational for shuttle train and passsenger vehicles) will link terminals near Folkestone and at Coquelles (near Calais). Construction began in 1988 on both sides of the Channel; the two ends are scheduled to meet any day now, and the system is due to open to passenger service in mid-1993. A major problem so far has been deciding which side of the road motorists will use.

From Australia and New Zealand

Due to *Let's Go's* distance from Down Under, we are regretfully not as omniscient about budget-travel opportunities there as in North America. A native of Australia or New Zealand is best advised to visit a local branch of one of previously-mentioned budget travel agencies. **STA Travel** is probably the largest international agency you will find: they have offices in Sydney (1A Lee St., Railway Sq., Sydney 2000, tel. (02) 212 1255), Melbourne (222 Faraday St., Carlton 3053, Melbourne, tel. (061) 347 4711), and Auckland (10 High St., Basement, Auckland, tel. (09) 309 9723). **British Airways** (tel. (02) 258 3300, (800) 247-9297 in U.S.) and **Qantas** (tel. (800)

227-4500 in U.S.) both fly direct from Australia to Britain, but obviously you pay for convenience: in the summer of 1991, the Sydney-London return route was AUS$2299 on B.A. and AUS$3440 on Qantas. Luckily, flying direct is but one (very expensive) way of getting to the British Isles. Any national airline between Australia and Britain can offer somewhat cheaper connecting flights on one part of the route; most travelers reportedly take Singapore Air or other Far East-based carriers during the initial leg of their trip. Check with STA or another company for more comprehensive information.

Once There

Getting Around

In general, fares on all modes of public transportation in Britain and Ireland are either "single" (one way) or "return" (round trip). "Period returns" require you to return within a specific number of days; "day returns" means you must return on the same day. Always keep your ticket when you travel, as it will sometimes be inspected on the journey or collected at the station when you arrive.

Trains

Britain's nationalized **British Rail** service is extensive but somewhat expensive. If you plan to travel a great deal within Britain, the **British Rail Pass** is a good buy. (N.B.: Eurailpasses are not applicable in Britain.) Passes are only available in the U.S. and Canada; *you must buy them before traveling to Britain.* They allow unlimited travel in England, Wales, and Scotland; British Rail does not operate in Northern Ireland or the Republic of Ireland. Passes are not valid for ferry, jetfoil, or Hovercraft transportation, although British Rail does offer fare packages for rail service combined with one or more of these options. In 1991, "Silver Passes" (economy class) cost $209 for eight days, $319 for 15 days, $39 for 22 days, and $465 for one month. However, British Rail does offer discounts for seniors, students/youth, and children. Those over 60 can purchase a Senior Railcard for substantial discounts; be aware that these are only available for purchase *in Britain,* usually at any British Rail Travel Centre in the country. Alternatively, seniors without Senior Railcards can buy Silver Passes for $189 for eight days, $289 for 15 days, $359 for 22 days, and $419 for one month. People between the ages of ages 16 and 25 pay $169 for eight days, $255 for 15 days, $319 for 22 days, or $375 for one month; those aged 5 to 15 can purchase any of these passes for about half of the standard adult price. The **Young Person's Railcard** (£16) offers the best reductions on individual rail fares—1/3 off most fares, as well as discounts on Sealink Stena Line to the Continental and Irish ports. Again, you can only buy the pass *in Britain.* If you're between 16 and 23 (or a full-time student over 23 at a British school), you must show proof of age (a birth certificate or passport) or student status at a British school, and submit two passport-sized photos; the card is valid for one year. Families have their own Railcard, as do disabled travelers (for further information on the latter, see Special Concerns: Disabled Travelers above). British Rail also offers "Flexipasses," which allow travel on a limited number of days within a particular time period. For more information on different pass options, current prices, and additional discounts (on tours, rental cars, etc.) available with the pass, talk to your travel agent or contact British Rail at one of the addresses below.

Passes are available from most travel agents (including Let's Go Travel Services, CIEE, and Travel CUTS) or BritRail Travel International's Reservation Centre, 1500 Broadway, 10th Floor, New York, NY 10036-4015 (tel. (212) 382-3737, fax (212) 575-2542). In Canada, write to 409 Granville St., Vancouver BC, V6C 1T2 (tel. (604) 683-6896) or 94 Cumberland St., Toronto M5R 1A3 (tel. (416) 929-3333).

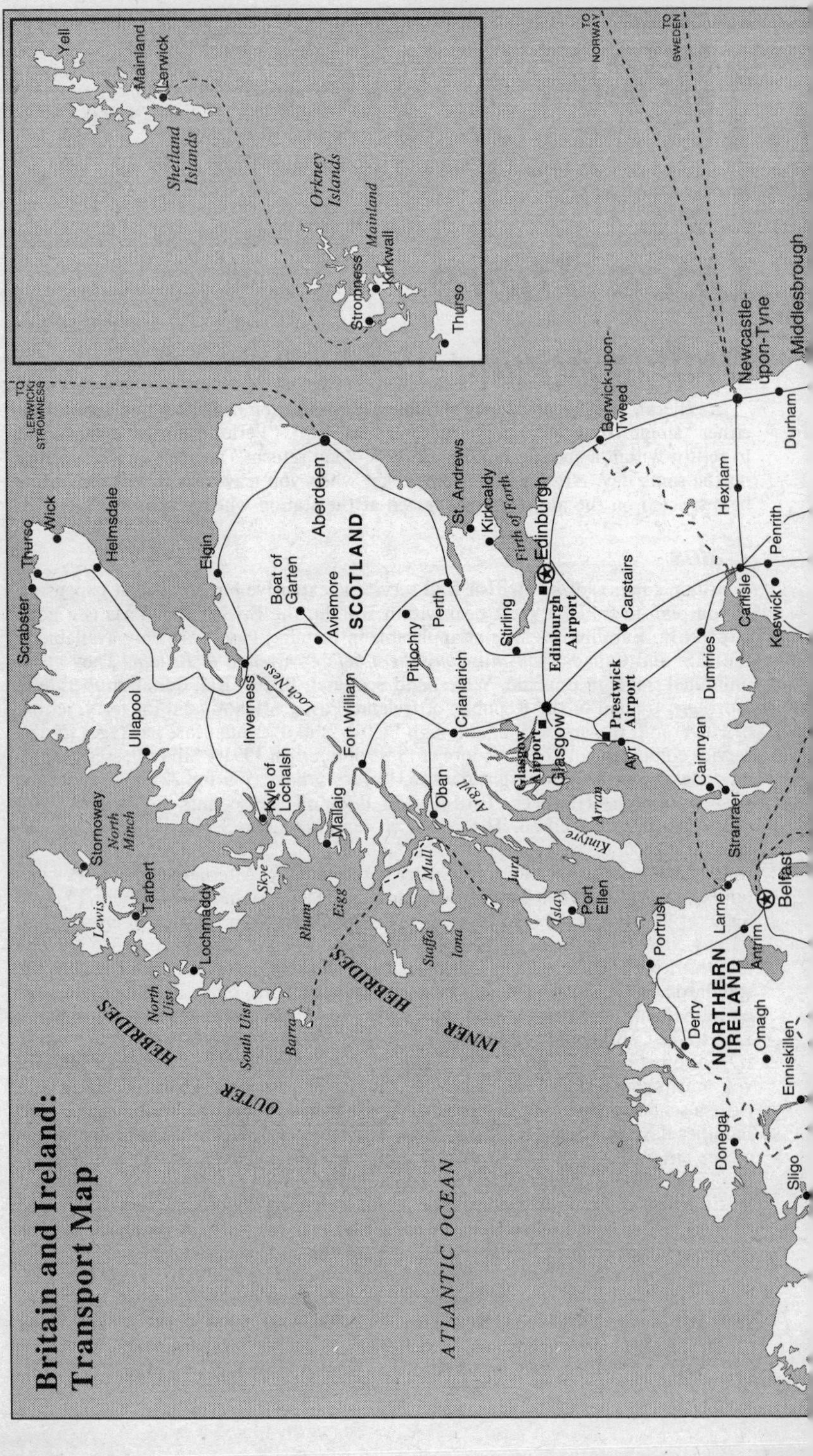

Britain and Ireland: Transport Map

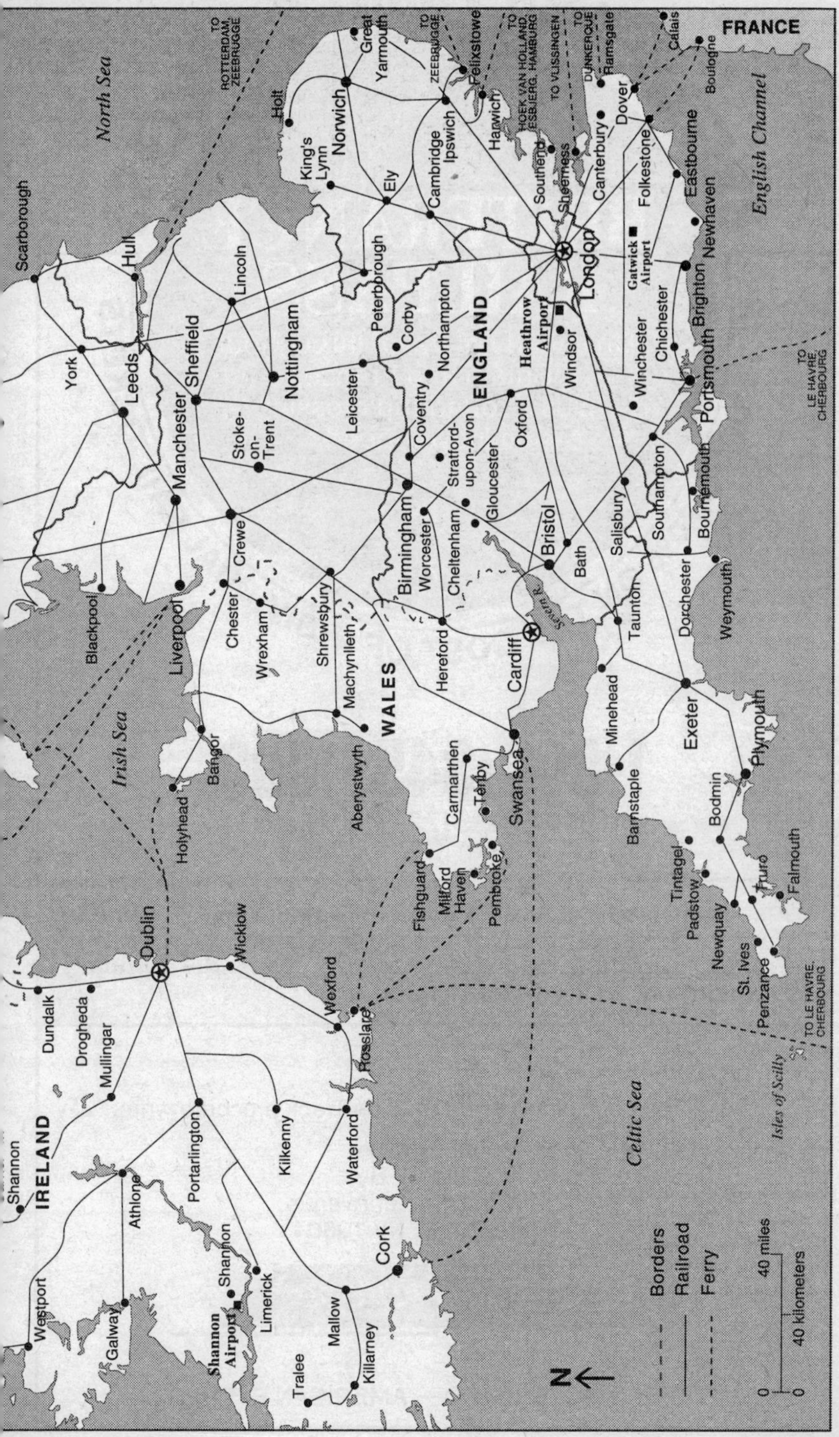
North Sea
TO ROTTERDAM, ZEEBRUGGE
TO ZEEBRUGGE
TO HOEK VAN HOLLAND, ESBJERG, HAMBURG
TO VLISSINGEN
TO DUNKERQUE
FRANCE
Calais
Boulogne
English Channel
TO LE HAVRE, CHERBOURG
TO LE HAVRE, CHERBOURG
Celtic Sea
Isles of Scilly
Irish Sea
IRELAND
WALES
ENGLAND
Scarborough
Hull
York
Leeds
Sheffield
Lincoln
Nottingham
Manchester
Blackpool
Liverpool
Stoke-on-Trent
Crewe
Chester
Wrexham
Shrewsbury
Machynlleth
Aberystwyth
Bangor
Holyhead
Fishguard
Milford Haven
Pembroke
Tenby
Carmarthen
Swansea
Cardiff
Hereford
Birmingham
Worcester
Cheltenham
Gloucester
Stratford-upon-Avon
Coventry
Leicester
Corby
Northampton
Peterborough
Oxford
Bristol
Bath
Severn R.
Heathrow Airport
Windsor
London
Gatwick Airport
King's Lynn
Holt
Norwich
Great Yarmouth
Ely
Cambridge
Ipswich
Felixstowe
Harwich
Southend
Sheerness
Canterbury
Ramsgate
Dover
Folkestone
Eastbourne
Newhaven
Brighton
Chichester
Winchester
Portsmouth
Southampton
Salisbury
Bournemouth
Dorchester
Weymouth
Taunton
Minehead
Exeter
Barnstaple
Plymouth
Bodmin
Tintagel
Padstow
Newquay
Truro
Falmouth
St. Ives
Penzance
Dublin
Wicklow
Wexford
Rosslare
Dundalk
Drogheda
Mullingar
Shannon
Athlone
Portarlington
Kilkenny
Waterford
Westport
Galway
Shannon
Shannon Airport
Limerick
Mallow
Cork
Tralee
Killarney
N
Borders
Railroad
Ferry
0 40 miles
0 40 kilometers

Different passes are available for extended travel in Wales, Scotland, or Northern Ireland (see the Getting There and Getting Around sections in the relevant introductions). In addition, a careful check of prices can often save you money. Returns usually cost slightly less than two single tickets, day returns often cost little more than singles, and weekend returns can save you up to 35% of the cost of two single tickets.

While the **Eurailpass** is not accepted in Britain, it is accepted in Ireland. Fares for 1991 were as follows: regular Eurailpass $390 (15 days), $498 (21 days), or $616 (1 month); Youthpass (for those under 26) $425 (1 month) or $560 (2 months); Flexipass (variable number of days to travel) $230 (5 days within 15 days), $398 (9 days within 21 days), or $498 (14 days within 1 month). However, this may only be a realistic and economical alternative if you plan to visit other countries in Europe that use the Eurail system; rail routes in the Republic of Ireland are not extensive and probably won't take you where you want to go. For more information on rail service in Ireland, see Getting There in the Ireland introduction below.

Coaches and Buses

The British distinguish between **buses,** which cover short local, rural, and city routes, and **coaches,** which cover long distances with few stops. Despite the somewhat chaotic system left in the wake of the 1986 denationalization of bus and coach companies, long-distance coach travel in Britain is more comprehensive and extensive than in most European countries, and definitely the least expensive option for travel within the United Kingdom. **National Express** is the principal operator of long-distance coach services (for information contact the National Express Coach Travel Centre, 13 Regent St., London SW1 (tel. (071) 730 0202)); each county or region also has its own company for rural service. Some coaches require advance reservation. **Student Coach Cards** (£3.90) are valid on National Express, reducing standard fares by 33%. **Magic Bus,,** a pan-European coach travel company, has a local office at Eurolines, 52 Grosvenor Gardens, Victoria Station SW1 (tel. (0582) 265 45). They can also be reached at 20 Filellinon St., Syntagma, Athens, Greece (tel. 323 7471/4, fax 323 0219), or through any National Express Travel Bureau.

Local intra-city services (mostly fast and frequent minibus services) are provided by local companies in conjunction with county councils. In towns where two or three inter-city rural-services companies link up (such as Glastonbury), the confusion can be incredible, so head for the local tourist office or bus station for help.

The major coach company in Ireland is **Bus Éireann,** which features an impressive network of criss-crossing routes. They offer several ticket options, including the **Rambler,** which allows you to travel anywhere in Ireland for a specified number of days (adult 3-day pass IR£24, 15-day pass IR£85.00). Tickets and information are available from the various Bus Éireann Travel Centres in major cities around the country. For more specific information on coaches and buses in Ireland, see Getting Around in the Ireland introduction below.

Cars and Caravans

The advantages of car travel speak for themselves. Disadvantages include high gasoline prices (around £1.85, or $3.50, per gallon in 1991), the unfamiliar laws and habits associated with driving in foreign lands, and the heinous exhaust that slips by lax British emissions standards. The major difficulty that most North American drivers seem to have in Britain and Ireland is driving on the "wrong" side—i.e. sitting on the right-hand side of the car and driving on the left-hand side of the road. Be particularly cautious at roundabouts (rotary interchanges); give way to traffic from the right. In both countries, the law requires drivers and front-seat passengers to wear seat belts; a new 1991 law in Britain mandates that rear-seat passengers are also required to belt up when belts are provided.

Great Britain is covered by a skeletal but adequate system of limited-access expressways ("M-roads" or "motorways"), connecting London with Birmingham,

Liverpool, Manchester, Cardiff, and Southern Scotland. The M-roads are supplemented by a tight web of "A-roads" and "B-roads" that covers every pocket of England, Scotland, Wales, and Northern Ireland. Speed limits are 60mph (97km/h) on single carriageways (non-divided highways), 70mph (113km/h) on motorways (highways) and dual carriageways (divided highways), and usually 30mph (48km/h) in urban areas. (Speed limits are always marked at the beginning of town areas; upon leaving, you'll see a circular sign with a slash through it, signalling the end of the speed restriction.) Speed limits aren't rabidly enforced; remember though, that many British roads are sinuous and single-track, so drivers should use common sense, especially in rural/mountainous areas. A few major bridges and tunnels require tolls.

In the Republic of Ireland, roads numbered below N50 are "primary routes," which connect all the major towns; roads numbered N50 and above are "secondary routes," similar to Britain's A-roads; regional "R-roads" are comparable to Britain's B-roads. Most of these are two-lane; four-lane two-way roads are not common. The general speed limit is 55mph (90km/h) on the open road and either 30mph (50km/h) or 40mph (65km/h) in town. Signs on roadways are usually in both English and Gaelic.

Hiring (renting) an automobile is the least expensive autokinetic option if you plan to drive for a month or less. For more extended travel, you might consider **leasing** instead. Major rental companies with agencies almost everywhere in Britain and Ireland include **Avis, Budget Rent-A-Car, Geoffrey Davis Europcar, Hertz, Kenning,** and **Swan National.** Prices range from £150 to £300 per week with unlimited mileage, plus VAT; for insurance reasons, renters are required to be over 21 and under 70. However, **Europe by Car** (see listing below) will rent to younger people if the paperwork is done in advance, in the U.S. All plans require sizable deposits unless you're paying by credit card. Make sure you understand the insurance agreement before you rent; some agreements require you to pay for damages that you may not have caused. Automatics are generally more expensive to rent than manuals (stick shifts). Several U.S. firms offer rental and leasing plans for Britain and Ireland; try **Kemwel Group,** 106 Calvert St., Harrison NY 10528-3199 (tel. (800)

678-0678 or (914) 835-5454); **Auto-Europe,** P.O. Box 1097, Camden, ME 04843 (tel. (800) 223-5555 or (207) 236-8235, fax (207) 236-4724); or **Europe by Car,** 1 Rockefeller Plaza, New York, NY 10020 (tel. (800) 223-1516 or (212) 581-3040; student and faculty discounts available on rentals). CIEE and Let's Go Travel Services have discount rental and leasing plans for students and faculty members. The **American Automobile Association (AAA),** 1000 AAA Drive, Box 75, Heathrow, FL 32746-5063 (tel. (800) AAA-HELP (222-4357) or (407) 444-8000), can offer general information on repairs and purchasing an international driver's permit.

Purchasing a car in Britain may in the end save you money if you travel for extended periods. The car must conform to safety and emission standards should you bring it back to the U.S. If you know what you're doing, buying a used car or van and then selling it before you leave can provide the cheapest wheels on the islands. *Europe by Van,* available for $6.50 ($8.50 from overseas) from David Guterson, 13024 Venice Loop, Bainbridge Is., WA 98110, explains the intricacies of buying and selling a van in London. David Shore and Patty Campbell's *Europe Free!: The Car, Van, & RV Travel Guide* or *Europe by Van and Motorhome* ($13.95) offers advice on similar topics; they are available from Shore/Campbell Publications, 1842 Santa Margarita Dr., Fallbrook, CA 92028 (tel. (619) 723-6184), as are other publications and information.

A brand-new organization called **Eurothumb G.B.** attempts to provide an economical and fun alternative to prohibitively expensive or dangerous forms of travel. Billing itself as "Britain's first commercial car-sharing agency," the Brighton-based company charges passengers a flat fee of £2, then 1p per mile plus ¼ of the gas expenses. The resulting one-way prices can be astounding, including £19.51 to Edinburgh (from Brighton), £5.77 to Oxford and £5.40 to Paris. You have to pay for you own ferry as well as your own food and accommodations, travel is slow and limited, and a return trip is not always available right away; still, this is probably the cheapest travel option you can find in Britain. Yearly registration is £3; write for an application and a journey request form to P.O. Box 792, Brighton, East Sussex BN1 9TG (tel. (0273) 566 668). They screen all potential travelers.

Biking

If you have ever biked down a deserted country road in the cool morning air, you will agree that cycling can be a uniquely satisfying means of travel. For information about touring routes, independent cyclists can consult tourist offices or any of the numerous books on cycling in Britain and Ireland. Rodale Press (33 E. Minor St., Emmaus, PA 18908 (tel. (215) 967-5171)) publishes *Mountain Biking Skills, Cycling for Women, Basic Maintenance and Repair* (all $4.95) and other general publications on prepping yourself and your bike for an excursion. *Bike Touring* ($10.95), from the Sierra Club, 730 Polk St., San Francisco, CA 94109 (tel. (415) 776-2211), offers similar advice on outfitting yourself and your itinerary. The **Cyclists' Touring Club,** Cotterell House, 69 Meadrow, Godalming, Surrey GU7 3HS England (tel. (0483) 417 217, fax (0483) 426 994) provides information, maps, and a list of bike rental firms in Britain. Annual membership is £22.50, under 21 £11.25, and family £37.50. The club's bi-monthly magazine, *Cycletouring and Campaigning,* is a valuable resource; they also publish an annual *Tours Brochure* for Great Britain.

If your only experience with biking is the old 10-min. ride to school, you should be aware that **touring** is an entirely different story. Much of Britain's countryside is well-suited for cycling; many roads are not heavily traveled. Ireland is much the same way, although one *Let's Go* reader found that after a while it seemed that the country was all uphill. Even well-traveled routes will often cover highly uneven terrain. We recommend that you take some reasonably long rides before you leave, both to get in shape and to assure yourself you're not in over your head. You must pack an absolute minimum of luggage. Be sure the gear range on your bike is adequate; you'll need extremely low gears to get a loaded bike up a steep hill. Have Greg LeMond or a reputable, well-equipped bike shop tune up your bike before you go.

Bringing a beloved bike from home involves considerable worry, work and expense. Every airline has its own regulations. Some carriers will include your bike as part of your baggage allowance if it is under a certain size (usually 62 inches), but some charge a fee. The amount of disassembling and crating you have to do also varies from airline to airline. Many bike stores sell airline bike-boxes, and some airlines will give you one; you will have to remove the handlebars, pedals, and front wheel. Another option is to buy a bike in Britain and Ireland. A bike bought new overseas is subject to customs duties if brought into your home country; used bikes, however, are immune from taxation.

Whatever the origin of the bike, be sure to purchase adequate **touring equipment.** Riding a bike with a heavy pack on your back is about as safe (and intelligent) as pedaling blindfolded on glare ice. The first thing necessary is a good **helmet.** At about $50-60, the best helmets—a Bell V1Pro or Bell Tourlite is frequently suggested—are an investment but much cheaper than critical head surgery or a tastefully appointed funeral. You should also obtain pairs of back and front panniers (saddlebags), with proper connecting attachments for the frame; they can run anywhere from $30-80. A selection of tools is essential, as well as a repair book that explains what to do with them. To secure your bike, purchase a U-shaped **lock** made by (among others) Nashbar or Kryptonite ($20-30). Selected models of both locks have a one-year $1000 anti-theft guarantee. British law states that at night your bike must show a white light at the front of the cycle and a red light and red reflector on the back. Adequate **maps** are also a necessity; Ordnance Survey maps (1 in. to 1 mi.) or Bartholomew maps (½in. to 1 mi.) are available in most bookstores. Though the sun might not always be a problem, carrying a hat or sunglasses is a good idea. A waterproof cape or poncho, on the other hand, is an absolute must in this part of the world.

Most of your bike needs can be taken care of by **Bike Nashbar,** 4111 Simon Rd., Youngstown, OH 44512 (tel. (800) NASHBAR (627-4227). If you can find a nationally advertised lower price, they will beat it by 5¢. Call their toll-free number (open 7am-midnight) and the order will usually be on its way the same day. They regularly ship anywhere in the U.S. and Canada and will also ship overseas. They also have a technical line (216-788-6464) to answer questions about repairs and such. Another exceptional mail-order firm specializing in mountain bikes is **Bikeology,** P.O. Box 3900, Santa Monica, CA 90403 (tel. (800) 326-2453).

If you plan to explore several widely separated regions, you can combine cycling with train travel. British Rail lets you put your bike in the luggage compartment of most trains free of charge and store your bike at most stations for a nominal fee. In addition, bikes ride free on all ferries leaving from Britain and Ireland. A pamphlet on bike/train travel is available from British Rail and at most stations; the maze of regulations and restrictions will scare you at first, but in real life many of these are not enforced. Renting a bike is preferable to bringing your own if your touring will be confined to one or two regions. A three-speed will cost anywhere from £8-20 per week, a mountain bike up to £30. Check specific town listings for Britain and Ireland for bike rental shops, or contact the Irish Tourist Board for a list of more than 100 dealers in Ireland who rent bikes; if you call or write ahead of time, you can arrange to have a bike waiting for you at Shannon Airport.

Hiking

The British maintain an extensive system of long-distance paths that range from the gently rolling footpaths of the South Downs Way to the rugged mountain trails of the Pennine Way. These paths are well-marked and well-maintained, and in many cases, youth hostels are conveniently located within a day's walk of each other. If you plan to do any serious hiking, be sure to bring adequate maps. Explorers will enjoy the Ordnance Survey 1:25,000 Second Series maps, which mark almost every house, barn, standing stone, graveyard, and pub. Less ambitious hikers will want the 1:50,000 scale maps. Other essentials include a waterproof jacket, compass, sturdy shoes, thick woolen socks, a first-aid kit, a flashlight, and, for long distance hikers, a whistle. Several specific organizations provide information for the self-propelled traveler. The **Ramblers' Association,** 1/5 Wandsworth Rd., London SW8 2XX (tel. (071) 582 6878), publishes a *Yearbook* on walking and places to stay, as well as offering free newsletters and color magazines (membership £13, family £16.25). The **Backpackers' Club,** P.O. Box 381, Reading, Berkshire RG3 4RL England (tel. (04917) 739; 24 hr.) offers its members (membership £17) site and pitch lists for most distance paths in the U.K., a quarterly magazine, camping equipment, insurance services, and best of all a Clothpatch to sew on your gear, identifying you as a Backpacker for all the world to see. The Sierra Club (see address above) publishes an *Annual Outing Catalog* ($2) for hiking and backpacking, and Wilderness Press (see address in Traveling With Children above) offers up both *Backpacking Sourcebook* ($7.95) and *Backpacking Basics* ($7.95), as well as regional guides. For more information on national trails and recreational paths, contact the **Countryside Commission,** John Dower House, Crescent Place, Cheltenham, Gloucestershire GL50 3RA (tel. (0242) 521 381). For *Walking in Britain, Out in the Country,* and *Heritage Coasts of England and Wales,* write to Countryside Commission Publications, 19/23 Albert Rd., Manchester M19 2EQ.

Hitchhiking

> *Let's Go* urges you to seriously consider possible risks before you decide to hitchhike. *Let's Go* does not recommend hitchhiking as a means of transport, and the routes listed below and elsewhere in the book are not intended to do so.

A wait of more than an hour is rare on major roads in summer. People who travel light usually garner more charity rides; they stand at places where drivers can stop easily and get back on the road safely: such places include the areas on or near a roundabout (rotary interchange), near the entrance to an M-road (see Cars and Caravans above), at an intersection where cars must slow down anyway, or on a lay-by (paved shoulder). Many carry a sign boldly lettered with their destination. You should never accept rides in the back of a two-door car; try to keep the door unlocked, with your luggage handy—don't let it be thrown in the trunk. In emergencies, some people open the door; this usually surprises the driver enough to make him slow down. Those who feel uneasy about the ride for any reason get out at the first opportunity or firmly demand to be let off, no matter how unfavorable the spot appears for further hitching.

Hitch-Hikers' Manual: Britain contains practical information on the laws concerning hitching, tips on techniques, and advice about the best places to hitch in 200 British towns. It is available from Vacation Work (see address in Alternatives to Tourism above) for £3.95. You might also try the Britain section of Ken Welsh's *Hitchhiker's Guide to Europe.*

Accommodations

Tourist information centers can provide invaluable aid in the search for accommodations. These offices often have free or inexpensive lists of available accommodations in town, which they will post on their doors after hours. For about £1, most offices will book you a place to stay. (*All* offices in Scotland provide this service; it's free, except in Edinburgh, where it costs £1.) Occasionally, it's cheaper to call listed B&Bs yourself; some accommodations may inflate prices in response to the finder's fee commissions charged them by tourist boards. Most offices also offer a "book-a-bed-ahead" service; for a fee of about £2 (less in Wales), they will reserve you a room in the next town on your itinerary. In many places, tourist offices only list proprietors who've paid a hefty fee to become members of the tourist board organization; the owners of other accommodations may have chosen for political or financial reasons to remain independent, which means they also remain somewhat invisible. The best way to find out about accommodations is simply by talking to other travelers and keeping your ear to the ground (and, of course, *Let's Go* has listed some choice spots that we've been able to find).

Making advance reservations (preferably secured with a deposit) may be inconvenient but will greatly lessen the anxiety of arrival, especially in the summer and particulary for single rooms. Write to a hotel or hostel, specifying the date of arrival and the length of your stay (commit yourself only to a minimum stay, since you may wish to move elsewhere). The proprietor will write back to confirm availability, whereupon you should send a deposit of one night's rent, preferably in the form of a signed traveler's check in pounds. Some places accept money orders in dollars or a personal check (possibly for a fee). You might want to phone the establishment before leaving home to confirm availability. A few hotels will accept credit card reservations over the telephone.

Hostels

Britain and Ireland have 400 IYHF-affiliated hostels in all major cities and towns. In Ireland, there are two non-IYHF hostel organizations—**Independent Hostel Owners (IHO)** (tel. (073) 301 30) and **Irish Budget Hostels** (tel. (065) 740 06). As well, many hostels throughout Britain and Ireland are not associated with any organization. Prices are similar at most of these accommodations, but many travelers find the independent hostels more amiable than the IYHF variety.

To stay in an IYHF hostel, you must be a member of the International Youth Hostel Federation (see Useful Addresses above). Alternatively, nonmembers may ask at hostels for an "International Guest Card." When they visit a hostel, an overnight fee plus one-sixth of the annual membership charge buys one stamp; a card with six stamps is proof of full IYHF membership. The IYHF hostels in Britain and Ireland are organized into the four regional groups listed below, and each group publishes a detailed directory of hostels in its area. These regional directories and the two volumes of the *International Youth Hostel Handbook* ($9.95 each) are available from the hostel association in your home country.

Some hostels are strikingly beautiful; others are little more than run-down barracks. Hostels and their grounds are usually closed from 10am to 5pm, and there is an evening curfew (usually about 11pm) at all but a few hostels. All hostels require sheet sleeping sacks, which they rent or sell at a small cost (usually about 80p). These regulations are often not strictly enforced. Many hostels have laundry facilities, ranging from washing machines to troughs in the backyard (in Scotland, only those marked "Grade 1," out of three, have such facilities; see Scotland introduction for further explanation of the grading system). Most large hostels offer hot evening meals, and almost all provide kitchen facilities and utensils at no extra charge. Some house small stores, where canned goods and camper's "food" are sold.

Bed and Breakfasts

The Bed-and-Breakfast is a type of accommodation native to Britain, although the concept has now spread the world over. Conceived originally as an inexpensive alternative to high-priced hotels, the term "bed-and-breakfast" generally menas a small place that offers basic accommodations and breakfast at a reasonable price. The type of accommodation often varies, but usually B&Bs are private homes whose owners have room to spare or guest houses. Not the place for those expecting room service and valet parking, B&Bs often provide nothing more than comfortable accommodations and British charm. The hospitality of British bed-and-breakfast establishments is celebrated the world over—with good reason. Those used to the impersonal management of budget motel chains will often be pleasantly shocked by the geniality of B&B proprietors. Just as often, however, you will be given a thoroughly businesslike reception. Do not expect to be welcomed everywhere like a wealthy long-lost relative. Outside London, most B&Bs have fewer than four rooms available, but since they often cluster together on one street or in one section of town, owners will direct you to a neighbor when their own rooms are full.

B&Bs are usually quite clean, particularly in rural areas. In London and other large cities they can be cramped and rather shabby, as well as painfully expensive. Most of the places *Let's Go* lists have central heating, but if you are traveling in the fall or winter, be sure to ask about its existence and nature. Before committing yourself to a place, see the room and test the bed. Also make sure the charges are clear to you; quoted fees may conveniently exclude the 15% VAT. Solitary travelers may have trouble finding space in rural areas, where proprietors try to fill their doubles with two people who know each other, waiting until the last minute to offer their rooms as singles. In large cities, strangers may be put in the same room, alleviating the problem. Prices generally decline as you travel farther from London. Expect to pay anywhere from £16-60 in London (almost always in advance), and about £10-12 in the rest of England. Some proprietors grant considerable rate reductions to guests who pay by the week or in advance; others may impose finicky restrictions and unreasonable check-out times. Prices between September and May are often reduced. In Scotland, Wales, and Ireland, rates will run slightly lower, and you'll frequently be offered extras, such as evening tea and cakes. An "English breakfast" should include eggs, bacon, toast, and tea or coffee, while a "Continental" breakfast includes only some form of bread and hot caffeine. Breakfasts vary as much as rooms in quality. These organizations can book your entire trip before you leave home:

Auntie's (Great Britain) Limited, 56 Coleshill Terrace, Llanelli, Dyfed, Wales SA15 3DA (tel. (0554) 770 077). £13-17/person (under 13 half price) for family B&Bs. Covers London suburbs and other areas of England, Scotland, and Wales. Specializes in catering for vegetarians.

Bed and Breakfast (GB), P.O. Box 66, Henley-on-Thames, Oxon, England RG9 1XS (tel. (0491) 578 803, fax (0491) 410 806). The most comprehensive service, covering all of England, Scotland, and Wales for £12 and up per night. Telephone reservation service. Write for free brochure and rate schedule. Publishes the helpful annual pamphlet *How to Book a Bed & Breakfast in Britain,* which includes information on prices, reservations, and host locations.

ACCOMMODATION

Central London

Budget Prices

WESTPOINT HOTEL

170 Sussex Gardens, Hyde Park,
London W2 1PT. Tel: 071-402 0281 (Reservations) Fax: 071-224 9114
Open all year. Central heating.
Most rooms with private shower & toilet, radio/intercom & colour T.V.
Children welcome. TV lounge

This hotel has long been a popular choice amongst tourists because of its central location, being near to Hyde Park and only 2 minutes from Paddington and Lancaster Gate tube stations. The West End's tourist attractions, including theatres, museums and Oxford Street stores are within easy reach. Individuals, families and groups are all welcome.

★ PRIVATE CAR PARK ★ PARKING ★

Rates:	Low Season	High Season
	Singles from £18 per person.	Singles from £22 per person.
	Doubles from £11.50 per person.	Doubles from £13 per person.
	Family rooms from £10 per person.	Family rooms from £11 per person.

SASS HOUSE HOTEL

Sass House Hotel is situated 2 minutes from Hyde Park and 10 minutes from Oxford Street.
Budget prices in Central London.
Open all year - Central heating - TV lounge - Radio/intercom in all rooms.
Bed & Breakfast room from - Single £14.00; Double £11.00 per person; Family £9.50 per person.
11 CRAVEN TERRACE, HYDE PARK, LONDON W2 3QD
Tel: 01-262 2325

ABBEY COURT HOTEL

Open all year. Colour TV lounge. Centrally heated. Car park. Centrally located near Lancaster Gate, Paddington Station and Hyde Park. Within easy reach of London's most important tourist attractions. Most rooms with private toilets and showers and colour TV. Single room from £22.00 per night; Double room from £17.00 per person nightly; Family room from £14.00 per person nightly.
174 SUSSEX GARDENS, HYDE PARK, LONDON W2
Tel: 01-402 0704

Bath

The Old Mill Hotel & Restaurant

TOLLBRIDGE ROAD, BATH, AVON. BA1 7DE ☎(0225) 858476 Fax: (0225) 852600.

The Old Mill Hotel is a unique setting on the banks of the river Avon overlooking the tollbridge and the Weir, yet only two miles from the centre of Bath. New riverside restaurants with a rotating base turned by the huge water wheel offering varied menus. Delightful garden with fishing and boating available for guests. Luxurious refurbished en-suite accommodation, most with river views four poster beds, all with colour TV, tea and coffee making facilities and telephone. Ample parking. Enquire for short break discounts. Sgl. from **£35.00**. Dbl. from **£22.00** p.p.

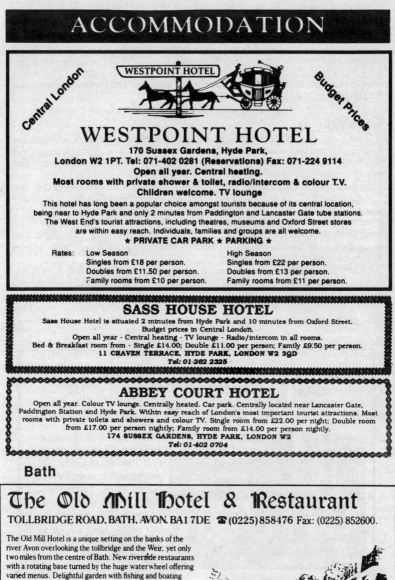

Independent Traveller, Dinneford Spring, Thorverton, Exeter EX5 5NU (tel. (0392) 860 870, fax (0392) 860 552). Offers cottages, house and apartments for rent all around the United Kingdom. Various price ranges, short or long stays. Also books B&Bs throughout Britain.

Cheap hotels, or guest houses as they are often called, can sometimes offer even better bargains than B&Bs. (In Scotland, accommodations fall loosely into three categories: B&Bs, the least expensive after hostels; guest houses; and budget hotels, the most expensive. In general, only in very small towns might hotels be better budget options than B&Bs.) The quality of these establishments varies widely, but for those on the run, hotels offer fewer restrictions and more flexible arrangements than B&Bs.

Camping

Britain has over 2500 campsites, more than most countries on the Continent; Ireland is similarly well endowed. Most campsites are open from April through October, though some stay open all year. While a few youth hostels have camping facilities (the charge is usually half the hostel charge; hostel card required), most campsites are privately owned and designed for people with caravans rather than tent-dwellers. You can legally set up camp only in specifically marked areas unless you get permission from the owner on whose land you plan to squat. It is legal to cross private land by **public rights of way;** any other use of private land without permission is considered trespassing. For more information about camping in Britain, send for the British Tourist Authority's free brochure *Caravan and Camping Parks* (see Useful Addresses below).

Unless you're camping in sub-zero temperatures, your **sleeping bag** need not be of hand-plucked down—a good synthetic fiber is almost as warm and will dry much more quickly should you encounter dismal weather. For three-season camping (spring, summer, fall), a 3½-lb. synthetic bag (around $110) or a 2½-lb. down bag (no less than $135) should suffice. Simple Ensolite pads (warmer and drier than foam) cost about $13.

Good **tents** have become very expensive (up to $150 for a 2-person nylon tent with a rain fly). Such modern accoutrements as the rain fly, bug netting, lightweight materials, and built-in frame and suspension will make your life much more comfortable. A good tent should weigh no more than 3½kg. Synthetic fabrics are more water-resistant than cotton. Make sure that the floor of your tent extends several inches off the ground at the edges, to prevent rainwater from seeping in. Cyclists and backpackers should consider investing in a sophisticated, lightweight tent; some two-person tents weigh only 1kg. Other camping basics include a battery-operated lantern (never gas) and a simple plastic groundcloth to protect the tent floor. A small campstove ($25-80) that runs on butane or white gas is also very useful, especially where no firewood is available. Always bring waterproof matches. The European-made propane product GAZ has also been highly recommended; it is available where finer camping accessories are sold.

Alternative Accommodations

Most British universities open their **dormitories** to groups and individuals during the long school vacations (mainly July-Sept., though some places are available from mid-March to mid-April). Accommodations usually consist of self-catering facilities in flats or single study bedrooms. B&B or full board is sometimes available for short stays; and you may gain convenience at the cost of charm. This service is most helpful for groups staying in a town for a week or more. Write well in advance to the British Universities Accommodation Consortium (BUAC), P.O. Box 581, University Park, Nottingham, England NG7 2RG (tel. (0602) 504 571).

Servas is an international cooperative system of hosts and travelers. Travelers may stay free of charge in host members' homes in 100 countries for 2-3 months. You must be genuinely interested in sharing with your hosts; you must also be willing to contact them in advance and fit into the household routine. Participation in the program costs $45 plus a refundable $15 fee. (Hosts receive no money.) Travelerscompleting a successful interview will receive a directory of host members in countries they'll be visiting, with short self-descriptions of those listed. For more information, contact the U.S. Servas Committee at 11 John St., #407, New York, NY 10038 (tel. (212) 267-0252).

Staying in Touch

Mail

Air mail from Britain or Ireland to anywhere in the world (except possibly Koala Paroondi) is speedy and dependable, especially if sent from a major post office. A letter will reach the East Coast of the U.S. or urban Canada in about a week and may arrive in as few as three days if sent from London. **Surface mail,** while much cheaper than airmail, takes up to three months to arrive. It is adequate for getting rid of books or clothing you no longer need in your travels. (See Customs above for details.) Overseas mail is not cheap, however; at 31p for letters not over 20g, you may have to keep people at home in suspense.

If you have no fixed address while in Britain or Ireland, you can receive mail through the British and Irish post offices' *Poste Restante* (General Delivery) service. Mark the envelope "HOLD," and address it like this (for example): "Marlies Morsink, c/o *Poste Restante,* Glastonbury, Somerset, England BA6 9HS." Include the county and the postal code if you know them. (Don't worry about using postal codes for Ireland—they do not exist.) Try to have your *Poste Restante* sent to the largest post office in a region; smaller offices may be mystified by them French words. When in London, Canadian visitors are encouraged to have mail sent to Visitor Mail, Canada House, Trafalgar Sq., London SW1Y 5BJ (tel. (071) 629 9492). American Express Travel Offices will accept mail free for their traveler's check and cardholders, as long as the envelope is no larger than 8½×11 (no care packages, please).

When writing to Britain and Ireland for information, you may have to send an "International Reply Coupon" with your request. This coupon, available from all post offices, can be exchanged for postage stamps and will cover charges on bulk packages sent back to you.

Telephones

Important numbers in Britain include **999 for police, fire, or ambulance emergencies,** 100 for the telephone operator, 142 for London directory inquiries, 192 for directory inquiries elsewhere, and 153 for international directory assistance. Area codes for individual countries or cities in Britain are listed in telephone directories. *Let's Go* provides codes for large towns in Britain and Ireland in the Orientation and Practical Information sections. Telephone area codes range from two to six digits, and local telephone numbers range from three to seven. The rarely-seen code (0800) indicates a toll-free number.

The newer, more polite **British pay phone** lights up with the words "Insert Money" as soon as you lift the receiver. Start with 10p; when the initial time period is exhausted, a series of annoying beeps warns you to insert more money. For the rest of the call, the digital diplay ticks off your credit in 1p increments so that you can watch and plan ahead when to insert more money. Change is returned; phones don't accept 1p or the new 5p coins. The dial tone is a continuous purring sound; a repeated double-purr means the line is ringing. In the unlikely case that you run across one, dial before inserting any coins; when the connection is made, desperately feed your coin down the slot. When your money is running out the beeps will resume; at this point, you have 15 seconds to feed the beast before your connection will be broken off. In addition to these classics, British Telecom boasts some less flashy open-air kiosks, and several private companies have begun to compete for your business with their own designer payphones.

The procedure for making **international calls** is as follows: dial the international code (011), the country code, the city code if necessary (without the "0"), and then the local number. The country code for the U.S. and Canada is 1; Australia's 61; New Zealand's 64; Britain's 44; Ireland's is 353. For international calls from Britain, the most convenient option is a British Telecom **Phonecard,** available in denominations of £2, £4, and £10. Cards are available everywhere; main post offices and almost any newsagent or John Menzies (the ubiquitous stationery chain) stock them. It's also possible, but more of a hassle, to make international calls from special phones that accept 50p and £1 coins; these are found at airports, train stations, and almost all town squares and post offices in Britain. Phonebooths that use calling cards are labeled in green, and those that take coins in yellow; the green signs are extremely common, except in rural areas. Another option is to persuade your B&B proprietor to let you dial direct. Ask the international operator ahead of time what the rate per minute will be; time your call and pay the proprietor. Consider calling through U.S. long-distance companies, which offer significantly cheaper rates. To access a U.S. AT&T operator from Britain, dial their "USA Direct" number, 0800-8900-11. You can then call collect or with an AT&T calling card—be warned that calling collect is a *significantly* more expensive option. Call AT&T at (800) 222-0300 to order a card and garner more specific information about prices. Rates vary with time (in Britain) called; overnight rates are cheaper than afternoon, and morning is the most expensive. Using an MCI calling card will also reduce your costs; from Britain, access an operator at (0800) 890 222. You can only use this service if you have an MCI calling card; call MCI ahead of time to get one (in the U.S., call (800) 444-3333). Rates are the same at all times and on all days of the week. British Telecom publishes a simple pamphlet telling visitors how to call collect or by calling card from any phone (available at tourist offices and most hotels, printed in several languages).

Reduced rates for most international calls from Britain apply from 8pm to 8am Monday through Friday, and all day and night on Saturday and Sunday. The low-rate period to Australia and New Zealand is from midnight to 7am and 2:30pm to 7:30pm daily. Within Britain, three rate periods exist: the lowest rates are from 6pm to 9am Monday through Friday, and all day and all night Saturday and Sunday; calls are slightly more expensive from 1pm to 6pm Monday through Friday, and most expensive on weekday mornings (9am-1pm).

In **Ireland,** old-fashioned coinboxes take 2p, 5p, and 10p coins. Pick up the receiver, wait for the dial tone, and deposit a coin. If the party answers, immediately press the button marked "A," which deposits your coin into the box. If there is no answer, push button "B," which returns your coin. In some remote areas, you may find telephones without dials; pick up the receiver and wait for an operator to come on the line and connect you. Although AT&T's least expensive calling plan (USA Direct) is not yet available in Ireland, you can use an AT&T card to charge calls at U.S. rates; access an Irish operator at 114 and recite the number on your card. MCI doesn't yet operate in Ireland.

An alternative to calling or writing home is **Overseas Access,** a telephone message service offered by EurAide, Inc., P.O. Box 2375, Naperville, IL 60567 (tel. (708) 420-2343). You and your "folks" can leave messages for each other by calling at the Munich office ($15 initial registration, $15 a week or $40 a month).

Weights and Measures

1 kilogram (kg) = 2.2 pounds
1 meter (m) = 1.09 yards
1 kilometer (km) = about 0.62 mi.
1 liter = 1.05 quarts
1 liter = 0.88 Imperial quarts
1°C = 3.8°F

Clothing Conversions

Women's Dresses, Coats, Skirts

USA	4	6	8	10	11	12	13	14	15	16	18
Continental	36	38	38	40	40	42	42	44	44	46	48
GB	8	10	11	12	13	14	15	16	17	18	20

Women's Blouses, Sweaters

USA	10	12	14	16	18	20
Continental	38	40	42	44	46	48
GB	32	34	36	38	40	42

Women's Shoes

USA	5	6	7	8	9	10
Continental	36	37	38	39	40	41
GB	3½	4½	5½	6½	7½	8½

Men's Suits

USA	34	36	38	40	42	44	46	48
Continental	44	46	48	50	52	54	56	58
GB	34	36	38	40	42	44	46	48

Men's Shirts

USA	14	15	15	16	16	17	17	18
Continental	37	38	39	41	42	43	44	45
GB	14	15	15	16	16	17	17	18

Men's Shoes

USA	7	8	9	10	11	12	13
Continental	39½	41	42	43	44½	46	47
GB	6	7	8	9	10	11	12

Men's Hats

USA	6⅞	7⅛	7¼	7⅜	7½
Continental	55	56	58	59	60
GB	6¼	6⅞	7⅛	7¼	7⅜

Children's Clothing

USA	3	4	5	6	6X
Continental	98	104	110	116	122
GB	18	20	22	24	26

Children's Shoes

USA	8	9	10	11	12	13	1	2	3
Continental	24	25	27	28	29	30	32	33	34
GB	7	8	9	10	11	12	13	1	2

ENGLAND

Though the once-supreme Empire is a vanishing ghost, and England has politically and economically retreated to its own small corner of Europe, this land holds to its past tenaciously. Its public life continues to include conspicuous observances of tradition: pageants of royalty, the bearing of the mace in Parliament, the pacing of Oxford and Cambridge graduates down the corridors of power. This is the country of the dear Queen Mum, heathered moors, and Alistair Cooke's weekly Miss Marple. This is also the country of Soho, football hooligans, and page-3 pinups, provided every morning by Rupert Murdoch. Birthplace of the Brontës and the Beatles, Monty Python and Virginia Woolf, Benjamin Britten and Benny Hill—"this blessed plot, this earth, this realm" is phenomenally diverse.

History

However isolationist today, Britain's island status did not protect it from intrusive foreign legions. Stonehenge and the stone circles of Avebury bear mute witness to the Isles' earliest inhabitants; recorded history began with the Celts. The Romans occupied Britain from the first century AD until the middle of the fifth century AD, their territorial claim extending as far north as Hadrian's Wall (built by the Roman Emperor Hadrian between AD 117 and 138); however, Caesar's legions failed to subdue the Celts in Wales and Cornwall in the west. Christian missionaries began arriving with the Romans, proselytizing beyond the limits of the Empire into Scotland and Ireland. With the dawning of the Christian era, the regions currently defined as Wales, England, Scotland, Northern Ireland and Ireland began to develop divergent identities.

With the decline of the Roman Empire in the 4th century, Britain was raided from northern Europe, mainly by the Angles (hence the name 'England'), Saxons and Jutes. These tribes established settlements and Kingdoms alongside those of the resilient Celts (also known as Britons) in Wales and Cornwall. Abbot Augustine, archbishop of Cantebury, set about the conversion of the Anglo-Saxons in the latter part of the 7th century.

Vikings invaded from the 9th to the 11th centuries, with varying degrees of success. The first wave of Danes managed to create settlements but were defeated by Alfred the Great of the Saxon Wessex dynasty in 878. A second wave of invasions led to a short-lived Danish Dynasty in England (1017-1042), after which the Wessex line again restored local control.

The Vikings were more successful in France, establishing a duchy owing only nominal allegiance to the French king. Duke William of Normandy ventured across the Channel and defeated the English at the Battle of Hastings in 1066. William promptly set about cataloguing his recent acquisitions in the epic sheepskin Domesday Book. The Norman influence burgeoned during the next three centuries: French became the language of the nobility, and continental legal and social structures were adopted in England. The monarchy established by William and his successors successfully established its authority over increasingly wide areas of the British Isles.

Henry II, of the House of Anjou-Plantagenat, ascended to the throne in 1154, initiating the conquest of Ireland. The ruling sovereign was forced to sign the Magna Carta in 1215, a document whose emphasis on preserving the rights of the Church and respect for laws earned it recognition as the "Bible of the Constitution." The first Parliament was convened in 1265, and Wales bacame a principality of the English crown in 1284.

The Hundred Years War between England and France commenced in 1339. The ensuing era fostered an English nationalism that gave birth to English as the official language in the courts of law, as well as a distinctly English literature—Chaucer

Regional Key
Thurso
Shetland Islands
Orkney Islands
OUTER HEBRIDES
INNER HEBRIDES
Inverness
Aberdeen
SCOTLAND
Oban
St. Andrews
Edinburgh
Glasgow
Derry
Larne
Stranaer
NORTHERN IRELAND
Sligo
Belfast
Newcastle-upon-Tyne
NORTH ENGLAND
Carlisle
Middlesbrough
Blackpool
York
Hull
Galway
Dublin
Bradford
Leeds
Liverpool
Manchester
Holyhead
IRELAND
Limerick
CENTRAL ENGLAND
Rosslare Harbor
Aberystwyth
Birmingham
EAST ANGLIA
Norwich
Peterborough
Cambridge
Cork
Fishguard
WALES
Stratford-Upon-Avon
HEART OF ENGLAND
Oxford
Cardiff
Swansea
London
Canterbury
N
Bath
Salisbury
SOUTHWEST ENGLAND
SOUTHEAST ENGLAND
0
100 miles
0
100 kilometers
Plymouth
Exeter
Portsmouth
Brighton
Penzance
FRANCE

started writing his *Canterbury Tales* in 1340 and the Bible was first translated into English by Wyclif in 1380.

The Wars of the Roses pitted the house of Lancaster against that of York from 1455-85; it was Henry VII who restored law and order, inaugurating the rule of the House of Tudor which lasted until 1603. Henry VIII waged wars against France and Scotland, and proclaimed himself king of Ireland in 1542. Elizabeth I ruled during the latter half of the 16th century. During her reign, the English defeated the Spanish Armada to become the leading Protestant power in Europe, and established themselves as a colonial power.

The unification of England, Wales (already united administratively, politically and legally with England by the Acts of Union of 1536 and 1542) and Scotland effectively took place in 1603, when Protestant James VI of Scotland ascended to the English throne and became James I of England. Religious and political tensions came to a head in the English Civil War (1642-48), triggered by the Irish Catholics rising in protest against the 1641 massacre of Ulster. Under the influence of Oliver Cromwell and his Parliamentary army, the monarchy was abolished and a rather short-lived Commonwealth was founded in 1649. (The monarchy was restored in 1660.)

Naval and trade wars against the Dutch and another war with Spain, largely over colonial interests, dominated British foreign policy during the latter part of the 17th century. After the Peace of Utrecht in 1713, Britain emerged as the "Arbiter of Europe." Domestically, the relatively bloodless Glorious Revolution erupted in 1688 to ward off the possibility of a Catholic monarchical dynasty: Catholic James II turned tail when confronted with the Protestant William III of Orange, who also led the campaign against the Irish Jacobites. During the next century, industrialization insidiously and irreversibly altered the texture of English (and global) society; Adam Smith wrote *The Wealth of Nations* in 1776.

The British Empire flourished from 1814-1914, spurred to ever greater heights by the likes of Benjamin Disraeli, Cecil Rhodes, and Joseph Chamberlain. Weakened by the two World Wars, the Empire was forced to relinquish almost all her colonies in the decades following 1945. A reluctant member of the European Economic Community, Britain nurtures a self-image contorted by memories of global dominance.

The Media

English journalism is spirited and frequently irreverent. Major papers in England have a national circulation; the goal of every aspiring journalist is to finish his required apprenticeship in the provinces as quickly as possible and become one of the "hacks of Fleet Street." The influence of the papers on daily life is much greater than in cultures addicted to the tube; *The Sun,* a daily Rupert Murdoch-owned tabloid better known for its page-3 pinup than for its reporting, was widely credited with delivering victory to Margaret Thatcher in her re-election campaign. *The Times,* for centuries a model of thoughtful discretion and mild infallibility, has recently turned Tory under the leadership of Rupert "Buy It" Murdoch. The correspondence section still carries on eccentric exchanges for weeks on end, and personal ads were only recently demoted from the first page.

The intellectual and slightly left-of-center *Guardian,* based in Manchester, is the only local paper ever to go national. *The Financial Times,* printed on orange paper, does more elegantly for the City what the Wall Street Journal does for Manhattan. The *Daily Telegraph* (dubbed "Torygraph") is fairly conservative and old-fashioned, but rigorously fair. The *Independent* lives up to its name. *The Observer* is a polished Sunday paper. Of the tabloids, *The Daily Mail, The Daily Express,* and *The Standard* (the only evening paper) make serious attempts at popular journalism, while *News of the World,* the *Star,* the *Daily Mirror,* and *Today* are as bilious as *The Sun.* The best international news shows up in *The Times, The Guardian,* and *The Independent.*

The magazine *Punch,* dating from the days of Dickens, has retained its urbanity through a recent rejuvenation, and it continues to parody England and the world with vaguely eccentric delight. *Private Eye* is subversive and hilarious, an upstart, overtly political rival to the more puckish *Punch.* World affairs are covered with a surreptitious wit by *The Economist; The New Statesman* on the left and *The Spectator* on the right cover politics and the arts with verve and sense. *The Listener,* which dates from the BBC's earliest days, includes both transcripts of radio programs and articles that sustain the Beeb's reputation for scrupulous fairness.

The BBC established its reputation for fairness and wit with its radio services: BBC1 has ceded resposibilities of news coverage to its cousin BBC4, but continues to feature rock and roll institution John Peel on weekdays from 8:30-10pm. BBC2 has easy listening and light talk shows; BBC3 broadcasts classical music (undoubtedly the finest station of its kind in the world). Be aware that AM is called Medium Wave (MW) in England. Along with the national services, each town and region in England are equipped with a variety of commercial broadcasting services.

TV-owners in England have to pay a tax; this supports the advertisement-free activities of BBC TV. Its quasi-governmental associations have not hampered innovation. Home of *Monty Python's Flying Circus,* BBC TV broadcasts on two national channels. BBC1 carries news at 1pm, 6pm, and 9pm as well as various Britcoms. Sheep-dog trials are telecast on BBC2, along with various "cultural" programs. ITV, Britain's established commerical network, carries much comedy along with its own McNews. Channel 4, the newest channel, has highly respected arts programming and a fine news broadcast at 7pm on weeknights—Salman Rushdie once worked for them. This web of national programming is supplemented by local stations. Parliament was introduced to television in late 1989: try to catch a session of Question Time, the regular, frequently hostile, parliamentary interrogation of the prime minister. (It's a far cry from the rehearsed, banal press conferences aired in the U.S.)

Music

No more buttered scones for me, Mater, I'm off to play the grand piano!

—Graham Chapman

England was long considered "a land without music," for while Europe expanded into the fervid creativity of 19th-century Romanticism, England withdrew, less producers of musical genius than connoisseurs of and hosts to Europe's best talent. The lion's share of English musical achievement was produced during the Renaissance, Restoration, and the 20th century.

Under the reign of Elizabeth I, the arts in England flourished as never before. Byrd's magnificent pieces for both the Anglican and Roman Churches vividly represent a country torn by religious differences but secure in its sense of might. Morley, Weelkes, and Wilbye took up the madrigal just as it was about to be abandoned in its native Italy, and infused it with a new expressiveness. Perhaps the most famous composer of the Elizabethan Age was the lachrymose lutenist John Dowland (1563-1626). Henry Purcell (1659-1695), England's only well-known composer through the 18th and 19th centuries, was the pride of England after the Restoration, and his opera *Dido and Aeneas* remains one of the masterpieces of the musical stage. Handel considered England his home after 1713, and the English certainly consider Handel theirs. J.C. Bach arrived in England in 1762 and promptly was claimed as "the English Bach." Mozart composed his first symphony in Chelsea; Haydn's last was named the "London."

In the late 19th century, the grand operettas of W.S. Gilbert and Arthur Sullivan satirized contemporary political blunders and social mores. In spite of their personal animosity, the two collaborated successfully on such perennial favorites as *The Mi-*

kado, H.M.S. Pinafore, and *The Pirates of Penzance.* Serious music began a "second renaissance" under Edward Elgar, whose moments of bombast are usually outweighed by passages of quiet eloquence—"Nimrod" in the *Enigma Variations,* for example. Frederick Delius created his own version of impressionism, while Gustav Holst *(The Planets)* adapted the methods of neoclassicism to folk materials and a Romantic temperament. Arnold Bax was unabashedly Romantic, writing lush and at times silly symphonies.

William Walton and Ralph Vaughan Williams created a modernist tradition in English music. Walton's *First Symphony* and Vaughan Williams's *Sixth* are two of the century's finest scores, along with Havergal Brian's *Gothic.* Benjamin Britten's *Peter Grimes* made modern opera accessible to a wide range of audiences; Britten wrote an extended series of operas, ending with a voluptuously doom-laden version of *Death in Venice.* Michael Tippett followed Britten's lead in opera while composing four powerful symphonies and *A Child of Our Time.* Peter Maxwell Davies, Harrison Birtwistle, Brian Ferneyhough, and Robert Simpson are the most important composers of the post-war era.

England's contribution to the popular music of the last half-century is immeasurable. The Beatles are modern icons, and their later music, particularly, is rich with mildly sarcastic commentary on English life. The Rolling Stones have energetically resisted the norms of polite society for nearly thirty years now—their gaunt faces and public prancing recall the England not of picnic baskets from Harrod's, but of football stampedes and racial riots.

For a brief few years in the late 60s, the London Underground did not refer to mass transit but to the center of Europe's avant-garde culture. The groups included Cream and Pink Floyd—but in the mass consumption of the 70s, Cream dissolved and Pink Floyd evolved into a corporate entity. One day in 1976, while Paul McCartney slept and Pink Floyd lay in a collective trance, rock music was stolen from its regular custodians by a political theorist and Chelsea sexshop owner named Malcolm McLaren. Soon thereafter, McLaren's clients the Sex Pistols released their fiercely indifferent anthems of negation "Anarchy in the U.K." and "God Save the Queen," the latter reported on the BBC charts as a blank space. Within weeks, this ominous void was filled by an entire punk subculture and musical syntax. Thousands of bands surfaced from the depths, recorded primitive and brutal denunciations of their sinking island, and vanished. McLaren eventually handed rock back to the authorities, scattering behind only a few rusty safety pins and corroded celebrities as evidence of his crime. The transition into the 80s once again reminded the world of the energy of the English club scene—emerging from it not only the pseudo-intellectual blather of The Police and later Sting, high priest of his own religion, but also many fine experimental groups. The angst-laden outpourings of the New Order, Siouxsie and the Banshees, and the Smiths have renewed the English presence on a pop scene otherwise populated by Samantha Foxes and various irretrievably vulgar heavy metal bands.

Food

> *English cooking, like the English climate, is a training for life's unavoidable hardships.*
>
> *—R. P. Lister*

The modest reputation of English cuisine is redeemed by the acknowledged, cholesteroly splendor of the English breakfast. This famous repast, still served in the best B&Bs, consists of orange juice, eggs, bacon, sausage, toast, butter, marmalade, grilled tomatoes and mushrooms, kippers, and (in winter) porridge. You will probably want to choose tea to wash all this down; unlike its French and Italian counterparts, English coffee is not exceptional.

The rest of English cuisine is not all boiled blandness. Dairy products from southwestern England are excellent, especially fresh Devonshire cream. The English are a nation of carnivores, and the best native dishes are roasts—beef, lamb, and Wiltshire hams. Beef roasts have a perfect side-dish in Yorkshire "pud," an airy batter baked in the meat drippings. Many proprietors will prepare vegetarian meals on request, if the incessance of meat's too much for you. *In addition, when you get to Britain, ask about the status of "mad cow disease" (bovine spongiform encephalopathy, or BSE)—in 1990, fear that it might possibly be transmissible put a crushing dent in the demand for beef.* Vegetables, usually boiled into a flavorless, textureless, colorless mass, are the weakest part of the meal; ask for a salad instead. The English like their desserts exceedingly sweet, but even if you shy from sugar you should try one of the glorious English puddings. "Boiled in a pail, tied in the tail of an old bleached shirt, so hot that they hurt," some of the best varieties are Christmas pudding, treacle tart, Spotty Dick, and steamed castle pudding, all served with thick jams and syrups. Perhaps the most blatant misnomer in the English language is trifle, a wondrous combination of the best things in life—cake, custard, jam, pudding, whipped cream, and fresh fruit. Crumpets, scones, shortbread, Jaffa cakes, and rich Dundee fruitcake are all tasty side-effects of the English sweet tooth.

Pub grub (food served in bars) is fast, filling, and a good option when all else is closed or vandalishly expensive. Hot meals vary from Cornish pasties (meat and vegetable wrapped in a pastry) and toad-in-the-hole (sausages baked in a batter) to steak and kidney pie with vegetables. The inexpensive "ploughman's lunch" is simply cheese, bread, pickle, chutney, and a tomato or two. Contrary to common belief, it is not traditional English country fare but the product of a 60s advertising campaign. Fish and chips, traditionally served in newsprint and dripping with grease, now face competition from McNuggets and the Whopper.

Outdoor markets and supermarkets (Safeway, Sainsbury, the Co-Op, and Tesco) sell suitable fare for picnics. Buy some cheese (Stilton and Double Gloucester are sharp, Cheddar the cheapest), apples (Cox's pippins are good), and a piece of English chocolate, and then find a suitably picturesque view. As an alternative to English food, try Chinese, Greek, and Indian cuisines. English restaurants (especially those in London and Birmingham) serve some of the best *tandoori* food outside of India.

Tea

English "tea" refers to both a drink and a social ritual. Tea the drink is the preferred remedy for exhaustion, ennui, a row with one's partner, a rainy morning, or a slow afternoon. English tea is served strong and milky; if you want it any other way, say so. Tea anywhere—in plush hotels or railway cars—tastes more or less the same until you graduate into the higher echelons of Jackson's or Fortnum & Mason's teas.

Tea the social ritual centers around a meal. Afternoon high tea includes cooked meats, salad, sandwiches, and pastries. "Tea" in the north of England refers to the evening meal, often served with a huge pot of tea. Cream tea, a specialty of Cornwall and Devon, includes toast, shortbread, crumpets, scones, and jam, accompanied by delicious clotted cream (a cross between whipped cream and butter). Most Brits take short tea breaks each day, mornings ("elevenses") and afternoons (around 4pm). Sunday takes the cake for best tea day; the indulgent can while away a couple of hours over a pot of Earl Grey, a pile of buttered scones, and the Sunday supplements.

Pubs and Beer

"As much of the history of England has been brought about in public houses as in the House of Commons," said Sir William Harcourt. As a transient, you may not witness history in the making, but you will certainly absorb the spirit of the land. The pub's importance as a social institution is reflected in its careful furnishings. Mahogany walls are ancient and often intricately carved; the benches are velvet-covered. Many pubs are centuries old, and each has a distinctive history, ambience, and clientele. Pub crawls are the English equivalent of bar hopping; some of the larger cities put out pub guides, available in bookstores. The Campaign for Real Ale (CAMRA) publishes a guide to pubs that serve real ale; write to 34 Alma Rd., St. Albans, Herts., England AL1 3BR (£4.50 plus postage).

In June 1987, Parliament voted to scrap a 1915 liquor law that required English pubs to close in the afternoon from 3pm to 6pm. Now pubs may stay open daily from 11am to 11pm. The hallowed cry of the publican, "Hurry up, please; it's time," leaves patrons 10 minutes to finish their pints.

Beer—not wine or cocktails—is the standard pub drink. Young's and Fuller's are widely available brands, and Samuel Smith and Tetleys, although less common, are superb ales. All beers except lagers are served at room temperature. Varieties include bitter, pale and brown ales, lager, and Guinness—a rich, creamy, and very dark Irish brew.

Cider, a fermented apple juice served either sweet or dry, is one alternative to beer. Those who don't drink alcohol should savor the pub experience all the same; Cidona, a non-alcoholic cider, and BritVic fruit juices are served. Along with food and drink, pubs often host games. Traditional pub games include darts, pool, and snooker (billiards played on a larger table with smaller balls). More recently, a brash and bewildering array of video games has invaded many pubs, as has piped-in music.

Sports

The English take their sports seriously. Football (known as soccer in the U.S.) is a chaotic and rowdy spectacle of chanting, urinating, crowds, fierce loyalties, and sudden violent outbursts. It is bet upon energetically. Cricket, a game of great subtlety and languorous civility, involves England and former members of its empire in intricate matches that last either one or five days. Rugby—"rugger" to its players—is a random *melée* of blood and drinking songs, incomprehensible to the outsider. Horse-racing is integral to English leisure; the Grand National Steeplechase in Liverpool in March, and the Royal Ascot and the Derby, in June are the highlights of the equestrian year. If English sports leave you bored, take solace in the fact that Monday Night Football is now often relayed from the U.S. to television screens all over Britain.Snooker

Language

Some English dialects are almost indecipherable to the unattuned ear. Some of the expressions favored by the English are listed below:

banger	sausage
bap	a soft bun, like a hamburger bun
baxfest	general mirthfulness
bedsitter, or bedsit	one-room apartment, sometimes with kitchen
bill	check (in restaurants)
biro	ball-point pen
biscuit	if sweet, a cookie; if not, a cracker
bladdered, blitzed	drunk
bobby	police officer
bonnet	car hood
boot	car trunk
boozer	pub
brick	a sport, a good person
brilliant	nifty, "cool"

caravan	trailer, mobile home
car park	parking lot
cheers, or cheerio	goodbye, sometimes thank you
chemist	pharmacist
chips	french fries
coach	bus
court shoes	women's pumps
crisps	potato chips
crumpets	like English muffins, slightly different
dicey, or dodgy	problematic
digs	lodgings
dinner	lunch
dosh	money
dual carriageway	divided highway
dustbin	trash can
first floor	first floor up (second floor)
flannel	washcloth
flat	apartment
fortnight	two weeks
grotty	grungy
hire	rental
hoover	vacuum cleaner
iced lolly	popsicle
in the high street	on Main Street
jam	jelly
jelly	Jell-O
jumble sale	yard sale
jumper	sweater
kip	sleep
knackered	tired, worn out
lavatory, "lav"	restroom
lay-by	paved shoulder or roadside turnout
leader (in newspaper)	editorial
leaflet	pamphlet, brochure, flyer
to let	to rent
lift	elevator
loo	restroom
lorry	truck
mate	pal
motorway	highway
naff	uncool
nappies	diapers
narg	geek, nerd
off-license	retail liquor store
pants	underwear
petrol	gasoline
phone box, call box	telephone booth
piss (take the piss out of)	make fun of
pissed	drunk
plimsolls	sneakers
pudding	dessert
pull	to "score"
quid	pound (in money)
queue up	line up
return ticket	round-trip ticket
ring up	telephone
roundabout	rotary road interchange
rubber	eraser

self-catering	(accommodation with) kitchen facilities
self-drive	car rental
single carriageway	non-divided highway
single ticket	one-way ticket
sleeping policeman	speed bump
smarties	M&Ms, without the M's
spotted dick	steamed sponge pudding with raisins
stalls	orchestra seats
stone	14 pounds (in body weight)
subway	underground pedestrian passage
sultanas	raisins
sweets	candy
swish	swanky
ta	thank you
ta-ta	good-bye
tights	nylons
toilet	restroom
torch	flashlight
trainers	sneakers
trunk call	long-distance telephone call
Tube, or Underground	London subway
verge	edge of road, shoulder
vest	undershirt
wellies	boots
W.C.	restroom
zed	letter "Z"

London

When a man is tired of London he is tired of life.
—Samuel Johnson

Through nursery rhymes, songs, and stories, we absorb London before we are even aware it exists; arriving in the city for the first time can be an odd homecoming, an eerie *déjà vu.* There are the red double-decker buses; the bobbies and the impassive guards at Buckingham in their enormous bear-skin hats; Westminster Abbey, rising more from the haze of memory than from the morning fog; and the notes of Big Ben, knelling through the mists as we have come to believe all bells must toll.

Orientation

Arriving and Departing

By Air

With planes landing every 47 seconds, **Heathrow Airport** (tel. 759 4321), in Hounslow, Middlesex, is the world's busiest international airport. The banks in each terminal are open daily: Thomas Cook, Terminal 1 (open 24 hrs.); International Currency Exchange, Terminal 2 (open 6am-11pm); and Travellers' Exchange Corporation, Terminals 3 and 4 (open 24 hrs.). The easiest way to reach central London from Heathrow is by **Underground** (about 70 min.), with one stop for terminals 1, 2, and 3 and one for terminal 4. A single ticket into the city costs £2.30, but if you plan on making more than one tube ride in a day, invest in a Travelcard for £3.10. To reach **Victoria Station,** transfer at Earl's Court or Gloucester Rd. to a District Line or Circle Line train heading east. At Victoria, you'll find a blue **Tourist Information Centre** with an accommodations service, a currency exchange office, and information about transportation connections (see Getting Around London below).

London Regional Transport's **Airbus** (tel. 222 1234) makes the one-hour trip from Heathrow to central points in the city, including hotels (departures every 30 min. 6am-3pm, every hr. 3pm-6am; £5, children £3). A **National Express** bus (tel. 730 0202) goes from Heathrow to Victoria coach station approximately every half hour until 9pm (1 hr., £6.75). A **Green Line** bus (tel. 668 7261) also makes the trip. After midnight, you can avoid the £30 taxi fare to Central London by taking night bus #N97 from Heathrow bus station to Piccadilly Circus (every hr. just before the hr. until 5am). National Express makes the 1-hr. trip from Gatwick to Heathrow every hour for £6.75.

Most charter flights land at **Gatwick Airport** in West Sussex (tel. 668 4211 or (0293) 228 22). From there, take the BR **Gatwick Express** train to Victoria Station (30 min., £7). Taxis take twice as long and cost almost five times as much. National Express coaches (#777) run hourly between Gatwick and Victoria from 6am to 8pm (75 min., £6).

By Train

If you are leaving London by train, find out from which of the eight major stations (Charing Cross, Euston, King's Cross, Liverpool Street, Paddington, St. Pancras, Victoria, or Waterloo) you will depart. The subway system, the **London Underground** or **Tube,** conveniently links these stations, and the tube stops bear the same names as the train stations. For information about particular destinations in Great Britain, consult the display pages in the British Telecom Yellow Pages phonebook (under the heading "British Rail"). For inquiries about rail services to Europe, call 834 2345.

British Rail runs **Travel Centres** at its mainline stations and at 12-16 Regent St. (Tube: Piccadilly Circus); The Strand (Tube: Charing Cross); Victoria St.; and King William St. (All open Mon.-Fri. 9am-5pm.) For **lost property,** check the property offices at mainline terminals.

To get a **Young Person's Railcard** (£16), you must be under 24 or a full-time student in the UK. A **Senior Railcard** for persons over 60 also costs £16. Both will save you 1/3 on off-peak travel for one year. A **Network Card** (£8) gives the same discount for travel in the Network South East area. Further details can be obtained from any mainline station.

By Coach

Victoria Coach Station (Tube: Victoria), located on Buckingham Palace Rd., is the hub of Britain's denationalized coach network. **National Express** coaches service an expansive network which links cities big and small. Coaches are considerably less expensive than trains but also take longer. (See Day Trips for rates and frequency of train and coach services to towns near London.) National Express offers a **Discount Coach Card** (£5) to students, disabled, and elderly. The card gives a 30% discount off normal fares at any time. Other coach companies compete with National Express; their routes often overlap and their prices are almost identical.

By Thumb

Let's Go strongly urges you to seriously consider the risks before you choose to hitch. We do not recommend hitching as a means of travel.

Should you decide to hitch, the Tourist Information Centre publishes a list of route suggestions. The University of London Union's ride board, on the ground floor of 1 Malet St. (Tube: Russell Sq.) lists a number of possibilities. Hitching can be quite difficult within central London and easier from places like Cambridge and Oxford to the city.

Layout of Greater London

Greater London is a colossal aggregate of distinct villages and anonymous suburbs, of ancient settlements and modern developments. As London grew, it swallowed adjacent cities and nearby villages, chewed up the counties of Kent, Surrey, Essex, and Hertfordshire, and digested all of Middlesex. Names such as the "City of Westminster" are vestiges of this urban imperialism. "The City" now refers to the ancient, and much smaller, "City of London," which covers but one of the 620 square miles of Greater London. The traveler's most useful navigational aids are the *London A to Z* and Nicholson's *London Streetfinder* (both available from newsagents and bookstores for £2-2.50).

Touring

Seeing all of London? Guess again. You'll never finish. London is a city of details and discovery. Don't feel that you must visit every monument of Western Civilization; they'll all still be there when you come back. Some tours can breeze you through the highlights enabling you to decide where to focus your energies.

The London Transport Sightseeing Tour (tel. 222 1234), provides a convenient and reasonable overview of London's maze of attractions. Tours lasting 1½ hrs. depart from Baker St., Haymarket, near Piccadilly Circus, Marble Arch, and Victoria St. (near the station), and include Buckingham Palace, the Houses of Parliament, Westminster Abbey, the Tower of London, St. Paul's, and Piccadilly Circus. (Tours daily every ½ hr. 10am-5pm; £8, under 16 £4, or £7 and £3 in advance from the British Travel Centre, a London Tourist Board Information Centre, or a London Transport Information Centre.) Longer day trips are also available. For half the

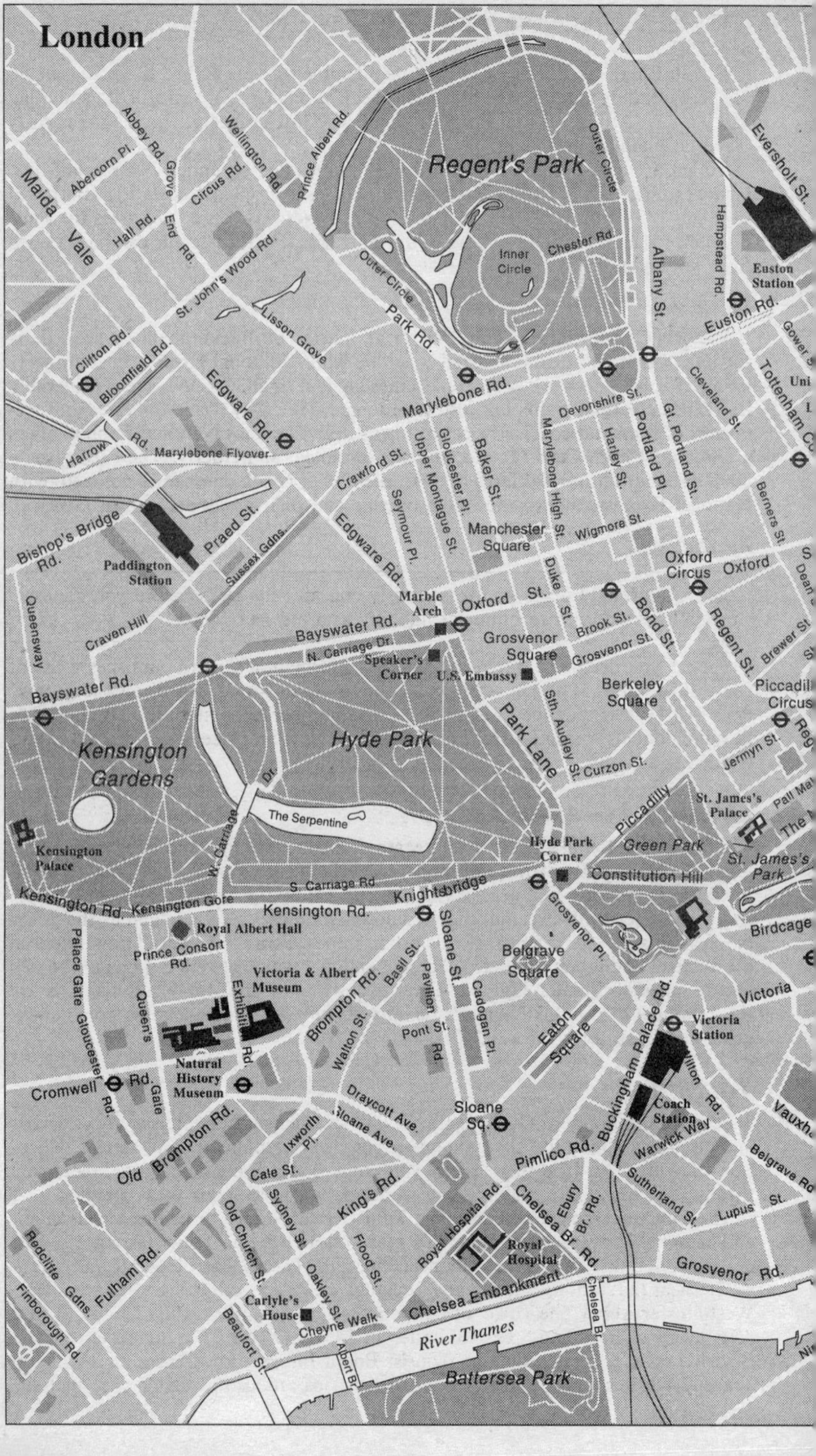
London
Regent's Park
Outer Circle
Inner Circle
Chester Rd.
Abbey Rd.
Abercorn Pl.
Maida Vale
Grove End Rd.
Circus Rd.
Wellington Rd.
Prince Albert Rd.
Hall Rd.
St. John's Wood Rd.
Lisson Grove
Park Rd.
Clifton Rd.
Bloomfield Rd.
Edgware Rd.
Harrow Rd.
Marylebone Flyover
Marylebone Rd.
Albany St.
Hampstead Rd.
Eversholt St.
Euston Station
Euston Rd.
Gower St.
Tottenham Ct.
Devonshire St.
Cleveland St.
Portland Pl.
Gt. Portland St.
Harley St.
Marylebone High St.
Baker St.
Gloucester Pl.
Upper Montague St.
Crawford St.
Seymour Pl.
Berners St.
Bishop's Bridge Rd.
Praed St.
Sussex Gdns.
Paddington Station
Manchester Square
Wigmore St.
Oxford Circus
Oxford St.
Marble Arch
Duke St.
Bond St.
Regent St.
Queensway
Craven Hill
Bayswater Rd.
N. Carriage Dr.
Speaker's Corner
U.S. Embassy
Grosvenor Square
Brook St.
Grosvenor St.
Brewer St.
Berkeley Square
Piccadilly Circus
Park Lane
Sth. Audley St.
Curzon St.
Jermyn St.
Kensington Gardens
Hyde Park
The Serpentine
W. Carriage Dr.
Kensington Palace
Piccadilly
St. James's Palace
Pall Mall
Green Park
St. James's Park
Hyde Park Corner
Constitution Hill
S. Carriage Rd.
Kensington Rd.
Kensington Gore
Knightsbridge
Sloane St.
Grosvenor Pl.
Birdcage
Royal Albert Hall
Prince Consort Rd.
Palace Gate
Victoria & Albert Museum
Exhibition Rd.
Basil St.
Pavilion Rd.
Belgrave Square
Brompton Rd.
Cadogan Pl.
Victoria
Victoria Station
Queen's Gate
Gloucester Rd.
Walton St.
Pont St.
Eaton Square
Buckingham Palace Rd.
Hilton Rd.
Cromwell Rd.
Natural History Museum
Draycott Ave.
Sloane Ave.
Sloane Sq.
Coach Station
Vauxhall
Ixworth Pl.
Warwick Way
Old Brompton Rd.
Pimlico Rd.
Belgrave Rd.
Cale St.
King's Rd.
Royal Hospital Rd.
Chelsea Br. Rd.
Ebury Br. Rd.
Sutherland St.
Lupus St.
Redcliffe Gdns.
Fulham Rd.
Old Church St.
Sydney St.
Flood St.
Royal Hospital
Grosvenor Rd.
Finborough Rd.
Oakley St.
Carlyle's House
Chelsea Embankment
Chelsea Br.
Beaufort St.
Cheyne Walk
River Thames
Albert Br.
Battersea Park

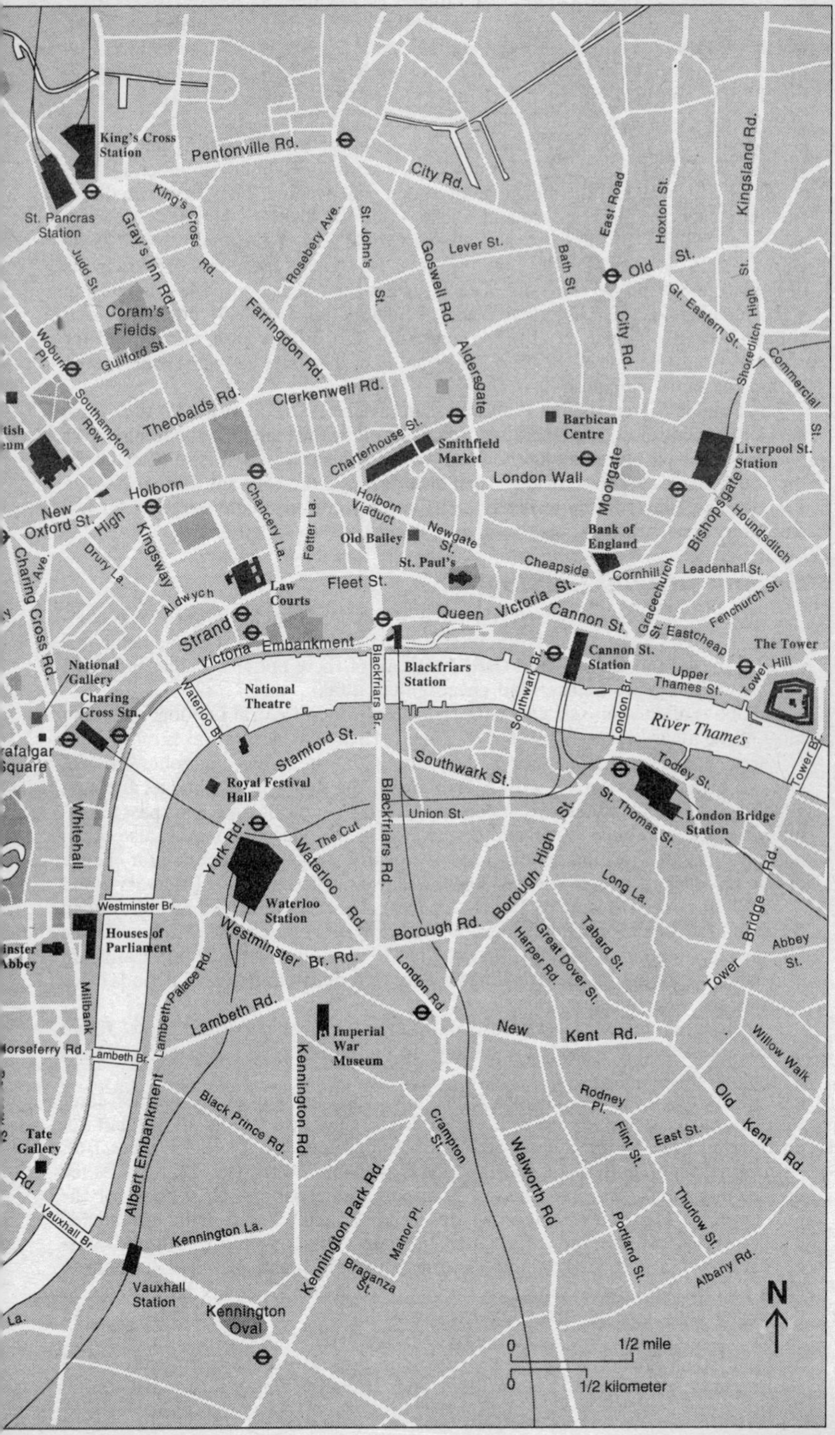
King's Cross Station
St. Pancras Station
Pentonville Rd.
City Rd.
King's Cross Rd.
Gray's Inn Rd.
Judd St.
Rosebery Ave.
St. John's St.
Goswell Rd.
Lever St.
Bath St.
East Road
Hoxton St.
Kingsland Rd.
Old St.
City Rd.
Gt. Eastern St.
Shoreditch High St.
Commercial St.
Coram's Fields
Guilford St.
Woburn Pl.
Southampton Row
Farringdon Rd.
Aldersgate
Theobalds Rd.
Clerkenwell Rd.
Barbican Centre
Charterhouse St.
Smithfield Market
London Wall
Moorgate
Liverpool St. Station
Bishopsgate
Houndsditch
Holborn
New Oxford St.
High
Chancery La.
Fetter La.
Holborn Viaduct
Newgate St.
Old Bailey
St. Paul's
Bank of England
Cheapside
Cornhill
Leadenhall St.
Gracechurch St.
Fenchurch St.
Eastcheap
Drury La.
Kingsway
Charing Cross Rd.
Ave.
Aldwych
Law Courts
Fleet St.
Queen Victoria St.
Cannon St.
Strand
Victoria Embankment
Blackfriars Station
Blackfriars Br.
Southwark Br.
Cannon St. Station
London Br.
Upper Thames St.
The Tower
Tower Hill
River Thames
Tower Br.
National Gallery
Charing Cross Stn.
National Theatre
Waterloo Br.
Trafalgar Square
Stamford St.
Southwark St.
Tooley St.
Royal Festival Hall
Union St.
St. Thomas St.
London Bridge Station
Whitehall
York Rd.
The Cut
Waterloo Rd.
Blackfriars Rd.
Borough High St.
Long La.
Westminster Br.
Waterloo Station
Borough Rd.
Tabard St.
Tower Bridge Rd.
Houses of Parliament
Westminster Abbey
Westminster Br. Rd.
Great Dover St.
Harper Rd.
Abbey St.
Lambeth Palace Rd.
London Rd.
Millbank
Lambeth Rd.
Imperial War Museum
New Kent Rd.
Willow Walk
Horseferry Rd.
Lambeth Br.
Kennington Rd.
Black Prince Rd.
Albert Embankment
Rodney Pl.
Flint St.
East St.
Old Kent Rd.
Crampton St.
Walworth Rd
Tate Gallery
Rd.
Vauxhall Br.
Kennington La.
Kennington Park Rd.
Manor Pl.
Portland St.
Thurlow St.
Albany Rd.
Braganza St.
Vauxhall Station
Kennington Oval
La.
N
0
1/2 mile
0
1/2 kilometer

price and a different perspective, London Transport also operates **London by Night,** which whizzes by London's floodlit landmarks. It departs 9pm from Victoria Station, 9:10pm from Park Lane, 9:15pm from Lancaster Gate, 9:20 pm from Paddington Station, and 9:35 pm from Piccadilly Circus (£3.50, under 14 £2).

A walking tour can fill in the hidden nooks that bus tours run right over; with a good guide, it can be as entertaining as it is informative. **The Original London Walks** (tel. 435 6413; £4, £2.50 for students, accompanied children under 15 free) conducts 2 hr. walks in the morning, afternoon, and evening. They have two different tours each for Shakespeare and Dickens and for Sherlock Holmes's London, as well as "Ghosts of the City" and others. **City Walks of London** (tel. 837 2841) allows you to discover "Beatles London" or revisit some of the more horrific aspects of the late 1880s in "On the Trail of Jack the Ripper." Tours cost £4, students and YHA members, £2.50. **Historical Walks of London** (tel. 668 4019), offers the usual jaunts (Dickens, Ripper, et al.) (£4, concession £3). In any case, ask around for opinions from veterans of the tours. The quality of the walks can vary widely, even within the same company.

The **London Silver Jubilee Walkway** map (available free at any LTB tourist office) circles central London in a ring of sights. Follow the map (and the round silver plaques in the pavement along the way) from Trafalgar Sq. to Westminster, along the South Bank to Tower Bridge, then back through the City and Bloomsbury to Trafalgar Sq. The 12-mile walkway easily breaks up into smaller sections for less ambitious types.

Getting Around London

London's public transit system, operated by **London Regional Transport,** is comprehensive. The Tube alone is impressive in its coverage, and it is supplemented by LRT buses and **British Rail (BR).** With all of these options, public transport will very often prove quicker and cheaper than a taxi.

London is divided into six concentric transport zones. Central London, including most of the major sights, is covered by Zone 1; Heathrow Airport takes off in Zone 6. Fares depend on the distance of the journey and the number of zones crossed, and are high. Arm yourself with a **Travelcard,** the savior of the budget traveler, which will prove a bargain if you make more than a couple of trips. This pass allows unlimited rides on buses, tube, and British Rail in the relevant zones. It also eliminates the hassle of waiting on long lines in crowded stations or fumbling for change on the top deck of a lurching bus. The one-day Travelcard (£2.30 for zones 1 and 2, £2.70 for zones 1-4, and £3.10 for all zones) is not valid before 9:30am Monday through Friday or for night buses (see Buses below). The seven-day card is available for any combination of zones (from zone 1, £7.80, to all zones, £22.00). Cards are also available for month- or year-long periods, or for custom-designed periods (they pro-rate the weekly rate).

For the seven-day or longer cards, you will need one passport-sized photo. Photo booths are located at major tube stations, including Victoria, Leicester Sq., Earl's Ct., and Oxford Circus.

If you want a Travelcard before 9:30am on a weekday, you can buy an LT card. More expensive than the One-Day Travelcard, the LT card is valid all day, but not on BR trains (£3.50 for zones 1 and 2, £4.50 for zones 1-4, £5.50 for zones 1-6).

Information on both buses and the tube is available 24 hrs. (tel. 222 1234). Pick up free maps and guides at London Transport's information offices (look for the lower-case "i" logo at information windows and on signs). You can find well-staffed booths with free maps and information on buses, Underground trains, and tours at Heathrow Airport, Euston and Victoria rail stations, and six major tube stops: King's Cross (open Sat.-Thurs. 8:15am-6pm, Fri. 8:15am-7:30pm); Piccadilly Circus (open daily 8:15am-6pm); Oxford Circus (open Mon.-Sat. 8:15am-6pm); St. James' Park (open Mon.-Fri. 9am-5:30pm); Liverpool St. (open Mon.-Fri. 9:30am-6:30pm, Sat. 8:30am-6:30pm, Sun. 8:30am-3:30pm); Heathrow Terminals 1, 2, 3 station (open Mon.-Sat. 7:15 am-6:30pm, Sun. 8:15am-6:30pm); Euston BR station

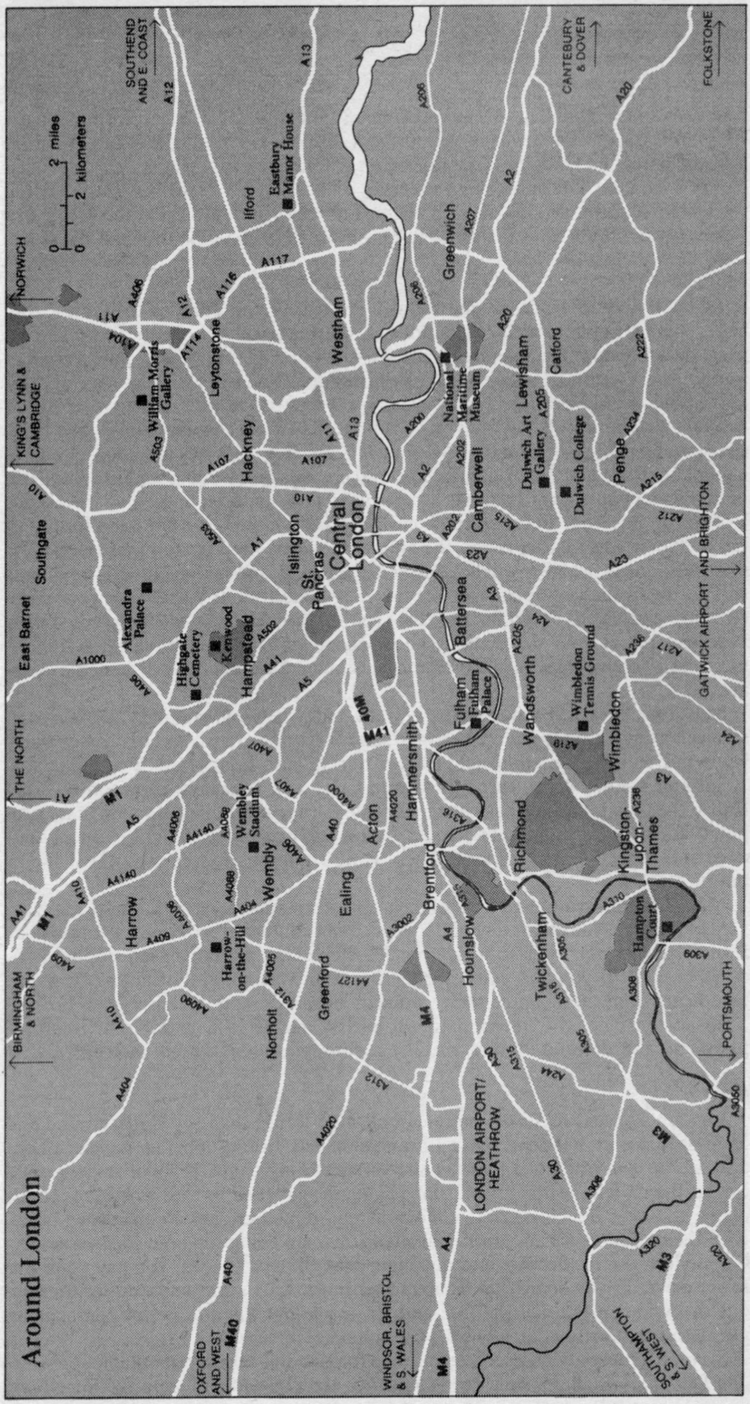
Around London
0 2 miles
0 2 kilometers
SOUTHEND AND E. COAST
NORWICH
KING'S LYNN & CAMBRIDGE
THE NORTH
BIRMINGHAM & NORTH
OXFORD AND WEST
WINDSOR, BRISTOL, & S WALES
LONDON AIRPORT/ HEATHROW
SOUTHAMPTON & S WEST
PORTSMOUTH
GATWICK AIRPORT AND BRIGHTON
FOLKSTONE
CANTEBURY & DOVER
Ilford
Eastbury Manor House
Westham
Greenwich
National Maritime Museum
Lewisham
Catford
Leytonstone
William Morris Gallery
Hackney
Islington
St. Pancras
Central London
Camberwell
Dulwich Art Gallery
Dulwich College
Penge
Southgate
East Barnet
Alexandra Palace
Highgate Cemetery
Kenwood
Hampstead
Battersea
Fulham
Fulham Palace
Wandsworth
Wimbledon Tennis Ground
Wimbledon
Hammersmith
Acton
Wembley Stadium
Wembly
Harrow
Harrow-on-the-Hill
Ealing
Brentford
Richmond
Kingston-upon-Thames
Hampton Court
Twickenham
Hounslow
Greenford
Northolt
M1
M4
M3
M40
M41

(open Mon.-Thurs. 7:15am-6pm, Fri. 7:15am-7:30pm, Sat. 7:15am-6pm, Sun. 8:15 am-6pm); Victoria BR station (open daily 8:15am-9:30pm); Heathrow Terminal 1 arrivals (open Mon.-Fri. 7:15am-10:15pm, Sat. 7:15am-9pm, Sun. 8:15am-10pm); Terminal 2 arrivals (open Mon.-Sat. 7:15am-9pm, Sun. 8:15am-10pm); Terminal 3 arrivals (open Mon.-Sat. 6:30am-1:15pm, Sun. 8:15am-3pm); and Terminal 4 arrivals (open Mon.-Sat. 6:30am-6:30pm, Sun. 8:15am-6:30pm). For information on how the buses and Underground trains are currently running, phone 222 1200 (open 24 hrs.). London Transport's **lost property office** (tel. 486 2496) lies just down the road from Sherlock at 200 Baker St. (Tube: Baker St.; open Mon.-Fri. 9:30am-2pm). Allow two working days for articles lost on buses or the tube to reach the office.

Underground

The color-coded **Underground** railway system, or the **Tube,** is the easiest way to get around London, with 269 stations on 11 lines (Bakerloo, Central, Circle, District, East London, Hammersmith and City, Jubilee, Metropolitan, Northern, Piccadilly, and Victoria). **Fares** depend on the number of zones passed through. A journey wholly within central zone 1 costs 80p; one from zone 1 to zone 2 £1.10. A trip to a distant suburb may set you back up to £3.80. On Sundays and Public Holidays, trains run less frequently. All transfers are free. Bicycles are allowed on the Circle, District, and Metropolitan lines except during morning and evening rush hours. Riders under age 16 travel at a reduced fare; children under five travel free.

You can buy your ticket either from the ticket window or from a machine. The ticket allows you to go through the automatic gates; keep it until you reach your final destination, where it will be collected or eaten by another machine. Travelcards will not be swallowed by the gates or taken by collectors. If you change your mind en route and decide to go farther than you've paid for, you will have to pay the "excess fare" at your destination. Those people convicted of traveling without a ticket can receive fines of £200 or more. Similar fines apply to dishonesty about age.

Most tube lines' **last trains** leave Central London between midnight and 12:30am; service resumes around 6am. The gap in service is bridged by Night Buses (see Buses below). The Tube, unremittingly packed during rush hour (Mon.-Fri. roughly 7-10am and 4:30-7:30pm), earns its share of flak due to delays, dirt, and diverted trains; the Northern Line has been nicknamed "the misery line" because of its rush hour bedlam. Bear in mind that some distant suburban tube stations close on Sundays and other off-peak periods. There is no smoking anywhere on the Tube or buses.

Many stations feature endless tunnels and steep staircases, so if you're carrying a lot of luggage, you might fare better on a longer route that requires fewer transfers. Fitness zealots may wish to tackle the 331-step climb at Hampstead station, London's deepest. If you find yourself suffering from vertigo on the endless escalator, take heart from the example set by wooden-legged Bumper Harris. When London Transport installed the first escalators at Earl's Court in 1911, they hired "Bumper" to ascend and descend all day, thereby encouraging weak-kneed passengers.

Buses

London's buses are a little more complicated to use than the Underground and invariably slower, but often prove more economical. In addition, the tunnels of London are far less attractive than its streets, and being shuttled about underground can hardly match the majesty of rolling along the street enthroned on the front seats of the top of a double-decker. Unfortunately, double-decker **Routemaster** buses, with their conductors and open rear platforms, are being replaced to save money. On modern double-deckers and on single-deck "hoppa" buses, you pay your fare to the driver as you board. On Routemaster buses, take a seat and wait for the conductor, who can tell you the fare and let you know when to get off. Smoking is not permitted on London's buses.

London Transport issues a free bus map for London called, remarkably, the *London Bus Map,* which is available at some tube stations and LRT information offices.

The *Central Bus Guide* is a more manageable pamphlet, describing only bus routes in zone 1. Bus stops are marked with route information; at busy intersections or complicated one-way systems, maps tell where to board each bus.

On stops marked "request," buses stop only if you flag them down (to get on) or pull the bell cord (to get off). While waiting, you must form a queue (line up); bus conductors may refuse some passengers at the stop during crowded periods. One stop may be served by a whole selection of buses. Completely ignore any daytime bus timetables you may come across, as the service has a notoriously sporadic nature. Ask Londoners what they'll be doing in the year 2000 and they'll reply, "still waiting for a 214 bus." Within zone 1, fares range from 50-70p. Other journeys cost from 30p-£3. A Travelcard is a worthwhile investment if you plan to make more than a couple of trips. **Bus passes** are valid only on buses and thus are not as versatile as Travelcards. Regular buses run from about 6am to midnight, although they can be impossibly slow during rush hour. **Night buses** (the "N" routes) now run frequently throughout London. All night bus routes run through Trafalgar Sq. (Tube: Charing Cross), so as the time of the last train approaches, head there. Victoria, King's Cross, and Liverpool St. stations are also good spots to catch one. Travelcards are not valid on night buses. London Transport's 24-hr. information line (tel. 222 1234) can tell you about all routes. Alternatively, pick up their free brochure about night buses, which includes times of the last British Rail and Underground trains, from a London Transport information office.

British Rail

Most of London is fully served by buses and the tube. Some districts, however, notably southeast London, are most easily reached by train. Travelcards are valid on Network South East (the portion of the BR system covering London) within the zones. The North London Link, stretching across north London from North Woolwich to Richmond is a handy line seldom used by visitors: trains (every 20 min.) scoot from Hampstead Heath to Kew in 25 minutes. Information on Network South East services is available at all mainline stations. The travel and information center at Waterloo (open Mon.-Sat. 8am-9pm, Sun. 9am-9pm) has full timetables of all services (20p for each section of London). *London Connections,* a map of all tube and Network South East lines, is free and available at any tube station or information office.

Taxicabs

London taxicab drivers must pass a rigorous exam and demonstrate intimate knowledge of the city to earn a license. The route taken by the cabbie is virtually certain to be the shortest and quickest; the massive London cabs are surprisingly maneuverable and dart in and out (mostly out) of traffic jams unperturbed. A taxi is available if its yellow light is aglow. You can catch a cab yourself or call a radio dispatcher for one (tel. 286 0286, 272 0272, 253 5000, or look in the Yellow Pages under "taxi"). Drivers are required to charge according to the meter for trips under 6 mi., but for longer distances, you must negotiate the price. A 10% tip is expected, with a surplus charge for extra baggage or passengers.

Apart from the licensed cabs, there are countless "minicab" companies, listed in the Yellow Pages. "Ladycabs" (tel. 254 3501) has only female cabbies (Mon.-Thurs. 7:45am-12:30am, Fri. 7:45am-1am, Sat. 9am-2am, Sun. 10am-12:30am). Be sure to ask the price when you order a minicab, and reconfirm it before you start the trip. Reclaim **lost property** (tel. 833 0996) you have left in a taxi at 15 Penton St., Islington, N1 (Tube: Angel; open Mon.-Fri. 9am-4:30pm). If you left something in a minicab, contact the company.

Bicycles

London's roads are in excellent condition, but on weekdays both the volume and temper of its traffic may seem homicidal. However, bicycling has its advantages, and there are few better ways to spend a Sunday than pedaling through the parks of the city. Great deals on secondhand bikes can be found at the General Auction (see below). Also check outdoor markets, classified ads in the local press, *Exchange and Mart,* and the University of London's bulletin board at 1 Malet St. (Tube: Russell Sq.). Bikes are allowed on BR trains; you may take a bike onto the Circle, District, and Metropolitan line Underground trains (Mon.-Fri. 10am-4:30pm and after 7:30pm, Sat.-Sun. all day) but you will be charged a child's fare for it.

General Auctions, 63 Garrat Lane, Wandsworth, SW18 (tel. (081) 874 2955). Tube: Tooting Broadway, then bus #44, 77, 220, or 280. Police auction as many as 100 used bikes here every Mon. at 11am. Prices range from £1 to £250. Examine bikes Sat. 9:30am-3pm, Mon. 10-11am. Examine the £1 ones with particular care.

On Your Bike, 22 Duke St. Hill, SE1 (tel. 357 6958). Tube: London Bridge. Ten-speeds £8 per day, £14 per weekend, £30 per week. £50 check or credit card deposit required. Mountain bikes £15 per day, £20 per weekend, £60 per week, steep £200 deposit. MC and Visa accepted. Open Mon.-Fri. 9am-6pm, Sat. 9:30am-4:30pm.

Mopeds and Motorcycles

Scootabout Ltd., 59 Albert Embankment, SE1 (tel. 582 0055). Tube: Vauxhall. Mopeds from £23.65 per day, £84.75 per week, including helmet, insurance, panniers, and unlimited miles but excluding VAT. Credit card or £100 deposit required. Call ahead. Open Mon.-Fri. 9am-6pm, Sat. 9am-2pm.

Cars

Renting a car will not save you time, money, or hassle compared to public transport in London. If you must rent, note that big rental firms like Avis and Hertz may be convenient, but they are quite expensive. Small cheap companies can be dodgy. Drivers must usually be over 21 and under 70. Make sure you understand the insurance agreement before you rent; some agreements require you to pay for damages that you may not have caused. If you are paying by credit card, check to see what kind of insurance your company provides free of charge. Automatics are generally more expensive to rent than manuals. You have been warned.

Boats

London's main artery during the Middle Ages, the **River Thames** no longer commands as much traffic, but if you venture out on to it in a boat you can still sense the pulse of a major lifeline. Boats make the half-hour trip from Westminster Pier (Tube: Westminster) to the Tower of London every 20 minutes from 10:20am to 5pm (tel. 930 4097; £2.60, £3.60 return). Voyages downstream to Greenwich (tel. 930 4097; every ½ hr. from 10:30am-5pm; £3.80, £4.80 return) and the Thames Barrier (tel. 930 3373; daily at 10am, 11:15am, 12:45pm, 1:45pm, and 3:15pm; £3.10, £4.80 return) take in fine industrial dockland scenery. Boats also chug upstream (tel. 930 4721) to Kew Gardens (£4, £6 return), Richmond (£5, £7 return) and Hampton Court (3-4 hr.; £6, £8 return). **The River Bus** (tel. 512 6555) offers speedy transport on the Thames from Charing Cross Embankment to Greenwich (daily, every 20 min. until 8pm; £3.60, £7.20 return).

Practical Information

Tourist Offices

LTB Tourist Information Centre: Victoria Station Forecourt, SW1 (tel. 730 3488, phone answered Mon.-Fri. 9am-6pm but difficult to get through). Run by the London Tourist Board; has information on London and England, a well-stocked bookshop, theatre and tour bookings, and an accommodations service (a hefty £5 booking fee, £12 refundable deposit). Expect to take a number and wait at peak hours, around noon. You can book a room by mail if you write to them at least 6 weeks in advance. With a Visa or Mastercard, you can book a room by phone on much shorter notice (tel. 824 8844, answered daily 9am-6pm). Victoria Station center open April-Nov. daily 8am-7pm; Dec.-March Mon.-Sat. 9am-7pm, Sun. 9am-5pm. Bookshop open April-Nov. Mon.-Sat. 8am-6:30pm, Sun. 8am-3:30pm; Dec.-March Mon.-Sat. 9am-6:30pm, Sun. 9am-3:30pm. Additional tourist offices are located at **Heathrow**

Airport, (open daily April-Nov. 9am-6pm; Dec.-March 9am-4:30pm), and **Harrods** and **Selfridges** department stores.

British Travel Centre: 12 Regent St., SW1 (tel. 730 3400). Tube: Piccadilly. Down Regent St. from the Lower Regent St. tube exit. Run by the British Tourist Authority and ideal for travelers bound for destinations outside of London. Combines the services of the BTA, British Rail, and American Express with an accommodations service. For the latter, you pay a booking fee (£5) and a deposit (either one night's stay or 10-15% of the total stay depending on the place; does not book for hostels). The office contains very helpful tourist information services of Wales, Ireland, and Northern Ireland (see below for slightly different hours). Also sells maps (an excellent selection), theatre tickets, and books, and can give you every pamphlet known to Englishkind, translated into many languages. Pleasantly relaxed compared to LTB, but the shortage of staff sometimes makes for a long wait. Open May-Oct. Mon.-Fri. 9am-6:30pm, Sat. 9am-5pm, Sun. 10am-4pm; Nov.-April Mon.-Sat. 9am-5pm.

City of London Information Centre: St. Paul's Churchyard, EC4 (tel. 606 3030). Tube: St. Paul's. Specializes in information about the City of London but answers questions on the whole of London. Helpful, knowledgeable staff and mountains of brochures. Open April-Oct. daily 9:30am-5pm., Nov.-March Mon.-Fri. 9:30am-5pm, Sat 9:30am-12:30pm.

London Transport Information Offices: (24-hr information line, tel. 222 1234). At the Heathrow, Victoria, Piccadilly Circus, Oxford Circus, Euston, and King's Cross Tube stops. Officials there answer inquiries regarding Underground and bus travel and push free bus route maps (see Getting Around London).

Irish Tourist Board (Bord Fáilte): 150 New Bond St., W1 (tel. 629 7292). Tube: Bond St. Open Mon.-Thurs. 9:15am-5:15am, Fri. 9:15am-5pm. Also has a combined desk with the Northern Ireland tourist board inside the British Travel Centre on Regent St. (tel. 839 8417), open May-Oct. Mon.-Fri. 9am-6pm, Sat.-Sun. 10am-4pm; Nov.-April Mon.-Sat. 9am-5pm.

Northern Ireland Tourist Board: 12 Regent St., SW1 (tel. 839 8417). Tube: Piccadilly Circus. Inside the British Travel Centre. Open May-Oct. Mon.-Fri. 9am-6pm, Sat.-Sun. 10am-4pm; Nov.-April Mon.-Sat. 9am-5pm.

Wales Tourist Board: 12 Regent St., SW1 (tel. 409 0969). Tube: Piccadilly Circus. Inside the British Travel Centre. Open May-Oct. Mon.-Fri. 9am-6:30pm, Sat. 9am-5pm, Sun. 10am-4pm; Nov.-April Mon.-Sat. 9am-5pm.

Scottish Tourist Board: 19 Cockspur St., SW1 (tel. 930 8661). Tube: Charing Cross. Open May-Sept. Mon.-Fri. 9am-6pm; Oct.-April 9:30am-5:30pm.

Budget Travel Organizations

The organizations listed below specialize in student discounts, youth fares, and other discounts. (See the Getting There section of the General Introduction for more information.) All of them sell ISIC cards at £5 each.

STA Travel: 74 and 86 Old Brompton Rd., SW7 3LQ (tel. 938 4711). Tube: South Kensington. Offices also at King's Cross (117 Euston Rd., NW1; tel. 465 0485) and Russell Sq. (University of London Student Union, 1 Malet St., WC1; tel. 636 1788). Cheap flights and tours all over the world. Long lines. Open Mon.-Fri. 9am-6pm, Sat. 10am-4pm.

YHA Travel Office: 14 Southampton St., WC2 (tel. 836 8541). Tube: Covent Garden. Travel services for free-wheeling, independent types, young or old. Bookshop offers a great selection of travel guides to every country under the sun, including *Let's Go.* Can sell you everything you need for your globe-trotting, bike-camping adventure holiday. Information on student discounts for those under 26. Open Mon.-Wed. and Fri. 10am-6pm, Thurs. 10am-7:30pm, Sat. 9am-6pm. The Kensington Branch is also well-stocked, at 174 Kensington High St., W8 (tel. 938 2948), open Mon.-Wed. and Fri 10am-6:30pm, Thurs. 10am-7:30pm, Sat. 10am-5:30pm.

Council Travel: 28a Poland St., W1 (tel. 437 7767). Tube: Oxford Circus. Affiliated with the pan-U.S. Council Travel group, selling cheap plane, rail, and bus tickets to any chosen destination. Humming with activity. Open Mon.-Fri. 9:30am-6pm.

Trailfinders: 42-48 Earls Court Rd., W8 (tel. 937 5400). Tube: High Street Kensington. Huge and dependable clearing house for cheap airline tickets for Europe and the rest of the world. Information and vaccination section for those using London as a base for long haul flights. Open Mon.-Sat. 9am-6pm; telephone only Sun. 10am-2pm.

Victoria station is a jungle of travel services. Skip the agencies inside the station and cross the street to get to Terminal House, at 52 Grosvenor Gardens, SW1.

London Student Travel: (tel. 730 3402). Tube: Victoria. Competitive rail, coach, and air fares all over the Continent and beyond. No age limit for many of their offers. Come early to avoid long lines. Open June-Oct. Mon.-Fri. 8:30am-6:30pm, Sat. 10am-5pm; Nov.-May Mon.-Fri. 9am-5:30pm, Sat. 10am-5pm.

National Express: (tel. 730 8235). Tube: Victoria. Specializes in coach and train travel in Western Europe. Additional office at Piccadilly (13 Regent St., SW1; tel. 925 0189). Open Mon.-Fri. 9am-5:30pm, Sat. 9am-4pm.

Touropa: (tel. 730 2101). Tube: Victoria. Yet another student travel center. Does most of its business in charter flights to the continent and European rail travel. Not nearly as busy as London Student Travel next door. Open June-Oct. Mon.-Fri. 9am-6pm, Sat. 10am-5pm; Nov-May Mon.-Fri. 9am-5:30pm, Sat. 10am-5pm.

Embassies and High Commissions

All embassies and high commissions close on English national holidays. Check the telephone book for other nationalities, or consult the *London Diplomatic List* for a complete list of embassies (available in the Her Majesty's Stationery Office, 49 High Holborn, WC1; tel. 211 5656; Tube: Holborn).

United States Embassy: 24 Grosvenor Sq., W1 (tel. 499 9000). Tube: Bond St. Someone will always answer the phone, but after 3pm on Sat. almost all counselors will have left. Embassy Travel Services at 22 Sackville St., W1. Tube: Piccadilly Circus. Travel Service office open Mon.-Fri. 10am-4pm.

Australian High Commission: Australia House, The Strand, WC2 (tel. 379 4334; in emergency, tel. 438 8181). Tube: Aldwych or Temple. Visa and passport inquiries tel. 438 8818. Open Mon.-Fri. 10am-4pm.

Canadian High Commission: MacDonald House, 1 Grosvenor Sq., W1 (tel. 629 9492). Tube: Bond St. or Oxford Circus. Visa services open Mon.-Fri. 8:45am-2pm. Information office open Mon.-Fri. 9:30am-5pm.

French Embassy: 58 Knightsbridge, SW1 (tel. 235 8080). Tube: Knightsbridge. For French visas (not necessary for U.S. citizens), contact the **French Consulate,** 6a Cromwell Pl., SW7 (tel. 823 9555). Tube: South Kensington. Open Mon.-Fri. 9-11:30am for applications, 4-4:30pm for collection of passports only.

Irish Embassy: 17 Grosvenor Pl., SW1 (tel. 235 2171). Tube: Hyde Park Corner. Open Mon.-Fri. 9:30am-5pm.

New Zealand High Commission: New Zealand House, 80 Haymarket, SW1 (tel. 930 8422). Tube: Charing Cross. Open Mon.-Fri. 10am-noon and 2-4pm.

Money

The number of travelers who throw money away by using the omnipresent *bureaux de change* is astonishing. If for some reason you're caught with only foreign currency, shop around at different banks for the best rates. Banks which do not have "window charges" often extort higher commissions. Even better, take your foreign currency into a bank and buy traveler's checks. The usual 1% commission is bound to be better than the *bureau* alternative, and checks are far safer to carry than cash. Don't be lured by *bureaux* that scream "No Charge—No Commission." If it makes you wonder how they make their money, just look at the rates.

American Express: 6 Haymarket, SW1 (tel. 930 4411). Tube: Piccadilly Circus. Message and mail services open Mon.-Fri. 9am-5pm, Sat. 9am-noon. Currency exchange open Mon.-Fri. 9am-5pm, Sat. 9am-6pm, Sun. 10am-6pm. Go to side door Sat.-Sun. Bring ID to pick up mail (60p; free for Amex check or cardholders). Other offices at Victoria Station (147 Victoria St., SW1; tel. 828 7411); Cannon St. (54 Cannon St., EC4; tel. 248 2671); Knightsbridge (78 Brompton Rd., SW3; tel. 584 6182); and at the British Tourist Centre above. Lost or stolen traveler's checks should be reported immediately (tel. 0800 52 1313; 24-hr.).

24-hr. Currency Exchange: If you must, you can find such places at major tube stations. **Thomas Cook,** 15 Shaftesbury Ave. Tube: Piccadilly Circus. **Exchange International** Victoria Station. Tube: Victoria. Expect to pay a hefty fee.

Emergency, Social, and Miscellaneous Services

Emergency medical care, psychological counseling, crash housing, and sympathetic support can often be found in London free of charge.

Emergency (Medical, Police, and Fire): Dial 999; no coins required.

Hospitals: In an emergency, you can be treated at no charge in the casualty ward of a hospital. You have to pay for routine medical care unless you work legally in Britain, in which case NHS tax will be deducted from your wages and you will not be charged. The advent of socialized medicine has lowered fees here, so you shouldn't ignore any health problem merely because you are low on cash. Try the **Westminster Hospital** at Pimlico (Dean Ryle St., Horseferry Rd., SW1; tel. 828 9811), the **University College Hospital** (Gower St., WC1; tel. 387 9300), the **London Hospital** at Whitechapel (Whitechapel Rd., E1; tel. 377 7000); or the **Royal Free Hospital** at Belsize Park (Pond St., NW3; tel. 794 0500). For others, the phone book has listings at the front, or for a more complete list look under "Hospitals."

Pharmacies: Every police station keeps a list of emergency doctors and chemists in its area. **Bliss Chemists** at Marble Arch (5 Marble Arch, W1; tel. 723 6116) is open daily, including public holidays, 9am-midnight. **Boots Chemists** has branches throughout London. Oxford Circus location (tel. 734 4646) open Mon.-Wed. and Fri.-Sat. 9am-6:30pm, Thurs. 9am-7:30pm. Victoria Station branch (tel. 834 0676) open Mon.-Fri. 7:30am-9pm, Sat. 9am-7pm.

Police: Stations in every district of London, including: Headquarters, New Scotland Yard, Broadway, SW1 (tel. 230 1212). Tube: St. James's Park; West End Central, 27 Savile Row, W1 (tel. 434 5212). Tube: Piccadilly Circus; King's Cross, 76 King's Cross Rd., WC1 (tel. 837 4233). Tube: King's Cross; Kensington, 72-74 Earl's Court Rd., W8 (tel. (081) 741 6212). Tube: Earl's Court.

Samaritans: 46 Marshall St., W1 (tel. 734 2800). Tube: Oxford Circus. Highly respected 24-hr. crisis hotline helps with all sorts of problems, including suicidal depression. A listening rather than advice service.

Rape Crisis Line: London Rape Crisis Centre, P.O. Box 69, WC1 (tel. 837 1600, 24 hr.). Call anytime, emergency or not, to talk to another woman, receive legal or medical information, or obtain referrals. Will send someone to accompany you to the police, doctors, clinics, and courts upon request.

Family Planning Association: 27-35 Mortimer St., W1 (tel. 636 7866). Tube: Oxford Circus. Informational services: contraceptive advice, and pregnancy test and abortion referral. Open Mon.-Thurs. 9am-5pm, Fri. 9am-4:30pm.

Alcoholics Anonymous: Tel. 352 3001. Information on meeting locations and times. Hotline answered daily 10am-10pm; answering machine from 10pm-10am.

Disabled Travelers' Information: Phone the **Disability Advice Service** (tel. (081) 870 7437), **RADAR** (tel. 637 5400), or the **Greater London Association for the Disabled** (tel. 274 0107) for general information. Perhaps the two most useful guides to London for the disabled are Nicholson's *Access in London,* available in any well-stocked travel shop and *Door to Door,* published by Her Majesty's Stationery Office (49 High Holborn, WC1; tel. 211 5656; Tube: Holborn). Disabled persons traveling by Underground should pick up the booklet *Access to the Underground,* available at any Transport Information Center for 70p or by mail for £1 from the Unit for Disabled Passengers (London Regional Transport, 55 Broadway, London SW1H 0BD). London Transport's 24-hr. travel information hotline is also useful for disabled travelers (tel. 222 1234). For transportation by car, call **London Dial-a-Ride Users Association** at 482 2325. The "Arts Access" section at the beginning of the new London telephone books details special services available for the disabled at theatres, cinemas, and concert halls around London.

Gay and Lesbian Travelers' Information: London Lesbian and Gay Centre, 67-69 Cowcross St., E1 (tel. 608 1471). Tube: Farringdon. The 5 floors house a bar, café, disco, bookshop, a women-only floor, exhibits, and theatre. Open daily noon-11pm. **London Lesbian and Gay Switchboard** (tel. 837 7324) provides a 24-hr. general advice, information, and support telephone service; mailing address BM Switchboard, Box 1514, London WC1N 3XX. **London Lesbian Line** (tel. 251 6911) operates sporadically in the evenings before 10pm; mailing address LLL, P.O. Box 1514, London WC1N 3XX.

Salvation Army: 101 Queen Victoria St., EC4 (tel. 236 5222). Tube: Mansion House or Blackfriars. Good reputation for advice and emergency short-range shelter.

Legal Trouble: Release, 388 Old St., EC1 (tel. 729 9904; 24-hr. emergency number 603 8654). Tube: Liverpool St. or Old St. Specializes in criminal law and advising those who have been arrested on drug charges. Also psychiatric and abortion referrals. Open Mon.-Fri. 10am-6pm. **Legal Advice Bureau,** 104 Roman Rd., E2 (tel. (081) 980 4205). Tube: Bethnal Green. May provide legal advice and representation for minimal fees.

Discrimination: National Council for Civil Liberties, 21 Tabard St., SE1 (tel. 403 3888). Tube: Borough. Advising and campaigning organization for prevention of all types of discrimination and protection of civil rights. Advice through letters only. Open Mon.-Fri. 10am-1:15pm and 2:15-5:30pm.

Automobile Breakdown: AA Breakdown service, tel. (0800) 887 766; 24-hr. RAC Breakdown service, tel. (0800) 828 282; National Breakdown, tel. (0800) 400 600.

Lost Property: If you've lost something on the **Underground** or on a **bus,** go in person to the Lost Property Office, 200 Baker St., W1. Tube: Baker St. Open Mon.-Fri. 9:30am-2pm. For articles lost in a **taxi,** write to the Metropolitan Police Lost Property Office, 15 Penton St., N1. Articles lost on **British Rail** should be reported to the destination station of your train. In all other cases, inquire at the nearest police station.

Baggage Storage: Dozens of cheap storage companies in the London area charge £3-4 per item per week (check the Yellow Pages for one in your area). Lockers in train stations and airports are seldom available because of frequent bomb threats.

Speaking Clock: tel. 123

Accommodations

London has not been blessed with large numbers of cheap, decent places to stay. Many budget lodgings make the heart sink, and the rest fill up to the rafters. B&Bs, hostels, and halls of residence all pack them in during the summer; you should plan ahead to nab one of the more desirable rooms.

Be forewarned: your London B&B may disappoint you. Don't look for a welcoming family home or a homemade breakfast. If you expect a small, shabby room with minimal furnishings (bed, light, sink, chair), you may not be disappointed.

If you don't mind sharing a room with ten strangers, London's YHA hostels provide a cheerful alternative, though you should be aware that they, too, will raise their summer rates (by £1). YHA hostels make up in friendliness what they lack in privacy, and can be marvelous places for swapping travel information and finding traveling companions.

Halls of residence of the London colleges and polytechnics offer privacy, but often in the form of small, boxy singles. Some have fantastic locations and beautiful grounds, but rooms generally become brighter and more spacious the farther you move from the center of town. Well-managed and secure, halls are an unadventurous but safe bet.

The Tourist Information Centre Accommodations Service, at Victoria Station (accommodations service tel. 824 8844, answered daily 9am-6pm), bustles during high season. Their least expensive rooms cost about £18 plus an unnerving £5 booking fee. Most rooms cost about £21. Callers carrying a Visa or Mastercard can make bookings by phone. Otherwise bookings can be made in person or by mail at least six weeks in advance. They also sell a booklet, *Where to Stay in London* £2.95, half-geared toward budget travelers.

Youth Hostels

Each of the eight IYHF/YHA hostels in London requires an **International Youth Hostel Federation (IYHF)** or **Youth Hostel Association of England and Wales (YHA) membership card.** Overseas visitors can buy one at YHA London Headquarters and often at the hostels themselves for £9. An **International Guest Pass** (£1.50) permits residents of places other than England and Wales to stay at hostel rates without joining the hostel association. After you purchase six of these Guest Passes, you attain full membership. A membership card for residents of England and Wales costs £8.30 for seniors (ages 21 and over), £4.40 for juniors (16-20) and £1.90 for youths (5-15).

The cheerful staff members, often international travelers themselves, invariably keep London YHA hostels clean and refreshingly well-managed. They can also often provide a range of helpful information on the environs of the hostel. Plan ahead, since London hostels are crowded. During the summer, beds fill up months in advance. In recent years, hostels have not always been able to accommodate every written request for reservations, much less on-the-spot inquiries. But hostels frequently keep some beds free until a few days before—it's always worth checking for vacancies the week before, the day before, or the morning of your intended stay. To secure a place, show up as early as possible and expect to stand in line. With a Visa or Mastercard, you can book in advance by phone. Or you can write to the warden of the individual hostel. Off-season, finding a place will not require such of a strain. But always phone ahead before you schlep across town.

For hostel information, visit the jumbo-market **YHA London Headquarters,** 14 Southampton St., WC2E 7HY (tel. 240 5236; tel. 240 3158 for membership inquiries; Tube: Covent Garden; open Mon.-Wed. and Fri. 10am-6pm, Thurs. 10am-7pm, Sat. 9am-6pm); or the new **YHA Kensington,** 174 Kensington High St., W8 (tel. 938 2948; Tube: High St. Kensington; open Mon.-Wed. and Fri. 10am-6pm, Thurs. 10am-7pm, Sat. 10am-5:30pm).

All permanent hostels listed here are equipped with large lockers that require a padlock. Bring your own or purchase one from the hostel for £2.50.

Prices below are listed by age group: seniors (ages 21 and over); juniors (16-20); and youths (5-15). Prices include rental of a sleeping sack.

Holland House (King George VI Memorial Youth Hostel), Holland Walk, Kensington, W8 (tel. 937 0748), next to Holland Park. Tube: Holland Park or High St. Kensington. The walk from High St. Kensington, while slightly longer, stays better lit at night. Restored Jacobean mansion in a palatial setting on the east side of Holland Park. Londoners play cricket in the park while befuddled squirrels and hostelers look on. Daily pick-up soccer games. Just renovated in 1991: new bathrooms and showers. Bright and clean, including a cafeteria featuring McDonald's chairs. 190 beds. Kitchen facilities and currency exchange available. Reception open 7am-11:30pm. Fills very quickly. No curfew. £14, £12, £10. Breakfast from £2.30. Evening meals from £3.

Oxford Street, 14-18 Noel St., London W1 (tel. 734 1618). Tube: Oxford Circus. Bang in the heart of London. 87 beds in small, plush rooms of 2-4. Microwave available. No laundry. No curfew and 24-hr. security. Currency exchange available. Monitored baggage room during the day. Reception open 7am-10:30pm. Fills up in a flash. Superb location makes up for the expense: £15, £13, and £11. Continental breakfast £1.90. (Walk east on Oxford St. and turn right on Poland St.; the hostel stands next to a rather bleak mural.)

Earl's Court, 38 Bolton Gdns., SW5 (tel. 373 7083). Tube: Earl's Ct. A converted townhouse in a leafy residential neighborhood, peacefully set just off the Earl's Ct. one-way system. 124 beds in rooms of about 10 each. Extensive kitchen amenities. Ongoing modernization should provide expanded shower facilities. Laundry. Currency exchange available. Reception open 7am-midnight in summer, 7am-11pm in winter. No curfew. £12, £11, £9. Breakfast and dinner £2-3; optional vegetarian meals. (Exit from the tube station onto Earl's Court Rd. and turn right; Bolton Gardens is the fifth street on your left.)

Hampstead Heath, 4 Wellgarth Rd., Hampstead, NW11 (tel. (081) 458 9054). Tube: Golders Green, then ½-mi. walk along North End Rd. Serenely positioned at the edge of Hampstead Heath extension and round the corner from The Bull and Bush. Despite its peaceful surroundings, this hostel often falls victim to the school parties that barrage the hostels of Central London. The only wheelchair-accessible hostel in London. 220 beds in surprisingly sumptuous dorms. Cooking and laundry facilities. Currency exchange. Reception open 7am-11pm. No curfew—code-operated doors. £12, £11, £9.

Highgate, 84 Highgate West Hill, N6 6LU (tel. (081) 340 1831). Tube: Archway, then a ¾-mile walk up Highgate Hill and Highgate High St., or take bus #210 or 271 from tube to Highgate Village. Walk down South Grove, which becomes Highgate West Hill. A Georgian house in the middle of historic Highgate village. The walk up the hill can prove strenuous, but you can restore yourself with a pint at The Flask. Out-of-the-way location and pleasant neighborhood make for a homey hostel. 74 beds. Kitchen stocks remarkable crockery. Reception open 7am-10am and 5-11pm. Doors locked 10am-5pm. £9.50, £8, £7.

Wood Green, Wood Green Halls of Residence, Brabant Rd., N22 (tel. (081) 881 4432). Tube: Wood Green, then walk 2 min. west on Station Rd. 157 single rooms in a modern Middlesex Polytechnic building, taken over each summer by the YHA. Laundry and self-catering facilities. No curfew. All-night security guard. £10, regardless of age. Open mid-July to mid-Sept. and 3 weeks at Easter. For advance bookings and enquiries during the closed period, contact the Hampstead Heath hostel.

White Hart Lane, All Saints Halls of Residence, White Hart Lane, N17 8HR (tel. (081) 885 3234). Tube: Seven Sisters, then BR to White Hart Lane, or BR direct from Liverpool St.; or tube to Wood Green, then bus #W3. Travelcard will undoubtedly be the cheapest way here. Women should avoid walking alone to the hostel from the tube at night. More completely unremarkable Middlesex Poly Halls, in a solidly working class district reminiscent of Coketown in *Hard Times.* Two kestrels nest in an adjacent house. 170 beds, mainly in plain, decently sized singles, with wash basins. Bathtubs only. Self-catering and laundry facilities. Reception open 7am-2pm and 5pm-midnight. No curfew. £10, regardless of age. Open mid-July to Aug. 31. Contact Hampstead Heath hostel during closed period.

Epping Forest Youth Hostel, Wellington Hall, High Beach, Loughton, Essex 1G10 4AG (tel. (081) 508 5161). Tube: Loughton (zone 6, 45 min. from central London), then a good 2-mi. walk (have a map handy) through the forest. A taxi from the tube station costs £2.70 for 1 or 2 people—about 60p extra for additional passengers. A marvelous retreat from London havoc and London prices. Set remotely in the heart of 6000 acres of ancient woodland. Simple washing facilities and no laundry, but large and well-equipped kitchen. Cheap and utterly rural. Reception open 7-10am and 5-11pm. £5.50, £4.40, £3.50. Open April-Oct.

Carter Lane, 36 Carter Lane, London EC4V 5AD (tel. 236 4965). Tube: St. Paul's or Blackfriars. Closed for refurbishment and due to reopen in early 1992, but call ahead for up-to-date information.

Private Hostels and Halls of Residence

Private hostels, which do not require an IYHF card, almost always have a youthful clientele and often contain coed dorms. Some have kitchen facilities. There are usually no curfews.

London's university residences often accommodate visitors for limited periods during the long summer break (usually July-Aug.), and often during Christmas and Easter vacations. Many of these halls are not exceptionally pleasant—unless you enjoy tall, barren buildings and box-like rooms. Most charge £10-20, although some have student discounts. Reliable, well-maintained, and well-located, they substitute convenience for character. Write to the bursar of the hall several months before your arrival. (Contact individual halls for London University residences.) These places frequently have short-term openings.

Bloomsbury

Passfield Hall, 1 Endsleigh Place, WC1 (tel. 387 3584 or 387 7743). Tube: Euston Sq. A London School of Economics hall between Gordon and Tavistock Sq. Lots of long-term residents and a boisterous atmosphere. Rooms vary tremendously in size, but all have desks and high ceilings. Laundry and cooking facilities. Singles £16. Doubles £25. Triples £33, breakfast included. Open July-Sept. (rooms scarce July and early Aug.), and for 1 month around Easter.

Carl Saunders Hall, 18-24 Fitzroy St., W1 (tel. 580 6338). Tube: Warren St. A newer LSE building west of Tottenham Court Road. Laundry facilities, TV lounge. 96 single study bedrooms, 12 doubles. Singles £18-34. Doubles £36-68. Breakfast included. Self-catering apartments across the street also available, min. stay 1 week. Weekly: doubles £217, triples £335, quads £434, quints £542, excluding VAT. Open July-Sept.

Rosebery Avenue Hall, 90 Rosebery Ave., EC1 (tel. 278 3251). Tube: Angel, also buses #19 and 38 from Piccadilly. Further out of the way than the other halls, and plainer. Carpeted, compact study bedrooms with sink, desk, wardrobe, and shelves. Bar, game lounge, kitchens, laundry facilities, TV room, and small garden. Singles £16.50-19. Doubles £25. Breakfast included. Discounts for stays over 5 weeks. Open June-Sept., and for 5 weeks around Easter.

John Adams Hall, 15-23 Endsleigh St., WC1 (tel. 387 4086), off Tavistock Sq. Tube: Euston Sq. Elegant London University building. High-ceilinged rooms come in different sizes; some have small balconies overlooking the street. 124 singles, 22 doubles. Laundry facilities, TV lounge, requisite ping-pong table, and quiet reading room. Reception open Mon.-Fri. 8am-1pm and 2-10pm, Sat.-Sun. 9am-1:30pm and 5:30-10pm. Singles £19. Doubles £34. English breakfast included. Weekly: singles £123, doubles £222. Open July-Sept. and at Easter. Book well in advance and confirm in writing; usually no deposit required.

Central University of Iowa Hostel, 7 Bedford Pl., WC1 (tel. 580 1121). Tube: Holborn or Russell Sq. On a quiet B&B-lined street near the British Museum. Bright, spartan rooms. Laundry facilities, TV room. 2-week max. stay. Reception open May-Aug. 8am-1pm and 3-8pm. Dorm rooms £13.50 per person. Doubles £29. All-you-can-eat continental breakfast included. Write as soon after April 1 as possible.

Museum Inn, 27 Montague St., WC1 (tel. 580 5360), off Bloomsbury Sq. Tube: Holborn, Tottenham Court Rd., or Russell Sq. Great location and young international clientele compensate for the drab dorms. Rock music plays at reception. No curfew. Dorm rooms £9-11 per person. Doubles £29. Triples £35. Quads £45. Continental breakfast included. Weekly rates available Oct.-April.

Helen Graham House (YWCA), 57 Great Russell St., London WC1B (tel. 430 0834). Tube: Holborn or Russell Sq. 289 beds, but only 20 or so for men. TV lounge. Laundry and kitchen facilities. Employment and long-term housing advice given. Both singles and doubles, but singles scarce because women already sharing rooms receive preference over newcomers. Watch out for the 6-month min. stay rule. 6-month waiting list. Weekly: singles £45, doubles £34 per person.

Tonbridge School Clubs, Ltd., (tel. 837 4406). Corner of Judd and Cromer St., 2 blocks south of St. Pancras station. Tube: King's Cross/St. Pancras. The price is right for desperadoes. Iffy neighborhood, but then you won't be around the club in the day—lockout 10am-10pm. Students with non-British passports only. Men sleep in basement gym, women in karate-club hall. Blankets and foam pads provided, hot showers, TV lounge. Storage space for backpacks during the day, but safety is not guaranteed. Student ID required. Arrive 10-11:30pm, leave by 10am. £2.50 per person.

London University Halls, Cartwright Gdns., WC1H 9EB (tel. 387-1477, -5526, -0311). Tube: Russell Sq. Organized groups get the lion's share of accommodations but some individual rooms free up during the summer. One bathroom with bathtub for 2 singles. Squash and tennis, laundry facilities, ping pong, TV lounges, library, music rooms, and a pleasant bar (pint of beer, £1.20). No curfew. No student ID required. No inquiries before June. Singles £17-20; students, £14. Breakfast and evening meal included. Open July-Aug.

Paddington and Bayswater

Centre Français, 61 Chepstow Place, Notting Hill Gate, W2 (tel. 221 8134). Tube: Notting Hill Gate or Bayswater. A delightful Gallic atmosphere pervades this immaculate hostel. In a chic residential area—look out for Princess Di delivering her sons to school round the corner. Bilingual staff welcomes a vibrant international clientele, half of whom hail from France. No curfew. 180 beds. All but 2 rooms have washbasins. Free lockers. Singles £21. Doubles £18 per person. Triples/ Quads £15 per person. Off-season prices drop £1-2. Dorm rooms £12 per person. Weekly: singles £126, doubles £110 per person, triples and quads £89 per person, dorm rooms £82 per person. Further reductions after 5 weeks. Breakfast included. Book at least 2 months in advance, if possible—phone reservations by Visa and MC accepted.

Palace Hotel, 31 Palace Ct., W2 (tel. 221 5628). Tube: Notting Hill Gate or Queensway. Young community atmosphere and big bright dorm rooms make this a great deal for hostelers. TV lounge and pool table. 8 beds per room. £8, weekly £ 50.

Quest Hotel, 45 Queensborough Terrace, W2 (tel. 229 7782). Tube: Queensway. A terraced house on an intermittently renovated street. Standard hostel accommodation in rooms of 4-8 beds. Central location. Kitchen facilities, snack bar, and free music videos. No curfew. £8.50-10per person. Key deposit £2.

Lancaster Hall Hotel Youth Annexe (YMCA), 35 Craven Terrace, W2 (tel. 723 9276). Tube: Lancaster Gate. For persons under 25, basic hostel facilities at the German YMCA in London. All rooms have washbasins. Singles £18. Doubles £32. Triples £40. Quads £50.

Kensington, Chelsea and Victoria

King's College, part of the University of London, controls summer bookings for the residence halls listed below. Their locations are often hard to beat. Accommodations include continental breakfast, linen, soap, towel, cooking and laundry facilities, and sometimes even tennis courts. There are no curfews. To reserve a room from July through September, write before May 1 to Elspeth Young, King's Campus Vacation Bureau, 552 King's Rd., London SW10 0UA (tel. 351 6011). A £5 deposit is required for each week reserved. For last minute arrangements, call the halls directly. Prices vary slightly according to location, but hover at £21-23 per person in single and double rooms. Accommodations are available in 1992 from January 2-7, March 26 to April 26, July 9 to September 30, and December 20-23 at Queen Elizabeth Hall, Campden Hill Rd., W8 (tel. 333 4255) (tube: High St. Kensington); **Lightfoot Hall,** Manresa Rd. at King's Rd., SW3 (tel. 351 2488) (tube: Sloane Sq. then bus #11 or South Kensington then bus #49); **Ingram Court,** 552 King's Rd. (no tel.) (tube: Fulham Broadway, then a 10-min. walk); **Wellington Hall,** 71 Vincent Sq., Westminster, SW1 (tel. 834 4740) (tube: Victoria, then walk one long block along Vauxhall Bridge Rd. and left on Rochester Row to Vincent Sq.) The following cost less than the residence halls listed above (about £16-18 per person), but are less convenient: **King's College Hall,** Champion Hill, SE5 (tel. 733 2167; BR to Denmark Hill); and **Malcolm Gavin Hall,** Beachcroft Rd., SW17 (tel. (081) 767 3119; Tube: Tooting Bec).

Other private residence halls and hostels include:

Curzon House Hotel, 58 Courtfield Gdns., SW5 (tel. 373 6745). Tube: Gloucester Rd. A *Let's Go* home away from home. Charles, the owner, has a knack for hiring the friendliest of managers and staff. Kitchen facilities, TV lounge, and no curfew. Book at least 1 month in advance. Continental breakfast included. Dorms £13 per person. Singles £26. Doubles £34. Triples £45. Quads £64. Reduced weekly rates in winter.

Queen Alexandra's House, Kensington Gore, SW7 (tel. 589 3635 or 589 4053), by the Albert Hall. Tube: South Kensington. Women only. Ornate Victorian building next to the Proms. Welcoming, with a touch of class. Cozy rooms, window seats. Kitchen and laundry facilities, sitting room, Tyler tiara, and sunny dining hall. All this and an English breakfast too. Rooms available mid-July to mid-Aug.; send written reservations weeks in advance to Mrs. Makey. £20 per person.

Albert Hotel, 191 Queens Gate, SW7 (tel. 584 3019). Tube: South Kensington or Gloucester Rd. Bus #2 from South Kensington. Large, smoke-free, but spartan rooms in an elegant Victorian building. Most rooms have private facilities. Great location, near the Kensington museums and Hyde Park. TV lounge includes pool table. Deposit valuables at reception. 24-hr. reception. Continental breakfast included. No reservations; call when you arrive in London. Dorms £8. Singles £18. Doubles £28. Weekly: bed in four-person dorms £51, in six-person dorms £45; singles £100, doubles £120.

Anne Elizabeth House Hostel, 30 Collingham Pl., SW5 (tel. 370 4821). Tube: Earl's Ct. Caters to the needs of travelers on extended stays: kitchen, laundry, and ironing board. Right around the corner from the biggest supermarket in London. Dorm-style rooms. No curfew. Continental breakfast heaped on. Prices vary depending on the exact dates of stay. Singles £14-17, doubles £23-29, triples £31-39. Larger rooms available. Weekly rates 10% off; longer-term rates 12% off. Reserve 1 month in advance for the summer.

North London

International Student House, 229 Great Portland St., W1 (tel. 631 3223), at the foot of Regent's Park. Tube: Great Portland St. 60s building lacks architectural merit but compensates with great location. A thriving metropolis with its own films, discos, study-groups, expeditions, parties, and mini-markets. Use of multi-gym costs 60p per hour. Well-stocked information desk. 300 beds in doubles and singles. Well-maintained but uninspiring rooms, although many in the second building at 10 York Terrace East have views of Regent's Park. Lockable cupboards. No curfew. Singles £20. Doubles £17 per person. Triples £14 per person. Quads £10 per person. English breakfast included. Reserve through main office on Great Portland St. at least 1 month ahead, earlier for academic year. Letter of confirmation required.

James Leicester Hall, Market Rd., London N7 9PN (tel. 607 3250 or 607 5417). Tube: Caledonian Rd. A Polytechnic of North London residence hall right around the corner from the tube station. 156 beds. Bright, modern buildings clustered around a courtyard. All rooms have wash basins. Licensed bar. No curfew. Singles only, £16.35. English breakfast included. Advance reservations compulsory—phone at least 5 days in advance and send a letter of confirmation to the Bookings Officer at the above address. Open July-Sept and Easter.

Tufnell Park Hall, Huddleston Rd., Tufnell Park N7 (tel. 607 3250). Tube: Tufnell Park. The second Polytechnic of North London residence hall. A modern tower block set in the residential area of Tufnell Park, reportedly the editorial center of the universe. 207 not unfriendly single rooms. Licensed bar. Prices, opening times, and reservation details same as for James Leicester Hall—all bookings taken through the James Leicester office. (Walk down Tufnell Park Rd., turn left, and go to the end of Huddleston Rd.) Open July 8-Sept. 22.

Bed and Breakfast Hotels

Bloomsbury

Despite its proximity to the West End, Bloomsbury manages to maintain a quiet residential atmosphere. Hotels here cost a pound or two more than those in less gracious areas, but you're paying for location and style. Feel the knowledge from the British Museum diffuse into you as you lie in bed. Budget hotels cram along Gower ST. (Tube: Goodge St.); an invariably pleasant set of Bloomsbury B&Bs blooms in **Cartwright Gardens** (Tube: Russell Sq. or King's Cross/St. Pancras); and the cheapest B&Bs cluster around tiny Argyle Sq. (Tube: King's Cross/St. Pancras).

Regency House Hotel, 71 Gower St., WC1 (tel. 637 1804). Clean, fresh, cool blue rooms with TV. Small garden. Book well in advance to be guaranteed a room. Singles £25, with shower £45. Doubles £35, with shower £55. Triples £48. Quads £58. Quints £68. Several pounds cheaper in winter.

Ridgemount Hotel, 65 Gower St., WC1 (tel. 636 1141). Bright, agreeable rooms with flowery wallpaper and firm beds, lovingly maintained by gracious owners. Comfy TV lounge. Doubles £36. Triples £47.25. Quads £60.

Jesmond Hotel, 63 Gower St., WC1 (tel. 636 3199). Cozy and neat, if slightly worn-looking rooms. TV lounge. Electric hot pots with coffee and tea in all rooms. Singles £24. Doubles £37. Triples £57. Private bath £12-15 extra.

Thanet, 8 Bedford Pl., WC1 (tel. 636 2869). Family-run hotel with speckless, spacious rooms. Color TV, radio, and hot pots with tea and coffee in every room. Rooms in the back overlook a peaceful patio. Singles £33. Doubles £45, with private bath £55. Triples £55, with shower £65. Quads £70. Good breakfast menu. To book in advance, send a personal check or your credit card number for the first night.

Repton House, 31 Bedford Pl., WC1 (tel. 636 7045). Cheaper and only slightly less ornate than its neighbors. Back rooms overlook a rose garden. Continental breakfast included. Singles £25. Doubles £35. Triples with private bath £55.

Hotel Crichton, 36 Bedford Pl., WC1 (tel. 637 3955). Has its share of peeling paint, but standard rooms come with TV, phone, tea-making facilities, and private safe. Singles £28. Doubles £45-50. Triples £57. Quads £69. With shower, £2.50 extra. Major credit cards accepted.

Jenkins Hotel, 45 Cartwright Gdns., WC1 (tel. 387 2067). Quiet, genteel family-run B&B. Bright, tidy rooms with soft pastel wallpaper, floral prints, phones, teapots, color TV, hairdryers, and mini-refrigerators. Some with charming coal-burning fireplaces. Small singles £30. Doubles £44, with private bath £53. Triples with bath £67.

Euro Hotel and George Hotel, 58-60 and 51-53 Cartwright Gdns., WC1 (tel. 387 1528 or 387 6789). Ornate rooms with TV, radio, and telephone. Reserve well in advance. Children under 13 sharing parents' room £8. Singles £29.50, with shower £35. Doubles £43, with shower £47. Triples £52, with shower £57.

Crescent Hotel, 49-50 Cartwright Gdns., WC1 (tel. 387 1515). Family-run with care; proprietor lives here. Attractive and homey, with full English breakfast and TV lounge. Singles £30, with shower £35. Doubles £44, with shower and toilet £53. Family rooms (for four) £66, with shower and toilet £74.

Grange House Hotel, 5 Endsleigh St., WC1 (tel. 380 0616), off Tavistock Sq. Tube: Euston Sq. Just on the other side of Upper Woburn, this B&B is more expensive but truly pristine. Immaculate, newly-furnished rooms with cool blue interiors. Second-story rooms open onto an ornate wrought-iron balcony. Breakfast served in your room. Singles £29.50. Doubles £47.

Near Victoria Station

Victoria Station is a traveler's purgatory. In exchange for your penitence in fairly expensive accommodation, you will be rewarded with an ideal location, within walking distance from London's major attractions. To get a room for the summer, make reservations at least two weeks in advance, for some places even earlier. Most B&Bs require a deposit—usually the price of one night's stay—to secure your reservation. Be sure to ask the manager how to send the deposit, as few places accept foreign currency.

Most rooms include a sink, a color TV, and a full English breakfast. Private bathrooms and showers are normally, but not always, available, and cost extra. Also, if you know that you will be arriving after 11pm, let the proprietor know. Banging on the door in the middle of the night is rude and ineffectual.

All of these places charge lower rates in the winter. Furthermore, the competition grows fierce enough around here that many will negotiate a reduced rate for long stays, especially in low season. Show reluctance to take a room, and you may see prices plummet.

Forage for B&Bs along **Belgrave Road** (Tube: Victoria or Pimlico), a noisy thoroughfare south of the station; **St. George's Drive,** a quieter road parallel to Belgrave rd. and one block south; **Warwick Way,** which crosses them both near Victoria Station; or historic **Edbury St.,** west of Victoria Station in the heart of Belgravia. Some suggestions are: **Luna House Hotel,** 47 Belgrave Rd., SW1 (tel. 834 5897), **Sidney Hotel,** 74-76 Belgrave Rd., SW1 (tel. 834 2738), **Melbourne House,** 79 Belgrave Rd., SW1 (tel. 828 3516), **Belgrave House Hotel,** 30-32 Belgrave Rd., SW1 (tel. 834 8620), **Georgian House Hotel,** 35 St. George's Dr. (tel. 834 1438), **Arden House Hotel,** 10-12 St. George's Dr., SW1 (tel. 834 2988), and **Greystones Hotel,** 73 Warwick Way, SW1 (tel. 834 0470).

For a hotel off the main thoroughfares, but still within easy walking distance of Victoria Station, try one of these:

Oxford House, 92-94 Cambridge St., SW1 (tel. 834 6467), **Windsor Guest House,** 36 Alderney St., SW1 (tel. 828 7922), **Melita House Hotel,** 33-35 Charlwood St., SW1 (tel. 828 0471), **Ebury House Hotel,** 102 Ebury St., SW1 (tel. 730 1350), **Eaton House Hotel,** 125 Ebury St., SW1 (tel. 730 8781), **Westminster House,** 96 Ebury St. (tel. 730 4302), and **Pyms Hotel,** 118 Ebury St., SW1 (tel. 730 4986).

Kensington and Chelsea

Times have certainly changed since Gilbert and Sullivan's day, when one of their characters had a nightmare that a swarm of relations who "all had got on at Sloane Square and South Kensington stations" invaded his coach. These days, the Royal Borough of Kensington and Chelsea is much more posh, and the few hotels here tend to the luxurious.

Vicarage Hotel, 10 Vicarage Gate, W8 (tel. 229 4030). Tube: High St. Kensington. Just like home—if you happen to live in a palace. Fabulous value. Dignified, friendly, newly renovated, and very clean. A cozy TV lounge, with cushions and old photos. Around the corner from Kensington Palace and Millionaires' Row. Singles £26. Doubles £48. Triples £57. Quads £62. Book 3 months ahead in the summer.

Abbey House Hotel, 11 Vicarage Gate, W8 (tel. 727 2594). Tube: High St. Kensington. Guests return year after year, drawn by charming owners, a superb location, and an English breakfast *par excellence.* Recently renovated rooms, each with color TV. Magnificent entrance hall does good impression of a palm house. All rooms have color TV. Singles £38. Doubles £48. Triples £58. Quads £68.

More House, 53 Cromwell Rd., SW7 (tel. 589 6754 or 589 8433). Tube: South Kensington. Unmarked Victorian building across the street from the National History Museum. In between the Yemeni Embassy and the Brunei High Commission. Attractive old wooden furniture. New shower units. Relaxed student atmosphere. Cheap laundry and a small library. Open July-Aug. Singles £20. Doubles £35. Triples £45. £5 supplement for one night stands, 10% weekly discount.

Still farther south you can stay in **Chelsea,** home of the trendy-chic, but you'll have trouble finding moderately priced hotels south of the King's Rd. To get to Oakley St., sandwiched neatly between the river and King's Rd., take the tube to Sloane Sq., then bus #11, 19, or 22; or the tube to South Kensington, then bus #49.

Oakley Hotel, 73 Oakley St., SW3 (tel. 352 5599). Comfortable, youthful, and friendly. Cheerful Australasian staff. Cooking facilities; tea and coffee readily available. Videos, games, and travel magazines in lounge. Singles £19, £100 per week. Doubles £34. Triples £42. Beds in quads £9.50, £59 per week. Book in advance.

Earl's Court

A slightly tawdry bargain basement of accommodations spreads east of the monstrous Earl's Court Exhibition Building. The area feeds on the budget tourist trade, overdosing on travel agencies, souvenir shops, take-away eateries, and the vile *bureaux de change.* The accents of tireless, globe-trotting Australians dominate the neighborhood, sometimes known as "Kangaroo Court." Singles generally run £20-30, and doubles £30-40. Try to avoid late-night solo strolls in the area. (Tube: Earl's Ct.)

Philbeach Gardens, a quiet, tree-lined crescent north of the exhibition hall, offers the best B&B accommodations in the area, including two gay B&Bs. Reserve rooms here in advance. Leave Earl's Ct. station at the exhibition hall's west exit. The following are worth looking into: **York House Hotel,** 28 Philbeach Gdns., SW5 (tel. 373 7519), **The Beaver Hotel,** 57-59 Philbeach Gdns., SW5 (tel. 373 4553), and **Philbeach Hotel,** 30-31 Philbeach Gdns., SW5 (tel. 373 1244), the largest gay B&B in England, popular with both gay men and women.

Guest houses and B&Bs dot all of the avenues branching off Earl's Court Rd. Most survive on the sheer volume of tourist traffic rather than on the quality of their services. Shop selectively and ask to see a room before you plunk down your money. Possibilities include **The Henley House Hotel,** 30 Barkston Gdns., SW5 (tel. 370 4111), **Merlyn Court Hotel,** 2 Barkston Gdns., SW5 (tel. 370 1640), **Half Moon Hotel,** 10 Earl's Court Sq., SW5 (tel. 373 9956), **Mayflower Hotel,** 26-28 Trebovir Rd., SW5 (tel. 370 0991), **Oxford Hotel,** 24 Penywern Rd., SW5 (tel. 370 5162), **Mowbray Court Hotel,** 28-32 Penywern Rd., SW5 (tel. 373 8285), and **Hotel Flora,** 11-13 Penywern Rd., SW5 (tel. 373 6514).

Somewhat distanced from the tourist trade of Earl's Court, the area around **Gloucester Road** proves quieter, more expensive, and comparably convenient to the Kensington museums, Kensington Gardens, and all of Chelsea.

Abcone Hotel, 10 Ashburn Gdns., SW7 (tel. 370 3383). Tube: Gloucester Rd. Close to the station. Plush hotel facilities: photocopying and wordprocessing facilities, in-house movies, and bright pink toilet paper. Continental breakfast. Singles £35-49. Doubles £48-59. Triples £64-78.

Queensbury Court Hotel, 7-11 Queensbury Pl., SW7 (tel. 589 3693). Tube: South Kensington. Cheap, well-used rooms. Clean bathrooms. In the center of the museum area, and right across from the College for Psychic Studies. TV lounge, prominent pool table. Singles £25-30. Doubles £36-42. Triples £48-52, with facilities £55.

Camping

Camping in London is not the most convenient of options. Even with a travelcard, the cost of shuttling in and out might better be spent on a cheap (and rain-proof) hostel. In summer months, even the few campsites near London fill up; make reservations one to two weeks in advance. If you decide to buy outdoor equipment, try **Blacks Camping & Leisure,** 53 Rathbone Place, W1 (tel. 636 6645), or the **Youth Hostel Association,** 14 Southampton St., WC2 (tel. 836 8541).

Hackney Camping, Millfields Rd., Hackney Marshes, E5 (tel. (081) 985 7656). Bus #38 or 55 from Victoria via Piccadilly Circus, or bus #22a from Piccadilly Circus. An expanse of flat green lawn in the midst of London's ethnic East End. Free hot showers, baggage storage, snack bar, and laundry facilities. No caravans. Open June-Aug. daily 8am-11:45pm. £2.50 per person, children under 12 £1.50.

Tent City, Old Oak Common, East Acton, W3 (tel. (081) 743 5708). Tube: East Acton. Your tent is already set up and waiting for you here. Extremely friendly campsite, full of backpackers. Deservedly popular. Open April-Sept., £4 per person.

The Housing Crunch

Don't head blythely into the Great Outdoors; sleeping in parks is unsafe and illegal. Impromptu campers are usually asked, urged, or forced to move along. If you are absolutely desperate, call the **Housing Advice Switchboard** (tel. 434 2522; Mon.-Fri. 10am-6pm, emergencies at any time). Solitary travelers who are really absolutely desperate should call the **Alone in London Service** (tel. 278 4224; Mon.-Tues. and Thurs.-Fri. 9am-4pm, Wed. 9am-12:30pm), or the **Salvation Army** (tel. 236 5222; usually open Mon.-Fri. 9am-4pm).

Food

London has few rivals in its range of foreign food—Lebanese, Greek, Indian, Chinese, Thai, Italian, Cypriot, African, and West Indian. But variety costs. In too many places, you pay a premium price for a minimum of atmosphere and service. Watch the fine print: perfectly innocent entrees that appear inexpensive on the menu often end up supplemented with side dishes, shamefully priced drinks, VAT, minimum per-person charges, and an occasional (and outrageous) £1-2 cover charge. You don't have to tip in those restaurants that include service charge (10-12½%) on the bill. And if the service has disappointed you, you can complain to the manager and then legally subtract part or all of the service charge. You may run into a puzzling sign saying something like, "Service included but individual gratuities are discretionary"—but don't be misled.

If you eat only one ethnic meal while in London, make it Indian. The Indian restaurants in London nearly outnumber the pubs. Most are quiet and candle-lit (except for the ever-popular Khan's, listed below), if a little on the garish side. In general, Indian restaurants are cheaper around Westbourne Grove (Tube: Bayswater) than in Piccadilly and Covent Garden.

For a cheaper alternative to restaurant dining, try a meal in a **café** (often pronounced and occasionally spelled "caff")—something akin to a U.S. diner. Caffs serve an odd mix of inexpensive English and Italian specialties (£4-5 for a full meal). Interiors range from the serviceable to the dingy, and tables may be shared, but the food is often very good. The owner is usually called Mick. Recently, diners actively styled to look and feel American have grown popular (most conspicuously Ed's Easy Diner). These sparkling formica hotspots breed a semi-surreal atmosphere: English youth crowd the booths and counters, downing English-brewed Budweiser and English-bottled Coke and eating cholesterol-laden U.S. favorites.

London's wealth of foreign restaurants shouldn't deter you from sampling Britain's own famous (or infamous) cuisine. While there are some dedicatedly British restaurants, like Porter's (listed below), **pubs** are your best bet for cheap, filling English fare. Those who object to meat pastries and potatoes can take refuge in the salads and sandwiches available in most pubs. The farther you get from central London, the greater your chances of encountering such authentic cockney favorites as jellied eels, cockles, mussels, smoked mackerel, and Scottish Arbroath smokies. Pubs are best for lunch. The **fish-and-chip shops** on nearly every street vary little in price but lie oceans apart in quality. Look for queues out the door and hop in line.

Not surprisingly, groceries cost less in supermarkets than in charming little corner shops. **Tesco** has branches at Goodge St., Portobello Rd. (Tube: Notting Hill Gate), and near Paddington and Victoria stations. **Safeway** stores squat on King's Rd., High St. Kensington, Edgware Rd. (not too far from Paddington), in the Barbican CEntre, and in the Brunswick Shopping Centre (Tube: Russell Sq.; open daily until 8pm). Beneficent **Sainsbury** has branches on Victoria Rd., not far from Victoria Station, on Cromwell Rd. (Tube: Gloucester Rd.), and on Camden Rd. (Tube: Camden Town), as well as an immense "SavaCentre" Hypermarket in Merton (Tube: Collier's Wood). **Marks & Spencer** (the department store) sells reliable produce for a bit more than Sainsbury; they have two branches on Oxford St. (one near

Marble Arch, one on Poland St.) and others all over the city. Both Sainsbury and "Marks and Sparks" sell satisfying prepared dishes (Sainsbury chicken pasty 65p, quiche lorraine £2.10 per lb, chicken tandoori £1.50). Fine fresh produce and excellent deli and bakery goods make Sainsbury and M&S your best bet for picnics and kitchen meals. Avoid supermarkets from 6-8pm and on Saturdays when the lines grow prohibitively long. The ubiquitous **Europa** groceries charge more but stay open until 11pm (look for the yellow sign). The enormous, regal foodhalls of **Harrods,** on Brompton Rd., offer almost everything under the sun at out-of-the-budget-world prices; visit if only to gawk. For the thrill of shopping outdoors, try **open-air markets** (see Shopping below). **Berwick Market,** near Piccadilly, sells cheap fruits and vegetables. Fruit markets pop up all over central London, offering fresh and healthy snacks at reasonable prices. The numerous small **grocery shops** stay open two or three hours later than supermarkets and also stay open on Sunday.

All these alternatives should make it easy to avoid the Anglicized versions of U.S. steak houses and the numerous fast-food chains (the mildly sinister Wimpy Bars, for example) that infest areas such as Piccadilly and Leicester Sq. For more advice or help finding little-known ethnic restaurants, contact the free **Restaurant Switchboard** (tel. (081) 888 8080, Mon.-Sat. 9am-8pm).

The West End

Soho, Piccadilly and Covent Garden offer an inexhaustible jumble of food. Prices in the West End are high; you may want to order your food to take away. Free seating reposes at Leicester Square (halfway between the Leicester Sq. and Piccadilly Circus Tube stops), under the Eros fountain at Piccadilly Circus, or by the lions in Trafalgar Sq. Don't overlook **Berwick Market** on Berwick St. for fresh fruit during the day. Piccadilly Circus, Leicester Sq., Covent Garden, and Charing Cross Tube stations are all within easy walking distance of most of the West End. Oxford Circus station is only a 10-min. walk north from Piccadilly. Tottenham Court Rd. station requires a similar stroll from Leicester Sq.

Soho and Piccadilly Circus

Pollo, 20 Old Compton St., W1 (tel. 734 5917). Tube: Leicester Sq. or Tottenham Court Rd. Popular and inexpensive Italian cuisine. Squeeze in early for dinner. Spaghetti from £2.20. *Chicken cacciatore* and 2 vegetables £4. *Tortellini carbonara* £2.90. Open Mon.-Sat. noon-11:30pm.

Gaby's, 30 Charing Cross Rd., WC2 (tel. 826 4233). Tube: Leicester Sq. Low on atmosphere but up there on great Middle Eastern and vegetarian food. Don't be put off by the steaming food photos out front. Large *latkes* £1. Smoked salmon sandwich £2.60. Large spinach egg rolls £1.50. Salads to go. Open Mon.-Sat. 9am-midnight, Sun. 11am-10pm.

Rabin's Nosh Bar, 39 Great Windmill St., W1 (tel. 434 9913). Tube: Piccadilly Circus. Small restaurant serving fresh, delicious food. Kosher dishes. Hot salt beef sandwich £2.60. Roast turkey bagel £1.85. Boiled or fried *gefilte* fish £1.80. Walls covered with photos of British and U.S. boxing legends. Open Mon.-Sat. 11am-8pm, occasionally later.

The Wren of St. James's, 35 Jermyn St., SW1 (tel. 437 9419). Tube: Piccadilly Circus or Green Park. When will you have another chance to eat turkey and ham pie (£1.95) in the courtyard of a church designed by Sir Christopher Wren? *Carpe diem.* Casserole of the day with roll and butter £3. Quiche from £1.85. Open Mon.-Sat. 8am-7pm, Sun. 10am-4pm.

Alpha One Fish Bar, 43 Old Compton St., W1 (tel. 437 7344). Tube: Piccadilly Circus. Look for the green neon sign. No drunken trout, just good, greasy fun. Big fish and great chips. Large cod only £2.40. Chips 65-85p. Large shish kebab and salad £2.50. Tartar sauce extra. Open Mon.-Thurs. 11:30am-1am, Fri.-Sat. 11:30am-2am, Sun. 11:30am-midnight.

Passage to India, 5 Old Compton St., W1. Tube: Leicester Sq. Serene, low-priced, but cramped Indian restaurant. Half a *tandoori* chicken £4. Vegetable dishes in the orbit of £3. Service charge 10%. Open Mon.-Thurs. noon-midnight, Fri.-Sat. noon-1am.

Chinatown

London's Chinatown (Tube:Leicester Sq.) may disappoint those familiar with the splendors of the Chinese districts of New York, San Francisco or Vancouver. Nevertheless the few blocks north of Leicester Sq. remain a fine place to eat. Because of the Hong Kong connection, Cantonese cooking dominates here, but Chinese food from every region can be found. Despite the Chinese tradition of eating *dim sum* only on Sundays, most Cantonese restaurants serve it every afternoon. A piece of fruit and a pork bun (70p) or a curry beef bun (60p) from a Chinese bakery makes a delicious and inexpensive lunch. The meat is a flavoring, not a filling. Try the **Garden Restaurant** (51 Charing Cross Rd., W1; open Mon.-Sat. 10am-11:30pm. Sun. 10am-11pm) or the olfactorily sensational **SuperCake Shop** (21 Wardour St., W1; open Mon.-Sat. 11am-8pm.).

Chuen Cheng Ku, 17 Wardour St., W1 (tel. 437 3433). Some consider it one of the planet's best restaurants. Certainly one of the largest menus. Look out for the dragon. *Dim sum* dishes £1.50. Try the dried and fried *Ho-Fun* noodles with beef £4. Open daily 11am-midnight.

Covent Garden

Covent Garden offers an enticing—but often expensive—array of eateries to playgoers in the heart of London's theatre district. Tube: Covent Garden.

Palms, 39 King St., WC2 (tel. 240 2939). A smaller and less crowded branch of the Italian restaurant on High St. Kensington. A lively mix of scrumptious Italian dishes and loudish pop music. Pastas £3-5, service included. Open daily noon-midnight.

Food for Thought, 31 Neal St., WC2 (tel. 836 0239). Expect a line at noon. Generous servings of delicious vegetarian food straight from the pot in a tiny downstairs restaurant packed with plants. Daily specials £3, flapjacks and granola 60p, cake £1. Take-away after 3pm. Open Mon.-Sat. 9am-7pm.

Calabash Restaurant, 38 King St., WC2 (tel. 836 1976). In the basement of the Africa Centre. Authentic African restaurant serving dishes from all over the continent. Entrees £4.10-7.50. *Doro Wat* (chicken stew served with eggs and rice or ingera) £6.50. Open Mon.-Fri. 12:30-3pm and 6-11:30pm, Sat. 6-11:30pm.

Porter's, 17 Henrietta St., WC2 (tel. 836 6466). It's delightful, it's delicious, it's Dickensian, it destroys your budget. But worth the price to learn how fine British food can be. Huge assortment of hot pies with traditional crust (turkey-chestnut, steak-mushroom, lamb-apricot, fish) and vegetables or salad £7.10. Sausage and mash £6.40. Minimum charge £4. Open Mon.-Sat. noon-3pm and 5-11:30pm, Sun. 5:30-10:30pm.

Bhatti, 37 Great Queen St., WC2 (tel. 831 0817). Award-winning Indian cuisine served in the center of theatreland. *Tandoor bater* (quail) £4.75. Very inexpensive vegetable dishes. Three-course pre-theatre set menu £9 per person (served 6-7:15pm). Make reservations. Service charge 15%. Open daily noon-2:45pm and 5:45-11:30pm.

Café Pasta, 2-4 Garrick St., WC2 (tel. 497 2779). A pleasant Italian café with a cozy downstairs bar and sidewalk seating. Pasta dishes £4. Open Mon.-Sat. 9:30am-11:30pm, Sun. 9:30am-11pm. Also at 184 Shaftesbury Ave., WC2 (tel. 379 0198).

Grunt's Chicago Pizza Company, 12 Maiden Lane, WC2 (tel. 379 7722). Lots of greenery and a 34-ft. mural of the Windy City. Big screen TV. Chicago-style pizza £5.45 for 2 people. Open Mon.-Sat. noon-11:30pm, Sun. noon-9pm.

Frank's Café, 52 Neal St., WC2 (tel. 836 6345). Somewhat spare. Homestyle pasta about a pound cheaper than anyplace else. Open Mon.-Sat. 8am-8pm.

Scott's, corner of Bedfordbury St. and New Row, WC2 (tel. 240 0340). Office workers queue up on the sidewalk at lunchtime to get into this delicious *patisserie* and sandwich shop. Rustic tables and chairs counterpoint a cool ceramic interior. Smoked salmon platter £4.50. Open daily 8am-11:30pm.

Bloomsbury and Euston

Superb Italian and Middle Eastern restaurants line **Goodge Street** and **Charlotte Street,** and the vegetarian restaurants in the area offer some of the best values around. Intriguing, authentic Indian food can be had farther north, in the area near

Euston Rd. (Drummond St., for example). Near the University of London, cushy outdoor cafés and colorful pubs clutter the secluded pedestrian pathways of **Cosmo Place,** off Queen Sq., and **Woburn Walk.** The cheapest food cooks at the student refectories of the University of London. Officially, you need a Union Card to eat there.

Near Euston

Diwana Bhel Poori House, 121 Drummond St. NW1 (tel. 387 5556). Tube: Warren St. Quick and tasty Indian vegetarian food in a clean and airy restaurant worth the wait. Try *samosas* or *thali* (an assortment of vegetables, rices, sauces, breads, and desserts meant to be shared). Meals £1.50-5. BYOB. Open daily noon-midnight. Another branch at 50 Westbourne Grove (Tube: Bayswater). **Gupta Sweet Centre,** across the street at 100 Drummond St., has excellent Indian take-away sweets and savories at half the sit-down price. Try their delicious *chum-chum,* a moist orange pastry sweetened with honey. Open daily Mon.-Thurs. 11am-7pm, Fri-Sat. 10am-7pm, Sun. noon-7pm.

Rhavi Shankar Bhel Poori House, 133-135 Drummond St. (tel. 338 6488). Tube: Euston Sq. An inconspicuous Indian-vegetarian restaurant renowned as one of London's finest. Most entrees £2.50-3. *Paper Dose* (paper-thin, crispy rice pancake served with rich vegetable filling, spicy-sweet *sambhar* sauce, and coconut chutney) £3.25. Open daily noon-11pm.

Great Nepalese Restaurant, 48 Eversholt St., NW1 (tel. 338 5935). Tube: Euston. Great indeed. Huge lunch of tandoori chicken, vegetable curry, rice, nan bread, papedam and drink £5.50. Good vegetarian dishes under £3. Minimum charge £5. Open Mon.-Sat. noon-2:45pm and 6-11:45pm.

Near Goodge Street

Cranks Health Food, 9-11 Tottenham St, W1 (tel. 631 3912). Tube: Goodge St. Large portions of vegetarian food served in cheerful surroundings. Delicious carrot cake £1.05. Many selections £1.50-2.25, large salad £3.25. Open Mon.-Fri. 8am-8pm, Sat. 9am-6pm.

Greenhouse Vegetarian Restaurant, basement of 16 Chenies St., WC1 (tel. 637 0838). Tube: Goodge St. Very fresh food that you choose by sight. Main courses £3.40, salad 85p, thick pizza £1.85, desserts 75p-£1.25. BYOB. Open Tues.-Fri. noon-9pm, Mon. and Sat. noon-8pm.

NatRaj, 93 Charlotte St., W1 (tel. 637 0050). Tube: Goodge St. Quiet, modestly decorated tandoori restaurant. Cheap curries £3-4. 4-course set menu for 2, £13. *Shak Suka* (minced lamb cooked in a mild cream sauce with eggs) £4. Minimum charge £4.50. Open daily noon-3pm and 6pm-midnight.

Shuler's Sandwiches, 35 Goodge St., W1 (tel. 636 4409). Tube: Goodge St. Perfect fixings for a picnic lunch. Incredibly cheap sandwiches and baked goods. Sandwich with any filling £1. Huge French loaves 70p. May run out of food early on Fri. Open Mon.-Fri. 8am-4pm.

Champagne, 16 Percy St., W1 (tel. 636 4409), off Tottenham Court Rd. Tube: Goodge St. Popular Chinese restaurant with candles and wax roses at every table. Filling 3-course lunch special (soup, entree, fried rice, and sherbet) £4.50. Open daily noon-midnight.

Trattoria Mondello, 36 Goodge St., W1 (tel. 637 9037). Tube: Goodge St. An array of zesty pasta dishes served in a rustic dining room with open-beam ceilings and hanging ferns. *Lasagna Pasticciata* £3.80. 50 p cover. Open Mon.-Wed. noon-3pm and 5:30-11:30pm, Thurs.-Fri. noon-3pm and 5:30-midnight, Sat. noon-midnight.

Around Russell Square

Wooley's Wholefood and Take-Away, 33 Theobald's Rd., WC1 (tel. 405 3028). Tube: Holborn. Good place for healthy and delicious picnic fare. Interesting sandwiches (apple and brie £1.85), provocative salads. Also a wide selection of breakfast snacks. Outdoor seating. Open Mon.-Fri. 7am-3:30pm.

The Fryers Delight, 19 Theobald's Rd., WC1. Tube: Holborn. One of the best chippies around, always crowded with Londoners. Fish or chicken with chips £2-3. You pay for the food, not the decor. Popular with British Library scholars. Open Mon.-Sat. noon-11pm.

My Old Dutch Pancake House, 131-32 High Holborn, WC1 (tel. 242 5200). Tube: Holborn. 107 varieties of giant Dutch pancake, thin and 18 in. in diameter. Popular toppings include ham, chicken, salami, chili, and curry. Vegetarian pancakes also available. All from £2.90. May be crowded. Open daily noon-midnight.

Café Dot, 42 Queen Sq., WC1, on the ground floor of the Mary Ward Center (tel. 831 7711). Tube: Russell Sq. No sign on the street. Look for the 18th-century townhouse next to the Italian Hospital. Barely visible behind the window, a life-size, papier-mâché dowager leans eternally over her bowl of soup. Good, hot food at rock-bottom prices. Scampi and chips £2. Assorted jacket potatoes with cheese and beans £1.20. Sandwiches £1. Open Mon.-Fri. 11am-3pm and 4-9pm, Sat. 11:30am-5pm.

Kensington and Chelsea

Knightsbridge and Hyde Park Corner

Growling stomachs fed up with window shopping may groan with disappointment at the dearth of eateries near Knightsbridge. Knightsbridge Green, northwest of Harrods off Brompton Rd., hides several sandwich shops (**Mima's Café** open Mon.-Sat. 6:30am-6pm and the **Knightsbridge Express** open Mon.-Sat. 7am-5:30pm). Coffee shops and expensive bistros also lurk between the antique boutiques along Beauchamp Place, southwest of Harrods.

The Stockpot, 6 Basil St., SW3 (tel. 589 8627). Tube: Knightsbridge. One of 3 branches of this restaurant serving palatable and inexpensive English cuisine. Salads from £2.10. Tasty escaloped chicken or steak and mushroom pie, £2-3. Handsome English breakfast (£2.10) served until 11am. Quick service may make you feel rushed. £1.70 minimum charge. 10% service charge. Open Mon.-Sat. 8am-11:30pm, Sun. noon-10:30pm. Other branches at Sloane Sq. (273 King's Rd., SW3) and Piccadilly (40 Panton St., SW1).

Hard Rock Café, 150 Old Park Lane, W1 (tel. 629 0382). Tube: Hyde Park Corner. Hype! The *Financial Times* reports rumors that areas of the Café are closed off to ensure lines of people on the street on slow afternoons. But behind the PR you'll find a damn good hamburger (from £5-7). Wide selection of American beers. Jimi Hendrix's guitar dangles over the bar. Arrive before 5pm to avoid the long "wait." Paraphernalia sold to queues of patient tourists up the street. Restaurant open Sun.-Thurs. 11:30am-12.30am, Fri.-Sat. 11:30am-1am.

South Kensington

Old Brompton Rd. and **Fulham Rd.** are the main thoroughfares in this graceful area of London. South Kensington tube station lies closest, but some of the restaurants below require a substantial hike from there. Old Brompton Rd. is served by bus #30; Fulham Road by bus #14 or #45.

Up-All-Night, 325 Fulham Rd., SW10 (tel. 352 1996). Ferns, art-deco fans, and Swedish sauna-style wooden booths—stop in after a late-night double bill at the Paris Pullman cinema. ¼-lb. burgers with fries, salad garnish from £3.40. Banana splits £2.65. Service charge 10%. Open daily noon-5:30am.

Johnny Rocket's, 140 Fulham Rd., SW10. Zippy new burger joint American-chrome-style, with limited counter seating. Burgers from £3.50. Great shakes and fries (£1). Open daily 11:30am-midnight.

Caffé Nero, 66 Old Brompton Rd., SW7. Polished chrome and a plethora of choices on big blackboards. Stand-up joint; best for a cappuccino (80p) on the run. Double espresso to go £1.10. Superb ricotta cheesecake from £1.30 per slice. Fudge brownies (90p) remarkably similar to solid blocks of chocolate. Open Mon.-Sat. 7:30am-8pm, Sun. 10am-7pm.

High St. Kensington

Inexpensive meals won't come running to greet you at High St. Kensington. Shoppers looking for a coffee break should stop at the **Café Gstaad** in the Kensington Arcade (sandwiches under £1.70; lunchtime £1.50 minimum; open Mon.-Sat. 7am-6:15pm). If coffee and a sandwich won't cut it, head to Henry's (see Wine Bars) or a wine bar on Kensington Church St.

Stick and Bowl, 31 High St. Kensington, W8 (tel. 937 2778). Cheap Chinese cuisine; seating scarce. Crispy beef £3.40. Try a special mixed dish for £4 (includes spring roll, sweet and sour pork, fried rice and vegetables, and 1 exploding prawn). Special dishes made upon request. £2 minimum. Open daily 11:40am-11:15pm.

Palms Pasta on the Hill, 17 Campden Hill Rd., W8. Café-style Italian restaurant popular with trendies young and very young. Spaghetti *carbonara* £4.60. *Fettucine con funghi e prosciutto* £4.65. Italian newspapers bedeck the ceiling. Happy Hour 5:30-7pm. Service charge 12.5%. Open daily noon-11:30pm. Another branch at Covent Garden (39 King St., WC2).

Chelsea

King's Road, a private thoroughfare until the middle of the 19th century, extends leisurely through Chelsea. Bus #11 runs the length of the road from the Sloane Sq. Tube station. Almost every destination along King's Rd. requires a bus ride or a considerable walk.

Chelsea Kitchen, 98 King's Rd., SW3 (tel. 589 1330). A 5-10 min. walk from the tube station. Locals rave about this place and its cheap, filling English and continental food: gazpacho, curried eggs, steak and kidney pie, and shish kebab. Head downstairs and acquire a booth for a cozier atmosphere. Expect to wait at meal times. Lunch £3-4, dinner £4-5. Breakfast served 8-11:25am. Open Mon.-Sat. 8am-11:30pm, Sun. noon-11:30pm.

Chelsea Pot, 356 King's Rd., SW3 (tel. 351 3605). Another Anglo-Italian adventure. Generous helpings. Lasagna £3.50. Omelettes from £2.40. Open Mon.-Fri. noon-3pm and 6-11:30pm, Sat.-Sun. noon-11:30pm.

Bamboo Kitchen, 305 King's Rd., SW3 (tel. 352 9281), at Beaufort St. Cheap Chinese take-away; no seating. The ultimate in chintz: bring your own utensils. Chopsticks cost 40p, spoons and forks 5p. Sweet and sour pork or Singapore-style chow mein £2.50. Call ahead for convenience. Open Mon.-Sat. noon-midnight, Sun. 5pm-midnight.

La Bersagliera, 372 King's Rd., SW3. Some of the best homemade pizza and pasta in London (both £4-5). Cozy atmosphere. Very Italian clientele. Friendly owner. Open Mon.-Sat. 12:30-3pm and 7pm-midnight.

Earl's Court

Earl's Court and **Gloucester Road** eateries generously cater to their tourist traffic. Earl's Court, a take-away carnival, revolves around cheap, ethnic, and palatable food. Groceries in this area charge reasonable prices; shops stay open late at night and on Sunday. The closer you get to the highrise hotels around Gloucester Station, the more expensive restaurants become. Look for the scores of coffee shops and Indian restaurants on Gloucester Rd. north of Cromwell Rd. (especially around Elvaston Place).

Benjy's, 157 Earl's Court Rd., SW7. Tube: Earl's Ct. Like the menu and the foil walls say, this is not the Ritz. Filling "Builder Breakfast" (bacon, egg, chips, beans, toast, 2 sausages, and all the coffee or tea you can drink) £2.80. Oodles of burly Australian types mirror the huge plates. Expect to share a table during mealtimes. Open daily 7am-9:30pm.

Vecchiomondo Ristorante Italiano, 118 Cromwell Rd., SW7. Tube: Gloucester Rd. Comfy Italian restaurant with wine flasks hanging from the ceiling and profuse greenery. Spaghetti *carbonara* £3. Pizza from £2. Open daily 10am-3pm and 5pm-1am.

Green Village Chinese Restaurant, 15 Kenway Rd., SW5. Tube: Earl's Ct. Tidy and tranquil Chinese restaurant, away from the roar of the tourist traffic. Set menu for 2 means tons of food (£10 per person). Fried rice £2-2.80. Open Mon.-Fri. and Sun. noon-2:30pm and 6-11:30pm, Sat. 6-11:30pm.

Notting Hill and Bayswater

This area is chock-full of high-quality, reasonably-priced restaurants, especially around Notting Hill Gate. Head to Westbourne Grove (Tube: Bayswater or Royal Oak) for large concentrations of decent, if rather unremarkable, Indian and Pakistani places.

Khan's, 13-15 Westbourne Grove, W2 (tel. 727 5240). Tube: Bayswater. Unlike many other Indian restaurants in London, Khan's is noisy and bustling. Excellent for a party. Great *tandoori* £4-5. Good-sized meals £4-6. Minimum order £4.50. Open daily noon-3pm and 6pm-midnight. Take-away available. 10% service charge.

Geale's, 2 Farmer St., W8 (tel. 727 7969). Tube: Notting Hill Gate. Efficient service. Consummately crisp fish and chips (from £3.50). Order the homemade fish soup instead of the canned crab soup. Three-course set lunch £5.50. Often a wait—sit it out in the bar upstairs. Take-away available. Overwhelming 15p cover charge. Open Tues.-Sat. noon-3pm and 6-11pm.

Malabar, 27 Uxbridge St., W8, (tel. 727 8800). Tube: Notting Hill Gate. Crowded, with wide ranging Indian cuisine. *Murg Dansak* £4.35. Open Mon.-Sat. noon-2:45 pm and 6:30-11:30pm, Sun. buffet lunch 1-2:45pm, dinner 6:30-11pm.

The City of London

This area is splendid for lunch (when food is fresh for the options traders) and disastrous for dinner (when the commuters go home and the food goes stale). The City overflows with pubs, wine bars, sandwich bars, and the odd trendy vegetarian place, filled each lunchtime with brogues and ties.

The Place Below, in St. Mary-le-Bow Church crypt, Cheapside, EC2 (tel. 329 0789). Tube: St. Paul's. Attractive and generous vegetarian dishes served to the hippest of City folks in a unique location. Quite super. Quiche and salad £4.45. Meals about £1 cheaper take-away. Open Mon.-Fri. 7:30am-3pm, plus Thurs. evenings 6-10:30pm.

Ye Olde Cheshire Cheese, 145 Fleet St., EC4 (tel. 353 6170 or 353 4388). Tube: Blackfriars. Closed for refurbishment, due to reopen in summer of 1992. Samuel Johnson's old watering hole, just 100 steps from his home. Famous for solid English cooking such as steak and kidney pie.

The City, 1 Seething Lane, EC3 (tel. 488 4224). Tube: Tower Hill. This seething pub-restaurant-wine-bar-nightclub is perfect after a day at the Tower. Hefty sausage with vegetables, £3.60. Open Mon., Wed. 11:30am-9pm; Tue, Thurs. 11:30am-10:30pm; Fri. 11:30am-11pm. Dinner Mon.-Thurs. only, until 8:30pm.

The East-West Restaurant, 188 Old St., EC1 (tel. 608 0300). Tube: Old St. Sublime macrobiotic cooking. Buy a small loaf of bread next door to go with the extra-large portions of hummus. Meals £4-5, side dishes £1 each. Tofu cheesecake £1.50. Open Mon.-Fri. 11am-8:30pm, Sat.-Sun. 11am-3pm.

North London

Indian Veg Bhelpoori House, 92 Chapel Market, N1. An unmistakable bargain—all-you-can-eat lunch buffet (noon-3pm) of Indian vegetarian food for a startling £3.25. Cheap evening meals (around £4) 6-11pm.

Upper St. Fish Shop, 324 Upper St., N1. A well-known chippy offering daily specials varied according to the catch. Take-away substantially cheaper than eat-in—cod and chips £3, mushy peas 40p. Open Mon. 5:30-10pm, Tues.-Fri. 11:30am-2pm and 5:30-10pm, Sat. 11:30am-3pm and 5:30-10pm.

Marine Ices, 8 Haverstock Hill, NW3 (tel. 485 3132). Tube: Chalk Farm. The savior of ice cream devotees. Superb Italian ice cream (40p per scoop) and sundaes—the top of the range. *Vesuvius* (£4.20) can defeat even the most Herculean appetite. Start off with a subtly flavored pizza (*quatro stagioni* £4). Massively popular with the north London *cognoscenti.* Ice cream counter open Mon.-Sat. 10:30am-10:45pm, Sun. noon-8pm. Restaurant open Mon.-Fri. noon-2:45pm and 6-10pm, Sat. noon-10:15pm.

Le Petit Prince, 5 Holmes Rd., NW5 (tel. 267 0752). Tube: Kentish Town. Tucked away in a side street off Kentish Town Rd. Left out of station, then first right onto Holmes past McDonalds. Loyal following swears by the *couscous.* French/North African flavored food and decor. Vegetable *couscous* £4.50, with chicken £6.50. Open daily noon-3pm, 7-11:30pm.

Crepe Van, outside the King William IV pub, 77 Hampstead High St., NW3. Tube: Hampstead. A Hampstead institution. Paper-thin Brittany crepes made in front of your eyes in the tiniest van imaginable. Sweet fillings (including banana and Grand Marnier) £1.50-2.50, savory £1.45-2.60. Open Mon.-Sat. 1-11pm, Sun. 1:30-11pm.

Pubs

I would give all my fame for a pot of ale
—Shakespeare, Henry V

London's 7000 pubs are as colorful and historic as their counterparts throughout England, with clientele varying considerably from one neighborhood to the next. Pubs in the City pack in tourists and pin-stripes at lunch. The taverns up in Bloomsbury tend to draw a mix of tourists and students, while those in Kensington and Hampstead cater to the trendy element. Around the wholesale markets, tradesmen grab early morning pints. Pub crawling, the English equivalent of bar hopping, can easily be done on all fours given the concentration of alehouses in London. Taverns and inns no longer play the role of staging post for coach and horses; but pubs remain meeting-places, signposts ("turn left at The Porcupine"), bus stops, and bastions of Brittania.

Beer is the standard pub drink. You may be surprised by the number of brews on tap in London pubs. Some stock as many as a dozen ales and two ciders. Pubs owned by one of the giant breweries, e.g. Courage, Ind Coope, or Taylor Walker, are compelled to sell only that brewery's ales. Independents, called "Free Houses," can sell a wider range of beers. **Bitter** is the staple of English beer, named for the sharp hoppy aftertaste. Young's, Fuller's, Ruddle's, Tetley's, John Smith, Courage Director's, and Samuel Smith are all superb ales. "Real ale," naturally carbonated and drawn from a barrel, retains its full flavor. Brown, mild, pale, and India pale ales—less common varieties—all have a relatively heavy flavor with noticeable hop. **Stout** is rich, dark, and creamy. **Guinness,** the national drink of Ireland, is the quintessential Stout beer—try standing a match on the amazing head of silky foam. All draught ales and stouts are served "warm"—at room temperature—and by the pint or half-pint. If you can't stand the heat, try a **lager,** the European equivalent of American beer. Budweiser and Miller, where available, cost at least 30% more than German and British brews. **Cider,** an alcoholic apple drink, can prove as potent as the ales; a few pints of it will make you Brahms and Liszt, as cockneys say. Those who don't drink alcohol should savor the pub experience all the same; fruit juices and colas are served (but tend to get expensive), and low-alcohol beers have become more widely available. Buy all drinks at the bar—bartenders are not usually tipped. While the last pint for less than a pound in London has probably been poured a long time ago, prices vary greatly with area and even clientele. Generally, a pint will set you back £1.30-1.55, but in the very center of London this could rise to as much as £1.70. Along with food and drink, pubs often host traditional games, including darts, pool, and bar billiards, an ingenious derivative of billiards played from only one end of the table. More recently, a brash and bewildering array of video games, trivia quiz machines, and fruit (slot) machines has invaded many pubs. CD jukeboxes extort music lovers at 50p a play.

In general, avoid pubs within a half-mile radius of an inner-city train station (Paddington, Euston, King's Cross/St. Pancras, and Victoria). They prey upon tourists by charging 20-40p extra per pint. For the best pub prices, head to the East End. Stylish, lively pubs cluster around the fringes of the West End. Many historic alehouses lend an ancient air to areas swallowed up by the urban sprawl, such as Highgate and Hampstead. Some pubs have serious theatre groups performing upstairs, while others are meeting places for community groups, readings, and other entertainment.

In June 1987, Parliament voted to scrap a 1915 liquor law that required English pubs to close in the afternoon from 3-6pm. Now, publicans have the option of keeping their establishments open throughout the day (Mon.-Sat. 11am-11pm and Sun noon-10:30pm), but most still close from 3-7pm on Sundays. A bell 10 minutes before closing time signifies "last orders." A second bell and the publican's hallowed cry, "Time, gentlemen, PLEASE" right at closing time give patrons 10 minutes to finish their beers. Most pubs are fairly relaxed about the drinking-up time but there are those that will kick you out at 11:10pm on the dot (10:40pm on Sun.).

The West End

Lamb and Flag, 33 Rose St., WC2. Tube: Covent Garden or Leceister Sq. A formerly obstreperous pub where a mob of angry readers seized Augustan poet John Dryden and nearly beat him to death—just one of the events that earned it the name "Bucket of Blood." Today a more docile crowd poised on window seats drinks in Regency calm.

Globe, 37 Bow St., WC2. Tube: Covent Garden. Right by the Royal Opera House—ideal for killing the ringing in your ears, along with orchestra members. Depicted in Hitchcock's *Frenzy.*

Round House, New Row at Bedford St., WC2. Tube: Covent Garden. *Let's Go* researchers and editors are believed to have been meeting here since Saxon times. The scarcity of seats forces patrons to drink and mingle with the hurly-burly post-5pm office-worker crowd.

The Chandos, 29 St. Martin's Lane, WC2. Tube: Charing Cross. A warm place to quaff tea after the National Gallery or the English National Opera; tiled interior and semi-enclosed alcove booths.

Nag's Head, 10 James St., WC2 (tel. 836 4678). Tube: Covent Garden. Not a tacky North Carolinian beach resort, but a favorite of London's theatre elite. The round, light beige "booths" recall airport seating.

The French House, 49 Dean St., W1. Tube: Piccadilly. Diminutive pub with grand liaisons, an unofficial H.Q. for the Free French forces during World War II. Decent French fare served in lieu of the usual English pub goodies: better wine selection than beer. Charles de Gaulle and Dylan Thomas both downed a few here.

The Porcupine, Great Newport St. at Charing Cross, WC2. Tube: Leicester Sq. The West End's most schizophrenic pub: young folks on the first floor generate smoke and noise, while a sedate older crowd (perhaps their parents) pecks at tasty pub meals (£4-5) upstairs before the theatre.

Kensington and Chelsea

Admiral Codrington, 17 Mossop St., SW3. Tube: South Kensington. From the station head east on Pelham St. and then on Draycott Ave., and turn left on Mossop St. This old, handsome pub with a peaceful patio off the back is a favorite watering hole for young Sloane Rangers. No silver bullets served here. Over 100 different kinds of whiskey.

The Antelope, 22 Eaton Terrace, SW1. Tube: Sloane Sq. A quiet, friendly pub that retains a provincial 17th-century ambience.

Cadogan Arms, King's Rd. near Old Church St., SW3. Invigorating and jovial. A good stopping place before a movie at the Cannon Chelsea across the street.

The Goat in Boots, 333 Fulham Rd., SW10. Tube: South Kensington. Perenially popular sloanepoint, with a wide range of beers. No one knows about the name.

Royal Court Tavern, Sloane Sq., SW1. Tube: Sloane Sq. Patronized by a proto-intellectual sloany crowd. Philosopher Andrew Deemer is known to quaff a pint or two here. Food served daily noon-2:30pm and 6-10:15pm.

The Zetland Arms, 2 Bute St., SW7. Tube: South Kensington. Were it not for its food, the Zetland Arms would be just another pub. Popular for its delicious shepherd's pie £2.30 and inexpensive, traditional pub grub. Ploughman's lunch £2.60. Food served all day.

Earl's Court

The Scarsdale, 23 Pembroke Sq., W8. Tube: Earl's Ct. Walk up Earl's Court Rd. 3 blocks past Cromwell Rd., and turn left at Pembroke Sq. More like a private party than a pub: jovial, stylish, and inexpensive. Unfettered by slot machines and pop music, this place leaves you only one option: to chat over a few delightful pints at vine-covered tables out front.

The King's Head, Hogarth Pl., SW5. Tube: Earl's Ct. From Earl's Court Rd., head west on Childs Way or Hogarth Pl. A quality pub in a quiet location, fireplace included. If you don't feel like ale, order champagne or hot chocolate.

Bloomsbury

Princess Louise, 208 High Holborn, WC1. Tube: Holborn. This big pub isn't big enough to contain the huge, jovial crowd that assembles after office hours. The Victorian men's room possesses its own preservation order.

The Lamb, 94 Lamb's Conduit St., WC1. Tube: Russell Sq. E.M. Forster and other Bloomsbury luminaries used to do much of their tippling here. Discreet, stained-glass "snob screens"—holdovers from Victorian times—render this pub ideal for nose-picking or dangerous liaisons.

Museum Tavern, 49 Great Russell St., WC1. Tube: Tottenham Court Rd. Karl Marx sipped ale here after banging out his *Das Kapital* across the street in the British Museum reading room. The Star Tavern, which formerly occupied this site, was one of Casanova's rendezvous spots. Thirteen beers on tap.

Queen's Larder, 1 Queen Sq., opposite St. George the Martyr, WC1. Tube: Russell Sq. or Holborn. A pleasant pub with coffered ceilings, dark mahogany paneling, and a fine restaurant upstairs. Queen Charlotte used the cellar of this building to store sweetmeats for her ailing (read: insane) husband, George III.

Rugby Tavern, corner of Rugby St. and Great St. James, WC1. Tube: Holborn. A light, quiet, elegant pub with a rare, working fireplace. Just off the bustling shopping strip of Lamb's Conduit St., an oasis of local good cheer.

The Water Rats, 328 Grays Inn Rd., WC1. Tube: King's Cross/St. Pancras. Ordinary appearance belies radical historical connections. A favorite haunt of Marx and Engels. Drinkers of the world, unite.

Grafton Arms, 72 Grafton Way, W1. Tube: Warren St. Off the tourist trail, near Regent's Park, and one of the best central London pubs for a relaxed pint. Caters to a London University student crowd. Wine bar on roof-top patio.

The City

Ye Olde Cheshire Cheese, Wine Office Court, 145 Fleet St., EC4. Tube: Blackfriars or St. Paul's. An authentic 17th-century pub with sawdust on the floors and Yorkshire beers flowing from the tap. Famous as Dr. Johnson's hangout, and home of a blue parrot whose death (of a cold) was reported worldwide by the BBC. Closed for renovation until summer 1992.

Black Friar, 174 Queen Victoria St., EC4. Tube: Blackfriars. Witty art nouveau monument in marble and bronze to the medieval monks, including a back room called "the Side Chapel."

Dirty Dick's, 202-204 Bishopgate, EC2. Tube: Liverpool St. Named after Nat Bentley from the old English folk ballad. Pub "decorated" with a pair of stuffed felines and cobwebs.

Cartoonist, 76 Shoe Lane, EC4. Tube: Chancery Lane. Headquarters for the Cartoonist Club of Great Britain; decorated with appropriate hilarity.

The Ship and Blue Ball, 13 Boundary St., E2. Tube: Old St. A snug, convivial pub with a prime selection of beers and ales from the Pitfield Brewery, including the organic "Dark Star."

Hampstead and Highgate

The Flask Tavern, 77 Highgate West Hill, N6, near the youth hostel. Tube: Archway. Enormously popular on summer evenings and at Sun. noon. Standing on the terrace outside, you can drink a toast to Karl Marx, Yehudi Menuhin, or any other Highgate luminary whose name flits through your giddy brain.

Spaniards Inn, Spaniards End, NW3, on the north edge of Hampstead Heath. Tube: Hampstead, then bus #210 along Spaniards Rd. Pub has provided garden in summer and fire in winter since 1585. The inn and outhouse prevent any road widening; traffic must crawl past the pub. Highwayman Dick Turpin and Dickens were patrons.

The Bull and Bush, North End Way, NW3. Tube: Golders Green. Immortalized in the classic music hall song "Down at the old Bull and Bush," though the spiffy young gentlemen who crowd the bar seem unlikely to break into chorus. A fine watering hole for Hampstead hostelers.

Tea

London hotels serve afternoon teas, often hybrids of the clotted and high variety, which are expensive and sometimes disappointing. A full set meal may induce the same after-effects as three bags of M & M's. But the food is terribly British and often delicious. You might order single items from the menu instead of the full set. Most upscale hotels and department stores have some kind of afternoon tea.

Terrace Bar, Harrods, Knightsbridge (tel. 730 1234). Tube: Knightsbridge. Revel in bourgeois satisfaction as you demurely enjoy your expensive set tea inside or out on the terrace (£9). Tea served daily 3-5:30pm.

The Orangery Tea Room, Kensington Palace, Kensington Gardens, W8. Light meals and tea served in the marvelously airy Orangery built for Queen Anne in 1705; architecture by Wren and Hawksmoor. Two fruit scones with clotted cream and jam £3. Pot of tea £1.25. Morning pastries served 9:30-11:30am, lunch 11:30am-2pm, tea 3-5pm.

Sights

The vast mass of London itself, fought street by street, could easily devour an entire hostile army.
—Sir Winston Spencer Churchill, radio broadcast, 1940

Most Londoners shun the major sights of their hometown, possibly fearing some dread encounter with the camera-toting masses. True travelers, however, are made of sturdier stuff, and realize that sight-seeing in a tourist Mecca such as London can yield a two-fold fascination: that of the sights themselves and that of looking at the tourists looking. To enlightened eyes, the contrast between the superhuman scale of London's celebrated palaces, parks, churches, and tombs and the stream of humanity shuffling through them is striking.

The landmarks of London that attract those on foot and in ever-lengthening coaches face an onslaught of up to five million visitors a year. These stampedes tend to concentrate from the late morning onwards, so try to down your bangers and mash as early as possible. London's most famous sights are those intimately connected with the royal family in all of its guises: while the Tower is no longer any use in defense of the royals, they are still baptised and buried in Westminster Abbey, reside in the Palace, are married in St. Paul's, and preside over the opening of Parliament every year. Pacing any assault on these particular sights will allow a much more thorough exploration of the various districts that make up the city. Hidden in and around the main sights can be found a serene chapel or an immense carnival, a museum of clocks, a deer park, an Indian film festival, or an exhibition of Masai arms. Modern day tourists are only the latest in a long line of arrivals to try to find out how the city fits together, and where they fit into the puzzle.

Westminster Abbey

This is the repository of the British kings and nobility, and very fine monuments are here seen over the graves of our ancient monarchs; the particulars are too long to enter into here, and are so many times described by several authors, that it would be a vain repetition to enter upon it here; besides, we have by no means any room for it.
—Daniel Defoe

That Westminster Abbey has become the city's most prized sight indicates just how heavily the weight of the past bears on London. Plaques honoring the most prominent of England's dead line the grey walls of the Abbey, an extraordinary arsenal of English history. Neither a cathedral nor a parish church, the abbey is a "royal peculiar," controlled directly by the crown and outside the jurisdiction of the Church of England. Death doesn't get any better than this; burial in the abbey is the greatest and rarest honor the British Crown can bestow. Byron was refused burial here because of his unconventional morals (though a plaque now honors him). Over the last 200 years, space has become so limited that many coffins stand upright under the pavement. The late Laurence Olivier is due to be honored in Poet's Corner in the next year or so, when the approval process is finally completed.

Just inside the abbey, in the **nave,** rests a memorial to Churchill, a piece of green marble engraved with the immortal words "Remember Winston Churchill." Parliament placed it here 25 years after the Battle of Britain, perhaps prompted by pangs of regret that Churchill's body lay buried in Bladon and not in the Abbey's hall of fame. The grave of the Unknown Warrior, a few paces beyond, commemorates the anonymous legions of WWI war dead. The tomb contains the body of a nameless British soldier transported from Flanders in 1920 and buried "among the kings because he had done good toward God and toward his home." At the foot of the Organ Loft, a memorial to Sir Isaac Newton sits next to the grave of temperate physicist Lord Kelvin. Franklin Roosevelt, David Lloyd George, Lord and Lady Baden-Powell of Boy Scout fame, and the presumptuous David Livingstone number among the elect remembered in the nave. On the hour, the Dean of the Abbey climbs the stairs of the pulpit and offers a timely prayer to this distinguished captive audience.

To see the rest of the Abbey, visitors must enter through a gate at the end of the north aisle of the nave and pay admission (see below). **Musician's Aisle,** just beyond this gate, contains the graves of the Abbey's most accomplished organists, John Blow and Henry Purcell, as well as memorials to the composers Elgar, Britten, Vaughan Williams, and William Walton. **Statesman's Aisle,** in the early Gothic north transept, has the most eclectic collection of memorials. Prime Ministers Disraeli, Gladstone, and Palmerston rub elbows with other statesmen in monuments of varying grandeur. The north wall features a cumbersome monument to William Pitt, confidently waving the peace sign that Churchill and, later, millions of hippies emulated. Sir Francis Vere's Elizabethan tomb in the southeast corner of the transept features the cracked shells of his armor held above his body. A strange paving stone in front of the memorial bears no exalted name, only the cold inscription, "Stone coffin underneath." The **High Altar,** directly south of the north transept, has been the scene of coronations and royal weddings since 1066. Anne of Cleves, Henry VIII's fourth wife, lies in a tomb on the south side of the sanctuary, just before the altar.

Behind the High Altar, in the **Chapel of St. Edward the Confessor,** rests the Coronation Chair, on which all but two English monarchs since 1308 (Edward V and Edward VIII) have been crowned. The chair rests on the ancient Stone of Scone, not to be confused with scones of stone served by teashops everywhere. The stone has been kidnapped twice—first by James I of England, who snatched it from Scotland, and again by anti-royalist students in the 1950s. During the Second World War, it was hidden from possible capture by Hitler, and rumor has it that only Churchill, Roosevelt, the Prime Minister of Canada, and the two workers who moved the stone knew of its whereabouts. For coronation convenience, the chair sits next to the seven-foot long State Sword and the handy-dandy shield of Edward III. The chapel contains a hodgepodge of kings and queens, from Henry III (d. 1272), to George II (d. 1760). Sick persons hoping to be cured would spend nights at the base of the Shrine of St. Edward the Confessor, at the center of the chapel. The king purportedly wielded healing powers during his life, and used to dispense free medical care to hundreds with the laying on of his hands. Tiny spiral staircases within small towers at the entrance to the shrine lead up to a higher chapel where Henry V's wife lies.

Visitors befuddled by the graves of obscure English monarchs will be relieved to find recognizable names on the graves and plaques located in **Poet's Corner.** This little shrine celebrates everyone dead, canonized, and anthologized in the annals of English lit. It begins early, with the short Gothic tomb of Geoffrey Chaucer, placed on the east wall of the transept 150 years after his death. Floor panels commemorate Alfred Lord Tennyson, T.S. Eliot, Dylan Thomas, Henry James, Robert Browning, Lewis Carroll, racy Lord Byron, and poets of World War I, all at the foot of Chaucer's tomb. Each one bears an appropriate description or image for puzzle solvers: D.H. Lawrence's publishing mark (a phoenix) or T.S. Eliot's symbol of death ("the fire and the rose are one"). The south wall bears a misspelled medallion of rare Ben Jonson as well as memorials to Edmund Spenser and John Milton. A partition wall divides the south transept, its east side graced with the graves of Samuel Johnson and actor David Garrick, its west side with memorials to an ever-pensive William Wordsworth, Samuel Taylor Coleridge, a tiny Jane Austen, and the granddaddy of them all, William Shakespeare. Plaques mounted just above the Shakespeare memorial romanticize Keats and Shelley, though both poets already had excessively romantic burials in Rome. Memorials to Robert Burns and the Brontë sisters cover the south walls. Handel's massive memorial, on the west wall of the transept, looms over his grave next to the resting place of prolific Charles Dickens. On this side of the wall, you'll also find the grave of Rudyard Kipling and a memorial to that morbid Dorset farm boy, Thomas Hardy.

The abbey's **cloister** rests in a special peace of its own. The entrance in the north-east corner dates from the 13th century, the rest of it from the 14th. The **Chapter House,** east down a passageway off the cloister, has one of the best-preserved medieval tile floors in Europe. The round, spacious room offers some relief from the hectic Abbey: you may find someone reading a novel on the side benches. The windows in the ceiling depict scenes from the abbey's history. The king's council used the room as its chamber in 1257, and the House of Commons used it as a meeting place in the 16th century. Even today, it is the government and not the abbey that administers the Chapter House and the adjacent Pyx Chamber, once the Royal Treasury and now a plate museum.

Those who enjoy amazingly informative discussions about architecture or a little fun gossip about the dead should take the excellent all-inclusive Abbey Guided Super Tour, lasting 1¼ hour and costing £6. (Tours depart from the Enquiry Desk in the nave Mon.-Fri. at 10am, 10:30am, 11am, 2pm, 2:30pm, and 3pm; Sat. at 10am, 11am, and 12:30pm.) To book one, inquire at the abbey desk, call 222 7110, or write to Super Tours, 20 Dean's Yard, London SW1P 3PA. Photography is permitted only on Wednesday from 6-7:45pm. (Westminster Abbey open Thurs.-Tues. 8am-6pm, Wed. 8am-7:45pm; free. Chapels and transepts open Mon.-Tues. and Thurs.-Fri. 9am-4:45pm, Wed. 9am-4:45pm and 6-7:45pm, Sat. 9am-2:45pm and 3:45-5:45pm; admission £2.60, students £1.30, children 60p. All parts of abbey free Wed. 6-7:45pm.)

Westminster

In the environs of Westminster Abbey, **St. Margaret's,** the parish church of the House of Commons, provides shelter from the storm. John Milton and Winston Churchill were married here (at different times to different people). The stained glass window to the north of the entrance depicts a blind Milton dictating *Paradise Lost* to one of his daughters. Some scenes from *Paradise Regained* surround the window. The John Piper windows on the south side of the Church, built after the war, are entitled "Spring in London." The stunning east window, made in Holland in 1501, honors the marriage of Catherine of Aragon to Prince Arthur. Beneath the high altar lies the headless body of Sir Walter Raleigh, who was executed across the road in 1618. The inscription on his memorial calls upon readers respectfully not to "reflect on his errors." (Open daily 9:30am-4:30pm.)

On the south side of the abbey group the buildings of the **Westminster School,** founded as a part of the Abbey. References to the school date as far back as the 14th century, but Queen Elizabeth officially refounded the school in 1560. The arch in Dean's Yard is pitted with the carved initials of generations of England's most privileged schoolboys. Alums include Ben Jonson, John Dryden, John Locke, Christopher Wren, Edward Gibbon, A.A. Milne, and Matt Jones.

A few blocks down Victoria Street from Westminster proper is **Westminster Cathedral.** Not to be confused with the Anglican Abbey, the Cathedral is the headquarters of the Roman Catholic church in Britain. Finished in 1903, the cathedral is a mix of banded brick, swirling marble, and a starker ceiling, and features a startling rocketlike tower. A lift inside takes visitors up for an unadorned view of the

Houses of Parliament, the river, and Kensington (lift open daily 9:30am-5pm, 70p; cathedral open 7am-8pm.)

The Houses of Parliament

The Houses of Parliament (Tube: Westminster), oft imagined in foggy silhouette against the Thames, have become London's visual trademark. For the classic view captured by Claude Monet, walk about halfway over Westminster Bridge, preferably at dusk and in purple fog.

Like the government offices along Whitehall, the Houses of Parliament occupy the former site of a royal palace. A few portions of the Palace of Westminster (notably Westminster Hall) have survived, but most of it went up in picturesque smoke on October 16, 1834. Sir Charles Barry and A.W.N. Pugin won a competition for the design of the new houses. From 1840 to 1888, Barry built a hulking, symmetrical block that Pugin ornamented with tortured imitations of late medieval decoration. "Tudor details on a classic body," Pugin later sneered, before dying of insanity.

The immense complex blankets eight acres and includes more than 1100 rooms and 100 staircases. Space is nevertheless so inadequate that Members of Parliament (MPs) can not have private offices or staff, and the archives—the original copies of every Act of Parliament passed since 1497—are stuffed into Victoria Tower, the large tower to the south. A flag flown from the tower (a signal light after dusk) indicates that Parliament is in session. You can hear **Big Ben** in the slightly smaller northern tower but you can't see it; it's actually neither the tower nor the clock but the 15-ton bell that tolls the hours. The immortal nickname has a prosaic origin; the bell was cast while a robustly proportioned Sir Benjamin Hall served as Commissioner of Works. Each of the Roman numerals on the clock face measures two feet in length; the "big hand," 14 feet. Over the years Big Ben (the bell) has developed a crack. The mechanism moving the hands is still wound manually.

Destroyed during the Blitz and rebuilt during the austere late 1940s, the modest room now housing the Commons preserves most features of the Old Chamber, including thin red lines fixed two sword-lengths apart. Members may not cross these lines during debates. The government of the day occupies the benches to the Speaker's right, with the Prime Minister sitting just opposite the Despatch Boxes. During votes, members file out of the chamber and into the "division lobbies" according to how they have voted: ayes into west lobby, and nays to the east. As they enter the Commons, members must pass through **Churchill's Arch,** the chipped and half-destroyed stone doorway that the statesman insisted be left untouched as a reminder of England's losses during World War II. One of the most haunting images of the war is a hurried snapshot that shows Churchill standing, head bowed, amid the rubble of the old House.

Until 1825, high treason trials were conducted in **Westminster Hall,** first built in 1097 but derided as a "mere bedchamber" by William II. The hall was rebuilt around 1400, at which time the hammerbeam roof was added. The long list of those condemned to death here includes Sir Thomas More, Guy Fawkes, and Charles I. A plaque marks the spot where Charles sat during his trial. After Charles' ill-fated attempt to arrest five MPs in 1641, no monarch even tried to enter the chamber until 1950, when George VI peeked in on the hall's reconstruction. The last of the public trials took place here in 1806. Today the hall is used primarily for the lying-in-state ceremonies of prominent personages.

Unfortunately, access to Westminster Hall and the Houses of Parliament has been restricted since an IRA bomb killed an MP in 1979. To get a guided tour (Mon.-Thurs.) or a seat at Question Time when the Prime Minister attends (Mon.-Thurs. at 2:30pm), you need to obtain tickets—available on a limited basis from your embassy—or an introduction from an MP. Because demand for these tickets is extremely high, the most likely way of getting into the building is to queue to attend a debate when Parliament is in session. The House of Commons Visitors' Gallery (for "Distinguished and Ordinary Strangers") is open during extraordinary hours (Mon.-Thurs. 4-10pm, Friday 10am-3pm). The more staid House of Lords

Visitors' Gallery is often easier to access (open Mon.-Wed. 2:30pm-late, Thurs. 3pm-late, Fri. 11am-late). Visitors should arrive early, and be prepared to wait in the long queues by Victoria Tower (on the left for the Commons, on the right for the Lords. Free.) Those willing to sacrifice the roar of the debate for smaller, more focused business can attend meetings of any of the various Committees when they are in session by jumping the queue and going straight up to the entrance. For times of committee meetings each week, call the House of Commons Information Office (tel. 219 4272).

Whitehall

In 1698, Henry VIII's Palace of Whitehall, "the biggest and most hideous place in all Europe," burned to the ground. England's royalty then began the roaming that took successive royal families to the palaces of Kensington and St. James's and finally to Buckingham Palace. Meanwhile, Whitehall (Tube: Westminster or Charing Cross), stretching from Parliament Street to Trafalgar Square, became the center of civil administration.

The **Banqueting House** (corner of Horse Guards Ave. and Whitehall), built in 1625, one of the few intact masterpieces of Inigo Jones, was the first true Renaissance building in England, and the only part of Whitehall to survive the fire that consumed the palace. This Palladian hall achieved notoriety on January 27, 1649 when King Charles I, draped in black velvet, was led out its doorway and beheaded. The allegorical paintings on the 60-ft.-high ceiling (ironically the story of the happy monarchy of James I and Charles I) are the handiwork of Rubens. A cautious James II supposedly placed the weather vane on top of the building to see if a favorable wind was blowing for William of Orange. From 1724 to 1890, the Banqueting House served as a Chapel Royal. These days the hall sees no executions, just some harmless state dinners (behind bulletproof glass) and the occasional concert. (Open Mon.-Sat. 10am-5pm, admission £2, students £1.50, children £1.35.)

Henry VIII's wine cellar was one of the few parts of the palace spared in the fire of 1698. In 1953, the government erected the massive Ministry of Defence Building, just south of the Banqueting House, over Henry's cache. The cellar had to be relocated deeper into the ground to accommodate the new structure. Technically, visitors may view the cellar, but permission is dauntingly difficult to obtain (apply in writing to the Department of the Environment or the Ministry of Defence with a compelling story). Near the statue of General Gordon in the gardens behind the Ministry of Defence Building, you'll find the remnants of Queen Mary's terrace, built for Queen Mary II. The bottom of the steps leading from the terrace mark the 17th-century water level.

Some of Whitehall's major attractions stand off the main street. **Scotland Yard** will probably fall short of crime-hounds' expectations. The home of so many correct but unimaginative detectives humbled by Sherlock Holmes and Hercule Poirot is nothing more than one large and one small building connected by an arch at 6 Derby Gate. The old buildings now contain government offices. The official residence of the British Prime Minister, **10 Downing Street** boasts the most recognizable door in England. Margaret Thatcher's contribution to the local architecture takes the form of large iron gates that now protect the street from terrorists and tourists alike; even the motorcycle messengers have to hand their papers through the gates. Behind the famous exterior of No. 10 beyond the security spreads an extensive political network, one of the centers of British government. The Chancellor of the Exchequer resides at No. 11 Downing St., the Chief Whip of the House of Commons at No. 12. Together, these three houses contain more than 200 rooms. Recently, the Cabinet room overlooking the back garden of No. 10 survived an IRA mortar attack launched from a nearby parked van with its roof cut out. In the middle of Whitehall as it turns into Parliament St. stands the rigorously formal **Cenotaph** honoring the war dead, usually decked with crested wreaths.

On the west side of Whitehall north of Downing St. stand the **Horse Guards,** where two photogenic mounted soldiers keep watch daily from 10am to 4pm. At

Whitehall's changing of the guard, as opposed to Buckingham Palace's, you can witness the pageantry without a large crowd in tow. (The head guard meticulously inspects the troops Mon.-Sat. at 11am, Sun. at 10am. The guard dismounts, with some fanfare, daily at 4pm.) Through the gates lies Horse Guards Parade, a large court (opening onto St. James's Park) from which the bureaucratic array of different styles of architecture that make up Whitehall can be seen. In early June, the Beating Retreat that takes place here is a must for lovers of pomp and circumstance (for information on tickets, call 218 3955).

Charing Cross and Trafalgar Square

The original **Charing Cross,** last of 13 crosses set up to mark the stages of Queen Eleanor's royal funeral procession in 1291 ("charing" comes from "beloved queen" in French), was once the center of Trafalgar Square. It has since been moved to the front of Charing Cross railway station. This spot used to be the true focus of London life as well as the geographical center of the city. "Why, Sir, Fleet Street has a very animated appearance," Samuel Johnson once remarked, "but I think the full tide of human existence is at Charing Cross." Now the full tide of traffic engulfs the place, and the bronze statue of King Charles drowns in the ebb and flow of automobiles.

Unlike many squares in London, **Trafalgar Square,** sloping down from the National Gallery to Charing Cross, has been public land ever since the razing of several hundred houses made way for its construction in the 1830s. **Nelson's Column,** a fluted granite pillar, commands the square, with four majestic, beloved lions guarding the base, and troops of pigeons everywhere. The monument and square commemorate brilliant Admiral Nelson, killed during his greatest victory off Trafalgar in Spain. Floodlights bathe the square after dark. Every year, Norway donates a giant Christmas tree for the square in thanks for Britain's help during World War II; in 1990, it and two policemen were nearly cut down by a man armed with a chainsaw protesting strict Norwegian drugs laws. Enthusiastic, even rambunctious New Year's celebrations take place here, including universal indiscriminate kissing.

At the head of the square squats the ordering façade of the National Gallery, Britain's collection of the Old Masters (see Museums below). A competition to design a new extension to the gallery ended in Prince Charles' denouncement of the winning entry as a "monstrous carbuncle" on the face of London, and the subsequent selection of a new architect. Robert Venturi's wing to the west of the main building has just been opened; the mock columns and pillars that echo the old building and even Nelson's Column are much discussed and generally liked.

The church of **St. Martin-in-the-Fields,** on the northeastern corner of the square opposite the National Gallery, dates from the 1720s. Designer James Gibbs topped its templar classicism with a Gothic steeple. St. Martin, which has its own world-renowned chamber orchestra, sponsors lunchtime and evening concerts, as well as a summer festival in mid-July. (Box office in the bookshop open Mon.-Sat. 11:30am-7:30pm, Sun. 11am-6pm; telephone bookings open 12:30am-2:30pm and 4:30-6:30pm; tel. 702 1377; tickets £4-12.50.) At the **Brass Rubbing Centre** in the church, you can replicate images of England's past from brass tablets. (Prices from £1. Open Mon.-Sat. 10am-6pm, Sun. noon-6pm.) The suitably dark, atmospheric café in the Crypt serves cappuccino with a Baroque flair (open daily 10am-8:30pm; church open daily 7:30am-7:30pm).

St. James's

Just north of Buckingham Palace and the Mall, up Stable Yard or Marlborough Rd., stands **St. James's Palace,** the residence of the monarchy from 1660 to 1668 and again from 1715 to 1837. King Charles I passed his last night in the palace's guardroom before crossing St. James's Park to be executed at the Banqueting House in 1649. History does not record whether he slept soundly. Only Henry VIII's gateway and clock tower and a pair of parading guards at the foot of St. James's St.

still hark back to the Tudor palace. You can visit Inigo Jones' fine **Queen's Chapel,** built in 1626, by attending Sunday services at 8:30 and 11:15am (Oct.-July).

The fashionable area around the palace has also come to be called St. James's. Bordered by St. James's Park and Green Park to the south and Piccadilly to the north, it begins at an equestrian statue of George III on Cockspur Street off Trafalgar Sq. **St. James's Street,** next to St. James's Palace, runs into **Pall Mall**—the name derives from "pail-mail," a predecessor of the 17th-century noble game of croquet. Many of the storefronts along the two streets have remained relatively unchanged since the 18th century, among them wine merchants Berry Bros. & Rudd and Lock & Co. (with rotting hats in the window), both on St. James's St. They rub storefront elbows with a number of famous London coffeehouses-turned-clubs. The chief Tory club, the Carlton, at 69 St. James's St., was recently bombed by the IRA. The chief Liberal club, the Reform at 104 Pall Mall, served as a social center of Parliamentary power. In 1823, a Prime Minister and the presidents of the Royal Academy and the Royal Society founded the Athenaeum, on Waterloo Place, for scientific, literary, and artistic men. Gibbon, Hume, Burke, and Garrick belonged to the Whig Brooks, founded in 1764 (60 St. James's St.). The offices of *The Economist* loom on St. James's St. in a modern highrise, though not as modern as the brand new office block (nicknamed the blackbird after a military jet) at no. 66.

Off Pall Mall, a statue of "The Grand Old Duke of York" perches on a tall column in Waterloo Place. In nearby St. James's Square, a statue of William III stands surrounded by a beautiful (and unapproachable) lawn. At the northeast corner of the square a memorial marks the spot where a policewoman was shot dead in 1984 by a submachine-gun-wielding diplomat in the adjacent Libyan embassy.

Between fashionable Jermyn St. and Piccadilly, you can enter **St. James's Church,** a post-war reconstruction of what Wren considered his best parish church. Blake was baptized here amidst the typical Wren single room interior, with galleries around the main space. The rector of the parish encourages "Protest through Prayer," and the church community sponsors encounter groups, musical recitals, and films on South Africa. (Tube: Green Park or Piccadilly Circus. Open Mon.-Sat. 10am-6pm, Sun. noon-6pm.)

Buckingham Palace

When a freshly-crowned Victoria moved from Kensington Palace in 1837, Buckingham Palace, built in 1825 by John Nash, had faulty drains and a host of other leaky difficulties. When the flag is flying, the Queen is at home, but don't plan on paying her a visit; no part of Buckingham Palace ever opens to the public. The Palace's best side, the garden front, is seldom seen by ordinary visitors as it is protected by the 40-acre spread where the Queen holds her garden parties. Nasty-looking spikes appeared four years ago on top of the wall surrounding the area; recently barbed wire was added, in an effort to stop occasional forays by admirers who managed to reach the Queen's bedroom and ask for a cigarette.

The oft-photographed **Changing of the Guard** takes place daily from April to July, and on alternate days from August to March. The "Old Guard" marches from St. James's Palace down the Mall to Buckingham Palace, leaving at approximately 11:10am. The "New Guard" begins marching as early as 10:20am. When they meet at the central gates of the palace, the officers of the regiments then touch hands, symbolically exchanging keys, et voilà—the guard is changed. The soldiers gradually split up to relieve the guards currently protecting the palace. The ceremony moves to the beat of royal band music and the menacing clicks of thousands of cameras. In wet weather or on pressing state holidays, the Changing of the Guard does not occur. To witness the spectacle, show up well before 11:30am and stand directly in front of the palace. You can also watch along the routes of the troops prior to their arrival at the palace (from 10:40-11:25am) between the Victoria Memorial and St. James's Palace or along Birdcage walk. Throughout the day, a couple of guards pace back and forth methodically in front of the palace.

In the extravagant **"Trooping the Colour"** ceremony, held on the Queen's official birthday, a Saturday in early June, the colors of a chosen regiment are paraded ceremonially before the royals. The parade in honor of the Queen brings out luminaries mounted on horses while somewhat less influential types putter about in limousines with little golden crowns on top. The best view of all this is on TV, but you might catch a glimpse of the Queen in person as she rides down the Mall. Tickets for the event must be obtained in advance through the mail. Write to the Household Division HQ, Horse Guards, SW1 before March 1. If you don't get a ticket for the event, you may receive one for one of the rehearsals on the two preceding Saturdays. Since the Queen does not need to rehearse, these tend to be noticeably less crowded.

Nearby, you can drop in on the **Guards Museum** at Wellington Barracks on Birdcage Walk, off Buckingham Gate. (Open Mon.-Thurs., Sat.-Sun. 10am-4pm. Admission £2, students and children £1.) The courtyard outside Wellington Barracks is probably the only place where you'll ever see the Guards at relative ease. Also off Buckingham Gate stands the curious **Royal Mews Museum,** which houses the royal coaches and other historic royal riding implements. (Open July-Sept. Wed.-Fri. noon-4pm, Oct.-Apr. Wed. noon-4pm. Admission £1.30, students £1, children 70p.)

Piccadilly

All of the West End's major arteries—Piccadilly, Regent Street, Shaftesbury Avenue, The Haymarket—merge and swirl around Piccadilly Circus, one of the world's great meeting places and the bright, giddy hub of Nash's 19th-century London. Today the circus earns its place on postcards with towering bluffs of neon, circular traffic congestion, and an absurd statue everyone calls "Eros," though it was intended to be the Angel of Christian Charity in memory of the reformer, Lord Shaftesbury. Despite the misleading romantic title of the statue, don't try to meet your lover here—you'll only lose each other in the crowds.

The circus became a center of popular entertainment during Victoria's reign, and while the old stages no longer stand, the façades of the great music halls remain, propped up against contemporary tourist traps and commercial ventures. Statues of Michael Jackson, Madonna, and Tina Turner wave to passersby from the balcony of the **London Pavillion,** 1 Piccadilly Circus, a historic theatre recently converted to house the Tussaud Group's latest enterprise, **Rock Circus** (tel. 734 8025; Tube: Piccadilly Circus), an impressive wax-work museum and revolving theatre dedicated to the history of rock-and-roll. Elvis, the Beatles, David Bowie, the Stones, Sid Vicious, and Sting stand among the 50 rock and pop artists eerily re-created as life-like wax effigies and androids. Infrared headsets trigger a CD soundtrack for each display as you wander through the exhibits. Unfortunately there is also commentary, haughtily informing us that Sting wrote "perceptive lyrics about real life and real love." It's pretty high-tech, though, and a *Let's Go* researcher fave. (Open July-Sept. Wed.-Mon. 10am-10pm, Tues. noon-10pm; Oct-June Wed.-Mon. 11am-9pm, Tues. noon-9pm. Admission £5.95, students and seniors £4.95, children £3.95.) Rainy afternoons can be whiled away in the glitzy galleries, shops, arcades and eating emporia of the adjacent **Trocadero Centre,** (entrance on Coventry St.), an oh-so-trendy mall and entertainment complex housed within a giant, triple-tiered atrium. On the third floor of the much-hyped centre you can find a campy, multimedia shrine to the *Guinness Book of World Records'* wide range of superlative accomplishments and aberrations. (Tel. 439 7331; open daily 10am-10pm. Admission £4.50, seniors and students £3.60, children £2.85.)

Aristocratic mansions once lined Piccadilly, a broad mile-long avenue stretching from Regent St. in the east to Hyde Park Corner in the west. The name derives from Piccadilly Hall, the 17th-century home of Robert Baker, an affluent tailor who did brisk business in the sale of "pickadills," frilly, lace collars that were much in fashion in his day. The only remnant of Piccadilly's stately past is the formidable **Burlington House,** built in 1665 for the Earls of Burlington and redesigned in the 18th century by Colin Campbell to accommodate the burgeoning **Royal Academy**

of Arts (tel. 439 7438; Tube: Piccadilly or Green Park). Founded in 1768, the Academy consists of 40 academicians and 30 associates who administer the exhibition galleries and maintain a free school of art (see Museums). Reynolds, Gainsborough, Constable, and Turner are a few of the many eminent names associated with the academy, while Romney, Blake, and Rossetti head up an equally impressive list of English artists whom the academy overlooked. The annual summer exhibition is an always noteworthy and often controversial mix of established masters and newer artists, hoping for recognition. The ambitious **Museum of Mankind** backs onto Burlington House behind the Royal Academy (see Museums).

A quiet courtyard just east of the Academy opens onto **Albany,** an 18th-century apartment block widely renowned as one of London's most prestigious addresses. Built by William Chambers in 1771 and remodeled in 1812 to serve as "residential chambers for bachelor gentlemen," Albany has evolved into an exclusive enclave of literary excellence. Swinger-soldier Lord Byron wrote his epic "Childe Harold" here. Other eminent men of letters associated with Albany include Macaulay, Gladstone, Canning, "Monk" Lewis, J.B. Priestley and Graham Greene.

Piccadilly continues south and west, running past imperious Bond Street, past the Ritz Hotel with its distinctive arcade and cluster of bright lights, and past a string of fashionable men's clubs on the rim of Green Park. At the gateway of the Wellington Museum in **Apsley House,** described by its first owner as "No. 1, London," the avenue merges into the impenetrable Hyde Park corner. Apsley House was built by Robert Adam in the 1780s as a residence commemorating Wellington's victory at Waterloo.

Running north from Piccadilly Circus are the grand façades of **Regent Street,** leading to Oxford Circus. The buildings and street were built by John Nash in the early 19th century as part of a processional route for the Prince Regent to follow from St. James' Park north through Oxford Circus to his house in Regent's Park. The façades have changed since Nash's time, and today the street is known for the crisp cuts of Burberry raincoats and Aquascutum suits as well as Hamley's, the giant warehouse of Santa's goodies.

Soho and Leicester Square

For centuries, Soho was to sex what the Houses of Parliament are to affairs of state. It has, however, undergone a well-funded renaissance, and the few porn shops that remain merely add an illicit edge to the newly recovered area. Many of London's most fashionable clubs, restaurants, and shops now occupy buildings that once housed massage parlors. As a result of strict vice laws, prostitutes can only sell their wares from upper-story windows, leaving the sidewalks free for more subtle forms of seduction. The area is loosely bounded by Oxford Street in the north, Piccadilly and Coventry St. in the south, Charing Cross Road in the east, and Regent Street in the west.

Wardour Street runs north through the offices of Britain's film industry from the eerie ruins of **St. Anne's Soho.** German bombers leveled most of this church in 1940; only Wren's anomalous tower of 1685 and the ungainly, green, bottle-shaped steeple added by Cockerell in 1803 emerged unscathed. William Hazlitt (who died two blocks away at no. 6 Frith St.) lies buried somewhere in the old churchyard; his memorial rests below the tower wall. A quiet garden spreads around the base of St. Anne's. Its park benches and surrounding lawns fill up with vagrants and rapacious pigeons.

Just to the north, a blue plaque above Leoni's Quo Vadis restaurant at **28 Dean Street** locates the austere, two-room flat where the impoverished Karl Marx lived with his wife, maid, and five children while writing *Das Kapital.* Running parallel to Dean St., Frith and Greek St. end at **Soho Square.** A breeding ground for mansions in the 17th century, the square has become a center of the film industry. Blurred by rough weather and cracked with age, an ancient statue of Charles II (1681) presides over the **Soho Village Green.** The ill-fated Duke of Monmouth once commissioned a palatial house on this site; according to local legend, the district's current name comes from his rallying cry at the battle of Sedgemoor, *"Soe-hoe."*

On weekdays, the fruit and vegetable market on **Berwick Street** rumbles with trade and far-flung Cockney accents. Brewer Street and Greek Street to the southeast retain the most seedy trappings of Soho's recent past. Near Regent Street, the neighborhood calms down, and **Meard Street** yields an impression of Soho in its earlier, more residential days. **Carnaby Street,** a notorious hotbed of 60s sex and sedition, has since lapsed into a lurid tourist trap crammed with stalls of junky gimmicks and souvenirs.

Leicester Square, just south of Shaftesbury Ave. (and Chinatown) between Piccadilly Circus and Charing Cross Rd., is an entertainment nexus, framed by the giant billboards of grand, expensive first run cinemas. The square is a pedestrian area, once called "Leicester Fields" and owned by descendants of the flashy Renaissance poet, Sir Philip Sidney. Current park remodelling is due to be completed in late 1992. A plaque on the west side of the square marks where Royal Academician Joshua Reynolds lived and died. On the north side, on Leicester Place, the French presence in Soho manifests itself in **Notre-Dame de France.** This church may not be anything to exclaim over architecturally, but it rewards visitors who go inside with an exquisite Aubusson tapestry lining the inner walls. And don't miss the tiny chapel built into the western wall, which features an arresting, cartoon-like mural by Jean Cocteau (note Judas's uncanny resemblance to the Creature From the Black Lagoon).

Mayfair

The center of London's glamorous *beau monde* was named for the 17th-century May Fair (held on the site of Shepherd's Market), a notorious haunt of prostitutes. Modern Mayfair, especially on Hill St. and Chesterfield Hill and among the shop windows on Bond St., Burlington Arcade and Jermyn St., has a distinctly patrician atmosphere; it is the most expensive property in the London version of *Monopoly.* Mayfair is bordered by Oxford St. to the north, Piccadilly to the south, Park Lane to the west and Regent St. to the east. Tube: Green Park, Bond St., or Piccadilly Circus.

Park Lane, the western border of Mayfair at Hyde Park, is famous for the astronomically priced and overwhelmingly tasteful hotels which grace its length, running north from Wellington's Apsley House and the newer Hard Rock Café. The Hilton, Grosvenor House Hotel, and the Dorchester can be found here, while Claridges is hidden further inside Mayfair on Brook St.

Grosvenor Square, between Brook and Grosvenor St., is the largest of its breed in central London. Developed by Sir Richard Grosvenor in 1725, the central garden spreads across the site of Oliver's Mount, a makeshift barricade erected by the people of London in 1643 to repel the invading armies of Charles I. Once a fashionable residential area and home to Shelley, the square has gradually evolved into an American military and political enclave. Future President John Adams lived at no. 9 while serving as the first American ambassador to England in 1785. Almost two centuries later, General Eisenhower established his wartime headquarters here at no. 20, and memory of his stay persists in the area's postwar nickname, "Eisenhowerplatz." A statue of Franklin Roosevelt—freed from his wheelchair by the sculptor, Reid Dick—towers above a white pedestal on the north side of the green. From here you can see the streamlined **U.S. Embassy** rising in the west, where protesters occasionally assemble to denounce the latest American indiscretion.

Shepherd's Market, the tiny village-like area just above Piccadilly, has become expensive and respectable since the 60s. Its web of little streets teems with inviting restaurants and pubs. P.G. Wodehouse's fictional aristocrat Bertie Wooster and insightful butler Jeeves lived in foreboding **Half Moon Street.** Blake saw mystical visions for 17 years on South Molton Street, Händel wrote the *Messiah* on busy Brook Street, and the reigning queen was born in a house (recently demolished) at no. 17 Bruton Street. Laurence Sterne ended his life and adventures in poverty on haughty Bond Street (no. 39).

The connoisseur will be drawn to the storefronts of **Bond Street** by the discreet promise of luxury: *haute couture* and handmade shotguns, emerald tiaras and platinum swizzle sticks, antique furniture and objets d'art. An array of art dealers and auctioneers with public galleries frequently offer special shows of exceptional quality. Try Marlborough (entrance by Albemarle Street) for the biggest contemporary names, Agnews (no. 43), or Colnaghi's (no. 14). For the Old Masters and even some nouveau excitement visit **Sotheby's** at no. 34: wander through art works on exhibit before auction, or desperately try not to sneeze during an auction (open Mon.-Fri. 9am-4:30pm). Modern art aficionados should also note the rugged Henry Moore frieze high up on the crest of the **Time/Life Building** (corner of Bruton St.), and duck inside for a glance at the splendid mural by Ben Nicholson.

Hyde Park and Kensington Gardens

Totalling 630 acres, **Hyde Park** and the contiguous **Kensington Gardens** constitute the largest open area in the center of the city, earning their reputation as the "lungs of London." Environmentally unsound Henry VIII used to hunt deer here. At the far west of the Gardens, you can drop your calling card at **Kensington Palace** (tel. 937 9561), originally the residence of King William III and Queen Mary II and recently of Princess Margaret. Currently, the Prince and Princess of Wales, the little Princes, and other stray members of the Royal Family live in the palace. A museum of uninhabited royal rooms and regal memorabilia includes a Court dress collection, with Di's wedding gown prominently displayed. Although Queen Victoria was born here, with characteristic propriety she left few traces of herself, aside from a nondescript statue outside the palace grounds. The palace gift shop appears to be the happening place to purchase Beatrix Potter memorabilia. (Palace open Mon.-Sat. 9am-5:30pm, Sun. 11am-5:30pm. Admission £3.75, students and OAPs £2.80, children £2.50.) A walk west of the palace along Kensington Palace Gardens, one of London's most opulent thoroughfare, reveals the homes of a crew of millionaires and embassies.

Remind yourself that parks were meant for children by walking north or east of the palace. The Round Pond east of the palace plays the ocean for a fleet of toy sailboats on weekends. In the playground north of the palace, younger children frolic around a fairy tree adorned with elves. Roughly at the center of the gardens, G.F. Watts' 1904 Physical Energy statue, a muscle-bound man, rides an equally muscular steed off into the sunset. The ramshackle Italian Gardens, farther north, is a hotspot for sunbathers and derelict waterfowl.

The Serpentine, a lake carved in 1730, runs from these fountains in the north, near Bayswater Rd., south to Knightsbridge. From the number of people who pay the £2 (children £1) to sunbathe at the fenced-off Serpentine beach (the Lido), one would think the sun shone more brightly there than anywhere else in London. Harriet Westbrook (P.B. Shelley's first wife) numbers proudly among the famous people who have drowned in this man-made "pond." The **Serpentine Gallery** (tel. 402 6075), in Kensington Gardens, often hosts interesting exhibitions of contemporary works, as well as art workshops. (Gallery open daily 10am-6pm. Parks open Mon.-Fri. 10am-6pm, Sat.-Sun. 10am-7pm; off-season Mon.-Fri. 10am-dusk, Sat.-Sun. 10am-4pm. Free.) On the southern edge of Kensington Gardens, the Lord Mayor had the **Albert Memorial** built to honor Victoria's beloved husband, whose death Victoria mourned for nearly 40 years. Considered a great artistic achievement when first unveiled in 1869, the extravagant monument now seems an embarrassing piece of imperial Victorian excess. Unfortunately, you will be unable to judge for yourself since the Albert Memorial will be under designer scaffolding for another six years as it undergoes restoration. The **Albert Hall,** with its ornate oval dome, hosts the Promenade Concerts (Proms) in summer (see Entertainment below; no tours). Also built to honor the Prince Consort, the hall is simpler than the memorial, and features a frieze of the "Triumph of the Arts and Sciences" around its circumference.

Avoid the east-west path through southern Hyde Park at night. Called Rotten Row, from a corruption of *Route du Roi* (King's Rd.), the walk can be dangerous.

Speakers' Corner, in the northeast corner of Hyde Park (Tube: Marble Arch, not Hyde Park Corner), is the finest example of free speech in action anywhere in the world. On Sundays from late morning to dusk, and on summer evenings, soapbox revolutionaries, haranguers, madmen and visionaries scream about anything from Kierkegaard to socialism to knitting. Test your patience and your vocal chords and go heckle with the best of them. At the southern end of Hyde Park cluster a group of statues: a Diana fountain, the "family of man," a likeness of Lord Byron, and London's first nude statue (1822), an Achilles molded from cannonballs. Royal park band performances take place in the bandstand 200 yards from Hyde Park Corner, in the direction of the Serpentine (June-Aug. every Sun. at 3 and 6pm).

Kensington, Knightsbridge and Belgravia

Kensington, a gracious and sheltered residential area, reposes between multiethnic Notting Hill to the north and trendy Chelsea to the south. Kensington High Street, which pierces the area, has become a shopping and scoping epicenter. Antique and obscure specialty shops fill the area along Kensington Church Street in the north, Victorian-era museums and colleges dominate South Kensington, while the area around Earl's Court has mutated into something of a tourist colony.

Take the Tube to High St. Kensington to reach **Holland Park,** a rabbit-ridden, peacock-peppered garden. Beyond the cricket pitches and tennis courts (open to the public), a block west of the park's southern entrance on the High St., stands the curious **Leighton House,** 12 Holland Park Rd. (tel. 602 3316). Devised by the imaginative Lord Leighton in the 19th century, the house is a bold and amusing pastiche. (House open Mon.-Sat. 11am-5pm, until 6pm for some exhibitions. Free.)

To reach the grandiose South Kensington museums, take the Tube or the #49 bus from Kensington High St. The Great Exhibition of 1851 funded many of these buildings built between 1867 and 1935. North of Cromwell Rd., the various royal institutions of learning and culture include the Imperial College of Science, the Royal College of Music, the Royal College of Art, the Albert Hall, the august Royal School of Needlepoint, and **Royal Geographic Society.** Inside the Geographic Society, just east of the Albert Hall, can be seen 800,000 maps, and the explorer Stanley's boots (open Mon.-Fri. 10am-1pm and 2-5pm. Free). Museums cluster between and around these institutions, bringing younger folk into the area to dilute the high concentration of professors and graduate students. The massive Museum of Natural History cathedral, the more modern Science Museum, and the eminently Victorian Victoria and Albert Museum all exhibit themselves at Cromwell and Exhibition Rd. (See Museums below.)

While **Knightsbridge** may be wealthy and stylish, its snooty reputation rests more on tradition than on practice. Knightsbridge is defined most of all by London's premier department store, **Harrods.** Founded in 1849 as a grocery store, by 1880 Harrods employed over 100 workers. In 1905 the store moved to its current location; today it requires 5000 employees to handle its vast array of products and services. Besides an encyclopaedic inventory, Harrods also has a pub, several restaurants, and naturally, a tourist information center. (Open Mon.-Tue. and Thurs.-Sat. 9am-6pm, Wed. 9am-8pm. See Shopping below.)

Chelsea

From Thomas More to Oscar Wilde to Johnny Rotten and the Sex Pistols, Chelsea has a checkered past and remains the flashiest district in London. Few streets in London scream louder for a visit than the **King's Road.** Mohawked UB40s and silk-scarved or pearl-necklaced Sloane Rangers (awfully loosely the English equivalent of preppies) gaze at trendy window displays, probably looking no further than the glass. Optimal viewing time is Saturday afternoon. The tube is practically nonexistent around here, so you'll have to rely on buses (like #11 or #22)—or better yet, your feet—along King's Rd. and Fulham Rd.

Any proper exploration of Chelsea begins at **Sloane Square.** The square takes its name from Sir Hans Sloane (1660-1753), one of three collectors whose artifacts made up the original collections of the British Museum. The nearby Royal Court Theatre debuted many of George Bernard Shaw's plays. Until 1829, King's Rd., stretching southwest from Sloane Square, served as a private royal thoroughfare from Hampton Court to St. James's. Hidden among the trendy boutiques lurk cheap restaurants, historic pubs, and the **Chelsea Antique Market** (where one can purchase first editions of Gibbon's *Decline and Fall*).

Off King's Rd., things become more peaceful. Hardly touched by the Underground, Georgian Chelsea remains a world apart from the rest of London. By the river stands Wren's **Royal Hospital,** of 1691, founded by Charles II for retired soldiers and still inhabited by 400 army pensioners. Ex-soldiers welcome visitors to the spacious grounds, dressed in uniform adapted only slightly to the present day. (Open Mon.-Sat. 10am-noon and 2-4pm, Sun. 2-4pm. Free.) East of the Hospital lie the **Ranelagh Gardens** (usually open until dusk). The **Chelsea Flower Show** blooms here in mid-May (in 1992, May 19-22), but even members of the Royal Horticultural Society have trouble procuring tickets for the first two days. The **National Army Museum** stands directly west of the hospital, along Royal Hospital Rd (see Museums below).

Cheyne Walk, Cheyne Row, and Tite Street formed the heart of Chelsea's artist colony at the turn of the century. Watch for the blue plaques on the houses. J.M.W. Turner moved into a house in Cheyne Walk, and Edgar Allan Poe lived nearby. Mary Ann Evans (a.k.a. George Eliot) moved into #4 just before her death. Dante Gabriel Rossetti kept his highly disreputable *ménage* in #16, where he doused himself with chloral hydrate and hammered the image of the artist as nonconformist into the public mind. Mick Jagger searched for satisfaction on the Walk in the 60s. The area's most notorious resident, Oscar Wilde, lived at 16 Tite St. and was arrested for homosexual behavior at Chelsea's best-known hotel, the Cadogan. John Singer Sargent, James MacNeill Whistler, Augustus John, and Bertrand Russell also lived on Tite Street. Today, fashionable artists' and designers' homes line the street.

Thomas Carlyle, the Victorian-era social critic, churned out his epic tomes on Cheyne Row. On this miraculously quiet street colored by flowers and tidy houses, **Carlyle's House,** 24 Cheyne Row (Tube: Sloane Sq.), has remained virtually unchanged since the Sage of Chelsea expired in his armchair. Glass cases shield his books and manuscripts; family portraits and sketches ornament the walls. In his attic study Carlyle wrote and rewrote *The French Revolution* after John Stuart Mill's chambermaid accidently burned Carlyle's first finished draft. The hat of this extraordinary man hangs on the peg of the garden door, and the water pitcher still stands ready for his cold morning showers. (Open Apr.-Oct. Wed.-Sun. 11am-5:30pm. Admission £2.30, children £1.15.)

Camden Town and Regent's Park

Waves of Irish, Cypriot and Portuguese immigrants brought a diversity to the Camden area that remains today. Trends are instigated and terminated at **Camden Lock market,** now London's fourth largest tourist attraction, which draws 200,000 funky visitors each weekend. Opened in 1974 with only four stall holders, the market now crams in 400 bohemian vendors. Still, Camden Town remains very much down-to-earth, as the dilapidated warehouses along Regent's Canal testify.

Just south of Camden Town lies the 500-acre **Regent's Park.** Larger than either Hyde Park or Kensington Gardens, and full of gardens, lakes, promenades, and Dakotan open spaces, the park has become a popular spot for family cricket matches and the scene of many tribulations of two-year-old future football champs. On summer evenings, American expatriates, enthusiastic British architects, and civil servants slug away at softball. On Sunday from June through August, you can hear tubas and trumpets entertain at the bandstand or see performances in the **Open Air Theatre** near Queen Mary's Gardens (see Entertainment). If you're feeling energetic or romantic, rent a boat on the park's lake (£5 an hour, open daily 10am-dusk).

The park's most popular attraction, the privately owned **London Zoo** (tel. 722 3333), commands a high admission price and large crowds, but can charm you nonetheless. Although low on funds, the zoo expects to remain open, possibly in a scaled-down form. The menagerie has an endless playlist of stars, including the ever-popular sweet-smelling elephants. Allow a good four hours to really do this place justice. The zoo's innovative design makes the animals feel right at home—the Mappin Terraces of 1913 (currently being rebuilt) offer a most natural habitat for bears and hogs. Children can ride camels, ponies, or llamas for 60p. The Snowdon Aviary, looking somewhat like an early-warning radar station, allows wonderfully close contact with its inhabitants. (Open March-Oct. Mon-Sat. 9am-6pm, Sun. 9am-7pm; Nov.-Feb. daily 10am-dusk. Admission £5.30, students £4.40, children £3.30, under 4 free.) Tube: Camden Town. Regent's Park, Great Portland St., and Baker St. stations are all on the south edge of the park—walk north through to the zoo (about 20 min.). Bus #74 brings you from Baker St. Station to the door.

Within the Inner Circle at the heart of the park, the delightful **Queen Mary's Gardens** erupt in color in early summer. The rose garden dazzles with 20,000 blooms. (Open until dusk.) North of Regent's Park stands **Primrose Hill,** long a favorite spot for picnics and kite-flying, and location of an epic scene from the once-popular British TV show *Minder.* On a clear day you can see as far as the Surrey Downs.

Marylebone

Located between Regent's Park and Oxford St., the grid-like district of Marylebone is dotted with decorous late-Georgian town houses. The name derives from "St. Mary-by-the-bourne," the "bourne" referring to the Tyburn or the Westbourne stream, both now underground. The eternally dammed Westbourne now forms the Serpentine in Hyde Park. Wimpole Street housed the reclusive poet Elizabeth Barrett until she eloped with Robert Browning. Britain's most eminent private physicians have Harley Street addresses. 19 York Street has been the home of John Milton, John Stuart Mill, and William Hazlitt (at different times, of course—they would have made an unfortunate rooming group). The area's most fondly remembered resident is undoubtedly Sherlock Holmes who, although fictitious, still receives about 50 letters per week addressed to his 221B Baker Street residence. The Abbey National Building Society currently occupies the site and employs a full-time secretary to answer requests for Holmes' assistance in solving mysteries around the world. One imagines the appeal for help from the American embassy in Beijing must have been tongue-in-cheek. The official line is that Holmes has retired from detective work and is keeping bees in the country. The **Sherlock Holmes Museum,** located at 239 Baker St. (marked "221b") is singularly steep at £5 (children £3) but Holmes enthusiasts will be thrilled by the meticulous re-creation of the detective's rooms. Upstairs is a passable display of "artifacts" from the stories, and a hilarious selection of letters Holmes has received in the last few years.

Ever since the redoubtable **Madame Tussaud,** one of Louis XVI's tutors, jetsetted from Paris in 1802 carrying wax effigies of French nobles decapitated in the Revolution, her eerie museum on Marylebone Rd. (tel. 935 6861; Tube: Baker St.) has been a London landmark. Nelson Mandela, Cher, Archbishop Desmond Tutu, Benny Hill, and Voltaire number among the luminaries re-created in life-size wax models. Most seem disconcertingly life-like, a few disappointingly uncharacteristic. The Chamber of Horrors downstairs shows grisly scenes of London from the time of Jack the Ripper and features the heads of Marie Antoinette and company; Adolf Hitler stands guard. You may enjoy a stroll among the famous personages, but be prepared to be accompanied by hordes of tourists and schoolchildren. Avoid the horrific queues by forming a minyan with at least nine fellow sufferers and using the group entrance. (Open June-Sept. daily 9am-5:30pm; Oct.-May 10am-5:30pm.

Admission £5.95, under 16 £3.95.) The distinctive green dome of the **Planetarium** (tel. 486 2242), next door, encloses a mini-universe. (Planetarium open June-Sept. daily 10:20am-5pm; Oct.-May 12:20-5pm. Shows every 40 min. Admission £3.60, under 16 £2.30. Joint admission to Madame Tussaud's and the Planetarium £7.75, under 16 £5.10.)

Bloomsbury

Today, very little of the famed intellectual gossip, literary argot, and modernist snobbery still emanates from 51 Gordon Square, where Virginia Woolf lived with her husband Leonard. Leonard always insisted that the brilliant novelist he married maintained a strong presence, stronger than her image "as a frail invalidated lady living in an ivory tower in Bloomsbury and worshipped by a little clique of aesthetes." The clique in question, the overrated Bloomsbury Group, included biographer Lytton Strachey, novelist E.M. Forster, economist John Maynard Keynes, art critic Roger Fry, painter Vanessa Bell (sister of Virginia Woolf) and, on the fringe, T.S. Eliot, the eminent British poet from St. Louis.

The **British Museum** makes an appropriate Bloomsbury centerpiece; forbidding on the outside but quirky and amazing within, the collection contains a near-complete account of Western civilization (see Museums below). Nearby, close to the former houses of Strachey and Keynes stands the **Percival-David Foundation of Chinese Art,** 53 Gordon Sq. (tel. 387 3909; Tube: Russell Sq. or Goodge St.), a connoisseur's hoard of fabulously rare ceramics presented in 1950 to the University of London. You may dally before pots depicting "a scholar standing on the head of a dragon fish," but do save time for the illuminating Ming Gallery on the top floor. Waft by the intricate fan given in 1930 by the last emperor of China to his English tutor, Sir Reginald Johnston. (Open Mon.-Fri. 10:30am-5pm. Free.)

To the south of the museum looms the massive, shrapnel-scarred Corinthian portico of Hawksmoor's 18th-century church, **St. George's Bloomsbury** in Bloomsbury Way. A contemporary statue of George I crowns the heavy steeple. Inside, novelist Anthony Trollope was baptized before the magnificent, gilded mahogany altar, where Dickens set his "Bloomsbury Christening" in *Sketches by Boz.* (Open sporadically: "We try to keep the church open all day, but we can't leave it unattended.") **St. Giles in the Fields,** a modest rectangular church surmounted by a beautiful Flitcroft tower (1731), rises above a 1687 Resurrection relief over a lush churchyard on St. Giles High St. John Wesley and his brother Charles preached from the pulpit here between 1743 and 1791. George Chapman, the celebrated translator of Homer and inspirer of Keats, lies buried beneath a heroic tomb attributed to Inigo Jones in the north aisle. The children of numerous London literati came here to be baptized-including Milton's daughter (and patient reader) Mary, Byron's daughter Allegra, and William and Clara Shelley, Percy and Mary's kids. (Open Mon.-Fri. 9am-4pm.)

Charles Dickens lived at 48 Doughty St. from 1837 to 1839, scribbling parts of *The Pickwick Papers, Nicholas Nickleby, Barnaby Rudge,* and *Oliver Twist.* Now a museum and library of Dickensia, the **Dickens House** (tel. 405 2127; Tube: Russell Sq. or Chancery Lane.) contains an array of prints, photographs, manuscripts, letters, and personal effects. The handsome drawing room has recently been restored to its original appearance. The rusty iron grill mounted on a basement wall was salvaged by the author from the Marshalsea Jail, a notorious debtor's prison where Dickens' father did time for three months in 1824, while his young son labored in a shoe-black factory. (Open Mon.-Sat. 10am-5pm. Admission £2, students £1.50, children £1, family £4.)

Further north, **St. Pancras Station** (Tube: King's Cross/St.Pancras) rises as a monument to Victorian prosperity over a neighborhood of present-day decay. This neo-gothic fantasy was completed in 1867, and is due to be refurbished along with the whole King's Cross/St. Pancras area. The station may become the Channel Tunnel rail terminal; planning continues ad nauseam. Next door, in stylistic contrast but in harmonious brick, the new British Library nears completion, amidst royal controversy over insufficient reading space.

Up St. Pancras Road, past the station's red brick effluvia, **St.Pancras Old Church** sits serenely in its large and leafy garden, where Mary Godwin first met Shelley in 1813. Parts of the church date from the 11th century.

Covent Garden

The beguilingly chic Covent Garden of today seems much different from the unruly marketplace where Fielding, Hogarth, Goldsmith, and even the Prince of Wales met with their cronies. Fruit and vegetable carts have left the **Central Market Building** for Nine Elms, south of the Thames. They have been replaced by fashionable, expensive restaurants and shops in a tourist-oriented but tasteful redevelopment. Crowds and street performers offer a modern version of the jostling convivality of the 18th century: watch for the rubbish-bin drummers and cobble-stone breakdancers.

The area's name recalls the ancient convent garden tended by the monks of Westminster Abbey. When he abolished the monasteries in 1536, Henry VIII bestowed this land upon John Russell, first Earl of Bedford. The Earl's descendants developed it into a fashionable *piazza* (designed by Inigo Jones) in the 17th century; the sixth earl had the Market Building built in 1830. Jones' **St. Paul's Church,** the "actor's church," is the only part of the original square to survive and testifies to the poor-little-rich-boy minimalism of the Bedford dynasty. Gouged by heavy taxes levied on his family by Charles I, the Duke of Bedford warned Jones to keep building costs down even if the church ended up looking like a barn. Following these instructions, Jones built what he called "the handsomest barn in England," his version of a Greek temple, free of classical ornamentation. Although a fire destroyed the original structure in 1795, the replacement was reconstructed faithfully, true to the character of Jones' work. The church can be entered through the heavy gates on Bedford St. Several famous artists lie entombed in the austere interior. Restoration playwright William Wycherly is buried here, along with Restoration sculptor Grinling Gibbons and Restoration painter Sir Peter Lely. Plaques throughout the church commemorate the achievements of Boris Karloff, Margaret Rutherford, Vivien Leigh, and Noel Coward. A silver casket set into the south wall holds the ashes of Ellen Terry. An inscription on the portico marks the first known performance of a Punch and Judy puppet show, recorded by Samuel Pepys in 1662. (Open Mon.-Fri. 9am-4pm.)

In the 18th century, Covent Garden began to fill the void left by the suppression of entertainments in Southwark. King George granted the first theatre charter in 1728, and for over a century the royal playhouses in Covent Garden and on adjacent Drury Lane held a virtual monopoly over theatre in London. The present buildings of the **Theatre Royal** and **Royal Opera House** both date from the 19th century. The present Theatre Royal replaced a 1674 Wren building, the site of attempted assassinations of Kings George II and III. As it burned in 1809, playwright Sheridan drank and watched, commenting, "Surely a man may take a glass of wine by his own fireside." (See Entertainment.)

The **London Transport Museum** and the **Theatre Museum** (see Museums) bloom in the old Flower Market building in the southeast corner of the *piazza.*

At the **Cabaret Mechanical Theatre,** 33-34 The Market, Covent Garden (enter via Punch and Judy's or the nearby stairways leading to the basement level; tel. 379 7961), you can watch miniature wooden machines perform amusing actions when you insert a coin—a whimsical way to rid yourself of all that heavy British change rattling around in your pockets. (Admission £1.75, students and children £1. Open Mon. noon-6:30pm, Tues.-Sat. 10am-6:30pm, Sun. 11am-6:30pm.)

Holborn and the Inns of Court

The historical center of English law lies in a small area straddling the precincts of Westminster and The City and surrounding long and litigious High Holborn,

Chancery Lane, and Fleet Street. The Strand and Fleet St. converge on the **Royal Courts of Justice** (tel. 936 6000), a formidable Gothic structure designed in 1874 by architect G.E. Street for the Supreme Court of Judicature. The cavernous central hall with fine mosaic floors outshines the tiny display of legal costume that makes financial law seem interesting by comparison. (Courts and galleries open to the public Mon.-Fri. 10:30am-4:30pm.)

Barristers in The City are affiliated with one of the famous **Inns of Court** (Lincoln's Inn, Middle Temple, Inner Temple, and Gray's Inn), four ancient legal institutions which provide lectures and apprenticeships for law students and regulate admission to the bar. The tiny gates and narrow alleyways that lead to the inns are invisible to most passersby. Inside, the Inns are organized like colleges at Oxford, each with its own gardens, chapel, library, dining hall, common rooms, and chambers. Most were founded in the 13th century when a royal decree barred the clergy from the courts of justice, giving rise to a new class of professional legal advocates. Today, students may seek their legal training outside of the Inns, but to be considered for membership they must "keep term" by dining regularly in one of the halls.

Named after Henri de Lacy (Earl of Lincoln), an advisor to Edward I and an early champion of legal studies, **Lincoln's Inn** (Tube: Holborn) was the only Inn to emerge unscathed from the Blitz. New Square and its cloistered churchyard (to the right as you enter from Lincoln's Inn Fields) appear today much as they did in the 1680s. The **Old Hall,** east of New Square, dates from 1492; here the Lord High Chancellor presided over the High Court of Chancery from 1733 to 1873. The most well-known chancery case is that of Jarndyce and Jarndyce, whose life-sapping machinations are played out in the pages of *Bleak House.* Dickens knew well the world he described, having worked as a lawyer's clerk in New Court just across the yard. To the west, **New Hall,** an impressive, Tudor-style building, houses a fine 19th-century mural by G.F. Watts and a lugubrious collection of legal portraits. Built in 1497, the adjacent library—London's oldest—holds over 70,000 volumes in its stacks. John Donne, William Pitt, Horace Walpole, and Benjamin Disraeli number among the many luminaries associated with Lincoln's Inn. (See the porter at 11A Lincoln's Inn Fields for admission to the halls. Whimsical opening policies.) On the north side of Lincoln's Inn Fields smugly sits **Sir John Soane's Museum;** it's the house bedecked with sculpture amidst a row of plain buildings (see Museums).

Gray's Inn (Tube: Chancery Lane), dubbed "that stronghold of melancholy" by Dickens, stands at the northern end of Fulwood Pl., off High Holborn. Reduced to ashes by German bombers in 1941, Gray's Inn was restored to much of its former splendor during the 1950s. The Hall, to your right as you pass through the archway, retains its original stained glass (1580) and most of its ornate screen. The first performance of Shakespeare's *Comedy of Errors* took place here in 1594. Francis Bacon maintained chambers here from 1577 until his death in 1626. Bacon supposedly designed the magnificent gardens, the most extensive of any Inn north of Field Court.

Of the nine Inns of Chancery, only **Staple Inn's** building survives (located where Gray's Inn Road meets Holborn) (Tube: Chancery Lane). The half-timbered Elizabethan front dates from 1586. Devoted son Samuel Johnson wrote "Rasselas" here in one week to pay for a funeral for his mother.

But none of these Inns can compare with the **Temple** (Tube: Yes, Temple). South of Fleet St., it houses both the Middle and Inner Temples, the other two Inns of Court. Its name derives from the crusading order of Knights Templar who embraced this site as their English seat during the 12th century. The bellicose order dissolved in 1312, and this property, then forfeited to the crown, was eventually passed on to the Knights Hospitallers of St. John, who leased it to a community of common law scholars in 1338. Virtually leveled by enemy action in the early 1940s, only the church, crypt, and buttery of the Inner Temple survive intact from the Middle Ages.

Held in common by both the Middle and Inner Temples, the **Temple Church,** also known as the Church of St. Mary the Virgin, should appear near the top of every list of sights in London. The finest of the few round churches left in England, it contains a handsome 12th-century Norman doorway, an altar screen by Wren (1682), and nine arresting, armor-clad effigies of Knights Templar dating from the 12th and 13th centuries. Author Oliver Goldsmith, whose late-night revelry at the Temple often irritated his staid neighbor, Blackstone, lies buried in the yard behind the choir. (Open Oct.-July Mon.-Sat. 10am-4pm, Sun. 2-4pm.) According to Shakespeare (*Henry VI*), the red and white roses that served as emblems throughout the War of the Roses were plucked from the Middle Temple Garden. On Ground Hog day in 1601, Shakespeare himself supposedly appeared in a performance of *Twelfth Night* in **Middle Temple Hall,** a grand Elizabethan dining room now open to the public whenever it's not serving as a student refectory. (Usually open Mon.-Fri. 10am-noon.) **Fountain Court,** just north of Middle Temple Hall, was the setting of Ruth Pinch's incestuous liaison with her brother Tom in Dickens' novel, *Martin Chuzzlewit.* Nearby, a handful of London's last functioning gaslamps line Middle Temple Lane.

North of the Temple and east of Lincoln's Inn stands the

The Strand and Fleet Street

Hugging the ancient embankment of the River Thames, **The Strand** (Tube: Charing Cross, Temple, or Aldwych—rush hours only) has not fared well through London's growth. Once lined with fine Tudor houses, this major thoroughfare now pierces a jumbled assortment of lame commercial buildings and suffers from incessant traffic jams. **Somerset House,** a magnificent Palladian structure built by Sir William Chambers in 1776, stands on the site of the 16th-century palace where Elizabeth I resided during the brief reign of her sister Mary. Formerly the administrative center of the Royal Navy, the building now houses the exquisite **Courtauld Collection** (see Museums) and the less exquisite offices of the Inland Revenue.

Farther east, the impeccable **St. Mary le Strand,** with its slender steeple and elegant Ionic portico, rises above an island of decaying steps in the middle of the modern roadway. Designed by James Gibbs and consecrated in 1724, the church overlooks the site of the original Maypole, where London's first hackney cabs assembled in 1634. Inside, the baroque complexities of the barrel vault and ornamental altar walls reflect Gibb's architectural training in Rome. The intricate floral moldings were crafted by two brothers, John and Chrysostom Wilkins, who received a mere 45p for each elaborate bloom. Isaac Newton was an early parishioner, and Dickens' parents got married here in 1809. (Open Mon.-Fri. 11am-3:30pm.) Across the north side of The Strand, cultured newsreaders pompously intone "This is London" every hour from Bush House, the nerve center of the worldwide radio services of the BBC.

To the east stands **St. Clement Danes** whose melodious bells get their 15 seconds of fame in the nursery rhyme "Oranges and lemons, say the bells of St. Clement's." Designed by Wren in 1682, the church was built over the ruins of an older Norman structure reputed to be the tomb of Harold Harefoot, leader of a colony of Danes who settled the area in the 9th century. In 1720, Gibb replaced Wren's original truncated tower with a slimmer spire. Although German firebombs gutted the church in 1941, the white stucco and gilt interior has been restored to its former splendor by the Royal Air Force (RAF), which adopted St. Clement's as its official church after World War II. RAF commemorations strafe the reconstructed church. Note the marble floors inlaid with brass squadron medallions. A quiet crypt-*cum*-prayer-chapel houses an eerie collection of 17th-century funereal monuments. Samuel Johnson worshipped here, and a paunchy bronze statue of the great Doctor (sculpted in 1910 by Fitzgerald) stands outside the east apse of the church. (Open daily 8am-5pm.) The nearby Gothic giant houses the Royal Courts of Justice (see Holborn and Inns of Court section above). **Twining's Teas** (tel. 353 3511) brews at 216 The Strand. It is both the oldest business in Britain still operating on original premises and the narrowest shop in London. The building dates from 1787. Just east stands the only Strand building to survive the Great Fire: the **Wig and Pen Club,** 229-230 The Strand, constructed over Roman ruins in 1625. Frequented by the best-known barristers and journalists in London, the Wig and Pen is, in the sage words of the *Baltimore Sun,* "a window through which you can see Fleet Street in all its aspects." The club is open to members only, though a passport-toting overseas traveler can apply for free and immediate temporary membership. Walk up the ancient, crooked staircase—the only remnant of the original 17th-century house. Backpackers beware: the doorman will haughtily reject denim-bedecked budget travelers. The **Temple Bar Monument** stands in the middle of the street where the Strand meets Fleet Street, marking the boundary between Westminster and the City. The Sovereign must still obtain ceremonial permission from the Lord Mayor to pass the bar and enter the City here.

Fleet Street, named for the one-time river (now a sewer) that flows from Hampstead to the Thames near Blackfriar's Bridge, was until recently the hub of British journalism. Before the late 1980s, all of London's major papers had their offices on the "Street of Shame," lampooned by Evelyn Waugh through the *Daily Beast* in his 1938 novel *Scoop.* All have left, led by the *Times,* which moved to cheaper land at Tobacco Dock, Docklands, in 1986. The *Daily Telegraph* vacated its startling Greek and Egyptian revival building, moving to Marsh Wall in 1987. The *Daily Express,* once the occupant of an art deco monster of chrome and black glass on Fleet Street, now headlines in Blackfriars.

Both Johnson and Bolt Courts lead north to Gough Square, and **Samuel Johnson's House** at No. 17 (tel. 353 3745). Remarkably enough, this is where Dr. Johnson lived, from 1749 to 1758. Follow the signs carefully; Carlyle got lost on his way here in 1832. Here Johnson completed his *Dictionary,* the first definitive English lexicon, even though rumor insists that he omitted "sausage." (His closest predecessor, Nathaniel Bailey, defined the heart as "a most noble part of the body" in 1717.) Johnson scholars will not find many original documents here but may be touched by the sparseness of the decor, a reminder of the poverty in which Johnson lived. Tours are self-guided, but the curator, a knowledgeable and charming woman, will supplement your visit with anecdotes about the Great Cham and his hyperbolic biographer, James Boswell. (Open May-Sept. Mon.-Sat. 11am-5:30pm; Oct.-April Mon.-Sat. 11am-5pm. Admission £2, students, children, and senior citizens £1.50.)

The spire of Wren's **St. Bride's** (1675), south of Fleet St. near Ludgate Circus, became the inspiration for countless English wedding cakes, via a copy-cat local baker. Excavations of the ancient crypt beneath the church (called the "printer's church"), have revealed traces of a late Saxon cemetery, the foundation of a 6th-century Roman structure, and the ruins of several earlier churches. A gentle, intriguing museum, housing a musty collection of relics and rocks, has been improvised in the lower chambers, alongside an exhibit detailing the evolution of printing in Fleet Street and an interesting array of manuscripts and literary memorabilia. (Open daily 8:15am-4:45pm.)

To the south, the **Embankment** runs along the Thames, parallel to The Strand. Between the Hungerford and Waterloo Bridges stands London's oldest landmark, **Cleopatra's Needle,** an Egyptian obelisk from 1450 BC presented by the Viceroy of Egypt in 1878. A sister stone stands in Central Park in New York.

The City of London

Once enclosed by Roman walls, the one-square-mile City of London is the financial center of Europe. Each weekday 350,000 people surge in at 9am and out again unfailingly at 5pm, leaving behind a resident population of only 6000. At the center of the City, the massive Bank of England controls the nation's finances, and the Stock Exchange makes the nation's fortune. At the heart of the area is Cheapside; "cheap" derives from the Old English for "purchase," and many street names here pay homage to commerce: Bread Street, Milk Street, Poultry Street, and Threadneedle Street. Proliferating cranes, office building sites, and rising share indices bear witness to the British economic resurgence of the late 80s.

The City owes much of its graceful appearance to Sir Christopher Wren, who was the chief architect working in the City after the fire of 1666 almost completely razed it. In his *Diary,* Samuel Pepys gives a most moving first-hand account of the fire that started in a baker's shop in Pudding Lane and leapt between the o'erhanging houses to sweep the City with destruction. Afterwards, Charles II issued a proclamation that City buildings should be rebuilt in brick and stone, rather than highly flammable wood and thatch. Wren's studio designed 51 churches to replace the 89 destroyed in the fire, and the surviving 24 churches are some of the only buildings in the City from the period immediately following the Great Fire. A host of variations on a theme, they gave Wren a valuable chance to work out, in stone rather than on paper, problems of design that came up as he rebuilt St. Paul's. Inside his churches, light plaster, dark carved oak, and an abundance of gilt create an airy elegance. The original effect of a forest of steeples surrounding the great dome of St. Paul's must be reckoned his greatest contribution to London's cityscape; unfortunately, the modern skyscrapers so energetically condemned by Prince Charles now obscure the effect.

Many of the churches have irregular or random opening times. The **City of London Information Center,** St. Paul's Churchyard (tel. 606 3030); Tube: St. Paul's) can give you up-to-date details on all of the City's attractions, and sells John Betjeman's guide, *City of London Churches,* for £1.75. (Open May-Oct. daily 9:30am-5pm; Nov.-April Mon.-Fri. 9:30am-5pm, Sat. 9:30am-12:30pm.)

The buildings of the Livery Companies represent perhaps the most important secular structures of the City. Originally organizations with a broad range of social and political obligations, the guilds also played a role in fixing trade standards; now many contribute to charity and education. Wealthier guilds such as the Haberdashers and the Merchant Taylors maintain schools. The twelve "great companies" are the Mercers (textile dealers, chartered in 1393), Grocers (1345), Drapers (1364), Fishmongers (1364), Goldsmiths (1327), Skinners (1327), Merchant Taylors (1326), Haberdashers (1448), Salters (1558), Ironmongers (1454), Vintners (1436), and Clothworkers (1528). The phrase "at sixes and sevens" arose from an argument between the Skinners and the Merchant Taylors as to who should march in sixth place in City processions. The 84 **livery halls,** many distinguished, are scattered around the square mile. Most halls do not open to the public; those that do require tickets. The City of London Information office (see above) receives a batch of tickets in March, but they disappear rapidly. Inquire there for the current opening situation. Some halls sponsor spring celebrations, and a few hold fascinating exhibits—for example, of the finest products of London's goldsmiths.

Until the 18th century, the City of London *was* London; all the other boroughs and neighborhoods now swallowed up by "London"—even Westminster—were neighboring towns or outlying villages. Enclosed by Roman and medieval walls, the City had six gates, whose names survive: Aldersgate, Aldgate. Bishopsgate, Cripplegate, Newgate, and Ludgate. The **London Wall Walk** runs along the course of the old wall from the Museum of London to the Tower, passing a few exposed remains. Start just outside the Tower Hill tube station and follow the signs and historical panels. Today's City hums with activity during the work week, is dead on Saturdays, and ghostly on Sundays. To catch the flavor of the City, visit on a weekday. Everyone you see will either be in a suit and working in a bank, or in a hard hat and building a bank. Endless blocks of mediocre modern architecture are lent life by these nine-to-five crowds; the city turns eerie when the workers go home. However, the area's museums and some of the Wren churches remain open Sundays, and you can contemplate the good and the evil of City architecture without being crushed by umbrellas and briefcases.

From Bank to Ludgate—the Western Section

The few remaining stones of the Roman **Temple of Mithras,** Queen Victoria St., dwell incongruously in the shadows of banal modern structures. Discovered during construction work and shifted a few yards from its original location, the temple still retains a recognizable outline. Down the road, **St. Mary Aldermary** (so called because it is older than any other St. Mary's church in the City), towers over its surroundings. (Open Tues.-Fri. 11am-3pm.) A rare Gothic Wren, it is especially notable for its delicate fan-vaulting. The bells that recalled Dick Whittington to London rang out from the church of St. Marie de Arcubus, replaced by Wren's **St. Mary-le-Bow,** Cheapside, in 1683. The range of the Bow bells' toll is supposed to define the extent of true-blue Cockney London. Being a Bow bell has never been easy—the first lot were annihilated by the Great Fire, the second destroyed by the Blitz. (Open Mon.-Fri. 8:15am-5:45pm.) Up Aldermanbury huddles the **Guildhall,** a cavernous space where dignitaries were once tried for treason. The building now accommodates the town clerk, a library, offices, and the clock museum (see Museums). The Great Hall houses excessive monuments to Nelson, Wellington, Pitt, and others. (Open Mon.-Sat. 10am-5pm; May-Sept. daily 10am-5pm.) The **Public Library,** founded in 1420, opens to the public on weekdays from 9:30am to 5pm.

St. Paul's dominates the cathedral scene in the western end of the City (see St. Paul's below), but Wren groupies should check out three fine churches in the environs. **St. James Garlickhythe** gets its name from the garlic sold nearby. Its modest but pleasing Hawksmoor steeple is dwarfed by the huge Vintners Place development across the street. West on Upper Thames St. stands a rare red brick Wren church, **St. Benet's,** with an elegant cupola. The burial place of Inigo Jones and site of one of Henry Fielding's marriages, **Benet's** survived an arson attempt in 1971.

Just to the north the **College of Arms** rests on its heraldic authority behind ornate gates. The College regulates the granting and recognition of coats of arms, and is directed by the Earl Marshal, the Duke of Norfolk. The officer-in-waiting at the Earl Marshal's stately paneled Court Room can address your claim to the throne. (Open Mon.-Fri. 10am-4pm.)

St. Andrew-by-the-Wardrobe was originally built next to Edward III's impressive closet. Now the church cowers beneath the Faraday building, the first building allowed to exceed the City's strict height limit.

Queen Victoria's Street meets New Bridge Street in the area known as Blackfriars, in reference to the darkly-clad Dominican brothers who built a medieval monastery here. Shakespeare acted in James Burbage's theatre here in the late 1500s. Ludgate Circus, to the north, is now the noisy site of a major redevelopment. A peaceful haven is offered by **St. Martin-within-Ludgate,** a Wren church untouched by the Blitz. The square interior boasts some fine Grinling Gibbons woodwork, and the slim spire still pierces the dome of St. Paul's when seen from Ludgate Circus, just as Wren intended. (Open Mon.-Fri. 10am-4pm.) Around the corner, the **Old Bailey** (tel. 248 3277), technically the Central Criminal Courts, crouches under a copper dome and a wide-eyed figure of justice on the corner of Old Bailey and Newgate St.—infamous as the site of Britain's grimmest prison. Trial-watching persists as a favorite occupation, and the Old Bailey fills up whenever a gruesome or scandalous case is in progress. You can enter the public Visitors' Gallery and watch bewigged barristers at work (Mon.-Fri. 10am-1pm and 2-4pm); it can be a touch depressing. When court is not in session (from the last week in July to Sept. 15), the building opens from 11am to 3pm. The Chief Post Office building, off Newgate to the north, envelops the stunning, nay mind-blowing, **National Postal Museum** (see Museums).

The Barbican and the Northern Section.

The **Barbican Centre,** covering 60 acres and opened in 1982, stands as one of the most impressive and controversial post-Blitz rebuilding projects. Widely considered a symbol of the brutalism of the postwar landscape, the Barbican is also universally acknowledged as a vital cultural centre. A city unto itself, the complex of apartments and offices houses the **Royal Shakespeare Company,** the **London Symphony Orchestra,** and the **Museum of London** (see Museums). (For information on the Festival of the City of London, see Music below.)

St. Bartholomew The Great, off Smithfield, one of London's oldest churches, is reached through a delightfully narrow Tudor house. Parts of the church date from 1123, although 800 years of alteration have much embellished it. (Open Mon.-Thurs. 8am-4:30pm, Fri. 10:45am-4:30pm, Sun. 8am-8pm.) For an early pint, try one of the pubs around **Smithfield,** a meat and poultry wholesale market. (Market open daily 5am-noon; some surrounding pubs open 6:30am.) Smithfield's associations with butchery go back further than the meat market. Scotsman William Wallace and rebel Wat Tyler rank among those executed here in the Middle Ages. Smithfield was a favorite site for burning Protestants under Queen Mary I.

Just north of the square, now in Islington, stands **St. John's Gate,** St. John's St. On the ground floor, a museum commemorates the volunteer St. John Ambulance Brigade, the savior of thousands of people who have fainted at Rolling Stones concerts, among others. (Open Mon.-Fri. 10am-4:30pm, Sat. 10am-4pm.) The **Clerkenwell Centre** (tel. 250 1039), at St. John's St. and Clerkenwell Rd., can give you further information about this area. (Open Mon.-Fri. 10am-6pm.)

From Bank to the Tower—the Eastern Section

The massive windowless walls and foreboding doors of the Bank of England enclose four full acres. The present building dates from 1925, but the eight-foot thick outer wall is the same one built by eccentric architect Sir John Soame in 1788. The only part open to the public is the plush **Bank of England Museum** (see Museums). The **Stock Exchange** next door is no more welcoming. Struck by an IRA bomb in 1990, the Visitors' Gallery is no longer open. **St. Margaret Lothbury** (down Throgmorton St.), Wren's last church apart from St. Paul's, contains a sumptuous carved wood screen (1689). Most of the church's furnishings come from other City churches which have been demolished. A couple of blocks north, the **National Westminster Tower** hovers at over 600 ft. The City is getting a run for its money from the Docklands, and in the latest encroachment the Canary Wharf tower surpassed NatWest's as Britain's tallest. Back through the land of threading needles and throgging mortons, behind the imposing, tautological Mansion House, home of the Lord Mayor, stands **St. Stephen Walbrook.** Arguably Wren's finest, and allegedly his personal favorite, the church combines four major styles: the old-fashioned English church characterized by nave and chancel; the Puritan hall church, which lacks any separation between priest and congregation; the Greek-cross-plan church; and the domed church, a study for St. Paul's. The Samaritans, a social service group that advises the suicidal and severely depressed, was founded here in 1953. The mysterious cheese-like object in the center is actually the altar, sculpted by Henry Moore, and is as controversial as you think. Unfortunately, St. Stephen's is completely surrounded by six-story buildings. (Open Mon.-Fri. 9am-4pm.) The church of **St. Mary Woolnoth,** at King William and Lombard St., may look odd without a spire, but the interior proportions and the black and gilt reredos confirm the talents of Wren's pupil Nicholas Hawksmoor. The only City church untouched by the Blitz, it "kept the hours" in Eliot's *The Waste Land.* **Mary Abchurch,** off Abchurch Lane, provides a neat domed comparison to St. Stephen's, its mellow, dark wood and baroque paintings contrasting with St. Stephen's bright airy interior. (Opening times vary. Usually open Thurs. 10am-4pm.)

Before even the most basic rebuilding of the city, Wren designed a tall Doric pillar, completed in 1671 and named simply the **Monument,** at the bottom of King William St. Supposedly, the 202-ft. pillar stands exactly that many feet from where the Great Fire broke out in Pudding Lane on September 2, 1666 and "rushed devastating through every quarter with astonishing swiftness and worse." High on Fish Street Hill, the column offers an expansive view of London. Bring stern resolution and £1 to climb its 311 steps. (Tube: Monument. Open April-Sept. Mon.-Fri. 9am-6pm, Sat.-Sun. 2-6pm; Oct.-March Mon.-Sat. 9am-4pm.)

The current **London Bridge** succeeds a slew of ancestors. The famed version crowded with houses stood from 1176 until it burned in 1758. The most recent predecessor didn't fall down as the nursery rhyme prophesied; worse, it was sold to an American millionaire for £1.03 million and shipped, block by block, to Lake Havasu City, Arizona. **St. Magnus Martyr,** on Lower Thames St., stands next to the path to the somewhat older 12th-century London Bridge, and proudly displays a chunk of wood from a Roman jetty. According to T.S. Eliot, the walls of the church "hold inexplicable splendor of Ionian white and gold," a soothing contrast to the forlorn Billingsgate fish market next door. The deserted trading floors there pine for the bustle and carp transported to the new Billingsgate in Docklands. (St. Magnus Martyr open Tues.-Fri. 9am-4pm, Sat.-Sun. 9:30am-1pm.)

Pepys witnessed the movement of the Great Fire from the tower of **All Hallows by the Tower.** Just inside the south entrance is an arch from the 7th-century Saxon church, discovered in 1960. To the left, the baptistery contains a striking wood font cover by Grinling Gibbons. William Penn was baptized, and John Quincy Adams married, in All Hallows. Another victim of the bombing, **St. Olave's** in Hart St., underwent restoration after the war. It was one of the few City churches to survive the fire of 1666. An annual memorial service is held for Pepys, who is buried here with his wife. (Open Mon.-Fri. 8am-3:30pm.) Don't be frightened by the name of Seething Gardens across the street; the lush spot is perfect for a take-away lunch.

The 1986 **Lloyd's** building and **Leadenhall Market,** off Leadenhall St., supply the most startling architectural clash in the City. The ducts, lifts, and chutes of Lloyd's would not look out of place on the *Brazil* set; one almost expects racing air-conditioning repairmen rather than stockbrokers to emerge from its doors. The futuristic setting houses the **Lutine Bell,** which is still occasionally rung—once for bad insurance news, twice for good. (Viewing gallery open Mon.-Fri. 10am-12:30pm.) Across a narrow alley, one looks for Jack the Ripper to emerge from the ornate cream and maroon of Victorian Leadenhall Market. A market has stood here since the middle ages.

St. Paul's Cathedral

Sir Christopher Wren's domed masterpiece dominates its surroundings even as modern usurpers sneak up around it. The third cathedral to stand on the site, St. Paul's has become a grand and moving monument, at once a physical and spiritual symbol of London. The first cathedral was founded in 604; fire destroyed it in 1089. The second and most massive cathedral was a medieval structure, one of the largest in Europe, topped by a spire ascending 489 feet. Falling into almost complete neglect in the 16th century, the cathedral became more of a marketplace than a church, and plans for its reconstruction were in the works well before the Great Fire. Wren had already started drawing up his grand scheme in 1666 when the conflagration demolished the cathedral, along with most of London, and gave him the great opportunity to build from scratch. Like his Renaissance predecessors, Wren preferred the equal-armed Greek cross plan, while ecclesiastical authorities insisted upon a traditional medieval design with a long nave and choir for services. Wren's final design compromised by translating a Gothic cathedral into baroque and classical terms: a Latin Cross floor plan with baroque detailing. The huge classical dome, second in size only to St. Peter's in Rome, towers at 365 feet.

Both the design and the building of the cathedral were dogged by controversy. Wren's second model received the king's warrant of approval (and is thus known as the "Warrant Model") but still differed from today's St. Paul's. The shrewd architect won permission to make necessary alterations as building proceeded and, behind the scaffolding, Wren had his way with it.

In December 1940, London burned once again. On the night of the 29th, at the height of the Blitz, St. Paul's stood in a sea of fire. This time it survived. Fifty-one firebombs landed on the cathedral, all swiftly put out by the heroic volunteer St. Paul's Fire Watch. Two of the four high-explosive bombs that landed did explode, wrecking the north transept; the clear glass there bears silent testimony. A small monument in the floor at the end of the Nave honors the Firewatch. St. Paul's is a majestic and durable place, saturated with tough British pride and crowded with monuments of imposing generals affectedly dressed as Roman senators. The cathedral held the wedding of Prince Charles and Lady Diana, who chose St. Paul's for its spaciousness and excellent acoustics, breaking the 200-year tradition of holding royal weddings in Westminster Abbey.

The stalls in the **Choir,** carved by Grinling Gibbons, narrowly escaped a bomb, but the old altar did not. It was replaced with the current marble "High Altar," covered by a St. Peter's-like *baldacchino* of oak, splendidly gilded. Above looms the crowning glory, the ceiling mosaic of Christ Seated in Majesty.

The **ambulatory** contains a shrouded statue of poet John Donne (Dean of the cathedral from 1621-1631), one of the few monuments to survive from old St. Paul's. Amble through the ambulatory to see Henry Moore's *Mother and Child* and the American Memorial Chapel (formerly Jesus Chapel), restored after the Blitz, and dedicated to U.S. servicemen based in Britain who died during World War II. Note the graceful and intricate choir gates, executed by Jean Tijou early in the 18th century.

The **Crypt,** stuffed with tombs and monuments, forms a catalogue of Britain's great figures from the last couple of centuries. (A few remnants made it through the Great Fire, including a memorial to Francis Bacon's father Nicolas.) The massive tombs of Wellington and Nelson command attention; Nelson's coffin, placed directly beneath the dome, was originally intended for Cardinal Wolsey. A bust of George Washington stands opposite a memorial to the ultimate romantic hero, Lawrence of Arabia. Around the corner lounges Rodin's fine bust of Henley. **Painter's Corner** holds the tombs of Sir Joshua Reynolds, absurd romantic Sir Lawrence Alma-Tadema, and J.M.W. Turner, along with memorials to John Constable and William Blake. Nearby, a black slab in the floor marks Wren's grave, with his son's famous epitaph close by: *Lector, si monumentum requiris circumspice.* This instruction to seek Wren's memorial in the glory of his creation was bombed through to the Crypt from the north transept. The display of **models** of St. Paul's details the history of the cathedral in all of its incarnations. Creating the star exhibit, the great model of 1674, cost as much as constructing a small house. In these models you can see how the upper parts of the exterior walls are mere façades, concealing the flying butresses which support the nave roof. Audio-visual presentations are shown every ½ hr. from 10:30am to 3pm.

Going up St. Paul's proves more challenging than going down: 259 steps lead to the suicidal, vertiginous **Whispering Gallery,** on the inside base of the dome. Words whispered against the wall whizz round the sides. Take in the overwhelming prospects up into the dome and down into the church. A further 118 steps up, the first external view glitters from the **Stone Gallery,** only to be eclipsed by the uninterrupted and incomparable panorama from the **Golden Gallery,** 153 steps higher at the top of the dome. Wren's church spires fight with building cranes for supremacy over the City; the monolithic Bankside power station dominates the South Bank; and the Gothic extravaganza of St. Pancras station struts to the north, laced with the greenery of Hampstead Heath. Before descending, take a peek down into the cathedral through the small glass peephole in the floor; Nelson lies over 400 feet directly below. (Open Mon.-Sat. 9am-4:15pm; ambulatory open Mon.-Sat. 9:30am-4:15pm; crypt open Mon.-Fri. 9:30am-4:15pm, Sat. 11am-4:15pm; galleries open Mon.-Sat. 9:45am-4:15pm. Admission to cathedral, ambulatory, and crypt £2, students £1.50, children and seniors £1; galleries £2, students £1.50, children and seniors £1. Comprehensive 1½-hr. guided tours include the crypt and some sections not open to the public: Mon.-Sat. at 11am, 11:30am, 2pm, and 2:30pm; £4, students, children, and seniors £2.)

St. Paul's Churchyard, a fine picnic spot popular since Shakespeare's day, is surrounded by railings of oft-unappreciated interest; they were one of the first uses of cast iron. The modern St. Paul's Cross marks the spot where the papal pronouncement condemning Martin Luther was read to the public.

The Tower of London

The Tower of London, the largest fortress in medieval Europe and the palace and prison of English monarchs for over 500 years, is soaked in blood and history. Its intriguing past and striking buildings attract over two million visitors per year. To cope with these sneaker-clad hordes, highly entertaining, informative (and free!) 45-minute tours are led by Beefeaters, departing every half hour from the Byward tower; miss the tour and you'll miss *really* seeing the tower.

The oldest continuously occupied fortified building in Europe, "The Tower" was founded by William the Conqueror in 1066 in order to protect—and command—his subjects. Not one, but 20 towers stand behind its walls, though many associate the image of the **White Tower,** the oldest one, with the Tower of London. Completed in 1097, the White Tower overpowers all the fortifications that were built around it in the following centuries. Originally a royal residence-*cum*-fortress, it was last lived in by James I, and subsequently served as wardrobe, stonehouse, public records office, armory, and prison.

Although more famous for the prisoners who languished and died here, the Tower has seen a handful of spectacular escapes. The Bishop of Durham escaped from Henry I out a window and down a rope. But the unfortunate Welsh Prince Gruffyd ap Llewelyn, prisoner of Henry III in 1244, apparently had not learned his knots properly—his rope of knotted sheets broke and he fell to his death. The prisoners may be gone (except for a few hapless tourists locked in after hours), but the weapons and armor remain. An expansive display from the **Royal Armouries,** testifying to Henry VIII's fondness for well-melded metal suits, takes up three floors. Both brutal and ornate, the collection mirrors its surroundings. Notice the early examples of firework launchers. To find a serious glut of arms and weaponry, also visit the **Oriental Armoury** in the Waterloo barracks, north of the White Tower, or the **New Armouries** to the east. The former features a full suit of elephant armor, captured by Clive at the Battle of Plassey in 1757. On the first floor of the White Tower nests the **Chapel of St. John,** dating from 1080, the finest Norman chapel in London. Stark and pristine, it is the only chapel in the world with an "aisled nave and encircling ambulatory", whatever that means. Beneath this chapel Guy Fawkes of the Gunpowder Plot was tortured.

The towers connect by massive walls and gateways, forming fortifications disheartening to visitors even today. Richard I, the Lionheart, began the construction of defenses around the White Tower in 1189. Subsequent work by Henry III (1216-72) and Edward I (1272-1307) brought the Tower close to its present condition.

Two rings of defenses surround the White Tower. On the **Inner Ward,** the **Bell Tower** squats on the southwest corner. Since the 1190s, this tower has sounded the curfew bell each night. Sir Thomas More spent some time here, courtesy of his former friend Henry VIII, before that same former friend had him executed in the Tower Green.

Along the curtain wall hovers the **Bloody Tower,** arguably the most famous, and certainly the most infamous, part of the fortress. Once pleasantly named the Garden Tower, due to the officers' garden nearby, the Bloody Tower supposedly saw the murder of the Little Princes, the uncrowned King Edward V and his brother (aged 13 and 10), by agents of Richard III. The murder remains one of history's great mysteries; some believe that Richard was innocent and that the future Henry VII arranged the murders to ease his own ascent. Two children's remains found in the grounds in 1674 (and buried now in Westminster Abbey) have never been conclusively identified as those of the Princes. Sir Walter Raleigh did some time in the prison here off and on for 15 years and occupied himself by writing a voluminous *History of the World Part I.* Before he got around to writing Part II, James I had him beheaded. Henry III lived in the adjacent **Wakefield Tower,** largest after the White Tower. The crown kept its public records and its jewels here until 1856 and 1967 respectively, although unsuprisingly, the Wakefield Tower also has a gruesome past. Lancastrian Henry VI was imprisoned by Yorkist Edward IV during the Wars of the Roses and was murdered while praying here. Students from Eton and Cambridge's King's College, founded by Henry, annually place lilies on the spot of the murder. Counter-clockwise around the inner **Wall Walk** come the **Lanthorn, Salt, Broad Arrow, Constable, and Martin** towers, the last scene of the inimitable self-styled "Colonel" Thomas Blood's bold attempt in 1671 at stealing the Crown Jewels. Martin's lower level now houses a small, boring exhibit of **Instruments of Torture.** The inner ring comes full circle, completed by the **Brick, Bowyer** (where, according to Shakespeare's constantly accurate *Richard III,* the Duke of Clarence died after being drowned in Malmsey wine), **Flint, Devereux,** and **Beauchamp** towers.

Within the inner ring adjoining the Bell Tower lurks the Tudor **Queen's House** (which will become the King's House when Prince Charles ascends to the throne). The house has served time as a prison for some of the Tower's most illustrious guests: both Anne Boleyn and Catherine Howard were incarcerated here by charming hubby Henry VIII; Guy Fawkes was interrogated in the Council Chamber on the upper floor; and in 1941, Hitler's Deputy Führer Rudolf Hess (or, as some believe, an imposter) was brought here after parachuting into Scotland. The only prisoners remaining today are the clipped ravens hopping around on the grass outside the White Tower; tradition has it that without the ravens the Tower would crumble and the British Empire disintegrate. Charles II hoped to banish the pests, but superstitions are superstitions and under pressure from advisers he granted them Royal protection. Unfortunately ravens mate only in flight, so new recruits have to be imported each time an old stager dies (a separate item in the national budget wisely provides for their upkeep and replacement). The ravens even have a tomb and gravestone of their own in the grassy moat near the ticket office.

Prisoners of the highest rank sometimes received the honor of a private execution rather than one before the spectators' benches of Tower Hill, just east of the present tube station. A block on the Tower Green, inside the Inner Ward, marks the spot where the axe fell on Queen Catherine Howard, Lady Jane Grey, and the Earl of Essex, Queen Elizabeth's rejected suitor. Fearing long wooden handles, Anne Boleyn chose to die by French sword instead. Sir Thomas More, "the king's good servant but God's first," was beheaded in public. The nearby **Chapel of St. Peter ad Vincula** (St. Peter in Chains) was once called "the saddest place on earth" by Lord Macaulay; the remains of prisoners were transported here after their executions. The decapitated bodies of Henry VIII's two executed queens lie beneath the altar and in the crypt. (Entrance to the chapel by Yeoman tour only. See below.)

Visitors enter the Tower through the **Byward Tower** on the southwest of the **Outer Ward,** which sports a precariously hung portcullis. The password, required for entry here after hours, has been changed every day since 1327, so bring your dictionary. German spies were executed in the Outer Ward during World War II. Along the outer wall, **St. Thomas's Tower** (after Thomas à Becket) tops the evocative **Traitors' Gate,** through which boats once brought new captives. The low gateway still has a dispiriting atmosphere.

The whole castle used to be surrounded by a broad **moat** dug by Edward I. Cholera epidemics forced the Duke of Wellington to drain it in 1843. The filled land became a vegetable garden during World War II but has since sprouted a tennis court and bowling green for inhabitants of the Tower.

The prize possessions of the Tower and of England, the **Crown Jewels,** pull in the crowds. Oliver Cromwell melted down much of the existing royal loot; most of the collection dates from after Charles II's Restoration in 1660. You may have seen thousands of pictures of the crowns and scepters before, but no camera can capture the dazzle. The **Imperial State Crown** and the **Sceptre with the Cross** feature the Stars of Africa, cut from the Cullinan Diamond. Scotland Yard mailed the precious stone third class from the Transvaal to London in an unmarked brown paper package, a scheme they believed was the safest way of getting it to England. **St. Edward's Crown,** made for Charles II in 1661, is only worn by the monarch during coronation.

The Tower is still guarded by the Yeoman Warders and the Yeomen of the Guard, *Beefeaters.* (The name does actually derive from "eaters of beef"—well-nourished domestic servants.) To be eligible to become a Beefeater, a candidate must have at least 22 years honorable service in the armed forces. Free, entertaining tours of about 45 minutes, given every half hour by Yeomen, start outside Byward Tower. (Tower of London open March-Oct. Mon.-Sat. 9:30am-5pm, Sun. 2-5pm; Nov.-Feb. Mon.-Sat. 9:30am-4pm. Admission £6, students £4.50, under 15 £3.70) Try to avoid the phenomenal Sunday crowd—queues start around noon. The best times to visit are Mondays and Tuesdays. Once inside, expect to queue for 20 to 30 minutes for entry to the Crown Jewels. For tickets to the **Ceremony of the Keys,** the nightly ritual locking of the gates, write in advance to Resident Governor, Tower of London, EC3 (Enquiries, tel. 709 0765).

Tower Bridge, a granite and steel structure reminiscent of a castle with a drawbridge, is a familiar sight. To walk across the upper level of the bridge costs a steep £2.50 (under 16 £1) but affords a spectacular view of the dirty Thames, the cluttered skyline, and the latest London Bridge. The roadway is occasionally raised (in less than 90 seconds) to allow taller ships to pass. (Open April-Oct. daily 10am-5:45pm; Nov.-March 10am-4pm.)

Southwark

Across London Bridge from the City lies Southwark, a distinctive area with a lively history of its own. The neighborhood has strong historical associations with entertainment, from Elizabethan bear-baiting to the even more vicious pleasures of Defoe's Moll Flanders. But the greatest "vice" of Southwark was theater. Shakespeare's and Marlowe's plays were performed at the **Rose Theatre,** built in 1587 and rediscovered during construction in 1989. The remnants are to be preserved and displayed underneath a new office block at Park St. and Rose Alley. Shakespeare's **Globe Theatre** lay nearby; a project is underway to build a new Globe on the riverbank. The **Shakespeare Globe Museum,** 1 Bear Gardens Alley (tel. 928 6342), a gallery devoted to Southwark history, concentrates on the Globe and less respectable neighborhood entertainments. (Open Mon.-Sat. 10am-5pm, Sun. 2-5:30pm. Admission £2, students £1.)

Near the bridge rises the tower of **Southwark Cathedral** (tel. 407 2939), probably the best Gothic church in the city after Westminster Abbey. Mostly rebuilt in the 1890s, the original 1207 choir and retro-choir survive. The glorious altar screen is Tudor, with 20th century statues. The church is dotted with interesting stone and wood effigies, with explanatory notes. Medieval poet John Gower is buried here in a colorful tomb, as is a pillmaker named John Lockayer, he of the humorous epitaph. This was the parish church of the Harvard family, and a chapel was dedicated to the memory of John Harvard in 1907. For reasons which remain unclear, the Harvard chapel also contains a memorial to lyricist Oscar Hammerstein.

Just a couple of blocks southeast, your hair will rise and your spine will chill at **St. Thomas's Old Operating Theatre** (tel. 955 5000), a carefully preserved 19th-century surgical hospital. (Open Mon., Wed., Fri. 12:30-4pm. Admission £1, concessions 60p.) If your appetite for destruction is stronger, the **London Dungeon** awaits at 28 Tooley St. Not for the squeamish, this museum recreates horrifying historical scenarios of execution, torture, and plague. Deadpan historical comments accompany the scenes of hanging, drawing and quartering, as if to justify and apologize for the stomach-churning reconstructions. (Tube: London Bridge. Open daily April-Sept. 10am-5:30pm, Oct.-March 10am-4:30pm. Admission £5, under 14 £3.)

Moored on the south bank of the Thames just upstream from Tower Bridge, the World War II warship **HMS Belfast** (tel. 407 6434) led the bombardment of the French coast during D-Day landings. The labyrinth of the engine house and the whopping great guns make it a fun place to play sailor. Mind your head. You can take the ferry that runs from Tower Pier on the north bank to the Belfast whenever the ship is open, or take the tube to London Bridge. (Open daily April-Oct. 10am-5:20pm, Nov.-March 10am-4pm. Admission £3.60, seniors, students, and children £1.80. Admission and ferry £4.40, seniors, students, and children £2.40.) East of Tower Bridge, the bleached Bauhaus box of the **Design Museum** perches on the Thames (see Museums).

The South Bank

A hulk of worn concrete and futuristic slate, the South Bank gestures defiantly at the center of London from across the Thames. The massive **South Bank Arts Complex** is the modern, more respectable descendant of the brothels and theatres that flourished in medieval Southwark. Until the English Civil Wars, most of this area fell under the legal jurisdiction of the Bishop of Winchester, and was thus protected from London censors. The region stayed almost entirely rural until the 18th-century Westminster and Blackfriars bridges were built. The current development began in 1951 during the Festival of Britain, the centenary celebration of the Great Exhibition of 1851. Current plans that call for a demolition and replacement of the Queen Elizabeth Hall and the Hayward Gallery have prompted many to reveal their fondness for the complex. The concrete blocks of the Royal Festival and Queen Elizabeth Halls, the Hayward Gallery, the National Film Theatre, and the National Theatre dominate the riverbank. The 3000-seat **Royal Festival Hall** is home to the Philharmonia and London Philharmonic Orchestras and host to countless others. The **National Theatre,** Waterloo Rd. (tel. 633 0880; Tube: Waterloo), opened by Lord Olivier in 1978, has become London's liveliest cultural center. The complex promotes "art for the people" through convivial platform performances, foyer concerts, lectures, and workshops. Excellent backstage tours are given regularly. (1¼-hr. tours Mon.-Sat. at 10:15am, 12:30pm, 12:45pm, 5:30pm, and 6pm. Admission £2.50, students £2.25. Book in advance.) The **Hayward Gallery** on Belvedere Rd. (tel. 928 3144; Tube: Waterloo) houses imaginative exhibitions primarily devoted to 20th-century artists. (Open during exhibits Thurs.-Mon. 10am-6pm, Tues.-Weds. 10am-8pm. Admission £4, students and seniors £2; £2 for all Mondays.) Multicolored posters displaying Russian titles and Asian warriors distinguish the entrance to the **National Film Theatre** (tel. 928 3232; Tube: Waterloo), directly on the South Bank. This cinema shows 2000 films per year and hosts most of the **London Film Festival** every November. (Films at festival £4. £10.25 annual membership required for advance priority bookings. See Entertainment for more details.) The Film Theatre also operates the innovative **Museum of the Moving Image** (see Museums).

The jumbled stalls of the **Cut Street Market** sprawl around the entrances to Waterloo station, London's busiest railway terminal. The station is at the end of "the drain," a BR line that shuttles commuters directly to and from the City. The market's old character has waned as ambitious development projects consume more of the area's residential neighborhoods. But prices have stayed low, and used-book sellers and curiosity stands have maintained the district's flavor. Farther along Waterloo Road, the magnificently restored **Old Vic** (tel. 928 7616), former home of Olivier's National Repertory Theatre, now hosts popular seasons of lesser-known classics and worthy revivals. (Box office open Mon.-Sat. 10am-8pm. Tickets £10-30.)

Emblazoned with the Stars and Stripes in memory of President Lincoln, the **Christ Church Tower** of 1876 rises above a mundane block of office buildings at the corner of Kennington Rd. Farther north, the refreshing **Jubilee Gardens,** planted for the Queen's Silver Jubilee in 1977, stretch along the Embankment to **County Hall,** a formidable Renaissance pile with a massive riverfront façade. The Hall was headquarters of the London County Council from 1913 until 1965, and of the Greater London Council, until it was controversially abolished in 1986. The building that once housed "Red" Ken Livingstone may be redeveloped into a hotel.

Lambeth Palace (Tube: Lambeth North), on the Embankment opposite the Lambeth Bridge, has been the Archbishop of Canterbury's London residence for seven centuries. Although Archbishop Langton founded it in the early 13th century, most of the palace dates from the 1800s. The palace's notable exterior features include the entrance at the 15th-century brick Morton's Tower, and Lollard's Tower, where John Wyclif's followers were thought to be imprisoned. (Open by prior arrangement only. Enquire to Lambeth Palace, Lambeth Palace Road, SE1.) West on Lambeth Road is the **Imperial War Museum** (see Museums).

Hampstead and Highgate

The urban villages of Hampstead and Highgate, poised on hills north of Regent's Park, seem entirely detached from central London. The very air is different, and the fragrance of roses steals over the red brick walls that line the streets.

Nestled in the midst of Hampstead, the **Keats House,** Keats Grove, is one of London's finest literary shrines. To get there, take the Underground to Hampstead, turn left down High St., and follow the signs. Before dashing off to Italy to breathe his last consumptive breath and die in true Romantic poet style, John Keats spent the last years of his life in Hampstead, pining for his fianceé, Fanny Brawne, who lived next door with her widowed mother. He allegedly composed "Ode to a Nightingale" under a plum tree here—the distant ancestor of the one growing in the garden today. The house is furnished as it was during Keats's life, complete with his manuscripts and letters. (Open April-Oct. Mon.-Fri. 2-6pm, Sat. 10am-1pm and 2-5pm, Sun. 2-5pm; Nov.-March Mon.-Fri. 1-5pm, Sat. 10am-1pm and 2-5pm, Sun. 2-5pm. Free.) The **Keats Memorial Library** next door contains a unique collection of books on the poet's life, family, and friends. (Open by appointment only. Tel. 435 2062.)

Now a National Trust property open to the public, **Fenton House,** Windmill Hill (tel. 435 3471) conserves a marvelous collection of 18th-century porcelain and of early keyboard instruments still used for occasional concerts. (For permission to play them, apply in writing to the Warden, Windmill Hill, London NW3 6RT.) You can see the walled garden and orchard free of charge. (House open April-Oct. Sat.-Wed. 11am-6pm; March Sat.-Sun. 2-6pm. Admission £2.) Round the corner, the **Admiral's House,** Admiral's Walk, tries to look like a ship, but doesn't quite cut it. **Church Row,** off Heath St., vehemently retains its 18th-century style; horseless carriages look out of place in front of its dignified terraces. The painter John Constable lies buried in St. John's churchyard down the row. At the bottom of Flask Walk, another cozy lane incongruously crammed with cars, **Burgh House** contains the interesting little exhibitions of the Hampstead Museum. Stop for lunch or a genteel cup of tea at The Buttery in the basement. (House open Wed.-Sun. noon-5pm. Buttery open Wed.-Sun. 11am-5:30pm.)

Hampstead Heath separates the two villages from the rest of London. Once a hangout for outlaws, it now attracts harmless picnickers and somewhat more dangerous kite flyers. You can get lost here; the heath remains the wildest patch of turf in London. On a hot day, take a dip in **Kenwood Ladies' Pond, Highgate Men's Pond,** or the outlandish **Mixed Bathing Pond.**

Presiding over the heath stands **Kenwood House,** Hampstead Lane, a picture-perfect example of an 18th-century country estate. This airy mansion now houses the **Iveagh Bequest,** an outstanding collection of 18th-century British portraiture and furniture, with a few fine works by Dutch masters, including Vermeer's *Guitar Player* and the last of Rembrandt's self-portraits. The original owner of Kenwood, influential chief justice Lord Mansfield, decreed the end to slavery on English soil. Mansfield's progressive policies did not win him universal popularity and, after destroying his abandoned townhouse in Bloomsbury, the Gordon Rioters pursued him north to Hampstead. Luckily for him (and for Kenwood House), his pursuers stopped for a drink at the **Spaniard's Inn** on Spaniards Rd., and a considerate publican made sure they got too drunk to continue. In summer, Kenwood hosts a hugely popular series of **outdoor concerts** (see Entertainment below) in which top-flight orchestras play from a bandshell across the lake. (Tube: Archway or Golders Green, then bus #210 to Kenwood. Kenwood open mid-April to Sept. daily 10am-6pm, Oct. to mid-April daily 10am-4pm. Free.)

Parliament Hill, on the southeastern tip of the heath, marks the southern boundary between Hampstead and Highgate and commands a Laurieresque view of London, sweeping from the docklands to the Houses of Parliament. The height of the hill, some say, owes much to the piles of corpses left here during the Plague. The bones of Queen Boudicca also reputedly lie here. It was toward this hill that Guy Fawkes' accomplices fled after depositing explosives under the House of Commons in 1605 to watch the big bang. (The explosives were discovered and the men captured, much to the disappointment of pyromaniacs everywhere. Britons commiserate on November 5 of every year by shooting fireworks at each other and burning effigies of Fawkes.)

To get from Hampstead to Highgate, walk across the heath or up Hampstead Lane. **Highgate Cemetery,** Swains Lane, is a remarkable monument to the Victorian fascination with death. Its most famous resident, rather inaptly, is Karl Marx, buried in the eastern section in 1883. An unmistakably Stalinist bust, four times life size, was placed above his grave in 1956 and attracts pilgrims from everywhere. Death makes for strange bedfellows; novelist George Eliot lies buried nearby. The magically spooky, and far wilder, western section contains some of the finest tombs. The zealously conscientious staff of the Friends of Highgate Cemetery (FOHC) provide a slice of Highgate life in themselves. (Tel. (081) 340 1834 or (081) 348 0808. Eastern Cemetery open April-Oct. daily 10am-5pm; Nov.-March 10am-4pm. Admission £1. Western Cemetery access by guided tour only in summer Mon.-Fri. at noon, 2pm, and 4pm, Sat.-Sun. 11am-4pm; in winter Mon.-Fri. at 11am, 2pm, and 3pm, Sat.-Sun. 11am-3pm. Admission £2. Camera permit £1, valid in both sections. No tripods, video cameras, or machine guns allowed. Times subject to change.)

Waterlow Park affords a gorgeous setting in which you can shed the urban grime of London and the Victorian gloom of the graveyard next door. The sociable ducks never turn down a good feed. By the eastern entrance, **Lauderdale House,** supposedly once home to Nell Gwyn, mistress of Charles II, now serves light snacks and lunches.

Highgate Village stands 424 ft. above the River Thames. You can climb Highgate Hill from Archway Tube station for a breathtaking view across London. On the way up, you will pass **Dick Whittington's Stone,** where 600 years ago the young, poor Dick heard the Bow Bells calling him back to London—"Turn again Whittington, thrice Lord Mayor of London." He turned, went back to London, and was thrice Lord Mayor. His petrified cat stands guard. The base of Highgate's parish church, **St. Michael's,** South Grove, is at the same level as the top of the cross on St. Paul's Cathedral dome. Opposite the church hides The Grove, an avenue of late 17th-century houses secluded behind magnificent elms. Poet and critic Samuel Taylor Coleridge lived at No. 3 for the last 18 years of his life, entertaining Carlyle, Emerson, and sundry other visitors.

To get to Hampstead, take the tube to Hampstead or Belsize Park, or the BR North London Line to Hampstead Heath. To reach Highgate, take the tube to Archway or Highgate. Either trip takes about half an hour from the center of London.

Greenwich and Blackheath

Greenwich means time. Charles II authorized the establishment of a small observatory here in 1675 "for perfecting navigation and astronomy," and the Royal Naval College moved here from Portsmouth in 1873. Successive royal astronomers perfected their craft to such a degree that they were blessed with the prime meridian in 1884.

Only select parts of the **Old Royal Observatory** (tel. (081) 858 4422; BR: Greenwich), designed by Sir Christopher Wren, remain open to the public. Flamsteed House covets an excellent collection of early astronomical instruments: astrolabes, celestial globes, and orreries. Jump from one hemishpere into the next across the **prime meridian,** marked by a brass strip in the observatory courtyard. Greenwich Mean Time, still the standard for international communications and navigation, is displayed on a 120 year old clock. The red time ball, once used to indicate time to ships on the Thames, drops daily at 1pm. (Open Mon.-Sat. 10am-6pm, Sun. 2-6pm; winter hours until 5pm. Planetarium shows on Sat. at 2:30 and 3:30pm. Admission £3.25, children £2.25.)

At the foot of the hill is the **National Maritime Museum** (see Museums), housed in 17th-century **Queen's House.** Designed by Inigo Jones and built for Charles I's wife Henrietta Maria, the house now exhibits sumptuous 17th-century furnishings and rich silk hangings. (Open Mon.-Sat. 10am-6pm, Sun. 2-6pm; in winter until 5pm. Admission £3.25, children £2.25.)

Opposite the Queen's House lies the **Royal Naval College,** also commissioned by Charles I and built by Wren, is decorated with James Thornhill's frescoed optical illusions. In the chapel hangs Benjamin West's painting of a shipwrecked St. Paul. (Open Fri.-Wed. 2:30-5pm. Free. Services Sun. at 11am.) By the River Thames in Greenwich, the *Cutty Sark,* one of the last great tea clippers on the route from China to Britain, anchors in dry dock. (Open Mon.-Sat. 10am-6pm, Sun. noon-6pm; winter hours until 5pm. Admission £2.50, children £1.25.) The *Gypsy Moth IV,* in which Sir Francis Chichester sailed around the globe, rests nearby. (Open April-Sept. Mon.-Sat. 10am-6pm, Sun. noon-6pm; Oct. daily 10am-5pm. Last admission ½hr. before closing. Admission 50p, children 30p.)

In summer, bands perform at Greenwich Park as a part of the Royal Park Band performance series. (3 and 6pm every Sun. June-Aug. 1½ hr.) and take place in the bandstand north of the gardens. From the last week of July to the middle of August, puppets perform in the playground at the northeast corner of the park (Mon.-Sat. at 11:30am and 2:30pm), and the season at the **Greenwich Theatre** (Croom's Hill, SE18) runs from April to August. (Box office tel. (081) 858 7755 from 10am-8:30pm. Performances Mon.-Fri. at 7:45pm, Sat. at 2:30 and 7:45pm. Tickets £6-10, £4 for students and seniors.)

The most picturesque (and appropriate) passage to Greenwich is by boat. Cruises to Greenwich pier depart from the Westminster, Charing Cross, or Tower piers (every ½ hr. 10:30am-4pm, 1 hr., £3.80, £5 return). The crew provides commentary on the major sights along the voyage. Trains leave from Charing Cross, Cannon St., and Waterloo (East) for Greenwich (25 min., £1.50 day return). The Docklands Light Railway whizzes from Tower Gateway to Island Gardens (16 min.). From there Greenwich is just a 10-minute walk through the foot tunnel. Bus #188 runs between Euston and Greenwich stopping at Kingsway, Aldwych, and Waterloo. One-day passport admission to the Observatory, Museum, Queen's House, and the Cutty Sark costs £6 (seniors and students £3.95, families £12). The **Greenwich Tourist Office,** 46 Greenwich Church St., SE10 (tel. (081) 858 6376; open daily 10am-6pm) conducts a variety of afternoon tours (£2.50-3, 1-1½ hr.).

On the south side of Greenwich Park lies the steel and concrete **Thames Barrier,** the world's largest movable flood barrier and the reason that London no longer enjoys the exciting high tides of yesteryear (tel. (081) 854 1373; open Mon.-Fri. 10:30am-5pm, Sat.-Sun. 10:30am-5:30pm; admission £2.20, seniors and children £1.35). From Charing Cross take BR to Charlton Station; from there it's a 15-min. walk. Alternatively take the boat from Greenwich pier (25 min.; 75 min. from Westminster pier). Call 930 3373 for details of Westminster service; (081) 305 0300 for Greenwich.

Richmond

Henry I rowed up the Thames in the 12th century, and though Richmond Palace was demolished during the Commonwealth, the town continues to preen its royal pedrigree. The **Richmond Tourist Information Centre,** in the old Town Hall on Whittaker Ave., has complete information on Richmond and surrounding areas (tel. (081) 940 9125; open Mon.-Fri. 10am-6pm, Sat. 10am-5pm, Sun. 10:15am-4:15pm; BR or Tube: Richmond).

The 2500 acres of Europe's largest city park, hilly **Richmond Park,** lap at the village fringe. Once a royal hunting ground, the park is still home to several hundred nervous deer. Across Richmond Bridge on Richmond Road perches the gleaming Inigo-Palladio **Marble Hill House** amid vast trimmed lawns. Gilt, carvings by James Richards, and the original Panini paintings of ancient Rome adorn the interior. During the summer, a series of outdoor concerts are held on the grounds (see Entertainment). (Tel. (081) 892 5115; house open April-Sept. daily 10am-6pm; Oct.-March daily 10am-4pm. Admission free). Next door, the remains of the 18th-century **Orleans House** (tel. (081) 892 0221) house local art and artifacts. (Open April-Sept. Tues.-Sat. 1-5:30pm, Sun. 2-5:30pm; Oct.-March Tues.-Sat. 1-4:30pm, Sun. 2-4:30pm. Admission free.) A ferry crosses the river here to **Ham House,** a restored 17th-century mansion, closed in 1992 for refurbishment.

Kew Gardens

The **Royal Botanic Gardens** at Kew, founded by Princess Augusta in 1759, foster thousands of flowers, plants, bushes, fruits, trees, and vegetables from all over the world, spread over 300 perfectly maintained acres. Not far from the main gate stands **Kew Palace,** built in 1631 as a summer residence of King George III and Queen Charlotte now houses a small museum depicting the vagaries of late 18th-century monarchical life. (Open daily 11am-5:30pm. Admission £1, students and seniors 75p.)

Kew's glasshouses are just a stone's throw away from the palace: the pyramidal **Princess of Wales Conservatory** allows you to browse through tropical climates among your favorite plants; the 1848 **Palm House,** though Kew's most graceful, is dwarfed by its younger Victorian sibling, the **Temperate House,** which calmly nurtures 3,000 species in its 50,000 square ft. Kew would not be complete without its simulated ruins of a Roman gate or unusual **pagoda** in the southeast corner of the park; the southwest corner of the park rambles on in a controlled but highly scenic state of wilderness.

The best way to reach Kew is by boat from Westminster pier (every 30 min. 10:30am-3:30pm, 1½ hr., £6, £8 return) and the cheapest way is by tube or BR North London line (Kew Gardens station, 50 min.). Ample parking space is available outside the gardens should you choose to drive. (Tel. (081) 940 1171. Gardens open Oct.-Jan. daily 9:30am-4pm; Feb.-Sept. Mon.-Sat. 9:30am-6:30pm, Sun. 9:30am-8pm. Glasshouses open daily 10am-4:30pm. Call to confirm closing times. Admission £3, students and seniors £1.50, children £1.)

Across the river at Kew Bridge, the **Kew Bridge Steam Museum** once was the proud water pumping station for West London. The engines still pump it up for ecstatic steam enthusiasts on weekends and Bank Holidays. (Tel. (081) 568 4757. Open daily 11am-5pm. Admission £1.50, children and seniors 75p.)

Hampton Court

Built by Cardinal Wolsey in 1519, Hampton Court was confiscated ten years later by Henry VIII when Wolsey fell out of favor. Henry's monumental Anglican Great Hall, Wolsey's Renaissance (and vaguely Catholic) designs, and later modifications by Wren unite to produce a unique and harmonious blend of 16th-century motifs and 18th-century classicism. Notice the clock on the south side, where the sun revolves around the earth.

Inside, you can see two curiosities of Renaissance art: the tapestries woven from the Raphael cartoons in the Victoria and Albert Museum, and a roomful of grisaille work originally by Mantegna but poorly repainted in the 18th century. The grounds of Hampton Court contain some highly celebrated amusements: the famous maze (open March-Oct.), first planted in 1714, a hedgerow labyrinth that served as the prototype for such later structures as Stanley Kubrick's Overlook Hotel; the great vine planted in 1796 that still produces grapes but now encloses a whole room with its foliage; and Henry VIII's tennis court (built in 1529), still used by "real tennis" purists. Also note the exhibit of Tijou's ironwork gates, left freestanding for the most part, and admirable from all sides. (Hampton Court open mid-March to mid-Oct. daily 9:30am-6pm; mid-Oct. to mid-March daily 9:30am-4:30pm. Tel. 977 8441. Admission £4.50, under 16 £2.90. Entry to the maze included in admission price.)

BR runs trains from Waterloo to Hampton Court every half hour (35 min., £3.10 day return). Green Line coach #718 makes the journey from Eccleston Bridge behind Victoria daily every hour from 9:40am (40 min., £2.70) whilst #715 leaves Oxford circus and then Marble Arch for the Palace (Mon.-Sat. every hr. from 10am, Sun. every 2 hrs., 55 min.). A boat runs from Westminster Pier to Hampton Court from June to September 4 times every morning (3-4 hr. one way, £6 single, £8 return).

Windsor and Eton

Royalty is an English national obsession, and **Windsor Castle,** (tel. (0753) 868 286)—where virtually everyone royal has been born, married, or imprisoned—has become one of its most visible symbols. Built by William the Conqueror as a fortress rather than as a residence, the castle stretches over and around one extended hill. Saunter in and out of its labyrinthine terraces, and enjoy beautiful views of the Thames Valley. As you enter the castle, **St. George's Chapel** rises across the courtyard, a sumptuous 15th-century building with delicate fan vaulting and stained glass. (Open Mon.-Sat. 10:45am-4pm, Sun. 2-4pm, £2, children £1). Inside, Henry VIII rests in a surprisingly modest tomb near George V, Edward IV, Charles I, and Henry VI. Dedicated to the Order of the Garter, the chapel hosts an annual ceremonial procession of the Knights of the Garter every year. Past the gargoyles of the (not really) Norman Gate, built by Edward III, at the top end of the castle, await the elegantly furnished **state apartments** (£2.90, child £1.25), and **Queen Mary's giant dolls' house** (£1.45, child 60p). Windsor's impressive changing of the guard takes place at 11am. (Grounds open April-Sept. daily 10:15am-6:15pm, Oct.-March daily 10:15am-4:15pm. Free. State apartments and dolls' house open April-Sept. Mon.-Sat. 10:30am-5pm, Sun. 12:30-5pm; Oct.-March Mon.-Sat. 10:30am-4pm, Sun. 12:30-4pm.)

The castle dominates a river town of cobbled lanes, small antique stores, and quaint tea shops, surrounded by the 4800-acre park. The old town is directly across the road from the castle gate, and the road that bears left around the royal grounds leads to the entrance to **Windsor Great Park.** The Long Walk leads from the castle towards the Copper Horse; at the other end of the park lie Savill Garden and the Smith's Lawn polo fields.

About 15 minutes down Thames St. and across the river is **Eton College,** a preeminent public (that is, private) school founded by Henry VI in 1440. Eton boys still wear tailcoats to every class, and solemnly raise one finger in greeting to any teacher on the street. Wellington claimed that the Battle of Waterloo was "won on the playing fields of Eton": catch a glimpse of the unique and brutal "Wall Game" and see why. Wander around the schoolyard, a central quadrangle featuring a statue of Henry VI, and the chapel, an unfinished cathedral. This route leads to the dreamy **cloisters** beyond, and an intriguing museum explaining some of the antiquated traditions that obscure the completely modern educational task of the school. (Yard, cloisters, and museum open April and July-Sept. 10:30am-4:30pm, May-June and Oct.-March daily 2-4:30pm. Admission £2.20, children £1.40.) A tour of the school costs a couple pounds.

The railway serves Windsor and Eton Central station and Windsor and Eton Riverside station). Trains leave from Paddington via Slough or directly from Waterloo (every 30 min., £4 cheap day return). Green Line coaches #700, 701, 702, and 718 also make the trip from Victoria Station (£3.80 day return). The tourist office (tel. (0753) 852 010) is in the Central station.

Museums

Rainy days, although quite numerous here, will not suffice for London's museums. You may find yourself indoors in the best of weather. London has more than its fair share of world-class institutions of art, archaeology, and science, and a host of smaller, more specialized collections.

Weekday mornings tend to be the most peaceful. Admission is usually free, but many museums, no longer heavily subsidized by the government, now charge or request a £1-2 donation. Most charge for special exhibits and offer student and senior citizen discounts. Many museums sponsor free films and lectures. A number have recently begun scrambling to modernize, with an eye toward attracting tourists.

British Museum

The British Museum is the British Museum is the British Museum. What more can one say about the greatest collection of far-flung artifacts in the world? Wandering randomly can be rewarding, if you've got about a month to spare. It's definitely worth investing in the £2 short guide to lead you through the maze; for a more in-depth look, guides to each collection are available for about £5. Guided tours (£5) cover the highlights of this mega-museum.

To your right as you enter are the **British Library** galleries. The **Manuscript Saloon** contains the English Literature displays, including manuscripts of *Beowulf* (c. 1000) and the *Canterbury Tales* (1410), and scrawlings form nearly every figure in English Literature up to Philip Larkin. Biblical displays include some of the oldest surviving fragments (the *Codex Sinaiticus* and the *Codex Alexandrinus*), third-century Greek gospels, and the Celtic *Lindisfarne Gospels.* Händel, Beethoven, and Stravinsky are represented in the music cases. You can read Henry VIII's complaint to Cardinal Wolsey that he found writing "sumwhat tedius and payneful," but probably not as much as did his predecessor King John, when assenting to the *Magna Carta,* of which the library has two copies. The highlight of the printed books in the **King's Library** is the Gutenberg Bible. The circular reading room, where Marx wrote *Das Kapital,* is open to visitors only on tours, Mon.-Sat. every hour on the hour from 11am to 4pm.

The ancient **Egypt** collection, housed on both floors of the museum, is outstanding. Entering the ground floor gallery, one is greeted by two of the many imposing statues of Amenophis III. To the left rests the **Rosetta Stone,** discovered in 1799 by French soldiers. Its Greek text enabled Champollion to finally crack the hieroglyphic code. Among the sculptures, the sublime, unidentified royal head in green schist (1490 BC) and the colossus of megalomaniac pharaoh Ramses II stand out. In the side gallery 25a, don't miss three of the finest and best known Theban tomb paintings, including *Nobleman hunting in the marshes.*

The upstairs Egyptian gallery contains brilliant sarcophagi and grisly mummies, and an ancient body "dessicated by the dry, hot sand." Delicate papyri include the famous *Book of the Dead of Ani.*

The **Greek antiquities** are rightly dominated by the white pieces of the Parthenon that reside in the spacious Duveen Gallery. In 1810, Lord Elgin, an enterprising British ambassador to Constantinople, procured the statues and pieces of the Parthenon frieze from the Sultan of Turkey. Later, for reasons of financial necessity, he sold them to Britain for £35,000 (they had cost him £75,000). Every so often, the Greeks renew their efforts to convince the British government to return the **Elgin Marbles.** The marbles, carved under the direction of ancient Greece's greatest sculptor, Phidias, comprise three main groups: the frieze, which portrays the most important Athenian civic festivals; the metopes, which depict incidents from the battle of the Lapiths and Centaurs (symbolizing the triumph of civilization over barbarism); and the remains of large statues that stood in the east and west pediments of the building. Keats, Byron, and Shelley all wrote a few stanzas to these inspiring stones.

Other Greek highlights include the complete Ionic façade of the Nereid Monument, one of the female caryatid columns from the Acropolis, and two of the Seven Wonders of the Ancient World: fragments of the **Mausoleum and Halicarnassus** and the Ephesian **Temple of Artemis.**

Among the many sculptures of the **Roman antiquities,** the dark blue glass of the **Portland Vase** stands out. The vase, which was the inspiration for ceramic designer Josiah Wedgwood, was shattered by a drunken museum-goer in 1845, but has been twice beautifully restored. A crisp second-century mosaic from France is outdone only by the Roman Christian mosaic upstairs found by a Dorset farmer in 1963. Nearby crouches **Lindow Man,** an Iron Age Celt killed in a ritual, and preserved by peat-bog.

The museum is located at Great Russell St., WC1 (tel. 636 1555; Tube: Tottenham Court Rd. or Holborn). Open Mon.-Sat. 10am-5pm, Sun. 2:30-6pm.

National Gallery

The National Gallery maintains one of the finest collections of European painting in the world, especially well-known for works by Rembrandt, Rubens, and 15th- and 16th-century Italian painters. The Berggruen collection of works from the turn of the 20th century, including many Impressionist masterpieces and a large selection of Picassos, has recently been loaned to the National for five years. The Tate Gallery has joint custody of the British collection.

The National Gallery's collection is undergoing a complete renovation and re-hanging, which will probably be finished sometime in spring 1992. Until then, you may have to check with the information desk to the right of the entrance to find your favorite paintings. You can spend days in this maze of galleries.

The National's collection is now split into four color-coded sections, and paintings within these sections are arranged by school. The collection starts in the new Sainsbury wing, to the west of the main building, designed by postmodernist Robert Venturi. Amid much-discussed fake ceiling supports and false perspectives hang works painted from 1260 to 1510. Early Italian paintings such as Paulo Uccello's grand fluorescent battle scene, *The Battle of San Romano,* Botticelli's *Venus and Mars,* Raphael's *Crucifixion,* and Leonardo da Vinci's famous *Virgin of the Rocks* are framed by the arches and columns of the new building.

Paintings from 1510 to 1600 are exhibited in the West Wing, to the left of the main entrance on Trafalgar Sq. These include paintings by late Renaissance masters such as Michelangelo, Venetians Titian (such as the beautiful *Bacchus and Ariadne*) and Tintoretto, and stormy pastels by El Greco. In the North Wing, further back behind the West Wing, are works of the 17th century. Rembrandt's gripping *Belshazzar's Feast* and graceful *Woman Bathing* are here, near a sprinkling of Vermeer and Hals. Serene Claude and Poussin landscapes are routed by the startling chiaroscuro of Caravaggio's *Supper at Eumaeus,* and the romanticism of Velázquez's *Toilet of Venus.*

The East Wing of the National Gallery, to the right of the main entrance, is devoted to painting from 1700 to 1920, including the recent arrivals from the Berggruen collection. The natural lighting provides the perfect setting for viewing the paintings; many, such as Turner's *Rain, Steam, and Speed* (note the tiny jackrabbit running alongside the train), seem to acquire a special luminosity. Gainsborough's tight *Mr. and Mrs. Andrews,* and Gerard Honthorst's compelling *Christ before the High Priest* whet the appetite before the Impressionists clamor for attention. Impressionist works include a number of Monet's most lavender and poignant waterlilies, Cézanne's *Les Grandes Baigneuses,* and Rousseau's rainswept *Tropical Storm with a Tiger.* Picasso's *Fruit Dish, Bottle, and Violin* (1914) represents the National Gallery's first foray into the abstract, complemented by a roomful of Picassos recently added to the collection.

The National Gallery holds frequent special exhibitions in the basement galleries of the new Sainsbury Wing. A large Rembrandt exhibition is planned for March-May 1992. Free hour-long guided tours of the collection start at 11am, 1pm, and 3pm Monday through Saturday. The National shows free films every Monday at 1pm in the lower-floor theatre, and lectures take place in the afternoons (Tues.-Fri. at 1pm, Sat. at noon). Each summer Wednesday the Gallery offers "Picture Promenade" lecture tours (July-Aug.; start at 6:30pm, 45 min.). Call for information regarding topics and times of lectures or films. The Gallery Shop sells detailed books and reproductions of many works in sizes ranging from postcard to poster.

The gallery is located at Trafalgar Sq. WC2 (tel. 839 3321, recorded information 839 3526; Tube: Charing Cross or Leicester Sq). Disabled access at Orange St. entrance. Open July-Aug. Mon.-Sat. 10am-8pm, Sun. 2-6pm. Sept.-June Mon.-Sat. 10am-6pm, Sun. 2-6pm. Free.

National Portrait Gallery

This unofficial *Who's Who in Britain* began in 1856 as "the fulfillment of a patriotic and moral ideal"—namely to showcase Britain's most noteworthy citizens. Alternatively you can think of the NPG as a response by the artistic community to Madame Tussaud's. The museum's declared principle of looking "to the celebrity of the person represented, rather than to the merit of the artist" does not seem to have affected the quality of the works displayed—many are by such top portraitists as Reynolds, Lawrence, Holbein, and Sargent. The 9000 paintings have been arranged more or less chronologically, though the order gets garbled on the lower floors. The earliest portraits hang in the top story—maligned Richard III, venerated Elizabeth I, and canny Henry VII. Charles II is here, surrounded by his wife and mistresses (Nell Gwyn is the one with the lamb).

Follow the flow of British history through the galleries: from the War of the Roses (Yorks and Lancasters), to the Civil War (portraits of Cromwell and his buddies), to the American Revolution (George Washington), to imperial days (Florence Nightingale), and on to modern times (Margaret Thatcher). On the first floor the emphasis shifts from crowned to creative heads: the Brontë sisters, painted by their brother Branwell, and William Blake. Famous geologists, politicians, reformers, and eccentric fops populate the Victorian section, along with literary figures including Tennyson, Thackeray, and Dickens. Portraits of Queen Elizabeth II and the present Royal Family are displayed on the mezzanine. (The likeness is better here than at Madame Tussaud's.) The basement shelters relatively modern portraits, including a sketch of W.H. Auden and a bust of Sir Alec Guinness. The annual British Portrait Award brings out a selection of works from England's most promising artists (on display June-Sept.). Visit the gift shop and buy classy postcards of your favorite personalities to send home to your friends or worship on your walls. Informative lectures transpire at 2:10pm Tuesday through Friday, at 5pm on Saturday. Check the monthly schedule for locations.

The gallery portrays at St. Martin's Pl., WC2 (tel. 306 0055; Tube: Charing Cross or Leicester Sq.). Museum open Mon.-Fri. 10am-5pm, Sat. 10am-6pm, Sun. 2-6pm. Free, except for some temporary exhibits £1-3.

Tate Gallery

The Tate Gallery opened in 1897 expressly to display modern British art. Since then, the gallery has widened its scope, obtaining a superb collection of British works from the 16th century to the present and a distinguished ensemble of international modern art. Like the National Gallery, the Tate has recently been completely reorganized; work should be completed by early 1992. The new captions and introductory notes in each gallery are particularly helpful.

The Tate's British collection is organized chronologically into schools, starting with a room at the far end of the gallery devoted to the Age of Hogarth. The parade of Constables includes the famous views of Salisbury Cathedral, and a bunch of Hampstead scenes, many dotted with the requisite red saddle splashes. George Stubbs' landscape and sporting portraits are enlivening, and lead up to Gainsborough's landscapes and Sir Joshua Reynolds' portraits. The haunting and visionary works of poet, philosopher, and painter William Blake are not to be missed, especially his marvelous illustrations of the Bible and of Dante's *Divine Comedy.* The psychological state of man is terrifyingly portrayed in his crawling *Nebuchadnezzar.*

The Tate's outstanding modern collection confronts you in the central halls with sculptures by Henry Moore, Epstein, Eric Gill, and Barbara Hepworth. The paintings include works of Monet, Degas, Van Gogh, Beardsley, Matisse, and the Camden Town Group (Sickert, Bevan), to the left of the entrance. The Bloomsbury Group, Francis Bacon, and the styles that have dominated since the 1950s (constructivism, minimalism, pop, super-realism, and process art) lie to the right of the main halls. Visit the extraordinary room of Rothko's studies in maroon and black.

The Tate's J.M.W. Turner collection has been moved to the **Clore Gallery,** an extension of the main building designed by the noted architect James Stirling. This vast display of 300 oil paintings and selected drawings and watercolors ranges from the early dreamy landscapes, such as *Chevening Park,* to the late visionary works, in which the subject gets lost in a sublime array of light and color. The natural light from above, cleverly allowed to filter through by the architect, illuminates scenes from the serene *Peace—Burial at Sea* to the furious depictions and raging paint of rain and snowstorms on the ocean.

Tours run Monday through Friday at 11am for the British collection, noon for Impressionism to expressionism, 2pm for expressionism to the present day, 3pm for the Turner collection. Lectures are given Mon.-Sat. at 1pm, Sun. at 2:30pm. The Tate puts on some of the most important special exhibitions in the world, both in the main building and in the Clore Gallery (admission usually £4-5, half price for students and children). Exhibitions scheduled for 1992 include the works of Otto Dix (March-May), pop artist Richard Hamilton (June.-Aug.) and English portraiture from Van Dyck to Augustus John (Oct.-Jan. 1993).

The Tate is located at Millbank, SW1 (tel. 821 1313; Tube: Pimlico). Open Mon.-Sat. 10am-5:50pm, Sun. 2-5:50pm. Free.

Victoria and Albert Museum

Housing the best collection of Italian Renaissance sculpture outside Italy, the greatest collection of Indian art outside India, and the world center for John Constable studies, the mind-boggling V&A specializes in fine and applied arts from every epoch and region of the world. Take an eight mile trek through art history in its 12 acres of galleries, divided among Art and Design galleries, Special Collections, and Materials and Techniques Collections.

The stars of the Renaissance art collection are the famed *Raphael Cartoons*—seven of the 10 large, full-color sketches (scenes from the Acts of the Apostles) done by Raphael and his apprentices as tapestry patterns for the Sistine Chapel. The endless galleries of Italian sculpture include Donatello's *Ascension* and *Madonna and Child.* The Medieval Treasury, in the center of the ground floor, features well-displayed vestments, plate, stained glass, and illuminations. The most spectacular treasure is the domed Eltenburg Reliquary. Plaster cast reproductions of European sculpture and architecture (the 80-ft.-tall Column of Trajan from Rome; the façade of the Santiago Cathedral in Spain; Michelangelo's *Moses, Dying Slave, Rebellious Slave,* and *David*) occupy rooms 46A-B on the ground floor. Next door, test the knowledge you've gained here to tell imposters from the real things in the Fakes and Forgeries gallery. Don't feel bad if you're fooled—in many cases, the V&A was too. The Dress Collection, also on the ground floor, traces popular clothing fashions from 17th-century shoes to the latest Armanis.

The first floor holds the large collection of British art and design. Shakespeare immortalized the immense Great Bed of Ware (room 54) in *Twelfth Night.* Cool, dim room 74, "1900-1960," exhibits the best in modern British design, including works by Wyndham Lewis, Charles Rennie Mackintosh, and Eric Gill. International design classics—mostly chairs—grace "Twentieth Century Design." The jewelry collection (rooms 91-93), so unwieldy that it has been annotated in bound catalogues instead of posted descriptions, includes pieces dating from 2000 BC. The National Art Library, located on the first floor, houses numerous Beatrix Potter originals as well as first editions of Pooh Bear adventures.

The V&A's formidable Asian collections have recently been beefed up by the new Nehru Gallery of Indian Art and the T.T. Tsui Gallery of Chinese Art. The Nehru Gallery contains splendid examples of textiles, painting, Mughal jewelry and decor, and enlightening displays about Europeans and Indians. You can see Tippoo's Tiger, a life-sized wooden model in the act of consuming a European gentleman, alluded to by consumption-obsessed John Keats in his poem *The Cap and Bells.*

John Constable's prodigious collection of weather studies resides on the sixth floor of the Henry Cole Wing. For those whose tastes run smaller, room 406 showcases English and Continental portrait miniatures (including Holbein's *Anne of Cleves* and *Elizabeth I*).

The V&A offers scores of special events. Introductory tours of the museum start Mon.-Sat. at 11am, noon, 2pm, or 3pm; Sun. at 3pm. Theme tours begin Mon.-Sat. at 11:30am, 1:30pm, and 2:30pm. Both last approximately one hour. Individual lectures of V&A summer courses can be attended for partial tuition: contact the Education Services Department (tel. 938 8638). Numerous free lectures throughout the summer cover anything from Impressionism to Japanese quilt technique. The V&A society hosts members' evenings on summer Wednesdays. Membership costs £25 (three-month membership £12); nonmembers may attend meetings for £2. Bookings can be made with the Box Office (tel. 938 8407), Victoria & Albert Museum, South Kensington, London SW7 2RL.

The V&A is located at Cromwell Rd., SW7 (tel. 938 8500; Tube: South Kensington). Open Mon.-Sat. 10am-5:50pm, Sun. 2:30-5:50pm. Donation £2, seniors and students 50p.

Other Major Collections

Cabinet War Rooms, Clive Steps, King Charles St. (tel. 930 6961 or 735 8922). Tube: Westminster. Churchill's secret underground headquarters during the Blitz present a fascinating glimpse into a world at war. The entrance is hidden; look for the queue. See the room where Churchill made his famous wartime broadcasts and listen to cuts of some of his speeches. Spot the 20-ton transatlantic hotline disguised as a loo. Free cassette guides available in English, French, German, Italian, Japanese, and Spanish. The 21-room narrated exhibit lasts about an hour. Open daily 10am-6pm. Last entrance 5:15pm. Admission £3.60; students, seniors, and under 16 £2.70, children £1.80. Additional discounts for groups of 10 or more.

The Design Museum, Butlers Wharf, Shad Thames, SE1 (tel. 403 6933). Tube: Tower Hill, then river shuttle from Tower Pier. In an appropriately Bauhausy box on the river, this museum is dedicated to mass-produced classics of culture and industry, such as the automotive bombshell dropped by the Citroen DS in the 1950s. Happily, you *can* sit in some of the century's most influential chairs. Open Tues.-Sun. 11:30am-6:30pm. Admission £3, students and children £2.

Institute of Contemporary Arts, the Mall, SW1 (tel. 930 3647). Tube: Piccadilly Circus or Charing Cross. Institutional outpost of the avant-garde in visual and performance art. Three galleries, a cinema featuring first-run independent films (£5), experimental space for film and video, theatre (from £5.50), seminars and lectures (£3), video library, and poetry readings (call for schedule). Day membership £1.50, students £1 (included in other ticket prices). Student art pass (£10) gets ½-price on any ticket for a year; normal membership £20. Galleries open daily noon-11pm.

The London Toy and Model Museum, 21/23 Craven Hill, W2 (tel. 262 7905.) Tube: Paddington or Queensway. On Sundays, the mini railway in the garden gives rides to small children (and, presumably, small adults). Inside, legions of dolls and cars inhabit cabinets. Open Tues.-Sat. 10am-5:30pm, Sun. 11am-5:30pm. Admission £2.70, students £1.70, children £1.20, families £6.

London Transport Museum, 39 Wellington St., WC2 (tel. 379 6344), on the east side of the Covent Garden flower market. Tube: Covent Garden. Traces the history of London transport from horse-drawn carriage to double-decker to Tube. Even non train- or bus-spotters will be impressed by the collection of old vehicles. Absorbing details on how London and its transport system grew up around each other. First-class museum shop sells stylish old (and new) London Transport posters and postcards at low prices. Museum open daily 10am-6pm, last admission 5:15pm. Admission £3, students, seniors, and children £1.50, families £7. Shop open daily 10am-5:45pm.

Museum of London, 150 London Wall, EC2 (tel. 600 3699). Tube: St. Paul's or Barbican. Located amongst old Roman walls and chaotic building sites, exhibits in themselves. The museum traces the metropolis from its beginnings as Londinium to the present. The flashiest new acquisition, the Lord Mayor's 1757 coach, steals the show from the prehistoric artifacts and the Great Fire animation. Cross-sectional models of Victorian sewers and Roman floors beneath a modern basement can mesmerize even the most blasé of tourists. Historical lectures given Wed.-Fri. at 1:10pm. Open Tues.-Sat. 10am-6pm, Sun. 2-6pm. Open Bank Holiday Mon. 10am-6pm. Free.

Museum of Mankind, 6 Burlington Gdns., W1 (tel. 437 2224). Tube: Green Park or Piccadilly Circus. Behind the Royal Academy. The ethnography collection of the British Museum, it includes a mass of engrossing artifacts, primarily from nonwestern cultures. Changing exhibits re-create the lifestyles of ancient and modern tribes, featuring everything from everyday tools to ritual objects. Useful introductory gallery gives a cross-section of the permanent collection, which includes Mexican turquoise mosaics, African pipes, British Columbian stone carvings, and Sioux war bonnets. Many exhibits appear sinister to Western eyes. Take a look at the amazing feathered image, found by Captain Cook, representing a Hawaiian god with a mohawk. Films Tues.-Fri. at 1:30pm and 3pm. Open Mon.-Sat. 10am-5pm, Sun. 2:30-6pm. Free.

Museum of the Moving Image (MOMI), South Bank Centre, SE1 (tel. 928 3232). Tube: Embankment or Waterloo. An outgrowth of the adjoining National Film Theatre, this entertaining museum charts the development of image-making with light, from 2000-year-old Chinese shadow puppets to present-day film and telly. Costumed actor-guides lead you through interactive exhibits—act out your favorite western, or read the TV news. The camera-shy will equally enjoy countless clips and famous props, from the gaudy days of the silents to the gaudy days of "Dr. Who." Open June-Sept. daily 10am-8pm, Oct.-May Tues.-Sat. 10am-8pm, Sun. 10am-6pm. Last admission 1 hr. before closing. Admission £4; students, seniors, and children £2.75.

Natural History Museum, Cromwell Rd., SW7 (tel. 938 9123). Tube: South Kensington. The original collection, 1 of 3 founding collections of the British Museum, was purchased from Sir Hans Sloane in 1753 for the nominal fee of £20,000. Today the museum's personality is split between a glorious but ultimately dull Victorian past (the encyclopedic frenzy only slightly subsided) and a modern, technological present (buttons, levers, and microscopes galore). In the "Life Galleries," the dinosaur exhibit mixes the best of new and old with its fierce robotic reconstructions and huge plaster skeletons. Other notable exhibits include Human Biology (useful for parents wondering how much their children really know), and Discovering Mammals (learn the truth behind "Superhog, could it really happen?"). The Geological Museum has recently become the "Earth Galleries" section. Shake and quake in the Earthquake room, and follow the Story of the Earth's interactive exhibits. Lectures and films presented summer Wed. and Sat. at 1 or 2pm; check at the information desk as you enter. Open Mon.-Sat. 10am-6pm, Sun. 11am-6pm. Admission £3.50, students and senior citizens £2, children £1.75, families (up to 2 adults and 4 children) £8. Free Mon.-Fri. 4:30-6pm, Sat.-Sun. 5-6pm.

North Woolwich Old Station Museum, Pier Road, North Woolwich, E16 (tel. 474 7244). BR: North Woolwich. Beneath walls crowded with colorful railway signs, ads, and signals, exhibits recall the glory that once was the British railway. An engine at back is occasionally steaming. Open Mon.-Wed., Sat. 10am-5pm; Sun. 2-5pm.

Royal Academy, Piccadilly, W1 (tel. 439 7438). Tube: Green Park or Piccadilly Circus. The academy frequently hosts traveling exhibits of the highest order: exhibition space has recently been enlarged by high-tech architect Norman Foster. The annual summer exhibition is a British institution where the works of contemporary artists are reviewed at the uncompromising rate of 10 per minute. Open daily 10am-6pm. Admission usually £3-5, students about £2, children £1. Summer exhibition admission: £3.60, students £2.10, under 18 £1.50. Advance tickets are occasionally necessary for popular exhibitions.

Science Museum, Exhibition Rd., SW7 (tel. 938 8000). Tube: South Kensington. The Science Museum can enlighten you on subjects ranging from the exploration of space to papermaking to basic topology. The museum's introductory exhibit romps through a "synopsis" of science since 6000 BC. Well-executed exhibits; the hands-on Flight Lab is interactive heaven for kids. Launch Pad, a special hall of child-run experiments on the first floor, is irresistible to kids of all ages: toddlers and *Let's Go* researchers alike. The Science Museum has recently absorbed the gloomy Wellcome Museum of the History of Medicine (on the 4th and 5th floors). Spock would no doubt find the museum's "Glimpses of Medical History" unbearably fascinating. Open Mon.-Sat. 10am-6pm, Sun. 11am-6pm. Admission £3.50, seniors £2, students and children £1.75.

Sir John Soane's Museum, 13 Lincoln's Inn Fields, WC2 (tel. 405 2107). Tube: Holborn. Soane was an architect's architect, but the home he designed for himself will intrigue even philistines. The anonymous façade hides an interior of funny angles and weird distortions. The famous breakfast room and the "Monk's Parlor" downstairs typify the house's individuality. The columns in the "Colonnade" room are actually supporting a room-within-a-room above. Important artifacts include Hogarth paintings and the massive sarcophagus of Seti I, which Soane put here after the British Museum inexplicably rebuffed his offer to donate it. Those who enjoy Soane's architectural imagination can glimpse his unexecuted designs in the drawings room. Open Tues.-Sat. 10am-5pm; lecture tour Sat. at 2:30pm.

Theatre Museum, 1E Tavistock St., WC2, public entrance on Russell St. (tel. 836 7891). Tube: Covent Garden. Britain's richest holding of theatrical memorabilia, such as the golden angel or "Spirit of Gaiety" rescued from the apex of Gaiety Theatre in Aldwych. See numerous 19th-century Shakespearean daggers before you. Evocative photograph collection and eccentric temporary exhibits. Box office just inside the door sells tickets to London plays, musicals, and concerts. Box office open Tues.-Sat. 11am-8pm, Sun. 11am-7pm. Museum open Tues.-Sun. 11am-7pm. Museum admission £2.50; students, seniors, and under 14 £1.50.

Entertainment

On any given day or night, Londoners and visitors can choose from the widest range of entertainment a city can offer. Broadway bluff aside, the West End is still the world's theatre capital, supplemented by an unpredictable "fringe." Music scenes range from the black ties of the Royal Opera House to Wembley mobs and nightclub throbs. Rep and new films, dance, comedy, sports, and countless unclassifiable happenings can leave you poring in bewilderment over the listings in *Time Out* (£1.30), *City Limits* (£1), and *What's On* (70p). **Kidsline** (tel. 222 8070) answers queries on children's events. **Artsline** (tel. (081) 388 2227) provides information about disabled access at entertainment venues across London.

Theatre

The focus of a national dramatic tradition dating from Shakespeare's day, London maintains lofty theatrical standards. London has respect for acting, and most of its actors have studied their craft seriously in some intensive drama program or other. You can visit any one of a charming slew of velvety playhouses with baroque balconies and see some of the world's best-trained actors joust or emote. Thanks to government subsidies, tickets are relatively inexpensive; the cheapest seats in most theatres cost about £5, progressing upward to £25 for orchestra seats. British theatres are small so you can see and hear well from almost anywhere. Previews and matinees offer even less expensive tickets, and many theatres (indicated by the letter "S" or some abbreviation of the word "concessions" in the *Evening Standard, Time Out,* and *City Limits*) offer rush tickets or student discounts on evening performances (tickets about £5 shortly before the performance—students must show ID); come to the theatre two hours ahead of curtain time to be certain of a seat. Most theatres also offer senior citizen discounts, especially on weekday matinees. For information on discounts offered by the Society of West End Theatres, call 836 0971. For the latest information on student standbys, listen to Capital Radio (95.8 FM) Mon.-Fri. at 6pm.

The **Leicester Square Ticket Booth** sells tickets at half-price (plus £1 booking fee, £1.25 for tickets over £5) on the day of the performance, but carries only expensive tickets, for selected plays. (Open for matinees Mon.-Sat. noon-2pm, for evening performances 2:30-6:30pm. Cash only.) If you schlep to the box office in person, you can select your seats from the theatre seating plan. (Box offices are usually open 10am-8pm.) Seats may also be reserved by phone by calling the box office directly and paying by post or in person within three days. Credit card-holders can charge the tickets over the phone but should be prepared to produce the card when picking up the tickets. Patronize ticket agencies only if you're desperate—they charge up to 20% commission. Not all plays start at 8pm—some curtains go up at 7:30 or 7:45pm.

Theatre schedules are published in *Time Out* and *City Limits.* You can obtain a fortnightly *London Theatre Guide* free from information centers and ubiquitous leaflet racks. Avoid the package-deal specials cooked up for tourists, and be aware that many of the shows around Piccadilly are tawdry farces and sex shows. For big-name shows, try to get tickets months in advance. Write or call first to the theatre box office; failing this, try **Keith Prowse** (tel. 793 1000), London's largest ticket agency (which also has an office at 234 W. 44th St., New York, NY 10036; tel. 1-800-669-7469), **Ticketmaster** (tel. 379 4444), or other agencies advertising in the SWET *London Theatre Guide.* These agencies charge a standard fee. Beware of other agencies you see congregating around Piccadilly and tube stations—they can, and will, charge whatever they like. If you have to buy a ticket from an agent, make sure you ascertain the exact face value and fee.

Aside from what's going on inside them, many West End theatres themselves form part of the city's fabric. A restored Victorian music hall, the **Old Vic** currently houses an excellent repertory company. The **Theatre Royal Drury Lane** dates from 1812 and even has a ghost. The **Theatre Trust** has protected many historic theatres from demolition; noteworthy landmark theatres include the Theatre Royal, Haymarket, the Albery, the Palace, the Criterion, the Duke of York, Her Majesty's, the Shaftesbury, the Savoy, and the Palladium.

National Theatre: Tel. 928 2252 for box office and information on standby tickets. Tube: Waterloo or Embankment. Excellent summer standby scheme. All unsold seats in the **Olivier, Lyttleton,** and **Cottesloe** theatres reduce to £9-12.50 at 10am on the day of performance; 40 seats in the first two rows are also sold at that time, to ensure that the most enthusiastic patrons occupy these seats. General standby seats sold from 2 hr. before performance at £8.50; student standby 45 min. before show, £5. Senior citizen Sat. matinees £8. The brilliant repertory companies in the Olivier and Lyttleton theatres generally put up classics from Shakespeare to Ibsen as well as mainstream contemporary drama. The Cottesloe plays with more experimental works. Platform performances (lectures or selections from plays) presented as pre-play appetizers (£2). The complex features live music, exhibitions, and other free activities. Tours offered Mon.-Sat. at 10:15am, 12:30pm, 12:45pm, 5:30pm and 6pm (£2.50; booking tel. 633 0880).

Barbican Theatre: Tel. 628 2295 for information; tel. 638 8891 for reservations. Tube: Moorgate or Barbican. London home of the Royal Shakespeare Company. Tickets £5-15; standby seats available from 90 min. before curtain at £10, £5 for students and seniors. Fascinating futuristic building; patrons enter their rows in the large auditorium through a side door (there are no aisles), and the forward-leaning balconies guarantee that no one sits farther than 65 ft. from center stage. Some of the funkiest productions take place in the smaller space, **The Pit** (matinees £10, evenings £12, senior citizen matinees £8, student standbys £5 from ½hr. before performance). Try to leave time after the show to look around the complex, which some observers berate as a glorified airport lounge and others laud for its innovative use of space. Box office on Level 7 of the Centre open daily 9am-8pm.

Open Air Theatre: Regent's Park (tel. 486 2431 or 486 1933 for credit card bookings). Tube: Baker St. Mostly Shakespeare; you have to sit close to catch every word. Bring a blanket and a bottle of wine. Open in summer only; tickets £6-13.50, student tickets 1 hr. before performance (£5). Call to check on availability.

Fringe

London's fringe, born in the late 1960s, mixes the intimate with the avante-garde. The renaissance of experimental drama abides in London's **fringe theatres,** presenting low-priced, high-quality drama. Check the fringe listings in *Time Out* or *City Limits,* and phone the theatre in advance for details. Most tickets run £3.50-10; all have student discounts. Some may require that you buy membership 48 hours in advance. One of the newest theatre companies, **Arts Threshold,** won first place in the fringe competition at the Edinburgh theatre festival, and has since toured Poland, Romania, Hong Kong, and Singapore. (Call (081) 994 4681 for information on their current London shows; tickets £4-5.)

These are some of the more prominent theatres in the greater London area: **Almeida Theatre,** 1A-1B Almeida St., N1 (tel. 359 4404). Tube: Angel or Highbury and Islington. **Battersea Arts Centre,** Old Town Hall, Lavender HIll, SW11 (tel. 223 2223). BR: Battersea Park or Clapham Junction. **Bloomsbury Theatre,** Gordon St., WC1 (tel. 387 9629). Tube: Euston Sq. **Bush Theatre,** Bush Hotel, Shepherd's Bush Green, W12 (tel. (081) 743 3388). Tube: Goldhawk Rd. **Drill Hall Arts Centre,** 16 Chenies St., WC1 (tel. 637 8270). Tube: Goodge St. **Hampstead Theatre,** Avenue Rd., Swiss Cottage Centre, NW3 (tel. 722 9301). Tube: Swiss Cottage. **Holland Park Theatre,** Holland Park, W14 (tel. 602 7856). Tube: Holland Park. **Institute of Contemporary Arts (ICA) Theatre,** Nash House, The Mall, W1 (tel. 930 3647). Tube: Charing Cross. **King's Head Pub Theater,** 115 Upper St., N1 (tel. 226 1916). Tube: Highbury and Islington or Angel. **Lyric Hammersmith,** King St., W6 (tel. (081) 741 2311 or (081) 741 8701.) Tube: Hammersmith. **New End Theatre,** 27 New End, NW3 (tel. 794 0022). Tube: Hampstead. **Shakespeare Globe Site,** Bankside, SE1 (tel. 620 0202). Tube: London Bridge. **Soho Poly,** 16 Riding House St., W1 (tel. 636 9050). Tube: Oxford Circus. **Theatre Royal Stratford East,** Gerry Raffles Sq., E15 (tel. (081) 534 0310). Tube: Stratford (not *that* Stratford). **Theatre Upstairs,** Royal Court, SW1 (tel. 730 2554). Tube: Sloane Sq. **Tricycle Theatre,** 269 Kilburn High Rd., NW6 (tel. 328 1000). Tube: Kilburn. **Young Vic,** 66 The Cut, SE1 (tel. 928 6363). Tube: Waterloo.

Lunchtime theatre productions are generally less serious than evening performances, but at £1.50-3 they're a great way to start the afternoon. (Most productions start around 1:15pm.) The **Kings Head** (see above) is probably the most successful theatre in this group. For courtyard performances of Shakespeare in June and July, check **The George Inn,** 77 Borough High St. (tel. 609 1198; Tube: London Bridge). **St. Paul's Church,** at the central marketplace in Covent Garden, often has lunchtime theatre on its steps. In the summer, call **Alternative Arts** for information on their street theatre around the city; recent shows include a performance of *War and Peace* entirely inside a motorcycle sidecar. If you can scrape together a group of 12-17 on a weekday evening, you can try London's largest theatre—the Underground. Follow a **Tube Theatre** comic posing as a bumbling commuter onto the trains and watch the real-life reactions. (Tel. 586 6828; tickets £11 per person.)

Film

Hollywood blockbusters can be seen at the many multi-screen, chain cinemas throughout the West End and Central London. The degenerate heart of the celluloid monster and the place to see 100-foot images of Stallone and Schwarzenegger battling for the audiences is Leicester Square. The most recent hits premiere here a day before hitting the chains around the city: they are expensive, however.

Other cinemas around London tend to have one screen only, and you may find youself inside a converted theatre, complete with gilt boxes for the audience. The film on the Nepalese fashion industry you have always wanted to see will probably be on soon: thousands of films pass through the capital every year, old and new. Newspapers have listings, while *Time Out* and *City Limits* include unbeatable guides both to expensive, commercial films and to the vast range of cheaper, more varied alternatives— including late-night films, free films, "serious" films, and repertory cinema clubs. Cinema clubs charge a small membership fee (usually 30p-£1.50), which entitles cardholders and one guest to reduced admission; some cards can be used at more than one theatre. For evening performances it's wise to buy your ticket early, or book in advance, especially on weekends. Most London moviehouses charge £5-6, but many charge only £3 all day Monday and for matinees Tuesday through Friday.

Repertory theatres include:

National Film Theatre, part of the South Bank Arts Complex, SE1 (tel. 928 3232). Tube: Waterloo or Embankment. Open to members only; yearly membership £10.25, £7.50 for students (of British schools only). Monthly membership £4. Daily 40p. Encyclopedic schedule (up to 6 films daily) with first runs, topical and directors' series, and special events. Hosts the London Film Festival in November. Best restaurant on the South Bank, too. Tickets £4.95, students £3.50.

The Institute of Contemporary Art (ICA) Cinémathique, Nash House, The Mall, W1 (tel. 930 3647). Tube: Piccadilly or Charing Cross. First-run films and esoteric *cinématique* offerings at £3. Day membership £1.50.

Scala Cinema Club, 275-277 Pentonville Rd., N1 (tel. 278 8052). Tube: King's Cross/St. Pancras. Great European double features, but in a sleazy neighborhood. Noted film-maker Matt Jones is known to frequent this establishment. Membership 50p per year; all-day tickets are £4, students £2.50 before 4:30pm.

Renoir, Brunswick Centre, Brunswick Sq., WC1 (tel. 837 8402). Tube: Russell Sq. British bohemian and popular foreign-language films (subtitled). Tickets £5, students £2.30 for first showing.

Phoenix, 52 High Rd., N2 (tel. (081) 883-2233). Tube: East Finchley. Double bills mix and match European, American, and Asian mainstream hits and classics. Cozy auditorium. Children's cinema club on Sat. mornings. Tickets £4, students £2.80 (except on weekends), children and seniors £1.70.

Minema, 45 Knightsbridge, W1 (tel. 235 4225). Tube: Hyde Park Corner. Small screen behind a tiny door, showing reborn art classics and popular foreign films. Tickets £6.25, students £3.50.

Electric Cinema, 191 Portobello Rd., W11 (tel. 792 2020). Tube: Ladbroke Grove or Notting Hill Gate. Great classics in a fantastic theatre. Tickets £4.50, students £3 before 4:30.

Gate Cinema, Notting Hill Gate, W11 (tel. 727 4043). Tube: Notting Hill Gate. Recent foreign language and art films. Tickets £5.50, students £3 before 6pm.

Lumière, St. Martin's Lane, WC2 (tel. 836 0691). Tube: Leicester Sq. Slightly offbeat Spanish and French films. Tickets £6.

Ritzy Cinema Club, Brixton Rd., SW2 (tel. 737 2121). Tube: Brixton. Good all-night triple features. Bring beer, sandwiches and a toothbrush. Membership 50p; tickets £4, students with ID £2.80, children £1.70.

Everyman Cinema, Hollybush Vale, Hampstead, NW3 (tel. 435 1525). Tube: Hampstead. Double and triple bills based on either a theme or an obscure celluloid figure. Special seasonal runs; membership 60p per year. Tickets £4.20, students £3.20 Mon.-Sat. before 4:30pm. Children £2.20.

Music

Everyone from punk-rocker to opera-head can exploit the richness of the London music scene. Unparalleled classical resources include five world-class orchestras, two opera houses, two huge arts centers, and countless concert halls. The rock scene, home of the London Underground of the late 60s, birthplace of the Sex Pistols and punk in the 70s, and lately blessed with Billy Bragg and Soul II Soul, has taken its most recent step ahead (and to the side of) the world with a strange lurching dance from Camden Town.

Summer is the best time for festivals and outdoor concerts, but the entire year offers enough music to satisfy and deafen you. Check the listings in *Time Out* or *City Limits.* Keep your eyes open for special festivals or gigs posted on most of the city's surfaces, and for discounts posted on student union bulletin boards.

Classical

London's five world-class orchestras make the city unique even among musical Shangri La-Ti-Do's. Yet they provide only a fraction of the notes that fill London's major music centres, and those are only a fraction of the concert venues of the city.

London has been the professional home of some of the greatest conductors of the century—Sir Thomas Beecham, Otto Klemperer, and Andre Previn, as well as fertile ground for Britain's greatest composers (who are well represented on London playlists). The venerable **London Symphony Orchestra,** led by Michael Tilson Thomas, inhabits **Barbican Hall** in the **Barbican Centre.** (Tube: Moorgate or Barbican; tel. 638 4141 for information. Box office open daily 9am-8pm, tel. 638 8891. Tickets £5-25; student standbys, when available, sold shortly before the performance at reduced prices.)

Klaus Tennstedt's **London Philharmonic** and Giuseppe Sinopoli's **Philharmonia Orchestra** play in the vast **Royal Festival Hall** in the grim labyrinth of the **South Bank Centre.** (Tube: Waterloo, or Embankment and walk across Hungerford Bridge; information tel. 928 3002, box office tel. 928 8800; open daily 10am-9pm. Tickets £3-25; student standbys, when available, sold 2 hr. before performance at lowest ticket price.) Vladimir Ashkenazy's **Royal Philharmonic Orchestra** performs at both the Barbican and the South Bank, and the **BBC Symphony Orchestra** pops up around town as well. These two main venues, as well as the South Bank's smaller halls, the **Queen Elizabeth** and the **Purcell Room** (both slated for demolition and replacement), play host to a superb line-up of other groups, including the Academy of St. Martin-in-the-Fields, the London Festival Orchestra, the London Chamber Orchestra, the London Soloists Chamber Orchestra, the London Classical Players, and the London Mozart Players, in addition to diverse national and international orchestras. Although the regular season ends in mid-July, a series of festivals on the South Bank in July and August take up the slack admirably, offering traditional orchestral music along with more exotic tidbits (tickets £3-20).

Exuberant and skilled, the **Proms (BBC Henry Wood Promenade Concerts)** never fail to enliven London summers. For eight weeks from July to September, an impressive roster of musicians performs in the **Royal Albert Hall** with routinely outstanding programs of established works and annually commissioned new ones. A special atmosphere of camaraderie and craziness develops in the long lines for standing room outside Albert Hall. (Gallery £2, arena £2.50—join the queue around 6pm; tickets £4-10.) The last night of the Proms traditionally steals the show, with the massed singing of *Land of Hope and Glory,* and closing with a rousing chorus of *Jerusalem.* Don't expect to show up at the last minute and get in; a lottery of thousands determines who will be admitted and allowed to dress up in Union Jack T-shirts and "air-conduct" along with the music. (Box office tel. 823 9998; open daily 9am-9pm; or try Ticketmaster at 379 4444. Tube: South Kensington.)

During the first three weeks or so of July, the **Festival of the City of London** explodes in activities around the city's grandest monuments: music in the livery halls, singing in churches, plays at various venues, grand opera, art exhibitions, and a trail of dance winding among the monuments. (Contact the Box Office, St. Paul's Churchyard, London EC4; tel. 248 4260; open Mon.-Fri. 9:30am-5:30pm. Many events free, other tickets £2-25. Information from early May at box office. Tube: St. Paul's.)

Artists from the **Royal College of Music** (Prince Consort Rd., SW7; tel. 589 3643) and the **Royal Academy of Music** (Marylebone Rd., NW1; tel. 935 5461) play at their home institutions and at the main city halls. Concerts at these schools are often free—call for details. Check with the **University of London Union** (1 Malet St., WC1; tel. 580 9551) for on-campus music there (Tube: Goodge St.).

Outdoor concerts in summer are phenomenally popular and relatively cheap. The **Kenwood Lakeside Concerts** at Kenwood, on Hampstead Heath present top-class orchestras, often graced by firework displays. (Tube: Golders Green or Archway, then bus #210; for information tel. 973 3427, for booking tel. Ticketmaster, 379 4444—no booking fee.) On Saturdays at 7:30pm, music floats to the audience from a performance shell across the lake. (Reserved deck chairs £7-9, students and seniors £3.50-4.50. Grass admission £4.50-6, students and seniors £3.50-4.) If the "outdoor" part is more important to you than the "concert," you can watch from afar for free. The grounds of stately **Marble Hill House** also host concerts, on summer Sundays at 7:30pm. (Tube/BR: Richmond, then bus #33, 90, 290, H22 or R70; information tel. 973 3427, booking tel. Ticketmaster, 379 4444—no fee.) Bring a blanket and picnic. Members of the audience eat anything from cheese sandwiches in Tupperware to salmon on alabaster.

Opera and Ballet

London's major opera companies have limited runs in summer. The **Royal Opera,** Box St. (tel. 240 1911 or 240 1066; Tube: Covent Garden), performs in the grand old Royal Opera House at Covent Garden. (Tickets run as high as £90; standbys—"amphitheatre" seats in back with a decent view—£7.50-12 from 10am on the day of the performance; when available, student standbys about £10 1 hr. before performance; tel. 836 6903 for recorded standby information; upper slips—on uncomfortable benches with a view of about half the stage—from £1.50.) Covent Garden has taken up the practice of "surtitling" all non-English works in the repertoire, which means subtitling, with a twist. (Box office 48 Floral St.; open Mon.-Sat. 10am-8pm.) For all its populism, the **English National Opera** commands no less respect. The repertoire leans more towards the contemporary, and all works are sung in English. Seats in the Opera's London Coliseum on St. Martin's Lane (tel. 836 6161; Tube: Charing Cross or Leicester Sq.) range from £4 to £40; standby tickets £10-15 available from 10am on day of performance. (Box office open Mon.-Sat. 10am-8pm.)

The ENO was founded as the Sadler's Wells Opera, and the current **Sadler's Wells Theatre** (Rosebery Ave, EC1; tel. 278 8916) presents a spring series called **"Opera 80."** (Tickets £5-20; 40 standby stalls seats available at £5 from 10:30am on performance day. Tube: Angel.) The **Holland Park Theatre** (Holland Park; Tube: Holland Park) presents open-air productions from a number of companies in June and July, in both English and the original languages. (Box office in the Visitor Centre, tel. 602 7856. Tickets £7.50-12, concessions £4-6.) On the cutting edge, the Royal Opera's **Garden Venture** stages new chamber opera at Riverside Studios in Hammersmith, from the end of May. (Crisp Rd., W6; tel. (081) 748 3354. Tickets £10, concessions £5.50. Tube: Hammersmith.)

The **Royal Ballet** performs at the Royal Opera House in Covent Garden. The box office stands around the corner at 48 Floral St. (tel. 240 1066 or 240 1911; open Mon.-Sat. 10am-8pm). Tickets cost £1.50-50. At 10am on the day of the show, 65 amphitheatre seats go on sale (strictly 1 per person; lines often long; £6-8.50). When available, standbys for students and senior citizens are sold from one hour before curtain; call 836 6903 for information. In the summer, when the English National Opera is off, the **English National Ballet** and visiting ballet companies perform in the London Coliseum, St. Martin's Lane, WC2 (tel. 836 3161; Tube: Leicester Sq.; tickets £5-55. Student and senior citizen discounts available by advance booking only). Visiting companies also grace the stage of the **Royal Festival Hall** in the South Bank Centre year-round (tel. 928 3002).

Sadler's Wells Theatre serves as the principal stage for visiting troupes ranging from Twyla Tharp to national folk companies. Tickets cost £4-20; student discounts are available. In summer, you can see dance outdoors at the Holland Park Theatre (tel. 602 7856; tickets £7.50-8.50, concessions £4-4.50).

For two weeks in July, the **Dance Days** festival puts on a diverse and energetic show of contemporary and folk dance; call the Battersea Arts Centre (tel. 223 2223) for details. London borough festivals also sponsor dance programs—most are widely publicized on tube station posters and at tourist offices. Fringe and experimental work is the focus of **The Place,** 17 Duke's Rd., WC1 (tel. 387 0031; Tube: Euston), and the **Institute of Contemporary Art,** Carlton House Terrace, SW1 (tel. 930 3647; Tube: Charing Cross; see Museums above). Some of the best fringe works make their way to the **Royal Court Theatre** in Sloane Square (tel. 730 1745. Tickets £5-12, standby £4. Tube: Sloane Sq.).

Jazz, Rock, Pop, Reggae, Folk, and Indie

London generates and attracts almost every type of performer under the sun: while the charts may be filled with the kind of wax performance idolized in the Rock Circus, the clubs and pubs of the capital offer a wider, stranger, and more satisfying variety of musical entertainment.

Time Out, What's On, and *City Limits* have extensive listings and information about bookings and festivals. You can make credit card reservations for major events by calling **Ticketmaster** (tel. 379 4444).

Rock and Pop

Major venues for rock concerts include the indoor **Wembley Arena** and the huge outdoor **Wembley Stadium** (Tube: Wembley Park or Wembley Central; tel. 902 1234 for both), the **Marquee,** and the **Town and Country Club** (see below). In the summer, many outdoor arenas such as **Finsbury Park** become the venues for major concerts and festivals. (For more rock listings, see Dance Clubs.)

Town and Country Club, 9-17 Highgate Rd., NW5 (tel. 284 0303). Tube: Kentish Town. Hot, hard-rocking bands, wild dancers, cheap drinks, and great sound make this club ideal for late-night weekend blow-outs. Big-name acts use this stage to tune up before nationwide tours. Admission £7-10. Open Mon.-Thurs. 8-11pm, Fri.-Sat. 7:30pm-2am.

The Marquee, 105 Charing Cross Rd., WC2 (tel. 437 6603). Tube: Leicester Sq. A loud, busy showcase for the latest bands: hundreds churn through each month. Admission £5-6:50. Open daily 7pm-midnight.

Powerhaüs, 1 Liverpool Rd., N16 (tel. 837 3218). Tube: Angel. Quirky mix of live rock and folk music in a converted pub. Admission £4-6. Open Mon.-Sat. 8pm-3am, Sun. 7-10:30pm.

Borderline, Orange Yard, Manette St., WC2 (tel. 497 2261). Tube: Leicester Sq. or Tottenham Court Rd. British record companies use this basement club to test new rock and pop talent. Admission £5. Open Mon.-Sat. 8pm-3am.

Academy Brixton, 211 Stockwell Rd., SW9 (tel. 326 1022). Tube: Brixton. Time-honored and rowdy venue for the harder end of popular rock. Admission (advance tickets) £9-12. Open daily 7-11pm.

Rock Garden, the Piazza, Covent Garden, WC2 (tel. 240 3901). Tube: Covent Garden. Great new bands play nightly—send them your demo tape. Admission £8. Open Mon.-Sat. 7:30pm-3am, Sun. 7:30pm-midnight.

Odeon Hammersmith, Queen Caroline St., W6 (tel. (081) 748 4081). Tube: Hammersmith. Large theatre featuring starry rock and pop acts. Admission (advance tickets) £9-15.

Le Palais, 242 Shepherds Bush Rd., W6 (tel. (081) 748 2812). Tube: Hammersmith. Large venue for rock and pop, with dance floor. Admission (advance tickets) £6-12.

Mean Fiddler, 24-28 Harlesden High St., NW10 (tel. (081) 961 5490). Tube: Willesden Junction. Formerly renowned as London's premiere spot for country western and folk, the Fiddler now specializes in indie rock. Cavernous club with high balconies and good bars. Admission £4-6. Open Mon.-Sat. 8pm-2am, Sun. 8pm-1am. Music nightly 10pm-closing.

Half Moon, 93 Lower Richmond Rd. (tel. 788 2387). Tube: Putney Bridge. Rocking pub with a mix of rock, jazz, and folk. Admission £3-5. Open daily from 8:30pm.

T&C2, 20-22 Highbury Corner, N1 (tel. 700 5716). Tube: Highbury & Islington. Rawish acts in a happy atmosphere. Open daily from 7:30pm.

Jazz

Jazz clubs tend to open and close down very quickly in London, apart from a few honored favorites. In the summer, hundreds of jazz festivals appear in the city and its outskirts, including the heavy-hitting Capital Radio Jazz Parade (July; tel. 379 1066), the North London Festival (June-July; tel. (081) 449 0048), and the City of London Festival (July; tel. 248 4260).

Ronnie Scott's, Frith St., W1 (tel. 439 0747). Tube: Leicester Sq. or Piccadilly. The most famous jazz club in London. Expensive food and great music. Rock/soul/world music on Sun. Admission £12, students £6. Book ahead or arrive by 9:30pm. Open Mon.-Sat. 8:30am-3am.

Bass Clef, 35 Coronet St., N1 (tel. 729 2476), off Hoxton Sq. Tube: Old St. Hosts British jazz and Latin performers, as does its sister venue, Tenor Clef. Call for a reservation or arrive early. Admission £4.50-7. Open daily 7:30pm-midnight.

Jazz Café, 5 Parkway, NW1 (tel. 284 4358). Tube: Camden Town. Top new venue in a converted bank. Classic and experimental jazz; groups sometimes last all week. Admission £7-10. Open daily from 8:30pm.

Jazz at Pizza Express, 10 Dean St., W1 (tel. 439 8722). Tube: Tottenham Court Rd. Packed, dark club hiding behind a pizzeria. Fantastic groups, and occasional greats; get there early. Admission £6-8. Music 9:30pm-1am.

Pizza on the Park, 11 Knightsbridge, SW1 (tel. 235 5273). Tube: Knightsbridge. Another smoky basement hideaway beneath another restaurant in the chain. Often sold out. Admission £5-8. Music 9:15pm-1am.

100 Club, 100 Oxford St., W1 (tel. 636 0933). Tube: Tottenham Court Rd. Strange mix of traditional modern jazz, swing, and rockabilly. Admission £5-8. Open Mon.-Sat. 7:30pm-1am, Sun. 7:45-11:30pm.

Palookaville, 13a St. James St., WC2 (tel. 240 5857). Tube: Covent Garden. Relaxed restaurant and wine bar with cool live jazz ensembles and an intimate dance floor. Admission free. Music nightly 8:45pm-1:30am.

Bull's Head, Barnes Bridge, SW13 (tel. (081) 876 5241). Tube: Hammersmith, then bus #9. A waterside pub renowned for good food and fine, traditional jazz. Admission £3-6. Open Mon.-Sat. 11am-11pm, Sun. noon-3pm and 7-10:30pm. Music starts at 8:30pm, and at lunchtime on Sun.

Africa Centre, 38 King St., WC2 (tel. 836 1973). Tube: Covent Garden. The centre of the world. Music and dance from Africa, including jazz and world music. Admission £7. Open Mon.-Sat. 8:30pm-3am.

Folk

To a large extent, folk music in London means Irish music. But there is some variation on the Celtic theme: folk rock, English ballads, and even English country-and-western. Many pub events are ephemeral: check weekly listings. Some of the best are free, but welcome donations or consumption.

Archway Tavern, Archway Roundabout, N19 (tel. 272 2840). Tube: Archway. Sponsors a mix of groups with a Gaelic accent (but rock only Mon.-Tues.). Admission from £2.50. Open Mon.-Sat. from 9:30pm.

Bunjie's, 27 Litchfield St., WC2 (tel. 240 1796). Tube: Covent Garden. Packed, with lively, dancing audience. Admission £2-2.50. Open Mon.-Sat. from 8:30-11pm.

Sir George Robey, 240 Seven Sisters Rd., N4 (tel. 263 4581). Tube: Finsbury Park. Varied schedule with Celtic rock and country rock, as well as traditional English and Irish folk. Occasional all-day festivals. Admission £2-3. Open daily from 7:30pm.

Dance Clubs

London happens to dance to anything. Clubs in the capital pound to Unbelievable 100% groovy Liverpool tunes, ecstatic Manchester rave, hometown soul and house, and imported U.S. rap and funk. Check out the 12" bins at record stores for the obscure Dub mixes that dominate the playlists. Fashion evolves and revolves: acid-hoods and sneakers are giving way to flares and platforms.

Many clubs host a variety of provocative one-nighters (theme parties, like "Leather and Old Spice Night") throughout the week. Call ahead and ask about the club's dress code, since your gold-sequined transparent catsuit may not be adequately appreciated. When you pay the cover, you are buying a one-night "membership" (subject to the club's approval). Remember that the Tube shuts down two or three hours before most clubs and that taxis can be hard to find in the wee hours of the morning. Arrange transportation in advance; otherwise, try London Regional Transport's extensive network of night buses (for information call 222 1234). As always, check the listings in *Time Out, What's On,* and *City Limits.*

The Fridge, Town Hall Parade, Brixton Hill (tel. 326 5100). Tube: Brixton. A serious dance dive with a multi-ethnic crowd, abandoned home of Jazzie B from Soul II Soul. Dress for heat and come prepared to move to house funk. Dress code: wear anything. Telly psychedelia. Admission £5-7. Lively mixed-gay night on Tues. and some Thurs. Open Mon.-Thurs. 10pm-3am, Fri.-Sat. 10pm-4am.

Africa Centre, 38 King St., WC2 (tel. 836 1973). Tube: Covent Garden. On weekends, "Club Limpopo" features DJ Wala's African grooves and a live set. Admission £6-7. Open 9pm-3am.

Camden Palace, 1a Camden High St. NW1 (tel. 387 0428). Tube: Mornington Crescent on weekdays, or Camden Town on weekends. Enormously popular with tourists and Brits alike, especially on Wednesdays, when "Twist and Shout," and 50s-60s music predominates. Gothic night on Tuesdays. Get hold of discount tickets handed out around the tube station and High St. Admission variable: Wed. £4, Thurs. free for women. Fri and Sat. £6. Go early.

The Electric Ballroom, 184 Camden High St. (tel. 485 9006). Tube: Camden Town. Cheap and fun; catch Gothic tunes on Fri., or funk and hip hop on Sat. Admission £5.

Crazy Larry's, 533 King's Rd., SW10 (tel. 376 5555). Tube: Fulham Broadway or Sloane Sq. A posh, civilized club with a fine restaurant and good sound. Popular feeding and breeding ground for Sloane Rangers and Mayfair trendies. Admission £5-7. Open Mon.-Wed. 9pm-1am, Fri.-Sat. 9pm-2:30am, Sun. 6pm-midnight.pen 10pm-3am.

Hippodrome, Charing Cross Rd. (tel. 437 4311). Tube: Leicester Sq. Infamously enormous, expensive, loud, and tourist-ridden. Admission £6-12 for the spectacle; leave your blue jeans and trainers behind. Witching-hour laser shows. Open Mon.-Sat. 9pm-3:30am.

Gay and Lesbian Nightlife

London's gay scene ranges from the flamboyant to the outrageous to the cruisy to the mainstream. The 24-hr. **Lesbian and Gay Switchboard** (tel. 837 7324) is an excellent source of information. Bars particularly popular among gay men are **Brief Encounter,** 42 St. Martin's Lane, WC2, and **Comptons of Soho,** 53 Old Compton St., W1; both are fairly touristy (Tube: Leicester Sq.). The wilder **London Apprentice,** 333 Old St. EC1 (Tube: Old St.) has a macho male crowd (leather nights Fri.-Sun.; £2.50 after 11pm). Women-only nights can be found at **Heds,** at HQ, Camden Lock, NW1, on Sundays from 9pm to 3am (Tube: Camden Town), or at the **Fallen Angel,** 65 Graham St., N1, on Tuesday nights from 7:30pm to midnight (Tube: Angel). Both *Time Out* and *City Limits* (the "Out" section) have a plethora of detail on bars, nightclubs, and special events.

Heaven, Villiers St., W2 (tel. 839 3852), underneath The Arches. Tube: Embankment. One of the coolest places to dance: gay/straight club with capacity of nearly 4000. Large dance floors, high-tech lighting, pool tables, and bars. Men only on Wed. ("Pyramid") and Sat. nights. Mixed/straight nights Fri. ("Garage"). Admission £4-6. Open Tues.-Wed. 10:30pm-3am, Fri.-Sat. 9:30pm-3am.

The City Apprentice, 126 York Way, N1 (tel. 278 8318). Tube: King's Cross. Adventurous, mainly male disco with amateur strippers on Mon., mud wrestling on Tues., and male strippers on Fri.

Black Cap, 171 Camden High St., NW1. Tube: Camden Town. Oldest gay bar in London, with a mixed male/female crowd and an olde worlde atmosphere. Admission £2-3 (Mon. free). Open Mon.-Sat. 3pm-2am, Sun. noon-3pm and 7pm-midnight.

Madame Jo-Jo, 8-10 Brewer St., W1 (tel. 734 2473). Tube: Piccadilly Circus. A fun, flamboyant cabaret club featuring raucous drag reviews. Small, crowded dance floor. Reserve tables well in advance. Admission £8-10. Open Mon.-Sat. 10pm-3am.

Club Copa, 180 Earl's Court Rd., SW5 (tel. 373 3407). Tube: Earl's Ct. Amiable and relaxed, this popular gay club is a good place to wind down after an evening out in Earl's Court. Men only. Admission £2.50-4.50. Open Mon.-Sat. 10:30pm-2am.

Comedy Clubs

Ten years after the "alternative" scene hit town, the London comedy circuit remains vibrant and original. These clubs tend to be informal, good for a great laugh or at least a fine night out. After seeing a few shows, though, you may find the alternatives wearing a little thin, and the gut-wrenching bouts of guffaws becoming less frequent. Comedy listings appear under "Cabaret" in *Time Out* and *City Limits.*

Comedy Store, 28a Leicester Sq., WC2 (tel. 839 6665). Tube: Leicester Sq. The most famous comedy venture in London, and birthplace of the alternative comedy revolution. The Comedy Store Players appear on Wed. and Sun., top guests on other nights. Shows at 8pm, plus midnight on Fri.-Sat. Arrive early. Admission £7.

Jongleurs, The Cornet, 49 Lavender Gardens, SW11 (tel. 924 2766). BR: Clapham Junction. Lively melange of mime, clowning, and humor; renowned for audience food-throwing. Shows Fri.-Sat. Admission £8, concessions £6.

Banana Cabaret, The Bedford, Bedford Hill, SW12 (tel. 081) 673 8904). Renowned stand-up and musical comedy in both the domed cabaret room downstairs and the cozy space upstairs. Admission £4, concessions £3.

Comedy Café, 66 Rivington St., EC2 (tel. 739 5706). Tube: Old St. Open Spot nights on Wed.—less risky comedy and magic the rest of the week. Admission £2-4.

Red Rose Cabaret, Red Rose Club, 129 Seven Sisters Rd., N7. (tel. 281 3051). Tube: Finsbury Park. The cream of the London circuit, hosted by Ivor Dembina. Shows Fri.-Sat. at 9:30pm. Admission £4.75, concessions £3.50, occasional discounts with a copy of *Time Out.*.

Offbeat Entertainment

The College of Psychic Studies, 16 Queensberry Place, SW7 (tel. 589 3292). Tube: South Kensington. Eager for you to become their newest subject. Unlock your true self through graphoanalysis, harness universal wisdom and release life blocks (karmic or otherwise) with regression therapy, or achieve that eternally-sought-after harmony between body and spirit through aromatherapy. Open Mon.-Thurs. 10am-7:30pm, Fri. 10am-4:30pm, closed most of August.

London Skydiving Centre, Cranfield Airport, Cranfield, Bedfordshire, MK43 (tel. (0234) 751 866). Two-day static-line training courses with jump for £95, plus £17 per each additional dive. Open Tues.-Sun. 9am-dusk.

Porchester Baths, Queensway, W2 (tel. 798 3689). Tube: Bayswater. A Turkish bath with steam and dry heat rooms and a swimming pool. Built in 1929, the baths charge high rates (£11.35 for 3 hr.), but devoted fans keep taking the plunge. Open daily 7am-8pm. Men only Mon., Wed., and Sat.; women only Tues., Thurs., and Fri.; Sun. mixed (couples only).

Vidal Sassoon School of Hairdressing, 56 Davies Mews, W1 (tel. 629 4635). Tube: Bond St. Become your own offbeat entertainment. Cuts, perms, and color at the hand of a Sassoony. Cut and blow dry £6.50, with student ID £3. All-over tint £9.25. Call ahead for an appointment.

Tube Theatre, (tel. 586 6828). Follow a comedian acting as a bumbling commuter onto the Underground, and keep a poker face as you savor the hilarious situations. Group bookings (12-17) only. £11.

Conway Hall, Red Lion Sq., WC1 (tel. 242 8032). Tube: Holborn. Atheist lectures Sun. morning, chamber music Sun. evening.

Speaker's Corner, in the northeast corner of Hyde Park. Tube: Marble Arch. Crackpots, eccentrics, political activists, and more crackpots speak their minds and compete for the largest audience every Sun. 11am-dusk. (See Hyde Park under Sights.)

Crafts Council, 12 Waterloo Place, Lower Regent St., SW1 (tel. 930 4811). Tube: Piccadilly Circus. Amiable, hospitable. Exhibitions, advice, conversation, and more. Books and slides on crafts, too. Open Tues.-Sat. 10am-5pm, Sun. 2-5pm.

Design Council, 28 Haymarket, SW1 (tel. 839 8000). Tube: Piccadilly Circus. Free exhibitions and information on the best and brightest of British design of absolutely everything. Open Mon.-Sat. 10am-6pm, Sun. 1-6pm.

Victorian Society, 1 Priory Gdns., W4 (tel. (081) 994 1019). Tube: Turnham Green. Genial company, historical knowledge, lectures, and guided walks through London. Membership £15, but the sneaky can probably join a walk without paying. Open Mon.-Fri. 9am-5:30pm.

Daily Mail and *Evening Standard.* Northcliffe House, 2 Derry St., W8 (tel. 938 6000). Tube: High St. Kensington. See an issue of one of these aspiring tabloids in production. For information write to the Personnel Administrator, Hammondsworth Quays Ltd., Surrey Quays Rd., SE16 1PJ.

Spectator Sports

Football

Many evils may arise which God forbid.
—King Edward II, banning football in London, 1314

It's a game of two halves, Brian.
—anon.

Football (soccer) has stirred passion and controversy for centuries. In its modern form, it draws huge crowds—over half a million people attend professional matches in Britain every Saturday. Each club's fans dress with fierce loyalty in team colors and make themselves heard with remarkable ritual songs and chants. At games, you can hear the uncanny synchronized singing of such simple but tuneful classics as "Ere we go" or "There's only one Michael Thomas." In recent years, the sport has been plagued by the violent outbursts of "football hooligans"; while stricter policing and booze-free stadiums have gone some way to reduce outbreaks of trouble, you should probably spend the extra cash to get a seat, and avoid the rowdier standing-(or staggering)-room-only "terraces".

The season runs from August to April. Most games take place on Saturday, kicking off at 3pm. Allow time to wander through the crowds milling around the stadium. London has been blessed with 13 of the 92 professional teams in England.

The big two are the League champions **Arsenal,** Highbury, Avenell Rd., N5 (tel. 359 0131; Tube: Arsenal) and the F.A. Cup holders **Tottenham Hotspur,** White Hart Lane (tel. (081) 808 1020; BR: White Hart Lane). Some of the others are **Chelsea,** Stamford Bridge, Fulham Rd., SW6 (tel. 381 6221; Tube: Fulham Broadway); and **Crystal Palace,** Selhurst Park, Whitehouse Lane, SE25 (tel. (081) 653 4462; BR: Selhurst or Norwood Junction). Tickets are available in advance from each club's box office; many now have a credit card telephone booking system. Seats cost £5-20. England plays occasional international matches at Wembley Stadium, usually on Wednesday evenings (tel. (081) 902 8833); Tube: Wembley Park).

Cricket

Cricket, which Robin Williams has likened to "baseball on valium," remains a confusing spectacle to most North Americans. A game of great subtlety, cricket fuses Caribbean calypso with Old-World decorum. Once a synonym for civility, cricket's image has been dulled by intimidating bowling, time-wasting, and arguments with umpires. The much-used phrase "It's just not cricket" has recently taken on an ironic edge.

London's two grounds stage both county and international matches. **Lord's,** St. John's Wood Rd., NW8 (tel. 289 1615; Tube: St. John's Wood), is *the* cricket ground, home turf of the Marylebone Cricket Club, the established governing body of cricket. An archaic stuffiness pervades the MCC; women have yet to see the inside of its pavilion. **Middlesex** plays its games here (tickets £5-6). Tickets to international matches cost £12-34. The **Oval,** Kennington, SE11 (tel. 582 6660; Tube: Oval), home to **Surrey** cricket club (tickets £5), also fields Test Matches. (Tickets for internationals £14-25.)

Rowing

The **Boat Race,** between eights from Oxford and Cambridge Universities, runs from Putney to Mortlake on a Saturday in late March or early April. Bumptious crowds line the Thames and fill the pubs. (Tube: Putney Bridge or Hammersmith. BR: Barnes Bridge or Mortlake.) Cambridge has won only once in the last 15 years.

Tennis

For two weeks in late June and early July, tennis buffs all over the world focus their attention on **Wimbledon.** The English take pride in their Wimbledon and keep everything about it highly polished. Most Brittanically, the grass-court tennis is unsurpassed and the traditional snack is strawberries and cream. If you want to get in, arrive early—9am the first week, 6am the second; the gate opens at 10:30am (get off the tube at Southfields, before Wimbledon proper). Entrance to the grounds (including lesser matches) costs £6, less after 5pm. If you arrived in the queue early enough, you will be able to buy one of the few show court tickets that were not sold months before. Depending on the day, center court tickets cost £10-30, court 1 tickets £9-24. If you fail to get center and court 1 tickets in the morning, try to find the resale booth (usually in Aorangi Park), which sells tickets handed in by those who leave early (open from 2:30pm; tickets £2).

For details of the 1992 championships call the All England Club (tel. (081) 946 2244) or send a self-addressed stamped envelope between Aug. 1 and Dec. 31 to The All England Lawn Tennis and Croquet Club, P.O. Box 98, Church Rd., Wimbledon SW19 5AE. Topspin lob fans mustn't miss the **Wimbledon Lawn Tennis Museum** (tel. (081) 946 6131), located right on the grounds. (Open Tues.-Sat. 11am-5pm, Sun. 2-5pm; call ahead to check near tournament time.)

Participatory Sports

If you fancy something a little more adventurous than a kickaround in the park or kite flying on Parliament Hill, then just do it. London provides a satisfyingly wide variety of sporting opportunities. *Time Out's Guide to Sport, Health, & Fitness* (£5) can give you more complete information. For general fitness during your visit,

London Central YMCA, 112 Great Russell St. (tel. 637 8131; Tube: Tottenham Court Rd.), has a pool, gym, weights, and offers weekly membership for £25.50, off-peak weekly membership (use after 4pm prohibited) £17. (Open Mon.-Fri. 8am-10pm, Sat.-Sun. 10am-10pm.) The Sportsline answers queries on a vast range of clubs and locations (tel. 222 8000; Mon.-Fri. 10am-6pm).

Shopping

London does sell more than royal commemorative mugs and plastic police helmets. However, many visitors to London do not buy anything but royal commemorative mugs and plastic police helmets. First-time shoppers may be disappointed by the amount of junk thrown at them; but dodge the barrage and you'll be able to satisfy any purchasing urge, be it for shortbread or howitzers.

For department stores and fashion outlets, try Oxford St., Knightsbridge, and Kensington; for expensive designer goods, Sloane St., Bond St., and Piccadilly; for hip young clothes, Soho, Kensington, Chelsea, and Camden; for specialty stores, Bloomsbury and Covent Garden. London Transport's handy *Shoppers' Bus Wheel* instructs bus-loving shoppers on the routes between shopping areas (available free from any London Transport Information Office). *Nicholson's Shopping Guide and Streetfinder* (£2.50) should suit bargain hunters seeking further guidance. Serious shoppers should read *Time Out's* massive *Directory to London's Shops and Services* (£6) cover to cover.

Prices descend during sale seasons in July and January. Tourists who have purchased anything expensive should ask about getting a refund on the 17.5% VAT. But most shops have a VAT minimum; Harrods, for instance, requires you to spend £150 before refunding VAT. Many shops stay open late on Thursday; almost all close on Sunday.

Department Stores

Occupying an entire turreted, terracotta block, **Harrods** (tel. 730 1234) remains the ultimate department store. They can do everything from finding you a live rhinoceros to arranging your funeral. They stock more than 450 kinds of cheese. Harrods also pours a rather elegant afternoon tea (see Teas, under Food). (Open Mon. and Thurs.-Sat. 9am-6pm, Tues. 9:30am-6pm, Wed. 9am-8pm.)

Except during sales, comprehensive department stores tend not to be the cheapest places to shop. The ubiquitous **Marks and Spencer** (tel. 935 7954), also known as Marks and Sparks, sells its own British staples in a classy but value-conscious manner. The clothes err on the side of frump; Margaret Thatcher buys her underwear here. (Branches near Bond St., Marble Arch, and Kensington High St. Tube stations. Open Mon.-Wed. and Fri. 9am-7pm, Thurs. 9am-8pm, Sat. 9am-6pm.) Also near the Bond St. Tube station on Oxford St. is **Selfridges** (tel. 629 1234), an enormous pseudo-Renaissance building with a vast array of fashions, homewares, and foods. (Open Mon.-Tues. and Fri.-Sat. 9am-7pm, Wed.-Thurs. 9am-8pm.) **Debenham's** (tel. 580 3000) at 334 Oxford St. (Tube: Oxford Circus) is a bit staider but cheap (open Mon.-Tues. 9am-6pm, Wed.-Fri. 9am-8pm, Sat. 9am-7pm).

South of Oxford Circus on Regent St. stands **Liberty and Co.** (tel. 734 1234; Tube: Oxford Circus). A prime exponent of the 19th-century arts and crafts movement, Liberty peddles silk scarves, fine cotton fabrics, elegant fashions, and furnishings in unusual Renaissance and Tudor buildings. Bargain hunters can get their Victorian wares on sale at the beginning of July and after Christmas. (Open Mon.-Wed. and Fri.-Sat. 9:30am-6pm, Thurs. 9:30am-7:30pm.)

At the renowned **Fortnum & Mason,** 181 Piccadilly (tel. 734 8040; Tube: Green Park or Piccadilly Circus), liveried clerks serve expensive foods in red-carpeted and chandeliered halls. Queen Victoria naturally turned to Fortnum & Mason when she wanted to send Florence Nightingale 250 lbs. of beef tea for the Crimean field hospitals. Visit the costly but satisfying tea shop, or splurge on an ice cream sundae in the fountain room. (Open Mon.-Sat. 9:30am-6pm.)

Clothing

Those who'd rather not swap a cherished limb for some new clothes should explore some of London's second-hand clothing stores. **The Frock Exchange,** 450 Fulham Rd., SW6 (tel. 381 2937; Tube: Fulham Broadway) sells second-hand designer items in excellent condition and at low prices. (Open Mon.-Sat. 10am-5:30pm.) The rage for second-hand American fashions has produced a number of cheap clothing outlets: **American Classics,** 400-404 King's Rd., SW10 (tel. 351 5229; Tube: Sloane Sq., then bus #11; open Mon.-Sat. 10am-6:30pm); **Flip,** 125 Long Acre, WC2 (tel. 836 7044; Tube: Covent Garden; open Mon.-Wed. and Fri.-Sat. 10am-7pm, Thurs. 10am-8pm, Sun. noon-7pm); and **High Society,** 46 Cross St., N1 (tel. 226 6863; Tube: Angel; open Mon.-Sat. 10:30am-6:30pm). **Kensington Market,** (49-53 Kensington High St., W8), has some better bargains (including second-hand clothes) and even wilder stalls, including a tattoo parlor. (Open Mon.-Sat. 10am-6pm.) Along the same lines, try **Camden Lock** market (see Street Markets), or the **Garage,** 350 King's Rd., SW3 (tel. 351 3505); Tube: Sloane Sq., then bus #11; open Mon.-Fri. 10am-6pm, Sat. 10am-7pm). Small secondhand shops of the same ilk dot the King's Rd. between Sloane Sq. and the Chelsea Town Hall.

For the latest in beat-tapping inexpensive shoes, try **Shelly's Shoes,** 159 Oxford St. (tel. 437 5842; open Mon.-Sat. 9:30am-6:30pm, Thurs. until 8pm; branches throughout London), the spiritual home of Doc Marten. **Russell and Bromley, Saxone** and **Dolcis** have shops across the capital.

Bookstores

In London, even the chain bookstores are wonders. Mammoth independents and countless specialized gems make up the capital's catalogue. An exhaustive selection of bookshops lines Charing Cross Road between Tottenham Court Rd. and Leicester Sq. and many vend second-hand paperbacks. Shops along Great Russell Street stock esoteric and specialized books on any subject from Adorno to Zemlinsky. The best place to look for maps is **Stanford's,** 12 Long Acre (open Mon. and Sat. 10am-6pm, Tue.-Wed. and Fri. 9am-6pm, Thurs. 9am-7pm; Tube: Covent Garden); also try Harrods and the YHA shop (see Specialty Shops below).

Hatchards, 187 Piccadilly, W1 (tel. 437 3924). Tube: Green Park. Oldest and most comprehensive of London's bookstores, undergoing expansion in 1991. Tremendous selection of travel narratives. Also at 150 King's Rd. (tel. 351 7649); 390 The Strand (tel. 379 6264); 63 Kensington High St., (tel. 937 0858); and Harvey Nichols in Knightsbridge (tel. 235 5000). Open Mon.-Fri. 9am-6pm, Sat. 9am-5pm.

Foyles, 119 Charing Cross Rd., WC1 (tel. 437 5660). Tube: Tottenham Court Rd. or Leicester Sq. The largest bookstore in London, stockpiling over 6 million books. Come roam through this amazing colossus, but don't expect too much guidance. Open Mon.-Sat. 9am-6pm, Thurs. 9am-7pm.

Dillons, 82 Gower St., WC1 (tel. 636 1577), near University of London. Tube: Goodge St. The most graceful bookstore in London. Easier to navigate and almost as complete as Foyles, though with a more academic focus, particularly on history and politics. Fair selection of reduced-price and second-hand books, plus classical CDs and tapes. Open Mon.-Fri. 9:30am-7pm, Sat. 9:30am-6pm.

Waterstones, 121-125 Charing Cross Rd. WC1 (tel. 434 4291), next door to Foyles. Tube: Leicester Sq. An extensive and well-ordered selection of paperbacks; calmer and friendlier than its neighbor though also a little cramped. They mail books to the US. Also at 193 Kensington High St. (tel. 937 8432); 99 Old Brompton Rd. (tel. 581 8523); 68-69 Hampstead High St. (tel. 794 1098). Open Mon., Wed.-Sat. 9:30am-8pm; Tue. 10am-8pm, Sun. 11am-6pm. Kensington High St. open until 10pm Mon.-Fri.

Art bookstores splatter the streets around the British Museum (Tube: Holborn or Tottenham Court Rd.) and Christie's (Tube: Green Park or Piccadilly). Close to Christie's, **Thomas Heneage & Co.,** 42 Duke St. St. James's (Tube: Green Park), houses a truly outstanding collection of art books (tel. 930 9223; open Mon.-Fri. 10am-6pm). Art books also adorn **Zwemmers,** 80 Charing Cross Rd. (tel. 379 7886; open Mon.-Fri. 9:30am-6pm, Sat. 10am-6pm), while 50s magazines and film posters clutter **Vintage Magazine Market,** on the corner of Brewer and Great Windmill

St. near Piccadilly Circus (tel. 439 8525; open Mon.-Sat. 10am-7pm; Sun. noon-7pm). For theatre and opera books, try **Samuel French's,** 52 Fitzroy St. (tel. 387 9373; open Mon.-Fri. 9:30am-5:30pm). Parents should stop in at the **Children's Book Centre,** 229 Kensington High St. (tel. 937 7497; open Mon.-Sat. 9:30am-6pm), or the **Puffin Bookshop,** The Market, Covent Garden (tel. 379 6465; open Mon.-Sat. 10am-8pm).

Record Stores

If a record can't be found in London, it's probably not worth your listening time. London, for years the hub of the English music scene, has a record collection to match. The Big Three, **HMV, Virgin,** and **Tower Records,** fall over each other in claiming to be the world's largest record store. Crammed with records, tapes, CDs, videos, T-shirts, and intimidating security apparatuses, they all offer a broad and comprehensive selection from rock, soul, and reggae, to jazz and classical. Don't expect any bargains or rarities, and remember that when it comes to records, "import" means "rip-off." For rarities, second-hand, and specialist records, try the wealth of diverse shops scattered throughout the West End and the suburbs. At **Camden Town, Brixton,** or **Ladbroke Grove/Notting Hill,** you can have a good afternoon's browse in search of an obscure *Steve Seligman Power* 12-inch or some Ska standards.

Markets

Street Markets

Many street markets sell modern junk or ordinary produce at non-bargain prices; an exceptional handful push offbeat styles and unique trinkets. Entertaining salespeople and an informal atmosphere make the markets livelier and more invigorating than shopping malls. With some luck and ingenuity, you may find cheap, unusual goods—come prepared to haggle and to participate in some cheerful, often incomprehensible, banter.

London has over 70 street markets, the majority of them unremarkable local shopping centers. Listed below is the more entertaining minority. Opening times vary considerably—Saturday is usually the busiest and best day.

Camden Lock, NW1, by Regent's Canal and along Camden High St. Tube: Camden Town. One of the funkiest, trendiest places to tap those Doc Marten soles. Plastic Pollock ties, wicked leather gear, crafts, grub, and seas of music. Camden Town Bootleggers do a roaring trade—check the quality of the tapes before buying. Open Sat.-Sun. 9am-6pm.

Brixton Market, Electric Ave., Brixton Station Rd. and Popes Rd., SW2. Tube: Brixton. Covered market halls and outdoor stalls sprawl out from the station. The wide selection of African and West Indian fruit, vegetables, fabrics, and records make Brixton one of the swingingest markets. Open Mon.-Sat. 8am-5:30pm; closed Wed. afternoons.

Portobello Road, W11. Tube: Notting Hill Gate or Ladbroke Grove. High-quality antiques at high prices. Some Londoners call this "a place to visit your stolen silver;" others consider it nothing more than a tourist trap. Immortalized by Paddington Bear. Watch out for pick-pockets. Over 2000 dealers; prices from £10-10,000. To the north, tourists thin out as antiques give way to produce and general secondhand. Antique market Sat. 7am-5pm.

Petticoat Lane, E1. Tube: Liverpool St., Aldgate, or Aldgate East. A London institution—street after street of stalls, mostly cheap clothing and household appliances. The real action begins at about 9:30am. The street called Petticoat Lane (Middlesex St. on some maps) proves the least interesting part of the market; for better buys and second-hand stuff, head north toward Brick Lane. Open Sun. 9am-2pm; starts shutting down around noon.

Camden Passage, Islington High St., N1. Tube: Angel. Turn right as you come out of the Underground, then bear right on Islington High St. One of the biggest antique markets, plus prints and drawings on Thurs. and some cheaper junk. Open Wed.-Thurs. 7am-4pm, Sat. 8am-5pm.

Merton Abbey Mills, Meranton Way, SW19. Tube: Colliers Wood or South Wimbledon. An excellent, earthy crafts and clothes market on the river Wandle: brown rice yogurt, and Chi-

LET'S PACK IT UP

Let's Go® Backpack/Suitcases

Innovative hideaway suspension with internal frame turns backpack into carry-on suitcase. Detachable daypack makes it 3 bags in 1. Water-proof Cordura® nylon. Lifetime Guarantee. 3750 cu. in. Navy, teal or black. **Supreme** adds lumbar support pad, torso and waist adjustment, two daypack pockets, leather trim, and *FREE shoulder strap.*

A1.	**Supreme**	**$154.95**
A2.	**Backpack/Suitcase**	**114.95**
A3.	**Shoulder Strap**	**4.50**

A1

A2

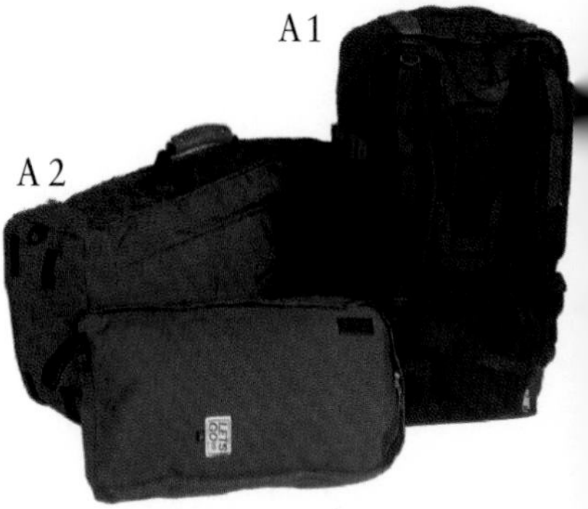

B

C

D

B. Chateau

Top-opening rucksack pack. Drawstring closure. 3 compartments. Taped inseams. Lifetime Guarantee. 1310 cu. in. Black.

$34.95

C. Undercover Neck/Waist Pouch

Secure & comfortable. Ripstop nylon with soft Cambrelle® back. 2 pockets. 6 ½ x 5" Lifetime Guarantee. Black or tan.

$7.95

D. Passport/Money Case

Waterproof nylon with zippered pouch. 7 ½ x 4 ½" Navy or gray.

$6.95

Duffles

Tough, capable, and appealing. 11 oz. waterproof Cordura-Plus® with 3" nylon web. Lifetime Guarantee. Red, black, purple, or blue.

E1.	**XL–36 x 15 x 15"**	**$69.95**
E2.	**L–30 x 15 x 15"**	**59.95**

H. Travel Case

Perfect carry-on luggage. Large compartment with 2 side pouches. Mesh pocket. No-sag bar and shoulder strap. Lifetime Guarantee. 20 x 16 x 9" Black or blue.

$94.95

E2

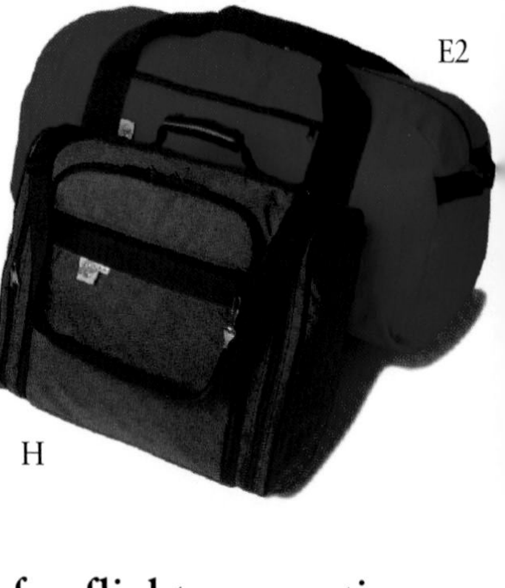

H

Call 1-800-5LETS GO for flight reservations.

J1

T1 T2

ET'S GO HOSTELING

92-93 Youth Hostel Card (AYH)
equired by most international hostels. ust be U.S. resident.

.	Adult (ages 18-55)	$25
.	Youth (under 18)	10

. **Sleepsack**
equired at all hostels. Washable durable ly/cotton. 18" pillow pocket. Folds to uch size. $13.95

. **1992-93 International Youth Hostel uide (IYHG)**
sential information about 3900 hostels Europe and Mediterranean. $10.95

FREE map of hostels worldwide.

et's Go® Travel Guides
urope; USA; Britain/Ireland; France; Italy; rael/Egypt; Mexico; California/Hawaii; ain/Portugal; Pacific Northwest/Alaska; reece/Turkey; Germany/Austria/Switz-land; NYC; London; Washington D.C.

1.	USA or Europe	$14.95
2.	Country Guide (specify)	13.95
3.	City Guide (specify)	9.95

$1.00 off the cover price.

LET'S SEE SOME I.D.

1992 International ID Cards
Provides discounts on accommodations, cultural events, airfares and accident/medical insurance. Valid 9-1-91 to 12-31-92.

T1.	Teacher (ITIC)	$15
T2.	Student (ISIC)	14
T3.	Youth International Exchange Card (YIEE)	14

FREE "International Student Travel Guide."

LET'S GO BY TRAIN

Eurail Passes
Convenient way to travel Europe. Save up to 70% over cost of individual tickets. Call for national passes.

First Class

V1.	15 days	$430
V2.	21 days	550
V3.	1 month	680
V4.	2 months	920

First Class Flexipass

V5.	5 days in 15 days	$280
V6.	9 days in 21 days	450
V7.	14 days in 1 month	610

Youth Pass (Under 26)

V8.	1 month	$470
V9.	2 months	640
V10.	15 days in 2 months	420

FREE Eurail Map, Timetable, & Travelers' Guide with passes.

LET'S GET STARTED

PLEASE PRINT OR TYPE. Incomplete applications will be returned.

International Student/Teacher Identity Card (ISIC/ITIC) (ages 12 & up) enclose:

1. Letter from registrar or administration, transcript, or proof of tuition payment. FULL-TIME only.
2. One picture (1 ½ x 2") signed on the reverse side.

Youth International Exchange Card (YIEE) (ages 12-25) enclose:

1. Proof of birthdate (copy of passport or birth certificate).
2. One picture (1 ½ x 2") signed on the reverse side.
3. Passport Number ______________________ 4. Sex: M F

Last Name ______ First Name ______ Date of Birth __/__/__

Street ______ We do not ship to P.O. Boxes. U.S. addresses only.

City ______ State ______ Zip Code ______

Phone ( ) ______ Citizenship ______

School/College ______ Date Trip Begins __/__/__

Item Code	Description, Size & Color	Quantity	Unit Price	Total Price

Shipping & Handling			
If order totals:	Add	Total Merchandise Price	
Up to $30.00	$4.00	Shipping & Handling (See box at left)	
30.01-100.00	6.00	For Rush Handling Add — $8 for Continental U.S. $10 for AK & HI	
Over 100.00	7.00	MA Residents (Add 5% sales tax on gear & books)	
		Total	

ENCLOSE CHECK OR MONEY ORDER PAYABLE TO: HARVARD STUDENT AGENCIES, INC.

Allow 2-3 weeks for delivery. Rush orders delivered within one week of our receipt.

LET'S GO® Travel

Harvard Student Agencies, Inc., Harvard University, Thayer B, Cambridge, MA 02138

(617) 495-9649 1-800-5LETSGO (Credit Card Orders Only)

Prices subject to change.

nese food galore. Morden Hall Park (National Trust) just along the river. Open Sat.-Sun. 10am-5pm.

Chapel Market, N1. Tube: Angel. Turn left off Liverpool Rd. Emphasis on produce, but also household goods, those dubious electronics, and clothes, spiced with nuts and African music. Open Tues.-Wed. and Fri.-Sat. 8am-6:30pm, Thurs. and Sun. 8am-12:30pm.

South and Southeast England

The lovely counties of Kent, Sussex, and Hampshire, with their seaside villages, wooded wealds, and green hilly downs, have seduced outsiders for centuries. Two especially tenacious tourists, Julius Caesar in 55 BC and William of Normandy in 1066 AD, left lasting marks during their vacations, dotting the coast with Roman and Norman ruins. The southeast has a dappled charm: Victorian mansions lining the shores punctuate gentle green countryside; hilly areas, such as the North Downs and High Weald, contrast with the low-lying regions of Low Weald and Romney Marsh. Known as the "garden of England" for its many orchards, Kent is also rich in archaeological sites, castles, and fortifications.

Getting Around

Public transportation pampers the area within 90 mi. of London and facilitates daytrips to the towns of Southern England. **British Rail** offers day return tickets to many points in the southeast for little more than the cost of single tickets. You can easily make short hops from one town to another, especially along the coast. Some local bus companies offer their own travel passes. The **Explorer** ticket (£3.80), which can be purchased from any local ticket office or on the bus, allows one day's unlimited travel on virtually all bus routes in East Kent, Maidenstone, Hastings, and Southdown. A **Sunday Rover** ticket, which can be purchased from the driver in advance, allows unlimited travel for a day on nearly all Sunday bus services in Kent. The **Freedom** ticket, available for periods of one, four, and 13 weeks, allows travel on most buses within a defined zone. The **National Bus Company** has offices in all major cities in the southeast; in summer, it's a good idea to reserve seats for Friday and Saturday trips. The **South Coast Express** #025 serves coastal towns between Kent and Devon. Unfortunately, there is no good cheap map of both rail and coach routes; you may want to combine a Railrover pamphlet and a Green Line Bus Map.

You can best enjoy the scenically undulating terrain on foot, bike, or moped. Walkers need not carry their packs the entire way; a fine group of youth hostels—particularly along the South Downs Way—make excellent bases for day hikes. Tourist offices have regional Camping Directories.

Canterbury

In the Middle Ages, England's most heavily traveled road was the one from London to Canterbury, lined with pilgrims striding to the shrine of Thomas à Becket. Becket clashed with Henry II over the clergy's freedom from state jurisdiction. Henry cried in exasperation, "Who will deliver me from this turbulent priest?" In December 1170 four loyal knights answered their king's query and murdered Becket in the cathedral. A shrine was born. Becket became a martyr and a saint; Henry died a mere mortal.

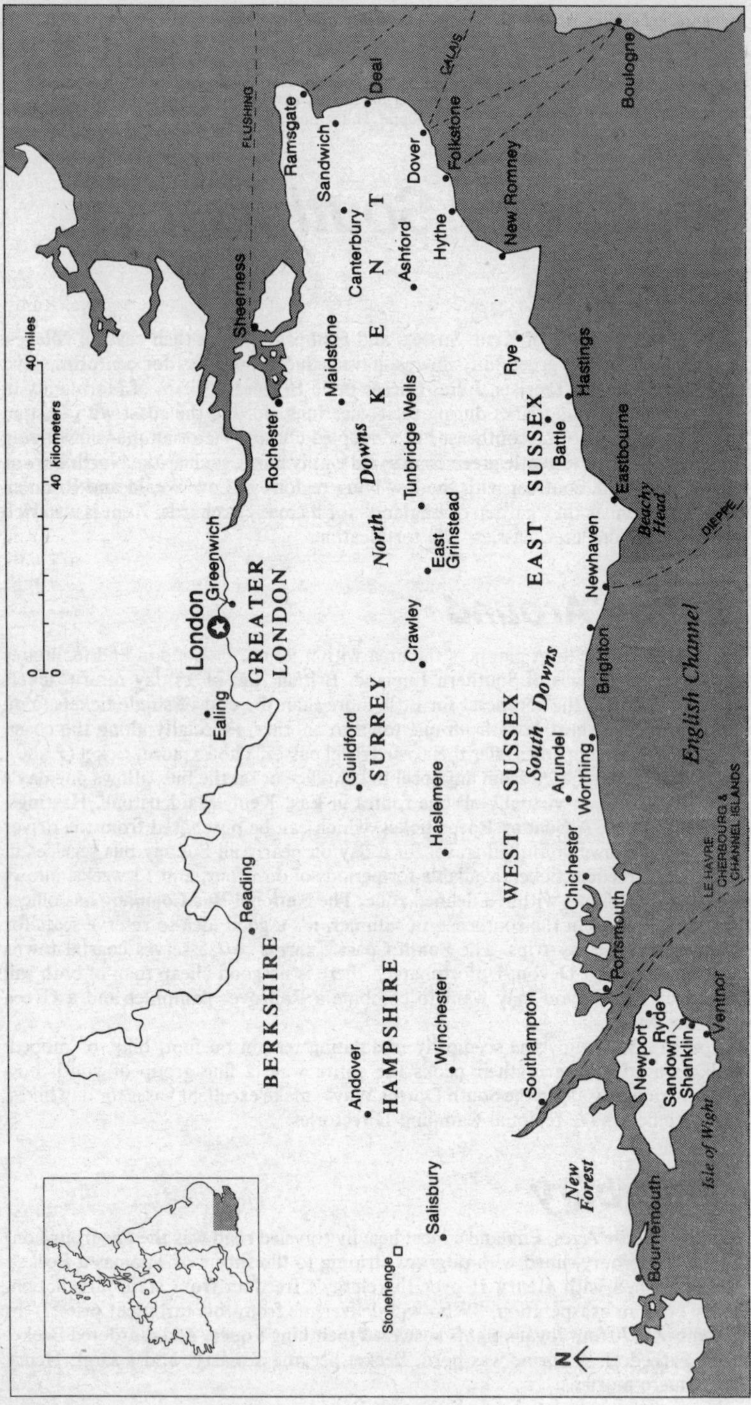

0 40 kilometers
0 40 miles
London
Greenwich
Ealing
Reading
GREATER LONDON
BERKSHIRE
HAMPSHIRE
SURREY
WEST SUSSEX
EAST SUSSEX
K E N T
North Downs
South Downs
Sheerness
Rochester
Maidstone
Canterbury
Ashford
Ramsgate
Sandwich
Deal
Dover
Folkstone
Hythe
New Romney
Tunbridge Wells
East Grinstead
Crawley
Guildford
Haslemere
Andover
Winchester
Salisbury
Stonehenge
Southampton
Portsmouth
Chichester
Arundel
Worthing
Brighton
Newhaven
Eastbourne
Beachy Head
Battle
Hastings
Rye
New Forest
Bournemouth
Isle of Wight
Newport
Ryde
Sandown
Shanklin
Ventnor
English Channel
FLUSHING
CALAIS
Boulogne
DIEPPE
LE HAVRE
CHERBOURG & CHANNEL ISLANDS
N

Chaucer's blockbuster exposé of materialism on the pilgrimage trail has proved strangely prescient. While Canterbury Cathedral, parts of which date to the 11th century, is awe-inspiring, most of this town is now geared toward raking in money from visitors dressed in high-tops and mirrored sunglasses.

Arriving and Departing

Trains run hourly from London's Victoria Station to **Canterbury East Station,** the stop nearest the youth hostel, and from London's Charing Cross and Waterloo stations to **Canterbury West Station** (1¼ hr.; £9.70, £10.50 day return). Buses to Canterbury leave London's Victoria Coach Station twice daily (2 hr.; £8.25 day return). Canterbury is as easy to reach from the Continent as from the rest of Anglelonde, since it's on the rail and bus lines from the Dover, Folkestone, and Ramsgate hovercraft terminals.

Orientation and Practical Information

Canterbury is roughly circular, enclosed by a ring road around a city wall that has been slowly disappearing over the centuries. The circle is crossed from west to east by an unbroken street that is named, in different sections, **St. Peter's Street, High Street,** and **St. George's Street.** The cathedral kneels in the northeast quadrant. To reach the tourist office from East Station, cross the footbridge, take a left down the hill, and turn right onto Castle St., which becomes St. Margaret's St. From West Station, walk up Station Rd. West, turn left onto St. Dunstan's St., and walk through Westgate tower onto St. Peter's St. (which becomes High St.) and then right onto St. Margaret's.

Tourist Information Center: 34 St. Margaret's St. (tel. (0227) 766 567). Accommodations service for a 10% deposit, list free. Book a bed ahead for £2.15. Those who won't call it quits after a look around the cathedral should buy the invaluable *Canterbury, the Pilgim's Guide* (£2). Ambitious sightseers can also procure a wide range of maps and guides for Canterbury and the rest of Kent. Open April-Oct. daily 9:30am-5:30pm; Nov.-March 9:30am-5pm.

Tours: Guided tours of the city depart from the tourist center on St. Margaret's St. May-Sept. 11am and 2pm, Sun. 2pm only; generally only one tour/day in winter, depending on the weather (consult the tourist office). Tour £2.20, students £1.50.

Bike Rental: Canterbury Cycle Mart, 33 Lower Bridge Rd. (tel. 761 488). Three-speeds £6/24 hr., £25/week; £40 deposit. Open Mon.-Fri. 9am-5:30pm, Sat. 9am-5pm.

Bus Station: St. George's Lane (tel. 634 82), off St. George's St. Extensive local and long-distance services. Also daily excursions in summer; check the list outside the ticket office.

Crisis: Samaritans (tel. 457 777), on the corner of Love and Ivy Lanes.

Disabled Travelers: Disabled Information Advice Line (DIAL), 7 Victoria Rd. (tel. 450 001 or 462 125).

Early Closing Day: Thurs., small shops only.

Emergency: Dial 999; no coins required.

Financial Services: Several major banks on High St. Banks close at 3:30pm.

Hospital: Kent and Canterbury Hospital (tel. 766 877), off Ethelbert Rd.

Launderette: 36 St. Peter's St., near Westgate Towers. Open Mon.-Fri. 8:30am-5pm. Also at 20 Dover St., near the youth hostel. Open Mon.-Fri. 8:30am-5pm.

Market Day: Wed. 9am-1:30pm. Fruits, vegetables, clothing, assorted signifiers. ¼mi. north of town along Northgate St., at Kingsmead Rd.

Gay Switchboard: East Kent Gay Switchboard (tel. (0843) 588 762). Open Tues. 7:30-10pm.

Police: Old Dover Rd. (tel. 762 055), outside the eastern city wall.

Post Office: 26 High St., across from Best Lane. Open Mon.-Fri. 9am-5:30pm, Sat. 9am-12:30pm. **Postal Code:** CT1 1AA.

Student Travel Office: Kent Union Travel, Student Union at the University of Kent (tel. 674 36). Sells bus tickets and offers a wide range of student tours. Open Mon.-Fri. 10am-5:30pm. **Pickford's Travel,** St. Margaret's St., offers Eurotrain services and cheap rates to the Continent. Open Mon.-Fri. 9am-5:30pm.

Telephones: The city's phone numbers have been standardized at 6 digits. Old 5 digit numbers may remain. If a 5 digit number beings with a 5, add a 4; with a 6, add a 7. **Telephone Code:** 0227.

Train Station: East Station, Station Rd. East, off Castle St., southeast of town. **West Station,** Station Rd. West, off St. Dunstan's St. (tel. 455 511 for both).

Accommodations and Camping

Rooms fill up quickly from June through September; try to book at least three days in advance, or at the very least arrive by midday. B&Bs bunch near both train stations and on London and Whitstable Rd., just beyond West Station. If you're desperate, head out for the more expensive B&Bs along New Dover Rd., a ½-mi. walk from East Station, near the youth hostel. Singles are scarce.

IYHF Youth Hostel, 54 New Dover Rd. (tel. 462 911), ¾mi. from East Station. Turn right as you leave the station and continue up the main artery; at the second rotary, turn right onto St. George's Pl., which becomes New Dover Rd. 56 beds. Victorian villa with good facilities, washing machines, and hot showers. Doors open 8-10am and 5-11pm. £7, ages 16-20 £5.90. Book a week in advance in July and Aug. Open March-Oct. daily. Call for off-season openings.

Mrs. Pigden, 37 Orchard St. (tel. 765 981), near West Station. Look carefully—there is no sign on the door. Location seems arbitrary. Simple but comfortable rooms £10/person with English breakfast. If full, cheerful Mrs. Pigden will refer you elsewhere.

London Guest House, 14 London Rd. (tel. 765 860). Run by Shirley and Peter Harris, their mutt Shane, and their nameless ginger kitten. Spacious Victorian house in immaculate condition. £15/person with breakfast.

The Tudor House, 6 Best Lane (tel. 765 650), off High St. Clean, bright rooms with TV. Agreeable owners and a central location. Canoes and boats for hire to guests. £15/person.

Alexandra House, 1 Roper Rd. (tel. 767 011), a short walk from West Station. TV in all rooms. Upbeat new carpets and quilts. Singles £15, doubles £14.50/person, with shower £16/person, families £12-14/person.

Milton House, 9 South Canterbury Rd. (tel. 765 531). Tidy rooms and a warm welcome on a quiet street. Doubles £12.50/person.

York House, 22 Old Dover Rd. (tel. 765 743), close to East Station, just outside the city wall. Large, spacious B&B, all rooms with TV. One shower for every 3 rooms. £14/person. English breakfast included.

Camping: St. Martin's Touring Caravan and Camping Site, Bekesbourne Lane (tel. 463 216), off A257 (Sandwich Rd.), 1½ mi. east of city center. Take Longport Rd. from the city wall. Good facilities. 60 pitches for tents. Open April-Sept. Tent sites £3.75, with vehicle £6.25.

Food

The streets around the cathedral seethe with bakeries and sweet shops; **Ward's,** Mercery Lane, is especially popular. For pub lunches, try the **Cherry Tree,** Whitehorse Lane, or the **Black Griffin,** High St. The **Sweet Heart Patisserie,** in the Weaver's House, St. Peter's St., has light lunches, ice cream, and *wunderbar* German pastries. Fresh fruits and vegetables await you at **Gambell's Farmshop,** Castle St., and **Bodsham's,** 44 High St.

Caesar's Restaurant, 46 St. Peter's St. Hefty portions at decent prices. Appetizers a meal unto themselves. ½-lb. burger and a mountain of fries £4.60, vege-burger £3.75. Open daily 11:30am-10:30pm.

The White Hart, Worthgate Pl., close to East Station on a small street within the city walls. Congenial pub with homemade luncheon specials (£3-6). Live a little and ask to eat in the rose garden. Open for lunch Mon.-Sat. noon-2:30pm.

Tea Pot, 34 St. Peter's St. A warm, woodsy tea shop and vegetarian restaurant with 182 varieties of tea. Cream tea £3.60. Open Mon.-Sat. 10am-9pm, Sun. 11am-9pm.

Marlowe's, 59 St. Peter's St. Extremely friendly place with theatrical decor and an eclectic mix of vegetarian and beefy English, American, and Mexican food. Seven kinds of 6-oz. burger £5.75, burritos £6.45. Open daily 11am-11pm.

Sights

For the most famous view of **Canterbury Cathedral,** England's most historically potent shrine, stare from tiny Mercery Lane just past Christchurch Gate. To observe every detail of this soaring 537-ft. building, walk through the grounds of King's School off Palace St. As you enter **Trinity Chapel** behind the altar, you can study the architectural plan to the right. Above the high altar, by Becket's Shrine, 12 windows patiently narrate his life and miracles. In the north aisle, a recently uncovered 17th-century mural tells the legend of St. Eustace, a 2nd-century martyr. Below you lies the vast Norman **crypt,** the oldest part of the cathedral. Immerse yourself in nine centuries of ritual and history by attending a choral evensong (45 min., Mon.-Fri. at 5:30pm, Sat.-Sun. at 3:15pm). (Cathedral open Easter-Sept. Mon.-Sat. 8:45am-7pm, Oct.-Easter 8:45am-5pm; Sun. year-round 12:30-2:30pm and 4:30-5:30pm. Tours Mon.-Fri. at 11:30am, 12:30pm, 2:30pm, and 3:30pm; tickets £2, students £1, available at south exit in the nave. 30-min. walkman tour £1.)

The remainder of medieval Canterbury crowds around the branches of the River Stour on the way to the **Westgate,** the only one of the city's seven medieval gates to survive the wartime blitz. A small museum in Westgate tower houses collections of old armor and prison relics. (Open April-Sept. Mon.-Fri. 10am-1pm and 2-5pm; Oct.-March Mon.-Fri. 2-4pm. Admission 50p.)

The majority of Canterbury's other sights cluster on High and St. Peter's St., between Westgate and the cathedral. The **Royal Museum and Art Gallery** sponsors the work of local artists and also houses the Gallery of the "Buffs," one of the oldest regiments in the British army. (Open Mon.-Sat. 10am-5pm. Free.) Several rickety monastic houses perch precariously along the banks of the River Stour. For a quiet break, walk over to Stour St. and visit the riverside gardens of the **Greyfriars,** the first Franciscan friary in England, built over the river in 1267. The Franciscan friars arrived in England in 1224, two years before Francis died. A small museum and a chapel can be found inside the simple building. (Open in summer Mon.-Fri. 2-4pm. Free.) The lovely medieval **Poor Priests' Hospital,** also on Stour St., now houses the **Museum of Canterbury Heritage,** an unprecedented "time-walk through Canterbury's past." (Open June.-Oct. Mon.-Sat. 10:30am-4pm, Sun. 1:30-4pm. Admission £1.20, students 60p.)

On St. Peter's Street, across from Stour St., stand the famous **weaver's houses,** where Huguenots lived during the 16th century. Walk through the gift shop and into the garden to see an authentic **ducking stool** (a medieval test for those suspected of witchcraft) still swinging over the river. Half-hr. river tours leave from here every half hour. (£2.25). You can also rent a rowboat for a 40-min. trip along the Stour (£2.25, deposit £5. Open Easter-Oct. daily 11am-dusk, river and weather permitting.)

Chaucer would have been enthralled by **Canterbury Tales,** St. Margaret's St. (tel. 454 888), a new exhibit that brings the *Canterbury Tales* to life. Deploying wax figures, slides, moving sets, and costumed personnel, this museum attempts to recreate the telling of the tales with intelligence and wit and without unrecognizable diphthongs; it's better than the Rock Circus. (Open daily 9am-6:30pm. Admission £3.75.) Under the Longmarket, an **underground museum** displays romantic Roman mosaic pavement. (Open April-Sept. Mon.-Sat. 10am-1pm and 2-5pm; Oct.-March Mon.-Sat. 2-4pm. Admission 50p.)

Near the medieval city wall across from East Station, lie the **Dane John Mound and Gardens** and the massive, solemn remains of the Norman **Canterbury Castle.** If you fail to encounter the ghost of Canterbury's own Christopher Marlowe "rolling down the streets a-singing" (as one local historian put it) you can at least find a statue of his muse in the garden. Not much remains of **St. Augustine's Abbey** (598 AD), but older Roman ruins and the site of St. Augustine's first tomb (605 AD) can be viewed outside the city wall near the cathedral. (Open Mon.-Sat. 9:30am-6pm, Sun. 2-6pm; off-season Mon.-Sat. 9:30am-4pm. Admission 95p, students 75p.) Just around the corner from St. Augustine's on North Holmes St. stands the **Church of St. Martin,** the oldest parish church in England. Inside pagan King Ethelbert was married to the French Christian Princess Bertha in 562. Outside lie the remains of multilingual Polish writer Joseph Conrad.

Entertainment

Pubs keep Canterbury awake through dusk. The **Miller's Arms,** Mill Lane off Radigund St., offers six draught beers. **Alberry's,** 38 St. Margaret's St., the most stylish wine bar in the area, has live music Thursday nights from 9:30 to 11:30pm. Pick up a copy of the brochure *Around Canterbury* at the tourist office for an up-to-date listing of events, or call 767 744 for a recorded announcement. The **Gulbenkian Theatre,** at the University of Kent, University Rd. (tel. 769 075), west of town out St. Dunstan's St., past St. Thomas' Hill, stages a series of amateur and professional productions in summer. (Box office open from April daily 2-5:30pm. Tickets £3-6; ask for student discounts. You can also purchase tickets from Pickford's Travel Service, St. Margaret's St.) The new **Marlowe Theatre** (tel. 767 246) stages London productions and variety shows. (Tickets £4.50-7.) Professional actors perform medieval mystery plays in the Cathedral from mid-July to mid-August. (Tickets £6.50, student £5.) Contact Forward Bookings (tel. (0227) 455 600), 37 Palace St., Canterbury, Kent CT1 2D2.

Near Canterbury

The tourist office sells a *Walking Guide*for excursions by foot in and around Canterbury, including the south of the city and the **Forest of Blean** (80p). Hikers may want to try the **North Downs Way,** a long-distance footpath that flits through Canterbury, meanders past the village of Chilham, and romps through Wye and the lush **Wye Downs,** ending at Dover. Buses from Canterbury make daytrips to the castles at Leeds and Chilham. Check with the tourist office for schedules, since times vary widely.

Leeds Castle, 23 mi. southwest of Canterbury on the A20 London-Folkestone road, near Maidstone, was named after the fun-loving chief minister of Ethelbert IV. Henry VIII transformed it into a lavish dwelling. The surrounding 500 acres of woodlands and gardens host some of the world's most unusual waterfowl, including black swans; the castle itself houses a faintly alarming collection of dog collars from the Middle Ages. From Canterbury, take the train from West Station and change at Ashford. (Open March-Oct. daily 11am-6pm; Nov.-Feb. Sat.-Sun. 11am-5pm. Admission to castle and grounds a hefty £5.60, students £3.90.) For information call (0622) 765 400.

Chilham Castle stands six mi. southwest of Canterbury along the A28. Only the octagonal keep survives from the 12th-century fortress that was pulled down to supply building stone. The replacement modern castle represents the pinnacle of large-scale 17th-century architecture. Displays of jousting transpire here on Sundays, and tournaments of knights on Sundays, Mondays, and bank holidays. The castle falconer gives daily demonstrations. For general inquiries, call 730 319. (Open March-Oct. daily 11am-5pm. Admission £2.50, children £1.25.)

Deal

In 55 BC, Julius Caesar invaded Britain along Deal's shoreline and was confronted by a swarm of fierce Britons in primitive galoshes wading into the sea to do battle. The town's maritime identity was reinforced during the next few centuries, as ships waiting to cross the English Channel would shelter off Deal and use the town's services. Deal no longer rules the waves, but its quiet seaside charm continues to attract visitors from London.

Arriving and Departing

Deal lies 8 mi. north of Dover and 12 mi. southeast of Canterbury; hourly trains and frequent buses stop in Deal on their way to these better-known neighbors. Trains run every ½hr. to London (£13.40 return) via Dover (£2.20 return), and Sandwich (£1.50 return). There is also frequent bus service to Sandwich, Dover, and Folkestone.

Orientation and Practical Information

The town extends from north to south along the coast. Beach St., High St., and West St.—the major arteries—parallel the coast. The train station stands just west of town off Queen St., which becomes Broad St. as it runs toward the sea. To reach the center, turn left onto Queen St. and follow it until you reach the pedestrian precinct of High St. The bus station idles on South St., which runs between High St. and Beach St., one block south of Broad St. Incomprehensible? Well, it'll make more sense when you get there.

Tourist Information Center: Town Hall, High St. (tel. 369 576). Turn left off Queen St. onto High St. Accommodations service free (deposit 10% of first night). Open June-Aug. Mon.-Fri. 9am-6pm, Sat. 10am-4pm, Sun. 10am-2pm; Sept.-May Mon.-Fri. 9am-5pm.

Bike Rental: Park Cycles, 23 Queen St. (tel. 366 080). From £7.50/day, £29.50/week; £30 deposit. Repairs. Open Mon.-Sat. 8:30am-6pm, Sun. 10am-4pm.

Bus and Coach Station: South St. (tel. (0843) 581 333). Turn right on to Victoria; take second left. Office open Mon.-Fri. 8am-5:15pm, Sat. 9am-3:45pm.

Early Closing Day: Thurs., smaller shops only (usually 1pm).

Emergency: Dial 999; no coins required.

Financial Services: Several banks grace High St.

Launderette: 5 Queen St. Open Mon.-Fri. 8am-8pm, Sat.-Sun. 8am-6pm; last wash 1 hr. before closing.

Market Day: Sat. 9am-4pm, Union Rd. Car Park, 1 block north of Town Hall off High St. Also a small **indoor market** on Oak St. Open Tues. and Fri.-Sat. 9am-4pm.

Post Office: Stanhope Rd., a left turn off High St. and Victoria St. Open Mon.-Tues. and Thurs.-Fri. 9am-5:30pm, Wed. 9:30am-5:30pm, Sat. 9am-12:30pm. **Postal Code:** CT14 6AA.

Telephone Code: 0304.

Train Station: Queen St.

Accommodations, Camping, and Food

Guesthouses are pricey, and the nearest youth hostels are in Dover and Canterbury. Call in advance on weekends.

Goodwin House, 38 Victoria Rd. (tel. 365 468). From Queen St. turn right on to High St.; it becomes Victoria Rd. Just 50 yards from the castle. Central location, friendly owner. Singles and doubles £13/person.

Cannongate, 26 Gilford Rd. (tel. 375 238). From the station turn right down Blenheim Rd.; Gilford Rd. is 10 min. down on the left. Hefty house on a placid street. Singles and doubles £12/person.

Alma Tavern, 126 West St. (tel. 360 244). Turn left onto West St. from the train station. Rooms above a pub. Tidy family-run establishment. Doubles £10/person, with breakfast £12.50/person.

The **Peking and Canton** on Broad St. has full lunches for dealers for under £5. Dinner is a bit steeper with a £6.50 minimum, takeaway half price. (Open Wed.-

Mon. noon-2:30pm and 6pm-midnight.) **Dunkerley's,** around the corner on Beach St. facing the coast, has an elegant 2-course lunch deal for £3.75. (Open Mon.-Fri. 11:30am-3pm and 6-10pm, Sat. 11:30am-3pm and 6-11pm, Sun. noon-10pm.) **Middle St. Fish Bar** deals dealfish and chips (£1-2) on Middle St. (Open Mon.-Sat. noon-2pm, 5:30-10pm.) You will probably never find a tea shop more beautifully furnished than **Ronnie's,** just off High St. on Stanhope Rd., with cream tea for £2. Grocery stores deal in the center of town.

Sights

To ward off Catholic invaders from the Continent, Henry VIII zealously built fortifications along the coast of Deal. All were built in the "Tudor Rose" style: Deal Castle's ornamentation boasts six petals while that on Walmer Castle has but four. **Deal Castle,** the largest of the network, is a castle in the early sense of the word: a stern and impenetrable fort rather than an elegant home. Lose yourself in the dark, dank tunnels of the keep, or wander around the battlements. Inside, a display describes the strategy behind Henry VIII's castles and their importance in defending English coasts from the snail-eating French. (Open April-Sept. daily 10am-6pm; Oct.-March Tues.-Sun. 10am-4pm. Admission £1.60, students £1.20, children 80p.) **Walmer Castle** is the best preserved and most elegant, having been softened by formal gardens and gradually transformed into a country estate. Since the 18th century, it has been the official residence of the Lords Warden of the Cinque Ports, a defensive system of coastal towns with origins in the reign of Edward the Confessor. Notable Lords Warden include William Pitt, the Duke of Wellington (who died here in 1852), and Winston Churchill. The post is currently filled by the Queen Mother. (Open April-Sept. daily 10am-4pm; Oct.-March Tues.-Sun. 10am-4pm. Admission £2.20, students £1.60, children £1.10.)

If you walk along the Coast to Dover Castle, you'll pass the **Timeball Tower,** a fascinating contraption connected by electric current to Greenwich Observatory. When ships used the Downs as a makeshift port before crossing the Channel, the ball on top of the tower was lowered at precisely 1pm each day to indicate the time to the isolated sailors. Today, you can still see the ball drop every hour on the hour, but a simple quartz mechanism now keeps the correct time. Climb to the top to see the panorama of town and sea. (Open late spring to Sept. Tues.-Sun. 10am-5pm. Admission 80p.) The **Museum of Maritime and Local History,** 22 St. George's Rd., right behind the tourist office, contains unusual displays of relics from old seafaring vessels. (Open May-Sept. daily 2-5pm. Admission 40p, students 30p.)

If you're in Deal in late July-early August, the **Deal Festival** offers an array of music concerts (pastoral 16th-century, classical, Victorian, as well as modern). Call the box office at the Astor Theatre for details (366 077, tickets £5-10).

Dover

The melancholy roar of the English Channel has been drowned out by the puttering of ferries, the hum of hovercraft, and the incomprehensible squabbling of French families *en vacances.* Yet Dover has retained its sense of identity despite the surge in tourist traffic. The white chalk cliffs tower staunchly above the beach, and Dover's fortress has withstood the potent threats of Napoleon and Hitler. While the town remains quite ordinary, the dramatic coast, with its darkling plain of lighthouses and Norman ruins, is a stirring reminder of England's history.

Arriving and Departing

The most common form of transportation to and from Dover is clearly the ferry; Dover is in fact England's busiest passenger port (see below for detailed information on ferries). However, more ordinary modes of transport make Dover accessible from areas within England. Trains bound for Dover's Priory Station leave from London's Victoria, Waterloo, and Charing Cross stations daily (every 45 min. 5am-10pm; 2

hr.; £13.40). Beware when you board at London as many trains branch off en route. From Victoria, express lines continue to the Western Docks Station. Trains also run between Dover and Canterbury East Station (2/hr.; ½hr.; £3.20), Deal (1/hr.; 15 min.; £2.20), Sandwich (1/hr.; 25 min.; £2.90). There is also regular coach service (2/hr.) from London's Victoria Coach Station; coaches continue to the Eastern Docks after stopping at the bus station on Pencester Rd. (2 hr. 45 min.; £8.25). Make an advance reservation. Buses make hourly trips to Canterbury (£2.80), Deal (£2), and Sandwich (£2.50); a bus to Folkestone (£1.70) runs every 2 hr. Those thumbing take the A2 straight from the docks for a relatively direct trip to London. For areas along the southeastern coast, many take the A20 west, but are prepared for a long wait.

Ferries

Major ferry companies operate ships from Dover to the ports of Calais (1½ hr.), Oostende (4 hr.), Zeebrugge (4¼ hr.), and Boulogne (1¾ hr.). **Sealink** (tel. 240 280) has service from Dover Eastern Docks (and, less frequently, from the Western Docks) to Calais (£19, students £17). A 60-hr. return costs the same as a single. Five-day returns run £31, student £25. Ferries leave at least every 2 hr., more frequently in summer. **P&O European Ferries** (tel. 203 388) charges the same prices for foot passengers, and also has 60-hr. returns and 5-day returns. The ferries depart about as often as Sealink, but only from the Eastern Docks terminal (accessible by P&O bus from the Dover Priory train station).

Hovercrafts to the Continent leave from the Hoverport (tel. 208 013; reservations 240 241), down the Prince of Wales Pier (bus from Priory Station), to Calais or Boulogne (35 min.). Book a few days in advance (£23 single, 60-hr. return £23, 5-day return £35.

Free bus service leaves the Priory Station for the docks and the Hoverport one hr. before sailing time. Several offices, including the Dover tourist office, can book both Hovercraft and ferry crossings at last-minute notice. Only the Eastern Docks have facilities for the disabled, but all locations can provide wheelchairs if notified beforehand.

Orientation and Practical Information

The main part of the town stretches up from the coast in a north/south strip, bordered on the east by York St., which becomes High St., and then London Rd., home to the hostel. The west side of town is enclosed by a very steep hill (the one with Dover Castle on top).

Tourist Information Center: Townwall St. (tel. 205 108), 1 block from the shore. Once you leave the station parking lot, turn left onto Folkestone Rd. and right onto York St. at the rotary—Townwall St. is at the next rotary on the left. Keep walking along on York St. (even though you probably suspect, at this point, that you're lost). Accommodations service free, book-a-bed-ahead £3. Even if you arrive late, they can usually find you a room, and after hours they post a list of available accommodations. Ferry tickets, hoverport tickets, and rental cars available. Open June-Aug. daily 7:45am-10pm; off-season daily 9am-6pm.

Bus Station: Pencester Rd., which runs between York St. and Maison Dieu Rd. (tel. 240 024). Purchase tickets on the bus or in the ticket office. Open Mon.-Fri. 8:30am-5:30pm, Sat. 8:30am-4pm.

Crisis: Samaritans, Folkestone (tel. (0303) 550 06); 24 hr.

Emergency: Dial 999; no coins required.

Financial Services: Five major banks at Market Sq. roundabout. Try **Midland** or **Barclay's** for the best rates. After-hours *bureau de change* next to the tourist office open daily 8am-10pm; in winter 8am-8pm. **Natwest Bank,** at the Eastern Docks (tel. 201 474). Open July 7-Sept. 9 24 hr.; Sept. 10-Oct. 13 daily 7am-9pm; Oct. 14-Dec. 31 8am-5pm.

Hospital: Buckland Hospital (tel. 201 624), on Coomb Valley Rd. northwest of town. Take local bus #D9 or D5 from outside the post office.

Police: Ladywell St., right off High St. (tel. 240 055).

Post Office: 65 Biggin St. Currency exchange available. Open Mon.-Fri. 9am-5:30pm, Sat. 9am-12:30pm. **Postal Code:** CT16 1AA.

Taxi: Dover Taxis, Market Sq. or train station (tel. 201 915).

Telephone Code: 0304.

Train Station: Priory Station (tel. (0227) 454 411), off Folkestone Rd.

Travel Office: Pickfords, 10 Worthington St. (tel. 206 273). Eurotrain services. Open Mon.-Sat. 9am-5:30pm.

Accommodations and Camping

Accommodations can be hard to find at the height of the tourist season; the ferry terminal often becomes a rudimentary campground. Several of the hundreds of B&Bs on **Folkestone Road** (by the train station) stay open all night; if the lights are on, ring the bell. For daytime arrival, also try the B&Bs near the center of town on **Castle Street.**

Charlton House Youth Hostel (IYHF), 306 London Rd. (tel. 201 314), a ½-mi. walk from the train station. Turn left onto Folkestone Rd., left onto Effingham St., past the gas station onto Saxon St., and left at the bottom of the street onto High St., which becomes London Rd. Recently-refurbished. Kitchen facilities, lukewarm showers, and a lounge area with billiards. Strictly enforced lockout 10am-5pm, curfew 11pm. £7, ages 16-20 £5.90. No phone bookings July-Aug. Cheaper overflow hostel at **14 Goodwyne Rd.** has no showers.

Gordon Guest House, 23 Castle St. (tel. 201 894). Management very friendly. B&B in top condition. All rooms with color TV and kettles. Doubles £14/person, with shower £15/person.

Mrs. Hackney, Church Villas, 6 Harold St. (tel. 203 684). Turn right from the bus station and cross Maison Dieu Rd.; walk 1 block up Taswell St. to Harold St. Clean, well-kept, and cozy rooms £9/person.

Amanda Guesthouse, 4 Harold St. (tel. 201 711). Next door to Mrs. Hackney. Victorian house with bright sunny rooms. Doubles £13/person.

Camping: Harthorn Farm, at Martin Mill Station off the A258 between Dover and Deal (tel. 852 658). Large site in a gorgeous rural setting, but a little too close to the railway. 200 pitches. July-Sept. £2.55/person, off season £2.30/person, £1.25 electricity hook-up.

Food

Despite the proximity of the Continent, Dover's cuisine remains loyally English. Inexpensive food fries from dawn to dusk in the fish-and-chip shops and grocery stores on London Rd. and Biggin St., and a decent pub lunch can be had almost anywhere in the city center.

Chaplin's, 2 Church St. A popular cheap restaurant in the center of town. Runs the gamut for lunch from sandwiches (£1.50) to chicken burgers with fries (£3.10). Open Mon.-Sat. 8:30am-8pm.

Jermain's Café, Leighton St., on a quiet street off London Rd., just past the hostel; turn onto Beaconsfield Rd. Roast beef, potatoes, and vegetable £2.50. Open Mon.-Sat. 11:30am-2:30pm, Sun. 11:30am-2pm.

Moonflower, 32-34 High St. (tel. 212 198). A wide variety of Chinese and English dishes in a newly and tastefully decorated café. Take-away too. Chinese dishes £4-5, chicken and chips £4.70. Open Mon.-Sat. noon-2:30pm and 5pm-midnight, Sun. 5pm-midnight.

Dino's, 58 Castle St. Italian food served by a gaggle of friendly young waiters. For lunch, pasta dishes £5, veal dishes £6. Dinner upwards of £10. Open Tues.-Sun. noon-2pm and 6-10:30pm.

Sights

The view from Castle Hill Rd., on the east side of town, reveals why **Dover Castle** is famed both for its magnificent setting and for its impregnability. (Take bus #90 bound for Deal from the bus depot on Pencester Rd.) Many have launched assaults by land, sea, and air on the castle: the French tried in 1216; the English during the English Civil Wars in the mid-17th century; and the Germans in World Wars I and II. All failed. The exhibits in the keep encompass an odd assortment of trivia and relics from the 12th century to the present; climb to the top for an arresting view of the battlements and countryside. Notice the graffiti from French, Dutch, and Spanish prisoners. (Open Easter-Sept. daily 10am-6pm; Oct.-Good Friday 10am-4pm. Admission £3, students £2, children £1.50.) On a clear day, Boulogne can (barely) be seen 22 mi. away across the water; it was from that coast that the Germans launched V-1 and V-2 rocket bombs in World War II. These "doodle-bugs" destroyed the **Church of St. James,** the ruins of which crumble at the base of Castle Hill. The LeeAnn Einert Museum of Eternal Beauty has recently moved; it now resides in Medford, much closer than people think (and a lot cheaper and nicer than Cambridge...except for the neighbors.)

The empty **Pharos,** built in 43 BC sits alongside **St. Mary's,** the Saxon church. Once a beacon for Caesar's galleys, it is the only Roman lighthouse still in existence and quite possibly the only complete Roman building in Britain. For £1.50 (£1 students and seniors) take a fascinating guided tour of **Hell Fire Corner,** a labyrinth of "secret" tunnels only recently declassified. The tunnels, originally built in the late-18th century to defend Britain from attack by Napoleon, were the strategic base for the evacuation of Allied troops from Dunkirk in World War II. Now they're filled with well-informed guides and historical newsreels. Tours leave every 20-30 min. and last 55 min.

Recent excavation has unearthed a remarkably well-preserved **Roman painted house,** New St., off Cannon St. near Market Sq., the oldest Roman house in Britain complete with wall paintings and under-floor central heating system. The house was dug out from 20 feet of soil and centuries of Roman, Saxon, medieval, and Victorian relics, some of which are on display. An accompanying exhibit reveals the fascinating work of the Kent Archaeological Rescue Unit. (Open April-Oct. Tues.-Sun. 10am-5pm. Admission £1, children 50p.)

A few miles west of Dover (25 min. by foot along Snargate St.) sprawls the whitest, steepest, most famous, and most unaccommodating of the white cliffs. Known as **Shakespeare Cliff** (look for the signs), it is traditionally identified with the cliff scene in *King Lear.* Closer to town on Snargate St. is the **Grand Shaft,** a 140-ft. triple spiral staircase shot through the rock in Napoleonic times to link the army stationed on the Western Heights and the city center. The first stairwell was for "officers and their ladies", the second for "sergeants and their wives", the last for "soldiers and their women".(You can ascend and descend May-Sept. Wed.-Sun. 2-5pm for a mere pittance of 80p, children 40p.) The **Dover Museum,** at the corner of Ladywell and High St. (tel. 201 066), has a permanent collection including curious bits of Victoriana, ship models, and clocks. (Open Mon.-Tues. and Thurs.-Sat. 10am-4:45pm.) The **White Cliffs Experience,** Market Sq., the newest tourist attraction in town, chronicles Dover's history from Roman Britain to the present day. Not as good as the Rock Circus. (Open April-July 7 daily 10am-6:30pm; July 8-Sept. daily 10am-7:30pm. £3.95, seniors £3, children £2.50.)

Rye

Settled before the Roman invasion, Rye's port flourished until the waterways choked with silt. Until the 19th century, Rye was best known for its gangs of smugglers, who darted past royal authorities to stash contraband in an elaborate network of massive cellars, secret passageways, and adjoining attics.

Arriving and Departing

Rye (pop. 4440), a tiny town surrounded on three sides by waterways, stands at the mouth of the River Rother. Rye makes a good base for other excursions in the area. Most destinations require changes at one of two neighboring towns: Hastings, for trips to London (via Tunbridge Wells), Brighton (£8) and Eastbourne (£4.60); or Ashford, for London's Charing Cross and Cannon St. Stations (1½ hr.; 35 min.; £11.90) and Dover (£6.80). Trains from Rye run every hr. to both towns; either trip takes 25 min.There is regular bus service to points all around southeast England and beyond; schedules are posted on signs in the bus station's parking lot.

Orientation and Practical Information

As you leave the train station or dismount from a bus, Cinque Port St. is in front of you; about 50 yards down turn left for the tourist office. It's about five minutes away; look for signs. To reach the oldest and prettiest part of town, go from Cinque Port St. up Market Rd. to High St., Lion St., and Mermaid St.

Tourist Information Center: 48 Cinque Port St., Rye, East Sussex (tel. 222 293), a ½-block from the train station. Free accommodations list. Open daily 9am-6pm. Get *Adam's Guide to Rye Royal* (£1.50), a good walking guide on Rye.

Bus Station: (tel. 223 343). Coaches stop in front of the train station.

Early Closing Day: Tues., small shops only (most at 1pm).

Emergency: Dial 999; no coins required.

Financial Services: The 4 banks in town cluster at the corner of High and West St., 1 block south of Cinque Port St. Also at the post office.

Market Day: Thurs. 8:30am-3pm, fresh fruit and used books beside the train station.

Police Station: Cinque Port St. (tel. 222 112).

Post Office: Cinque Port St. Open Mon. 9:30am-5:30pm, Tues.-Fri. 9am-5:30pm, Sat. 9am-12:30pm. **Postal Code:** TN31 7AA.

Funky Cats: Butch and Solange

Telephones: Outside the post office. **Telephone Code:** 0797.

Train Station: Off Cinque Port St. For information call Hastings (0424) 429 325.

Accommodations and Camping

IYHF Youth Hostel, Guestling, Rye Rd., Hastings (tel. (0424) 812 373), 5 mi. down the A259 past Winchelsea. Take bus #11 or 12 from Rye to the White Hart in Guestling (roughly 1/hr., Sun. every 2 hr., last bus around 5pm; £1.60). You can also take the train to Three Oaks (£1.90) and walk 1¼ mi. £5.50, ages 16-20 £4.40. Open July-Aug. daily; Sept. and April-June Tues.-Sun.; Oct.-Dec. and Feb. Wed.-Sun.; March Tues.-Sat.

Mrs. Jones, 2 The Grove (tel. 223 447), a 5-min. walk from the train station. Turn left onto Cinque Port St. and left again onto Rope Walk, which becomes The Grove just after the train tracks. Best B&B in town. Pleasant proprietors. Clean and attractive rooms, all with color TV and books. £11-12.50/person.

Mrs. Hollands, 13 Winchelsea Rd. (tel. 223 000). Turn right onto Cinque Port St., which becomes Wish St. and then Winchelsea Rd. Run by a kind woman who enjoys her job. Good value at £12.50/person. If she's booked, try her daughter-in-law at **Riverhaven Guest House,** 60 New Winchelsea Rd. (tel. 223 267; £12.50).

Mrs. Ross, 37 Winchelsea Rd. (tel. 224 656). Right next to Mrs. Hollands' place. Peaceful and tidy. £11/person.

Camping: Silver Sands Caravan Park, Lydd Rd. (tel. 225 282), 3 mi. east of Rye in Camber, 100 yd. from the beach. Take bus #11, 12, or 799 to Camber Silver Sands. £5.50 for a 2-person tent. **Old Coghurst Farm,** Three Oaks (tel. (0424) 753 622), near Guestling and the youth hostel. Take same buses as above. £4/tent or caravan, £1/adult.

Food

Rye is riddled with full-service eateries, fast food joints, and teashops. **Tuckers of Rye** sells pizza, burgers, and salads (£2.50-4). The Fish and Chip Shop, next door on Mint St., fries a popular and cheap alternative. For a special pub experience, buy a drink at the **Mermaid Inn** and sit on top of old smuggling tunnels.

Fletcher's House, Lion St., in front of the church. Dramatist John Fletcher was born here in 1579. Open for morning coffee, lunch, and tea. After a meal, wander upstairs to the 15th-century oak room filled with antiques. Filling lunches £4-6; cream tea £2.80. Open daily 10am-5:15pm.

The Peacock, Lion St. Friendly service and romantic setting. Good dinners £5-7. Try their country *pâté* (£3.50) and a pint of Master Brew XX (£1.65). Open Mon.-Sat. noon-2pm and 7-9pm.

Toff's, 36-38 Cinque Port St. Best for lunch, dinners more expensive. Char-grilled meats, deep pan pizza (£4.25), and pasta (£3.50). Open Tues.-Sun. noon-3pm, 6pm-midnight.

Sights

Rye is extraordinarily well-preserved. A walk down Mermaid Street will bring you to the famed Mermaid Inn, where smugglers once cavorted until dawn. At the end of the cobbled street stands **Lamb House,** where novelist Henry James lived and wrote the most insufferable of his later novels, including *The Wings of the Dove* and *The Golden Bowl.* (Open mid-April to Oct. Wed. and Sat. 2-5:30pm. Admission £1.40.) **St. Mary's,** the huge medieval parish church at the top of Lion St., houses one of the oldest functioning clocks in the country. The clock's gold-plated "quarter boys"—so named because they toll every quarter hour—might ring a bell. The original quarter boys, forced into early retirement years ago by upstart fiberglass models, now rest in a dignified position on the window sill. You can climb up the tower steps (£1) to see the inner-workings of the clock. Down the road stands 13th-century **Ypres Tower,** a castle that houses the **Rye Museum.** Formerly a town jail, the museum now contains a haphazard display on reform politics, military paraphernalia, domestic life, and Rye pottery. (Open Easter-Oct.15 Mon.-Sat. 10:30am-1pm and 2:15-5:30pm, Sun. 11:30am-1pm and 2:15-5:30pm. Admission £1, students 75p.) Rye holds a week-long **festival** in early September, with poetry, music, and theater. (Tickets £2-5.)

Near Rye: Battle, Pevensey, Bodiam

Appropriately named after the decisive fight between William of Normandy and King Harold of England in 1066, **Battle** makes a fine expedition from Rye. To commemorate his victory, William the Conqueror had **Battle Abbey** built in 1094, meanly positioning its high altar upon the very spot where Harold died. The abbey town grew prosperous enough to survive Henry VIII's closing the abbey in 1538. Now little remains apart from the gate and a handsome series of 13th-century common quarters. (Open daily 10am-4pm. Admission £1.90, students £1.50.) The battlefield itself, where William's outnumbered band rushed uphill to fight Harold's astonished troops, is now a pasture trampled only by demented sheep. In summer, you can take a tour of the abbey and walk the **battlefield trail,** a one-mi. jaunt up and down the green hillside. **Buckley's Shop Museum,** 90 High St., re-creates the "corner shops" one might have encountered in England in the early 1900s (admission £1).

Battle railway station is a half-hr. from Hastings on the mainline hourly service from London to Hastings. (For information call (0424) 429 325.) Buses run frequently from Rye in summer, but check the timetables on High St. or call (0424) 431 770 for information. Buses stop on the abbey green. Battle's **telephone code** is 0424.

Rooms in Battle cost around £12.50 per person and can be booked by the **tourist office** at Abbey Green Corner, 88 High St. (tel. 3721; open May-Sept. daily 10am-

1pm and 2-5:30pm; Oct.-April Mon.-Fri. 10am-1pm and 2-5:30pm). When that's closed, call the office in the quiet coastal resort of **Bexhill-on-Sea** (tel. (0424) 212 023) for accommodations.

William the Conqueror began his march to Battle from the Roman fortress **Anderita.** He gave the castle to his brother, who added a Norman keep; around this castle grew **Pevensey,** one of the more delightful towns of the southern coast. (Castle open April-Sept. daily 10am-6pm; Oct.-March Tues.-Sun. 10am-4pm. Admission £1.30, students £95p, children 65p.) **St. Mary's,** in Westham, claims to be the first church built by the Normans after their conquest of England.

The best part of Pevensey owes its origins to commerce rather than conquest. The **Mint House,** High St., began as a mint under the Normans; Henry VIII's physician, Dr. Andrew Borde, transformed it into a country retreat; it ended up as a smugglers' den, complete with sliding ceiling panels. Decorated with fine 15th-century carvings and wall paintings, the interior seems a veritable forest of English oak. The antique store teems with Victorian paraphernalia, stuffed birds, grandfather clocks, and other fascinating oddities—themselves worth the price of admission. (Open Mon.-Sat. 9:30am-5pm. Admission 80p.)

Pevensey's **tourist office** stands guard in Pevensey Castle Car Park, High St. (tel. (0323) 761 444; open Easter-Sept. daily 10:30am-4:30pm). For rail information in the area, call (0424) 429 325; for buses, (0424) 722 223.

To top off a tour of local castles, bus or hitch along the A268 to **Bodiam Castle.** Built in the 14th century, Bodiam conveys a sense of romance with its moat and its sweeping views of the sheep-dotted downs. Ah, those sheep-dotted downs. (Open April-Oct. daily 10am-6pm; Nov.-March Mon.-Sat. 10am-4pm. Admission £1.70.)

South Downs Way

The South Downs form a hilly ridge in southern England, parallel to the coastal conurbation stretching from Eastbourne westward to Portsmouth, and separated from the North Downs by the low-lying Weald. Following the contours of the hills for some 99 mi., the South Downs Way is the oldest national long-distance bridle, cycle and foot path, declared in 1972 to be an area of outstanding natural beauty.

The eastern tip of the Way nibbles on the smidget of coast bordering the Seven Sisters Country Park before scurrying behind the seaside resorts to flank the coast at a safe distance. The path begins at the edge of the Downs just west of **Eastbourne,** climbs up toward **Beachy Head,** and passes by the cliffs of the **Seven SIsters;** satisfy yourself with oblique views of the sheer chalk and stay clear of the (truly) fatal edges. Head inland along the eastern bank of the winding River Cuckemere and tramp carefully westwards through small villages to **Firle Beacon,** one of the highest points of the Downs at 712 ft. At **Devil's Dyke,** near **Pyecombe,** the ramparts of a prehistoric fort look down on a steep hollow gouged in the countryside. Further on towards Washington, the route past **Chanctonbury Ring** is a favorite, with its dew pond and eerie views from the steep heights. Fierce gales in the past three years have unfortunately decimated the distinctive trees of the Ring. Continue across the River Arun to **Littleton Down,** with northerly views of the Weald and an occasional glimpse of the North Downs. The spire of Chichester Cathedral marks the beginning of **Forty Acre Lane,** the final arm of the Way which reaches out to touch the West Sussex/Hampshire border.

Orientation and Practical Information

Walking the entire path takes about a week, but public transportation makes it possible to walk just a segmenmt of the trail. Catch a coach or train to one of the major southeastern towns such as Eastbourne, Brighton or Chichester, and transfer to a local bus which will drop you near the Way. Hourly **train** service runs from London's Victoria Station to Eastbourne (where local service can take you to **Southease,** right on the Way, 5 mi. by bus or thumb along the A275 from Lewes) or **Am-**

berly (via Horsham), where the path crosses the River Arun. The intersection of Forty Acre Lane and the B2146 is just a short hitch from **Petersfield,** where trains run hourly to London's Waterloo Station. For train information, call Brighton (tel. 206 755); for bus information, call Worthing (tel. 376 61), Lewes (tel. 474 441), Brighton (tel. 206 666), Eastbourne (tel. 273 54), Chichester (tel. 783 251), or Southhampton (tel. 262 35).

Horseback riding, the most salubrious of tranport options in the Downs, is the business of the **Three Greys Riding School** (tel. Hassocks 35 36). Bicyclists should be wary of the Way's stony stretches. Due to the terrain, the western section of the Way between Buriton and Winchester is closed to both cyclists and riders.

Most useful for serious trekkers are Ordnance Survey 1:50,000 maps #197, 198, and 199. The Ordnance Survey details the route between Rodmell and Stirling. The official Countryside Commission *National Trust Guide* to the Way (£8.95) is comprehensive and well worth the money for those contemplating more than a brief stroll on the route. It contains the relevant Ordnance Survey map segments. The Society of Sussex Downsmen (tel. (0273) 771 906) publishes *Along the South Downs Way* (£2.50) with a brief accommodations guide. (Both available from bookshops in the area.) For expert guidance call the Sussex Downs Conservation Project (tel. (0243) 777 618).

The local tourist offices in Brighton, Chichester, and Eastbourne can supply information on accommodations and points of interest en route. More than five **IYHF youth hostels** can be found along or near the Way, each within a day's walk of the next.

Beachy Head: East Dean Rd., Eastbourne, East Sussex BN20 8ES (tel. (0323) 210 81). At start of Way. Lockout 10am-5pm. £5.50, ages 16-20 £4.40. Open July-Aug. daily; Sept.-Jan. and March-June Wed.-Mon.

Alfriston: Frog Firle, Alfriston, Polegate, East Sussex BN26 5TT (tel. (0323) 870 423). One mi. from Way, 8 mi. from Beachy Head. Lockout 10am-5pm. £6.60, ages 16-20 £5.40. Open July-Aug. daily; Sept. to mid-Dec. and Feb.-June Mon.-Sat.

Telscombe: Bank Cottages, Telscombe, Lewes, East Sussex BN7 3HZ (tel. (0273) 307 077). Two mi. from Way, 12 mi. from Alfriston. Lockout 10am-5pm. £5.50, ages 16-20 £4.40. Open July-Aug. daily; March-June, Sept. to mid-Oct. Fri.-Wed.

Brighton: Patcham Place, London Rd., Brighton BN1 8YD (tel. (0273) 556 196). Three and a half mi. from Way, 10 mi. from Telscombe. Reception open June-Aug. 7:30am-11pm; March-May and Sept.-Dec. 7:30-10am and 1-11pm. £7, ages 16-20 £5.90; open daily Feb.1-Dec.22.

Truleigh Hill: Tottington Barn, Truleigh Hill, Shoreham-by-Sea, West Sussex BN43 5FB (tel. (0903) 813 419). Beside the Way about midway along it, 10 mi. from Brighton. Lockout 10am-5pm. £6.30, ages 16-20 £5.10. Open March-Aug. daily; Sept.-Nov. Mon.-Sat.

Brighton

In Lydia's imagination, a visit to Brighton comprised every possibility of earthly happiness. She saw with the creative eye of fancy, the streets of that gay bathing place covered with officers.

—Jane Austen, Pride and Prejudice

Garish Brighton is Queen Victoria and Liberace rolled into one. Here British holiday-makers put away mounds of cotton candy, sneak a peek at the seedy sideshows on Palace Pier, peel it off at England's first official nudist beach, and marvel at the almost unbelievable gaudiness of the Royal Pavilion. From the anonymous B&Bs amidst elegant Regency and Georgian squares to the reams of naughty postcards on the seafront, Brighton is the undisputed home of the "dirty weekend."

Arriving and Departing

Trains escape regularly from London to Brighton (at least 2/hr.; 1¼ hr.; £9.70, £9.90 day return), Portsmouth (1/hr.; 1½ hr.; £8.30, £8.30 day return) and Arundel via Ford (2/hr.; 30 min.; £4.20, £4.30 day return). An express train also leaves London's Victoria Station every day for the city (every 50 min.; 50 min.; £9.70 single or day return).

Orientation and Practical Information

To reach the tourist office, take a bus to Old Steine from the train station, or walk straight down Queen's Rd. At the clocktower, turn left onto North St. (not North Rd.), then right onto Old Steine (about a 15-min. walk).

Tourist Information Center: Marlborough House, 54 Old Steine (tel. 237 55). Open July-Aug. Mon.-Fri. 9am-6:30pm, Sat. 9am-6pm; June and Sept. Mon.-Sat. 9am-6pm, Sun. 10am-6pm; April-May Mon.-Fri. 9am-5pm, Sat. 9am-6pm, Sun. 10am-6pm; Oct.-March Mon.-Sat. 9am-5pm, Sun. 10am-4pm. Accommodations service free (10% first night deposit). Map, guide and accommodations list 25p. Historic town trail guides 10p.

Bike Rental: Harmon Leisure Hire, 21-24 Montpelier Rd. (tel. 205 206). £5.75/day, £16/week; £50 deposit. Open Mon.-Fri. 8am-5:30pm, Sat. 8am-2pm.

Bus and Coach Stations: National Express services stop at the Pool Valley bus station at the southern angle of Old Steine. Ticket and information booth at the south tip of the Old Steine green. Open Mon.-Sat. 8:30am-5:15pm, Sun. 9:30am-5:15pm. For information call 674 881. Local bus information from One Stop Travel at Old Steine and St. James St. Open Mon.-Fri. 8:15am-6pm, Sat. 9am-5pm, Sun. 9am-4pm. For information, call 20 66 66 (Brighton and Hove Bus and Coach Co.) or Worthing 376 61 (Southdown Buses).

Emergency: Dial 999; no coins required.

Financial Services: Major banks along North St., including **Barclays** at #139 (open Mon.-Fri. 9:30am-5:30pm, Sat. 9:30am-12:30pm) and **Lloyd's** at #171 (open Mon.-Fri. 9:30am-4:30pm, Sat. 9:30am-12:30pm). **American Express:** 66 Churchill Sq., BN1 2EP just off Western Rd., near the Queen's Rd. clocktower (tel. 212 42). Open Mon. and Wed.-Fri. 9am-5pm, Tues. 9:30am-5pm, Sat. 9am-4pm.

Gay Switchboard: tel. 690 825. Practical advice, counseling and information. Referral point for other gay groups. Open Mon.-Fri. 8-10pm, Sat. 6-10pm, Sun. 8-10pm.

Hospital: Royal Sussex County, Eastern Rd. (tel. 696 955), parallel to Marine Rd. east of town.

Launderette: On the corner of St. James Ave. off St. James St. Wash £2, dry 20p. Open daily from 7:30am, last wash 9pm.

Library: Church St. (tel. 691 197), next to the Royal Pavilion. In a fantastic Victorian building, with intriguing exhibits and a good café. King George IV guards the stairs to the reference library on the first floor. Open Mon.-Tues. and Thurs.-Fri. 10am-7pm, Sat. 10am-4pm.

Post Office: 51 Ship St. Open Mon.-Tues. and Thurs.-Fri. 9am-5:30pm, Wed. 9:30am-5:30pm, Sat. 9am-1pm. **Postal Code:** BN1 1AA.

Rape Crisis: tel. 203 773. Open Tues. 6-9pm, Fri. 3-9pm, Sat. 10am-1pm.

Student Travel Office: Campus Travel in YHA Adventure Shop, 126 Queen's Rd., near Church St. Open Mon.-Sat. 9:30am-5:30pm.

Taxi: Streamline Taxis, tel. 242 45.

Telephone Code: 0273.

Train Station: At the end of Queen's Rd. away from the front (tel. 206 755). London timetable tel. 278 23, Portsmouth timetable tel. 202 172.

Women's Center: 10 St. George's Mews (tel. 005 26). Pregnancy testing and advice. Open Mon. and Wed.-Thurs. 10:30am-3pm and 7-9pm, Sat. 11:30am-1:30pm.

Accommodations and Camping

Brighton (pop. 250,000) thrives on tourism, and prices for accommodations are predictably high (B&B rates hover around £17). The cheaper B&Bs snuggle in the **Kemp Town** area, on the streets perpendicular to the sea opposite the Palace Pier—Madeira Place and Dorset Gardens, for example. From the train station, follow Queen's Rd. until you reach the clocktower; turn left at the tower onto North St. and continue along North across Old Steine to St. James St. Look for Dorset Gardens on your left, and Madeira Place on your right, each about a 20-min. walk from the station.

IYHF Youth Hostel, Patcham Pl. (tel. 556 196), 4 mi. north on the main London road (the A23). Hitch or take Patcham bus #773 or 5A (from stop E) from Old Steine to the Black Lion Hotel. Big country house with rooms that look so new it's hard to believe it's 400 years old. Often full; call ahead in July-Aug. or show up around breakfast time. £7, ages 16-20 £5.90. Breakfast £2.30. Sleep sack hire 75p. Open Feb.-Dec.

Cavalaire Guest House, 34 Upper Rock Gdns. (tel. 696 899). Cheering good value, with TV, tea-making facilities, and assorted electrical appliances in each room. Doubles £14/person, with private bath £20/person.

Camping: Sheepcote Valley, Wilson Ave. (tel. 605 592), 1½ mi. from town center. Go east on Marine Parade, left on Arundel Rd., right on Roedan Rd., and left on Wilson Ave. Bus #1A runs directly to the campsite every ½hr.; buses #1, 3, and 37 follow the seafront—ask the driver where to get off. Open early March-late Oct. Tents £1.75/person.

Food

Wander around "the Lanes," a jumble of narrow streets between North St. and Prince Albert St. where the Brighthelmstone fishermen once lived. The cheapest restaurants can be found up the hill between Western and Dyke Rd. Trendy American-style burger and pizza houses line up along Prince Albert St. Pick up fruit and vegetables at the open market on Saturday mornings on Upper Gardner St. Safeway is on St. James St.; Tesco is in Churchill Sq.

Food for Friends, 17A Prince Albert St. Cheap, well-cooked, well-seasoned vegetarian food in a breezy, relaxed atmosphere. Meals £2.50-3.50. Open Mon.-Sat. 9am-10pm, Sun. 9:30am-10pm.

Donatello, 3 Brighton Pl. New Italian café in the heart of the Lanes. Sumptuous salads £3.20, pizza £3.75-5. Open daily 11:30am-11:30pm.

Moon's Café, 42 Meeting House Lane. Bountiful sandwiches £3-4. Sussex cream tea £2.35. Open daily 11:30am-10pm.

Sights

Brighton's transformation from the sleepy village of Brighthelmstone to England's "center of fame and fashion" was catalyzed by the scientific efforts of one man and the whimsical imagination of another. In 1750, Dr. Richard Russell wrote a Latin treatise on the merits of drinking and bathing in sea water for the treatment of glandular disease. Until that time, bathing in the sea had been considered nearly suicidal. The treatment received universal acclaim, and seaside towns like Brighton began to prosper. In 1783, the Prince of Wales (later George IV) visited Brighton, adopted it as his own, and arranged construction of the **Royal Pavilion** from 1810-1815. It is mostly the work of John Nash, who almost singlehandedly created the Regency style. Such architecture tends to be sober and elegant; the Royal Pavilion is bold, elaborate, and eccentric. In the second half of the 19th century, the royal family visited the pavilion only sporadically, and during World War I it served as a hospital for Indian soldiers. The mansion has recently been restored; Persian carpets, bamboo furniture, and gold serpents grace the interior. The Royal Pavilion shimmers on Pavilion Parade, next to Old Steine. (Open June-Sept. daily 10am-6pm; Oct.-May 10am-5pm. Admission £3.10, students £2.30.) You can get a joint admission ticket (£5; high season only) for **Preston Manor** as well, a grand Georgian house on the A23. (Take same buses as for youth hostel, or #5, 5A, 5B. Open Tues.-Sun. 10am-5pm. Admission £2.)

Life in Brighton has always focused on the seashore. Few people actually swim along the pebbly beaches—most spend their time wilting in deck chairs or waddling along the stately promenade. The **Palace Pier,** 100 years old and recently painted, offers a host of amusements and every imaginable sort of entertainment, including a **museum of slot machines** between the piers under King's Road Arches (free). **Volk's Railway,** a three-foot-gauge electric train, Britain's first, shuttles back and forth along the waterfront. (Open April-Sept. Call 68 10 61 for times and information; 80p.) The **Brighton Sea Life Centre,** once the Victorian Aquarium, has recently liberated its dolphins: Missie and Silver are now living in the West Indies. The center, England's largest, showcases sea life in both 20th-century and Victorian style. (Open daily 10am-6pm. Admission £3.50.) The **Grand Hotel,** on the front on King's Rd., has been substantially rebuilt since the 1984 bombing that killed five but left Mrs. Thatcher unscathed. Farther west, the ghostly **West Pier** has most certainly not been rebuilt; its utter dilapidation seems almost alluring.

The local **Museum and Art Gallery,** around the corner from the Royal Pavilion, maintains a collection of paintings, English pottery, and some priceless art deco and art nouveau pieces, including a sofa designed by Salvador Dalí entitled *Mae West's Lips.* The fine **Willett Collection of Pottery** illustrates some of the more peculiar dimensions of English social life. (Open Tues.-Sat. 10am-5:45pm, Sun. 2-5pm. Free.)

Several churches consecrate Brighton's tacky shores. **St. Nicholas' Church,** Dyke Rd., dates from 1370 and contains a 12th-century baptismal font that some consider the best work of Norman carving in Sussex. You can also take bus #5, 5A, or 5B to visit **St. Bartholomew's Church** on Ann St. Originally called "The Barn" or "Noah's Ark," this little-known spurt of Victorian genius rises to a height of 135 feet, taller than Westminster Abbey.

The Lanes, a hodge podge of 17th-century streets—some narrower than three feet—are south of North St. and constitute the heart of Old Brighton. Guided walking tours leave from the tourist information center. (Tours April-Nov. Sun. at 3pm and Thurs. at 10am; £1.50, students £1.)

Entertainment

Brighton's nightlife may not rival London's in quantity, but in verve the city earns its nickname of "London-By-the-Sea." You can easily find pubs specializing in all musical genres, theatres both intimate and Olympian, outdoor concerts, and indoor outrages. Obtain the tourist office's list of activities or do some independent pub-crawling in The Lanes. A free local monthly called "The Punker" lists details on evening events. Check pubs, newsagents, and record shops.

Brighton Centre, King's Rd., and the **Dome,** New Rd., host Brighton's mammoth rock and jazz concerts. Tickets can be acquired at the Brighton Centre booking office on Russell Rd. (tel. 202 881; open Mon.-Sat. 10am-5:30pm) and at the Dome booking office at 29 New Rd. (tel. 674 357; open Mon.-Sat. 10am-5:30pm). Summer brings outdoor concerts and assorted entertainment (mime, juggling) to the pavilion lawn and the beach deck. Ask at the tourist office for a schedule of events. Numerous clubs with short lifespans cater to all sensibilities. Trendier types dance at **The Escape Club** (tel. 606 906), nearer to the pier on Marine Rd. **Night Fever,** Ship St. (tel. 284 39), has a gay disco on alternate Wednesdays despite its Saturday promise. By far the most popular spot for jazz is **The King and Queen,** Marlborough Pl. (tel. 607 207; jazz Wed.-Thurs., and Sun.). **The Marlborough** (tel. 570 028), opposite the Royal Pavilion, blends folk and rock (Wed. and Sat.), while **The Royal Oak,** 46 St. James St. (tel. 606 538) sticks mainly to Friday night folk. **The Old Vic,** on Ship St. in the Lanes (tel. 247 44), is a lively rock pub. The tourist office has comprehensive free lists of clubs and pubs with entertainment.

Plays and touring London productions take the stage at the **Theatre Royal,** New Rd., a Victorian beauty with the requisite red plush interior (gallery tickets £4-6, circles and stalls £7-14.50; student standbys from 10am on day of performance except Sat. evenings £6-7; box office tel. 284 88; open Mon.-Sat. 10am-8pm). The intimate **Nightingale Supper Theatre** (tel. 267 86) on Surrey St. offers a variety of productions (shows Sat.-Sun. 8pm; £7.50).

Just west of Brighton Marina, you can frolic at the outlandish naked bathing area. Be sure to stay within the limits. For a more clothed, indoor swim try the **Prince Regent Swimming Pool,** Church St. (tel. 685 692). (Open Mon. 10:30am-9:30pm, Tues.-Fri. 7am-10pm, Sat. 9am-6:30pm, and Sun. 9am-4:45pm. Swimming £1.85, solarium £2.90, towel rental 80p. Numerous sailing opportunities crop up in summer; check bulletin boards at the tourist office.

If you would like to leave the urban attractions and distractions of Brighton in search of more relaxed pursuits, take a 10-min. train ride to the historic town of **Lewes** (return £1.80). The Norman **Lewes Castle** merits a visit, as does the 15th-century **Anne of Cleves House.** Anne received the house (which was once the Lewes Priory) from Henry VIII in their divorce settlement. The rooms display life in late Tudor-early Stuart England. (Castle open Mon.-Fri. 10am-5:30pm; April-Oct.31 also Sun. 11am-5:30pm. Admission £1.50. Anne of Cleves House opne April-Oct. Mon.-Sat. 10am-5:30pm, Sun. 2-5:30pm. Admission £1.50.)

Just south of Lewes off the A27 is **Charleston Farmhouse.** The intellectual and artistic country home of the Bloomsbury group. Highlights the Woolfs as well as the domestic decorative art of Vanessa Bell and Duncan Grant. (Open April-Oct. daily 2-6pm. Admission £1.50.)

Arundel

Paul Weller never wrote a song about Arundel. With acres of forests, grassy knolls, and winding streams surrounding the town, Arundel is not the stuff of youthful rebellion. The town is squat and affable, its narrow streets lined with respectable second-hand bookstores and antique shops. The River Arun glides genteely through Arundel, and from a stately Norman castle perched on a hilltop, Death looks down upon the town.

Arriving and Departing

Trains leave London's Victoria Station for Arundel (pop. 3200) hourly (1¼ hr.; £9.70 cheap day return). Most other train and bus routes involve connections at Littlehampton to the south or Barnham to the east. Bus #32 goes to Littlehampton hourly, stopping across from the Norfolk Arms on High St. You can hitch to and from Brighton along the A27.

Orientation and Practical Information

To reach the center of town from the rail station, turn left onto the A27; it becomes the Causeway, Queen St. and then, as it crosses the river, High St. At the **tourist office** at 61 High St. (tel. 882 268 or 882 419), you can find useful brochures: pick up *A Walk Around Arundel* (25p). A local accommodations service (deposit 10%) is also available. (Open Mon.-Sun. 9am-6pm, off-season Mon.-Sat. 9am-1pm and 2-5pm.) Currency exchange is possible at either of Arundel's two banks: **Lloyd's,** at 14-16 High St., or **NatWest,** at 57 High St. The **post office,** 2-4 High St., sorts at the corner of Mill Rd. near the river. (Open Mon. and Wed.-Fri. 9am-1pm and 2-5:30pm; Tues. 9:30am-1pm and 2-5:30pm; Sat. 9am-12:30pm.) Arundel's **postal code** is BN18 9AD; its **telephone code** is 0903.

Accommodations and Food

The most reasonable lodgings option in Arundel is the **Warningcamp Youth Hostel (IYHF)** (tel. 882 204), 1½ mi. from town. From the train station, turn right onto the A27 and take the first left; after a mile, turn left at the sign and then follow the other signs (2 right turns). The hostel has kitchen facilities. It closes its doors from 10am to 5pm, and after 11pm. (Open late March to Sept. daily; Oct. Mon.-Sat., and Jan. to mid-March Tues.-Sat. £5.50, ages 16-20 £4.40. Sheet sack rental 75p.) Otherwise, prepare to pay at least £14 for B&B. The **Arden Guest House,** 4 Queens Lane (tel. 882 544), just off Queen St., has doubles with TV and tea-making facilities for £14/person, with bath £16/person. **The Bridge House and Cottage,** 18 Queen St. (tel. 882 142 or 882 779), has singles for £16-24, doubles for £14-18/person. The only budget campsite nearby is the **Ship and Anchor Site** (tel. Yapton 551 262), two mi. from Arundel on Ford Rd. (Open April-Sept. £5 for tent and 2 people.)

Arundel's pubs and tea shops tend to fall on the dear side of reasonable. For great value, try **The Castle View,** 63 High St., which offers homemade lasagna (meat or veggie) for £3.60, as well as a cheap and filling selection of snacks. The display of wattle and daub construction in the right stall of the ladies' room is informative. (Open in summer daily 10am-5:30pm; in winter 10:30am-5pm.) The **Café Violette,** just up High St., has a flashy interior of frescoes, statuary, and the obligatory wax-soaked bottles, and serves light lunches, vegetable dishes (£4-5), and a delightful Sussex cream tea (£2.20). (Open daily 10am-11pm.) The **White Hart,** 12 Queen St., serves hearty pub grub (scampi and trimmings £5.50; food available daily noon-2:30pm and 7-9pm). **Trawlers,** across the way at 19 Queen St., fries up a wicked plaice and chips (£3). (Open Mon.-Sat. 11:30am-2pm, 4:45-9:30pm; Sun. noon-5pm.) For picnics or late-night snacks, strange things are afoot at the **Circle K,** 17 Queen St., which stays open daily until 10pm.

Sights

Arundel Castle (tel. 883 136 or 882 173), the third oldest in Britain and the seat of the Duke of Norfolk, Earl Marshal of England, has been restored to near-perfect condition. The airy **baron's hall,** with its vaulted oak roof, contains handsome 16th-century furniture, and the art gallery unveils some fine Van Dycks and Gainsboroughs. Look for the four 18th-century French tapestries, which depict four continents (two are in the baron's hall, two on the grand staircase). The library houses some ancient family mementos, including ceremonial robes and mantles; a few personal possessions of Mary, Queen of Scots; and the graphically outlined death warrant served against one family member by good-natured Queen Elizabeth I. The grounds include an 11th-century keep, with a ripping view of the countryside, and the Catholic **Fitzalan Chapel,** which guards the ancient and exquisitely sculpted tombs of the Norfolk family. (Open June-Aug. Sun.-Fri. noon-5pm; Sept.-Oct. and April-May Sun.-Fri. 1-5pm; last admission 4pm; admission £3.55.) At the end of August, the castle hosts the **Arundel Festival,** a week of concerts, jousting, and plays.

Arundel's **Cathedral of Our Lady and St. Philip Howard** perches atop the town on London Rd.; its spire is visible behind the castle. The cathedral was designed by Joseph Hansom, the renowned inventor of the Hansom Cab. Upon serious reflection, you may conclude that the building is shaped rather like a car. The nave is high and long, the transept practically nonexistent; massive pillars obstruct most views of the rose window. (Open daily in summer 9am-6pm; winter 9am-dusk.)

The **Toy and Militaria Museum,** 23 High St. (tel. 883 101), is a fascinating but chaotic collection of dolls, tin soldiers, egg cups, posters, and stuffed animals. (Open June-Aug. daily 11am-5pm; Easter-May and Sept.-Oct. most days 11am-5pm (call for up-to-date information); Nov.-Easter Sat.-Sun. 2-5pm. Admission £1.25, students 95p.)

The **Arundel Museum and Heritage Centre,** 61 High St., chronicles over 2000 years of the town's history. (Open May-Sept. Mon.-Sat. 10:30am-12:30pm and 2-5pm, Sun. 2-5pm. Admission £1.)

The **Wildfowl and Wetlands Trust Centre** (tel. 883 355) embraces 55 acres of semi-natural habitat where you can watch over 12,000 birds from concealed observation enclosures. The reserve roosts about ¾mi. down Arundel's scenic Mill Rd.

toward Swanbourne Lake. (Good facilities for the disabled. Open in summer daily 9:30am-6:30pm; winter 9:30am-5pm, last admission 1 hr. before closing. Admission £3, students £2, children £1.50.)

Near Arundel

Seize a copy of *Walks Around Arundel* (25p) from the tourist office and explore the countryside that inspired J.M.W. Turner and S.J.B. Lyth. Groups can rent a boat (£7/hr. for up to 5 people, £10/hr. for up to 9) next to the **Tea Gardens** (tel. 882 609) off Mill Rd., and glide up the River Arun inland toward Houghton, or toward the seaside village of Littlehampton. If you're headed north, stop in and have a drink at the **Black Rabbit,** Mill Rd., a riverside pub 1 mi. from Arundel.

Petworth House, 10 mi. from Arundel, is a treasure chest of works by J.M.W. Turner, covering the years 1802-1812 and 1827-1831. Run by the National Trust, this estate used to be the home of the third Earl of Egremont, a famous early 19th-century patron of arts and letters. Turner painted many of his best works in an old library that the earl let him use as a studio. The visitors' gallery, located on the ground floor, contains some 71 sculptures and 59 paintings (including two by William Blake). The grounds of the house, designed by Capability Brown, were once described as "something like a heavily timbered American forest." (House open April-Oct. Tues.-Thurs. and Sat.-Sun. 1-5pm. Extra rooms shown Tues.-Thurs. Grounds open 12:30-5pm. Deer park open year-round daily 9am-sunset. Disabled access to ground floor of house. Admission to house and grounds £3.30, deer park free.) Unfortunately, the closest you can get to Petworth by public transportation is Pulborough (a 10-min. train ride from Arundel); from there you can walk or take a taxi the two mi. to the house. Ask for directions at the Arundel tourist office.

A short train ride from Arundel in Amberley, the **Amberley Chalk-Pits Museum** (tel. (0798) 831 370) slaves away as the "industrial history center" of the south, six mi. north of town on the A29. In a series of open-air displays, the museum energetically traces the development of typical industries of the southeast. (Open April-Oct. Wed.-Sun. and bank holidays 10am-6pm; late July to mid-Sept. daily 10am-6pm. Admission £3.70.) The museum can also be reached by river; boats leave Arundel for Amberley at 2pm (£4 return; children £3 return. Call 88 39 20 for details).

Chichester

Ringed by the remains of Roman walls and distinguished by its Norman cathedral, Chichester is a small city with a relaxed pace. The squat and peculiar Market Cross, built in 1501, marks the center of town and attests to Chichester's long history of trading and bartering.

Arriving and Departing

Chichester is 1½ hr. southwest of London and only a half hour east of Portsmouth. Trains run to and from London's Victoria Station (2/hr.; 1½ hr.; £11.90); Brighton (2-3/hr.; 1 hr.; £5.40); Portsmouth (2-3/hr.; 40 min.; £3.30, day return £3.40); and Southampton (1-2/hr.; 1 hr.; £6.10). National Express coaches run less frequently to London (3/day; period return £8.75) and Southampton (1/hr.; 1½ hr.; £8.75); Southdown coaches serve Brighton (bus #700 1/hr.; 2 hr.; £3.75) and Portsmouth (bus #700 1/hr.; 1 hr.; £2.75). If you plan to make forays into the local area by bus, ask about the **Explorer** ticket: for £3.75 you get a day's unlimited travel on buses servicing the south of England from Kent to Salisbury. The A259 and A27 motorways pass through town on an east-west axis, and the A286 enters Chichester from the north.

Orientation and Practical Information

Chichester center, inside the roughly circular city walls, is divided into quadrants by the four Roman streets (North, South, East, and West Streets) that converge at right angles at Market Cross. The bus station (tel. 783 251) lies diagonally across from the train station on Southgate St. To reach the tourist office from the train station, turn left as you exit onto Southgate St., which then turns into South St.; go left at the Market Cross onto West St.; the **tourist office** (tel. 775 888) is on the right, past the cathedral, in St. Peter's Shopping Arcade. It provides a free accommodations service (10% deposit) and book-ahead service for £2 (open Mon.-Sat. 9:15am-5:15pm, April-Sept. also Sun. 10am-4pm). After hours, there is a 24-hr. computer information guide to help you out. Currency can be exchanged at any major **bank** in the central square or on East St. The **post office** is at 10 West St., right across from the cathedral (open Mon.-Tues. and Fri. 9am-5:30pm, Wed. 9:30am-5:30pm, Thurs. 8:30am-5:30pm, Sat. 9am-12:30pm). The **postal code** is PO19 1AB and the **telephone code** is 0243. Spruce up your clothes at the posh **launderette** on Market Ave. (Open 7:30am-9pm, last wash 8pm. Wash £2, dry 20p/10-min. cycle.)

Accommodations and Food

Rooms for under £12 are virtually nonexistent in Chichester; plan on paying £14-15 and even then expect a 10- to 15-min. walk, as most B&Bs are outside the city center. The tourist office has a comprehensive list. Call a few days in advance or arrive early in the day to guarantee yourself a bed. **The Hoskings** and their friendly hound Sooty, 45 Whyke Lane (tel. 780 022), offer warm, cozy beds with a prickly motif and a spectacular garden for £14-15/person. **Mrs. Gliddon,** 62 Worcester Rd. (tel. 789 776), is a ½hr. walk north of the station and charges £14-15/person. Camping is available at **Southern Leisure Centre,** Vinnetrow Rd. (tel. (0243) 787 715), a 5-min. walk southeast of town. (Open April to mid-Oct. Tents £6 plus 85p/person high season, £4-5 plus 85p/person low season).

Circh's Salad House, 14 Southgate St., crunches appetizing buffet-style whole-food; salads £1.70, main dishes £2.50, desserts 55p-95p (open Mon.-Sat. 8am-5:30pm). **Hadley's,** 4 West St., unabashedly lavishes lasagna (meat or vegetarian for £3.25) and a vast array of sandwiches (£2-3) on its customers, in full view of the cathedral (open 10am-6pm.) The **Cathedral Pub,** on South St. near Southgate St., has a congenial atmosphere and filling entrees, both provided by locals. Try the ham and chicken pie with chips and 4 vegetables (£3.50), and top it off with homemade apple pie with cream (£1.50). Bakeries congregate on North St. while the **Tesco Supermarket** is on East St.

Sights

Just west of Chichester's center, the **Cathedral,** begun in 1091, is primarily Norman in design. Later architectural styles have been grafted on, and the interior conflates Romanesque austerity with Norman motifs. There are many fine medieval sculptures and paintings, notably the carvings of Christ and of *Mary at the Raising of Lazarus* in the south aisle, and the oils by Barnard. A **Marc Chagall stained glass window** crowns the south aisle. (Open daily 7:40am-7pm; in winter 7:40am-5pm. Free, donation of (£1) encouraged. Guided tours mid-April to Oct. Mon.-Sat. at 11am and 2pm.)

Chichester's other attractions include a city-within-the-city called the **Pallants** in the southeast quadrant. Once the special preserve of the bishop, it is now a quiet area with elegant 18th- and 19th-century houses. The newly opened **Pallant House Gallery,** 9 North Pallant, a historic house-*cum*-art gallery, shelters the Walter Hussey collection of paintings and sculptures in a restored Queen Anne townhouse. (Open Tues.-Sat. 10am-5:30pm. Admission £1.50.) The brown signposted **Walls Walk** winds around the city and bounds the Roman remnants. The most fashionable avenue in town, **North Street,** has a long row of Georgian houses, including **John Nash's Market House** near the Market Cross.

Entertainment

Chichester is home to professionals and artists who enjoy tranquil pastimes and cultural events. The **Chichester Festival Theatre** (tel. 781 312), multi-faceted gem of Chichesterian nightlife, lies north of town; walk up North St. which turns into Brogle Rd. and look for signs to your right. Founded by the late Sir Laurence Olivier, this is perhaps the best theater in England outside London with productions ranging from Restoration Comedy to Theater of the Absurd. The festival runs from May to September. (Tickets £7-12. Student standbys £3 after 6pm on the day of the performance; unreserved tickets available at box office 10am day of performance.) The theater restaurant and café cater to patrons from 12:30pm on matinee days and from 6pm for evening performances. The spanking new **Minerva Studio Theatre** next to the Festival adds even more spice to the dramatic offerings (tickets £5-8). **Chichester Festivities,** held during the first two weeks of July in celebration of the cathedral's founding, is one of the finest spells of concentrated creativity in all of England, featuring concerts in the cathedral, recitals, art exhibitions, films, and outdoor events. (Tickets from £2. Schedule of events available from the box office behind St. Peter's, the tourist office, or the Festival Director, Hammick's Bookshop, 65 East St.; call 78 01 92. Open Mon.-Sat. 9:30am-5:15pm.) **Chichester Harbor Water Tours** (tel. 786 418) runs boat tours around the harbor (2/day; 1½ hr.; £3). Take bus #252 or 253 to Itchner Crossroads (15 min.; £1.50 return); from there it is a 2½-mi. hike. If you feel the need to get in the water, the new **Westgate Leisure Centre,** Avenue de Chartres (tel. 785 651), has indoor swimming for £1.60. (Open Mon. 9am-10:30pm, Tues.-Sat. 7:30am-10:30pm, Sun. 9am-6pm. Some times may be reserved for schools or members.)

Near Chichester

The **Fishbourne Roman Palace** (tel. 785 859), built in 75 AD, is the largest Roman residence yet excavated in Britain. From the time of King Cogidubnus (an ally of Rome) until a fire in 285 AD, Fishbourne was the palace of local chieftains. At one point, the owner of this villa had the full rights of a Roman senator; the ornate mosaic floors testify to the luxury of this position. The vast area now open to the public was discovered by trench-diggers in 1965. More than three-quarters of the original building remains buried under the houses along Salthill Rd. (Palace open May-Sept. daily 10am-6pm; March-April and Oct. daily 10am-5pm; Nov. daily 10am-4pm; Dec.-Feb. Sun. 10am-4pm. Admission £2.50, students £1.80.) The **Fishbourne Museum** has an exceptional display of Roman remains. **Fishbourne** is an easy walk from the Avenue de Chartres roundabout in Chichester; go west along Westgate, which becomes Fishbourne Rd. (the A259) for 1½ mi., or take bus #66 or 700 from Chichester center. The buses let you off at Salthill Rd., a 5-min. walk from the palace.

Three mi. northeast of Chichester stands **Goodwood House** (tel. 774 107), ancestral home of the Duke of Richmond and Gordon. In this 18th-century country home, splendid Canalettos, Reynolds, and Stubbs vie for attention. (Open Aug. Sun.-Thurs. 2-5pm; May-July and Sept.-Oct. Sun.-Mon. 2-5pm, including Easter Sunday and Monday. Admission £3.20; take bus #268 or 269, £1.50 return.)

The **Weald and Downland Open Air Museum** (tel. (0243) 633 48), 6 mi. north of Chichester, is an ensemble of historic buildings rescued from southeast England, including a medieval farmhouse and a working watermill. (Open April-Oct. daily 11am-5pm; off-season Wed., Sun., and bank holidays 11am-4pm. Admission £3, students £1.50.) Take bus #260 from Chichester.

Portsmouth

Don't talk to me about the naval tradition. It's nothing but rum, sodomy, and the lash.
—Winston Churchill

Base of the D-Day armada, Portsmouth is the overlord of British maritime history. Henry VIII's **Mary Rose,** which sank in 1545 and was raised 437 years later (in 1982), crowns an incomparable array of naval heritage. Nowhere else would Nelson's triumphant flagship, **HMS Victory,** have to fight to gain top billing.

Arriving and Departing

Portsmouth (pop. 180,000) lies on the south coast 75 mi. southwest of London. Trains from London Waterloo stop at both Portsmouth and Southsea station (the "town station") and Portsmouth harbor station (2/hr.; 1½ hr.; £13.20 day return). National Express coaches run from London every 1½ hr. (2½ hr.; £8.50 single or day return).

Orientation and Practical Information

Two tourist offices are open year-round on the Hard and in town on Commercial Rd.; two more open during the high season.

Tourist Information Center: The Hard (tel. 826 722), right next to entrance to historic ships; 102 Commercial Rd. (tel. 838 382), next to the town station. Open daily 9:30am-5:30pm. Seasonal offices at the Continental Ferry Port (tel. 838 635) and at the Pyramids Resort Centre, Clarence Esplanade, Southsea (tel. 832 464). Open July-Sept. daily 9:30am-5:30pm. A sea of free maps and leaflets. Free accommmodation list. Accommodations booking service (deposit of 10% of first night's cost, deducted from final payment). Currency exchange available sometimes (£2.50 min. commission).

Bus and Coach Station: The Hard Interchange, The Hard, next to the Harbour station. Local routes (enquiries tel. 738 570 or 815 452) and National Express services (tel. (0329) 230 023). National Express tickets sold at Sealink office (open July-Aug. daily 8am-5pm; Oct.-June Mon.-Sat. 8am-5pm).

Emergency: Dial 999; no coins required.

Ferries: Isle of Wight passenger ferry leaves from Harbour station (1/hr., 2/hr. in summer; 15 min.; £3.90, £5.40 day return; tel. 827 744). For continental services call 64 70 47.

Financial Services: Major banks cluster in Commercial Rd. shopping precinct just north of Portsmouth and Southsea station, including **Midland** (open Mon.-Fri. 9:30am-5pm, Sat. 9:30am-3:30pm) and **Barclay's** (open Mon.-Fri. 9:30am-5pm, Sat. 9:30am-noon). Currency exchange also available at tourist office (see above).

Hospital: Queen Alexandra Hospital, Southwick Hill Rd. (tel. 379 451).

Police: tel. 321 111.

Post Office: Slindon St. (tel. 833 201), near the town station. Open Mon.-Thurs. 9am-5:30pm, Fri. 9:30am-5:30pm, Sat. 9am-12:30pm. **Postal Code:** PO1 1AA.

Student Travel Office: Student and Youth Travel Centre, Portsmouth Polytechnic Union, Alexandra House, Museum Rd. (tel. 816 645). Open Mon.-Wed. and Fri. 10am-4pm, Thurs. 12:15-5:15pm.

Taxi: Streamline Taxis, tel. 811 111.

Telephone Code: 0705.

Train Station: Portsmouth and Southsea Station, Commercial Rd. Travel center open Mon.-Sat. 8am-8pm. **Portsmouth Harbour Station,** The Hard, ¾ mi. away at the end of the line. To Cosham, for the hostel, every 20 min.; £1.20, £1.40 day return. Trips between town and harbor cost 80p, day return £1. Call 82 57 71 for information.

Accommodations

Moderately priced B&Bs clutter Southsea, Portsmouth's contiguous resort town 1½ mi. east along the coast from the Hard. Take Southdown Portsmouth bus #6, 43, or 44 to South Parade. Cheaper lodgings lie two or three blocks inland—Whitwell, Granada, St. Roman's, and Malvern Rd. all have a fair sprinkling.

IYHF Youth Hostel, Wymering Manor, Old Wymering Lane, Medina Rd., Cosham (tel. 375 661). The old home of Catherine Parr now houses those somewhat less likely to be the sixth spouse of a fat English monarch. Take bus #1, 12, or 22 from the Hard to Cosham post office and walk left on Medina Rd., or train to Cosham then right out of the station to the post office. Open July-Aug. daily; April-June and Sept. Mon.-Sat.; mid-Feb. to March and Oct.-Dec. Tues.-Sat. £5.90, ages 16-20 £4.70; July-Aug. £6.30, ages 16-20 £5.10.

Portsmouth Polytechnic Halls of Residence, Bellevue Terrace (tel. 843 178), overlooking Southsea common, 15 min. from the Hard. Single and twin rooms available July 10-Sept. 27. **Burwell House** has small modern rooms with puritanically narrow beds; older **Rees Hall** shows more signs of age and character. £12/person.

Testudo House, 19 Whitwell Rd., Southsea (tel. 824 324). Comfortable rooms in quiet surroundings. Mrs. Parkes, the landlady, proudly displays her collection of American table mats. Singles and doubles £13/person, triples £10.30/person.

YMCA, Penny St. (tel. 864 341), 10 min. from the Hard. Basic worn rooms; those on higher floors look out over the sea wall to the Solent. Singles £10.25, doubles £9.25/person.

Camping: Southsea Caravan Park, Melville Rd., Southsea (tel. 735 070). At the eastern end of the seafront, 3 mi. from The Hard. Tent with 2 adults £9 in high season, £6 shoulder, £5-8 low season. Call in advance.

Food

Decent restaurants with a dash of style bunch along Osborne, Palmerston, and Clarendon Rd. in the Southsea shopping district (buses #6, 43, and 44 all stop at Palmerston Rd.). Standard fast-food joints abound around Commercial Rd. near the town station. The town is awash in pubs; try **The Gorge** at 85 Queen St. for a hearty fillet of plaice (£3).

Brown's, 9 Clarendon Rd. Solid English food in relaxed low-key surroundings. Steak, kidney, and Guinness pie £4, desserts 95p. Open daily 9:30am-9:30pm.

HMS Victory Buffet, in the Historic Dockyard. The only food to be had while boarding the boats. Clean and tidy with a nautical flair. No mealy pudding or salt beef here. Light meals and snacks 40p-£2.

Sights

Portsmouth overflows with engrossing ships, relics, and museums. Head first to the spectacular **Naval Heritage Centre,** in the Naval Base (entrance right next to the Hard tourist office; follow brown signs to Historic Ships.) The **Mary Rose** grabbed Britain's attention when she was raised from the Solent in 1982. Henry VIII's best-loved ship set sail from Portsmouth in July 1545 amidst much ballyhoo to engage the French fleet. In one of the greatest anti-climaxes in history, the overloaded vessel keeled over and sank in front of him. Centuries later, divers and underwater engineers raised up the starboard side. On display in a special **ship hall,** sprayed by chilled water to prevent crumbling, the hulk is an eerie, compelling sight.

An enthralling collection of Tudor artifacts, salvaged along with the wreck but displayed in a separate exhibition hall, give an unsurpassable picture of 16th-century life. The backgammon board and dice belie their age, although the horrific syringe used for urethral injections makes a clear statement about medical knowledge 400 years ago. An Elizabethan manicure set includes a natty little ear-wax remover. Ornate bronze and iron guns, including two fine Bastard Culverins, guard the exhibits. (Open March-Oct. daily 10:30am-5:30pm; Nov.-Feb. daily 10:30am-5pm. Last admission 1 hr. before closing—a general rule in Portsmouth. Admission £3.60, students and children £2.30. Ship hall is behind HMS Victory, 300 yd. from exhibition hall.)

Two 100-foot masts lead the way to Admiral Horatio Nelson's flagship **HMS Victory,** the oldest surviving Ship of the Line in the world. While winning the decisive Battle of Trafalgar against the French and Spanish in 1805, Nelson was shot in the fighting and died beneath deck—a small plaque marks the spot where he fell. Active sailors and marines conduct tours. The ship, 30% genuine Trafalgar vintage, conveys a vivid impression of the dismal cramped conditions for press ganged recruits—just eight toilets for 850 men. Some rich and strange equipment has been restored: versatile hammocks, variously used as sandbags, life jackets, or coffins; dummy wooden guns ("Quakers"), to fool the enemy; and bendy gun rammers for use in a tight spot. (Open March-Oct. daily 10:30am-5:30pm; Nov.-Feb. daily 10:30am-5pm. Admission £3.60, children and students £2.20. Tickets include entrance to Royal Naval Museum.)

HMS Warrior, somewhat eclipsed by its famous neighbors, nevertheless provides an intriguing companion to the Victory. The pride and joy of Queen Victoria's navy and the first iron-clad battleship in the world, Warrior has never seen battle. The restored innards (it took eight years to transform the ship from makeshift oil tank to pristine battleship) detail Victorian naval technology. (Open March-Oct. Mon.-Sat. 10:30am-5:30pm; Nov.-Feb. 10:30am-5pm. Admission £3.50, students and children £2.) The five galleries of the **Royal Naval Museum** fill in the gaps (historically) between the three ships; the collection of grotesque figureheads in the first gallery is the stuff of nightmares. (Open daily 10:30am-5pm. Admission £1.50, students and children £1.10. Admission to Victory includes free entry to museum.)

In the **D-Day Museum,** along Clarence Esplanade, the Overlord Embroidery, a latter-day Bayeux Tapestry, recounts the invasion of France. (Open daily 10:30am-5:30pm. Admission £3.10, children and students £1.90; low season £2.30, children and students £1.40.) Next door, the **Sea Life Centre** displays aquatic exhibits with a finful of verve. Look down, up, or across at tiddly sharks and sinister sting-rays. (Open daily 10am; tel. 734 461 for closing times. Admission £3.50, students £3.)

The **Royal Marines Museum,** in Eastney barracks, relentlessly traces the glory of the Navy's soldiers. The regimented ranks of the medal collection might overwhelm even the enthusiast. Archaic syringe fanatics will be satisfied with one particularly gruesome item. (Open Easter-Sept. daily 10am-5:30pm; Oct.-Easter 10am-4:30pm. Admission £2, students and children £1.) The **Eastney Industrial Museum,** three mi. east from the Hard, on Bransburg Rd., steams up its two James Watt beam engines each weekend during summer and displays sundry polished metal. (Open April-Sept. daily 1:30-5:30pm, in steam on weekends; Oct.-March first Sun. in month 1:30-5:30pm in steam. Admission £1, students and children 60p (in steam); 60p, students and children 35p (non-steam).)

Charles Dickens was born in 1812 at 395 Old Commercial Rd., ¾mi. north of the town station. The house has been done up in the Regency style. Morbidly enough, the only authentic Dickens artifact is the couch on which he died. (Open March-Oct. daily 10:30am-5:30pm. Admission 80p, students and children 50p.)

Winchester

Throughout the Dark and Middle Ages, Winchester was a seat of ecclesiastical, political and economic power: both William the Conqueror and Alfred the Great made Winchester the center of their respective kingdoms, and it was here that the *Domesday Book* was compiled and written. Though surpassed in power, pace, and prestige by its predecessors, 20th-century Winchester retains its majestic grace.

Arriving and Departing

Strategically located in the center of southern England, just north of Southampton, Winchester makes an excellent base from which to take daytrips to Salisbury

(25 mi.), Portsmouth (27 mi.), or even London (63 mi.). Trains leave for London (hourly; 1 hr.; £11.90 cheap day return), Chichester (1 hr., change at Southamption; £6.80), Portsmouth (45 min.; £4.80), and Bath (hourly, change at Southampton; 1½ hr.; supersaver return £12.50). **National Express** coaches run to London (8/day; 2 hr.; £10). The **Hampshire** bus makes the trip to Salisbury (14/day; 1½ hr.; £3), Portsmouth (12/day; 1½ hr.; £3), and Southampton (every ½hr.; 40 min.; £2.30). **Day rover** tickets (£3.50) are available for travel in Hampshire and Wiltshire counties.

Some travellers hitch into town along the A34 and the M3 from the north, the A33 from the south, the A31 and the A272 from the east, and the A272 from the west.

Orientation and Practical Information

The heart of Winchester is a compact square bounded by the North Walls, Eastgate St. (which runs along the River Itchen), College St. (which turns into Canon St.), and Southgate St. (which becomes Jewry St.). The train station, Station Hill, is northwest of the city center, near the intersection of City Rd. and Sussex St.; the city center is an easy 10-min. walk (down City Rd., right on Jewry St., then left on High St.). If you're loaded down with luggage, catch any bus (34p) from City Rd. as it makes its way back to the bus station which idles on Broadway, in city center. High St., Winchester's major axis, becomes Broadway and then Bridge St. as it stretches east.

Tourist Information Center: The Guildhall, Broadway (tel. 840 500 or 848 180), near King Alfred's statue. Accommodations service (10% deposit). Book-a-bed-ahead £2. Substantial visitors' guide with accommodations list £1. Foreign exchange (£2 commission). Several pamphlets (30p-£1) on walking tours. 1½-hr. guided tours at 10:30am and 2:30pm (£1.50). Open May-Sept. Mon.-Sat. 9:30am-6pm, Sun. 2-5pm; Oct.-April Mon.-Sat. 9:30am-5pm.

Bus and Coach Station: Broadway (tel. 852 352 for schedule information), across from the Guildhall. All local buses and National Express coaches leave from here. Open Mon.-Fri. 8:30am-5:30pm, Sat. 8:30am-1pm.

Crisis: Samaritans, 10 Parchment St. (tel. 606 33), off the pedestrian area of High St.

Financial Services: Thomas Cook, 30 High St. (tel. 841 661). Open Mon.-Tues. and Thurs.-Fri. 9am-5:30pm, Wed. 9:30am-5:30pm, Sat. 9am-5pm. Major banks cluster around the junction of Jewry and High St. Most open Mon.-Fri. 9:30am-4:30pm, Sat. 9:30am-12:30pm.

Emergency: Dial 999; no coins required.

Hospital: Royal Hampshire County, Romsey Rd. (tel. 863 535), at St. James Lane.

Library: District Library, Jewry St. (tel. 853 909). Reference branch, with an excellent local history collection, at 81 N. Walls (tel. 846 059/60). Open Mon.-Fri. 9:30am-7pm, Sat. 9:30am-4pm.

Market Day: Wed., Fri., and Sat. 8am-5pm behind Marks and Spencer.

Police: N. Walls (tel. 868 100), near the intersection with Middle Brook St.

Post Office: Middle Brook St. (tel. 854 004), off High St. Open Mon.-Tues. and Thurs.-Fri. 9am-5:30pm, Wed. 9:30am-5:30pm, Sat. 9am-12:30pm. **Postal Code:** SO23 8AA.

Taxi: Wintax, tel. 866 208. **'A' Tax,** tel. 840 717. £1.20 flat rate, 20p every ¼mi.

Telephone Code: 0962.

Train Station: Station Hill (tel. (0703) 229 393), northwest of the city center, near the intersection of City Rd. and Sussex St. Travel Centre open Mon.-Fri. 8:30am-6pm, Sat. 8:30am-5pm, Sun. 11:15am-6:30pm.

Accommodations and Camping

Winchester's many B&Bs cluster ½mi. southwest of the tourist office on the sections of Christchurch Rd. and St. Cross Rd. near Ranelagh Rd. Buses #44, 47, and 48 go from the town center to Ranelagh Rd.

IYHF youth hostel, 1 Water Lane (tel. 853 723). Cross the bridge past the statue of Alfred the Great and turn left. Super location in a converted 18th-century watermill, flanked and undermined by the rushing water of the River Itchen. Kitchen facilities. Lockout 10am-5pm, curfew 11pm. £6.30, ages 16-20 £5.10. Breakfast £2.30. Sleep sack rental 80p. Open April-Sept. daily; Feb.-March and Oct.-Dec. Tues.-Sun.

Mrs. Tisdall, 32 Hyde St. (tel. 851 621), a 5-min. walk from town (Jewry St. becomes Hyde St.). Large comfortable rooms and a filling breakfast in a family house with very friendly proprietors. Doubles £12/person.

Mrs. P. Patton, 12 Christchurch Rd. (tel. 854 272), between St. James Lane and Beaufort Rd. Lovely garden. Breakfast served in the observatory. Large doubles with washbasins £11/person. Open April-Oct; call ahead.

Mrs. Farrell, 5 Ranelagh Rd., just off St. Cross St. (tel. 869 555). Large rooms with firm mattresses. One shower and 1 bathtub; TV lounge. £13/person.

Camping: River Park Leisure Centre, Gordon Rd. (tel. 869 525). A 5-min. walk from town off North Walls, left onto Hyde Abbey, and right onto Gordon Rd. £2/person per night; maximum stay 3 nights. Open June-Sept.

Food

High St. and St. George's St. are home to several food markets and fast food venues. More substantial restaurants line Jewry St., and most of Winchester's many pubs serve good fare. **The Wykeham Arms,** 75 Kingsgate St., is the best (open Mon.-Sat. noon-2pm, Tues.-Sat. 6:30-8:45pm); the **Eclipse** is Winchester's smallest public house; and the **Royal Oak** claims fame as the oldest. (See Entertainment below for further information.) **Avocados,** on the Broadway next to the statue of Alfred the Great, serves pizza (from £3.50), pasta (from £4.50), and burgers (from £4). Sunday brunch comes with a newspaper and unlimited coffee (£4.50). Tuesday is vegetarian day. (Open daily noon-3pm and 6:30-11pm, Fri.-Sat. 6pm-midnight.)

Sights

The **Buttercross,** High St., is a good starting point for a walking tour of the town. Duck through the archway (note the Norman stones from William the Conqueror's palace), pass through the square, and behold **Winchester Cathedral,** set in a peaceful field of tombstones. Famed for its nave, the 556-ft. cathedral is the longest medieval church in Europe. Originally built in just 14 years (1079-1093), it was revamped by each successive Bishop of Winchester until 1486. The heavy Norman piers inside were pared down to form complex Gothic columns that matched the new rib-vaulted ceiling. Along the northern aisle a memorial stone marks Jane Austen's sepulchre (no mention is made of her writing). Near the high altar, Tudor mortuary chests hold the remains of a few Saxon kings of England, including Canute, Egbert, and Egwyn, and other pre-conquest monarchs. The stained glass window in the rear of the cathedral seems oddly Cubist—Cromwell's soldiers smashed the original window in the 17th century, and though the original glass pieces have been reinserted, the pattern got lost in the shuffle.

The **Norman crypt,** one of the finest in England, can only be viewed in summer by guided tour as it floods in winter. Most interesting for its ingenious engineering, it also stores statues of two of Winchester's most famous figures: Bishop William of Wykeham, founder of Winchester College, and St. Swithun, patron saint of weather. Swithun, King Alfred's tutor, requested to be buried where the rain might fall on him. One July 15, however, his remains were exhumed and reinterred inside the cathedral. Legend has it that this angered the saint so much that he brought torrents down on the cuplrits for forty days. Custom holds that if it rains on July 15 (St. Swithon's Day) it will rain for 40 days.

St. Ethelwald designed the delicate calligraphy used on the pages of the 12th-century ***Winchester Bible,*** a glorious, illuminated Vulgate which required the hides of 250 calves. The Bible is in the cathedral library. The **Triforium Gallery** contains some fine relics including some marvelous 14th-century figures from an altar screen. (Gallery and library open Easter-Sept. Mon. 2:30-4:30pm, Tues.-Sat. 10:30am-12:30pm and 2:30-4:30pm; Oct.-Dec. Wed. and Sat. 10:30am-12:30pm and 2:30-4:30pm; Jan.-Feb. Sat. 10:30am-12:30pm and 2:30-4:30pm. Admission £1.50, students 50p. Crypt tours Easter-Sept. Mon.-Sat. at 10:30am and 2:30pm, water level permitting. Tour 50p, 25p children. Cathedral open daily 7:15am-6:30pm. Donation £1.50.)

The **Cathedral Close** is a magnificent collection of medieval buildings, including the Deanery, Dome Alley, and Cheyney Court. Pilgrim's School choirs still sing in Pilgrim's Hall, a 14th-century hall with a wooden hammerbeam roof. (Close open daily, when not in use by schoolchildren.) South of the cathedral, tiny **St. Swithun's Chapel,** rebuilt in the 16th century, is nestled above **King's Gate,** one of the two surviving city gates (the other is Westgate).

King's Gate leads to **Winchester College,** founded in 1382 as England's first "public" school; most of its 14th-century buildings remain. The chapel, **War Memorial Cloister,** is open to the public, as are the Old Cloisters and chantry during term. The cloister is carved with the names of famous Wykehamists who lived by the school's motto: "Aut disce, aut discede, maner sors tertia caedia" (manners maketh the man). The moving and beautiful War Memorial Cloister commemorates more than 500 Men of College who died during the Great War and World War II. (Very good guided tours April-Sept. Mon.-Sat. at 11am, 2pm, and 3:15pm. £2, children £1.50.) A short stroll further down College St. will bring you to **Wolvesey Palace,** where the Bishop of Winchester lives, and **Wolvesey Castle,** where the Norman bishop used to dwell. (Open Easter-Sept. daily 10am-1pm and 2-6pm. Admission 95p, students 75p.) You can see most of the ruins from the entrance without paying the 80p admission. Make your way from the end of College St. back to Bridge St. via Riverside Walk, a fine footpath along the River Itchen.

At the end of High St., atop Castle Hill, the **Great Hall** has witnessed and withstood much of England's history. It was here that Henry III built his castle on the remains of a fortress erected by William the Conqueror, and where Henry V met with the French ambassador in 1415 before launching the campaign that brought England's greatest glory at Agincourt. The unfortunate Sir Walter Raleigh was tried for treason and sentenced to death in 1603; less than 50 years later Oliver Cromwell destroyed part of the castle during the Civil War. In 1655 Judge Jeffreys presided over one of his "Bloody Assizes" here following the Monmouth Rebellion. The above is all true, which is more than can be said for the "King Arthur's Round Table" that hangs on the West Wall. The table can be dated only to the 13th century and Henry VIII probably posed for the painting of Arthur in the 16th century. (Hall open daily 10am-5pm; Nov.-Feb. Mon.-Fri. 10am-5pm, Sat.-Sun. 10am-4pm. Free.) A gaggle of regimental museums honk in the Peninsula Barracks just outside Westgate. The brand new **Gurkha Museum** depicts, with unusually gruesome tableaux, the history of the Nepalese regiments from 1815 to the Falklands War (open Tues.-Sat. 10am-5:30pm; £1.50, children 75p); in the magnificent **Royal Green Jackets Museum,** a vast diorama (22'× 11') tells the story of the Battle of Waterloo. (Open Mon.-Sat. 10am-5pm, Sun. noon-4pm. Admission £1.50, children £1.) The **Crusades Experience** never quite manages to convince you that you are not still in the 20th century. (Open daily 10am-5pm; admission £2.70, students £2.20.)

One mi. south of the town center, via either St. Cross Rd. or some beautiful water-meadows, rests the **Hospital of St. Cross,** England's oldest functioning almshouse. One can still receive the traditional Wayfarer's Dole (in very small portions) upon request, and visit the picturesque hospital buildings, including the 12th-century church. Several buses run to the hospital. (Open Mon.-Sat. 9:30am-12:30pm and 2-5pm; Oct.-March 10:30am-12:30pm and 2-3:30pm. Admission £1, students 50p.)

Another scenic walk from the town center follows St. Giles Hill; cross the bridge behind the statue of Alfred the Great, go up Magdalen Hill Rd., and climb the steps.

Entertainment

The pubs in Winchester do a roaring business. Most popular is the **Royal Oak,** down Royal Oak Passageway, next to Godbegot House on High St. Reputedly the oldest pub in this area, it has a splendid oak bar, a good variety of real ales, and live jazz on Mondays and Thursdays. The **Guildhall Tavern,** in the Guildhall on the Broadway, comes alive with house music on Tuesdays and Thursdays (no cover).

The Edwardian glory of the **Theatre Royal,** Jewry St. (box office tel. 843 434), hosts many London-based theatrical companies. The town also welcomes a **Folk Festival** in early May. Similarly, the **Hat Fair** in mid-July fills a weekend with theater, street performances, and peculiar headgear. The famed Bonfire Night procession and fireworks on Guy Fawkes Day (Nov. 5) is excellent.

Near Winchester

Jane Austen dwelled in the meek village of **Chawton,** 15 mi. northeast of Winchester, from 1809 to 1817. In these years she produced *Pride and Prejudice, Emma, Northanger Abbey,* and *Persuasion.* The author's house (tel. (0420) 832 62) now displays many of her personal belongings. (Open April-Oct. daily 11am-4:30pm; Nov.-Dec. and March Wed.-Sun. 11am-4:30pm; Jan.-Feb. Sat.-Sun. only. Admission £1.50.) Take bus #251 from Winchester (1 hr.; return £3.20). Back in Winchester, you can pass by and tip your cap (but not enter) the house where Jane died (College St.).

The **New Forest,** covering 145 sq. mi. of heath and woodland 17 mi. southwest of Winchester, was William the Conqueror's personal hunting ground. The **Rufus Stone** (near Brook and Cadnam) marks the spot where Norman King William II met his untimely end in a "hunting accident." The park is now a protected area in which wild ponies, donkeys, and cows frolic freely. Hikers find refreshment at the **William-Farrel Pub,** 1 mi. from the Rufus Stone. No buses run to the park; it is possible to hitch along the A31.

Spend a morning or afternoon in **Romsey,** a small market town southwest of Winchester. Romsey was built around an exquisite Norman **abbey,** burial place of Earl Mountbatten of Burma and home to a 900-year-old Saxon crucifix depicting Christ as king and the Cross as the Tree of Life. In St. George's chapel, Crusaders adorn the brilliant tiles. (Open daily 7:30am-dusk. Donation 50p.) Across the street, **King John's House,** actually the abode of a late 13th-century noble, has kept its original roof timbers, decorated wall plaster and intriguing graffiti drawn in 1306 by members of Edward I's court. (Open May-Sept. Mon. 2-4pm, Tues.-Sat. 10:30am-12:30pm and 2-4pm; Oct.-Nov. and March-April Sat. 2-4pm. Admission 40p, students 20p.) Bus #66, 900, or 901 leaves Winchester for Romsey (Mon.-Sat. every hr.; 45 min.; £2.70). You can also take the train from Winchester to Bournemouth and change at Southampton for Romsey (every hr.; return £2.90).

About a ½-mi. from Romsey along the A31 road lies **Broadlands,** the Palladian mansion that was the home of the Victorian Prime Minister Lord Palmerston and the late Lord Mountbatten. The newly added Mountbatten Exhibition highlights the life of the last viceroy of India, uncle of Prince Philip and great uncle to Prince Charles. Broadlands is more recently famed for being the sight of Prince Charles and Lady Diana's honeymoon. (Open April-July Sat.-Thurs. 10am-4pm; Aug.-Sept. daily 10am-4pm. Admission £4.50, children £3.)

Salisbury

Unlike many other English medieval cities, Salisbury did not grow haphazardly into a jumble of streets. Rather, the "City of New Sarum" was built according to a rectangular grid pattern (five streets running north to south and six running east to west) devised by Bishop Poore in the early 13th century. The heart of the city, despite its 20th-century commercial chaos, retains its 13th-century logic. Not far from the din and tumult of the city center, Salisbury Cathedral remains quiet and secluded, walled off from the clamor by the buildings around the close and wreathed in an expanse of green meadow.

Arriving and Departing

Salisbury (pop. 38,000) lies 80 mi. southwest of London. Trains leave at 15 min. past each hour from London's Waterloo Station (£15.10 cheap day return). BR also runs to most of the other major towns in the region, including Winchester (2/hr., change at Southampton; 1½ hr.; £6.80), Southampton (2/hr.; 40 min.; £4.80), and Portsmouth (1/hr.; 1½ hr.; £8.50). National Express coaches run from Victoria (every 3 hr. 9am-6pm; 2½ hr.; £11.25 day return). Wilts and Dorset service #X4 runs from Bath, 40 mi. northwest of Salisbury (6/day; 2 hr.; £2.65); buses also move along to Stonehenge (Mon.-Fri. 5/day, Sat.-Sun. 4/day; ½hr.; £3.05 return).

Orientation and Practical Information

You'll find the Salisbury bus and coach station in the center of town; the train station is a 10-min. walk. To reach the tourist office from the train station, turn left out of the station onto South Western Rd., bear right onto Fisherton St. (which becomes Bridge St.), pass over the bridge, and cross High St. Walk straight ahead onto Silver St., which becomes Butcher Row and then Fish Row.

Tourist Information Center: Fish Row (tel. 334 956), in the Guildhall in Market Sq. Extremely helpful. Accommodations service (10% deposit), book-a-bed-ahead service £2.10. List posted. Guided tours mid-April to mid-Oct. Mon.-Sat. at 11am; also June to mid-Sept. at 2:30pm and 8:30pm (£1). Currency exchange, commission £3. Open July-Aug. Mon.-Sat. 9am-7pm, Sun. 11am-5pm; June and Sept. Mon.-Sat. 9am-6pm, Sun. 11am-4pm; Oct.-May Mon.-Sat. 9am-5pm.

Bike Rental: Hayball and Co., Rollestone St. (tel. 411 378). £5/day, £25/week; £25 deposit. Cash only. Open Mon.-Sat. 9am-5:30pm.

Bus and Coach Station: 8 Endless St. (tel. 336 855). It's not an end, it's a beginning. Booking office open Mon.-Fri. 8:15am-5:45pm, Sat. 8:15am-5:15pm. Explorer ticket £3.50, child £1.75; good on Wilts and Dorset, Hampshire bus, Provincial or Solent Blue.

Crisis: Samaritans, 42 Milford St. (tel. 233 55); 24 hr.

Early Closing Day: Wed. at 1pm (small shops only).

Emergency: Dial 999; no coins required.

Financial Services: Barclay's, on the corner of High and Bridge St. Open Mon.-Fri. 9:30am-4:30pm, Sat. 9:30am-noon. **Thomas Cook,** 5 Queen St. Open Mon.-Tues. and Thurs.-Sat. 9am-5:30pm, Wed. 9:30am-5:30pm. **Lloyd's,** on Minster St. across from Market Sq. Open Mon.-Fri. 9:30am-5pm, Sat. 9:30am-1pm. **National Westminster,** on Blue Boar Rd. Open Mon.-Fri. 9:30am-4:30pm, Sat. 9:30am-1pm.

Hospital: Salisbury General Infirmary, Fisherton St. (tel. 336 212), just over the bridge.

Launderette: Washing Well, 28 Chipper Lane. Drop-off Mon.-Fri. 8:30am-6pm. Wash, dry, and fold £3.30/load. Open daily 8am-9pm.

Library: Salisbury Library, Market Pl. (tel. 324 245). Open Mon., Wed., and Fri. 10am-7pm; Tue. 9:30am-7pm; Thurs. 10am-5pm; Sat. 9:30am-5pm.

Market Days: Tues. and Sat., in Market Sq. (roughly 6am-3pm).

Police: Wilton Rd. (tel. 411 444).

Post Office: 24 Castle St. (tel. 413 051), at Chipper Lane. Open Mon.-Tues. and Thurs.-Fri. 9am-5:30pm, Wed. 9:30am-5:30pm, Sat. 9am-1pm. **Postal Code:** SP1 1AB.

Taxi: tel. 334 343. Taxi stands at train station (for Stonehenge) and New Canal (near the cinema).

Telephone Code: 0722.

Train Station: South Western Rd. (tel. 275 91), west of town across the river. Information and ticket office open Mon.-Sat. 5:45am-9pm, Sun. 8am-8:45pm.

Accommodations and Camping

IHYF Youth Hostel, Milford Hill House, Milford Hill (tel. 327 572). From the tourist office, turn left on Fish Row, right on Queen St., left on Milford St., and walk ahead a few blocks under the overpass. A beautiful old house amid 2 acres of garden. Lockout 10am-1pm. Curfew 11:30pm. £6.60, ages 16-20 £5.40. Camping £3.30. Breakfast £2.30.

Ron and Jenny Coats, 51 Salt Lane (tel. 327 443), just up from the bus station. A welcoming and clean 400-year-old house. Hostel-type lodgings in mellow 3- and 6-bed rooms. Centrally located. £6.50, £8.30 with breakfast, 80p sleepsack rental, 10p for 2-min. shower.

Mrs. Spiller, Nuholme, Ashfield Rd. (tel. 336 592), 10 min. from the train station. Bear right out of station; cross the car park straight ahead; turn right onto Churchfields Rd. then turn right again onto Ashfield. Very friendly place run by an elderly woman who can recite Shakespeare over a cuppa. £11, students £10.

Camping: Hudson's Field of the **Camping Club of Great Britain,** Hudson's Field, Castle Rd. (tel. 320 713). On the way to Old Sarum. 100 pitches. Curfew 11pm. £3.70/person. Open April-Oct.

Food and Pubs

From 6am to 3pm on Tuesdays and Saturdays the town center throbs with vendors hawking clothes, fresh local produce, and homemade jams. Satisfy your sweet tooth with tea and homemade chocolates at **Michael Snell's,** 5 St. Thomas Sq., near Bridge St. (open Mon.-Sat. 9am-5:30pm). Grocery stores include Tesco on Castle St. and Safeway in the Malting Shopping Centre.

Mo's, 62 Milford St., on the way to the youth hostel. Favored by locals for its tasty food at low prices. Carnivores can devour burgers (£4.05) or ribs (£5.40) while vegans can ruminate over lentil creations (£4.05) or veggie burgers (£4.05). Mo's milkshake is magnificent (£1.75). Open daily 11:30am-11pm.

The Golden Curry, 7 Minster St. Bargain 3-course lunch £4. Dinner a tad more pricey with £5 minimum. Open daily noon-2:30pm and 5:30pm-midnight.

Don Giovanni's, 44 St. Catherine St. Wide range of pasta dishes (£3.50-5.50). Open Mon.-Sat. 11:30am-2pm, 6-9:30pm.

The Old House Restaurant, 47 New St. A range of English favorites: bar lunches £3-5; cream teas £2; roast beef with Yorkshire pudding £4.50. Open Sun.-Mon. 11am-3pm, Tues.-Fri. 10am-5:30pm, and Sat. 10am-8pm.

With sixty-seven pubs in the city, you're sure to find one that suits you. The venerable **New Inn,** New St., was one of the first non-smoking pubs in Britain. Try also **Burke's Bar and Buttery,** New St., or **The Oddfellows Arms,** Milford St. Live music has been known to descend upon the **Cathedral Hotel,** Milford St. The **Haunch of Venison,** Minster St., a 600-year-old beauty, serves real ale, mostly to tourists. The pub displays a replica of a hand that was severed from the arm of a dishonest poker player and mummified for posterity. Salisbury's younger crowd hunts their game at **The Pheasant,** on Salt Lane.

Sights

Rising monolithically from its grassy close, **Salisbury Cathedral** ascends to the neck-breaking height of 404 feet. The bases of the marble pillars near the entrance to the choir are buckling under the strain of 6400 tons of limestone; if a pillar rings when you knock on it, you should probably move away. The flying buttresses supporting the tower both inside and out were added to ease the problem, and the inverted arches above the choir keep the walls from caving in. Despite these measures, nearly 700 years of use and weathering have left the cathedral in need of structural and aesthetic repair. (Sir Christopher Wren calculated that the spire leaned 29½ inches.) The spire, the tower, and the west front of the cathedral are shrouded in scaffolding. During guided tours in the summer and on Tuesdays you can ride up to the roof and the base of the spire on the outdoor contruction workers' elevator. Tour and hard hats are free. (Tours June-Aug. Mon.-Sat. at 11am, noon, 2pm, 3pm; March-May and Sept.-Oct. Mon.-Sat. at 11am, 2:30pm). The oldest working clock in Britain, dating from 1386, stands by the North Door. Several tombs of crusaders line the sides of the nave. The most colorful is that of William Longespée, bastard son of Henry II, who was instrumental in writing the *Magna Carta.* Longespée brought what is now one of four surviving copies of the famous document to Salisbury (two are stored in the British Museum, the fourth in Lincoln); today it rests in the cathedral's **Chapter House.** (Open Mon.-Sat. 9:30am-4:45pm, Sun. 1-4:45pm; Nov.-Feb. Mon.-Sat. noon-3:15pm, Sun. 1-3:15pm. Donation 50p.) The **cloisters** adjoining the cathedral somehow grew to be the largest in England, although the cathedral never housed any monks. Bump, nudge, and rub brass here (Mon.-Sat. 10am-5pm, Sun. 2-5pm). (Cathedral open Aug.-June daily 8am-6:30pm; July 8am-8:15pm. Donation £1, virtually mandatory; students 50p. Evensong Mon.-Sat. at 5:30pm.)

The open lawns of the **cathedral close** flank some beautifully preserved old homes, including **Malmesbury House,** where Handel once lived, and reputedly now haunts. (Open for guided tours April-Sept. Tues.-Thurs. every ½hr. 10am-5pm. Admission £2, children £1.) **Mompesson House,** another sumptuous residence, has fine plasterwork, a Queen Anne interior, and an inspiring collection of 18th-century drinking glasses. (Open April-Oct. Sat.-Wed. 12:30-5:30pm. Admission £2.30.)

The **Salisbury and South Wiltshire Museum** is housed in the King's House, 65 The Close. Tantalizing exhibits trace the development of Salisbury, show aerial photographs of ancient cities and burial mounds, and present the latest crackpot theories on Stonehenge. (Open April-Sept. Mon.-Sat. 10am-5pm, Sun. 2-5pm; Oct.-March Mon.-Sat. 10am-4pm. Admission £1.80, students £1.20.)

Entertainment

Salisbury's repertory theater company presents a variety of high-quality productions at the **Playhouse,** Malthouse Lane (tel. 320 333), over the bridge off Fisherton St. Tickets start at £5; student seats at £4.10 are available in advance for first nights, matinees, and Monday shows. (Rush seats at the same price available 5 min. before curtain.) The **Salisbury Festival** features dance exhibitions, music, and a separate wine tasting festival at the Salisbury library during the first two weeks of September. (Tickets from £2.50. Write to the Festival Box Office, Salisbury Playhouse, Malthouse Lane, Salisbury SP1 7RA; tel. (0722) 325 173.) The **Salisbury Arts Centre,** in St. Edmund's Church, Bedwin St. (tel. 321 744), promotes a wide range of events, including punk musicals, jazz bands, and Shakespearean tragedies. (Box office open Mon.-Sat. 10am-6pm, and evenings of most performances. Tickets from £2.50.)

Near Salisbury

The germ of Salisbury, **Old Sarum,** lies 1½ mi. north of the town. Here, an Iron Age hill fort evolved into a Saxon town and then into a Norman fortress. In the 13th century, friction with Richard I goaded church officials into moving the settlement and building a new cathedral. Gradually, New Sarum replaced the old town as the prominent trading and religious center.

Deserted today, Old Sarum was the most notorious of the "rotten boroughs" eliminated by the Reform Act of 1832. Until then, it had continued to send two members to Parliament although no one had lived there for centuries; the MPs were chosen by the owner of the land. Today Old Sarum is a lonely windswept mound that is home to the bishop's palace, a castle, a Norman castle moat, the foundations of the original cathedral, and the ruins of the original fort. (Open April-Sept. daily 10am-6pm; Oct.-March Tues.-Sun. 10am-4pm. Admission 95p, students 75p.) Old Sarum is off the A345, on the way to Stonehenge. Buses #5-9 run every 15 min. from the Salisbury bus station.

Declared by James I to be "the finest house in the land," **Wilton House,** three mi. west of Salisbury on the A30, exhibits paintings by Van Dyck, Rembrandt, Rubens, and others, and has an impressive, almost outrageous interior design. The Double Cube Room is one of eight extraordinary 17th-century state rooms. (Open April to mid-Oct. Tues.-Sat. 11am-6pm, Sun. 12:30-6pm. Admission £4.20, students £3.50, grounds only £1.60.) Catch the bus outside Marks and Spencer (every 10 min., Sun. every hr.).

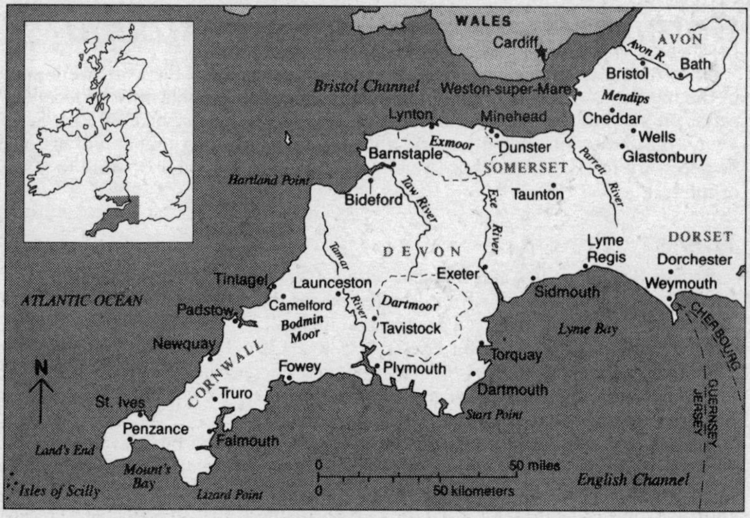

Southwest England

Mists of legend shroud the counties of Somerset, Dorset and Cornwall in England's **West Country.** King Arthur is said to have been born at Tintagel on Cornwall's northern coast and to have battled Mordred on Bodmin Moor. One hamlet purports to be the site of Camelot, another village claims to be the resting place of the Holy Grail, and no less than three small lakes are identified as the final resting place of Arthur's sword Excalibur. The ghost of Sherlock Holmes still pursues the Hound of the Baskervilles across Dartmoor, in Devon, and St. Michael's Mount in Cornwall's Marazion is believed to have held the terrible giant Cormoran hostage in its well. Indeed, entering the West Country is like stepping into another era; the jagged coastline hems in a land of misted moors, wooded valleys, and grassy hillsides, where seafarers and farmers alike have made their homes. In Avon and Somerset, the smoothly rounded Mendip Hills press out of the fertile farmland, while in the high country of Devon and northern Cornwall, the Rivers Tamor, Taw and Exe score verdant cliffs in the upland plateaus. The cities and towns sprinkled throughout the grasslands are as diverse as the terrain; industrial cities like Bristol and Plymouth puff alongside lithe cobblestone villages like Clovelly or Fowey. The southern coast of Cornwall, especially the Penwith Peninsula at England's southwestern tip, receives so much sunshine that it has become something of a resort (the "Cornish Riviera"). Each summer, tens of thousands of pale Brits make the pilgrimage west to walk along the narrow streets of Cornwall's seaside fishing villages like Mousehole or surfing meccas like Newquay and bake their bodies on sandy beaches.

A diversity of nations found an enclave in West Coutry's varied terrain. Bronze Age barrows (burial mounds), Stone Age quoits (chamber tombs), and peregrine megaliths of unknown significance add to the celestial refuse. The Celts maintained a stronghold in Cornwall, even as the Romans and Normans over-ran the rest of the country. Abbey ruins list like ships in an earthen sea of heather and bracken. Of all the languages introduced, the Celtic spoken in Cornwall has proven to be the most tenacious after English. The last native speaker of Cornish died some time ago, but a few committed souls are attempting a revival, currently stalled by a bitter debate over whether the language should be taught in the original or with a simpler phonetic spelling system.

Getting There and Getting Around

Unfortunately, no single rail or coach pass will cover all of the worthwhile spots in the region, as many of the more remote towns are accessible only by local bus; count on visiting the moors and National Trust areas by car, bike or foot. Select a pass that best suits your itinerary, with the understanding that it will at times be necessary to take a local bus (usually under £2), rent a bike, or walk to a spot of interest.

Trains

British Rail offers fast and frequent service from London and the north. The region's primary east-west line from London passes through Taunton, Exeter, Plymouth, and Truro, and ends at Penzance. Trains roll to: Penzance (1/hr.; 5½ hr.; £39); Plymouth (3½ hr.; £36); Exeter (2½ hr.; £30). The north-south line from Edinburgh passes through Bristol, Taunton, and Exeter before continuing through Plymouth to Penzance. Branch lines connect St. Ives, Newquay, Falmouth, and Barnstaple to the network.

Special fares make rail travel competitive with coach and bus travel; ask about cheap day-return fares, which, as elsewhere in Britain, are often marginally more expensive than single fares. Holders of a Young Person's, Senior Citizen's, or Disabled Person's Railcard (£16, valid for 1 yr., available at British Rail offices) receive a 34% selected fare reduction. British Rail also offers a variety of Rail Rover passes in the West Country: the **Freedom of the Southwest Rover** allows unlimited travel inclusive of Bristol Parkway and the line through Salisbury and down to Weymouth, covering all of Cornwall, Devon, Somerset, and part of Avon and Dorset (7 days, £45); the **Devon Rail Rover,** is bounded by and includes the Taunton-to-Exmouth line on the east and the Gunnislake-Plymouth line in the west (7 days, £30; **FlexiRover,** valid 3 of 7 days, £22); and the **Cornwall Rail Rover,** is bounded by and includes the Gunnislake-Plymouth line (7 days, £30; FlexiRover, valid 3 of 7 days, £19). For rail information, call British Rail in Bristol at (0272) 29 42 55, in Plymouth at (0752) 22 13 00, or in Penzance at (0736) 658 31.

Coaches and Buses

National Express coaches run to major points along the north coast via Bristol, and to points along the south coast (including Penzance) via Exeter and Plymouth. For journeys within the region, local bus service is less expensive and more extensive than the local trains, passing through towns that are not large enough to have train stations.

All of the large regional bus companies—Cornwall Busways, Western National (in eastern Cornwall and south Devon), Southern National (in Somerset and West Dorset), Devon General, and the curiously-named Badgerline (in Avon and Somerset)—offer **Explorer** or **Day Rambler** tickets, allowing a full day's travel on any bus within their region for £3-4 (prices vary by company). The weekly **Key West** ticket (£19.50, seniors £15) is good on all Devon and Cornwall routes for a week. For information about regional bus services or National Express coaches, call Cornwall Busways in Penzance at (0736) 694 69, Western National in Plymouth at (0752) 22 13 00, or Badgerline in Bristol at (0272) 29 29 00. In the off-season, be sure to phone ahead; branch-line rail service on Sundays shuts down for the winter, and many bus lines don't run at all between September and March.

Hiking and Biking

Distances between towns are so short in England's southwest that it is feasible to travel throughout the region on your own power. The narrow roads and hilly landscape can make bicycling difficult, but hardy cyclists will find the quiet lanes and countryside rewarding terrain. If you're walking or cycling, on- or off-road, bring along a large-scale Ordnance Survey map and an impregnable Gore-Tex body prophylactic to shield you from foul weather. If you'll be hiking through countryside, it is important to be respectful of the local residents whose livelihood depends on the land you're crossing. Stay on public paths as much as possible; don't pollute streams or troughs that may be used for the watering of livestock, and be sure to close every gate that you open. Remember as well to leave your name and proposed route with the local police or ranger station.

The longest coastal path in England, the **South West Peninsula Coast Path,** originates in Dorset and passes through South Devon, Cornwall, and North Devon, ending in Somerset. The path, which would take several months to walk in its entirety, winds past cliffs, caves, beaches, ports, and tourist-infested resorts; walkers should expect to run into crowds of sheep or camera-carrying couples. Many rivers cross the path on their way to the sea, so you will have to take a ferry or wade through the crossings. Check ferry times carefully to avoid being stranded. Some sections of the trail are so difficult as to dissuade all but the most invigorated, and it is important to check your route with a tourist information center official before you set out to make sure that the area you want to visit is well-marked.

The path is divided into four parts based on the national parks and the counties through which it passes. The **Dorset Coast Path,** famous for its cliffside fossils, runs from Poole through Lyme Regis to Exmouth. The **South Devon Coast Path** picks up near Paighton and continues through Plymouth, winding around spectacular cliffs, wide estuaries, and remote bays set off by lush vegetation and wildflowers. The **Cornwall Coast Path,** which includes some of the most rugged stretches of the route, starts in Plymouth (a ferry service takes you on to Cremyll), rounds the southwestern tip of Britain, and continues up the northern Atlantic coast all the way to Bude. The magnificent Cornish cliffs in this stretch of the path harbor a great range of birds and sealife. The final section, the **Somerset and North Devon Coastal Path,** travels from Bude through Exmoor National Park to Minehead. The least arduous of the four sections, it still offers magnificent coastal scenery in North Devon and the highest seaside cliffs in The West Country.

Most of the path is easy to cover on a bike, as some areas have been eroded to an appropriate smoothness. Often bike rental shops will offer suggestions for 3-day to week-long routes along the coast. Journeys of any length are possible along any part of the path, as buses serve most points along the route, and youth hostels and B&Bs are spaced out 5-25 mi. intervals along it. One excellent guidebook to the path, updated every year, is the South West Way Association's *Complete Guide to the Coastal Path* (£1.80, available at tourist offices and national park offices). For more information, contact The South West Way, c/o Mrs. D.Y. Lancey, "Kynance," Old Newton Rd., Kingskerswell, Newton Abbot, Devon. The Countryside Commission sells extremely useful guides and Ordnance Survey maps covering each section of the path (for address see Getting Around in the General Introduction), as do most tourist offices.

Dorchester

Famed as the inspiration for Thomas Hardy's "Casterbridge," Dorchester is sleepy, bordering on narcolepetic. The town, one quickly realizes, has changed little since Hardy's departure in 1928; shops and antique dealers still peddle their wares along its High St., and the neolithic and Roman oddities sprinkled around Dorchester, notably Maiden Castle and the Maumbury Rings, remain intact.

Arriving and Departing

Dorchester (pop. 14,000), the county seat of Dorset, is 120 mi. southwest of London. Trains leave **Dorchester South Station,** Weymouth Ave., for points north and east, including London's Waterloo (1/hr.; 2½ hr.; £22.50) and Weymouth (22/day; 15 min.; £1.80 return). Trains from **Dorchester West Station,** off Maumbury Rd.

near Damers Rd., connect to points west, such as Bath (10/day; 1 hr. 40 min.; £11.50) and Bristol (14/day; 2½ hr.; £12.50). Buy tickets on the train.

The **Wilts & Dorset bus** connects Dorchester with Salisbury, while **Bere Regis,** 7 Bridport Rd. (tel. 262 992), provides service within the local perimeter; Bere Regis also sells tickets for **National Express** coaches to London's Waterloo Station and Exeter.

For those hitching from Salisbury to Dorchester, take the A354 to the A35; from Exeter, the A30 to the A35. From Dorchester to London, walk down West High St. and over Greys Bridge. To Exeter, walk west to the intersection of Bridport Rd. and Damers Rd. To Bristol, walk north on The Grove just past Millers Close to New Rd.

Orientation and Practical Information

The intersection of High West St. with South St. (Cornhill St. on some maps) serves as the unofficial center of town. The main shopping district extends southward along South St. The Top o' Town roundabout lies at the nexus of High West St., Bridport Rd., The Grove, and Albert Rd. Both rail stations are off Weymouth Ave., which runs southwest from the bottom of South St. To reach the tourist office from the Dorchester South train station, walk straight out of the station onto Weymouth Ave., right onto South Walks and left onto Acland Rd. The office is on your left. From Dorchester West Station, turn left out of the station onto Maumbury Rd., right onto Great Western (which becomes South Walks Rd.), then left onto Acland.

Tourist Information Center: 1 Acland Rd. (tel. 267 992), behind the Hardye Arcade off South St. opposite the large parking lot. Accommodations booking (10% first night's stay; outside of Dorchester £2.15). The *Historical Guide to Dorchester* (30p) includes a map, brief history, and 4 leisurely walking tours. Ask about pamphlets (10p) that detail paths through areas in Hardy's novels. Guided tours of Dorchester (£1.50; 1½ hr.) every Wed. at 11:15am and 2pm. (Open Mon.-Fri. 9am-6pm, Sat. 9am-5pm.)

Bike Rental: Dorchester Cyles, 31A Great Western Rd. (tel. 268 787). Mountain bikes £10/day, £30/week, £50 deposit. Tandem £20/day, £90/week, £100 deposit. Open Mon.-Sat. 9am-5:30pm.

Bus and Coach Depot: Buses depart from the lettered bus stops sprinkled like pixie dust about town. **Bere Regis,** 7 Bridport Rd. (tel. 262 992), sells both National Express and Bere Regis tickets and provides schedule information. Open Mon.-Fri. 7am-4:50pm, Sat. 8am-6pm.

Emergency: Dial 999; no coins required.

Financial Services: Compare rates at the cluster of banks near the town center. **Barclay's,** 10 South St.; **Midland,** 15 Cornhill; **Lloyds,** 1 High West St.; and **National Westminster,** 49 South St. All open Mon.-Fri. 9:30am-3:30pm. Some branches operate limited hr. Sat.

Hospital: Dorset County Hospital, Princes St. (tel. 263 123), near the town center.

Launderette: Park Launderette, 40 Coburg Rd. Open Mon.-Fri. 8:30am-8pm, Sat.-Sun. 8:30am-5pm. Wash £2, dry 20p/10 min. cycle.

Market Day: Wed. about 8:30am-2pm, at the Corn Exchange on Weymouth Ave.

Pharmacy: Boots, South St. Open Mon.-Sat. 9am-5:30pm.

Police: Weymouth Ave. (tel. 251 212).

Post Office: 43 South St. Open Mon. and Wed.-Fri. 9am-5:30, Tues. 9:30am-5:30pm, Sat. 9am-12:30pm. **Postal Code:** DT1 1DH.

Telephones: at the Top o'Town roundabout on Weymouth Ave. **Telephone Code:** 0305.

Train Station: Dorchester South, Weymouth Ave. for points north and south; **Dorchester West,** off Maumbury Rd. near Damers Rd. for points west.

Accommodations

Dorchester has no IYHF youth hostel; the nearest one is 10 mi. away at Litton Cheny (tel. (03083) 340).

Clovelly, 19 Cornwall Rd. (tel. 266 689). Follow Albert Rd. south from the Top o' Town roundabout. Remote-control TVs and comfortable beds. Meaty breakfasts, but can cater to vegetarians. Singles £14, doubles £12.50/person.

Victoria Hotel, Dagmar Rd. off Damers Rd. (tel. 262 808). From town center head down South St., turn right on Great Western Rd. Genial pub with B&B. Large garden. £12.

Westin House, 53 Icenway (tel. 642 25), off High East St. Three spacious and well-decorated rooms with dinosaurs next door. £14.

Wollaston Lodge, Acland Rd. (tel. 265 952), the continuation of Church St. off High East St. Many amenities (coffee/tea and TV) in a sumptuous Victorian home. Gregarious proprietors offer insights into local events. £14.

Camping: Giant's Head Caravan and Camping Park, Old Sherborne Rd., Cerne Abbas, (tel. (03003) 242) 7 mi. north of Dorchester; head out of town on The Grove, bear right onto Old Sherborne Rd. 2 folks and tent from £3; open March-Oct.

Food

Food in all its glorious permutations can be enjoyed in eateries along High West and High East St. Several places slice sandwiches for 60p-£1, such as **County Stile,** 10 Hardye Arcade, which creates oversized sandwiches for under £2. (Open 8am-4:30pm.) **Tesco** on South St., the **Borough Arms** on East St. and the **Judge Jeffrey's** on High West St. pack in the indigenous for pints.

Potter In, 19 Durngate St. off South St. Crunchy wholefood restaurant ideal for light lunches, snacks, and tea. Meals (£3-4) served noon-2pm. Browse through the selection of local crafts sold upstairs before you leave. Open Mon.-Sat. 10am-5pm.

Gorge Café, South St., serves Dorset's finest eggburgers (£1.95). Popular for evening coffee. Open Mon.-Sat. 7am-8pm, Sun. 8am-8pm.

Sights and Entertainment

Dorchester's sights are far from riveting; you would do better to hike around outside the village. The **Dorset County Museum,** High West St., houses a strange but interesting hodgepodge of planetary leftovers, as diverse as fossils of 192-million-year-old quasi-carnivorous pseudo-dolphin-like reptiles and a detailed reconstruction of Thomas Hardy's study. (Open Mon.-Sat. 10am-5pm. Admission £1.50, seniors and children 75p.) Dorchester's other museums seem to have been created for post-apocalyptic rainy days. The three rooms of the **Dinosaur Museum** senselessly obfuscate rambunctious children with complicated dinosaur terminology. (Open daily 9:30am-5:30pm; admission £2.30, children £1.65.) Dorchester's **Military Museum,** Bridport Rd., displays an unexceptional collection of military paraphenalia from the past 300 years. (Open Mon.-Sat. 9am-1pm and 2-5pm. Admission 50p, children 25p.)

Several ruins in and around Dorchester attest to Dorchester's Roman origins. Near the Dorchester South railway station are the **Maumbury Rings,** a Bronze Age monument along the lines of Stonehenge and Avebury; however, it is the grassy maw of the amphitheater, later used by the Romans, which rises most visibly from the site. The complete foundation and one mosaic floor of a **Roman Town House** are at the back of the County Hall complex near the Top o' Town roundabout (enter the parking lot and walk all the way back; the gate is unlocked during daylight hours). The only remaining fragment of the old **Roman Wall** is on Albert Rd., a short walk to the south. On the way you will pass a statue of Thomas Hardy grumpily surveying the roundabout.

The most significant of Dorchester's ancient ruins is **Maiden Castle,** a fortification dating from 3000 BC captured by the Romans in 44 AD. The "castle" consists of a hilltop fortified by a series of steep ridges. A climb up to the top reveals how effectively the sculpted land tired attackers. After the Roman victory, the fortification became a religious center, and a Roman temple (the ruins still extant) was erected on top. Today only sheep hold the fort. There is no bus to the monument, but the local shuttle to Vespasian Way will take you half-way (every 15 min. from Trinity St.); otherwise, it is a scenic 2-mi. hike from the center of town down Maiden Castle Rd.

The rolling fields extending in every direction from Dorchester make any walk out of the village stunning. The **Dorchester Ramblers Association** rambles throughout the summer, usually on Sunday afternoons. Check the bulletin board at the Town Hall (High East St. at North Sq.; tel. 262 911). More interesting is the **Morris Dancing,** originally performed as part of pagan fertility rites to ensure good harvests and ward off evil spirits (from April to October; schedule at the tourist office).

Dorchester doesn't offer much in the way of entertainment. If you feel the urge to dance, try **The Buzz Inn** on High West St. (open Thurs.-Sat; admission £3-5). The **Plaza Cinema** on Trinity St. is small but functional and shows first-run flicks (tel. 262 488).

Near Dorchester

Three mi. east of Dorchester lies the tiny village of **Higher Bockhampton,** where Thomas Hardy was born in 1840. Thanks to an observant midwife, young Thomas was rescued after having been declared dead on arrival, a fact which perhaps accounted for the lugubrious nature of his later prose. The modest "seven-roomed rambling house" was the setting for his first two novels, *Under the Greenwood Tree* and *Far from the Madding Crowd.* In childhood the already peculiar lad lived close to nature, experiencing "sheep-ness" by munching on grass with the flock. Appointments are necessary to see the house's interior (tel. 262 366). A delightful flower garden fronts the house, and Thorncobe Wood and the Blackheath Trails are at the rear. (Garden and trails open April-Oct. Wed.-Mon. 11am-1pm and 2-5:30pm, Tues. noon-5:30pm.) No bus goes to Higher Bockhampton, but a footpath runs along the River Frome. Pick it up at the bottom of London Rd. at Grey's Bridge. For a more direct but less scenic route, go down High St. until it turns into London Rd., then follow it for ½mi. to Bockhampton Rd.; turn left at the crossroads. The lane to Hardy's cottage is about 800 yd. up on the right.

Weymouth

Surrounded by the rolling Dorset hills, Weymouth is a small resort town with a spectacular sandy beach. First made fashionable by King George III, Weymouth still draws bathing beauties to its welcoming waters.

Weymouth's best side can be seen from a deck chair facing south towards the sea (chair rental 75p, 50p deposit). The town itself is small and has but a few attractions. The **Deep Sea Adventure and Shipwreck Centre,** 9 Custom House Quay, houses three floors of interesting exhibits tracing the development of diving science and salvage techniques from the 17th century to the present. (Open daily 10am-10pm; Sept.-June daily 10am-5:30pm. Admission £2.95, seniors and students £2.50, children £2. Extensive facilities for disabled people.) Be sure to visit the special exhibit on the Titanic. King George's Bathing Machine is the grand centerpiece of an otherwise mundane collection of historical artifacts at the **Weymouth Museum,** now housed in the Time Warp on Brewers Quay. The **Time Warp,** Weymouth's most popular attraction aside from the English Channel, transports visitors back into Weymouth's past. See the horrors of the Black Plague, walk aboard a Spanish Galleon, and cavort in a smuggler's cove. (Open daily 10am-9pm; Sept.-June daily 10am-6pm. Admission £2.95, seniors and children £1.75.) Bask in historical splendor at the **Tudor House,** 3 Trinity St., an authentically furnished early 17th-century merchant's house. (Open June-Sept. Mon.-Fri. 11am-4:15pm; Oct-May Sun. 2-4pm.

Admission £1, students 40p, children 30p.) A 15-min. walk along the harbor lands you in **Nothe Gardens,** a well-manicured park bursting with color.

From the quieter south side, a 4-mi. peaceful cliffside stroll along the **Underbarn Walk** leads to the island town of **Portland.** Frequent buses (every 20 min.) run to Portland from the King's Statue near the Weymouth tourist office; pick up an information leaflet at the office before you go. Visitors to the **Portland Bill Conservation Area,** at the southern tip of the island, should climb up the steps of the lighthouse for a spectacular view and a morsel of respite from the madding crowds on the **Esplanade.** During July and August, Monday nights are filled with exploding fireworks over the water. Grab a blanket and some beach. (Open daily 11am-dusk. Free.)

The **tourist information center** is on the Esplanade at the King's Statue (tel. (0305) 785 747; open Aug. 9:30am-9pm, June-July daily 9:30am-7pm, Sept.-May daily 10am-5pm). Banks ready for currency exchange line St. Mary's St. Weymouth's **telephone code** is 0305.

A very friendly staff in the cramped tourist office will book a bed in town (£2.75) or out of town (£3.25). Pick up the local guide (£1). Sunbathing crowds soak up all the rooms in summer; reservations are essential. **B&Bs** on the Esplanade are the most expensive and rare (£14 or more). **Lennox Street** and **Ranelagh Road** are quieter and cheaper (£12-14). **Greenacre,** 83 Preston Rd. (tel. (0305) 832 047), has rooms from £12.50, with breakfast.

Back in the Old Town area, the heart of Old Weymouth, a variety of food awaits you. **The House at Pooh Corner,** 50 St. Mary St., serving pizza and Piglet, is affordable. Pizza £3.50, Piglet is priceless (open Mon.-Fri. 9am-7:30pm, Sat. 9am-5:30pm, Sun. 10:30am-3pm). **Ye Olde Sally Lunne Shoppe,** on the corner of Maiden and St. Alban St., has a variety of Bak'd Goodes which ye can take out to the beach—try the bloomer loaf (£1.20). (Open Mon.-Sat. 8:30am-5pm.) **Ming Wah,** 86 St. Thomas St., serves a 3-course lunch for £3.50 (open Mon.-Thurs. 11:30am-2:30pm and 5:30-11:30pm, Fri.-Sat. 11:30am-2:30pm and 5:30pm-midnight). The **Tesco Supermarket** is on St. Thomas St. across from the post office. There are five noisy pubs on Custom House Quay, Weymouth's pub central. The brightly lit **White Heart,** on Bond St., or **Golden Lion,** on St. Mary St., are quieter. All pubs serve meals from noon-2:30pm and 6-10pm.

The **train station,** on Ranelagh Rd., connects Weymouth with London (£24 return), Chichester (£17), Bath (£9.70), Brighton (£21.70), and Dorchester (£1.80). **National Express** bus tickets can be bought at the Southern National office on the Esplanade, across from George III's brightly painted statue. (Open Mon.-Fri. 9am-5pm, Sat. 9am-3:45pm.)

Exeter

The Romans ventured as far west as the River Exe in 50 AD, founding the town that still in the Middle Ages was considered the last outpost of civilization before the wild and desolate moors of the Southwest Peninsula. Exeter (pop. 103,000) remains a cosmopolitan cynosure of culture amid the smaller villages of the West Country, with one of the few universities in the area and a choice of theaters.

Arriving and Departing

Frequent trains, coaches, and local buses serve this transportation gateway to the West Country, where passengers from London and Bristol transfer to vehicles bound for the rest of Devon and Cornwall. National Express buses are the least expensive access to Exeter, especially once you reckon in the 1/3 discount from the student coach card (£5, available at any National Express office; buses from London 8/day; 4 hr.; £20.50). Trains from London reduce the length of the trip for a price (7/day; 3 hr.; £33).

Orientation and Practical Information

The bus and train stations are located just outside the city walls. To reach the town center from St. David's Station, where most trains unload, follow the footpath and turn right onto St. David's Hill (which becomes Iron Bridge and then North St.) and turn left after the Guild Hall Shipping Centre onto High St. From Central Station, take Queen St. down to High St. Coaches and buses stop in the coach station on Paris St.; walk through the arcade to Sidwell St. and turn left to reach High St.

The majority of sights in Exeter are inside the old city walls, remnants of which have endured centuries of erosion and a few days of heavy German bombing in World War II. **High Street** bisects the walled-in area and the **cathedral** is planted at its center. **Nipper buses** shuttle inner city areas. A *Freedom of Exeter* pass allows unlimited travel on the Nippers (£1.20/day). Unassertive passengers might as well walk—the Nippers will skip stops unless warned.

Tourist Information Center: Civic Centre, Paris St. (tel. 265 700 or 265 297). Across the street from the steps at the rear of the bus and coach station. Accommodations service £1.50; list of B&Bs free. Ordnance Survey maps of Dartmoor, Exmoor, Plymouth, Land's End (£3.35-3.75); copies of *Exmoor Visitor* and *Dartmoor Visitor* free. *What's On* lists movies, live entertainment, and sporting events. Open Mon.-Fri. 9am-5pm, Sat. 9am-1pm and 2-5pm.

Tours: Free walking tours (30-90 min.) leave 5 times/day, twice on Sun., from the Royal Clarence Hotel, Cathedral Yard. Check also at the tourist office for 90-min. walking theme tours of "Haunted Exeter."

Bike and Camping Rental: Flash Gordon, 1A Old Park Rd., off Longbrook St. (tel. 213 141). Three-speeds £5/day, 5-speeds £6, and 10-speeds £8. Week rentals £20, £22, £25/week, respectively. Insurance 50p. Bike packs, mountain bikes, camping and hiking gear. Open Mon.-Sat. 9am-6pm, Sun. occasionally—phone first.

Bus and Coach Station: Paris St., off High St. just outside the ancient city walls (tel. 562 31). Lockers available 24 hr. (50p, £1, or £2, depending on size). Open daily 7:45am-6:30pm.

Crisis: Samaritans, 2 Wynards, Magdalen St. (tel. 411 711); 24 hr.

Emergency: Dial 999; no coins required.

Financial Services: Thomas Cook, 77 Sidwell St. Fee £2; Cook checks exchanged free. Open Mon.-Tues. and Thurs.-Sat. 9am-5:30pm, Wed. 9:30am-5:30pm. **Barclay's,** 20 High St. Fee £2. Open Mon.-Fri. 9:30am-4:30pm, Sat. 9:30am-noon. **Lloyd's Bank,** 234 High St. £4 fee on traveler's checks, £2 on cash. Open Mon.-Fri. 9:30am-4:30pm, Sat. 9:30am-12:30pm.

Hospital: Royal Devon and Exeter, Barrack Rd. (tel. 411 611). Bus #H through High St.

Launderette: St. David's Laundrette, St. David's Hill. Open daily 8am-9pm. Last wash 8pm. £1.60 wash, 20p dry. 15% off for students.

Market: St. George's Market, 91 High St. Open Mon.-Tues. and Thurs.-Sat. 9am-5pm, Wed. 9am-noon.

Pharmacy: Boots, 250 High St. Open Mon.-Wed. and Fri.-Sat. 8:45am-5:30pm, Thurs. 8:45am-8pm. Late night pharmacists are open on a rotational basis—check the roster in any chemist's window.

Police Station: Heavitree Rd. (tel. 521 01).

Post Office: Bedford St. (tel. 531 22). Mark *Poste Restante* "Bedford St." Open Mon.-Thurs. 9am-5:30pm, Fri. 9:30am-5:30pm, Sat. 9am-1pm. **Postal Code:** EX1 1AA.

Rape Crisis: tel. 430 871; 24 hr.

Taxi: City Taxi, right outside Debenham's on High St. (tel. 434 343).

Telephones: Opposite the post office and between the bus station and tourist office. Several in kiosks on High St. **Telephone Code:** 0392.

Train Station: Exeter St. David's, St. David's Hill (tel. 433 551), several blocks from the center of town. Trains from London's Waterloo go through the smaller **Exeter Central Sta-**

tion, on Queen St. next to Northernhay Gardens (every 2 hr.) Phone inquiries Mon.-Sat. 7:30am-9pm, Sun. 9am-9pm.

Accommodations and Camping

Exeter's B&Bs include all the comforts of Buckingham Palace but are far less pretentious. Many of the less expensive B&Bs flourish on St. David's Hill, near the train station; others group around Pinhoe Rd., on the opposite side of the center. (Take bus #K, T, or G until just past Mt. Pleasant Inn for the latter.)

IYHF youth hostel, 47 Countess Wear Rd. (tel. 873 329), 2 mi. southeast of the city center, off Topsham Rd. Take minibus #K or T from High St. to the Countess Wear post office (65p). Follow Exe Vale Rd. to the end and turn left at the beswanned lake. The large, clean hostel is at the top of the hill. £6.60. Evening meal £3; hearty English breakfast, £2.30; self-catering kitchen also available. Sheets 75p, towels 20p. Open daily Feb.-Oct.; Nov. and Jan. Thurs.-Mon.

Telstar Hotel, 77 St. David's Hill (tel. 724 66). Between the downtown and St. David's rail station. Welcoming family coddles you in their cozy, crimson-colored cove. Singles £12.50, doubles £23, doubles with bath £26.

Clocktower Hotel, 16 New North Rd. behind Central Station. All rooms heated, with color TV; pithy moral epigraphs on wall. Singles £12.50, single with bath £14.50, doubles £21, doubles with bath £25.

Camping: Hill Pond Camping Site, Sidmouth Rd. (tel. 324 83). Take the Sidmouth bus and ask to be let off past the Cat & Fiddle Pub; the site is up on the left. £3.

Food and Pubs

Many restaurants are clustered around the cathedral.

Tinley's of Exeter, Cathedral Close (tel. 728 65), sells baked goods and wholefood. Shop open Mon.-Sat. 10am-5pm, restaurant daily noon-2:30pm and Tues.-Sat. 7-10pm.

Mad Meg's, Fore St. (tel. 221 225), across from St. George's Market. Mammoth portions served in medieval style. Get your palm read upstairs by Madame Rio, clairvoyant. The spirits recommend the lasagna ("Exeter's best") and 2 vegetables £4.45. Open daily 11:30am-2:15pm and 7pm until late.

Herbie's, 14 North St. As in herbivorous. Vegetarian food (£1-3) and artwork. Browse through peace journals while you eat. Mon.-Fri. 11am-2:30pm, Sat. 10:30am-4pm; dinner Tues.-Sat. 6-9:30pm.

Capel's, 21 Heavitree Rd. Fish and grilled meat served cafeteria-style in ozone-friendly packaging. Steak and kidney pie, 85p. Full course dinner, £2.80. Open Mon.-Thurs. 11:30am-2pm, 5pm-midnight; Fri, 11:30am-2:30pm, 5pm-1:30am; Sat. 11:30am-2:30pm, 5pm-12:30am; Sun. 6-9pm.

Sandwich House, 46 Bedford St. 117 varieties of sandwiches, from pb & banana to tongue and cucumber (£1-2). Open Mon.-Sat. 8am-3:30pm, dinner 7pm, last order at 9:30pm.

Pubs are on parade in Exeter and are usually open Mon.-Sat. 11:30am-2:30pm, 5-9pm. Most of the popular pubs line the alleyways off High St. The skeleton of a plague victim guards the Roman-era well in the basement of the **Well House Tavern** (annexed to the ancient **Royal Clarence Hotel**), while hearty ale flows upstairs. Sir Francis Drake frequented the **Ship Inn** (tel. 720 40), on St. Martin's Lane off High St. (beef and veggie burgers £1.70 in pub and snack bar downstairs; the upstairs is more plush and expensive), while Charles Dickens installed himself between installments at the **Turk's Head Hotel,** by the guildhall.

Sights

Magnificent **St. Peter's Cathedral** (tel. 555 73), reputed to be the best-preserved in England, rises above the central city High St. malls. Hundreds of faceless stone figures on the west front guard the interior with its lofty Gothic vaulting. The **Bishop's Throne,** made without nails, was disassembled in 1640 and again during WWII to save it from destruction. A collection of manuscripts, donated to the cathedral in the 11th century by the munificent Bishop Leofric and known to modern scholars as the **Exeter Book,** is the richest treasury of Anglo-Saxon poetry in the world. The book is on display in the cathedral library. The cathedral continues to hold choral evensong services Mon.-Fri. 6:30pm, Sat. 3pm. The library is open daily for tours. Call the cathedral (tel. 555 73) or stop by for more information.

William the Conqueror took Exeter in 1068 after an 18-day siege. To keep the natives in check, he built **Rougemont Castle.** The remaining ruins between High St. and Central Station include a gatehouse from 1070. (Open Mon.-Fri. 2-5pm. Free tours, 2:30pm.) Two gardens almost surround the castle site. The immaculate flower beds of the Regency-era **Rougemont Gardens,** on Castle St., are attached to the **Rougemount House Museum,** home to an exquisite collection of costumes and lace. (Open Mon.-Sat. 10am-5:30pm. Admission £1.50, children and students 75p; Nov.-April £1, children and students 50p. Free every Friday.) The expansive 17th-century **Northernhay Gardens** unfold just beyond the Rougemount and the preserved **Roman city walls.** Medieval authorities dug subterranean ducts to transport pure water into the city; **underground passages** (tel. 265 858) are accessible from Princesshay St., off High St. (Passages open Tues.-Sat. 2-5:30pm; last tour 5pm. Admission £1.25, children 75p.) The **Royal Albert Memorial Museum,** (tel. 265 058) across the way on Queen St., maintains an extensive collection of historical English finery (open Tues.-Sat. 10am-5:30pm; free), and the **Maritime Museum** (tel. 580 25) encourages visitors to climb aboard a Chinese junk, sail a Portuguese fishboat, and manipulate marine fixtures from every continent. (Open daily 10am-5pm, July-Aug. 10am-6pm. Admission £3.25, students and children £1.90.)

Entertainment

The **Exeter and Devon Arts Centre** on Gandy St. (tel. 219 741) and the **Arts Booking and Information Centre** on Princesshay St. supply monthly listings of cultural events in the city. The **Northcott Theatre** at the **University of Exeter** showcases its own and visiting drama troupes (tel. 548 53). The immense campus of the University of Exeter sprawls just over a rise to the north of town. To reach the university, walk up Longbrook St., which becomes Pennsylvania Rd.; take a left at the traffic light at the top. Minibus #G saves the trek from High St.

The most popular dance spot in town is the **Timepiece** wine bar (tel. 780 70). The club spins disco and punk music and features occasional live bands. (Open Wed.-Sat. 7pm-1am. Admission free until 8pm, then £1-2 plus £1 "membership" fee.) **Humphrey B's** admits only the smartly dressed to its Casablanca-style dance den. (Open nightly, admission from 9:30-10:30pm £2.50, after 10:30 £3-5, depending on the night.)

Exeter hosts a bevy of revelries—the **Devon County Show** in mid-May, the **Sailing Regatta** in July, and the **Autumn Festival** in October. From the middle to the end of June, the **Exeter Festival** fills the cathedral close with crafts, dancing, and music, and the cathedral itself with choral and orchestral concerts (for information call 718 88). Later in the summer, the **Sidmouth Folk Festival** highlights international folk dancers in a multi-cultural smorgasbord of food and dance lessons for all. (Contact the Festival Office, Civic Centre, Exeter EX1 1JN for details, available two months before the festivals.)

Lyme Regis

Known as the "Pearl of Dorset," Lyme Regis is an exquisite beach resort which has retained the charm of an 18th-century fishing village. Built into the face of a hillside, Lyme Regis (pop. 3500) is a town of steep climbs, startling views, and prodigious natural beauty. The River Lym generates soothing white-noise. Lyme's secluded beaches and lovely crescent have attracted a number of artists over the years. It was here that Jane Austen worked and vacationed and that Whistler painted both *The Master Smith* and *The Little Rose.* More recently, John Fowles set his neo-

Victorian, post-modern novel *The French Lieutenant's Woman* in Lyme Regis, and the movie was filmed in part in the town.

Most of the action in Lyme occurs near the seafront. The **Marine Promenade** backs broad beaches extending from the mouth of the River Lym westwards to the protuberate **Cobb,** an arm of land which cradles Lyme's harbor. Sunbathing resumes west of the Cobb. The **Marine Aquarium** (tel. 443 678), on the Cobb, exhibits an array of sea-harvesting tools and indigenous marine life ranging from sea mice to giant conger eels. (Open May-Oct. daily 10am-5pm, July-Aug. until dusk. Admission £1, children 50p.) The fisherman who runs the aquarium offers boat tours on the *Donna Marie.* (Summer hours depend on the weather; £3; check chalkboard by the aquarium for changes.) Chalk notices on the Cobb advertise fishing trips as well (mackerel, £3; night deep-sea fishing, £6). The Town Crier does live advertising for his very own, an Exteter's newest museum, the **Lyme Regis Experience.** Located on the Marine Parade, the museum (tel. 443 039) uses wax figures to retrace the history of the town. Other exhibits include pictures of town criers around the world and a world-famous fossil collection. (Open daily 10am-5pm; July-Aug. 10am-9pm. Admission £1.90; guided tours through town with town crier, Tues. 3pm; £1.) Coombe St. and Broad St. head inland from the north of the Lym, each with its own attractions. The gargantuan **Dinosaurland** (tel. 443 541), on Coombe St., presents the dangerous captive cromagno-lapin and reveals the intimacies of Brontosaurus procreation. (Open Easter-Oct. daily 9am-5pm. Admission £1.95, children 95p.) The **Lyme Regis Philpot Museum,** on Bridge St. next to the Guild Hall, contains rather dull exhibits on the history and geology of Lyme. (Open April-Oct. Mon.-Sat. 10:30am-1pm and 2:30-5pm, Sun. 2:30-5pm. Admission 50p, children 25p.)

Coffee shops and greengrocers line Broad St., the central artery of the town, and excellent fish-and-chip shops can always be found on Cobb St. (The Cobb becomes Cobb St. after it crosses Marine Parade.) Try the family-run **Lyme's Fish Bar,** 34 Coombe St., for the best fish-and-chips (£2) and a taste of neighborhood charm. (Open daily noon-2pm, 5-10pm; summer, noon-midnight.) Dorset cream teas (£2.30 for tea, scones, jam, and "clotted cream") are a specialty at the **Smuggler's Restaurant,** 30 Broad St (tel. 442 795; open daily 9am-10pm). The **Pancake Restaurant,** hidden in the rear of 2616 Sherwood Lane at the top of Main St. across from the cinema, serves crepe and wholefood dinners from 6-10pm.

Lodges and B&Bs huddle expectantly on Silver St. (the continuation of Broad St.), Hill Road, and Woodmead (going inland, Hill is the first right and Woodmead the second right off Silver). Expect to pay around £13-15. Down the hill, closer to the center of town, is the **Lym Guest House,** at 1 Mill Green, a merciful 5-min. walk "on the level" from the beach. (July-Aug. £15-17.50, Nov.-April £12.50-15. Showers, TV and teakettle included with every room.) **The Happy Friar,** 7 Church St. (tel. 442 379) is open for food and accommodations daily 8am-10pm. (June-Sept. £13, Oct.-May £11.) Camping is available for £5-6 at **Hook Farm** (tel. 442 801), a 15-min. walk from the coast.

Lyme Regis makes a fine—though carefully planned—day trip from Exeter. National Express bus #705 runs once a day in the summer (9am; 1¾ hr.; £6.20, students £4.50; return trip is at 6:25pm only) and only on weekends in winter. Bus #31/X31 from Axminster (just north of Lyme Regis on the A35) runs hourly. To get to Axminster, take the London-Exeter rail line (from Exeter's St. David's and Central Stations daily every 1-2 hr.) Buses stop on **Broad Street,** with its three banks, Boots Pharmacy, and **post office** (open Mon.-Wed. and Fri. 9am-12:30pm and 1:30-5:30pm, Thurs. 9am-1pm, Sat. 9am-12:30pm). The **tourist center** (tel. 442 138) is on Church St., left at the bottom of Broad St. after a short stretch of Bridge St. (Open Mon.-Fri. 10am-6pm; Sat.-Sun. in summer only 10am-5pm.) **Early closing day** is Thursday at 1pm. The **telephone code** is 0297; the **postal code** is DT7 3JH; in **emergency** call 999 or visit the **police** on Hill Rd., the continuation of Coombe St.

Exmoor National Park

Once the English royal hunting preserve, Exmoor is one of the smallest of Britain's 11 National Parks, covering an area of 265 sq. mi. on the north coast of England's southwestern peninsula. Dramatic cliffs plunging into the sea fringe tranquil woodlands and purple-heathered moorland where sheep and cattle graze. Countless ancient bridges span over 300 mi. of rivers full of trout and salmon, and thatched hamlets dot the valleys. Wild ponies still roam freely here, and the last great herds of red deer graze in woodlands between the river valleys. R.D. Blackmore's novel *Lorna Doone* (1869), based on the exploits of a band of smuggling brigands, takes place in the heart of Exmoor; a 6-mi. path leads from Oare, the scene of Lorna's shooting, to the Doone Valley.

Though over 80% of Exmoor is privately owned (as is the case with most National Parks), the territory is open to respectful hikers, bikers and nature enthusiasts.

Getting There

Access to Exmoor is made easy by frequent buses and trains from Exeter and Plymouth, the two closest cities, as well as from Bristol and London. Many lines pass through Taunton on their way to the park. The towns of Barnstaple and Minehead are Exmoor's western and eastern gateways; to get into the park you'll probably have to pass through one or the other. **Barnstaple,** at the end of a branch line from Exeter, is easy to reach by rail (4/day; 1½ hr.; £7.10). By coach, catch the #75/77 from Exeter to Ilfracombe; Barnstaple is close to the end of the line (4/day, Sun. 2/day; 2 hr.; £3.95). National Express #734 runs two afternoon trips from Bristol (2½ hr.; £16). From London, British Rail offers 8 trips daily (3 hr.) and National Express runs for £23.50 from London's Victoria Station (7 trips/day; 5 hr.). From Plymouth, catch the North Devon Expressway #85/86 coach (8:45am; 2hr. 45 min.) or one of British Rail's 6 trips (2 hr.; £14). Call the bus station in Exeter (tel. (0392) 433 551) or Plymouth (tel. (0752) 221 300) for information. Bus services to both cities change often—check ahead of time to confirm details.

The surest way to **Minehead,** by rail or by coach, is via Taunton, accessible by the main Penzance-London rail line and by frequent coach services from Exeter and Plymouth. From Taunton, you have several options for reaching Minehead: the hourly Southern National coach #28 (7/day, 1 on Sun.; 1 hr.; £2.55); **Scarlet's Coaches,** 53 the Avenue (tel. (0643) 704 204), which offers competitive services and prices (3/day; £3); or the **West Somerset Railway** (tel. (0643) 704 996), a private line that runs to Minehead from Bishops Lydeard, a town not far from Taunton (July-Aug. 5/day; May-June and Sept.-Oct. Sun.-Fri. 4/day, Sat. 5/day). Buses shuttle to Bishops Lydeard from the Taunton rail station. As bus service to both Minehead and Taunton is erratic, call ahead to confirm routes and times.

Getting Around

Although getting to the outskirts of Exmoor by public transport is easy, exploring the park by bus is nightmarish. Buses are infrequent and unpredictable, changing from season to season and from year to year. Crossing the park from Barnstaple to Minehead can take all day if you have to wait for the infrequent connecting bus in Lynton. Although it will cost £4-5 extra, you may actually save time by taking the train to Exeter, changing to a Taunton train, and then taking the Minehead bus from Taunton. The meagre offerings of the area's sundry coach companies have been collected in a booklet that is available at the tourist and park offices.

The park is best visited on foot or by bike. Two long-distance paths are the **Somerset and North Devon Coast Path** for hikers, and the coastal path which follows the ghost of the Barnstaple railroad, for bikers. Both of these pass through or near the towns of Barnstaple, Ilfracombe, Combe Martin, Lynton, Portlock Weir, Minehead and Williton, traveling from west to east (see Sights for more information). For those who insist on making quick time on sections of the coastal routes, the following buses do run, though infrequently: **Southern National** coaches (tel. (0823) 272 033) run from Minehead, to Porlock Weir (3/day) and Williton (6/day), and offer coach tours to **Ilfracombe** and Barnstaple (each £3.35). Taking these tours one-way is a plausible transport option. **North Devon Bus** (tel. (0271) 454 44) also runs frequent service to Ilfracombe from Barnstaple (Mon.-Sat. every hr.). From Ilfracombe there is a daily bus to **Combe Martin. Dunster** and **Williton** (Mon.-Fri. 7/day) lie on a continuation of the Scarlet's Coaches line from Taunton via Minehead.

Practical Information

The National Park Information Centres listed below supply detailed large-scale Ordnance Survey maps of the region (about £3) and bus timetables. Also pick up a free copy of the *Exmoor Visitor,* an annual park publication that includes a map and a detailed accommodations list (50p-£1). The centers offer guided walks from 1½ to 10 mi. The tourist information centers also book B&Bs for free (deposit required). Always be prepared for a sudden rainstorm in Exmoor. Sea winds create unpredictable weather, and thunderstorms blow up without warning. Be sure to purchase food and equipment in the larger towns, as supermarkets and camping stores in the tiny villages along the coast have a smaller selection of goods.

Exmoor National Park Information Centres

Combe Martin: Seacot, Cross St. (tel. (027188) 33 19), 3 mi. east of Ilfracombe. Open April-Sept. daily 10am-5pm.

Countisbury: County Gate (tel. (05987) 321), 2 mi. east of Lynton. Open April-Oct. daily 10am-5pm.

Dulverton: Exmoor House, Dulverton, Somerset (tel. (0398) 238 41). Headquarters of Exmoor National Park. Handles all postal inquiries. Open April-Oct. daily 10am-4:30pm; Nov.-March Mon.-Fri. 10am-4pm.

Dunster: Dunster Steep Car Park (tel. (0643) 821 835), 2 mi. east of Minehead. Open March to mid-Nov. and Christmas week daily 10am-5pm.

Lynmouth: The Esplanade (tel. (0598) 525 09). Open April-Oct. daily 10am-5pm.

Tourist Information Centers

Barnstaple: North Devon Library, Tuly Sheet, Devon, EX32 7EJ (tel. (0271) 471 77). Turn left at bus station and follow signs for library. Open April-Sept. Mon.-Sat. 10am-7pm; Oct.-March Mon.-Sat. 10am-6pm.

Ilfracombe: The Promenade, EX34 9BX (tel. (0271) 863 001). Open July-Sept. Mon.-Fri. 9:30am-5:30pm, Sat. noon-6pm, Sun. 10am-noon; May-June Mon.-Fri. 9:30am-5pm, Sat. noon-5:30pm, Sun. 10am-noon; April and Oct. Mon.-Fri. 9:30am-5pm, Sat. 2-5pm, Sun. 10am-noon; Nov.-March Mon.-Fri. 9:30am-4pm.

Lynmouth and Lynton: Town Hall, Lynton, EX35 6BT (tel. (0598) 522 25). Open April-Sept. Mon.-Sat. 10am-4:30pm.

Minehead: Town Hall, The Parade, TA24 5NB (tel. (0643) 702 624), corner of Bancks St. Open April-Oct. Mon.-Sat. 9am-1pm and 2-5pm; Nov.-March. Mon.-Sat. 2-5pm.

Accommodations and Camping

Check tourist office listings for accommodations; the *Exmoor Visitor* includes several pages of detailed listings, including B&Bs (starting at £9-9.50) scattered through the park. Call to reserve, as hostels and B&Bs tend to fill up quickly, rain or shine. Camping may be the best way to see the park without worrying about accommodations. The *Exmoor Visitor* lists several caravan parks that accept tents, but campsites that don't advertise are easy to find, especially near the coastal towns.

Before pitching a tent, ask the landowner's permission; most of Exmoor is private property.

IYHF Youth Hostels

The quality of hostels tends to vary wildly according to proprietor and location. In general, however, guests can expect accommodations with kitchen and laundry facilities, a day lockout (usually 10am-5pm), and a curfew (11pm-midnight).

Crowcombe Heathfield: Denzel House, Crowcombe Heathfield, Taunton, Somerset TA4 4BT (tel. (09847) 249), on the Taunton-Minehead road, 2 mi. from village below Quantock Hills. Turn opposite the road marked "Crowcombe Station & Lydeard St. Lawrence"; *don't* make the turn by Flaxpool Garage signposted "Crowcombe Station and Crowcombe Heathfield." Large house in woodland setting. £5.50, ages 16-20 £4.40. Open mid-March to Oct. Sat.-Thurs.; Feb. to mid-March and Nov. Fri.-Tues.

Exford: On Withypoole Rd., Exe Mead, Exford, Minehead, Somerset TA24 7PU (tel. (064383) 288); Southern National bus #39, or Scarlet Coaches from Minehead, next to the River Exe bridge. Superior grade, in the center of the park's moorland. £6.30, ages 16-20 £5.10. Open July-Aug. daily; March-June and Sept.-Oct. Mon.-Sat.; Feb. and Nov. Tues.-Sat.

Hartland: Elmscott, Hartland, Bideford, Devon EX39 6ES (tel. (02374) 416 37), 3 mi. southwest of Hartland village by footpath. No meals provided. £4.40, ages 16-20 £3.50. Open daily July-Aug.; March-June, Sept. Fri.-Tues.

Holford: Sevenacres, Holford, Bridgwater, Somerset TA5 1SQ (tel. (027874) 224). Past Alfoxton Park Hotel 1½ mi. west of Holford—keep right after passing through gate by hotel stables. In forest overlooking Bridgwater Bay, with riding stables nearby (special rates for YHA members). £5.50, ages 16-20 £4.40. Open March-Oct. Mon.-Sat.; Nov. Fri.-Sat. only.

Ilfracombe: Ashmour House, 1 Hillsborough Terrace, Ilfracombe, Devon EX34 9NR (tel. (0271) 653 37); Red Bus #6, 62, or 306 from Barnstaple, just off the main road. Georgian terrace house with view of Welsh coast. Superior grade. £6.30, ages 16-20 £5.10. Open July-Aug. daily; April-June and Sept. Mon.-Sat.

Instow: Worlington House, New Road, Instow, Bideford, Devon EX39 4LW (tel. (0271) 860 394); Red Bus #1, 2, or B from Barnstaple. A Victorian house with a view across Torridge Estuary. £6.30, ages 16-20 £5.10. Open April-Aug. Sat.-Thurs.; Feb.-March and Sept.-Oct. Sat.-Wed.

Lynton: Lynbridge, Lynton, Devon EX35 6AZ (tel. (05985) 32 37); Red Bus #310 from Barnstaple. Small former hotel in valley of River Lyn West. Well-recommended. £5.90, ages 16-20 £4.70. Open March-Oct. Tues.-Sun.; Nov.-Dec. Thurs.-Mon.

Minehead: Alcombe Combe, Minehead, Somerset TA24 6EW (tel. (0643) 25 95), 2 mi. from the town center. Follow Friday St., which becomes Alcombe Rd., turn right on Brook St. and continue to Manor Rd. From Taunton, take Minehead bus to Alcombe stop (1 mi. from hostel). Spacious grounds. £5.50, ages 16-20 £4.40. Open April-Aug. Tues.-Sun.; Jan.-March and Sept.-Oct. Tues.-Sat.

Sights and Activities

Although **Barnstaple** does not make a good hiking base unless you want to set out on the coastal path, it is the largest town in the region (much larger than Minehead), a transportation center, and the best place to get camping and hiking gear, as well as a good pre-trip meal. **Marden Arches,** on Marden St. just off High St., offers squid and pasta dishes for under £3, and on Tuesdays and Fridays, two markets grace the town: both the **market** at Butcher's Row and the glass-roofed **Pannier Market** sell locally-grown vegetables and fruits, and delectable Devonshire clotted cream. Cheap camping equipment can be bought at **Cassie's Surplus,** 19 Tuly St., across from the tourist office (tel. (0271) 50 79). Bikes can be hired from **Tarka Trail,** conveniently located at the head of the coastal bike path; from the center of town, cross the bridge, and Tarka's is by the railroad station (tel. (0271) 242 02, £3.50-6/day). The path provides level cycling for 15 mi. along the coast, where the old Barnstaple railroad tracks used to run.

Two good places to begin traipsing into the forest close to Barnstaple are Blackmoor Gate, 9 mi. northwest of Barnstaple, and **Parracombe,** 2 mi. further. Both are on the Barnstaple-Lynton bus line.

Minehead is only a mile from the park's eastern boundary. It prides itself on having a **nature trail** designed for disabled visitors that winds past labeled trees and shrubs. A guided trail (25p) begins off Parkhouse Rd. Other well-marked paths weave through North Hill, an easy walk from the town center. Bikes, horses and fishing boats can be rented on Warren St., along the water, at the **West Somerset Booking Office** (mountain bikes £8/day).

Three mi. east of Minehead lies the village of **Dunster. Dunster Castle** (tel. (0643) 821 314) towers over the 17th-century yarn market, still going strong today. Home to the Luttrell family for 600 years, the castle has seen its share of battles, especially during the English Civil Wars. The demolished sections were remodeled in the 19th century, and today the National Trust maintains the elaborate interior, which includes a not-to-be-missed 16th-century portrait of Sir John Luttrell wading buck-naked through the surf. (Open March-Sept. Sat.-Wed. 11am-5pm; Oct.-Nov. Sat.-Wed. noon-4pm. Subtropical gardens and shrubs open daily March-Nov. 11am-5pm. Admission £3.50, children £1.50; admission to the garden and grounds only, £1.70, children 70p.) The castle and English Heritage sponsor a week-long medieval archery festival the second week of June. Tickets are available the day of the event. (For information on English Heritage events, call 973 3457.) Buses from Minehead stop at the base of Dunster Village every hour in the summer. Four mi. farther east, near Washford, the ornamentation of the ruined 12th-century **Cleeve Abbey** (tel. (0984) 403 77) is still discernible. (Open April-Sept. daily 10am-6pm; Oct.-March Tues.-Sun. 10am-4pm. Admission £1.50, seniors £1.)

Four mi. west of Minehead, **Selworthy** is a beautiful thatched-roof village built around Selworthy Green. The National Trust now owns most of the village and maintains an information booth and shop that blends in nicely with the surroundings (tel. (0643) 862 745; open Mon.-Sat. 10am-5pm; April-Oct. Sun. 2-5pm also).

Somerset and North Devon Coast Path

This coastal stretch is the highest of England's Cliff Walks, but the least arduous of the four sections of the Southwest Peninsula Coast Path, which hugs cliffs and shore all the way around Cornwall and back to South Devon. It runs 87 mi. from Minehead west through Porlock, Lynmouth, Ilfracombe, and Marshland Mouth at the Devon/Cornwall border, passing within 2 mi. of the IYHF youth hostels at Minehead, Lynton, Ilfracombe, Instow, and Hartland. The hostels are about 20 mi. apart, an ambitious but not impossible day's walk. Along the way, the path passes **Culbone,** with England's smallest church, the 100-ft. dunes of **Saunton Sands,** and the precipitously steep cobbled streets of **Clovelly Village** on Hartland Point, with its pubs dating back to the 1500s. Consider hiking or bicycling along the coastline and visiting some of these less-traveled towns. Pick up the Countryside Commission's leaflet on the path at any tourist office, and bring along a large-scale Ordnance Survey map, also available at tourist information centers—some stretches of the path are not yet marked.

Dartmoor National Park

To the south of Exmoor, 10 mi. west of Exeter and 7 mi. east of Plymouth, Dartmoor lives up to its name: valleys gouged by branches of the River Dart divide up the 365 sq. mi. of high, peaty moorland. The moors have been inhabited for more than 10,000 years, and historic remains in the park date back to 4000 BC. Standing stones, chambered tombs, and stone rows stand unguarded and mysterious all over the moor, and ravens perched on giant tors of weathered granite watch over stone circles and burial cairns, as well as Iron Age hill forts. Remains of the tin-mining industry which once flourished on the moors, are the most recent entry in the archaeological anthology. Such remnants of abandoned civilization lend the park a grim charm; Dartmoor's haunting atmosphere inspired Sir Arthur Conan Doyle whose horror story "Hound of the Baskervilles" is set in the misty peatlands.

Dartmoor's hellhound failed to frighten away its 30,000 permanent residents, among them the registered commoners who have retained the feudal "Common Rights" that allow them to graze their ponies and sheep, cut peat, and collect heather for thatching on public land. Although this "common land" makes up much of the park, the central moorland remains largely uninhabited.

Getting There and Getting Around

Dartmoor is most easily accessible from either Plymouth or Exeter. Buses link these two large towns on the peninsula's southern coast with various towns on the park's perimeter (such as Ivybridge, Tarrstock, Okehampton, Moretonhampstead, Bovey Tracey, and Ashburton), as well as a few in the central moorlands (Princetown and Postbridge).

The **Transmoor Express** (National Express bus #82) cuts through the middle of the park on its southwest-northeast route between Plymouth and Exeter, passing through Yelverton (at the southwest corner of the park), Princetown, Postbridge, Moretonhampstead, and Steps Bridge (at the park's northeast corner). (3/day mid-May to mid-Sept. No buses 2nd week of July and 1st week of Sept., tel. (0392) 562 31 Exeter or (0752) 222 221 Plymouth.) Exeter and Plymouth are also linked by #X38/39, which follows a route along the park's southern edge, stopping in Buckfastleigh and Ashburton (every hr., Sun. every 2 hr.). Plymouth runs 31 buses to Ivybridge (service #188, X80, or 88 Mon.-Sat.; ½hr.); to Tavistock, on the western edge of the park, north of Yelverton, take #83, 84, or 84A (Mon.-Fri. 3/hr. until 6pm, then every hr.; 1 hr.; one additional bus runs on Monday afternoon (#98A) and Tuesday afternoon (#96)); to Okehampton, on the park's northern edge, catch #86 (Sat. evening passing through Tavistock; 1 hr. 45 min.) or #X86 (Sun. evening continuing on to Barnstaple). Services change seasonally and routes are not permanent; check all schedules at the bus station. For more information, contact the **Exeter coach station** at (0392) 562 31; the **Plymouth coach station** at (0752) 66 40 11; the Devon County Council's Public Transportation Helpline (Mon.-Fri. 8:30am-5pm; tel. (0392) 382 00); or any National Park Information Centre (see below).

Hiking, cycling, and hitching are the best ways to traverse the park once you've reached its perimeter,as making bus connections requires careful planning. In the winter, snow will often render the park and its tortuous roads impenetrable.

Orientation and Practical Information

The *Dartmoor Visitor,* available free at National Park Information Centres and at the Exeter and Plymouth tourist offices, is essential for any trip into the park. The newspaper lists the park rangers, facilities for the disabled, firing hours of the shooting ranges on the North Moor, addresses of the information centers, and provides a basic map of the area. Walking-talking tours on the archaeology, folklore, or fauna of the region depart from the information centers, and are also delineated in leaflets. (2 hr. tours £1, up to 8 hr. £2.20; leaflets 25p.) The *Dartmoor Visitor* lists the times and themes. The British Telecom weatherline (tel. (0898) 141 203) broadcasts climate changes in Dartmoor and Exmoor.

Visitors should not underestimate the capricious Dartmoor weather and terrain. An Ordnance Survey map scaled 1:50,000 or 1:25,000 (£2.75-4), a compass, and truly waterproof garb are essential; mists come down without warning, and there is no shelter away from the roads. The footpaths marked on the map are not signposted on the high moor; invest in the better Ordnance Map with terrain markings. Walking alone is never wise, but if solitude is your only solace, leave word of your intended route and expected time of return with the local police or youth hostel warden. The sinister Stapleton of Doyle's story has not been the only Dartmoor wanderer to vanish in the bogs.

Most of Dartmoor's roads are good for bicycling, though the dips and hills can send you hurtling. Fishing, canoeing, and climbing, are also possible; for canoeing arrangements, contact Mr. K. Chamberlain, **Mountain Stream Activities,** Hexworthy (tel. (03643) 215). The National Park Information Centres and the *Dartmoor Visitor* can elaborate on various programs, including horse-riding camps that take live-in volunteers for a few weeks at a time (arrange in advance). It is wise to book ahead at riding stables if you want to get on your high horse in high season. Try the following establishments:

Ilsington: Smallacombe Farm Riding Stables, Newton Abbot (tel. (03646) 265). £4/hr., £15/day. Day trekking by arrangement, instruction available.

Mary Tavy: Cholwell Farm and Riding Stables near Tavistock (tel. (082281) 526). Escorted rides and instruction. £3/hr., £5.50/half day, £10/day.

Sticklepath: Skaigh Stables, Skaigh Lane, near Okehampton (tel. (0837) 840 429). £5/hr., £19 day. Escorted rides, open Easter-Oct.

Warning: The Ministry of Defense uses much of the northern moor for target practice; consult the *Dartmoor Visitor* or an Ordnance Survey map for the boundaries of the danger area, and then check the weekly firing timetable (available in park and tourist offices, hostels and campsites, police stations, and local pubs), or call (0837) 529 39 from Okehampton, (0752) 70 19 24 from Plymouth, or (0392) 701 64 from Exeter for recorded information.

National Park Information Centres

Dartmoor National Park Tourist Information Centre, Town Hall, Bedford Square, Tavistock PL19 0AE (tel. (0822) 612 938). The central moor information center. Books accommodations and has information about all of southwest England. Open April-Oct. Mon.-Sat. (occasionally Sun.) 10am-5pm.

Okehampton (tel. (0837) 530 20). On Main St. in the courtyard adjacent to the White Hart Hotel. Similarly books accommodations and has information about all of southwest England. Open July-Aug. daily 10am-5pm; April-June and Sept.-Oct. Mon.-Sat. 10am-5pm.

Newbridge (tel. (03643) 303). In a caravan at Spitchwick Common, on the Two Bridges road from Ashburton. Open April-Oct. daily 10am-5pm.

Parke Barn tel. (0626) 832 093). Bovey Tracey. Headquarters of the Dartmoor park service. Open April-Oct. 10am-5pm.

Postbridge (tel. (0822) 882 72). In a car park off the B3212 Moretonhampstead-Yelverton road. Open April-Oct. daily 10am-5pm; Nov.-Dec. Sat.-Sun. 10am-5pm.

Princetown (tel. (082289) 414). In the town hall, midway between the shops and the prison. Open April-Oct. daily 10am-5pm.

Steps Bridge (tel. (0647) 520 18). On the Dartmoor side of the River Teign bridge. Caravan center in a car park off the B3212. Convenient to the Steps Bridge youth hostel. Open April-Oct. 10am-5pm; Nov. 10am-4pm.

Some useful **telephone codes** are Ashburton (0364), Bovey Tracey (0626), Christow (0647), Okehampton (0837), Princetown (082289), Tavistock (0822), and Yelverton (082285). Princetown, Newbridge, and Postbridge are located deeper in the Dartmoor forest than the rest, which ring the edges.

Accommodations and Camping

B&B signs are frequently hung in pubs and farmhouses along the roads, but the less adventurous can check the *Dartmoor Visitor,* the *Guide to Dartmoor* (published by the Dartmoor Tourist Association), and the *West Devon Holiday Guide*—all available at park information offices and in Plymouth and Exeter—for accommodations listings . The Dartmoor National Park Information Centres can give you an accommodations list for free, and the Tavistock and Okehampton offices will book you a room for 85p. If you arrive late at an information center, check the "Out of Hours" notice board in the window. If all else fails, call the Dartmoor Tourist

Association for help (northwestern area, tel. (082281) 411; northeastern area, tel. (0364) 526 79; eastern area, tel. (0626) 832 422; southern area, tel. (082285) 35 01).

Youth Hostels

Steps Bridge, Dunsford, Exeter EX6 7EQ (tel. (0647) 524 35), 1 mi. southwest of Dunsford village on the B3212. Take the Exeter-Moretonhampstead bus. Simple grade IYHF hostel; a cabin in wooded surroundings with warm showers. £5.10, ages 16-20 £4. Open June-Aug. Mon. and Wed.-Sun., April-May and Sept. Mon. and Thurs.-Sun.

Bellever, Postbridge, Yelverton, Devon PL20 6TU (tel. (0822) 882 27), 1 mi. southeast of Postbridge village, the nearest bus stop (ask the driver to let you off closer). An IYHF hostel in the heart of the park and very popular. Showers and evening meal available. Standard grade. £5.90, ages 16-20 £4.40. Open April-Oct. Tues.-Sun.

Gidleigh, Castle Farm, Gidleigh, Chagford, Newton Abbot, Devon TQ13 8HR (tel. (06473) 24 21), 3 mi. west of Chagford village, the nearest bus stop. A wooden hut on a tiny farm. Simple grade: no meals or showers. £2.30, ages 16-20 £1.90. No phone bookings. Open April-Sept. Fri.-Wed.

Camping

Although official campsites exist, it is common practice to camp on the open moor. Remember that most Dartmoor land is privately owned. If you suspect that land is owned, ask permission before crossing or camping on it. Backpack camping is permitted on the unenclosed moor land more than ½mi. away from the road or out of sight of inhabited areas and farmhouses. Hikers should not climb fences or walls, nor build fires in the moors; stick to the marked paths.

Ashburton: Ashburton Caravan Park, Waterleat, Ashburton (tel. (0364) 525 52). 1½ mi. from town. £4.50 for site. **River Dart Country Park,** Holne Park, Ashburton (tel. (0364) 525 52). £5.50/2-person tent. Open April-Sept.

Okehampton: Yertiz Caravan and Camping Park, Exeter Rd. (tel. (0837) 522 81). £2.25/2-person tent.

Tavistock: Higher Longford Caravan Park, Moorshop, Tavistock (tel. (0822) 613 360). 2 mi. from Tavistock toward Princetown. £5.50 for 2-person tent. Open March-Nov.

Sights

Both **Postbridge** and **Princetown** hover at the southern edge of the park's north-central plateau. Princetown, the larger of the two, is dominated by Dartmoor's forbidding maximum-security prison, where Frenchmen from the Napoleonic Wars and Americans fighting to annex Canada in 1812 once moldered. Prehistoric remains are scattered about the moor around Princetown, the area where the finest of Sir Arthur Conan Doyle's Sherlock Holmes tales was set. The *Hound of the Baskervilles* had its origin in an ancient Dartmoor legend of a gigantic, fire-mouthed hound. The northern moor is crowned by several peaks, the highest of which is **High Willhays** (2038 ft.).

The eastern part of the park is the rugged area around **Hay Tor.** Dartmoor's celebrated medieval ruins at **Hound Tor,** where excavations unearthed the remains of 13th-century huts and longhouses, lie 2 mi. north of Hay Tor village. Guided walks on the mound are available; check the **Dartmoor Visitor** for times.

To the west, **Tavistock** is Sir Francis Drake's birthplace. South of Tavistock lies **Yelverton,** where Cistercian monks built **Buckland Abbey** (off Milton Combe Rd.) in 1278. Drake later bought the abbey with his booty and transformed it into his private palace. While the Tudor and Georgian interiors of the abbey are unspectacular, the exterior and grounds, including the huge **Tithe Barn,** are impressive. (Open April-Oct. Mon.-Wed. and Fri.-Sun. 10:30am-5:30pm; Nov.-March Sat.-Sun. 2-5pm.)

Near **Buckfastleigh,** at the park's southeastern edge, is **Buckfast Abbey** (tel. (0364) 437 23), restored by the monks themselves. One of the monks, Brother

Adam, is world-famous for his bee-keeping. The 90-ft. **White Lady** waterfall plunges through the Devil's Cauldron to **Lydford Gorge.**

Plymouth

One of England's major naval ports and the largest city in the West Country, Plymouth claims to be the only place in the area that knows how to have fun. Its modern city center and happening nightlife act as a magnet to the youth of southwest England. 75,000 buildings in Plymouth were destroyed in one night during WWII, and the new city center, designed with the pedestrian in mind, features broad shopping malls, grassy courts, and car-free underpasses. The elevated promenade along the coast gives a panoramic sweep of the dockyards below and waters beyond.

Plymouth made its mark on world history as a maritime center. Both Sir Francis Drake and the *Mayflower* began their famous voyages from Plymouth's Barbican, where restored Elizabethan buildings now house shops and pubs which cater to those of tourist ilk.

Arriving and Departing

Plymouth lies on the southern coast of the southwest peninsula between Dartmoor National Park and the Cornwall peninsula, on the east-west rail line between London and Penzance (at England's southwestern tip). Trains run every hour to: London's Paddington (3½ hr.; return £36); Exeter (2 hr.; return £8.50); Bristol (3½ hr.; return £23); and Penzance (return £8.70). National Express buses serve London (6 hr.; £24), Exeter (2½ hr.; £5), and Bristol (2½ hr.; £19). Western National buses #X38/39 connect Plymouth and Exeter by running around Dartmoor (1¼ hr.; day return £2.90), while the Transmoor Link #82 goes through the park.

Orientation and Practical Information

Plymouth city center, wedged between two river inlets (the Tamar in the west and the Plym in the east), boasts two divergent characters. The gardens and restored forts of the Hoe (the area along the coastal road), and the Barbican's cobblestone streets and fisherman's pubs by historic Sutton Harbor yield to a more modern metropolitan center further inland, based around the Royal Parade and the pedestrianized shopping streets of Armada Way, which run perpendicular to the Parade and the coast. **Hoppa** buses shuttle from Royal Parade, the center of the city where you'll find the tourist office and bus and coach station, to most areas of the city (50p-£1.50).

Tourist Information Center: Civic Centre, Royal Parade (tel. 264 849/51), in the main entrance hall. Open June-Sept. Mon.-Fri. 9am-5pm, Sat. 9am-4pm; Oct.-Nov. and April-May Mon.-Thurs. 9am-5pm, Fri. 9am-4:30pm, Sat. 9am-noon; July-Sept. Sun. 10am-4pm. Accommodations booking for £1.50, city maps (10p) and free *What's On* listing of cultural events.

Tours: A *Plymouth Historic Walk* pamphlet (available at the tourist office, 10p) is packed with information and guides a sensible journey from St. Andrew's Church to The Hoe. Plymouth Gin, Southside St., gives tours 10:30am-4pm (£1.25, under 18 75p). 1 hr. cruises (£2.50, children £1.25) around the Hoe and the dockyards leave daily from Phoenix Wharf (tel. 822 202), near the Barbican at the eastern end of town, every ½hr. 10am-5pm. Check the wharf for additional ferries in the summer.

Bike Rental: Plymvale Mountain Bikes, Queen Anne's Battery (tel. 268 328). £10/day. Open Mon.-Sat. 9:30am-5:30pm, Sun. 10am-4pm.

Bus and Coach Station: Bretonside Station, near St. Andrew's Cross, a square at the eastern end of Royal Parade (tel. 664 011). To get to the city center, exit stairs onto Exeter St. to St. Andrew's Cross, continue to Royal Parade.

Crisis: Samaritans, 20 Oxford Place (tel. 221 666; 24 hr.), off North Rd. Western Approach. Doors open daily 9am-10pm.

Emergency: Dial 999; no coins required.

Ferries: Millbay Docks, Brittany Ferries (tel. 221 321). Take city bus #34 to docks, to the west of the city center at the mouth of the River Tamar, and follow signs to ferry stand. Quite a haul. Tickets must be booked at least 24 hr. in advance. Ferry to: **Roscoff, France** (1-4/day; 6 hr.; £30); **Santander, Spain** (1-3/day; 24 hr.; £70). Check-in an hour before departure.

Financial Services: Midland Bank and **Thomas Cook,** 1 Old Town St., by the post office. Fee £2.50. Mon.-Fri. 9:30am-5:30pm, Sat. 9:30am-3:30pm. Royal Parade and Armada Way burst with banks. **American Express:** 7 Raleigh St. (tel. 228 708), opposite Theatre Royal by the Derry's Cross rotary. Mail held; currency exchange (fee £1.50). Open Mon.-Fri. 9am-5pm, Sat. 9am-noon.

Hospital: Derriford Hospital, Derriford (tel. 777 111). Take bus #50 from Royal Parade stop.

Launderette: Mayflower Launderette, 12 Mayflower St. W (tel. 229 082). Open daily 8am-9pm, last wash 8pm.

Pharmacy: Boots, 76 New George St. by post office. Open Mon.-Fri. 9am-9pm, Sat. 9am-6pm, Sun. 4-8pm.

Police: Charles St. (tel. 701 188), near Charles Cross bus station.

Post Office: St. Andrew's Cross (tel. 665 776). *Poste Restante,* Plymouth, at stamp counter. Open Mon.-Thurs. 9am-5:30pm, Fri. 9:30am-5:30pm, Sat. 9am-12:30pm. **Postal Code:** PL1 2EW.

Telephones: Phonecard and pay phones at junction of Royal Parade and Armada Way. **Telephone Code:** 0752.

Train Station: Milehorse, North Rd. (tel. 221 300), north of city center. Take Western National bus #80 or 81 to the city center.

Accommodations and Camping

A fountain of luxurious, low-priced B&Bs irrigates Citadel Rd. and Athenaeum St., between the north end of Royal Parade and the Hoe; all include color TV, tea-making facilities, and continental breakfast. Standards are uniformly high, and prices run from about £11.50 to £16. Consult *Welcome to Plymouth* for accommodations listings, or check on B&B availability at the tourist office. Book in advance at the hostel and YWCA, which fill up quickly.

IYHF youth hostel, Belmont House, Devonport Rd., Stoke, Plymouth PL3 4DW (tel. 562 189), 2 mi. from city center. Take bus #15 or 15A (70p, day return £1) to Molesworth St. Left at traffic light, and eventually left into gates. Clean and spacious rooms in a former banker's mansion. £5.90, ages 16-20 £4.70. The showers are as hot and delicious as the chicken curry dinner (evening meals £1.70-2.10, breakfast £1.10). Curfew 11pm, lockout 10am-5pm. Open March-Oct. daily; Dec.-Jan. Wed.-Sun.

YWCA, 9-13 Lockyer St. (tel. 660 321), at Notte St. A stone's throw from the Hoe and the Royal Parade. A clean and secure place that takes transients of all types and nationalities. Laundry facilities and continental breakfast included. No curfew. Singles £9.50, doubles £8.50/person, dorm room £6. Continental breakfast included. £10 key deposit.

St. Rita Hotel, 76/78 Alma Rd. (tel. 667 024), just up the hill from the railroad station. Slot in with this eccentric, loveable couple and their rad vending machines. £11.50-15.50.

Food and Pubs

The cobbled streets of the Barbican and the city center quake with shoppers during the day. At night, the pubs are lively with locals; the restaurants in the Barbican depend largely on tourists and are commensurately expensive. Pick up picnic fixings at **Plymouth Market** at the west end of New George St. Open Mon.-Tues. and Thurs.-Sat. 7am-5:30pm, Wed. 7am-2pm.

The Gorge Café, Royal Parade (tel. 262 552), diagonally across from the Theatre Royal. Wash down a block of Nelson Square (a fruity bread pudding, 28p) with an Italian-quality ice coffee

(65p) in this surreal and spacious Victorian-fixtured melon-colored cavern, also famous for its homemade Cornish pasties (65p). Open Mon.-Sat. 7:30am-6pm, Sun. 9:30am-5:30pm.

Plymouth Arts Centre Restaurant, 38 Looe St. (tel. 660 060), Kinterbury St. from St. Andrew's Cross. Homemade for herbivores. Fill up on an à la carte meal (£2) after catching a flick. Quiche with wholemeal shell 75p. Lunch Mon.-Sat. noon-2pm, dinner Tues.-Sun. 5-8pm.

Cap'n Jaspers, a stand by the Barbican side of the Harbor, sells local catch and Breton crepes to locust-like hordes of tourists. Puppets and pop-ups fail to amuse. Burgers under £1. Open Mon.-Sat. 6:30am-11:45pm, Sun. 10am-11:45pm.

Marianna's Kitchen, Higher Lane (tel. 226 753) corner of Buckwell St. Homemade cakes and eccentric specialties. Try the pasty with steer meat (£1). Open flexibly Mon.-Sat. 6:30am-late evening.

Southside St. demands a crawl through its pubs en route to the Barbican; try **The Ship** or **The Navy** for seaside spirits. **The Abbey,** on Higher Lane, is a popular spot for drinks and dinner, while **The Minerva Inn** on Looe St. is one of the most experienced buildings in Plymouth (open 2-11pm daily). An older crowd frequents the **Queen's Arms** by the harbor.

Sights

The kernel from which Plymouth grew, a Saxon parish church, was built on the site of **St. Andrew's Church** on Royal Parade. Little remains of the 13th-century structure, which was restored to its 15th-century incarnation after being gutted by fire during the bombing raids of 1941. **Pryston House,** behind the church, cherishes its 11th-century tapestry. (Open April-Oct. Mon.-Sat. 10am-4pm. Admission 50p; seniors and children 15p.) In 1762, the Jewish community constructed a **synagogue** on Catherine St. behind St. Andrew's Church (ring and the caretaker will show you around). Still in use today, it is the oldest Ashkenazi (Eastern European-rite) synagogue in continuous use in the English-speaking world.

Merchant's House, former home to the town's 17th-century mayors located near St. Andrew's, illustrates "Tinker, Tailor, Soldier, Sailor, Rich Man, Poor Man, Apothecary, Thief" in the context of Plymouth history. The pharmacy on the top floor captures the mystery and ignorance of 1930s medicine, leeches and all. (Open Tues.-Sat. 10am-1pm and 2-5:30pm. Admission 80p, children 20p.) On the other side of the Barbican, **Elizabethan House** on New St. is a sea-captain's home frozen in the 16th century. (Open Tues.-Sat. 10am-1pm and 2-5:30pm, Sun. 2-5pm. Admission 80p, children 20p.)

A plaque on the Barbican marks the spot where the Pilgrims set off in 1620 for their historic voyage to America. Subsequent departures have been marked as well, including Sir Humphrey Gilbert's voyage to Newfoundland, Sir Walter Raleigh's attempt to colonize North Carolina, and Captain Cook's voyage to Australia and New Zealand. Plymouth's most celebrated native, Sir Francis Drake, left in 1577 to carry out Queen Elizabeth's scheme to circumnavigate the globe. Three years later Drake returned in triumph, with enough booty to satisfy the Virgin Queen and purchase Buckland Abbey for himself.

Legend has it that Sir Francis was playing bowls on the green of the fortress on the Hoe in 1588 when he heard that the Spanish Armada had entered the English Channel. Displaying classic British phlegm, Drake finished his game before hoisting sail. The looming **Royal Citadel** currently houses the Royal Navy and excludes the clamoring public. Plebs may climb the spiral steps and four ladders of **Smeaton's Tower** for a magnificent view of Plymouth and the remains of the fortress on the now unvisitable **Drake's Island.** (Open May-Oct. 9am-6pm, 65p.) While a prison, the island held Major General John Lambert, Cromwell's intended successor.

The Dome, (tel. 603 300) beneath the tower, is a new multi-media museum that tickles your sensory organs with the olfactory history of Plymouth—note the stench of Elizabethan England and the maid emptying a chamberpot overhead. (Open daily 10am-7pm. £2.10, children £1.45, seniors £1.85.)

Entertainment

The **Theatre Royal** has discount tickets for students and under 18s on Monday and Tuesday (£2). Student standbys purchased a half hour before the show are only £3. **Plymouth Art Centre,** at 38 Looe St., shows art-circuit films. (£2.50; tel. 660 060; check a brochure from the tourist office.) Rambunctious **Union Street** barely contains Plymouth's wild nights. From **Boobs** (be warned: the name says it all) to the buzzing **Grapevine** in the New Continental Hotel, Plymouth has something for every taste, every night of the week.

Bodmin Moor

Equidistant between the north and south coasts of the peninsula, Bodmin Moor is high country, like Dartmoor and Exmoor to the east, containing Cornwall's loftiest points—Rough Tor (1311 ft.; ROH-tor) and Brown Willy (1377 ft.). Unlike Exmoor and Dartmoor, Bodmin Moor is not a national park, and so officially *any* hiking and camping in this scenic area must be done with the permission of the private owners of these lands. Be sure to keep to designated paths. The region is rich in lore and legend, most notably Arthurian legend; some say that Camelford, at the moor's northern edge, is the site of Arthur's Camelot, and that Arthur fought his last battle at the Ancient Slaughter Bridge a mile north of town.

Getting There and Getting Around

Bodmin Moor spreads north of Bodmin town towards Tintagel (on the coast), Camelford, and Launceston (both inland from Tintagel). Bodmin is the park's point of entry, accessible from all directions, though not a particularly good place to start hiking. The town is served directly (Mon.-Fri.) by buses from Padstow on the north coast (6/day) and St. Austell on the southern shore (every hr.). Three daily National Express buses arrive from farther afield: from Plymouth in the southeast (afternoons only; 1 hr.; £3.50) and from Newquay in the west (mornings). For bus information, call the station in Truro (tel. (0872) 404 04). Trains stop hourly at the Bodmin Parkway Station on the Plymouth-Penzance line (from Plymouth, 40 min.; £5.80). Call 87 38 78 for train information.

Buses run from Bodmin to various towns on the moor. **Fry's Bus Services** (tel. (0840) 770 256) is a private company that sporadically connects Bodmin with Camelford, Tintagel, and Launceston. The schedule is not well circulated and changes annually; call for specifics.

Orientation and Practical Information

Since Bodmin is not a national park, it is devoid of information centers dedicated to the area. Visitors are advised to visit the tourist office in Bodmin for information on the moor. Like the other moors around the West Country, Bodmin Moor is best seen by foot, bike, or car. Bikes are for hire in Bodmin and the towns around it.

Accommodations

Book accommodations through the Bodmin tourist office, or hope to happen upon evidence of the B&B rash which mottles the moor; **Mennabroom** in Warleggan (tel. 822 72), which nestles deep in the park by Colliford Lake's trout-ridden waters (£10), or the quiet 13th-century monk's fishery at **St. Anne's Chapel Hayes,** next to the River Camel (tel. 727 97) on the road between Bodmin and Wadebridge (£10.50), are examples of the gems you are bound to find.

There are many sanctioned camping sites throughout the moor, as well as a number of youth hostels.

IYHF Hostels

Boscastle Harbour, Palace Stables, Boscastle PL35 0HD (tel. (08405) 250 287); take Fry's bus from Bodmin or Plymouth. £5.90, ages 16-20 £4.70. Open daily July-Aug.; March-June, Sept.-Nov. Tues.-Sun.

Tintagel, Dunderhole Point, Tintagel PL34 0DW (tel. (0840) 770 334). Take Fry's Services from Bodmin or Plymouth to Tregatta Corner. £5.90, ages 16-20 £4.70. Open daily July-Aug.; March-June, Sept.-Nov. Wed.-Mon.

Sights

The unremarkable town of **Bodmin** is the last supply stop before tumbling onto Arthurian stomping grounds. The **tourist office** at the Mount Folly Car Park (tel. (0208) 766 16) provides free accommodations listings, a booking service (£1.50), Ordnance maps of the area (£2.99-3.70) and supplementary reading. (Open Mon.-Fri. 9:30am-1pm and 2-4pm. July-Aug. also Sat. 9:30am-4pm.) The **police station** (tel. 722 62) is up Priory Rd., past the ATS car parks, and the **post office** (tel. 726 38) is beyond the tourist information center. (Open Mon.-Thurs. 9am-5pm, Fri. 9:30am-5pm.) Bodmin's **postal code** is PL31 1AA, and the **telephone code** is 0208. For food head to Fore St., where grocers and bakers hawk digestibles. The **Take a Bite Cafe,** 59 Fore St. (tel. 734 94) fuels the body electric with cheap and greasy servings for take out (fish or pasty and chips £1.45; open Mon.-Sat. 7:30am-8pm, Sun. 8am-7pm). **P&R,** a daily supermarket, has competitive proices with the least expensive bakers and produce shops (open daily 8am-10pm), and Saturdays are market day in Bodwin.

To get to the center of town from the Bodmin Parkway Station, 4 mi. out of town, hop a Hoppa bus. Efficient two-wheeled transport (as opposed to the inefficient 4-wheeled version) is available at the **Bodmin Trading Co.** at the bottom of Mt. Folly and Fore St. (tel. 725 57). (Ten-speeds £2.50/day; mountain bikes £5. Refundable deposit of £25. Open Mon.-Fri. 9am-5:30pm, Sat. 9am-5pm.) Bed down at **Scrumptious,** a 10-min. walk from town (£10). **Yewberry,** 5 Berry Lane, is cheap and closer to the hub (£9). Camping closest to Bodmin is a mile north of the town at the **Camping and Caravaning Club,** Old Callywith Rd. (tel. 738 34; equipped with laundry, showers and shop; open March-Sept.; £3.35/night, children £1).

Thirteen mi. north of Bodmin, the smaller town of **Camelford** is a better but less accessible base for hiking, as it is closer to the moors. The Camelford **tourist office,** in the North Cornwall Museum and Gallery, The Clease, Camelford (tel. (0840) 212 954), can direct you onto the moor. (Open April-Oct. Mon.-Sat. 10:30am-5pm.) You can rent a bike from **Bridge Bike Hire** (tel. (0208) 813 050), immediately off the Camel Trail, the old railroad track that has been turned into a biking and hiking path. (3-speeds £3.50/day. £10/week; mountain bikes £4.50/day, £23/week.) Camelford claims to be "Camelot": one mi. north of town, **Slaughter Bridge** and **King Arthur's Tomb** mark the site where Arthur battled his nephew Mordred, and where **Excalibur** was last seen. **Dozmary Pool** to the east, near **Bolventor** and the Jamaica Inn, is believed to caress the sword in its depths.

Tintagel Castle, 5 mi. northwest of Camelford, is the promontory fortress of Arthurian legend. You may climb through the ruins of the 5th-century castle to Merlin's cave below for £1.60, seniors and students £1.20. (Open April-Sept. 10am-6pm, Oct.-March Tues.-Sun. 10am-4pm.) The **IYHF youth hostel** (tel. (0840) 770 334) at Dunderhole Point will provide lodgings. (£4.60, ages 16-20 £3.70. Open March-Oct. Wed.-Mon.)

St. Breward on the west side of the park and Minions on the east each claim to be the highest village in Cornwall. Near **St. Breward's,** take a footpath to **King Arthur's Downs,** two Bronze Age stone circles. The curious stone enclosure called **King Arthur's Hall** is nearby. The Hall's purpose remains a mystery, and guesses as to the time of its origin have ranged from the Neolithic to the distant future. In contrast, **Candra Hall** (tel. 850 415), near St. Breward, quite clearly caters to sleepy visitors for £10. Rough Tor challanges ambitious hikers who spend the night. **Mrs. Muriel Wilton** at Wetherham Lane (tel. 850 096) in St. Tudy (off the B3266 north of Bodmin) is closer to the Tor, Arthur's last stab. The house also has facilities for the disabled (£9). From **Minions,** hike to the granite-looped Cheesewring and the **Hurlers,** a Bronze Age stone circle of men metamorphosed to roquefort as punishment for sporting on a Sunday. **St. Cleer,** between Minions and Liskeard, is hemmed by Trethevy Quoit, a megalithic chamber tomb, and King Doniert's stone.

If you can get there, the hillside market town of **Launceston** (LAWN-ston) is a pleasant place to spend a day. The ruins of Norman Launceston Castle (tel. (0566) 23 65), preside over Dartmoor and Bodmin from a hill at the center of town. (Open April-Sept. 10am-6pm; Oct.-March Tues.-Sun. 10am-9pm; 85p, seniors and students 65p.)

Falmouth

Seven rivers flow into the sea at Falmouth's harbor, and the rocky stretch of Pendennis Head sweeps out to the open sea. Falmouth's Pendennis Castle commands the heights, overlooking winding roads above huge cliffs and gorgeous rocky beaches. Luxury mansions, hotels and beachfront cottages tumble down to the third-largest natural harbor in the world, where a jumble of small craft dance on the water. A refuge for pirates and privateers under the ruthless governorship of the Killigrew family, Falmouth enjoyed its heyday from 1689 to 1840 as England's foremost mail-packet station. Today the town is still obsessed by its harbor, with most of the activity focusing on the quays and on the seashore.

Arriving and Departing

About 60 mi. west of Plymouth along the southern coast of England, Falmouth (pop. 18,600) is accessible by rail from any stop on the London-Penzance line (including Exeter and Plymouth); change at Truro and go one stop to Falmouth (1/hr.; 25 min.; £3.50). By bus, take National Express from London (2/day 11:30am or 1:30pm; 6½ hr.), Newquay, Plymouth, or Penzance (every 2 hr.) From Penzance, Western National #2 will take you straight to Falmouth.

Orientation and Practical Information

Falmouth has three train stations. **Penmere Halt** is a 10-min. walk from town; the **Dell-Falmouth Town**is east of the center and convenient to area ripe with budget B&Bs; **Falmouth Docks**is nearest the Pendennis Castle area and hostel. Out-of-town coaches and local Hoppa buses stop just outside the tourist office at **The Moor,** a large traffic island on Killigrew St., which runs perpendicular to the harbor. The post office, three banks, and a bike rental surround The Moor. At the bottom of Killigrew St. is a narrow thoroughfare of shops and pubs. As it climbs toward Pendennis, it is successively renamed High St., Market St., Church St., Arwenack St., Bank Pl., Grove Pl., Bar Rd., and Castle Dr. Cars hurtling through force pedestrians into hieroglyphic poses of self-preservation.

Tourist Information Center: 28 Killigrew St. (tel. 312 300), on The Moor. Follow signs to beaches or moor, turn down Kimberly Park Rd. to Killigrew. Accommodations service £1.50. Free accommodations lists and town maps. Open June-Sept. Mon.-Thurs. 8:45am-5:15pm, Fri. 8:45am-4:45pm, Sat. 9am-5pm; Oct.-May Mon.-Fri. 8:45am-1pm and 2-5:15pm; July-Aug. Sun. 10am-4pm.

Bike Rental: Aldridge Cycles, Swanpool St. (tel. 318 600), by the Custom's Quay. £4/day, £10 deposit. Open Mon.-Sat. 9am-5:30pm.

Boats and Ferries: check signs on Custom House Quay and Prince of Wales Pier. **Enterprise Boats,** Prince of Wales Pier (tel. 374 241), offers 2-hr. tours around the River Fal daily at 10:30am (£3.50, children £1.75) as well as trips to **Truro** and **Malpas. Princessa** sails daily through the bay and a ferry travels to St. Mawes (every ½hr. in summer, every hr. in winter; ½hr.; £3 return). Both boats are owned by the **St. Mawes Ferry Co.** (tel. 313 813). Rent your own aquatic pleasure tools at Custom House Quay (tel. 311 434 day, (0247) 235 09 evenings.)

Buses and Coaches: Buses and coaches stop next to the tourist office at The Moor. Call 404 04 for information. For schedules and tickets, contact Newell's Travel Agency, 17-18 Killigrew St. (tel. 312 620), on The Moor, or the tourist office.

Car Rental: Fiesta Motors, Castle Dr. (tel. 319 357).

Crisis: Samaritans, tel. (0872) 772 77; 24 hr.

Early Closing Day: Wed. at 1pm.

Emergency: Dial 999; no coins required.

Financial Services: Barclays, Killigrew St., The Moor. Open Mon.-Fri. 9:30am-4:30pm. Fee £4. **Lloyd's,** The Moor. Open Mon.-Fri. 9:30am-5:30pm. Fee £4. **Midland Bank,** Market St. Open Mon.-Fri. 9:30am-3:30pm. Fee £3.

Health Center: Trescobeas Rd. (tel. 317 317). Take Falmouth Hoppa B from the library to Trescobeas.

Hospital: Truro City Hospital, Trescobeas Rd., Truro (tel. (0872) 742 42).

Pharmacy: Boots, 4749 Market St. (tel. 312 373). Open Mon.-Sat. 9am-5:30pm. Late night pharmaceutical duties rotate.

Police: Commercial Rd., Penryn (tel. 722 31).

Post Office: The Moor (tel. 312 525). Open Mon.-Thurs. 9am-5:30pm, Fri. 9:30am-5:30pm, Sat. 9am-12:30pm. **Postal Code:** TR11 3RB.

Telephones: Next to the post office. **Telephone Code:** 0326.

Train Stations: Penmere Halt, up Killigrew St. and Rd., right on the roundabout to Chard Terrace, left up Penmere Hill. **The Dell/Falmouth Town station:** at the juncture where Grove Pl. curves into Bar Rd., turn up Avenue Rd. **Falmouth Docks:** at the foot of Castle Dr. (tel. 762 44).

Accommodations and Camping

B&Bs cluster along Melville Rd. Those on Cliff Rd. and Castle Dr. have spectacular views of the foliage and cliffs that touch the water, but expect to pay for the thrill (£14-16). B&Bs closer to town, surprisingly, are cheaper. The exceptionally accommodating tourist office will book a bed within your budget.

IYHF youth hostel, Pendennis Castle, Falmouth (tel. 311 435). Follow the signs for a scenic ½-mi. uphill hike. This most beautiful and historic hostel has brand-new facilities and an exquisite sunset view of Falmouth. A 15-min. walk along the water from the docks' train station—look for signs. Open March-Nov. daily; Dec. Mon.-Fri. £6.60, ages 16-20 £5.70.

Castleton Guest House, 68 Killigrew St. (tel. 311 072). Hotel-quality accommodations in a 200 year-old house. Vegetarians may request alternatives to the English breakfast. £10.50; no singles.

Afton Guest House, 91 Trevethan Rd. (tel. 316 770). Mr. & Mrs. R.J. Pierce will make you feel right at home. Singles £10.50.

Camping: Tremorvah Tent Park, Swanpool Rd. (tel. 312 103), just past Swanpool Beach. A lovely secluded hillside spot. TV, laundry and showers available. Hoppa #6 runs near every half hour. £2-2.60/tent.

Food and Pubs

Simply Sugar, Church St. at the rear of the confectionary shop, entrance through alley toward the harbor. Appetizer, salad, entree (including fresh fish), dessert, and a pot of tea is £4.95. Cream teas £1.40. Fresh cakes 90p. Mrs. White has baked for Princess Anne. Her frivolous confections are famous. (Open Mon.-Sat. 9:30am-5pm, Tues.-Sun. 6:30-9:30pm, Sun. 11am-5pm.)

De Wynn's 19th Century Coffee House, 55 Church St. Tiny Arabian coffee den serves up exotic teas and baked specialties. Open Mon.-Sat. 10am-5pm, Sun. 11am-4pm.

Laughing Pirate, 7 Grove Pl. (tel. 311 288). Sit on a barrel stool for a feast of Gammon Steak (pig rump), chips, peas, mushrooms, and pineapple rings £4.25. All-you-can-eat lunch £3.50. Open Mon.-Fri. noon-3pm and 6:30-11pm, Sat. 11am-11pm, Sun. noon-3pm and 7-10:30pm.

Falmouth's pubs, like a besotten chorus line of high-stepping pirates, share a ribald maritime theme. Located on the quay and in the alleyways along Church St., they generally open sometime after 11am with last orders at 10:30pm. Many serve snacks and light meals up through dinnertime. The lounge of dimpled velvet divans in **The Globe** overlooks the harbor. Plush **King's Head** on the corner of Church St. is a local favorite. (Open daily to 11pm.) Note the entrance, fortified with English porcelain potties overhead. Climb the 111 steps of **Jacob's Ladder** (next to Lloyd's Bank) and earn a certificate suitable for framing from Jacob, proprietor of the technicolor dream pub at the top. Falmouth evenings rock at **Club International,** upstairs at **St. George's Market** and at **Shades Night Club** on the Quay (both open until 1am).

Sights

Pendennis Castle (tel. 316 594), on Pendennis Head, is Falmouth's highest attraction. Built by Henry VIII in his attempt to fortify England's coast, it was later the site of a spirited resistance movement against Cromwell's soldiers. (Open daily 10am-6pm; Oct.-March Tues.-Sun. 10am-4pm. Admission £1.50, seniors and students £1.20, children 75p.) The interior underwhelms with talking dioramas of military defenses; walk the grounds instead. From the ramparts of Pendennis, another of Henry VIII's forts, **St. Mawes Castle** (tel. 270 526), is visible. (Same hours; £1, seniors and students 75p, children 50p.)

The Arwenack House, Grove Pl., is on the way to the beaches. This 16th-century manor, now a condominium complex, was once the residence of Sir John Killigrew, the first governor to lodge at Pendennis Castle. Across the street stands Falmouth's granite **Killigrew Monument,** erected in 1737 by Martin Killigrew who, it reads, "never stated specifically the purpose of it." The **Maritime Museum** at 19 Chapel St. (tel. 318 107 or 150 507) documents life on the high seas from the pirating Killigrews to the present. (Open Mon.-Sat. 10am-5pm. Admission £1.50, students and children 75p.) The **Royal Cornwall Polytechnic Society,** on Church St., offers free art and history exhibits. (Open Mon.-Sat. 10am-4pm.)

To taste the surf, head to one of the three beaches on Falmouth's southern shore. **Castle Beach,** on Pendennis Head, is too pebbly for swimming or sunbathing, but low tide reveals a labyrinth of seaweed and tidepools writhing with life. The waters of **Gyllyngvase Beach** are popular with windsurfers and families. **Swanpool Beach,** west of Gyllyngvase, is the sandiest. The town slips into a tizzy each summer for **Carnival Week** and **Regatta Week** during the first two weeks of August.

Lizard Peninsula (Landewednack)

Sunning itself lazily between Falmouth and Penzance lies the National Trust area of the **Lizard Peninsula** (signposted as "The Lizard"). Originally a leper's colony, the Lizard remains in social quarantine. A swath of unspoiled coastline, quiet coves, and rugged scenery ends at Lizard Point, the most southerly point in England. Gweek, at the innermost cut of the River Helford, houses the **Cornish Seal Sanctuary,** where sick and injured seal pups found on the beaches are nursed back to health and returned to the sea. On the west shore of the Lizard, **Mullion Cove** is justifiably the most-photographed of Cornwall's fishing villages. Hundreds of seabirds nest on **Mullion Island,** three hundred yards off Mullion Cove. Purple serpentine rock and Cornish heath are unique to the **Goonhilly Downs** between Mullion and Coverack.

South along the coastal path, **Coverack,** above Black Head, has the only **IYHF hostel** on the Lizard (tel. (0326) 280 687; £5.90, ages 16-20 £4.70; open April-Oct.; take Truronian bus #311 from Helston, then to Parc Behan on School Hill). B&Bs are like luxury hotels; try the **Most Southerly House** (tel. (0326) 290 300) by the point, overlooking 4 acres of rugged cliffs, or spectacular **Tregominium Farm** (tel. (0326) 290 408), a wicker, window-lit home with the entire sea at its doorstep (£12).

For a charge of glamor, pay the extra £2 or £3 to sit in one of the exclusive hotel lounges for a bite to eat. The views are spectacular, and the cheaper cafés are equally touristy. The **Top House** pub in the center of town is open daily until 11pm for meat or vegetarian meals; have a sip on one of the 19 types of malt whiskey, 18 wines, or multiple ales for £1.20-1.75. Down the road towards Helston, the **Lizard Centre** plays live music Wednesdays and weekend nights.

The relative inaccessibility of the Lizard Peninsula, source of its secluded charms, can also be a source of frustration. The Penzance bus station provides guided tours to the Lizard from Penzance and St. Ives (leaves Penzance Tues. and Thurs. 11:30am, leaves St. Ives noon; 6 hr.; £4.50, children £3.50). Otherwise, take the National Express bus from Falmouth or Penzance to Helston, and then take the Truronian down to the Lizard. On Tuesdays and Thursdays, a morning bus runs from Helston to Gweek and returns in the early afternoon. For information on bus service into the peninsula, call Truro (tel. (0872) 404 04). Driving access is by the A3083 via A394.

Penwith and The North Cornish Coast

You know you've hit the Cornish "Riviera" when every cottage has a name like "Sunshine Daydream" or "Shore Enuf." The region at England's Southwest tip has some of the broadest, sandiest beaches in northern Europe; the surf is up year-round whether or not the sun decides to break through. The peninsula's riches are no secret. Every year hundreds of thousands of British and foreign tourists jockey for rays on the beaches of Penzance, St. Ives, and Newquay. Penwith is also home to a rich collection of Stone Age and Iron Age monuments; the region has apparently attracted partially naked people for thousands of years.

Getting Around

By far the best base for exploring the region is Penzance, terminus of British Rail's Cornish Railways service and of Cornwall Busways Cornwall Express coach service from Plymouth. The main rail line from Plymouth to Penzance bypasses the coastal towns, but there is connecting rail service to Newquay (change at Par, 6/day; £12.50), Falmouth (change at Truro, 12/day, 6 Sun.; £7), and St. Ives (change at St. Erth, 1-2 every hr.; £2.90). Trains are frequent, and distances are short enough that you can easily make even Newquay a day trip from Penzance. Pick up the free Cornish Railways timetable at any station, or call British Rail in Truro (tel. (0872) 762 44) for information. Cheap **day returns,** (not available on some trains), are often a better deal than single tickets. Those making three or more trips (or even fewer, provided one of them is long distance, such as Plymouth-Penzance) should consider purchasing a **Cornish Rover** ticket, valid for unlimited travel on all trains west from Plymouth for seven days (£30, £20 for holders of a Young Person's, Senior Citizen's, or Disabled Person's Railcard) or a **Cornwall FlexiRover,** valid for unlimited travel on three out of seven days (£19, with Railcard discounts £12.60).

The **Cornwall Busways** network is similarly thorough. Buses run frequently Monday through Saturday from Penzance to Land's End (every hr.), St. Ives (3/hr.), and from St. Ives to Newquay (2/day), stopping in the smaller towns along these routes. Pick up a set of timetables at any Cornwall bus station, or call the company in Truro (tel. (0872) 404 04) or Penzance (tel. (0736) 649 469) for information. Most buses don't run on Sundays, and many run only from May through September. Summer service varies from year to year, and the starting and ending dates may vary from what's printed on the timetable, so call to check. Although fares are already quite low (most Penwith day returns are under £3), **Explorer** tickets are an excellent value for those making long-distance trips or hopping from town to town (£4-5). Cyclists may not relish the narrow roads, but cliff paths with their evenly spaced youth hostels are ideal for easy hikes.

Penzance

Penzance, the largest town on Cornwall's Penwith peninsula, manages to integrate Cornish Market Town and Mediterranean Resort. The climate is unusually sunny and mild for England, allowing some incongruous tropical plants to thrive on the heather-covered cliffs. Penzance's narrow roads and small refurbished homes create a comfortable base for your visit to the rest of the Penwith peninsula and western Cornwall.

Arriving and Departing

Just 10 mi. from England's southwesternmost point, Penzance is the last stop on a long train ride from London (5½ hr.; £58), via Plymouth (1½hr.; £8.70) and Exeter (2½ hr.). Change at St. Erth for St. Ives (£3); change at Truro for Falmouth (£7); change at Par for Newquay (£12). Get a Cornish Railways timetable at the tourist office. British Rail offers special bargain tickets for travel in this area: the Southwest 7-Day Rover (£45); the Cornish 7-Day Rover (£30), which allows unlimited travel in all areas west of Gunnislake and Plymouth; or the FlexiRover for the same region (any 3 days out of 7, £19).

Nine National Express Rapide coaches make the trip to London daily (8 hr.; £29, stop at Heathrow), and there is coach service to Plymouth via Truro (2/hr.; 3 hr.; £5.25). Local service to St. Ives (3/hr.; 35 min.; £2.10), Land's End (bus #1 or 4 every hr.; 50 min.; £2.50), Mousehole (every ½hr.; 20 min.; 95p), Falmouth (Western National bus #2 or 2A every ½hr.; 1½ hr.; £3.35), and Helston (Hoppa #2 hourly; 45 min.; £2.50; change here for Lizard).

National Express, Western National, and local Cornwall buses offer guided tours of the region and bargain Explorer passes. Guided tours include weekly trips to King Arthur's County, Boscastle, and Tintagel (Mon. 9:15am; £6, children and seniors £4.50), Cornish fishing village (Fri.; £6, children and seniors £4.50), and Newquay and Lizard Peninsula (times subject to change; £4.50, children and seniors £3.25). Check the bus station for details on tours and discounts.

Orientation and Practical Information

Penzance's rail station, bus station, and tourist information center stand together in the same square, adjacent to both the harbor and the town. **Market Jew Street** rises up from the harbor, laden with bookstores, bakeries, and colorful craftshops. **Chapel Street,** the cobblestone row of antique shops and traditional pubs, connects the markets with the rest of the town.

Tourist Information Center: Station Rd. (tel. 622 07), beside the train and coach station. Accommodations service £2, list of B&Bs and information about the area in *The West Cornwall Holiday Magazine* (free). Map of Penzance 15p. Open late May-early Aug. Mon.-Sat. 9am-6pm, Sun. 10am-1pm; May and Sept. Mon.-Sat. 9am-5:30pm; Oct.-Dec. Mon.-Thurs. 9am-5:30pm, Fri. 9am-5pm.

Bike Rental: Penwith Bikes, 51 Causewayhead (tel. 625 84). 3-speeds £4/day, £20/week; 10-speeds £5/day, £25/week; mountain bikes £6/day, £30/week. Open Mon.-Fri. 9am-5pm. **Bike About,** 1 Mount St. (tel. 503 45), up Leskinnick Place and turn left. An experienced cyclist offers touring tips for interesting routes along the North Coast and free panniers, tool kits, and maps (50p). Mountain bikes £6/day, £32/week. Insurance included. Open daily April-Oct. Flexible hours.

Bus Station: Wharf Rd. (tel. 649 469), at the head of Albert Pier. Information and ticket office open Mon.-Fri. 8:30am-5:30pm, Sat. 8:30am-1:30pm.

Crisis: Samaritans, tel. (0872) 772 77; 24 hr.

Early Closing Day: Wed. at 1pm. Suspended during summer.

Emergency: Dial 999; no coins required.

Financial Services: Barclay's, Market Jew St. Visa checks free, others £2. Currency exchange £1.50. Open Mon.-Fri. 9:30am-4:30pm, Sat. 9:30am-noon. **Lloyd's,** Market Jew St. American Express checks £4.

Hospital: West Cornwall Hospital, St. Clare St. (tel. 623 82). Bus #D, 10, or 10A to St. Clare St.

Launderette: Dr. Cleaning Polyclean Centre, 43 Leskinnick Pl., across from the rail and bus stations. Superior valet facilities. One load £2, dryers 20p. Dry cleaning. Open daily 9am-9pm (last wash 7:45pm).

Market Day: Tues. and Thurs., at the top of Causeway Rd.

Moped Hire: Blewett & Pender, Albert St. (tel. 641 57). £12/day.

Pharmacy: Boots, 100-102 Market Jew St. (tel. 621 35). Open Mon.-Sat. 8:45am-5:30pm.

Police: Penalverne Dr. (tel. 623 95), just off Alverton St.

Post Office: corner of Market Jew St. and Jennings St. Open Mon.-Thurs. 9am-5:30pm, Fri. 9:30am-5:30pm, Sat. 9am-12:30pm. **Postal Code:** TR18 2LB.

Taxi: Harvey's Taxi, tel. 666 66.

Telephones: In front of **Lloyd's** bank on Market Jew St. **Telephone Code:** 0736.

Train Station: Wharf Rd. (tel. (0872) 762 44), at the head of Albert Pier. Station is open Mon.-Sat. 6am-8pm, Sun. 9am-7pm, but you can board trains at any hour.

Accommodations and Camping

Penzance's robust tribe of B&Bs occupies the hills above the esplanade and beach mainly on Morrab Rd. between Alverton St. and Western Promenade Rd. You should also look on the side streets off Chapel St., and on Alexandra Rd., farther down Western Promenade. Prices are generally £11-15. Camping areas blanket the west Cornwall peninsula; check the tourist office for lists.

IYHF youth hostel, Castle Horneck (tel. 626 66). Perambulate up Market Jew St. and then Alverton St. (or take Hoppa B and ask to be let off at the Pirate Inn), turn right onto Castle Horneck, and take the left fork up the hill. Inside an 18th-century mansion reputed to have a smuggler's tunnel. Though the showers disappoint, enlivening British witticisms fly among the staff. Well-stocked hostel shop behind the kitchen. £7, ages 16-20 £5.90. Meals available. Curfew 11pm.

YMCA, Orchard Ct. and Alverton Rd. (tel. 650 16), past the Alexandra Rd. roundabout. Coed dorm accommodations with sinks in each room. Lockout 9:30am, curfew 11:30pm. With your own sleeping bag £5.25; without £7.25. Breakfast £2.75, evening meal £4.05.

Inyanza, 36 Chapel St. (tel. 609 67), left at the top of Market Jew St. A hidden gem at the bottom of Antique Row. Clean, classy and very comfortable. English or vegetarian breakfast graciously served. £12.

Ocean View, Chyandour Cliff (tel. 517 70). Frilly, flowery, and fairly expensive. Singles £13, doubles £11-12/person.

Cornerways, 5 Leskinnick St. (tel. 646 45). One block from the rail station. You're in luck—you'll get a warm welcome from the entire royal family, past and present. Very accommodating owners. £10.50.

Camping: Tourist office a has list of sites. **River Valley Caravan Park,** Relubbus, Penzance (tel. 736 398). Quiet camping in sheltered valley. £4-6.

Food and Pubs

Expect to pay at least £6 for Penzance's excellent seafood dinners along the Quay. Market Jew St.'s fare is unexciting and expensive. The best buys are in coffee shops and local eateries on smaller streets and alleys, far from the hustle-bustle of town.

The Mill House, Victoria Pl. (tel. 666 68), in a narrow alley between Morrab Rd. and Queen St. near Alverton St. Incredible smorgasbord lunch (£2.70) includes moussaka, kasha, gado gado, suki yaki, and ratatouille, among other vegan delights. Open Mon.-Wed. 9:30am-6:30pm, Thurs.-Sat. 9:30am-8:30pm.

Snatch-a-Bite, 45 New St. (tel. 668 66), right off Market Jew St. Sumptuous salad and choice of meat on wholemeal or french bread, £1.30 (30p cheaper to take away). Open Mon.-Sat. 9am-4:30pm.

The Turk's Head, 46 Chapel St. The first pub by this name in all of imperialist England. Delicious food in a consummately English pub. Lunch £5, seafood dinners from £5.10. Open Mon.-Sat. 11am-11pm, Sun. noon-3:45pm and 7-10pm.

On the waterfront, the **Old Dolphin Inn** on The Quay enthusiastically preserves the piratical tradition of heavy drinking. On Chapel St., you can spit and cuss as smugglers once did in the 400-year-old **Admiral Benbow** or swill elderberry wine and Cornish mead by candlelight in the medieval dungeon of **The Meadery** (tel. 629 46; open Oct.-April Wed.-Sun. 6:30-10pm). Pubs serve light meals and snacks regularly, but food is usually less expensive elsewhere. After 11pm, try **Club Zero,** off Chapel St., for after-hours drinking and dancing.

Sights

You can see most of the town's sights by walking down **Chapel Street** from Market Jew St. to the docks. Near the top of the street is the bizarre **Egyptian House.** Its façade is a rare example of the 1830s craze for Egyptian ornamentation. The House now contains a National Trust office that can tell you about other historic sites (tel. 643 78; open Mon.-Sat. 9am-5pm). The **Maritime Museum,** in the center of Chapel St., recreates life at sea in 1730 and features gruesome mannequins of wounded sailors and a busy surgeon (open Mon.-Sat., £1.50). The proprietor of **The Little Gallery,** 58 Chapel St., keeps busy by making foot-high historical dolls and dressing them by hand in authentic period costumes. You can buy any or all of Henry VIII's six wives for £8.50 apiece. If you aren't completely satisfied, feel free to behead them. (Open Mon.-Sat. 9am-6pm.)

Land's End to St. Ives

The Penwith Peninsula culminates its majestic scroll into the Celtic Sea at **Land's End** with granite cliffs so dramatic that, once upon a time, the Countryside Commission declared Land's End an Area of Outstanding Natural Beauty. The commission's efforts to protect the area unfortunately could not prevent it from being purchased and transformed into an area of outstanding commercial booty. Now, Land's End is a tourist holiday park of rides, historic displays, and other plastic phenomena. Seen from the cliff path that circles the Peninsula, the complex rears up out of the barren landscape like a tortured carousel stallion. Buses run every hour to Land's End from Penzance (1 hr.; £4.50) and three times daily from St. Ives.

The same busline will take you to **St. Just,** just north of Land's End on Cape Cornwall. Its craggy coast remains unpurchased and remarkably beautiful. Small (2-4 mi.) day walks are outlined in leaflets in most tourist offices, but the dramatic cliff path winding around the entire coast unveils the best of Cornwall. The **St. Just Youth Hostel (IYHF)** at Letcha Vean is said to be among the nicest in the region (tel. (0736) 788 437; £5.90, ages 16-20 £4.70; from the bus station's rear exit, turn left and follow the lane past the chapel and farm to its end).

Inland on the Penwith Peninsula, some of the best-preserved Stone and Iron Age monuments in England lie along the Land's End-St. Ives bus route. The *quoits* (also called cromlechs or dolmens), are post-and-lintel structures composed of a flat stone laid on two or three stones standing on end. Once covered by mounds of earth, the structures are believed to be burial chambers dating back to 2500 BC. The **Zennor Quoit** (on the Land's End-St. Ives bus route) is named for the town where a mermaid, drawn by the singing of a young man, happily returned to the sea with him in tow. The **Lanyon Quoit** (off the Morvah-Penzance road about 3 mi. from each) is one of the best preserved megaliths in the area. The famous stone near Morvah (on the Land's End-St. Ives bus route), with a hole through the middle, has the sensible Cornish name **Mên-an-Tol,** or "holed stone." The stone doughnut is the focus of a number of myths that attribute magical powers and curative capabilities to it. Climbing through the aperture supposedly remedies backache, assures easy childbirth, or induces any physiological change you choose to believe. The best-preserved Iron Age village in Britain is at **Chysauster** (tel. (0736) 618 89), between Penzance and Zennor (about 4 mi. from each). Parts of four pairs of oval stone houses remain erect. Take the footpath off the B3311 near Gulval. (Open mid-March to mid-Oct. Mon.-Sat. 9:30am-6:30pm, Sun. 2-6:30pm; mid-Oct. to mid-March Mon.-Wed. and Sat. 9:30am-4pm, Thurs. 9:30am-noon, Sun. 2-4pm.) The countryside is also punctuated by the ghostly remains of chimneys from old tin miners' engine houses.

St. Ives

These days it seems everybody and her teenage schnauzer is going to St. Ives. Ten mi. north of Penzance, the town looks over a breathtaking bay. Peaked roofs line the hillside and hundreds of sea gulls dip and whirl towards the harbor. St. Ives has provided a remove for artists since Whistler arrived in 1880, and today, still grants a partial reprieve from the rampant commercialization of neighboring towns. Several small galleries adorn this artists' town, but the finest display of art in St. Ives is the **Barbara Hepworth Museum,** set up in the late artist's studio. Her sculptures in wood, stone, and bronze are sheltered within a perfectly tended garden. (Open July-Aug. Mon.-Sat. 10am-6:30pm, Sun. 2-6pm; April-June Mon.-Sat. 10am-5:30pm; Oct.-March Mon.-Sat. 10am-4:30pm. Admission 75p; seniors, students, and children 50p.) In the car park off Fish St., near the end of Fore St., is the **Sloop Craft Market** (tel. (0736) 796 053). There is usually someone at work from 9am to 10pm daily. When the surf's up, head to **Porthmeor Beach,** one of St. Ives' beautiful, sandy but packed beaches.

The **tourist information center,** in the Guildhall at Street-an-Pol (tel. (0736) 797 600 or 796 297), gives weekly hour-long walking tours of the town (Wed. 8pm; £1.50). (Free list of accommodations. Booking £2. Map 15p. Open mid-May to mid-Sept. Mon.-Sat. 9am-6pm, Sun. 10am-1pm; mid-Sept. to mid-May Mon.-Thurs. 9am-5:30pm, Fri. 9am-5pm.) Bikes and surfboards can be hired or repaired at **Windansea Surf Shop** at 11 Fore St. (tel. (0736) 796 560). (Surfboard or wetsuit £8/day, £24/week. Mountain bikes £7/day. Deposit £5/item plus ID. Repairs. Open daily 10am-8pm.)

Although the closest youth hostel and YMCA to St. Ives are in Penzance, there are scads of B&Bs in town for £11 and up. Prices are usually lower for rooms farther from the water and higher up the gusty hillside. Try **Belmont Place, Barnoon Hill,** or **Park Avenue. Tregowan Guest House,** Porthmeor Hill (tel. (0736) 797 185), and **Seagull's Guest House,** 4 Godreavy Terrace (tel. 797 273) charge £11 or £12 respectively for a comfy nest above Porthmeor Beach, straight up the hill from the bus station. Camping is abundant in Hayle—check the tourist office for listings. Try **Trevalgan Camping Park,** with laundry and cooking facilities, and access to the coastal path (tel. (0736) 796 433).

Fore St. is densely packed with small bakeries, each with its own interpretation of the Cornish pasty (PAH-stee). The miniscule **Ferrell's Bakery,** at 15 Fore St. (tel. (0736) 797 703), bakes a delicious Cornish pasty (large size £1) or saffron bun (reputedly Cornwall's best). But come early—the pasties and buns are usually sold out by early afternoon. (Open Mon.-Sat. 9am-5:30pm.) **Hazelnut Wholefoods,** up the hill, cooks up fat- and animal-free cuisine (pizza provençale, £1; open Mon.-Fri. 9am-6pm, Sat. 9am-4pm). Stock up on groceries at **LoCost,** Treganna Place, and **Co-Op Supermarket,** Royal Place. Serving beer since 1312, **The Sloop,** on the wharf at Fish St., is the oldest pub in Cornwall, serving ale and food Monday to Saturday until 11pm (tel. (0736) 796 584).

The small St. Ives branch rail line meets the main Plymouth-Penzance line at St. Erth. Trains run daily during the summer (Oct.-March Mon.-Sat. every hr.) between St. Erth and St. Ives (10 min.), and St. Erth connects to Penzance (£3) and Truro. Three buses an hour run from Penzance (daily; in off-season Mon.-Sat.), and six daily Cornwall Express buses between Plymouth and Penzance stop in St. Ives year-round. From the bus and train stations, walk down to the foot of Treganna Hill and turn right on Street-an-Pol to the tourist office. Take Hoppa bus #16 or 17 to Carbis Bay for the **hospital,** on Edward Hain (tel. (0736) 795 044). The **post office** is on High St., at the foot of Treganna Place. St. Ives' **postal code** is TR26 1AA; the **telephone code** is 0736, same as Penzance.

Newquay

In 1989, Newquay's favorite son Martin Potter shredded his way through the pro tour to become Britain's first World Surfing Champion. The relentless waves on which Potter honed his chops have made Newquay an outpost of surfer subculture and the peninsula's most popular beach resort. Over Newquay's endless summer, most shops and restaurants stay open late into the evening, and people are out strolling well into the night. The town overlooks six beaches that pout in a thick lip around the bay at low tide, each with its own particular crowd and reputation. Porth Beach, Lusty Glaze, Tolcarne Beach, Great Western, and Towan Beach are cut off from one another at high tide, when the surfers rise from their beach chaises and hit the water in large numbers.

Arriving and Departing

Getting to or from Newquay (pop. 20,000) by rail from the main London-Penzance line requires a quick stopover in the small town of Par. Trains go to Par (5/day; 50 min.; approx. £4.50), Plymouth via Par (every hr.; 1 hr.; approx. £7.50) or Penzance via Par (every hr.; 1 hr.; approx. £14). By coach, catch National Express to Plymouth via Bodmin (2/day; 2 hr.; approx. £4.50), St. Austell (daily, in off-season Mon.-Sat. only; 2/hr.; 45 min.; approx. £3.75), St. Ives (June-Sept. daily, 3/day; 2 hr.; approx. £4.75).

Orientation and Practical Information

The tourist information center and bus station are just off East St. on Marcus Hill Rd., where day-glo surf shops and fish-and-chip shacks exuberantly overflow onto the street. Fore St. leads down to the amusement centers and shops on the shore.

Tourist Information Center: Marcus Hill (tel. 871 345/6/7), off East St. 2 blocks from the train station; down the hill from the bus station. Helpful lists of discos, tide tables, and accommodations (50p). They'll book a bed for £1. Open Mon.-Fri. 9am-5pm, Sat. 9am-1pm.

Bike Rental: Cycle Revolutions, 7 Beach Rd. (tel. 872 364). Mountain bikes £11/day, £55/week. Full insurance included. **Bilbo 2000,** Cliff Rd. (tel. 844 501), by the train station.

Bus Station: East St. (tel. 871 186).

Crisis: Samaritans, tel. 772 77; 24 hr.

Early Closing Day: Wed. at 1pm.

Emergency: Dial 999; no coins required.

Financial Services: Barclay's, 55A Bank St. (tel. 871 272). £3 fee. Open Mon.-Fri. 9:30am-4:30pm.

Hospital: St. Thomas' Rd. (tel. 871 345). Hoppa bus #E from East St. to Trenance Rd.

Launderette: Cornish Coinomatic, 1 Beach Rd. (tel. 875 901). Digital dryers. Open Mon.-Sat. 9am-5:30pm. Last washorama 4:30pm.

Pharmacy: Boots, East St. Open daily 9am-5:30pm.

Police: Tolcarne Rd. (tel. 872 263).

Post Office: East St. (tel. 873 364). Open Mon.-Thurs. 9am-5:30pm, Fri. 9:30am-5:30pm, Sat. 9am-12:30pm. **Postal Code:** TR7 1BU.

Surfing Rental: Bilbo 2000, Cliff Rd. (tel. 844 501) by the train station. Surfboards and wet suits, £6/day, £24/week; boogie boards £5/day. Open 9am-6pm.

Surfing Lessons: Newquay Surfing School, Clevedon Rd. (tel. 850 450). Initiation into rad-dom. £9, £13 with equipment. Open daily 10am-6pm.

Taxi: Taxi Rank, at the bus station (tel. 872 487).

Telephones: across from the bus station on Marcus Hill. **Telephone Code:** 0637.

Train Station: Station Parade, off Cliff Rd. (tel. 877 180). Station staffed Mon.-Sat. 8:15am-noon and 12:50-4:10pm.

Accommodations and Camping

Despite the fact that Newquay looks like a B&B colony, it's hard to find a place to stay in July and August. The accommodations list available at the tourist office is well worth the 10p. There are at least 100 B&Bs within a 2-mi. radius, charging between £10 and £15. Check Marcus Hill, Beachfield Ave., Grosvenor Ave., and Berry Rd. near the bus station. Tolcarne Rd. and Edgecombe Ave. near the train station are also bountifully supplied. Farther out, beyond Narrowcliff Rd., nearly every house on Henver Rd. offers lodgings. Expect to compromise space for proximity to the beach; rooms are little more than storage boxes for your gear. Book as far in advance as possible.

IYHF youth hostel, Alexandra Court, Narrowcliff (tel. 876 381), at the top of Narrowcliff (eastern extension of Cliff Rd.), next to the petrol station, 10 min. from the bus station. Sensational showers, and a pool table in the common lounge. Open daily July-Aug.; Feb.-April and Sept.-Nov. Tues.-Sat.; approx. £8, ages 16-20 £6.50.

Towan Beach Backpackers, 15 Beachfield Ave. (tel. 874 668). Cramped hostel lodgings, but the ideal location and lack of curfew will free up your nights anyway. Foreign travelers only. Approx. £8. Sauna (£3) and laundry facilities available.

Parma Family Guest House, 23 Grosvenor Ave. (tel. 850 408). Gregarious hosts, massage shower-heads, and, if you're lucky, a king-sized bed. Approx. £12.

Quebec Guest House, 34 Grosvenor Ave. (tel. 874 430). Luxury rooms with cable TV, tea-making facilities, and riotous hosts. Approx. £12-15.

Maresa, Berry Rd. (tel. 874 033). Elegant B&B with pool table and bar in the lounge. Approx. £12, evening meal approx. £3.50.

Camping: Trevelgne Caravan and Camping Park, Porth (tel. 873 475). Approx. £7-8. **Hendra Tourist Park**(tel. 875 778), about 2 mi. east of town beyond the Lane Theatre. From Trenance Gardens, go under viaduct and past the boating lake, turn turn left. For families and couples only. Approx. £3-5/person.

Food

The restaurants in Newquay cater mostly to tourists who want a quick, bland fill-up and are willing to pay more than it's worth. Keep your eye out for signs advertising a three-course "early bird special." **Food for Thought,** on Beachfield Rd., offers take-away California-style salads and sandwiches. **Gannets' Barn,** at 41 Bank St. (tel. 871 326), combines a wholefoods grocery store with a cozy tea shop and café. **Ellery's Bakery,** 58 East St. (tel. 872 832), serves full meals for under £5 in an elegant atmosphere. Open daily 10am-4pm and 7pm-1am. Live jazz Fridays.

Sights and Entertainment

On a sunny day, Newquay's streets seethe with tourists and wetsuit-clad surfers headed for the town's 7 mi. of **beaches.** You can avoid the crush if you hit the beaches at low tide; high tide reduces the beaches to one-fourth of their maximum size. There are two beach areas at Newquay—**Fistral,** which is often considered Cornwall's best surfing beach, and the stretch of beach adjacent to the harbor, which at high tide is subdivided into four separate beaches. Surfboards are available for rental all over town.

Newquay is notorious in Cornwall for its after-hours activities. Stores extend their hours well into the night, and droves of 18-30 year olds scavenge the town in search of loud music and good sweaty fun. **Tall Trees** on Tolcarne Rd. (tel. 873 894) is the acknowledged giant of the Newquay club scene (disco Tues., Thurs.-Sat.). **Steamers** on Marcus Hill (tel. 872 194) has black walls and is more anonymous (disco Mon.-Sat.). **The Newquay Arms** pub on East St. pulses with loud music even in the afternoon. Almost every hotel offers some type of dancing. Follow your ears and look around early to avoid the cover charge. Other activities are also open in the evening hours. The **Lane Theatre** (tel. 876 945) presents midsummer night's drama (tickets from £5), and comedians and musicians often entertain by the beach. **The Gallery of Old Newquay** (tel. 872 878) shows exhibits of local history during the calmer hours of the day. (Open Easter-Oct. Mon.-Fri. 10am-4pm; winter, Wed. mornings. £1.)

Near Newquay

Fourteen mi. north of Newquay, **Padstow** retains the atmosphere of a traditional fishing village—something of a relief after the neon brouhaha of Newquay. Check it out, my friend.

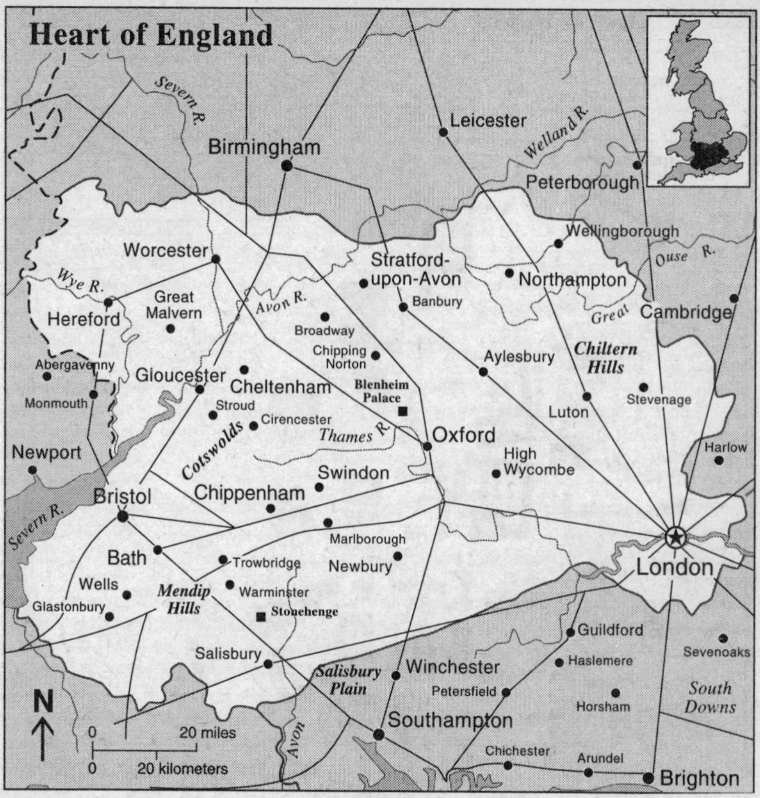

Heart of England

After London, the **Heart of England** contains the largest number of "must-sees" in England. Extending from London west to Salisbury and Bath and north to the Cotswolds and Stratford-upon-Avon, the Heart of England centers on Oxford, England's oldest university town. The region is warm and inviting, brightened by the light yellow Cotswolds stone. Though Shakespeare's literary preeminence shielded Stratford-upon-Avon from industrialization, it doomed the town to crass commercialization; the tranquil country scenery and groomed flowerbeds only occasionally peek from under the morass of tourists. Bath and Stonehenge, though overrun with people in the hot summer months, retain an air of ancient dignity, seemingly undisturbed by the masses.

Oxford

Shrouded in 800 years of tradition, Oxford's forty colleges and halls are a soft sheltered world. A measure of mayhem, squealing coach brakes, foreign language students, and rattling bicycle chains have, however, forced directors of BBC dramas to shoot Oxford's "dreaming spires" from very select camera angles. Oxford enjoys the attention but wishes seats on the buses were easier to find.

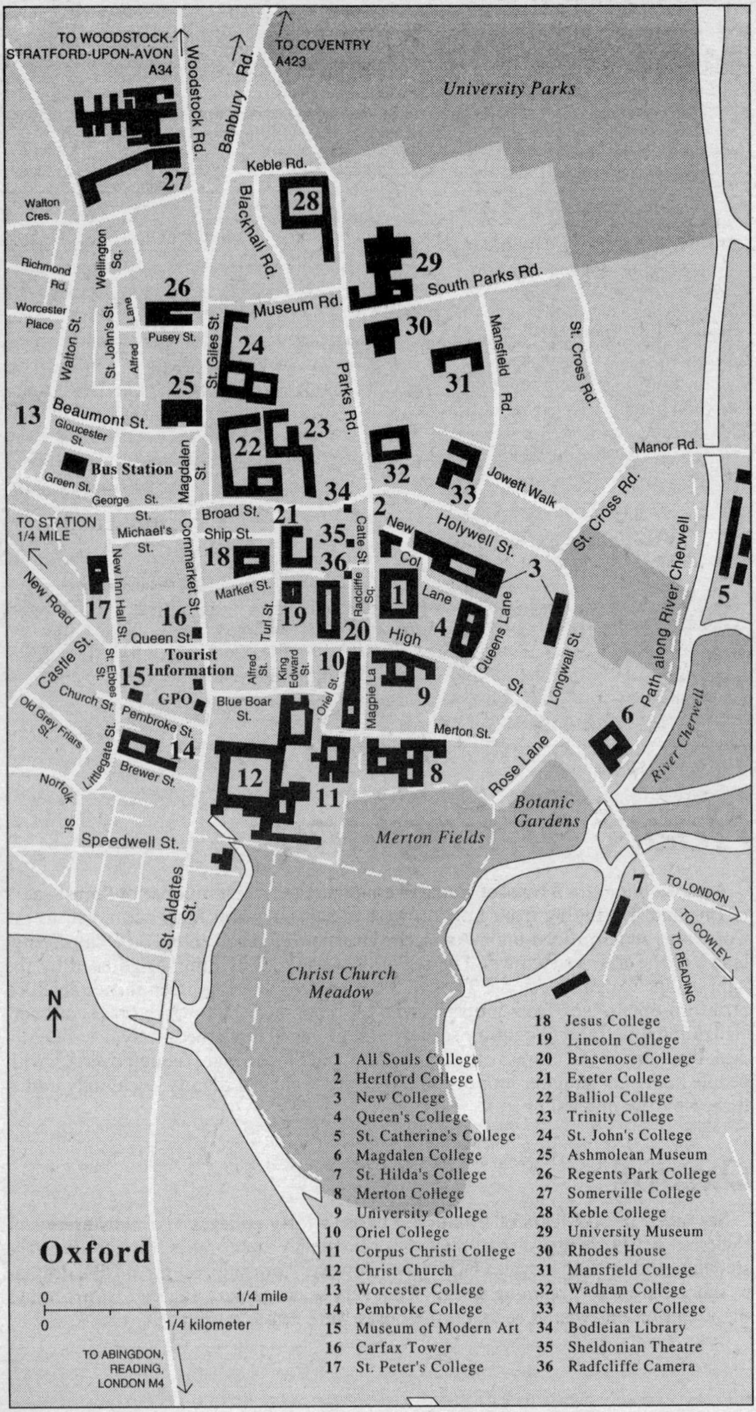

Oxford
TO WOODSTOCK, STRATFORD-UPON-AVON A34
TO COVENTRY A423
University Parks
Woodstock Rd.
Banbury Rd.
Keble Rd.
Blackhall Rd.
Walton Cres.
Richmond Rd.
Wellington Sq.
Worcester Place
Walton St.
St. John's St.
Lane
Alfred
Pusey St.
St. Giles St.
Museum Rd.
South Parks Rd.
Parks Rd.
Mansfield Rd.
St. Cross Rd.
Beaumont St.
Gloucester St.
Bus Station
Green St.
George St.
Magdalen St.
Broad St.
Manor Rd.
Jowett Walk
Holywell St.
New Col Lane
TO STATION 1/4 MILE
St. Michael's St.
Ship St.
Catte St.
Radcliffe Sq.
Market St.
Turl St.
New Inn Hall St.
Cornmarket St.
Queen St.
High St.
Queens Lane
Longwall St.
Path along River Cherwell
River Cherwell
New Road
Castle St.
St. Ebbes St.
Tourist Information
GPO
Alfred St.
King Edward St.
Oriel St.
Magpie La
Blue Boar St.
Church St.
Pembroke St.
Old Grey Friars St.
Littlegate St.
Brewer St.
Merton St.
Rose Lane
Botanic Gardens
Norfolk St.
Speedwell St.
Merton Fields
St. Aldates St.
TO LONDON
TO COWLEY
TO READING
Christ Church Meadow
N
0 1/4 mile
0 1/4 kilometer
TO ABINGDON, READING, LONDON M4
1 All Souls College
2 Hertford College
3 New College
4 Queen's College
5 St. Catherine's College
6 Magdalen College
7 St. Hilda's College
8 Merton College
9 University College
10 Oriel College
11 Corpus Christi College
12 Christ Church
13 Worcester College
14 Pembroke College
15 Museum of Modern Art
16 Carfax Tower
17 St. Peter's College
18 Jesus College
19 Lincoln College
20 Brasenose College
21 Exeter College
22 Balliol College
23 Trinity College
24 St. John's College
25 Ashmolean Museum
26 Regents Park College
27 Somerville College
28 Keble College
29 University Museum
30 Rhodes House
31 Mansfield College
32 Wadham College
33 Manchester College
34 Bodleian Library
35 Sheldonian Theatre
36 Radfcliffe Camera

Arriving and Departing

From London, trains run from Paddington (every hr., 1 hr., £9.50 not-so-cheap day return, £17 period return). The **Oxford Tube** (every 20 min., 1¼ hr., £4.50 day return, £6.50 period return) and **Oxford CityLink** (3 per hr., 1½ hr., £4.50 day return, £6.50 period return) provide competing coach services between Oxford's bus station and London's Victoria coach station.

Orientation and Practical Information

Queen, High, St. Aldates, and Cornmarket St. intersect at right angles in **Carfax,** the town center. The colleges surround Carfax; the bus and train stations lie to the west. Past the east end of High St. over Magdalen Bridge, the neighborhoods of **East Oxford** stretch along **Cowley Road** (marked "To Cowley" on the map) and **Iffley Road** (marked "To Reading"). To the north along **Woodstock** and **Banbury Roads,** leafier residential areas roll on for miles.

The **Oxford Bus Company** (tel. 711 312) operates the red double-deckers and the lime-green "City Nipper" minibuses, as well as the CityLink service to London; **Oxford Minibus** (tel. 771 876) operates the checkered-flag minibuses, as well as the Oxford Tube London service. Masses of minibuses scoot around Oxford, and cut-throat competition makes for swift and frequent service. **South Midlands** (tel. 262 368) also runs some Oxford services. Most local services board on the streets immediately adjacent to Carfax; some longer-distance buses depart from the bus station. Abingdon Rd. buses are often marked "Red Bridge;" some Iffley Rd. buses are marked "Rose Hill." Fares are low (most about 80p return). Some companies issue Compass tickets, good for one day's travel (about £4), but companies disdain each other's tickets. The signs all over town reading "No Cycles Here" do little to prevent cyclists from riding whereever they like, even in heavy traffic. Stop in one of Oxford's cycle shops and pick up a copy of the free 45-page guide *Cycling in Oxford,* which includes 17 pages of cycling maps of the city and outlying areas. Bikes are especially not permitted on Cornmarket St. or in college parklands or quads.

Tourist Information Centre: St. Aldates St. (tel. 726 871), just south of Carfax. Their *Welcome to Oxford* guide (50p) is a valuable resource. If you're staying for the day, just pick up a map (20p). Local accommodations service £2.30. Accommodations list 35p. Open Mon.-Sat. 9:30am-5pm, Sun. 10:30am-1pm and 1:30-3:30pm. **Thames and Chilterns Tourist Board,** The Mount House, Church Green, Whitney (tel. (0993) 778 800). Covers surrounding countryside. Open Mon.-Sat. 9am-5:30pm, Sun. 1-4pm.

Tours: Good daily tourist office walking tours (11-11:30am and 2-3pm every ½ hr.; tickets £3, children £1.50). Alternatively you could support student life and take a tour from one of the many student groups that offer them (£2.50, students £2). Some students will regale you with stories you won't hear on the official tours and will give your money back if you're dissatisfied. Others won't. Often the more reliable student guides hang out right near the tourist office.

Accommodations Bureau: Bravalta House, 242 Iffley Rd. (tel. 241 326 or 250 511). When the tourist office is closed, call Mrs. Downes, the city's Secretary of Accommodations and a B&B owner herself. Phone before 10pm. No fee. Or check in the window of the tourist office.

Discount Student Travel: Campus Travel, 13 High St. (tel. 242 067). Eurotrain tickets, ISICs, railcards, discount airfare, coaches, insurance. Open Mon.-Fri. 9:30am-5:30pm, Sat. 10am-5pm. **STA Travel,** 19 High St. (tel. 240 547). Open Mon.-Fri. 9am-5:30pm, Sat. 10am-4pm.

Financial Services: Try one of the many banks near Carfax: **Barclay's,** Cornmarket St. (Open Mon.-Fri. 9:30am-4:30pm, Sat. 9:30am-noon); **National Westminster,** Cornmarket St. (open Mon.-Fri. 9:30am-4:30pm, Sat. 9:30am-3:30pm); **Lloyd's,** in Selfridge's, Queen St. (open Mon.-Sat. 9:30am-4:30pm); and **Thomas Cook,** at 5 Queen St. (open Mon.-Sat. 9am-5:30pm) and at the train station (open daily 9am-5pm). **American Express: Keith Bailey Travel Agency,** 98 St. Aldates St. (tel. 790 099), a few doors down from the tourist office. Mail held; postal code OX1 1BT. Open Mon. and Wed.-Fri. 9am-5:30pm, Tues. 9:30am-5:30pm, Sat. 9am-5pm.

Bike Rental: Thakes Cycles, 55 Walton St., Jericho (tel. 516 122), about 1 mi. north of town. Cheapest 3- or 10-speeds £5 per day, £10 per week; £25 deposit. Open Mon.-Sat. 9am-6pm. **Pennyfarthing,** 5 George St. (tel. 249 368). Closest to town center. Rental £5 per day; 3-speeds £10 per week; £20 deposit. Open Mon.-Sat. 8am-5:30pm. **Beeline Bicycles,** 33 Cowley Rd. (tel. 246 615). Three-speeds £5 per day, £9 per week; £25 deposit. Open Mon.-Sat. 9am-6pm.

Boat Rental: Hubbock's Boat Hire, Folly Bridge (tel. 244 235), south of Carfax, along St. Aldates St. Punts £5.50 per hr.; £20 deposit. Open June-Sept. daily 10am-7pm. **C. Howard & Son,** Magdalen Bridge, east of Carfax at end of High St. Punts £6 per hr.; £15 deposit. Open daily 10am-dusk. Arrive early, especially on sunny days, to avoid a long, long wait. **Salter Brothers,** Folly Bridge (tel. 243 421). Runs cruises to Abingdon (at 2:30pm, 1 hr., £7.15 return, children £5), Rose Island (2 per day, 90 min., £3.50 return, children £2.50), and Iffley (5 per day, 20 min., £2.75 return, children £1.65). Open May-Sept. Mon.-Sat. 9am-6pm, Sun. 9am-4pm.

Bookstores: Blackwell's, 48-51 Broad St. (see Sights below). Oxford's largest. Open Mon.-Sat. 9am-6pm, Sun. noon-5pm. **Music department,** 38 Holywell St. Open Mon.-Sat. 9am-6pm, Sun. noon-5pm. **Dillon's,** William Baker House, Broad St. Blackwell's competition. Open Mon.-Fri. 9am-8pm, Sat. 9am-6pm, Sun. 10am-5pm. **Thornton's,** Broad St. Used student books. Open Mon.-Thurs. 9am-6pm, Fri.-Sat. 9am-4pm. **EOA Books,** 34 Cowley Rd. Good selection of alternative and radical titles. Open Mon.-Sat. 10am-5:30pm.

Bus and Coach Station: Gloucester Green. **Oxford Tube** (tel. 772 250); **Oxford CityLink** (tel. 711 312); and **National Express** (tel. 791 579). **National Travelworld** (tel. 726 172), at Carfax, books for National Express. Open Mon.-Fri. 9am-5pm, Sat. 9am-1pm.

Camping and Hiking Supplies: YHA Shop, on Magdalen Bridge roundabout (tel. 247 948). Youth hostel membership available. Open Mon. and Wed.-Fri. 10am-6pm, Tues. 10am-7pm, Sat. 9am-5:30pm.

Crisis: Samaritans, 123 Iffley Rd. (tel. 722 122). Phone 24 hrs.; drop in 8am-10pm. **Drug and Alcohol Hotline,** tel. 244 447 or 248 591. 24-hr. answer phone. **The Women's Line,** tel. 726 295. Open Mon.-Tues. 7-9pm, Wed. 2-10pm, Thurs.-Fri. 2-4pm; answering machine other times; in emergency call London Rape Crisis Center at (071) 837 1600.

Emergency: Dial 999; no coins required.

Hospital: John Radcliffe Hospital, tel. 647 11. Take bus #10.

Launderette: Clean-o-Fine, 66 Abingdon Rd., South Oxford. Open daily 8am-9:30pm. **Valuematic,** 184 Cowley Rd., across Magdalen Bridge. Open Sun.-Fri. 8am-9pm, Sat. 8am-5pm.

Gay and Lesbian Switchboard: Tel. 726 893. Phone answered Tues.-Wed. and Fri. 7-9pm.

Pharmacy: Boots, Cornmarket St. Open Mon. and Fri.-Sat. 8:45am-6pm, Tues.-Wed. 9am-5:30pm, Thurs. 8:45am-8pm.

Police: St. Aldates and Speedwell St. (tel. 249 881).

Public Library: Westgate Shopping Centre (tel. 815 509). Fine local history collection. Open Mon.-Tues. and Thurs.-Fri. 9:15am-7pm, Wed. and Sat. 9:15am-5pm.

Ticket Office: Tickets-in-Oxford, tourist office (tel. 727 855). Tickets for local events and the Royal Shakespeare Company in Stratford. Open Mon.-Sat. 9:30am-5pm.

Post Office: 102/104 St. Aldates St. (tel. 814 783). **Bureau de change** inside. Open Mon.-Tues. and Thurs.-Fri. 9am-5:30pm, Wed. 9:30am-5:30pm, Sat. 9am-12:30pm. **Postal Code:** OX1 1ZZ.

Telephones: Banks of Phonecard and intercontinental phones at Carfax and on Cornmarket St. **Telephone Code:** (0865).

Train Station: Botley Rd. (tel. 722 333 or 249 055), west of Carfax. Travel Centre open Mon.-Fri. 8am-7:45pm, Sat. 8:30am-5:30pm, Sun. 11:15am-6:45pm. Station open Mon.-Fri. 5:50am-8:15pm, Sat. 6:30am-7:50pm, Sun. 7am-8:30pm.

Women's Center: 35 Cowley Rd. (tel. 245 923). Phone answered Mon.-Sat. noon-4pm.

Accommodations and Camping

Book at least a week ahead, especially for singles, and expect to mail in a deposit. B&Bs line the main roads out of town, all of them a vigorous walk from Carfax.

The No. 300s on **Banbury Road,** fern-laced and domestic, stand miles north of the center (catch a Banbury bus on St. Giles St.). You'll find cheaper B&Bs in the 200s and 300s on Iffley Rd. and from No. 250-350 on Cowley Rd., both served by frequent buses from Carfax. **Abingdon Road,** in South Oxford, is about the same price and distance, though less colorful. Wherever you go, expect to pay at least £15-18 per person.

IYHF Youth Hostel, Jack Straw's Lane (tel. 629 97). Catch any minibus departing from the job center south of Carfax (every 15 min., last bus 10:30pm). Remote but well-equipped, with showers, kitchen, and food shop. Lockout 10am-1pm. Curfew 11pm. £6.30, ages 16-20 £5.10. Breakfast £2.30. Sleepsack rental 80p. Open March-Oct. daily; Nov. and Jan.-Feb. Mon.-Sat.

YWCA, Alexandra Residential Club, 133 Woodstock Rd. (tel. 520 21), quite a walk up Cornmarket St. and down Woodstock Rd., or bus #60 or 60A. Women over 16 only. Bunk rooms, TV lounge, kitchen and laundry facilities. Limited accommodations in summer; fills up with students during term. Reserve about 2 weeks in advance for summer. Office open Mon.-Fri. 8:30am-1pm and 2:30-7:30pm, Sat. 10am-noon and 4-5pm, Sun. 11am-noon. Curfew: Sun.-Thurs. 2am, Fri.-Sat. 2:30am. Three-night max. stay. £6; 2 nights £11; 3 nights £15.

Tara, 10 Holywell St. (tel. 244 786 or 248 270). The best B&B in town, situated among the colleges. Kind hearing-impaired proprietors, Mr. and Mrs. Godwin, lip-read and speak clearly—no communication problems. Desks, basins, TVs, and refrigerators in every room; kitchenette on the 2nd floor. Breakfast room a virtual museum of academic regalia, college coats-of-arms, and other Oxford paraphernalia. Open July-Sept.; the rest of the year it fills up with students, but check anyway. Reserve at least 2 weeks in advance. Singles £18. Doubles £30. Triples £36.

White House View, 9 White House Rd. (tel. 721 626), off Abingdon Rd. Good-sized rooms only 10 min. from Carfax. Solicitous proprietors and excellent breakfasts. £14 per person.

Micklewood, 331 Cowley Rd. (tel. 247 328). Enchanting proprietor will shelter you in rooms decorated with excruciating detail. Comfort and cleanliness abound. Singles £16. Doubles £27.

Newton Guest House, 82-84 Abingdon Rd. (tel. 240 561), about ½ mile from town center; take any Abingdon bus across Folly Bridge. Antique enthusiasts will be taken with the monolithic wooden wardrobes in every room. Affable proprietor. No singles. Doubles £30, with bath £40.

King's Guest House, 363 Iffley Rd. (tel. 241 363). Spacious doubles in a modern, comfortable home. Helpful proprietors. No singles. Rooms £30, with bath £35.

Gables' Guest House, 6 Cumnor Hill (tel. 862 153). Oxford's finest pink B&B. One mile from train station, 2 mi. from city center. Best for motorists: lots of parking and close to the ring road. Gargantuan bathroom on first floor. Full English breakfast. Reserve ahead with 1 night's deposit. Comfortable rooms. £17 per person, £20 with facilities.

Camping: Oxford Camping International, 426 Abingdon Rd. (tel. 246 551), behind the Texaco Station. 129 nondescript sites on a manicured lawn. Laundry and warm showers. Open year-round. £6 for 2 people and tent. **Cassington Mill Caravan Site,** Eynsham Rd., Cassington (tel. 881 081), about 4 mi. northwest on the A40. Take bus #90 from the bus station. 83 pitches. £5.50 for 2 people and tent. Hot showers included. Neither of these places rents tents.

Food

Oxford brandishes innumerable restaurants and cheap cafés to distract students from disagreeable college food; expect an upbeat atmosphere at most places. During the summer, walk a few blocks away from the four major streets to escape coach tourists and generic food. For fresh produce and deli goods, visit the **Covered Market** between Market St. and Carfax. (Open Mon.-Sat. 8am-5:30pm.) For dried fruit, whole grains, and the like, head for **Holland & Barrett,** King Edward St. (Open Mon.-Sat. 9am-5:30pm.) Eat and run at one of the better take-aways: **Bret's Burgers,** Park End St., near the train station, with delectable burgers and chips from £2 (open Sun.-Thurs. noon-11:30pm, Fri.-Sat. noon-midnight); or **Parmenters,** High St., near Longwall St., the trendiest take-away in town (date flapjacks 60p, enormous slices of carrot cake £1.10; open Mon.-Fri. 8:30am-6:30pm, Sat. 9am-6pm, Sun. 9:30am-5pm).

Munchy Munchy, 6 Park End St., on the way into town from the rail station. Stark wooden decor and absurd name somehow redeemed by spirited cooking and an energetic proprietor. Different dishes daily, all Indonesian or Malaysian, at least 1 vegetarian (£5-8). BYOB but 50p corkage per person. Open Tues.-Sat. noon-2pm and 5:30-10pm.

Brown's Restaurant and Wine Bar, 5-9 Woodstock Rd. Renovation has somehow both diminished the chic atmosphere and improved the English cuisine. Large helpings of spaghetti, burgers, vegetable salad all under £6. Open Mon.-Sat. 11am-11:30pm, Sun. noon-11:30pm.

Poor Student Restaurant, Ship St., off Cornmarket St. Well, not utterly destitute. Student-style English food served in a bright, ritzy interior with art deco lamps. Pasta £5-5.35. Open daily noon-10pm.

Cherwell Boathouse, Bardwell Rd. (tel. 527 46), off Banbury Rd., 1 mi. north of town. Romantically perched on the bank of the Cherwell and run by amiable young proprietors. A good place to propose. Menu offers a choice of 3-course meals—1 vegetarian, both unorthodox. Well-loved wine list. Expect to spend the entire evening; book well in advance. Dinner usually under £20, and worth every penny. When you're finished, rent a punt next door (£5) and drift off into the watery evening. Open Mon. and Wed.-Sat. 7:30-10pm, Sun. 12:30-2pm.

The Nosebag, 6-8 Michael's St. Vegetarian and wholefood meals served in sauna-like surroundings for under £5. Open Mon. 9:30am-5:30pm, Tues.-Thurs. 9:30am-5:30pm and 6:30-10pm, Fri. 9:30am-5:30pm and 6:30-10:30pm, Sat. 9:30am-10:30pm, Sun. 9:30am-6pm.

Pastificio, George St. near Cornmarket St. and the Apollo Theatre. Deep-dish pizza (£3.75-4.75) and fresh pasta (£4.35-5.35) served in clean modern surroundings. Open daily noon-midnight.

Polash Tandoori Restaurant, 25 Park End St. Inexpensive and delicious Indian cuisine served in a quiet setting near the train station. Chicken curry £4.15. Vegetable dishes under £2.15. Lunch buffet £7.50 per person. Open Mon.-Thurs. noon-2:30pm and 6-11:30pm, Fri.-Sat. noon-2:30pm and 6pm-midnight, Sun. noon-11:30pm.

Pubs

The Perch, Binsey. From Walton St. in Jericho, walk down Walton Well Rd. and over Port Meadow, cross Rainbow Bridge, head north and follow the trail west. This pub will make your whole vacation worthwhile. Definitely worth the trouble of finding. The lovely garden makes an ideal place for Sunday lunch or twilight drinks. Lunch served noon-2pm, cold buffet Mon.-Fri. 6:30-8:30pm. Occasional do-it-yourself barbecues.

The Turf Tavern, 4 Bath Pl., off Holywell St. A rambling, 13th-century building, intimate and relaxed. Good selection of drinks: beers, punches, ciders, and country wines—mead, elderberry, apple, and red-and-white currant. Wine about £1. Great salad buffet and hot meals noon-2pm.

The Bear, Alfred St. and Bear Lane. Christ Church's local: a dyed-in-the-wool Oxford landmark since 1242. Wouldn't be the same without the collection of ties, some of them snipped from England's best, brightest, and most boastful. Lunch served 12:30-2:15pm, dinner 7-10:30pm.

Victoria Arms, Marston Rd., by the river. A student favorite. The Happy Mondays did not play here on their recent tour.

The King's Arms, Holywell St. at Parks Rd. The university's unofficial student union and center for saturnalia studies. Punks, drunks, and a few scholars. Crowded and charmless, but keen with students.

The Head of the River, Folly Bridge. Immense river pub popular with the young and available. Large patio and multitudinous tables provide a great variety of settings in which to enjoy your ale.

The Bakery and Brewhouse, Gloucester St., just down from the bus station. Fast and lively crowd. Jazz on Wed. evenings and Sun. afternoons. Lunch served noon-2:15pm, dinner 5:30-8:30pm. Try their home-brewed ale and home-baked bread.

The Blue Boar, Blue Boar St. The quintessential English pub—starting with the name. Excellent ale, and no piped-in music.

The Eagle and Child, 49 Giles St. An inn since the 17th century, popular with the likes of J.R.R. Tolkien and C.S. Lewis. The owner has adorned the walls with photos and newspaper clippings from his days as a stunt double for Peter Ustinov. Popular with tourists.

Sights

Oxford University, England's first, was founded in 1167 by Henry II. Until then, Englishmen had traveled to Paris to study, a fact that never sat well with the francophobic English king. After his tiff with Thomas à Becket, Archbishop of Canterbury, Henry ordered the return of English students studying in Paris, so that "there may never be wanting a succession of persons duly qualified for the service of God in church and state." Over 800 years, the university has flourished into an international center of learning. In the ever-fierce competition with that other university on the Cam, Oxford boasts among its graduates Sir Christopher Wren, Oscar Wilde, Indira Gandhi, 13 prime ministers, and Dudley Moore.

Oxford has no official "campus." The university's 40 independent colleges, where students live and learn, are scattered throughout the city; central libraries, laboratories, and faculties are established and maintained by the university. At the end of their last academic year, students from all the colleges come together for their "degree examinations," a grueling three-week process that takes place in the Examination Schools on High St. Each year, university authorities unsuccessfully undertake to prohibit the vigorous post-examination celebrations in the street. The tourist office guide *Welcome to Oxford* (50p) and the tourist office map (20p) list colleges' public visiting hours (often curtailed with neither prior notice nor explanation). Christ Church, Magdalen, and New College charge admission.

Before tackling the university on your own, you may or may not want to visit **The Oxford Story,** Broad St. This museum of sorts (visitors are hauled around roller-coaster style in medieval "desks") recreates various scenes of Oxford's history. Guide yourself through the exhibits by cassette (narrated by Sir Alec Guinness) and participate in the St. Scholastica's Day Riot in 1355 or the development of Boyle's Law. (Open July-Aug. 9:30am-7pm; April-June and Sept.-Oct. 9:30am-5pm; Nov.-March daily 10am-4pm. Admission £3.75, students and seniors £3, children £2.25.)

Start your walking tour at Carfax, the center of activity, with a hike up the 97 spiral stairs of **Carfax Tower** for an overview of the city. Before hitting the heights, get a map of the rooftops from the attendant at the bottom. (Open March-Oct. Mon.-Sat. 10am-6pm, Sun. 2-6pm. Admission 80p, children 40p.) Then head down St. Aldates Street to the **Museum of Oxford** (across from the tourist office at the corner of Blue Boar St.), probably the most comprehensive and complete local-history collection in Britain. The seemingly endless but nevertheless entertaining walk-through displays outline Oxford's growth from a Roman and Saxon river-crossing for oxen to a famed intellectual watering hole. (Open Tues.-Sat. 10am-5pm. Free.)

Just down St. Aldates St. stands **Christ Church,** an intimidating mass of sandy stone that dwarfs the other colleges. "The House" has Oxford's grandest quad and its most socially distinguished, obnoxious students. (Open Mon.-Sat. 9:30am-6pm, Sun. 12:45-5:30pm. Admission £1, seniors, students, and children 40p.) Christ Church's chapel is also Oxford's **cathedral,** the smallest in England. In the year 730, St. Frideswide, Oxford's patron saint, built a nunnery on this site, in thanks for two miracles she had prayed for: the blinding of an annoying suitor, and his recovery. In the **hall,** college students and faculty take their meals on long wooden tables in a solemn setting. The cathedral's right transept contains a stained glass window (c. 1320) depicting Thomas à Becket kneeling in supplication, just before being put to death in Canterbury Cathedral. The 20-minute film shown continuously in the vestry (free) gives a concise history of the college and cathedral.

The Reverend Charles Dodgson (who wrote under the name Lewis Carroll) was friendly with Dean Liddell of Christ Church—and friendlier with his daughter Alice—and used to visit them in the gardens of the Dean's house at the eastern end of the cathedral. From the largest tree in his garden, the Cheshire Cat first grinned and vanished. Dodgson, who also taught mathematics at Oxford, used to come here to photograph and chat with Alice and her sisters. Among the nonsensical in-jokes that populate his Wonderland (on subjects ranging from Disraeli to religious reform to the early tweedles) Dodgson inserted several subtle references complaining about dining hall food at Oxford.

Curiouser and curiouser, the adjoining **Tom Quad** sometimes becomes the site of undergraduate lily pond-dunking. The quad takes its name from **Tom Tower,** which looms over the gate and in turn takes its name from **Great Tom,** the seven-ton bell it houses, which has faithfully rung 101 strokes (the original number of students) at 9:05pm (the original undergraduate curfew) every evening since 1682. Sixty coats of arms preside over the ceiling under the tower. Nearby, the fan-vaulted college hall bears imposing portraits of some of Christ Church's most famous alumni—Charles Dodgson, Sir Philip Sidney, W.H. Auden, John Ruskin, and John Locke. Other stately faces peer down in stone from the trim of the building's exterior. If you can, visit the kitchens and see the spits used for roasting oxen.

Through an archway (to your left as you face the cathedral) lies **Peckwater Quad,** encircled by the most elegant Palladian building in Oxford. Look here for faded rowing standings chalked on the walls and for Christ Church's library, closed to visitors. The adjoining **Canterbury Quad** houses the **Christ Church Picture Gallery,** a fine collection of Italian primitives and Dutch and Flemish paintings. (Open Mon.-Sat. 10:30am-1pm and 2-5:30pm, Sun. 2-5:30pm. Admission 50p. Visitors to gallery only should enter through Canterbury Gate off Oriel St.) Spreading east and south from the college's main entrance, **Christ Church Meadow** helps compensate for Oxford's lack of "backs" (riverside gardens in Cambridge).

Across St. Aldates at 30 Pembroke St., the **Museum of Modern Art** exhibits works ranging from anti-war sculptures to a photographic history of Israel. (Open Tues.-Wed. 10am-6pm, Thurs. 10am-9pm, Fri.-Sat. 10am-6pm, and Sun. 2-6pm. Admission £2.50, children £1.50.)

Across the street from the entrance to Christ Church lives neurophysiology professor Roger Bannister, the master of **Pembroke College** and the first human to break the 4-minute mile. Less speedy Samuel Johnson graduated from Pembroke, and his teapot and portrait still reside in its Senior Common room. Visitors must apply at the lodge to see the College.

Oriel College (real name "The House of the Blessed Mary the Virgin in Oxford") is wedged between High and Merton St. Oriel became a hotbed of the "Tractarian Movement" in the 1830s, when college clergy such as Keble and Newman tried to push the Anglican church back toward Rome. (Open daily 2-5pm.) Behind Oriel, **Corpus Christi College** surrounds a quad with an elaborate sundial in the center, crowned by a golden pelican. (Open daily 1:30-4:30pm.) Next door, **Merton College,** off Merton St., features a fine garden; the college's 14th-century library holds the first printed Welsh Bible. The college is also home to the **Mob Quad,** Oxford's oldest, dating from the 14th century. (College open April-Sept. Mon.-Fri. 2-5pm, Sat.-Sun. 10am-5pm; Oct.-March until 4pm.) A peaceful stroll down Merton Grove leads to **Merton Fields,** a quiet dab of green adjoining Christ Church Meadow.

University College, obviously up Logic Lane from Merton St., dates from 1249 and vies with Merton for the title of oldest college, claiming Alfred the Great as its founder. (Open afternoons when conferences are not in residence.) Percy Bysshe Shelley was expelled from University for writing the pamphlet *The Necessity of Atheism,* but has since been immortalized in a prominent Godless monument inside the college (to the right as you enter from High St.). Farther down High St. on the right lies the **Botanic Garden,** a sumptuous array of plants that has flourished for three centuries. (Open daily 9am-5pm; in winter daily 9am-4:30pm. Glasshouses open daily 2-4pm. Free.) For an esoteric escape from the weight of Oxford's tradition, visit **Oxford Holographics,** 71 High St., an exhibition hall of over 65 holograms. (Open daily 9:30am-6:30pm. Admission 50p, children 35p.)

With flowers lining the quads, a deer park on its grounds, the river flanking its side, and Addison's Walk (a verdant circular path) framing a meadow at one edge, **Magdalen College** has traditionally been considered Oxford's handsomest. Its spiritual patron is probably alumnus Oscar Wilde—the place has always walked on the flamboyant side. Edward Gibbon declared the 14 months he spent here "the most idle and unprofitable of my whole career." Every May Day, the college choir climbs up Magdalen's open-air stone pulpit and the bell tower to serenade the crowd below. Perhaps the third most illustrious member of the college is, you guessed it, Meline Von Brentano. (Open daily 2-6:15pm. Admission 75p.) Just up High St. toward Carfax, a statue of Queen Caroline (wife of George II) crowns the front gate of **Queen's College.** Wren and Hawksmoor went to the trouble of rebuilding Queen's in the 17th and 18th centuries, with a distinctive Queen Anne style in glorious orange, white, and gold. With its neat lawns and military flowerbeds, the college approaches Magdalen's beauty. A trumpet call summons students to dinner; a boar's head graces the Christmas table. The latter tradition supposedly commemorates an early student of the college who, attacked by a boar on the outskirts of Oxford, choked his assailant to death with a volume of Aristotle. (Open daily 2-5pm.) Next to Queen's stands **All Souls,** a graduate college with a prodigious endowment. Candidates who survive the terribly difficult pre-admission exams get invited out to dinner, where it is ensured that they are "well-born, well-bred and only moderately learned." (Open daily 2-5pm.)

Turn up Catte St. to the **Bodleian Library,** Oxford University's principal reading and research library with over six million books and 50,000 manuscripts. Sir Thomas Bodley endowed the library's first wing in 1602 on a site that had housed university libraries since 1489; the institution has since grown to fill the immense **Old Library** complex, the round **Radcliffe Camera** next door, and two newer buildings on Broad St. As a copyright library, the Bodleian receives a copy of every book printed in Great Britain—gratis. Admission to the reading rooms is by ticket only (if you can prove you're a scholar and present 2 passport photos, the Admissions Office will issue a 2-day pass for £2). No one has ever been permitted to take out a book, not even Cromwell. Well, especially not Cromwell. The library's unusual and entertaining exhibition includes Shelley's guitar, a lock of his hair, the only folio copy of Shakespeare's *Venus and Adonis,* a manuscript of a Haydn sonata, and an illuminated Aztec scroll. (Library open Mon.-Fri. 9am-5pm, Sat. 9am-12:30pm.) Across Broad St. from the Bodleian you can browse at **Blackwell's,** the famous bookstore with a seemingly erudite clientele. Blackwell's extends to a vast music department on Holywell St., an art shop next door, and a paperback shop and children's bookshop across the street (see Practical Information above).

The **Sheldonian Theatre,** set beside the Bodleian, is a Roman-style jewel of an auditorium built by Wren as a university theatre and home of the University Press. Graduation ceremonies, which are conducted in Latin, take place in the Sheldonian and can be witnessed with permission from one of the "bulldogs" (bowler-hatted university officers on duty). At the *Encaenia* in June, a vast procession of robed academics and luminaries winds with great pomp through the streets toward the Sheldonian. The cupola of the theatre affords an inspiring view of the spires of Oxford. (Open Mon.-Sat. 10am-12:45pm and 2-4:45pm; Nov.-Feb. until 3:45pm. Admission 50p, children 25p.) The **Museum of the History of Science,** next to the Sheldonian, houses a bewildering miscellany of arcania; including antique microscopes, charming astrolabes, and a blackboard touched by Einstein. (Open Mon.-Fri. 10:30am-1pm and 2:30-4pm. Free.)

The gates of **Balliol College,** across Broad St. (open daily 10am-6pm), still bear scorch marks from the immolations of 16th-century Protestant martyrs (the pyres were built a few yards from the college). The martyrs' monument is sometimes identified to gullible tourists as Oxford's "famous sunken cathedral." Housed in flamboyant neo-gothic buildings, Balliol is a mellow place that recently had a Marxist master. Swinburne went here. Balliol students preserve some semblance of tradition by routinely hurling bricks over the wall at their arch-rival, conservative **Trinity College,** on Broad St. (open daily 2-5pm). Trinity, founded in 1555, has a perfectly baroque chapel, with a limewood altarpiece, cedar lattices, and angel-capped pediments. Trinity's series of eccentric presidents includes Ralph Kettell, who used to come to dinner with a pair of scissors and chop away at members' hair that he deemed too long.

Across Catte St. from the Bodleian, New College Lane leads to **New College.** So named because of its relative anonymity at the time of its founding by William of Wykeham in 1379, New College has become one of Oxford's most prestigious colleges. The accreted layers of the front quad—compare the different stones of the first and second stories—reveal the continuous architectural history of the college. The chapel contains Jacob Epstein's sculpture *Lazarus,* an El Greco painting, and some fine stained glass. Look for the exquisitely detailed misericords, carved by sympathetic carpenters into the pews to support the monks' bottoms. A peaceful eastern garden is encircled by part of the **old city wall,** and every few years the mayor of the City of Oxford visits the college for a ceremonial inspection to ascertain the wall's good repair. One of the more notable members of the college was Warden Spooner, former head and originator of the "spoonerism." This stern but befuddled Oxford academic would raise a toast to "our queer old dean," or rebuke a student who had allegedly "hissed all the mystery lectures" and "tasted the whole worm." (Open daily 11am-5pm; off-season 2-5pm. Admission 50p.)

The bridge over New College Lane reveals the obsession of British architects with replicating the *Bridge of Sighs* in Venice. Cambridge has a replica too, theirs more appropriately straddling a river.

Turn left at the end of Holywell St. and then bear right on Manor Rd. to see **St. Catherine's,** one of the most striking of the colleges. Built between 1960 and 1964 by the Danish architect Arne Jacobsen, "Catz" has no chapel, and its dining hall was funded by that curmudgeonly eccentric, Esso Petroleum. (Open daily 9am-5pm.) At the corner of St. Cross and South Parks Rd., the **Zoology and Psychology Building** looms like a great concrete ocean liner. Many colleges hold sporting matches nearby on the **University Parks,** a refreshing expanse of green.

If, for some reason, you want to see over 1000 bees within an inch of your nose, visit the **University Museum,** Parks Rd. (Open Mon.-Sat. noon-5pm. Free.) Walk through to the **Pitt Rivers Museum** and examine a wonderfully eclectic ethnography and natural history collection that includes shrunken heads and rare butterflies. (Open Mon.-Sat. 1-4:30pm. Free.) Just up Banbury Rd. on the right, the **Balfour Buildings** house 1400 musical instruments from all over the world. (Open Mon.-Sat. 1-4:30pm. Free.)

Keble College, across from the University Museum, was designed by architect William Butterfield to stand out from the sandstone background; the intricate and multi-patterned red brick, known as "The Fair Isle Sweater," was deemed "actively ugly" by Sir Nikolaus Pevsner. (Open daily 10am-dusk.) Through a passageway to the left, the **Hayward** and **deBreyne Buildings** squat on the tarmac like a black plexiglass spaceship ready for takeoff.

The imposing **Ashmolean Museum,** Beaumont St., was Britain's first public museum when it opened in 1683. Its outstanding collection includes drawings and prints by Leonardo da Vinci, Raphael, and Michelangelo; copious French impressionist and Italian works; and Rembrandts, Constables, and assorted Pre-Raphaelites. The Ashmolean also houses mummies, a Stradivarius violin, and the lantern carried by Guy Fawkes as he tangoed through the cellars of Parliament. (Open Tues.-Sat. 10am-4pm, Sun. 2-4pm. Free.) Ashmolean's **Cast Gallery,** behind the museum, stores over 250 casts of Greek sculptures. (Open Tues.-Fri. 10am-4pm, Sat. 10am-1pm. Free.)

A few blocks up St. Giles, as it becomes Woodstock Rd., stands **Somerville College,** Oxford's most famous women's college. (The oldest is Lady Margaret Hall.) Somerville's alumnae include Dorothy Sayers, Indira Gandhi, Margaret Thatcher, Ena Franey, and Shirley Williams. Women were not granted degrees until 1920—Cambridge held out until 1948. Today, women comprise 38% of the student body.

At the remote end of Beaumont St., you'll reach **Worcester College.** Derisively called Botany Bay, the college has attracted some of Oxford's more swashbuckling students, including essay fiend and opium addict Thomas De Quincey and handsome poet Richard Lovelace. Worcester enjoys a large and dreamy garden and a lake shore that stages summertime plays. (Open daily 2-6pm; also 9am-noon during vacations.) At the very end of Beaumont St., on the north side, look for a stone tablet on the wall marking the birthplace of King Richard I in 1157.

By far the most self-indulgent of Oxford's neighborhoods is the five blocks of **Cowley Road** nearest the Magdalen Bridge roundabout. The area is a living version of the *Whole Earth Handbook,* a fascinating clutter of alternative lifestyles, Marxist bookstores, jumble shops, and scruffy wholefood and ethnic restaurants. Check out **Rainbow's End,** a comic-book shop at 78 Cowley Rd. (tel. 251 140; open Mon.-Thurs. and Sat. 10am-12:45pm and 1:30-6pm, Fri. 10am-12:45pm and 1:30-5:30pm), and **Jeremy's,** a stamp-collector's, used-paperback and postcard shop at 98 Cowley Rd. (tel. 241 011; open Mon.-Fri. 10am-12:30pm and 2-5pm). The **women's center** is nearby (see Practical Information above). To the north of Worcester College along Walton St., past the palatial **Oxford University Press** complex, lies the neighborhood of **Jericho.** A working-class suburb in the 19th century, the area has been redeveloped and today houses a varied ethnic population.

Entertainment

No teeming student carnival, the town closes down fairly early. Posters plastered around advertising upcoming events make the best entertainment guide. Check the bulletin boards at the tourist office or pick up a free copy of *This Month in Oxford.* Keep in mind that public transport peters out by 11pm.

The university itself offers marvelous entertainment. Throughout the summer, college theatre groups stage productions in gardens or in cloisters. Music at Oxford is a particularly cherished art; try to attend a concert or an evensong service at one of the colleges, or a performance at the **Holywell Music Rooms,** the oldest in the country. **City of Oxford Orchestra,** the city's professional symphony orchestra (tel. 240 358), plays a subscription series ("Beautiful Music in Beautiful Places") in the Sheldonian Theatre and college chapels throughout the summer. (Shows at 8pm. Tickets £3.50-9, students £2.50-8.) The year-long **Music at Oxford** series plays in halls throughout the city; for information, call 864 056 or write to 6a Cumnor Hill, Oxford OX2 9HA. The annual **Dorchester Abbey Festival** (music, drama, and poetry readings) runs for two weeks beginning in late June in Dorchester-on-Thames, nine miles south of Oxford. Coach transportation is available from Oxford. Call 240 358 or write to Dorchester Abbey Festival, Oxford OX1 2BR. The **Apollo Theatre,** George St. (tel. 244 544), presents a wide range of performances, including comedy, drama, rock, jazz, and the Royal Ballet. (Tickets from £6, student and senior discounts.) The **Oxford Union,** St. Michael's St., hosts modern productions performed by the small, avante-garde Mayfly theatre company in July and August. Tickets are available from Tickets-in-Oxford (tel. 727 855). Ask at the tourist office about student and community theatre productions in Oxford and environs.

The best cinema in Oxford is the **Penultimate Picture Palace,** better known as the **PPP,** Jeune St. (tel. 723 837), off Cowley Rd. Different double features play every day (one show £2.75). **The Phoenix,** Walton St. (tel. 549 09), shows mostly serious (read: foreign) films. (Tickets £2.75.) *What's On In Oxford* lists the clubs and pubs that play music. The less student-oriented **Jericho Tavern,** at the corner of Walton and Jericho St. (tel. 545 02), features local rock and jazz bands. (Open Mon.-Sat. until 2:30am, Sun. noon-2pm and 7-10:30pm.)

A favorite pastime in Oxford is **punting** on the River Thames (known in Oxford as the Isis) or on the River Cherwell. (See Boat Rental under Practical Information above.) Punters receive a long pole and a small oar, and are advised not to fall into the river. The flat-bottomed boat is propelled by pressing the pole against the river floor. It is very easy to end up in the river; if you're afraid to punt yourself, at least take a seat on the deck of the Head of the River pub at Folly Bridge and watch braver souls go by. Also, don't be surprised if you suddenly come upon **Parson's Pleasure,** a small riverside area where men sometimes sunbathe nude. Female passersby are expected to open their parasols and tip them at a discreet angle to obscure the view.

The university celebrates **Eights Week** at the end of May, when all the colleges enter crews in the bumping races, and beautiful people gather on the banks to sip strawberries and nibble champagne. In early September, **St. Giles Fair** invades one of Oxford's main streets with an old-fashioned carnival, complete with Victorian roundabout and whirligigs. Daybreak on **May 1** brings one of Oxford's loveliest moments: the Magdalen College Choir greets the summer by singing madrigals from the top of the tower to a crowd below, and the town submits to morris dancing, beating the bounds, and other age-old rituals of merrymaking—pubs open at 7am.

Near Oxford

The largest private home in England and birthplace of Winston Churchill, **Blenheim Palace** was built to reward the Duke of Marlborough for defeating Louis XIV's armies at the Battle of Blenheim in 1704, and in appreciation of his wife Sarah's friendship with Queen Anne. The palace's rent is currently one French franc, payable each year to the Crown. Sir John Vanbrugh's design is at once immense and coherent. Blenheim has wonderful rambling grounds designed by Capability Brown, as well as a lake and a fantastic garden center. Whilst attending a party here, Churchill's mother gave birth to the future cigar smoker and Prime Minister; the historic event transpired in a closet. (Palace open mid-March to Oct. daily 10:30am-5:30pm, last entrance 4:45pm. Grounds open daily 9am-5pm. Admission £4.50, children £2.20) Blenheim sprawls in **Woodstock,** eight miles north of Oxford on the A34; South Midlands (tel. (0993) 776 679) runs an express coach from Oxford's Gloucester Green (3 per day, 20 min., £1, children 50p). Woodstock, a tidy little village, chirps and hops with shops and pubs. Geoffrey Chaucer once lived here, and Winston Churchill is buried in the nearby village churchyard of **Bladon.**

Cotswolds

The Cotswolds are a band of medium-sized hills (highest elevation 1000 ft.) stretching across the west of England from the River Humber to the Dorset coast. From this ruggedly arching landscape, the famed Cotswold stone (properly termed *oolite* after the microsopic sea creatures that comprise it) has been extracted for centuries and shipped throughout the country. The warm golden buildings in Roman and Georgian Bath and medieval Oxford owe their distinctive look to the Cotswold quarries. The Cotswolds are a land of old settlement, made gentle with long civilization. The towns dating back to Saxon times tend to be small; only Cirencester has noteworthy substance.

Getting There and Getting Around

The Cotswolds lie mostly in Gloucestershire, bounded by Banbury in the northeast, Bradford-upon-Avon in the southwest, Cheltenham in the north and Malmesbury in the south. The range hardly towers: a few areas in the north and west rise above 1000 ft. but the majority of hills only ascend to between 400 and 900 ft., the average being 600 ft. The western reaches of the Cotswolds' dramatic landscape is dominated by the **Edge,** an unbroken ridge that runs for 52 mi. in a southwesterly direction.

While the Cotswolds ought not to be omitted from any itinerary, they are not easily accessible by public transportation. Major cities within the area (Cheltenham, Bath, Gloucester, and Cirencester) can be reached by train or coach; the smaller villages are linked by a bus service that is infrequent, slow, and patchy. Thankfully, the Gloucestershire Cotswolds (most of the range) are serviced by many different companies which operate under the auspices of the local county government. The inclusive and far-reaching *Connection* timetable is free and available from all area bus stations and tourist information centers; it is absolutely indispensible.

The **Cotswold Way** appeals to those interested in hiking the hills and staying in unspoiled villages. This 97½-mi. walk can easily be done in less than a week (shoot for 15 mi. a day); only certain sections of the path are suitable for biking and riding. The uncrowded way is well marked and affords glorious vistas of hills and dales. The following books are all available at tourist centers: the *Cotswold Way Handbook* (90p) provides a basic guide; Mark Richard's *Cotswold Way: A Walker's Guide* (£1.50) has maps and explicit directions. For additional reference, consult Ordnance Survey Maps 1:50,000 sheets #151 (Stratford); 150 (Worcester and the Malverns); 163 (Cheltenham); 162 (Gloucester); and 172 (Bath and Bristol). Check listings for local festivities like cheese rolling or woolsack races, where participants dash up and down hills laden with 65 lbs.

Practical Information

Tourist offices in the area (listed in a north to south direction) include:

Chipping Camden: Woolstapler's Hall Museum, at High St., Glos. GL55 6HB (tel. (0386) 840 101). Open April-Sept. only.

Broadway, 1 Cotswold Court, Worc. WR12 7AA (tel. 0386) 852 937). Open April-Sept. only.

Cirencester, Corn Hall, Market Pl., Glos. GL7 2NW (tel. (0285) 654 180).

Cheltenham, 77 Promenade, Glos. GL50 1PP (tel. (0242) 522 878).

Gloucester, St. Michael's Tower, The Cross, Glos. GL1 1PD (tel. (0452) 421 188).

Bath, the Colonnades, Avon BA1 1SW (tel. (0225) 462 831).

Accommodations and Food

The **Cotswold Handbook** (90p) lists B&Bs along the Way; they are generally spaced 3 mi. apart in villages and hamlets, and offer friendly lodgings to trekkers. Call ahead in the morning to reserve lodging for the same evening.

The IYHF has a number of hostels in the Cotswolds. The distance to the next closest hostel is indicated in brackets.

Charlbury: The Laurels, The Slade, Charlbury, Oxford 0X7 3SJ (tel. (0608) 810 202). 1 mi. north of Charlbury, 5 mi. northwest of Blenheim Palace, 13 mi. northwest of Oxford. Off the Oxford-Worcester rail line. (12 mi. from Stow-on-the-Wold hostel.) £5.50; ages 16-20 £4.40. Open April-Aug. daily; March and Sept.-Oct. Tues.-Sat.; Jan.-Feb. Fri.-Sat.

Cleeve Hill: Rock House, Cleeve Hill, Cheltenham, Glos. GL52 3PR (tel. (0242) 672 065), 4 mi. northeast of Cheltenham. Castleways (Winchcombe) bus from Royal Well in Cheltenham stops on demand at hostel gate, though hitching is easy on the A46. ½mi. from Way. Buy a guide (45p) to the surrounding countryside. (14 mi. from Duntisbourne hostel.) £5.50; ages 16-20 £4.40. Open July-Aug. daily; March-June and Sept.-Oct. Tues.-Sun.

Duntisbourne Abbots: Cirencester, Glos. GL7 7JN (tel. (0285) 821 682), off the A417, 5 mi. northwest of Cirencester. (14 mi. from Cleeve Hill hostel.) £5.50, ages 16-20 £4.40. Open March-Oct. Mon.-Sat. 19th century rectory set in 2 acres of grounds.

Inglesham: "Littleholme," Upper Inglesham, Highworth, Swindon, Wilts. SN6 7QY (tel. (0367) 525 46), 2 mi. south of Lechlade on the A361. Small store. Simple-grade. (20 mi. from Duntisbourne hostel.) £4.40, ages 16-20 £3.50. Open March-Sept. Wed.-Mon.

Slimbridge: Shepherd's Patch, Slimbridge, Glos. GL2 7BP (tel. (0453) 890 275), across from the Tudor Arms Pub, next to the slug bridge. Comes complete with its own ponds and wild fowl. Off the A38 and the M5, 4 mi. from the Cotswold Way and ½mi. from the Wild Fowl Trust Reserve. 50 beds; showers and dinner; small store. (22 mi. from Cleeve Hill hostel.) £7, ages 16-20 £5.90. Open April-Sept. daily; Jan. to March and Oct.-Dec. Mon.-Sat.

Stow-on-the-Wold: The Square, Cheltenham, Glos. GL54 1AF (tel. (0451) 304 97 or 307 40). In the market square of this hilltop village. On the A424 highway; Pulham's bus passes about every hr. from Cheltenham (17 mi.), Bourton-on-the-Water, and Moreton-in-Marsh (4 mi.). Comfortable rooms, knowledgeable warden. (12 mi. from Charlbury hostel.) £5.50, ages 16-20 £4.40. Open March to Oct. daily; Nov.-Dec. Fri.-Sun.

Camping is plentiful around Cheltenham but rather sparse elsewhere. Pick up a free copy of **The Cotswolds and Gloucestershire Caravan and Camping Guide** from local tourist centers.

You'll never starve in the Cotswolds. Large towns like Cheltenham and Cirencester have supermarkets, fast food and full-fledged restaurants; you can carbo-load in the hamlets or villages every 3 mi. or so along the Way at the plentiful country pubs.

Cotswold Villages

At the far northern edge of the Cotswolds, **Broadway** has welcomed visitors since it became a coach stop on the London-Worcester route in the 16th century. The town is now a museum of restored Tudor, Jacobean, and Georgian buildings, roofed with traditional Cotswold tile or thick thatch. From the top of **Broadway Tower,** a folly built in 1800, you can see 14 counties.

Three mi. east of Broadway, pristine **Chipping Campden** was once the capital of the Cotswold wool trade. Later, the village became a market center ("chipping" means "market"). The town is currently famous for its **Dover Games** in late May and early June, highlighted by the obscure "sport" of shin-kicking. This sadistic activity was prohibited from 1852 to 1952, but has since been enthusiastically revived to the glee of local orthopedists. (Tickets available the day of the game.)

Stow-on-the-Wold ("where the winds blow cold"), is quintessential Cotswolds—it flourished with the sheep trade and its buildings are of honey-colored stone. There is an **IYHF youth hostel** in the center of town. Just a few miles southwest lie the **Slaughters, Upper and Lower,** tranquil villages that epitomize the Cotswolds. A tributary of the River Windrush trickles underneath stone footbridges in Lower Slaughter, and an Elizabethan manor house dominates the peaceful cottages of Upper Slaughter. West of Stow-on-the-Wold and 6 mi. north of Cheltenham on the A46, **Sudeley Castle** (tel. (0242) 604 357) dominates **Winchcombe.** Once the manor estate of King Etheldred the "Unready," the castle was a prized possession in the Middle Ages, with lush woodland and a royal deer park. The Queens Garden is streamlined by a pair of yew hedge corridors leading to rose and herb beds.

Archaeologists have found prehistoric tracks and some 70 habitation sites across the Cotswolds. **Belas Knap,** a laterally chambered long barrow built 4000 years ago, stands about 1½ mi. southwest of Sudeley Castle. The exterior of this sealed tomb shows the distinctive Cotswold stone in an unusual setting. The **Rollright Stones,** off the A34 between Chipping Norton and Long Compton, comprise a 100-ft.-wide ring of eleven stones. Other sites are scattered throughout the Cotswolds; consult Ordnance Survey Tourist Map #8 (£4.25).

Charles I's four-poster bed sits in carved glory among the rich furnishings, armor, and paintings that ornament the castle's interior, and landscapes by Glover are scattered throughout, culminating in Constable's *The Lock* in the final room. The best-restored part of the castle is St. Mary's church, containing the tomb of Queen Katherine Parr. There are also regular falconry shows. Visit Sudeley on a weekday to avoid the crowds. (Open April-Oct. daily noon-5pm. Admission £4.50, seniors £3.25, children £2.25.)

The Cotswolds contain some of the best examples of Roman settlements in Britain—most notably **Cirencester** and **Chedworth** in the center. Cirencester, sometimes regarded as the capital of the Cotswolds, is the site of "Corinium", founded in 49 AD and second in importance only to "Londinium." Although only the amphitheater now remains, the **Corinium Museum,** Park St. (tel. (0285) 655 611), houses a formidable collection of Roman artifacts. (Open Mon.-Sat. 10am-5:30pm, Sun. 2-5:30pm; Oct.-March Tues.-Sat. 10am-5pm, Sun. 2-5pm. Admission 70p, seniors and students 50p, children 40p.) On Fridays, the entire town turns into a bedlamic marketplace.

Tucked away in the Chedworth hills southwest of Cheltenham is a well-preserved **Roman villa** (tel. (024289) 256), equidistant from Cirencester and Northleach off the A429. The famed Chedworth mosaics were discovered in 1864, when an observant gamekeeper noticed fragments of tile uncovered by clever rabbits. (Open March-Oct. Tues.-Sun. 10am-5:30pm; Nov. Wed.-Sun. 11am-6pm. Admission £2.25.)

Slimbridge, 12½ mi. southwest of Gloucester off the A38, is the largest of the Wildfowl Trust's seven centers in Britain. Sir Peter Scott has developed the world's largest collection of wildfowl here, with a total of over 180 different species. All six species of flamingos nest here, and white-fronted geese visit from their Siberian homeland. In the tropical house, hummingbirds and tanagers skim through jungle foliage. The visitors center has exhibitions, films, and food, glorious food (tel. (0453) 893 33; open daily 9:30am-6pm, or until dusk; admission £3, children £1.50). The **IYHF youth hostel** benefits from Sir Peter's avarian efforts, shepherding a flock of wildfowl on its grounds.

Cheltenham

Cheltenham epitomizes elegance. Beautifully manicured gardens, expensive shops, and immaculate terraces attest to the town's past as a posh spa. The budget traveler need not be dismayed by the Laura Ashleyesque quality of this town; its flower-lined streets, plush gardens, and free waters offer an affordable respite from the heavily touristed centers of Bath and Stratford, or the gloomy industrial megaliths of Bristol and Birmingham.

Arriving and Departing

Cheltenham (pop. 86,500), lies between Birmingham and Bristol, 43 mi. from each. Trains run regularly to London (1/hr. 5am-9:25am; 2½ hr.; £22), Bristol (1/hr. 6am-9:25pm; 1 hr. 45 min.; £6.30), Bath (1/hr. 6am-8:25pm; 1½ hr.; £9), and Exeter (every 2 hr. 7:30am-9:25pm; 2 hr.; £21).

Frequent coaches pull into **Royal Well,** behind the tourist office. **National Express** runs to London (1/hr. 6am-6:35pm; 3 hr.; £16); Bristol (every 2 hr. 9:30am-6pm; 1 hr. 15 min.; £6.75), Bath (2/day 1:30-3:30pm; 2½ hr.; £7.50), and Exeter (every 2 hr. 9:35am-6pm; 3½ hr.; £17).

Orientation and Practical Information

Cheltenham is a compact town; the majority of attractions slightly overflow a square area bounded by Albion St. to the north, Bath Rd. to the east, Oriel Rd. to the south, and Royal Well Rd. to the west. The **Promenade** is the main street in town and home to the tourist office. To reach the tourist office from the train station, walk down Queen's Rd. and bear left onto Lansdown Rd.; bear left again at the Rotunda onto Montpellier Walk, which leads to the Promenade. Alternatively, jump on one of the frequent F or G buses (78p return). From the bus station, Royal Well, walk around the block. Cheltenham's train station lies west of the town center, 15 min. by foot or a short ride on the F or G bus.

Tourist Information Center: Municipal Offices, 77 Promenade (tel. 522 878), 1 block east of the bus station. Accommodations service free with a 10% credited deposit; book-a-bed-ahead service £2. Free list filled with Cotswolds info. Open Mon.-Fri. 9:30am-6pm, Sat. 9:30am-5pm, Sun. 10am-4pm; Oct.-May Mon.-Sat. 9:30am-5pm.

Bike Rental: Crabtrees, 50 Winchcombe St. (tel. 515 291). 3-speeds £5/day, mountain bikes £7/day. £50 deposit. Open Mon.-Sat. 9am-5:30pm, Sun. 10am-4pm.

Bus and Coach Station: Royal Well (tel. 584 111), Royal Crescent. National Express has a temporary office there, but tickets can also easily be bought at **National Travel World,** 229 High St. (tel. 522 021). Open Mon.-Fri. 9am-5:30pm, Sat. 9am-4:30pm. Bus schedules posted.

Crisis: Samaritans, 3 Clarence Rd. (tel. 515 777).

Financial Services: Thomas Cook, 21 Promenade (tel. 233 601), at Clarence St. Open Mon.-Tues. and Thurs.-Fri. 9am-5:30pm, Wed. 9:30am-5:30pm, Sat. 9am-5:30pm. **Barclay's,** 128 High St. Open Mon.-Fri. 9:30am-4:30pm and Sat. 9:30am-noon. **National Westminster,** 31 Promenade. Open Mon.-Fri. 9:30am-4:30pm and Sat. 9:30am-3:30pm.

Early Closing Day: Wed., small shops only (most at 1pm).

Emergency: Dial 999; no coins required.

Hospital: Cheltenham General, Sandford Rd. (tel. 222 222), southeast of the town center, next to the college.

Launderette: Soap-n-Suds, 312 Lower High St. Soap 40p, n' suds £1.50. Dry 20p/10 min. cycle. Open daily 8am-8pm.

Market Day: Sun. 9am-2pm, open-air market at the race course; Tues.-Sat. 9am-5:30pm, in-door market at Winchcombe St.

Pharmacy: Boots, on the Promenade. Open Mon. and Wed.-Sat. 8:30am-5:30pm, Tues. 9am-5:30pm.

Police: Lansdown Rd. (tel. 521 321). Go west down Promenade onto Montpellier walk; Lansdown is on the right.

Post Office: 227 High St. (tel. 526 056). Open Mon.-Thurs. 9am-5:30pm, Fri. 9:30am-5:30pm, Sat. 9am-1pm. **Postal Code:** GL50 1PP.

Telephones: neat red rows in the pedestrian area of the Promenade. **Telephone Code:** 0242.

Train Station: Lansdown Station, Queen's Rd. at Gloucester Rd. (tel. (0452) 295 01 for schedule information). Information and tickets Mon.-Sat. 8am-8pm, Sun. 9am-6pm.

Accommodations and Food

Cheltenham's B&Bs are slightly expensive, but standards are high. The tourist office issues a pamphlet listing those under £13. B&Bs don't cluster along any particular streets, but instead blossom individually on the edges of town.

IYHF youth hostel, Cleeve Hill (tel. 672 065), 4 mi. out of town. Castleways buses (tel. 602 949) run every hr. 8:30am-10pm, Sun. 3/day. £6.60, ages 16-20 £4.95. Open July-Aug., March-June, and Sept.-Oct. Tues.-Sun.

YMCA, Vittoria Walk (tel. 524 024). At Town Hall, turn east off Promenade and walk 3 blocks—it's on the right. Men and women. A large, well-located "Y" with standard rooms and a helpful staff. Caters mostly to long-term tenants, but singles occasionally available for £11.55. Continental breakfast included.

The Bayshill Inn, St. George's Place (tel. 52 43 88) behind Royal Well Bus Station. Very basic accommodations above a pub. English breakfast included. £10.

Cheverel, Western Rd. (tel. 517 159) at the corner of St. George's Rd. Grandfather clocks and somber antiques. Ask for the attic room if it's available. English breakfast. £13.50 first night, £13 thereafter.

Hamilton House, 65 Bath Rd. (tel. 527 772). High-ceilinged rooms with antiques and TVs. English breakfast, but French and German spoken. £13.

Camping: Longwillows, Station Rd., Woodmancote (tel. (0242) 674 113), 3½ mi. off the F3 north of Cheltenham. Take the A435 (Evesham Rd.) north toward Evesham and turn off at Bishops Cleeve onto Station Rd.; it's on the left after the railway bridge. 50 sites. Bar and restaurant on grounds. £4.50-5.20. Open March-Oct.

Food in Cheltenham runs the gambit from fast food to haute cuisine; supermarkets and the aptly named **Fruity Fruit Store** locate on High St. and Clarence St. The **Barleycorn Cafe** at 317 High St. (tel. 241 070) cultivates vegetarian dishes on its outdoor patio (open Mon.-Sat. 9am-5:30pm). The **Orchard Restaurant** (tel. 521 300), in Cavendish House on the Promenade, serves a "Shopper's Special" 3-course lunch for £4.25 between 11:30am and 12:30pm. Cream teas £1.75. (Open Mon.-Wed. and Fri. 9am-5:30pm, Thurs. 9am-8pm, and Sat. 9am-6pm.) **Pastificio,** 21 Promenade, is one of a chain that dishes up pasta and pizza for £3-5 (open Mon.-Sat. noon-11pm). The tourist office serves up *What's Cooking in Cheltenham* (free), a food guide indexed by type of cuisine and price range.

Sights

Cheltenham proudly possesses the only naturally alkaline water in Great Britain. King George III took the waters in 1788, and in the 19th century the Duke of Wellington claimed that the spring cured his "disordered liver." Enjoy the diuretic and laxative effects of the waters at the Town Hall (Mon.-Fri. 9am-1pm and 2:15pm-5pm; free) or at the **Pittville Pump Room** (tel. 512 740), which also houses a museum and Gallery of Fashion. (Open all year Tues.-Sat. 10:30am-5pm; April-Oct. also Sun. 10:30am-5pm. Admission to pump room free; to museum 55p, children 30p.) Pittville Park hosts Sunday concerts and brunches in the summer. The Pump Room and Town Hall occasionally showcase entertainment, from symphony to cabaret to big band music (tel. 523 690 for info and tickets).

The **Gustav MacCallum Holst Birthplace Museum,** 4 Clarence Rd. (tel. 524 846), presents an interesting picture of the astronomical composer's early life. Follow the signs in the general direction of the coach station, then walk 1 block farther to Clarence Rd. Born here into a family of musicians, Holst enjoyed only a brief period of popularity during his lifetime. Items are arranged in typical Regency and Victorian rooms, and reveal as much about middle-class family life in those periods as about the Holster himself. (Open Tues.-Fri. noon-5:30pm, Sat. 11am-5:30pm. Free.) From High St., follow Pittville St. (which becomes Portland St.) to the end. The Cheltenham **Art Gallery and Museum** (tel. 237 431), on Clarence St. (not Clarence *Road,* where the Holst Museum is), 2 blocks from the bus station, houses an impressive collection of pottery, momentos of the Arts and Crafts movement, and curious curios like a pewter collection, a late 18th-century Ewbank carpet sweeper, and wooden bird-scares. (Open Mon.-Sat. 10am-5:30pm; May-Sept. also Sun. 2-5:30pm. Free.) The 12th-century **Parish Church of St. Mary,** off High St. by the museum, features a curious tombstone that begins its lament, "Here lies John Higgs,/A famous man for killing pigs./For killing pigs was his delight./Both morning, afternoon, and night."

If you're traveling with your Gold Card, stroll down Regent's Arcade between Regent St. and Rodney Rd. For continental ambience promenade along **Montepellier Walk,** where *caryatids* (female figures used as pillars) guard everything from banks to tobacconists.

Entertainment

Cheltenham hosts cultural events that draw people from throughout the district; most notable is the **Cheltenham International Festival of Music** in early July, now celebrating its 47th year of classical music, opera, dance, theater, and professional singers. Fringe concerts feature jazz and folk music. Full details are available in March from the box office, Town Hall, Imperial Sq., Cheltenham, Glos. GL50 1QA (tel. 523 690). Tickets are available on a first come, first serve basis; prices range from £1.50-18. The **Cheltenham Cricket Festival** is held in early August, with a carnival and flower show later in the month. October heralds a week-long **Festival of Literature,** the longest-running purely literary festival in England, which includes readings, lectures, and seminars. For a full program of events, write to the Town Hall (address above). Tickets are generally available in advance and range from £1.50-4.

The monthly *What's On,* free from the tourist office, will fill you in on concerts, plays, and evening hotspots. **Everyman's Theatre** on Regent St. (tel. 572 573) is a stop for traveling performers, such as dancers from the London City Ballet. The **Playhouse Theatre,** Bath Rd. (tel. 522 852), runs amateur productions on Monday nights. Experimental drama and dance have a home in the **Shaftesbury Theatre** on St. George's Place (tel. 222 795).

For a relaxing pint and good conversation try **Peter's Bar** on Montpellier Walk or **Dobell's** on the Promenade. (Both open Mon.-Sat. 11am-11pm and Sun. noon-2:30pm and 7-10:30pm.) If you'd prefer to dance, head to **Gas,** St. James Square (tel. 527 700), or **Ritzy** on the Bath Rd. (tel. 242 751). Every day has its own theme (house, funk, 60s, hip hop, alternative); cover charge and dress code vary with the tunes (£1 to £7; open 9pm-2am).

Near Cheltenham: Tewkesbury

10 mi. northwest of Cheltenham, on the A38 to Worcester and at the confluence of the Rivers Avon and Severn, lies **Tewkesbury.** Stately **Tewkesbury Abbey,** consecrated in 1121, is surrounded by expansive grounds leading out into the countryside. The abbey still stands today after townsfolk subscribed £453 to save it from Henry VIII's planned dissolution. (Open Mon.-Sat. 7:30am-5:30pm, Sun. 7:30am-6pm. Abbey services held Sun. at 8am, 9:15am, 11am, and 4pm; matins and evensong daily.) The **Old Baptist Chapel,** Church St., dating from 1480, is newly restored (open daily 9am-dusk; free). The **Country Park,** Crickley Hill (tel. (0684) 863 170), once an Iron Age fort, has ethereal views and many items of archaeological interest.

Several museums dot the town: **Tewkesbury Museum,** Barton St., displaying a model of the town and another of the Battle of Tewkesbury (open April-Oct. daily 10am-1pm and 2-4:30pm; admission 50p); the **John Moore Museum** on Church St., with rustic exhibits and an emphasis on nature conservation (open Easter-Oct. Tues.-Sat. 10am-1pm and 2-5pm; admission 40p, children 20p); and the **Little Museum,** Church St., a medieval merchant's cottage built in 1450 and restored in 1970 (open Easter-Oct. Tues.-Sat. 10am-5pm; free).

Stop by the town's **tourist office,** 64 Barton St. (tel. (0684) 295 027), for details on sights or accommodation bookings. (10% deposit on B&Bs; open June-Aug. Mon.-Sat. 10am-5pm.) Stay at **Mrs. Warnett's,** Crescent Guest House, 30 Church St. (tel. 293 395) for £13 or **Mrs. Wells,** Hanbury Terrace (tel. 299 911) for £11 (non-smokers only). Tewkesbury's **telephone code** is 0684.

Marchant's Coaches (tel. 522 714) run from Cheltenham through Bishop's Cleeve (Mon.-Fri. 5/day 9am-6pm, Sat. 2/day, Sun. 4/day; 35 min.). **Cheltenham District** buses (tel. 522 021) depart every hour until 5pm Monday through Saturday; only two buses run on Sunday.

Worcester

Halfway between Cheltenham and Birmingham, Worcester (WOOS-ter) has neither the gentility of the former nor the frenetic urban pace of the latter. Sight of the last battle of the Civil War and home of the unpronouncable Worchestershire sauce, Worcester is a commercial city with a captivating (though crumbling) cathedral.

Arriving and Departing

Worcester (pop. 90,000), 100 mi. northwest of London, is connected by train to the Big Fig (1/hr.; 2½ hr.; £22), Birmingham (1/hr.; 1 hr.; £3.50), Oxford (1/hr.; 1½ hr.; £6.70), and Cheltenham (1/hr.; 15 min.; £4.30). Buses arrive and depart from the station on Angel Pl.: **National Express** runs to London (2/day; 4 hr.; £14), Birmingham (1/hr.; 1 hr.; £4.50), and Bristol (2/day; 1½ hr.). A **Midland Red West Day Rover** ticket costs £3.20 (seniors £2.80).

For those traveling on their feet, the main roads into town are the A449 and A38 from the north, the A44 and A422 from the east, the A38 from the south, and the A44 and A449 from the west.

Orientation and Practical Information

The center of the city is shaped like an I. The north is bounded by the train station at Foregate St., the south by the cathedral. Running between the two is the pedestrianized main street which changes its name from Foregate to The Cross to High St. To get to the town center from the train station, proceed straight down Foregate St./The Cross/High St. until you see the Guildhall on your right. A highly informative staff and a slew of pamphlets awaits you in the **tourist office.** From the bus station, turn left out of the station, left onto Broad St. and right onto The Cross.

Tourist Information Center: The Guildhall, High St. (tel. 726 311). Enter through the unobtrusive blue door on the front left. Quiet and packed with pamphlets. Take your pick of several free maps. Local accommodations service free (10% deposit); booking elsewhere in England £2. Open June-Sept. Mon.-Sat. 9:30am-6:15pm; Sept.-Oct. and March-June Mon.-Sat. 9:30am-5:30pm; and Nov.-Feb. Mon.-Sat. 9:30am-4pm.

Tours: 1½-hr. tours leave from the Guildhall daily at 11am and 2:30pm Wed. and Sat. in the summer. £1.50, seniors and students £1.

Bike Rental: Cadence Café and Cycle Hire, platform #1 at the train station (tel. 613 501). The Rolls-Royce of rental. 3- and 5-speeds £6/day, 12-speeds £8/day; £50 deposit. Also tandems, trikes, and mountain bikes. Open Mon.-Sat. 9am-6pm.

Bus Station: Angel Place (tel. 252 55), off Broad St. Depot at Newport St. For information call Midland Red West (tel. (0345) 212 555) or National Express (tel. 232 96 or 248 98).

Financial Services: Thomas Cook, 16 High St. (tel. 282 28), across from the Guildhall. £2 fee. Open Mon.-Wed. and Fri. 9am-5:30pm, Thurs. 9:30am-5:30pm, Sat. 9am-5pm. **Lloyds** and **National Westminster,** The Cross. Open Mon.-Fri. 9:30am-3:30pm.

Early Closing Day: Thurs., small shops only (most at 1pm).

Emergency: Dial 999; no coins required.

Hospital: Royal Infirmary, Castle St. (tel. 763 333). Bus #354.

Launderette: Severn Laun-Dri, 22 Barbourne Rd., across from the Esso station. Open 9am-9pm. Wash £1.50, 20p dry cycle.

Market Day: Cattle Wed., General Market. Fri. and Sat., Cornmarket, 9:30am-4pm.

Pharmacy: Boots, 72-74 High St. (tel. 726 88). Open Mon.-Sat. 8:30am-5:30pm.

Police: Deansway (tel. 723 888), directly behind the Guildhall, across from St. Andrew's Park.

Post Office: 8 Foregate St. (tel. 726 131), next to the train station. Open Mon.-Fri. 9am-5:30pm, Sat. 9am-12:30pm. **Postal Code:** WR1 1AA.

Telephone Code: 0905.

Train Station: Foregate St. (tel. 272 11; open daily 8am-7pm), next to the post office. Ticket window open Mon.-Sat. 6am-8pm; in summer also Sun. 9am-8pm. Travel Centre open Mon.-Fri. 9am-5pm, Sat. 9am-4pm.

Accommodations and Camping

B&B prices in Worcester are high, as proprietors cater to Londoners looking for a weekend in the country; the beginning and end of the summer tend to be the busiest times of the year. Call ahead or try your luck on Barbourne Rd., north of Foregate St.

IYHF youth hostel: the closest one is 7 mi. away in Malvern (see Near Worcester: Malvern below).

Osbourne House, 17 Chestnut Walk (tel. 222 96). Homey decor and caring proprietor. The best in the city. £13.50.

Mrs. Woods, 11 Battenfall Rd. (tel. 350 158). Nurturing host suckles close to the center. Open Feb.-Oct. Doubles £12.50/person.

Abbeydore, 34 Barbourne Rd. (tel. 267 31). One of many on B&B row just north of Foregate St. Tidy rooms, nourishing breakfast. £13.

Shrubbery Guest House, 38 Barbourne Rd. (tel. 248 71). Plush rooms with TVs and tea- and coffee-making facilities. £13.

Camping: Worcester Racecourse, Pitchcroft (tel. 239 36), off Castle St. and Croft Rd., ¼ mi. from town. Caravans and tents. £4.50/person. Open April-Oct.

Food

You can satisfy your appetite on Friar St. or at Sainsbury's Supermarket in **The Shambles** on High St.

Heroes, 26-32 Friar St. (tel. 254 51), near the Tudor house. Stocks a boundless supply of food. Ham or quiche platter £3.50. Open Sun.-Thurs. 11am-11:30pm, Fri.-Sat. 11am-midnight.

Hodson Coffee House and Patisserie, 100-101 High St. (tel. 210 36). Cafeteria-style interior and café-style garden. Tasty pastries. Chicken curry or seafood pie £3.25, gooseberries with cream £1.25. Open Mon.-Sat. 9:30am-5:30pm.

Farrier's Arms, 9 Fish St. (tel. 275 69), off High St. Fresh bar meals served under wooden beams or in the light and airy beer garden. Choice of lunch dishes with vegetable (£2.75). Open daily 11am-2pm and 5:30-9:45pm.

Bottles Wine Bar & Bistro, 5 Friar St. (tel. 219 58), at the corner of Charles and Friar St. Rich red decor, wooden barstools, and a dress code. Quiche, herring, chicken, and the like £3-4, vegetarian dish of the day £2.90. Passion cake and other nifty desserts £1.50. Live music Sun. and Tues. nights. Open Mon.-Sat. noon-7pm for meals; bar open Mon.-Sat. noon-11pm, Sun. 7am-10:30pm.

Natural Break, 17 Mealcheapen St. (tel. 264 17), also at 4 The Hopmarket (tel. 266 54). Vegetarian meals cheap 'n' clean. Open Mon.-Sat. 9:30am-6pm.

Sights

Worcester Cathedral (tel. 288 54) stands majestically at the southern end of High St. by the river, cloaking a frail internal structure: the buttresses supporting the central nave are deteriorating and the central tower is in danger of collapsing. Though steel rods have been inserted into the base of the tower, the renovation efforts fail to detract from the quietly awe-inspiring detail of the nave and quire. The Lady Chapel, begun in 1224, is a stunning example of the Early English style. King John of Magna Carta fame rests downstairs in the the longest Norman crypt in England. Worth a closer look are the pulpit, carved from four different types of marble; the cloister garden, where the walls have alcoves and squints, used to supervise the Benedictine monks assiduously copying manuscripts during the 10th and 16th centuries; the bell display; and the tower. (Cathedral open daily 8am-6:30pm. Donation £1.50.) From Nash's passage, look over Perry Wood, where Cromwell allegedly danced with the devil under pale moonlight to insure his success in the battle of Worcester. His elfine steps paid off; you can retrace the history of the 1651 Battle of Worcester at the **Commandery,** Sidbury Rd. (tel. 355 071), Charles II's former headquarters. (Open Mon.-Sat. 10am-5pm, Sun. 1:30-5:30pm.)

Southeast of the cathedral, on Severn St., the **Worcester Porcelain Company** manufactures some of the finest bone china in England. A showroom on the premises sells high-quality pieces, while another shop sells seconds at greatly reduced prices. (Both open Mon.-Sat. 9am-5pm.) A few works in the adjacent **Dyson Perrins Museum** (tel. 232 21) merit a quick look. (Open Mon.-Sat. 9:30am-5pm. Free.) The **porcelain factory** gives tours explaining the manufacture of porcelain. (45-min. tours begin at the museum at 10-min. intervals, Mon.-Thurs. 10:15am-12:15pm and 1:15-3:15pm, Fri. 10:15am-12:15pm and 1:15-2:15pm. £2.50.)

A trip to Worcester wouldn't be complete without acknowledging the birthplace of the fiesty **Worcestershire Sauce:** a blue wash building on Bank St. Lea and Perrins later moved their factory to Midland Rd., near the Shrub Hill rail station. To the south, behind the Guildhall, all that remains of the demolished St. Andrew's Church is the 245½-ft. spire that stands at the entrance to the gardens. It is known locally as the **Glover's Needle** because of its shape and the area's association with glove-making. Left of the garden, turn onto the riverwalk that leads over the bridge to the **Worcestershire Cricket Ground** (tel. 748 474). A sign warns visitors to "enter at your own risk," but if you can spare a few hours, go in. Matches proceed at a sloth's pace from 11am to 6:30pm; admission is £3.25, £1.75 for county matches, though the gatekeeper may let you pay half-price to watch for an hour or so.

The **Worcester Museum and Art Gallery,** Foregate St. (tel. 253 71), near the post office, highlights the history of the city; the military history exhibits are especially well-done. (Open Mon.-Wed. and Fri. 9:30am-6pm, Sat. 9:30am-5pm. Free.)

Six mi. south of town lies the **Elgar Birthplace Museum** (tel. 662 24) filled with manuscripts and memorabilia. Midland Red West bus #312, 317, 419/420 make the journey (10 min., £1.10 return). Alternatively, you can cycle the six mi. along the Elgar trail based on the composer's own cycle routes. (Museum open May-Sept. Thurs.-Tues. 10:30am-6pm; Oct. to mid-Jan. and mid-Feb. to April Thurs.-Tues. 1:30-4:30pm.)

Near Worcester: Malvern

The name **Malvern** refers collectively to the contiguous towns of Great Malvern, West Malvern, Malvern Link, Malvern Wells, and Little Malvern, which hug the base and the eastern side of the **Malvern Hills.** The Malverns are accessible from Worcester via British Rail and bus (Mon.-Sat. every ½hr., less frequently on Sun.).

The tops of the Malvern Hills peek over the A4108 southwest of Worcester and offer the hiker 8 mi. of accessible trails and quasi-divine visions of greenery. The **Worcestershire Way** passes through the Malverns, 36 mi. to Kingsford County Park in the north. The Countryside Service (tel. 766 475) in the County Hall in Worcester provides additional information on hiking in the area. The Malvern **tourist office** (tel. (0684) 892 700) at the Winter Gardens, Grange Rd., will assist in hill-navigation (short distance walk pamphlets, 15p) and finding accommodations. (Open June-Sept. Mon.-Sat. 9:30am-6:30pm; Oct.-May Mon.-Sat. 9:30am-4pm.)

Great Malvern was built around an 11th-century parish church. Benedictine monks rebuilt the structure in the mid-15th century and added narrative stained glass windows. On the hillside above town, **St. Ann's Well** supplies the restorative "Malvern waters" that fueled Great Malvern's halcyon days as a spa town. The **priory** in Little Malvern, noted for its chancel and 15th-century stained glass, also harbors whimsical carvings of three rats attempting to hang a cat, and of a monk driving away the devil with a pair of bellows. The **Festival Theatre** (tel. 892 277), built in the 1920s, hosts recitals and large-production plays as well as famous celebrities like Frankie "Mule Train" Laine and Prunella "Fawlty Towers" Scales. The IYHF hostel in Malvern, **Hatherly,** sits at 18 Peachfield Rd. in Malvern Wells (tel. (0684) 569 131). Take citibus #42 from Great Malvern. (£5.90, ages 16-20 £4.70. Open April-Oct. daily, Feb.-March Thurs.-Mon.)

Stratford-upon-Avon

It is something, I thought, to have seen the dust of Shakespeare.

—Washington Irving

In 1930, the owners of the Great Texas Fair cabled Stratford-upon-Avon: "Please send earth Shakespeare's garden water River Avon for dedication Shakespeare Theater Dallas Texas July 1," revealing a classic case of obsession with Shakespeare's hometown. The soil of Stratford has been a totem of literary ritual ever since David Garrick's 1769 Stratford jubilee. England and this town have made an industry of the bard, emblazoning him on £20 notes and casting him and all of his long-lost twin brothers in beer advertisements. Yet this rich and strange form of relic-worship has more to it than another ill-begotten encounter with Polonius in polyester. Mary Arden's house, described as the home of Shakepeare's mother, may be a complete fiction, but despite—or perhaps because of—its unverifiable or imagined associations, Stratford keeps itself in the tourist limelight. There's no business like Bard business, and this helluva town may even upstage London as the center of England's cultural consciousness.

Arriving and Departing

Stratford performs 2¼ hours from London by rail or by the coach/rail "Shakespeare Connection," which runs from London's Euston Station (4/day, Sun. 2/day, coach connections at Coventry; 2 hr.; £24.50, £27 return. Only the Shakespeare Connection operates at night after plays.) Other trains run to London's Paddington Station (every 1½ hr., change at Reading and Leamington Spa; 2¼ hr.; £15, £15 return), Oxford (every 1½ hr.; £7.90, £7.90 return), and Warwick (12/day; £2.60 return). **National Express** coaches run to and from London's Victoria Station (8/day; 2¾ hr.; £12.75 single or day return, £15.50 period return); local Midland buses head to Warwick and Coventry (every 15 min.; explorer ticket £3.50) and to Birmingham (1/hr.; 1 hr.; £2.20).

Orientation and Practical Information

The closest thing Stratford has to a bus or coach station is the **Travel Shop** office (tel. 204 181; open daily 9am-5pm), at the corner of Warwick Rd. and Guild St. Here most National Express and Midland Red South buses and coaches arrive and depart. You can purchase tickets for coaches run by both of these companies at the Travel Shop office. Tickets can be bought on buses.

Tourist Information Center: Bridgefoot (tel. 293 127). Local accommodations service 10% of first night's stay (deducted from final bill). Open Mon.-Sat. 9am-5:30pm, Sun. 2-5pm; Nov.-March Mon.-Sat. 10:30am-4:30pm.

American Express: Bridgefoot CV37 6GW (tel. 415 784), in the tourist information center.

Bike Rental: Clarke's Gas Station, Guild St. at Union St. (tel. 205 057). Look for the Esso sign. £5.50/day, £25/week; £50 deposit. Open daily 7am-9pm. **Rent-a-Bike,** Guild St. (tel. 292 603). Free delivery of bike to wherever you need it. £5/day. £50 deposit. Open Mon.-Sat. 9am-6pm.

Boat Rental: Stratford Marina, Clapton Bridge (tel. 696 69). £5/hour. Across from the Dirty Duck pub. At the same dock you can chug across the Avon on the last of England's chain ferries (20p).

Bus and Coach Station: Corner of Warwick Rd. and Guild St.

Emergency: Dial 999; no coins required.

Launderette: Fountain Cleaners, 18 Greenhill St. wash £1.20; dry £1. Senior discount days on Wed. and Thurs. Open Mon.-Fri. 8am-9pm, Sat. 8am-6pm, Sun. 9am-2pm.

Market Day: Fri., at the intersection of Greenhill, Windsor, Rother, and Wood St.

Police Station: Rother St. (tel. 414 111), up Greenhill St. from American Fountain, turn left.

Post Office: 24 Bridge St. Open Mon.-Fri. 9:30am-5:30pm, Sat. 9am-12:30pm. **Postal Code:** CV37 6AA.

Royal Shakespeare Theatre Box Office: Tel. 295 623. Standby tickets may be available immediately before the show at the RST and the Swan for students and seniors (£6-12). Open Mon.-Sat. 9am-8pm. 24-hr. ticket information: tel. 691 91.

Telephone Code: 0789.

Train Station: Alcester Rd. (tel. 204 444). Inform Guide Friday Ltd. (tel. 294 466) in advance if you plan to travel on late-night Shakespeare Connection. Discount rail fares can be had by purchasing both rail and theatre tickets from **Theatre and Concert Travel** (tel. (0727) 411 15).

Accommodations and Camping

To B&B or not to B&B? This hamlet has tons of them, but singles are hard to find. Finding doubles involves less toil and trouble. In summer, 'tis nobler to make advance reservations by phone. Guesthouses (£14-18) line **Grove Road, Evesham Place,** and **Evesham Road.** (From the train station, walk down Alcester Rd., take a right on Grove Rd., and continue to Evesham Place, which becomes Evesham

Rd.) If these fail, try **Shipston Road** across the river. The tourist office describes local farms that take paying guests (£12.50-16).

IYHF Youth Hostel, Hemmingford House, Wellesbourne Rd., Alverton (tel. 297 093), 2 mi. from Stratford. Follow the B4086; take bus #518 from the Travel Shop (every hr.), or walk. Large; attractive 200-year-old building; recently renovated bath facilities. Kitchen facilities available. Curfew 11pm (11:30pm after a show). Lockout 10am-1pm. £3.90-5.60. Very crowded; call ahead. Open March-Dec.

The Hollies, 16 Evesham Pl. (tel. 668 57). Exceptionally warm and attentive proprietors, for whom the guest house is a labor of love. Green prevails. TV and tea-making facilities in every room. Spacious doubles; no singles. £15-18/person.

The Glenavon, 6 Chestnut Walk (tel. 292 588), off the end of Evesham Place. Prime location and comfortable rooms. English breakfast. Singles and doubles £14/person.

Nando's, 18 Evesham Pl. (tel. 204 907) Delightful owners, homey rooms. £14.50-16/person.

Strathcona, 47 Evesham Rd. (Tel. 292 101). Lovely gardens, caring owners. £13/person with full English breakfast.

Carlton Guesthouse, 22 Evesham Pl. (tel. 293 548). Elegant proprietor serves original English breakfasts in an antique-laden breakfast room. TV in every marvelous room. Come just to meet Saba, the gentle "bacon hound." Singles and doubles £16-19/person.

Greensleeves, 46 Alcester Rd. (tel. 292 131). On the way to the train station. Mrs. Graham will dote on you in her cheerful home. £14/person with breakfast.

Bradbourne Guest House, 44 Shipston Rd. (tel. 204 178). Easygoing proprietors. Charming rooms in a quiet location only ¾mi. from the center of town. Doubles £14/person.

Compton House, 22 Shipston Rd. (tel. 205 646). Small comfortable house run by the ever-helpful Mrs. Bealing. £14.50-17.50/person.

Camping: Elms, Tiddington Rd. (tel. 292 312), 1 mi. northeast of Stratford on the B4056. Open April-Oct. Tent and 1 person £2.50, each additional person £1.50. **Dodwell Park,** Evesham Rd. (tel. 204 957), 2 mi. from Stratford on the A439. Open year-round. Tent and 1 person £4.50, each additional person £1.50. Both have showers available.

Food

Imitation-Tudor fast food places mock the Bard's hometown. Check out the half-timbered Pizza Hut with extra cheese. Supermarkets are on Greenhill St.

Kingfisher, 13 Ely St. A take-away that serves chips with everything (fish, chicken, eggs). Cheap, greasy, and very popular; lines form outside. Meals £1-3.10. Open Mon. 11:30am-2pm and 5-9:30pm, Tues.-Thurs. 11:30am-2pm and 5-11pm, Fri.-Sat. 11:30am-2pm and 5-11:30pm.

Café Natural Wholefood Vegetarian Restaurant, Greenhill St. Lurking behind a health food store, this highly acclaimed café serves elaborate vegetarian foods. 10% discount on Tues. for students and seniors. Entrees £1.25-3.25. Open Mon.-Thurs. and Sat. 9am-5:30pm, Fri. 9am-7:30pm.

Hussain's Indian Cuisine, 6a Chapel St. Probably Stratford's best Indian cuisine; a slew of tandoori specialties. A favorite of Ben Kingsley. Chicken tikka £6.75.

Elizabeth the Chef, Henley St., opposite the Birthplace. Cafeteria-style lunch (£1.55-3.25) in a setting reminiscent of Holly Hobby. Open daily 10am-6pm.

Vintner Bistro and Cafe Bar, Sheep St. Satisfying ham, beef, and turkey salads (£4.25-4.75). Dinner about £4.75. Desserts may render you suddenly sockless. Open daily 10:30am-11pm.

Dirty Duck Pub, Southern Lane. Soothing river view. Indulge. Pub lunch £1-4.25. Fancy dinners more expensive. Chicken *Provençale* £8.95. Photos of actors adorn the walls.

Sights

Stratford's sights are most pleasant before 11am (when the herds of daytrippers have not yet arrived) or after 4pm (when most have left). Bardolatry peaks at 2pm. A ticket to all five **Shakespeare properties** costs £6, a savings of £2.50 if you manage to make it to every shrine. They are: Shakespeare's Birthplace and BBC Costume Exhibition, Anne Hathaway's cottage, the fictitious Mary Arden's House and Countryside Museum, Hall's Croft, and New Place or Nash House. You might not want to visit them all—dark timbered roof beams and floors begin to look the same no matter who lived between them. (Skip the "World of Shakespeare.")

The least crowded way to pay homage to the institution himself is to visit his grave in **Holy Trinity Church,** Trinity St., although the little arched door funnels massive tour groups at peak hours. (Admission 40p, students 20p.) In town, start your walking tour at **Shakespeare's Birthplace** on Henley St. (Enter through the adjoining museum.) The Birthplace, half period recreation and half Shakespeare life-and-work exhibition, includes an admonishment to Will's father for putting his rubbish in the street. Amazingly, half a million visitors shuffle each year through these narrow corridors and twisting staircases. The adjacent **BBC Costume Exhibition** features costumes used in the BBC productions of the Shakespeare plays, complete with photo stills. Avoid this exhibition if the idea of a Disney plastic show turns your stomach; one half expects the mannequin cast of Hamlet to launch into a chorus of "Zip-a-Dee-Do-Dah." (Birthplace and BBC exhibition both open Mon.-Sat. 9am-6pm, Sun. 10am-6pm; Nov.-March Mon.-Sat. 9am-4:30pm, Sun. 1:30-4:30pm. Admission £2.20, children 90p.) On High St., you can see another example of humble Elizabethan lodgings in the **Harvard House** (so called because Katherine Rogers, John Harvard's mom, grew up here). Period pieces sparsely punctuate this authentic Tudor building. The caretaker can tell you many truths about how the Rogers family passed the time in the 16th century. (Open Mon.-Sat. 9am-1pm and 2-6pm, Sun. 2-6pm. Admission £1.25, students 75p.) **New Place,** Chapel St., was Stratford's hippest home when Shakespeare bought it back in 1597. Also visit the **Great Garden** at the back. (Open Mon.-Sat. 9am-6pm, Sun. 10am-6pm; Nov.-March Mon.-Sat. 9am-4:30pm. House admission £1.50, children 60p. Garden free.)

Shakespeare learned his "small Latin and less Greek" at the **Grammar School,** on Church St. To visit, write in advance to the headmaster, N.W.R. Mellon, King Edward VI School, Church St., Stratford-upon-Avon, England CV37 6HB (tel. (0789) 293 351). The **guild chapel,** next door, is open daily. Shakespeare's eldest daughter once lived in **Hall's Croft,** Old Town Rd., an impressive building with a beautiful garden in tow. (Open Mon.-Sat. 9am-6pm, Sun. 10am-6pm; Nov.-March Mon.-Sat. 9am-4:30pm. Admission £1.50, children 60p.)

Head down Southern Lane and stroll through the **theatre gardens** of the Royal Shakespeare Theatre. You can fiddle with RSC props and costumes at their **gallery** museum. (Gallery open Mon.-Sat. 9:15am-8pm, Sun. noon-5pm. Admission £1.50, students and seniors £1.) The shed in the gardens houses a **brass-rubbing studio,** an alternative to plastic Shakespeare memorabilia. (Admission free, but materials cost 60p-£6.)

The modern, well-respected **Shakespeare Centre,** Henley St., has a library and a bookshop (across the street) and archives open to students and scholars. The center exhibits 16th-century books, holds madrigal concerts, and hosts a fine poetry festival in July and August. (Concerts £1-£1.50. Festival tel. 204 016. Poetry readings Sun. at 8pm; tickets £3.50-5.50.)

Anne Hathaway's Cottage, the birthplace of Shakespeare's wife, lies about a mile from Stratford in Shottery; take the footpath north from Evesham Place or the bus from Bridge St. The cottage exhibits portray the swinging Tudor rural lifestyle. (Open Mon.-Sat. 9am-6pm, Sun. 10am-6pm; Nov.-March Mon.-Sat. 9am-4:30pm, Sun. 1:30-4:30pm. Admission £1.80, children 80p.) **Mary Arden's House,** the lettice 'n lovage style farmhouse home that a 19th-century entrepreneur determined to be that of Shakespeare's mother, stands four mi. from Stratford in Wilmcote; a footpath economically connects it to Anne Hathaway's Cottage. (Open April-Oct. Mon.-Sat. 9am-6pm, Sun. 10am-6pm; Nov.-March Mon.-Sat. 9am-4:30pm. Admission £2.50, children £1.)

Entertainment

RSC spells relief. After enduring the cultural commodity-fetishism of the tourist hot spots, seek solace in a performance by the skillful and often sublime **Royal Shakespeare Company.** To reserve seats (£5-28), call the box office (tel. 295 623; 24-hr. recorded information tel. 691 91); they hold tickets for three days only. The box office opens at 9:30am. Good matinee seats are often available after 10:30am on the morning of a performance, and some customer returns and standing-room tickets may be available on the day of an evening performance (queue up 1-2 hr. before curtain). Student standbys for £6-12 just before curtain exist, but are rare. The company does not perform in Stratford in February or the first half of March. You can take a 45-min. **backstage tour** at 1:30 and 5:30pm and after performances, Monday through Saturday (except matinee days) or Sunday at 12:30, 2:15, 3:15, and 4:15pm (tours £3.50, students and seniors £2.50).

The new **Swan Theatre** has been specially designed for RSC productions of plays written by Shakespeare's contemporaries. The theatre is located down Waterside, in back of the Royal Shakespeare Theatre, on the grounds of the old Memorial Theatre. (Tickets £8-19, standing room £3.) It's smaller and often more crowded than the RST; line up early for tickets.

The **Stratford Festival** (July 13-Aug. 4) refreshingly celebrates artistic achievement other than Shakespeare's. The festival typically features world-class artists from all aspects of performance art (the likes of Simon Rattle to the anachronistic theatrical troupe Regia Anglorum). Tickets (when required) can be purchased from the Stratford Festival box office (2 Chestnut Walk, tel. 679 69). The theme for 1992 is Europe.

Near Stratford

Within an hour's drive of Stratford cluster dozens of stately homes and castles, testimony to England's "teeming womb of royal kings." Assorted historians, architects, and ad copy writers regard **Warwick Castle,** between Stratford and Coventry, as England's finest medieval castle. Its magnificent battlements loom over gracious, meandering grounds. A collection of wax models by Madame Tussaud occupies the castle's private apartments; the dungeon and torture chamber feature gruesomely detailed exhibits. (Castle and grounds open daily 10am-5:30pm; Nov.-Feb. 10am-4:30pm. Admission £5.75, children £3.50.) A Midland Red bus journeys from Stratford to Warwick every hour (#18 or X16, 15-20 min.), and trains make the trip frequently (£2.60).

Ragley Hall, eight mi. west of Stratford, a Palladian mansion, is home to the Marquis and Marchioness of Hertford. The estate boasts a fine collection of paintings, including Graham Rust's modern mural, "The Temptation," which took 15 years to paint. The 400-acre park includes a captivating maze. (Open in summer Tues.-Thurs. noon-5pm, Sat.-Sun. 1:30-5:30pm.) Take a bus (Mon.-Sat. 5/day) from Stratford to Alcester, then walk one mi. to the gates of Ragley Hall and then another ½mi. up the drive. (Admission £4, children £3.)

Bath

A visit to Bath remains de rigueur, even though this elegant Georgian city is now more of a museum than a resort. Immortalized by Fielding, Austen, and Dickens, Bath was at one time the second social capital of England. Aristocrats came here in search of something calmer than the metropolis and livelier than the country. Heavily bombed during World War II, Bath has since been painstakingly restored. Aristocratic patronage has graced the city with glorious buildings, a long roster of famous residents, and many minor artistic treasures.

Legend ascribes the founding of Bath to King Lear's leper father Bladud, who wandered the countryside bemoaning his banishment from court. He took work as a swineherd, but his pigs soon caught the affliction. The devoted and decompos-

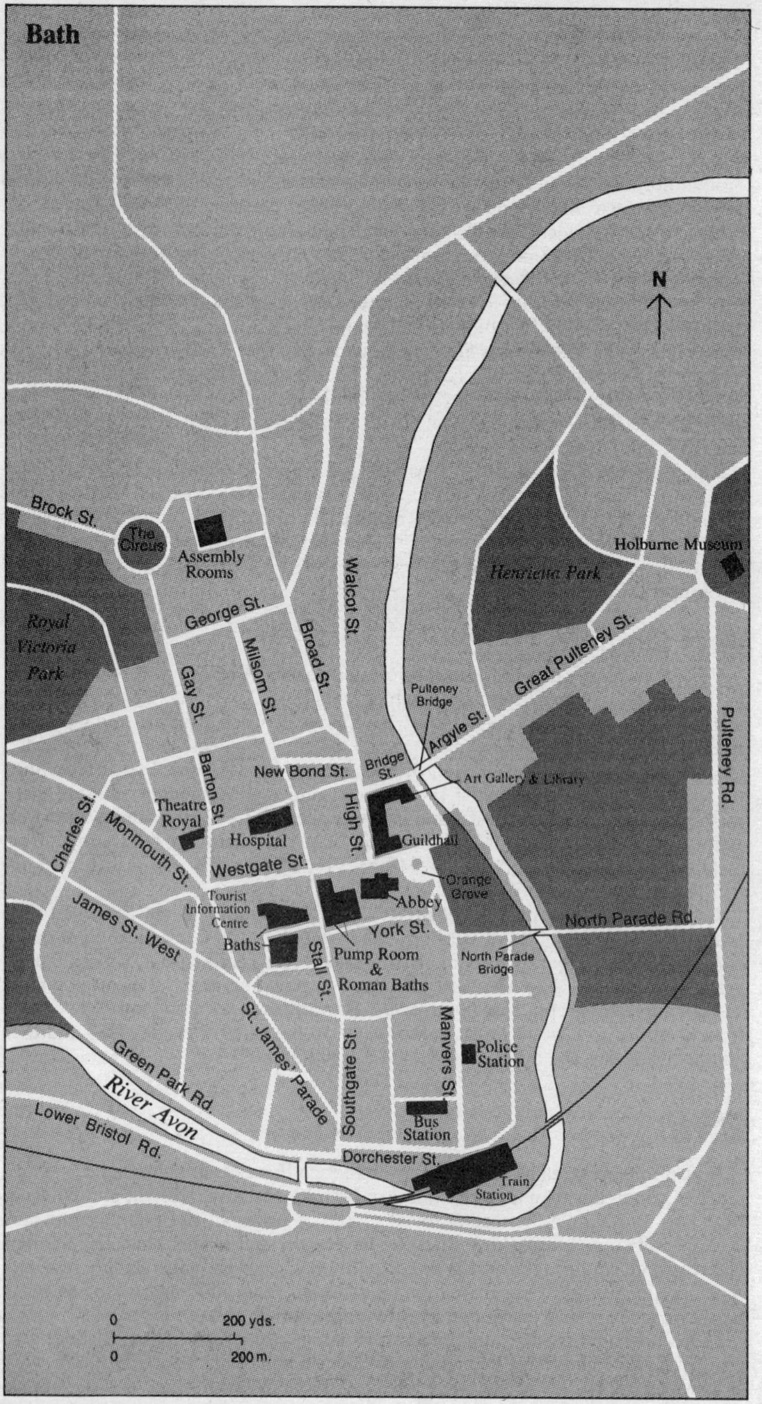
Bath
N
Brock St.
The Circus
Assembly Rooms
Royal Victoria Park
George St.
Gay St.
Milsom St.
Broad St.
Walcot St.
Henrietta Park
Holburne Museum
Great Pulteney St.
Pulteney Bridge
Argyle St.
Pulteney Rd.
Bridge St.
New Bond St.
Barton St.
Theatre Royal
Charles St.
Monmouth St.
Hospital
High St.
Art Gallery & Library
Guildhall
Westgate St.
Orange Grove
Tourist Information Centre
Abbey
North Parade Rd.
James St. West
Baths
York St.
Stall St.
Pump Room & Roman Baths
North Parade Bridge
St. James's Parade
Southgate St.
Manvers St.
Police Station
Green Park Rd.
River Avon
Bus Station
Lower Bristol Rd.
Dorchester St.
Train Station
0 200 yds.
0 200 m.

ing swine led their king to a therapeutic spring; out of gratitude, Bladud founded a city on the site of the healing waters. Tragically, Bladud's attempt to heal his faithful herd resulted only in a large amount of cold pork stew.

The Romans built an elaborate complex of baths here early in their occupation of Britain. The success of the spa was sealed when Queen Anne paid a visit in 1701. From then on, a parade of distinguished visitors and residents—Pitt, Burke, Johnson, Defoe, Austen, and innumerable bathing-beauty high-society types—came here to indulge themselves in the healing powers of the spa. Unfortunately, the baths were far from therapeutic for one 11-year-old girl who visited them a few years ago and contracted a fatal case of cerebral meningitis. Although much mystery surrounds the exact source of the disease, the baths have been reopened to visitors for viewing, although not for bathing.

Arriving and Departing

Bath (pop. 83,000) is served by direct rail service from London's Paddington Station (1/hr.; 1½ hr.; supersaver return £23), Exeter (22/day; 1¾ hr.; £16), and Bristol (60/day; 15 min.; £3.50). **National Express** coaches depart for London's Victoria Station (1/hr., 3 hr., £16.50), Oxford (6/day; 2 hr.; £11.50), and Salisbury (4/day; 1½ hr.; £4.15). **Badgerline** buses offer an **Explorer** ticket (£3.90) which gives unlimited travel for one day (to Bristol every ½hr.; 50 min.; £1.95).

Orientation and Practical Information

Bath is 107 mi. west fo London and 12 mi. east of Bristol. The Pultney Bridge and North Parade Bridge span the **River Avon,** which runs through the city from the east. The Roman Baths, the Abbey, and the Pump Room are all in the city center. The Royal Crescent and the Circus lie to the northwest. The train and coach stations are near the south end of Manvers St., at the bend in the river. From either terminal, walk up Manvers St. to the Orange Grove roundabout and turn left to the tourist office in the Abbey Churchyard.

Tourist Information Center: The Colonnades, (tel. 462 831 for information and accommodations). Exceptionally efficient staff, although the office gets crowded in summer. Reams of useful information. Accommodations service with 10% deposit, list free. Book-a-bed-ahead £2. Map and mini-guide 25p. Pick up a free copy of Bath Events. Open Mon.-Sat. 9:30am-7pm, Sun. 10am-6pm.

Tours: Several available. Excellent free 1¾-hr. guided walking tours leave from the Abbey Churchyard Mon.-Fri. at 10:30am and Sun. at 10:30am and 2:30pm; extra tours May-Sept. Tues. and Fri.-Sat. at 7pm and Wed. at 2:30pm; Oct. Wed. at 2:30pm. Bus tours of city (every ½hr. 10am-5:30pm; 1 hr.) cost £3, students £2.50.

Bike Rental: Avon Valley Bike Hire, Railway Pl. (tel. 461 880), behind train station. £5-11 for 4 hr., £8-17 for 8 hr.; £15-50 deposit. Open daily 9am-6pm.

Boating: Bath Boating Company, Forester Rd. (tel. 466 407), about ½mi. north of town. Punts £2.50/person per hr., rowboats £3/person per hr. £30 deposit required. One-hr. guided river tours from Pulteney Bridge £2.50, children £1.50.

Bookstore: George Gregory, 23 Mawes St. (tel. 466 000) in the basement. Established in 1845. Open Mon.-Fri. 9am-1pm and 2-5pm, Sat. 9:30am-1pm.

Bus and Coach Station: Manvers St. (tel. 464 446).

Crisis: Samaritans, tel. 429 222; 24 hr.

Emergency: Dial 999; no coins required.

Financial Services: Barclay's on Stall St. (tel. 462 521), behind the Abbey Churchyard, will exchange Visa checks for free. Open Mon.-Fri. 9:30am-4:30pm, Sat. 9:30am-noon. **Thomas Cook,** 20 New Bond St. (tel. 463 191), charges £2; open Mon.-Wed. and Fri. 9am-5:30pm, Thurs. 9:30am-5:30pm, Sat. 9am-5pm. **Lloyd's** on Milsom St. will exchange American Express checks for free. Open Mon.-Fri. 9:30am-4:30pm. **American Express:** Bridge St. (tel. 444 767), just before Pulteney Bridge. Open Mon.-Wed. and Fri. 9am-5pm, Thurs. 9:30am-5pm, Sat. 9am-2pm, Sun. 10am-2pm.

Gay and Lesbian Concerns: Gay West, tel. (0272) 425 927.

Launderette: Self Serve Laundry, George St. Open daily 8:30am-7:45pm. Wash £2, 10-min. dry 20p.

Library: Bath Central Library, 10 the Podium (tel. 428 144). Open Mon. 10am-6pm, Tues.-Fri. 9:30am-8pm, Sat. 9:30am-5pm.

Pharmacy: Boots, Southgate St. Open Mon.-Wed. and Fri.-Sat. 9am-5:30pm, Thurs. 9am-8pm.

Police: Manvers St. (tel. 444 343), just up from the train and bus stations.

Post Office: New Bond St. (tel. 825 211), at Broad St. Open Mon.-Fri. 9:30am-5:30pm, Sat. 9am-1pm. **Postal Code:** BA1 1AA.

Taxi: Stands near stations. **Abbey Radio,** tel. 465 843, **Rainbow,** tel. 460 606.

Telephone Code: 0225.

Train Station: At the south end of Manvers St. (tel. 463 075). Booking office open daily 6am-9:30pm.

Accommodations and Camping

Bath has traditionally catered to the well-heeled. Don't try to find a bargain basement room (some are quite frightening). Instead, dig deep, expect to pay £12-17, and enjoy Bath's gracious style. B&Bs cluster on **Pultney Road** and **Pultney Gardens.** From the stations, walk up Manvers St., which becomes Pierrepont St., right on to N. Parade Rd and past the cricket ground to Pulteney Rd.. For a more relaxed setting continue past Pulteney Gdns. (or take the footpath from behind the rail station) to **Widcombe Hill**—a steep climb, with prices to match (from £14).

IYHF Youth Hostel, Bathwick Hill (tel. 656 74). From N. Parade Rd., turn left onto Pulteney Rd., then right onto Bathwick. A footpath takes the hardy up this steep hill to the hostel (20-min. walk). Badgerline "University" bus #18 (5/hr. until 11pm, 75p return) runs from the bus station or the Orange Grove roundabout. The hostel crowd seems out of place in this gracious Italianate mansion overlooking the city. 112 beds, shower, TV, laundry. Curfew 11pm. Reception open 7:30-10am and 1-10:30pm. July-Aug. £7, ages 16-20 £5.90; Sept.-June £6.60, ages 16-20 £5.40.

YMCA International House, Broad St. Place (tel. 460 471). Walk under the arch and up the steps from Walcot St. across from Beaufort Hotel. Men and women allowed. More centrally located than IYHF hostel (3 min. from tourist office), with free hot baths or pulsating showers and no curfew. Heavily booked in summer. Singles £12. Doubles £21.50. Dorm rooms £9/person. £5 key deposit. Continental breakfast included; hot breakfast 50p extra.

The Shearns, Prior House, 3 Marlborough Lane (tel. 313 587). Great location on west side of town beside Royal Victoria Park. Take bus #14 or 15 from bus station (every 15 min.). Far and away the best value in Bath. Warm, wonderful proprietors treat guests well. No singles. £12/person. English breakfast included.

Mrs. Guy, 14 Raby Pl. (tel. 465 120). From N. Parade, turn left onto Pulteney Rd., then right. Comfortable rooms in an elegant Georgian house with light, cool interiors and superior views of the city. Fresh seasonal fruits and yogurts complement a generous English breakfast. No smoking indoors. Singles £14. Doubles £28.

Mrs. Rowe, 7 Widcombe Crescent (tel. 422 726). In the southeastern area, up the hill from the stations. The height of elegance—they don't make 'em like this anymore—and a view to match. Management quite particular, and atmosphere decidedly staid. Blissfully quiet neighborhood. Full bath and TV. Singles £14-16. Doubles £24-34.

Avon Guest House, 1 Pulteney Gdns. (tel. 313 009), at Pulteney Rd. Large rooms, each with full bath, color TV, and tea-making facilities. Friendly owners. £16/person. Fine English breakfast included.

Pulteney Guest House, 14 Pulteney Rd. (tel. 460 991). Well-appointed rooms with a myriad of electrical conveniences. Singles £15-18, doubles £32-40.

Camping: Newton Mill Touring Centre, Newton St. Loe (tel. 333 909), 3 mi. west of city center off the A36/A39. Take bus #5 from bus station (5/hr.; 75p) to Newton Rd. 105 sites. Laundry; free warm showers. £6.70/pitch. £3/person.

Food and Pubs

For budget-priced fruits and vegetables, visit the **Guildhall Market,** between High St. and Grand Parade. (Open Mon.-Sat. 9:30am-5:30pm.) **Harvest Wholefoods,** 27 Walcot St., stocks a tremendous selection of organic produce, including some exotic items. (Open Tues.-Sat. 9:30am-5:30pm, Mon. 11:30am-5:30pm.) **Seasons,** 10 George St. (tel. 697 30), has a small deli and also offers a good selection of natural foods. (Open Mon.-Sat. 9am-5:30pm.) Grab picnic fare at **Waitrose** in the Podium on High St. across from the Post Office.

Pub meals are a particularly good alternative on Sunday nights. For take-away, try **The Kitchen** (a.k.a. **Bake and Take**), on Upper Borough Walls near Barton St.—cheap, reliable, and open late (daily until 11pm). Splash out for an elegant cream tea (£4.25) in the **Pump Room,** Abbey Churchyard, a palatial Victorian restaurant (open Mon.-Sat. 10am-noon and 2:45-5pm).

Scoff's, corner of Monmouth and Westgate St. Memorable, freshly baked wholefood pastries and filling lunches served in a warm, woody dining room with high ceilings and a fine view of shady Kingsmead Sq. Take-away too. Big *tandoori* burger and salad £2.50. Open Mon.-Sat. 9am-5pm.

The Walrus and The Carpenter, 25 Barton St., uphill from the Theatre Royal. No cabbages or kings, just your basic bistro: carefully casual, cramped but intimate, candle-stuffed wine bottles, checked tablecloths, drowsy waiters . . . you know the rest. Good burgers with creative toppings £5-7. Smattering of vegetarian entrees £5-8. Open Mon.-Sat. noon-2pm and 6-11pm, Sun. 6-11pm.

Pasta Galore, 31 Barton St., just over from the Walrus and Carpenter. A big (albeit very good) franchise successfully masquerading as a cozy little Italian café with a walled garden off the back. Wide selection of homemade pastas and rich desserts. *Canneloni* with a choice of 3 sauces £5.40. Open Mon.-Thurs. noon-2:30pm, Fri.-Sat. 6-11pm.

Huckleberry's, 34 Broad St., down the street from the Y. Bath's only vegetarian restaurant, and it's good. Walls as green as the politics. Full meals from £3.50. Open Mon.-Thurs. 9am-4:30pm, Fri. 9am-9pm, Sat. 9am-5:30pm.

The Crystal Palace, 11 Abbey Green, behind Marks and Spencer. A sprawling, 18th-century pub-*cum*-restaurant with an outdoor patio. Ploughman's lunch 12 different ways (£3-4.50). Open Mon.-Thurs. 10:30am-2:30pm and 6-10:30pm, Fri.-Sat. 10:30am-2:30pm and 6-11pm, Sun. noon-2pm and 7-10:30pm.

Salamander Restaurant and Free House, 3 John St. Good pub grub at good pub prices. Paul Weller never wrote a song about this place. Open Mon.-Sat. noon-3pm and 6-11pm, Sun. noon-11pm.

Fagin's Restaurant, Queen St. A range of dishes with a twist. Mr. Bumble's bolognese £4, Dickens or Beadle burger £4, Toff's Chicken Curry £5.

Maxson's Diner, Argyle St. at Laura Pl. Beef burgers in a bebop joint (£4.50-5). Vegans should try the spinach and lentil lasagna (£5.40). Open daily noon-11pm.

Among Bath's many pubs, **The Grapes,** Westgate St., attracts an energetic student throng. The **Regency Bar,** Sawclose, complete with video screen, also draws a crowd. The Green Room at **The Garricks Head,** beside the Theatre Royal, is a calm, pleasant gay pub. The **Saracen's Head,** on Broad St., Bath's oldest dating from 1713, inspired Dickens to pen the *Pickwick Papers.*

Sights

As the Roman spa city of Aquae Sulis, Bath flourished for nearly 400 years, and the **Roman Baths** retain their prominence in the town center. Sewer-diggers first uncovered the site inadvertently in 1880, and recent intentional excavation has yielded a splendid model of advanced Roman engineering. Make your way through a maze of tunnels interrupted by dripping and fenced-off segments of the bath. Also on display within the corridors lurk a gilded bronze head of Minerva, a heap of Roman pennies tossed into the baths for good luck, and *ligulae,* bronze ear wax removers. (Open March-June and Sept.-Oct. daily 9am-6pm; July 9am-7pm; Aug. 9am-7pm and 8:30-10:30pm; Nov.-Feb. Mon.-Sat. 9am-5pm, Sun. 10am-5pm. Admission £3.60, ages 5-16 £1.70, under 5 free.) Excellent guided tours of the baths leave twice per hour from beside the main pool.

In 1703, professional gambler Richard "Beau" Nash, grabbing the opportunity of developing a luxury tourist trade in the area, promoted Bath as a status spa with resort facilities. The **Pump Room** above the Roman Baths (see Food and Pubs above) exemplifies the elegant atmosphere he created. The city's residential northwest corner is another, in which Nash's contemporaries John Wood, *père et fils,* transformed the Georgian row house into an element of design. Though bus tours run regularly from the bus station and from Kingsmead Sq. (see Practical Information above), you may want to stay on foot to see the city. Walk up Gay St. to **The Circus,** which has attracted illustrious residents for two centuries. Blue plaques mark the houses of Thomas Gainsborough, William Pitt, and David Livingstone. Proceed from there up Brock St. to **Royal Crescent** and its great upended saucer of a lawn. Note that there are precisely 114 giant Ionic columns. The interior of **No. 1 Royal Crescent** has been painstakingly restored by the Bath Preservation Trust to a near-perfect replica of a 1770 townhouse, authentic to the last teacup and butter knife. (Open March-Oct. Tues.-Sat. 11am-5pm, Sun. 2-5pm; Nov.-Feb. Sat.-Sun. 11am-3pm. Admission £2.50, children £1.50.) **Royal Victoria Park,** next to Royal Crescent, contains one of the finest collections of trees in the country, and its botanical gardens nurture 5000 species of plants from all over the globe. (Open daily 9am-sunset. Free.)

The famous **Assembly Rooms,** Bennett St., just east of The Circus, staged fashionable social events in the late 18th century. Royalty, musicians, and other self-absorbed characters frequented the balls and concerts held here. Although the ravages of World War II pretty much decimated the rooms, renovations duplicate the originals in fine detail. Between the Assembly rooms and the Baths, at the engaging **National Centre of Photography,** you can buy picture-perfect postcards, catch contemporary exhibits, and follow the history and growth of the camera. (Open Mon.-Fri. 10am-6pm, Sat. 10am-5pm. Admission £2.50, children £1.25.)

The 15th-century **Abbey Church** seems an anomaly among Bath's first-century Roman and 18th-century Georgian sights. Inside the church, tombstones cover the walls and floor (the center benches were added in the 1800s, covering the stones). A stone just inside the entrance commemorates Reverend Dr. Thomas Malthus (1766-1834), founder of modern demographics and inspiration to family planners everywhere. (Open Mon.-Sat. 9am-6pm, Sun. 1-2:30pm, 4:30-5:30pm. 50p donation.)

The **American Museum** (tel. 460 503) perched high above the city at Claverton Manor, houses a fascinating series of furnished rooms transplanted from historically significant homes in the United States. The exhibits reflect a wide range of period and regional styles of architecture; among the most impressive are a 17th-century Puritan Keeping Room, a Shaker Meeting House, an ornate Greek Revival dining room, and a cozy Revolutionary-War era tavern kitchen complete with a working beehive oven. The #18 bus (£1.20) can save you a steep two-mi. trudge up Bathwick Hill. (Open Tues.-Sun. 2-5pm. Admission £4, students £3.25, children £2.50.)

Entertainment

Classical and jazz concerts enliven the **Pump Room** (see Food and Pubs above) during morning coffee (Mon.-Sat. 10:30am-noon) and afternoon tea (3-5pm). In summer, buskers (street musicians) perform in the Abbey Churchyard, and a brass band often graces the Parade Gardens. Beau Nash's old pad, the magnificent **Theatre Royal,** Sawclose (tel. 448 844), at the south end of Barton St., sponsors a diverse dramatic program (tickets £5-25, matinees £5-7; student discounts available). **The Tier Garten** (tel. 425 360), under Pulteney Bridge near Tilley's Bistro, has a good mix of local rock and jazz bands, comedy, and DJ nights (open nightly 9pm-2am; cover £3). **The Little Theatre,** St. Michael's Pl. (tel. 466 822), shows offbeat movies and oldies (tickets £2.70, seniors and children £1.60). High-energy dance tracks draw a young crowd to the **Players Club,** on the corner of Pierrepont and North Parade (open nightly 9pm-2am; cover £5).

The renowned **Bath International Festival of the Arts,** a 17-day program of concerts and exhibits, takes place all over town from late May to early June. The festival opens with the **Contemporary Art Fair,** including the work of over 700 British artists. Musical offerings range from major symphony orchestras and choruses to chamber music, solo recitals, and jazz. For a festival brochure and reservations, write to the Bath Festival Office, Linley House, 1 Pierrepont Pl., Bath BA1 1JY. The concurrent **Fringe Festival** celebrates music, dance, and liberal politics—and proves just as much fun as the established gala, with no advance booking required.

Wells

Named for the five natural springs at its center, the small town of Wells orbits a splendid Gothic cathedral. Its streets, lined with petite Tudor and golden sandstone shops, fade gently into quiet meadows.

Rail routes don't get around to Wells (pop. 9000), but Badgerline buses run regularly to Bath (#173 or 773, 1/hr., Sun. every 3 hr.; 80 min; £3.30 return) and Bristol (#376 or 676, 1/hr., Sun. every 3 hr.; 1 hr.; £3); bus #376 rambles to Glastonbury and Street. If you'll be skipping from place to place, a day **Rambler** (£3.90) is a good investment.

Orientation and Practical Information

Buses stop in the **Princes Road Depot.** To reach the tourist office in the Market Place, walk out to Market St. (ahead and to the left as you face the bus information window), then turn left onto Queen St. and right onto High St., which runs into the Market Place. The center of town is a rectangle bounded on the north by Chamberlain St., the south by High St., and the east by the cathedral and the Market Place.

Tourist Information Center: Town Hall (tel. 672 552), in the Market Place, to the right as you face the cathedral grounds. Accommodations service £1, list 35p. Book-a-bed-ahead £1.85. Maps of Wells 5p, area bus timetables free. Open April-Oct. Mon.-Fri. 9:30am-5:30pm, Sat.-Sun. 10am-5pm; Nov.-March daily 10am-4pm.

Tours: Well's town crier, the fashionably-attired Freddy Gibbons, gives excellent hour-long guided tours of the city including the cathedral district, Thurs. at 3pm (£1). Groups leave from the tourist center. In addition, the knowledgeable Blue Badges lead 1¼-hr. tours July-Sept. Fri at 1pm (£1.50).

Bike Rental: Wells City Cycles, 80 High St. (tel. 675 096). Three-speeds £4.50/day, mountain bikes £9/day; £25-50 deposit. Repairs too. Open Mon.-Tues. and Fri.-Sat. 9am-5:30pm, Wed. 9am-1pm.

Buses: Badgerline buses from Avon and Somerset stop in the Princes Rd. depot. Call 67 30 84 or pick up a timetable at the tourist center.

Early Closing Day: Wed., at 1pm. Not observed by many shops during tourist season.

Emergency: Dial 999; no coins required.

Financial Services: Barclay's, Market Place, next to the Conservative Club. Visa checks exchanged free, others for £2. Open Mon.-Fri. 9:30am-3:30pm. **Thomas Cook,** High St., near Market Place. Cook checks exchanged free, others for £3. Open Mon. 9:30am-5:30pm, Tues.-Fri. 9am-5:30pm, Sat. 9am-5pm. **Lloyd's,** High St., exchanges American Express checks for free. Open Mon.-Fri. 9am-4:45pm. **National Westminster,** High St. Open Mon.-Fri. 9am-5:30pm. **Midland,** High St. Open Mon.-Fri. 9:30am-3:30pm.

Hospital: Cottage Hospital, St. Thomas St. (tel. 673 154).

Launderette: Wells Laundrette, St. Cuthbert St. Wash £1.50, 10-min. dry cycle 20p. Open daily 8am-8pm. Last wash 7pm.

Police Station: Glastonbury Rd. (tel. 673 481).

Post Office: Market Place (tel. 677 825). Open Mon. and Wed.-Fri. 9am-5:30pm, Tues. 9:30am-5:30pm, Sat. 9am-12:30pm. **Postal Code:** Somerset, BA5 2RA.

Taxi: Wells Taxi (tel. 672 387).

Telephones: Three phone boxes including a Phonecard phone in Market Place. Three more by the bus station. **Telephone Code:** 0749.

Accommodations

The closest **IYHF youth hostels** are in Cheddar (10 mi.) and Street (6 mi.; see Glastonbury). During the summer, accommodations fill up early. A number of B&Bs (rates about £13-15) line **Chamberlain Street,** and others cluster on St. Andrews St., behind the cathedral.

IYHF Youth Hostel, Hillfield, Cheddar (tel. (0934) 742 494), off the Hayes, three blocks from Cheddar bus stop (walk up Tweentown Rd.), and one mi. from Cheddar Gorge. Frequent buses from Wells (#126-129, Mon.-Sat. every hr. until 5:40pm; £1.20). Stone Victorian house, a bit worn. Lockout 10am-5pm. Open July-Aug. daily; Sept.-Oct. and Feb.-March Tues.-Sat.; and April-June Mon.-Sat. £5.50, ages 16-20 £4.40. Breakfast £2.10, evening meal available.

Mrs. J. Ollis, 1 St. Thomas Terrace (tel. 675 361), across from St. Thomas Church. Immaculate, elegantly decorated rooms. Down comforters on every bed. Warm, accommodating proprietor. English breakfast to top it off. £12/person.

The Old Poor House, 7a St. Andrew St. (tel. 675 052). One need not be a pauper to stay here. Mrs. Hazelwood is perfectly charming and the rooms are quite posh. £13.50/person.

Bridge House, 5 St. John St. (tel. 677 074), near the bus station. A stony stream teeming with eel runs alongside this tranquil, 16th-century home. Ancient flagstone floors, working fireplaces, caring owners. Rooms come with color TV, tea-making facilities, firewood, and the blessing of an Anglican priest. No smoking indoors. Doubles only £24-26.

Richmond House, 2 Chamberlain St. (tel. 676 438). Large rooms and friendly proprietors. Vegetarian breakfast available. From £15.

Camping: In **Wookey Hole** and **Cheddar** (see Near Wells).

Food

Assemble a picnic at the Market Place (Wed. and Sat. 8:30am-4pm) or try **The Cheese Board,** at the top of High St. (open Tues.-Sat. 9am-5pm). Health-conscious **Holland & Barrett,** up the block, sells wholefood (open Mon.-Sat. 9am-5:30pm), while **Read's Bakery,** High St., specializes in fattening fare (open Mon.-Sat. 8:30am-5pm, Sun. 10am-4pm). Greengrocers flourish on busy Broad St. **Crispin's Fish and Chips,** at #17, is a popular, Tudoresque chippie serving up cheap, daily lunch specials (open Mon.-Thurs. 11:30am-11pm, Fri.-Sat. 9:30am-11:30pm). In the evening, you may want to step in on one of Well's many pubs; the best of the lot, **Bishop's Kitchen** and the **Penn Eating House,** near the Market Place, serve hot bar food until 9pm. Take-away pizza is available from **Toppings** (7-in. pizza £2.50, 14-in. £4.50; open Tues.-Thurs. noon-2pm and 5-10:30pm, Fri.-Sat. noon-2pm and 5pm-midnight, Sun. 7-11pm).

Sights

The 13th-century **Cathedral Church of St. Andrew** is one of the best surviving examples of a full cathedral complex: bishop's palace, vicar's close, and chapter house. Entering any of the medieval gateways, you will face the quiet western front, adorned with 293 of the original 400 medieval sculptures. Their bright colors now faded, the statues depict the nine angelic orders and the dozen apostles; notice their division into six tiers according to sacred and secular history. A thorough restoration effort involving sandblasting the front's blackened stone, has restored it to its proper golden shade. Each piece of stained glass has been removed, cleaned, and reinserted.

Inside, the magnificent scissor arches sweeping up from the time-worn flags to the vaulted ceilings of the nave encompass some of the most fluid masonry of medieval England. Massive yet graceful, these ingenious, hourglass-shaped structures were devised by some anonymous architect to displace the thrust of the central tower, relieving the cathedral's cracking foundation. Atop the fanciful 14th-century clock in the north transept, a pair of jousting, mechanical knights spur on their chargers and strike at each other every 15 minutes—the same unfortunate rider is unseated every time. Cradled in the arms of umber angels on the clockface below, the bodiless heads of the four winds hurl their breath into the corners of a confidently ordered universe; the moon is depicted in its proper cycle and the sun revolves around the earth. The gold sandstone pillar in the center spreads across the ceiling like a tree trunk crowned with interlacing branches. (Cathedral open daily 9:15am-8:30pm. Expert tour guides will educate you for free, daily at 10:30am, 11am, 11:30am, 2pm, and 2:30pm. Suggested donation £1.50, students 75p.) During term time (Sept.-April), the renowned **Wells Cathedral School Choir** gives evensong recitals weekdays (except Wed.) at 5:15pm and Sundays at 3pm in the cathedral.

The **Bishop's Palace** to the right of the cathedral (entrance from Market Place) evokes the power wielded by medieval bishops. One of the oldest inhabited houses in England, it has served as palace, castle, and country house. Bishop Ralph of Shrewsbury (1329-63), alarmed by village riots in the 14th century, built the moat and walls to protect himself. No fighting transpired, but when rioting Chartists destroyed the bishop's palace in Bristol in 1831, the bridge here was drawn up just in case. Today, with less to fear from the villagers, a cement walkway bridges the moat. (Open Easter-July and Sept.-Oct. Thurs. and Sun., Aug. daily 2-6pm. Admission £1.) The mute swans in the moat have been trained to pull a bell-rope when they want to be fed. A note asks that only brown or wholemeal—heavens, not white—bread be given to the new-age designer swans. **Vicar's Close,** behind the cathedral, is the oldest street of houses in Europe; the houses date from 1363, their chimneys from 1470.

Just north of the cathedral green, the **Wells Museum** displays plaster casts of the figures on the cathedral's west front. The shop of miniature antiques has every detail exquisitely reproduced. (Open April-Oct. daily 11am-5pm; Nov.-March Wed.-Thurs. and Sat.-Sun. 11am-4pm. Admission £1, children 50p.)

Near Wells

You need only venture a short distance from the simplicity and serenity of Wells to encounter crass commercialized settings. If you plan to see both Wookey Hole and Cheddar, save money and buy a **Day Rambler** ticket (£3.90).

Wookey Hole, only two mi. northwest of Wells, is home to the **Wookey Hole Caves and Mill** (tel. (0749) 722 43; open May-Sept. daily 9:30am-5:30pm; Oct.-April 10:30am-4:30pm). The admission price of £4.50 (seniors £4, children £3), 50p cheaper at the tourist center in Wells, includes the subterranean caves, a tour of the working paper mill, and a spectacular collection of wooden carousel animals from Britain, the Continent, and the U.S. The gold lion is worth over $50,000. Steel yourself to the somewhat tawdry and distracting man-made elemnts, and appreciate the natural ones. **Camping** is available at **Homestead Park** (tel. (0749) 730 22) beside a babbling brook (£7/tent and 2 people). For lunch, stop at the **Wookey Hole Inn.** (Open daily 10:30am-2pm and 7-10:30pm.)

Cheddar, as in the cheese, is an overcrowded mélange of touristy tea-shops and tired cheezwhizardry; a day trip here is justified only by the two mile-long **Cheddar Gorge,** formed by the River Yeo in the hills just northeast of town. The bus from Wells (every hr. Mon.-Sat.; 20 min.; £1.50) lets you off below the thicket of tourists at the gorge's mouth. From the bus stop follow the signs to Jacob's Ladder, a 322-step stairwell to the top (75p, seniors and children 50p). The unsullied view of the hills to the north and the broad expansive plain to the south rewards the climber. At the foot of the cliffs huddle the **Cheddar Caves,** the finest show caves in England. Note the different mineral colors of the stalagmites and stalactites: rust-red is iron; green is manganese; and grey is lead. (Caves open Easter-Sept. daily 10am-5:30pm, Oct.-Easter 10:30am-4:30pm. Admission to all caves, Jacob's Ladder, and museum £4, children £2.50.)

The Cheddar **tourist office** is located in the town library on Union St. (tel. (0934) 742 769; open Mon. and Wed. 10am-1pm and 2-5:30pm, Fri. 10am-1pm and 2-7:30pm, Sat. 10am-12:30pm). From June to September, there's another tourist information office at the base of Cheddar Gorge (tel. (0934) 744 071). **Camping** is available at **Froglands Farm** (tel. (0934) 742 058), just outside of town toward Wells (£3.50 for tent and 2 people). The town also boasts an **IYHF youth hostel** (see Accommodations in Wells).

In 1170 Henry II declared Cheddar cheese the best in England. Wine and cheese enthusiasts can sate their appetite at the **Chewton Cheese Dairy,** just north of Wells on the A39. Take the bus toward Bristol and get off at Cheddar Rd., just outside Wells (tel. (076 121) 666; shop open April-Dec. Mon.-Fri. 8:30am-5pm, Sat.-Sun. 9am-5pm; Jan.-March Mon.-Fri. 8:30am-4pm, Sat.-Sun. 9am-4pm; cheese-making around noon, but call first). Ask at the Wells or Glastonbury tourist office about vineyard tours.

Glastonbury

The reputed birthplace of Christianity in England and the seat of Arthurian myth, Glastonbury has evolved into an intersection of Christianity and mysticism. According to ancient legend, Jesus traveled here with his merchant uncle, Joseph of Arimathea. Other myths hold that the area is the resting place of the Holy Grail; that Glastonbury Tor is the Isle of Avalon, with the bones of Arthur and Guinevere still beneath Glastonbury Abbey; and that the Tor contains a passage to the underworld. Grow your hair, suspend your disbelief, and join hands with Glastonbury's subculture of hippies, spiritualists, and mystics.

Arriving and Departing

Fast, frequent Badgerline buses come from Bristol (#376, 1/hr., Sun. every 2 hr.; 1½ hr.; £3.45) and from Wells (#167, 168 or 378; 25 min.; £2). From Bath, change at Wells (£3.75).

Orientation and Practical Information

Glastonbury lies 6 mi. southwest of Wells on the A39 and 22 mi. northeast of Taunton on the A361. Glastonbury is a compact town bounded by Manor House Rd. in the north, Bere Lane in the south, Magdelene St. in the west, and Wells Rd. in the east. Shopping and services are concentrated on High St.

Tourist Information Center: Marchants Bldg., Northload St. (tel. 329 54), 1 block from the Market Cross (about 50 yd. down Northload St.) near the parking lot in a side alley (entrance through small archway). Accommodations service 60p. Free maps. Open April to mid-Nov. Mon.-Sat. 9:30am-5pm, Sun. 10am-4pm.

Bike Rental: Pedlars Cycle Shop, 8 Magdalene St. (tel. 311 17). Repairs and rentals. Bikes £5/day plus £20 deposit. Open Mon.-Sat. 9am-5:30pm.

Buses and Coaches: Badgerline (tel. (0749) 730 84) and **Southern National** (tel. (0823) 272 033). Both stop in front of the town hall on Magdalene St. National Express tickets are sold at the travel agency on High St.

Early Closing Day: Wednesday at 1pm.

Emergency: Dial 999; no coins required.

Financial Services: Barclay's, Midland, and **Natwest** cluster on the High St. Open Mon.-Fri. 9:30am-3:30pm.

Launderette: Glastonbury Launderette, 46A High St. Wash £1.40; dry cycle 20p. Open daily 8am-9pm. Last wash 8pm.

Market Day: Tuesday from 8:30am to 5:30pm.

Pharmacy: Andrew Bond, at the top of High St. Emergency prescriptions tel. 506 89. Open Mon.-Fri. 9am-1pm and 2-6:30pm, Sat. 9am-1pm.

Police: Benedict St. (tel. 321 12).

Post Office: High St. (tel. 314 82). Open Mon.-Fri. 9am-5:30pm, Sat. 9am-1pm. **Postal Code:** BA6 9HS.

Telephones: In front of town hall, Magdalene St. **Telephone Code:** 0458.

Accommodations

Singles are hard to find in Glastonbury. Stop by the tourist information office for a free list. Some B&Bs are located in the hilly hinterlands of town.

IYHF Youth Hostel, The Chalet, Ivythorn Hill, Street BA16 OT2 (tel. (0458) 429 61), 2 mi. south from Street off the B3151. Take Badgerline bus #376, alight at Leigh Rd., and walk 1 mi. Swiss-style chalet with views of Glastonbury Tor, Sedgemoor, and Mendip Hills. Lockout 10am-5pm. Open March-Oct. Mon.-Sat. £5.50, ages 16-20 £4.40.

Tamarac, Mrs. Talbot, 8 Wells Rd. (tel. 343 27 or 320 36). A spiffy modern house on a central residential street. Plush, comfortable rooms with color TV and teapots. Primarily doubles, though families can get a lovely cottage out back. Generous breakfast. £11/person.

The Bolthole, 32 Coursing Batch (tel. 328 00), opposite the Chalice Well. Bright, flowery rooms with basins, TVs, and teapots. Proprietor keeps healing well water on hand. Singles and doubles from £11/person.

Mr. and Mrs. Knight, 1 Northload St. (tel. 310 39). Knock on the white door opposite the tourist center; if no one answers, inquire next door at Knight's Pub. Though larger, more expensive, and less intimate than many of the B&Bs outside of town, the central location, colorful rooms, and breezy rooftop terrace make Knight's an excellent choice for travelers on foot. Singles £15. Doubles £30.

Tor Down Guest House, Mrs. Parfitt, 5 Ashwell Lane (tel. 322 87), a steep mile from the town center, at the base of Glastonbury Tor. Sunny and spotless rooms, all with basins and tea-making equipment. Vegetarian breakfast available. Small but cheerful singles £12.50. Doubles £26.

Little Orchard, 2 Ashwell Lane (tel. 316 20), a short drive or 20-min. trudge from the center; access from Shepton Mallot as well. Luminous rooms with tall windows and fine views of the Vale of Avalon. Singles and doubles from £10/person.

Camping: Ashwell Farm House, Ashwell Lane at Edgarley End (tel. 323 13). Take the first left after Ashwell Lane. Impeccably maintained sites with nothing but green void between you and Avalon. £2.50/person. Electricity hookup £1.

Food

Try a picnic by the Tor; **Truckle of Cheese,** 33 High St., has a good selection of luncheon fare. (Open Mon.-Sat. 8:30am-5:30pm.) High St. also has greengrocers, two supermarkets, a wholefood store, a bakery, and reasonably priced restaurants.

Rainbow's End, 17A High St. Whole-food buffet table on earthenware dishes in pleasant atmosphere. Try the ratatouille and garlic bread (£1.80) or pizza (£1.10). Wear your Birkenstocks. Open Mon.-Sat. 10am-4:30pm.

Market House Inn, 21 Magdalene St., near the town center. Huge helpings at bargain prices. Sweet and sour pork (£2.75); cottage pie with fresh veggies (£2.75). Open Mon.-Sat. 11am-11pm, Sun. noon-2pm. No meals Tues. nights.

Abbey Tea Room, Magdalene St. Quiet and correct lunch for under £3 and delicious cream teas with scones and jam for £1.75.

Deacon's Coffee House, 24 High St. Ploughman's lunch (£2.75) or Coronation chicken (£3). Roast beef with horseradish sauce £2.75. Skip lunch and feast on Somerset Cream tea (£2.30). Open Mon.-Fri. 10am-5:30pm, Sat. 9:30am-5:30pm, Sun. 11:30am-5:30pm.

Sights

Behind the archway on Magdalene St. lurk the ruins of **Glastonbury Abbey,** the oldest Christian foundation and once the most important abbey in England. It now consists of one steeple surrounded by green lawns marked with the outline of the old abbey. Joseph of Arimathea supposedly built the original wattle-and-daub church on this site in 63 AD; larger churches were successively raised over the next millenium. Erected in 1184, the stone abbey flourished until the Reformation. Its sixth and last abbot, Richard Whiting, disobeyed Henry VIII's order that all Catholic churches dissolve. Not known for his sense of humor, Henry had Whiting hanged, drawn, and quartered on Glastonbury Tor.

Two national patron saints, Patrick of Ireland and George of England, have been claimed by the abbey—Patrick is said to be buried here and George to have slain his dragon just around the corner. But King Arthur most captivates the legend-makers. In 1191, the monks dug up a coffin they claimed contained the remains of Arthur and Guinevere; in 1276, in the presence of King Edward I, they reinterred the pair before the high altar. (Abbey open daily 9am-6pm. Admission £1.50, children £1.)

The tower visible across Somerset's flatlands from miles away is **Glastonbury Tor** or, more properly, the remains of St. Michael's Chapel. Glastonbury Tor is the site of the mystical Isle of Avalon, where the Messiah is slated to reappear. From the top of the hill, you survey the Wiltshire Downs, the Mendips and, on a clear day, the distant spires of Bristol Cathedral. To reach the Tor, turn right at the top of High St. and continue up Wellhouse Lane. Take the first right up the hill.

On the way down from the Tor, visit the **Chalice Well,** at the corner of Wellhouse Lane, the supposed resting place of the Holy Grail. Legend once held that the well ran with Christ's blood; in these post-Nietzschean days, rust deposits at the source turn the water red. The water gurgles from the well down through a tiered garden of hollyhocks, climbing vines, and dark, spreading yew trees. You can drink the water from the lion's head on the second tier. When the grounds are shut down, you can still get well water from a tap on the outside wall. (Open March-Oct. daily 10am-6pm; Nov.-Feb. daily 1-3pm. Admission 40p, children 20p.)

Take a short walk down Chilkwell St. to the 14th-century **Abbey Barn,** part of the **Somerset Rural Life Museum** (tel. 311 97). Exhibits depict the rural industries of Somerset, such as cider-making and peat-digging. Notice the elegant roof in the Abbey Barn; it supports 80 tons of stone tiles. (Open Easter-Oct. Mon.-Fri. 10am-5pm, Sat.-Sun. 2-6pm. Admission £1.20, seniors 80p, children 30p.)

Head down Bere Lane to Hill Head to reach **Wearyall Hill,** where legend has it that Joseph of Arimathea's staff bloomed and became the **Glastonbury Thorn.** The Thorn, a grove of trees native to Palestine, has grown on Wearyall Hill since Saxon times. The Thorn should, according to legend, burst into bloom in the presence of royalty. Horticulturists here and abroad (where offshoots of the thorn are planted) have wasted considerable time on making the trees bloom each time the Queen comes to visit.

Stonehenge

You may put a hundred questions to these rough-hewn giants as they bend in grim contemplation of their fellow companions; but your curiosity falls dead in the vast sunny stillness that shrouds them and the strange monument, with all its unspoken memories, becomes simply a heart-stirring picture in a land of pictures.

—Henry James

Stonehenge is a potent reminder that England seemed ancient even to the Saxons and Normans. Surrounded by imperturbable cows and swirled by winds exceeding 50mph, the much-touted stones, only 22 feet high, may initially be disappointing. Consider, however, that they were lifted by a simple but infinitely tedious process of rope-and-log leverage. Built over many lifetimes, Stonehenge represents an enduring religious and aesthetic dedication that defies modern explanation. Buffeted by nonsensical theories and ludicrous fantasies, Stonehenge has yielded none of its ageless mystery.

The most famous Stonehenge legend holds that the circle was built by Merlin, who magically transported the stones from Ireland. (Actually, the seven-ton Blue Stones are made of rock quarried in Wales.) Other stories attribute the monument to giants, Romans, Danes, Phoenicians, Druids, Mycenaean Greeks, and—most recently—to aliens. In any case, whether they traveled by land or water, the Bronze Age builders would seem to have possessed more technology than anthropologists can explain. Archaeologists now date construction from approximately 2800 to 1500 BC, dividing the complex into three successive monuments. The relics of the oldest are the Aubrey Holes (white patches in the earth) and the Heel Stone (the isolated, rough block standing outside the circle). This first Stonehenge may have been a worship and burial site for seven centuries. The next monument consisted of about 60 stones imported from Wales around 2100 BC to mark astronomical directions. The present shape was formed by 1500 BC; it may once have been composed of two concentric circles and two horseshoes of megaliths, enclosed by substantial earthworks.

Many different peoples have worshipped at Stonehenge: from late Neolithic and Early Bronze Age chieftains to contemporary mystics. In 300 BC the Druids arrived from the Continent and claimed Stonehenge as their shrine. The true Druids have died out, but the Druid Society of London (ordinary folks who like to wrap themselves up in sheets) still honor the sun's rising over the Heel Stone on Midsummer's Day. The summer of 1988 saw a bizarre confrontation between hippie-pagan celebrants and police amid spotlighting, a haze of tear gas, and barbed wire. The finest view of the monument can be captured from Amesbury Hill, 1½ mi. up the A303. On some winter Tuesdays and Fridays, in clear weather, the ropes around the monument are taken down to allow a closer view. (Stonehenge open daily April-Sept. 10am-6pm; Oct.-Easter 10am-4pm. Admission £1.90, students £1.50.

Getting to Stonehenge takes little effort. Several buses run daily from the center of Salisbury and from the train station (£3.05 return). The first bus leaves Salisbury at 8:45am, and the last one leaves Stonehenge at 4:15pm (40 min.). A taxi to Stonehenge from Salisbury station costs £26. Amesbury is a short hitch along the A345 from Salisbury. The most scenic walking or cycling route to Stonehenge follows the **Woodford Valley Route** through Woodford and Wilsford. Go north from Salisbury on Castle Rd., bear left just before Victoria Park onto Stratford Rd., and follow the road over the bridge through Lower, Middle, and Upper Woodford. After about 9 mi., turn left onto the A303 for the last mile to Stonehenge.

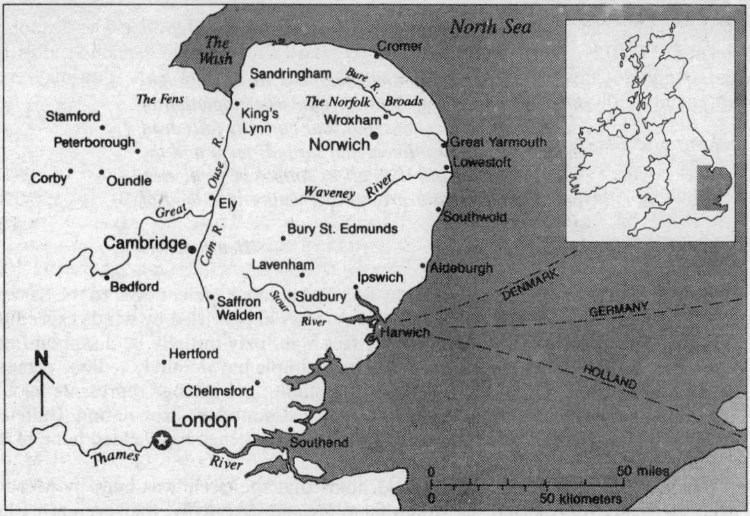

East Anglia

The plush green farmlands and dismal watery fens of East Anglia stretch northeast from London, cloaking the counties of Cambridgeshire, Suffolk, and Norfolk. High-tech industry may be transforming the economies of Cambridge and Peterborough, but college town and cathedral city are still linked by flat fields that extend to the horizon, sliced into irregular tiles by windbreaks, hedges, and stone fences. In the low-lying northwest quarter, rivers flow between raised embankments that pen the water from the drained swamps of the Fens. From Norwich east to the English Channel, water has flooded huge areas of medieval peat bogs, creating the lakes and rivers of the Norfolk Broads. Visitors either love or hate the Fens; Graham Swift wrote in defence of his native land, curiously embracing the sense of desolation and alienation it provoked in him.

East Anglia bears witness to the changing tides of history with its Roman towns (like Colchester) and medieval cathedral cities (like Ely). Skirting the north coast between Great Yarmouth and Cromer, the Weaver's Way footpath once led Roman traders through dozens of market towns. On the elevated mound at Ely, Norman invaders built a magnificent cathedral from stone transported by boat over the flooded fenland. In a minor village along the River Cam, renegade scholars from Oxford established a new university, and were later granted the imprimatur of extravagant royal building projects.

Getting There and Getting Around

Cambridge and Norwich, both of which have excellent hostels, are the most convenient bases for touring the region. Ely and Bury St. Edmunds make ideal daytrips from Cambridge, and Peterborough and Grantchester are not far from Cambridge or King's Lynn. The dignified natural preserves among the sand dunes and salt marshes of the north coast and the unspoiled fishing towns of Southwold and Aldeburgh on the Suffolk coast provide opportunities for rest and relaxation. The resorts farther south (Harwich and Felixstowe) have a quicker pace and a more international feel, thanks to frequent ferry traffic.

An **Anglia Rover** ticket (£27, with Railcard £17.80), available only at rail stations within East Anglia, entitles you to one week's unlimited travel on all rail routes in the region. These tickets also carry other transportation discounts. The **Explorer** ticket (£37.50) is good for one day's travel on all Eastern Counties bus routes in East Anglia, which serve many areas not covered by British Rail. You may end up paying with your time, however, since buses are infrequent.

Hiking and Biking

East Anglia's flat terrain and relatively low annual rainfall are a boon to bikers and hikers. A leisurely trip through pastures and tiny villages recalls the painted landscapes of natives Constable and Gainsborough. Rental bicycles are readily available in Cambridge and Norwich, but more elusive elsewhere.

The area's two longest and most popular walking trails, together covering 200 mi., are **Peddar's Way** (which includes the **Norfolk coast path**) and **Weaver's Way,** a newly extended trail that runs from Cromer to Great Yarmouth. Every 10 mi. or so, each walk passes through a town with a bus or rail station. You can get free route guides for the Weaver's Way from tourist offices in Norwich, Bury St. Edmunds, and several Suffolk villages. For the Peddar's Way, pick up the *Peddar's Way Guide and Accommodations List* (£1.75) or Bruce Robinson's *Peddar's Way and Norfolk Coast Path* (£5.25) at the King's Lynn or Norwich tourist office. Written inquiries about Peddar's or Weaver's Way should be addressed to LDR Manager, Director of Planning and Property, County Hall, Martineau Lane, Norwich, England NR1 2DH; enclose an International Reply Coupon.

Cambridge

Cambridge the town has been dominated by Cambridge the university for 700 years. Each term, battalions of bicycle-riding students invade this quintessential university town. Competing in everything with Oxford, Cambridge loses in age and boat races but wins on charm and spectacle; the terribly beautiful Backs, along the River Cam, imbue both Cantabrigians and visitors with an understandable sense of self-indulgence. Cambridge has ceased to be the exclusive preserve of upper-class sons, although roughly half of its students still come from independent schools, and only 35% are women. Most of the students are refreshingly down-to-earth; only a few, bedecked with brogue, cravat, and cane, strive to preserve the old image.

Cambridge University itself exists mostly as a bureaucracy that handles the formalities of lectures, degrees, and real estate. The individual colleges within the university provide the small tutorials and seminars that form the crux of a Cambridge education. Third-year finals alone determine the academic future of many students; during the official "quiet periods" of May and early June, students disengage themselves from the social mêlée, and most colleges close to visitors. At the end of exams, the University explodes with gleeful gin-soaked revelry. Mayweek—logically enough, a week in mid-June—ushers in a dizzying schedule of cocktail parties and mirth, starting with a health-threatening number on aptly named Suicide Sunday.

Arriving and Departing

Trains to Cambridge run frequently, from both London's King's Cross and Liverpool Street stations (every ½ hr.; 1 hr.; £10.60 day return, £9.50 period return with railcard); they also from Cambridge to Ely (1/hr.; 20 min.; £2.90 day return) and King's Lynn (every 2 hr.; 1 hr.; £10.50 day return). National Express coaches travel hourly between London's Victoria Station and Drummer St. Station in Cambridge (2 hr.; £8 single or day return). Buses travel between Oxford and Cambridge every two hours from 8:40am to 4:40pm (3 hr.; £11.75 single or day return). **Cambus,** the town's bus service, also runs numerous local and regional routes from Drummer St.

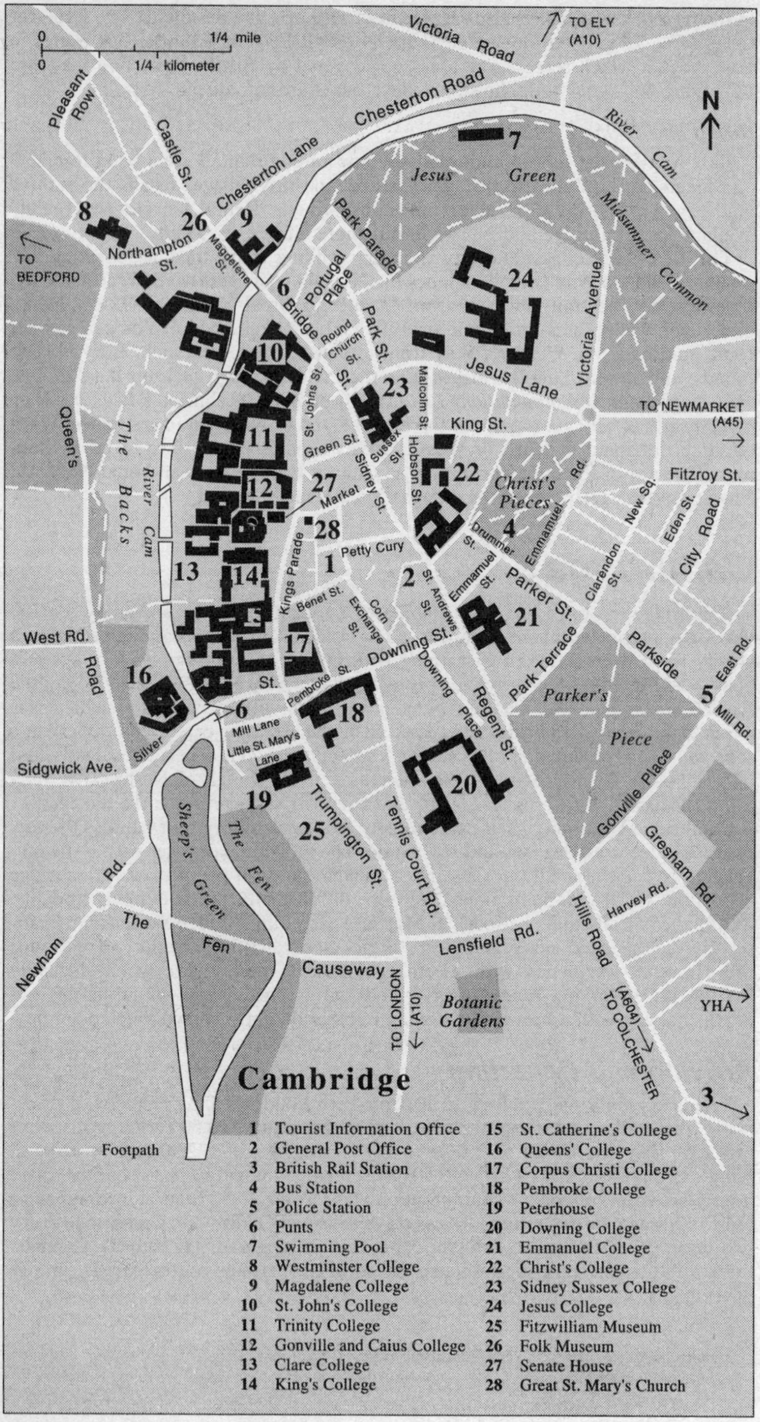

Cambridge

1	Tourist Information Office	15	St. Catherine's College
2	General Post Office	16	Queens' College
3	British Rail Station	17	Corpus Christi College
4	Bus Station	18	Pembroke College
5	Police Station	19	Peterhouse
6	Punts	20	Downing College
7	Swimming Pool	21	Emmanuel College
8	Westminster College	22	Christ's College
9	Magdalene College	23	Sidney Sussex College
10	St. John's College	24	Jesus College
11	Trinity College	25	Fitzwilliam Museum
12	Gonville and Caius College	26	Folk Museum
13	Clare College	27	Senate House
14	King's College	28	Great St. Mary's Church

Orientation and Practical Information

Cambridge (pop. 102,000), about 60 miles north of London, has two main avenues. The main shopping street starts at Magdalene Bridge and becomes Bridge Street, Sidney Street, St. Andrew's Street, Regent Street, and finally Hills Road. The other—St. John's Street, Trinity Street, King's Parade, Trumpington Street, and Trumpington Road—is the academic thoroughfare, with several colleges lying between it and the River Cam. To get to Market Sq. in the city center from the train station, take a Cityrail Link bus (Mon.-Sat. daytime every 8 min., Sun. and evenings every 15 min.; 50p) or walk down Hills Road (20 min.).

Tourist Information Center: Wheeler St., Cambridge (tel. 322 640), 1 block south of the marketplace. Railway and coach schedules available. Accommodations service £1.25. Accommodations list (40p) posted. Mini-guide 30p. Maps of the town 10p. Open July-Aug. Mon.-Tues. and Thurs.-Fri. 9am-7pm, Wed. 9:30am-7pm, Sat. 9am-5pm; March-June and Sept.-Oct. Mon.-Tues. and Thurs.-Fri. 9am-6pm, Wed. 9:30am-6pm, Sat. 9am-5pm; Nov.-Feb. Mon.-Tues. and Thurs.-Fri. 9am-5:30pm, Wed. 9:30am-5:30pm, Sat. 9am-5pm. Also open Easter-Sept. Sun. 10:30am-3:30pm. Information on Cambridge events also available at Corn Exchange box office (tel. 357 851), Corn Exchange St., opposite the tourist office.

Tours: Unbeatable 2-hr. walking tours of the city and some colleges leave the main tourist office daily. April-June at 11am and 2pm; July-Aug. every hr. 11am-3pm and at 6:30pm; Sept. every hr. 11am-3pm. Tours less frequent during the rest of the year. Sun. and bank holidays, first tour at 11:15am. £2.85. 1½-hr. tours focusing on the town rather than the university leave the tourist office July-Aug. daily at 6:30pm. £2.85.

AIDS Helpline: tel. 697 65. Open Tues.-Wed. 7:30-10pm.

Bike Rental: University Cycle, 9 Victoria Ave. (tel. 355 517). £4 per day, £10 per week; £25 cash deposit. Repairs. Open Mon.-Fri. 9am-6pm, Sat. 9am-5pm. **Geoff's Bike Hire,** 65 Devonshire Rd. (tel. 656 29). £5 per day, £12 per week; £20 deposit. Open daily 9am-5:30pm. **C. Frost,** 188 New Market Rd. (tel. 356 464). £4 per day, £12 per week; £20 deposit. Open Mon.-Fri. 9am-1pm and 2-6pm, Sat. 9am-1pm and 2-5pm. Most bike rental firms cater to block bookings of more than 2 weeks from groups of language students.

Bookstores: Heffers. Main branch at 20 Trinity St. (tel. 358 51), maps at 19 Sidney St. (tel. 358 241), and paperbacks at 31 St. Andrew's St. (tel. 354 778). Assorted other branches. Most open Mon.-Sat. 9am-5:30pm. **Sherratt and Hughes,** 1 Trinity St. (tel. 355 488). Site of a bookshop since 1581. Open Mon.-Sat. 9am-5:30pm, Sun. 11am-6pm. **Galloway and Porter,** 30 Sydney St. (tel. 678 76). Cheap second-hand books in great condition upstairs. Open Mon.-Fri. 8:30am-5:30pm, Sat. 9am-5:15pm. Second-hand bookstalls cluster around St. Edward's passage and the marketplace.

Bus and Coach Station: Drummer St. Station. **National Express** tel. 460 711. **Cambus** (tel. 423 554) handles city and area service (fare 50p-£1). Some local routes serviced by **Miller's** or **Premier** coaches. **Whippet Coaches** run daytrips from Cambridge. Travel Centre open Mon.-Sat. 8:15am-5:30pm.

Emergency: Dial 999; no coins required.

Financial Services: Most banks open Mon.-Fri. 9:30am-3:30pm; some stay open until 4:30 or 5pm. **Barclay's,** Market Sq., also open Sat. 9am-noon. **Thomas Cook,** 5 Market Hill, open Mon.-Fri. 9am-5:30pm, Sat. 9am-5pm. No exchange facilities open Sun. **American Express: Abbot Travel,** 25 Sydney St. (tel. 351 636). Open Mon. and Wed.-Fri. 9am-5pm, Tues. 9:30am-5pm, Sat. 9am-4pm.

Hospital: Addenbrookes, Hills Rd. (tel. 245 151). 1½ mi. southeast of the train station; follow Station Rd. to Hills Rd. and turn left.

Launderette: Coin-Op Laundry, 28 King St. Wash £1.20, dry 20p. Open daily 7am-10pm. One closer to the hostel can be found **underneath the painted bull** at 44 Hills Rd. Wash £1.20, 7-min. dry 10p. Open daily 9am-9pm.

Library: 7 Lion Yard (tel. 652 52). Reference library with helpful information desk on 2nd floor sells comprehensive *Citizen's Guide* (23p). Open Mon.-Fri. 9:30am-7pm, Sat. 9:30am-5pm.

Police: Parkside (tel. 358 966). From the train station, follow Hills Rd. to Gonville Place. Turn right onto Gonville and then left onto Parkside. The station will be on your right.

Post Office: 9-11 St. Andrew's St. (tel. 351 212). Open Mon.-Tues. and Thurs.-Fri. 9am-5:30pm, Wed. 9:30am-5:30pm, Sat. 9am-12:30pm. **Postal Code:** CB1 1AA.

Rape Crisis Group: Tel. 358 314. Open Mon. 7-9pm, Wed. 6pm-midnight, Sat. 11am-5pm.

Student Travel Office: STA Travel, 38 Sydney St. (tel 669 66). Open Mon.-Fri. 9am-6pm, Sat. 10am-4pm. **Campus Travel,** 5 Emmanuel St. (tel. 324 283). Open Mon.-Sat. 9am-5:30pm.

Taxi: Camtax (tel. 313 131). Open 24 hr. Ranks overrun St. Andrew's St. and Market Sq.

Telephone Code: 0223.

Train Station: Station Rd. (tel. 311 999; recorded London timetable Mon.-Fri. 359 602, Sat. 467 098, Sun. 353 465). Travel Centre open Mon.-Sat. 5am-11pm, Sun. 6:30am-11pm. Free timetables.

Accommodations and Camping

Cambridge has no shortage of rooms for visitors, but it's advisable to book ahead during high season. Many of the cheap B&Bs around Jesus Lane convert into student housing during the academic year and only open to visitors during the summer. If one house is full, ask for other accommodations in the neighborhood (B&Bs are often not labeled as such). Check the comprehensive list in the window of the tourist office.

IYHF Youth Hostel, 97 Tenison Rd. (tel. 354 601), entrance on Devonshire Rd. Extremely close to the train station; walk straight ahead and then right on Tenison Rd. Relaxed, welcoming atmosphere; boppy music in reception, well-equipped kitchen, laundry room, TV lounge, game room, and store. 125 bunks in 5-bed rooms, a few doubles. Couples may share a room, space permitting. Three-night max. stay when busy. Lockout 10am-1pm, but early arrivals can leave their bags in the morning. Curfew 11:30pm. £8.30, ages 16-20 £7. £1 surcharge June-Aug. Sleepsack rental 80p. English breakfast £2.30, packed lunch £2.50, evening meal £3. Open all year and crowded March-Oct.; call a few days in advance and arrive by 6pm.

Mrs. Connolly, 67 Jesus Lane (tel. 617 53). A recently refurbished house decorated in sunny shades. Open year-round. £12.50 per person.

Mrs. Bennett, 70 Jesus Lane (tel. 654 97). Visitors can reap the benefits of extensive renovations carved out by Christ's College. 2 doubles, 2 twins, 2 singles. Open June-Sept., Easter, and Christmas. £12 per person.

Mrs. French, 42 Lyndewode (tel. 316 615), off Tenison Rd. One of the best buys near the train station. £10 per person.

Mrs. Fesenko, 15 Mill Rd. (tel. 329 435). Decent rooms with schizophrenic wallpaper. Charming proprietor natters away in a bewildering *mischung von Englisch and German.* A good buy. £10 per person.

Mrs. West, 2 Malcolm St. (tel. 359 814). Cheerful rooms cared for by maternal owner. Open June-Sept. £12.50 per person.

Tenison Towers, Mrs. J. Tombo, 148 Tenison Rd. (tel. 639 24). A touch of the Mediterranean near the train station. Clean and comfy. Singles £15. Doubles £24.

Camping

Highfield Farm Camping Site, Long Rd., Comberton (tel. 262 308). Head west on A603 for 3 mi. then left on B1046 for another mile. Or take Cambus #118 from the Drummer St. bus station (every 45 min.). Flush toilets, showers, and a washing machine. Open April-Oct. £6 per tent. Call ahead.

Camping and Caravaning Club Ltd., 212a Cambridge Rd., Great Shelford (tel. 841 185), 3 mi. south on A10, then left onto A1301 for ¾ mi., or take Cambus #103. Flush toilets, showers, washing machine, and facilities for the disabled. No unaccompanied children under 16. Open April 12-Oct. 30. £3.50, children £1.50; off-season £3, children £1.25. Call ahead.

The tourist office also has a list of 16 other camping sites in the Cambridge vicinity (25p).

Food

Market Square has bright pyramids of fruit and vegetables for the hungry budgetarian. (Open Mon.-Sat. approximately 8am-5pm.) For vegetarian and wholefood groceries, try **Arjuna,** 12 Mill Rd. (Open Mon.-Wed. and Fri. 9:30am-6pm, Thurs. 9:30am-2pm, Sat. 9am-5:30pm.) The local branch of the **Holland and Barrett** wholefood chain, in Bradwell's Court off St. Andrew's St., carries a more extensive but more expensive selection. (Open Mon.-Tues. and Thurs.-Sat. 9am-5:30pm, Wed. 9:30am-5:30pm.) Students buy their gin and cornflakes at **Sainsbury's,** 44 Sydney St., the only grocery store in the middle of town. (Open Mon.-Tues. 8:30am-7pm, Wed.-Fri. 8:30am-8pm, Sat. 8am-6pm.) The food section in **Marks and Spencer,** 8 Sydney St., includes some high-class picnic items. (Open Mon. 9:15am-5:30pm, Tues. 9:30am-5:30pm, Wed. 9am-8pm, Thurs. 9am-6pm, Fri.-Sat. 8:30am-6pm.) On Sundays, pick up groceries at the **Nip-In General Store,** 30 Mill Rd. (open daily 8am-10pm); **H.T. Cox,** 67 Regent St. (open daily 8am-9pm); or **Spenser's,** 33 Hill Rd. (open daily 8am-11:45pm).

Cambridge turns up its nose at most restaurant chains—though pizza parlors grace almost every block, hamburger take-aways are limited to **Burger King.** Cambridge has some fantastic ethnic food, including a wealth of satisfying curry restaurants (before ordering, make sure that Christ's College football club has not arrived on their ritual curry night out). Both Hills Rd. and Mill Rd., south of town, brim with good, cheap restaurants just becoming trendy with student crowds.

Nadia's, 11 St. John's St. The best bakery in town, and one of the cheapest. Wonderful filled rolls and quiches 70p-£1.30. Stuff your face for £2. Take-away only. Open Mon.-Fri. 7am-5:30pm, Sat. 8am-5:30pm, Sun. 8am-5pm.

Nettles, 5 St. Edward's Passage, off King's Parade. A tiny place with seating for 10 tiny people. Delicious wholefood dishes, dirt cheap. Hot casseroles £1.75-2.30. Large sandwiches 80p. Take-away even cheaper. Open Mon.-Sat. 9am-8pm.

Rajbelash, 36-38 Hills Rd. A bewildering array of curries, *tandooris,* and *biryanis* £2.60-6.40. Give your mouth some relief with a chewy unleavened *naan* bread (£1.10). Take-away available. Open daily noon-2:30pm and 6pm-midnight.

Corner House Restaurant, 9 King's St. Generous portions and low prices make up for the vinyl-fluorescent atmosphere. Spaghetti and chips £3.25. Open Mon.-Fri. 11:30am-2:30pm and 5-9:30pm, Sat.-Sun. 11:30am-9:30pm.

Clown's, 52 King St. A meeting place for foreigners, bozos, and beautiful people. Affable, entertaining proprietor. Practice your Esperanto over cappuccino (90p), quiche (£1.25), or cake (£1.15). Open daily 9:30am-10pm.

Hobbs' Pavillion, Parker's Piece, off Park Terrace. Renowned for imaginative, overpowering pancakes. (Note that the English like their pancakes thin, like French crepes.) Bacon, eggs, and maple syrup pancake £3.90. Mars Bar and cream pancake £3.50—expect not to feel like eating again for 2 weeks. Open Tues.-Wed. and Fri.-Sat. noon-2:30pm and 7-10pm, Thurs. noon-2:30pm and 8:30-10pm.

King's Pantry, 9 King's Parade. A vegetarian restaurant popular with the 90s-alternative crowd. Concerned allergics can examine a list of ingredients for each dish. Deep south pecan pie £4. Open Mon.-Sat. 8am-5:30pm. Dinner served Wed.-Sat. 7-9:30pm.

The Little Tea Room, 1 All Saints' Passage, off St. John's St. Not as hopelessly generic as it sounds; tip-top teas served in a fun basement room. Scone, jam, and cream with a pot of tea £2.20. Open Mon.-Sat. 9:30am-5:30pm.

Auntie's Tea Shop, 1 St. Mary's Passage, off King's Parade. Lace tablecloths, clinking china, and triangular sandwiches. Egg-and-cress sandwich £1.05, carrot cake £1.25. £1.50 min. after noon. Don't expect to see many students. Open Mon.-Fri.. 9am-6:30pm, Sat. 9:30am-6:30pm, Sun. noon-5:30pm.

Mr. Chips, 78 King St. Fish-and-chip connoisseurs may sneer at the polystyrene trays that pathetically substitute for classic greaseproof bags and newspapers, but the product is as satisfying as ever. Cod and chips £2.40. Battered sausage 50p. Open Mon.-Thurs. 11:30am-midnight, Fri.-Sat. 11:30am-12:30am, Sun. 5:30pm-midnight.

Pubs

Cantabrigian hangouts offer good pub-crawling year-round, though they lose some of their character and their best customers in summer. Most pubs stay open from 11am to 11pm, noon to 10:30pm on Sundays. A few close from 3 to 7pm, especially on Sundays. The local brewery, Greene King, supplies many of the pubs with the popular bitters IPA (India Pale Ale) and Abbott. Along the river, try the **Anchor,** Silver St., or **The Mill,** Mill Lane, off Silver St. Bridge. Their tranquil river views contrast sharply with the bustle inside. The **King Street Run,** King St., a down-to-earth towny pub, is named after a historic pub crawl. Two stops on "the run" along King St. are the **Cambridge Arms,** a large renovated brewery, and the **Champion of the Thames,** a miniscule, charming closet of a pub—groups of more than five might not even fit. (King St. gets a bit dicey around closing time on Sat. nights.) A favorite with Magdalene men and women from Cambridge secretarial colleges, the **Pickerel** on Bridge St. is Cambridge's oldest pub. Down the road, the lively town pub **Baron of Beef,** 19 Bridge St., has resisted the onset of flashy décor. **The Maypole,** Park St., sports one of the few bar-billards tables in the center of town. Locals and Christ's College crew members pack the **Free Press,** Prospect St.; tourists might not feel comfortable walking in alone. The **Sir Isaac Newton,** Cattle St., is one of the few pubs in town with facilities for the disabled.

Sights

Cambridge is an architect's dream, packing some of the finest examples of English architecture over the last 700 years into less than one square mile. You should see the world-famous King's College Chapel—but if you explore some of the more obscure courts (quads), you'll discover gems unseen by the majority of visitors.

If you are pressed for time, visit at least one chapel (preferably at King's College), one garden (try Christ's), one library (Trinity's is the most interesting), and one dining hall (difficult without befriending a Cambridge undergrad, although no one will prevent you from taking a surreptitious peek). Most of the historic university buildings line the east side of the River Cam between Magdalene Bridge and Silver St. On both sides of the river, the gardens, meadows, and cows of the **Backs** lend Cambridge a pastoral air. If you have time for only a few colleges, **King's, Trinity, Queens', Christ's, St. John's,** and **Jesus** should top your list, though the whistle-stop traveler could manage 12 or 14 colleges in a few hours. The pamphlet *Cambridge, a Brief Guide for Visitors* (available at the tourist office) includes a street plan and basic information about the colleges and museums.

Cambridge University has three eight-week terms: Michaelmas (Oct. 9-Dec. 7), Lent (Jan. 15-March 15), and Easter (April 23-June 14). Most of the colleges are open daily from 9am to 5:30pm, though most close to visitors during the Easter term, and virtually all are closed during exam period (mid-May to mid-June). Unlike many U.S. campuses, Cambridge has no armed University police. Security is maintained by plump ex-servicemen called Porters, who wear bowler hats. Look and act like a student (i.e. wear no backpack, no camera and, for heaven's sake, no Cambridge University sweatshirt) and you should be able to wander freely through most college grounds—but not on the preciously tended lawns. In the summer, a few undergrads stay to work or study, but most abandon the town to the mercies of mobs of teenage language students. Some university buildings shut down over vacations.

King's College, on King's Parade, is the proud possessor of the university's most famous chapel, a spectacular Gothic monument. In 1441, Henry VI cleared away most of the center of medieval Cambridge for the foundation of King's College, and he intended its chapel to be England's finest. Although Hank wanted the inside of the chapel to remain unadorned, his successors ignored his wishes and spent nearly £5000 and three years carving an elaborate interior. If you stand at the southwest corner of the courtyard, you can see where Henry VI's master mason John Wastell (who also worked on the cathedrals of Peterborough and Canterbury) left off and where later work under the Tudors began—the earlier stone is off-white, the later, dark. The interior of the chapel consists of one huge room cleft by a carved wooden choir screen, one of the purest examples of the early Renaissance style in England.

Wordsworth described the fan-vault ceiling as a "branching roof self-poised, and scooped into ten thousand cells where light and shade repose." Stained glass windows depicting the life of Jesus were preserved from the iconoclasm of the English Civil War, allegedly because John Milton, then Cromwell's secretary, groveled on their behalf. On the walls, alternating Tudor rose and portcullis pendants symbolize Henry VI's reign (look for the grinning pendant on the left). Behind the altar hangs Ruben's magnificent *Adoration of the Magi* (1639), protected by an electronic alarm since a crazed would-be stonemason attacked it with a chisel several years ago. (Chapel open during the term Mon.-Sat. 9am-3:45pm, Sun. 2-3pm and 4:30-5:45pm; during vacation Mon.-Sat. 9am-5pm, Sun. 10:30am-5pm. Free. Chapel exhibition open during the term Mon.-Sat. 9:30am-3:30pm; during vacations Mon.-Sat. 9:30am-5pm, Sun. 11am-5pm. Admission £1, students 60p.) Take in the classic view of the chapel and of the adjacent **Gibbs Building** from the river.

In early June, in the Georgian **Senate House** opposite the chapel, the university posts the names and final grades of every student; about a week later, degree ceremonies are held here. Cambridge graduates are eligible for the most readily available master's degrees in the world; after spending three and a third years out in the world, a graduate sends £15 to the university to receive one without further ado, provided that said graduate is not in the custody of Her Majesty's Prison Service.

Trinity College, on Trinity St., is Cambridge's largest and wealthiest. Founded in 1546, Trinity used to specialize in literature (alums include George Herbert, John Dryden, Lord Byron, and Lord Tennyson), but in this century has instead spat forth scientists and philosophers (Ernest Rutherford, Ludwig Wittgenstein, G.E. Moore, and Bertrand Russell). The heir apparent, Prince Charles, was an average student in anthropology. The **Great Court** is the largest yard in Cambridge, so huge that its utter lack of straight lines and symmetry is hardly noticeable. Inside the courtyard, in a florid fountain built in 1602, Byron used to bathe nude. The eccentric young poet who lived in Nevile's Court also shared his rooms with a pet bear, which he claimed would take his fellowship exams for him. Although the movie was filmed at Eton College, the story behind *Chariots of Fire* took place here. What William Wordsworth called the "loquacious clock that speaks with male and female voice" still strikes 24 times each noon. Sir Isaac Newton, who lived on the first floor of E-entry for 30 years, first measured the speed of sound by stamping his foot in the cloister along the north side of the court. Underneath the courtyards lie the well-hidden, well-stocked Trinity wine cellars. Recently the college purchased over £20,000 worth of port that won't be drinkable until 2020. The college's wealth is legendary—myth-mongers hold that it was once possible to walk from Cambridge to Oxford without stepping off Trinity land.

Walk through the college toward the river to reach the reddish stone walls of the stunning **Wren Library.** Notable treasures in this naturally lit building include A.A. Milne's handwritten manuscript of *Winnie-the-Pooh* and less momentous works such as John Milton's *Lycidas.* The collection also contains works by Byron, Tennyson, and Thackeray. German-speakers should look for Wittgenstein's journals. His phenomenal *Philosophical Investigations* was conceived here during years of intense discussion with G.E. Moore and students in his K-entry rooms on the top floor. (Library open year-round Mon.-Fri. noon-2pm; also Sat. 10am-2pm during the term. Free. Trinity's courtyards close at 6pm. Closed during exams.)

Established in 1511 by Lady Margaret Beaufort, mother of Henry VIII, **St. John's College,** is one of seven Cambridge colleges founded by women. The striking brick and stone gatehouse bears Lady Margaret's heraldic emblem. St. John's centers around a paved plaza rather than a grassy courtyard, and its two best buildings stand across the river from the other colleges. A copy of Venice's Bridge of Sighs connects the older part of the college to the towering neo-Gothic extravagance of New Court, likened by philistines to a wedding cake in silhouette. Next door, you can see more adventurous college architecture, the modern **Cripps Building,** with clever bends that create three distinct courts under the shade of a noble willow. The **School of Pythagoras,** a 12th-century pile of wood and stone rumored to be the oldest complete building in Cambridge, hides in St. John's Gardens. (Courtyard and some buildings open until 6pm. Closed during exams.)

Queens' College, founded in 1448 by two queens, Margaret of Anjou and Elizabeth Woodville, has few rivals in the "cute" department. It possesses the only unaltered Tudor courtyard in Cambridge, containing the half-timbered President's Gallery. The **Mathematical Bridge,** just past Cloister Court, was built in 1749 without a single bolt or nail, relying only on mathematical principle. A meddling Victorian took the bridge apart to see how it worked and the inevitable occurred—he couldn't put it back together without using a steel rivet every two inches. (College open daily 1:45-4:30pm; during summer vacation also 10:15am-12:45pm. Closed during exams.)

Clare College, founded in 1338 by the thrice-widowed, 29-year-old Lady Elizabeth de Clare, has preserved an appropriate coat of arms: a shield with golden teardrops on a black border. Across Clare Bridge (the most elegant on the river) lie the **Clare Gardens.** (Open Mon.-Fri. 2-4:45pm.) Walk through Clare's Court (open during exams to groups of less than three) for a view of the University Library, where 82 miles of shelves hold books arranged according to size rather than subject. George V called it "the greatest erection in Cambridge;" more recently it appeared in the cinematic masterpiece *Brazil.*

Christ's College, founded in 1505, has won fame for its gardens (open Mon.-Fri. 2-4pm) and its connection with John Milton—a mulberry tree reputedly planted by the "Lady of Christ's" still thrives here. The gardens are also home to Blyth's Footprint, planted some 350 years later. To reach the gardens, walk under the lovely neoclassical Fellows Building dubiously accredited to Inigo Jones. New Court, on King St., is one of the most impressive, horrible modern structures in Cambridge; its strikingly symmetrical white stone walls and black-curtained windows look like the cross-bred offspring of an Egyptian pyramid, a Polaroid camera, and a typewriter. Charles Darwin survived among the fittest at Christ's, taking his undergraduate degree. His rooms (closed to visitors, and unmarked) were on G staircase in First Court. The entire college closes during exams, except for access to the chapel during services and concerts. (Inquire at the porter's desk.)

Built on a more secluded site than most back in 1496, **Jesus College** has preserved an enormous amount of unaltered medieval work. Beyond the long, high-walled walk called the "Chimny" lies a three-sided court fringed with colorful gardens. Through the archway on the right lie the remains of a gloomy medieval nunnery. The Pre-Raphaelite stained glass of Burne-Jones and ceiling decorations by William "Wallpaper" Morris festoon the chapel. (Courtyard open until 6pm. Closed during exams.)

Magdalene College (MAUD-lin), founded in 1524, has acquired an unsavory, aristocratic reputation. The **Pepys Library,** in the second court, displays the noted statesman and prolific diarist's collection in the original cases. You can see the dining hall on the left as you walk to the second court. (Library open Mon.-Sat. 2:30-3:30pm; also Easter-Aug. 11:30am-12:30pm. Free. Courtyards closed during exams.)

In **Peterhouse** (1284), the oldest college, Thomas Gray wrote his *Elegy in a Country Churchyard.* The newest of Cambridge's colleges is **Robinson College,** on Grange Rd. Founded in 1977, this mod-medieval brick pastiche sits just behind the university library. Bronze plants writhe about the door of the college chapel, which features some interesting stained glass. James Stirling's **History Faculty building,** between West Rd. and Sidgwick Ave., once provoked much debate about its aesthetic merits; of its leaky roof, there were never any doubts.

Corpus Christi College, founded in 1372, contains a dreary but extremely old courtyard forthrightly called Old Court, unaltered since its 1352 enclosure by town merchants. The library maintains the snazziest collection of Anglo-Saxon manuscripts in England, including the Parker Manuscript of the *Anglo-Saxon Chronicle.*

The 1347 **Pembroke College** next door harbors the earliest architectural effort of Sir Christopher Wren. (Courtyards open until 6pm. Closed during exams.)

A chapel designed by Wren dominates the front court of **Emmanuel College.** Emmanuel, founded in 1584, on St. Andrew's St. at Downing St., and **Downing College,** founded in 1807, just to the south along Regent St., are both pleasantly isolated. (Courtyards open until 6pm. Chapel open when not in use.) Downing's austere neoclassical buildings open onto an immense lawn. (Open daily until 6pm. Dining hall open when not in use. Closed during exams.)

The **Round Church,** Bridge St., one of five round churches surviving in England, was built in 1130 (and later rebuilt) on the pattern of the Church of the Holy Sepulchre in Jerusalem. The pattern deserves comparison with **St. Benet's Church,** a rough Saxon church on Benet St. The tower of St. Benet's, built in 1050, is the oldest structure in Cambridge.

You can easily get caught up in the splendor of the colleges, but try to take the time to explore a few museums. The **Fitzwilliam Museum,** Trumpington Rd. (tel. 332 900), a 10-minute walk down the road from King's College, dwells within an immense Roman-style building. Inside, a cavernous marble foyer leads to a collection that includes paintings by Leonardo da Vinci, Michelangelo, Dürer, Corot, Monet, and Seurat. A mixture of Egyptian, Chinese, and Greek antiquities bides its time downstairs, coupled with an extensive collection of 16th-century German armor. Check out the interesting illuminated manuscripts under their protective cloths. The drawing room displays William "Barmy" Blake's books and woodcuts. (Open Tues.-Sat. ground floor 10am-2pm, upper floor 2-5pm, Sun. both floors 2:15-5pm. Free. Call to inquire about lunchtime and evening concerts. Guided tours Sat.-Sun. at 2:30pm, £1.50.) The **Museum of Zoology** (tel. 336 650), off Downing St., houses a fine collection of dead wildlife specimens in a modern, well-lit building. (Open Mon.-Fri. 2:15-4:45pm. Free.) Across the road, opposite Corn Exchange St., the **Museum of Archaeology and Anthropology,** Downing St. (tel. 333 516), contains an excellent collection of prehistoric artifacts from American, African, Pacific, and Asian cultures, as well as exhibits from Cambridge through the ages. (Open Mon.-Fri. 2-4pm, Sat. 10am-12:30pm. Free.) If you're near Magdalene College, stop by the **Folk Museum,** 2 Castle St. (tel. 355 159), at Northampton St., an appealing junk heap. (Open Mon.-Sat. 10:30am-5pm, Sun. 2-5pm. Admission £1, children 50p.) **Kettle's Yard,** at the corner of Castle and Northampton St., houses a collection of early 20th-century art. (Open Tues.-Sat. 12:30-5pm, Sun. 2-5:30pm. Free.) The **Scott Polar Research Institute,** Lensfield Rd. (tel. 336 540), commemorates icy expeditions with photographic and artistic accounts, equipment, and memorabilia. (Open Mon.-Sat. 2:30-4pm. Free.)

The **Botanic Gardens** (tel. 336 265; enter from Hill Rd., Trumpington Rd., or Bateman St.) are a xerox copy of Eden. The gardens were ingeniously laid out by Henslow, Sir Joseph Hooker's father-in-law, in 1856. When the wind gets friendly, the scented garden turns into an olfactory factory. The adders (poisonous snakes) in the gardens have yet to bother visitors; keep to the path nevertheless. (Open Mon.-Sat. 8am-6pm, Sun. 10am-6pm. Admission £1 on Sun., free Mon.-Sat.)

Entertainment

On a sunny afternoon, bodies sprawl on the lush banks of the River Cam. The Cam is almost always stocked with narrow, flat-bottomed **punts,** England's retort to the gondola. Punting is the sometimes stately, sometimes soggy pastime of propelling a flat little boat (a punt) by pushing a long pole into the river bottom. If your pole gets stuck, leave it in the mud instead of taking a plunge. Punters can take two routes—one from Magdalene Bridge to Silver St., and the other from Silver St. along the River Granta (the name given to the Cam as it passes out of town) to Grantchester. On the first route—the shorter, busier, and more interesting one—you'll pass the colleges and the Backs. The art of punt-bombing, in which students jump from bridges into the river right next to a punt, thereby tipping its occupants into the Cam, has been largely discontinued since the advent of increased river policing a few years ago. You can rent a punt from **Scudamore's Boatyards,** at Magdalene Bridge or Silver St. (tel. 359 750); hourly rates are £6 for punts, rowboats, and canoes, plus a £30 cash deposit. (Open daily 9am-6pm.) Upstart **Tyrell's,** Magdalene Bridge (tel. 352 847), has punts and rowboats for £5.20 per hour, plus a £25 deposit. Tyrell's offers chauffered rides (45 min.) for £15 per group.

You can expect long lines for punts on weekends, particularly on Sunday—rowboats and canoes are easier to come by. To avoid bumper-punting, go late in the afternoon when the river traffic dwindles, but remember that boats must be returned by 6pm. Guided tours, punted by students, offer a cop-out option to those unwilling to risk a plunge. Inquire at the tourist office.

During the first two weeks of June, students celebrate the end of the term with **May Week** (this is, perhaps, a May of the mind), crammed with concerts, plays, and elaborate balls which feature anything from hot air balloon rides to lying utterly drunk face down in the street to breakfast on the Seine. Along the Cam, the college boat clubs compete in an eyebrow-raising series of races known as the **bumps.** Crews line up along the river rather than across it, and attempt to ram the boat in front before being bumped from behind. May Week's artistic repertoire stars the famous **Footlights Revue,** a collection of comedy skits; its performers have gone on to join such troupes as Beyond the Fringe and Monty Python. John Cleese, Eric Idle, and Graham Chapman graduated from the Revue. (At the Arts Theatre box office, tel. 352 000.)

During the rest of the summer, entertainment is geared more toward tourists than students, but the **Cambridge Festival,** a series of concerts and special exhibits culminating in a huge **folk festival,** brightens the last two weeks of July. (The 1992 festival is scheduled for July 10-26.) Tickets for the weekend (around £32) include camping on the grounds. (For the main festival, call the Corn Exchange box office, tel. 357 851; for the folk festival, tel. 463 359.)

During the third week of June the **Midsummer Fair,** which dates from the early 16th century, appropriates Midsummer Common for about five days. The **Strawberry Fayre,** Cambridge's answer to Glastonbury, takes place the first Saturday in June. (Address all festival inquiries to the tourist office.)

John Maynard Keynes, the resident economic voodoo-master of Cambridge during the first half of this century, took time off from his dubious science to found the **Arts Theatre Club** (box office tel. 352 000; open Mon.-Sat. 10am-8pm), which sponsors drama, film, and dance. The theatre is located at 6 St. Edward's Passage. Students pay £5.50 for advance tickets and £4.50 for any ticket still unsold an hour before the show starts. Tickets usually cost £8-12.50. The **Arts Cinema,** Market Passage (tel. 352 001), screens comedy classics and undubbed foreign films and holds a film festival during the Cambridge Festival. (Tickets £2.50-3.50. Box office open Mon.-Fri. 1-9:15pm, Sat. 11am-9:15pm, Sun. 1:30-9:15pm.) During the term and the Cambridge Festival, the **ADC Theatre** (Amateur Dramatic Club), Park St., offers lively entertainment, including student-produced plays (£2.50-6) and movies (£3). Call the box office (tel. 359 547) for the latest schedule. The best source of information on student activities is the *Varsity,* free to undergrads, 25p in a news shop; or enquire at the tourist office.

You can get an earful of concerts at the **Cambridge Corn Exchange,** at the corner of Wheeler St. and Corn Exchange, a venue for band, jazz, and classical concerts. (Box office tel. 357 851; tickets £5.50-12.50, 50% off for student standby 30 min. before performances. Box office open Mon.-Sat. 10am-6pm.) The **Cambridge Union,** a private debating club, sponsors social activities during the summer (officially only for people enrolled in language courses, but check anyway). The clubhouse orates on Round Church St., off Sydney St. Students pack the **Anchor,** Silver St. (tel. 353 554), on Tuesday and Thursday nights, when live bands play hot jazz. **Flambard's Wine Bar,** Rose Crescent, has jazz on Friday nights. To the east, **The Geldart,** 1 Ainsworth St. (tel. 355 983), features Irish folk music on Tuesday and Sundays. **Route 66,** Benet St., draws a house crowd on Wednesdays and motor traffic on bank holiday weekends.

The Junction, Clifton Rd., off Cherry Hinton Rd. south of the town, proves a popular alternative dance venue on Friday nights, and hosts top local bands such as *The First Five Minutes of Betty Blue.* **Cinderellas Rockefellers,** Lion Yard, right in the center draws a gay crowd from throughout East Anglia on Sunday nights. Popular night spots change constantly; students, bartenders, and the latest issue of *Varsity* will be your best sources of information.

Near Cambridge

Not easily visited, **Grantchester** is worth the effort. Immortalized by Rupert Brooke in 1912 with his clumsy verse "Stands the Church clock at ten to three? And is there honey still for tea?", Grantchester is a mecca for Cambridge literary types. When the clock was stopped for repairs in 1985, its hands were left frozen pedantically at ten to three. You can see the church clock tower next to Brooke's home at the Old Vicarage (closed to the public).

To reach Grantchester Meadows from Cambridge, take the path that follows the River Granta (about 45 min.). Grantchester itself lies about a mile from the meadows; ask the way at one of the neighborhood shops. If you have the energy to pole or paddle your way to the meadow, rent a punt or canoe from **Scudamore's Boatyards** on Silver St. (tel. 359 750). After tying up your boat (no one will steal it), follow the signs to the road. The **Rupert Brooke** and the **Green Man** will reward the famished and parched trekker (lunch £3.75-5.50; both open Mon.-Sat. 11:30am-2:30pm and 6-11pm, Sun. noon-3pm and 7-10:30pm). Before returning to Cambridge, stop by the charmingly weathered **Parish Church of St. Andrew and St. Mary,** on Milway. Some of its fragments date to the 14th century.

Ten mi. southwest of Cambridge lies **Wimpole Hall,** Cambridgeshire's most spectacular mansion in an elegant 18th-century style. Among works included are by Gibbs, Flitcroft, and Joane, and gardens sculpted by Capability Brown. Don't miss **Wimpole's Home Farm,** complete with Longhorn and Gloucester cattle, Soay sheep and Tamworth pigs. (Open April-Nov. Tues.-Thurs. and Sat.-Sun. 10:30am-5pm. Admission to farm only £3, hall and gardens only £4, joint hall and farm £5.)

Slightly farther from Cambridge, 12th-century **Anglesey Abbey** (tel. 811 200) has been tastefully remodeled to house the priceless exotica of the first Lord Fairhaven. One of the niftiest clocks in the universe sits inconspicuously on the bookcase beyond the fireplace. In the 100-acre gardens, trees punctuate lines of closely clipped hedges and manicured lawns. (Abbey open April-Oct. Wed.-Sun. 1:30-5:30pm; mid-July to mid-Sept. daily 11am-5:30pm. Gardens open mid-April to July and mid-Sept. to mid-Oct. Wed.-Sun. 11am-5:30pm. Admission £4.50, gardens only £2.) The abbey lies only 6 mi. from Cambridge on the B1102 (off the A1303, if you want to hitch from Cambridge). Buses (#111 or 122) run hourly from Drummond St. Station; ask to be let off at Lodge Crossroads.

Dating from the days of the Saxon invasions and possibly the Neolithic and Bronze Ages, the market town of **Saffron Walden** (pop. 12,515; 15 mi. south of Cambridge) retains a medieval street layout that few towns in England can match. From Cambridge, take Cambus #112 (Mon.-Sat. every 2 hr.; 50 min.; £20) or Cambus #122 (leaves Cambridge Mon.-Sat. at 12:15, 2:40, and 5:35pm; last return 1:05pm) or Cambus #9 (Sun. only, every ½hr. 10am-6pm, last reurn 7:10pm). Trains leave Cambridge hourly for nearby **Audley End,**bout a mile from town. Audley End is a magnificent Jacobean hall set in grounds designed by Capability Brown. (Open April-Sept. daily noon-5pm. Admission £4, students £3.) Saffron Walden's name comes from the saffron that used to be sold there, and from the Anglo-Saxon for "wooded valley." The town is best known for the "pargetting" (plaster moulding) that adorns many of the town's Tudor buildings.

The **tourist office** (tel. (0799) 242 82) has a free mini-guide. (Open April-Oct. Mon.-Sat. 9:30am-5pm; Nov.-March 10am-4:30pm. Walking tours given April-Oct. Thurs.-Sun. at 11am and 2:30pm; £1.) The **IYHF youth hostel,** 1 Myddylton Place (tel. (0799) 231 17), in the north part of Saffron Walden on the A130, occupies one of the oldest buildings in the village. (Open April-June Fri.-Tues.; July-Aug. daily; Sept.-Oct. Fri.-Tues.; Nov. ot mid-Dec. and Freb. Fri.-Sat.; March Fri.-Tues. £5.50, ages 16-20 £4.40.) Within the **Eight Bells** pub on Bridge St. beats the heart of the town's social life. (Open noon-2pm and 6-11pm.) Don't leave town without traipsing across the green to the town **maze,** laid out with bricks set in the ground. Hedge-hunters will be disappointed.

Ely

Legend has it that in the area just north of Cambridge, St. Dunstan saw fit to turn the local monks into eels as punishment for their lack of proper piety—a sacred transformation that earned one town the name Ely (EEL-ee). Here too, brave Hereward the Wake defended himself against Norman invaders, earning the title "the last of all the English." Things have quieted down in this age of golf and television, but the beautiful cathedral and restful atmosphere make for a good stopover between London or Cambridge and cities farther north.

The massive **cathedral,** nicknamed the "Ship of the Fens," was founded in 1081 on the spot where St. Etheldredats had formed a hilltop religious community 4 centuries earlier. In 1322, the original Norman tower collapsed and the present octagonal **lantern tower** was constructed. Macabre masks grin with bared teeth from the intersection of the inner buttresses. (Disabled access on the north side.) In 1986, Ely was the first city in England to charge admission to its cathedral, earning national notoriety. Tours of the cathedral are usually given only to groups, but you can probably tag along. (Open Mon.-Sat. 7am-7pm, Sun. 7:30am-5pm; off-season Mon.-Sat. 7:30am-6pm, Sun. 7:30am-5pm. Evensong Mon.-Sat. 5:30pm, Sun. 3:45pm. Admission £2.40, students £1.70, free during services.) The cathedral's separate **stained glass museum** overlooks the nave. (Open Easter-Oct. Mon.-Fri 11am-4pm, Sat. 11am-4:30pm, Sun. noon-3pm. Admission £1, students 50p.) Admission to the brass-rubbing center is free—you pay for materials only.

The monastic buildings that surround the cathedral are still in use: the **infirmary** now houses the Dean of Ely, and the **bishop's palace** is a school for disabled children. The rest of the buildings are used by the **King's School,** one of the older public schools in England. (School buildings sometimes open July-Aug. Apply to the seneschal at the door.) For a rigorous architectural tour of the town, consult the overwhelmingly detailed **Town Walks** pamphlet from the tourist office (45p). Standing in the shadow of Ely Cathedral, **Oliver Cromwell's House,** 29 St. Mary's Street, has recently been refurbished in period decor. (Open May-Sept. daily 10am-6pm; Oct.-April Mon.-Sat. 10am-5:15pm. Admission £1.) The **Ely Museum,** 28c High St. (tel. 66 31 35), tells the fascinating story of a fenland city and its people. Ely was an island until the fens were drained in the 17th century. (Open Tues.-Sat. 10:30am-1pm and 2:15-5pm, Sun. 2:15-5pm. Admission 80p.)

The **tourist information office,** 29 St. Mary's St. (tel. 662 062), just west of the Cathedral, occupies the house Oliver Cromwell lived in for 10 years. The enthusiastic staff will flabbergast you with free maps and accommodations lists and book a room for £1. (Open daily 10am-6pm; Oct.-April Mon.-Sat. 10am-5:15pm. Guided tours of the town and cathedral leave the tourist office twice a week July-Aug. on Thurs. at 2:30pm and Sat. at 11am; £2.75, children £2.25. Winter tours of the city and cathedral must be booked in advance.) The **post office** (tel. 662 727) is in the market place. Ely's **postal code** is CB7 4AA; the **telephone code** is 0353. The **police** can be reached on Nutholt Lane (tel. 66 23 92).

Ely's B&Bs hover slightly out of reach of the budget-minded (at £12-15), but the **IYHF youth hostel,** Ely Sixth Form Centre, St. Audrey's, Downham Rd. (tel. 667 423), in a large, clean school building, usually has space. (Lockout 10am-5pm. Curfew 11pm. Small kitchen and store. TV lounge. £5.50, ages 16-20 £4.40. Open June-Aug. daily.) From the cathedral, follow the Gallery to Egremont St., turn left, then right on Downham Rd.—the hostel is 3 blocks away on the right. **Mrs. Wheeler,** St. David's, 19A Egremont St. (tel. 662 217), offers two singles and one double to nonsmokers (£14). About a mile down Downham Rd. from the hostel, **Jane Hull and Bill Jackson** rent rooms on their working farm (tel. 662 316). An extremely gregarious hostess, Mrs. Hull is happy to lend her horse to anyone interested in hacking through the nearby Chettisham Woods. (Free transporation from station. £9/person.) You can camp among potatoes and sugarbeet for only 90p per person at **Braham Farm,** Cambridge Rd. (tel. 662 386), off the A10 just past the golf course (toilets, bath, and cold water available).

Tea houses are everywhere in Ely, but good cheap meals are hard to find. On Thursdays from 8:30am to 4:30pm, stock up on provisions at the general **market** in Market Pl. The **Minister Tavern,** Minister Pl., around the corner from the tourist office, is popular. (Lunches £2-4.) **The Steeplegate,** on 16-18 High St. across from the cathedral, serves tea and light snacks in two rooms built over a medieval undercroft; fall into a romantic reverie over a pot of Earl Grey (70p). **Mother Nature,** High St., purveys wholefoods (open Mon.-Fri. 9am-5pm, Sat. 8:30am-5pm). A lunch of roast beef, Yorkshire Pudding, two vegetables, and potatoes for £3 awaits you at the crowded, vaguely elegant restaurant above **Bonnet's Bakery** on High St. (open Tues.-Sat. 10am-5pm). On the banks of the Great Ouse (OOZE), the pub at the **Maltings,** a restored brewery building, serves bar meals on its patio (£1.50-3.50; open daily noon-2pm and 6-9pm). Watch the elaborately painted pleasure boats go by as you down a plate of roast wild boar (£3.50). **Surma,** 80 Broad St., serves good, affordable curries and *tandooris* (around £4.50; open daily noon-3pm and 6pm-midnight).

Ely is a junction on the train lines between London, King's Lynn, Norwich and Peterborough, with frequent connections to each of these cities. Trains run between Cambridge and Ely (every hour; 20 min.; £2.90 day return) and Norwich (hourly; 1½ hr.; £8 return). To reach the cathedral and the tourist office from the train station, walk up Station Rd. and continue onto Back Hill, which becomes The Gallery. St. Mary's St. is on the left just past the cathedral.

Suffolk

In the 14th century, Suffolk County was a thriving center of wool production and trade. The imposing houses, halls and magnificent "wool churches" that dominate the landscape of southeast East Anglia attest to the impressive wealth accumulated in bygone centuries. The frenetic pace in the numerous small towns has slowed, leaving an air of quiet serenity amongst the hundreds of crooked timber-framed buildings.

Getting There and Getting Around

A short hop from metropolitan London, Suffolk is served by frequent train and coach service. Bury St. Edmunds makes an excellent daytrip from either Norwich or Cambridge, especially if you include a jaunt to Lavenham, Sudbury, Lona, Melford, or any of the other historic villages scattered throughout Western Suffolk.

Trains leave London's Liverpool St. station for Bury St. Edmunds (£14); Harwich (£16); Felixstowe (£16); and Colchester (£13.75). Trains also run between Cambridge and Norwich via Bury (every hour, Sun. every 2 hr., change at Stowmarket; 1¼ hr.; £8.50 single or day return). **National Express** coaches leave from London's Victoria Station for Bury St. Edmunds (£10.25). Cambus #X2 runs on weekdays every 2 hours (Sun. every 3 hr.) from Drummer St. Station in Cambridge to St. Andrew's Station in Bury (50 min.; £3.25 return). The Young Person's Card (£16) and the Network Southeast Card (£12) both reduce train fares by 1/3, and the National Express Card (£5) offers discounts on buses.

Regional bus service is provided by **Eastern Counties** (for information, call the office in Bury St. Edmunds at (0284) 766 171.) Eastern Counties' #141, 142, 143, 144 leave Bury's St. Andrew's Station to Horringer and Ickworth. (Mon.-Sat. 6/day; 15 min.; day return £1.25. Last return from Horringer at 4:30pm weekdays and Sat. 5:30pm.) **H.C. Chambers'** buses #20 and 27 leave Bury from St. Andrew's for Lavenham (Mon.-Sat. 7/day, 20 min.; £1; call (95) 22 72 33 for information); Sudbury is 10 mi. further along this bus route. An H.C. Chambers' bus also leaves Bury for Melford (Mon.-Sat. 7/day; 45 min.; £1.25). Bury lies on the A45, and Melford is allegedly an easy 12-mi. hitch south of Bury on the A134.

The region is eminently explorable by bike. **Cycle King,** 26 Mustow St. (tel. (0284) 769 902), downhill from the tourist office in Bury, repairs and rents bikes (£8/day, £30/week, £50 deposit) and tandems.

Accommodations

B&Bs provide a comfortable base from which to explore the area, and there are several conveniently located youth hostels. In **Alpheton** there is a simple-grade **IYHF youth hostel** (tel. (0284) 828 297) at Monk's Croft, Bury Rd., near the A134. (Open April-Oct. Wed.-Mon. £3.20, ages 16-20 £2.60.) The hostel, 3 mi. north of Long Melford, 4 mi. northwest of Lavenham, and 10 mi. south of Bury St. Edmunds, makes a good base for touring the region if you have a bicycle or if you are totally insane. **Colchester,** famed as England's oldest town on the books, is home both to England's finest cricketer, Gregory St. John Munby, and an **IYHF youth hostel.** The large Georgian house is often crowded with ferry-riders. (East Bay House, 18 E. Bay; tel. (0206) 867 982. Lockout 9am-1pm. £5.90, 16-20 £4.70. Open March-Aug. daily; Sept. Mon.-Sat.; Feb. and Oct.-Nov. Tues.-Sat. Call ahead, although phone reservations not accepted if nearly full.)

For B&B in Lavenham, try graciously Victorian **Mrs. Morley's,** 48 Water St. (tel. (0787) 248 422), for £14. The **George and Dragon** (tel. (0787) 712 85), in Long Melford, offers bed and board above a country pub. The elegant, Edwardian **Cottage,** 1 Melford Rd., Sudbury (tel. (0787) 881 184) welcomes carnivores and herbivores alike to its exquisite gardens. (£12.50).

Bury St. Edmunds

Bury St. Edmunds is an appropriate name for the small town where invaders beheaded Saxon King Edmund in 869 AD after tying him to a tree and using him for target practice. According to besotted legend, a voice crying "Here I am!" led Edward's faithful subjects to the place in the brush where his severed head rested between the paws of a wolf. The busy commercial and administrative center that has grown up around Edmund's mythical burial place attracts few travelers, in welcome contrast to the neighboring crowds of Cambridge or Norwich.

A few hours of unsupervised wandering will reveal Bury's modest charms. Along Crown St., across from the tourist office on the soggy banks of the River Lark, lies the beautifully ruined **abbey,** home to cadres of foraging ducks. Only low crumbling walls and three massive pillars remain where 25 English barons met in 1214, a year before they forced Bad King John to sign the *Magna Carta.* The elaborate formal gardens next to the remains of the abbey won a special award in the annual "Britain in Bloom" competition. (Abbey and gardens open daily 7:30am-sunset. Free.) Next door to the abbey, the 16th-century **St. Edmundsbury Cathedral** sports a recently repainted hammerbeam roof flanked by guardian angels. (Open daily 7am-7pm. Free. Inquire at tourist office about summer organ concerts.) To the right of the cathedral rise the ruins of an old Norman tower, which guards a decadently overfoliated cemetery. For a free atonal concert, show up at the **Gershom Parkington Collection of Clocks and Watches** at noon. This small Georgian house opposite the abbey contains dozens of synchronized timepieces, including a replica of the first rolling-ball clock. (Open Mon.-Sat. 10am-5pm, Sun. 2-5pm. Free; donation requested.) The **Moyses' Hall Museum,** Corn Hill, in the marketplace, houses a wonderful collection of historical junk, including a violin made out of a horse's skull, a 19th-century jukebox, and yet more clocks. (Open Mon.-Sat. 10am-5pm, Sun. 2-5pm. Free.)

Market days in Bury are Wednesday and Saturday (about 8am-4pm)—£710 will buy you a cow at Wednesday's cattle market. In late July and early August, the town applies its collective—and usually quite successuful—green thumb to the "Britain in Bloom" competition.

Laid out according to the regular Roman four-square plan, Bury's streets are easier to untangle than those of its East Anglian neighbors. The **tourist office,** Athenaeum, Angel Hill, Bury St. Edmunds 1P33 1LY (tel. (0284) 764 667), distributes the usual handy maps and leaflets, as well as the voluminous *Bury and District Visitor Guide.* (Open Easter-Oct. Mon.-Fri. 9am-5:25pm, Sat. 10am-4pm; in July and Aug. also Sun. 10-11:30am; Nov.-Easter Mon.-Fri. 9am-5pm, Sat. 10am-noon.) To reach the office from the train station, follow Outnorth-gate past the roundabout onto Northgate St. Turn right onto Mustow St. and walk up to Angel Hill. The tourist office books B&Bs in town or on a nearby farm for £12.50-15 (10% deposit). The **post office** is on Comhill; the **postal code** is IP33 1AA. Any day of the week except Sunday, £1.30 will buy you a pint at the pint-sized **Nutshell,** the smallest—and it often seems the most popular—pub in England. **The Harvest Bakery,** Abbeygate St., sells inexpensive sandwiches, salads, and rolls (60p-£2) in a comfortable cafeteria and busy take-away (open Mon.-Sat. 8am-5pm).

Other Sights

Just 3 mi. southwest of Bury in the village of **Horringer** is **Ickworth** (tel. (0284) 735 270), the massive home of the Marquis of Bristol. Dominated by a 106-ft. rotunda, the opulent 19th-century state rooms are filled with 18th-century French furniture and more than a few portraits (including some by Reynolds and Gainsborough) of the mansion's founding family, the Harveys of Bristol Cream fame. The classical gardens are as splendid as one would expect, considering their proximity to the florid glory of Bury. (House open May-Sept. Tues.-Wed. and Fri.-Sun. 1:30-5:30pm; April and Oct. Sat.-Sun. 1:30-5:30pm. Admission £3.50, park only £1, children half-price.)

The medieval village of **Lavenham** lies 15 mi. south of Bury on the A1141. Lavenham **Guildhall,** in the marketplace (tel. (0787) 247 646), displays an exhibition on the ancient wool trade under its 450-year-old timbers. (Open April-Oct. daily 11am-1pm and 2-5:30pm. Admission £1.50, children 50p.) The **tourist office** (tel. (0787) 248 207) provides information on sights in and around the village (open Easter-Sept. daily 10am-4:45pm).

Ten mi. further along the bus route is the village of **Sudbury** and **Thomas Gainsborough's House** (tel. (0787) 729 58; open Tues.-Sat. 10am-5pm; Oct.-Easter Tues.-Sat. 10am-4pm; admission £2, students £1).

Turrets and moats await those who visit **Long Melford,** a Suffolk village near Sudbury well known for its Tudor architecture. **Melford Hall** (tel. (0787) 880 286) has been maintained in style over the past century—the panelling of the banquet hall is original. The most impressive display, the Chinese porcelain, was stolen from a Spanish galleon. The octagonal garden house is unique. (Principal rooms and garden open May-Sept. Wed.-Thurs. and Sat.-Sun. 2-5:30pm; April and Oct. Sat.-Sun. only, bank holidays also 2-5:30pm. Admission £2.40.) Just north of the village green stands the other red brick Tudor mansion, **Kentwell Hall** (tel. (0787) 310 207), which is surrounded by a broad moat. Most of the house is open to view. (Open July 17-Sept. 29 Mon.-Fri.; Oct. 6-27, Sun. noon-5pm; April Mon.-Fri. 2-5pm; April-May Sun. 2-5pm; May 28-June 2 Mon.-Fri. 2-5pm; June 9-16 Sun. 2-5pm. Admission £3, £2 for park and gardens only.)

Just 8 mi. south of Cambridge on the A505 and southwest of Bury, **Duxford Airfield** exhibits aircraft, military vehicles, tanks, and guns used during the Battle of Britain. (Open daily 10am-6pm. Admission £4.50, students £2.25.) Unspoilt **Woodbridge,** on the bank of the River Deben to the southeast of Bury, is home to England's up-and-coming tennis pro Sandra Lloyd. Woodbridge also boasts a rare 19th-century **Tide Mill.** When the tide comes in (late afternoon) you can see the mill grind the meal into flour. (Open May-Sept. daily 10am-5pm. Admission 80p.)

Harwich

Harwich (HAR-idge) is a popular ferry depot for trips to Holland, Germany, and Scandanavia. **Sealink** (tel. (0255) 240 965) sails twice daily (except Dec. 25-26) between Harwich and the **Hoek van Holland.** Boats leave Harwich at 11:30am (arriving at 7pm) and at 9:30pm (arriving at 7am). Boats depart from Hoek van Holland at noon (arriving at 5:45pm) and 10:30pm (arriving at 6:45am). Single tickets (£30, children under 14 £15), two-day returns (£30, £15), and five-day returns (£47, £24) are available. Children under 4 always sail free. Cabins, deck chairs, and vehicles cost extra. Bicycles cost £6-12 for a return trip. For Sealink reservations, call (0255) 243 333 or (0233) 647 022.

DFDS Seaways (tel. (0255) 240 240) operates boats to **Esbjerg,** Denmark (Mon., Wed., Fri., and Sun. 5pm; 20 hr.; £107 single); **Gothenburg,** Sweden (2-3/week on an erratic schedule; 24 hr.; £135 single); and **Hamburg,** Germany (3-4/week 3:30pm; 23 hr.; £90 single). There is a half-price discount with an ISIC card; prices are lower off-season. Both the Sealink and the DFDS docks are opposite the train station.

Close to Harwich, **Felixstowe** offers ferry service to **Zeebrugge,** Belgium. **P&O Ferries** offers "Whileoway" (£10), "Escapade" (£10), and "Moonlighter" (£14) ferry trips; boats depart Felixstowe at 11am or 11pm, arriving in Zeebrugge 5:45pm or 8am, respectively; return ferries leave Zeebrugge at midnight or noon and arrive at 7am or 4:45pm, respectively. Call P&O at (0394) 604 802 for information.

Norwich

One of England's largest cities before the Norman invasion, Norwich remains distinctly medieval. The skyline is dominated by an 11th century cathedral and a 12th century castle keep, and the central district is girdled by the weighty remains of the city's walls. Norwich's mazelike streets, whose twists and dead ends suggest an era when life was lived mainly by pedestrians, wind through a city which would rather convert its medieval churches into restaurants and sports centers than knock them down in overt deference to a demythified modernity. Norwich lies on the River Wensum at the southern edge of the Norfolk Broads, and was an important port until sea-going vessels got too big to sail up the river and had to dock in Yarmouth instead. The city makes an excellent base for touring both urban and rural East Anglia.

Arriving and Departing

Norwich (NOR-ridge) is easily accessible by bus, coach, and train. **Eastern Counties** buses run to Yarmouth (buses #717, 718, and 705/626, 6 per day 10:15am-6:20pm, Sun. 4 per day 10:30am-7:30pm; find price), King's Lynn ((buses #435, 438, and 794, 6 per day 7am-8:15pm, Sun. 4 per day noon-8:15pm; £3.50), and Peterborough ((bus #794, 4 per day 8:30am-5:30pm, Sun. 8:30am and 4pm; £3.80), and other Norfolk villages. **Explorer** tickets are good for one day's unlimited travel on Eastern Counties and can be purchased at the bus station or on the bus (adults, £3.80, children £2.40, seniors £3.10, family (up to 2 adults and 2 children) £7.50).

National Express coaches run to Cambridge (10 per day 8am-7pm; 2 hr. 20 min.; £5.75, economy return £6, period return £7.50), London (10 per day 7:40am-7:30pm; 3 hr.; £11.50), and many other destinations.

Trains go to Yarmouth (Mon.-Fri. 23 per day 6:20am-11pm, Sat. 15 per day 8:14am-10:25pm, Sun. 8 per day 8:30am-10:30pm; 30-40 min.; £2.30, day return £4.10), Peterborough (Mon.-Fri. 18 per day 5:09am-6:40pm, Sat. 18 per day 5:09am-6:34pm, Sun. 8 per day 10am-7:15pm; 90 min.; £11, saver return £9.20 for departures after 9:30 am), Cambridge (18-19 per day 5:09am-9:02pm, Sun. 11 per day 11:03am-8:10pm; 80-110 min.; £7.70, saver return £8.60 for departures after 9am), and London (19 per day; 2 hrs.; £23, saver return £22, not valid Mon.-Fri. 5:30am-8:05am).

For hitching to King's Lynn, take Dereham (King's Lynn) Rd. (near the youth hostel) west to the A47. To Cambridge, take St. Stephen's St. (near the bus station) to Newmarket Rd. to the A11.

Orientation and Practical Information

Although the street plan of Norwich's old city is the antithesis of a rational gridwork, imbuing destinations with an elusive character, most of the city's sights are fairly close together and quite manageable on foot. The hostel and many bed-and-breakfasts lie outside the city walls to the west, in a much more modern and more easily navigable part of town.

Tourist Information Centre: Guildhall, Gaol Hill, Norwich NR2 1DF (tel. (0603) 66 60 71), on the westward continuation of London St. in front of City Hall. The center offers a plentiful variety of brochures and sells books about Norwich and Norfolk. Accommodations service (10% deposit), free list. City guide 25p. Luggage storage 50p with £1 key deposit. Open Mon.-Sat. 9:30am-6pm, Sun. and bank holidays 9:30am-1pm; Oct.-May Mon.-Sat. 9:30am-5:30pm. 1½hr. Guided tours leave from the tourist office June-Oct. Mon.-Sat. 2:30pm, Sun. 10:30am; in Aug. also Mon.-Sat. 10:30am (£1, under 16 free).

Bike Rental: Dodgers, 69 Trinity St. (tel. 62 24 99). £3 per day, £20 deposit. Reserve ahead. Repairs. Open Mon.-Sat. 10:30am-5:30pm.

Bus and Coach Station: Surrey St. (tel. 62 04 91), off St. Stephen's St. southwest of the castle. Information center and ticket desk open Mon.-Fri. 8:30am-5pm, Sat. 8:30am-4pm. Additional information at the **Norfolk Bus Information Centre (NORBIC),** 4 Guildhall Hill (tel. 61 36 13), behind the tourist office. Open Mon.-Fri. 9am-5pm.

Bookstores: Waterstone's, 30 London St. (tel. 63 24 26). Good selection of maps and travel books. Open Mon.-Fri. 9am-7pm, Sat. 9am-5:30pm.

Currency Exchange: Thomas Cook, 23 St. Andrew's St. Open Mon.-Fri. 9am-5:30pm. **Western Trust and Savings,** 10 Dove St. Open Mon.-Fri. 9:30am-4:30pm, Sat. 9:30am-12:30pm. Major banks on London St. include **Barclay's.**

Emergency: Dial 999; no coins required.

Hospital: Norfolk and Norwich Hospital, St. Stephen's St. (tel. 62 83 77). ¼mi. from the castle. Follow Castle Meadow south to Red Lion St., which becomes St. Stephen's St. The hospital is on the right beyond the Chapelfield-Queen's intersection.

Late Night Pharmacy: Different each night. Check list at tourist office or in local press, or inquire at police station.

Launderette: Laundromat, 179A Dereham Rd. (tel. 62 66 85), near the hostel. Wash £1.60. Open Mon.-Sat. 8am-8pm, Sun. 8am-7pm, last wash an hour before closing. **Clean Machine,** 134 Unthank Rd. (tel. (0638) 66 82 22), call for other locations. Wash £1.20, dry 20p. Open daily 6:30am-10pm, last wash 9pm.

Market: In the square facing City Hall and the tourist office. Open Mon.-Sat. about 8am-4:30pm.

Police: Bethel St. (tel. 62 12 12); around the corner from the town hall.

Post Office: Main branch at 13/17 Bank Plain, ½block north of the castle. *Poste Restante* branches on Davey Pl. and St. Stephen's St., near the bus station. Open Mon.-Wed. and Fri. 9am-5:30pm, Thurs. 9:30am-5:30pm, Sat. 9am-12:30pm. **Postal Code:** NR2 1AA.

Rape Crisis: (tel. 66 76 87).

Taxi: Beeline & Dolphin, (tel. 76 76 76/62 33 33), 24 hrs.

Telephone Code: 0603.

Train Station: (tel. 63 20 55) at the corner of Riverside and Thorpe Rd., 15-min. walk uphill to the town center. Outrageously expensive **lockers for luggage storage** (£1-3).

Accommodations and Camping

The most conveniently located and reasonably priced accommodations are the YMCA and YWCA, a few blocks west of the tourist office. Earlham, Unthank, and Eaton Rd., radiating to the west of the city center, have loads of B&Bs in the £10-14 range, but they are at least a 20-min. hike from the center and even further from the train station. From the tourist office, follow St. Giles St. to the Ring Rd. rotary and cross the footbridge; Unthank Rd. branches off to the left, Earlham Rd. to the right. To reach **Eaton Rd.,** turn sharply left and follow the main road about ½mi. The guesthouses appear when the house numbers reach the 100s.

IYHF Youth Hostel, 112 Turner Rd. (tel. 62 76 47), 1½miles from the center. Take bus #19 or 20 (#37 or 38 after 6pm and on Sundays) from the train station, walk across the river and wait at the shelter in front of the Multiyork Furniture Store; or, take Castle Meadow to the Earl of Leicester pub at the corner of Dereham and Bowthorpe Rd. and turn right onto Turner Rd. Very clean rooms in a quiet residential neighborhood; good kitchen facilities. Opens at 5pm, 1pm in July and August. Adults £6.60, ages 16-20 £5.40, under 16 £4.40. Curfew 11pm. Open April-Aug. daily, Sept.-Nov. and Feb.-April Sun.-Thurs. Often filled in July and August.

YMCA, 46-52 St. Giles St. (tel. 62 02 69). Central location. Simple and clean rooms. Separate wings for men and women. Laundry facilities. TV lounge. No curfew. B&B £12.05. Weekly £56.54 with two evening meals. Key deposit £5. Often full, so call ahead.

YWCA, 61 Bethel St. (tel. 62 59 82). Women only. Central location. Rooms are clean, but not plush. No prepared meals, but a very well-equipped kitchen. Laundry facilities. Minimum age 16. Men allowed on main floor until 10pm. No curfew; porter lets you in after 10:30pm. Singles and twins £6.96-8.35 per person. Weekly rates £32.50-39. Key deposit £10. Definitely call ahead.

Aberdale, 211 Earlham Rd. (tel. 50 21 00), 15-min. walk from the center. Relaxed, unpretentious B&B. £12 per person, children sharing adults' room £7.

Androse House, 272 Unthank Rd. (tel. 542 76). Walk 20 min. from city center, or take bus #5 from Castle Meadow. Thankfully gracious family house and delightful garden. Singles £14.50, doubles £28.

Camping: Closest is the new **Lakenham** campsite, Martineau Lane (tel. 62 00 60), 1 mi. south of the center. From the train station, follow Riverside Rd. south to Carrow St. Cross river and turn left onto King St. Turn left again at Martineau Lane. Eastern Counties #29, 31, 32 stop nearby. Toilets and showers. Facilities for the disabled. £2.90 per person. Open April-Sept. Call ahead. Also close is **Scouts Headquarters** (tel. 50 22 46), though it's sometimes full. Take St. Stephen's St. to Newmarket Rd. and continue past the roundabout; take the 1st left onto Church Lane and watch for signs. Otherwise take bus #1,2 or 6 from the train station or Castle Meadow to Cellar House Pub and turn left onto Church Lane. £1.50 per person, showers 10p.

Food and Pubs

The stalls of one of England's largest and oldest open-air **markets** (Mon.-Sat. roughly 9am-4:30pm) offer everything from the obligatory fresh fruit and cheeses to pet hamsters and custom-cut foam rubber.

Don Miller's Hot Bread Kitchen, 21 White Lion St., off Red Lion St. Watch the fresh loaves roll out of the oven. Sandwiches 88p-£1.45. Excellent doughnuts 6 for 66p. Open Mon.-Sat. 7am-5:30pm.

Linzer Vienna Patisserie, 67 London St. Rum-drenched truffles (65p) are the specialty at this elegant eatery. Open Mon.-Fri. 8:30am-5:30pm, Sat. 9:30am-5:30pm.

The Mecca, 5 Orfond Hill, off Bell Ave. A good deli, wholefood grocer, restaurant, and tea-and-coffee specialty shop occupy several floors. Lots of teas. Vegetarian meals. Open Mon.-Sat. 8:30am-5:30pm; breakfast 8:30-11:30am, lunch noon-2:30pm (average cost £3), and tea 2:30-5:30pm. Noon-2:30pm £2 minimum charge at restaurant.

The Waffle House, 39 St. Giles St., near the YMCA and YWCA. Stylish place very different from the American chain. Belgian waffles with sweet or savoury fillings 95p-£3.60. Not just for breakfast. Open Mon.-Thurs. 11am-10pm, Fri.-Sat. 11am-11pm, Sun. noon-10pm.

Cafe La Tienda, 10 St. Gregory's Alley, off Charing Cross St. Pleasant, pocket-sized place tucks cheese, tuna, and other delicious fillings into warm pita (£2.40). Open Mon.-Sat. 10am-5pm.

The Briton Arms Coffee House, 9 Elm Hill. The perfect place for afternoon tea on picturesque Elm Hill. Good salads and sandwiches (£1.50). Tea 45p, scones and cakes about 50p. Open Mon.-Sat. 9:30am-5pm. Tea served 3:30-5pm.

The Assembly House, Theatre St. An 18th-century building with beautiful chandeliers and columns. Light meals and teas in a gray panelled gallery at cafe prices. Sandwiches and buffet lunch £2.50-3.65. Adjacent cinema. Open Mon.-Sat. 10am-7:30 pm. Bar open Mon.-Sat. 11:30am-2pm, 6-10pm. Lunch noon-2pm, dinner 5-7:30pm.

The Reindeer, 10 Dereham Rd, just beyond the city walls and near the hostel. Offers three varieties of home-brewed ales and a lively atmosphere. Open Mon.-Fri. 11am-3pm and 5-11pm, Sat. 11am-11pm, Sun. noon-3pm and 7-10:30pm.

The Adam and Eve, Bishopgate, at the Palace St. end of Riverside Walk. The oldest pub in Norwich and one of its most pleasant watering holes. Open daily 11am-3pm and 6-11pm.

One of the most charming places for an evening drink is not a pub. **Cinema City,** St. Andrew's St. (tel. 62 20 47), in the old Suckling House, is an "exhibition center" that includes a movie theater, bookshop, information desk, and a fantastic 14th-century bar. Open Mon.-Sat. 11am-11pm, Sun. noon-10:30pm. The theater shows good second-run and foreign films (call 62 20 47 or check at tourist office for schedule).

Sights

The original **Norwich Castle** was a wooden structure built in 1089 by a Norman monarchy intent on subduing the Saxon city. In 1160 the stone keep was erected, but its current exterior dates from the 1830s, when the keep was refaced in a restoration effort. The signing of the Magna Carta in 1215 saw royal power checked, and the castle was then used as a jail from 1345 until 1887. It has been a museum since 1894.

The **Castle Museum** (tel. 62 11 54), which occupies the castle keep, contains a jumble of art, archaeology, history, and natural history—everything from bits of armor to a prized chunk of 12,500-year-old mammoth excrement. While the museum allows you to see the inside of the keep, the battlements and dungeons may be seen only on guided tours. (Tours Mon.-Sat. 10:30am-3:30pm on the ½-hr.; Sun. 2:15, 3, and 3:45. Adults £1.20, children 60p, under 5 free. Museum open Mon.-Sat. 10am-5pm, Sun. 2-5pm. Admission £1.30, ages 5-16 50p, students and seniors £1). Admission to the museum includes admission to the **Royal Norfolk Regimental Museum,** on nearby Castle Meadow (tel. 62 84 55). (Open Mon.-Fri. 10am-5pm, Sat. 2-5pm. Admission to this museum only (not to the castle) 60p, ages 5-16 30p, seniors and students 40p).

The Norman **Norwich Cathedral,** which is most easily found by walking toward its distinctive spire, was built by an 11th-century bishop as penance for having bought his episopacy. The beautiful two-story cloisters are the only ones of their kind in England, and the interior boasts a beautiful 15th-century nave roof. On the east side of the building, behind the high altar, the French-style flying buttresses help support the second tallest spire in the country. Outside the cathedral is the grave of Edith Cavell, a Norfolk-born nurse who in 1915 was shot by the Germans for overstepping her role as a non-combatant. In the summer, the cathedral frequently hosts orchestral concerts and small art exhibitions. Call the Visitors' Office for information (tel. 62 62 90). (Open mid-May to mid-Sept. daily 7:30am-7pm; mid-Sept. to mid-May daily 7:30am-6pm. Free. Guided tours June-Sept. Mon.-Fri. 11:15am and 2:15pm, Sat. 11:15am. Disabled access.)

Two blocks north of the tourist office is **Stranger's Hall,** a folk museum which displays furnishings and items of daily life since the Tudor period (tel. 61 12 77; entrance on Charing Cross west of St. Andrew's St.). Formerly home to prosperous citizens of Norwich, the Tudor-style building is furnished in a variety of styles dating from the 16th-century onward. The room to the right of the entrance contains changing costume exhibitions. (Open Mon.-Sat. 10am-5pm. Admission 50p, students 25p, children 20p, ½-price in winter.)

Two blocks down St. Andrew's St., in Bridewell Alley, is the **Bridewell Museum** (tel. 61 12 77). From 1583 to 1828, this medieval merchant's house was a prison for tramps and beggars (named for one in London on Bride's Well St.). Dates and initals carved by prisoners are still visible in the far left corner of the courtyard above the bench. The museum now contains exhibits on clog-making, canary-breeding, silk-weaving, ale-brewing, and other bygone industries. A mock-up of a 1920s pharmacy sells sea sponges and bedpans. (Open Mon.-Sat. 10am-5pm. Admission 50p, students 25p, children 20p, half-price in winter.) Further down the street, the **Coleman Mustard Shop,** 3 Bridewell Alley (tel. 62 78 89), chronicles the rise and fall of one of old Norwich's most esoteric industries. Among the photographs of East Anglian mustard-plant fills and series of evolving mustard containers, you will find an interesting account of the innovative "Mustard Club" advertising scheme authored by mystery writer Dorothy L. Sayers. (Open Mon., Wed., and Fri.-Sat. 9am-5;30pm, Tues. 9:30am-5:30pm.)

Out at the University of East Anglia, 3 mi. west of town on Earlham Rd., is the **Sainsbury Centre for Visual Arts** (tel. 50 60 60). (Eastern Counties buses #526 and 527 leave from Castle Meadow every 15 min.; 25 min. ride; 75p). Sir Robert Sainsbury, former chairman of the supermarket chain, donated a superb personal collection of 20th-century and primitive art to the university in 1973. The collection includes works by Picasso, Moore, Degas, and young contemporary artists. (Open Tues.-Sun., noon-5pm. Admission 75p, students 40p.)

One of the prettiest sights in Norwich is the view of the city from **St. James Hill** near **Mousehold Heath,** a large public park about 1½mi. northeast of the city center, on the other side of the River Wensum. Alternatively, ascend **Kett's Heights,** just across Kett's Hill. The **Riverside Walk** follows the curving Wensum from Palace St. to Prince of Wales Rd. (Free pamphlet detailing walk available from tourist office.)

Entertainment

The best resources for entertainment information are the tourist office's publication *What's On in Norwich* (free) and the prescient *Preview,* available at newsagents (85p). Located next to the Assembly House on Theatre St., the **Theatre Royal** is being renovated, but should be open by late 1992.

The home of the Norwich Players, **Maddermarket Theatre** has revived the tradition of high-quality amateur drama. A beautiful building just behind Stranger's Hall, it marks the spot where, in 1599, Will Kemp (the great clown in Shakespeare's comedies) reached Norwich after a nine-day Morris dance from London. (Box office tel. 62 09 17. Tickets £1.50-5; matinees and student standbys (available after 7pm) £1.50. Open daily 10am-5pm, before performances until 7pm.) The **Norwich Puppet Theatre,** Whitefriars, puts on sophisticated and ingenious productions that appeal to adults and children alike. (Box office tel. 62 99 21. Tickets £3-3.50, children £2-2.50. Open Mon.-Sat. 10am-6pm, Sun. 10am-3pm, on performance days only. Check specifics with tourist office).

The Norwich Arts Centre, in Reeve's Yard off St. Benedict St. (tel. 66 03 52), presents jazz, cabaret, dance, concerts, and theater workshops. (Box office open Mon.-Fri. 10am-5pm, Sat. 2-5pm. £1.50-4, students £1 off most tickets.) Open only during the summer, the **Whiffler Theatre** presents a series of outdoor plays and concerts, as well as special afternoon performances for children in the colorful Castle Gardens. Norwich's several outdoor parks host a stream of festivals and folk fairs. Inquire at the tourist office about all outdoor events.

Few pubs or clubs in Norwich feature live music. The **Wilde Club** (tel. 66 03 52), attached to the Arts Centre, risks experimental bands on most Monday nights (£2-3). The **Festival House,** a pub at the intersection of St. George's, St. Andrew's and Prince's St., schedules live jazz on Friday and Saturday nights. **Henry's,** Rose

Lane (tel. 62 77 01), is a Samantha Fox-soaked disco frequented mostly by the under-20 crowd. Clubs metamorphose as fast as tadpoles—consult *Preview for the latest toads.*

Norfolk Broads

The **Norfolk Broads,** a network of channels and tributaries formed in the 14th century by the natural flooding of peat bogs, spread east and north of Norwich to the English Channel. This Environmentally Sensitive Area, rich in wildlife and nature reserves, is easily explored on foot or by boat. Five **nature trails** pass through different sections of the Broads. Pleasure boats of all sizes cruise the canals; it's possible to sail from one pub to the next all the way from Norwich to Great Yarmouth. The tourist offices in Norwich, Great Yarmouth (South Quay, tel. (0493) 84 21 95), and other villages in the area sell a helpful mini-guide to the Broads that describes various trails, waterways, and nature reserves (20p).

Wroxham, 7 mi. northeast of Norwich, is a good base for exploring the more remote areas of the Broads. You can get information from the **Hoveton Tourist Office,** Station Rd. (tel. (0603) 78 22 81; open Easter-Sept. daily 9am-1pm, 2-5pm; Oct. Tues.-Sat. 9am-5pm). It also has lists of boat-rentals and of the many campsites scattered through the area. From Wroxham, **Broads Tours** (tel. (0603) 78 22 07), the Bridge, run one- to 3½-hour cruises through the Broads. (Most at 11am amd 2:30pm; more frequent hours in high season. £2.25-4.50, children £1.75-3.25.) In Norwich, **Southern River Steamers** (tel. 50 12 20) offers cruises to Surlingham Broad in the summer and autumn, departing from quays near the cathedral and train station. (Leave Elm Hill Quay 2:15pm; leave Foundry Bridge Quay (near train) 7:30pm. 2½hrs. Disabled access. Adults £4.95, children £2.95). **Cley-next-to-the-Sea** is particularly popular among birdwatchers. Inquire at the Royal Society for the Protection of Birds, Aldwych House, Bethel St., Norwich NR2 1NR (tel. (0603) 61 59 20).

To reach the Broads, take a train from Norwich, Lowestoft, or Great Yarmouth to the smaller towns of Beccles, Cantley, Lingwood, Oulton Broad, Salhouse, or Wroxham. From Norwich, Norwich Cityline #51 leaves from St. Stephen's St. (Mon.-Sat. every hour 8:30am-5:41pm, last return at 5:38pm; about ½hr.; £1.20). Only Eastern Counties' #718 makes the trip on Sundays (4 per day 10:30am-7:30pm, last return at 7pm; ½hr.; £1.20).

King's Lynn

King's Lynn confronts the earth tones of the East Anglian countryside with a somber brick facade. This dockside city on the banks of the Great Ouse (pronounced, aptly enough, ooze), once a member of the Hanseatic League (a 17th-century version of the E.E.C.), borrows its Germanic look from such trading partners as Hamburg and Bremen; its architecture is dominated by straight lines in blackened red brick and slate roofs.

Arriving and Departing

In the county of Norfolk, King's Lynn (pop. 38,000) lies at the end of the main rail route from London's Liverpool St. Station via Cambridge and Ely. The train station (tel. 77 20 21) is on Blackfriars Rd., to the east of most attractions. Ten to twelve trains make a 2½-hr. day run between Lynn and London (single £16.14; saver return £20; change at Cambridge. From Cambridge, 1 hr.; single £6.20, day return £10.50).

Rail and coach links run from the train station to Peterborough for connections to other lines (6 per day, Sun. 2 per day; 65 min.; single £4.90, ages 5-16 £2.45, day return £5.80, ages 5-16 £2.90; discounts available with Railcards). Check the dispenser at the entrance to the station for free city maps. To get to the Tourist Office, walk half a block south on Blackfriars Rd. to St. John's Terrace, turn right and walk 3 blocks to High St. and turn left.

Buses from Cambridge, Norwich, Ely, and Peterborough arrive at **Vancouver Centre** (tel. 77 23 43), also east of the city center. To get to the tourist office, walk out the rear entrance onto Broad St. and turn left. Turn right onto New Conduit St., then left onto High St. The walk is a total of about 4 blocks.

Orientation and Practical Information

King's Lynn's western boundary is the Great Ouse, the endpoint of one of England's five major river systems (others are those terminating at Hull, London, Bristol, and Liverpool). One block inland are King St. and Queen St. (a single hermaphroditic thoroughfare), which run from the Tuesday Market Place (a square) at the north edge of town to the Saturday Market Place (a street), near the tourist office. One more block inland, and also connecting the two markets, is High St., which, together with New Conduit St., Broad St., and a stretch of Norfolk St. forms a bustling quadrilateral pedestrian-only precinct. This area takes on the air of Dodge City in the evening after shops have closed. Just south of the Tuesday Market, Norfolk St. runs perpendicular to the river and becomes Gaywood Rd.

The **tourist office** (tel. 76 30 44), housed in the Trinity Guildhall on the Saturday Market Pl., gives out free accommodations lists, books rooms (£1), provides bus and train information, and houses exhibits (see Sights). (Open Mon.-Thurs. 9:15am-5pm, Fri. 9:15am-4:30pm, Sat. 9:15am-5pm; May-Sept. also Sun. 10am-3pm.) For **currency exchange,** try Barclay's in Tuesday Market (open Mon.-Fri. 9:30am-4:30pm, Sat. 9:30am-noon) or any of the banks along New Conduit St. The **post office** is at the corner of Broad St. and New Conduit St. Lynn's **postal code** is PE30 1AA; its **telephone code** is 0553. The **hospital** (tel. 76 62 66) is on Gayton Rd. In an **emergency** dial 999 (no coins required).

Accommodations and Food

A very pleasant **IYHF youth hostel** (tel. 77 24 61) occupies part of the 16th-century Thoresby College, on College Lane, just opposite the tourist office. (Open July-Aug. daily; Sept.-Oct. Fri.-Tues.; Feb.-March and Nov. to mid-Dec. Fri.-Sat.; April-June Fri.-Wed. Lockout 10am-5pm. Curfew 11pm. £5.90, ages 16-20 £4.70, under 16 £3.80.) B&Bs are a bit of a hike from the city center; the least expensive are clustered along Gaywood Rd., near the hospital. From the train station, turn right and walk along Blackfriar's Rd. When you reach Norfolk St., turn right and walk about ½mi. **Mrs. D.E. Child,** of "Oakview," 1-7 Tennyson Rd., a road off Gaywood after the stadium (tel. 77 11 80), runs a relaxed and friendly B&B. Say hello to Billy the Parrot (£12 per person). **Maranatha Guest House,** 115 Gaywood Rd. (tel. 77 45 96), has comfortable rooms with TV and washbasins. Singles £12, doubles or twins £20. The hostel often fills, so call a few days ahead. Late arrivals should consult the list of guesthouses posted outside the tourist office.

Some restaurants are closed Sunday and Monday evenings (look for a take-away or grocer instead), but are open on Wednesdays, when shops close early. The pink and plastic **La Mama's,** 110 High St. (tel. 69 15 12), one of the only places open Mondays, bakes decent pizzas (£3.15-10.15, open daily, 9:30am-11:30pm). Behind the Guildhall of St. George, 27-29 King St., spreads the **Riverside Restaurant,** with both indoor and outdoor seating. The carefully prepared food makes up for the rather less appetizing view of the Ouse. Quick, inexpensive lunches £3.15-8. Dinner entrees are £12, and on theater evenings (the Guildhall also houses the King's Lynn Arts Centre) supper for about £6 is available 6-10:30pm. Open Mon.-Sat. noon-2pm and 7-10pm.

In the basement of the hall, cavernous **Crofter's Coffee House** serves sandwiches and hot items (£1.15-3). Open Mon.-Sat. 9:30am-5pm.

The **Tudor Rose,** St. Nicholas St., off the Tuesday Market Pl., has a popular bar menu, including vegetarian specials (£1.50-3.25). **Holland and Barrett,** on the corner of Chapel and Norfolk St., has tasty take-away wholefood. Open Mon.-Sat. 9am-5:30pm.

For fresh fruits and vegetables, try the **markets** (roughly 8:30am-4pm) on Tuesday and Friday at the larger Tuesday Market Pl. on the north end of High St., or on Saturday at the Saturday Market Pl., across from the tourist office. You can pick your own fruits and berries at farms one to 5 mi. outside town. Check the *Lynn News and Advertiser* or the tourist office to see what's in season.

Sights

King's Lynn's most interesting buildings lie on the western edge of the city, not far from the Ouse. The huge 15th-century **Guildhall of St. George,** 27-29 King St., near the Tuesday Market, said to be the last surviving building in England where Shakespeare appeared in one of his own plays, is now home to the **King's Lynn Arts Centre,** which hosts performances, films, and art exhibits.

During the last week in July, the guildhall is home to the **King's Lynn Festival,** an orgy of classical and jazz music, along with ballet, puppet theater, and film presentations. (Tickets from £2.50-9, student standbys available 30 min. before curtain time for half-price. Get schedules from the Festival Office, 27 King St., King's Lynn, Norfolk PE30 1HA; tel. 77 35 78). The guildhall hosts theater and dance events and concerts during the rest of the year. (Box office open Mon.-Fri. 10am-5pm, Sat. 10am-1pm amd 2-4pm. Guildhall open Mon.-Fri. 10am-5pm, Sat. 10am-4pm. Free.)

The tourist office, in another 15th-century guildhall, holds two good exhibitions, the **Regalia Rooms** and the **Heritage Exhibition and Watercolour Collection,** which spice up the usual bus timetables and accommodations lists with some of the city's treasures. (Regalia Rooms open Mon.-Fri. 10am-4pm, Sun. 10am-3pm; Oct. and May, Mon.-Fri. 10am-4pm; Nov.-April Fri.-Sat. 10am-4pm. Heritage Exhibition and Watercolour Collection open Mon.-Sat. 9:15am-4:30pm, Sun. 10am-3pm; Oct.-May, Mon.-Sat. 9:15am-4:30pm. Admission for both 45p, children, students, and seniors 25p.) Across the street is **St. Margaret's Church** (tel. 77 28 58), bits of which date from the 13th century. The northwest tower inside slouches alarmingly, the result of a poor foundation. High water marks notched in stone outside the west door are reminders of East Anglia's vulnerability to flooding. The little **Lynn Museum,** Old Market St. (tel. 77 50 01), adjacent to the bus station, exhibits historical tidbits such as medieval shoes, old chamberpots, and an ancient bone wool-carder in the shape of a hand. (Open Mon.-Sat. 10am-5pm. Admission 60p, ages 5-16 30p, students and seniors 50p). The **Museum of Social History,** 27 King St., more interesting than the Lynn Museum, reveals what seems in retrospect to have been the drudgery of medieval and Victorian home life. (Open Tues.-Sat. 10am-5pm. Admission 50p, students 40p). Although it looks like a space rocket, the octogonal **Greyfriars Tower,** St. James St., is in fact the final remnant of a 14th-century monastery.

Glass-blowing in this area dates from the 14th century, and a visit to the **Caithness Crystal Factory** (tel. (0553) 76 51 11/6) illustrates the process. The factory lies just east of King's Lynn at the Hardwick Industrial Estate on Scania Way. From July 25-Sept. 3 you can get there on the bus to Heachum. (Tours Mon.-Fri. 9:30am-4:30pm, 70p.)

Near King's Lynn

The territory of the wealthy, punctuated by sumptuous (and visitable) mansions, gives way to wildlife country as the road leading north from King's Lynn bends east to flank the northern Norfolk coast.

A holiday home of the Royal Family since 1862, **Sandringham** (tel. (0553) 77 26 75) and its grounds are open to the public except when in use by the Royal Family. Sandringham's extensive gardens and two nature trails attract many British holiday-makers to this spot just 10 mi. north of King's Lynn. The best time to visit is during the **flower show** in the last week of July. Write to Mr. J. Annison, The Dene, West Newton, King's Lynn (tel. Dershingham 54 05 75). (Open late April-Sept. Mon.-Thurs. 11am-4:45pm, Sun. noon-4:45pm; grounds open ½hr. before house and close ¼hr. later. Admission to house, grounds, and museum £2.20, seniors £1.70, children £1.40; to grounds and museum only £1.70, seniors £1.30, children £1.) The house and grounds are closed for a couple of weeks in July; check with the Lynn tourist office before you set off. Eastern Counties bus #411 serves Sandringham from King's Lynn (Mon.-Sat. 8 per day, last return 6pm, Sun. 5 per day, last return 7:30pm; 25 min.).

Castle Rising, a solidly intimidating keep on top of massive earthworks, was once home to Queen Isabella after she had plotted the murder of her husband, Edward II. (Open daily 10am-6pm; Oct.-March Tues.-Sun. 10am-4pm. Admission 95p, seniors and students 75p, children 45p. Eastern Counties buses #410 and 411: Mon.-Sat. 22 per day, plus a few that don't stop at the castle, last return 8:46pm, Sun. 5 per day, last return 6:25pm; 15 min.)

Built in the mid-18th century for Sir Robert Walpole, the first prime minister of England, **Houghton Hall** is a magnificent example of Palladian architecture, with lavish paintings, tapestries, and "the most sublime bed ever designed." The manor, 14 mi. northwest of King's Lynn, is occupied today by the Marquess of Cholmondeley (CHUM-ley). House open Easter-late Sept. Thurs., Sun., and bank holidays 1-5:30pm; grounds open ½hr. earlier. Admission to house and grounds £3, seniors £2.50, children 5-16 £1.50, under 5 free. Either take a bus (Mon.-Sat. 2 per day, last return 5:30pm; 45 min.) or hitch from King's Lynn to Harpley, then walk 2 mi. north to Houghton village.

The northern **Norfolk coast,** with its expanses of beach, sand dune, and salt marsh, stretches from **Hunstanton,** 16 mi. north of Lynn, to **Wells-next-the-Sea** and beyond. Bird sanctuaries and nature preserves abound; the **Scolt Head Island** reserve and the **Holme Bird Observatory** are superb. Buses #410 and #411 run from Vancouver Centre in King's Lynn to Hunstanton (Mon.-Sat. every ½hr., Sun. every 2 hr.). An **IYHF youth hostel,** 15 Avenue Rd., Hunstanton, Norfolk PE36 5BW (tel. (0485) 53 20 61) is in the center of Hunstanton near the Wash. (£5.60, ages 16-20 £4.70. Open July-Aug. daily; April-June Mon.-Sat.; Feb.-March and Sept.-Oct. Wed.-Sun.; Nov. Fri.-Sat.) Holme is 3 mi. to the east. Scolt Head Island is accessible from Brancaster on the Staithe (an Anglo-Saxon word meaning "pier") 10 mi. east along the A149. **Mervyn Nudds** (tel. 21 06 38) runs a boat from the Staithe to Scolt Head.

The **National Trust Information Centre** (tel. (0485) 21 07 19), next to the Dial House, rents bikes (£3.50 per day, £10 deposit; tandems £7 per day). Open April-June Sat.-Sun. 10am-6pm; July-Aug. 10am-6pm. The King's Lynn tourist office has some information on excursions to surrounding areas.

Peterborough

A stop in Peterborough given the city's position at the juncture of several rail lines, with the A1 Motorway passing through it, is hardly inconvenient. While perhaps not a destination in its own right, the city and its cathedral provide a pleasant diversion from the road.

As you enter the gate of the **cathedral** (tel. (0733) 433 42), you will pass under the little chapel of St. Nicholas and emerge to a spectacular view of the 13th-century Norman west front, added onto a 12th-century main structure. The painted ceiling is one of the oldest and finest in England. The diamond shapes that fill its wooden span enclose figures of saints, bishops, and devils. At the far end of the sanctuary, John Wastell's 15th-century addition, the **New Building,** features the fan vaulting he also used in King's College Chapel at Cambridge. Also in the cathedral are the tomb of Catherine of Aragon, first of Henry VIII's six wives, and the one-time tomb of her great-niece, Mary, Queen of Scots. Displays tell the stories of these unfortunate women. (Open May-Sept. daily 10am-4pm; cathedral open in summer daily 7am-8pm; in winter 7am-evensong. Tours of cathedral May-Sept. Sat. at 11am. £1 donation requested. Evensong is held Mon.-Tues. and Thurs.-Fri. at 5:30pm, Sat.-Sun. at 3:30pm.)

The **Peterborough Museum and Art Gallery,** Priestgate (tel. 55 50 98), has a varied collection, including elaborate artwork crafted from cheap materials by some creative prisoners of war detained near Peterborough during the Napoleonic Wars. Open Tues.-Sat. 10am-5pm. Free.

On the outskirts of town, the **Flag Fen Bronze Age excavation** (tel. 31 34 14), proves conclusively that rotting 3000-year-old timbers can be interesting. The ongoing project has dug out bits of a Bronze Age raised village, inconsiderately covered by Roman road builders. (Open April-Oct. 11am-4pm. Admission adults £2.15, seniors £1.95, ages 5-17 £1.50, under 5 free. 20 min. guided tour. Take Viscount bus #30 from Bay 14, every 2 hr. 10:30am-4:30pm; 55p. The site is a 15. min. walk from the bus stop.)

At the center of the city is a pedestrianized area composed of Cowgate, Long Causeway, and Bridge St. The **tourist office,** 45 Bridge St. (tel. 31 73 36) has an accommodations service (£1.10) and a list of places to stay posted in the window. A free map and other brochures are available. (Open Mon.-Fri. 9am-5pm, Sat. 10am-4pm). Exchange money at any of the banks near the tourist office (open Mon.-Fri. 9:30am-3:30pm, Sat. 9:30am-noon). On the north and west sides of the pedestrain zone is the enormous Queensgate Shopping Centre, which also houses the **bus station** (tel. 23 71 41). Buses to London (every 2 hrs., 2½hrs., single or day return £7.75) and Portsmouth, changing at London (every 2 hr.; 6½hrs.; single or day return £15.50). The **train station** (tel. 681 81) is on the other side of the shopping center from the tourist office and across Bourges Blvd. (to London every ¼hr.; single £14.50, saver return £17). The cathedral lies to the east of the center. To reach the cathedral and tourist office from either station, cut through the mall to the pedestrian precinct and follow the signs. The **post office** is in Cathedral Sq.; Peterborough's **postal code** is PE1 1AA; the **telephone code** is 0733.

Mrs. J. Paylor, 3 Scotney St. (tel. 542 32), has B&B singles or twins for £9 per person. Walk about 2 mi. north on Lincoln Rd. and take the last right onto Scotney St., or take the Queensgate-Walton minishuttle from Bay 10A (Mon.-Sat. 8:30am-5:30pm every ½hr.). The basic but friendly **Minister** hotel, 15-17 Eastfield Rd. (tel. 34 63 41), east of town, has singles for £12 and doubles for £22 per person. The nearest **IYHF youth hostel** is in the village of **Thurlby** (tel. (0778) 42 55 88) about 15 mi. north on the A15, at 16 High St. (Lockout 10am-5pm. Curfew 11pm. £4.60, ages 16-20 £3.70. Open Fri.-Wed.; Nov.-March Fri.-Sat.) The Delaine bus runs to Thurlby from Bay 14 Mon.-Sat. 7:30am-11pm, 20 per day; Sun. 12:05-6pm, 4 per day (45 min.; £1.30, return £1.70); however, transport back to Peterborough from Thurlby might make the hostel an inconvenient place to stay unless you have a car. The unusually attractive branch of **Holland and Barrett,** 33 Long Causeway, serves wholefood take-away (open Mon.-Tues. and Thurs.-Sat. 9am-5:30pm, Wed. 9:30am-5:30pm).

Near Peterborough

Two of the statlier homes in England lie close to Peterborough. **Kirby Hall** (tel. (0536) 20 32 30), about 25 mi. west of Peterborough, once rivaled the grandest homes of Italy. The house is a fine Elizabethan structure, and the 17th-century gardens are well-maintained. (Open Tues.-Sun. 10am-6pm; Oct.-March Tues.-Sun. 10am-4pm. Admission 95p, seniors and students 75p, children 45p.) Hitch from Peterborough to Oundle on the A605, then take the A427 to Weldon and walk the remaining 2 mi., or take a National Express coach from Peterborough to Corby (daily at 9:10am, return at 7:15pm; 45 min.; single or day return £3.59) and walk the remaining 3 mi.

Burghley House (tel. (0780) 524 51) claims to be "the largest and grandest house of the first Elizabethan age." Built in the mid-16th century by William Cecil, the first Lord Burghley and, suspiciously, Lord High Treasurer under Queen Elizabeth I, the house is lavishly furnished with 17th- and 18th-century furniture. (Open Easter-Sept. daily 11am-5pm. Admission £3.80, children £2.30, tour included.) Burghley is easily accessible from Peterborough. Hitch 13 mi. on the A1 or take the Delaine bus from Bay 9 (Mon.-Sat. every 2 hr.; 45 min.; £1.10, day return £1.50). Trains also run daily to Stamford (6am-9pm every hr.). From Stamford, turn off St. Martin's St. onto Bornack Rd. The house itself is over a mile away, but an entrance to the grounds lies just outside town.

The national historic landmark of **Stamford** (pop. 20,000) is a sight in its own right. Centuries without interference have left hundreds of fine Georgian and Jacobean houses lining the town's narrow streets. The churches of **St. Martin** and **St. Mary** merit particular attention. The **Stamford Brewery Museum** (tel. (0780) 521 86), in the old brewery on All Saints' St., demonstrates the beer-making process; you can taste the results during serving hours. (Open April-Sept. Wed.-Sun. 10am-4pm. Admission £1.20.) In June and July, the **Stamford Shakespeare Company** (tel. (0780) 561 33) performs in an outdoor amphitheatre at Tolethorpe Hall, 2 mi. north of Stamford on the A6121. Tickets £5-7.50. The company also sometimes takes on-stage help. The **tourist office,** Broad St., Stamford Museum PE9 1PJ (tel. (0780) 556 11), books B&Bs (90p) or gives out free lists (open April-Sept. Mon.-Sat. 10am-5pm, Sun. 2-5pm).

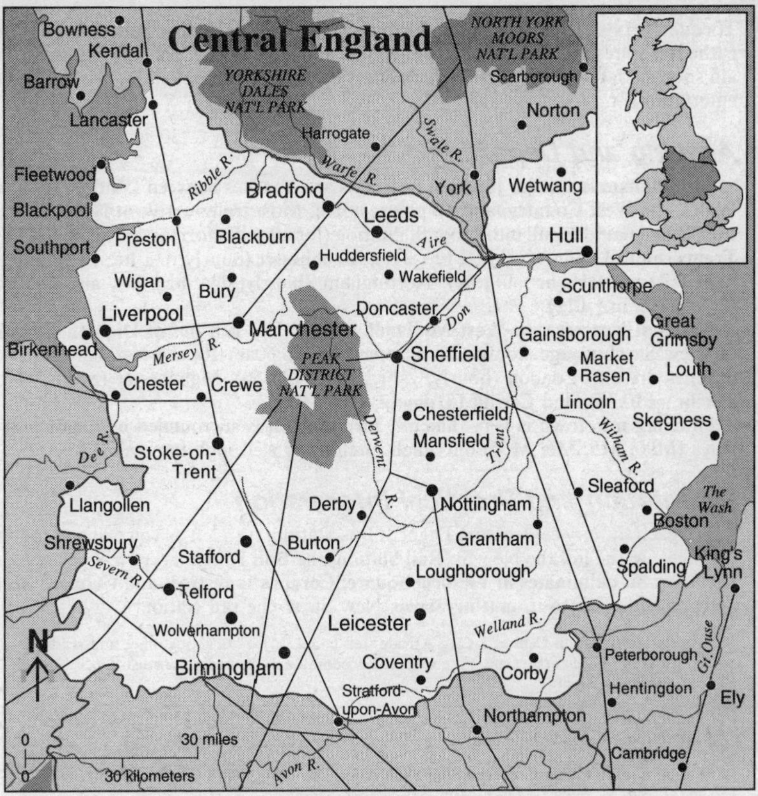

Central England

In 1800 there were two cities in England; by 1913 there were 50. When England was the "workshop of the world," much of the shop floor was located in a region of rapidly growing cities in the middle of the country. The "dark Satanic Mills" that William Blake foresaw did indeed overrun the Midlands, but they repaid the region with prominence and prosperity. Wool, automobiles, bicycles, and armaments were the pillars of the region's economy for more than 150 years. The area remains the industrial heart of England despite growing unemployment and a dwindling population. However, the description "industrial" should not automatically disqualify this region from your route: Bradford has a terrific photography museum, Leeds some wonderful architecture, and Sheffield. . .well, Sheffield is near the Peak District. Besides, not all of this region is rooted in industry—cities like Lincoln and Chester tell some of their stories in Latin. Unfortunately, though the Liverpool-Manchester-Leeds-Sheffield metropolis is served by an efficient network of interlocking commuter rail lines, receding as far as the center of the Peak District, most of these modern cities lack youth hostels and cheap B&Bs.

Birmingham

Home of the Industrial Revolution, Birmingham is geared more towards commerce and industry than tourism. Although no longer the "vast forge" that De

Tocqueville visited in the 1830s, Birmingham boasts a skyline punctured not by cathedral spires but rather by a rotund glass and steel Coca-Cola building. As Britain's second largest city, Birmingham offers bargain-filled markets and rich cultural entertainment.

Arriving and Departing

Birmingham is a major junction for trains and coaches between London, Central Wales, the West Country, and all points north. Most trains arrive at **New St. Station;** the remainder pull into Moor St. Station (for all rail information call 643 2711.) Trains run to London (3/hr.; 2 hr.; £17), Manchester (hourly; 1½ hr.; £12), Liverpool (12/day; 1½ hr.; £11.50), Nottingham (hourly; 1¼ hr.; £7), and Oxford (2/hr.; 1¼ hr.; £12).

National Express and **West Midlands** bus services run out of **Digbeth Station** on New St. (Luggage storage £1.10, open daily 6:50am-10pm.) National Express coaches drive to London (hourly; 2 hr.½ hr.; £11.50), Manchester (every 2 hr.; 2¼ hr.; £10.25), and Cardiff (5/day; 2¼ hr.; £16).

Hitching into town is very difficult: Birmingham is surrounded by major highways (M90, M5, M6, M54) on which hitching is well nigh impossible.

Orientation and Practical Information

To reach the city center from Digbeth Bus Station, turn left as you exit and follow the signs up the hill the New St. Rail Station; the Bull Ring market will be on your left. New St. culminates in **Victoria Square; Corporation Street** and **Colmore Row** are perpendicular to it, cutting across New St. at the rail station.

Tourist Information Center: 2 City Arcade (tel. 643 2514). A ticketing office and scads of information on the arts scene. Free map and accommodations booking or list. Open Mon.-Sat. 9:30am-5:30pm.

Tours: 1¼-hr. tour of the city center, departing every ½ hr. between 10:30am-3pm from the tourist office. £2.

Budget Travel: Campus Travel, in the YHA Adventure Shop, 90-98 Corporation St. (tel. 233 4611), Bull St. Subway. Open Mon.-Sat. 9:30am-5:30pm.

Buses: Digbeth Station (tel. 622 4373). **West Midlands** (tel. 236 8313) serves Coventry and Wolverhampton. Office open Mon.-Thurs. 8:10am-7:15pm, Fri. 8:10am-8:15pm.

Financial Services: Barclay's, 56 New St. (tel. 632 5721). Open Mon.-Fri. 9am-4:30pm, Sat. 9am-noon. **Thomas Cook,** Corporation St. (tel. 236 9711) or New St. (tel. 643 3120). Open Mon.-Sat. 9am-5:30pm. **American Express,** 17 Martineau Sq. (tel. 233 21 41), through the arcade, across from Rackhams's. Open Mon.-Fri. 9am-5:30pm, Sat. 9am-5pm.

Emergency: Dial 999; no coins required.

Hospital: General Hospital, Steelhouse Lane (tel. 236 8611).

Pharmacy: Boots, Big Top, 2 New St. (tel. 631 2322). Open Mon.-Fri. 8:45am-9pm, Sat. 8:45am-6pm, Sun. 10am-2pm.

Police: Steelhouse Lane (tel. 236 5000).

Post Office: Victoria Sq. (tel. 644 8652). Open Mon.-Fri. 9am-5pm, Sat. 9am-noon. **Postal Code:** B2 4TX.

Telephone Code: 021.

Train Station: New St. or **Moor St.** (all rail info, tel. 643 2711). Most trains go through New St. **Public Transportation Office:** In the New St. Station (information tel. 200 2700). Local transit map and bus schedules. Day bus and train pass £2.25; bus only £1.50. Open daily 6am-11pm.

Accommodations and Food

Hotels in the city mainly serve convention-goers, and budget B&Bs are rare—try to book through the tourist office. Call ahead to reserve a place at the YMCA or YWCA—they are often booked solid. The hostel may seem eerily deserted because of its high price.

IYHF youth hostel, Cambrian Halls, Brindley Dr. (tel. 233 3044). Take any bus (50p) from Rackham's (#3,10,21,22,23,25,29) to the Botanical Gardens; ask to be let off at the Polytechnic. Single-rooms and dorms with gourmet kitchens. Lockout 10am-5pm. £9. Key deposit £5. Open July 10-Sept. 25. To book before July 9, call the Stratford-Upon-Avon hostel (tel. (0789) 297 093).

YWCA, 27 Norfolk Rd. (tel 454 8134). Take bus #9 from Colmore Row. Singles for women and men £6.50/day, £33/week. £10 key deposit, 50p "membership" fee required. A second one at 5 Stone Rd. (tel. 440 2924). Take bus #61-63 to the stop after Belgrave Rd. £8.

YMCA, 300 Reservoir Rd. (tel. 373 19 37). Take bus #104 to Six Ways in Erdington. Another **YMCA** is at 200 Bunburg Rd. (tel. 475 62 18). Take bus #61-63 to Church Rd., Northfield. Singles in a B&B for men and women, £11.75/night. Dinner £2.95. £55/week includes full board.

Grasmere Guest House, 37 Serpentine Rd., Harborne (tel. 427 4546). Tidy rooms. To get there, take bus #3 or 21 from Coronation St. £13.

Lyby, 14/16 Barnsley Rd., Edgbaston (tel. 429 4487). Spacious and well-equipped rooms. Take bus #9 from Corporation St. to King's Head Pub, walk up the street across the road from King's Head, and ask directions at the next pub on your left. £13.

Stirling Lodge, 66-68 Stirling Rd., Edgbaston (tel. 456 2079). Firm mattresses and soft pillows for £12- 5.

Birmingham's eateries vacillate between cheap 'n fast, and expensive 'n executive. Though there are no supermarkets in town, bakeries and fruit stores surround the markets. The **Little Pub Company,** a basic foodstuffs chain with burgers for £3.50-5.50, has outlets throughout the city. (Open 11am-2pm and 6-11:30pm.) The **Belvedere,** at the Pallasades Shopping Centre, convenient to New St. Station, concocts pasta dishes under £3.65 and good pizza specialties for around £3.25. (Open Mon.-Sat. 8am-9pm.) The **Amazon Cafe,** 54 Allison St., is a decidedly green vegetarian restaurant. They even grow their own vegetables. Lunches £2-4. (Open Mon.-Sat. 8am-6pm.)

Sights

Birmingham is a commercial city that pays small tribute to its industrial heritage, instead drawing bargain-hunting Britons from across the country to its many markets. When markets are open, the area from New St. Train Station to Digbeth Bus Station becomes a psychedelic ant farm of fruit, fish, and fabric mongers. The covered **Bull Ring Market** mainly sells edibles (Mon.-Sat. 9am-4:30pm); farther on, the **flea market** (Tues., Fri., or Sat.) purveys more cheap items than used goods; the indoor **Rag Market** is probably the most entertaining of the three, with rows of inexpensive vintage clothing and antiques up for lively barter.

At the end of Newhall St. artisans work in the historic Jewellery Quarter, a monument to the city's metalworking past. The **City Museum and Art Gallery** at Chamberlain Sq. off Colmore Row (tel. 235 2834), boasts Big Brum, a cousin to London's Big Ben clock tower. Exhibits include pre-Raphaelite art as well as archaeological, ethnographic, and local history rooms. (Open Mon.-Sat. 10am-5pm, Sun. 2-5pm. Free.) Off Colmore Row on Newhall St., the **Museum of Science and Industry** (tel. 236 1022) wholeheartedly acknowledges the city's woefully ignored industrial past. Exhibits include the only surviving working James Watt engine built in 1779. (Open Mon.-Sat. 9:30am-5pm, Sun. 2-5pm. Free.) The **Barber Institute of Fine Arts,** at the University of Birmingham, University Rd., displays a stunning array of works from many eras, schools, and countries. Artists include Bellini, Canaletto, Rubens,

Turner, Gainsborough, Monet and Degas. Take bus #61, 62 or 63. (Open Sept.-June Mon.-Fri. 10am-5pm, Sat. 10am-9pm. Free.)

The **Botanical Gardens and Glasshouses,** Westbourne Rd. (tel. 454 1860), is a 12-acre green oasis in this exhaust-tinctured city. (Open daily 10am-dusk or 8pm, whichever is earlier. £1.35; seniors and ISIC-toting students 65p. Take bus #3, 10, 21, 22, 23, 25, or 29.) **Aston Hall** (tel. 327 0062) showcases a "long hall" of Jacobean architecture flanked by heavy tapestries. There are cannon marks on the Great Staircase, dating from the Civil War attacks. (Open March 24-Nov. 4 daily 2-5pm. Take bus #7.) Those who never tire of castle ruins can take bus #21 or 29 to the **Weoley Castle Ruins,** once a fortified manor dating to the 13th century. (Open late March-Oct. Tues.-Fri 2-5pm.)

Entertainment

The **Hippodrome Theatre,** Hurst St., applauds Birmingham's rich theatrical tradition. Originally a variety music hall that featured big-name vaudevillians, the Hippodrome recently underwent major renovations and is now one of Britain's leading opera houses. (Box office tel. 622 7486. Open Mon.-Sat. 10am-8pm. Half-price senior, student, and standby tickets. Two-for-one tickets on first-night performances, £5-20.) Less grandiose but justly celebrated theaters in Birmingham are the **Alexandra,** on Suffolk St. next to the Albany Hotel (box office tel. 633 3325), which hosts comedies and Broadway hits, and the **Birmingham Repertory Theatre,** on Broad St. (box office tel. 236 4455; open Mon.-Sat. 10am-8pm; student tickets for weekday performances). The experimental theater and cinema at the **Midland Arts Centre** shows avant-garde art. Seats range from £2.50 to 6.50, and discounted films are offered in the afternoon (4pm, 5:30pm, 6pm; £1.95; box office tel. 440 3838). Aston University's **Triangle Cinema** (tel. 359 3979) shows hearty-arty films (£2.70; seniors £2; students £2.50; matinee £2), and has a pleasant café for cakes and conversation (open daily 2:30-8:30pm). Ticket information for all Birmingham theaters is available from the Convention and Visitor Information Bureau (tel. 643 2514). Pick up a **Birmingham Entertainment Bulletin** at the tourist information center.

'Tis the season to be jazzy during the first two weeks in July. The **Birmingham Jazz Festival** brings over 200 bands, singers, and instrumentalists to town. (For information call 454 70 20.) The world-class **City of Birmingham Symphony Orchestra,** in the new Symphony Hall at the Convention Centre, is conducted by the extremely talented and outstandingly young Simon Rattle (tickets £5-18). A Youth Savers Card (£3; available with student ID) is valid for a year of half-price tickets. The box office is in the town hall (Victoria Sq.; tel. 236 3889). **Bobby Brown's The Club,** 52 Gas St. (tel. 643 2673), attracts an energetic student crowd. Industrial cities breed good music; the leaflets plastered all over town are the best guide to local bands.

Near Birmingham

Abraham Darby first smelted iron using coke as a catalyst in 1709 at **Ironbridge Gorge,** 35 mi. northwest of Birmingham in **Telford,** between Wolverhampton and Shrewsbury. You can still see the furnace where Darby's innovation sparked the Industrial Revolution; the bridge spanning the gorge was the first ever built of iron.

A number of sights and museums champion the era of industry, including **Blists Hill,** an open-air Victorian museum. (£4.75, seniors £4, students £3.50. Open April-Oct. daily 10am-6pm; off-season hours fluctuate—call (095 245) 35 22 weekdays, 27 51 weekends.) A "Passport" to all sights related to the Industrial Revolution (Blists Hill, Coalport China Museum, Jackfield Tile Museum, Tar Tunnel, Museum of Iron, and Rosehill House Museum) admits you to any of them in any order at any time. (£7, seniors £5.75, students £4.)

The **Iron Bridge youth hostel (IYHF)** (tel. (0952) 433 281) is 1 mi. from the gorge. Walk up the B4380 towards Shrewsbury, turn right onto Coalbrookdale, and right again at Paradise. Evening meal available. (£7, ages 16-20 £5.90. Open March-Oct. daily; Feb. and Nov.-Dec. Mon.-Sat.)

Lincoln

To explore Lincoln is to unfold the quilt of English history since Roman times. Cobbled medieval streets climb uphill past half-timbered Tudor houses to Lincoln's imposing 12th-century cathedral. The towering Minster and the Norman castle which crown the hill are relative newcomers to a city which was built as a settlement for retired Roman legionnaires and paid tribute to the Danes.

Arriving and Departing

Lincoln sits on one of the rail routes from London to York, and has decent connections with each. (To London: 22/day 6am-9:45pm, Sun. 8/day 11:10am-9:05pm; single £26, saver return £34. To York: 14/day 6:56am-8:42pm, Sun. one at 12:05pm; single £12.50, return £15-19.) There are some direct trips to London, but usually you'll have to take the fairly slow local train from Lincoln to Nottingham, Doncaster, or Newark (about 1 hr. from each) and change there. National Express runs coaches to London (3/day; 4 hr.; single or economy return £14.75).

Orientation and Practical Information

Roman and Norman military engineers were attracted to the summit of Castle Hill; the later engineers who put in the railway preferred its base. As a result, Lincoln is somewhat split between its historic and affluent acropolis to the north, and the lower town which largely consists of cottages built near the railway for industrial workers. There are two tourist offices, one centered between castle and cathedral on the hill, the other near the rail and coach stations below. To reach the lower tourist office, turn left from the train station and right onto High St.; from the bus station go through the shopping arcade onto High St. High St. is renamed the Strait, Steep Hill, and eventually Bailgate as it climbs; along it are both tourist offices, most attractions, and many shops and restaurants.

Tourist Information Center: Main Office, 9 Castle Hill, LN1 3AA (tel. 52 98 28), near cathedral. About a 10-min. walk up High St. to the top of the fairly steep Steep Hill. Accommodations service £1.10, plus a list of guesthouses. Several free publications are available, including *Where to Stay* and the very detailed *Places of Interest.* An extremely helpful staff provides information about the city, Lincolnshire, and nearby counties. (Open Mon.-Thurs. 9am-5:30pm, Fri. 9am-5pm, Sat.-Sun. 10am-5pm.) The downhill office at Cornhill (tel. 51 29 71), off High St., provides the same services, but is not open on Sundays.

Tours: July-Sept. Thurs.-Sat. at 2:30pm, 1½ hr., £1. Leave from Exchequergate, across from the main tourist office.

Bus and Coach Station: National Express (tel. 53 44 44) stops at the **City Bus station** off St. Mary's St. opposite the railway station. Local and regional buses serve both the City and **St. Mark's Bus Stations** off High St. Grantham buses leave from St. Mark's (open Mon.-Fri. 8:30am-5pm, Sat. 8:30am-4pm).

Currency Exchange: Thomas Cook, 4 Cornhill Pavement, off High St. near the tourist office. Open Mon.-Tues. and Thurs.-Sat. 9am-5:30pm, Wed. 9:30am-5:30pm. **Barclay's,** 316 High St., near lower tourist office. Open Mon.-Fri. 9:30am-4:30pm, Sat. 9:30am-noon.

Emergency: Dial 999; no coins required.

Hospital: County Hospital, St. Anne's Rd. (tel. 51 25 12).

Launderettes: Maytag, 8 Burton Rd., at Westgate near the cathedral. Wash £1, dry 20p. Open daily at 8:30am; Mon.-Fri. last wash 7pm, Sat.-Sun. last wash 4pm.

Pharmacy: Boots, High St. Open Mon.-Tues. and Thurs.-Sat. 8:45am-5:30pm, Wed. 9am-5:30pm.

Police: Beaumont Fee, near City Hall (tel. 299 11).

Post Office: Guildhall St. (tel. 322 88). Open Mon.-Tues. and Thurs.-Fri. 9am-5:30pm, Wed. 9:30am-5:30pm, Sat. 9am-12:30pm. **Postal Code:** LN1 1AA.

Telephone Code: 0522.

Train Station: Central Station, St. Mary's St. (tel. 53 95 02), near High St. Lockers 30-50p. Travel Centre open daily 8:30am-5:30pm.

Accommodations

Carline Rd. and Yarborough Rd., west of the castle and cathedral, have many B&Bs. To get to Yarborough Road from the lower tourist office, walk up High St., under the stonebow, to Corporation St. Turn left, and Corporation will become West Parade. Bear right at the traffic triangle and you will be on Yarborough. Carline Road feeds into Yarborough halfway up the hill. Call ahead from June through September.

IYHF youth hostel, 77 S. Park (tel. 52 20 76), opposite South Common at the end of Canwick Rd. Veer left from the train station, then go right onto Pelham Bridge, which becomes Canwick Rd. Take the first right after the traffic lights at South Park Ave. A 10-15 min. hike. A top-notch, relaxing hostel across the street from a park and golf course, somewhat removed from the main tourist area. Open July-Aug. daily; April-June and Sept. to mid-Dec. Mon.-Sat.; Feb.-March Tues.-Sat.; reception closed 10am-5pm; available beds posted outside. Curfew 11pm. £7, ages 16-20 £5.90. Cafeteria meals 5-8pm.

YMCA, St. Rumbold's St. (tel. 281 54), near the bus and train stations. Rooms in modern block are quite comfortable with a dash of luxury; those in the older building are basic and rather grotty. No curfew. Men and women. Singles B&B £10. A few twins £7/person. Room deposit £2.

Mayfield Guest House, 213 Yarborough Rd. (tel. 53 37 32). From the rear entrance on Mill St. it's a short, level walk to the castle. Cheerful rooms and gracious hosts. B&B £13/person for single, double, or twin, most with toilet and shower.

Carline Guest House, Mrs. Pritchard, 3 Carline Rd. (tel. 53 04 22). Affable, welcoming atmosphere halfway up the hillside. Some rooms with TV, tea, clock radio, and hair dryer, most with private shower. B&B £14 for a single with hall bath, £16.50/person in a double.

Admiral Guest House, Mrs. Robertson, 18 Nelson St. (tel. 54 44 67) in the lower part of town. Follow Newland Rd., which becomes Newland St. W. after the Avenue; pass the Vine Inn, and turn left. Cheery proprietor has small but pleasant rooms with TV and tea in each, and a shower in most. Renovations planned for 1992. £11.50/person. Call ahead.

Bradford Guest House, 67 Monks Rd. (tel. 52 39 47). Terraced house on a busy, grey street, 5 min. from High St. Soulful pink rooms with TV, tea, hot and cold water. Singles £14, other rooms £11/person.

Food

The Sincil St. Markets, by the bus station, sell fresh produce, as well as clothing and other goods. The outdoor section is open Mon.-Sat. 8:30am-about 4:30pm; the indoor market keeps the same hours but is closed on Wednesdays.

Lion and Snake, 79 Bailgate, up by the cathedral. A fine restorative pint and meal (£3.50-5). Open Mon.-Sat. 11am-11pm, Sun. noon-3pm, and 7:30-10:30pm. Food served noon-2pm, 6-8pm.

Wig and Mitre, 29 Steep Hill, near the cathedral in a 14th-century building. Downstairs, sandwiches and breakfast items are available at all hours. Upstairs serves more elegant meals (£7-14).

Stokes High Bridge Café, 207 High St. (tel. 51 03 33). Busy tearoom in a house built on a medieval bridge. Leg of lamb with vegetable £3. Cream teas £1. Open Mon.-Wed. 9:30am-5pm, Thurs.-Sat. 9:30am-5:30pm; meals only 11:30am-2pm (£3-4).

The Spinning Wheel, 39 Steep Hill (tel. 52 24 63), one block south of Guildhall in a leaning half-timbered building. Basic entrees with chips and peas (£3.25-5); mind-blowing desserts. May be your only chance to eat in a fireplace. Open daily 10am-9pm.

Sights

France has Chartres, Spain has Santiago, and England has Lincoln as the home of its great Gothic cathedral. Built beginning in the twelfth century on the ruins of a Norman structure, **Lincoln Minster** (tel. 54 45 44) was for many centuries the tallest building in Europe, and its position at the top of Castle Hill makes it visible from as far away as Boston (only on clear days). The elaborately carved interior is impressive, containing several styles of Gothic architecture, plus some curiosities, such as the internal organs of Edward I's Queen Eleanor, which would have rotted had they been transported to London after she died near Lincoln in 1290. Don't miss the cloisters, with their humorously carved wooden vaulting and the library designed by Christopher Wren. (Open Mon.-Sat. 7:15am-8pm, Sun. 7:15am-6pm. Winter Mon.-Sat. 7:15am-6pm, Sun. 7:15am-5pm. Suggested donation £1; seniors, students and children 50p. Guided tours May-Sept. 11am, 1pm, and 3pm; March-April and Oct.-Nov 11am and 2pm. Roof tours must be booked in advance and cost £2.50/person.)

William I was a very practical conqueror, and he did not grant a charter for the cathedral until 1072, four years after he had ordered the construction of **Lincoln Castle** (tel. 51 10 68), which shares Castle Hill. Though heavily restored, the Norman walls remain, enclosing a vast area. They are sturdy enough that one can walk along the battlements, and the panoramic view from Observatory Tower includes the cathedral, the river, and most of Lincolnshire. Informative guided tours start daily at 11am and 2pm. Everything from weddings to jousting tourneys occur on the castle grounds; pick up a free events calendar in the gift shop. (Castle open Mon.-Sat. 9:30am-5:30pm, Sun. 11am-5:30pm. Winter Mon.-Sat. 9:30am-4pm. Last admission ½hr. before closing. Admission 80p; children, seniors, and students 50p.)

On the far side of the castle from the cathedral is **The Lawn,** Union Road (tel. 56 03 30). This newly-opened complex occupies the building and grounds of what used to be Lincoln's mental hospital. Exhibits include a display on the history of psychiatric treatment, an archaeology center, and a greenhouse with tropical plants. (Open Mon.-Thurs. 9am-5:30pm, Fri. 9am-5pm, Sat.-Sun. 10am-5pm. Winter Mon.-Thurs. 9am-5:30pm, Fri. 9am-5pm, Sat.-Sun. 10am-4pm. Free.) Also near the castle is the **Museum of Lincolnshire Life,** Burton Rd. (tel. 52 84 48), which has exhibits on the social history of Lincolnshire, as well as the collections of the Royal Lincolnshire Regiment. (Open daily 10am-5:30pm; Oct.-April Mon.-Sat. 10am-5:30pm, Sun. 2-5:30pm. Admission 80p, children 40p.)

Many of Lincoln's smaller historic buildings can be found along a single street, albeit one with many names. On top of the hill, where it is known as Bailgate, the street is spanned by the remnants of the Roman north gate of Lindum Colonia. The pile of stones known as **Newport Arch** is nothing like the marble triumphal arches the Romans erected in Southern Europe. Past the tourist office, the street becomes **Steep Hill,** which passes by several medieval buildings. At the bottom of the hill the street is called High Street, and it passes beneath the **Stonebow,** which was built in the 15th century as the southern gate of the city and now houses the **Guildhall** (tel. 51 15 11) and the Civic Insignia. (Guildhall open first Saturday of each month, 10am-noon and 2-4:30pm, or by appointment. Free.) Farther down the street, the **High Bridge** is the last one in Britain still to provide a foundation for medieval houses. The buildings are currently occupied by a china shop and the High Street Café (see Food above). For a good view of the houses and bridge, drop down the Glory Hole, a narrow alleyway to the right of the café, and walk along the murky canal. Farther along the canal, at Brayford Wharf, is the **National Cycle Museum** (tel. 54 50 91). Exhibits chronicle cycling through the ages, from the Boneshaker and the Penny Farthing to the BMX, and provide a tame diversion from medieval Lincoln. (Open daily 10am-5pm. Admission 60p, children 30p.) On the other side of High St., near the bus station, the **City and County Museum,** Broadgate (tel. 53 04 01) houses one of the four extant original copies of the Magna Carta, as well as archaeological finds from the area, an entire legion of toy Roman soldiers, and a collection of quite dead Lincolnshire wildlife. (Open Mon.-Sat. 10am-5:30pm, Sun. 2:30-5:30pm. 50p, children 25p. Free on Thursday.)

Entertainment

Both *What's On in Lincoln* and *Broadsheet* (the Lincolnshire and Humberside arts leaflet) are good sources of information, both free from the tourist office. During the first weekend of June, the **Lincoln Carnival** comes to the West Common. You can sample wines from Neustadt, Lincoln's German sister city, at the **Wine Festival,** usually held the first week in June. Lincoln's **Arts Festival** features exhibitions and touring theater companies in May. For a comprehensive listing of summer arts and entertainment activities in the castle, pick up a copy of *Lincoln Castle Events 1992* at the tourist office. The **Theatre Royal,** Clasketgate (tel. 52 55 55), between High St. and Broadgate, stages drama all year round. (Tickets £2.50-6.50. Student discounts are sometimes available depending on the program. Box office open daily 10am-6pm.) **The Ritz Theatre,** High St. (tel. 54 63 13) puts on recent films and "live stage entertainment" of all varieties. (Tickets £3.50-£12.50; box office open Mon.-Sat. 10:30am-5:30pm.)

Club names in Lincoln change constantly. **Vienna,** on Newland Ave. and **Ritzy,** Silver St., currently supply music and a flat surface.

Near Lincoln

About 25 mi. south of Lincoln, in **Grantham,** Sir Isaac Newton attended the **King's School** on Brook St. and carved his schoolboy signature into the windowsill. (Visitors by appointment; tel. (0476) 631 80.) The **Grantham Museum** (tel. (0476) 687 83), off High St. next to the tourist office, features exhibits on Newton's life and work, as well as a video exhibit on another Grantham spawn, Margaret Thatcher. (Open Mon.-Sat. 10am-5pm, Sun. 2-5pm; Oct.-March Mon.-Sat. 10am-12:30pm and 1:30-5pm. Admission 25p, children 10p. Free on Wed.) The Thatchers' legendary grocery store is now a restaurant (vandalized after England lost in the World Cup semi-final find out when and where). Seven mi. farther south is **Woolsthorpe Manor** (tel. (0476) 86 03 38), Newton's birthplace. It was here under an apple tree that the scientist was first struck by the idea of gravity, and also here (on a 1665 visit to escape the plague in Cambridge) that he dreamt up calculus. (Open April-Oct. Sat.-Wed. 1-5:30pm. Admission £2, children £1.) The town of Grantham is accessible by rail from Lincoln (every hr.; 50 min.; day return £5.30), or by bus from St. Mark's Bus Station (every hr.; 75 min.; day return £2.45).

East of Grantham, near the mouth of the River Witham, life goes on in tiny **Boston,** despite the departure of a band of Puritans for New England in 1630 find out exact history. Originally planning to depart for Holland in 1607, they were betrayed and imprisoned in the Guildhall (now a museum). Holding no grudges, they named their quite remarkable new settlement on Massachusetts Bay after the Lincolnshire town that had held them prisoner. From the top of **Boston Stump** (the 272-ft. tower of **St. Botolph's Church**), you can see all the way to Lincoln on a clear day. (Church open in summer daily 8:30am-4:30pm, in winter Mon.-Sat. 8:30am-4:30pm, Sun. 8:30am-noon. Tower open Mon.-Sat. 10am-4pm. £1, children 50p.) Boston can be reached by rail from Lincoln, changing at Sleaford (every hr.; 1 hr.; £5.90 day return). The **tourist office** in the Assembly Rooms (tel. (0205) 35 66 56) can give you information about the area and the fine local soccer team, Boston United. (Open Mon.-Fri. 9am-5pm, Sat. 9am-1pm.)

Nottingham

It was once a flourishing center of lace production, and has a canal and several free museums. Situated on the highest navigable point of the Trent, Nottingham has had a fairly interesting existence since the days when Prince John was Earl and Sherwood Forest didn't have its own visitor center. Indeed, the city has more to recommend it than the memory of a semi-legendary medieval proto-socialist bowman (...Robin Hood), though tourist officials might try to make visitors believe otherwise.

The current incarnation of **Nottingham Castle,** on Castle Road, bears little resemblance to the Norman structure in which Prince John was beseiged by his brother, Richard I, and upon which Charles I raised his standard against Parliament to start the Civil War. That structure was demolished in 1651 in an attempt to limit Cromwell's power, and the current building is a 1674 palace built for the Duke of Newcastle. In 1831, after the fourth Duke helped defeat an election reform law, a revolution-minded mob stormed and burned the palace. Repaired in the 1870s, the mansion now houses the **Castle Museum** (tel. 48 35 04), which has exhibits on the history of Nottingham, some mediocre Victorian art, the regimental memorabilia—medals, uniforms, and trophies—of the Sherwood Foresters, and some interesting temporary exhibits. (Museum open daily 10am-5:45pm, Oct.-March 10am-4:45pm. Grounds open Mon.-Fri. 8am-dark, Sat.-Sun. 9am-dark. Museum and grounds are free Mon.-Sat., on Sun. and bank holidays admission 40p, children 20p.)

Across Castle Road from the entrance to the castle and down Castle Gate is the **Museum of Costume and Textiles,** (tel. 48 35 04). The museum displays several furnished rooms with mannequins dressed in period costume, as well as an exhibit of hundreds of pieces of lace from the Continent and Nottingham, where the production of lace was mechanized at an early date. (Open daily 10am-5pm. Free.) Nearby, at the base of the castle's hill, the **Brewhouse Yard Museum** (tel. 48 35 04 ext.3600) stocks items of everyday life from the past 300 years, so you can see how toothpaste was packaged during the reign of Queen Victoria. (Open daily 10am-5pm. Free.)

Closer to the train station is the topical **Canal Museum** (tel. 28 46 02), Canal Street. The waterway was opened in 1796 to transport coal but was made largely obsolete by the coming of the railway in the mid-19th century. The museum has displays on the history of the canal and the Trent, and is the starting point for boat tours of the canal. (Museum open Wed.-Sat. 10am-noon and 1-5:45pm, Sun. 1-5:45pm. Oct.-Easter Wed.-Thurs. and Sat. 10am-noon and 1-5pm, Sun. 1-5pm. Free.)

If the castle museum does not sate your appetite for lingerie and doilies, **Lace Hall,** High Pavement (tel. 48 42 21), uphill from Broad Marsh Centre has still more. The exhibit tells the history of lace, and demonstrates how it is made. (Open daily 10am-5:30pm, winter 10am-5pm. Admission £1.95; children, seniors, and students £1.)

Nottingham's enormous **tourist office,** 16 Wheeler Gate (tel. 47 06 61), keeps its excellent free maps and "Places of Interest" brochures behind the counter, so ask for them. Accommodations are booked for £1.05 9am-4:30pm; a list of hotels is posted outside. (Open Mon.-Fri. 8:30am-5pm, Sat. 9am-5pm, Sun. 10am-4pm.) The **train station** (tel. (0332) 32 05 1) is on Garrington St., across the canal. Trains run to Lincoln (24/day, Sun. 11/day; £3, day return £4.80), Sheffield (about every ½hr., Sun. every hr.; £7.80, return £8.30), and London's St. Pancras (28/day, Sun. 15/day; £25.50, saver return £22-28). To get from the train station to the tourist office, turn right on Carrington St. as you leave the station; continue on Carrington over the canal until you reach Broad Marsh Centre, a shopping mall. Walk straight through the center and along two pedestrianized blocks to Wheeler Gate. The tourist office is marked by a pillar with a large "I" on it. **Coaches** stop at the **Victoria Shopping Centre** (tel. 58 53 17) on the north side of town. Coaches run to London (8/day 2:20am-6:05pm; single £12.75, return £13.25-19.50), Sheffield, Manchester, and other destinations. To get to the tourist office, walk through Victoria Centre and exit at the corner of Milton St. and Lower Parliament St. Walk down the pedestrianized Clumber St., continue for one block on High St., and turn right onto South Parade. Turn left at the intersection with Barclay's, and you will be on Wheeler Gate. Luggage lockers at the Victoria Centre coach station cost 50p-£2. You can also store luggage at the local bus station in Broad Marsh Centre for 50p, but you must retrieve it before the office closes. The **post office** is on Upper Parliament St., the continuation of Lower Parliament St. in the direction of the tourist office. The **telephone code** is 0602. Several banks lie along South Parade.

The **YMCA,** 4 Shakespeare St. (tel. 47 30 68), near the coach station, offers B&B for £11.50 plus £4 key deposit. Exit Victoria Centre through the Mansfield St. doors, near the food court, and you will be directly across from the Y. The **Newcastle Arms,** 68 North Sherwood St. (tel. 47 46 16), also near the coach station, offers quiet rooms above a pub for £14 per person. From Victoria Centre, turn right on Mansfield Road and left on Bluecoat St.; the pub is at the end of Bluecoat.

Getting a cheap meal is a challenge. Try the food court in Victoria Centre. **Fellows, Clayton, & Morton, Ltd,** next to the Canal Museum, brews its own beer and sells bar meals Mon.-Sat. 11:30am-2pm (£2.50-4).

Near Nottingham

Wollaton Hall (tel. 28 13 33) is a Tudor mansion west of Nottingham with a deer park and natural history museum. On the grounds of the hall is the **Industrial Museum** (tel. 28 46 02), which displays steam engines, lace machines, and assorted technology. (Hall and Natural History Museum open Mon.-Sat. 10am-7pm, Sun. 2-5pm. Oct.-March Mon.-Sat. 10am-dusk, Sun 1:30-4:30pm. Industrial Museum open Mon.-Sat. 10am-6pm, Sun. 2-6pm. Oct.-March Thurs. and Sat. 10am-4:30pm, Sun. 1:30-4:30pm. Free except on Sun. and bank holidays, then 40p, children 20p.) North of Nottingham, in the village of Linby, is **Newstead Abbey** (tel. (0623) 79 35 57), the ancestral home of Lord Byron. The abbey is filled with poetic memorabilia. (Grounds open daily dawn-dusk. House open daily noon-6pm. Admission to house and grounds £3, children and seniors £1.40. House only, £2, children and seniors £1. Grounds only, £1.20, children and seniors 60p.) Even further to the north is the famous **Sherwood Forest,** considerably thinned since the 13th century. The **Sherwood Forest Visitor Centre** (tel. (0623) 82 32 02) is the bull's eye of all things Robin-Hoody and Merry-Manly. Call the Nottinghamshire Buses Hotline (tel. (0602) 24 00 00) for information on public transit to these sites.

Liverpool

Athens had its Piraeus, Rome its Ostia, and Manchester its Liverpool. Liverpool was on its way to becoming an important port as early as 1715, when it opened England's first commercial dock, but it was the growth of the Lancashire cotton industry that allowed Liverpool to export more cargo than London itself by 1900. In addition to raw cotton coming in and textiles flowing out, people came and went from Liverpool, among them many emigrants to America. After World War I, both the decline of the British Empire and the advent of air travel dealt serious blows to the city's once-prosperous shipping industry. Economic hardship is still visible here, and some areas of the city should be explored with caution. Despite its grim surroundings, Liverpool (pop. 500,000) is a remarkably pleasant place to visit. Native Liverpudlians, known for their nasal "scouse" accent, are an energetic, outgoing lot with a keen sense of humor. The city that clings tightly to its status as the birthplace of the Beatles maintains a thriving cultural life that has diminished little since the 1960s, when Allen Ginsberg described it as "the center of human consciousness."

Arriving and Departing

Trains connect Liverpool to most major cities in North and Central England. They run to: Manchester (every ½hr. 5:42am-12:45pm; 1 hr.; £4.70, day return £5); Birmingham (every hr. 6am-11:25pm; 1¾ hr.; £14.50, day return £11.50, £18 on Fri.); and London (evry hr. 6am-8pm, Sun. 12/day 8:58am-midnight; 3 hr.; £37.50, return £25-33). APEX return fares to London (£18) are available on certain trains if purchased 7 days in advance at Lime St. or by calling (051) 709 28 94 with a credit card.

Coaches run to: London (5 Rapide/day, every 2½ hr. 7:30am-5:30pm; 4½ hr., plus one regular coach at 11:25pm for 7½ hr.; £16.50, return £17-22); Manchester (every hr. 6:15am-11pm; 1 hr.; £3.50, return £3.50-4.50); and Birmingham (6/day 8am-11:25pm; 21/3 hr.; £8.25, return £8.50-11).

Northern Ireland can be accessed by **Belfast Car Ferries** (tel. 922 62 34) from Liverpool to Belfast (leave daily at 11am, arrive 7:45pm; £18-23 single, seniors £16-20.50, students with Travelsave stamp £15-18, children £9-11.50; bikes free; cabins £7.25-14/berth; reservations urged). Shuttles to the dock are available from Liverpool Lime St. rail station and Liverpool Port Terminal starting at 9:30am; arrive at the docks no later than 10am. The journeys provide an excellent opportunity to get acquainted with Irish easy listening music.

Orientation and Practical Information

Although Liverpool is part of a vast conurbation which sprawls across the River Mersey, its central district is pedestrian-friendly. Two clusters of museums flank the central shopping district: those on William Brown St. near the train station, and those at Albert Dock, on the river. Both the train and the bus stations are near the center of town. Coaches stop on Brownlow Hill, opposite the Adelphi Hotel, near the train station.

Tourist Information Center: Merseyside Welcome Centre, Clayton Sq. Shopping Centre, L1 1QR (tel. 709 3631). From the train station, exit onto Skelhorne St. and turn right. Clayton Sq. is the brick building with horizontal bands of sandstone. From the coach stop, walk downhill and turn right on Lime St.; walk about a block until you can see the center, identified by a green and blue "W" rather than the standard red rose. Pick up an accommodations list and the *Pocket Guide to Merseyside,* which contains lists of things to see in the county and a lousy map (both free). Accommodations booked with a 10% deposit. There is also a *bureau de change,* and Beatles souvenirs up the wazoo. Open Mon.-Sat. 9am-5:30pm, Sun. 10am-5pm. A smaller branch at **Atlantic Pavilion,** Albert Dock (tel. 708 88 54), has much of the same information, and will also book accommodations (open daily 10am-5:30pm).

Tours: One-hr. Beatles "Magical History Tour" leaves from tourist office at 2:30pm (£4). Request a Japanese-speaking Beatleguide for an alternative linguistic perspective on the Fab Four. 19 different coach tours (from £3) and 35 different walking tours (£1) rotate throughout the summer; the tourist office has the leaflets if you have the feet.

Bike Rental: Greenbank Cycle Shop, 232 Smithdown Rd. (tel. 733 66 66). Three mi. outside the city center. Open Mon.-Tues. and Thurs.-Fri. 9am-6pm, Wed. and Sat. 9am-5:30pm. £23/week, £70 deposit, cash only.

Bookstores: W.H. Smith, Church St. at Williamson St. (tel. 709 14 35). Carries *Let's Go* guides. Open Mon.-Wed. and Fri. 9:00am-5:30pm, Thurs. and Sat. 9am-6pm. **News From Nowhere,** 112 Bold St. (tel. 708 72 70). Radical and feminist bookshop with a wide selection. Gay and lesbian periodicals, bulletin board with women's and gay/lesbian groups and events. Disabled access. Open Mon.-Sat. 10am-5:30pm.

Coach Station: The "office" is a shack on the sidewalk (tel. 709 64 81).

Emergency: Dial 999; no coins required.

Financial Services: Thomas Cook, Church St. (tel. 709 38 45), facing Barclay's. Open Mon.-Wed and Fri. 9am-5:30pm, Thurs. 9:30am-5:30pm, Sat. 9am-5pm. On Sun. the **tourist office** will exchange up to £50 per person for a £1.50 fee. **Barclay's,** 84 Church St. Open Mon.-Fri. 9:30am-4:30pm, Sat. 9:30am-noon. **American Express:** 54 Lord St. (tel. 708 92 02). Mail held up to 3 mos. for cardholders. Open Mon.-Tues., Thurs.-Fri. 9am-5pm, Wed. 9:30am-5pm, Sat. 9am-4pm.

Friends of Merseyside: To chat or arrange a visit with a hospitable Liverpudlian, call 336 66 99.

Hospital: Royal Liverpool Hospital, Prescot St. (tel. 709 01 41), ½ mi. from the railroad station.

Launderette: Liver Laundrette, 107 Park Rd., about a mile south of the city center. Take bus #32 or 82 from Renshaw St. Yes, this really is the most convenient launderette in Liverpool. Wash £1.20-2, dry 20p. Open daily 9am-8pm, last wash 7:15pm.

Merseytravel (tel. 236 76 76) runs buses, trains, and ferries throughout Merseyside. Information is available at the Welcome Centre (see Tourist Office), at the Ferries Centre on the docks, and elsewhere. The information phone line is open daily 8am-8pm.

Pharmacy: Em-Ess Chemist, 68170 London Rd. (tel. 709 52 71). Open daily 9am-11pm.

Police: Canning Place (tel. 709 60 10).

Post Office: 23-33 Whitechapel (tel. 242 41 65). Disabled access. Open Mon.-Thurs. 9am-6pm, Fri. 9:30am-6pm, Sat. 9am-12:30pm. **Postal Code:** L1 1AA.

Student Travel Office: Liverpool Student Travel, Student Union, 2 Bedford St. N. (tel. 708 07 21). Open Mon.-Fri. 9:30am-5pm.

Telephone Code: 051.

Train Station: Lime St. Station. Make schedule inquiries at Lime Street Travel Centre (tel. 709 96 96) in the station. Open daily 8am-8:30pm. Left luggage office is open daily 6:30-10am, 10:30am-6pm, and 6:30-9:30pm.

Accommodations

Relatively cheap accommodations are available at the YMCA and YWCA, and some modest but decent hotels line **Lord Nelson Street,** adjacent to the train station, and **Mount Pleasant,** one block from Brownlow Hill and the coach stop. Demand for accommodations is highest in early April when jockeys and gamblers gallop into town for the Grand National Race; call ahead for reservations.

YMCA, 56-60 Mt. Pleasant (tel. 709 95 16), near the city center. Men and women. The rooms are fine, the common areas less attractive: the smell of cigarettes lingers in the corridors, and the laundry facilities have been known to be out of order. Singles £10.20, doubles £9.20/person, full breakfast included. Key deposit £2.

YWCA, 1 Rodney St. (tel. 709 77 91), 1 block up Mt. Pleasant from the YMCA. Single women and a few families only. Kindly proprietor. Adequate, spare singles and multi-bed rooms. Two kitchens, laundry room, TV lounge, free baths and showers. Singles £6, £24 weekly; doubles £10/person, £40 weekly. Key deposit £10.

University of Liverpool, Roscoe and Gladstone Halls (tel. 794 64 40), just past the top of Mt. Pleasant. Turn left before the concrete building with the columns. B&B £9.25/person. Open June-Sept. **Philharmonic Court** (call 794 64 40 and ask for Paul Beesley) is a self-catering hall of residence—bring your own sheets and food. Open mid-July to late Sept. £4.50, students £3.35.

Hardman House, 13-15 Hardman St. (tel. 708 83 03), parallel to Mt. Pleasant. Unluxurious but clean rooms with high ceilings. Singles and doubles £12.50/person. Continental breakfast £1.50. Free jazz concerts on Tues. evenings.

Atlantic Hotel, 9 Lord Nelson St. (tel. 709 11 62). Clean rooms and a good location, with a full or vegetarian breakfast. Singles £15, doubles £11/person.

Ridgway's Hotel, 11 Lord Nelson St. (tel. 709 18 25). Not elegant, but sunny. One single (£15) and several doubles (£12/person); the price includes a continental breakfast.

Camping: Wirral Country Park, Thurstaston (tel. 648 43 71). Take Mersey Ferries across the river to Woodside, then take bus #71 (every ½hr.), which passes within a mile of the site. £4.50/tent and 2 people. **Abbey Farm,** Ormskirk (tel. (0695) 57 26 86), on the northern rail line from Lime St. Station (£4).

Food

Try **St. John's Market** (above the shopping mall) for fresh produce and local color. **Holland & Barrett** on Whitechapel (open Mon.-Tues. and Thurs.-Sat. 9am-5:30pm, Wed. 9:30am-5:30pm) has a large selection of health foods. Liverpool has many an ethnic restaurant, especially along Hardman St. These close on Sundays, however; the hotel meals or fast-food joints on Lime or Lord St. may seem like your only hope, but **Chinatown,** near the corner of Great George and Nelson St., is both affordable and open on Sundays (ask for your food to be prepared without MSG).

Everyman Bistro, 9-11 Hope St. (tel. 708 95 45), off Mt. Pleasant, near the university. A bouncy student hangout below the theater. Although the food is microwaved, interesting herbs and preparation set this bistro apart from standard cafeterias. A large vegetarian selection. Hot meals run about £4. Open Mon.-Sat. noon-midnight.

Kirkland's, 13 Hardman St. (tel. 707 01 32). Lunch and dinner of various ethnic origins £3. Pleasant atmosphere. Open Mon. and Wed. 10am-midnight, Tues. and Thurs.-Sun. 10am-1am. Food served until 7pm.

New Capital, on Great George, in Chinatown. A good variety of dishes "with rice," meaning a lot of rice and a fair portion of meat and vegetables (£4.30). Open Sun.-Thurs. noon-11:30pm, Fri.-Sat. noon-1am.

Black Horse and Rainbow, Berry St., in Chinatown. A noisy pub named after the two bitters brewed on the premises. Open Mon.-Sat. 11:30am-1am, Sun. noon-3pm, 7-10:30pm.

Sights

Liverpool's efforts to bring its waterfront out of the rusty age of freight and into the brave new world of the service economy have yielded **Albert Dock,** an 1846 series of warehouses transformed into a complex of shops, offices, apartments, restaurants, and museums. A cornerstone of this development is the **Tate Gallery,** Albert Dock (tel. 709 32 23), a branch of the London institution. The Liverpool Tate doesn't have a permanent collection, relying instead on temporary exhibitions of the top artists of the 20th century. An exhibition of postwar European art will do a three-year stint in 1992, and from April-Aug. 1992 American abstract expressionism will show its colors. The museum café produces desserts that are themselves works of art. (Museum and café open Tues.-Sun. 11am-7pm. Free, except for some special exhibitions which cost £1, seniors, students, and children 50p.) Questions about the original function of Albert Dock or about Liverpool shipping in general can be answered at the **Merseyside Maritime Museum** (tel. 207 0001), which displays an astounding number and variety of ship models. Admission to the museum includes entrance to a pilot cutter, the piermaster's house, and an exhibit on the over nine million emigrants (mostly Irish) who passed through Liverpool during the 19th century. (Open Mon.-Sat. 10:30am-5:30pm. Last entry 4:30pm. Admission £1.50, students, seniors, and children 75p.) On Aug.16 1992, the regatta of tall ships at the Liverpool waterfront will celebrate the discovery of America and subsequent departure of all manner of undesirables (tel. 709 36 31). Among the other attractions at Albert Dock is **The Beatles Story** (tel. 709 19 63), which presents a chronological look at the once prominent string and percussion quartet. (Open daily 10am-6pm. £3, students, seniors and children £2, families £7.50.)

For more locales associated with these musicians, pick up the **Beatles Map** (£1) at the tourist office, which gives directions to Strawberry Fields and Penny Lane. The original Cavern on Mathew St., the famous club where the group first gained prominence, has been replaced by a shopping mall. Nearby, the **Beatles Shop,** 31 Mathew St. (tel. 236 80 66), is stuffed to the gills with disappointingly tasteful souvenirs and memorabilia. (Open Mon.-Sat. 9:30am-5:30pm.)

While Albert Dock may be flashier, the three museums on William Brown St., near the train station, merit a look. The **Liverpool Museum** presents a truly bewildering collection: lunar soil, Victoria Crosses, horse-drawn carriages, Anglo-Saxon spearpoints, and living lungfish are all housed under one roof. Within the museum, the innovative **Natural History Centre** encourages adults and children to examine pre-selected specimens with the appropriate instruments (open Tues.-Sat. 1-4:30pm, Sun. 2-4:30pm); there is also a **planetarium** (shows Tues.-Fri. at 3:15pm, Sat. 1:15, 2:15, 3:15, and 4:05pm, Sun. 2:20, 3:15, amd 4:05pm, often other shows on weekdays; £1, seniors and children 50p). Next door, the **Walker Art Gallery** covers the bases of European art since the Middle Ages without revealing anything too remarkable. Further down the block, the **Merseyside Museum of Labour History** has an important story to tell, but the exhibits rely so heavily on text and photographs that you might as well read the book. (All three museums open Mon.-Sat. 10am-5pm, Sun. 2-5pm. Free; information on any of them can be acquired from the National Museums and Galleries on Merseyside by calling 207 00 01.) Not far away, near the tourist information center on School Lane, the **Bluecoat Arts Centre** houses both a gallery with intriguing exhibitions which rotate about once a month (tel. 709 56 89; open Tues.-Sat. 10:30am-5pm; admission free) and the **Merseyside Film Institute** (tel. 709 42 60, mostly recent films, Mon.-Fri. 6pm and 8:15pm). Look for the attractive Georgian building, formerly a school for poor children.

Liverpool has two 20th-century cathedrals, both outside the city center and connected by Hope St. The Anglican **Liverpool Cathedral** (tel. 709 62 71), begun in 1904 and completed in 1978, is—in a word—vast. Designed by the 22-year-old Giles Gilbert Scott, it presides over an abandoned quarry. A Trumpian wonder, it has the highest Gothic arches ever built (107 ft.), the largest vault and organ (10,000 pipes), and the highest and heaviest bells in the world. Climb to the top of the tower for views to north Wales. (Cathedral open daily 9am-6pm; tower open daily 10am-4pm, weather permitting. Admission to tower £1.50, seniors and students £1, children 50p. Free organ recitals Fri. 12:30pm.) The cathedral refectory, overlooking the quarry, serves delicious teas and brunches. (Open Mon.-Sat. 10am-4:30pm, Sun. noon-5pm.) The inside of the Roman Catholic **Metropolitan Cathedral of Christ the King** (tel. 709 92 22), dubbed "Paddy's Wigwam" by local blasphemers, looks more like a rock concert hall than the setting for a mass. The steel and concrete walls entomb a dramatic stained-glass Lantern Tower. Multicolored rays frolic about inside when the sun is shining. (Cathedral open daily 8am-6pm. Disabled access.)

Entertainment

Liverpool's somewhat grim surroundings are brightened by a thriving arts scene and an energetic nightlife. The Merseyside Arts Council's *Look Alive* has more complete information than the City Council guide *What's On.* The most reliable guide to clubs and discos is the *Liverpool Echo.* For local "alternative" events, check the bulletin board in the Everyman Bistro (see Food). They often host bohemian happenings in their own **Third Room.**

Fight your way inside **Flanagan's Apple,** Matthew St., which has the best Irish music in town most nights. Free jazz (in the sense of *gratis,* not Cecil Taylor) on Tuesdays (8:30-11pm) graces the **Hardman Hotel,** Hardman St. Its **Club Corinto** frequently hosts Latin and African bands. **Daley's Dandelion,** on Dale St., has launched a few local bands, including the popular Mojo Filter. **Kirkland's** wine bar and disco, Hardman St., is popular, though more sedate types might prefer **The State,** Dale St., an upscale version owned by the same people. **The Crown** and **The Central** are lively pubs in the town center. **The Slaughterhouse Tavern,** Fenwick St., opened in 1750 and proudly displays the ledgers signed by the first customers. **Spencer's,** London Rd., is a lively spot with disco (Thurs.-Sat.). Aficionados of those modern Messiaens will be disappointed that no Beatles impersonators play on a regular basis, although many pubs play a steady (and stale) stream of their hits.

The **Royal Liverpool Philharmonic Orchestra,** one of the finest English orchestras outside of London, performs at Philharmonic Hall, Hope St. (tel. 709 37 89; tickets from £5, students 25% off). Theater in Liverpool is extremely good, and cheap: the **Liverpool Empire,** on Lime St. (tel. 709 15 55), hosts drama and comedy, welcoming such famous troupes as the Royal Shakespeare Company. (Box office open Mon.-Sat. 10am-8pm. 50% student discounts sometimes available ½hr. before curtain. Prices start at £3.50 without concessions. Disabled access.) The **Everyman Theatre,** Hope St. (tel. 709 47 76), presents contemporary plays (tickets from £3, students 25% off); the **Playhouse Theatre** (tel. 709 83 63) caters to both adults and children (tickets £4-6, children's shows £2-2.50). If that isn't enough art for you, the **Neptune Theatre** (tel. 709 78 44), Hanover St., hosts touring companies and produces small-café shows; the **Unity Theatre** attracts the avant-garde, and the **Royal Court** (tel. 709 43 21), Roe St., holds big-name rock concerts.

Liverpool hosts a **Festival of Comedy** in late June, during which comedians of all shapes and sizes invade all available spaces. (Tickets start around £2.50. For information and tickets, contact the Festival Box Office (tel. 709 83 63; *c/o* Liverpool Playhouse, Williamson Sq., Liverpool 1).

Chester

With fashionable shops tucked away in half-timbered medieval houses, guides in full Roman armor leading tours around the city's walls, and Barclay's bank occupying a wing of the cathedral, Chester at times resembles an American theme-park pastiche of Ye Olde English Village and daringly tacky commercialism. Originally the Roman fortress of Deva on the River Dee, Chester thrived between the 5th and 10th centuries after the Romans left. The town withstood sieges, became a base for Plantagenet campaigns against the Welsh, and expanded its web of trading connections all the way to the Baltic, France, Spain, Portugal, and the Low Countries. When, over the course of the 17th century, the silting-up of the River Dee interfered with Chester's harbor and rival Liverpool supplanted it as a commercial center, Chester could only age gracefully. Crowded but charming, the city now conspires to keep foreigners inside its fortified walls, while keeping a watchful eye on Wales, just 3 mi. away.

Arriving and Departing

Chester (pop. 60,000) serves as a rail gateway to North Wales; a rail line hugs the north coast (passing through Flint, Colwyn Bay, and Bangor on its way out to Holyhead), and another branches down into Snowdonia. You can travel by train from Chester via Shrewsbury to central and south Wales. Frequent and quick rail service makes Chester a very plausible day trip from Liverpool (every ½hr.; 45 min.; £2.10, day return £3.70). Other trains run to London's Euston (every hr.; 3 hr.; £24 saver return), Holyhead (every 2 hr.; £9.70), Manchester (every 1½ hr.; 2 hr.; £5), Birmingham (every ½hr.; 1½ hr.; £12), and Shrewsbury and Hereford (change at Crewe).

National Express coaches run to London (4 Rapide/day 8:25am-3:10pm; 4½ hr., plus one standard at 12:20am for 6½ hr.; £16.50, return £17-22), Birmingham (5/day 8:25am-12:20am; 2 hr.; £8.25, return £8.50-11), Manchester (3/day 8:50am-5:15pm; 1¼ hr.; £4.50, return £4.75-6), and Bristol (3/day 9:45am-3:10pm; 5 hr.; £15, return £15.50-20).

Orientation and Practical Information

Chester's city center is encircled by a medieval **city wall,** broken by seven gates. The rail and bus stations are both to the north, outside the walls. From the rail station, which is about ¾mi. out of town, proceed straight ahead onto City Rd. and turn right onto Foregate St. at the huge roundabout; trot through Eastgate and turn right at The Cross to get to the tourist office. From the bus station, trundle left onto Upper Northgate St. and patter through Northgate to the tourist office. Frequent buses (20p) run from both stations to the Market Square Bus Exchange, near the tourist office. Otherwise, it's a 20-min. walk from the rail station.

Tourist Information Center: Town Hall, Northgate St., Cheshire (tel. 31 31 26 or 31 83 56). Accommodations service with a 10% deposit. The *Town & Heritage Map* (£1.10) has clever color-coding allowing rapid calculation of restaurants per meter. Open Mon.-Sat. 9am-7:30pm, Sun. 10am-4pm; Oct.-May Mon.-Sat. 9am-5:30pm. A similar range of services is available at the information desk in the **Chester Visitor Centre,** Vicars Lane, opposite the Roman amphitheater (tel. 35 16 09; open daily 9am-9pm; Nov.-Feb. 9am-7pm). The center is a nine-ring circus of souvenir shops, videos, and brass-rubbing centers. Both centers have enough information on Wales to equip a legion.

Tours: "Pastfinder" tours of the cathedral and walls leave from town hall at 10:45am and 2:30pm. A legionnaire sweating in full armor leads the Roman tour (June-Sept. Thurs.-Sat. 11:30am and 2:30pm). Each tour costs £1.80, seniors, YHA members, students, amd children £1. The **Chester Visitor Centre** also sponsors tours, including evening walks (Easter-Oct. Mon.-Sat., Thurs.-Sat. are the evenings for the popular Ghost Walk, same prices). Coach tours run every 20 min. 9:40am-4:20pm from various stops; passengers can alight and reboard when they choose. £2.50, seniors and children £1.25, families £6. Call 34 74 52 for details.

Bike Rental: Davies Bros. Cycles, 6-8 Cuppin St. (tel. 31 92 04), off Grosvenor St. near Bridge St. 3-speeds £6/day, £25/week; mountain bikes £10/day, £45/week, £60 deposit. Some panniers available. Open Mon.-Sat. 9am-5:15pm.

Boat Rental: Several places by the river between Bridgegate and Queen's Park Bridge rent motorboats (3/¼hr.), pedal boats, and rowboats (£3/hr.). Cheapest rowboats (£2/hr.) and pedal boats (£2/½hr.) at **Bramston Launches** (tel. 426 94).

Buses: Some stop at the coach station; most stop at the **bus exchange** in Market Sq., around the corner from the town hall. Call 60 26 66 (Mon.-Fri. 8:30am-6pm, Sat. 10am-2pm) for information about all local services in Chester and Cheshire. Attendant staffs the Crosville booth Mon.-Sat. 9:30am-5:30pm.

Coach Station: Delamere St. (tel. 38 15 15), just north of the city wall, off Northgate St. Long-distance and county coaches and buses; local service into North Wales. Office open Mon.-Fri. 9am-5pm, Sat. 9am-5pm.

Crisis: Samaritans, 36 Upper Northgate (tel. 37 79 99).

Early Closing Day: Smaller shops close at noon Wed.

Emergency: Dial 999; no coins required.

Financial Services: Thomas Cook, 10 Bridge St. (tel. 32 30 45). Open Mon.-Tues. and Thurs.-Sat. 9am-5:30pm, Wed. 9:30am-5:30pm. **Barclay's,** in the west wing of cathedral and on Eastgate St. Open Mon.-Fri. 9:30am-3:30pm, Sat. 9:30am-noon. The tourist office has a **bureau de change** with less competitive rates. **American Express: Apollo Travel Agency,** 23 St. Werburgh St. (tel. 34 83 15). Traveler's checks, emergency check cashing, mail held. Open Mon.-Fri. 9am-6pm, Sat. 9am-5pm.

Hospital: Countess of Chester (West Chester) Hospital, St. Martin's Way (tel. 36 50 00).

Hospitality Service: Chester at Home. Overseas visitors can spend the evening in an English home free of charge, and enjoy tea, biscuits, and conversation. Phone any day 5-7:30pm; Mr. and Mrs. Richardson (tel. 67 88 68) or Mr. and Mrs. Brockley (tel. 38 07 49) will find you a host (8-10:30pm). Pick-up from hotel arranged.

Launderette: Leighton's, 71 St. Anne St., near Northgate Arena. £1 wash, 20p dry. Open Mon.-Fri. 8:30am-9pm, Sat.-Sun. 8:30am-8pm.

Market: Mon.-Sat., covered market by bus exchange, Princess St.

Pharmacy: Boots, 47-55 Eastgate (tel. 328 42). Open Mon.-Fri. 8:45am-6pm, Sat. 8:45am-6pm. Late-night dispensing rotates.

Police: Grosvenor Rd. (tel. 35 02 22).

Post Office: 2 St. John St. (tel. 34 83 15), off Eastgate St. Open Mon.-Tues. and Thurs.-Fri. 9am-5:30pm, Wed. 9:30am-5:30pm, Sat. 9am-12:30pm. **Postal Code:** CH1 1AA.

Telephone Code: 0244.

Train Station: City Rd. (tel. 34 01 70; office open Mon.-Fri. 8:10am-7:30pm, Sat. 8:10am-6pm, Sun. 9:40am-6pm).

Accommodations and Camping

The highest concentration of decent B&Bs (average price £12) is along **Hoole Road,** a five-minute walk from the train station (turn right from the exit, climb the steps to Hoole Rd., and turn right over the railroad tracks). Buses #C21, C30, C46, and C53 run to this area from the city center.

IYHF youth hostel, Hough Green House, 40 Hough Green (tel. 68 00 56), 1½ mi. from the city center. Cross the river on Grosvenor Rd. and turn right at the roundabout, or take bus #16, 19, A8, B2, B4, or B25. A beautiful Victorian house on a quiet street. Exceptionally jovial staff and thunderous showers restore lost youth and vitality. £7, ages 16-20 £5.90, children £4.60. Open Jan.-Nov.

YWCA, City Rd. (tel. 201 27), a 2-min. walk from the train station. For women 16 years and over. Singles and doubles £6/person; no meals, but a well-stocked kitchen, washer and dryer, free baths, and TV. No curfew.

Davies Guest House, 22 Cuppin St. (tel. 34 04 52), off Grosvenor St. near Bridge St. Cheerful rooms with floral decor and TV. Located on the better side of the city walls—inside. Singles £12, doubles £11.50/person.

Camping: Chester Southerly Caravan Park, Balderton Lane, Marlston-cum-Lache (tel. (0829) 27 06 97), 3 mi. south of town on the A483 towards Wrexham. Space for 70 caravans and 20 tents. Take bus #D1 from the bus exchange (every ½hr.), or cross the river on Grosvenor Rd. to hitch from the roundabout. £4.50/tent and 2 people.

Food and Pubs

All the indoor shopping malls off Northgate, Eastgate, and Bridge Streets contain supermarkets and bakeries. For cheeses and fresh produce, stop at the indoor **market** beside the Town Hall. **Dutton's Health Foods,** 8 Godstall Lane, near the cathedral entrance, has packed lunches—a roll with cheese or paté, apple, and Brazil nuts—for a pittance (50-60p). (Open Mon.-Sat. 9am-5:30pm.) For a smaller range of the same, try **Owen Owen,** on Bridge St. (Open Mon.-Wed. and Fri. 9am-5:30pm, Thurs. 9am-8pm, Sat. 9am-6pm.) Most restaurants line the main thoroughfares: Watergate/Eastgate, which runs east-west, and Northgate/Bridge St./Lower Bridge St.

No. 14, Lower Bridge St. (tel. 31 86 62). A surprisingly diverse number of cultures are represented in their vegetarian offerings. Lunch £2.50-3.50, dinner entrees about £5. Open Mon.-Sat. 11am-2:30pm and 7-10:30pm, Sun. 11am-4pm and 7-10:30pm.

Chester Rows, 24 Watergate Row (tel. 31 60 03), on the upper tier of Watergate. Eat cheap at this swanky joint by ordering the early bird special: a delicious entree, including bread and vegetables, plus either a starter or dessert, all for £6 (available before 7pm, Sun.-Fri. in summer). Lunches run about £5, dinner entrees £6-10. Open daily noon-2:30pm and 6-10pm.

Francs, Cuppin St. (tel. 31 79 52). Menu of inexpensive gourmet lunches. Break away from chips and cholesterol. Open Mon.-Sat. noon-11pm, Sun noon-3pm and 6:30-10pm.

Chester has 32 pubs to annihilate thirst and hunger. The **Coach and Horses** on Northgate St. serves a limited menu of light meals under £3 on white linen tablecloths. The concentration of comfortable and interesting watering stops is higher on Lower Bridge St.: **The Falcon** and **Ye Olde King's Head** are restored 17th-century family houses, and **Claverton's Wine Bar** is lively and genial with a large array of salads—a good stop on an evening constitutional down to The Groves along the river. Further down Lower Bridge St., **The Bear and Billet** occupies an 18th-century townhouse that the Earls of Shrewsbury once called home. Join in the steady conversation at the friendly **Dublin Packet** in Town Hall Sq., which has large booths and hot bar snacks from £2.20 at lunchtime. The **Boat House** glitters along the River Dee at night, while **Telford's** by the canal is favored by more grungy university students. (In general, pubs open Mon.-Sat. 11am-11pm, Sun. noon-10:30pm, with some places closed 3-7pm.)

Sights

The architectural hodgepodge (some of the medieval-style buildings are actually Victorian pastiches) effectively masks the fact that the center of Chester is really one vast outdoor shopping mall. On summer Saturdays, the already thick crowds coagulate, and a bizarre variety of street musicians, from cowpoke trios to accordion-wielding matrons, sets up shop. The famous **castle walls** completely encircle the town, and you can walk around them for free. A submerged Roman-era shopping cart from the Battle of Sainsbury's is visible in the river below.

Many pathways slither over and under the city walls and pass through unimaginatively named gates. The original **Northgate,** with a fine-grained view of the Welsh hills, was rebuilt in 1808 to house the city's jail, 30 ft. below ground level. The bridge outside the gate, euphemistically dubbed the Bridge of Sighs, connected the jail with the chapel to prevent convicts from escaping on the way to their last service.

Just outside Newgate lie the half-unearthed foundations of the largest **Roman amphitheater** in Britain. Excavated in 1960, it once accommodated the 7000-strong Roman legion at Deva. (Open daily 10am-6pm, Oct.-March Tues.-Sun. 10am-1pm and 2-4pm. Free.) The Romans are credited with the layout of Chester's streets, but their character is medieval. The **rows** of Bridge St., Watergate St., and Eastgate St., and some other streets are unique to Chester: above the street-level shops, a walkway gives access to another tier of storefronts. Some historians theorize that Edward I imported the idea from Constantinople, which he had visited while on crusade. Many of the buildings in the rows were substantially restored, and more were built during the Victorian era.

Chester's brooding and massive gothic **cathedral** began its life in the 11th century as the burial place for St. Werburgh, a Mercian abbess and one of the early founders of the northern monasteries. Her shrine became a center for pilgrimages during the Middle Ages. Fine examples of medieval architecture remain; look for the Norman arches hidden in the north transept. For those last-minute donations, there is a Barclay's bank branch tucked away conveniently in the west wing. The cathedral will be 900 years old in 1992, highlighting its anniversary celebration with two weeks of mystery plays in July. (Cathedral open daily 7am-6:30pm.)

The **Grosvenor Museum,** 27 Grosvenor St. (tel. 32 16 16), flaunts Chester's archaeological and natural history, with an emphasis on the Roman occupation. Inside, the **Castle Street Period House** is a townhouse with paneled rooms furnished in Stuart, mid-Georgian, and Victorian styles. (Museum open Mon.-Sat. 10:30am-5pm, Sun. 2-5pm. Free.) Visit the **Toy Museum,** 13A Lower Bridge St. Row (tel. 34 62 97), to see which match-box cars your collection lacked—the museum has the largest collection in the world. (Open daily 11am-5pm. Admission £1.50, seniors, students and children 70p.)

For a look at some Cheshire cats, primates, and reptiles, head to the **Chester Zoo** (tel. (0244) 38 02 80) in nearby Upton-by-Chester. Moats and low walls divvy up the 110-acre site, proffering unhindered views of the creatures. This zoo has been very successful at breeding endangered species, and maintains a large population of that most fearsome of all wild beasts—the screaming English schoolchild. From the Chester bus station, bus #40 runs to the zoo every 8 minutes Mon.-Sat., every 30 min. on Sun. A mini-bus also runs from the Bache station on the Chester-Liverpool rail line. (Zoo open daily 10am-dusk, last admission 5pm. Admission £5, ages 3-15 and seniors £2.50, families £15.)

Entertainment

The **Chester Gateway Theatre,** The Forum, Hamilton Pl. (tel. 34 03 92/3), presents a varied if somewhat limited season. Tickets cost £4-8, but there are student discounts and free admission to wheelchair-users (space permitting) for all weekday and matinee performances. (Box office open on performance days Mon.-Sat. 10am-8pm, other days 10am-6pm.)

The **Sports and Leisure Fortnight,** held each year during the last week in June and the first week of July, centers around a river carnival and a raft race on the Dee. A huge crowd turns out for such under-appreciated fun as dinghy-racing and hang gliding. Write the tourist office for tickets, which are often free and are available two months before the festival (see Practical Informations above). On sporadic spring and summer weekends, England's oldest horse races are held counterclockwise on the **Roodee** (tel. 32 73 71), formerly the Roman harbor. The races replaced an early version of football, banned in the 16th century for its excessive violence. B&Bs fill up quickly on these weekends; write to the tourist office for schedules and advance booking information.

An event begun in the 18th century as a forum for Chester's minstrels to audition, the **Chester Summer Music Festival** draws orchestras and musical groups from across the country. Held during the third week of July and promoted by the Chester Music Society, the festival schedules several events daily, including lunchtime recitals and late evening shows (tickets £3 and up). A full program leaflet is available in May from the Chester Summer Music Festival Office, Gateway Theatre, Hamilton Pl., Chester CH1 2BH (tel. 34 03 92). The **Chester Fringe** has a much wider range of events; contact the tourist office or the Gateway Theatre Box Office (see above).

For current listings of musical and special events, pick up the free monthly *What's On* from the tourist office. **Rendezvous,** Northgate St. (tel. 27 71 41; open Thurs.-Sat. 9:30pm-2am), and **Blimper's,** City Rd. (tel. 31 47 94; open Wed. and Fri.-Sat. 9:30pm-2am), both blast a good variety of music, live and recorded. **The High Society Love St.** (tel. 434 48) keeps up with university trends—check for alternative nights (open Tues.-Sat. 9pm-2am).

The finest pleasure in Chester is also the simplest: strolling beside the River Dee. You can rent a boat or simply take tea and watch vessels as they float by at the **Rex Café,** beside the Queen's Park Footbridge, the street which runs along the water (open daily 10am-dusk). You might catch a band concert in The Groves (summer Sun. 3:30 and 6:30pm).

Manchester

While manufacturing in Birmingham and coal production in Yorkshire grew gradually, Manchester's cotton mills sprang up overnight. Its clattering factories and crowded streets provided the most tangible evidence that an industrial revolution was well underway. Gentry and yeomen were replaced by unsentimental industrialists devoted to the rawest form of capitalism and angry laborers who terrified the middle classes. Manchester avoided the severe depression of other Midlands cities by developing its financial services sector, but its traditionally leftist political climate has persisted. Anti-apartheid, anti-nuclear, and Marxist movements thrive in Manchester, as do a fine university and an exceptional public library. Outwardly grim and industrial, Manchester's sprawling landscape conceals an intense cultural core; one of the most vibrant arts communities in England flourishes under the soot. Though the scarcity of accommodations and tourist services makes the city a diffidult place to visit, Manchester spruced up in a bid for the 1996 Olympics and is well worth a look, if not a stay.

Arriving and Departing

Besides Heathrow and Gatwick, **Manchester International Airport** is the only airport in England that serves North America. Bus #757 express (every ½hr.; £1.60) connects the airport with Piccadilly Bus Station in the center of town.

Manchester (pop. 570,000) is served by two main rail stations, Manchester Piccadilly (primarily for trains from the south and east), and Manchester Victoria (primarily for trains from the west and north), are connected by Centreline minibus #4 (every 7 min. 7am-7pm, Sun. every 15 min.; 10 min.; 30p). Trains run to: London (every hr.; 2½ hr.; Intercity saver £23); Liverpool (every ½hr.; ¾hr.; day return £4.80); Chester (every hr.; 1 hr.; day return £5); and York (every ½hr.; 1 hr.; day return £9.10). There is also service to Sheffield (via the Peak District), West Yorkshire (on the Leeds line), the Lake District, and the west coast. A third rail station, Manchester Oxford Rd., near the university, is served mostly by local and regional trains.

Coaches stop in the Chorlton St. Coach Station. National Express serves Birmingham (8/day 3:45am-11:50pm, with an additional coach at 7pm on Fri. and

Sun.; 2-3 hr.; £8, return £8.25-10.50), Sheffield (every 2 hr., 1½ hr., single or day return £4.79), Glasgow (5-7/day; 4-5 hr.; £14, return £15-17.50), and London (7 Rapide/day 7:30am-11:50pm; 5 hr.; £15.50, return £16-20.50).

Orientation and Practical Information

The **tourist office** is in the annex across the street from the town hall in Albert Sq. From Piccadilly Bus Station, the hub of Manchester's gargantuan network of local and regional services, turn left onto Mosley St. then right onto Princess St. to the town hall. From Piccadilly Rail Station, just two blocks south and 1 block east of the Piccadilly Bus Station, walk straight ahead onto Piccadilly and turn left on Portland St. to Princess St. From Chorlton Coach Station, turn left onto Portland St. to Princess St. From Victoria Rail Station, take virtually any bus to Piccadilly Bus Station and walk from there, or walk down Corporation St. for about a ½mi. and cross.

Manchester reveals its youth by allowing some streets to run several blocks without changing their names. Mosley St. runs southwest from Piccadilly bus station to the G-Mex, passing within a block of Town Hall. It is roughly paralleled by Deansgate/Victoria St., to the west, and the River Irwell, further west. Important cross streets are Liverpool Rd., which connects the G-Mex and the Museum of Science and Industry, and Oxford St., which runs southeast from the library to the university, about a ½mi. away.

Tourist Information Center: Town Hall Extension, Albert Sq. on Lloyd St. (tel. 234 31 57/8), to the right and across the street as you face the town hall entrance. Accommodations service 95p. In addition to the free hotel guide on display, a free list of B&Bs is kept under the counter and provided on request. Free maps and leaflets, including the *Manchester Attractions Guide,* which lists hours, prices, and the extent of disabled access, and *A Stroll Around Manchester.* Open Mon.-Fri. 9am-5pm, Sat. 10am-5pm.

Tours: Tourist office offers dozens of guided walks (£1.50, seniors, students and children £1) on such topics as "Dickens in Manchester," "Canals Under the City's Streets," and "Children's Manchester." Some tours must be booked at least ½hr. in advance; most are given about once per day June-Aug., less frequently other months. The tourist office has a free schedule with full details about walking and coach tours (£3-10).

Bookstore: Waterstone's, 91 Deansgate (tel. 832 19 92), between St. Ann's St. and King St. Large selection of everything good, including *Let's Go* guides. Fantastic section of real travel literature. Open Mon.-Fri. 8:45am-9pm, Sat. 8:45am-7:30pm, Sun. 10:30am-6:30pm.

Bus Station: Piccadilly Bus Station, consists of about 50 bus stops around Piccadilly Gardens. Immense fold-out route map (free) can be picked up from the information desk in the station. For further information, call 228 78 11. Piccadilly Information Office open Mon.-Sat. 7am-6:30pm; information line open daily 8am-8pm.

Coach Station: Chorlton St. (tel. 228 38 81). 2 blocks south and 1 block east of the Piccadilly Bus Station.

Emergency: Dial 999; no coins required.

Financial Services: Thomas Cook, 2 Oxford St., off Peter Sq. Open Mon.-Wed. and Fri. 9am-5:30pm, Thurs. 9am-5pm, Sat. 9am-1pm for *bureau de change* only. **Barclay's,** 51 Mosley St. Open Mon.-Fri. 9:30am-4:30pm. **American Express:** 10-12 St. Mary's Gate, at Deansgate and Blackfriars. Mail held for cardholders. Open Mon.-Tues. and Thurs.-Fri. 9am-5pm, Wed. 9:30am-5pm, Sat. 9am-1pm.

Hospital: Royal Infirmary, Nelson St. (tel. 273 33 00). Buses #119, 120 and 189-191 run from Piccadilly down Oxford Rd.

Launderette: Buckingham Laundry, 418 Wilbram in Chorlton. Facing Chorlton post office, turn left; it's 3 blocks up, on your left. Wash 70p-£1, dry 20p. Open Mon.-Wed. and Fri. 9am-7:30pm, Thurs. and Sat. 9am-3:30pm.

Pharmacy: Enterprise Dispensing Chemist, 7 Oxford St. (tel. 236 14 45), off St. Peter's Sq. Open daily 8am-midnight.

Police: Chester House, Chester Rd., Stretford.

Post Office: 26 Spring Gardens (tel. 837 82 53), near Market St. *Poste Restante* (separate entrance) opens at 7am. Open Mon.-Fri. 8:30am-6pm, Sat. 8:30am-1pm. **Postal Code:** M2 1BB.

Student Travel Office: YHA Adventure Centre, 166 Deansgate (tel. 833 20 46). Hostel memberships, ISIC, *Let's Go* books, Travelsave stamps (£6). Books ferries, trains, and coaches. Good deals on flights. Also, camping and hiking supplies. Open Mon.-Wed. and Fri. 10am-6pm, Thurs. 10am-7pm, Sat. 9am-5:30pm.

Telephone Code: 061.

Train Stations: Piccadilly Station, on London Rd. Travel Centre open daily 7:30am-8:30pm. **Victoria Station,** on Chapel St. Travel Centre, open Mon.-Fri. 8:30am-9pm, Sat. 8:30am-8pm, Sun. 8:30am-8:30pm. Both stations open 24 hr. For 24-hr. information on all stations call 832 83 53.

Accommodations and Camping

According to the economic theories of the Manchester School, a high demand for cheap rooms in Manchester should produce an abundant supply. No such luck. While there are plenty of expense-account hotels for business travelers, tourists will have to search harder and must probably resign themselves to taking a bus out to their lodgings. A few of the pubs along **Chapel St.,** which runs roughly parallel to and northwest of Deansgate, have B&B from £12.50. A few B&Bs and small hotels are a 15- to 20-min. bus ride outside the city center in an area called **Chorlton;** buses #85-86 and 102-103 pass by or near the Chorlton post office on Wilbraham Rd.

University of Manchester, Wolton Hall (tel. 224 72 44), 2 mi. past the university. Take bus #40-46 or 49; get off at Owens Park. Mostly singles, some doubles. Standard, nondescript dorm-like dwellings. Often filled with groups. B&B £13.

Ilkeston, 6 Chelford Rd. (tel. 860 68 87), off Upper Chorlton Rd., about 2 mi. from the city center. Take Bus #47, 84, or 86 from downtown to the "T.A. Depot." Pleasant rooms and amiable hosts who don't mind a bit if you want to visit clubs all night and sleep all day. B&B £12.

The Black Lion, 65 Chapel St. (tel. 834 19 74), at Blackfriars. Singles, doubles, and family rooms above a cheerful pub. All with TV and teamakers. B&B £13.

Food and Pubs

Downtown is an arid plain of fast-food places and cheap, charmless cafés. Chinatown, bounded by Portland, Mosley, Charlotte, and Oxford St., is a disappointingly uniform agglomeration of pricey Cantonese restaurants, though you can save a few quid by eating a multi-course "Businessman's Lunch," offered by most Mon.-Fri. noon-2pm (£4-7.50). A more heartening source of ethnic food is the Rusholme area, past the university, where numerous Middle Eastern and South African restaurants and take-out counters line Wilmslow Rd., near the intersection with Dickenson Rd.

Basta Pasta, Mosley and York St. Friendly joint with a gleaming black and white interior. Pizza for around £4, large portions of various pastas with your choice of toppings £3.10-4.40. Bring your own beer or wine. Espresso and mediocre gelato. Open Mon.-Sat. 11am-11pm.

Mark Addy, 3 Stanley St. (tel. 832 4080), on the far bank of the River Irwell, off New Bailey Bridge. Choose one of 46 varieties of cheese (or a paté) and get a good slab of it, plus bread, onion and pickle for about £3. Indoor or outdoor seating overlooking the river.

Camel One, 107 Wilmslow St. (tel. 257 2282), in Rusholme. Snazzier than its take-away brethren, with a more interesting menu. £3 gets you a kebab or curry and a fluffy naan, to take away or eat at the counter. Open daily 11am-5am.

Cornerhouse Café, 70 Oxford St. On 2nd floor of arts center. Trendy, collegiate crowd. Panoptical view of the street and its crawling inhabitants. Quiche and salad £1.60, hot vegetable dishes and salad from £1. Scrumptious desserts from 55p. Hot meals served noon-2pm and 5-7pm. Open daily noon-8pm.

Pizza Express, S. King St. and Ridgefield off Deansgate. Nouvelle and elegant with a touch of light jazz; no need to feel rushed. Specialty pizzas (with artichokes and stuff) £4-5. Open daily 11:30am-midnight.

The French Window, King's St. pedestrian mall. Great cheese and pastry selection. "Beigels" filled with cream cheese 55p. Open Mon.-Sat. 8am-5:30pm.

Royal Exchange Theatre Café, Cross St. Great atmosphere; busy and cluttered, but elegantly so. Cold salads £1.30, sandwiches from 80p. Open Mon.-Sat. 10am-9:30pm.

Manchester is a fortress of real ale. The tourist office can supply a list of pubs that brew and serve ale the genuine way and includes pub tours among its guided walks. The **Lass-O-Gowrie,** Charles St., serves two versions of their own brew to a rambunctious crowd. (Open Mon.-Fri. 11:30am-11pm, Sat. 11:30am-3:30pm and 9:15-11pm, Sun. noon-3pm and 7-10:30pm.) For a more sedate crowd and great beer, pound at **The Circus Tavern** on Portland St. (Open Mon.-Sat. 11am-11pm, Sun. noon-3pm, 7-11pm.)

Sights

Presiding over the city is the **Manchester Town Hall,** a phenomenal neo-Gothic structure designed by Alfred Waterhouse and opened in 1877. Ford Madox Brown murals in the great hall depict the history of Manchester from the establishment of a Roman fort to local industrial inventions in the 17th and 18th centuries; an inflatable tribute to Father Christmas clings to the tower in December. (Free guided tours: Mon. 10am, Wed. 10am and 2:30pm, Thurs. 10am. Confirm with tourist office.) Behind the building, the **Peace Garden** attests to Manchester's status as a nuclear-free city. Behind the Town Hall Extension is Manchester's jewel, the **Central Library.** One of the largest municipal libraries in Europe, it was opened by George V in 1934. Among many other fine collections, the domed building houses a music and theater library, an exceptional language and literature library, and England's most extensive Jewish-studies library outside London. (Open Mon.-Wed. and Fri. 10am-8pm, Sat. 10am-noon and 1-5pm.) The **Museum of Science and Industry** (tel. 832 2244), on Liverpool Rd. in the spruced-up area of Castleton, comprises five buildings displaying technology past and present. Working steam engines and looms provide a more dramatic sense of the awesome speed, power, danger, and noise of Britain's industrialization than any diagram or description ever could. In addition, its **Xperiment! Gallery** has many physics toys to play with, including a polished bowl that allows you to thumb-wrestle with a ghostly image of your hand; the **Air and Space Gallery** houses a 1942 Spitfire. Many of the exhibits emphasize the history of Manchester. (Open daily 10am-5pm. Admission £2.60, students, seniors and disabled £1.30; includes entrance to all galleries for one day, which may not be enough.) Also in Castleton, **Granada Studios** (tel. 832 9090) on Water St. holds particular appeal for devotees of the long-running series "Coronation Street," though it also features mock-ups of New York, the House of Commons, and 221B Baker St. (Open April-Sept. Tues.-Sun. 9:45am-7pm, last admission 4pm; Oct.-Dec. and Feb.-March Wed.-Sun., Jan. Sat.-Sun. 9:45am-5:30pm, last admission 3pm. Admission £7.95, children £5.45.)

The **City Art Galleries** (tel. 236 5244) consist of two adjacent buildings with entrances on different streets. The Mosley St. building houses a permanent collection of mostly 19th-century English works, weighted towards classical and biblical subject matter. Touring shows are curated next door at the Princess St. building. (Both buildings open Mon.-Sat. 10am-5:45pm, Sun. 2-5:45pm. Free. Difficult disabled access.) The Spanish and Portugese Synagogue turned **Manchester Jewish Museum,** 190 Cheetham Hill Rd. (tel. 834 98 79 or 832 73 53), north of Victoria Station, traces the history of the city's sizeable Jewish community. (Open Mon.-Thurs. 10:30am-4pm, Sun. 10:30am-5pm. Admission £1, seniors, students, and children 50p.) The brown land of the Ardwick and Rusholme neighborhoods south of the city center is gilded by **Manchester University** and its two fine museums. **Manchester Museum,** on Oxford Rd., houses the university's natural history collections, including extensive prehistoric and anthropological exhibits. (Open Mon.-Sat. 10am-5pm. Free.) The **Whitworth Art Gallery,** 1½ mi. from the city center down Oxford Rd., features British watercolors, a few stray Warhols, and a large collection of international textiles. (Open Mon.-Wed. and Fri.-Sat. 10am-5pm, Thurs. 10am-9pm. Admission free. Complete disabled access.) To see what Manchester really cares about, ask at the tourist office about tours of the city's football grounds.

Entertainment

Hardworking, obstreperous Mancunians have furnished themselves with a lively nightlife, especially near the university during the term. Pick up a copy of the bi-weekly *City Life* (90p, available at the tourist office or at most news agents) for a comprehensive schedule of arts events (from Mozart to dance clubs) before entering the whirlpool. You can phone or visit the **Arts and Entertainment Booking and Information Service** (tel. 236 70 76) in the tourist information center. Buses run to outlying areas regularly until 11pm; less frequent night service runs until 2:30am.

The **Royal Exchange Theatre,** Cross St. (tel. 833 98 33), performs an exciting and diverse program in a space-age theater-in-the-round inside the 1809 Exchange Building. (Box office open Mon.-Sat. 10am-6pm or until performance begins. Tickets from £3.40. Student standbys (£3.50), senior and disabled person discounts (both £3) available Mon.-Thurs. Can be purchased up to 3 days in advance.) The **Library Theatre** (tel. 236 71 10), in the intimate former lecture hall of the Central Library, St. Peter's Sq., is an active and offbeat professional company; the **Palace Theatre,** Oxford St. (tel. 236 99 22), caters to more bourgeois tastes in theater, opera, and ballet. The university's **CONTACT Theatre,** Oxford St. (tel. 274 44 00) showcases its own performances and occasionally hosts touring companies in its auditorium (tickets start at £4, students £2.50). The **Cornerhouse,** 70 Oxford St. (tel. 228 24 63), features foreign films on its three screens. (Tickets £2.75, students £1.75, matinees £2.50 and £1.50.) A small upstairs gallery frequently has exhibits with a strong experimental and political slant. For some radical cabaret, join the carbuncular crowd down the street in **The Green Room,** 54-56 Whitworth St. (tel. 236 16 77), a comfortable café/bar/theater tucked inside an old industrial building. (Open Tues.-Sat. noon-11pm, Sun. noon-6pm.) The **Nia Centre,** Chichester Rd. (tel. 227 9254), presents black theater and music.

The Free Trade Hall, Peter's St., is now the home of the superb **Hallé Orchestra** from October to May (booking office on Cross St., tel. 834 17 12). Pop, jazz, and classical concerts are frequently held at the **G-Mex** (Greater Manchester Exhibition and Event Centre; tel. 834 27 00), a renovated former train station on Lower Mosley St. Students stampede to **Band on the Wall,** 25 Swan St. (tel. 832 66 25), to hear quality jazz, blues, reggae, and rock performed "exceptionally live" Monday through Saturday.

Manchester's club scene sets the nation's trends, and it centers on **Hacienda,** 11-13 W. Whitworth St., close to G-Mex. The club that launched The Smiths, New Order, and the Stone Roses continues with ecstatic all-night "raves" of house music. (For concert information call 236 50 51. Open 9pm-2am.) Similar music is played by DJs at **The Venue,** also on Whitworth St. (tel. 236 0026; open 9pm-2am). For a variety of house, hip-hop, and quasi-disco in a subterranean setting, check out **Konspiracy,** 55 Fennel St. Nightclubs in the center of town can be a bit seedy.

Sheffield

God gave man teeth and fingers, but Sheffield gave him cutlery. While Manchester was clothing the world, Sheffield was setting the table, first with hand-crafted flatware, then with mass-produced goods and eventually stainless steel, which was first widely used here. The city's population skyrocketed in the boom years of the mid-19th century, and now Sheffield is England's fourth-largest city. Though itself a thoroughly urban center, Sheffield is just a short bus trip from the tiny village and open moors of the Peak District.

Arriving and Departing

Sheffield lies on the M1 Motorway, about 30 mi. east of Manchester and 25 mi. south of Leeds. It is connected by frequent direct train service to Manchester (through the Peak District's Hope Valley), Liverpool, York, and Birmingham. For the Lake District and the northwest, change at Preston or Stockport; for Chester, change at Stockport. **Trains** run to Manchester (every ½hr. 6:27am-10:06pm, Sun. every hr. 8:55am-10:35pm; 1-1½ hr.; £6.20-7.30 depending on the time of travel), Birmingham (26/day all night, Sun. 12/day 10:06am-9:26pm; 2 hr.; £14, return £15.50-22), London's St. Pancras (30/day 5:13am-8:54pm, Sun. 10/day 8:40am-8:52pm; 2-3 hr.; saver return £28-34).

National Express Rapide coach service is less frequent than the Hourly inter-city trains to London, but cheaper.National Express **coaches** run to London (every 2 hr. 6:30am-10:15pm; 3½ hr.; £17, economy return £17.50), Birmingham (every 2 hr. 8:30am-6:35pm; 2 hr.; £10), and Nottingham (every 1-2 hr. all night; 1 hr.; £4.75). The office in the Sheffield Interchange is open Mon.-Sat. 8am-6pm, Sun. 9:30am-6pm (tel. 75 49 05).

Orientation and Practical Information

Coaches, local buses and buses to the Peak District arrive at the marvelously designed Sheffield Interchange between Pond St. and Sheaf St. The train station is one block south on Sheaf St. (24-hr. train information, tel. 72 64 11; recorded timetable tel. 73 85 55). The **Transport Executive Office** (tel. 76 86 88) is located in the Interchange opposite the coach office, and has information on local buses. (Open Mon.-Sat. 8am-6pm, Sun. 9am-5pm.) You can also get bus information from **South Yorkshire's Transport** (tel. 75 56 55).

The **tourist office,** Town Hall Extension, Union St. (tel. 73 46 71/2) has an accommodations service (£1) and distributes free accommodations lists, places of interest leaflets (including the *Peakland Post,* which has information on the Peak District), and plenty of entertainment brochures. After hours, an accommodations list is posted in the window. (Open Mon.-Fri. 9:30am-5:15pm, Sat. 9:30am-4:15pm. Accommodations booking closes 1 hr. earlier.) To reach the office from the Interchange, exit the Interchange at Pond St., cross Pond, turn right, and walk uphill to the end of the enormous white-tiled building. There turn left and go up the concrete steps and through the subway. Turn left upon emerging, onto Norfolk St. The office is at the far end of the modern, tan building which has a causeway leading to Town Hall. The post office lies on Fitzalan Sq. (tel. 73 35 25), one block uphill from the interchange. Address *Poste Restante* to "Head Post Office" at postal code S1 1AA. (Open Mon.-Tues. and Thurs.-Fri. 8:30am-5:30pm, Wed. 9am-5:30pm, Sat. 8:30am-12:30pm.) The telephone code is 0742.

Accommodations

The tourist office list, posted in the window, is fairly comprehensive; unless you can get a room at the YMCA, B&Bs run at least £14. Most places are quite a hike from the city center and fill up quickly, especially during summer weekends. Call in advance.

YMCA, 20 Victoria Rd. (tel. 68 48 07) between Broomhall and Victoria Rd. Take bus #60 to Hallamshire Hospital; bear left on Clarkehouse Rd. to Park Lane and turn left again. Alternatively, take buses #81-84 to Collegiate Crescent, then walk up and turn right on Victoria Rd. Clean, comfortable rooms. Men and women. Singles £11, doubles £10/person. Continental breakfast included. Key deposit £3.

Mr. and Mrs. Chambers, 17 Sale Hill (tel. 66 29 86). Take bus #60 to the beginning of Manchester Rd., then climb 1 block to Sale Hill. Flower garden overlooking the city is worth the hike. Singles £15, doubles £13/person.

Peace Guest House, 92 Brocco Bank (tel. 68 51 10), at Ecclesall Rd. Take buses #81-84. Singles £15, doubles £14/person.

Food

For meat and fish, head for **Castle Market** on Exchange St.; **Sheaf Market,** across the street, has fruit and vegetables. (Both open Mon.-Wed. and Fri.-Sat. roughly 8am-5pm.)

Mamas and Leonies, 111-115 Norfolk St., near Town Hall. Serves pasta and pizza to businessmen. Most entrees around £4.50. (Open Mon.-Sat. 10am-11:30pm.)

Bebek Kebab, 14 Norfolk Row (tel. 72 06 95). Take-away kebabs grilled to order, £2.30-3.50, slightly more for table service. Open Mon.-Wed. 11am-midnight, Thurs.-Sat. 11am-3am, Sun. 6pm-midnight.)

Sights and Entertainment

Vulcan stands proudly atop Town Hall's 193-ft. tower, the symbol of Sheffield's industry. The city's industrial heritage is more extensively recalled at the **Abbeydale Industrial Hamlet,** 4 mi. south on the A621 (Abbeydale Rd. S.; tel. 36 77 31; take bus #24 or 42 from High St., every ½hr). Here, a complete water-powered scythe works, including a water-driven tilt forge and grinding wheel, blacksmith's forges, and one of the few surviving crucible steel furnaces in Britain, has been restored in all its 18th-century glory. (Open Mon.-Sat. 10am-5pm, Sun. 11am-5pm. Admission £1.80, seniors and children 90p, disabled people free.) The **Kelham Island Industrial Museum,** Alma St. (tel. 72 21 06), displays some of the iron, steel, silverware, and unusual metal products manufactured in Sheffield over the past 300 years. It also houses a working 12,000 horsepower steam engine (Britain's most powerful). (Open Wed.-Sat. 10am-5pm, Sun. 11am-5pm. Admission £2, seniors and children £1. Take bus #47 or 48 from the interchange every hr.; alight at Nursery St.)

In 1875, the Victorian critic and artist John Ruskin established a museum to show the working class that "life without industry is guilt, and industry without art is brutality." What emerged was the Guild of St. George Collection, now displayed in the **Ruskin Gallery,** Norfolk St. in the center of town (tel. 73 52 99). The gallery contains paintings, mineral formations, and illuminated manuscripts. The local crafts gallery is also worth a glance. (Both open Mon.-Fri. 10am-6pm, Sat. 10am-5pm; free.) Nearby is the **Graves Art Gallery,** Surrey St. (tel. 73 47 81), at the top floor of the Central Library building, which houses contemporary British art and the Grice collection of Chinese ivories. (Open Mon.-Sat. 10am-6pm. Free.) **The Untitled Gallery,** Brown St. (tel. 72 59 47), near the train station, has changing photography exhibits, often with a local theme. (Open Tues.-Sat. 10am-5:30pm; Jan.-March Tues.-Sat. noon-5:30pm. Free.)

Two museums share a building in the beautifully landscaped Weston Park, west of the city center and adjacent to the university. **The Mappin Art Gallery** (tel. 72 62 81), Weston Park, holds a large collection of Victorian painting. (Open Tues.-Sat. 10am-5pm, Sun. 2-5pm. Free. The **City Museum,** (tel. 76 85 88), focuses on ancient British artifacts, many from the Bronze Age, and has in addition a room full of cutlery from Sheffield and elsewhere. (Open Tues.-Sat. 10am-5pm, Sun. 11am-5pm. Free. Disabled access.) Take bus #52 from High St. to the Children's Hospital.

At night, the **Crucible Theatre,** Norfolk St. (tel. 76 99 22), offers musicals, plays, and concerts; in past years presentations have included *American Buffalo, The Cherry Orchard,* and the Lindsay String Quartet. Those under 26 can get tickets for £2 after 10am on the day of the show, Mon.-Fri. For two interminable weeks in April, the **World Snooker Championship,** in all its infinite subtlety, elbows its way onto the stage and into the hearts of British and tourists alike. (Tickets £2-7, students £3-4.) The lavishly restored **Lyceum Theatre,** next to the Crucible, will, when completed, hold touring West End shows (call 76 99 22 for details).

For a lively student atmosphere, try **The Leadmill** (tel. 72 15 57), near the train station. Their *Gig Guide,* available at the tourist office, will tell you when to catch jazz, acid house, and Agropop (cover £1-5). **Isabella's,** on Eyre St., has a student night on Wednesdays (cover £3-4). If you'd rather spend the evening on your feet, head for **The Club with Two Brains,** Charter Sq. (Open weekends 10pm-2am, cover charge £2, £1.50 before 10:30pm.)

Peak District National Park

The Peak District lies at the southern end of the Pennines, covering a rough square with Manchester, Sheffield, Nottingham and Stoke-on-Trent at its corners. Remarkably devoid of mountain peaks, the area derives its name from the Old English *peac,* meaning hillock. In the northeastern Dark Peak area, deep "groughs" (gullies) gouge the hard peat moorland against a backdrop of gloomy cliffs while gray stone villages and patches of forest break up the rolling hills in the limestone plateau of the southern White Peak. Here the landscape is pastoral rather than wild, with low stone walls crawling over fields of grass well-nibbled by sheep and Friesian cattle.In the Derbyshire Dales, rivers have chiseled white limestone into deep gorges.

The tiny villages here host annual "well-dressing" festivals, which have nothing to do with clothing. Rather, elaborate mosaics of flower petals are pressed onto clay slabs near local wells, signifying gratitude for yet another year's supply of water. Because such decorative venerations of a pagan life source are scheduled according to the church calendar, the dates vary when reckoned by the standard calendar. Exact dates are published in *Peak District and Derbyshire Events,* available from tourist centers after February.

Wedged between large urban centers, the Peak District receives over 20 million visitors per year, more than any other national park in England. Exceptional public transport and commercial coach tours facilitate mob movement on sunny weekends; catch the infrequent buses to the bleaker northern moors, out of the reach of the commuter-rail lines for a moer peaceful visit. Although protected from development by national park status, the land is still privately owned, so be respectful and stay to designated rights-of-way. By far the best ramblers' guidebooks are Mark Richards' *High Peak Walks* and *White Peak Walks* (£7.95 each). These books, and many other useful publications, are available at National Park Information Centres and can be ordered by mail. Write to Peak Park Joint Planning Board, National Park Office, Aldern House, Bakewell DE4 1AE for a list of publications. *Places of Interest Around Sheffield,* available for free from the Sheffield Tourist Office, is a good list of non-trail attractions, such as caverns and castles, within the park.

Getting There and Getting Around

Many would say that walking is the essence of the park and that your feet are all you need to get from one village to the next. Nevertheless, there is fairly good bus and even rail service between the villages. If you plan on using buses or trains to get around, Derbyshire County Council's *District Timetable* (50p) is an excellent investment; it includes all bus and train information and comes with a good map. You can get a copy at the Transport Executive in the Sheffield interchange, the Bakewell tourist office, and elsewhere. The Council also staffs a bus inquiries line (tel. (0298) 230 98, 7am-8pm daily). Transport services actually improve on Sundays—special buses are added to cart nature lovers far out into the country.

Two rail lines originate in Manchester and enter the park in the northwest: the Hop eValley train runs hourly and terminates at **Buxton** near the park's western edge, while the second line (also hourly service) continues across the park to Sheffield (via **Edale**), **Hope** (near **Castleton**), and **Hathersage.** Both rail lines enter the park at New Mills, alebit stopping at two different stations within a 20-min. walk of each other. A third rail line leaves from Nottingham and runs north via Derby to Matlock, located on the southeastern edge of the Peak District.

Bus #252, the "Transpeak," makes the 3½-hr. journey through the park from Manchester to Nottingham every two hours, stopping at Buxton, Bakewell, Matlock, Matlock Bath, and Derby; this mainline service is a counterpart to the north's Hope Valley rail line. Evening buses may not cover the whole route, so check the timetable.

If you plan to do a great deal of riding, buy a **Greater Manchester Wayfarer** (£4.50, seniors and children £3.25) or a **Derbyshire Wayfarer** (£6, seniors and children £3). Each ticket covers virtually all rail and bus services within the Peak District for a day. The former also covers services to, from, and around Manchester; the latter also covers services to and from Sheffield. If you're traveling strictly within the park, the ticket will be worth your while if you board three or more buses or trains.

Orientation and Practical Information

Facilities in the Peak District generally stay open through the winter, due to the proximity of large cities. Some B&Bs and youth hostels stay open into December. The *Peakland Post,* a free newspaper available at the Sheffield tourist office and park tourist offices, is loaded with information on sights and events in the park. For an information pack on the Peak District, write to the Tourism Officer, Town Hall, Matlock, Derbyshire, DE4 3NN.

Tourist Information Centers

Ashbourne: 16 Market Pl. (tel. (0335) 436 66). Open daily 9:30am-1pm, 2-5pm; Oct.-March, reduced hours but always open on Thurs. and Sat.

Bakewell: Market Hall (tel. (0629) 81 32 27). Also a National Park Information Centre. Books accommodations with a deposit of 10% of the first night's payment, which is applied to the bill, until 5pm. Comprehensive exhibit on local life and the park's history. Sells a good selection of maps and guides. Open daily 9am-5:30pm; Sat., Sun., bank holiday and in Aug. until 6pm; Nov.-March Fri.-Wed. 9:30am-5pm.

Buxton: The Crescent (tel. (0298) 251 06). Books accommodations for 95p. Open daily 9:30am-5pm; Nov.-March Mon.-Sat. 10am-12:30pm and 1:30-4pm, Sun. noon-4pm.

Matlock Bath: The Pavilion (tel. (0629) 550 82), along the main road. Free accommodation-booking service (10% deposit) until 4:30pm. Open daily 9:30am-5:30pm.

National Park Information Centres

National Park Centres display the park's symbol of a circle above a horizonal rectangle.

Bakewell: See Tourist Information Centers above.

Castleton: On Castle St. (tel. (0433) 206 79), near the church. Open daily 10am-5:30pm; Nov.-March Sat.-Sun. 10am-5pm. From the bus stop, follow the main road into town and turn left at the youth hostel sign.

Edale: Fieldhead (tel. (0433) 67 02 07), between the rail station and village. Open daily 9am-5:30pm; Nov.-Easter daily 9am-5pm.

Fairholmes: In Upper Derwent Valley, near Derwent Dam (tel. (0433) 509 53). Open daily 10:30am-5:30pm; Oct.-Easter Sat.-Sun. 10:30am-5pm.

Hartington: In the signal box at Hartington Old Station, 1½ mi. from the village. Open Easter-Sept. Sat.-Sun. around 11am-5pm.

Torside: In Longendale Valley. Open Easter-Sept. Sat.-Sun. around 11am-5pm.

Accommodations and Camping

Information centers in the park distribute free park-wide and regional accommodations guides; a camping guide costs 30p. B&Bs are plentiful and cheap (from £8), as are youth hostels (about £6). Many farmers allow camping on their land, sometimes for a small fee; remember to leave the site just as you found it. The nine park-operated **camping barns** are simple night shelters for hikers and bikers, providing a sleeping platform, water tap, and toilet for £2/person. Book and pay ahead with the Peak National Park Centre, Losehill Hall, Castleton, Derbyshire S30 2WB (tel. (0433) 203 73).

IYHF Youth Hostels

The *IYHF Guide*(£4, or free with IYHF membership) provides a complete listing of all IYHF youth hostels in the park, most of which are within an easy day's hike of one another. In most cases, the hostels are locked 10am-5pm, have an 11pm curfew, and cost between £3.50 and £6.50. Hostels often fill with school and youth groups, so call ahead and watch where you step: Bakewell (tel. (0629) 81 23 13); Bretton (tel. (0742) 88 45 41); Buxton (tel. (0298) 222 87); Castleton (tel. (0433) 202 35); Crowden-in-Longdale (tel. (0457) 85 21 35); Dimmingsdale (tel. (0538) 70 23 04); Edale (tel. (0433) 67 03 02); Elton (tel. (0629) 88 394); Eyam (tel. (0433) 303 35); Gradbach Mill (tel. (0260) 22 76 25); Hartington Hall (tel. (0298) 84 223); Hathersage (tel. (0433) 504 93); Ilam Hall (tel. (033529) 212); Langsett (tel. (0742) 88 45 41); Matlock (tel. (0629) 58 29 83); Meerbrook (tel. (053834) 244); Ravenstor (tel. (0298) 87 18 26); Shining Cliff (tel. (062988) 394); Youlgreave (tel. (0629) 63 65 18).

Camping Barns

Abney Barn: Ivy House Farm (tel. (0433) 504 81), about 5 mi. southwest of Hathersage. Sleeps 8.

Bakewell Barns: Bank Top House Farm (tel. (062981) 26 92). Sleeps 13.

Birchover Barn: Barn Farm (tel. (062988) 245), between Bakewell and Matlock off the B5056. Sleeps 10.

Butterton: Near the southern end of the park, along the mainfold track. Sleeps 12.

Edale Barn: Catefield Farm (tel.(0433) 702 73), close to the beginning of the Pennine Way. Sleeps 8.

Losehill Barn: Near Castleton (tel. (0433) 203 73). Sleeps 8.

Nab End Barn: Between Hollinsclough and Longnor. Sleeps 16.

Old Glossop: In the northern part of the park, near the terminus of a rail line to Manchester. Sleeps 12.

One Ash Grange: Above Lathkill Dale National Nature Reserve (tel. (062986) 291). Sleeps 12.

Upper Booth Barn: Near the head of Edale (tel. (0433) 702 50). Well situated for exploring Kinder Scout and ridgewalking above Edale. Sleeps 12.

Warslow: Near Warslow (tel. (029884) 602) on the edge of the Manifold Valley. Sleeps 16.

Hiking and Biking

The central park is marvelous territory for rambling or light hiking. Small villages, B&Bs, and IYHF youth hostels are within an easy day's walk of one another. Settlement is sparser and buses are fewer north of Edale in the land of the Kinder Scout plateau, the great Derwent reservoirs, and the gritty cliffs and waterlogged peat moorlands. From Edale, the Pennine Way (see below) runs north to Kirk Yetholm, across the Scottish border.

If you hike, be particularly careful not to contaminate livestock water supplies and to close gates so that animals can't wander through and escape. Stick to marked paths or public rights-of-way. Bring a large-scale Ordnance Survey map, your own water and food, and waterproof clothing. The Peak District is on the same latitude as Siberia and Labrador, and people have died in the mist on Bleaklow and Kinder

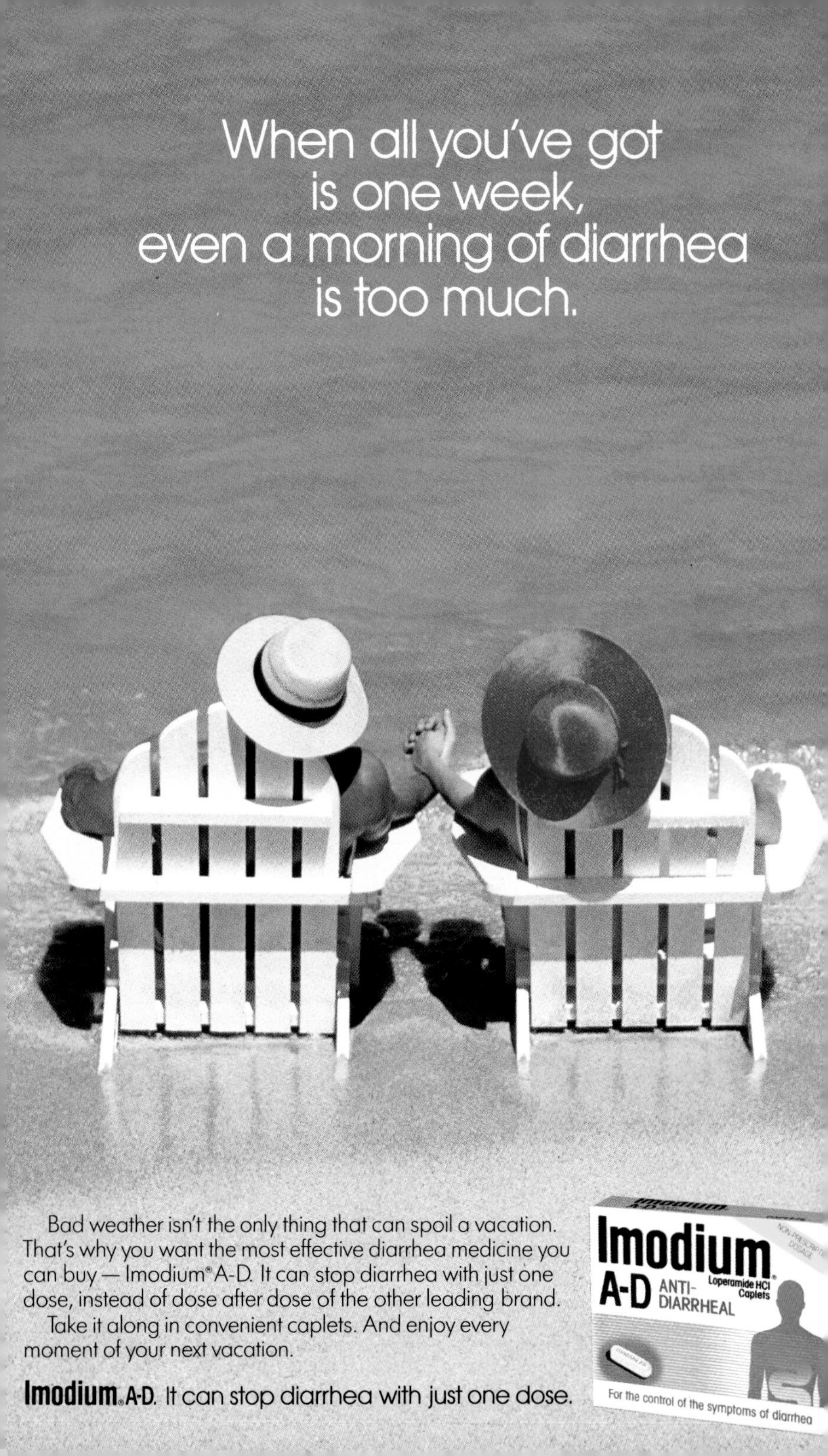
When all you've got
is one week,
even a morning of diarrhea
is too much.
Bad weather isn't the only thing that can spoil a vacation. That's why you want the most effective diarrhea medicine you can buy — Imodium® A-D. It can stop diarrhea with just one dose, instead of dose after dose of the other leading brand.
Take it along in convenient caplets. And enjoy every moment of your next vacation.
Imodium® A-D. It can stop diarrhea with just one dose.
Imodium
A-D
ANTI-
DIARRHEAL
Loperamide HCl
Caplets
For the control of the symptoms of diarrhea

Scout, just a half-hour outside two large cities. National Park Centres distribute leaflets on mountain safety.

The park authority operates seven **Cycle Hire Centres,** where you can rent a bike. (£5/day, £3 for 3 hr.; under 16 £3.50/day, £2.50 for 3 hr.; £5 deposit; 10% discount for YHA members and Wayfarer ticket holders; centers open in summer daily 9:30am-6pm, varying hours the rest of the year.) You can usually rent cycles from one center and return them to another.

Ashbourne: Mapleton Lane (tel. (0335) 431 56).

Derwent: Near the Fairholmes information center (tel. (0433) 512 61).

Hayfield: Near New Mills on the Sett Valley (tel. (0663) 462 22).

Middleton Top: Near Matlock on the High Peak Trail (tel. (0629) 82 32 04).

Parsley Hay: Near Buxton (tel. (0298) 844 93).

Shipley Country Park: Near Heanor off the A608 (tel. (0773) 71 99 61). Open in summer 9:30am-5pm daily.

Waterhouses: Between Ashbourne and Leek near the southern end of the Manifold Truck (tel. (0538) 30 86 09).

YHA also offers **Interpeak Cycling,** which lets you rent bikes from one hostel and return them to another. Daily cycle hire is available at Castleton and Edale Youth Hostels. Contact Keith Hannah, P.O. Box 177, Derby DE3 7PP (tel. (0332) 76 04 47); £4/day, £8 for mountain bikes; book ahead).

Southern Peak District

The Southern Peaks are better served by buses and trains than the Northern Peak District, and as a result are also more trampled.

Buxton

Mary Queen of Scots used Buxton's waters to treat her rheumatism, and restorative pools are still open (open Mon.-Tues. and Fri. 12:30-6:30pm, Wed.-Thurs. 12:30-8pm, Sat. 9am-3:30pm, Sun. 9am-4:30pm; Sept.-April Mon. and Fri. 12:30-6:30pm, Wed.-Thurs. 12:30-8pm, and Sat.-Sun. 9am-3:30pm. Admission £1, weekdays 90p, seniors 45p, children 50p.) Another remnant of Buxton's fashionable past is the **Buxton Opera House** (tel. (0298) 721 90), whose performances include opera and stage drama. (Box office open Mon.-Sat. 10am-6pm.) The **Buxton Micrarium** (tel. (0298) 786 62) claims to be "the world's first inner space centre." You may witness the birth of a tiny water flea on their hands-on large-screen microscope projections. (Open April-Oct. daily 10am-5pm. Admission £2, seniors £1.50, children £1.) If insect breeding does not fascinate you, try **Poole's Cavern** (tel. (0298) 269 78), just outside of town, one of the many stalagmite-studded showcaves scattered throughout the Peaks. (Open June-Aug. daily 10am-5pm; April-May and Oct. Thurs.-Tues. 10am-5pm. Admission £2.20, seniors £1.80, children £1.20. YHA discount.)

The **Buxton Festival,** to be held from approximately July 23 to August 22 in 1992, unleashes an avalanche of operas, concerts, comedy, drama, and readings from Voltaire. For information and booking, contact the Festival Box Office, Opera House, Buxton, Derbyshire SK17 6XN (tel. (0298) 721 90). Tickets start at £5. The **Festival Fringe** features exhibitions, recitals, and alternative theater; contact the tourist office for a program. Buxton's **well-dressing** festival, during which flower mosaics adorn local water sources and an even more local carnival enlivens the main square, is held the second weekend in July.

The **tourist office** books accommodations for free and gives guided walks of the town (1½ hr., £1, seniors 75p, children 50p; reservations required). The **IYHF youth hostel** (see Accommodations) is a good 25-minute hike from the station. Turn right out of the station, go to the Market Pl., and follow the main road until you reach Harpers Hill. **Mrs. Oliver,** Burbage (tel. (0298) 232 42), 1 mi. from the center of Buxton, is the cheapest B&B in the Buxton area (3 doubles, £12/person). In town, try the **Old Manse Guesthouse,** 6 Clifton Rd. (tel. (0298) 56 38; £ 12.50). **La Terraza,** in the excessively cute Cavendish Arcade, has decent pizza (from £2.85) and pasta (from £3.20). (Open daily noon-2:30pm and 5:30-10:30pm.)

Buxton (pop. 20,750) is the last stop on one rail line from Manchester and as such acts as something of a gateway to the southern part of the Peak District, although techincally it does not lie within the park's boundaries. Trains run from Manchester (at least hourly 6:48am-11:25pm, Sun. at least hourly 8:56am-10:56pm). Numerous buses connect this busy tourist spot with towns further south such as Bakewell (buses #X23, 282, and others) and Matlock (bus #232), both 5-8/day.

Bakewell

Fifteen mi. southwest of Sheffield and 30 mi. southeast of Manchester, Bakewell (pop. 4000) is the best base for exploring the southern portion of the park and a transfer point for more elaborate bus trips. Located near several scenic walks through the White Peaks, the town itself is best known for Bakewell pudding (created when a flustered cook in the Rutland Arms, trying to make a Bakewell tart, poured egg mixture over strawberry jam instead of mixing it into the dough).

Although most visitors to Bakewell stalk around in wool socks and hiking boots preparing to hit the trails, the town itself does have a few things to see. **All Saints Church,** on the hill above town, is a picturesque repository of Anglo-Saxon gravestones and carved-cross fragments. Nearby sits a 16th-century house which has aptly been transformed into the **Old House Museum** (tel. 81 36 47). (Open Easter-Oct. daily 2-5pm. Admission £1, children 50p.) In 1330, the king granted Bakewell permission to hold a weekly **market.** Livestock are still traded in the marketplace every Monday from 10am until the food vendors pack up their stalls. Bakewell's **well-dressing** festival occurs during the last week of June.

Bakewell's **tourist office** doubles as a National Park Information Centre, and displays informative exhibits on the history of Bakewell and the Peaks. Walkers can pick up the standard *6 Walks Around Bakewell* (60p) or trail leaflets for the surrounding area (£1.30-1.50). An accommodations service is available before 5pm, for a 10% deposit. A map of Bakewell is free. Bakewell also provides banking and other services less convenient in smaller towns. The **Bakewell Laundorama** on Water St., behind the Red Lion, has wash (£1.20-1.50) and dry (20p/round). (Open Mon.-Fri. 7:30am-3:30pm, Sat.-Sun. 7:30am-6pm.)

Bakewell has an **IYHF youth hostel** and numerous B&Bs, many of which lie on or near Haddon Road, the continuation of Matlock St. Try **The Mount** on Yeld Rd. (tel. (0629) 81 21 98) beyond the church overlooking the town (doubles £13/person), or **Avenue House** (tel. (0629) 81 24 67), which has spacious twins and doubles for £13/person. Single rooms in town are harder to find. Numerous sandwich shops offer provisions for hikers. Near the tourist office on Water Lane, the upstairs **By-Ways Café** serves lunch amid sunny wicker and dark wood. (Welsh rarebit with pineapple £2.60. Open Mon.-Sat. 10am-6pm, Sun. 1-6pm.) On Rutland Sq., **The Original Bakewell Pudding Shop** sells overpriced lunches and delicious desserts (pudding £1.50 with custard or cream), in a paneled restaurant above the shop. (Open daily 9am-6pm; Nov.-April daily 9am-5pm.)

2½ mi. northeast of Bakewell, off the B6012, **Chatsworth House** is immensely popular. The Duke and Duchess of Devonshire's palatial residence is surrounded by 100 acres of creative landscaping by Capability Brown, and tends to attract gaggles of gawking Americans. (Open April-Oct. daily 11am-4:30pm. Admission £4.50, seniors and students £3.50, children £2. Grounds only £3.75, seniors and students £3.) The house is not wheelchair accessible. Only buses #254, 256, and 257 (summer Sundays and bank holiday Mondays only) run to the house itself, but bus #X23 (from Sheffield and Buxton) and 170 (from Bakewell) run to Edensor, ½ mi. from the house.

Matlock Bath

2 mi. south of the transit hub of Matlock is the former spa town of **Matlock Bath,** which straggles along the A6 between the River Derwent and the steep hills above it. With a rail station of its own, a cable car ride, and several nearby theme parks, Matlock Bath is more likely to attract tour coaches than serious hikers, as evidenced by the video game parlors and fish-and-chip shops.

The high ground above the town, which offers the best views of the gorge and secrets two caverns has been staked out by a private company and incorporated into the **Heights of Abraham** Country Park (tel. (0629) 58 23 65). A cable car runs to the heights from a point across the river. (Return trip on cable car and admission to all attractions £4.50, children £2.50, seniors £3.75. Pedestrian access—up a steep hil—£2.50, children £1.75 includes attractions, £1 for grounds only.)

In the same building as the tourist office is the **Peak District Mining Museum** (tel. (0629) 38 34). (Open Feb.-Nov. Mon.-Fri. 10am-5pm, Sat.-Sun. 11am-4pm. Admission £1; seniors, students, and children 80p, families £2.50.) Rowboats are for rent nearby (tel. (0629) 557 47; open 11:30am-6pm July-Aug. daily, weekends during rest of summer; £1/person, 50p for children,/½hr.).

The nearest **IYHF youth hostel** is in Matlock, but Matlock Bath's **tourist office** books accommodations in town for 95p. There are five or six B&Bs near the cable car entrance, starting around £8.50; try **Tor View** (tel. (0629) 562 62), with singles, doubles, and family rooms with a tea machine in each for £9.50/person. **Beano's,** on Holme St., just up the hill from the bend in the river, is a wholefoods shop. (Open Mon.-Fri. 10am-6:30pm, Sat. 10am-5:30pm.) On the main road, **La Caverna** serves pizza and pasta for about £4, but you may have to order side dishes to fill up. (Open Tues.-Sat. 11am-2pm and 6:30-10pm, Sun. 11am-10pm.)

About 3 mi. south of Matlock Bath, near Cromford, the **High Peak Trail** sets out westward for 18 mi. along the defunct Cromford and High Peak Railway. All southbound buses from Matlock and Matlock Bath stop at Cromford, and most (including #252 and most #139-141 services) continue south along the A6 or the Holloway Rd. to the trailhead near High Peak Junction. Get off bus #139-141 just before it turns away from the canal toward Lea Bridge.

An abandoned quarry about 4 mi. farther south near Crich is the unlikely site of the **National Tramway Museum** (tel. (0773) 85 25 65). Most of the 40 vintage streetcars run, and two or three of them are driven daily. (Open April-Aug. Mon.-Fri. 10am-5:30pm, Sat.-Sun. 10am-6:30pm; Sept. Mon.-Thurs. 10am-5:30pm and Sat.-Sun. 10am-6:30pm; Oct. Sat.-Sun. only. Last entry 1 hr. before closing. Admission £3.30, seniors £2.90, children £1.90, includes unlimited tram rides.) The museum is on bus #139-141 from Matlock and Matlock Bath (every hr., ½hr.), and can also be reached by a 1-mi. uphill walk from Whatstandwell train station (trains between Matlock and Derby, Mon.-Fri. every hour, Sat.-Sun. every 2 hr.).

Northern Peak District

The northern Dark Peak area contains some of the wildest and most rugged hill country in England, with vast areas like **Kinderscout** and **Bleaklow** entirely undisturbed by motorized traffic. In these desolate mazes of black peat hags and deep groughs, even paths are scarce. The few towns and villages in the Dark Peak nestle into the valleys, incognizant of the ravages of the tourist trade.

Edale

Cradled in the deep dale of the River Noe, with gentle grey-green hills sweeping straight up on two sides, Edale has little in the way of civilization besides a church, café, pub, school and IYHF youth hostel. Its natural environs, however, are arguably the most spectacular in Northern England. On summer weekends this tranquil village comes alive with hikers and campers readying themselves to tackle the Pennine Way (which passes out of the Peak District and into the Yorkshire Dales after a 3-4 day hike) or trek one of the shorter (1½-8½ mi.) walks closer to Edale proposed by the National Park Authority's *8 Walks Around Edale* (60p). If you disdain acting as your own pack mule, head for the **Lady Booth Riding and Trekking Centre** (tel. (0433) 702 05), next door to the hostel, and canter up the 2000-ft. Kinder Scout Plateau for a refreshing view. (£8 for half-trek 10am-12:30pm or 2-4:30pm; £14/day; £5/hr. Book in advance.) Stop at the huge **National Park Information Centre** (see listing below) for weather forecasts, free videos of the Hope Valley, training with a map and compass, and information on mountain rescue.

Your tent could be your best friend in this town where the only alternative is the large, 140-bed **youth hostel,** alive on summer weekends with a large population of squabbling young children. The hostel does try to redeem itself with a permanent open-door policy and strong showers. (Ask at the Park Centre about the 30 min. shortcut through the fields to the hostel.) The prices of campgrounds increase with the level of convenience offered. **Ollerbrook Farm** (tel. (0453) 6702 35), five minutes across the fields, is cheap at £1 per person. Near the school, **Cooper's Camp and Caravan Site** (tel. (0433) 6703 72), Newfold Far, asks £1.25. The campground next to the **National Park Centre** tops them all at £1.80 (children £1.15).

Of the three establishments in Edale that serve food, most popular among hikers is the **Old Nag's Head Inn,** which churns out steak and kidney pie and the Hiker's Special (both £4.50). (Open Mon.-Fri. noon-3pm and 6:30-11pm, Sat. 11am-3pm and 6-11pm, Sun. noon-3pm and 7-10:30pm.) A small café next to the general store has delicious home-baked pastries and meat pies for less than £1. (Open in summer Sat.-Sun. 9am-5:30pm.)

Edale lies on the Manchester-Sheffield rail line, and is served every 2hr. (£3.50, saver return £3.80).

Castleton

Two mi. southeast of Edale, Castleton is the most commodified of the area's villages but lovely nonetheless. Its main attractions include several caverns and Blue John stone, a rich blue and brown variety of spar quarried here and found nowhere else in the world. Souvenir shops unfortunately feel compelled to impress upon the visitor that Blue John stone is the village's primary source of income. The **Blue John Cavern** (tel. (0433) 206 38) and **Treak Cliff Cavern** (tel. (0433) 205 71) are about 1½ mi. west of town on the A625. (Both open daily 9:30am-6pm; shorter hours in winter. Admission to Blue John £3.60, ages 5-15 £1.30, seniors £2; to Treak Cliff £2.95, ages 5-14 £1.45, seniors £2. YHA and student discounts at both.) Treak Cliff cavern is the loveliest and holds the most Blue John. At **Speedwell Cavern** (tel. (0433) 205 12), closer to town along the same road, visitors are taken by boat to the rim of the "Bottomless Pit." (Open daily 9:30am-5:30pm. Admission £3.50, under 14 £2.) Gigantic **Peak Cavern** (tel. (0433) 202 85), right in town, was tastefully known in the 18th century as the "Devil's Arse." The cavern features the second-largest opening in the world (the first is in New South Wales, Australia), which is unfortunately obscured by the entrance structures. (Open Easter-Sept. daily 10am-5pm. Admission £2, children and seniors £1, 20p off with flier from tourist office.)

The dramatic ruins of **Peveril Castle** (tel. (0433) 206 13), built in the 11th century by Jeremy Maltby, one of William the Conqueror's knights, stand high on the hill just above the town. (Open April-Sept. daily 10am-6pm; Oct.-March daily 10am-4pm. Admission 95p, seniors and students 75p, children 45p.) If you're in luck, you might catch **Mam Tor** in action: this shale mound periodicly crumbles onto the A625 below, earning it the nickname "Shivering Mountain" (the Celtic name means "mother mountain"). The **National Park Information Centre** in town offers guided walks of the city (Mondays at 2pm; £1, seniors 35p, students 50 p). Hikers looking for a more strenuous challenge can set off southwards on the 26 mi. **Limestone Way** Trail to Matlock.

The **IYHF youth hostel** (see Accommodations) by the castle entrance has an open lounge. The several guest houses nearby include Mr. and Mrs. Skelton's **Cryer House** (tel. (0433) 202 44), across from the tourist office (£11). The tearoom downstairs is a great place for a snack (tea and Black Forest cake £1.25).

Castleton lies 2 mi. west of the Hope rail station. Bus #272 runs daily from Sheffield interchange to Castleton via Hathersage and Hope. (Departs Castelton about once an hour.) Sporadic service between Castelton and Bakewell is provided by buses #173, 174, and 181; there is no service on Saturdays.

Hathersage

Only Brontë diehards should spend an hour or two in the village that probably corresponds to the "Morton" to which Jane Eyre fled from Thornfield Hall. The excellent guide *Jane Eyre and Hathersage* (available at any tourist office in the park for 80p) will help you find your way around and identify sights from the novel.

The **IYHF youth hostel,** in a 44-bed Victorian Gothic building, is a good place to stay if the hostel in Castleton is full (see Accommodations).

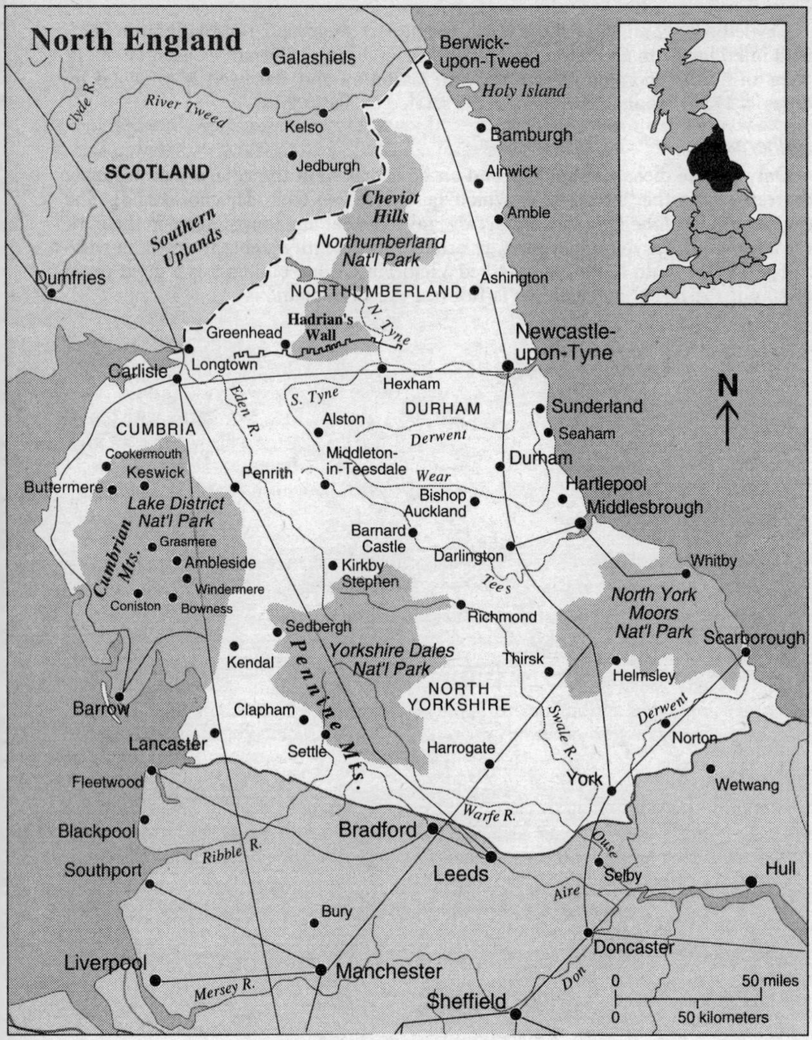

North England

Between Central England's industrial belt and Scotland is a quiet area of natural beauty; vertically sliced by the Pennine Mountains, North England's main attractions lie enshrined in four national parks. Even before the Victorians invented tourism, local and foreign travelers were drawn to this particularly varied countryside, fleeing the smoke of the increasingly industrialized transportation hubs to kick up their own clouds of dust on rural trails. The English today are rabid walkers, and no trail tests their stamina more than the Pennine Way, the country's first official long-distance path and still its longest. Extensive systems of shorter paths traverse the grey and purple moors that captured the imagination of the Brontës, the emerald green dales that figure so prominently in the stories of James Herriot, and the stunning crags and lakes that inspired Wordsworth's philosophy of the sublime. Isolated villages along the trails continue a pastoral tradition that contrasts with the extravagance of England's big cities.

Sink your teeth into such regional specialties as Yorkshire pudding, Cumberland sausage, Wensleydale and Cheshire cheeses, and "fat rascal" scones. Northumbria's Craster kippers can't be beat for hearty seafood, and the Lake District's Kendal Mint Cake is a quick pick-me-up for climbers. Eccles cakes (raisins, and spices wrapped in flaky pastry) can be found only in Lancashire and Yorkshire; char, a cross between trout and salmon, is unique to the Lake District.

Getting Around

In the far north, there are two sets of north-south rail lines, one via Crewe to Carlisle (west of the Pennines), and the other via York to Newcastle (east of the Pennines). Near the Scottish border, an east-west line connects Newcastle with Carlisle. There are also express inter-city trains. British Rail's **Rail Rover** tickets are a great buy for this area. The **North East Rover** offers a week of unrestricted travel on all British Rail-operated lines in the rectangular region bounded by Sheffield, Carlisle, Newcastle, and Cleethorpes (including the scenic Settle-Carlisle line) for £32, £21.20 with a railcard. The North West Rover includes fewer lines, bounded by Carlisle, Bradford, Manchester, Liverpool, and the coast, costing only £25, £17.50 with a railcard. Here, as everywhere, the cheapest ticket will often be a day return, especially near major cities. Buses run between some of the scattered hamlets of agricultural England, but not with the frequency of their urban cousins; plan detailed itineraries and check them twice to avoid being stranded for a week in Hathersage. **Wayfarer, Explorer,** and **Day Rambler** tickets (each about £3.50) are issued by various local authorities for a day's travel on all bus companies' routes within a given region and often on rail routes as well; some companies issue their own.

Compiled timetables for most national parks are available from tourist offices, rail stations, and bus depots. In general, the most helpful tourist offices are in the Northumbrian Coast-Newcastle area and in York. In the national park areas, National Park Information Centres are better equipped to help you with transportation schedules and other semiotic devices.

Pennine Way

The Pennine (PEN-eyen) Peaks are England's spine, arching down the middle of Britain from the Scottish border in the north through the Peak District in the south. The **Pennine Way,** the Countryside Commission's 250-mi. path, crowns the central ridge of the watershed. To hike the whole path, set out from Kirk Yetholm in Scotland or Edale in the Peak District. The path traverses the massive, boggy plateau on top of **Kinder Scout** in the south and then passes into the Yorkshire Dales at Malham, reemerging at Pen-y-Ghent. The northern part of the path crosses the area known as the High Pennines, a 20 mi. stretch reaching from below Barnard Castle to Hadrian's Wall in the north. Turbulent rivers cut gentle dales into the mountain sides up and down the chain, from the southernmost Derwent Valley to Teesdale, Weardale, and Allendale, generating landscapes of spacious moorland and arbored slopes, dotted by mild stone villages.

Although some hikers are rumored to have finished the walk in ten days and lived to tell about it, most will probably need two and a half to three weeks. Hiking the path from end to end remains an achievement almost exclusively of British walkers, although foreigners find themselves richly rewarded when they take up the challenge. Countless shorter loops along the route also make good trips. The segments near Edale, in the High Pennines, and north of Hadrian's Wall are lovely, though every experienced wayfarer will recommend a different stretch.

The classic Wainwright's *Pennine Way Companion* (£6.50), a pocket-sized volume compiled by a team of ramblers just after the path was opened in 1965 (available from the Peak District Information Centres) is a worthwhile supplement to Ordnance Survey maps. Sudden mist and rain on the Peaks can reduce visibility to under 20 ft. After a storm, the low-level paths can become boggy, and some paths will leave you knee-deep (or worse) in hungry peat. At some points (especially in the Yorkshire Dales) and in ominous weather, you should stay on the narrow roads that run nearby. In England, six blasts on a whistle (or six of anything recognizable), repeated at regular intervals, is a generally recognized distress signal. Leave word of your intended route with a hostel warden or the local police, even if it's short and simple.

IYHF youth hostels are nominally spaced within a day's hike (7-27 mi.) of one another; note which are closed on certain nights. Any National Park Information Centre can supply details on trails and alternate accommodations in this area. The *Pennine Way Accommodations and Camping Guide* (£1) will come in handy. YHA now also offers the invaluable "Pennine Way Package," to make booking in the 18 or more youth hostels along the walk as easy as falling into a bog. From July to mid-September, you can book a route (30p/hostel) and obtain useful advice on paths and equipment. Write to the **YHA,** Bowey House, William St. South Gosforth, Newcastle-Upon-Tyne NE3 1SA (tel. (091) 284 74 71) to obtain the Pennine Way Central Booking Service Information Pack (£1.50).

The following hostels are located on the route. Lockout is 10am-5pm unless otherwise noted.

Alston Youth Hostel, The Firs, Alston, Cumbria CA9 3RW (tel. (0434) 38 15 09), 22 mi. from Dufton. Breakfast, evening meal, and shop. £5.90, ages 16-20 £4.70, under 16 £3.80. Open July-Aug. daily; late March-May, June, and Sept.-Oct. Mon.-Sat.; Jan. to mid-March Fri.-Sat.

Baldersdale Youth Hostel, Blackton, Baldersdale, Barnard Castle, Co. Durham DL12 9UP (tel. (0833) 506 29), 15 mi. from Keld. Shop, but no meals. £5.50, ages 16-20 £4.40, under 16 £3.50. Open mid-March to Aug. Fri.-Wed., Sept.-Oct. Fri.-Tues.

Bellingham Youth Hostel, Woodburn Road, Bellingham, Hexham, Northumberland NE48 2ED (tel. (0660) 203 13), 14 mi. from Once Brewed. No shop or meals. £5.10, ages 16-20 £4, under 16 £3.10. Open July-Aug. daily; March-June and Sept.-Oct. Mon.-Sat.

Byrness Youth Hostel, 7 Otterburn Green, Byrness, Newcastle Upon Tyne NE19 1TS (tel. (0830) 202 22), 15 mi. from Bellingham. Café and store nearby. £5.10, ages 16-20 £4, under 16 £3.10. Open July-Aug. daily; March-June and Sept.-Oct. Thurs.-Tues.

Crowden-in-Longendale Youth Hostel (Peak National Park), Crowden, Hadfield, Hyde, Cheshire SK14 7ZH (tel. (04574) 21 35), 15 mi. from Edale. Evening meal, breakfast, and shop. £5.50, ages 16-20 £4.40, under 16 £3.50. Open March-Oct. Thurs.-Tues.

Dufton Youth Hostel, Redstones, Dufton, Appleby, Cumbria CA16 6DB (tel. (07683) 512 36), 12 mi. from Langdon Beck. Breakfast, evening meal, and shop. £5.90, ages 16-20 £4.70, under 16 £3.80. Open July-Aug. daily; mid-Jan. to March Thurs.-Mon.; mid-April to June and Sept. to mid-Nov. Wed.-Mon.

Earby Youth Hostel, Glen Cottage, Birch Hall Lane, Earby, Colne, Lancashire BB8 6JX (tel. (0282) 84 23 49); 17 mi. from Haworth. No meals served. £5.10, ages 16-20 £4, under 16 £3.10. Open April-Oct. Tues.-Sun.

Edale Youth Hostel, Rowland Cote, Nether Booth, Edale, Sheffield S30 2ZH (tel. (0433) 703 02), 2 mi. from start of the Pennine Way. A YHA activity center. Open all day. £7, ages 16-20 £5.90, under 16 £4.60. Evening meal and breakfast available. Open daily Jan. to mid-Dec.

Greenhead Youth Hostel, Greenhead, Carlisle, Cumbria CA6 7HG (tel. (06972) 401), 17 mi. from Alston. Breakfast, evening meal, and shop. £5.50, ages 16-20 £4.40, under 16 £3.50. Open April-Aug. daily; Sept. to mid-Nov. Tues.-Sun.; Feb.-March Wed.-Sun.

Hawes Youth Hostel, Lancaster Terrace, Hawes, North Yorkshire DL8 3LQ (tel. (09697) 368), 19 mi. from Stainforth. Breakfast, evening meal, and shop. £6.30, ages 16-20 £5.10, under 16 £4. Open mid-March to Sept. daily; Oct. to mid-Dec., Feb. to mid-March Thurs.-Mon.

Haworth Youth Hostel, Longlands Hall, Longlands Drive, Lees Lane, Haworth, Keighley, West Yorkshire BD22 8RT (tel. (0535) 422 34), 12 mi. from Mankinholes. Evening meal, breakfast, and shop. £6.30, ages 16-20 £5.10, under 16 £4. Open March-Oct. daily; mid-Jan. to Feb., Nov. Mon.-Sat.

John Dower Memorial Youth Hostel, Malham, Skipton, North Yorkshire BD23 4DE (tel. (07293) 321), 15 mi. from Earby. Evening meal and breakfast available. £6.30, ages 16-20 £5.10, under 16 £4. Open mid-March to Sept. daily; Jan.-Feb. and Nov. Tues.-Sat.; Oct. and early March Mon.-Sat.

Keld Youth Hostel, Keld Lodge, Richmond, North Yorkshire DL11 6LL (tel. (0748) 862 59), 13 mi. from Hawes. Evening meal, breakfast, and shop. £5.50, ages 16-20 £4.40, under 16 £3.50. Open July-Aug. daily; March-June and Sept.-Oct. Tues.-Sun.; Jan.-Feb. and early Nov. Wed.-Sun.

Kirk Yetholm Youth Hostel, Kelso, Roxburyshire, Scotland (tel. (057382) 631), 27 mi. from Byrness (the home stretch). Open April-Oct. daily. For information, call (0786) 511 81 or contact the Scottish Youth Hostel Association, 7 Glebe Crescent, Stirling FK8 2JA.

Langdon Beck Youth Hostel, Langdon Beck, Forest-in-Teesdale, Barnard Castle, Co. Durham DL12 0XN (tel. (0833) 222 28), 15 mi. from Baldersdale. Breakfast, shop, and evening meal. £6.30, ages 16-20 £5.10, under 16 £4. Open July-Aug. daily; April-June and Sept.-Oct. Mon.-Sat; Jan. to mid-Feb. Fri.-Sat.; mid-Feb. to March Tues.-Sat.

Mankinholes Hall Youth Hostel, Mankinholes, Todmorden, Lancashire OL14 6HR (tel. (0706) 81 23 40), 24 mi. from Crowden. Evening meal, breakfast, and shop. £5.50, ages 16-20 £4.40, under 16 £3.50. Open April-Sept. Thurs.-Tues.; March, Oct. to mid-Dec. Thurs.-Mon.

Once Brewed Youth Hostel, Once Brewed, Military Road, Bardon Mill, Hexham, Northumberland NE47 7AN (tel. (04984) 360), 7 mi. from Greenhead. Shop and cafeteria. Open after 1pm. £6.60, ages 16-20 £5.40, under 16 £4.40. Open March-Oct. daily; Feb. and Nov. Mon.-Sat.

Stainforth Youth Hostel, Taitlands, Stainforth, Settle, North Yorkshire BD24 9PA (tel. (07292) 35 77), 8 mi. from Malham. Breakfast, evening meal, and shop. £5.90, ages 16-20 £4.70, under 16 £3.80. Open July-Aug. daily; April-June and Sept.-Oct. Mon.-Sat.; mid-Feb. to March and Nov.-Dec. Tues.-Sat.

Leeds

Leeds' textile prosperity blossomed in the late Victorian period, an era fond of ornament. As a result, building facades in the downtown areas are crowded with a delightful army of stone lions, griffins, and cherubim. Particularly beautiful are enclosed **shopping arcades** that run between Briggate and Vicar Lane, a few blocks north and east of the train station. Leeds also has several interesting museums to recommend it. Although larger than its neighbor Bradford, Leeds is even less hospitable—the utter lack of cheap accommodation near the center of town may make a day trip from Manchester a better idea than an overnight stay.

While the city's art gallery, the **Headrow** (tel. (0532) 47 82 48), does not bulge with works by the most famous artists in history, the museum displays some very intriguing pieces, including many by contemporary artists. (Open Mon.-Tues., Thurs.-Fri. 10am-6pm, Wed. 10am-9pm, Sat. 10am-4pm, Sun. 2-5pm. Free.) In the same building, the **Henry Moore Centre for the Study of Sculpture** (tel. 47 82 77) has the rounded work of its eponymous Yorkshireman, plus sculpture, models, and drawings, by an array of lesser-known sculptors, both historic and comtemporary. (Open Mon.-Fri. 10am-1pm and 2-6pm, Wed. evenings and Sat. by appointment.)

At the east end of the Headrow, near the arcades, **Shebab,** 2 Eastgate (tel. 48 89 88) has a wide variety of Indian entrees (£4.50-6). The most fun is the "Thali" lunch, in which you get small portions of 5 dishes, plus yoghurt, puri, and rice, which you can mix to taste (£4.50). (Open Mon.-Fri. 11:30am-2:30pm and 6-12pm, Sat. 11:30am-11:45pm, Sun. 6-11:45pm.)

The **tourist information center,** 19 Wellington St (tel. (0532) 46 24 54/5), provides a free map of the city center, as well as an accommodations list and brochures about Leeds' museums. Accommodations service is £1. From the rail station, turn left and follow the signs; from the coach station, turn left onto Wellington St. (Open Mon.-Fri. 9:30am-4pm.) The coach station can be reached at tel. 46 00 11; the rail station (tel. 44 81 33) is open for business Mon.-Sat. 8am-8pm, Sun. 9am-8pm (tickets available for Mon.-Sat. 4am-11:50pm, Sun. 6:30am-11:30pm). To keep in touch with the folks at home, visit the **post office** at City Square (tel. 44 76 03; open Mon.-Tues., Thurs.-Fri. 9am-5:30pm, Wed. 9:30am-5:30pm, Sat. 9am-12:30pm); Leeds' **postal code** is LS1 2VH. Finally, to catch up on your reading, spend some time at the excellent **Austick's Maps and Travel Bookshop,** 64 the Headrow (tel. 45 23 26), which stocks an impressive selection of maps and guides for the Yorkshire Dales and elsewhere, as well as the ever-popular *Let's Go* series.

Leeds is about 50 mi. northeast of Manchester and 10 mi. east of Bradford, midway between the South Pennines and the Yorkshire Dales. Direct trains and coaches run to Leeds from most major cities, including Bradford (about 4/hr. 6:10am-midnight, Sun. about every ½hr. 8:30am-midnight; 20 min.; £1.20, off-peak 65p, day return), Manchester, York and London (many in the early morning, then about 1/hr. 8:34am-7:47pm, Sun. 9/day 10am-8pm; 3 hr.; £39, saver return £48, supersaver £39.)

South Pennines

Brownish-gray gorse-covered moorland covers eroded layers of grit and sandstone to form the peaks and valleys of the South Pennines. The bleakness and desolation of the landscape bring peace to the hiker's soul. In addition to the Pennine Way, numerous short- to medium-distance footpaths traverse the area. The best short trips into the area are to **Haworth** or **Hebden Bridge** from Bradford or Manchester. **Yorkshire Rider** operates infrequent bus service between Hebden Bridge and Haworth (#500, May-Sept. daily, Oct.-April Wed. & Sat.) and between Bradford and Haworth; call (0274) 73 22 37 for information.

Single bus fares within West Yorkshire are all 50p except during weekday rush hours; rail fares are also discounted. A **Day Rover** ticket is good for a day's unlimited bus and rail travel in West Yorkshire after 9:30am (train and bus £1.90, children 95p, families £3.20; bus only £1.50, children 75p).

The Haworth tourist office is alive with trail guides. The **Worth Way** traces the 5½ mi. from Keighley and Ovenhope; hop the steam-train back to your starting point. Paul Hannon's *Walks in Brontë Country* (£2.85 at Haworth, £2.45 at Hebden Bridge) and the free leaflet *How to Stop Yourself Dying on the Moors,* available at regional information centers, will guide you through the sisters' beloved moors.

Hebden Bridge

A historic gritstone village built on the side of a hill, Hebden Bridge lies in Calderdale, close to the Pennine Way and the 50-mi. circular Calderdale Way. From Hebden Bridge, you can make the several shorter hikes to the nearby villages of Blackshaw Head, Cragg Vale, or Hepstonstall, where you'll find the ruins of a 13th-century church. **Walkley's Waterbus** (tel. (0422) 84 48 33) gives tours of the recently restored Rochdale Canal and other sites. (Aug. daily; July and Sept. Thurs. and Sat.; Easter-July Sat. only. Departs Hebden Bridge Marina at 1 and 3pm. £2.95, children £1.75; longer cruises available.) An interesting stop on the Walkley's Waterbus tour is the **Clog Factory Museum,** which celebrates England's last working clog mill. The **tourist office** at 1 Bridge Gate (tel. (0422) 84 38 31) is equipped with maps, guides, and an accommodations service (95p; open Mon.-Sat. 9am-5pm, Sun. 10am-5pm.) For B&B, try **The Birchcliffe Centre,** in a former Baptist chapel on Birchcliffe Rd. (tel. (0422) 84 36 26; singles £11.75, doubles £8.25/person, triples £6/person). **Watergate Tea Shop,** on Bridge Gate near the tourist office, is worth breaking into (meals from £2.60, desserts £1.15).

Hebden Bridge is about halfway down the Manchester-Leeds rail line, with service in both directions every hour (for Bradford, change at Leeds).

Haworth

> *I can hardly tell you how the time gets on at Haworth. There is no event whatever to mark its progress. One day resembles another . . .*
>
> *—Charlotte Brontë*

Those underwhelmed by Brontë-sister stories might be a bit bored by Haworth. The town is plain, Ye Olde Shoppes along Main Street fall short of quaint, and the whole area is enveloped in a death shroud of tourists. The bleak moorland, purple with heather only in August, makes the town's austerity at least escapable.

The **tourist office,** 2 West Lane (tel. (0535) 423 29; open daily 9:30am-5:30pm), at the top of Main St., stocks plenty of maps and guides. Most useful to the daytripper are *Three Walks from the Centre of Haworth* (20p) and the town's miniguide (20p). The **IYHF youth hostel,** Longlands Dr. (tel. (0535) 422 34), tops another hill 1 mi. from the tourist office. It's a lovely Victorian mansion (red carpets, wood paneling, and stained glass), and you don't have to marry wealth to get inside. (£6.30, ages 16-20 £5.10, under 16 £4. Open March-Oct. daily; mid-Jan. to Feb. and Nov. Mon.-Sat.)

If you set out to make the rounds of Brontëbilia, begin at the **parsonage** (tel. (0535) 64 23 23) on the edge of town, where Emily, Charlotte and Anne lived with their father and brother Branwell. The bleak Georgian building is now an excellent museum that houses such relics as postage-stamp-sized books written and illustrated by the Brontës, in their childhood years. (Open April-Sept. daily 10am-5pm, Oct.-March 11am-4:30pm; £2.50, seniors and students £1, ages 5-16 50p. On your way to the parsonage take a look at the village church, the final resting-places of Charlotte and Emily.

Behind the church, a footpath leads up the hill toward **Brontë Falls,** a 2½-mi. hike over the moor. The tourist office's leaflet lists alternative routes. In the town cemetery, just outside Penistone Hill Country Park, pause by the grave of Lily Cove, Britain's first woman balloonist/parachutist. Her grave overlooks the spot where she plummeted to her death during a 1906 exhibition. The walk (Brontë Way) continues 4 mi. to **Top Withens,** a ruined farmhouse rumored to have been the inspiration for *Wuthering Heights;* here the path meets the Pennine Way. (The trail continues 5 more mi. and ends at **Wycoller Hall,** a building deserted since the 16th century and said to be *Jane Eyre's* Ferndean Manor.) Farther north along the Pennine Way is Pondon Hall, a.k.a. Thrushcross Grange. If you stay on the Way into the Yorkshire Dales National Park, you'll find the next **IYHF youth hostel** (tel. (0282) 84 23 49) in Earby, 17 mi. away. (Open April-Oct. Tues.-Sun. £5.10, ages 16-20 £4, under 16 £3.10.)By rail to Haworth, take the train from Leeds (or from Bradford's Forster Sq. Station, across town from the main Bradford Interchange Station) to Keighley (KEETH-lee), and change to the private **Keighley and Worth Valley Railway** (June Sat. 7/day, Sun. 13/day; July to mid-Sept. Mon.-Fri. 4/day, Sat. 7/day, Sun. 13/day; late Sept. Sat. 7/day, Sun. 13/day.) Some weekday trains run in spring; call (0535) 436 29 or 452 14 to check. (£1.80, return £2.40, seniors and children half-price. YHA discounts.) **West Yorkshire bus** #663-5 runs a lumpy route every half hour between Haworth and Keighley. West Yorkshire's **off-peak fares** for bus and train can be incredible money savers.

Yorkshire Dales National Park

The York District National Park is centrally located between the southerly Peak District, the Lake District to the west, the northerly Northumberland National Park, and th North York Moors on the east coast. The National Park occupies only one-third of the area of the dales (680 sq. mi.), excluding such scenic areas as Nidderdale in the southeast, Teesdale in the north, and the Forest of Bowland in the southwest. Nevertheless, the York District National Park has its fair share of dales: valleys gouged into bog and moor (or "fell") forming misshapen hills dusted with green, brown, and purple, Wharfedale, Wensleydale and Swaledale contain some glorious scenery, and popular areas, such as the Pennine Way, the Three Peaks Walk, and Malham, tend to be well-traveled. This huge upland area, encompassing the Pennine Hills and the surrounding valleys, remains one of Northern England's genuine idylls.

Geological marvels in the Park include stunning waterfalls, towering white limestone pinnacles, and "scars" (gorges) carved eons ago by swift rivers and lazy glacial flow. Historical curiosities abound: Bronze and Iron Age tribes traced "green lanes" (footpaths that still remain upon the moorland tops), while the Romans built straight roads and stout hill-forts and the Vikings influenced the local dialect. The remains of **Bolton Priory, Easby Abbey,** and **Jervaulx Abbey** bear witness to industrious Cistercian builders who bred racehorses and created Wensleydale cheese. Ancient drystone fences still make good neighbors for the hill farmers and their sheep (mascots of the National Park), and agriculture in the northern dales remains far more traditional than in the Midland valleys. For a true taste of the Dales, try some Yorkshire pudding, Chorely Cakes, Yorkshire Parkin, or Yorkshire Curd Tarts.

Getting There and Getting Around

In the south of the park, **Skipton** acts as a transportation hub and provides goods and services not available in the smaller villages. **Grassington** or **Linton** farther north are more scenic bases for exploring southern Wharfedale. **Malham** is a good starting point for the western part of Wharfedale. To explore Wensleydale farther north, move out from **Hawes. Richmond** provides solid access to Swaledale.

The most convenient way to penetrate the park is to take a bus or train from Bradford or Leeds to Skipton, only then switching to the local buses which serve the smaller villages. Trains run from Bradford and Leeds to Carlisle, Morecambe, or Barrow via Skipton (Mon.-Sat. every ½hr.; 40 min.; £6.60 return; buses from Bradford #666, 667, and 668 Mon.-Sat. about 2/hr., Sun. about 1/hr.; 1½ hr.; from Leeds bus #784 about 1/hr.; 1½ hr.). Other options for getting to Skipton include catching a bus from York (**Mountain Goat Bus Co,** tel. (09662) 51 61), which runs to the Lake District via Skipton, Settle, and Ingleton (May-Oct. Mon., Wed., and Fri.-Sat. 1 in each direction), taking a coach from Bradford via Keighley, or hopping the daily National Express Rapide coach from London (£22, period return £29).

From Skipton, West Yorkshire Road Car's **Keighley and District** line (tel. (0756) 79 55 31) connects to **Grassington** (Mon.-Sat. as many as 9/day, Sun. 4/day, single £1.80, return £3.30) and occasionally Kettlewell. **Pennine Motor Services** (tel. (0756) 74 92 15) connects from Skipton to **Settle** (#580 Skipton-Settle every hr., less frequent on Sun.), **Ingleton** (4/day, Sun. 2/day), and **Malham** (#210; 3/day; Sun. in summer). Settle is also served by some Carlisle-bound trains from Leeds. The train from Skipton to **Windermere** (with two transfers) is just as fast as the Mountain Goat bus from York. Each of these companies has a daily **Wayfarer** ticket for £3.20-4 on its own routes.

Other villages are served less regularly. Inter-village buses tend to run infrequently, often only on certain days of the week. To complicate things further, denationalized bus service means that nearly a dozen companies vie for your business. You cannot do without the **Dales Connection's** compiled timetable (free at any tourist office or National Park Information Centre). Note that in the winter, bus service dries up considerably.

Hitching is unreliable—be willing to accept a ride that will get you only part of the way to your destination.

Hiking

Since bus service is scant and hitching is poor, hiking is the best way to get around the Dales.

The park's Information Centres can help you prepare for a trek along one of the three long-distance footpaths through the park. The **Pennine Way** runs from Gargrave in the south (on the rail line just west of Skipton) to Tan Hill in the north, passing Malham, Pen-y-ghent, Hawes, and Keld. The **Dales Way** runs from Bradford and Leeds past Ilkley, Grassington, Whernside, and Sedbergh on its way to the Lake District; it crosses the Pennine Way near Dodd Fell. The **Coast-to-Coast Walk** runs through the top of the park from Richmond to Kirkby Stephen, sweeping through Reeth and Keld.

Alternative routes are described in Wainwright's *Walks in Limestone Country* (£6); Paul Hannon's *Walks in Wensleydale* and *Walks in the Craven Dales* (£2.85 each) are also excellent. His *Dales Way Companion* (£3.45) will take you through several areas of the park. The park authority encourages you to keep to their "walks" in order to protect grasslands and avoid falling into hidden mineshafts. They offer leaflets (35p, available at National Park Information Centres) describing over 30 unmarked walks. Four trail leaflets (50p) describe easier three-hour marked trails. Trails begin at Ingleton, Longstone Common, Malham, and Aysgarth Falls. Park Information Centres also supply brochures detailing the Yorkshire Dales Cycleway, a series of six 20-mi. routes connecting the dales, and listing places where cycles can be rented. The area is hilly, but feasibly biked.

Here, as in other English countryside, bring along sturdy footwear and warm clothing, raingear, water, maps, and a compass. Stay on public rights-of-way (marked on maps). In an **emergency,** dial 999 (no coins required) from any telephone and ask for fell rescue. Six blasts on a whistle (or six of any sharp sound), repeated at one-minute intervals, is an acknowledged signal of distress in Natinal Parks all over the U.K.

Most of the smaller paths aren't waymarked, making detailed maps of the area essential. Ordnance Survey map #98 (1:50,000 "Wensleydale and Wharfedale," £3.35) covers much more of the district than its title suggests (it includes Swaledale, the Three Peaks, and Upper Ribblesdale as well). Sheets #91 and 92 cover Teesdale, and #104 covers Nidderdale and east Wharfedale. Arthur Gemmel's *Stile Maps* series (50-90p each) is more geared to hikers than the Ordnance Survey maps, and Outdoor Leisure sheets #2, 10, and 30 (£4 each) cover the park in more depth.

Orientation and Practical Information

The following **National Park Information Centres** are staffed by well-informed Dales devotees. The centers also sell maps, guidebooks, and leaflets of all textures. Many also offer guided walks; call for details. Pick up *The Visitor* (free). As a rule, all of the centers are open at least from 10am to 4pm daily.

Aysgarth Falls: tel. (0969) 66 34 24. Open April-Oct. daily 10am-5:30pm.

Clapham: tel. (04685) 419. Open April-Aug. daily 9:30am-4:30pm; Sept.-Oct. daily 10am-4pm.

Grassington: "Colvend," on Hebden Rd. (tel. (0756) 75 27 74). Open daily 9:30am-5:30pm; Nov.-April Sat.-Sun. 9:30am-5:30pm.

Hawes: Station Yard. (tel. (0969) 66 74 50). Open July-Aug. 9:30am-4:30pm; April-June and Sept.-Oct. 10am-4pm.

Malham: tel. (07293) 363. Open daily 9:30am-4pm.

Sedbergh: tel. (05396) 201 25. Open April-Oct. daily 9:30am-5:30pm.

Accommodations and Camping

Overnight options in the Park include hostels, converted barns, tents, or B&Bs. Twelve **IYHF youth hostels** are scattered throughout the Yorkshire Dales area. **Hawes Stainforth, Keld,** and **Malham** hostels are on the Pennine Way, and the **Ingleton** hostel is on the edge of the park, convenient also to the Lake District. The **Linton, Kettlewell, Dentdale, Aysgarth Falls,** and **Grinton Lodge** hostels lie a few miles off the Pennine Way. **Ellington,** near Ripon, and **Kirby Stephen,** north of Hawes and served by rail, are a bit more removed.

The association of **Dales Barns** offers cheap accommodations in converted barns: £3.50-4/night in dorm rooms in converted barns (up to 30 people/barn; bunkhouse accommodations, no livestock). The barns generally cater to small groups, but they are ideal for hikers exploring the Pennine or the Dales Way. Bookings should be made to each individual barn well in advance: Airton (tel. (07293) 263); Barden Tower (tel. (075676) 630); Camm Farm (tel. (0860) 64 80 45); Catholes (tel. (05396) 203 34); Chapel-le-Dale (tel. (05242) 414 77); Dub Cote (tel. (07296) 238); Grain House Farm (tel. (0200) 283 66); Grange Farm (tel. (075676) 259); Hazel Bank Farm (tel. (075676) 312); Hill Top Farm (tel. (07293) 320); Manor Farm Barn (tel. (075677) 241); North Cote Farm (tel. (0756) 75 24 65); Ravenstonedale (tel. (05873) 254); Stacksteads Farm (tel. (05242) 413 86); Walden (tel. (0969) 66 33 41); West Scarfton (tel. (0969) 406 01).

Campgrounds may only be easily accessible by car, so consider asking a farmer if you can sleep on his bit of moor. The *Yorkshire Dales Accommodation Guide* (30p) is available at National Park Centres and at the York tourist center. It lists both B&Bs and camping sites. *Yorkshire and Humberside Caravan & Camping Guide* is also available at National Park Information Centres.

Grassington: Wood Nook Caravan Park, Skirethorns, Threshfield, Skipton, North Yorkshire BD23 5NU (tel. (0756) 75 24 12). 2 mi. from Grassington. Open March-Oct.

Hawes: Bainbridge Ings, Hawes, North Yorkshire DL8 3NU (tel. (0969) 66 73 54). Open April-Oct. **Brown Moor Caravan & Camping Site,** Hawes, North Yorkshire DL8 3PS (tel. (0969) 66 73 38). Open Easter-Oct.

Richmond: Brompton on Swale Caravan Park, Richmond, North Yorkshire DL10 7EZ (tel. (0748) 4629). Open April-Oct. **Swaleview Caravan Park,** Reethe Road, Richmond, North Yorkshire DL10 4SF (tel. (0748) 3106). Open March-Oct.

Settle: Flying Horseshoe Hotel, Clapham, North Yorkshire LA2 13ES (tel. (04685) 229). Open April-Nov.

Skipton: Dalesway Caravan Park, Marton Rd., Gargrave, Skipton, North Yorkshire BD23 3NS (tel. (0765) 74 95 92). Open April-Oct.

Airedale

Although **Skipton** (pop. 13,000) is more plausible as a transfer point than a destination, it has a number of sights and plenty of lodging. To reach the **tourist office** (tel. (0756) 79 28 09), turn right from the **train station** (tel. (0756) 25 43) and walk about a ½mi. to the pedestrian plaza off High St. (Open Mon.-Sat. 10am-5pm, Sun. 2-5pm. Accommodations service with 10% deposit.) **Skipton Castle** (tel. (0756) 79 24 42) is an extremely well preserved, if unfurnished, medieval home of the Earls of Comberland, with plenty of arrow slits and a good field of fire (should you decide to attack the other visitors). A self-guided tour describes the function of each room, connected to each other in some cases only by very worn stone steps. (Open Mon.-Sat. 10am-6pm or sundown if earlier, Sun. 2-6pm or sundown if earlier. £2.20, ages 5-18 £1.10.) For a good night's rest, try **Gateway House,** 39 Gargrave Rd., the continuation of Water St. (tel. (0756) 79 25 28), with teamakers in each room. (Singles and doubles £13/person.) Up the street at **Peace Villas,** 69 Gargrave Rd. (tel. (0756) 79 06 72), nicely furnished singles and doubles are only £11 per person. You can pitch your tent at Mr. Harrison's **Sixpenny Syke Farm,** Carlton (tel. (0756) 20 25), about 1½ mi. outside of Skipton (call first). Stock up on camping and hiking supplies at **The Dales Outdoor Centre** on Coach St. (tel. (0756) 43 05; open Mon.-Fri. 9am-5pm, Sat. 9am-5:30pm, closed Tues. in winter). At 5 Albert St., the **Tom Jones Carvery** (tel. (0756) 79 87 99) dishes out hearty roasts, potatoes, and two vegetables for £3.85 (Wed.-Mon. noon-2pm, 5:30-10pm). **Healthy Life,** on High St. near the town hall, is a wholefood shop (open Mon. and Wed.-Sat. 9:30am-5pm, Tues. 10am-5pm) and café (sandwiches £1.35, salads £2.45; open Wed.-Mon. 9:30am-5pm). Load up on fresh fruit and vegetables at the **market,** which makes High St. and other streets nigh impasssable; every day except Tuesday and Sunday, count on wading through racks of floral housecoats and baskets of plimsolls to get to those prize tomatoes. For mountain bike rental, try **Mick Walker Cycles,** on Water St. (tel. (0756) 43 86; £10/day, £60/week; £50 deposit; ID required; open Mon. and Wed.-Sat. 9:30am-5:30pm). In the summer, **Pennine Cruises** (tel. (0756) 79 08 29) run from the Canal Basin on Coach St. (Check schedule, but usually Mon.-Sat. 1:30 and 3pm, Sun. 2 and 3:30pm, plus evening cruises at 7pm on Wednesdays and 6pm on Sundays. 1¼ hr.; return £2.40, seniors £2, children £1.50.) Skipton's **postal code** is BD23 1RH.

Wharfdale

With a Park Information Centre, many trails nearby, and regular bus service to Skipton, **Grassington** (pop.1500) makes a good base from which to explore the southern part of the region. The **National Park Information Centre,** on Hebden Rd. across from the bus station, books accommodations (90p) and offers two- to three-hour guided walks (March-Oct., £1, children 50p) on varying days of the week. (Open daily 9:30am-5:30pm; Nov.-April Sat.-Sun. 9:30am-5:30pm.) The immense rooms at **Kirkfield,** about 200 yd. beyond the information center on Hebden Rd. (tel. (0756) 75 23 85), offer unobstructed views of limestone-studded farmland (£12.50/person). **Florrie Whitehead,** 16 Wood Lane (tel. (0756) 75 28 41), supplies excellent B&B and impeccable hospitality for £8.50. **Paul and Cheryl's,** 14 Main St. (tel. (0756) 75 24 17), serves tasty pizza (about £4) and pasta (£3.50 with salad; open Mon.-Wed., Fri.-Sat. noon-2pm and 5:30-9:30pm. **Bike rental** is available at Cobblestone Café (tel. (0756) 75 23 03; 3-speed £3.50/day, mountain bike £10; £25 deposit; open daily 10:30am-5:30pm). **The Mountaineer** (tel. (056) 75 22 66), in Pletts Barn Centre on Garrs Lane at the northern end of town, sells camping gear and rents mountain bikes (£6 half day, £10 day) and hiking boots (£2.50/day). Follow the signs to Logan Gallery. (Open Mon.-Wed. and Fri.-Sat. 9:30am-5pm, Sun. 11am-4;30pm; shorter hours in winter.) In Grassington Town Square, the **Folk Museum** (tel. (0756) 75 28 00) displays an eclectic assortment of artifacts, including medieval mining equipment, baby gas masks, and a gum-chewing mechanical leech. (Open daily 2-4:30pm; Nov.-March Sat.-Sun. 2-4:30pm. Admission 40p, seniors and children 30p, families £1.)

Spectacular **Kilnsey Crag** is a 3½-mi. walk northwest of Grassington toward Kettlewell. **Stump Cross Caverns** (tel. (0756) 75 27 80), adorned with beautiful stalagmite columns and glistening curtains of rock, can be reached by a 5-mi. walk east toward Pataley Bridge; some travelers choose to hitch along the B6265. Dress warmly. (Open Easter-Oct. daily 10am-5:30pm; Nov.-Dec. Sun. 11am-4pm. Admission £2, children £1.)

Linton, a picturesque one-church, one-street village, is less than 10 mi. north of Skipton and 2 mi. south of Grassington. An **IYHF youth hostel** (tel. (0756) 75 24 00) occupies the town's 17th-century rectory. (£6.30, ages 16-20 £5.10, under 16 £4. Open April-Sept. Mon.-Sat.; Feb.-March and Oct.-Dec. Tues.-Sat. Address inquiries to the Old Rectory, Linton-in-Craven, Skipton, N. Yorkshire BD23 5HH.) The Skipton-Grassington bus #72 (see above) passes near the hostel.

Kettlewell, north through the peaceful forest of Langstrothdale, is another fine choice for touring the Dales. In the center of the village is an **IYHF youth hostel,**

Whernside House (tel. (075676) 232; £5.90, ages 16-20 £4.70, under 16 £3.80; open April-Sept. daily; Feb.-March and Oct.-Dec. Mon.-Fri.).

Malhamdale and Ribblesdale

Sights in **Malham** are consistently spectacular. Climb up to the stunning limestone pavement of **Malham Cove,** then walk through "Dry Valley," with its Iron Age caves, to **Malham Tarn,** Yorkshire's second-largest natural lake. Two mi. from Malham is the equally impressive **Gordale Scar,** cut by rampaging glacial melt water in the last Ice Age. Malham is the proud home of a **National Park Information Centre** and a superior-grade **IYHF youth hostel** (tel. (07293) 321) thronged by Pennine Way groupies. (£6.30, ages 16-20 £5.10, under 16 £4. Open March-Sept. daily; Oct. and Jan.-Feb. Tues.-Sat.) There is camping at **Townhead Farm** (tel. (07293) 310; 70p/person), and several B&Bs in town; try **Mrs. Boocock,** Town End Cottage (tel. (07293) 345; doubles £11/person.)

From Malham, the high peaks and cliffs of **Ingleborough, Pen-y-ghent,** and **Whernside** form the so-called "Alpes Pennina." The 24-mi. **Three Peaks Walk** connecting the Alpes begins and ends in **Horton-in-Ribblesdale** at the clock of the **Pen-y-ghent Cafe,** a hiker's haunt with mammoth mugs of tea. *Walks in the Three Parks* (£1.20) lays out the whole trail and recommends shorter circuits as well. The best place to break your journey is **Ingleton** (meaning "Beacon Town"; pop. 2000), where the local **tourist office** (tel. (0468) 410 49) has do-it-yourself accommodation booking with a free list and a 10p map. (Open May-Oct. daily 10am-4:30pm.) Several small B&Bs on Main St. charge about £10. The **Ingleborough View Guest House** (tel. (0468) 414 01) charges £20 for doubles; the **IYHF youth hostel** (tel. (0468) 414 44) is in the center of town. (£5.50, ages 16-20 £4.40, under 16 £3.50. Open April-Aug. daily; Sept.-Oct. and March Mon.-Sat.; Jan.-Feb. Wed.-Sun.) The breathtaking 4-mi. "Falls Walk" from Ingleton is well worth the 75p (students 30p, children 20p) charged by the enterprising Ingleton Scenery Company.

Wensleydale

As you venture north into Wensleydale, the landscape of potholes, caves, clints, and grikes melds into a broad strath of fertile dairyland. Charles Kingsley described Wensleydale as "the richest spot in all England, this beautiful oasis among the mountains." Make your forays from **Hawes,** which has a **National Park Information Centre** (tel. (09697) 450; open July-Aug. 9:30am-4:30pm; April-June and Sept.-Oct. 10am-4pm). Farther west along Ingleton Rd. is the **IYHF youth hostel** (tel. (09697) 368; £4.90, ages 16-20 £4; open late March-Sept. daily; late Sept. and Feb. to mid-March Tues.-Sat.).

Hardrow Force, England's waterfall altitude (not height) champion, spits and hisses 1 mi. north along the Pennine Way. To see this overrated and unimpressive natural sight, you must grease palms at the Green Dragon Pub with 20p. More worthwhile are the **Aysgarth Falls,** to the east, which rolls in successive tiers down the craggy Yoredale Rocks, and the natural terrace of the **Shawl of Leyburn.** A **National Park Information Centre** is in the car park above Aysgarth Falls, and a **tourist office** in the center of **Leyburn** (tel. (0969) 230 69). Both Aysgarth and Leyburn are served sporadically by United #26 and West Yorkshire #800; contact the bus companies for current timetables (see Getting There and Getting Around above). Both information centers are open only in summer; the latter will find you a bed for 70p. There is also an **IYHF youth hostel** (tel. (09693) 260) in a former private school 1 mi. east of Aysgarth on the A684. (£5.90, ages 16-20 £4.70, under 16 £3.80. Open April-Sept. daily; Nov. to mid-Dec. and Feb. to mid-March Fri.-Sat.) Eastward lies **Bolton Castle,** one of the myriad places throughout Britain where Mary, Queen of Scots was locked up. (Open March-Oct. daily 10am-5pm. Admission £1.50, seniors and children 75p.)

York

A well-preserved circuit of medieval walls ineffectually defend medieval cottages, Georgian townhouses, and Britain's largest Gothic cathedral from the vicissitudes of spot migration. York is a justifiably popular tourist destination that has learned to handle the hordes with grace, hiding them from each other in narrow alleyways and providing all the essentials at reasonable prices.

In 71 AD, the Romans founded "Eburacum" as a military and administrative base for Northern England, and the town remained important as Anglo-Saxon "Eoforwic" and Viking "Jorvik." After the Norman conquest, William I built the inevitable castle, and for several centuries York held the limelight as England's second city; it was graced with its own archbishop and, during the War of the Roses, its own royal house. In the 18th century, however, Hull took over most of York's port functions, and the older city was forced to shift its attentions from commerce and industry to social services and tourism.

Arriving and Departing

York is on the main London-Edinburgh Intercity rail line. Trains run to: London, King's Cross (every ½hr. morning rush hr.-9:17pm, Sun. every ½hr. 8:33am-8:44pm; 2½ hr.; £39, saver return £48, supersaver £39); Manchester (about every hr. 6:38am-10:10pm, Sun. about every hr. 8:30am-10:39pm; 1¾ hr.; £9.40, return £10-13); Newcastle (every ½hr. 7:30am-midnight, Sun. every hr. 8:09am-10:20pm; 1¼ hr.; £15, return £17.50-23); and Scarborough (every hr. 7:24am-10:35pm, Sun. 11/day 9:41am-10:30pm; 1 hr.; £6.80, return £10.50).

Coaches run less frequently to: London: (4/day 1:35am-4:30pm; 5 hr.; £23.50, return £25-31.50); Manchester (5/day 2:30am-5:55pm; 2½ hr.; £6, return £6.25-8); Edinburgh (1/day 10:20am; 7 hr.); and Bradford (5/day 2:30am-5:55pm; 2 hr.; £4.50, return £4.75-6).

Orientation and Practical Information

York is a fairly compact city, with most attractions lying within the walls or just outside. Surrounding the tangle of pedestrian streets at the city center are a few relatively straight thoroughfares. The ½mi. strip formed by Station Rd., the Lendal Bridge, Museum St., and Duncombe Pl. leads from the rail station to the Minster. The other important chain of streets runs perpendicular to this. Running southeast from the Minster, High Petergate, Low Petergate, and Colliergate lead towards the shops and restaurants concentrated at the heart of the walled city.

There is a small tourist office in the train station, and another on Rougier St., next to the coach stop, but the main one is near the Minster in the city center. From the train station, turn left down Station Rd. and cross under the city wall; with the wall on your left, cross over the river on Lendal Bridge. Rougier St. and the bus station are on the right just before the bridge. As you walk onto the bridge, the Minster is straight ahead; turn left 1 block before it onto St. Leonard's Pl. to reach Exhibition Sq. and the main tourist office.

Tourist Information Centers: Main Office in De Grey Rooms, Exhibition Sq. (tel. 62 17 56). Provides an extensive accommodations list and a useful brochure entitled *The Historic Attractions of York,* as well as all sorts of leaflets on tours, attractions, and entertainment. Accommodations booked with a 10% deposit; rent a Sony Walkman with a recorded tour for £3/day. Open Mon.-Sat. 9am-7pm, Sun. 11am-4pm; Oct.-May Mon.-Sat. 9am-5pm. The smaller office in the train station (tel. 64 37 00) is open Mon.-Fri. 9:30am-5:30pm, Sun. 11am-5pm); the one on Rougier St. (tel. 62 05 57) is open Mon.-Sat. 9am-6pm, Sun. 10am-5pm.

Bike Rental: Cycle Scene, 2 Ratcliffe St., off Barton Stone Lane (tel. 65 32 86). Open Mon.-Sat. 9:30am-5:30pm. £6/day, £40 deposit. Panniers £7/week. Repairs.

Boats: Several companies along the River Ouse near Lendal, Ouse, and Skeldergate Bridges offer 1-hr. cruises for about £2. **York Marine,** Skeldergate Bridge (tel. 70 44 42), rents motorboats (£11/hr., £10 deposit) and rowboats (£2/person/hr., £5 deposit). Open daily 9am-7pm.

Bookstores: Pick up a free guide to York's 15 antiquarian bookshops at any one of them; try **Ken Spelman,** 70 Micklegate (tel. 62 44 14; open Mon.-Sat. 9am-5:30pm). **One World,** 17 Goodramgate, is a rad anti-nuke, pro-peace book, card, and craft shop. Open Mon.-Sat. 9am-6pm.

Buses and Coaches: Go to Rougier St. for a piece of the action. National Express coaches board on Rougier St. (call (0532) 46 00 11 for information), and coach tickets are sold in the Rougier St. tourist office. **York City Rider** regional bus information office on Rougier St. (tel. 62 41 61). (Open daily 9am-1:30pm, 2-5pm.) Local buses board at the train station, Rougier St., or on Piccadilly. Buses to Scarborough, Harrowgate, and Castle Howard board at Rougier St. **Reynard-Pullman,** Exhibition Sq. (tel. 62 29 92), runs day tours to Castle Howard, Moors, and Dales from ABC Cinema, Piccadilly.

Crisis: Samaritans, 89 Nunnery Lane (tel. 65 58 88).

Financial Services: Barclays, St. Helen's Sq. (tel. 63 13 33). Open Mon.-Fri. 9:30am-4:30pm, Sat. 9:30am-noon. **Thomas Cook,** 4 Nessgate. Open Mon.-Wed. and Fri.-Sat. 9am-5:30pm, Thurs. 9:30am-5:30pm. Exchange in the **train station** open daily 9am-8pm. Exchange in the **main tourist office** open same hours as tourist office. Rates slightly higher than banks. **American Express:** 6 Stonegate. Rates slightly higher than Barclay's, but no commission on AmEx traveler's checks. Open Mon.-Fri. 9am-5pm, Sat. 10am-5pm; Nov.-March Mon.-Fri. 9am-5pm, Sat. 10am-1pm.

Early Closing Day: Wed., around 1pm. Smaller shops only.

Emergency: Dial 999; no coins required.

Hospital: York District Hospital, Wiggonton Rd. (tel. 63 13 13).

Launderette: Clifton Co-Op, Bootham at Queen Anne's Rd. Wash £1.10, dry 20p (10p coins only). Open Mon.-Fri. 8am-6pm, last wash 4:45pm; Sat-Sun. 8am-5pm, last wash 3:30pm. Attended after 9am. **Walmgate Bar Laundromat,** just inside the city walls. Wash £1.40-1.80, large drier £1.20. Attendant has change. Open Mon.-Wed. and Fri. 9am-8pm, Sat. 9am-6pm, Sun. 10am-2pm.

Market: Between Shambles and Parliament St. Mon.-Sat. about 8am-5pm.

Police: Fulford Rd. (tel. 63 13 21).

Post Office: 22 Lendal (tel. 61 72 85, ext. 210). Open Mon.-Tues. and Thurs.-Fri. 9am-5:30pm, Wed. 9:30am-5:30pm, Sat. 9am-12:30pm. **Postal Code:** YO1 2DA.

Telephone Code: 0904.

Train Station: Station Rd. (tel. 64 21 55). Information office open Mon.-Sat. 8am-7:45pm, Sun. 9am-7:45pm. Luggage lockers 50p-£1.50. Luggage office storage £1.30 for small articles, £2 for a pack. Open Mon.-Sat. 7:15am-9:15pm, Sun. 11:15am-6:45pm.

Accommodations and Camping

Competition for inexpensive B&Bs (from £9) can be fierce from June through August. The tourist office provides an accommodations service and leaves a list outside after hours. Try **The Mount** area (out past the train station and down Blossom St.), **Haxby Road** (take bus #2A, or walk from the tourist office out to the end of Gillygate and take the right fork), or any of the sidestreets along Bootham/Clifton. Book ahead during the summer, even for hostels and camping sites.

Bishophill House Youth Hostel, 11-13 Bishophill Senior Rd. YO1 1EF (tel. 62 59 04 or 63 06 13). Most bunk for the buck. Turn left out of the train station and follow Station Ave. Cross under the walls and continue onto Rougier and then George Hudson St., until you reach Micklegate. Turn right and make the next left onto the narrow St. Martin's Lane, which will bring you to Bishophill. The 29-bed Room 12 is an excellent place to meet fellow travelers of various nationalities; much of the rest of the building is often booked by youth groups. A bar opens after the pubs close and stays open until about midnight; there is also a TV lounge. Showers are free, and are hotter for early risers. Sheets are £1 unless you have your own, continental breakfast £1.30, full breakfast £2.30, bike rental £4.50, laundry £2 wash, 50p dry. Dorm beds £7-8.50 depending on the size of the room; singles £12.50-16, twin £10.25-14.40/person. Call ahead in summer.

IYHF youth hostel, Haverford, Water End, Clifton YO3 6LT (tel. 65 31 47), 1 mi. from the town center. From the Exhibition Sq. tourist office, walk about ½mi. out Bootham, which becomes Clifton. Superior-grade hostel: members' kitchen, TV room, and blazing hot showers. 158 beds with 4-8 beds/room; often fills with groups, so call ahead. A few beds are saved for walk-ins. Reception open 7am-11:30pm. Lockout 10am-5pm, curfew 11:30pm. £9.30, ages 16-20 £7, under 16 £5.50; Sept.-May £8.30. Breakfast £2.30, linen 80p. Open daily early Jan.-early Dec.

Maxwell's Hotel, 54 Walmgate (tel. 62 40 48). Good location. Clean dorm rooms with 4-6 beds, £8, including linen. Continental breakfast £1, full £2. Airy singles and doubles with full breakfast, £14.50, Oct.-April £12.50.

The Old Dairy, 10 Compton St. (tel. 62 38 16). Walk ½mi. up Bootham from Exhibition Sq or call to find out the current number of the bus from the train station to Clifton Green. Charming chambers with wrought iron beds, tea and coffee facilities. £11.

Queen Anne's Guest House, 24 Queen Anne's Rd. (tel. 62 93 89), a short walk out Bootham from Exhibition Sq. Spotless rooms with TV, £12-13, Nov.-June £11-12.

The Racecourse Centre: Racing Stables, Dinghouses (tel. (0904) 70 63 17). 192 dormitory beds available. Open March-July when not in use by jockeys. Take bus #3, 3A, 3B or 4. £7.63-8.63/person. Includes breakfast.

Camping: Caravan Club Site, Terry Av., York YO2 1JQ (tel. (0203) 69 49 95), beyond Skeldergate Bridge. £2.50-3/person. Book 3 mo. in advance. **Bishopthorpe** (tel. 70 44 42), 3 mi. south of York off the A64. Riverside site. Take bus #14, 15, or 15A to Bishopthorpe. Tent and 4 people £4, 1 person £3. Open Easter-Sept. **Post Office Site** (tel. 70 62 88), 4 mi. south of York off the A64, by the river. Take any Acaster Malbis bus. Tent, car, and 2 people £4.50. Additional person 75p. Open April-Oct. **Poplar Farm** (tel. 70 65 48), near Post Office Site. Tent and 2 people £5. Additional person 50p. Syke's bus leaves Skeldergate every 2 hr.

Food and Pubs

Expensive tea rooms, medium-priced bistros, and cheap eateries line even the remotest alleyways of York. Alternatively, there is a fruit and vegetable market behind the Shambles. (Open Mon.-Sat. 8am-5pm.)

The Blake Head, 104 Mickelgate (tel. 62 37 67), behind a bookstore. A sunny, relaxed vegetarian café, the perfect place to write a letter home—everyone misses you, you know. Delicious desserts, many low in sugar (£1.75). Lunch, including crisp salads, is served noon-2:30pm (£2.50-4). On Friday and Saturday evenings, dinner is served 6:30-9pm; call ahead for reservations. Open Mon.-Sat. 9:30am-6pm, Sun. 10am-5pm.

St. William's Restaurant, 3 College St. (tel. 348 30). Cafeteria inside the 15th-century building and cobbled courtyard outside St. William's College. Small but tasty portions. Salad 45p, hot dishes £2.50-4. Fancy tea 55p. Open Mon.-Sat. 10am-5pm, lunch served noon-2:30pm.

The Mogul, 39 Tanner Row (tel. 65 96 22), near the coach stop. Cheaper than many of the other Indian restaurants, with a wide selection of curries for £3.60 or less. Open daily noon-2:30pm and 6pm-midnight.

The York Pie Shop, 24 Pavement (tel. 64 44 14). Tasty meat pies covered with flaky crusts are almost enough to give English food a good name (£4.25-7.25). Open daily 10am-10pm.

Oscar's Wine Bar and Bistro, Little Stonegate (tel. 65 20 02), off Stonegate. A mixed salad (from £2) and coffee in the swank courtyard will keep you going for the day. A varied menu and a lively atmosphere. Open daily 11am-10pm.

Lew's Place, King's Staith (tel. 62 81 67), near Ouse Bridge. The food is fantastic and you get prodigious portions for £6.25-9. Open Mon.-Sat. noon-2pm and 6:30-10pm.

There are more **pubs** in the center of York than gargoyles on the east wall of the Minster. Whether half-timbered, Victorian or something in between, all are packed on weekend nights. The **Lowther Arms,** on King's South by the river, serves a wide variety of bar meals for around £3.50 (food served daily 12:30-2pm amd 5:30-8:30pm). The **Roman Bath,** St. Sampson's Sq., serves pints among the ruins. The **Punch Bowl,** Stonegate, is one of York's handsomest pubs, and its neighbor down the street, the **Old Starre,** is the city's oldest. The **Black Swan Inn,** Peasholme

Green, is more sedate—come here to avoid the droves of teenagers who queue up for a pint of 7-UP outside the pubs closer to St. Sampson's Sq.

Sights

The **York Visitor Card** (80p), available at the tourist office, offers discounts on many of the museums and buildings in York; it will pay for itself if two adults use it at just one or two places. The best introduction to York is a 2½-mi. walk along its medieval walls. Unless you go very early in the morning or at dusk to avoid the herd of tourists, however, you may feel like a cow being driven to market. Of the bewildering array of organized tours of York, a few merit attention: the free two-hr. **walking tour,** offered by the Association of Voluntary Guides, emphasizes York's architectural legacy (meet in Exhibition Sq.; April-Oct. daily at 10:15am and 2:15pm; June-Aug. also at 7pm); and a fascinating **haunted walk** covers some of York's ghostlier spots (meet at Exhibition Square Mon.-Fri. 8pm; £2, children £1; tel. 42 17 37). For information on the narrated open-top **Jorvick bus tour,** call 736 37. The Friends of Richard III (tel. 76 24 92) give a tour of **Richardian York** every Sunday at 2pm (meet at Library Sq., Museum St., £1), in an effort to dispel the king's undeserved reputation as a scheming murderer. A word of caution: be sure you are with the right tour before abdicating to the guide. The offbeat guide book *Snickelways of York* by Mark W. Jones (£3.50) is an excellent introduction to the city.

Everyone and everything in York converges on **York Minster,** the largest Gothic cathedral in Britain. The present structure, built from 1220 to 1470, was preceded by the Roman fortress where Constantine the Great was hailed emperor in 306 and the Saxon church where King Edwin was converted to Christianity in 627. The Minster is estimated to contain more than half of all the medieval stained glass in England. The **Great East Window,** constructed from 1405-08 and depicting the beginning and the end of the world in over a hundred small scenes, is the largest single medieval glass window in the world.

By the 1960s, the Minster's foundations had become so weak that the lantern tower threatened to collapse. A remarkable feat of modern civil engineering created the new supports visible in the **undercroft,** which you can tour for £1.50, seniors and students 75p, children 60p; admission to undercroft includes admission to the treasury. (Open Mon.-Sat. 10am-6:30pm, Sun. 1-6:30pm.) Despite this achievement, there is still a great deal of work to be done on the cathedral, and scaffolding will cover some part of the exterior until the next century. It is a mere 275 steps up to the top of the **Central Tower,** from which you can stare down at the red roofs of York. (Open daily 10am-6pm. Admission £1.50, children 70p.) A complete tour of the cathedral should cover the **chapter house** (same hr. as undercroft; admission 60p, children 30p), the **crypt** (inquire about admission at entrance desk), and the **Minster Library** (open Mon.-Fri. 9am-5pm; free). The Minster itself is open daily (7am-8:30pm, donation £1). A beautiful choral **evensong** is held weekdays at 5pm and Sundays at 4pm.

Behind the Minster on College St. stands 15th-century **St. William's College** (tel. 371 34). Charles I established the royal printing press and mint here when he moved to York just before the Puritan Revolution. (Open Mon.-Sat. 10am-5pm, Sun. 12:30-5pm. Admission 35p, children 15p.) The **Treasurer's House,** around the corner on Chapter House St., is a lavish invention of the 17th century. (Open April-Oct. daily 10:30am-6pm, last admission 4:30pm. Admission £2.30, children £1.) Nearby, **York Art Gallery,** in Exhibition Sq. across from the tourist office, has a fair selection of Continental work (including early Florentine and Siennese primitives) and a better selection of English painters. (Open Mon.-Sat. 10am-5pm, Sun. 2:30-5pm. Free.) Also in Exhibition Sq., the **King's Manor,** once the royal headquarters for the north of England, is now part of the University of York.

The **Yorkshire Museum,** Museum St. (tel. 62 97 45), contains a variety of artifacts dug out of the local soil, including a bust of Constantine the Great, Roman pottery, coins, and ichthyosaurus fossils. (Open daily 10am-5pm; Nov.-Easter Mon.-Sat.

10am-5pm, Sun. 1-5pm. Admission £2, seniors, students, and children £1.) In the museum gardens that slope down to the river, peacocks strut among the ruins of **St. Mary's Abbey,** once the most influential Benedictine monastery in northern England. Lascivious monks once cavorted there and controlled York's brothels, until the not-so-chaste-himself Henry VIII brought them to heel in 1539 and turned the Abbey into a quarry. Every four years, the skeletal monastery chapel becomes the backdrop for performances of the York Mystery Plays.

York has retained so many of its old buildings and streets that after a brief acquaintance with the city, it seems natural that a building should be 600 years old. The **guildhall** in St. Helen's Sq. (tel. 61 31 61), built in 1466 but partly destroyed by bombs in 1942 after the collapse of an Anglo-German agreement to spare historic cities, has been largely restored to its medieval state. (Open Mon.-Thurs. 9am-5pm, Fri. 9am-4pm, Sat. 10am-5pm, Sun. 2-5pm; Nov.-April Mon.-Thurs. 9am-5pm, Fri. 9am-4pm. Free.) Thankfully not restored to its medieval state is the **Shambles,** traditionally the street of butchers, where rotting animal parts mingled with living animals' wastes, and inspired the addition of a word for "scene of slaughter and destruction" to the English language. All that remain are flagstone streets connecting half-timbered houses which lean toward one another at crazy angles, shutting out sunlight and creating a triangular tunnel for pedestrians. **Whip-ma-whop-ma-gate,** at one end of the Shambles, has the most peculiar name east of Wales; it was originally called "Whitnourwhatnourgate" (meaning "What a street!"). Nearby, the colorful **Merchant Adventurers' Hall,** Fossgate, contains the relics of the once most powerful and wealthy company in the city. (Open daily 8:30am-5pm; Nov.-March Mon.-Sat. 8:30am-3:30pm. Admission £1.50, seniors £1.20, children 50p.) Also nearby, **St. Anthony's Hall** on Peasholme Green dates from 1453. In the 16th century, a weaving workshop was set up here to prevent "laytering and ydleness of vacabunds and poor follc." Today, a small but fascinating collection of ecclesiastical documents is displayed in the hall upstairs. (Open Mon.-Fri. 9:30am-12:50pm and 2-4:50pm. Free.)

Housed in a former debtor's prison, the huge York **Castle Museum** (tel. 65 36 11) contains everything from excavations to, quite literally, the kitchen sink. The museum was endowed with the vast collection of Dr. Kirk, a 19th-century physician who accepted antiques, relics, and bric-a-brac from his patients in lieu of fees. Visit **Kirkgate,** an intricately reconstructed Victorian shopping street, and the **Half Moon Court,** its Edwardian counterpart. More unusual folk reconstructions include a World War I trench scene and a functioning watermill that sells stone-ground flour. (Museum open Mon.-Sat. 9:30am-5:30pm, Sun. 10am-5:30pm; Nov.-March Mon.-Sat. 9:30am-4pm, Sun. 10am-4pm. Admission £3.20, seniors, students, and children £1.60.)

Across from the Castle Museum is the strange, squat silhouette of **Clifford's Tower** (tel. 64 69 40), one of the last remaining pieces of York Castle and a reminder of the worst anti-Semitic outbreak in English history. In 1190, Christian merchants tried to cancel their debts to Jewish bankers by destroying York's Jewish community. On the last Sabbath before Passover, 150 Jews took refuge in a tower that previously stood on this site and, faced with the prospect of starvation or butchery, committed collective suicide. Inside the tower there isn't much to see, but there is a good view from the walls. (Tower open daily 10am-6pm; Oct.-March Mon.-Sat. 10am-4pm. Admission 95p, seniors and students 75p, children 45p.)

The nearby **Jorvik Viking Centre** (tel. 64 32 11) runs a cleverly executed 20-min. ride into a subterranean Viking village re-created in superb detail. You may be able to beat the crowds if you line up before opening time. (Open daily 9am-7pm; Nov.-March 9am-5:30pm. Steep admission £3.20; Nov.-March only children £1.60, seniors £2.40.) The **National Railway Museum,** Leeman Rd. (tel. 62 12 61), doesn't purport to be an art museum, but its many titanic steam locomotives and plush passenger cars have been lovingly restored to such gleaming brilliance that they are nothing short of sculpture. On summer Wednesdays and Saturdays, these historic engines pull visitors in replica antique cars—call for an exact schedule. (Open

Mon.-Sat. 10am-6pm, Sun. 11am-6pm. Admission £3.30, seniors, students, disabled £2.10, children £1.65, family £8.)

As befits a tourist town, York is cluttered with smaller attractions, from historic Georgian townhouses to elaborate wax museums, each with an admission charge of £2-3. Stop by the tourist office for brochures on any and all.

Entertainment

For the most current information, pick up the weekly *What's On* guide and the seasonal *Evening Entertainment* brochure from the tourist office. The free, bimonthly *Artscene* is a good resource for arts information throughout Yorkshire.

The Black Swan Inn, Peasholme Green, hosts folk artists on Thursday nights at 8pm (£1.25-2.50). Housed in a beautifully preserved 15th-century merchant's house, this pub is worth visiting any day of the week. For free folk tunes, duck under the polished golden sheep that hangs over the door of the **Golden Fleece,** the Pavement, on Sunday evenings. At the **Punch Bowl,** 7 Stonegate, folk and blues on Wednesday and jazz on Thursday are free and begin at 9pm. The most eclectic concert in town is *al fresco.* In **King's Square,** barbershop quartets and recorder ensembles share the pavement with jugglers, magicians, politicians, and evangelists. In addition, the Minster and local churches host a series of summer concerts.

Near York

You can spend an uncrowded day only 2 mi. east of York in the open-air **Yorkshire Museum of Farming** (tel. 48 99 66) in Murton Park, where the beekeeper demonstrates honey extraction on weekends. (Open May-Sept. daily 10:30am-5:30pm; March-April and Oct. Tues.-Sun. Admission £2, seniors £1.25, children £1.) From June through August, bus #840 runs from York station to the museum (Mon.-Fri. only, 3/day in each direction, last return 2:55pm; 20 min.). Otherwise, take the local bus to Osbaldwick from the train station and walk 10 minutes to Murton.

Castle Howard (tel. (065384) 444) was the first structure ever built by Sir John Vanbrugh, a somewhat bawdy dramatist. Despite his dubious literary pedigree, he manipulated the technical language of architecture with an accent of unquestionable refinement. The building, still inhabited by the Howard family, made its TV debut in the grandiose soap opera *Brideshead Revisited.* Inside is a fine museum that houses *objets d'art* from all over the world. The famous hall is a lavish example of the English baroque—horses of the sun tumble out of the sky on the painted ceiling. Formal gardens stretch away through fountains and lakes to Hawksmoor's mausoleum, which contains the Howard bones. The stables have recently been remodeled into a **Costume and Regalia Gallery,** the largest private collection of its kind. The costumes range from pre-French Revolution *sacque-back* dresses to flapper bathing suits. (Castle and galleries open April-Oct. 11am-4:30pm, grounds open from 10am. Admission £4.50, seniors £3.50, children £2). Reynard-Pullman (tel. 62 29 92; booking office across from Exhibition Sq. tourist office) conducts afternoon tours to Castle Howard (Mon., Wed., Fri.; £3.50), and Yorkshire Coastliner (tel. (0653) 69 25 56; 1 bus/day; £2.30 return); as always, check at the tourist office; companies frequently change their schedules.

Set among woods and cliffs by the River Skell, **Fountains Abbey** (tel. (076586) 333) is one of Yorkshire's best-preserved. This abbey was founded in 1132 by monks who left the corrupting urban setting of York to settle in the wilderness. Henry VIII's dissolution of the monasteries in the early 16th century was bitterly resented in Yorkshire, and the "Pilgrimage of Grace" that ensued turned into a rebellion. The Tudors crushed the dissent, and the abbeys crumbled into disrepair. The undercroft of Fountains Abbey, supported by an endless row of columns, is an extraordinary architectural feat. (Abbey open April-June and Sept. daily 10am-7pm; July-Aug. 10am-8pm; Oct. 10am-6pm; Nov.-March Sat.-Thurs. 10am-5pm. Admission £2.70, children £1.20. 1-hr. guided tours April-Oct. daily at 2:30 and 3:30pm.) To reach the abbey, take bus #143 from the York train station to Ripon; then walk

4 mi. (via Westgate, Park St., the B6265, and the village of **Studley Roger**). The walk itself is entertaining, leading through the formal pleasure grounds of **Studley Royal,** an 18th-century Italianate garden complete with Temple of Piety and sham ruins (admission free with ticket to Abbey). **St. Mary's Church** in Studley Roger is a fine example of Victorian "muscle-bound Gothic" architecture. (Open Wed.-Sat. 9:30am-6:30pm, Sun. 2-6:30pm.)

North York Moors National Park

Those who have sampled the English countryside and determined that *moor* is a four-letter-word (along with *rain* and *peat*) may not find the paths here less boggy and the rainfall lighter than in the Peak District, Lake District, or the Cheviots, whatever the statistics may prove. The North York Moors National Park is a broad kidney-shaped chunk of heather-covered moorland, rock-walled farmland, and wooded dales in the east of England extending from Middlesbrough to Scarborough on the coast and to Thirsk. Topographically, the park includes the Vale of Pickering in the south, the Vales of York and Mowbray in the west, the flat Cleveland and Teeside Plains in the north, and the rugged North Sea coastline in the east.

The moors are undoubtedly at their best under a shroud of early-morning mist, haunted by the spirits that inspired the Brontë sisters, Bram Stoker, and Arthur Conan Doyle. Thirteenth-century flagstone paths (known as "trods" or "pannier-man's tracks") that were once used by monks carrying goods between religious houses still thread the moors, and wayfarers still find their way with the help of the famous stone moorland crosses—lonely markers rising up from the depths of the English bog. **Lilla Cross,** on Fylingdales Moor, is the oldest Christian monument in northern England, a tribute to the servant Lilla who in 626 used his own body to shield King Edwin from an assassin's dagger. The landscape is dotted with castles (at Helmsley, Pickering, and Scarborough) and the ruins of many medieval abbeys and hermitages. Some of the highest cliffs in England line the park's coastal border, interspersed with tiny harbors such as Straithes and Robin Hood's Bay.

Getting There and Getting Around

The park, about 25 mi. north of the city of York, is fringed by Middlesbrough and Guisborough to the northwest, Whitby to the northeast, Scarborough to the southeast, Pickering and Helmsley to the south, and Thirsk to the southwest. Any of these towns makes a suitable base for exploring the North York Moors, but Whitby and Pickering (connected to each other by a rail line through the park and to York by bus) are the most appealing.

There is no single town that serves as an obvious transport hub—Malton and Pickering, near the southern edge of the park and Middlesbrough to the north all have good connections. From Leeds and York, **Yorkshire Coastliner** runs frequent buses to Malton, continuing to Scarborough or Pickering and Whitby. **East Yorkshire** #802 runs from Hull to Malton and Pickering on Sundays in July and August. Bus #128 connects Scarborough and Pickering about every hour. Buses #93, 93A, 93C, and X93 link Middlesbrough, Whitby and Scarborough. A British Rail line runs about every hour northeast from York to Scarborough via Malton.

The essential document for transport within the park is the *Moors Connections* pamphlet, which covers both bus and rail service in delightful detail (available free at information centers or for 50p from Elmtree Publications, The Elms, Exelby, Bedale, North Yorkshire DL8 2HD). A **Tees Day Ranger** (£5.50, with railcard £3.65, children £2.75) is good for unlimited travel in the area bounded by Bishop Auckland, Darlington, Sunderland, and Whitby.

British Rail's **Esk Valley Line** runs four times a day through the northern part of the park from Darlington (midway between York and Newcastle) east through Middlesbrough, Danby, and Grosmont (GROW-mont), ending at Whitby on the coast. A private rail line, the **North Yorkshire Moors Railway** (tel. (0751) 725 08, recorded timetable 735 35), runs steam trains from Grosmont due south through the Newtondale Gorge to Pickering, about 8 mi. north of Malton. A coach link from Grosmont to Whitby is also available mid-June to Sept. Although the fares are almost as steep as the Newtondale Gorge itself, this is the only dependable north-south public transport within the region east of the Newcastle-York Intercity rail line (late March-early Nov. only; schedule varies from 3/day to every hr.; £5.20-6, seniors £3.55-6, children £2.60-3; return £6.50-7.50, £4.25-7.50, £3.10-3.60). Even if you don't care to board this obsolete iron horse, it is a treat to watch these beauties pull out of Pickering Station in a blast of steam and greenhouse gases.

The approach to the moors on bike is tough, but on the plateau the paths are pleasantly level. In Pickering, you can rent bikes at **A. Taylor & Son,** (tel. (0751) 721 43; Hungate £15/day for a mountain bike, £8 for a 3-speed (open Mon.-Sat. 8am-5pm); ask about other places at the Moors Centre (see below). For pony trekking, Mrs. R. Cook at **Beck Isle Ponies** (tel. (0751) 729 82), Wells Walk in Pickering, charges £5 for a 1-hr. ride in the forest. In Helmsley, **The Riding School** (tel. 0439) 703 55) caters to experienced riders only (£13 for 2 hr., £18.50/day). The *North York Moors Visitor* (available at any tourist office) contains an extensive list of places to rent bikes, mares, and stallions in each major town.

Practical Information

Along with the *Moors Connections,* the *North York Moors Visitor* (40p) is the other essential publication for the park. Available at information centers, it lists attractions, events, and accommodations.

Information Centers

Danby: The Moors Centre, YO21 2NB (tel. (0287) 66 06 54). The largest National Park Information Centre in the park, with many maps and guidebooks and nearby trails. 20 min. from Danby train station. On Sundays in July and August, bus #700 runs twice each way between Malton and Pickering and Stockton, stopping in Danby. If you plan to make a round-trip from Malton or Pickering, you will have only 2 hrs. in Danby. Open daily 10am-5pm, Nov.-March Sat.-Sun. 11am-4pm.

Sutton Bank: Near Thirsk (tel.(0845) 59 74 26). National Park Information Centre. Open daily 10am-5pm, Nov.-March Sat.-Sun. 11am-4pm.

Helmsley: Market Place (tel. (0439) 70 173). National Park Information Centre and Ryedale Tourist Information Centre. Open daily 9:30am-6pm, Nov.-March Sat.-Sun 10am-4pm.

Pickering: Eastgate Car Park (tel.(0751) 73 791). Tourist Information Centre. Books accommodations with a 10% deposit. Open daily 10am-5pm.

Scarborough: St. Nicholas Cliff (tel. (0723) 37 33 33). Open daily 10am-5pm.

Whitby: New Quay Rd. (tel. (0947) 60 26 74). Open daily 10am-5pm.

Accommodations

Ten youth hostels guarantee dry lodging in the moors at Boggle Hole (£6.30, ages 16-20 £5.10, children £4), Helmsley (£5.90, ages 16-20 £4.70, children £3.80), Lockton (£4.40, ages 16-20 £3.50. children £2.60), Malton (£5.50, ages 16-20 £4.40, children £3.50), Osmotherley (£5.90, ages 16-20 £4.70, children £3.80), Scarborough (£5.50, ages 16-20 £4.40, children £3.50), Saltburn (£5.50, ages 16-20 £4.40, children £3.50), Thixendale (£4.40, ages 16-20 £3.50, children £2.60), Westerdale (£5.10, ages 16-20 £4, children £3.10), Wheeldale (£4.40, ages 16-20 £3.30, children £2.60), and Whitby (£5.50, ages 16-20 £4.40, children £3.50). For detailed directions, opening times and phone numbers, buy the IYHF guide. You can also book B&Bs in towns throughout the park through any of the local tourist offices for a small fee.

Hiking

The best way to see the moors is to hike. Both the energetic and the leisurely can find trails to suit their stamina. They are not all well-defined or well-marked, however, and many of them intersect. *Always* carry a detailed map and a compass. The Ordnance Survey *Tourist Map 2* (£3.30), which covers the whole park, may not be adequately detailed for hikers; the 1:25,000 *Outdoor Leisure* sheets #26 and 27 (£4 each) are more helpful.

Also pick up the free *Moorland Safety* pamphlet, available from Helmsley, Damby, or Sutton Bank (they may not be available at other tourist offices). Sturdy footwear, warm pants (not jeans), a wind- and water-proof jacket, and extra clothing are essential; as well, an Ordnance Survey map and compass, flashlight, first-aid kit, polythene survival bag, and whistle just might save your life. The **international distress signal** is six long flashes or blasts in quick succession, repeated at one-min. intervals. The moors can be uncomfortably hot or bitterly cold in the summer—be prepared for sudden changes in weather. Check the weather forecast ahead of time (tel. (0898) 50 04 18), but be aware that it reports on all of northeast England, and that the weather can vary dramatically even within the park.

Hiking

The national park office produces a series of pamphlets (called *Waymark*, #1-30) (30p each) on 2- to 10-mi. circular walks in the park, all marked with blue or yellow arrows. The office also publishes a list of guided walks each season. Paul Hannon's *Walks on the North York Moors* (£2.85 for each of 3) is a chipper paperback series outlining circular walks. The spiral-bound *Bartholomew Map and Guide* lays out 40 short walks and, like all the best travel guides, is updated annually (£3.95). The free pamphlet *Facilities for the Disabled* outlines walks accessible to the disabled.

Ambitious hikers might consider tackling one of the three official, or one of the many unofficial, long-distance footpaths in the park. The 93 mi. **Cleveland Way** is outlined in Paul Hannon's excellent paperback *Cleveland Way Companion*, modeled after Wainwright's, with detailed hand-drawn maps and a humorous slant (£3.45). Bill Cowley's *The Cleveland Way* (£3.75) and the Dalesman *Cleveland Way Guide* (£3.75) are both useful. More information can be obtained from the *North York Moors Visitor* and the North York Moors National Park Information Office, The Old Vicarage, Bondgate, Helmsley, Y06 5BF. The official guidebook to the 79-mi. **Wolds Way** is a publication by the same name by Roger Ratcliffe (£2.50). Two unoffical paths are the **White Rose Walk** and the **Crosses Walk;** Malcolm Boyes has written a guide on the latter (£2.25), and the Moors Centre, Danby, Whitby Y021 2NB has more information. A fourth long-distance path is the famous **Lyke Wake Walk;** the official guide book can be obtained at the Danby, Sutton Bank, and Pickering. Finally Wainwright describes the 190-mi. **Coast-to-Coast Walk** in his excellent guide (£6).

The Northern Park

The **Moors Centre** in **Danby** is the moors' largest National Park Information Centre (tel. (0287) 66 06 54). As you come off the train platform, turn right down the driveway, left on the road, and then right at the crossroad before the Duke of Wellington pub. The Moors Centre is ½mi. ahead on the right. (Open daily 10am-5pm; Nov.-Easter Sun. noon-4pm, weather permitting.) The walk to the centre will refresh the cathedral-weary with naturally grandiose views of the Esk valley and moors. Several hiking trails, both short and long, originate at the centre; all are clearly marked and require no special equipment. With the help of a *Waymark* guide, you can ascend the 1400-ft. **Danby Rigg** (ridge) to the top of **Danby High Moor,** and continue on to **Castleton Rigg** or **Glaisdale Rigg** (these are also accessible from the train stations at Castleton, Glaisdale, or Lealholme). The walk to **Oakley Side** from Danby passes beautiful views of the undulating **Esk Valley** farmland. The entire Esk Valley walk, a series of 10 connecting trails, follows the River Esk from its source near the northwest edge of the park to its mouth in Whitby Bay. The official guide costs £1.50, but there are also free pamphlets describing each hike. **Danby Castle,** visible from the outside only, is an early 14th-century fortress built by the house of Latimer. The castle itself is quite unspectacular, but the gentle 2-hr. walk there and back is pleasant. Passers-through can leave their packs under the stairs in the information office. Farther afield, you can walk from the Little Ayton rail station (on the Esk Valley line) or from Newton-under-Roseberry (accessible by bus) to the summit of **Roseberry Topping** (not a dessert), overlooking the wide expanse of the western moors. *Waymarks* #3 and #4 describe 3½ hr. walks around the base of the mountain. No pamphlets describe the ascent itself, but signposts will direct you. Allow at least two to three hours to walk up and back down, plus some time to stop and enjoy the view. You can also hook up with the **White Rose Walk** here. For more information, inquire at Danby.

Just 3 mi. north of Newton along the A173, in the town of Guisborough (GIZ-ber-a), **Gisborough Priory**'s empty 11th-century window frames open onto rolling countryside (tel. (0287) 383 01; open daily 10am-6pm; Oct.-March. Tues.-Sun. 10am-4pm. 60p, seniors and students 45p, children 30p).

The Southern Park

Pickering (pop. 7500), at the southern end of the North Yorkshire Moors Railway, makes a good base from which to visit the southern part of the park. **Pickering Castle,** built in the time of William the Conqueror, was once a vacation house for monarchs who hunted boar and deer in a nearby royal forest. (Hr. same as Guisborough. Admission 85p, seniors and students 65p, children 40p.) The nearby **Church of St. Peter and St. Paul** displays medieval frescoes discovered and restored in the last century. On Bridge St., the **Beck Isle Museum** is an interesting and informal collection of the accoutrements of rural life, including a 19th-century printing press, cobbler's shop, and dairy. (Open July-Sept. daily 10am-5pm, April-June and Oct. 10am-12:30pm amd 2-5pm. Admission £1, children 50p.) A dazzling **tourist office,** 7 Eastgate Sq. (tel. (0751) 737 91), Pickering Y018 7DP, books accommodations for free with a 10% deposit. From the train station turn right, then left on Market Place; carry on through the Place veering right past the roundabout to the Eastgate Car Park on your left. (Open April-Oct. daily 9:30am-6pm.)

Many of Pickering's plentiful B&Bs are listed in the *North York Moors Visitor,* available at tourist offices and National Park Centres. The tourist office also has a list, which it posts outside after hours. **Mrs. Pocock,** 27 Burgate (tel. (0751) 732 24), offers large, tastefully decorated rooms with great views. From the train station, turn left, walk 50m, take a right up steep Brant Hill, then another right onto Burgate. (£12/person.) **Bon Appetit,** 2 Birdgate (tel. 749 85) near the tourist office, offers a great selection of local cheeses, plus some hot lunches (open Mon.-Sat. 9am-5pm). Across from the train station, **Jumbo Natural Foods** hawks wholefoods and has a café with tea garden. (Open Mon.-Tues. and Thurs.-Sat. 9:30am-5pm, Wed. 9:30am-noon.)

In Helmsley, 10 mi. directly west of Pickering, there is another **tourist office** (tel. (0439) 701 73), in the Market Place. **Rievaulx Abbey** (REE-vo), 3 mi. northwest of Helmsley by road or footpath, was once one of the largest and finest Cistercian abbeys in England. Founded in the 12th century by monks from Burgundy, it now lies in ruins. The choir loft and the refectory are considered two of the finest extant examples of early English architecture. (Abbey open daily 10am-6pm; Oct.-March Tues.-Sun. 10am-4pm. Admission £1.40, seniors and students £1.05, children 70p. Disabled access.) The Duncombe family built ½-mi. Rievaulx Terrace overlooking the abbey, with a classical 18th-century temple tastefully adorning each end. The terrace and temples are 2½ mi. northwest of Helmsley on the B1257. (Open April-Oct. daily 10:30am-6pm. Last entry 5:30pm. Admission £1.70, children 80p. Disabled access to the terrace.) Recently opened **Duncombe Park** (tel. (0439) 702 13) features an 18th-century estate with a Baroque mansion and 100 acres of landscaped gardens and forests. The park is 1 mi. from the center of Helmsley and accessible from York by **Yorktour** buses (tel. (0904) 64 17 37; Wed., Fri., and Sat. 9:30am; Wed. and Fri. 12:30pm). The greenery is especially impressive and includes well-tended 19th-century parterres, grass terraces, and the tallest lime and ash trees in Britain. (Open mid-April to Sept. Sun.-Thurs. 11am-6pm, last entry 5:30; admission to house and grounds £3.50, seniors £3.25, children £1.75; grounds only £2, children £1.)

From the Newtondale or Levisham stations on the North Yorkshire Moors Railway, explore the **Newtondale Gorge,** lined with ferns and pine forests, or take easy scenic strolls through the **Newtondale Forest.** The Pickering tourist office has *Waymark* guides (20-30p) for several two- to four-hr. hikes from town. The simple-grade **IYHF youth hostel,** near Levisham in **Lockton** at the Old School, is a convenient place to stay for gorge gazers. From Pickering you can take York City District bus #92 (tel. (0904) 62 41 61) and get off at the Fox and Rabbit. Three mi. southwest of the Moors Railway stop at **Goathland,** (past **Mallyan Spout,** a beautiful waterfall) is the secluded **Wheeldale youth hostel (IYHF).**

Another **IYHF youth hostel** is 10 mi. south of Pickering in **Malton.** Take bus #92 or #X49 from Pickering. From the rail and bus station, walk uphill to Yorkgate. Turn left and follow the road ¾ mi. out of town. The Malton **tourist office,** Ryedale House (tel. (0653) 60 06 66), Malton Y017 OHH, will guide you to walks in the area. (Open April-Oct. daily 9:30am-1pm and 1:30-5:30pm; Nov.-Dec. Sat.-Sun. only, same hr.) Ten mi. southeast of Malton near the Wolds Way is the simple-grade **Thixendale youth hostel (IYHF).** From Malton, take BritRail to Thixendale.

Coast from Whitby to Scarborough

The cliff-cropped stretch of the **Cleveland Way** from Whitby to Scarborough (about 25 mi.) is magnificent. The unused Whitby-Scarborough rail line has become a **footpath;** inquire at the Whitby tourist office for directions. Buses run from Whitby to Scarborough daily from 7am to 9pm at 25 minutes past the hour (£1.85 single, £3 return).

A tumble of red roofs spilling downward amid a maze of narrow streets, **Whitby** is a charming coastal town midway between Middlesbrough and Scarborough. Its large beach has a blessed paucity of amusement arcades; its harbor is rife with colorful fishing boats. The town is one of two in England where you can watch the sun both rise and set over the sea. At sunset, however, the streets begin to crawl with ghouls from Whitby's past. Atop the farthest cliff, the skeletal remains of **Whitby Abbey,** the inspiration for Bram Stoker's *Dracula,* haunt the town. After dark, the abbey is caught in a spotlight, and large blackbirds roost in its arched windows, with crosses and tombstones mingling in the shadowy graveyard at its foot. As the legend goes, Dracula arrived during a stormy night on a boat from Transylvania; he leapt out in the form of a wolf, bounded up the 199 steps to the cemetery, and disappeared into one of the graves. He used his new tomb as a base for his bloody sorties into the surrounding area. (Abbey open daily 10am-6pm, Oct.-March Tues.-Sun. 10am-4pm. Admission 85p, seniors and students 65p, children 40p.)

The intricately carved stone monument known as **Cædmon's Cross** was placed at the top of the abbey steps in the 19th century. The nine-line poem inscribed in both Anglo-Saxon and modern English is the *Creation Hymn* of Cædmon (an illiterate Anglo-Saxon herdsman), and the "Patriarch of English Sacred Song." The nearby **parish church** contains the body of King Edwin of Northumbria, whose head is in York Minster. Lucy's favorite spot was among the benches in the graveyard on the East Cliff, until Dracula drained her blood and put her six feet under.

From Whitby (pop. 13,403), try the pleasant cliffside walks west toward Staithes or east toward Robin Hood's Bay, or lounge on the vast sandy beach below the west cliff. Watch out for high tides, which can leave you dangerously stranded. A zestful walk takes you down to the lighthouses and up to the scenic **Captain Cook's Monument.** The captain was apprenticed to John Walker, a Quaker ship-owner, in 1746, and some of the ships he sailed to New Zealand and Eastern Australia were built here in Whitby. John Walker's 300-year-old house, now the **Captain Cook Memorial Museum,** Grape Lane (tel. (0947) 60 19 00), contains an outstanding collection of ship models, letters, and drawings by artists who traveled on Cook's voyages. (Open April-Oct. daily 9:45am-5pm, last entry 4:30pm. Admission £1, seniors and children 60p. No wheelchair access.)

Whitby hosts an annual **folk week** the week before the August bank holiday, with 200 hours of dance, concerts, and "fringe" events. (Contact Malcolm Storey, 26 Marine Ave., North Ferriby, East Yorkshire HU14 3DR (tel. (0482) 63 47 42) for more information.) It also holds a **Regatta** (for 1992 information, call (0947) 60 37 41).

The **tourist office,** New Quay Rd. (tel. (0947) 60 26 74) books rooms (£2) and sells accommodations guides (40p). In addition to the full series of *Waymark* walks, they have a useful street map that includes Scarborough. Store your luggage at the bus station (50p).

The town's standard-grade **IYHF youth hostel** occupies the old stables opposite the graveyard and beside the abbey, with spectacular views over the town. Be prepared to lug your pack up the abbey steps to your bed. B&Bs line Crescent Ave., Silver St., and the streets in between. **Ashford-Henry and Flora Collett,** 8 Royal Crescent (tel. (0947) 60 21 38), offer huge rooms in their seaside home. Just as friendly as their owners, the remarkably loud canines Peggy and Pebble will greet you with a good deal more saliva. (£11.50, students £10.50.) The freshly painted **Chiltern Guest House,** Noramby Ter. (tel. 60 49 81), has nine sunny rooms (B&B £11, bed only £9.50; call ahead). The small but very comfortable **Europa Private Hotel,** 20 Hudson St. (tel. 60 22 51) has tea- and coffee-making facilities and television in all rooms. Of the seven guest houses on East Crescent, **St. Catharine's,** 1 East Crescent (tel. (0947) 60 27 70), has the most breathtaking views. (Doubles £11/person; sometimes lets singles for £13. For family rooms, children pay half-price.) There are two campsites about 4 mi. south on the A171 in High Hawkser, with toilets, shower, laundry facilities, and a shop. (Both open April-Oct.) **Northcliffe Caravan Park** (tel. (0947) 88 04 77) charges £4.50, £24/week; **York House Caravan Park** (tel. (0947) 88 03 54) charges from £4 to 4.50 (£25/week). You are not allowed to camp on the Abbey Plain; the fierce winds would tip your tent over anyway. A **launderette** is on the corner of Church and Bridge St. (Wash £1.10, dry 20p. Open Mon.-Tues. and Thurs.-Sat. 8:30am-4pm; Wed. open 8:30am-noon.)

The **Circus Café,** 3 Flowergate, serves large portions of fish and chips (£2.15-3.35) in a faded but charming atmosphere (open daily 10am-9:30pm). The **Old Smuggler,** off Baxtergate through a small alley, emphasizes traditional Yorkshire fare. (3-course lunch £4.25. Open Mon.-Sat. 9:30am-5pm.) The **Whole Restaurant,** in Sander's Yard behind Shephard's Purse on 95 Church St., is a half-timbered room with samplers on the wall; it serves good vegetarian meals (main dish, potato, and salad for £3.80) and desserts that sneer at your diet. (Open Mon.-Wed. 10am-5pm, Thurs.-Sat. 10am-9pm.)

Seven mi. south of Whitby is **Robin Hood's Bay,** where the tiresome outlaw sought refuge from his pursuers. Go up to the headlands of North and South Cheek for a view of the windswept bay, with the village tucked away at the northern end. At low tide you can walk out on the mud and look for fossils. Pick the Robin Hood's Bay *Waymark* pamphlet in Whitby. The **IYHF youth hostel** at Boggle Hole is a good place to break your trip if you're doing the entire Whitby-Scarborough coastal hike; it's about a mile from Robin Hood's Bay on the Ravenscar Geological Trail.

Ravenscar, several miles farther, is a good place to get away from it all. Ravenscar was nicknamed "the town that never was" after a much-anticipated luxurious seaside resort failed to appear. Although the story itself is set in Whitby, Bram Stoker wrote *Dracula* in this smaller town. Pick up the Ravenscar Geological Guide at the **National Trust Centre** (tel. (0723) 870 138). (Open June-Aug. daily 10:30am-5:30pm; April, May, and Sept. weekends only 10:30am-5pm.) There is camping at **Middlewood Farm** (tel. (0947) 88 04 14; £2.50).

Durham

Located on a hairpin bend in the River Wear, Durham remains England's loveliest cathedral city. A daunting Gothic cathedral commiserates with the third oldest university in England, concealed within a Norman castle, and winding medieval roads crisscross the river.

Arriving and Departing

Durham lies just 20 mi. south of Newcastle on the A167 and an equal distance north of Darlington. Trains from Newcastle stop frequently at the main railway station, just north of town, *en route* to York and London. Trains run to London's King's Cross (every 15 min. daily 6:15am-10:30pm, 3 hr.; single £50, saver return £5), York (same times; 45 min.; single £13, saver return £15.50), and Newcastle (same times; 20 min.; single £1.80, saver return £3.10). A **Tyne Valley Day Ranger** ticket gets you unlimited travel by train in the area (£11.50).

A large number of companies serve local routes, stopping at the bus station on North Rd. **National Express** runs regularly to London (5/day; 4½ hr.; single or day return £21) and Leeds (9/day; 2 hr.; single or day return £11). **Go Ahead Northern** runs extremely frequently from the Durham bus station to Worswick St. station in Newcastle (every 20 min., 7am-11pm, 50 min.; day return £2.50), as do various other companies.

Orientation and Practical Information

The River Wear surrounds the town; you must approach and depart via Framwelgate Bridge. Maps of this easily navigable city can be found in the tourist office in Market Place, or in the back of the **Durham City Travel Guide,** distributed at the bus station. The bus station is in the center of town just to the west of the cathedral and castle, over Framwelgate Bridge. The rail station is also west of town; to reach the tourist office from there, descend the steps to your left just as you begin to descend the hill. Cross the street and continue over the bridge, then take the pedestrian path uphill on your right and turn right onto Market Place. From the coach station, walk downhill on North Rd., cross the river, and continue down Silver St.

Tourist Information Center: Market Place (tel. (091) 384 37 20). Information on Durham and Northumbria. Very helpful despite city's tourist onslaught. Local accommodations booking (£1), vacancies posted after hours, free map. Inexpensive walking tours (£2, consult the board in the Market Place). City Trust Walk guides 15p, free £Where to Stay. Open Mon.-Sat. 9:30am-6pm, Sun. 2-5pm; Oct.-May Mon.-Sat. 9:30am-5:30pm.

Bike Rental: Dave Heron Cycles, 6 Neville St. (tel. 384 02 87), near bus station. Ten-speeds and mountain bikes £5-10/day with VAT, £25-50/week with VAT. Open Mon.-Sat. 9am-5:30pm, Wed. occasionally closes early.

Boat Rental: Brown's, Elvet Bridge (tel. 386 42 92). Rowboats £1.70/person per hr., children 80p. Also river cruises. Open daily 10:30am-8pm.

Bus and Coach Station: North Rd. Information office open Mon.-Fri. 9am-5:30pm, Sat. 9am-4pm. Pick up the **Durham City Travel Guide** (free) with maps, sight listings and all bus and train schedules. National Express (tel. (0325) 431 447); **Go Ahead Northern** (tel. (091) 388 22 61) and **OK Travel** (tel. (0388) 604 581).

Emergency: Dial 999; no coins required.

Financial Services: Thomas Cook, Market Place. Open Mon.-Wed. and Fri. 9am-5:30pm, Thurs. 10am-5:30pm, Sat. 9am-5pm. **Barclays,** Market Place. Open Mon.-Fri. 9:30am-3:30pm, Sat. 9:30am-noon. **Lloyd's,** same place, same hr.

Hospital: Dryburn Hospital, Newcastle Rd., Framwelgate Moor (tel. 386 49 11). **Casualty branch** on North Road, beyond the rail.

Market: Off Market Place. Open Thurs.-Fri. 8am-4pm, Sat. 7am-5pm.

National Trust Information Centre: 64 Saddler St. Open Mon.-Sat. 10am-5pm.

Pharmacy: Boots, Market Place. Open Wed.-Sat. and Mon. 8:30am-5:30pm, Tues. 9am-5:30pm.

Police: Aykley Heads (tel. 386 49 29).

Post Office: Silver St. Open Mon.-Thurs. 9am-5:30pm, Fri. 9:30am-5:30pm, Sat. 9am-1pm. Mark *Poste Restante* "Silver St. Office." **Postal Code:** DH1 3RE.

Student Travel Office: Durham Student Union, Dunelm House, at New Elvet St. and Kingsgate Bridge. Sells Eurotrain and InterRail tickets and student flights. Open Jan.-July 24 and Sept.-Dec. Mon.-Wed. and Fri. 9:30am-5pm, Thurs. 9:30am-4:15pm.

Taxi: Paddy's (tel. 386 66 62 or 384 28 53). Average fare £1.30.

Telephone Code: 091, same as Newcastle.

Train Station: 24-hr. information tel. 232 62 62 (Newcastle).

Accommodations and Camping

B&Bs are neither particularly plentiful nor close to the center of town. To avoid the late-June graduation crunch, book accomodations far in advance. For a pound, the tourist office will search for you. Several colleges at the University of Durham rent their rooms to visitors during the summer; inquire at the tourist office for a free brochure.

IYHF youth hostel, Durham Sixth Form Centre, The Sands, Providence Row. Book to YHA Area Office, Bowey House, William St., South Gosforth, Newcastle-upon-Tyne NE3 1SA (tel. info. (091) 284 74 73). The camp beds at the hostel sometimes play musical chairs with different buildings in town; check at the tourist office for the hostel's current location. £5.50, ages 16-20 £4.40. Open late July-Aug.

University College, Durham Castle (tel. 374 38 63). Grandiose Norman staircase leads up to rather ordinary, but well kept, dorm rooms. Open June-Sept.; £15.28, children £8.81.

St. John's College, 3 South Baily (tel. 374 35 66), on a quiet cobbled street beside the river, behind Durham Cathedral. Vie for a room in the spacious theology students' section. Laundry facilities. £13.50. Open July-Sept.

Glück Auf, 6-7 Prospect Terr. (tel. 384 25 47), 1 mi. uphill out Crossgate on the right just past the second traffic light. Take bus #43, 49, 49A, or 50 and ask for the Neville's Cross Post Office—the house is opposite the bus stop. Delightful Mrs. Dunn serves breakfast in front of a roaring fire, even in June. £9.50.

Mr. and Mrs. J. Buxton, 1 Allergate Terr. (tel. 386 70 34). Cheery young couple lets rooms of all kinds on a quiet, convenient street. Bewitching floral prints. £15.

Camping: Finchale Abbey (tel. 386 65 28), 3 mi. north of Durham next to the Abbey. Take any Brass Side bus. Shower and laundry. £5 for tent and 2 people. **Grange,** Meadow Lane, Carrville (tel. 384 47 78), on the A690 just off the A1. Showers and hand laundry. £6.40/tent and 2 people.

Food

While you pay dearly for Northumbrian specialties like Kielder venison, Cheviot lamb, or smoked Craster kippers, look out for humble Cotherstone cheese or groveling snapdough gingerbread, a sticky slab that will last through at least two cups of tea. Or try some Lindisfarne mead, still made on Holy Island to the north. Most bakeries in town sell stottycakes, flat brown loaves often used to make jumbo *sa stotty* sandwiches. **Maggie's Farm,** 6 New Elvet St., is a wholefood shop with take-away sandwiches and savories at lunchtime (open Mon.-Fri. 9am-5:30pm, Sat. 9:30am-5pm). Fruits and vegetables fill the stands of the weekend **market** near the tourist office (open Thurs.-Sat.).

House of Andrews, 73 Saddler St. A cozy dining room with a timbered roof, tucked away behind an ancient commercial façade. Varied and inexpensive menu; £3 or less for a large meal. Hot apple pie á la mode £1.25. Open daily 9am-9pm; Jan.-March 9am-5:30pm.

The Almshouses Café, Palace Green, near cathedral. Bright, airy café serving light, elegant meals under £4. Blueberry *fromage frais (£1.65). Lunch served noon-2:30pm. Open daily 9am-8pm.*

Castle Tandoori, 28 Allergate. Take-away only. Excellent *tandoori* specialties £2.50-5, curry and *biryani* dishes £2.50-4. Veggie specials every Thurs. (£3). Open daily noon-2pm and 6pm-midnight.

Stones, Silver St. (tel. 386 07 22), as in the band. Jaggeresque theme wears thin but the menu remains robust. Veggie lasagna with salad and potato (£4.95), hot chili (£2.65). Open daily noon-10:30pm.

Sights

Durham's tourist attractions are sparse but spellbinding. The city itself has won several awards for self-preservation, banning cars and such from historic streets. Built in 1093, **Durham Cathedral** is the greatest Norman cathedral in England. Flamboyantly described by Sir Walter Scott as "half church of God, half castle 'gainst the Scot," the cathedral has withstood the siege both of northern warriors and the winds of change since it was founded by monks from Holy Island in 875. Crude "flying buttresses," which anticipated the soaring Gothic churches of France, make the cathedral an architectural adventure. The body of St. Cuthbert, carried by the monks from Holy Island, is entombed in the **Chapel of the Nine Altars** below the great window. The **Venerable Bede,** author of the oldest surviving English historical text, lies in the 12th-century **Galilee Chapel** at the west end under a simple stone slab. Off the cloisters, the cathedral treasury showcases sacred objects and manuscripts. (Treasury open 10am-4:30pm, Sun. 2-4:30pm. Admission 60p, children 10p.) Climb the tower for a fantastic view of the Durham peninsula fringed with green. (Open Mon.-Sat. 10am-4:30pm, Sun. 2:30-4:30pm; £1, children 50p.) Tours of the entire cathedral are possible only by written request to the cathedral vergers. Informal hour-long walks around the cathedral leave from the font inside the north door (July-Aug. Mon.-Fri. at 10:15am). Evensong is held weekdays at 5:15pm, Sunday at 3:30pm. (Cathedral open daily 7:15am-8pm; Sept.-May 7:15am-5:45pm.)

Across the palace green is **Durham Castle,** begun shortly after the Norman Conquest to protect William the Conqueror's somewhat unpopular prince-bishops. Once a key defensive fortress against Scotland, it has become, in these quieter times, a residence for male students at the University of Durham. The great hall retains marvelous hints of the pomp of medieval life, including two stone pulpits used by trumpeters. The tiny Roundhead suits of armor date from the English Revolution. The immense great kitchen is still in use. (Tours daily every hr. or so 10am-noon and 2-4:30pm; Oct.-June Mon., Wed., and Sat. sporadically. £1.30, children 50p.)

Below the cathedral on the riverbank lies the **Old Fulling Mill Museum,** which exhibits the region's archaeological finds. (Open daily 11am-4pm; Nov.-March 1-3:30pm. Admission 50p, seniors and students 25p, children free.) Try the view from which Turner painted Durham Cathedral on Prebends Bridge.

Entertainment

A young crowd fills the popular **Buffalo Head,** Saddler St., where a pub upstairs and a new-wave club downstairs accommodate drinkers and dancers alike. Young people also congregate at **Brodie's,** Gilesgate. The trendy riverside **Coach and Eight,** Framwelgate Bridge, has music on Friday and Saturday nights. (Open Mon.-Sat. 11am-11pm, Sun. noon-3pm and 6:30-10:30pm.) **Traveller's Rest,** Claypath St., is known for its wide selection of beer and real ale.

Durham Theatre Company (tel. 46 98 61) often performs in unusual settings, such as the Galilee Chapel in the cathedral. (Tickets at tourist office £2.50, students £1.50.) For a cheap evening thrill, £1 buys an hour in a rowboat. From Elvet Bridge, go around the horseshoe curve of the Wear, dodging scullers and ducks. The steep, overgrown banks of the river are a great place for a leisurely stroll; don't forget the insect repellent.

Durham holds a **folk festival** during the first weekend in August, with singing, clog dancing, mimes and musicians from all over the country. This is the only time when you can camp free along the river (Fri.-Sun.), so pitch your tent early. (Weekend festival tickets £12; call Jean Longstaff at 384 44 45 for more information.) During the last week of August or the beginning of September, Durham holds its **beer festival** in Dunelm House on New Elvet. (Season tickets £2.50; ring Jim McCaffery at 368 91 05 for more information.)

Near Durham

Northwest of Durham near Chester-le-Street is the **Beamish Open Air Museum** (tel. (0207) 231 811), a 200-acre park that re-creates the region's social and industrial lifestyle at the turn of the century. Exhibits include a model farm, functioning steam locomotives, and craft demonstrations. (Open daily 10am-6pm, last admission 4pm; Nov.-March Tues.-Sun. 10am-5pm, last admission 4pm. Admission £4.50, seniors and children £3.50; in winter £2.50 and £1.50.) Diamond bus #720 operates daily from Milburngate in Durham to Beamish Crossings, the entrance to the museum (Mon.-Sat. every hr.; call (0207) 232 430 or 232 735 for timetable). Many hitch along the A1 to the Chester-le-Street exit and then follow the signs along the A963 towards Stanley. British Rail runs from Durham to Chester-le-street very erratically, from Monday through Saturday only. Tynelinde buses #X1 or #X46 run from Durham's North St. station to Chester-le-Street from Monday through Saturday every hour. The museum itself is 2 mi. northwest along the A693. On your way to or from Beamish, take a free look at the new **Ankar's House Museum** (tel. Chester-le-Street 388 32 95), a few miles southwest of Beamish on the A693, which depicts the solitary religious life of an Ankerite. (Open Mon.-Sat. 10am-4pm.)

Northern (or High) Pennines

The area known as the **High Pennines** stretches north to south about 20 mi. west of Durham City, from below Barnard Castle in the south to Hadrian's Wall in the north. Unlike the neighboring Yorkshire Dales and Lake District, this region remains largely uninfested by tourists. Wide-open moorland, tree-lined slopes, quiet stone villages, and turbulent rivers greet the visitor in the Derwent Valley and the region's other dales: Teesdale, Weardale, and Allendale. The Pennine Way crosses each dale as it winds up to Hadrian's Wall and then to the Scottish border. The leaflet *The High Pennines,* available from the Northumbria National Park Centres, provides a good introduction to the area. (Also see Northumberland National Park section.)

Getting There and Getting Around

The area was made for hiking, and cars successfully navigate the roads; buses, however, tackle the region with distressing hesitancy. Four motorways delimit the region: the A66 in the south, hugging Darlington's latitude; the A6 or M6 from Penrith to Carlisle in the west; the A69 from Carlisle to Newcastle to the north; and in the east the A167 from Newcastle through Durham and Darlington. The B6277 cuts a diagonal through this quadrilateral, running northwest from Barnard Castle through Middleton-in-Teesdale to Alston. Hitching along these roads is not bad. Getting to Darlington by bus is easy enough, but heading northwest from there is like wading through treacle. A bus runs from Middleton to Barnard Castle as well as to Alston, though with reduced frequency.

Sights and Activities

Twenty mi. southwest of Durham along the River Tees, the charming town of **Barnard Castle** makes an excellent base for exploring the castles of Teesdale and the peaks and waterfalls of the North Pennine Hills. Along the river, the cryptic ruins of the 13th-century Norman **castle** spread over six acres. The major attraction in town is the anomalous **Bowes Museum** (tel. (0833) 690 606), a 17th-century-style French chateau set in a landscaped garden. Built in the 19th century by a wealthy local businessman and his French wife, the museum attempts to bring French "culture" to the heart of England. Inside are more than 30 galleries of French interior design. (Open May-Sept. Mon.-Sat. 10am-5:30pm, Sun. 2-5pm; March-April and Oct. Mon.-Sat. 10am-5pm, Sat. 2-5pm; Nov.-Feb. Mon.-Sat. 10am-4pm, Sun. 2-5pm. Admission £1.60, seniors and children 80p.)

The small though well-stocked **tourist office,** 43 Galgate (tel. (0833) 690 909), will book you a room (£1). Guided walks of the town leave from the office every Thursday (July-Sept.) at 2:30pm (60p, children 30p), while Tuesday (July-Sept.) is the day for longer, 3-4 mi. walks (free). **The Black Horse Hotel,** 10 Newgate (tel. (0833) 372 34) lets singles, doubles, and family rooms for £12 per person, breakfast included. The centrally located **Ruby Arms Hotel,** 17 Market Pl. (tel. (0833) 371 05) and the nearby **Turks Head Hotel,** 27 Market Pl. (tel. (0833) 313 96), both let rooms for £11; the latter come with coffee. Test the comfortable beds at **Netherdene,** 23 Wilson St. (tel. (0833) 381 10) by the Bowes Museum (£10). The **Castle Café** at the corner of Horsemarket and Galgate (tel. (0833) 385 43) serves café fare at reasonable prices (open Mon.-Sat. 7:30am-5:30pm, Sun. 10am-5:30pm); the **Market Place Teashop,** 29 Market Place (tel. (0833) 690 110), diversifies its selection with such vegetarian options as baked spinach, cheese and brown rice with bean salad (£2.05). (Open March-Dec. Mon.-Sat. 10am-5:30pm, Sun. 3pm-5:30pm.) Most of the pubs and restaurants along the Bank and the Market Place serve lunchtime and evening meals.

To reach Barnard Castle, either take British Rail to Darlington and catch a bus to Barnard, or hop United bus #6 from Durham to Bishop Auckland (every 15 min., Sun. every hr.; 30 min.; £1.40) and pick up bus #8 to Barnard Castle (Mon.-Sat. every 2 hr. 7am-10:15pm, 45 min.; £1.80).

If walks along the wooded riverside paths below Barnard Castle have piqued your interest in the rest of Teesdale, you might try covering some of the **Dickens' Drive,** a 25-mi. circular path tracing the route Dickens followed in 1838 while researching *Nicholas Nickleby.* The tourist office has pamphlets describing transportation along the route. Part of the trail leads 5 mi. southwest of Barnard Castle on the A66 to **Bowes Castle,** a 12th-century stone stronghold that overlooks the River Greta. From Barnard Castle you can get to Bowes Castle by catching the infrequent bus from Barnard Castle (11am daily; 10 min.).

A pleasant 12 mi. northwest along the Pennine Way lies **Middleton-in-Teesdale,** a mining town. The *Teesdale Accommodation Guide,* free at the Barnard Castle tourist office in the crafts shop, lists dozens of B&Bs in town. The **Hudeway Centre** hostel, Stacks Lane (tel. (0833) 400 12), has 18 beds available and windsurfing and canoeing options (£4, B&B £7.50). Return to Barnard Castle by bus #76, or carry on along the River Tees for the next 9 mi. of the **Pennine Way** to the **Langdon Beck youth hostel (IYHF),** Forest-in-Teesdale, Barnard Castle (tel. (0833) 222 28; open July-Aug. daily; March-June, Sept., and late Oct. Wed.-Mon.). During this idyllic stroll in the Tees Valley past **High Force Waterfall,** one of England's most spectacular falls, you should follow Wainwright's advice and " . . . tarry long in the presence of beauty, for so much in life is barren." (Admission 35p, children 15p.) United Bus #76 runs from Barnard Castle to the High Force Hotel Mon.-Sat. at 12:55 and 3:45pm (inquire about return times), also stopping at Middleton-in-Teesdale.

For some particularly dramatic scenery, walk about 15 mi. farther on the Pennine Way past the **Cauldron Snout Waterfall** to the **Dufton youth hostel (IYHF),** "Redstones," Dufton, Appleby (tel. (07683) 512 36). They serve excellent home-cooked food. (Open Jan.-March and July-Aug. daily; April-June and Sept.-Oct. Wed.-Mon. £4, ages 16-20 £3.20.) About 5 mi. before Dufton is **High Cup Nick,** a breathtaking, green gorge. Just northeast of Barnard Castle along the A688 looms **Raby Castle** (RAY-bee), an imposing 14th-century fortress with superb medieval kitchen and gardens. (Open July-Sept. Sun.-Fri. 1-5pm, Easter-June Wed. and Sun. 1-5pm. Admission £2.50, seniors and children £1.20.) Bus #8 stops near the entrance on its way between Bishop Auckland and Barnard Castle.

North of Teesdale, the Pennine Way traverses the other three dales of the High Pennines—the Derwent Valley, Allendale, and Weardale—as it winds its way north to Tynedale, the southern border of the Northumberland National Park. Each of these dales offers fine hiking and scenery but little public transportation or accommodation. If you're particularly industrious there is an 18-mi. walk along the old railroad tracks of the Derwent Valley Railway running from Swalwell to Conselt. Pick up a pamphlet at the Middleton-in-Teesdale tourist office.

The best base for exploration is **Alston,** reputed to be the highest market town in England. The **tourist office,** in the railway station (tel. (0498) 816 96), can find you a room for £1. (Open April-Oct. daily 10am-noon and 12:40-5pm.) As long as you're there you can also take a rather short ride in a steam train on England's highest narrow-gauge railway, the **South Tynedale,** to Gilderdale and back (1/hr. 11:15am-4pm daily; 50 min.; return £1.50, children 75p). Three quarters of a mi. from Alston along the Pennine Way stands a superior-grade **IYHF youth hostel,** The Firs, Alston (tel. (0498) 815 09). (Open July-Aug. daily; April-June and Sept.-Oct. Mon.-Sat.; Jan.-March Fri.-Sat. £5.50, ages 16-20 £4.) The **bus station,** ¼mi. from the hostel, has connections north to Hexham in Northumberland National Park, west to Penrith in the Lake District, and south to Bishop Auckland and Barnard Castle in the High Pennines. (Call (0498) 812 00 for timetable.)

Newcastle-upon-Tyne

However lowly its place on the average tourist's itinerary, Newcastle bills itself as a city of firsts. In addition to such utilitarian contributions to culture as the hydraulic crane and the steam locomotive, this gritty industrial capital also claims to have given the world its first beauty contest and dog show. Newcastle lacks the splendor of York and Durham to the south, and with their incomprehensible nasal accents Newcastle Geordies are the butt of many jokes. But it is not easy to dismiss this strangely grand city with its Tyneside Classical architecture, its proximity to Norman and Anglo-Saxon ruins, and its rich and enduring industrial history.

Arriving and Departing

Newcastle is the last of England's large towns before you cross the Scottish border. It lies an hour or so north of York on the A19 and about an hour and a half east of Carlisle on the A69. Edinburgh is a straight run up the A68. Newcastle is also accessible directly by ferry from Scandinavia.

Trains leave Central Station, Neville St. for York (Mon.-Fri. every 15 min. 5:45am-midnight, Sat. every 15 min. 6am-9:45pm, Sun. every ½ hr. 7:30am-10pm. 1 hr.; £15, saver return £23.50, supersaver return £17.50.), London's King Cross via Durham and Darlington (Mon.-Sat. 12/day 7am-11pm, Sun. 4/day 12:30pm-11pm; 4¼ hr.; £50, saver return £100, supersaver return £59), Edinburgh, at the other end of the Intercity line to York (Mon.-Fri. 20/day 7:50am-9:30pm, Sat. 23/day 8:30am-9pm, Sun. 18/day 9:30am-9:30pm; 1½ hr.; £21, saver return £30, supersaver return £30); and Carlisle via Hexham and Haltwhistle (Mon.-Sat. every 15 min. 6:30am-9pm, Sun. 8/day 10am-9:45pm; 1¾ hr.; £ 6.20, return £10). Several train passes cover the area around Newcastle: the **Northeaster Flexi Rover** offers 3 days of travel out of 7 consecutive days for £38, children £25.10. Serving only Northumbria, the **North Country Flexi Rover** gives 4 days travel out of 7 for the same prices. For a day of wandering, try the **Tees Day Ranger** (£8.20, children £4.10).

Buses to London, Glasgow and other far away places generally leave from the **Gallowgate Coach Station: National Express** runs buses to London (every 1½ hr. 6:30am-11:30pm; 5¼ hr.; single or day return £27) and Edinburgh (every 2 hr. 10am-6pm; 3½ hr.; single or day return £20). **Northeast Blue Line** runs to London a few times daily from the **Marlboro Crescent** stop (2-4/day, £17, return £20). From the Haymarket Station, the local **Northumbrian Line** runs regular buses to Berwick-upon-Tweed (Mon.-Sat., every ½hr. 7:05am-10:45pm,, Sun. 3/day

11:15am-10:15pm; 2¼ hr.) **Explorer** day tickets offer some discounts on sight admissions. National Express buses offer student discounts with an ID.

DFDS Seaways (tel. 296 01 01; open Mon.-Fri. 9am-5pm, Sat. 9am-noon) sails ferries to **Esbjerg, Denmark** (June 14-16 Fri.; couchette class single £85, midweek return £110; June 17-Aug. 20 Fri. and Sun.; couchette single £100, midweek return £149) and **Gothenburg, Sweden** (June 16-Aug. 27 Sun. only, couchette single £110. 50% off couchettes for students with ISIC; children ½price). **Norway Line** (tel. 296 13 13) departs to **Bergen, Norway.** (Mid-June to mid-Aug. Thurs. and Sat. Single couchette class £60, cabin £80; mid-May to mid-June and mid-Aug. to mid-Sept. Thurs. and Sat. only. Single couchette £45, cabin £60; mid-Sept. to Dec. Sat. Single couchette £25, cabin £40; 25% reduction for students with ISIC; seniors, children ½price.) All ferries leave from **Tyne Commission Quay.** Bus #327 serves all arrivals and departs from station 2½ hr. and 1¼ hr. before each sailing; the bus also stops at the hotel (£2, children £1; tel. 257 03 07).

Orientation and Practical Information

A good map of Newcastle is essential; streets tend to change direction and name every few blocks. The only thing you can be sure of is that the waterside lies at the bottom of every hill. The center of town is **Grey's Monument,** an 80-ft. pillar of stone dedicated to Charles Earl Grey, who pushed the 1832 Reform Bill through Parliament. Due west are the coach and bus stations; to the south, the rail station and the River Tyne; to the north, the university. From the rail station, turn right, then make a quick left onto Grainger St., which leads straight to the monument. From Gallowgate Coach Station, walk into and straight through the Eldon Sq. shopping mall for 2 blocks. From Haymarket Bus Station, walk down Northumberland St. and take a right at the first major intersection. The main tourist office is a block from the monument—face Eldon Sq., then turn around and walk past the monument to New Bridge St., just past the next intersection.

Newcastle's **Metro** is immaculate and efficient. The main line runs north from **Central Station** (the rail station) past **Monument, Haymarket,** and **Jesmond** (home to most B&Bs). Tickets within this zone are 30p. Look for the black-on-yellow "M" outside station entrances.

Tourist Information Center: Central Library, off New Bridge St. (tel. 261 06 91). Large, friendly (despite the chaos), and exceptionally well-informed. Free map, guide, events listings and accommodations list; booking service £1. Open Mon.-Thurs. 9:30am-8pm, Fri. 9:30am-5pm, Sat. 9am-5pm. June-Aug. Sun. 10am-4pm. Another office at **Central Station** (tel. 230 00 30) offers the same services, with only a little less literature. Open Mon.-Wed. and Sat. 10am-6pm, Thurs.-Fri. 10am-8pm, Sun. 10am-4pm.

Bike Rental: Cycle Centre, 165 Westgate (tel. 222 16 95); take your second right off Grainger St. from the Monument. Mountain bikes £10/day, £100/week, £30 deposit. Racing bikes £5/day, £50/week, £20 deposit. Open Mon.-Sat. 9am-5:30pm.

Coaches and Buses: National Express operates coaches out of the **Gallowgate Coach Station** (tel. 261 60 77), a few blocks east of the city center off Percy St. There's a ticket office and informal information desk. **Northeast Blue Line** (tel. 323 33 77) runs from Marlboro Crescent and **Northumbria** runs from the bus stand at **Haymarket Bus Station** beside the Metro Stop.

Emergency: Dial 999; no coins required.

Ferries: DFDS Seaways (tel. 296 01 01). Open Mon.-Fri. 9am-5pm, Sat. 9am-noon. **Norway Line** (tel. 296 13 13) All ferries leave from **Tyne Commission Quay.**

Financial Services: Barclay's, Market St. Open Mon.-Fri. 9:30am-4:30pm, Sat. 9am-noon. **Lloyd's,** Hood St. Good rates, plus lowest commission (£4). Open Mon.-Fri. 9:30am-4:30pm.

Hospital: Royal Victorian Infirmary, Queen Victoria Rd. (tel. 232 51 31). Take bus #10, 11, or 38 from Haymarket (in front of Civic Centre) or from rail station.

Launderette: Clayton Rd., near YWCA. Wash £1.40, dry 20p for 5 min.

Pharmacy: Boots, to the right of the monument; another huge one is in Eldon Sq. Open Mon.-Sat. 8:15am-9pm, Sun. 10am-4pm.

Police: Market St. at Pilgrim St. (tel. 232 34 51).

Post Office: Nicholas St., across from cathedral. Open Mon.-Tues. and Thurs.-Fri. 9am-5:30pm, Wed. 9:30am-5:30pm, Sat. 9am-12:30pm. Address *Poste Restante* to "Head Post Office." **Postal Code:** NE1 1AA.

Student Travel Office: Union Society Travel Bureau, Newcastle University (tel. 232 28 81). From Haymarket Metro station, walk past St. Mary's church and turn left up the steps; on the top floor of brick building on left. Open Mon.-Fri. 10am-4pm.

Telephone Code: 091.

Train Station: Central Station, Neville St. (tel. 232 662; 24 hrs.). Includes a full fledged tourist office (see above).

Accommodations

In **Jesmond,** just north of town and accessible by Metro (25p), there are several costly small hotels and guesthouses. A few slightly less expensive alternatives are scattered along bus routes, many a few blocks to the north of Jesmond on Osborne Rd. If you can't get into the youth hostels or YMCA, you'll have to pay at least £15, more for singles. Call in advance to secure a room.

IYHF youth hostel, 107 Jesmond Rd. (tel. 281 25 70). From Jesmond Metro station, turn left, then left again, and walk past the traffic lights—it's on the left next to RAC. This funky old town house attracts global packers. Kitchen a bit archaic but manageable; tasty baked goods on sale at desk (50p-£1). Very strict 11pm curfew. Lots of ferry traffic, so call several days in advance. £5.50, ages 16-20 £4.40. Open March-Oct. daily; Nov. to mid-Dec. Tues.-Sat.

Newcastle University, Leazes Terr. Student Houses, 10 Leazes Terr. (tel. 222 81 50). Convenient to center; walk 2 blocks from the non-monumented side of Eldon Sq. or 2 blocks north of Gallowgate Bus Station. Stadium across the street. Seems to attract large groups of travelers. £8.25. Open July-Sept.

YMCA, Jesmond House, on Clayton Rd. (tel. 281 12 33). Turn left just beyond the youth hostel onto Akenside Terr., then take the second left onto Clayton. Women and men. Affable. Spic-and-span modern rooms. Evening meal available. B&B £12.65, £62.70/week. Key deposit £5.

Food

Every other restaurant offers inexpensive pasta and pizza, and those in between serve *tandoori* specialties (popular with the late night crowd), enchiladas, veggie burgers, and peanut butter casserole. Chinese eateries line Stowell St. near Gallowgate. **Health Fayre,** opposite Haymarket Station, sells wholefood groceries, little pots of hummus (£1) and take-away sandwiches. (Open Mon.-Fri. 8am-5pm, Sat. 8am-3pm.) For just about everything else, head for the **Cloth Market/Bigg Market** area, northwest of the cathedral.

Super Natural Vegetarian Restaurant, Princess Sq. From the library go up the ramp to the right of Princess St. Upper level. Dreary interior spiced up by spooky posters. Entrees from £2. 10% student discount on hot dishes. Open Mon.-Wed., Fri-Sat. 10am-8pm, Thurs. 10am-9pm.

Heartbreak Soup, Quayside. Schizophrenic southwestern café. Famed for its delicious peanut and celery soup (£1.50) and veggie bake with cheese (£4.95). Non-nutty dishes also available. Open daily noon-3pm and 6pm-midnight.

Sights

Newcastle wears its monuments and towers particularly well. Grey's Monument is the tallest and can be climbed every Sat. for a view of the city (35p), but others hide near every wall and alley. In the civic center gardens behind **St. Mary's Church,** across from Haymarket Metro station, a huge iron tableau called **"The Response"** depicts troops marching off to defend their country from Teutonic Huns in 1914. The most elegant tower in Newcastle crowns the **cathedral** on Nicholas

St. This symmetrical set of small towers around a double arch, called "The Lantern," is meant to resemble Jesus's crown of thorns; it was copied by Sir Christopher Wren for a church in London. Many of the treasures inside survived Scottish incursions in the 1600s and the vicar's attempt to toss them out in 1783, though some got severely damaged. Of the many museums and galleries in Newcastle, the most unusual is the **Military Vehicle Museum** in Exhibition Park, which includes search lights and videos of contemporary war footage (tel. 281 72 22; open daily 10am-4pm; £1, children 50p). The **Laing Art Gallery** (tel. 232 77 34), behind the library, displays more conventional treasures. (Open Tues.-Fri. 10am-5:30pm, Sat. 10am-4:30pm, Sun. 2:30-5:30. Free.) At 9 The Side is the **Side Photographic Gallery,** one of the best in the country. (Open Tues.-Sat. 11am-5pm, Sun. 10am-4pm. Free.)

The variety of Newcastle's architecture is startling—ask the tourist office to point you toward some of the fine Victorian and Georgian buildings, or take one of their tours: walking (£1, children 50p), coach (£1.20, children 80p). Tyneside Classical is a sparse architectural style peculiar to Newcastle. **Byker Wall,** at the Byker Metro stop, is a huge, curving technicolor wall of low-income apartments; at the other end of the timeline yawns the **Keep,** part of the "New Castle," built by a son of William the Conqueror. (Open Tues.-Sun. 9:30am-5:30pm; Oct.-March Tues.-Sun. 9:30am-4:30pm. Admission 70p, seniors and students 30p.)

Entertainment

Newcastle has a thriving club and theater scene; unfortunately, hostelers with an 11pm curfew will enjoy little of it. Pubbing starts early, peaking at midnight when revelers roll downhill from the closing pubs of Bigg Market to the Quayside club scene. Pub popularity is closely related to sheer speaker size. The best underground bands from both sides of the Altlantic surface at **Riverside,** 57-59 Melbourne St. (tel. 261 43 86). On Fridays and Saturdays, flocks of trendies dance to recorded pop and funk. (Open 7:30pm-1am. £1-2 cover before 9pm.) Dance floors also pave **Julie's,** Manor House Chambers, The Close, Quayside (tel. 232 72 40; open Tues. and Thurs.-Sat.), and **The Mayfair** on Percy St. (tel. 232 31 09), which attracts queues of students every Thurs. night. **Tuxedo Royale,** in the large ex-cruise ship beneath the Tyne Bridge (tel. 477 88 99), stores liquor and disco balls in the hold. (Mon.-Sat. 9pm-2am, Mon.-Thurs. £3, Fri.-Sat. £6). **Rock 'n Doris,** upstairs at Redhouse, Quayside, has some gay and lesbian nights. For an exhaustive list of pubs and clubs with regular folk and jazz, peruse the indispensable *Paint it Red* (50p), available at the tourist office or at Volume Records, Ridley Pl.

The **Theatre Royal,** 100 Grey St. (tel. 232 20 61; box office open Mon.-Sat. 10am-8pm; tickets from £5, seniors and children half-price, student discounts Mon.-Thurs.), has been newly renovated. The **Gulbenkian Studio** (tel. 232 99 74), on King's Walk off Haymarket, hosts inexpensive experimental theater, dance, and music year-round. The **Tyneside Cinema,** 10 Pilgrim St. (tel. 232 15 07), shows foreign films (£2.90; seniors, children, and the disabled £1.50; all seats cheaper Mon.). For progressive and often politically astute acting out, try the **Live Theatre,** 27 Broad Chare, Quayside (tel. 261 26 94), which performs both music and theater (ticket office open Mon.-Fri. 9:30am-5:30pm; prices start at £2).) For more information on cultural offerings of all kinds, obtain the *Index* at the tourist office.

Near Newcastle

Greater Newcastle has absorbed several Anglo-Saxon and Norman ruins. While the sites' proximity to the city makes for a less than enchanting setting, they are easily accessible by Metro or British Rail.

The Venerable Bede (673-735), the most prolific and eloquent spokesperson of early Anglo-Saxon Christianity, might be distressed nowadays to find his name slapped onto everything from parkways to a Metro station near the dull suburb of **Jarrow,** 4 mi. southeast of downtown Newcastle. Bede was born and lived his entire life on the grounds of a serene monastery on the site of the present **St. Paul's Church,** now overshadowed by cranes and chemical storage tanks. Most of the original building was destroyed by Viking raids in the 8th century, but the layout of the original structure is marked out on the grass. From the Bede Metro station, turn left, then right, then left, then right—with any luck, the church will be on your right. (Open April-Oct. Mon.-Sat. 10am-4:30pm, Sun. 2:30-4:30pm. Free.)

Just across the green to the north is the **Bede Monastery Museum.** Here Bede wrote the *History of the English Church and People* (746), the first historical work to date events from the pastoral parturition of Jesus. (Open Tues.-Sat. 10am-5:30pm, Sun. 2:30-5:30pm; Nov.-March Tues.-Sat. 11am-4:30pm, Sun. 2:30-5:30pm. Admission 70p, students 50p, seniors and children 30p.)

East of Newcastle, also on the Metro, squats **Tynemouth Castle,** a stocky Norman fortification used as recently as World War I. The castle gatehouse and priory walls still stand, and the ceiling of the 15th-century chapel is particularly well preserved. (Open daily 10am-6pm; Oct.-March Tues.-Sun. 10am-4pm. Admission 95p, seniors and students 75p, children 45p. Disabled access.) The more spectacular castles further north along the Northumbrian Coast and the wild peaks and valleys of the Northumberland National Park make excellent daytrips from Newcastle. (See Northumberland National Park section.)

Northumbrian Coast

The coastal region from Newcastle north to the Scottish border has one of the highest concentrations of historic sites in England. The farther north you go beyond Seahouses, the higher the concentration of visitors and accompanying souvenir shops. Nearly every town has its Norman castle, a reminder of the centuries of fierce border conflicts between the English and the Scots. The coastal weather is usually better suited for ice-skating than swimming; even in July and August, the air chills and the freezing North Sea repels even the most well-insulated. But the region will endear itself to connoisseurs of rugged, windy coastlines and salty relics.

Getting Around

With careful planning and much stamina, one can leave Newcastle in the morning, see four or five sights on the coast, and spend the night in Berwick-upon-Tweed, on the Scottish border. Bus #X18 runs from Newcastle's Haymarket Station to Warkworth (every ½ hr. 6:40am-8:45pm, Sun. every hr. 9:45am-8:45pm; 1¼ hr.; £2.40), terminating inland at Alnwick. From Alnwick, bus #501 leaves every two hours for Craster, continuing up the coast to Dunstanburgh Castle, Seahouses and Bamburgh Castle. British Rail runs from Newcastle to Berwick (every 2 hr.; 1¼ hr.); Edinburgh is one hour farther north. Considerably less comfortable is the #505 bus from Newcastle via Alnwick (every 2 hr. 8:30am-6:30pm; 2 hr.). An **Explorer North East** pass, available at bus stations or from drivers, is good for one day of unlimited travel on most regional services and the Newcastle Metro (£4.10, seniors £3.10, under 14 £1.70, families £8). Save yourself from oblivion with the indispensable *Northumberland Public Transport Guide* (£1 from any tourist office or bus station), containing complete bus and rail timetables, telephone numbers of tourist offices and emergency services, and brief descriptions of sights.

Sights

Twenty mi. north of Newcastle, the evocative ruins of **Warkworth Castle** guard the mouth of the River Coquet. Centered on a labyrinthine 15th-century keep, the castle was home to the Percy family. Stand by the river to see its best side. (Open late March-Sept. daily 10am-6pm; Oct. to mid-April Tues.-Sun. 10am-4pm. Admission 95p, seniors and students 75p, children 45p.) Henry Hotspur, whom you might remember from Shakespeare's *Henry VI Part I,* was possibly baptized ½mi. upstream, in an enchanting 14th-century chapel carved out of the Coquet cliffs. To reach the hermitage from the castle, walk down to the river and turn left. About ½mi. up the river, a knowledgable Scottish couple will row you across to the **Hermitage,** hidden behind dense brush and trees, and give you a fascinating tour of the sight. (Hermitage open late March-Sept. Sat.-Sun. 10am-6pm. Admission 65p, seniors and students 50p, children 35p.) On summer afternoons, you can rent rowboats below the castle; follow the narrow path by the side of the castle (£1.25/person per hr., last boat at 5:30pm).

About 7 mi. northwest of Warkworth, magnificently preserved **Alnwick Castle** (tel. (0665) 510 777) is another former Percy-family stronghold. This rugged Norman fortification shields an Italian Renaissance interior, Titians and Van Dycks, and the Duke and Duchess of Northumberland. (Open early May-late Sept. Sun.-Fri. 1-5pm, last entry 4:30pm. Admission £2.20, seniors £1.70, children £1.30.) **Dunstanburgh Castle** lies just north of **Craster,** a tiny fishing village 8 mi. northeast of Alnwick and 10 mi. north of Warkworth known for its oak-smoked kippers. Follow the 1½-mi. coastal footpath from Craster to the skeletal ruin attesting to the mayhem of the War of the Roses. Perched atop a basalt crag, 100 ft. above the sea, Dunstanburgh Castle is now haunted by white gannets and mists. (Same hours and admission as Warkworth.) Somewhere on the way from Alnwick to Dunstanburgh Castle, in the minute village of **Rock,** lies the remote **Rock Hall Youth Hostel** (tel. (066579) 381). Look for the old stone manor house set back from the road. (Open March-Sept. and Nov. daily; Feb.-March and Oct. Mon.-Sat.; Nov. Tues.-Sat.; Jan to mid-Feb. Fri.-Sat.; £5.50, ages 16-20 £4.40.) Catch bus #501 from Newcastle to Charlton Mires, then walk or thumb the remaining 2 mi. to the hostel.

Henry VI chose **Bamburgh Castle,** 10½ mi. farther north, (tel. (06684) 208), as his royal capital during the War of the Roses; modern-day movie directors favor it as a shooting location. Competely restored in 1900, the castle displays fine collections of porcelain and armor. (Open July-Aug. 1-6pm; April-June and Sept. daily 1-5pm; Oct. 1-4:30pm, last admission ½ hr. before closing. Admission £2, students £1.60, children 80p.) Boats depart from **Seahouses,** a frenzied tourist mecca of pay toilets and souvenir shops 2½ mi. south of Bamburgh Castle, to the remote and rocky **Farne Islands,** breeding grounds for gray seals and 18 varieties of seabirds. Several different companies run a variety of narrated cruises (Easter-Oct. daily, weather permitting; 1½ and 2½ hr.; £3-5). The islands are owned by the National Trust (tel. (0665) 720 424), which charges landing fees (£2.90, children ½-price). Access may be restricted during the breeding season (May-July). Call the boat owners for details (W. Shiel, tel. (0665) 720 308; W. McKay, tel. (0665) 720 155); and H.J. Harvey, tel. (0665) 720 388).

Right on the Scottish border, **Berwick-upon-Tweed** (BARE-ick) has probably changed hands more often than any other place in Britain—14 times between 1100 and 1500 alone. Berwick's walls date from the 1560s; most of the castle is buried under the present railway station, although the 13th-century Breakneck Stairs are still standing. The **Berwick Barracks,** built in 1717, house a museum on the history of the British infantry. (Open daily 10am-6pm; Nov.-Easter Tues.-Sat. 10am-4pm. Admission £1.60, seniors and students £1.20, children 80p.)

Berwick's **tourist office** (tel. (0289) 307 187), in the town center in the Castlegate Car Park (open April-Oct. daily 10am-6pm), can book you a room locally (£1) or sell you an accommodations guide (£1). **Mrs. J.B. Russel,** 1 Loraine Terr. (tel. (0289) 306 194), lets rooms in a comfortable house conveniently located near the station, the town, and the waterfront (£10).

Just off the coast about 8 mi. south of Berwick lies romantically lonely and windswept **Holy Island.** The missionary Aidan came here from Iona in Scotland to set up England's first Christian monastery, **Lindisfarne Priory** (tel. (0289) 892 44), seven years after King Edwin converted. (Same hours as Warkworth. Admission £1.60, seniors and students £1.20, children 80p.) The **Lindisfarne Castle** (tel. (0289) 892 00), a tiny fort built in 1550, is now a private home. (Open April-Sept. Sat.-Thurs. 11am-4:30pm; Oct. Sat.-Sun. 11am-4:30pm. Admission £3, Sept.-May £2.) Getting there is half the fun; Holy Island is connected to the mainland by a 2¾-mi. causeway that submerges at high tide. A bus runs from Berwick to Beal and onto the island (mid-June to Aug. Mon.-Sat. 2/day); departure times depend on the tide. Call (0289) 307 283 for the timetable or pick it up at the tourist office.

Northumberland National Park

Battered by the sea and Scots, Northumberland endures on the English frontier. It feels ancient (maybe it's all the forts), war-torn (maybe it's the ruins), rugged (maybe it's the hilly, boggy landscape), and stoic (definitely it's the weather). As most people don't stray from the beaten path in the area north from London to Scotland, Northumberland remains largely unspoiled. In Roman times, Hadrian's Wall marked the northern limit of the *Pax Romana.* Later, the Anglo-Saxon kingdom of Northumberland, stretching from southern Scotland south to the River Humber (hence the name), included this region. Today, the Northumberland National Park stretches south from the grassy Cheviot Hills on the Scottish border through the Simonside Hills to the dolomitic crags of the Whin Sill, where it meets Hadrian's Wall. The information centers in the region can pelt you with free leaflets that cover Roman and Norman sites in detail. The *Guide to Anglo-Saxon Sites,* by Nigel and Mary Kerr (Granada, 1982; £2.95), will fill in the chronological gaps.

Getting There and Getting Around

The *Northumberland Public Transport Guide* (£1) is indispensable: it includes bus and rail timetables, the names, addresses, and opening hours of tourist offices and National Park Information Centres, and a brief listing of sights. Without it you might well end up unpleasantly stranded, although most towns have ample accommodations and at least one sight. Within the park itself, transportation can be frustratingly slow or even nonexistent. An **Explorer Ticket** is almost always a good deal (£4.10, children under 14 £1.70). Since buses run more frequently up the coast than within the park, **Newcastle, Morpeth,** and **Alnick** make the best bases for exploring the park. Of the cities on the very edge of the park, **Rothbury** (to the southwest of Alnwick) and **Wooler** (to the northwest of Alnwick) enjoy the most frequent connections (although that's not saying much). Rothbury has an expecially well-equipped **National Park Information Centre.** Here, disabled travelers can pick up the *Disabled Visitor's Guide.* Other important villages in the park include Bellingham, in the southeast, Kielder to the west, and Byrness, north of Kielder; all of these lie south of Rothbury and Wooler.

Hiking

The northernmost section of the Pennine Way plods through the park beginning at **Greenhead,** a meek village on Hadrian's Wall 25 mi. east of Carlisle and 40 mi. west of Newcastle. The path winds east 7 mi. to **Once Brewed,** then continues northeast 14 mi. to **Bellingham** (BELL-in-jum), due west of Morpeth, which has a simple-grade **IYHF youth hostel,** a ½mi. outside of town on Woodburn Rd. (tel. (0434) 22 03 13; £5.10, ages 16-20 £4; open mid-July to Aug. daily; March to mid-July and Sept.-Oct. Mon.-Sat.).

The Bellingham **visitors' center** on Main St. (tel. (0660) 206 16) details walks in this area, including a 1-mi. stroll through a woodland ravine to the **Hareshaw Linn Waterfall.** (Visitors' center open April-Oct. Mon-Sat. 10am-1pm and 2-6pm, Sun. 1-5pm; Nov.-March Tues.-Sat. 2-5pm.) From Bellingham, bus #814 runs west to **Kielder** (Mon.-Fri. 6/day 7:45am-6:05pm, Sat. 3/day 8:25am-4:30pm; ½hr.), located on the northern tip of **Kielder Water,** the largest man-made lake in Europe. The Kielder **forestry information center** (tel. (0434) 220 242) is in a Norman castle (open May-Sept. daily 10am-5pm). You can get acquainted with the lay of the lake at the **Visitors' center** at Tower Knowe, Falstone (tel. (0434) 240 398), on the lake's southeastern shore (open daily 10am-6pm) The **Leaplish Waterside Park,** located centrally on Kielder's southern shore, offers a wide range of water sports, including waterskiing and windsurfing. Bus #814 stops at all 3 of the above points. Tour the lake's 27 mi. of shoreline on a two-wheeler rented from **Kielder Bikes** just north of Falston (tel. (0434) 220 392; £7-15/day, mountain bikes come with instruction; open daily 10am-6pm).

The stretch from Bellingham northwest to **Byrness** (about 15 mi. on the Pennine Way) is bordered by an expanse of forest on the left and high hills on the right. There is a standard-grade **IYHF youth hostel** with a good drying room in Byrness at 7 Otterburn Green (tel. (0830) 202 22; £5, ages 16-20 £4; open mid-July to Aug. daily; March to mid-July and Sept.-Oct. Thurs.-Tues.). Here, Pennine Wayfarers rise before dawn and gird their loins. Bus #915 runs between Bellingham and Byrness (Mon.-Fri. 3/day, 7:25am-4:15pm; 45 min.).

The homestretch of the Pennine Way, unbroken by hostels, runs an uneven, boggy 27 mi. through the Cheviots from Byrness to **Kirk Yetholm** in Scotland. There is an **IYHF youth hostel** in Kirk Yetholm (tel. (057382) 631; £4.20, ages 16-20 £3.10; open mid-March to Sept.). The **Border Hotel** marks the official end of the Pennine Way and gives a free half-pint to anyone who has completed the Way and is carrying Wainwright's *Pennine Way Companion.*

At the northern end of the park, **Wooler** can serve as a base for less strenuous daytrips into the **Cheviots.** The **tourist office** in the Wooler bus station car park (tel. (0668) 816 02) books accommodations and describes uphill climbs in the Cheviots and gentler low-level walks through the Happy Valley. (Open July-Aug. 10am-1pm and 2-6pm; June and Sept. daily 10am-1pm and 2-5pm; April-May Sat.-Sun. 10am-5pm; Oct. Mon.-Wed. and Fri.-Sat. 10am-1pm and 2-4pm.) Wooler has a standard-grade **IYHF youth hostel** (tel. (0668) 813 65), 300 yd. from the bus station at 30 Cheviot St. with a nice warden and new showers. (£5.50, ages 16-20 £4.40. Open June-Aug. daily; April-May Mon.-Sat.; March and Sept.-Oct. Fri.-Wed.) Direct buses from the Haymarket depot in Newcastle run infrequently (2-3/day at varying times); try catching a connection at Alnick, north of Newcastle, instead (Mon.-Fri. 3/day 12:40-4:25pm, Sat. 4/day 9:40-5:45pm; 45 min.; £7.50.). Southbound bus #267 runs from Berwick-upon-Tweed to Wooler (Mon.-Sat every 2 hr. 7am-5:30pm, Sun. 2/day; 1 hr.; £3).

The nearest **National Park Information Centre** (tel. (0665) 782 48) is 7 mi. south of Wooler in **Ingram.** (Open May-Sept. daily 10am-6pm.) Gold Leaf Travel bus #940 runs a circular route between Wooler and Ingram twice daily on school days at 7:30am and 5:30pm (call (0668) 815 91 for timetable). During summer vacation, you must take bus #470 or #473 to Wooperton (Mon.-Sat. 4-5/day) and hike 4 mi. to Ingram.

Twenty-five mi. farther south of Wooler off the A697 on the B6341, the village of **Rothbury** sits in a narrow, densely wooded valley carved by the River Coquet halfway to Bellingham. The **National Park Information Centre,** on Church St. (tel. (0669) 208 89), describes beautiful walks on either bank of the river and posts the weather. (Open April-Sept. daily 10am-6pm.) To the north, a 2-mi. path up Bilberry Hill has fine views of the Cheviots before it veers east through a forest of purple rhododendrons (laminated trail guide 50p). Three mi. southwest along the Hexham road, three marked trails in the **Simonside Hills** run through a dense pine forest and along a rugged ridge. The view across Coquetdale from the top of the hill is dotted with hearty blackfaces and the peculiar hornless Cheviot sheep (trail guides free). To get to Simonside, walk south on the B6342 and turn right to Lordenshaws. The forest is 2 mi. across the moors. **Backwoods Mountain Biking,** Simonside House, Front St. (tel. (0669) 212 72) rents wheels and gives tours of the area. Buses run semi-regularly to Rothbury from Newcastle via Morpeth (Mon.-Fri. 8/day, 8am-6:45pm, Sat. 6/day 10am-6:45pm, Sun. 2/day at 12:15pm and 4:15pm; 1¼ hr.).

Cragside (tel. (0699) 203 33), on the road between Rothbury and Alnwick, was the former home of Lord Armstrong and the first house to be lit by hydroelectric power. Wander through the landscaped grounds to three lakes, three waterfalls, and three billion rhododendrons. (House open April-Sept. Tues.-Sun. 1-5:30pm; grounds open April-Sept. daily 10:30am-6pm; Oct. daily 10:30am-5:30pm; Nov.-March Sat.-Sun. 10:30am-4pm. Admission £3.50, park £2.) To reach the visitors' center from Rothbury, take the B6341 towards Alnwick and turn right at the Debdon entrance, or take the B6344 and turn left at the Dunkirk entrance. Most buses between Newcastle and Alnwick stop here on request. The tourist office will direct you to a 3-mi. riverside footpath to the grounds.

The wonderfully hospitable **Mr. and Mrs. Cummings,** 8 Silverton Terr., Rothbury (tel. (0669) 208 89), will keep you up half the night discussing every aspect of Northumbrian culture, from dialect poetry to bronze-age archaeology (£11). The tourist office also books rooms. Camping is available at the **Coquetdale Caravan Site** (tel. (0669) 932 05 49), ½mi. south of town along the main road that follows the south bank.

Ten mi. upriver from Rothbury, deeper in the park, lurks another **National Park Information Centre** in **Harbottle** (open May-Aug. Sat., Sun. and bank holidays 10am-6pm). To explore this remote area, rent a bike from **Cheviot Bikes,** 1 mi. north in Low Alwinton (tel. (0669) 502 24; usually open 10am-6pm, but call ahead). Bus #817 and 917 run between Rothbury, Harbottle, and Alwinton in early morning and late afternoon only (Mon.-Fri., ½hr.). Call (0669) 205 16 for an updated timetable.

Hadrian's Wall

Hadrian's Wall "Over the heather the wet wind blows,
I've lice in my tunic and a cold in my nose.
The rain comes pattering out of the sky,
I'm a Wall soldier, I don't know why."
—W.H. Auden, "Roman Wall Blues"

The Roman Emperor Hadrian visited Britain in 122 AD and decided that any people who painted themselves blue and fought as fiercely as the Picts were too much trouble to rule. So he found the narrowest part of Britain and built a wall across it—first a 27-ft.-wide V-shaped ditch, and then a stone barrier 15 ft. high and 8-9 ft. thick (wide enough for a chariot), surmounted every 1620 yd. by an outpost fort (a milecastle) and two turrets (watchtowers). Seventeen massive forts mounted the wall, manned by 5500 cavalrymen and 13,000 infantrymen from all parts of the empire. This tremendous structure duly separated the troublemaking Selgovae and Damnonii tribes of Southern Scotland from the Brigantes of northern England. The wall originally extended from coast to coast; today's ruins stretch only as far east as Bardon Mill, about 14 mi. west of Hexham. Although lengthy portions of the wall have been reduced to rubble, infrequent public transportation has managed to keep major tourist invasions away.

Getting There and Getting Around

Carlisle and **Hexham** serve as the two main bases for touring along the Wall; Carlisle caters to coach-potatoes while Hexham draws rugged individualists. Although slightly expensive, the easiest way to see the major sites along the Wall is to join a well-informed, 3-hr. **coach tour** leaving from the Carlisle tourist office in the Old Town Hall (tel. (0228) 512 444; June-Sept. daily at 1pm, return at 4 pm; £6, children £4; includes entry into Birdoswald Fort and a £1 discount on a Leed-Settle-Carlisle railway ticket). The coaches are timed to meet trains departing for Leeds, Settle and Carlisle. Hexham, 38 mi. east of Carlisle, is a tricky 14 mi. trek from the Wall. From Newcastle, bus #602 runs regularly to Hexham's bus station (every ½ hour 6:30am-10:30pm, Sun. 6/day 10:30am-8:30pm; 1½ hr.).

Both buses and trains shadow the wall. Bus #685 runs regularly from Carlisle to Hexham (1/hour 6am-9:45pm, Sun. 4/day 12:20am-7:20pm; 1 hr.). The Newcastle-Carlisle rail line passes through Hexham, running almost parallel to, but always more than a comfortable walk from, the Wall. Trains stop at key points along the Wall, including Bardom Mill (access to Vindolanda and Housesteads), Haltwhistle (access to Cawfields) and Brampton (access to Lanercost) en route to Carlisle (13/day 7am-10pm,Sun. 8/day 10:45am-9:30pm; 1 hr.). From late July to early September only, **Hadrian's Wall Coach Service** (tel. (0434) 604 011; bus #890) runs four times per day (10am-4pm) from Hexham to Acomb, Chesters Fort, Housesteads, Once Brewed, Vindolanda, Haltwhistle, and back. The Housesteads stop accesses the largest cluster of sights, but necessitates a 4-mi. trek. Be prepared to hike on to 4 mi. from each bus stop to the nearest fort or wall segment. During the offseason, British Rail trains and sporadic buses stop within a few miles of several sights.

Even a self-guided tour of the Wall can get expensive with admissions charges to many of the more important museums and forts (£1.60-2). If you plan to visit three or more tourist checkpoints over a period of days, a **Hadrian's Wall Pass** will help cut costs (£6, seniors £4.50, children £3).

Accommodations

There are two **IYHF youth hostels** practically on the wall. **Greenhead** (tel. (06972) 401), in a converted chapel very near the Roman Army Museum, lies 16 mi. east of Carlisle near the western end of Hadrian Wall's 12-mi. "high point," which runs west from Seingshields near Haydon Bridge. (£5.50, ages 16-20 £4.40; open mid-March to Aug. daily; Sept.-Oct. Tues.-Sun.; Feb. to mid-March Wed.-Sun.) **Once Brewed** (tel. (04984) 360; £6.60, ages 16-20 £5.40; open March-Oct. daily; Feb. and Nov. Mon.-Sat.), only a ½mi. from the Wall, 1 mi. from Vindolanda and 13 mi. west of Hexham, rents binoculars. To reach either Greenhead or Once Brewed, take bus #685 from Carlisle, Newcastle, or Hexham (every 2 hr.). Get off at Henshaw and walk 2 mi. north to Once Brewed; take a left onto Military Rd. (the B6318) and you're there. You can also take British Rail to Bardon Mill (along the Newcastle-Carlisle line) and walk 2½ mi. northwest to Once Brewed.

Hexham offers a number of B&Bs. **The Old Grey Bull,** on Battle Hill (tel. 603 438), provides functional doubles with teamakers (£13).

The spartan, simple-grade, converted stable of an **IYHF youth hostel** (tel. (0434) 602 864) in nearby **Acomb** has an outgoing and well-informed warden. (£4.40, ages 16-20 £3.50. Open July-Aug. daily; March-June and Sept.-Oct. Tues.-Sat.; Nov.-Feb. Fri.-Sat.) Tyne Valley buses #880 and 882 ("Acomb" or "Bellingham") run directly to the hostel from Hexham bus station and rail station. The last bus leaves around 5pm; otherwise it's an uphill, ill-marked 2-mi. walk north. A **campsite** (tel. (0434) 603 553) lies 1 mi. east of the hostel at Fallowfield Dene (open April to mid-Oct.), but there are no sites convenient to the Wall.

Sights

Hexham's tourist office (tel. (0434) 605 225), in the 14th-century Manor Office on Hallgate, tells you so much about the wall that you'll feel like you're coming home to it when you see it in the flesh. To reach the tourist office from the rail station, turn left as you face the sports field, follow the path along the left side of the field through the parking lot and up the hill. The office has an accommodations service (free; book-a-bed-ahead £1.75), a leaflet listing all accommodations (camping included) near Hadrian's Wall (40p), and transportation and hiking information. Also pick up your "Loo of the Year" award ballot. (Open Mon.-Sat. 9am-5pm; mid-May to mid-Sept. Mon.-Sat. 9am-6:30pm, Sun. 11am-5pm.)

Set off from Hexham and work your way west along the wall. Sights in town include a 12th-century **abbey,** built with graffitied Roman stone, dating back to 211 AD and containing a 7th-century crypt. You can request an informal guided tour. (Open daily 9am-7pm; Oct.-April 9am-5pm.) Next to the tourist office, the **Museum of Border History** vividly evokes life along the Scottish border in the 15th and 16th centuries, all set in Britain's first prison. (Open Easter-Sept. Mon.-Fri. 10am-4:30pm. Admission 90p, students and seniors 45p.) Four mi. north of Hexham, on the Hexham-Bellingham bus route, stands the **Chesters Fort and Museum** (tel. (043)

481 379). (Open daily 10am-6pm; Oct.-Good Friday daily 10am-4pm. Admission £1.60, seniors £1.20, children 80p.)

Once Brewed's **National Park Information Centre** (tel. (0434) 344 396) flashes excellent exhibits next to the hostel. (Open April-Nov. daily 10am-6pm.) From here, you can walk along the wall to the **Housesteads Roman Fort** (tel. (049) 363), one of the best-preserved sections of the wall. (Open daily 10am-6pm; Oct.-Good Friday daily 10am-4pm. Admission £1.60, seniors £1.20, children 80p.) **Vindolanda,** 2 mi. south, shelters the largest Roman museum outside London (tel. (049) 84 277). Excavations begun here in the early 1970s have revealed the entire fort and settlement. (Open July-Aug. daily 10am-6:30pm; May-June 10am-6pm; April and Sept. 10am-5:30pm; March and Oct. 10am-5pm; Nov.-Feb. 10am-4pm. Admission £2.50, students £1.75, children £1.25.)

The main part of the extant wall stretches for 7 mi. along the Pennine Way from Once Brewed to the excellent **Roman Army Museum** (tel. (06972) 485) at **Caravan,** just ½ mi. north of the Greenhead hostel. (Open March-Oct. daily 10am-5pm; Feb. and Nov. Sat.-Sun. 10am-4pm. Admission £2, seniors and students £1.50, children £1.) Several well-preserved milecastles and bridges lie between Greenhead and the **Birdsowald Roman Fort,** 4 mi. to the west (open any time). There is a **visitors' center** (tel. (06972) 602) with bathrooms, a café, and a few exhibits next to the fort. (Open Easter-Oct. daily 9:30am-5pm. £1.50, children 75p.)

Carlisle

Carlisle is Berwick-upon-Tweed's west coast counterpart; both towns bear the scars of countless Anglo-Scottish battles. Nicknamed "The Key of England," Carlisle unlocks the history and culture of the Northumbrian frontier and is one of the best bases from which to probe various sites along Hadrian's Wall. The city makes a perfect afternoon trip from either Newcastle or the Northern Lake District.

All of Carlisle's sights lie inside the remains of the **city walls,** built in the 12th century to enclose the Roman town of Luguvallium. The **Castle,** built in 1092 by William II using stones from Hadrian's Wall, stands at the heart of the city. An absence of barriers, guides, and crowds makes for an enjoyable, hassle-free romp of the castle's nooks and crannies. The battlements, cannons, turret, and 10 to 15-foot-thick walls will convince you that the castle is impenetrable. Tickets (£1.60 students, seniors and children £1.20) include admission to a museum of regimental history and an exhibition of over 900 years of Carlisle's history. (Open daily 10am-6pm; Oct.-Good Friday daily 10am-4pm.) The **Tullie House Museum and Art Gallery,** Castle St. (tel. (0228) 347 81), documents Border lore. Exhibits include a display devoted to the Border Reivers, Carlisle's lawless, pillaging Anglo-Scottish ancestors. (If your name is Armstrong, **Nixon,** Graham, Bell, or Milburn, you're descended from them too.) (Open daily 10am-5pm; April-Sept. 10am-7pm. £2.80, students £1.40.) The **Guildhall Museum,** to the left of the tourist office, currently houses Tullie's collection of Roman relics, drawings by Dante Gabriel Rossetti, and musical instruments. (Open Tues.-Sat. 11am-4pm; July-Aug. also Sun. noon-5pm. Free.) The modestly imposing **cathedral** across the street is known for its east window and starry blue and gold ceiling. (Open daily all year 8am-6:30pm; free guided tours can be arranged.)

You can leave your backpack at the **tourist office** in the Old Town Hall, Green Market (tel. (0228) 512 444), for only 30p and join one of the office's guided walks: town tours of 1½ hr. leave daily at 1:30pm (£1, children 50p). The office also books accommodations for free. (Open Mon.-Sat. 10am-7pm, Sun. 10am-5pm; Nov.-March Mon.-Sat. 10am-5pm.) To get here from the train station, turn left and walk through town; from the bus station at the corner of Lowther and Lonsdale St., cross the street and walk through the shopping center. Buses in town cost 48p (exact change required) and route information is available at the station.

In 1992 you'll be stranded among a sea of B&Bs without a youth hostel to guide you, since by that time the hostel at Etterby House will be closed. You can seek refuge at large, centrally located **Park View,** 38 Aglionby St. (tel. (0228) 335 99) for £11. From the railway station, hang a hard right down Botchergate, and then take the third left onto Tait St., which becomes Aglionby St. **Naworth Guest House,** 33 Victoria Pl. (tel. (0228) 216 4512) is similarly accessible and provides TVs to boot. From the train station, head straight round the citadel onto Lowther St.; your 2nd left will be Victoria Pl. From the bus station, take a left out of the entrance the buses come in onto Lonsdale St., turn left again onto Spencer St., and then right onto Victoria Pl.

Trains run regularly from Newcastle's Central Station to Calisle via Hexham (every 15 min. 6am-9:05pm, Sun. 8/day 10:05am-8:45pm; 1¾ hr.; £6.20, return £10). The **Leeds-Glasgow Line** passes through Leeds, Settle and Carlisle (6/day 7am-6pm, Sun. 4/day 9:50am-5:45pm; 1¾ hr. to Settle, 2¾ hr. to Leeds, 2 hr. to Glasgow). **Cumberland Motor Services** (tel. (0228) 732 00) bus #104 runs frequently to Keswick in the Lake District (7/day 7:50am-5:50pm, Sun. 10:10am; 1½ hr.).

Near Carlisle

Carlisle is a good starting point for taking in the 2000-year-old majesty of **Hadrian's Wall.** The Carlisle-Newcastle British Rail line runs roughly parallel to the wall, and the tourist office offers coach tours of all the wall sights. See Hadrian's Wall section for detailed information.

If you're sick of air-conditioned archaeology, consider touring some of Cumbria's less traveled areas via the circular **Cumbria Cycle Way.** The 259-mi. circular route runs from Carlisle in the north all the way around the outskirts of the Lake District. Pick up the information pamphlet from tourist office (£1.50), which includes a map, information on hostels, trains, and buses, and addresses of bike shops in each town along the road. The closest bike rental to Carlisle dwells in the town of **Further Afield** (no joke) Warcarr, Greenhead (tel. (06977) 473 58), a few miles west; someone from the shop will deliver a bike to you or meet you at the station with one if you call from nearby; Carlisle qualifies as "nearby." (Panniers £10/day, £50/week, £25 deposit). For more information, contact John Studholme, c/o County Planning Department, Cumbria County Council Offices. Kendal, Cumbria LA9 4RQ (tel. (0539) 220 00).

Lake District National Park

A patchwork of hill farms and mortarless cottages, built from the region's blue-green slate, cloaks the majestic Cumbrian Mountains and sparkling waters of the Lake District. The major lakes diverge like the spokes of a wheel from the hub town of **Grasmere,** south of Keswick and north of Ambleside on the A591. **Derwentwater,** by Keswick, is perhaps the most beautiful lake and **Wastwater,** halfway between Grasmere and the coast, the wildest; but even **Lake Windermere** (the longest lake in England), a 5-min. walk from crowded Windermere, is spectacular. Remote **Borrowdale** and more central Grasmere rank with the Peak District's Vale of Edale among the most breathtaking valleys in all of England.

Windermere, Ambleside, Grasmere, and Keswick all make sensible bases for exploring the Lake District. To enjoy the best of the region, however, get up into the hills and the smaller towns, especially those in the more remote northern and western areas; the farther west you go from the busy bus route serving the towns along the A591, the more countryside you'll have to yourself. These days, hikers, bikers and boaters are almost as numerous as sheep and goats, at least during the summer. The ratio is particularly disastrous in July and August, when tour buses spew their contents onto the lake shores.

Getting There

The best option for reaching the Lake District is either to take public transport straight to Windermere and Keswick or to penetrate the periphery of the park at Oxenholme and Penrith and connect from there to Windermere and Keswick.

Buses and trains from England and Scotland run directly to **Windermere** in the southern sector of the park. Supersaver return rail fares are available from London (4 hr.; £35), Birmingham (3½ hr.; £27), Manchester (3 hr.; £15.10), and Edinburgh (3 hr.; £12). **National Express** coach fares are slightly lower (return to London £22, Birmingham £16.50, Manchester £10.25), but service along the 7¾-hr. route to London is frustratingly infrequent (from Windermere, 3/day 6:55am-11:30 pm). Call the National Express office in Carlisle (tel. (0228) 484 84) for information.

Keswick, the largest town in the northern Lake District, is served by **Mountain Goat Bus** from York, which stops in Skipton, Settle, Ingleton, and Windermere (tel. (09662) 51 61 in Windermere); one bus a day makes the 3 hr. journey between York and Keswick in each direction. (May-Oct. Mon., Wed., and Fri.-Sat.; York-Keswick £16, period return £23.40; Ingleton-Keswick £9.50; Skipton-Keswick £12.30, period return £17.30.) Senior discounts of 25-50% and erratic YHA/ISIC discounts relieve some of the pain of high fares. CMS bus #555 from Keswick serves Ambleside and Windermere (1/hr. 9:25am-6:25pm, Sun. 5/day 10am-5:35pm; to Ambleside ¾hr., to Windermere 1 hr.).

Two rail lines flank the park: the **Preston-Lancaster-Carlisle line** (trains connect with Leeds at Lancaster) runs from south to north along the eastern edge of the park, while the **Barrow-Carlisle line** serves the western coast. If your first destination is the remote western or southern area, hiking from one of the stations along the Barrow-Carlisle line might be your best bet. Otherwise, catch the Preston-Carlisle line to either Oxenholme or Penrith. From **Oxenholme,** a short branch line covers the 10 mi. to Windermere (1/hr. 6:50am-9:25pm, Sun. 1/hr. 10:20am-10:15pm; 10 min.). CMS supplies regular service from Windermere to Ambleside, Grasmere and Keswick in the north on #555 (Mon.-Fri. 10/day 8am-5pm, Sat. 11/day 6:55am-5pm, Sun. 5/day 8:35am-4pm; 15 min. to Ambleside, ½hr. to Grasmere, 1 hr. to Keswick). If you decide to disembark at **Penrith,** just south of Carlisle, CMS bus #104 from Carlisle runs westward to Keswick (tel. (0228) 484 84 for bus times; Mon.-Fri. 7/day 7:50am-5:50pm, Sat. 6/day 7:50am-5:50pm, Sun. 10:10am; 1½ hr.).

Getting Around

Once in the park, a vast array of bus, rail, and lake steamer transport is at your disposal. **CMS** buses serve Hawkshead, Coniston, and Newby Bridge, and connect Keswick with Penrith, Carlisle, Seatoller, Whitehaven, and Cockermouth. Timetables can be found in the free *Guide to Lakeland by Bus and Coach.* An **Explorer** ticket (£4.20) gives unlimited 1-day travel and discounted admission to a few sights; period Explorers cost £12.20 for 4 days of unlimited travel.

British Rail serves the rugged western coast with its Carlisle-Barrow route and offers a **North West Rover** ticket (£39.50, £27.50 with railcard), good for a week's unlimited travel in the coastal region bounded approximately by Manchester, Leeds, Carlisle, and Liverpool. There are also two private rail lines in the area (not covered by the Rover ticket). The **Lakeside and Haverthwaite Railway** (tel. (05395) 315 94) can take you through the scenic River Leven Valley by steam locomotive (late April-Oct. 7/day 11:15am-5:45pm; £2.45 day return, children £1.25). The 15-min. trip begins in Lakeside, a town on the southwest shore of Lake Windermere that is connected by ferry to Bowness Pier. The **Ravenglass and Eskdale Railway** (tel. (0229) 717 171) is England's oldest and narrowest (11 in.) narrow-gauge railway, affectionately known as "t'laal Ratty" (5-10/day, mid-Nov. to March 3/day; 40 min.; return £4.90, children £2.45). Ravenglass is on British Rail's Barrow-Carlisle rail line.

To reach the more remote areas, particularly high points where hiking is difficult, take the **Mountain Goat Bus,** which runs mini-buses from Ambleside to Hawkshead, Coniston, Langdale, or Ullswater; from Windermere to Ullswater; or from Keswick to Ullswater, Buttermere, Penrith, Borrowdale, and Cockermouth. The company also organizes a series of friendly and occasionally bizarre minibus and coach tours (such as "Local Pub Towns" or "Goat and Boat"), which cost £9.50-18. Pick up free information and timetables at any tourist office in the region or at one of Mountain Goat's booking offices: the main office (tel. (09662) 51 61) is in Windermere, next to the tourist office and the train station (open Mon.-Sat. 8:30am-6pm); there is also a branch office (tel. (07687) 739 62) open only during the summer in Keswick, in Moot Hall on Market Sq. Ask about discounts for YHA members. **Fellbus** (tel. (0596) 724 03) operates two tour buses between Keswick and Seatoller via Braithwaite, Keskadale, Buttermere, Gatesgarth, and Honister (May-Oct.; £7.50 for ½day tour, £14 full day).

Practical Information

Note that many information centers, B&Bs, and nearly all campgrounds close for the winter. All major towns' **tourist offices** will find you accommodations and help with transportation, hiking, and recreation plans. Most offices have detailed trail pamphlets and Ordnance Survey maps. For an introduction to the area, including exhibits, talks, films, and special events, visit the beautiful landscaped grounds and house of the **National Park Visitor Centre** (tel. (09662) 66 01) in **Brockhole,** halfway between Windermere and Ambleside. Most Ribble or CMS buses will drop you off at the site. (Open July-Aug. 10am-10pm, Sept.-June 10am-5pm. Admission £1.90, children 90p.) The free newspaper, *Lake District Guardian,* includes a comprehensive calendar of guided walks and events in the park.

The following **National Park Information Centres** disseminate schemata and provide expert information on the Lakes, including a camping guide (95p).

Bowness Bay: tel. (09662) 28 95. Open Easter-Oct. daily 9:30am-7:30pm; Nov.-Dec. Mon.-Fri. 1-4pm, Sat.-Sun. 10am-12:30pm and 1:30-4pm. Write to National Park Information, The Glebe, Bowness, Cumbria LA23 1LJ.

Keswick: Blencartha Centre, Threlkeld (tel. (07687) 796 01), with the clock tower. Open daily 9:30am-7pm; Sept.-June daily 10am-5pm.

Grasmere: tel. (09665) 245. Open June-Aug. daily 9:30am-6:30pm; April-May and Sept. 10am-5pm daily. Write to National Park Information, Red Bank Rd., Grasmere, Cumbria LA22 9SW.

Ambleside (Waterhead): tel. (05394) 327 29. Open daily 9:30am-5pm; Oct. to Good Friday Mon.-Fri. 2-5pm, Sat. 9am-5pm. Write to National Park Information, The Car Park, Waterhead, Ambleside, Cumbria LA22 OEN.

Hawkshead: tel. (09666) 525. Open April-Oct. daily 9:30am-6:30pm.

Coniston: tel. (05394) 415 33. Open April-Oct. daily 9am-5pm.

Ullswater Information Centre at Glenridding: tel. (07684) 824 14. Open April-Oct. daily 9:30am-5pm.

Pooley Bridge: tel. (07684) 865 30. Open April-Oct. daily 9am-5pm.

Seatoller Barn: tel. (07687) 772 94.

Gosforth: tel. (09405) 285. Open April-Sept. daily 10am-1pm and 1:30-5pm.

Biking, Climbing, and Hiking

You can mount an assault on the Lake District by bike if you are prepared to confront hilly terrain. There are a number of rental establishments in each town. A selection from Ambleside, Keswick, Windermere and Ulverston are mentioned below, but go to the local tourist office for complete listings:

Ambleside Mountain Biker, Scotts Café, Waterhead by lake (tel. (05394) 320 14). £12/day, £60/week (ID deposit required). Open daily 9:30am-5pm.

Trackers Cycle Hire, 66 Main St. in Keswick (tel. (07687) 713 72). £10/day, £60/week. Open 9:30am-5pm.

J.D.'s Cycles, around the corner from the tourist office in Windermere (tel. (09662) 44 79). 3-speeds for £6.50/day, £35/week, panniers for £1.50/week, mountain bikes for £11/day, £50/week (£20 deposit). Open daily 9am-5:30pm.

Lakeland Leisure, near the rail station in Windermere (tel. (09662) 47 86). Rents panniers for £2/day, £8/week; bikes for £6-12/day, £30-70/week (£30 deposit). YHA discount. Open daily 9am-5pm, shorter hr. in winter.

Lowick Mountain Bikes, Red Lion Inn, Lowick Bridge in Ulverston (tel. (022985) 366). 3-speeds for £6/day, mountain bikes £12/day. Open daily 9:30am-5pm.

The Lake District is both a climber's dream and nightmare, presenting superb rock faces and treacherous, loose shale. Every town has a large number of climbing stores, such as **John Gaynor Sports,** beside the Ambleside bus station (open daily 10am-5pm), and **Stuart's Sports,** on the main road in Bowness (open daily 9am-9pm; winter Mon.-Sat. 9am-5:30pm, Sun. 10am-5pm). Any such store can describe the best climbs, advise on the necessary precautions and give you current weather reports. A few establishments also rent boots and backpacks. In Keswick, try **Keswick Mountain Sports,** 73 Main St. (Boots £5/week, no deposit; backpacks £5/week, £10 deposit. Open daily 9am-5:30pm.) In Ambleside, **Frank Davies' Climbers Shop,** on the corner of Rydal Rd. and Compston Rd., rents boots for £5/day (£20 deposit; open daily 9am-1pm, 2pm-5:30pm, shorter hr. in winter). In other towns, inquire at the tourist office.

Hikers will find an abundance of trails and often an overabundance of fellow walkers. If you plan to take a long or difficult hike, check with the Park Service, call for weather information (tel. (09662) 51 51) or ask at any tourist office or hiking store, and leave a plan of your route with your B&B proprietor or hostel warden before you set out. Equip yourself with woolen socks, boots or strong shoes, shirt, warm sweater, warm waterproof trousers, map, compass, whistle (6 blasts is the accepted distress signal), flashlight, first-aid kit, and extra food. Kendal Mint Cake, a slightly repulsive and highly addictive chocolate-covered sugar brick sold everywhere, is the jump starter of choice in Lakeland.

Wainwright's classic *Pictorial Guide to the Lakeland Falls* is probably a worthwhile purchase only for the most meticulous explorer (£6 each). Many libraries and some hostels have the series. Those covering more ground may prefer the Rambler's Association's *Walking in Lakeland* (3 volumes, £1.95 each). John Parker's *Walk the Lakes* details 40 short walks (£3.95). The National Park Authority also publishes the comprehensive *Walks in the Countryside.* All of these publications are available from National Park Information Centres, tourist offices, and bookshops. Most of the tourist offices also carry copies of the **Disabled Access Guide** (free).

Accommodations and Camping

Although plentiful, accommodations in the Lake District do fill up in July and August; book as far ahead as possible. B&Bs line every street in every town (£10-11)and the Lakes have the highest density of IYHF youth hostels in the world (34 at last count). You should call to reserve—most places will hold a bed until 6pm. Some hostels have short lock-out hours, reopening at 1 pm.

Ambleside: Waterhead, Ambleside, Cumbria LAZZ OEU (tel. 05394) 323 04), one mi. south of Ambleside on Windermere Rd. (the A591), 3 mi. north of Windermere in 6 Victorian townhouses on the Lake's shores. The Windermere bus stops right in front. £7, ages 16-20 £5.90. Open daily; late Sept.-late March Thurs.-Tues.

Arneside: Oakfield Lodge, Redhills Rd., Arnside, Carnforth, Lanes LAS OAT (tel. (0524) 761 781). One mi. south of Arneside on the coast in the southern tip of the region. £7, ages 16-20 £5.90. Open daily late March-Sept.; Jan.-March Mon.-Tues.

Black Sail: Black Sail Hut, Ennerdale, Cleator Cumbria CA23 3AY (no phone). Between Grasmere and the coast, but otherwise in the middle of nowhere. CMS #79 runs from Keswick to Seatoller and the hostel is another 3½ mi. walk from there. £5.10, ages 16-20 £4. Open mid-March to Oct. Tues.-Sun.

Buttermere: King George VI Memorial Hostel, Buttermere, Cockermouth, Cumbria CA13 9XA (tel. (07687) 702 45). Overlooking Lake Buttermere, ¼ mi. south of the village on the B5289. £6.30, ages 16-20 £5.10. Open late March-late Sept. daily; Jan.-late March and late Sept.-late Nov. Mon.-Sat.

Carrock Fell: High Row Cottage, Haltcliffe, Hesket Newmarket, Wigton, Cumbria CA7 8JT (tel. (06998) 325). Between Caldbeck and Mosedale in the northern area of the District. Good views of the Carrock Fell. £5.50, ages 16-20 £4.40. Open late May-late Aug. Tues.-Sun.; mid-March to late May and Sept-Oct. Wed.-Sun.

Cockermouth: Double Mills, Cockermouth, Cumbria CA13 0DS (tel. (0900) 822 561), in the town center. A converted 17th-century water mill. £5.50, ages 16-20 £4.40. Open late May-late Aug. Thurs.-Tues.; Sept.-late May Thurs.-Mon.

Coniston: Holly How, Far End, Coniston, Cumbria LA21 8DD (tel. (05394) 413 23), ¼ mi. north of Coniston village on the Ambleside Rd. Good cooking, including hearty vegetarian options. £5.90, ages 16-20 £4.70. Open daily; Sept.-June Mon.-Sat.

Coniston Coppermines: Coppermines House, Coniston, Cumbria LA21 8HP (tel. (05394) 412 61), 1 mi. west of the village overlooking the water. £5.50, ages 16-20 £4.40. Open July-Aug. Thurs.-Tues.; mid-Feb. to June and Sept.-Dec. Thurs.-Mon.

Derwentwater: Barrow House, Borrowdale, Keswick Cumbria CA12 5UP (tel. (07687) 772 46), 2 mi. south of Keswick on the B5289. Take the "Borrowdale" bus (CMS #79) to Seatoller (1/hr.). Opens at 1pm. £7, ages 16-20 £5.90. Open mid-March to mid-Sept. daily; Jan. to mid-March and mid-Sept. to mid-Dec. Mon.-Sat.

Elterwater: Elterwater, Ambleside, Cumbria LAZZ 9HX (tel. (09667) 245), 1 mi. west of High Close. CMS bus #516 from Ambleside passes within 1 mi. of the hostel. £5.90, ages 16-20 £4.70. Open April-Aug. Tues.-Sun.; mid-Feb. to March and Sept.-Nov. Wed.-Sun.

Ennerdale: Cat Crag, Ennerdale, Cleator, Cumbria CA23 3AX (tel. (0946) 861 237). Not especially easy to get to: 1¼ mi. west of Ennerdale water. Nearest bus drops 7 mi. away at Kirkland (bus #77 from Whitehaven) or at Seatoller (bus #79 from Keswick). £5.50, ages 16-20 £4.40. Open mid-March to Nov. Fri.-Wed.

Eskdale: Boot, Holmrook, Cumbria. In a quiet valley 1½ mi. east of Boot on the Ravenglass/Eskdale railway. £6.30, ages 16-20 £5.10.

Grasmere: Butharlyp How, Grasmere, Ambleside, Cumbria. North of Grasmere village; follow the road to Eastdale for 150 yd., then turn right down the sign-posted drive. £6.60, ages 16-20 £5.40.

Grasmere: Thorney How, Grasmere, Ambleside, Cumbria. ½ mi. northwest; follow the road to Eastdale, turn right at the fork, then turn left. In a farmhouse. £6.30, ages 16-20 £5.10.

Hawkshead: Esthwaite Lodge, Hawkshead, Ambleside, Cumbria. Overlooking the lake, this was once the home of novelist Francis Brett Young and houses a library of his works. Near hiking and cycling trails. Bus #505 from Ambleside drops you off at Hawkshead, 1 mi. north. £7, ages 16-20 £5.90.

Helvellyn: Greenside, Glenridding, Penrith, Cumbria. 900 ft. up and a mere 1½ mi. from Glenridding village, 3 mi. from Ulsterwater Lake. Buses from Keswick and Windermere will drop you at Glenridding. £5.90, ages 16-20 £4.70.

High Close: Langdale, High Close, Loughrigg, Ambleside, Cumbria. 4 mi. north of Loughrigg and semi-accessible by bus #516 from Ambleside; go ¾ mi. south of Elterwater, and the hostel lies ¾ mi. to the west. £6.30, ages 16-20 £5.10.

Honister House: Seatoller, Keswick, Cumbria, at head of **Honister Pass,** easy day trek from Keswick. 9 mi. to the north. Bus #79 from Keswick to Seatoller gets you within 1½ mi. of the hostel. £5.50, ages 16-20 £4.40.

Kendal: Highgate, Kendal, Cumbria. Right in town; convenient to both the bus and train stations. £6.60, ages 16-20 £5.40.

Keswick: Station Rd., Kewsick, Cumbria. Right near the town center, with balconies overlooking water. Open at 1pm. Lots of transport in and out of town. £7, ages 16-20 £5.90.

Longthwaite: Keswick, Cumbria. On the River Derwent's shores. The village of Rothswaite is ½mi. north. Bus #79 from Keswick gets you near. £5.90, ages 16-20 £4.70.

Patterdale: Goldrill House, Patterdale, Penrith, Cumbria. Only 1 mi. south of Ullsterwater and just off the A592, ¼mi. south of Patterdale village. £7, ages 16-20 £5.90.

Tebay: the Old School, Tebay, Penrith, Cumbria. No kitchen, but they've got a dryer. In Tebay village on the A685. £5.90, ages 16-20 £4.70.

Thirlmere: the Old School, Stanah Cross, Keswick, Cumbria. 5 mi. south of Keswick off the A591. About as simple as they come. £4.40, ages 16-20 £3.50.

Wasterwater: Wasdale Hall, Wasdale, Seascale, Cumbria. Right on the water and in good climbing territory. Bus #12 from Whitehaven to Seascale stops 5 mi. away in Gosforth. £6.30, ages 16-20 £5.10.

Windermere: High Cross, Bridge Lane, Troutbeck, Windermere, Cumbria. 1 mi. north of Windermere off the A591, this hostel has lots of rooms and views. The Ambleside bus stops in Troutbeck Bridge; walk the remaining ¾mi. to hostel. £5.90, ages 16-20 £4.70. Open late March-late Sept. daily; late Feb.-late March and late Sept. Wed.-Mon.

Campers should pick up the National Park Authority's comprehensive guide (95p), which includes listings of **camping barns** (£3-5) where you can stay high and dry in the big outdoors.

Windermere and Bowness

A first stop for most travelers, Windermere and Bowness (pop. 8500) together form an extended vacation town that becomes the Lake District's tourist center during the summer, when the water-ski *coterie* arrives *en masse.* Although the towns are pleasant enough, their popularity is due mostly to Windermere's **rail station** (tel. (0524) 323 33), and the spectacular **Lake Windermere** nearby.

To reach Bowness and the pier, turn left from Windermere's rail station and walk through the center of the town to New Rd., which becomes Lake Rd. and leads you to Bowness and the lake after a 20-min. downhill walk. You can also catch the CMS "Lakeland Experience" bus to Bowness from the rail station (every 20 min. 8:15am-8:15pm; 68p). For a shorter walk to a more deserted piece of lakeshore away from the pier, turn right from New Rd. and follow Birthwaite Rd. to its end near Queen Adelaide's Hill. **Bowness Bay Boating** (tel. (09662) 33 60) and the **Windermere Iron Steamboat** (tel. (05395) 311 88) run cruises from the Bowness Pier: boats sail ½hr. north to Ambleside (every hour 9am-5:55pm; £2.35, return £4.10, children ½price) or south to Lakeside (1/hr. 10:25am-6:30pm; same prices). A full lake tour from Bowness is £6.75. You can rent rowboats near the pier (£2.10/person per hr.).

The **Windermere Festival** takes place in the first week of July, and includes folk music, dancing, regattas, and traditional Westmoreland wrestling contests. For information, write to the tourist office, Gateway Centre, Victoria St., Windermere, Cumbria LA23 1AD or call David Smith at (09662) 45 02.

Tourist information is available in both towns: the **tourist office** near the Windermere rail station (tel. (09662) 64 99; open daily 9am-9pm, Nov.-March daily 9am-6pm) and the **National Park Information Centre** beside the Bowness Pier (tel. (09662) 66 01; open daily 10am-10pm, Sept.-Easter. daily 10am-5pm) both book beds (10% deposit) and sell accommodations lists (45p) and maps (10p). In Windermere, you can also pick up the *Vegetarian Directory,* a guide to the area's eats (20p), or a guide to lake walks (40p).

The nearest **IYHF youth hostel** (tel. (09662) 35 43) is in Troutbeck, 2 mi. north of Windermere off the A591 in a fantastic house with lovely grounds and beautiful views. Call a week or so in advance. The Ambleside bus stops in Troutbeck Bridge, but from there it's a ¾-mi. walk. (£5.90, ages 16-20 £4.70. Open late March-late Sept. daily; late Feb.-late March and late Sept. Wed.-Mon.) Both Windermere and Bowness are chock-full o' B&Bs, incredibly convenient to train and town. **Lingmore,** 7 High St. (tel. (09662) 49 47), is run by wonderful Mr. and Mrs. Austin who supply tea and candybars (£10/person). The rooms at the **Brendan Chase**

Guest House, College Rd. (tel. (09662) 56 38), are neat and come stocked with sewing kits, hairdryers and color TVs. (£10/person, £12.50 with bath; discounts for 3 or more days.) Color carpets **Norman Hogarth,** 5 Upper Oak (tel. (09662) 39 27; £11). The friendly young proprietors of **Kirkwood,** Princes Rd. (tel. (09662) 39 07), off the main road halfway down to Bowness, will pick you up from the station. They often include kippers and vegetarian dishes at breakfast (£12.50/person, £15 with private bath). The nearest campground, **Limefitt Park** (tel. (0966) 323 00), lies 4½ mi. south of Bowness on the A592 and has all the necessary amenities (£7.50/tent and 2 people).

The **Wild Oats Vegetarian Restaurant,** Main St. in Windermere, serves filling luncheon specials (£4.20) and filled rolls (£1.50; open daily 10am-5:30pm). In Bowness, try the **Hedge-Row Vegetarian Restaurant,** on the main road across from the Lakes Bookshop (meals about £4.75; open Sat.-Thurs. 9:30am-6pm, Fri. 9:30am-5pm). During the day, cheery pink decor brightens the simple but tasty offerings at the very, very small **The Coffee Pot,** 15 Main Rd., Windermere (baked potato with filling and salad £1.80, sandwiches from £1.65; open Tues.-Sat. 10am-5pm). Just up the road, the pub in the **Queen's Hotel** serves inexpensive meals (£3.50) all day (open Mon.-Sat. 11am-11pm, Sun. noon-3pm and 7-10:30pm).

Ambleside

Only 4 mi. from the town of Windermere, at Lake Windermere's northern tip, Ambleside (pop. 2600) is more handsome and less frenetic than its neighbor. Frequently served by buses and full of reasonably priced B&Bs and restaurants, the town makes a solid base for exploring more remote areas to the north.

Ambleside's only sight is the tiny **House on the Bridge,** off Rydal Rd.; actually, house and bridge are one and the same. About 4 paces long and 1 pace wide, it was once inhabited by a basket weaver, his wife, and six children. The best views of the surrounding fells are from the middle of the lake; rent a boat at the Waterhead pier (£3/hr., £4 for 2 people) and drift under the splendor of the Horseshoe fells. The town hosts two festivals in summer: **Rushbearing** on the first Saturday in July, in which flower-covered crosses are toted through the town; and **Ambleside Sports Festival,** the Thursday before the first Monday in August, with sheep-dog trials, running, and Cumberland wrestling. The sports are held on the grounds of Rydal Hall (admission about £1).

The **tourist information center,** Church St. (tel. 325 82), offers a free accommodations service (10% deposit) and can also book-a-bed-ahead for £2.15. One-hr. tours of town leave from the office every Thursday at 2:30pm (July-Aug.; £1.30, children 70p; office open daily 9am-6pm; Nov.-March Fri. 1-4pm and Sat. 10am-4pm). Change money at **Barclay's** near the post office (open Mon.-Fri. 9:30am-4:30pm), or in the **post office** itself on Market Place. (Open Mon.-Fri. 9am-5:30pm, Wed. 9:30am-5:30pm, Sat. 9am-12:30pm; Oct.-June Mon.-Tues. and Thurs.-Fri. 9am-12:30pm, Wed. 1:30-5:30pm, Sat. 9am-12:30pm.) Ambleside's **postal code** is LA22 9AA; the **telephone code** is 0966.

Accommodation seems to be Ambleside's principal industry; there are almost as many B&Bs and guesthouses here as private residences. Most B&Bs cost about £12.50 and fill up quickly in summer; call ahead in July and August, or at least arrive early in the day to hunt down a room. Some B&Bs cluster on Church St. and Compston Rd.; others line the busier Lake Rd. leading in from Windermere.

The closest **IYHF youth hostel,** in Waterhead, Ambleside, Cumbria LA22 0EU (tel. 323 04), resides near the steamer pier, a 15-min. walk south of Ambleside on the A591 to Windermere; the Windermere bus stops right in front of the hostel. Housed in a huge building, formerly a hotel, this is the country club of Lakeland hostels; you can even swim off the pier. (Small 2-6 bed rooms. Call a few weeks ahead; they may ask for a deposit. Wash 50p. £7, ages 16-20 £5.90; high season £8.30, ages 16-20 £7. Open daily; late Sept.-late March Thurs.-Tues.)

In town, the **YMCA,** Old Lake Rd. (tel. 323 40), is open to both women and men. Though they cater predominently to school groups, the wardens take the bunks down in July and August to create a B&B. Brew some tea in the small kitchen or feast in the cheery dining room (£11.75). Charming **Mr. and Mrs. Richardson,** 3 Cambridge Villas (tel. 323 07), serve herbivorous breakfasts on request (£11.50). **Raaesbeck,** Fair View Rd. (tel. 338 44), a fascinating 400-year-old cottage with solid oak floors and beams and comfortable beds, occupies a quiet spot above the main road (£11). Blue-eyed Ezra purrs appreciatively in the family atmosphere of the spacious **Thorneyfield,** Compston Rd. (tel. 324 64; one single £13; several doubles £15/person, £14 if you mention *Let's Go*). There's a laundrette on Kelsick Rd. (Wash £1.50, dry 20p, last wash 8pm. Open daily 9am-9pm.) You can camp at the basic **Hawkshead Hall Farm** (tel. (09666) 221), 5 mi. south of Ambleside off the B5286 (£3.20; open March-Oct.).

Ambleside's eateries tend to be superior to those of surrounding areas in terms of both quality and diversity, enhancing the town's attractiveness as a base for exploring the Lake District. **The Old Smithy,** The Slack, is the cheapest place in town; try the pie and chips for £1.80 (take-away £1.30; open Mon.-Thurs. 11:30am-2pm and 5-8:30pm, Fri.-Sat. 11:30am-2pm and 5-10:30pm, Sun. noon-2pm and 5-8pm). **Harvest Wholefood Vegetarian Restaurant,** Compston Rd., sells delicious vegetarian concoctions, such as meal-sized salads or hot dishes with salad (£5.60). Surprise your stomach with a banana-and-honey or a rosewater-and-yogurt whisked drink (£1.50). Herb teas, fresh fruits, and baked desserts are also available. (Open Mon.-Fri. 5-10pm, Sat. noon-2:30pm, 5-10:30pm, Sun. noon-2:30pm, 5-10pm.) The popular **Apple Pie Eating House,** Rydal Rd., next to the famous House on the Bridge, serves quiche with salad, or hot meat pies, for £3.50. You should try one of the unusual sandwiches (hummus sandwich £1.95) or treat yourself to the home-baked apple pie (£1.80 and £1.40; open daily 9am-5:30pm; in winter Fri.-Wed. 9am-5:30pm). The classical music at **Sheila's Cottage,** The Slack, entertains an upscale clientele that takes morning breakfast and coffee to the tune of £2.95 (10:30-11:30am), lunch for £5-6 (noon-2:30pm) and sips afternoon tea for £4.95 (2:30-5pm). Indulge in the Crazy Sticky Toffee Pudding and creme (£2.60). The interior decorator at **Zeffirelli's,** Compston Rd., does almost as good a job as the pastry chef (pastries £1.85). Start with a fresh salad or quiche for £3.25. (Open Mon.-Fri. 5-9:45pm, Sat.-Sun. noon-2:30pm and 5-9:45pm.) The **Golden Rule** has good local beer and a loyal following among residents. Young people frequent the **Sportsman** on Compston Rd., which has a disco and serves pizza.

Buses arrive and depart on King St., serving many areas in the Lake District. **CMS** (tel. (0539) 723 221) buses #555-557 run hourly to Grasmere (£1.40), Keswick (£3), and Windermere (£1.40). Bus #505 and 515 serve Hawkshead and Coniston (3/day, Sun. 2/day). You can store luggage at **Oxley's Stores,** Kelsick Rd. for 50p per bag. Tour the area on a bike rented from **Ambleside Mountain Bikes,** Scotts Café, Waterhead (tel. 320 14), by the lake. (£12/day, £60/week, ID deposit. Panniers. Open daily 9:30am-5pm.)

Near Ambleside

The **Brewery Arts Centre** in Kendal (tel. (0539) 251 33), about 10 mi. to the southeast past Windermere, hosts good theater, cinema, folk, and jazz festivals and has a permanent café and bar. (Open Mon.-Fri. 10am-8pm, Sat. 10am-2pm. Discounts for students and seniors; disabled access.) CMS buses #555-557 run to Kendal Mon.-Fri. hourly, summer Sun. every 2 hr.

North of Ambleside, the countryside becomes mountainous, but scenic walks are not always difficult. The fells to the northeast are most popular, but even the footpath leading northwest to Grasmere is superb. The tourist office's trail guide (20p) details a circular route (9½ mi., about 4 hr.). Two magnificent mountain **IYHF youth hostels** are a few miles away. The **High Close** hostel (tel. (09667) 313), 4 mi. north in Loughrigg, Ambleside, is comfortable and seldom full, so there is little competition for the pool and ping-pong tables. (£6.30, ages 16-20 £5.10. Open late March-late Sept. daily; Jan.-late March and late Sept.-Nov. Mon.-Sat.) For some reason, **Elterwater youth hostel,** Ambleside, Cumbria LA22 9HX (tel. (09667) 245) in Langdale, 1 mi. west of High Close, is more popular. (£5.90, ages 16-20 £4.70.

Open April-Aug. Tues.-Sun.; mid-Feb. to March and Sept.-Nov. Wed.-Sun.) CMS bus #516 from Ambleside passes within 1 mi. of each of these hostels; from Grasmere, it's a 1½-mi. walk southwest to High Close.

Coniston Water

The racey waters of this flourishing boating center flow parallel to those of Lake Windermere, separated from the larger lake and the busy towns of Windermere and Ambleside by a 5-mi. trek through the Grizedale Forest. Coniston Water is accessible by bus #505, which starts in Kendal and travels via Windermere (Bowness Pier), Ambleside and Hawkshead to the lake (8/day 10:10am-5:25pm, Sun. 3/day 10:10am-3:10pm; 1 hr.).

The **tourist office** (tel. (05394) 415 33) in Coniston provides an accommodations service (£1) and posts a list of vacancies. (Open April-Oct. daily 10am-12:30pm and 1:30-5pm.) You can stay at the **Holly How youth hostel (IYHF)** Far End, Coniston, Cumbria LA21 8DD (tel. (05394) 413 23), just north on Ambleside Rd. (Lockout 10am-5pm. £5.90, ages 16-20 £4.70.) The delirious **Coniston Coppermines youth hostel (IYHF),** Coniston, Cumbria LA21 8HP (tel. (05394) 412 61), is at the edge of the copper mines and overlooks the water. (Simple grade. £5.90, ages 16-20 £4.70. Open July-Aug. Thurs.-Tues.; mid-Feb. to June and Sept.-Dec. Thurs.-Mon.)

On Yewdale Rd., near Coniston, the **John Ruskin Museum** preserves existential relics of this writer-philosopher-art critic's life. (Open Easter-Oct. daily 11am-4:30pm. Admission 75p.) **Brantwood** (tel. (05394) 413 96), Ruskin's manor house from 1872, lies perfectly situated between Coniston and Hawkshead, containing Ruskin's art and works by Tolstoy, Gandhi and Proust. (Open daily 11am-5:30pm; mid-Nov. to mid-March Wed.-Sun. 11am-4pm. Admission £2.50, children £1.50.) The Coniston Steam Yacht "Gondola" stops at Brantwood twice daily on its circular route around the lake, and **Coniston Boating Centre** rents rowboats (£2.20/hr.), sailboats (£8/hr.) and motorboats (£9.50/hr.).

The small village of **Hawkshead,** several miles east of Coniston, was the boyhood home of Wordsworth. A new **Theatre in the Forest** offers folk and classical music, as well as drama, amidst a snarl of pine-trees and nature trails (tel. (022984) 291; box office open Tues.-Sat. 11am-4pm; theater season March-Dec.). The **Hawkshead youth hostel,** Esthwaite Lodge, Hawkshead, Ambleside, Cumbria LA22 0QD (tel. (05394) 362 93), overlooking the lake, was once the home of novelist Francis Brett Young; his works fill the hostel library. A number of hiking and cycling trails pass near the hostel. (Reception open 1-5pm. Lockout 10am-5pm. £7, ages 16-20 £5.90. Open late March-late Sept. daily; mid-Feb. to late March and late Sept.-late Nov. Mon.-Sat.)

Two mi. southeast of Hawkshead, in the hamlet of **Near Sawrey** on the shores of Esthwaite Water, Beatrix Potter's 17th-century house **Hilltop** (tel. (09666) 269) contains her furniture, china, and pictures. Take the Windermere ferry to Lakeside and walk about 1½ mi. (Open April-Oct. Sat.-Wed. 10am-5:30pm, last entry 4:30pm. Admission £2.50, children £1.40.) If you catch the Windermere bus from Ambleside and get off just past Hawkshead, a 10-min. hike will bring you to **Tarn Hows,** a small lake surrounded by mountains. The National Trust's footpath will take you through solemn pine groves carpeted with fern and misty green grass.

Grasmere

Grasmere is a rather bland little town, populated by wealthy, retired aficionados of spectacular landscapes. Every establishment in town tries, in relatively good taste, to cash in on William Wordsworth's legacy, occasionally falling back on the more easily digested Beatrix Potter. Though framed cross-stitches of *Daffodils* and excerpts from *The Prelude* can be seen just about everywhere, the poetic sublimity of the splendid lake and hills at Grasmere ultimately speak for themselves.

The 19th-century **Dove Cottage,** where Poet Laureate Wordsworth lived with his wife, his sister Dorothy, Samuel Taylor Coleridge, Thomas De Quincey, and up to a dozen assorted children, friends, and groupies from 1799 to 1808, is a relatively primitive affair. Its current caretakers will load you with as much Wordsworth lore as you can bear during their 20-min. guided tour. The tickets to the cottage (£3.50, children £1.75, sold at the shop nearby) also cover admission to the museum next door, which has an excellent exhibit on the life of Wordsworth, as well as manuscripts and portraits of Wordsworth, Coleridge, De Quincey, and Southey. (Cottage open daily 9:30am-5:30pm; museum open 9:30am-5:30pm.)

The Wordsworth trail continues back toward Ambleside and the poet's last and most comfortable home, **Rydal Mount,** where he lived from 1813 until his death in 1850. The attic study is now a showcase for his books, letters, and portraits, and three walls are covered with a family tree. Wordsworth himself designed the 4½-acre garden outside. (Estate open daily 9:30am-5pm; Nov.-Feb. daily 10am-4pm. Admission £1.75, seniors and students £1.25, children 60p.) The Wordsworths' graves are in the yard of St. Oswald's Church in Grasmere village.

Grasmere is ideal walker's country. Ambitious climbers might want to tackle the **Rydal Fells** or **Langdale Fells,** but even the paths around Rydal Water and Grasmere are scenic. Aquaphiles might walk down Langdale Rd. and hire a boat to row on the deep green lake (in summer daily 10am-5pm; £4/person per hr., £15 deposit required; lower rates for larger parties).

The **National Park Information Centre** (tel. (09665) 245), in town on Red Bank Rd., books accommodations (10% deposit) and sells maps and guides, including Ordnance Survey maps (£3.30-3.90) and Grasmere walking guides (15p each; center open late July-Aug. daily 9:30am-6:30pm; April to mid-July and Sept. daily 10am-5pm).

There are two **IYHF youth hostels** within ½mi. of Grasmere. **Butharlyp How,** Grasmere, Ambleside, Cumbria LA22 9QG (tel. (09665) 316), is a big stone house with a flowering garden north of Grasmere village; follow the road to Eastdale for 150 yd., then turn right down the sign-posted drive. (£6.60, ages 16-20 £5.40. Open late March-late Sept. daily; late Feb.-late March and late Sept. Tues.-Sun.) **Thorney How,** Grasmere, Ambleside, Cumbria LA22 9QW (tel. (09665) 591), a converted farmhouse planted squarely between a number of good walking routes, is ½mi. northwest; follow the road to Eastdale, turn right at the fork, then turn left. (£6.30, ages 16-20 £5.10. Open late March-late Sept. daily; Jan.-late March Wed.-Mon.) Both hostels accept telephone reservations within a week or so of arrival. All the B&Bs in town cost at least £15, but Grasmere is an easy daytrip from Windermere, Ambleside, or Keswick, where B&Bs are more reasonably priced.

Grasmere's restaurants are surprisingly good. The **Rowan Tree,** Langdale Rd., is a good place for a snack, with homemade soups (£1.50) and hot meals (£4-5; open daily 10am-8pm). Splurge at **Baldry's,** in the village center, serving Wensley rarebit (£3.50) and delicious Cumberland Rum Nicky, a pie laced with rum and filled with dates, roast ginger, and eggs (£1.25/slice; open Fri.-Wed. 9:30am-5:30pm). Sarah Nelson's famous Grasmere Gingerbread is a bargain at 16p per slice in **Church Cottage,** just by St. Oswald's.

Keswick

Set between high fell and crag by the side of northerly Lake Derwentwater, once-quiet Keswick (KEZ-ick) has come to rival Windermere as the Lake District's tourist capital; in summer, visitors indulging their tree and Kendal Mint Cake fetishes outnumber permanent residents. This former mining center is a hiker's springboard for the central and northern lakes; most of the lakes lie within a 10-mi. radius of the town and are accessible by road or hiking trail.

Arriving and Departing

Located 1½ hr. southwest of Carlisle and due west of Penrith on the A66, Keswick is northernmost in the string of "charming towns" well-served by public transport stretching south from Carlisle through Ambleside, Grasmere and Windermere. See the main *Getting There* section for the Lake District above for specific information. **Fellbus** (tel. (07687) 726 45) offers ½day and day tours of the area (10am; £7.50, fullday £14).

Orientation and Practical Information

Keswick (pop. 4700) is the queen's chamber in the beehive of the Lake District. To reach Keswick's tourist office, turn right from the front entrance of the bus station and walk down the road to the town center until you reach Market Square.

Tourist Information Center: Moot Hall, Market Sq. (tel. 726 45). Local accommodations service free, book-a-bed-ahead £2.15, accommodations booklet 50p, map 20p. National Park information. A 2-hr. guided walk departs daily at 10:20pm (£2.50, children £1). Pick up your own copy of *Mountain Biking in the Lakeland* by Michael Hyde (£2.75). Open Mon. 9:30am-7pm, Tues.-Sun. 9:30am-5pm; Sept.-June daily 10am-4pm.

Emergency: Dial 999; no coins required.

Financial Services: Barclay's, near the tourist office. Open Mon.-Fri. 9:30am-4:30pm. Currency exchange also at the **post office.**

Launderette: Main St., near the bus station. Open daily 7:30am-7:30pm. Last wash 6:30pm.

Market Day: Sat. 9am-5pm.

Mountain Rescue: tel. 720 04.

Police: Bank St. (tel. 720 04).

Post Office: 48 Main St. Open Mon.-Tues. and Thurs.-Fri. 9am-5:30pm, Wed. 9:30am-5:30pm, Sat. 9am-12:30pm. **Postal Code:** CA12 5JJ.

Telephone Code: 07687.

Accommodations and Food

A vast quantity of B&Bs, all charging about £11, lie sandwiched between the A591, Station St., St. John St. and Ambleside Rd. The July and August crowds inevitably exhaust this supply, so be sure to book ahead or arrive early in the day to press your luck.

Keswick youth hostel (IYHF), Station Rd., Keswick, Cumbria CA12 5LH (tel. 724 84). From the tourist office, bear left down Station Rd. and espy the YHA sign on the left. This former hotel has balconies over the river, spanking new rooms with lockers, and a decent kitchen. Laundry 50p and 20p. Opens at 1pm. Curfew 11pm. £7, ages 16-20 £5.90. Open late March-late Sept. daily; mid-Feb. to mid-March and late Sept.-Nov. 6 Thurs.-Tues.

Derwentwater youth hostel (IYHF), Barrow House, Borrowdale, Keswick, Cumbria CA12 5UR (tel. (059684) 246). Two mi. south of Keswick on the B5289. Take the "Borrowdale bus" (CMS #79) to Seatoller (every hr.). Worth the traveling inconvenience to stay in this 200-year-old house with a splendid view of Derwentwater, extensive grounds and trails, home-cooked meals, and its own 108-ft. waterfall. YHA activity center. Opens at 1pm. £7, ages 16-20 £5.90. Open mid-March to mid-Sept. daily; Jan. to mid-March and mid-Sept. to mid-Dec. Mon.-Sat.

Bridgedale, 101 Main St. (tel. 739 14), just outside the bus station; noisy buses rumble by. 17 rooms with teamakers, including 2 singles. £8 bed only, £1 continental breakfast, £2 cooked breakfast. Open all year.

Mr. and Mrs. Nixon, Grassmoor, 10 Blencathra St. (tel. 740 08). Vye for the red passion room. All rooms come with tea and TV. £11-12.

Mrs. Walker, 15 Acorn St. (tel. 741 65). Varied breakfasts, luxurious bathroom, and a warm welcome. Doubles £10.50/person. Discounts for extended stays.

Mrs. Peill, White House, 15 Ambleside Rd. (tel. 731 76). Bright spacious rooms with the feel of a quality hotel. Three doubles, 1 family room. Open March-Oct. £11/person, £14.50 with private bathroom.

Camping: Dalebottom Holiday Park (tel. 721 76; £5/tent and 2 people), 2 mi. southeast of Keswick. **Castlerigg Hall** (tel. 724 37; £5/tent and 2 people), 1 mi. southeast of Keswick. Both sites have telephones, flush toilets, and showers, and both are open April-Oct. The Windermere bus passes both. Call ahead.

Mayson's, Lake Road, serves heaping plates of veggie lasagna, stir fries, and other specials under a thicket of hanging plants (dinners £2.75-4.25, scones and jam 60p, homemade pizza £2.50; open daily 9am-9pm). **Trekker's Lodge,** Lake Rd., serves heaping portions under the frozen gaze of the Keswick Mountain Rescue Team in Nepal. (Sandwiches £1, full meals £2.60, enormous mugs of lemon tea 60p, bags of bread for the ducks 20p.) On Main St., near Moot Hall, try **The Loose Box** for pizza (£4.25) or pasta (£4.55, lunch specials £2.95; open daily noon-2:30pm and 6-10:30pm, Fri.-Sat. noon-2:30pm and 6-11pm). Also on Main St., **Sundance Wholefoods** has an above average selection. (Open daily 9am-5:30pm.) When the t'irst hits ye, join the lively young crowd at **Jennings',** Lake Rd. (Open Sun.-Thurs. 11:30am-2:30pm and 5:30pm-9:30pm, Fri.-Sat. 11:30am-2:30pm and 5:30-10pm.)

Sights and Activities

To sharpen your understanding of local industry, visit the scintillating **Cumberland Pencil Museum** (tel. 736 26), off Main St., just beyond the bus station, with both history and the World's Largest Pencil. (Open daily 9:30am-last entry 4pm. Admission £1.20, seniors and children 60p. Disabled access.) To see old manuscripts of Southey, Wordsworth, and Coleridge, and Downing-Fassett, stop in at the **Keswick Museum and Art Gallery** (tel. 732 63), across the bridge on Station Rd., 50 yards beyond the hostel. (Open April-Oct. Mon.-Sat. 10am-12:30pm and 2-5:30pm. Admission 75p, children and seniors 30p.)

The tourist office can give you a list of pony trekking centers, boat rentals, and hiking trails in the area. Many walks leave from the tourist office. Check their board or the free newspaper, *The Guardian.* (Two-hr. guided free walks Wed. and Sun.; day walks with a ranger £2.50, children £1; day-long Keswick Rambles £3.) Serious climbers should inquire at the tourist office about taking a guided daytrip with one of Lakeland's finest climbers, **Ray McHaffie** (tel. 742 90). **Keswick Launch** (tel. 722 63) stages frequent day and evening 50-min. narrated cruises around the lake. (10am-8pm; £3.85, children £1.90. YHA discount of 10%.) You might find a more secluded beach near one of the five landings. The Launch also rents streamlined rowboats (£2.50/person per hr., children £1.25) and motorboats (£8 for the first 2 people, £3/person after that) from Keswick and Lodore landings (9am-6:30pm). Try rowing out to **St. Herbert's Island,** a 7th-century hermitage.

The lakeside **Blue Box Theatre** (tel. 744 11) is housed in what looks like the world's largest—and bluest—trailer. The repertory company alternates every three nights among three contemporary plays. (Performances at 8pm; tickets £6.50, children £4.50. Book at Moot Hall kiosk June-Oct. Mon.-Fri. 10am-1pm and 2-6pm, and at theater box office Mon.-Sat. 6-8:15pm.)

Near Keswick

The best ridge hike in the entire Lake District starts only 1 mi. from Keswick. Ascend the **Cat Bells** from the west shore of Derwentwater at Hawse End and take a gentle 3-mi. stroll atop the ridge, passing **Maiden Moor** and **Eel Crags** on the way to **Dale Head.** For another excellent daytrip, walk southwest through the quiet village of **Portinscale** and over the Derwent Fells to **Buttermere** (returning by bus or thumb). The easy **Castlehead Walk** from Keswick's Market Place brings you to spellbinding **Friar's Crag,** praised by Ruskin, Wordsworth, and other luminous literati. The "Borrowdale Bus" to Seatoller follows an arresting route along Derwentwater and through the dramatic Jaws of Borrowdale Pass.

Just 1½ largely vertical mi. east of town stands the Bronze Age **Castlerigg Stone Circle.** The Scottish archaeoastronomer Alexander Thom claims that lines drawn between the stones indicate sunrises over certain peaks on certain days of the year. Although the circle is not as striking as some others, the hilltop view is sensational—nothing but mountains in every direction.

Western Lake District

A comfortable 9 mi. day's hike south of Keswick and Derwent Water lies the harrowing **Honister Pass,** gateway to the wildest parts of the Lake District: Wasdale, Eskdale, and Longdale. Catch CMS bus #79 from Keswick to Seatoller (8/day 7:25am-5:25pm, Sun. 6/day 10:30am-5pm; ½hr.), south of Keswick on the B5259 and 1½ mi. east of the pass. At the summit of the pass poses the **Honister Hause youth hostel (IYHF),** Seatoller, Keswick, Cumbria CA12 5XN (tel. (059684) 267; £5.50, ages 16-20 £4.40; open July-Aug. daily; mid-March to early June and Sept.-Oct. Fri.-Tues.).

Set in a splendid valley beside an icy mountain lake, **Buttermere,** 4 mi. northwest of the pass, makes a smashing base for touring the area. The town is directly accessible by Mountain Goat Bus (see the main Getting Around section for the Lake District above). Nearby **Sour Milk Gill Falls** plummet from the slopes of Red Pyke. The hike/climb to the top of **Haystacks** is difficult, but the summit allows bone-chilling views of the surrounding mountains. **Red Pyke, High Style,** and **High Cragg** are the three main challenges for ambitious hikers in the area. Others might take an afternoon constitutional up **Ranadale Knotts,** just behind the village. Another **IYHF youth hostel** (tel. (07687) 702 45) grants a hiker's reprieve. (£6.30, ages 16-20 £5.10. Open late March-late Sept. daily; Jan.-late March and late Sept.-late Nov. Mon.-Sat.) If the hostel is full, stay at the **Syke Farm** (tel. (059685) 222) for B&B (£12/person, family, or doubles; £11 for stays of two nights or more) or camping (£3/person); or spend the night at **Crag Foot Cottage** (tel. (059685) 220), a wonderfully friendly B&B (singles and doubles £11/person).

Wasdale cowers beneath the solemn **Great Gable** (2949 ft.) and its bulky twin, the **Green Gable** (2628 ft.). The climb from Honister to the summit (about 3½ hr.) is steep and invigorating. A mi. from the base of Green Gable is **Black Sail youth hostel (IYHF),** Ennerdale, Cleator, one of England's most remote hostels. The warden is a charming mountaineer who serves plenty of coffee, tea, and simple meals. (Simple grade. No phone or access for cars. Lockout 10am-1pm. £5.10, ages 16-20 £4. Open late March-Nov. Tues.-Sun.) Take CMS bus #79 from Keswick to Seatoller and then hike 3½ mi. Equally charming and inaccessible is the **Giltherwaite youth hostel (IHYF),** Cat Crag, Ennerdale, Cleator, Cumbria CA23 3AX (tel. (0946) 86 12 37), near 3 ridges and just off the Smithy Beck forestry trail, lies in a bucolic valley. (Open mid-March to Oct. Fri.-Wed.; £5.50, ages 16-20 £4.40.) The **Eskdale youth hostel (IHYF),** Boot, Holmrook (tel. (09403) 219), is approached by the Ravenglass-Eskdale railway, which stops in Boot, 1½ mi. away. (Open late March-early April, late May, and July-Aug. daily; April-late May and June Mon.-Sat.; Sept.-Dec. and mid-Feb. to mid-March Tues.-Sat.; £6.30, ages 16-20 £5.10.)

B&Bs cluster at **Wasdale Head:** try **Mrs K. Naylor,** Row Head Farm (tel. (09406) 244), or **Sandra Naylor,** Middle Row (tel. (09406) 306), for friendly lodging at £12/person (singles or doubles). Facing the famous and forbidding **Wastwater Screes,** a jumble of loose rock, is the standard-grade **Wastwater youth hostel (IYHF),** Wasdale Hall, Wasdale, Seascale, Cumbria CA20 1ET (tel. (09406) 222; open late March-late Sept. daily; Jan-late March and late Sept.-Nov. Tues-Sat.; £6.30, ages 16-20 £5.10). Climb the nearby **Whin Rigg,** or venture over to the many waterfalls of **Greendale Valley.** Take CMS bus #12 from Whitehaven or Seascale, get off at Gosforth, and walk 5 mi. southeast; alternatively, walk 5½ mi. from the Arton Rd. stop on the Ravensglass-Eskdale railway.

WALES

Though Wales has been fully integrated into the British economy, it clings steadfastly to its Celtic heritage, continuing a struggle for independence that has been going on for over a millenium. At the height of its power, the Roman Empire extended over part of Wales, but the English who took over in the 13th century had the more lasting influence. Welsh, a Celtic language, endures in conversations, in a revived literature, and on bilingual road signs. As churning coal and steel mills fall victim to the vicissitudes of Britain's economy, the unemployment rate has risen, and Wales has begun to turn its financial base from heavy industry to tourism. Largely unmarred by modern development, the landscape of Wales is unremittingly grand.

History

As the western terminus of many waves of emigration, Wales has been often invaded. The compact build and dark complexion of many Welsh people is a legacy of the Iberians, the area's original inhabitants. Tall, fair Celts conquered them and took the British Isles in 800 BC. When the Romans invaded Britain, they were forced to station two of their three legions at the Welsh border. The Romans departed in 410 AD, and for 700 years the Welsh were left to themselves. The Saxons pushed them back and built Offa's Dyke, a 168-mi.-long earthwork, to keep the Welsh in their hilly land. But even the Saxons could not subdue these Celtic tribes—they were foiled, perhaps, by the daring military tactics of the legendary Arthur. After a long campaign, Edward I of England finally conquered the rebellious country in 1282 by recapturing the bride of Llewelyn ap Gruffydd, the Prince of Wales. Edward constructed a series of massive castles—the fortresses of Conwy, Caernarfon, Harlech, and Beaumaris—at strategic points along the northern and western coasts.

In the 15th century, the bold guerilla warfare of Owen Glendower (Owain Glyndwr) temporarily freed Wales from English rule. "The great magician, damn'd Glendower," as Shakespeare's Henry IV calls him, succeeded in reigniting Welsh nationalism and rousing his compatriots to arms, but after 1409 he disappeared into the mountains, leaving only a legend to guide his people. Full union with England came in 1536, at which time Welsh customs, laws, and language were outlawed; ironically, the reigning Tudors were of Welsh descent.

In the early 19th century, the discovery of rich coal veins in the south catapulted Wales into modernity. The handsome area of Glamorgan was soon covered with ash, grit, and dust-covered workers; Carlyle described it as "a vision of Hell." The harshness of the era fermented a grim sobriety that paralleled the rise of religious fundamentalism. The organization of labor found perhaps its purest expression in the soaring men's choirs still found in many Welsh towns. Crushingly rapid industrialization in Wales contributed to the formation of a strongly leftist political consciousness. David Lloyd George, leader of Liberal reform in the first decade of the 20th century, began his career as a rabble-rousing Welsh rad-boy.

A vigorous campaign to save one of Europe's oldest living languages is part of the recent, sometimes prickly, revival of Welsh nationalism. A few years ago, a majority of Welsh community councils voted to make Wales a nuclear-free zone, a move that was as much a reaction against England as a protest against nuclear development. Prince Charles' office wrote a letter to the councils "denying the request," and the liberal Welsh have continued their crusade against conservatism and the English "imperialists" who have made Wales their summer holiday land.

Irish Sea
Liverpool
Amlwch
Holyhead
Anglesey
Beaumaris
Conwy
Llandudno
Colwyn Bay
Conwy R.
Clwyd River
Flint
Chester
Dee River
Bangor
Caernarfon
Llanrwst
Caernarfon Bay
Llanberis
Betws-y-coed
Wrexham
Mount Snowdon
Beddgelert
Blaenau-Ffestiniog
Llangollen
Criccieth
Porthmadog
Lleyn Pen.
Pwllheli
Harlech
Abersoch
Bardsey Island
Dolgellau
Barmouth
MOUNTAINS
Welshpool
Shrewsbury
Machynlleth
Tywyn
Dovey River
Severn River
Cardigan Bay
Newtown
ENGLAND
Aberystwyth
Devil's Bridge
CAMBRIAN
Llandrindod Wells
New Quay
Hay-On-Wye
Pembrokeshire Coast National Park
Builth Wells
Wye River
Cardigan
Strumble Head
Teifi River
Hereford
Llandovery
Fishguard
Brecon
Black Mountains
Wye Valley
St. David's
Broad Haven
Carmathen
Tywi River
Usk River
Brecon Beacons National Park
St. Bride's Bay
Haverfordwest
Taf River
Monmouth
Milford Haven
Abergavenny
Saundersfoot
Ystradfellte
Tintern Abbey
Dale
Merthyr Tydfil
Tenby
Swansea
Rhondda Valley
Chepstow
Pembroke
Carmarthen Bay
Gower Peninsula
Newport
St. Govan's Head
Rhossili
Mumbles Head
Caerphilly
Worms Head
Cardiff
Bristol
Bristol Channel
N
0
50 miles
0
50 kilometers

Literature

Wales, like other Celtic countries, has a long bardic tradition. The 12th-century *Mabinogion* contains the three tales that became the famous Arthurian romances of Chretien de Troyes and the 14th-century poetry of Dafydd ap Gwilym. In 1568, Queen Elizabeth was so concerned with the "intolerable multitude of vagrant and idle persons calling themselves minstrels, rhymers and bards" that she issued a Royal Commission for the establishment of an Eisteddfod where dawdlers could be put to the test. Today the National Eisteddfod is a huge annual festival and competition of singing, storytelling, and skits, the culmination of hundreds of smaller local and school *eisteddfodai.*

Well-known Welsh authors include Saunders Lewis, Kate Roberts, Richard Llewelyn (author of the best-selling novel *How Green Was My Valley*) and the brilliant Dylan Thomas.

Ffood

Traditional Welsh cooking relies heavily on potatoes and onions, dairy products, mutton and pork, and fish and seaweed. Welsh rarebit is buttered toast topped with a thick cheesy mustard beer sauce. Griddle cakes *(crempog)* are made with sour cream and topped with butter. Wales has quite a variety of unique and tasty breads—try *laver,* made with seaweed, or the scrumptious *bara brith,* a fruit and nut bread. **Cawl** is a thick broth with everything in it, served with a slab of bread. Soups are thick with leeks and generous helpings of lamb and beef.

Language

The word "Welsh" comes from the Old English *wealh,* or "foreigner," and the language does indeed seem utterly alien to English-speakers. Try to familiarize yourself with the lovely lilt of the language by learning the basics of Welsh pronunciation. *Ch* is the deep, guttural sound "kh" heard in "Bach" or the Scottish "loch." *Ll*—the oddest of Welsh consonants—is produced by placing your tongue against the top of your mouth, as if you were going to say "l," and blowing. Another common consonant *dd,* is pronounced like the "th" in "the." *C* and *g* are always hard. *W* is generally used as a vowel and sounds like the "oo" in "drool," and *y* sounds like either the "u" in "ugly" (especially when between hyphens), or the "i" in "ignoramus." *F* is pronounced like a "v," as in "vavoom." Emphasis usually falls on the next to last syllable. There are no silent letters in Welsh.

Most Welsh place names are quite sensibly derived from prominent features of the landscape. *Llan* or *betws* means church, *chepe* market, *stowe* town, *afon* river, *mynydd* mountain, *ffordd* road, *glyn* glen or valley, *pen* top or end, and *caer* fort. *Mawr* is big, *fach* is little. The Welsh call their land *Cymru* and themselves *Cymry.* Phrases that you should know include *ar gau* (closed), *ar agor* (open), *perygl* (danger), *cyhoeddus* (public), *preifat* (private), *dynion* (men), *merched* (women), *allan* (exit), *llwybr cyhoeddus* (public footpath), and *diolch yn far* (dee-OLCH een VAR, thank you).

South Wales

The transition from England to Wales is smoothest in the south, where calm hills ease into gritty harbors and seething market towns. Unemployment remains high, public transportation has been cut back alarmingly, and coal-mining strikes ravage morale. However, much has been done to repair the damage wrought by indiscriminate strip mining. Pine trees cover hillsides once bare and grey, and many miners' homes have been livened up with bright paint and new brick.

The Wye Valley forms a fertile and serene border between England and Wales while Brecon Beacons National Park, to the north of Cardiff, covets rugged hills, forests, limestone caves, and moorlands. Both the Gower Peninsula, jutting south at Swansea, and the far larger Pembrokeshire Peninsula to the west, flaunt unmatched coastal scenery and fine beaches. The further north you go, the more characteristically Welsh the terrain and the communities become; the rail line between Machynlleth on Wales's west coast and Shrewsbury in England marks the imaginary border with North Wales.

Getting Around

Transportation throughout South Wales is easiest by car, as train stations are few and far between. The rail system consists of two lines originating at Cardiff. One line sticks to the coast, passing through Tenby on its way to Pembroke on the southern coast of the Pembrokeshire Peninsula; the other runs inland across the peninsula, stopping in Carmarthen and terminating at Fishguard on the peninsula's northern coast. Ask for special Ranger passes at any BR office. The **Valley Lines Day Ranger** is valid on branches radiating from Cardiff to Barry, Penanth, Rhymney (via Caerphilly), and Treherbert, Aberdave, and Merthyr Tydfil (via Pontypridd) (£4.20). A **Heart of Wales Weekday Rambler** is good on the Swansea-Knighton line. Call the BR offices at Cardiff (tel. (0222) 228 000) or Swansea (tel. (0492) 467 777) for information.

The bus network provokes white-knuckle-level frustration. Take all bus schedules with a grain of salt—Welsh buses are often late. **National Welsh** (tel. (0222) 371 331) buses serve the area around Cardiff; **South Wales Transport** (tel. (0792) 475 511) buses serve the routes from Gloucester and Hereford in England west through the Wye Valley, past Abergavenny and Brecon in the north and Cardiff in the south, all the way to Neath (near Swansea) and Carmarthen and Haverfordwest in South Pembrokeshire in the west. Together, these two companies operate **Expresswest** buses, running from South Wales to Bristol with stops in Haverfordwest, Milford Haven, Pembroke, Tenby, Carmarthen, Swansea, and Cardiff. These buses run less frequently (6/day), but tend to be much faster than local service between towns. **Traws Cambria** (tel. (0222) 371 331) is a network of coach links connecting National Welsh buses in the south with Crosville buses in north and mid-Wales. On Trans-Cambria, you can travel easily from Cardiff or Swansea north to Aberystwyth, Machynlleth, and Bangor. Seniors receive a 25% discount, students and YHA members 15%.

Private bus companies fill in some of the gaps. **Silcox Coaches** (tel. (0834) 21 89) covers south Pembrokeshire, and a branch of South Wales Transport, locally called **Cleddau** (KLETH-eye; tel. (0437) 763 284), covers the Haverfordwest area. **Richard Bros.** (tel. (0239) 613 756) connects Haverfordwest north to St. David's, Fishguard, and Cardigan, where you can hook up with **Crosville** for travel north. Pick up a *Public Transport Map* for the area in which you will be traveling. Most local buses do not run on Sunday, though Expresswest does operate twice in the morning and twice in the afternoon on summer Sundays. If you leave from Cardiff, the bus station inquiries office (tel. 371 331) can provide invaluable help in planning your trip.

Passes simplify the bus fare system in the south. The **Roverbus** pass, which can be purchased from any driver, is valid for unlimited travel for one day on all National Welsh and South Wales Transport buses (£2.95, seniors and under 16 £1.90, children with adult holding a full-fare Roverbus pass 95p). For seven days of consecutive travel on these buses, buy a **Weekly Roverbus** (£12.50, children and seniors £8.50; also good on Expresswest West buses); the pass must be bought at a National Welsh or South Wales Transport office in a local bus station. (Bring a passport-sized photo.) Richard Bros. has a £2.30 day out ticket for its buses only.

Many find **hitchhiking** in summer is more efficacious in South Wales than farther north due to heavy traffic to the coast. Cars stop easily for hitchers who stand in lay-by (pull-off) areas along these narrow roads.

Hiking

Wales has hundreds of well-marked **footpaths.** Long-distance hikers should buy 1:50,000 Ordnance Survey maps and bring along proper equipment. For further advice, check the booklets *Walking in Wales,* available in Welsh tourist offices, and *Wales: Walking* (£1.10), available from the British Tourist Authority. The Offa's Dyke Path and the Pembrokeshire Coast Path are popular long-distance walks through glorious and often remote countryside. For more information, write to the Countryside Commission Dispatch Dept., 19-23 Albert Rd., Manchester, England M19 2EQ. The £1.20 Tourist Map available at all tourist offices and most bookstores gives a good sense of the layout of the region, as well as train and road lines.

Cardiff (Caerdydd)

The only truly urban center in a land of small villages, Cardiff (pop. 300,000) has a modern flair and a youthful culture. Its intense Welsh pride expresses itself through the lively arts scene and the beautifully restored architecture of both public buildings and homes. Residential buildings spread out around a center containing one of Britain's most lavish castles, classical buildings that house government offices and the National Museum, and the enormous Bute Park. The shopping in Cardiff is considered the best in Britain in terms of price and variety.

Arriving and Departing

National Express Rapide coaches (tel. 344 751) run between Cardiff and London's Victoria Station or Heathrow Airport (5/day; 3 hr.; £21.50), Penzance (2/day; 8 hr.; £33.25), Bristol (9/day; 1 hr.; £6.75), and Glasgow (3/day; 8½ hr.; £42). **BR** trains are faster and more frequent, leaving from London's Paddington Station (1/hr.; 2 hr.; £29) and stopping in Cardiff before heading west to Pembroke/Haverford and Fishguard. Trains also run from Bristol (½hr.; £6.20), Bath (via Bristol; 1 hr.; £10), Glasgow and Edinburgh (via Crewe; every hr.; 7 hr.; £52), and Birmingham (2½ hr.; £19.50). BR also services several other lines through Wales departing from Cardiff. **National Welsh** and **South Wales Transport** buses both offer Rover day passes and week passes, and British Rail offers a Freedom of Wales Rover. (See South Wales Introduction for more information.)

Orientation and Practical Information

The castle stands triumphantly in the city center, with the mantle of massive Bute Park stretching out behind it; to the east bow the Civic Centre, university buildings, and museums. Shops, pedestrian walks, and indoor arcades foray out to conquer the rest of the city.

BWS Caerdydd runs an extensive network of orange buses all over Cardiff and environs. Buses run less frequently Sun. mornings, and never after 11pm. Pick up a timetable for 30p. Regular fares run from 35p-£1.10; take advantage of the reduced fares Mon.-Fri. 9:15am-3:45pm. (Seniors and disabled persons ½fare; after 5:30pm on Thursdays and all day Sundays 12p. Day tickets £2.50; purchase on the bus. Party ticket (unlimited travel for up to 4 people on weekends and holidays) £3.40.)

Tourist Information Center: 8-14 Bridge St. (tel. 227 281), down the street from the Holiday Inn. Free accommodations service (10% deposit), list of B&Bs, and impressive *Visitor's Guide,* as well as currency exchange, car rentals, and love spoons. Open July-Sept. Mon.-Sat. 9am-6pm, Sun. 10am-4pm; Oct.-June Mon.-Sat. 9:30am-6pm.

Tours: The Cardiff Experience (tel. 395 173); 1-hr. bus tours of Cardiff, leaving from the tourist office. Mon.-Sat. noon and 2pm, £4.50, seniors and students £3.50. **National Welsh** (tel. 383 803); tours on several different themes; information and booking available at the Central Bus Station. **Bay Tours** (tel. 463 833); free tours 5 days/week, 11am and 2pm; call early to reserve a seat, as they fill up weeks in advance.

AIDS Line: tel. 223 443; open Mon.-Fri. 7-10pm.

Bike Rental: Mike Tane Garage, Caerphilly Rd. (tel. 623 854).

Budget Travel Office: Students' Union, Park Pl., 1st Floor, Cardiff University (tel. 382 350). Books BR, National Express, ferries, charter flights, etc. Student discounts. Open Mon.-Fri. 9am-3:30pm. **Campus Travel,** YHA Adventure Shop. See Camping Equipment below.

Bus Station: Wood St. (For National Welsh information, call 371 331; for National Express, call 344 751.) Booking office and Travel Centre open Mon.-Sat. 8am-6pm, Sun. 10:45am-6pm. BWS Caerdydd office, Wood St. (tel. 396 521 for information and lost and found daily 9am-11pm), across from the bus station. Open Mon. and Fri. 8am-5:30pm, Tues.-Thurs. and Sat. 8:30am-5:30pm.

Camping Equipment: Campus Travel, YHA Adventure Shop, 13-15 Castle St. (tel. 399 178). Student fares and a herring barrel's worth of backpacking, camping, and hiking gear. Open Mon.-Sat. 10am-6pm, Thurs. 10am-7pm.

Car Rental: Avis, 4 Saunders Rd. (tel. 342 111). Open Mon.-Fri. 8:30am-6pm, Sat. 9am-12:30pm. Call the tourist office for ADTEC (tel. 222 098).

Crisis: Samaritans tel. 344 022; 24 hr.

Emergency: Dial 999; no coins required.

Financial Services: Thomas Cook, 16 Queen St. (tel. 341 296). Open Mon.-Fri. 9am-5:30pm, Sat. 9am-noon. **American Express,** 3 Queen St. (tel. 668 858). Open Mon.-Sat. 9am-5pm.

Hospital: Royal Infirmary, Newport Rd. (tel. 492 233), off the end of Queen St., 10-min. walk from town center. 24-hr. accident and emergency care.

Launderette: Launderama, 60 Lower Cathedral Rd. (tel. 228 326).

Market: High St. Arcade, junction of St. Mary and High St. Mon.-Sat. 9am-5pm. **Open Air Market:** Charles St., behind the library.

Pharmacy: Boots, Queen St. (tel. 221 268). Open Mon.-Sat. 9am-9pm. **Late Night Pharmacy: Boots,** 5 Wood St. (tel. 234 043), across from the bus station. Open Mon.-Fri. 8am-10pm, Sun. 6-7pm.

Police: Cathay's Park, Civic Centre (tel. 344 111).

Post Office: 2-4 Hill St., The Hayes (tel. 227 363). Open Mon.-Fri. 9am-5:30pm, Sat. 9am-12:30pm. **Postal Code:** CF1 2ST.

Rape Hotline: 108 Salisbury Rd. (tel. 373 181).

Taxi: Metro Cabs, tel. 464 646; 24-hr. service.

Telephones: At Queen St. shopping precinct, St. David's Hall. **Telephone Code:** 0222.

Train Station: Central Station, Wood St. (tel. 228 000), behind the bus station. Luggage storage (until 9pm, £1.30) or lockers (£1-2; 24 hr.). Station and ticket window open 24 hr. Travel Centre open Mon.-Sat. 8am-9pm, Sun. 9am-7:45pm.

Accommodations and Camping

Budget accommodations are scarce at the center of Cardiff, but the tourist office lists reasonably priced B&Bs (£11-13) on the outskirts and will book you a room for free if you leave a deposit. Most of the B&Bs in the courtly Victorian houses along Cathedral Rd. are graciously decorated but sometimes rudely priced (£18-22). The smaller neighborhoods around Cathedral Rd. are the best bet for less expensive B&Bs (bus #32, 62, or a 15-min. walk from the castle). Across town, Newport Rd. harbors the **YMCA, YWCA,** and large guest houses and hotels.

Cardiff youth hostel (IYHF), Wedal Rd., Roath Park (tel. 462 303), 2 mi. from the city center; take bus #80 or 82 from Central Station. Comfortable, roomy dormitory with individual bed lights in each bunk. Helpful warden knows the bus timetable and stops by heart. "Mickrick" the mutt might nuzzle at the front desk. Meals available. £7, ages 16-20 £5.90. Open March-Oct. daily; Jan.-Feb. and Nov. Tues.-Sat. Open for check-in at 3pm. Curfew 11pm.

YWCA, 126 Newport Rd. (tel. 497 379). Women and married couples only. Mainly residential, but space is almost always available. Personal attention from resident "mother." No curfew. Kitchen facilities. B.Y.O.Utensils. £7.

YMCA, The Walk (tel. 497 044), 2 blocks down East Grove off Newport Rd. Men and women. Luxury living by "Y" standards . Curfew 10pm, but you can ring for the night porter. Single with continental breakfast £13.67, double £12.67/person. £5 key deposit.

Plasturton House, 1 Plasturton Ave. (tel. 383 188), off Cathedral Rd. Turn left at the Beverly Hotel. A home with 3 children, a golden retriever called Honey, and a pond of goldfish in the backyard. The proprietor can give you tips on clog-dancing. Singles £12, doubles £10/person.

Ty Gwyn, 5/7 Dyfrig St. (tel. 239 785), off Cathedral Rd. at the 120s. Luxurious rooms (shower in each) for 1-3 people in the home of a former fine arts professor. Beautifully decorated with antiques befitting a museum. £10-14.

Annedd Lon, 3 Dyfrig St. (tel. 223 349). Pure and elegant non-smoking household with a Victorian touch. £12.

Camping: Acorn Camping and Caravaning, Rosedew Farm, Ham Lane South, Llantwit Major (tel. (0446) 794 024). £3-5/tent or caravan.

Food

Central Cardiff is bereft of cheap markets. Stock up on produce at the indoor market off High St. (Mon.-Sat. 8am-5:30pm), or at the outdoor market at the end of Charles St. (off Queen St. and St. David's Centre). Relatively cheap food is usually tucked away in the corners of the indistinguishable pedestrian arcades.

Crumbs, 33 David Morgan Arcade (tel. 395 007), off Sidmaelly Rd. and The Hayes. Locals pack this vegetarian restaurant serving enormous, delicious salads (£2.05) and homemade breads in its wee wooden den. Open Mon.-Fri. 9:30am-3pm, Sat. 9:30am-4pm.

Dorothy's and **Tony's Fish Bar,** both on Caroline St., an alley that runs between St. Mary St. and The Hayes. Fish and not a few chips £1.55. Pasties, pies, and curries under £2. Open daily 10am-2pm. Sun. hr. somewhat arbitrary.

The Homade, 26 Dumfries Pl., at the end of Queen St., and **Bistro One,** Quay St., off St. Mary St. toward the castle. Large rolls enlivened by a variety of fillings and salad—try the Spanish omelette (£1). The cheapest place to sample Welsh rarebit (£1.30). Open Mon.-Sat. 7:30am-6pm.

Sights

The preposterously opulent interior of **Cardiff Castle** (tel. 822 083) is no less flamboyant than the peacocks that mewl inside the gates and pester tourists for food; the third Marquess of Bute employed William Burges, the most lavish of Victorian architect-designers, to restore the castle in the 19th century. (Castle open for tours every 20 min. May-Sept. 10am-12:30pm and 2-5pm, Oct.-Nov. and Feb.-April less frequently. Admission July-Sept. £3.05, seniors and children £1.55.) Though the castle's interior is its main attraction, you can also visit the gardens, the Norman keep, and the military museum (£1.70, seniors and children 85p).

Across North Rd. stands Cardiff's **Civic Centre,** a grand collection of government and university buildings separated by wide avenues and grassy squares. The 19th-century **City Hall** is an ornate, domed palace which was built when Cardiff was reaching the height of its coal-fired prosperity. The **War Memorial** gardens in the center strike a 17th-century balance with the monumental buildings around it. Through both its architecture and its collection, the **National Museum of Wales** (tel. 397 951) reinforces Cardiff's reputation as a repository of national culture. The museum attempts to cover just about everything indigenous to Wales, from art to industry: in the mining gallery, a life-sized mine tunnel displays the dangers and intricacies of work in the mines, while the second floor circular gallery displays the works of French impressionists. (Open Tues.-Sat. 10am-5pm, Sun. 2:30-5pm. Admission £1, seniors and children 75p.) The **Lovespoon Gallery,** 25 Castle St. (tel.

231 742) devotes itself exclusively to this stirring Welsh folk tradition. The managers will give you a full tour of the gallery. (Open Mon.-Sat. 10am-5:30pm.)

Entertainment

Cardiff's signature odor emanates from **Brains Brewery** in the middle of the city. Its specialty is Brains S.A. (Special Ale), known by locals as "Brains Skull Attack" and served by many pubs in the city center. The Motorhead crowd congregates at **Bogey's,** 3 Penarth Rd. (tel. 226 168), under the bridge past the Holiday Inn. The angst-chic brood at the **Stage Door,** 25 The Parade (tel. 838 145), and **CoCo Savannah** (tel. 377 014), across from the New Theatre (tidy dress required; £4). **The Student Union** (tel. 396 421) is probably the best bet for music and company (as well as cheap meals); on weekends go early or have a student take you in as a guest—also check the university for theatrical performances. When the pubs close, head to one of Cardiff's many writhing dance clubs. Boogie by the **Tom Tom Club,** on St. Mary's St., or **Ratcliff's,** Westgate St., by the bus station; upstairs is a gay club, downstairs slam dancing. The weekly magazine *Venue* provides all the information on social events and hotspots that you'll need.

If you'd rather sit back and spectate, pick up the Cardiff *Entertainments* guide, free at the tourist office. The **Chapter Arts Centre,** Market Rd. in Canton (tel. 399 666), features an eclectic program of dance, drama, gallery exhibitions, and film (from Joel Silver to *Help I'm Being Crushed to Death by a Black Rectangle).* The first-floor café is relaxed, and the Downstairs Bar has music nightly. (Open Mon.-Sat. 10am-11pm, Sun. noon-11pm. Late-night films Thurs.-Sat. at 11pm. Take bus #12 or 19 from Castle St. up Cowbridge.)

Adornments on the **John Bachelor Statue,** at the corner of Hill St. and The Hayes, are a happy gauge of the festive atmosphere in Cardiff. Scarves and hats signify rugby or football matches, and a clumsily held can of Brains S.A. is a sure sign of bacchanalia. Rugby is beyond doubt Wales' religion. Games are played in Cardiff at the **National Rugby Stadium,** Westgate St. (ticket office tel. 390 111); from September through April, try Entrance 4, near the souvenir stand, for international tournament tickets (standing room £4, best seats in the house £10-20). Watch for Saturday afternoon matches at the **Cardiff Rugby Club** (tel. 395 804) next door (admission £4-6).

Near Cardiff

The **Welsh Folk Museum** shares the 100 acres of **St. Fagan's Park,** 4 mi. west of Cardiff, with native trees and sculpted hedges (tel. 569 441). Nearly 20 buildings—ranging from a late 15th-century farmhouse to the 1760 Esgair woolen mill—have been transported piece by piece from different parts of Wales and reassembled here. There is someone (often a professional craftsperson) at each of these exhibits eager to answer questions and demonstrate a skill such as handweaving, leather-tanning, or blacksmithing. The main exhibition galleries display, among other things, a marvelous collection of Welsh lovespoons. (Open daily 10am-5pm; Nov.-March Mon.-Sat. 10am-5pm. Admission £3, seniors £2.25, children £1.50.) Take the hourly bus #32 (60p) from Central Station, or from any stop on Cathedral Rd.

Two mi. northwest of the city center near the River Taff, **Llandaff Cathedral** was built by the Normans, defaced by Oliver Cromwell's ale-swilling troops and bombed by German planes in 1941. Remarkably restored, the only remaining Norman features are the chapel near the west end and the beautifully embellished doorways leading into the choir. The interior is now dominated by a concrete Jacob Epstein sculpture of *Christ in Majesty.* Take bus #25 from Castle St. or #62 from the station (every ½hr., Sun. every hr.), or walk down Cathedral Rd. and through Llandaff Fields.

The third Marquess of Bute and the architect William Burges (the same pair that renovated Cardiff Castle) struck again at **Castell Coch** (Red Castle) (tel. 810 101),

5 mi. northwest of Cardiff, crafting a fairy-tale castle atop 13th-century ruins. Take the half-hour ride on bus #136 or X26 (1/hr.), or the A470 road northwest to the village of **Tongwynlais,** and then walk straight up the hill. (Open daily 9:30am-6:30pm; mid-Oct. to mid-March Mon.-Sat. 9:30am-4pm, Sun. 2-4pm. Admission £1.50, seniors and children 75p.)

Eight mi. north of Cardiff lie **Caerphilly** and **Caerphilly Castle** (tel. (0222) 883 143). The castle is the second-largest fortress in Europe (Windsor is the largest) and has the most elaborate water and land defense system in Britain, constructed by the Normans during the 13th century. Four centuries later, Cromwell thought it a good idea to drain the lakes and blow up the towers—or at least try; the famous leaning tower of Caerphilly is evidence of his attempts. (Open daily 9:30am-6pm; mid-Oct to mid-March. Mon.-Sat. 9:30am-4pm, Sun. 2-4pm. Admission £1.50, seniors and children 90p.) **Red and White Caerphilly Buslink** connects from Central Station in Cardiff to Caerphilly.

National Welsh bus #304 or 305 from Mill Lane will take you to **Barry Island** to bask on sandy beaches and promenade through lush gardens just 11 mi. outside of the city.

Wye Valley

The River Wye (Afon Gwy) wanders from its remote source in the hills of mid-Wales to its confluence with the broad River Severn at Beachley near **Chepstow.** The valley is shared by both England and Wales; on its way south, the river neatly sidesteps through England's **Hereford,** to the east of **Hay-on-Wye,** re-entering Wales north of **Monmouth.** The Normans saw this valley as a foothold for new conquests, building a series of castles (now in ruins) on the west side of the river, from which they launched attacks on the adjoining Welsh lowlands. Numerous walking paths lace through the valley, retaining most of the tranquility through which William Wordsworth once stumbled.

Getting There and Getting Around

Enter the valley from the south, at Chepstow; both buses and trains run to Chepstow from Cardiff or Newport, 20 mi. east of Cardiff (by bus: #X73 every hr. 8:30am-5:30pm; 1¼ hr.; by train: 6/day; 35 min.; £3.90). Trains also run from Cardiff or Newport to Hereford, north of Chepstow in England (7/day; 1 hr.; £9.90).

Red and White Buses (tel. (02912) 622 947) are the primary means of transport in the Wye Valley; be warned that there is no Sunday service. Bus #69 loops through Chepstow, Tintern, and Monmouth every two hours, and connecting buses run regularly from these towns to Hereford and Hay-on-Wye. Buy a **Roverbus Pass** (£3.80, seniors £2.70), available in the bus stations and on the buses, for daytrips between towns; it'll pay for itself with one return trip. The pass is good for all travel on Red and White and National Welsh buses within the area bounded by Swansea, Brecon, Hereford, and Gloucester; it is not valid on local Cardiff buses. Pick up a free timetable for information on additional services. Hitchikers say the going is good on the A466 in the summer; some stand near the entrance to Tintern Abbey or by the Wye Bridge in Monmouth.

Hiking

The valley coughs up walks of all difficulties and lengths. The **Wye Valley Walk** runs between the picturesque towns of Chepstow and Monmouth along cliffs, wooded hills, and farmland; the beautiful abbey and cathedral at Tintern and Hereford provide blessed diversions. Across the river, **Offa's Dyke Path,** runs the entire length of the English-Welsh border, offering over 150 mi. of hiking trails (Chepstow-Tintern, 5 mi.; Tintern-Monmouth, 11 mi.; Monmouth-Symonds Yat, 6 mi.). From Symonds Yat, the walk continues north to Hereford, in England, and Hay-on-Wye (78 mi. total). East of Symonds Yat, the 20,000-acre **Forest of Dean,** once the happy hunting ground of Edward the Confessor and Williams I and II, now forms the pupil of an ornithological nature reserve. A variety of trails leads to the Wye Valley Walk or Offa's Dyke Path; tourist offices sell pamphlets of these walks, which vary from 1½ to 10 mi. (30p). For information on Offa's Dyke Path, write to the Offa's Dyke Association, West St., Knighton, Powys, Wales LD7 1EW (tel. (0547) 528 753).

Chepstow (Cas-gwent)

Chepstow's strategic position at the mouth of the River Wye and the base of the English and Welsh border once made it an important fortification and commercial focus for the rest of the Valley.

Chepstow Castle (tel. (02912) 40 65) guards the mouth of the valley; its long, narrow structure and fine 11th-century Norman keep stretch out against the limestone cliffs. An impressive array of Norman defensive plans adorn the inner halls. (Open daily 9:30am-6:30pm; mid-Oct. to mid-March Mon.-Sat. 9:30am-4pm, Sun. 2-4pm. Admission £1.50, seniors and students 90p.) The **Chepstow Festival,** held during the first two weeks of July in every even year, is punctuated by the clash of full armor battles held within the grounds, a siege of the castle, and musical and dramatic events. The old **town wall,** in some places 7 ft. thick and 15 ft. high, was designed as an extension of the castle for the collection of tolls and nighttime protection from vagabonds. Across from the castle, the **Stuart Crystal Factory** conducts free tours on the fine art of crystal blowing which conveniently start and end at the factory outlet store. (Open daily 9am-8pm; Oct.-April 9am-5pm.) The **tourist office** (tel. (029162) 37 72), at the Gate House on High St., can direct you on walks around the area, past such landmarks as **Wintour's Leap,** a 300-ft. cliff from which the doomed Sir Geoffrey De Wintour supposedly leapt, and **Lancaut Church,** once a leper (not leaper) colony. (Free.)

The B&Bs in town do an impressive job of picking up the slack now that the Chepstow YHA hostel is closed; unfortunately, they remain somewhat expensive. **Lower Hardwick House,** Mt. Pleasant (tel. (0291) 622 162), is a gorgeous old mansion with enormous rooms (singles £15, doubles £12.50/person, triples £11/person) and an exquisite garden which accommodates campers (£5/tent, £3.50 full English breakfast). **Langcroft** is less expensive but just as homey. For more **camping,** continue north from the hostel up the A466 to **Chepstow Race Course** (tel. (02912) 37 10), site of the famous annual horse races (tel. (0291) 622 260 for details on upcoming races). Bus #69 will stop at the parking lot. **Beeches Farm,** Tidenham (tel. (0291) 689 257), 5 mi. north of Chepstow and just east of Offa's Dyke Path, is more convenient for walkers. (Both campsites £3-5/night.)

Chepstow's **train station** is on Station Rd., perpendicular to the main road. Buses stop above the town gate in front of the supermarket; schedules are posted at the Five Bays. Both stations are unstaffed, but you can ask about tickets at **Fowler's Travel** (tel. (02912) 30 31), on Moor St. (Open Mon.-Fri. 9am-5:30pm, Sat. 9am-4pm.)

Tintern

Five mi. north of Chepstow along the A466, **Tintern Abbey** raises its barren walls to the sky. Although swamped with tourists in the summer, the abbey is an impressive sight against the hills and cliffs that hug the Wye. Built by the Cistercian monks in the late 11th and 12th centuries, the abbey reflects a wish to re-create more austere forms of religious life. Stained glass, carved decorations, and church towers were banished; the builders' imagination found expression in Tintern Abbey's pointed arches. Now under restoration, the abbey is more complete than when Wordsworth saw it during his rambles through the Wye Valley. (Open daily 9:30am-6:30pm; October 16-March 14 Mon.-Sat. 9:30am-4pm, Sun. 2-4pm. Admission £1.75, seniors and under 16 £1.) The **tourist office** (tel. (0291) 689 431), in the abbey entrance across from the bus stop, verses wanderers on hiking paths and accommodations in Gwent. (Open late May to mid-Oct. daily 10am-6pm.) If the crowds in the village are overwhelming, cross the iron footbridge and head into the hills. Way-marked paths lead to **Offa's Dyke** (¾hr.) and **Devil's Pulpit** (1 hr.), an enormous pulpit-shaped stone from which the Nasty One is said to have tempted the monks from their prayers; ironically, the view from the Devil's Pulpit is the broadest and most beautiful view of the Abbey and the entire Wye Valley.

As the path winds through Tintern village, it passes the 400-year-old **Wye Barn Bed and Breakfast,** with a stellar view of its own (£13). Avoid the temptation of fast food at the tea shop in the Tintern parking lot and stroll into the village, where several of the hotels have wizard afternoon cream teas.

Monmouth (Trefynwy)

Just north of the confluence of the Rivers Wye and Monnow sits the market town of Monmouth. Birthplace of Henry V and Geoffrey of Monmouth (who gave what little historical credibility there is to King Arthur and Merlin in his *History of the Kings of Britain),* the town preserves its Norman character in its famous 13th-century toll bridge and chapel. The Norman castle, once a defense against intruders from Wales, now lies in ruins. **Agincourt Square,** the town center, frames Monmouth's **market** on Friday and Saturday, and the mooing and bleating **livestock market** on Monday.

The **tourist office** (tel. (0600) 713 899) in Shire Hall provides information on hiking and walks. (Open daily May-Oct. 9:30am-5:30pm.) The Forestry Commission (tel. (0594) 363 04) assists in finding accommodation in the Forest of Dean. Monmouth's **IYHF youth hostel,** Priory St. School (tel. (0600) 715 116), occupies a 15th-century building in the center of town. (Open March-Oct. daily. £5.10, ages 16-20 £4.) B&Bs lie mostly along Hereford Rd. and in St. James' Square. **Wye Avon,** along Dixton Road (tel. (0600) 713 322), provides board in a typically beautiful Monmouth mansion, with a typically high Monmouth price (£13). Bakeries, grocers, and tea rooms frost Monnow St.

Buses stop in a parking lot near the fortified bridge. Monmouth is the last stop for bus #69 from Chepstow and Tintern (see above); bus #65 also runs from Chepstow to Monmouth, via Trelleck rather than Tintern (Mon.-Sat. 5/day). Bus #X49 departs for Hereford (Mon.-Sat. 5/day), continuing to Newport (3/day), and Cardiff (1/day). Midland Red West (tel. (0345) 212 555) operates a line to Ross-on-Wye via Whitchurch (#61 every 2 hr.)

Hereford

Another 18 mi. north of Monmouth, Hereford is the only town in the Wye Valley accessible by BR; although itself in England, Hereford makes a good springboard for a trip through Wales. A modern city punctuated by a 17th-century "Old House," a Victorian gardens museum, and a cider factory, Hereford still confines itself to the ruins of its old Norman walls, built in 676 AD (a self-guided tour of walls takes 2 hr.). The 13th-century cathedral secrets the **Mappa Mundi,** a gem of a world map drawn in 1920, inside her library. (Cathedral open daily. Library and Mappa Mundi open Easter-Oct. Mon.-Fri. 10am-4:30pm. Free.) Joint tickets to the **Old House** on Broad St. and **Churchill Gardens** on Venn's Lane are available at the tourist office. (Churchill Gardens open Tues.-Sun. 2-5pm, winters Tues.-Sat. 2-5pm; Old House open Tues.-Fri. 10am-5pm, Mon. 10am-1pm, summers Sat. 10am-5:30pm. £1.20, seniors and children 35p.) The **Cider Museum,** Pomona Place, on Whitecross Rd. adjacent to the Cider Brandy Distillery (tel. (0432) 354 027), tells the story of traditional cider-making from the 17th century to the present. (Open April-Oct. daily 10am-5:30pm; Nov.-March Mon.-Sat. 1-5pm.) Art and music create a carnival atmosphere during the **Festival** of the first two weeks of August; and in late October, a craft exhibition comes to town.

The **tourist information center,** at the Town Hall Annex on St. Owen's St. (tel. (0432) 268 430), provides walk pamphlets (15p), tickets to some sights, and an accomodations service (£1.50, book-a-bed-ahead £2.50). (Open May-Oct. Mon.-Sat. 10am-5pm, Nov.-April Mon.-Sat. 10am-4pm.) Accommodations in town are both sparse and expensive. Call the tourist center for assistance, or try **Tenby Guest House,** 8 St. Nicholas St. (tel. (0432) 274 783), for huge rooms and a lounge with papsan chairs. (Singles £15, doubles £12/person.) You can windowshop along cobblestoned **Church Street,** or duck into **Jolly Roger,** 88 St. Owen St. (tel. (0432) 274 998), for some food and entertainment. Roger invites you to eat with your hooks in this pirate's den; Desperate Dan burgers £2, sandwiches and beer samples £2.75. Jazz strums on Fridays, while Tuesdays feature sing-alongs; bring your own instruments to this jam session. Full tours of the adjacent brewery are also available. (Open Mon.-Sat. 11am-11pm, Sun. noon-3pm, 7-10:30pm.)

Trains from London arrive every hr. and leave for London every ½hr. (3 hr.; £26). They also run to Abergavenny (1/hr.; 25 min.; £5.20), Shrewsbury (1 hr.; £9.50), Cardiff (1 hr.; £9.90), and Chepstow via Newport (£15). Hereford is connected by **Red and White** bus routes to the other Wye Valley villages as well as to Brecon, Abergavenny, and Newport (Red and White Rover Pass, £3.80). Sundays, the **Kilvert Connection** offers a service from Brecon to Hereford via Hay-on-Wye. The train station and bus station are at the end of Commercial Rd., near the **County Hospital,** Union Walk (tel. (0432) 355 444); Hopper bus #444 will take you there.

Hay-on-Wye

Home to the largest colony of second-hand bookstores in the world, Hay-on-Wye is a restless hotbed of esotericism. Glass-blowers, potters, and candlestick makers gather here to sell their wares along the narrow streets under the shadow of the beautiful 1880 town clock and the 17th-century Jacobean castle (not open to the public). Crafts and music abound during the annual jazz festival, held in late August, and in summer, book or craft fairs occur almost weekly.

The **tourist information center** (tel. (0497) 820 144) is as eccentric and loveable as the rest of the town. (Open daily Easter-Oct. 10am-5pm, Nov.-Easter 11am-4pm.) Head down Castle St. or Belmont Rd. to catch crafts. You can hire a bicycle from **DYG Sport** (tel. (0497) 821 446), opposite the tourist office (mountain bikes £8/day, £40/week; open Mon. and Wed.-Sat. 10am-5pm), and bike the Wye Valley Path (Offa's Dyke Path is unsuitable for biking).**The Granary,** Broad St. (tel. (0497) 820 790), bakes Welsh specialties like *Bara Brith* (a delicious buttered fruitcake) fresh every day.

The youth hostel nearest to Hay-on-Wye lies 8 mi. out of town at **Capel-y-Ffin,** along Offa's Dyke Path. (tel. (0873) 890 650; £ 5.50, ages 16-20 £4.40. Open March-Oct. Thurs.-Tues.; Nov. and Feb. weekends only.) National Welsh buses serving the Hereford-Brecon route stop outside the hostel, as do taxis from the center of town (£8; call (0497) 821 266 for minivan taxi). **Belmont House** (tel. (0497) 820 718), an antique-filled home, rubs noses with the bookshops and craftstores (singles £15, doubles £12/person). **Mrs. Jones,** on Garibaldi Terrace (tel. (0497) 820 351), charges £11 per person. It is easy to camp near Hay along the Wye Valley walk or Offa's Dyke. **Radnor's End Campsite** (tel. (0497) 820 780) is the closest to town; cross Bridge St. and go 300 yards to the left towards Clyvo (£2-4/tent).

The closest train station to Hay is in Hereford. **Red and White** buses arrive from both Hereford and Brecon (5/day, Sun. 2/day; £1.80; 55 min.). The **Kilvert Connection** runs only on Sundays between Hereford and Brecon via Hay, following a scenic route through the Black Mountains (2/day; £1.50-2.50).

Abergavenny (Y-Fenni)

Caught in a valley between the Wye Valley and Brecon Beacons National Park, Abergavenny makes a good touring base for either. Hikers following Offa's Dyke Path, which starts in the Wye Valley, often stop off in Abergavenny before continuing along the eastern border of the Brecon Beacons; the National Park Information Centre in town is well-equipped for hikers and nature lovers. In 1175, the Norman knight William de Breos killed the Welsh lords at his table in Abergavenny Castle; today, visitors tempt their own fate by hang-gliding off the cliffs at Blovenge.

Arriving and Departing

Abergavenny (pop. 10,000) is linked by rail to Hereford and Shrewsbury in the north, and to Newport (£4.50) in the south, with connections to Cardiff (£6.20), Chepstow, Bristol (£6.20), and London (£26). **Red and White Buses** run Mon.-Sat. to Hereford (#20, 4/day), Brecon (#21, 6/day; £3.80), Newport (#20 and 21 in the other direction; 12/day; about 1 hr.), and to Merthyr, continuing to Cardiff (#X4, 9/day; 2¼ hr.). Hitching on the A40 between Abergavenny and Brecon is unreliable, but not impossible.

Orientation and Practical Information

Abergavenny's rail station is on a hill southeast of town. Walk down Monmouth Rd. to reach the bus station and tourist office and from there jog into town. Monmouth Rd. segues into Cross St., High St., and Frogmore St.

Tourist Office and National Park Information Centre: Swan Meadow, Monmouth Rd., by the bus station. Tourist information tel. 775 88; accommodations information only tel. 777 78; National Park information tel. 32 54. Accommodations service free (with 10% deposit); book-a-bed-ahead to England £1.95. Open Easter-Oct. Mon.-Sat. 10am-6pm. After hours, consult showcases on High St. and Market St. for a list of stores carrying similar brochures.

tourist office

Bike Rental: Dave Brook Bikes, 9 Brecon Rd. (tel. 770 66). Mountain bikes £10/day; weekly rates available. Open Tues.-Sat. 10am-6pm.

Bus Station: At the foot of the main road where it becomes Monmouth Rd., near the castle. Get schedule information at Gwent Travel, 14 High St. (tel. 776 66; open Mon.-Fri. 9am-5:30pm, Sat. 9am-4pm) or the tourist office.To reach the center of town from the bus station, turn right and follow Cross St. for 200 yd.

Early Closing Day: Thurs. at 1pm, small shops only.

Emergency: Dial 999; no coins required.

Financial Services: Barclay's, 57 Frogmore St. (tel. 59 11). Fee £2; Barclay's checks free. Open Mon.-Fri. 9:30am-4:30pm.

Hospital: Nevill Hall, Brecon Rd. (tel. 20 91). Bus #21 to Brecon goes by every 2 hr.

Launderette: Chapel Rd., beyond Stanhope St., past the Family Food Store. Open Fri.-Wed. 9am-9pm, Thurs. 9am-noon, last wash Fri.-Wed. 8:15pm, Thurs. 11:15am.

Market Day: Tues. (cattle and produce) and Fri. (cattle on the 1st and 3rd Fridays of the month, produce every Fri.).

Pharmacy: Boots, 2 Cross St. (tel. 32 07). Open 9:30am-5:30pm Mon.-Sat. Check rota schedule for late night hours.

Police: Tudor St. (tel. 22 73).

Post Office: St. John's Sq. (tel. 28 33), to the left off the main street. Open Mon.-Fri. 9am-5:30pm, Sat. 9am-12:30pm. **Postal Code:** NP7 5EB.

Taxi: Lewis Taxi, tel. 41 40; 24 hr.

Telephone Code: 0873.

Train Station: Station Rd. (tel. 23 93), off Monmouth Rd. Open Mon.-Sat. 6am-8pm, Sun. 1:45-9pm.

Accommodations and Camping

Few B&Bs in town are affordable, and the closest youth hostel is at Capel-y-ffin, 16 mi. out of town and inaccessible by bus. The tourist office distributes a free list of accommodations, most of them wonderful rooms in farmhouses within 5 mi. of the city center, near the park. In some cases, the proprietors will arrange to pick you up in town if you call ahead.

Ivy Villa Guest House, 43 Hereford Rd. (tel. 24 73). A huge, wooly mammoth welcomes you with a bark into this hospitable den. £11.

Mrs. Bradley, 10 Merthyr Rd. (tel. 22 06), at the end of Frogmore St. Vast rooms on a noisy road. Singles, doubles, and triples £11/person with continental breakfast. Hot breakfast £2.

Bryn Usk, Monmouth Rd. (tel. 27 39), on the right, down from the train station. The rooms are like the front garden: spacious and immaculate. £13.50.

Great Tre-Rhew Farm, Llantherine (tel. 821 268). Mrs. Beavan works at the tourist office and will drive you to her home in the country, 6 mi. out of town. £12.50.

Camping: Pyscodlyn Farm (tel. 32 71). About 2 mi. from the town. Showers. From £3/site. Open April-Oct.

Food

On Tuesday and Friday, the **market** provides fresh produce, cheese, and baked goods. Otherwise, try the **Tesco's** on Frogmore St. or the **Safeway** off High St. (both open Mon.-Sat. 8am-6pm).

Iris' Cafe, 57 Cross St. (tel. 33 81). Delicious baked goods all under £2. Open Mon.-Sat. 7:30am-4:30pm.

Clam's Coffee House, Lion House, King St. (tel. 44 96). Enormous jacket potatoes with all sorts of fillings, all under £3. Open daily 10:30am-6pm.

Sights

Little is now left of **Abergavenny Castle,** but the grounds are a favorite spot for weekend hang gliders. The **Abergavenny Museum,** on a site just over the old dungeons, displays antique furnishings and relics of traditional crafts. (Open Mon.-Sat. 11am-1pm and 2-5pm, Sun. 2-5pm; Nov.-April Mon.-Sat. 11am-1pm and 2-4pm. Admission £1, seniors and children 50p. Castle grounds open dawn to dusk.) Walk the **Abergavenny Town Trail** (pamphlet 50p) to discover medieval streets and courtyards.

Abergavenny's real attraction lies in the hills around it. **Blorenge** (1811 ft.) is by far the most massive, a looming hump 2½ mi. southwest of town perfect for launching hang gliders. **Skystports Hangliding School,** 36 Hatherleigh Rd. (tel. 61 12) teaches 2-, 5-, and 7-day courses for novices and intermediate students. A path begins off the B4246, traversing valley woodlands to the upland area; it climbs the remaining 1500 ft. in 4½ mi. Climbers adore the sharp, arresting **Sugar Loaf** (1955 ft.), 2½ mi. north; the trailhead to the top starts about 1 mi. west of town on the A40. Hitch a ride to the car park and begin your hike from there to save your legs for the difficult but rewarding hike to the summit. The path to **Skirrid Fawr** (1595 ft.), northeast of town, starts about 2 mi. down the B4521. *Thirty Walks in the Abergavenny Area* (50p), available from the park office, details mountain climbs as well as gentler walks in the valleys. Pony trekking is popular in the farmlands around Abergavenny; pick up the free brochure on Outdoor Activities from the tourist center.

Near Abergavenny

The area around Abergavenny can be split into the Black Mountains, part of the Brecon Beacons National Park, and Offa's Dyke Path, a continuation of the Wye Valley area. The Rivers Usk, Wye, and Canal all run south from this region to the

Bristol Channel. Hiking is popular in the area, but most of the well-marked trails start at least 2 mi. outside of Abergavenny itself. As buses rarely emerge from their hidng places, drive or hitch to a trail head suggested by the tourist office.

All of the megaliths in the Black Mountains are believed to point toward the ruined **Llanthony Priory,** perhaps to help wandering friars find their way home. Founded in the 12th century by a group of dissenting Augustinian priests led by William de Lacy, the priory was dissolved in 1536 during the Reformation and sold, with its contents, for a measly £160. Roofless and abandoned since the 16th century, the lonely priory stands between two major ridges of the Black Mountains in the gentle curve of the Llanthony Valley. Look for signs on the B4423, 10½ mi. north of Abergavenny. Take the Hereford bus (#20) or the A465 to Llanfihangel Crucorney, where the B4423 begins. Most walk or hitch the last 6 mi. to the priory. (The **Capel-y-Ffin youth hostel (IYHF)** is an additional 4 mi. along.)

Partrishow Church lies in the neighboring valley of Grwyne Fawr, 6 mi. north of Abergavenny and 6 mi. northeast of Crickhowell. The church retains its original rood porch, which separated worshipers in the nave from the clergy in the sacristy. You can get the key to the church from the farm next door. Three mi. beyond Crickhowell, on the A479, **Tretower Court and Castle** (tel. (0874) 730 279) provides a concise history of fortified architecture in Wales; the side tower is Norman and the nearby manor house late medieval. (Open Mon.-Sat. 9:30am-6:30pm, Sun. 2-6:30pm; Oct. 16-March 14 Mon.-Sat. 9:30am-4pm, Sun. 2-4pm. Admission £1.50, seniors and children 90p.)

At the **Big Pit Mining Museum** (tel. (0495) 790 311), in Blaenavon, 5 mi. southwest of Abergavenny (take the B4246, then the B4248), you can ride down a 300-ft. shaft into a big pit and explore the subterranean workshops, stables, and coal faces of a 19th-century colliery that remained in operation until 1980. The mine is dark and cold, and the tour guides' stories are chilling. (Open March-Dec. daily. Tours 10am-3:30pm. Admission £4, children £3, children under 5 not allowed.)

Seven mi. east of Abergavenny off the B4521, **White Castle** (tel. (060085) 380) commands bold views of the valley and the Welsh border. Rebuilt in the 13th century atop Norman fortifications, the castle was abandoned in the 16th century. (Open Mon.-Sat. 9:30am-6:30pm, Sun. 2-6:30pm; Oct. 16-March 14 Mon.-Fri. 9:30am-4pm, Sun. 2-4pm. Admission £1, seniors, children and students 60p.)

Rising above the A40 halfway between Abergavenny and Monmouth, the hexagonal plan and elaborate drawbridge of **Raglan Castle** are more typical of Northern France than Wales. Cromwell's men penetrated the fortress only after "tediously battering the top thereof with pickaxes." (Open daily 9:30am-6:30pm; Oct. 16-March 14 Mon.-Sat. 9:30am-4pm, Sun. 2-4pm. Admission £1.50.)

Brecon Beacons National Park (Bannau Brycheiniog)

The Brecon Beacons National Park encompasses roughly 519 sq. mi. of varied terrain and wildlife. The park is divided by four mountain ranges: the rugged and challenging country around the remote western Black Mountain; Forest Fawr, containing the spectacular waterfalls of Ystradfellte; the Black Mountains to the east; and the impressive Beacon peaks where once signal fires warded off invaders. The market towns on the fringe of the park make pleasant touring bases, especially Brecon and Abergavenny. Since few people expect an area of such beauty in South Wales, the region is much less crowded than northern Snowdonia, and the bus service much patchier.

Getting There and Getting Around

The London (Paddington)-South Wales rail line runs to Abergavenny, at the southeastern corner of the park, and Merthyr Tydfil, on the park's southern side;

both of these towns offer the easiest access to other points in the Brecon Beacons. (The train also connects to Newport, Cardiff, Chepstow and Bristol on the coast, and Hereford and Shrewsbury inland.) The Central Wales rail line passes through Llandeilo and Llandovery, towns in the more remote Black Mountain region with little bus service. Bus service is patchy throughout the park; the Black Mountain, for instance, is inaccessible without a car. *Silverline* buses sporadically cross the park en route from Brecon, on the northern side of the park, to Swansea, west of Cardiff along the coast (3/day; 1 hr.; £4, student £2.50). **Red and White** buses stop in Merthyr Tydfil (£2.50, student £1.70), Abergavenny, and Hay-on-Wye. A Red and White Rover bus pass (£3.80/day, seniors £2.70, £11.80/week) covers the entire area and is a worthwhile investment. For bus information, call Red and White (tel. (06333) 51 18) or Silverline (tel. (0685) 824 06). For rail schedules, call (0222) 228 000. Information offices in the area will also provide time tables.

Practical Information

Stop at a **National Park Information Centre** before venturing forth. While tourist offices are helpful in planning a route by car or bus, the park centres provide pamphlets and advice on hiking, including updated weather reports. Free maps of the park are available, but serious explorers should pick up Ordnance Survey Map #11 (£4). You can buy leaflets outlining suggested walks in almost any region of the park (15p-£1). The free *Summer Walks and Events* outlines an assortment of lovespoon-carving and sheepdog demonstrations. Send inquiries to the National Park Office, 7 Glamorgan St., Brecon, Powys, Wales LD3 7DP (tel. (0874) 44 37); enclose a self-addressed envelope plus an International Reply Coupon (two for airmail return). In addition, the **Mountain Centre** in Libanus and the **Craig-y-nos Park** provide guided walks, lectures, and a leisurely cup of tea for travelers passing by along the mountain ridge. Yellow trail cards are available at the Mountain Centre; leave one with the police at your base town before setting out on a hike.

Abergavenny: Monmouth Rd. (tel. (0873) 32 54), opposite the bus station in the tourist office. Open April-Oct. Mon.-Sat. 9:30am-5:30pm.

Brecon: Watton Mount (tel. (0874) 624 437), at the bottom of the Watton. Open April-Oct. Mon.-Sat. 9:30am-1pm, 1:30-5pm. Main Park office around the corner on Glamorgan St.

Llandovery: Broad Street (tel. (0550) 206 93). Open April-Oct. Mon.-Sat.

Libanus Mountain Centre, Brecon Beacons (tel. (0874) 623 366). Catch the Silverline Brecon-Merthyr bus #43 to Libanus, 5 mi. southwest of Brecon (6/day, Sun. 3/day), and walk the remaining 1½ mi. uphill. Manages a covered picnic area and adjacent café with access for the disabled. (Open July-Aug. daily 9:30am-6pm; March-June and Sept.-Oct. daily 9:30am-5pm; Nov.-Feb. daily 9:30am-4:30pm.

Craig-y-nos: Pen-y-cae (tel. (0639) 730 395). Open Easter-Oct. daily 10am-dusk.

You can load up on gear south of Brecon at the **Tal-y-Bont Venture Centre** (The Old Shop), Tal-y-Bont-on-Usk, Brecon Powys LD3 7JD (tel. (087487) 458). Tal-y-Bont offers access to the Brecons by way of an enjoyable 6-mi. hike alongside the reservoir. The rivers flowing into it form an impressive string of waterfalls (the Blaen y Glyn) which rival those in Ystradfellte. Tal-y-Bont is accessible by National Welsh bus #21 from Abergavenny or Brecon (Mon.-Sat. 5/day; 1 hr.), which stops 20 yd. from the Venture Centre.

Safety

Like all of Britain's national parks, the Brecon Beacons is comprised of small, privately owned farms, and animal husbandry still sustains the local population. Walkers and cyclists are welcome to explore, but they are exhorted to stick to the marked paths; be sure to close all gates behind you, never light fires in open areas, and generally be considerate of the people and animals whose land this is.

The mountains are unprotected and in places difficult to scale. Hypothermia is the main threat, since the weather can change dramatically in a matter of minutes.

Never hike alone, and entrust particulars of your journey to a youth hostel warden or park officer; be sure to take along a good map and compass. In an emergency, summon help with six blasts on a whistle, six shouts, or six of anything recognizable repeated as necessary after a minute's pause. If you can reach a telephone, call **mountain rescue** in Brecon at (0874) 23 31; dialing 999 will also suffice.

Accommodations and Camping

Hosteling and camping are your two aces for accommodations. Five **IYHF youth hostels,** including Brecon's (see Brecon below) are spread through the park.

Llanddeusant hostel (IHYF) (tel. (05504) 634), in the isolated Black Mountain area, by Llangadog village, accessible from the Trecastle-Llangadog mountain road. £4.40, ages 16-20 £3.50. Open March-Oct.

Ystradfellte youth hostel (IYHF) (tel. (0639) 720 301), south in the waterfall district. A 3-mi. walk or hitch from the A4059 and 4 mi. from the village of Penderyn. Simple-grade hostel is a good base for those touring the cave and waterfall country without a car. £5.10, ages 16-20 £4. Open March-July and Sept. Fri.-Wed; Aug. daily.

Llwyn-y-Celyn youth hostel (IYHF), Brecon Beacons (HLOOEEN-uh-kel-in; tel. (0874) 624 261), 8 mi. south of Brecon and 2 mi. south of Libanus on the A470 midway between Libanus and Storey Arms. Take Silverline bus #43 from Brecon to Merthyr Tidfil (6/day, Sun. 3/day). Traditional Welsh farmhouse serves superior homemade food at a low price; order on arrival. £5.50, ages 16-20 £4.40. Open March.-Oct. Mon.-Sat.

Capel-y-ffin youth hostel (IYHF) (tel. (0873) 890 650), near the River Honddu, at the eastern edge of the Black Mountains. Hay-on-Wye is the closest town; catch Red and White Bus #39 from Hereford to Brecon, stop before Hay and walk uphill. A convenient base for ridge-walking. Allows camping on its grounds. £5.50, ages 16-20 £4.40. Open March-June and Sept.-Oct. Thurs.-Tues; July-Aug. daily; Feb. and Nov. Fri.-Sat.

Commercial campsites are plentiful and fairly evenly dispersed, but often difficult to access without a car. The brochure *Camping and Caravan Sites* (10p) maps 30 sites in the park, complete with grid references. Many offer laundry and shopping facilities, and all have parking and showers; prices range from £1.75-5 per tent. Farmers may let you camp on their land if you ask first and promise to leave the site as you found it; be prepared to make a donation toward the upkeep of the sheep.

The Brecon Beacons

At the center of the park, the Brecon Beacon mountain range provides some of the most popular and accessible hiking in the area. A splendid view of the range complements an exhibit on its history at the **Mountain Centre** just outside Libanus (see Practical Information above). From the Mountain Centre, an hour-long stroll among the sheep leads to the scant remains of an Iron Age fort and more views of the surrounding valleys and hills. Near the Mountain Centre, the path from **Storey Arms** (5 mi. south of the center on the A470) to 2907-ft. **Pen-y-Fan,** the highest mountain in South Wales, is so popular that the path has been eroded. A far more attractive hiking route starts in nearby Llanfaes (just to the south), following pleasant, narrow roads with little traffic, and ending in trailheads to the mountains. Take the trail that goes by way of **Llyn** (Lake) **Cwm Llwch** (koom-hlooch), a small pool at an altitude of 2000 ft. shadowed by **Corn Ddu** peak. The walk from Brecon to the trailheads is about 4 mi.; from the trailhead to Cwm Llwch is another 3¾ mi. The area is full of manageable walks; the National Park Information Centres will help you choose the road less traveled.

The touristy **Brecon Mountain Railway,** Pant Station, Merthyr Tydfil (tel. (0685) 48 54), gives a glimpse of the southern side of the Beacons. Take the narrow gauge steam train north to Pontsticill, where the station provides information on specific walks in the area. A return fare includes the 4-mi. round trip and admission to the **Locomotive Museum and Workshop.** (Train runs daily Easter week and May-Sept. 11am-4pm on the hr. £3, children £1.50.) Silverline Coaches (tel. (0685) 824 06) runs a Beacons Rambler daily in the summer starting from Merthyr, stopping in

Brecon and Talybont before returning to Merthyr. Guided walks link up with the coach route, or you can walk part of the Taff Trail on your own; free walks booklet provided with the ride (£2.50, seniors and children £1.50).

The Black Mountains

The Black Mountains, in the easternmost section of the park, are an unspoiled group of long and lofty ridges that offer 80 sq. mi. of uncompromising solitude. Such summits as **Waun Fach,** the Black Mountains' highest point (2660 ft.), are sometimes disappointingly rounded and boggy, but the ridge-walks are unsurpassed. A 1:25,000 Ordnance Survey Map #13 is essential.

Crickhowell, on the A40 and the bus route between Brecon and Abergavenny (Red and White bus #21, Mon.-Sat. every 2-3 hr.), is the easiest starting point for forays into the area. **Pony-trekking** centers based in Crickhowell and Abergavenny charge from £8 to 12 per day; pick up a copy of the pony-trekking pamphlet (10p) at any information center. You can also explore by bus: the route linking Brecon and Hay-on-Wye (National Welsh #39, from Brecon to Hereford) descends the north side of the Black Mountains. **Gospel Pass,** the highest mountain pass in the park, often leads to sunshine above the cloud cover. Nearby, **Offa's Dyke Path** (see Wye Valley section) runs along the easternmost boundary of the national park. The ridge valleys are dotted with a handful of impressive churches, priories, castles, and other ruins. Those who use public transportation will find these sights more accessible from Abergavenny (see Near Abergavenny section).

The Waterfall District (Fforest Fawr)

The Waterfall District, a modest area southwest of the Beacons, centers on Ystradfellte (uh-strah-FELTH-tuh) off the A4059. At **Porth-yr-Ogof** (Welsh for "mouth of the river"), less than a mi. from the IYHF hostel, the River Afon Mellte flows into a cave at the base of a cliff and reappears in a small, natural, ice-cold swimming pool. Much of the ground is rough and unstable, and the wet limestone is treacherously slippery; if you do decide to swim, be careful. Stick to more sure-footed terrain with a guide such as *Waterfall Walks in the Ystradfellte Area* (15p), available at Park Information Centres.

Near **Abercrave,** midway between Swansea and Brecon off the A4067, the **Dan-yr-Ogof Showcaves** (tel. (0639) 730 284) are huge and stunning, with enormous stalagmites. From the Ystradfellte youth hostel, 10 mi. of trails pass by Fforest Fawr (the headlands of the Waterfall District) on their path to the caves. **Silverline Coaches** (tel. (0685) 824 06) pause here three times per day on their way from Brecon (£2.60). Walk along the cemented pathways inside the caves, or slalom down the dry-ski-slope outside. (Open daily 10am-5pm, slightly later in peak season. Admission £3.50, seniors and children £2.75.) A large caravan/tent site nearby has full facilities (£2/tent). Relax from your caving adventures at the **Craig-y-nos Country Park** (tel. (0639) 730 395), ½ mi. away, which encompasses an information center, picnic tables, ponds, meadows, paths, and the grounds of opera singer Adelina Patti's personal castle, complete with restaurant. (Free. Brecon-Swansea bus stops at castle.)

Brecon (Aberhonddu)

Although not actually in the mountains, Brecon (pop. 7100) is the best base for hiking through the craggy Brecon Beacons that loom to the south. Accessible from the south coast via Abergavenny or Hereford, Brecon is an enchanting market town with ample and inexpensive accommodations, a National Park Information Centre, shops where you can stock up for your outdoor adventures, frequent craft and antique fairs, and an exceptional Jazz Festival.

Arriving and Departing

Brecon has no bus or train station, but buses arrive regularly from other spots in the area. Inquire about bus schedules and routes at **Holiday World,** 9 the Bulwark (tel. 625 678; open Mon.-Sat. 9am-5:30pm) or **Darron Travel,** 99 The Struet (tel. 624 948 or 625 045).

Silverline bus #63 (tel. (0685) 824 06) connects Brecon with Swansea (3/day, Sun. 1/day). Service #43 meets trains from Cardiff at Merthyr Tydfil (6/day, Sun. 3/day); the scenic drive highlighted by waterfalls every 100 yd. is worth the £2.50 day return (£1.70 students). **Red and White Buses** (tel. (0222) 371 331) runs four or five coaches (Mon.-Sat.) to Hereford via Hay-on-Wye (#39), Abergavenny, and Newport (#21). Red and White #X4 runs to Merthyr every hr. from Abergavenny and from Cardiff; to get to Brecon from Merthyr, you must rely on Silverlines coaches. **Williams Buses** (tel. (062) 730 289), based in Brecon, make two morning trips to Abergavenny. Along the A40 from Abergavenny or the A470 from Merthyr Tydfil, most hitchers stay near intersections where lorries can stop.

Orientation and Practical Information

Buses stop at the **Bulwark,** Brecon's main strip, which fans out to St. Mary St., Church Lane, High St. Inferior, and Lion St.; these streets in turn empty into a stretch dubbed, successively, Wheat St., High St. Superior and the Struet. The Watton leads out of town towards the youth hostel.

Tourist Information Center: Cattle Market Car Park (tel. 622 485 or 625 692). Take Lion Yard off Lion St. to the car park. Accommodations service free (10% advance deposit). Pamphlet *Where to Stay in Brecon Beacons National Park* is also free. Open Easter-Oct. daily 10am-6pm.

Brecon Beacons National Park Information Centre: Watton Mount, Brecon, Powys, Wales LD3 7DP (tel. 624 437), at the base of The Bulwark. National Park Service headquarters. Information on guided walks, hiking conditions, maps. Open Easter-Sept. Mon.-Sat. 9:30am-1pm and 1:30-5pm. Send National Park inquiries to 7 Glamorgan St. (enclose self-addressed envelope plus an International Reply Coupon).

Bike Rental: Talybon Venture Centre (tel. 628 7458), 6 mi. from Brecon. Mountain bikes £12/day. **Wales on Wheels,** Shandon House, 12 Bridge St. (tel. 625 519). Mountain bikes £12/day, £6/4 hr. Open daily.

Buses: Buses leave from The Bulwark, opposite St. Mary's Church. Schedules posted in three nearby locations, or ask at an information center.

Early Closing Day: Wed. at 1pm, small shops only.

Emergency: Dial 999; no coins required.

Financial Services: Barclay's, 9 The Bulwark, (tel. 625 333). Open Mon.-Fri. 9:30am-4:30pm. **Lloyd's,** 38 High St. (tel. 623 761). Foreign currency £2, traveller's checks £3. Open Mon.-Fri. 9:30am-4:30pm.

Hospital: Brecon War Memorial, Cerrichion Rd. (tel. 622 443), up the hill from Free St.

Launderette: Washeteria, Lion Yard, between car park and Lion St.; follow signs to "toilets." Wash £1.20. Open Mon.-Fri. 9am-7pm, Sat.-Sun. 9am-5pm. Last wash 1 hr. before closing.

Market Day: Tues. and Fri. Cattle market, last Fri. of month, Free St.

Pharmacy: Boots, 26 High St. Superior (tel. 622 917). Open Mon.-Sat. 9am-5:30pm.

Police: Lion St. (tel. 622 331).

Post Office: St. Mary St. (tel. 25 18) off The Bulwark. Open Mon.-Fri. 9am-5:30pm, Sat. 9am-12:30pm. **Postal Code:** LD3 7AA.

Taxi: Brecon Taxis, tel. 623 344; 24 hr.

Telephone Code: 0874.

Accommodations and Camping

Only a 3-min. walk from town, the Watton is ripe with B&Bs (£12-13). If you plan to visit during the third week in August, book far in advance—the Jazz Festival will claim every spare foot of room in town.

Ty'n-y-Caeau youth hostel (IYHF) (tin-uh-KAY-uh; tel. 628 6270), 3 mi. from town, on a lane leading from the A470 through the hamlet of Groesffordd to the A38 (Hay Rd.). A 2½-mi. footpath from Brecon reduces the distance; ask at the tourist office. The Brecon-Abergavenny bus stops right outside Groesffordd; from there, follow the signs. You may also be able to arrange a pick-up with the warden. A large country house, popular with cyclists and fell-walkers, which the friendly and helpful warden runs by the book. Well-stocked store and maps; equipment for rent. £5.90, ages 16-20 £4.70. Open daily April-Sept.; March and Oct. Mon.-Sat.

Mrs. J. Thomas, 13 Alexandra Rd. (tel. 624 551) behind the tourist office. The proprietor has traveled in 25 countries, lived in 15, and loves *Let's Go* users. Large rooms with exotic furnishings. £13.

Walker's Rest, 18 Bridge St. (tel. 625 993), across the bridge from Castle in Llanfaes. Breakfast is served in your own room, giving a whole new meaning to Bed and Breakfast. £12. Not affliated with Walker's Point nor any establishment in Kennebunkport.

The Grange Guest House, The Watton (tel. 624 038), next to the Presbyterian Church. Large, lacy rooms in a recently restored Georgian house. Doubles with TV £13/person.

£Camping: Brynich Caravan Park (tel. 623 325), 2 mi. east on the A40, just down the road from hostel. £2/person. Showers and laundry facilities. Open Easter-Oct.

Food

Gather your camping supplies while you may at the **Top Drawer,** 15 Ship St., which specializes in dried food and snacks. For fresh produce, head to **Top Drawer 2,** High St., or one of the supermarkets on High St.

Sarah Siddons Inn, 47 High St. (tel. 622 009). Order the "Double Decker Hunger Wrecker" (£1.60). Leviathan lunches with risqué names under £3. Open for lunch Mon.-Sat. noon-2:30pm.

The Brown Sugar Restaurant and Tea Garden, 12 The Bulwark (tel. 625 501). Light but excellent homemade food. Salads £3 and up; sandwiches £1 (toasted £1.30); hot and creamy soups £1. Tea garden. Open Mon.-Sat. 10am-5:30pm, Sun. 11am-5pm; Sept.-May Mon.-Sat. 10am-9:30pm.

The Blue Boar Inn, The Watton. Classic pub with food and amusement center for children in the back. Open Mon.-Sat. 11am-11pm, Sun. noon-2pm, 7-10:30pm.

Sights and Entertainment

Brecon Cathedral has been a cathedral only since 1923, but one parish church or another has occupied this site for over 800 years. Located by the river on Bridge St., the cathedral has been rebuilt on several occasions over the centuries, culminating in the restoration work of the Victorian architect Sir Gilbert Scott. The stone baptismal font is virtually the only remnant of the original Norman church. Of interest are a shoemaker's chapel, a cresset stone, several effigies, and a golden rodd (thought to have healing properties in the late Middle Ages). Concerts are held here on occasion throughout the summer. Take the well-marked path (to the left behind the cathedral) back to town via The Struet, a route blessed by ample greenery and the slow-moving River Honddu (Afon Honddu).

The **Brecknock Museum** (tel. 624 121), at the end of The Bulwark (across from the National Park Information Centre), is the finest of the town's museums. An Edwardian naturalist's study leads to an impressive natural history exhibit; upstairs, *Ogham* stones and early sewing machines give way to the town stocks (last officially used in 1826) and the assize court. (Open Mon.-Sat. 10am-5pm. Free.)

Further down The Watton, the **Borders Military Museum** (tel. 623 111) has a Zulu war room filled with guns and uniforms. (Open April-Sept. Mon.-Sat. 9am-

1pm and 2-5pm; Oct.-March Mon.-Fri. Admission 50p.) Boat trips down the tourist-jammed River Brecon (which flows into the River Usk) leave from the bottom of The Watton at 3pm Wed. and Sun. for tours of the mountains. (2½) hr.; £2.50, seniors £1.50; call 628 6382 for information.)

Brecon draws crowds to its **antique fairs** on the second Sunday of every month and craftspeople from all over South Wales hawk their wares in Market Hall on High St. at the **craft fairs** on the third Saturday of every month. The rarer **Jazz Festival,** on the third weekend of every August, really packs the streets for the likes of Gerry Mulligan and Cecil Taylor. Stroller tickets (£22 for the whole weekend, £7-14 for a single day) buy unlimited access to all shows except those separately ticketed (£5-10). You must arrive at least an hour early to guarantee admission to the popular shows, but walking the streets ("strolling") may prove just as entertaining. Additional campsites open on the farms during the festival and buses provide extra service to Cardiff. For more information, contact the Festival Office, Watton Chambers, Brecon, Powys, Wales LD3 7EF (tel. 625 557).

Swansea (Abertawe)

A sprightly coastal shopping town and gateway to the sublime Gower Peninsula, Swansea (SWAN-zee) has not always presented so fresh a face: not long ago, native son Dylan Thomas called Swansea "this ugly lovely town" as he contemplated the thick smoke that decades of copper smelting had draped over the city.

The **Swansea Market,** across the Quadrant from the bus station, provides welcome diversity in an area packed with suburban shopping malls; try the gooseberries or the *laver* bread, an ancient dish made from boiled seaweed which some locals eat lightly fried with bacon while others declare it unfit for human consumption. (Open Mon.-Sat. 8:30am-5:30pm.) Poetry fans should hike the **Dylan Thomas Upland Trail,** which passes by the poet's boyhood haunts. (Pick up the free pamphlet from the tourist office.) Elsewhere in the marina, you'll find the *Katie Ann,* a 500-ton oak trawler, and an array of stained glass studios and workshops. Regarded as the leading art gallery in Wales, the **Glynn Vivian Art Gallery and Museum,** Alexandra Rd. (tel. 550 06), houses an eclectic collection of paperweights, furniture, and clocks, in addition to a fine open-air sculpture park. (Open Mon.-Sat. 10:30am-5:30pm, daily in summer. Free.) For a nape-high dose of horticulture, **Plantasia** (tel. 302 454) in the Parc Tawe Complex off the Strand, maintains 700 varieties of intermittently exotic plants. Twenty pairs of paradisey birds garnish this displaced jungle. (Open daily 10am-7pm. Admission £1.70, seniors and students 85p.)

The new **Dylan Thomas Theatre** (tel. 473 238), along the marina, stages large-scale musical productions (tickets prices vary according to performance). For the entire month of October, the **Swansea Festival** presents a variety of concerts and recitals, while a simultaneous **Fringe Festival** diverts attention from the main event. In mid-August, the area moans and pines with folk musicians from all over the world attending the **Pontardawe International Music Festival,** held in the village of **Pontardawe,** 8 mi. north of Swansea. (Take bus #120 or #125)

For information on Swansea or the Gower Peninsula, visit the **tourist information center,** Singleton St. (tel. 468 321), next to the Quadrant Bus Station. The office books accommodations anywhere in Britain for £1, supplies free maps of the entire peninsula, and stocks the free, glossy *Summer Welcome* and *What's On*—pick up the latter for entertainment listings. (Open Mon.-Sat. 9:30am-5:30pm.) You can change currency at **Thomas Cook,** 3 Union St. (tel. 654 114; open Mon.-Sat. 9:30am-5pm), or at **Travelwise Foreign Exchange,** 1 Plymouth St., next door to the Quadrant Bus Station (tel. 458 072; open Mon.-Sat. 9:30am-5pm). *Samaritans* in Swansea will respond to crises around the clock (tel. 655 999). Swansea's **telephone code** is 0792; the **postal code** is SA1 3QG.

The only cheap accommodation in town can be found at the **YMCA,** 1 The Kingsway, (tel. 652 032), which supplies self-catering single rooms and an on-site fitness center (£8, YMCA Interpoint members £6). Otherwise, the closest youth hostel to Swansea is the **Port Eynon Hostel (IHYF)**, about 16 mi. (1 hr.) out of town by bus (see listing in Gower Peninsula section below). A colony of B&Bs lies west of Swansea, toward Mumbles along Eaton Crescent and Bryn-y-Mor. Catch the Mumbles bus to Oystermouth Rd. at Singleton Park and settle into the deluxe accommodations at the **Oyster Hotel,** 262 Oystermonth Rd. (tel. 654 345); snag a tumbler at the residential bar. (Open Easter-Sept. Singles £14, doubles £13/person.) Lacking a suitable alternative, many people opt to camp along the peninsula.

Swansea is directly connected to most major cities in Britain. **BR** (tel. 467 77) leaves the station on High St. for Cardiff (every ½ hr.; 1 hr.; £5.50), Birmingham (every hr.; £30), and London (every hr.; 2¾ hr.; £32). **National Express** coaches (tel. 470 820) leave every two hours for London (4 hr.; £26.50), Birmingham (4 hr.; £17.50), Manchester (7 hr.; £28), and Cardiff (1 hr. 10 min.; £8). **South Wales Transport** buses cover both the Gower Peninsula and the rest of Wales; a shuttle runs to Cardiff (£4.50). A bus runs between the train station and the Quadrant Bus Station (tel. 475 511) every 30 min. (25p). Various Rover Tickets are available; the **Master Rider** ticket covers most trajectories (£3.80/day, £11.80/week.) Swansea-Cork **ferries** leave from Keys Dock to Cork, in Ireland. (9pm, Sept.-May less frequently; £18, bikes £7. Call 456 116 for information.)

Gower Peninsula

Only 18 mi. long, the fist-like Gower Peninsula pummels the sea with a brute seductiveness even garish tourism cannot mask. Reaching westward from Swansea, its southern coast is dominated by sheer cliffs, headlands, and lovely bays and beaches. Suburbs alternate with tiny stone villages perched on dramatic cliffs. The **Gower Festival** during the last two weeks in July fills the churches all over the peninsula with music. (Call 468 321 for information or contact the Civic Information Centre, Singleton St., Swansea SA1 3QG.)

Getting Around

Buses from Swansea's Quadrant Station cover a fair amount of the peninsula. Buses #1, 2, and 3 depart every 6 min. for Oystermouth Sq. in Mumbles (20 min.; £1.65 return); South Wales Transport bus #18 serves Rhosilli Beach, stopping at Parkmill, Reynoldston, Port-Eynon and Rhosilli (up to 4/day). Frequent buses serve Port Eynon (last bus at 6:45pm; 1 hr.; £3.30 return.) Hitchhiking is perhaps more reliable and quicker than public transport, and it may allow you to see more of the coast. The **Swansea Bikepath** leads directly to Mumbles and continues around the peninsula; the pamphlet *30 Walks in Gower* by Roger Jones outlines scenic hikes.

Accommodations

Campsites and B&Bs cover the entire peninsula at high peak season. The farther west you go, the more likely you are to find camps that are not swarming with tents and caravans.

Guest houses in Mumbles charge £12-15 for B&B; ask at the tourist office for the typed list, not the glossy brochure. **Mrs. Clifton,** 47 Oakland Rd. (tel. 362 310), will make a fuss over you; alternatively, **Dolphin House,** 6 Cornwall Place (tel. 266 435) is 2 houses away from the gorgeous sandy beach (£12.50)

A relatively quiet spot for families and couples, **Three Cliffs Bay Caravan Park,** North Hills Farm, Penmaen, (tel. 371 218) has clean showers and a beautiful campsite overlooking the exquisite Three Cliffs Bay between Mumbles and Port Eynon. Fully equipped on-site shop. (£5.50-£6.50/tent.)

Port Eynon, west of Mumbles, offers both a no-frills hostel and camping right by the beach. The **Port Eynon Hostel (IYHF)** (tel. 390 706) is run by a wind-blown chap who adheres to self-catering, self-entertaining principles. (£5.90, ages 16-20 £4.70. Open March to mid-Oct. Tues.-Sun.) The **Carreglwyd Camping Site** (tel. 371 687) offers somewhat noisy camping amidst arcades (£4).

Sights

In the southeast corner of the Gower Peninsula rests **Mumbles,** a quiet fishing village by day and a raving Gomorrah of student self-indulgence at night. The short stretch of Mumbles Rd. at Mumbles Head is lined with 14 pubs, some of them former haunts of the area's most famous drinker, Dylan Thomas. To hang out on Mumbles Rd. is, in University of Swansea parlance, to "go mumbling," while to start at one end and have a pint at each of the pubs on the road is to "do the Mumble Mile." Flower's, Usher's, or Felin Foel are the local real ales. The **Lovespoon Gallery,** 492 Mumbles Rd. (tel. 360 132) will rap you on the knuckles for thinking that a Welsh lovespoon is a ritualistic wooden absurdity. (From £5. Open Mon.-Sat. 10am-5:30pm.) Standing on a hill that overlooks Mumbles, slack-jawed **Oystermouth Castle,** off Newton St., was built around 1280 by the De Breos family, the same vile clan that in 1175 killed the Welsh lords at Abergavenny Castle. (Open Easter-Sept. daily 11am-5:30pm. Admission 75p, children 35p.)

The Mumbles **tourist office** (tel. 361 302) and the bus stop ride abreast. (Open Mon.-Sat. 9:30am-5:30pm; March and Oct. Mon.-Sat. 10am-4pm.) You can rent bikes from **Mumbles Cycle Hire,** Village Lane, across from the Antelope (tel. 814 290. £1.50/hr., £9/day, £35/week; open daily 10am-sunset). **Gibson's Jetski** (tel. 896 910) stands next door; other types of bicycles and boats are for rent all along the Promenade. For inexpensive food, try the fish specials at the **Oyster Catcher** (tel. 368 286), Mumbles Rd. (open for lunch noon-2pm). **Roots Café,** Queen St. (tel. 366 006), advocates the BYOB (no, not broccoli) method of enjoying vegetarian cuisine (meals under £6; open Mon.-Tues. 11am-5pm, Wed.-Sat. 11am-9pm). Try the homemade traditional Welsh ice cream at **Joe's** on Mumbles Rd.

Three Cliffs Bay and **Southgate-on-Pennard,** on the south coast between Swansea and **Port-Eynon,** are particularly quiet beach areas. From Pennard, Three Cliffs is a 20-min. walk along the Coast Path to a secluded, cave-ridden beach that is utterly stupefying in its beauty. Caswell Bay is the most popular, and is a study in crowding behavior at high tide on a hot day. The walk to the **Parc Le Breos Burial Chamber,** over Green Cwm, is among the most interesting described in *30 Walks in Gower.* Built six millenia ago, the cairn is 70 ft. long and originally held only four bodies. Take the A4118, which will lead you around the peninsula, or bus #18 to the village of Parkmill and then the footpath ½mi. south of the village.

On the westernmost tip of the peninsula, **Rhosilli Beach** is renowned for its hang gliding. Not one for understatement, Dylan Thomas called it "the wildest, bleakest, barrenest" beach he knew. Its size at low tide makes it virtually impossible to overcrowd.

Pembrokeshire Coast National Park

The Pembrokeshire Coast National Park consists of 225 mi. of undisturbed inland scenery, swathed around a single 178 mi. coastal path from Amroth to Cardigan along the western peninsula jutting out into St. Georges Channel. The coast presents hikers with magnificent cliffs, craggy hiking terrain, sheltered beaches and islands teeming with wild birds and breeding seals. Inland, swaths of farmland separate villages like Tenby and St. David's, home of the best Welsh bakers and craftspeople; together, coast and croft capture what is most typical of traditional Welsh culture.

Getting There and Getting Around

The best place from which to enter the region is centrally located Haverfordwest, on the main rail line from London and Cardiff (served every 2 hr.). A rail line also runs to Fishguard, on the north coast (change at Clarbeston Rd.), and to Tenby and Pembroke Dock, on the south coast (change at Whitland). Buses offer more frequent and wide-ranging service than the albeit speedy trains that venture into this area. From Haverfordwest, inexpensive Richards Brothers and Southwest Transport buses run to St. David's (#340, 11/day, last one 6pm; 1 hr.), Tenby

(#358, 1/hr., last one 5:15pm, 1½hr.) and Pembroke (#358, 1/hour, last one 5:40pm; 15 min.). Tenby bus #361 runs to Pembroke (every 2 hr; last 5:15pm, 45 min.).

The Dale Peninsula, southwest of Haverfordwest, is rather poorly serviced by public transport. Your best bets are buses #314 or 315 from Milford Haven. Call Edward Brothers (tel. (0437) 890 230) for schedules. Buses serve the northern portion of the park more frequently, from Broad Haven and Little Haven to Poppit Sands. A-roads lead from Tenby west through Pembroke and then north to Haverfordwest and St. David's. Many hitchers rave about this area.

Practical Information

The **National Park Information Centres** listed below sell 10 annotated maps covering the entire path along the peninsula, printed on convenient plastic cards (20p each, complete set £3). Other pamphlets outline less demanding walks and pony trails in the area (10-20p). The park authorities publish their own coastal path mileage chart and *A Guide for Disabled Visitors* (60p). The free newspaper *Coast to Coast,* published each summer, has details on scheduled walks and tours (half day £1.20, full day £2), as well as on boat trips, park events, riding, fishing, and tide tables. Also available are the indispensable Ordnance Survey maps (£3-4). For walking, try Brian John's *The Pembrokeshire Coast Path* (£7.95). National Park officers can help you plan your hike, and will book you into area youth hostels. **Tourist information centers** also provide advice and book accommodations. Send mail inquiries and requests for publications to the administrative office at National Park Information Services, Country Offices, Haverfordwest, Dyfed, Wales SA61 1QZ (tel. (0437) 45 91, ext. 5133). For **weather information,** call (0834) 813 672, which will also put you in touch with rescue rangers. As always, dial 999 in an emergency.

Broad Haven: National Car Park (tel. (0437) 781 412).

Kilgetty: Kingsmoor Common (tel. (0834) 812 175).

Newport: Bank Cottages, Long St. (tel. (0239) 822 912).

Pembroke: The Drill Hall, Main St. (tel. (0646) 682 148).

Saundersfoot: Harbormaster's Office.

St. David's: City Hall (tel. (0437) 720 392).

Tenby: The Croft (tel. (0834) 24 02).

Fishguard Tourist Information: Hamilton St. (tel. (0348) 873 484).

Haverfordwest Tourist Information: The Old Bridge (tel. (0437) 763 110).

Milford Haven Tourist Information: Town Hall, Hamilton Terrace (tel. (0646) 692 501).

The park is also aflutter with Outdoor Activity Centres, which rent canoes, kayaks, ponies, bicycles and other archaic vehicles; most range from £5 to 15 per day. Pick up two extremely helpful brochures at the tourist office: *Sporting Preseli* and *Preseli on the Water.* Mountain bikes are a popular way to get around the park. Although they cannot be taken on the coastal path (not only illegal but extremely dangerous), paved one-lane roads make great riding and often lead directly to the most secluded beaches. Try **Preseli Mountain Bikes** (tel. (0348) 037 709), in Parcynole Fach) 77 09) outside Haverfordwest. In summer, book ahead (see Twr-y-Felin in St. David's).

Accommodations

IYHF youth hostels are conveniently spaced along the coastal path. The following are all within a reasonable day's walk of one another:

Pentlepoir (tel. (0834) 812 333), north of Tenby (£5.50, ages 16-20 £4.40).

Manorbier (tel. (0834) 871 803), the newly built space station by the Manorbier Castle (£6.60, ages 16-20 £5.40, see Near Tenby for more information).

Marloes Sands (tel. (06465) 662), near the Dale Peninsula (£5.10, ages 16-20 £4).

Broad Haven (tel. (0437) 781 688), on St. Bride's Bay (£6.60, ages 16-20 £5.40).

St. David's (tel. (0437) 720 345; £5.90, ages 16-20 £4.70).

Trevine (tel. (03483) 414), midway between St. David's and Fishguard (£4.40, ages 16-20 £3.50).

Pwll Deri (tel. (03485) 233), just around Strumble Head from Fishguard (£5.50, ages 16-20 £4.40).

The **Poppit Sands hostel** (tel. (0239) 612 936) is 30 mi. past Pwll Deri near Cardigan (£5.90, ages 16-20 £4.70). The popular Broad Haven hostel has 60 beds and the best facilities on the walk, including access for the disabled, as has Manorbier; the smaller hostels in farmhouses are homier and located in more striking locations. Book ahead for hostels in July and August; if you plan out your route in advance, you can book at all of the hostels except Pentlepoir through the Pembrokeshire Coast Central Booking Bureau, c/o Anna Daires, Warden, St. David's Youth Hostel, Whitesands Bay, St. David's, Dyfed, Wales SA62 6PR (tel. (0437) 720 345; £1.75 booking; allow at least 3 weeks).

The roads between Tenby, Pembroke and St. David's are seething with B&Bs which run from £10 for a basic bed to £16-20 for a fancy farmhouse. Yet B&Bs can be hard to secure in Pembrokeshire, especially for the summer. The coast is lined with **campsites,** as many farmers convert fields that are lying fallow into tent sites in summer (usually about £3/tent). Use common sense: always ask first. The youth hostels at Poppit Sands, Pwll Deri, and St. David's also allow camping.

Hiking

For short hikes, stick to the more accessible St. David's Peninsula, in the northwest. Otherwise, set out on the coastal path, which is marked with acorn symbols and covers mostly manageable terrain. The path begins in the southeast at Amroth and continues westward through Tenby to St. Govan's Head, the southernmost point in Pembrokeshire. From here to Elegug Stacks, birds cling to every nook in the rocks; the path passes natural sea arches, mile-wide lily pools at Bosherton, and great limestone stacks. Unfortunately, the 6-mi. stretch from St. Govan's Head past the Stacks to Freshwater West is sometimes used as a shooting range; it is closed to hikers except on weekends and certain evenings. (Contact Pembroke National Park Office.)

From Freshwater West to Angle Bay, the coastline is relatively easy to walk and exceptionally pretty. Some hikers cut directly across the inlet of Milford Haven from Angle or Pembroke, on the south shore of the waterway, to St. Ishmael's, on the Dale Peninsula. Others take a boat ride from Pembroke Dock to explore the magnificent wildlife of the mud flats and woodlands. There is a small break in the path at Milford Haven at the mouth of the extensive inland waterway, a channel which runs for over 25 mi. inland and is geologically known as a "ria" (a drowned river valley).

From the Dale Peninsula, the path passes by the long, clean beaches of St. Bride's Bay, turns up to Newgale, and arrives at the ancient St. David's Head, the site of pre-Cambrian formations and the oldest named feature on the coast of Wales. The spectacular trail continues—past Abereiddy's trilobite fossils, the quarry at Porthgain, the Strumble Head Lighthouse, and on to Fishguard along some of the highest cliffs in Britain. From Fishguard it runs up past Dinas Head and Newport Bay almost all the way to Cardigan, ending at the cliffs of Poppit Sands, just beyond Cemaes Head at the mouth of the River Teifi.

A number of islands freckle the coast. On **Grassholm,** farthest from the shore, 35,000 pairs of gannets nest and raise their young. **Dale Sailing Company** (tel. (0646) 601 636) runs daytrips from Martin's Haven (Mon. and Fri. only; £16, £3 landing fee; reservations required). They also sail to the islands of **Skomer** and **Skokholm,** both marine reserves and breeding grounds for auks and puffins. (Tues.-Sun.; £5, children £3; landing fee £3; no booking necessary.) Seals and rare seabirds live on **Ramsey Island,** farther up the coast. (See St. David's section for more information.) You can hire a boat in almost any harbor; owners who don't officially run services are often receptive to requests.

Tenby (Dinbych y Pysgod)

Nicknamed the "Welsh Riviera," Tenby lacks only a decent Bordeaux and *provençale* cuisine. Its golden, sandy beaches and coastal caves entice travelers from as far away as Cardiff while the scent of bashful perfume wafts over from the monastary on nearby Calday Island.

Arriving and Departing

Getting to Tenby is an unavoidably slow process. Short of driving yourself, catching a bus is probably your best bet; note that no buses run on Sundays. **South Wales Transport/Cleddau** bus #358 arrives hourly from Haverfordwest via Pembroke (Mon.-Sat. until 6pm; £1.60-3). An SWT **Day Tripper** from the Quadrant Bus Station in Swansea leaves at 10:15am in the summer and stops at Oakwood Leisure Park before getting to Tenby (2 hr.; £3.80, children £2.80). **Expresswest** (tel. (0792) 475 511) bus #612 links Tenby with Haverfordwest and Swansea (Mon.-Sat. 3/day) and **Silcox** coaches (tel. 21 89) cover most local routes in conjunction with SWT.

Trains stop at Tenby's meditative station every two hours on weekdays—seven per day on Saturday, and four on Sunday. **BR's** main southern line through Swansea branches at Carmarthen and continues on to Pembroke Dock. Trains arrive from Cardiff (2½ hr.; £10.30), Swansea (1½ hr.; £6.30), Pembroke (30 min.; £2.50), and Carmarthen (45 min.; £4).

Orientation and Practical Information

Tenby extends upwards from the lip of the cliffs to the old town walls known as the Five Arches. High St. runs along the promenade overlooking the beach and leads into Tudor Sq.; Upper Frog St. crouches between High St. and South Parade, which holds the main shopping district. If you walk from the rail station up Warren St. until you see the beach, the tourist information center will be to the left, shops to the right.

Tourist Information Center and National Park Information Centre: The Croft (tel. 24 04), overlooking North Beach. Map of Tenby and Pembroke (15p), bus timetables, and an assortment of coastal path information. Guided town walks and rambles (30p). Accommodations booking, 10% deposit. Open July-Aug. daily 10am-9pm; week before Easter-Oct. daily 10am-5pm.

Bus Station: Arcade, Upper Frog St. Open Mon.-Fri. 9am-5:30pm, Sat. 9am-1pm. Buses leave from the **multi-story car park** at Upper Park Rd. Looking at the posted schedules may be more helpful than calling for information. Open Mon.-Fri. 9am-5:30pm, Sat. 9am-1pm.

Emergency: Dial 999; no coins required.

Financial Services: Barclay's, Tudor Sq. (tel. 46 14). Open Mon.-Fri. 9:30am-3:30pm.

Hospital: Tenby Cottage Hospital, Church Park (tel. 23 03).

Launderette: Washeteria, Lower Frog St. (tel. 24 84). Wash £1.20, dry 20p. Open daily 8:30am-9pm, last wash 8:30pm; Sept.-May daily 10am-6pm.

Pharmacy: Boots, High St. (tel. 21 20), across from St. Mary's Church. Open Mon.-Fri. 9am-9pm, Sat. 9am-5:30pm, Sun. 9am-5:30pm; Sept.-June Mon.-Sat. 9am-5:30pm.

Police Station: Jones Terrace, Warren St. (tel. 23 03), near the church off White Lion St.

Post Office: Warren St. at South Parade (tel. 32 13). Open Mon.-Fri. 9am-12:30pm and 1:30-5:30pm, Sat. 9am-12:30pm. **Postal Code:** 5A70 7JR.

Taxi: Tudor Taxis, (tel. 43 10), 24 hr.

Telephone Code: 0834.

Train Station: Warren St. (tel. 22 48 for information). Open Mon.-Fri. 6:15am-2:30pm, Sat. 6:15am-6pm, Sun. 11:30am-7:30pm.

Accommodations

Ask at the tourist office for the *South Pembrokeshire Holiday Accommodation List* (includes campsites). **Warren Street** has several places in the £12-14 range; **Greenhill Avenue** and its sidestreets, as well as the streets off Esplanade and Trafalgar Rd., are almost as well-endowed. Should these fail you, go one train stop or take a short bus ride to Saundersfoot for a plethora of B&Bs.

Pentlepoir youth hostel (IYHF), The Old School, Pentlepoir (tel. 812 333). Four mi. north of Tenby near Saundersfoot. Take Silcox's Kilgetty bus from Tenby and ask the driver to let you off at the hostel; the last bus leaves Tenby at 6:30pm (½ hr.; 70p). Standard-grade. £5.50, ages 16-20 £4.40.

The Weybourne, 14 Warren St. (tel. 36 41). Spotless rooms with TV and a regular clientele. £11.50.

Frogmore House, Frogmore St. (tel. 45 90), yellow door next to Wishbone's. Right in the center of town, this is the perfect spot for nightlife lovers and walkers who prefer to stay close to the trail. £12.

Ivy Bank Guest House, Harding St. (tel. 23 11) and **Sunnybank Guest House** (tel. 40 34). Bright, flowery rooms, each in a different period style. Singles and doubles £10-15/person. Evening meal available upon request (£6).

Camping: Meadow Farm (tel. 48 29), at the top of The Croft, beyond the tourist office and overlooking North Beach. Plenty of other sites in the area. Follow The Croft up the hill. £4/person.

Food

Tenby has plenty of restaurants. To avoid paying £6 for pub grub, take a picnic to the tiny garden behind St. Mary's Church. You can find cheap eats and picnic supplies at any supermarket on St. Julian St. Open Mon.-Sat. until 5:30pm.

Pam Pam, 2 Tudor Sq. (tel. 29 46). Huge portions all under £5 in a friendly family restaurant with live music 4 nights a week. Open daily 10am-10pm.

Plantagenet Restaurant, Quay Hill (tel. 23 50). Hidden in a romantic 15th-century house on a narrow alley connecting Bridge St. and St. Julian St. Excellent vegetarian and continental fare; quiche with huge salad £4.60. Open daily noon-3:30pm and 6-10:30pm.

The Three Mariners (tel. 28 34), at the corner of St. George and St. Mary St. Tasty pub grub or BBQ burgers for under £1.50. Live music Sun. and Tues. Open Mon.-Sat. noon-11pm, Sun. noon-3pm, 7-10:30pm.

Candy, Crackwell St. (tel. 20 52), in full view of the ocean. Daily special of soup, entree, vegetable, and potato £3.95. Sandwiches £1.40. Open daily 9am-9pm.

Sights

On a sunny day, you'll be tempted to sprawl catatonically on sandy **North Beach** by The Croft or **South Beach,** overlooked by the Esplanade. If you're feeling more adventurous, try **Castle Beach** at the southern tip of Tenby, for cliffs and coastal caves. Just off Castle Hill sits the craggy spur of **St. Catherine's Island,** with an abandoned fort once used as an "early warning" outpost on top; you can wade to the island at low tide. Tide tables are available at the tourist office. A variety of trips are offered around the bay, leaving from the harbor. (45 min.-2 hr. Prices range from £3.50-7; check the boards for the offerings or call 31 79.)

Poised on Castle Hill facing South Beach, the eclectic **Tenby Museum and Picture Gallery** (tel. 28 09) exhibits hundreds of bird's eggs and watercolors of Tenby. (Open Easter-Oct. daily 10am-6pm; Nov.-Easter Mon.-Fri. 10am-4pm. Admission 60p, seniors 50p, children 30p.) The National Trust runs the **Tudor Merchant's House,** Quay Hill (tel. 22 79), a restored 15th-century home with period furnishings and fine early frescoes. (Open Easter-Oct. Mon.-Fri. 11am-6pm, Sun. 2-6pm. Admission £1.25, seniors and children 60p.)

To the south lies **Caldy Island,** site of an active Cistercian monastery that was established in the 5th century. Now the land harbors fish ponds, medieval buildings, and a community of monks who produce perfume, dairy products, and chocolate, sold on an island shop. Anyone may visit the island, but only men may enter the monastery. Free informal tours are available. Check at the post office, where the boat comes in; it acts as the island's tourist office. **Caldy Boats** (tel. 26 90) sail from the harbor to the island (late May-Sept. Mon.-Fri. every 15 min. 9:45am-5:30pm; £4, seniors and children £3). Check at the quay for fishing trips (tackle included in prices; call 29 49 for details).

Near Tenby

Five mi. northwest of Tenby, right in between Pembroke and Tenby, rest the imposing ruins of **Carew Castle** (tel. (0646) 651 782). A strange and handsome stronghold built in the late 11th-century, it was enlarged in the 15th century for use as a dwelling. Nearby, a **tidal mill** dating from 1558 (one of only three in Britain) turns quietly alongside a medieval bridge and a 13-ft. 11th-century Celtic cross. (Open Easter-Oct. Mon.-Sat. 10am-5pm. Admission to mill and castle £1.75, children £1.15. Admission to castle only 90p, seniors 60p.) Take Silcox bus #360 from Tenby to Carew Cross (Mon.-Sat., every 2 hr.).

B&Bs and camping sites line the roads between Tenby and Pembroke. In **Jameston,** the village next door to Manorbier, the **Elm House** (tel. 871 888), on the main road in the center of the village, will make you feel right at home; it is the least expensive accommodation in Pembrokeshire (singles £10, doubles £8/person). The national park organizes guided walks in the area, outlined in their free seasonal publication *Coast to Coast,* available at information centers in the main towns.

Manorbier Castle (tel. 823 94) lies 5 mi. southwest of Tenby with a beach below its ramparts. Take Silcox bus #59, South Wales Transport bus #358, or BR to the slightly more remote, unmanned train station. Trains run every 2 hours from Tenby, Pembroke and Haverfordwest. (Open Easter-Sept. daily 10:30am-5:30pm. Admission £1.20, seniors and children 60p.) Manorbier also has a new space-age, deluxe **youth hostel (IYHF)** at Skrinkle Haven (tel. 871 803). Spotless laundry facilities and rigorously hot showers might make a traveler wonder how this complex landed in the middle of the desolate Pembroke farmland. (Open daily; Feb.-June and Sept.-Oct. Mon.-Sat.; £6.60, ages 16-20 £5.40.) From the Manorbier train station, walk up past the A4139 to the castle, make a left onto the B4585 and then a right up to the army camp and follow hostel signs.

Pembroke (Penfro) and Pembroke Dock

A Norman castle towers above the town and trails an ancient, crumbling trickle of a wall through Pembroke. The twin town, Pembroke Dock, is not as blue-blooded; once a royal dockyard, today its greatest attraction is the ferry to Rosslare, Ireland. Both towns are stepping stones to the Pembrokeshire National Park, but Pembroke is the more popular spot to stay.

Arriving and Departing

Silcox buses leave from the front of the castle in Pembroke for Water St. in Pembroke Dock every half hour (Mon.-Sat.; last bus around 10pm). Silcox also runs bus #361 to and from Tenby (Mon.-Sat. 4-5/day). **Expresswest** buses leave for Tenby from the Gateway Supermarket, Main St., four times daily, with connections north to Haverfordwest and east to Swansea, Cardiff, and Bristol. Fares are more expensive than Silcox's, but the trips take less time. **Cleddau Buses** (tel. (0437) 32 84), the local branch of South Wales Transport, connects the Pembrokes with Haverfordwest more frequently, less expensively, and infinitely more slowly than Expresswest. Pembroke Dock lies at the end of a **BR** western branch line that splits at Whitland. Six trains run daily from Pembroke Dock to destinations in England, passing through Pembroke and Tenby. To get elsewhere in western Wales, take buses to avoid the rail back-track to Whitland.

Orientation and Practical Information

Beginning at the castle, Pembroke's Main St. writhes salmon-like up the hill; it ends at the train station and the road out of town to Tenby and the rest of Pembrokeshire. Main St. is lined on either side with craft shops, cafés and an occasional B&B.

National Park Information Centre: Pembroke Castle entrance (tel. 682 148), Drill Hall. Coastal path maps, guides, and pamphlets. Supplies the *South Pembrokeshire Holiday Accommodation List* (free). Open Easter-Sept. Mon.-Sat. 9:30am-1pm and 2-5:15pm.

Buses: Buses stop across from the castle in Pembroke and at **Silcox Garage,** Pembroke Dock (tel. 683 143). Call for information Mon.-Fri. 9am-5pm.

Cruises: Flying Fish, Pembroke Dock (tel. 685 627). 3½-hr. bay cruises £6, seniors £3.

Emergency: Dial 999; no coins required.

Ferries: B&I Line (tel. 684 161) runs 2 ships daily from Pembroke Dock to Rosslare, Ireland. Ferries depart at 2:45am and 2:15pm (4¼ hr.). Walk-on passengers £19.50 each way. Children under 16 ½-fare, under 5 free. Duty-free day trips, hand luggage only, £10 return/family, individual £5. Book at May's Travel, Pembroke Dock (see listing below), or call B&I.

Financial Services: Barclay's, Main St. (tel. 684 996). Open Mon.-Fri. 9:30am-4:30pm.

Hospital: South Pembrokeshire (tel. 682 114), Pembroke Dock.

Launderette: New Way, off Main St., Pembroke, just before East Back Rd. Open daily until 8pm.

Police: Water St. (tel. 682 121), Pembroke Dock.

Post Office: 49 Main St., Pembroke (tel. 682 737). Open Mon.-Fri. 9am-12:30pm and 1:30-5:30pm, Sat. 9am-12:30pm. **Postal Code:** SA71 4JT.

Telephone Code: 0646.

Train Station: Dimond St. E., Pembroke Dock (tel. 68 48 96). Staffed only around departure or arrival times. Pembroke station at the end of Main St., unstaffed.

Travel Information: May's Travel Agency, 53 Dimond St. E., Pembroke Dock (tel. 682 090), next to the train station. Train and ferry information and bookings. Open Mon.-Fri. 9am-5:30pm, Sat. 9am-noon. **Redwing Travel,** 4 Main St. (tel. 621 021). BR, buses and boats. Open Mon.-Fri. 9am-5:30pm, Sat. 9am-noon.

Accommodations and Food

Finding a room in Pembroke is difficult only during the height of the summer season when streams of spawning tourists and hikers heading for the coastal path crest the already steady wave of travelers arriving on the ferry from Rosslare. It is advisable to book ahead between July and September.

Try **Merton Place House,** 3 East Back (tel. 684 796), for pleasant rooms in a Georgian townhouse. The winsome walled garden off the back has private access to the handsome millpond (£15). The **High Noon Guest House,** Lower Lampley Rd. (tel. 683 736), is a 5-min. walk to town (£12.50). A ½-mi. trek from the town center, **Mr. and Mrs. Phillips,** The Glen, Lower Lampley Rd. (tel. 683 194), maintain one truly magnificent double and shower their guests with individual attention. (£11/person). In Pembroke Dock, the **Fleur de Lis Guest House,** 26 Water St. (tel. 684 778), has washbasins and evening meals in every room (£12.50).

The restaurants in Tenby know very well that hungry tourists will gobble anything within reach. Skip the "best fish and chips" next to the castle and check the faded lunch menu at the **King's Arms Hotel** (tel. 683 611), across the street. Enjoy shark in soy sauce or monkfish sautéed in garlic and butter with bread and salad for a mere £3.30. (Open daily; lunch between noon and 2pm.) **Richmond Restaurant** (tel. 685 460), next to the castle, serves tea, baked goods, and lunch, and sports an all-you-can-eat salad bar (£3.50). (Open Mon.-Sat. 9am-4:45pm, evenings Thurs.-Sat. 7-10pm.) **The Granary,** 16 Main St. (tel. 682 889), offers wholesome foods in a nonsmoking environment. At **Cromwell's Tavern,** you can admire the man's handiwork across the street. Supermarkets lie on Main St. and out by the train station.

Sights

Pembroke Castle (tel. 681 510), at the head of Main St., is the birthplace and home of Henry VII and among the most impressive fortresses in South Wales. Its 80-ft. keep dates from the 13th century. The cavernous **Great Keep** is now home to the Greater Horseshoe Bat; the **Wogan Cavern** is down several flights of stairs from the chancery entrance. The mill pond, directly beneath the castle walls, amuses coots and cormorants. (Castle open April-Sept. daily 9:30am-6pm; March and Oct. daily 10am-5pm; Nov.-Feb. Mon.-Sat. 10am-4pm. Admission £1.50, seniors 80p. Summer tours Mon.-Sat. 4 times/day; 50p.)

Pembroke swells with churches: have a look at 12th-century **St. Daniel's Church,** St. Daniel Hill, at the southern end of the town, by the train station; **St. Mary's Church,** on Main St., with its 13th-century windows; or **Monkton Priory Church,** Monkton St., which has a hagioscope—a wall-slit that enabled **leprous monks** to watch the service at the altar.

In the **Museum of the Home,** 7 Westgate Hill (tel. 681 200) past the castle, masses of household gadgets trace the history of the common home from the 16th century to the present. Items include an ivory and tortoise shell tongue-scraper ("for removing excesses of poor claret"). (Open Easter-Oct. 10:30am-5:30pm. Sun.-Wed. and Fri. Admission £1, seniors and children 70p.) And for only 50p, you can make your own medieval Welsh coin at the **History and Bronze Rubbing Shop,** Main St., next door to the tourist center.

St. David's (Tyddewi)

St. David's, one of the smallest villages in Great Britain, serenely occupies a picturesque area only slightly larger than the grounds of the magnificent cathedral for which it is named: **St. David's Cathedral** gently lures its visitors down the 39 steps that connect it to the town. (Cathedral open 7am-7pm. Suggested donation £1.) Explore the ruins of the gigantic **bishop's palace,** next to the cathedral, built by ambitious Bishop Gower in the 14th century and last used in 1633. (Open April-Oct. daily 9:30am-6:30pm; Oct.-March Mon.-Sat. 9:30am-4pm and Sun. 2-4pm. Admission £1.50, seniors, students and children 90p.) In summer, you can take a boat trip to **Ramsey Island** and observe the domestic chores of birds, seals, and red deer. Boats leave from the lifeboat station at St. Justinian's two to four times daily, depending on the season and demand, and sometimes according to posted timetables in town and at the dock (£5, £3 optional landing fee; tel. 721 423).

The **National Park Information Centre,** City Hall, High St. (tel. 720 392), at the corner of New St., has pamphlets on St. David's and the many beautiful walks in the vicinity of the town, photographic displays, and maps. (Open Easter-Oct. daily 9:30am-5:30pm.) St. David's postal code is SA62 6SW, its telephone code 0437. Stay the night at **St. David's youth hostel (IYHF),** Whitesands Bay (tel 720 345), 2½ mi. from town (open March-July and Sept.-Oct. Fri.-Wed.; Aug. daily. £5.90, ages 16-20 £4.70.) or at the **Trevine youth hostel (IYHF),** 11 Ffordd-y-Afon (tel. (0348) 834 14), in a village ½mi. from the coastal path; take fishguard bus Richards's #411. (Open March-July and Sept.-Oct. Sat.-Thurs., Aug. daily. £4.40, ages 16-20 £3.50.) B&Bs are clustered in the center of town on **High Street, New Street,** and **Nun Street.** You can camp at the **Glan-y-mor Tent Park,** Caerfai Bay Rd. (tel. 721 788), just off the A487, about ½mi. toward Haverfordwest. (£4/site.) Head to the tea rooms for an affordable opportunity to sample Welsh specialties. Try the **Iron Kettle Tea Room** on High St. for a Welsh tea (£2), which includes Welsh cakes (small versions of scones) and the ever-delicious, ever-adored Bara Brith.

To reach St. David's, take the A487 from Haverfordwest, or catch a Richards Bros. bus (#132; 8/day; 1 hr.). Buses from St. David's or Haverfordwest run to Fishguard (#411 every 2 hr.; 1 hr.), Cardigan (#412 every 2 hr.; 1½ hr.), and Aberystwyth. Buses rarely rev on Sundays.

St. David's to Cardigan

Though Cardigan itself is fairly inhospitable, multiple minor sights along the stretch of coast to the south of the town merit a visit. Five Richard Bros. buses run from Fishguard and Haverfordwest to Cardigan and back every day except Sundays (bus #412, 10/day until 6pm; 1½ hr. for the whole trip).

Cilgerran Castle (tel. 615 136), south of Cardigan off the A478, is fairly well preserved and open to the public. Its massive drum towers are visible high above the Teifi gorge. (Open April-Oct. Mon.-Sat. 9:30am-6:30pm, Sun. 2-6:30pm. Admission £1.25, seniors 75p.) Midway Motors (tel. (0239) 831 279) run five or six buses a day from Finch Sq. to the castle (10 min.).

The tiny town of **St. Dogmaels,** 2½ mi. west of town between Cardigan and Poppit Sands, houses the ruins of a 12th-century Benedictine abbey (open 24 hr.; free), **Y Felin** (a working flour mill), and the spunky **Sagram's Stone**—an *ogham* stone engraved with the old Irish alphabet translated into Latin. The post office holds the key to the church; anyone polite should be able to secure it. Bus #407 leaves Cardigan's Finch Sq. for St. Dogmael's 10 times per day till 6pm (15 min.).

Several miles west of Cardigan, past St. Dogmaels, you can eat your meals as you gaze out over the sea at the **Poppit Sands youth hostel (IYHF)** (tel. 612 936). The laid-back warden Mike will recount a multitude of local legends, wake you up with Tchaikovsky, and may even let you drop your pack during "lockout" hours (£5.90). Camping on the grounds is permitted, and the hostel rents mountain bikes (£5/day). From July through September, bus #404 leaves Finch Sq. in Cardigan at 11am, 1pm, 2:10pm, and 5:15pm, and drops you at the ½-mi. uphill stretch that leads to the hostel. Otherwise take the bus to St. Dogmaels, 1½ mi. away from the hostel; follow the beach to Poppit Sands and walk up the hill, and up, and up... Turn right at the snail-shaped bush. Farther down the road to Fishguard stands the Iron Age fort at **Castell Henllys** (tel. 319 023 979), where archaeologists are hard at work uncovering prehistoric coffee cups and other traces of life. (Open March-Sept. 10am-6pm.)

The castle in **Newcastle Emlyn,** southeast of Cardigan, is disappointingly ruined, but the **Felin Geri** flour mill offers various events from hot-air ballooning to falconry. The town crier announces Friday's market.

Cardigan (Aberteifi), allegedly the second poorest city in Britain, lies at the northeastern edge of the Pembrokeshire Coast National Park, 19 mi. northeast of Fishguard. The **tourist information center** (tel. 613 230) is housed in the Theatr Mwldan; the staff will book beds (10% deposit) or give instruction on Welsh taste and manners. (Open daily Easter-Oct. 10am-6pm; Nov.-Easter Mon.-Sat. 9am-5pm.) Check

Gwbert Rd., off the top of North Rd., for B&Bs. Cardigan's **telephone code** is 0239, and the **postal code** is SA43 1JH.

Aberystwyth

Positioned at the center of Wales' sweeping Cardigan Bay coastline, Aberystwyth's elaborate pier and promenade hark back to the town's heyday as a Victorian seaside resort. Unlike the castle ruins overlooking South Beach, the town has risen with the times; pastel townhouses accommodate the life and excitement of not-so-Victorian students. Nevertheless, the town remains a center of Welsh heritage, stored and perpetuated at the National Library and in the country's first college.

Arriving and Departing

Aberystwyth (abber-IST-with) is a hubcap for travel by bus or train to all of Wales. The city rests at the western end of the mid-Wales rail line that cuts across the land to Shrewsbury (7/day, Sun. 2/day; 2 hr.; £18.70). To rail destinations north along the coast, change at Machynlleth (8/day, Sun. 5/day; 30 min.; £3.50). **Crosville Buses** (tel. 617 951), headquartered in Aberystwyth, run south to Cardigan (#550, hourly until 6:30 pm; £2.90) and north to Machynlleth (#2 and #514, hourly till 9pm; £3.50). Crosville offers Day Rover tickets (£3.50) and the better-value Week Rover passes (£9.25). The North and Mid-Wales Rail Rover is valid on both buses and trains everywhere north of the imaginary Aberystwyth-Shrewsbury line (£28, £18 with Disabled, Senior, or Young Persons Railcards).

Orientation and Practical Information

Buses arrive and depart from outside the rail station on Alexandra Rd. From the station, walk up Terrace Rd. five short blocks to the ocean; the **tourist office** is at the top.

Aberystwyth's commercial center sprawls above the rocky coastline along Penglais Rd. to the east of town, somewhat removed from the university. The tourist center is back towards the beach, at the top of Terrace Rd. Great Darkgate St. and North Parade parallel the beach at the center of town. Terrace Rd. and Pier St. contain most of the shops and restaurants.

Tourist Information Center: Terrace Rd. (tel. 612 125). Chipper, helpful staff. Beds booked free within Wales, £1.95 outside Wales (10% deposit). Dossiers of B&B photos and current rates for your perusal. Open daily 10am-6pm; Nov.-Easter Mon.-Thurs. 10am-5pm, Fri. 10am-4:30pm.

Bus Station: Crosville Buses, Alexandra Rd. (tel. 617 951). Local bus information, National Express and Rover tickets. Pick up a newspaper of schedules in the tourist office. Buses arrive at and embark from points on Alexandra Rd.—check signs. Open Mon.-Fri. 8:45am-4:45pm, Sat. 9am-12:15pm.

Crisis: Samaritans, 5 Trinity Rd. (tel. 624 535).

Early Closing Day: Wed. at 1pm.

Emergency: Dial 999; no coins required.

Financial Services: Barclay's, corner of North Parade and Terrace Rd. Open Mon.-Sat. 9:30am-4:30pm.

Hospital: Bronglais General Hospital, Caradoc Rd. (tel. 623 131), uphill from the town.

Launderette: Wash-n-Spin-n-Dry, Bridge St. Wash (£1.20)-n-Spin-n-Dry (20p for 5 min.). Open Mon.-Sat. 8am-8:30pm, Sun. 9am-1pm.

Market Day: Mon.-Fri. in Market Hall, St. James' Sq., 9am-5:30pm; cattle on Mon.

Pharmacy: Boots, Pier St. (tel. 612 292). Open Mon.-Sat. 9am-5:30pm.

Police: tel. 612 791, off Victoria Terr.

Post Office: 8 Great Darkgate St. (tel. 612 298). Open Mon.-Fri. 9am-5:30pm, Sat. 9am-12:30pm. **Postal Code:** SY23 1AA.

Rape Crisis: tel. 61 11 24.

Taxi: Express tel. 62 3 19; 24 hr.

Telephones: Marine Terr., by the pier, and on almost every corner in town. **Telephone Code:** 0970.

Train Station: BR, Alexandra Rd. (tel. 612 377). Information window staffed Mon.-Fri. 9am-5pm, Sat. 10:30am-6:30pm. **Vale of Rheidol Railway** (tel. (0685) 48 54) in the BR Station.

Accommodations and Camping

Aberystwyth's waterfront swims with expensive B&Bs (£16-30); cheaper establishments lie closer to the town center. There is a fairly wide selection around Sea View Pl., Bridge St., and Rheidol Terrace.

IYHF youth hostel, 9 mi. north in Borth (tel. (0970 871 498). Surrounding beaches are good, but the hostel is often full. Take the train to Borth Station (Mon.-Sat. 10/day, Sun. 5/day; 10 min.) or Crosville bus #512 from Aberystwyth (Mon.-Sat. every hr.; £6.30, ages 16-20 £5.10). Open April-Sept. daily; March and Oct. Fri.-Wed.

YWCA, 28 North Parade (tel. 615 143), 2 blocks from the rail station. Women only. Hygienic, centrally-located dormitory. No curfew, but visitors must leave by 11pm. Access to superior kitchen, including microwave; showers (10p); bring your own toilet paper. Singles £6.

Mrs. E. V. Williams, 28 Bridge St. (tel. 612 550). Engaging proprietor prepares a full Welsh breakfast, tea, biscuits and Welsh cakes. Large, well-furnished rooms you can lose yourself in. £10.

Myrddin, 11 Rheidol Terr. (tel. 624 876). Cozy rooms in an old coastal house. The lounge overlooking the sea facilitates hours of contemplation. TV and tea-making facilities in all rooms, most with view. Open June-Aug. £12.

Alexandra Hall, Victoria Terr. (tel. 612 415), at the end by the Cliff Railway. Funk and grunge in a surreal shadowy dormitory built as the first housing for women students in Britain. Though the cheapest place, it is neither the cleanest nor the safest. Spectacular views over the ocean nonetheless. Access to kitchen and showers. £5 bed; £7 with linen 1st night, £6 each night thereafter. "Luxury suites" with TV and coffee-making equipment, £8.50.

Camping: Midfield Caravan Park (tel. 612 542), 1½ mi. from town center on the A4120, 200 yd. uphill from the junction with the A487. The most pleasant campsite in the area, with an excellent view of town and the hills. High season £4.80/tent, low season £3.80. Walkers and cyclists may be charged less. **Aberystwyth Holiday Village,** Pendarcan Rd. (tel. 624 211). Slightly closer to town and better suited to families and couples.

Food and Pubs

Take-away is both surprisingly cheap on Pier St. and open on Sundays. Try the two Chinese restaurants or the cafeteria-style **Dolphin Fish Bar** (take-away crunchy buttered fish and chips, £2.85). The **Lo-Cost Supermarket** on Terrace Rd. and **Gateway's,** behind the railway station, sell napkins.

Y Graig Wholefood Café, 34 Pier St. (tel. 611 606). Passionfruit juice in a colorful hole in the wall. Dishes for vegans, vegetarians, and carnivores (under £4). Tie-dyed T-shirts and political postcards for sale. Try the peace buns, Y Graig's answer to the popular "hot cross" variety. Open Mon.-Sat. 9am-11:30pm, Sun. 2pm-11:30pm.

The Cabin Coffee Bar, Pier St. (tel. 417 398) at Eastgate. The walls read like a history of Hollywood machismo—Bogie and Cagney glare into your gourmet coffee. Sandwiches (£1.50). Open Mon.-Sat. 9am-5:30pm; July-Aug. also Sun., same hours.

Connexion, Bridge St. (tel. 615 350). Macramé and Aubrey Beardsley. Vegetarian dishes £5. In a masticatory rage, get the "Carpet Bagger," a 9 oz. steak braised with oysters, for £9.50. Dinner daily 7-10pm.

As it's been a while since we tipped the old file cabinet, you might be pleased to learn that at last report there were 42 **pubs** in Aberystwyth. Aberystwyth's swarm of crazy college kids keep the pubs and multitudinous arcades along the pier buzzing. **T.J.'s Video Bar** on Great Darkgate St. blasts armor-piercing bullets of music at its clientele; for more of the same, try **Streets,** on Victoria Terr., or **Skinners,** off Great Darkgate St. The rowdy crowd vents spleen at the **Angel** next door, and the rugby team packs it in at the **Black Lion,** Bridge St.

Sights

Aberystwyth's charming *fin-de-siècle* pier has been abducted by the rogues of the tourist trade: arcades and unappealing restaurants. The beachfront and promenade remain much as they were in Victorian times, and pastel townhouses still lend the town a peaceful, aristocratic air. At the south end of the promenade stands the university's **Old College,** a Neo-Gothic patchwork structure opened in 1877 as Wales' first university. Next door stands **St. Michael's Church,** where you can climb the tower for a view of Cardigan Bay. If you haven't had enough of Victorian Aberystwyth, check out the "Aberystwyth Yesterday" exhibit above the train station. Once the site of a city dance hall, the building now houses a collection of luggage, clothes, pharmaceuticals and sepia photographs—there's even a stereoscope you can try (open daily 10am-5pm; free).

Edward I built **Aberystwyth Castle** in 1277 after defeating the last native prince of Wales, LLywelyn ap Gruffydd. Explosive-toting Cromwell dropped by in 1649 and made quick work of the diamond-shaped fortress. The ruins on the hill are perfect for climbing, hiding, and seeking, and they offer a free view of the coastline. At the other end of the promenade, the **Electric Cliff Railway** (tel. 617 642), "a conveyance for gentlefolk since 1896," will whisk you to the top of **Constitution Hill** to see the Camera Obscura gazebo, an enormous wide-lens telescope which offers dizzying views of the town. (Open daily 10am-6pm, July-Aug. 10am-9pm train every 10 min. Last entry to Camera Obscura 5:30pm. Railway fare return £1.85, seniors £1. Admission to Camera Obscura free.) You can climb halfway up the hill to the **Welsh National Centre for Children's Literature,** housed in a former monastery. (Call the Welsh Books Council at 624 455 for an appointment, Mon.-Fri. 9am-5pm.) Back in town, the **Ceredigion Museum,** Terrace Rd. next to the tourist office, has an eyebrow-raising collection of marquetry—pictures created from a mosaic of wood inlay and natural veneers. (Open Mon.-Sat. 10am-5pm. Free.)

The **National Library of Wales** (tel. 623 816), off Penglais Rd., houses nearly all books and manuscripts written in or pertaining to Wales, including almost all of the surviving medieval Welsh manuscripts, from the tales of the *Mabinogion* to the first Welsh translation of the Bible. (Open Mon.-Fri. 9:30am-6pm, Sat. 9:30am-5pm. Free.) A short climb farther up the hill brings you to the plush **Theatre Y Werin,** which sponsors a fine Welsh repertory company and a film program.

Near Aberystwyth

The **Vale of Rheidol Railway** (tel. (0685) 48 54), the only steam-operated line in the BR network, climbs and twists its way inland from Aberystwyth to the waterfalls and gorges of **Devil's Bridge** (Easter-Sept. 4 trains/ day; 8/day Mon.-Fri. in Aug.; 3 hr. round trip; £9). The two upper bridges were constructed in 1708 and 1901 over the waterfalls; the lower bridge, attributed to the Architect of Evil, was probably built by Cistercian monks from the nearby **Strata Florida Abbey** in the 11th century. Paths are turnstile operated, so take some change. The steps of Jacob's Ladder (50p) descend into the depth of the Devil's Punchbowl gorge, cross the torrent on an arched footbridge, and climb back beside the waterfall to the road. The hostel closest to the gorge is the **Ystumtuen youth hostel (IYHF)** (tel. (097085) 693), near the end of the railway off the A44 in Ponterwyd, with simple-grade accommodations. (£4.40, ages 16-20 £3.50. Open March-Oct.)

North Wales

North Wales is even more fiercely nationalistic, linguistically separate, and culturally independent of England than is South Wales. Its varied topography and vegetation enhance this sense of distinctiveness. From atop the hills of Snowdonia, the vast English flatlands appear soft and placid, in sharp contrast with the jagged and uneven Welsh hills to the west. You may want to avoid the crowded castles and resort towns of the northern coast by heading inland to the mountain footpaths and hamlets of Snowdonia National Park, which covers the larger part of North Wales. Mount Snowdon itself, at 3560 ft., is the highest, barest, and most precipitous peak in England or Wales. Other ranges, such as the Glyders or Cader Idris, challenge blissfully smaller numbers of serious hikers. To the southwest of Snowdonia, the largely unspoiled Llyn Peninsula attracts visitors to its sandy beaches; to the northwest the Isle of Anglesey sends ferries to Ireland; and to the east languishes the lush Vale of Conwy. Llangollen, near the English border, hosts the International Eistedfodd in July, a week-long singing festival attended by over 30 countries.

Edward I's castles form a ring, now more touristy than defensive, around North Wales. After defeating Llewelyn in 1282, Edward, the only native Prince of Wales, built these castles as quickly as he could, importing thousands of English laborers. Four fortresses—at Harlech on Cardigan Bay, Caernarfon and Beaumaris on opposite sides of the Menai Strait between the mainland and the Isle of Anglesey, and Conwy on the north coast—demonstrate the increasing sophistication of concentric fortification that gave the English such strength in hostile territory. Harlech Castle, briefly taken from the English by the rebel Welsh prince Owain Glyndwr, is the loveliest and least crowded of this ring of fortresses. The rubble of Criccieth and Dolbadarn mournfully mark Welsh defeats.

Getting Around

North Wales has impressively efficient bus service. If you plan to travel nearly every day, buy a **Crosville Rover** ticket, good north of Aberystwyth and as far east as Chester. (**Week Rover** £6.50; **Day Rover** £2.90.) Bear in mind that few bus routes operate on Sunday. Pick up the Crosville bus timetables for all of north and mid-Wales at any bus station or tourist office.

There are two main **rail lines** in North Wales. One runs from Holyhead on the Isle of Anglesey along the northern coast to Chester; the other begins in Pwllheli on the Llyn Peninsula and runs along the Cambrian coast south to Aberystwyth. Other **British Rail** lines run from Llandudno Junction near Conwy on the north coast to Blaenau Ffestiniog, where a narrow-gauge train runs through lyrical scenery to Porthmadog; and from Machynlleth on Cardigan Bay east across Wales to Shrewsbury in England. The **North Wales Day Ranger** (good Sun.-Fri. after 9:30am) includes travel between Holyhead and Chester and between Llandudno and Blaenau Ffestiniog (£10.50). The **Conwy Valley Evening Ranger** covers travel after 4pm between Bangor and Prestabyn and between Llandudno and Blaenau Ffestiniog (£3.20). The **Cambrian Coast Day Ranger** takes care of travel between Machynlleth, Aberystwyth and Pwllheli (£10). There are no reductions on regional tickets for railcard holders. The **North and Mid-Wales Rover** is valid for all travel within the Aberystwyth-Shrewsbury-Crewe area, including free travel on the Ffestiniog Railway. (Trains and buses £30, railcard holders £19.80.)

Bikers should obtain a copy of the indispensable *Cyclists Guide to North Wales;* bicycles can be rented from the occasional dealer. Betws-y-Coed, Llanberis, and Shrewsbury all make good bases.

There are 20 youth hostels in North Wales. Many of the hostels in Snowdonia are off the beaten track and primarily serve hikers, but Bangor, Llandudno, Llangollen, and Colwyn Bay all have hostels in easy range. You can book B&Bs at town tourist offices for 10% of the cost of a night, which will then be deducted from your bill.

Machynlleth

An 18 mi. ride north from Aberystwyth will take you through the lush Dovey valley to Machynlleth (ma-HUN-hleth; pop. 2000), a scenic market town at the head of the River Dyfi estuary. Since the 13th century, Machynlleth has thrived as the region's most important commercial center; more recently, the town has edged into the vanguard of Britain's technology industry. Here, where Owain Glyndwr crowned himself Prince of Wales and the land's first autonomous parliament was convened, the Centre for Alternative Technology calls attention to a future of conservation and green politics.

The town's architecture has been richly diversified by over seven centuries of prosperous inhabitants; its streets are studded with fine examples of late Georgian townhouses, quaint timber-built cottages, and a handful of medieval buildings constructed from shards of deep-blue rubblestone mined in the surrounding hills. The **Castlereagh Memorial Clocktower,** a fanciful bit of masonry bequeathed to the town in 1873 by the Marquess of Londonderry, stands at the corner of Penrallt St., just down the road from the rail station. Rub brasses or read up on Glyndwr's rebellion at the **Owain Glyndwr Interpretive Centre,** Maengwyn St. (tel. 28 27), in Owain Glyndwr's Parliament House of 1404 (50p-£2/rubbing; open daily 10am-5pm). The gates across the street open into **Plas Machynlleth,** a quiet path and picnic area redolent of grazing sheep. The weekly Wednesday **market** lines the town's two main streets, selling sweaters, food, and housewares.

Three mi. north of town hovers the innovative **Centre for Alternative Technology;** walk along the scenic, untraveled old road, or take Gwynedd bus #34, 59 or 2 and ask the driver to stop at the center. The 15-year-old center calls itself a "village of the future;" conservation, recycling, pollution-free power, and communal living bear this motto out. A wholefood **café** inside serves fabulous meals for about £2.80. (Open daily 10am-5pm. Admission £3, seniors and students £2.10, children £1.30. YHA members receive an extra discount.)

At the **tourist office,** (tel. 702 401) on Maengwyn St., down the road from the town's Clocktower, hitchhikers can get a cardboard sign that publicizes where they're going or book a B&B. (10% deposit. Open daily 9am-6pm; Oct.-Easter Mon.-Fri. 9am-5pm.) From the rail station, follow Doll St. and veer right at the church onto Penrault St. and continue until you see the clock tower. Everything you need is left on Maengwn St. The **post office** (tel. 25 23) stands opposite a row of exotic **telephone booths.** (Post office open Mon.-Fri. 9am-1pm and 2-5:30pm, Sat. 9am-12:30pm.) **Early closing day** is Thursday. Machynlleth's **postal code** is SY20 8AF; the **telephone code** is 0654. In an emergency, dial 999 (no coins required).

Though the youth hostel in nearby Corris has closed, you can still find reasonably priced accommodations in and around Machynlleth. **Pendre Guest House** (tel. 702 088), in town on Maengwyn St., charges £13 for huge rooms with friendy wicker furniture. **Mrs. A. Fleming,** Heol Powys (tel. 702 662), parallel to Maengwyn St., will cheerfully lead you to a comfortable paisley bedroom (£10). For camping, try Warren Park (tel. 702 054) in Penegoes (£8/tent), or head out on the Dolgeddan road to **Llwyngwern Farm** (tel. 702 492), near the Centre for Alternative Technology. You can rent **bikes** at Joyrides, The Old Station. (Touring bikes £9/day, £45/week; mountain bikes £10 and £50; open daily 9am-5pm; New Year's-Easter Sun.-Wed. and Fri. 9am-5pm.)

Machynlleth pubs offer nothing spectacular in the way of afforable gluttony. Stock up on oat groats at the **Quarry Shop Café,** 13 Maengwn St. (tel. 702 624), an environmentally-conscious vegetarian restaurant; daily specials (£3.50); baked potato with cheese (£1.20). (Open July-Aug. daily 9:30am-5pm, Sept.-June Fri.-Wed. 9:30am-4pm, Thurs. 9:30am-2pm.)

British Rail (call 702 311 for information) runs to Machynlleth from Shrewsbury (8/day, Sun. 4/day; 1½ hr.; £11), Aberystwyth (9/day, Sun. 5/day; ½ hr.; £3.50), and Harlech (6/day; 2½ hr.; £6.40). **Crosville** bus #2 connects Machynlleth and Aberystwyth (Mon.-Sat. 4/day; return £3.50; if you plan to go any farther, buy a bus pass at the same price); the scenic ride along the A487 is worth the extra time. For bus information, call 22 39. **Traws Cambria Bus** #701 travels daily to Cardiff at 12:34pm (5 hr.; £13.50).

Machynlleth to Harlech

During the summer, sunburned British tourists foxtrot to the town of **Barmouth,** 40 mi. north of Machynlleth and 10½ mi. south of Harlech. Inebriated revelers used to be locked up in **Ty Crwn,** The Round House, built under a 1782 Act of Parliament in the south end of town as a jail for drunken sailors. One door was for the men, the other for the women who helped celebrate the return of each ship. (Open summer Sun.-Fri. 10am-6pm.) The **Three Peaks Yacht Race,** held during the third week of June, is the current inspiration for townwide drinking. Racers work their way up the British coast, landing in Caernarfon (Wales), Ravenglass and Fort William (Scotland) and climbing a mountain each time they disembark (Mount Snowdon, Scafell Pike, and Ben Nevis respectively).

The Barmouth **tourist office** (tel. 280 787), directly across from the railroad station on Jubilee Rd., provides the usual. (Open Easter-Sept. daily 10am-6pm.) Most B&Bs in Barmouth charge over £12; the cheaper ones line King's Crescent. The main road into town has a swell launderette, a nifty fish-n-chip stop, and a soulful **Lo Cost Grocery. Bikes n' Boards** (tel. 381 263), opposite the post office, rents riders for £3 per hour. Barmouth's **telephone code** is 0341. Bus #38 runs 8 times per day from Harlech to Barmouth. Trains serve Barmouth less frquently; call 280 562 for rail information or 280 677 for bus information.

If you cross the estuary between Barmouth and Arthog on the **Railway Bridge,** you can take in the whole Cader Idris mountain range. For another view of the mountains, try the the 3-mi. **Panorama Walk;** the Barmouth tourist office supplies a detailed map (10p). The steam-engine **Fairbourne Railway,** the smallest of Wales's narrow-gauge railways, runs for 2 mi. along an attractive stretch of Cardigan Bay at Fairbourne, with ferry connections to Barmouth.

Bus #94 runs inland from Barmouth to the ancient stone town of **Dolgellau** (dole-GETH-lee), winding deep into the conifers of the Idris mountain range along the Mawddach Estuary. The town lies in the shadow of **Cader Idris,** literally "seat of Idris" and home to the Grey King (Brenin Llewyd) of Susan Cooper's *Dark is Rising* series. Three Roman roads once met here, and livestock is still traded along the Bala road on Fridays at 12:30pm. Dolgellau is a good base for a number of scenic walks: the **Precipice Walk** begins 3 mi. north of Dolgellau, near Llanfachreth; the **Talywaen Farm Trail,** which won the "Prince of Wales Award," takes you past an old Welsh farm; the **Penmaen Pool Walk,** 3 mi. from town, leads down the river's estuary to a bird observatory.

For further information on area walks, contact the **tourist office** at The Bridge (tel. (0341) 422 888), which doubles as a Snowdonia National Park Station. The office books B&Bs (£11-12) and provides excellent free brochures and maps. (Open daily 10am-6pm; Oct.-Easter shorter hours.) Four mi. away at Kings is an **IYHF youth hostel** (tel. (0341) 422 392); take bus #28 (6/day) from Dolgellau. Camping is available at **Tanyfron Caravan and Camping Site** (tel. 422 638), a 5- to 10-min. walk south of town off the A470. **B&B** (£9.50) is available in the campground owner's home.

Just 1 mi. south of Harlech on the A496 near Llanfair lie the **Old Llanfair Quarry Slate Caverns** (tel. 780 247). Although tiny in comparison to their northern Snowdonian cousins at Blaenau-Ffestiniog, these caves are much less crowded and more memorable. The "crypt" cavern delivers you to the "cathedral"; try to arrive in the afternoon, when sunshine filters through the ceiling (at Easter, the Llanfair choir sings a service here). (Open Easter-Oct. daily 10am-5:30pm. Admission £1.80, children 90p.) Take bus #R38 from Harlech to Llanfair (Mon.-Sat. 3-4/day).

Harlech

Harlech hovers just shy of the Llyn Peninsula, about 50 mi. north of Machynlleth along the coastal road. Harlech's clean, uncrowded beach is one of the safest and finest in Wales. **Harlech Castle,** Edward I's third masterpiece, commands a mesmerizing view of the Snowdonias merging with the Llyn Peninsula from bluffs 200 ft. above the sweeping bay. (Open daily 9:30am-6:30pm; Nov.-Feb. Mon.-Sat. 9:30am-4pm, Sun. 2-4pm. Admission £2, students and seniors £1.25.) **Theatr Ardudwy,** Coleg Harlech (tel. 780 667), is the town's cultural node, hosting films, plays, concerts, and exhibitions. (Some concerts are free; other performances range from £2.50-£8.)

The **tourist office,** Gwyddfor House, High St. (tel. 780 658), doubles as a **National Park Information Centre,** offering maps, pamphlets, and exhibits about Harlech and Snowdonia. (Open Easter week, early May, and June-Sept. daily 10am-6pm.) The small **post office** (tel. 780 231) and **Barclay's** (open Mon.-Fri. 9:30am-3pm) are on High St. Harlech's **postal code** is LL46 2YA; the **telephone code** is 0766.

The **Llanbedr hostel (IYHF)** (tel. (034123) 287) qualifies as the closest hostel to Harlech, only 4 mi. south; take the train or bus #38 and ask to be let off at the hostel. (£5.50, ages 16-20 £4.40. Open April-June, Aug., and Oct. Sat.-Thurs.; March Thurs.-Mon.; Sept. Thurs.-Tues.; Nov. Mon.-Thurs.) The B&Bs in and around Harlech might save you the trip; from the tourist office, turn right until you come to the surgery, then turn left onto Rock Terrace; the cheapest B&Bs will be right before your nose. **Mrs. Williams,** Ael-y-Garth, 6 Rock Terr. (no telephone), welcomes you into her home with a full breakfast for £7. If she's full, try **Mrs. Owen,** Greigle, by the school at 1 Rock Terr. (tel. 780 555), also for £7. **Pant Mawr** (tel. 780 226) provides elegantly lacey rooms with wardrobes that would have inspired C.S. Lewis (turn left at the car park; £11). For **camping,** try **Min-y-Don Park,** Beach Rd. (tel. 780 286). (Open Easter-Sept. £2.50/tent.)

The Yr Ogof Bistro, on the road to Talsarnau, offers the best bargains in town, with a wide range of homemade entrees and creative vegetarian dishes (spinach and nut pancake in a stilton sauce £3.25-4.50). Call ahead to reserve a table. (Open daily July-Sept. 11am-3pm and 7-10:30pm; Nov.-June 11am-3pm and 6-9:30pm.) The view from the **Plas Cafe,** High St. (tel. 780 204), is enough to inspire a visit for afternoon tea. (Savory chicken and fish dishes from £4, nightly vegetarian special. Open daily 9:30am-8:30pm. Reservations recommended.)

Harlech lies mid-way on the Cambrian coastal rail line; its **train station,** just below the castle, is a steep 15-min. walk from the upper town. Trains arrive at Harlech from Shrewsbury, to the east (every 2 hr.; 3 hr.; £13.40), and from Machynlleth, to the south (every 2 hr.; 2 hr.; £6.40), connecting to Pwllheli (every hr.; 45 min.; £4.30) and other spots on the Llyn Peninsula. Crosville bus #38 connects Harlech to Barmouth in the south and Porthamadog in the north.

Llyn Peninsula

English imperialists establish colonies of *tai-haf* (summer houses) in Llyn to better enjoy the sandy beaches between Pwllheli and Abersoch and the wilder, cliff-lined coast west of Abersoch. The huge breakers at southerly Porth Neigwl draw surfers and beachcombers, and the coves in northern Nefyn are great places to relax. While the sandy tip of the peninsula draws weekend tourists and fishing folk, it is in towns like Porthmadog (along the A487 at the base of the peninsula) and Criccieth (slightly to the west) that Welsh language and culture permeate everyday life.

Getting There and Getting Around

The northern end of British Rail's Cambrian Coast line reaches through Porthmadog (port-MAD-dok) and Criccieth (KRIK-key-ith) to Pwllheli (poo-THELL-ee), stopping at smaller towns in between. The line begins in mid-Wales at Aberystwyth; change at Machynlleth for northern destinations (7/day, Sun. 4/day; Machynlleth to Pwllheli about 2 hr.; £9.50 return). "Scenic" is the operative word; this is not rapid service. For one-way trips, don't bother getting a Cambrian Day Ranger (£12), as fares run from £1.50-£10. Steam trains link the Llyn Peninsula to Snowdonia Natinal Park. Porthmadog is the starting point of the justly famous **Ffestiniog Railway** (tel. (0766) 831 654), which runs northwest through the Ffestiniog Valley into the hills of Snowdonia, terminating in Blaenau Ffestiniog (March-Sept. daily; 1 hr.). British Rail's **Conwy Valley** line connects Blaenau Ffestiniog to Llandudno, on the northern coast of Wales.

A daily bus runs from London (£27) to Pwllheli, and service extends to Caernarfon, Aberdaron, and Porthmadog. **Bus Gwynedd** serves most spots on the peninsula with reassuring frequency for £1-£2. Catch bus #18 to Abersoch (every hr.) or #17 to Aberdaron (6/day).A **Gwynedd Red Rover,** bought from the driver, is good all the way from Chester down to Aberystwyth and offers discounts on many sites in the area (£3.50, children £1.75). The state of Sunday buses and trains ranges from unsteady to comatose; be sure to pick up timetables.

Accommodations and Sights

Porthmadog, resort town and travel hub, is the southeastern gateway to the peninsula. Though its principal attraction is the Ffestiniog Railway, **Porthmadog Pottery,** Snowdon St. (tel. 512 137), invites visitors to indulge their artistic angst; you can splatter paint on the largest mural in Wales, or torture your own bit of clay. (Open Easter-Sept. Mon.-Fri. 9am-5:30pm. Admission £1.20.) The **Brynkir Woolen Mill,** 3 mi. north of Porthmadog in Golan, demonstrates weaving in a former corn mill. (Take bus #1; 11/day. Open Mon.-Thurs. 8:30am-4:45pm, Fri. 8:30am-4pm.) You have to pay even to cross the threshold of the private Italianate village of **Portmeirion,** built by the late Sir Clough Williams-Ellis just 2 mi. east of Porthmadog. (£2.50; open daily April-Oct. 9:30am-5:30pm, Nov.-March 10am-5pm.) Mountains of pamphlets swamp Porthmadog's **tourist office,** at the end of High St. (tel. 512 981; open daily 9am-6pm). Check for small B&B signs in the windows along Madoc St. and Snowdon St.—rooms are generally uninspiring but reasonably priced (£12). **Hirgraig,** Morfa Bychan Rd. (tel. 512 836), promises sea views (£12); **Bryn Derwen** (tel. 513 316) has spacious doubles and breakfast overlooking the harbor (£13/person); and **Lleiron,** 1 Meadow Drive (tel. 512 064), keeps a huge collection of dolls from around the world (£12.50). The **launderette** at 34 Snowden St. is convenient to the B&B district; you can do your shopping at the end of Madoc St. in the gargantuan **Leo's,** so big they'll hand you a map when you arrive. (Open Mon.-Thurs. and Sat. 8am-8pm, Fri. 8am-9pm, Sun. 10am-5pm.) Porthamadog's **telephone code** is 0766.

Above the coastal town of **Criccieth,** 5 mi. west of Porthmadog, stand the remains of **Criccieth Castle,** built by Llewlyn in 1230 and destroyed by Owain Glyndwr in 1404. Its gatehouse, silhouetted against the skyline, glowers over Tremadog Bay, with Snowdonia to the northeast and Harlech across the water. (Open Mon.-Sat. 9:30am-6:30pm, Sun. 2-4pm; Oct. 25-March 24 9:30am-4pm, Sun. 2-4pm. Admission £1.50, children 90p.) **Llanystumdwy,** a tiny village 1½ mi. north of Criccieth, was the boyhood home of David Lloyd George. (Take hourly bus #3.) Aside from many monuments to him, the village boasts the **Dwyfor Ranch Rabbit Farm** on Cardiff Rd. (tel. 523 136), with 1000 rabbits to cuddle and feel sorry for. (Open Sun.-Fri. 10am-7pm, Sat. 9am-noon.) The Criccieth **tourist office** (tel. 523 303) is in the rear of The Sweet Shop, 47 High St. (Open Mon.-Sat. 9:30am-9:30pm; Sept.-June 9:30am-5:30pm.) B&Bs are scattered along the way to the castle; **Mrs. Jones,** the healer at Wern Ddu, will invite you into her potpourried den (£12). On the quieter side of town past the castle, **Dan-Y-Castell,** 4 Marine One Terr. (tel. 522 375), serenades the sea (£12).

Pwllheli, 8 mi. west of Criccieth, is the main town on the peninsula. While there is little to keep a traveler in Pwllheli, the town is a hub for buses to the more remote villages on the peninsula. The **tourist office,** Maes Sq. (tel. (0758) 613 000), books B&Bs (£10-11; open May-Sept. daily 10am-6pm). A short walk from the tourist office, **Bank Place Guest House,** High St. (tel. 612 103), has spacious rooms and huge breakfasts (£10.50). **Hendre** (tel. 613 416) offers **camping** near Pwllheli, on the road to Nefyn at Efailnewidd (£3-5/tent; laundromat and showers available); **Cae Bach Site** (tel. 612 536) lies ¾mi. from Pwllheli (£3-6 depending on group size; showers available; open July-Sept.). You can rent a bike in Pwllheli at the **Llyn Cycle Centre** (tel. 612 414) on Maes Sq. (10-speeds £8/day, £35/week; 4 days for £20; £20 deposit. Tandems too! Open Mon.-Wed. and Fri.-Sat. 9:15am-5pm.)

Just a mile outside of Pwllheli, **Starcoast World** (tel. 612 112) perpetuates Sir Billy Butlin's post-war, forget-the-war contribution to working-class holidays. After the war, barracks were converted to chalets, amusement rides replaced the armaments, and vacationers piled in from Birmingham, Manchester, and Liverpool. A day pass (£4.50, seniors £2) will give you access to all the rides and "leisure/sports" facilities, from the roller coaster to the tennis courts. (Open May-Oct. Mon.-Sat. 10am-10pm; check for Sunday hours. Hourly bus #3 will stop at the entrance.)

Farther west along the peninsula, **Abersoch** is a slightly snooty resort somnopolis with an overabundance of leisure boats. For all its airs, however, Abersoch has some surprisingly affordable B&Bs. Try **Tŷ Draw Guest House** (tel. (075881) 26 47) at £10-14.50 or **Aberview** (tel. (075881) 34 52) at £12. **Aberdaron** is an isolated village on the tip of the peninsula, where high hills surround a trickle of a creek, and a graveyard overlooks the beach. The white and yellow B&B overlooking the bay and Aberdaron village, **Bryn Mor** (tel. (075886) 344), is the best value at £10; other B&Bs average £11-12. **Bardsey Island,** the legendary "Island of 20,000 Saints" and one of the last Welsh Druid strongholds, lies off the southwest corner of the peninsula. **Elwyn Evans** (tel. (0758) 836 34) sails from Aberdaron; **David Thomas** makes the trip from Criccieth (tel. (0766) 522 239; call for sailing times).

Tre'r Ceiri (trair-KAY-ree), on the peninsula's north shore, is home to Britain's oldest fortress and city wall, dating back some 4000 years. Take the Pwllheli-Caernarfon bus to Llanaelhaearn, 7 mi. from Pwllheli (#12; Mon.-Sat. 10/day), then look for the public footpath signpost 1 mi. southwest of town on the B4417. The remains of over 200 circular stone huts are clustered within a double defensive wall. Wear warm clothing to protect yourself from the crosswinds at the top.

Caernarfon

The castle and walled city at Caernarfon, across the estuary from the Isle of Anglesey, once served as the center of English government in North Wales. For centuries, the Welsh were forced to live outside the walls, and the town withstood two sieges by Owain Glyndwr during the Welsh Rebellion of 1401-14. Even now the legacy of British dominion lives on: Prince Charles was appointed Prince of Wales at the castle in 1969.

Arriving and Departing

Caernarfon is the well-greased pivot for buses from South Wales and the southeasterly Llyn Peninsula heading northeast to Bangor and the Isle of Anglesey: buses #5 and X5 shuttle between Caernarfon and Bangor every 20 minutes (99p), and to Holyhead via Bangor (£3.50 Rover). The Snowdon Sherpa bus runs southwest to Beddgelert and Llanberis, both in Snowdonia National Park, every two hours. Bus #2 leaves the concrete bus islands in Castle Sq. and drives south to Porthmadog (every 2 hr.; £2.70) to connect with the coastal railway. Buses leaving before noon on Sunday are few and far between.

Orientation and Practical Information

The **tourist information center,** Castle Pitch, Oriel Pendeitsh (tel. 672 232), as well as the more expensive craft shops, lies opposite the castle entrance. An accommodations-booking service (10% deposit), free bus timetables, and a town map (10p) are all available. (Open Sept.-March daily 10:30am-5:30pm; April-June daily 10am-6pm; July-Aug. 9:30am-6pm.) For other necessities, head up the hill from the castle to Castle Sq. and the pedestrian area behind it. Note that in the winter, everything shuts down on Thursday afternoons at 1pm.

A market is held in the square every Saturday from 9am-5pm, the **post office** (tel. 21 16; **postal code** LL55 2ND; open Mon.-Fri. 9am-5:30pm, Sat. 9am-12:30pm) flanks the square, and a branch of **Barclay's Bank,** Bangor St. (tel. 672 396) can exchange your currency in the lego-block center. (Open Mon.-Fri. 9:30am-3:30pm.) The **telephones** outside the post office are wired to area code 0286. **Fourteenth Peak Outdoor Gear,** Palace St. (tel. 51 24), off Castle Sq., sells camping equipment and clothing; you can rent a tent for £18-26 per week. A coffee shop in the back sells Alabama Chocolate Fudge Cake (£1.25) and other goodies. (Open Mon.-Sat. 9am-5pm; July-Aug. occasionally Sun.) You can wash your clothes at the **launderette** on South Penrallt, off Bridge St. (Wash £1, dry 20p/6 min. Open Sun.-Fri. 8:30am-7:30pm, Sat. 8:30am-5:30pm.)

In a medical emergency, contact **Bangor General Hospital (Ysbyty Gwynedd** tel. (0248) 370 007); Bangor bus #5 or X5 will take you right there from Castle Sq. Otherwise contact the **police** at Pendeitsh Rd. (tel. 673 333), on the quay.

Accommodations and Food

Although slightly inconvenient to the city center (a 10-min. walk from the castle), the B&Bs lining St. David's Rd. are far and away Caernarfon's best values in budget accommodations (£12-14); other guest houses (£13.50-17) elbow in on Church St. **Mrs. Hughes,** Pros Kairon, Victoria Rd. (tel. 762 29), should be your first port of call. If you make it in, you will be treated like one of the family. Head toward the Segontium on Beddgelert Rd., then turn left on Dinorwic St. (£10). Situated in a row of blondstone Victorian townhouses, the **Marianfa** (tel. 55 89) offers bright, spacious rooms with ornate ceilings, color TV, and tea-making facilities. (Doubles and family rooms £11-12/person.) **Meirion** (tel. 34 70), on Victoria Rd., has minimalist but commodious rooms. (Singles £12, doubles £11/person.) Seven mi. south of Caernarfon on the A487, **Tanrallt Centre** (tel. 881 724) supplies dorm beds for under £5, mostly to groups (book in advance). **Camping** is available about ½mi. from town at **Cadnant Valley Park,** Llanberis Rd. (tel. 31 96); expect lots of caravans in the summer. (Campers with tents £5/person.)

For picnics, try Pool Street's **Lo Cost Supermarket** and bakeries, or the **Tesco's** on Eastgate St. **Cremepogau,** on the corner of Palace St. (tel. 672 552), serves dinner pancakes (stuffed with chili, £2.20; in mushroom sauce, £2). **Flintstone's Café,** a wholefood restaurant upstairs in the indoor market on Palace St., and the **14th Peak Café** in the sporting goods store, are more appealing than the cafés along the track to the castle.

Sights and Entertainment

Impregnable **Caernarfon Castle** was built by Edward I of England in 1283, and features the typically Middle Eastern double gatehouses and multi-angled arrow slits that he discovered while on Crusade. You can spend hours exploring the intricate passageways and chambers, or lounging on the inner courtyard: in the summer, choirs, musicians, and *Mabinogi* actors often perform here, and a "Fire and Fantasy" light show sparkles infrequently (check at the tourist office across the street for details). Several towers contain exhibits on the castle, Prince Charles' investiture, and regimental momentos. (Open daily 9:30am-6:30pm; mid-Oct. to mid-March Mon.-Sat. 9:30am-4pm. Admission £3, seniors and under 16 £2.) The foundations of the Roman fort **Segontium** (tel. (0286) 56 25) occupy a hill ½mi. southeast of town along the Beddgelert Rd. A **museum** at the entrance to the site enlightens visitors. (Segontium open Mon.-Sat. 9:30am-6pm, Sun. 2-5:30pm; Oct.-April shorter hours. Free.)

Folk music abounds in Caernarfon. **Y Mount Folk Club** hosts open shows Thursday nights, and **Merlin Music,** Old Market Hall (tel. (0766) 757 55), sells folk music instruments from around the world. On Saturday nights during the summer, folk musicians play at **Parc Glynllifon,** a craft, amusement and nature park outside of Caernarfon. (Take bus #91 to Dinas Dinlle.)

Bangor

The budget accoutrements of this university town suit travelers bent on exploring the Isle of Anglesey, just over the bay to the northwest, or the Vale of Conwy, to the east. Though less well endowed with historical alluvium than other towns in the area, Bangor boasts a smattering of attractions bursting with youthful energy and Welsh pride: one of the finest castles in Wales, a Victorian pier, a thriving Welsh arts scene, and a bustling pedestrianized shopping district.

Arriving and Departing

Bangor is the transportation depot for the Isle of Anglesey to the north, the Llyn Peninsula to the southwest, and Snowdonia to the southeast. Crosville bus #42 leaves Bangor for Llangefni and Holyhead via Llanfair P.G. (14/day; £3.55); for Conwy and Llandudno with connections to Rhyl in the east (bus #5 every 20 min.; £3.05); for Porthmadog with connections to all of the Llyn Peninsula (bus #2 16/day; £3.50); to Caernarfon direct (Rover every ½hr.; 99p); to Pwllheli direct (2/day); and to Llanberis at the foot of Snowdon on the Sherpa bus line (2/day). Bangor is also on the North Wales Coast rail line that connects Holyhead with Chester (every hr.; £8.40).

Orientation and Practical Information

The two main streets—Deiniol Rd. and High St.—run parallel to each other and bisect the city. Upper Bangor, up the hill from Deiniol Rd., marks the edge of the hip university area with its funky shops and cheap health food. Buses stop at the shelters down from the town clock—all schedules are posted. The rail station is at the end of Deiniol Rd.

Tourist Information Center: Theatr Gwynedd, off Deiniol Rd. (tel. 352 786). Accommodations service with 10% deposit. Loads of bus schedules, maps, and other good things. Open April-Sept. daily 10am-6pm.

Bus Station: Crosville Bus Co., Garth Rd. (tel. 370 295 for information), down the hill from the clocktower. All buses leave from Garth Rd. Station. Office open Mon.-Fri. 9am-noon and 1-4pm, Sat. 9-11:30am.

Camping Equipment: The Great Arrete, College Rd., Upper Bangor (tel. 352 710). Reasonably-priced, reasonably-stocked climbing and mountaineering shop run by knowing folk. Open Mon.-Sat. 9am-5:30pm.

Crisis: Samaritans, 7 Abbey Rd. (tel. 354 646); 24 hr.

Early Closing Day: Wed. at 1pm.

Emergency: Dial 999; no coins required.

Financial Services: Barclay's, High St. Open Mon.-Fri. 9:30am-5pm. **National Westminster** on High St. also open Sat. 9am-3:30pm.

Hospital: Ysbyty Gywnedd Hospital (tel. 370 007), off Penrhos Rd. Bus #9, 5, or 5A.

Launderette: P. Leung's Launderette, at the bottom of Hendrewen Rd., corner of Caernarfon Rd.

Market Day: Sun., at the end of High St.

Pharmacy: Boots, High St. Open Mon.-Sat. 9am-5pm.

Police: Lore Lane (tel. 370 333).

Post Office: 60 Deiniol Rd. (tel. 354 444). Open Mon.-Thurs. 9am-5:30pm, Fri. 9:30am-5:30pm, Sat. 9am-12:30pm. **Postal Code:** LL87 1AA.

Telephone Code: 0248.

Taxi: tel. 353 535; 24 hr.

Train Station: Holyhead Rd., at the end of Deiniol Rd. (tel. 353 201 or (0492) 851 51 for information).

Accommodations and Camping

Finding a room in Bangor during graduation (the first week of July) can be a hellish prospect without advance bookings. The best B&Bs occupy handsome Victorian townhouses near the tourist office on Garth Rd.

Tany y Bryn youth hostel (IYHF) (tel. 353 516), ½mi. from town center. Follow High St. to the water and walk uphill, turning right at the house with a three-headed dog at the base of the window; if your pack feels leaden, take the Maesgeirchen bus from the train station. Aristocratic view of Penrhyn Castle; Vivien Leigh and Sir Lawrence Olivier always chose room 7. Be one of the tune-humming warden's "locusts of the valley." Good showers and meals. £6.30, ages 16-20 £5.10. Open daily April-Sept.; Feb.-March and Oct. Tues.-Sat.

Mrs. S. Roberts, 32 Glynne Rd. (tel. 352 113), between Garth Rd. and High St. A bustling household you'll share with Dusty, Lucky, and Rusty. £10.

Mrs. Jones, Bro Dawel, Garth Rd. (tel. 355 242). Veer left at the end of the road. Tri-bedded doubles, winter colors, and a big sooty dog in a huge home. Singles £14, doubles £12/person.

Mrs. Sloane, 4 Green Bank, Garth Rd. (tel. 364 426). Colorful garden overlooking Anglesey. £13.50.

Camping: Dinas Farm, Halfway Bridge (tel. 364 227), 2 mi. from town on the A5. Sheltered sites on the bank of the River Ogwen. £1.10/person. Open April-Oct. Also **Nant Park,** Holyhead Rd. just past the National Tire Service, 20 min. from town. (£1. No facilities.)

Food

The usual plethora of bakeries make a basic sandwich and sweeten the cheapest take-away meal. The larger supermarkets lie at the lower end of High St., away from the cathedral. Wholefood and international cuisine is popular above the university, around College Rd.

The Sea Fresh, Dean St. (tel. 353 894). Probably the cheapest take-away meals in Wales, cooked by experts in hospital coats. Fish battered while you wait (90p), mound of chips (40p), burger (65p).

Cane's, 215 High St. (tel. 354 777). Upbeat student hangout with gargantuan burgers (veggie or beef) (£2), exotic salads with starfruit and kiwis (95p), and cascading ice cream desserts. Open noon-10pm.

Greek Taverna Politis, Holyhead Rd. Lunch from £1.90, dinner from £3.50; hummus or retsina £1.10. Open Tues.-Sat. 10:30am-2pm and 7-10:30pm.

Sights and Entertainment

The **University College of North Wales,** on the hill overlooking the town, is Bangor's most visible feature. For 1400 years, **Bangor Cathedral** (tel. 351 693), small and steepleless because of poor foundations, has been the ecclesiastical center of one quarter of Wales, keeping Welsh curs in their place with cast iron "dog tongs." (Open June-Sept. Sun.-Fri. 10:30am-4:30pm, Sat. 10:30am-2pm.) The nearby **Museum of Welsh Antiquities and Art Gallery** (tel. 353 368), on Fforth Gwynedd, models 19th-century Welsh costumes and antique furniture alongside modern contributions. (Open Tues.-Sat. noon-4:30pm. Free.)

Just outside Bangor, where the A55 splits off the A5 (walk about 2 mi., or catch any bus heading north), stands **Penrhyn Castle** (tel. 353 084), a 19th-century neo-Norman structure almost grotesque in its grandeur. Many of the furnishings were made from local slate, and the results are staggering—one bed weighs over a ton. (Open July-Aug. Wed.-Mon. 11am-5pm; April-June and Sept.-Oct. noon-5pm. Admission £3.50, YHA members £2, children £1.75. Grounds only £1.50, children 75p.)

The modern **Theatr Gwynedd** on Deiniol Rd. at the base of the hill (tel. 351 708) houses a thriving company that performs in both Welsh and English. (Box office open Mon.-Fri. 11am-3pm and 6-8pm. Films £2.70, plays £4-20, students 50p. Tickets available at most tourist offices on north coast.) The **Student Union** (Deiniol Rd., near the tourist office) is open all year long Mon.-Fri. 9:30am-6pm for coffee in the lounge upstairs. When school is in session, its basement bar often jams with sizzling rock, pop, folk, and reggae concerts. Check the Union and Cob Records on High St.

Isle of Anglesey (Ynys Môn)

Separated from the rest of Wales by the Menai Strait, Anglesey was the Welsh breadbasket during the period when Wales campaigned to rid itself of English overlords. Edward I built his castles at Caernarfon (on the mainland) and Beaumaris (on the island) to cut off Welsh supplies and isolate the region. Bronze Age and Roman ruins are common, especially near Holyhead and on the coast facing Caernarfon, but it is the beaches and resorts along the northeast and southwest coasts that lure most tourists to the Anglesey. Today, private farms cover most of the island, and ferries leave for Ireland from Holyhead.

Getting There and Getting Around

Crosville's Bws Gwynedd runs six bus lines across Anglesey. Bus #4, the major route, runs the width of the island from Bangor to Holyhead via Llangefni (every ½hr., Sun. 3/day; £3.55 return). Bus #53 follows the southeast coast north from Bangor to Beaumaris (every ½hr., Sun. 2/day; £1.60 return). Bus #62 runs northwest from Bangor to Amlwch, on the northern coast (2/hr., Sun. 2/day; £1.60 return). From Amlwch, bus #61 cruises across northwestern Anglesey and into Holyhead (Mon.-Sat. 6/day). Bus #32 runs north from central Llangefni to Amlwch (Mon.-Sat. 5/day). Bus #42 from Bangor curves along the southwest coast as far as Aberffraw, then heads north to Llangefni (Mon.-Sat. every hr.). British Rail runs from Bangor to Holyhead (express, 14/day; 25 min.; £4.30) and from Llanfair P.G. (8/day; 30 min.; £3.60).

Practical Information

Telford's **Menai Suspension Bridge** (1826) links Bangor with **Llanfairpwllgwyngyllgogerychwyrndrobwll Llantysiliogogogoch,** which has the longest village name in the U.K., meaning "Church of Mary in the Hollow of the White Hazel near the Rapid Whirlpool at the Church of Tysilio by the Red Caves." So named in the 19th century to attract publicity, the spot is known locally as Llanfair P.G. Today, it boasts a huge Pringle woolens factory as well as one of the two main **tourist centers** on the island. (The other is in Holyhead.) A less equipped **tourist office** is in the center of the island in Llangefni, at Pen yr Orsedd (tel. (0248) 724 666; 24-hr.; open Mon.-Fri. 9am-5pm).

Beaumaris

4 mi. northeast of the Menai Bridge on the southeasterly A545 stands **Beaumaris Castle,** the last and largest of Edward I's moat-encircled fortresses, overlooking Puffin Island to the north. Catch bus #56 from Bangor; the stronghold is at the end of Beaumaris' bustling Castle St. (Open daily 9:30am-6:30pm; Oct. 16-March 14 Mon.-Sat. 9:30am-4pm, Sun. 2-4pm. Admission £1.50, children 90p.) You can relive the past at the **Museum of Childhood,** Castle St. (tel. 712 498; open Easter-Christmas Mon.-Fri. 10am-6pm, Sun. noon-5pm; admission £2, children under 16 £1). Those of twisted mind may enjoy the treadmill and scaffold of the doomed at the old **Beaumaris Courthouse and Gaol,** the 1809 Victorian jailhouse on Bunker's Hill which features original cells and memoirs of local policemen (open June-Sept. 10am-6pm). Beaumaris hosts a week-long **Gwŷl Beaumaris Music Festival** at the end of May, which includes orchestral concerts, opera, theater, jazz, and street performances (programs £2); for further information, talk to Janet (see below).

Though the town can afford a majestic Šeaside Royal Anglesey Yacht Club, it refuses to invest in a tourist information center. A case outside Town Hall on Castle St. usually contains **tourist brochures,** and unofficial advice is best obtained from Janet in the **Nut House,** a health food store at 44 Castle St. (tel. (0248) 810 930).

The closest youth hostel to Beaumaris is in Bangor (£6.30, ages 16-20 £5.10; tel. (0248) 353 516). B&Bs in Beaumaris are quaint and comfortable, if pricey (£13-16). **Mrs. Pratt,** 5 Castle St. (tel. (0248) 811 475), provides a sunny, wooden home away from home right next door to the Museum of Childhood. Pretty bathtub but no showers (£13). Institutionalized camping is best at **Kingsbridge Caravan Park,** 3 mi. out of town towards Llangoed (tel. (0248) 786 36). Piping-hot pizzas (£3-3.30) are practically perfect in busy **Bottle's Bistro,** on Castle St.

Holyhead (Caergybi)

A narrow strip of land attached to the Isle of Anglesey by a causeway and a bridge, Holy Island has only one sure lure for the traveler: Holyhead (HOLLY-head) and its **ferries to Ireland.** The town has only weakly resisted the grim austerity of other ferry ports. If you have time on your hands, explore the many paths of Holyhead Mountain. Its **North** and **South Stacks** are good spots for birdwatching, and the closed lighthouse gazes nostalgically out over the sea.

Two ferry lines operate out of Holyhead: **B&I** and **Sealink Stena.** Book B&I (tel. (0407) 760 222) on the ferry itself or from a travel agent. B&I runs directly to Dublin daily at 4am and 3:45pm; return trips leave Dublin at 10am and 9:45pm. All trips take 3 hours (July-Aug. £21, return £42; other times £16, return £32). B&I offers a special strictly-enforced day-return ticket called the **Duty Free Fun Fare** (£10; May-July Mon.-Wed.; Aug. Tues.-Wed.; Sept.-Feb. only a few excluded days). Tickets are available from the Holyhead British Rail station, most North Wales coast travel agents, and at any tourist information center in north Wales.

Sealink (tel. (0407) 762 304) has a booking office at the train station on Turkeyshore Rd. (Open Mon.-Sat. 9:30am-6pm and 11pm-6am, Sun. 10:30am-5:30pm and 11pm-6am.) Ferries sail to **Dún Laoghaire** in Ireland (3½ hr.), with bus connections to nearby Dublin. Departures from Holyhead are at 3:15am and 2:45pm; return trips at 8:45am and 8:45pm; additional sailings leave in June at 11am, in July and August at llam and 11:30pm, and from May through August there is an additional return at 4:30pm. (£22, return £44; Sept. to mid-July £15, return £30.) Sealink offers a day-return fare for £14.50 (plus £6 duty-free voucher). Bicycles go free with both lines. Pick up complete schedules at the tourist office. (Open daily 11:30am-6pm and 11:30pm-6am.) 25% discounts for YHA members are available for single journeys on both lines, and the YHA offers special package deals (ferry, a week's hostels, and transportation in Ireland for under £70). Call the YHA for details (tel. (0727) 552 15).

If you are traveling in July and August, book at least several weeks in advance through the ferry office or a travel agency. For off-season trips, **Mona Travel,** 20 Market St. (tel. 45 56) in Holyhead, has fare, schedule, and booking information (open Mon.-Fri. 9:30am-5pm, Sat. 9:30am-1pm). Only car-ferry parties leave from the docks; foot passengers embark at the rail station. Arrive an hour in advance, and bring your passport.

If you arrive in Holyhead too late to continue on your route, check the list of B&B vacancies (from £11) posted at Holyhead's **tourist office,** Marine Sq., Salt Island Approach (tel. 762 622), in a caravan down the main road from the terminal. (Open daily 10am-6pm.) The Sealink staff at the car dock and railway station also has a B&B list. Avoid the high-priced hotels near the rail station; instead, leave the train station, go over the bridge and walk for about a mile along the main road until you see the B&B signs on the left before the dock. Holyhead's **telephone code** is 0407.

Holyhead can be reached by Crosville Bus #4 from Bangor via Llangefni (every hr., Sun. 3/day; 1 hr. 20 min.), and National Express runs up to Holyhead from most major cities. The town is also the terminus of the North Wales Coast rail line with hourly trains to Bangor (½hr.; £4.30), Chester (1½ hr.; £11), and London (5 hr.; £35). British Rail runs from Holyhead to Cardiff (£41 month return).

Snowdonia Forest and National Park

The park covers the larger part of northwestern Wales, stretching from Machynlleth in the south to Bangor and Conwy in the north. 840 sq. sheep-dotted mi. in total, Snowdonia encompasses coastal areas as well as the rugged hills of the interior. Numerous paths lead visitors through the mountains, while the Snowdon Mountain Railway and the slate mines of Llanberis and Blaenau Ffestiniog lure visitors to the towns of Snowdonia. Phenomenal popularity notwithstanding, the towns and the park remain largely unsullied by touristic excess.

Getting There and Getting Around

The **Snowdon Sherpa,** a service of Crosville bus lines on which all Crosville passes are valid, offers relatively easy access to the various Snowdon trailheads, where parking is almost impossible to find. A Day Rover ticket (£3.50) buys unlimited travel on the Sherpa buses and on any other bus in Gwynedd; individual trips tend to cost about £1.50. Most routes are serviced by one bus every two hours. Inform the driver if you intend to switch buses; connections often fail due to late or impatient buses. Be sure to pick up a Sherpa schedule in any tourist office.

Buses run to the interior from towns near the edge of the park, such as Porthmadog and Caernarfon at the root of the Llyn Peninsula to the west, Conwy on Wales' north coast, and Betws-y-Coed, just south of Conwy. Services connect Caernarfon with Llanberis and Beddgelert, stopping at Pen-y-Pass, Bryn Gwynant, and Snowdon Ranger youth hostels; Porthmadog with Beddgelert; and Betws-y-Coed and Conwy with Llanberis, Llanrwst, and Llandudno, stopping at Pen-y-Pass, Capel Curig, and Rowen youth hostels.

Narrow-gauge railway lines running through Snowdonia let you enjoy the countryside without enduring the masochism of a hike. The **Snowdon Mountain Railway** (tel. (0286) 870 223), opened in 1896 and still operated entirely by coal-fired steam locomotives, travels from Llanberis to the summit of Snowdonia (2½ hr. round-trip; 30 min. at the peak). Weather conditions and passenger demand rule the schedule from July to early September; on a clear day the first train leaves Llanberis at 9am (if there are at least 25 passengers), with subsequent trains about every half-hour until mid-afternoon (£8.50, return £12; tired hikers can try for a £5 standby back down). The **Ffestiniog Railway** romps through the mountains of Snowdonia from Porthmadog to Blaenau Ffestiniog (£4, return £7.80). You can travel part of its route to Minffordd, Penrhyndeudraeth, Tanybwlch, or Tdnygrisiau (8-11/day

8:40am-7pm; Oct.-May. 2-3/day). At Porthmadog, the narrow-gauge rail connects with the Cambrian Coast service from Pwllheli south to Aberystwyth in mid-Wales. **Llanberis Lake Railway** (tel. (0288) 870 549) runs a short and scenic jaunt through the woods (6/day, March-Oct. 4/day; 40 min.; £3.20).

Practical Information

Area tourist offices and National Park Information Centres all stock pamphlets on walks, drives and accommodations, as well as trusty Ordnance Survey maps. Contact the **Snowdonia National Park Information Centre,** Penrhyndeudraeth (pen-ren-DOY-dryth), Gwynedd, Wales LL48 6L5 for detailed information. Other National Park Information Centres are located at: Betws-y-Coed, Royal Oak Stables (tel. (06902) 426 or 665); Harlech, High St. (tel. (0766) 780 658); Blaenau Ffestiniog, Isaltt, High St. (tel. (0766) 830 360); Llanberis (tel. (0286) 870 765); Aberdyfi, The Wharf (tel. (065472) 321); and Bala, High St. (tel. 0678) 520 367).

The weekend and week-long residential programs listed below span every aspect of outdoor and mountain life; centers often provide special mountain sport practice facilities:

Snowdonia National Park Study Centre, Plas Tan-y-Bwlch, Maentwrog, Blaenau, Ffestiniog, Gwynedd, Wales LL41 3YU (tel. (076685) 324). Write the director at least 7 weeks in advance. Courses on naturalist favorites such as wildlife painting and geology.

Pen-y-Pass youth hostel (IYHF), Mountain Centre, Nant Gwydant, Gwynedd, Wales LL55 4NY (tel. (0286) 870 428). Canoeing, rock climbing, first-aid courses.

Plas-y-Brenin, Capel Curig, Gwynedd, Wales LL24 OET (tel. (06904) 214). Mountain activities for outdoor thrill seekers, with artificial ski slope, canoe-rolling pool, indoor climbing wall, and courses on how to do these activities for real in the wild.

Safety

In case of an **emergency** in the park, get to the nearest road or a **Mountain Rescue Post** (marked on most area maps) and dial 999.

Weather on the exposed mountains shifts quickly, unpredictably and wrathfully. Bring sturdy boots, warm clothing, extra food, rain gear, a flashlight, a whistle, and a first-aid kit. Two essential items, no matter which of the six trails up Snowdon you attempt, are the Ordnance Survey map of Snowdonia National Park (£3.95) and the individual path guides (20p each)—both available at Park Centres and most bookstores. A compass wouldn't hurt either. Leave details of your route with the hostel warden or the nearest police or ranger station before setting out; bright orange forms for this purpose are available at all National Park Information Centres and youth hostels. Hiking in the winter is especially perilous—check in at a ranger station for advice on the trouble spots. Get a detailed Snowdonia **weather forecast** by calling (0286) 870 120, or call **Mountaincall Snowdonia** (tel. (0839) 500 449) for the local forecast, information on ground conditions, and a national 3- to 5-day forecast.

Accommodations

The eight **IYHF youth hostels** in the mountain area are some of the best in Wales. They are marked clearly on Gwynedd bus schedules and on the more legible transport map. Summer school excursions can make getting into the hostels a challenge—book at least two days ahead.

At the hostel just above **Llanberis** (tel. (0286) 870 280), plenty of sheep, cows and bulls keep hostelers company as they take in the splendid views of Llyn Peris and Llyn Padarn below and Mt. Snowdon above. (£6.30, ages 16-20 £5.10. Open April-Oct. daily; March and Nov. Fri.-Tues.) **Bryn Gwynant** (tel. (076686) 251), above Llyn (Lake) Gwynant and along the road from Pen-y-Gwryd to Beddgelert (4 mi. from Beddgelert), is at the trailhead of the **Watkin's Path** to Snowdon. (£6.30, ages 16-20 £5.10. Open April-Sept. daily; March and Oct.-Nov. Mon.-Sat.) The **Pen-y-Pass** hostel (tel. (0286) 870 428) commands the most unusual and spectacular position of any hostel in Wales: 1170 ft. above sea level at the head of Llanberis Pass between the Snowdon and Glyders peaks. The hostel is 6 mi. from Llanberis and 4 mi. from Nant Peris. More sheep mindlessly block the front door. Two Snowdon ascents, the Pyg track and the Llyn Llydaw miner's track, leave from its door. (£7, ages 16-20 £5.90. Open April-Oct. daily; March and Dec. Mon.-Sat.) The **Snowdon Ranger,** at Llyn Cwellyn (tel. (028685) 391), is the starting point for the grandest Snowdon ascent—the **Ranger Path.** A path across the road leads to a quiet lake and views of the ranges. (£6.30, ages 16-20 £5.10. Open April-Sept. daily; Feb.-March and Oct. and Dec. Thurs.-Mon.)

The **Ffestiniog** hostel (tel. (076676) 27 65), in Ffestiniog (*not* Blaenau Ffestiniog), is only 2 mi. from the famous slate quarries and narrow-gauge railway. (£5.50, ages 16-20 £4.40. March-Oct.; call for days open.) **Capel Curig** (tel. (06904) 225) marks the crossroads of many mountain paths, only 5 mi. from Betws-y-Coed on the A5. (£6.30, ages 16-20 £5.10. Open April-Sept. daily; March and Oct.-Nov. Thurs.-Mon.) **Idwal Cottage** (tel. (0248) 600 225), just off the A5 at the foot of Llyn Ogwen in northern Snowdonia, lies within hiking distance of Pen-y-Pass, Llanberis, and Capel Curig. (£5.50, ages 16-20 £4.40. Open Feb.-July and Sept.-Oct. Mon.-Sat.; Aug. daily.) **Lledr Valley** (tel. (06906) 202) naps in the eponymous Valley, only 5 mi. from Betws-y-Coed on the bus line between Betws-y-Coed and Ffestiniog. (£5.90, ages 16-20 £4.70. Open April-Oct. daily; March and Nov. Mon.-Sat.)

The land in Snowdonia is privately owned—stick to public pathways and campsites or ask the owner's consent. In the high mountains, camping is permitted as long as you leave no mess, but lower in the valleys, owner's consent is required. Public camping sites spot the roads during peak seasons; check listings below for sites in specific towns.

Hiking

Park rangers lead day walks in Llanberis, Betws-y-Coed, Nant Gwynant, and elsewhere (£2.50, short walk £1.50; seniors £1.50, £1). Contact tourist offices and National Park Information Centres for more options, and check the free newletter, the *Snowdonia Star,* for goings-on and walking advice. Private mountain guides and other companies also advertise in the local youth hostels.

Lesser ranges, such as the **Glyders** or **Cader Idris,** will challenge any serious climber, but the highest peak, **Mount Snowdon** (*Yr Wyddfa,* or "burial place") at 3560 ft. remains the most popular; half a million climbers reach the summit every year. Because multiple trails make the mountain accessible to hikers of all strengths, Mt. Snowdon has become eroded and its nature distrupted. The Park officers request that all hikers stick to the well-marked trails to avoid further damage to the area. Since other climbs will be less crowded and probably more scenic, it might be wise to skip Snowdon altogether.

There are six principal paths up Snowdon. The **Llanberis Path** is the easiest, the longest (a 5-mi. ascent), and by far the most popular. The path begins on the first side road above the Snowdon railway station at the edge of Llanberis and also takes five hours round-trip. The **Snowdon Ranger Path** is, like the Llanberis Path, one of the easier ascents up Snowdon. The 3.1-mi. trek begins beside the Snowdon Ranger youth hostel, on the northern shore of Llyn Cwellyn, and also takes five hours round-trip. The **Watkin's Path,** with an ascent of 3300 ft., is the most difficult and also the most beautiful attack on the summit. The 3.4-mi. hike takes five hours up and three hours down; it begins at Pont Bethania on the A498, 3 mi. northeast of Beddgelert (on the Snowdon Sherpa bus line). The spectacular sunsets above the **Rhyd Ddu Path** make it a popular end-of-the-day descent. The trailhead of this five-hour path is at the end of a car park south of Rhyd Ddu on the Snowdon Sherpa line between Beddgelert and Caernarfon. Two other paths are the **Miner's,** an easy ascent only as far as Llyn Glaslyn, and the **Pyg Path,** an extremely difficult trail at the top. Both of these paths are 2.8 mi. and begin at Pen-y-Pass.

Llanberis

Distinguished mainly by the Mountain Railway, **Llanberis** is the largest town in the park and the best place to stock up on gear and food. The **Museum of the North** takes you on a Walkman-guided trip through rooms where Wales's history is dramatically narrated by, among others, Merlin and a talking tree. (Open daily June-Sept. 9:30am-6pm; March-May and Nov. 10am-5pm. Admission £4, seniors £3.) To reach the ruins of nearby **Dolbadarn Castle,** follow the River Hwch until the path crosses the footbridge and leads up through woods to the castle. From the castle, you can gaze at the industrial scabs on the shores of Llyn Peris. Nearby, at the end of a clearly marked path from the Lake Railway, and only 100 yd. from the bus park, lies the Vivian Quarry pool. To reach **Ceunant Mawr,** one of Wales's most impressive waterfalls, take the public footpath on Victoria Terrace by Victoria Hotel, then the first right and first left (about a mile). The path leads past smaller falls and pools to the tracks of the Snowdon Mountain Railway. The **Welsh Slate Museum** (tel. 870 630; open end of May-Sept. 9:30am-5:30pm; admission £1.50, seniors and children 90p) is embraced by the **Padarn Country Park;** walk 300 yd. from the tourist office, and the park is to the left on the road running between Llyn Padarn and Llyn Peris. **Craft workshops** (tel. 351 427) dot the park, and craftspeople demonstrate brass-molding (on request), harp manufacturing, screen printing, flower pressing, woodburning, and slate art. (Open Easter Week daily 9:30am-5:30pm; May-Sept. daily 9:30am-6:30pm.) The **Llanberis Lake Railway** (tel. (0286) 870 549) runs 2 mi. along Llyn Padarn. (March-Oct. Mon.-Fri. and Sun.; check for additional Sat. trips in July. £3.20, children £2.) The **Snowdon Mountain Railway** (tel. 870 223) whisks you up Mt. Snowdon from Llanberis (£8.50, return £12; see above). Postcards of the mountain often offer a less foggy view.

The **tourist office,** Museum of the North building (tel. (0286) 870 765), in the bypass at the end of High St., doles out tips on hikes and sights, in addition to running an accommodations-booking service. (Open Easter-Sept. daily 10am-6pm.) The bookstore across the street carries pamphlets on an assortment of local walks (20p). Plan your hike and pick up gear at **Joe Brown's Store** on High St., owned by one of the world's greatest pioneer climbers. (Open Mon.-Fri. 9am-6pm, Sat. 9am-8pm, Sun. 1-5pm.) Rent a mountain bike to struggle along the ridges from **Llanberis Mountain Bike Centre,** 57 High St. (tel. 870 052; open Mon.-Sat. 9:30am-6pm, Sun. 10am-4pm; £3/hr., £15/day, £50/week), or **The Bike Man,** 6 Goodman St. (tel. 771 80; open Mon.-Tues. and Thurs.-Sat. 9:30am-5pm). Bicycle riding through mountain pastures is not looked upon kindly by the farmers and local landowners. Follow trails, close all gates you open, and give walkers and horseback riders the right of way. Address the **post office** (open Mon.-Tues. and Thurs.-Fri. 9am-5:30pm, Wed. and Sat. 9am-12:30pm) with **postal code** LL55 4EU; Llanberis's **telephone code** is 0286.

You can stoke your engine with a dose of awe-inspiring chili (£3.15) at **Pete's Eats** (tel. 870 358; open daily 9am-8pm; off-season 9am-6:30pm), or stock up on groceries at the **Stop and Shop,** High St. (Open Mon.-Sat. 8am-8pm.) In town, there are several B&Bs (£10-12) and an **IYHF youth hostel,** ½mi. up Capel Coch Rd. (tel. 870 280; £6.30, ages 16-20 £5.10). **Hugh and Judy Walton** (tel. 870 744), experienced local climbers, run a bunkhouse on the road to Caernarfon that charges £4 per night (B&B £11.50); the Waltons also organize climbing expeditions. Campers can head 2 mi. north of Llanberis to the mammoth **Snowdon View Caravan Park** (tel. 870 349), which has great facilities and a heated swimming pool (£4-6/tent), or continue a bit farther to **Pritchard's Camp Site,** opposite the hotel in Nant Peris (tel. 870 494; toilets and running water, but no showers; £1.50/person).

Situated on the western edge of the park, Llanberis is a short ride from Caernarfon; catch Crosville bus #88 from Caernarfon (Mon.-Sat. every ½hr.) or one of the Sherpa buses.

Beddgelert

The landscape around Beddgelert, 8 mi. south and slightly east of Llanberis, is markedly different from that of the coast. Small streams spritz the lushly arbored mountain foothills, while the Rivers Glaswyn and Colwyn run through dark, forested vales before meeting in the center of the village. Situated at the foot of Moel Hebog (2566 ft.) and at the junction of three valleys, Beddgelert ("Gelert's Grave") makes an excellent base for hiking in the surrounding country. From the top of **Moel Hebog,** accessible by a path leading directly out of Beddgelert, you can view the coast on either side of the Llyn Peninsula as well as the surrounding peaks of Mt. Snowdon. Trails on Hebog are much less crowded than those on Snowdon, and only stone walls and sheep fortify the summit. The climb is about four hours round-trip, with some rocky patches near the top; get a hiking map in town before you leave.

The **visitors center** is in the National Trust building, Llewelyn Cottage (tel. 293), built on the foundations of Prince Llewelyn's hunting lodge. (Open daily Easter-Nov. 10am-6pm.) The **Y Warws Warehouse-Beddgelert,** a large camping store that carries compasses, Ordnance Survey maps, and a wide variety of tents and gear, lies opposite the Ael-y-Bryn B&B. (Open Mon.-Sat. 9am-6pm, Sat. 10am-6pm.) Maps are also available at **The Welsh Lady** (open 9:30am-5:30pm), across the bridge. The **post office** (tel. 201) sits on Caernarfon Rd. (Open Mon.-Tues. and Thurs.-Fri. 9am-5:30pm, Wed. 9am-1pm, Sat. 9am-12:30pm.) Beddgelert's **postal code** is LL55 4UY; the **telephone code** is 076686.

Accommodations in Beddgelert fill quickly in summer. **Plas Tan-y-Graig Guest House,** by the bridge into town (tel. 329), comes complete with views over the River Colwyn and a mountain of a dog (£12). **Plas Colwyn** (tel. 458), to the left over the bridge, offers a similar deal. Outside of town, 700 yd. along the Caernarfon Rd. across from the Y Warws camping store lies **Ael-y-Bryn** (tel. 310), with an outdoor terrace facing the mountains. (B&B £11-15 with private shower.) The **Beddgelert Forest Campsite** (tel. 288), run by the Forestry Commission, pitches its tents 1 mi. out of town, supplying lots of hot showers, extremely clean bathrooms, a launderette, and a well-stocked grocery store (sites £2.30). You can get a good clotted cream tea at the tea room above the antique shop just over the bridge (open daily 10am-6pm), and **Saracen's Head** (tel. 223) serves up huge portions of beef and vegetarian specials for £2 in a medieval atmostphere.

Cars travel frequently between Caernarfon and Beddgelert in July and August, and many hitchhike, making hitcher competition hot and heavy. The A4085 and bus #11 run from Caernarfon and the A498 or bus #97 from Porthmadog.

Blaenau Ffestiniog

Over the last 50 years, the emphasis of the Welsh economy has shifted from farming and mining to farming and tourism, and nowhere is this change more evident than in the old mining towns. Two large mining museums are the sole attractions of desolate **Blaenau Ffestiniog,** which rises defiantly from the broken slate. Beautiful in a grim and eerie way, the town recalls the unvoluptuousness of doom. The most interesting mine is probably **Gloddfa Ganol** (tel. (0766) 830 664), which paints a clear picture of the miner's dark lifestyle with a vast maze of tunnels and caverns (£2.75, children £1.50; open Mon.-Fri. 10am-5:30pm, July-August also Sun.). The **miner's path,** a sometimes treacherous shortcut back to town, with sliding slate heaps, starts opposite the mine's admission booth. **Llechwedd Slate Mine** (tel. (0766) 830 306) still produces small quantities of slate and offers two tours of the caverns: an underground tramway ghost train and a more strenuous walk into the Deep Mine. (Open daily 10am-5pm. Each tour £3.75, £5.75 for both; seniors and children £2.75, £4 for both. 1-mi. walk from town, or take the bus from Queens Hotel.) **The tourist office,** High St. (tel. (0766) 830 360), awaits next to the rail station. (Open Easter and June-Sept. daily 10am-5pm.) The **youth hostel at Ffestiniog** (tel. (0766) 762 765), 3 mi. away, is often booked at peak season, so call at least a week in advance if you are traveling in July or August. (Open March-Oct. and Dec.-Jan. £5.50, ages 16-20 £4.40.) Cheap B&Bs are sprinkled around town: **Madoc House,** High St., is right in the center of town, very clean, and equipped with tea and TVs (£9).

Bus #X84 runs sporadically to Blaenau Ffestiniog from Llanrwst in the north, as do bus #35 from Dolgellau, #38 from Barmouth via Harlech, and #1 from Porthmadog. Trains run along the Conwy Valley line eight times per day (Sun. 2/day). Bus #40 shuttles from the rail station to the slate mines seven times a day.

Conwy

The historical town of Conwy has surrendered its agelessness to clouds of auto exhaust and fallout from a brisk tourist trade. Fish-and-chip shops and boutiques engulf the town's old walls, buses carrying visitors to Conwy Castle scrape through 13th-century arches, and noise accrues into deafening dissonance between narrow rows of shops. Conwy does, however, provide a good base for exploring the northern coastline.

Arriving and Departing

Crosville buses #5 and X5 serve a northern coastal route, passing from Bangor (to the southwest) to Llandudno (across the broad mouth of the River Conwy) via Conwy (every 20 min.; £2 return). Conwy is also on the Sherpa bus line which serves the Vale of Conwy, stopping in Betwy-y-Coed and Capel Curig, and runs as far as the Llyn Peninsula, terminating in Porthmadog (3/day). **National Express** buses leave from Castle St. to London via Chester and Birmingham (3/day). The train station in Llandudno Junction connects to most other train stations in north Wales; Llandudno is an easy 20-min. walk alongside crawling traffic or a 4-min. infrequent train ride from the unstaffed Conwy station.

Orientation and Practical Information

Old Conwy is contained within the castle walls. The A5 enters the town through the castle, promptly dividing into Berry and Castle St. High St. crosses both these avenues at right angles. Rose Hill St. arcs to the left of the castle into Lancaster and becomes Bangor Rd. Watch out for speedy drivers; even the tiniest streets of Conwy are filled with thru-traffic to Bangor and Caernarfon.

Tourist Information Center: Conwy Castle Visitor Centre (tel. 592 248), at the entrance to the castle. Accommodations service (10% deposit) and map (10p). Open Easter-Oct. daily 9:30am-6:30pm.

Buses: Information and schedules from tourist office or visitors center.

Early Closing Day: Wed. at 1pm (off-season only).

Emergency: Dial 999; no coins required.

Financial Services: Barclay's, High St. (tel. 592 881). Open Mon.-Tues., Thurs.-Fri. 9:30am-4:30pm, Wed. 9:30am-3:30pm. Fee £2.

Hospital: Llandudno Hospital, Maesdu Rd. Bus #19 or 49.

Launderette: The closest is in nearby Llandudno Junction. **Launderette,** Conwy Rd. Wash £1, dry 20p. Open daily 8am-8pm. Last wash 7:30pm.

Market Day: Tues. (April-Aug.) and Sat. (year-round) 8:30am-5pm, in the train station car park.

Police: Lancaster Sq. (tel. 592 222).

Post Office: Bangor Rd. (tel. 596 294). Open Mon.-Fri. 9am-1pm and 2-5:30pm, Sat. 9am-12:30pm. **Postal Code:** LL32 8HU.

Telephone Code: 0492.

Train Station: Berry St. Buy tickets on train. Llandudno train station, tel. (0492) 585 151. Open daily 8am-5pm. Lockers 30-50p.

Accommodations and Food

For B&Bs, look around the **Cadnant Park** area (leave the town walls by the post office and turn left; it's a 10-min. walk).

IYHF youth hostel, Penmaenbach (tel. 623 476) on Bangor Rd., 5 mi. from Conwy. Take the shuttle to Bangor, the train to Penmaenmawr, or hitch on the A5. Sparsely furnished, but hot showers and great view. £5.50, ages 16-20 £4.40. Open Mon.-Sat.; Oct.-July Thurs.-Tues. Camping available—call ahead.

Colwyn Bay youth hostel (IYHF), Foxhill, Nant-y-Glyn (tel. 530 627), about 8 mi. from Conwy and 1 mi. from Colwyn Bay. Buses run every 20 min. to Colwyn Bay (#13, 14, 16, 22, or 26; Sun. every hr.). £5.50, ages 16-20 £4.40. Open April-Aug. daily; March and Sept.-Nov. Tues.-Sat.

Cadwern, 5 Cadnant Park (tel. 393 240). Sunny 1st-floor rooms braced by gardens and a riotous proprietor. Includes a mammoth, lilac-filled purple room with bay window for 3-4 people. £12.

Llwyn Guest House, 15 Cadnant Park (tel. 592 319). A warm and welcoming lounge with hosts to match. £12.

Myn-y-Don, Woodlands. Coming into town from Llandudno, turn left before the castle; ¼mi. up from town. Family fun and a teapot full of laughs, overlooking the town wall. £11.50.

Castle View, 3 Berry St. (tel. 596 888). Vast exotic bathrooms with Arabian design, smack dab in the center of town. £11.

Camping: Bwich Mawr Farm, Llanrwst Rd. (tel. 592 856). A steep mile or so outside town on a ridge overlooking the Conwy Valley. Follow Llanrwst Rd. and the posted signs. Equipped with launderette and showers. 2-person tent £5. Open Easter-Sept. Also **Tyddyn Du Farm,** at Penmaenmawr (tel. (0492) 622 300 or 623 830; £2/person).

Most restaurants cater to the tourist crowd. The blinding plastic and chrome take-away mart at the corner of Castle and High St. makes sure you won't miss their cheap and greasy fish-and-chips (open daily noon-9pm). Pack away some pies at the wall-to-wall carpeted **Conwy Steak and Pizza House** on High St. (tel. 593 391); burgers £2, specials £3. (Open daily 10am-10pm.) For afternoon tea, try the **Clemence Restaurant,** Castle St. (tea with scone and cream £1; open daily 9am-9pm), or the outdoor garden at **Castle Tea Gardens,** just up the street (open daily 10am-6pm).

Sights

Conwy Castle was built by Edward I to defend Conwy against the campaigns of Welsh Prince Llewelyn. The castle chapel witnessed Henry "Hotspur" Percy's famous betrayal of Richard II in 1399, and many prominent Normans and English rotted beneath the false bottom of the prison tower. Cromwell's fire ultimately deprived the Welsh of the castle in 1646. (Castle admission £2, seniors and students £1.25. Open daily 9:30am-6:30pm; mid-Oct. to mid-March Mon.-Sat. 9:30am-4pm, Sun. 2-4pm. Tours, when offered, 50p.) The **Conwy Festival,** held in late July, calls local musicians, dancers and medieval performers out into the streets and castle courtyard. Both Telford's elegant **suspension bridge** and the castle can be seen by boat; the ship's captain vociferously announces the departure of the *Queen Victoria* from the quay at the end of High St. (45 min.; £2.50, children £1.50).

In the 14th-century **Aberconwy House,** Castle St. (tel. 592 246), tilted floors and windows weirdly frame displays of armor and period furnishings, and a narrated slide show recounts the town's history. (Open April-Oct. Wed.-Mon. 11am-1pm and 2-5:30pm. Admission £1.20, seniors and children 50p.) Around the corner on High St. is **Plas Mawr** (tel. 592 284), an ornate Elizabethan townhouse laced with sordid stories. (Open daily 10am-5:30pm. Admission £2.20, students £1.25, children 25p.)

Head down High St. and out onto the quay to see if you can fit your pinky finger into **Ty Bach** (tel. 59 34 84), Britain's smallest house. With a total frontage of 72 in., this pill-box housed an elderly couple and then a 6'3" fisherman. (Open March to mid-Oct. daily 10am-6pm. Admission 50p, students and children 30p.) Festering with unkempt grass and satanic tombstones, the ancient walled enclosure of **St. Mary's Church** grumbles quietly to itself behind Conwy's loud streets. The **Butterfly House** (tel. 593 149), in the park outside the walls of Berry St., is just *covered* with butterflies. (Open daily Easter-Oct. 10am-5:30pm. Admission £1.80, seniors £1.20, students £1.) For more silliness, join the crowd at **Towers Restaurant Wishing Well,** opposite the castle, for "Conwy Ghost Tours" (Mon.-Thurs. 6:30pm; £1.50, children 60p).

Vale of Conwy

The soft, lush landscape of the Conwy Valley seems reluctant to make the transition to the harsh peaks of Snowdonia. Although lacking the striking beauty of Mount Snowdon, Conwy's gentle valley makes for far better cycling.

Getting Around

Most chartered coaches stop only at the two end-point cities, Betws-y-Coed and Llandudno, leaving the valley itself relatively undisturbed. One of the best ways to see the Vale is to buy the **Crosville Day Rover** (£4), which gives a day of unlimited travel throughout Gwynedd County, and hop on bus #19: the route winds from Betws-y-Coed up to Conwy and stops in most of the valley's tiny villages. The British Rail **Conwy Valley Day Ranger** ticket gives you a day of unlimited rail travel between Llandudno and Blaenau Ffestiniog, south of Betws-y-Coed, but you'll have to scurry like a squirrel on a hotplate to make it pay off (Mon.-Fri.; £10.50, no railcard discounts).

Sights

The Chilean Fire Bush mingles scandalously with eucrypheas and hydrangea at **Bodnant Gardens** (tel. (0492) 650 460), 8 mi. south of Llandudno off the A470. (Open mid-March to Oct. daily 10am-5pm. Admission £2.50, children £1.25.) The entrance is by the Eglwysbach Rd.; take Crosville bus #25 from Llandudno, Colwyn, or Llandudno Junction, or the Conwy Valley line to Tal-y-Cafn Station (every hr.). Buses run a circular route from Llandudno to the gardens six times per day from May through September.

On the other side of the River Conwy and farther south, the town of **Trefriw** lies along the River Crafnant. **Lake Crafnant,** 3 mi. uphill from town (along the road opposite the Fairy Hotel), is surrounded by some of the highest peaks in Snowdonia. You can hire a rowboat at the small quay during the summer or look on from the lakeside farmhouse café. The folks at the **Trefriw Woolen Mills** (tel. (0492) 640 462), on the banks of the River Crafnant, demonstrate the weaving of their tapestries and tweeds. The Queen Mum buys her frumpy *couture* here. Just outside of town, rock basins offer up the "richest charlybeate" spa waters at the **Trefriw Spa** (tel. 640 057). Originally found to be healthy treatment for anemia, today the water is used to treat rheumatism, eye disease, and homesickness. (A month's supply sells for £6.95. Open Easter-Oct. Mon.-Sat. 10am-5:30pm, Sun. noon-5:30pm. Free. Guided tours £2, seniors £1.80, children £1.) To get to Trefriw, take Crosville Sherpa bus #19 or 49 from Conwy, Llandudno, or Llandudno Junction. (Mills open Easter-Oct. Mon.-Fri. 9am-5:30pm. Free. Shop open Mon.-Fri. 9am-5pm, Sat. 10am-4pm; July-Aug. also Sun. 2-5pm.)

Tuesday is market day in nearby **Llanrwst,** the area's market town. A 15-min. walk takes you to **Gwydyr Castle,** the 16th-century manor of Sir John Wynne (tel.

648 261); the Betws-y-Coed tourist center can give you the low-down on a set of 6 walks through oak forests. Visit the **Queens,** at Station Rd., for an uproarious pint—quiz nights every other Wednesday. For one of the last authentic Welsh teas around, stop at **Tu-Hwnt-i'r-Bont,** an old, ivy-colored cottage across the Llanrwst Bridge on the banks of the River Conwy. (Open Tues.-Sun. 10:30am-5:30pm.) The **IYHF youth hostel in Rowen,** just north of Llanrwst, makes a perfect base for exploring the Vale; Snowden Sherpa bus #19 or 49 from Conwy (every hr., Sun. every 2 hr.) stops in front of the door. Rustic but flavorful. (tel. 231 370. £4.40, ages 16-20 £3.50. Open May-Aug. Wed.-Mon.)

Betws-y-Coed

Situated at the southern tip of the lush Vale of Conwy and the eastern edge of the Snowdonia Mountains, Betws-y-Coed (BET-us uh COYD) makes a convenient though crowded base from which to hike or bike either area. The houses and churches of navy blue hillstone, the ever-present sound of riverrun, and the surrounding tree-covered bluffs all hold their charm against the stiffest summer odds. The eight bridges in Betws deserve a look, especially Telford's 1815 **Waterloo Bridge,** built in the same year as the famous battle.

The cheerful and tireless staff at the self-proclaimed busiest **tourist office** in Wales (tel. (06902) 426 or 665) provides accommodations listings, sight information, bus and train timetables, a well-stocked bookshop, and the occasional lecture. The office faces the train and bus station (open daily 10am-6pm; summer 9am-6pm). Rent bicycles from **Beics Betws** (tel. (0690) 710 766), behind the post office and across from the Vicarage. (Mountain bikes £2.50/hr., £16/day. Tool kit, helmet and map included. Open Mon.-Sat. 9am-5:30pm.)

B&Bs in town charge £12 and up. Try Mr. Jones at **Mairlys** (tel. (06904) 337), next to the Spar Supermarket (£12), or **Bryn Conwy,** next door to the Vicarage (£12.50-13). Call ahead to the local hostels. **Lledr Valley hostel (IYHF)** (tel. 06906) 202) is on the #X84 route to Blaenau Ffestiniog, just past Pont-y-Pant Train Station (£5.90, ages 16-20 £4.70; open Feb.-Oct.). Four Sherpa buses (#19 or 95) per day head west for 5 mi. along the A5 to the luxurious **Capel Curig (IYHF)** (tel. (06904) 225), a favorite with climbers (£6.30, ages 16-20 £5.10; open April-Sept. daily, March and Oct.-Nov. Thurs.-Mon.). **Riverside Caravan Park** (tel. (0960) 310) ducks behind Betws rail station (£3.25/person). The **Dol Gam Campsite** (tel. (0690) 228), midway between Betws-y-Coed and Capel Curig on the A5, charges £2.50 per person. **Gwern Gof Isaf** (tel. 276), halfway to Capel Curig, provides similar grassy patches. Some people camp unofficially along the roads, trusting to security in numbers.

Most of the 30 restaurants in Betws-y-Coed are overpriced. Try the less formal hotels near Pont-y-Pair Bridge (lunch specials about £4), or stock up at the bakeries and small grocery stores lining Holyhead Rd. Take-away food is prohibited in Betws, as it is a National Park village; plastic containers and other litter are not welcome here, nor anywhere in North Wales.

Sherpa #19 connects Betws-y-Coed with Llanrwst, Conwy, or Llanberis, stopping at most of the area hostels four times per day. Betws-y-Coed lies halfway down the Conwy Valley Line between Llandudno and Blaenau Ffestiniog—trains pass through seven times per day Monday through Saturday (two trains on Sun. during high season); winter Sundays are practically silent.

Llangollen

Hidden from the English Midlands by steep tree-covered hills and limestone quarries, Llangollen (thlang-OTH-len) is the first characteristically Welsh town you will encounter if you enter North Wales from England.

Every summer, the town's population of 3000 swells to 80,000 during the **International Eisteddfodd** (ice-THETH-vod). Participants from over 30 countries compete in performances of folk songs, choral works, instrumental works, and folk dances. The festival is held the second week in July. Book tickets and accommodations far in advance through the International Musical Eisteddfod Office, Llangollen, Clywyd, Wales LL20 8NG (tel. 860 236). (Office open Mon.-Fri. 9:30am-12:30pm, 1:30-4:30pm. Unreserved seat and ground admission the day of performances all £2, seniors and children £1. Evening only £1.50, seniors and children £1. Concert tickets £4.50 or £6.50, season tickets £30-£80.) Pubs tend to be overrun during this week and some owners lock their doors after 8pm to avoid being trampled by merrymakers. The **tourist office,** Town Hall, Castle St. (tel. 860 828; open daily 9am-6pm; Oct.-May 9am-5pm) and Eisteddfod office keep an emergency list of accommodations, although some are as far as 15 mi. away. The town's postal code is LL20 8RW; its telephone code 0978.

The friendly wardens at the **IYHF hostel,** Tyndwr Hall (tel. 860 330), 1 mi. out of town, frequently plan days of climbing, archery (both £12), or water sports (£16). Expect to share this newly-renovated 138-bed activity center with a group of some sort. From town, follow the A5 towards Shrewsbury and bear right up Birch Hill. (£6.60, ages 16-20 £5.40. Open March-Oct.) For B&B in town, try the quiet, comfortable rooms at **Mrs. Lewis,** 1 Bodwen Villas (tel. 860 882) for £12.50. **Brynant Rose,** 31 Regent St. (tel. 860 389), has convenient and clean rooms (£12). Campsites abound; probe **Tower Farm,** Tower Rd. (tel. 860 798), at the far end of Eisteddfod campgrounds (£1.50/person) or **Wern Isa Farm,** Wern Rd. (tel. 860 632), with sites ¾mi. from town. Take Wharf Hill to Canal, then turn right up Wern Rd. (£3). The most exciting and the most Welsh of Llangollen's many restaurants is **The Good Taste,** Market St. (tel. 861 425), which serves huge vegetable cobblers "with every kind of bean imaginable." (Open Mon.-Sat. 10am-6pm.)

Though bus service to Llangollen is infrequent, cars passing through the town on the A5 regularly pick up hitchhikers. Most public transport from outside Wales comes as far as Wrexham, 10 min. from Llangollen; trains connect Wrexham with Shrewsbury, Birmingham, and London, and **National Express** buses depart for Birmingham and London (Mon.-Sat. 2/day). Welsh **Gwynedd** buses connect Llangollen to Wales's west coast at Barmouth via Dolgellau (5/day); **Crosville** buses travel north from Wrexham to Chester every 15 min. Local **Bryn Melyn** buses leave Llangollen for Chirk and Wrexham (Mon.-Fri. hourly 9am-5pm; £1.50-1.95 return). The **Bus Gwynedd Pass** (week £9.25) is a good bargain for travel in this area.

Near Llangollen

Perched on a hill overlooking the town are the lyrical ruins of **Dinas Brân** (Crow Castle). The footpath up the hill begins behind the canal museum, and the walk takes about an hour each way. The view from the castle stretches from the mountains near Snowdonia to the flat English Midlands. The 13th-century **Valle Crucis Abbey** (tel. 860 326), 2½ mi. west along the canal towpath (turn right onto the A542 for the last ½mi.), lies serene and roofless in a stunning valley. (Open daily 9:30am-6:30pm; Oct.-Easter 9:30am-4pm. Admission £1, seniors, students, and children 60p.) **Eliseg's Pillar,** just up the road, was once the base of the enormous crucifix from which the Valle Crucis derived its name.

More easily accessible by rail or bus than Llangollen, nearby Wrexham has a **tourist information center,** Lampit St. (tel. 357 845), that may prove particularly helpful in finding accommodations during Llangollen's Eisteddfod week. (Open Mon.-Sat. 10am-5pm.) Native son Elihu Yale founded a wretchedly substandard college in the dismally bland town of New Haven, Connecticut, where he replicated the tower of St. Giles Parish Church. Catch bus #4 to Wrexham from Llangollen.

When you're traveling abroad,
it's nice to hear a familiar voice.
Bobbi Coney
AT&T Operator
Pittsburgh, PA

The language may be difficult.
The food may be different.
The customs may be unfamiliar.
But making a phone call back to the States can be easy.
Just dial the special *AT&T* ***USADirect***® access number for the country you're in.
Within seconds, you're in touch with an *AT&T Operator* in the U.S. who can help you complete your call.
Use your *AT&T Calling Card* or call collect. And not only can you minimize hotel surcharges but you can also save with our international rates.

Only *AT&T* ***USADirect*** *Service* puts you in easy reach of an *AT&T Operator* from over 75 countries around the world.
And it's just another way that AT&T is there to help you from practically anywhere in the world.
So call **1 800 874-4000 Ext. 415** for a free information card listing *AT&T* ***USADirect*** access numbers.
And see how making a phone call from distant lands can become familiar territory.

AT&T ***USADirect***® *Service.*
Your express connection to AT&T service.

AT&T
The right choice.

Shrewsbury

Wales used to be something of a Wild West to the English, and Shrewsbury, east of Machynlleth on the English side of the "Marches," sometimes tended towards extreme violence. David, last Welsh Prince, was hung, drawn and quartered in the town center; this was the first such execution of its kind in Great Britain. In these tamer days, commuters jostle tourists to mount trains and buses to Wales.

Arriving and Departing

Shrewsbury is a whirlpool of rail, with trains spinning out to London (every 2 hr.; 3 hr.; £21), Machynlleth (7/day; 2 hr.; £11), Wolverhampton (every 2 hr.; 1 hr.; £1.80) and most of north Wales. Buses servicing the surrounding area are frequent and far less expensive. **Shearing** buses serve Shrewsbury and its immediate environs, while **National Express** buses go farther afield; call 241 166 for information on either company.

Orientation and Practical Information

The River Severn enters Shrewsbury (pop. 91,000) from the north and embraces the town center on three sides. The Welsh and English Bridges connect to the outskirts, and the castle sits defensively at the narrowest point between two branches of the river, next to the train station. Up the hill lie Pride Hill and Butcher's Row, where in medieval times 25 slaughterers turned their trade; these are still the town's central shopping and business areas. The tourist office is in the Music Hall on Old Market Hall Sq., off High St.

Tourist Office: Music Hall, Market St., The Square (tel. 350 761). Free town maps, accommodation guides and "Where to Eat" pamphlets. Summer walking tours of Shrewsbury's historic streets and architecture (daily 2:30pm, additional tours Sun. 11am; 80p). Office open Easter-Oct. Mon.-Sat. 9:30am-4pm, Sun. 10am-4pm; Nov.-Easter Mon.-Sat. 9:30am-5:30pm.

Bike Rental: Jack Davies, 22A Chester St. (tel. 353 093). £7/day, £35/week. £25 deposit. Open Mon.-Sat. 7:30am-5:30pm, Thurs. 7:30am-2pm.

Bus Station: Raven Meadows. Bus information available from the tourist office or from **Shearings,** Barker St. (tel. 241 166).

Crisis: Samaritans, tel. 369 696; 24 hr.

Emergency: Dial 999; no coins required.

Financial Services: Lloyd's, 1 Pride Hill (tel. 235 051). Open Mon.-Fri. 9:30am-4:30pm, Sat. 9:30am-12:30pm. Fee £2, travelers' checks £4. **Thomas Cook,** 36 Pride Hill (tel. 231 144). Open Mon.-Sat. 9am-5:30pm. Fee £2.50. **American Express:** 27 Claremont St. (tel. 236 387). Open Mon.-Fri. 9am-5:30pm, Sat. 9am-5pm.

Hospital: Shrewsbury Hospital, Copthorne Rd. (tel. 231 122). Bus #13 from Raven Meadows.

Launderette: New Monkmoor Road Launderette, Monkmoor Rd. over English Bridge. Wash £1.20-2; dry 20p; service wash 30p. Open daily 7:30am-7:30pm. Last wash 6:30pm.

Pharmacy: Boots, 7 Pride Hill (tel. 351 311). Open Mon.-Sat. 9am-5:30pm.

Police: corner of Raven Meadows and Roushill (tel. 232 888).

Post Office: St. Mary's St. (tel. 362 925). Open Mon.-Fri. 9am-5:30pm, Sat. 9am-12:30pm. **Postal Code:** SY1 1DE.

Taxi: Station Taxis, tel. 343 305.

Telephone Code: 0743.

Trains: Castle St. Ticket office open daily 5am-10pm. Information open daily 8am-6pm.

Accommodations

The **Shrewsbury youth hostel,** The Woodlands, Abbey Foregate (tel. 360 179), lies about 1 mi. from the rail station. From town, cross the English Bridge, pass the abbey, and follow signs to Shirehall; or catch bus #8 or 26 from the town center. Housed in a large Victorian ironmaster's house, the hostel offers laundry facilities, video games, and a mini-pool table. (Open daily March to mid-Sept.; mid-Sept. to Oct. open Mon.-Sat.; Nov.-Dec., Feb. open weekends. £6.30, ages 16-20 £5.10.) B&Bs in town tend to be fairly expensive (£14-18). **Sunbeams,** Bishop St. (tel. 357 495), off Monkmoor Rd., offers a ray of light: friendly proprietors scrub their simple lodgings and offer tea to tired backpackers for £11.50. **Abbey Lodge,** 68 Abbey Foregate (tel. 235 832), is a delightful, family-run, hotel-quality B&B which pampers its guests with TV, tea, and a car park (£13).

Food

Though Shrewsbury's streets sweat with every kind of fast food imaginable, slower food is also in good form. For cheap and delicious baked goods in a serve-yourself cafeteria, try **Stanton's,** 26 Claremont St. (Open Mon.-Sat. 8am-5pm.) **The Good Life Wholefood Restaurant,** Barracks Passage, Wyle Cop (tel. 350 455), downstairs from the Lion Hotel, occupies a restored 14th-century building (everything under £2; open Mon.-Fri. 9:30am-3:30pm, Sat. 9:30am-4:30pm). **The Little Gourmet** on Castle St. butters superb French-bread sandwiches for £1. (Open Mon.-Sat. 9am-5:30pm.) **Muswell's,** 49 Mardol (tel. 271 568), an elegant indoor/outdoor café with black and white photos and background jazz, brings a smile to American faces with their *iced* water. (Specials £1.50. Open Mon.-Sat. noon-10pm, Sun. noon-9pm.) Next door at 50 Mardol St., the family-run **Pizza Two Four** (tel. 344 834) is applauded by all of Shrewsbury; pizzas £3, pastas £4. (Open Mon.-Sat. 11:30am-2pm, daily 6-10pm.)

Sights

Shrewsbury overflows with stone buildings, timber-frame neighborhoods and huge Georgean townhouses that all claim to have sheltered famous men, including Charles Darwin. The daily tour from the Music Hall (80p) drags you through old alleyways (called "shuts" because they were used to keep out strangers) to the castle grounds, administering soporiphics along the way. The **Shrewsbury Castle** (tel. 358 516), just up from the train station, was built by Roger of Montgomery in 1083 only to be stripped of its stones for town building projects; rebuilt by Poultney in the 19th century, the castle looks quite hale today. The **Regimental Museum** inside the castle houses plenty of armor, war memorabilia, and a lock of Napoleon's hair. (Open daily 10am-5pm. Last admission 4pm. Admission 80p, grounds and gardens free.) Just behind the castle lies the **County Jail,** built in 1830 by Thomas Telford (the designer of the A5 to Holyhead and numerous bridges) as an innovative experiment in prison design. Then, inmates were housed in separate cells to prevent contagion; today, tourists are cordoned off entirely. (Free.)

According to local law, sheep are free to graze in the shuts (alleys) of the town; ignoring the protests of nearby bakers and grocers, a number even infiltrate the churyard at **St. Mary's,** across from the post office. The church boasts stained-glass windows from all over the world. The gardens and sarcophagi at the **Abbey** warrant a trip across the English bridge... of course, Abbys tend to be pretty cool.

SCOTLAND

Scotland at its best is a world apart, yet its modern cities often threaten to upstage the natural drama that surrounds them: exuberant Glasgow, the 1990 European City of Culture, is the most Scottish in character, and Edinburgh is transformed annually into an epicenter of culture during its International Festival. Over half the size of England with but one tenth its population, Scotland revels in open space that varies in character with the geography of the land. The kaleidescope of mountains and lochs along the west coast and under the luminescent mists of the western isles is divine, while the bucolic borders to the south, the level river valleys along the east coast, and the garden islands of Orkney in the north all display an intimate beauty not always present in the sweeping vistas of the mountainous regions.

The Scottish people will show you a rare blend of respect and geniality. Whether they greet you with the Scandinavian lilt of the northern isles or the Gaelic accent of the Hebrides, passersby still say "good morning," even in the crowded chaos of the Glasgow subway. Despite reluctant union with England in 1707, the Scottish continue to nurture a separate identity and retain control over certain social and political institutions, such as schools, churches, and the judicial system. At times the uniquely Scottish heritage seems overplayed, as with the famous kilts, clans and bagpipes; in fact, the popularity of these icons probably owes more to the clever marketing efforts of 18th century woollen merchants than to any local tradition.

Getting There

Both **Edinburgh** and **Glasgow Airports** handle flights from the continent, and Glasgow receives transatlantic flights. The cheapest way to Scotland from outside Britain is usually through London; although the coach trip from London's Victoria Station takes more than seven hours, fares are one half the cost of trains. Two companies, **Scottish Citylink** and **Caledonian Express,** offer service to Scotland (standard fares for both lines £27, return £29). Students should ride with Citylink (£19.50 return, valid 3 months); Caledonian Express has comparable discounts but to take advantage of them you must buy a £5 discount card which is unnecessary for discounts within Scotland. The cheapest non-student fare to Edinburgh is the standby on Caledonian Express (£22.50; no specific seat guaranteed); fares to Glasgow are similar. Buses depart London before 1pm (day service) and after 9pm (overnight service). Advance reservations are helpful; call (071) 636 9373 for Scottish Citylink, (071) 730 0202 for Caledonian Express Stagecoach.

From London, trains to Scotland take only 5 hr., but fares are steep: to Edinburgh (16-21/day, most from King's Cross Station; £55, 1 month return £65) and to Glasgow (5-9/day from Euston Station). Book one week in advance for the economical APEX fare (£44 return); you must return within one month of your departure. For enquiries in London call Euston Station (tel. (071) 387 7070) or King's Cross (tel. (071) 278 2477).

Air travel is even more expensive; APEX return fares (£99; 2 wk. advance booking required) between Heathrow and Edinburgh or Glasgow are available on **British Airways** (tel. (081) 897 4000), **British Midland** (tel. 589 5599), and **Air UK** (tel. (0345) 666 777). British Airways and British Midland also sell a limited number of APEX return tickets for £70, which stipulate that you must stay over a Sat. night; call far ahead and ask about the zed class flights. Air UK's **Skylink Singles** (from Gatwick £65; reservable day before departure only) are the choicest of the one-wayfares. **Dan-Air** (tel. (0345) 100 200) offers competitive direct flights to Inverness and Aberdeen.

Scotland is also linked by **ferry** to Northern Ireland (see Larne or Stranraer), and to Norway and the Faroe Islands (see Thurso and the Shetland Islands).

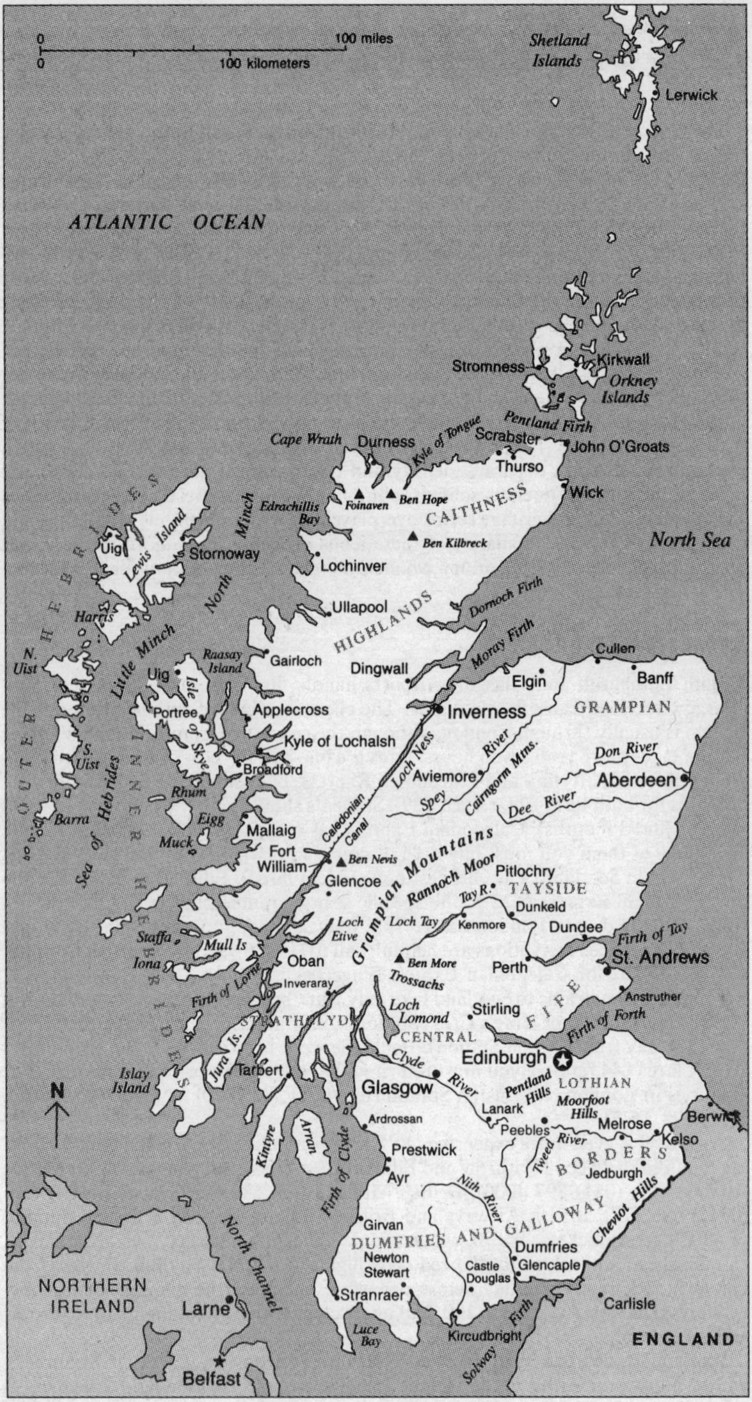
0 100 miles
0 100 kilometers
Shetland Islands
Lerwick
ATLANTIC OCEAN
Stromness
Kirkwall
Orkney Islands
Pentland Firth
Cape Wrath
Durness
Kyle of Tongue
Scrabster
John O'Groats
Thurso
Wick
Foinaven
Ben Hope
CAITHNESS
Edrachillis Bay
Ben Kilbreck
North Sea
Uig
Lewis Island
Stornoway
North Minch
Lochinver
OUTER HEBRIDES
Ullapool
Dornoch Firth
Harris
HIGHLANDS
Moray Firth
N. Uist
Little Minch
Raasay Island
Gairloch
Dingwall
Cullen
Elgin
Banff
Uig
Isle of Skye
GRAMPIAN
Portree
Applecross
Inverness
Kyle of Lochalsh
Loch Ness
River
S. Uist
Cairngorm Mts.
Don River
Broadford
Aviemore
Aberdeen
INNER HEBRIDES
Rhum
Caledonian Canal
Spey
Dee River
Barra
Sea of Hebrides
Eigg
Mallaig
Muck
Fort William
Ben Nevis
Grampian Mountains
Pitlochry
Glencoe
Rannoch Moor
TAYSIDE
Tay R.
Dunkeld
Loch Tay
Kenmore
Dundee
Loch Etive
Staffa
Mull Is
Firth of Tay
Iona
Oban
Ben More
Perth
St. Andrews
Trossachs
Inveraray
FIFE
Anstruther
Firth of Lorne
Loch Lomond
Stirling
STRATHCLYDE
CENTRAL
Firth of Forth
Jura Is.
Edinburgh
Clyde
Islay Island
Tarbert
River
Pentland Hills
LOTHIAN
Glasgow
Moorfoot Hills
N
Lanark
Berwick
Ardrossan
Peebles
Melrose
River
Kelso
Arran
Prestwick
Tweed
BORDERS
Kintyre
Firth of Clyde
Jedburgh
Ayr
Nith River
DUMFRIES AND GALLOWAY
Cheviot Hills
North Channel
Girvan
Newton Stewart
Dumfries
Castle Douglas
Glencaple
NORTHERN IRELAND
Stranraer
Larne
Carlisle
Luce Bay
Kircudbright
Solway Firth
ENGLAND
Belfast

Before you leave London, visit the **Scottish Tourist Board** office at 19 Cockspur St. (tel. 930 8661. Tube: Charing Cross or Piccadilly Circus.) They have buckets-full of books and free brochures and can book train, bus, and plane tickets at their travel desk (open Mon.-Fri. 9am-6pm).

Getting Around

No matter how you travel in Scotland, the *Touring Map of Scotland* (£2.95 at any tourist office) is a wise investment. *Getting Around the Highlands and Islands* (£4, available at all tourist offices in the Highlands) is an indispensable reference book for travel in the north of Scotland. This comprehensive timetable and map includes even the most obscure bus, ferry, and rail services in the Highlands. Unfortunately, no such crutch exists for other regions in Scotland.

Train or bus travel within the Lowlands (south of Stirling and north of the Borders) is much like travel in England. Rail connections are frequent, buses run almost everywhere, and transportation is relatively cheap. In the Highlands, though, trains snake slowly north on a few restricted routes, bypassing almost the entire Northwest region, and bus services, though extensive, are slow and infrequent. Public transport in this region virtually halts on Sundays. Even if you intend to do all your sightseeing by bus and train, it may not be physically possible to make the various rail and bus passes profitable; no single company offers a network comprehensive enough that their pass allows sufficient freedom or flexibility. A possible exception is the off-season **Travelpass '92,** which allows travel by ferry to Orkney and the Western Isles, unlimited train travel and discounted bus fares. (From Oct.-May, an 8-day pass goes for £40, a 15-day pass for £60; both are about £30 more from June-Sept.) Furthermore, intense competition in some regions has resulted in some extremely low fares, especially for students.

Bus travel in Scotland is a steal. Tickets often cost as little as half the train fare, and service is usually more frequent and almost as fast and comfortable. In addition, students receive a 1/3 fare reduction on medium and long-distance trips. **Scottish Citylink** and **Caledonian Express** are the main long-distance operators. Unfortunately, neither company has printed a comprehensive timetable. Bus stations are often closed or nonexistent, but tickets can always be bought on board. In rural areas, wave to signal the driver to stop.

ScotRail trains are clean and punctual, if not especially cheap. Pick up their comprehensive timetable (available at all stations). The £16 Student Coach Card (for ages 16-23 as well), available at major stations, reduces all fares by 1/3 for a one-year period; bring two photos.

Air travel is predictably expensive between major cities, but British Air offers a good deal in the north: a ½hr. flight between Orkney and Shetland costs about the same as the 8-hr. ferry, providing that you spend a night in a B&B after arriving.

Many **hitchhike** in Scotland, except in places like the Northwest and Inverness, where cars crammed full of namby-pamby tourists make up a large percentage of the traffic. Drivers tend to be most receptive in the least-traveled areas. Far to the northwest and in the Western Isles, the Sabbath is strictly observed, making it difficult or impossible to get a ride on Sundays.

Biking

Scotland offers scenic, challenging terrain for biking. You can usually rent bikes even in very small towns and transport them by ferry for little or no charge. In the Highlands, even major roads often have only one lane, and locals drive at high speeds—keep your eye out for the passing zones.

Bringing a bike to the Highlands by public transportation can be as difficult as pedalling there. Many Scotrail trains carry only three or fewer bikes; reservations (£3) are essential. Beginning in April, the **Bike Bus** (tel. (031) 229 6274) will take you and your bike from Edinburgh to different points north and south on summer weekends (£4-6). Hitching with a bicycle is often easier than it sounds.

Both the northern and western isles are of a negotiable scale and terrain for bicyclists. The area of Fife and regions south of Edinburgh and Glasgow offer gentle pastoral pedalling. Touring or mountain biking in the Highlands allows a freedom of access to the remote beauty of this area which easily compensates for the physically demanding cycling. *Mountainbiking in the Scottish Highlands* (£6) by Frances Fleming outlines many rides with meticulous maps and gradient profiles.

Hiking and Hill-walking

Two long-distance footpaths, the West Highland Way and the Southern Upland Way, were planned and marked by the Countryside Commission under the Countryside Act of 1967. The **West Highland Way** begins just north of Glasgow in Milngavie and snakes 95 mi. north along Loch Lomond, through Glencoe to Fort William and Ben Nevis ("from Scotland's largest city to its highest mountain"). The **Southern Upland Way** runs 212 mi. from Portpatrick on the southwest coast to Cockburnspath on the east coast, passing through Galloway Forest Park and the Borders. Most tourist offices distribute simple maps of the Ways as well as a list of accommodation options along the routes. For more information on these paths, write to the Scottish Tourist Board, 23 Ravelston Terr., Edinburgh EH4 3EU. Comprehensive guidebooks to both paths are available (£10 and £6 respectively) at most bookstores.

Scottish mountaineering is dominated by the frequently obsessive practice of Munro Bagging. Hugh T. Munro compiled the original list of Scottish peaks over 3000 ft. in 1891; today about 280 are recorded. Any addition sends thousands of hikers scrambling up previously unnoticed peaks to maintain their distinction of having "bagged every Munro." Some people accomplish this feat over a lifetime of hiking; others do it in a frenetic six months. Thankfully, only one Munro, the Inaccessible Pinnacle on Skye, requires technical rock-climbing skills. *The Munros* (£11), put out by the Scottish Mountaineering Club, presents a comprehensive list of the peaks along with climbing information. In *The First Fifty Munro Bagging Without a Beard* (£13), the irreverent peroxide blond Muriel Gray presents a humorous account of this compulsive sport.

Mountain areas like the Cuillins, the Torridons, Glen Nevis, and Glencoe all have hostels situated in the midst of the ranges, providing bases for spectacular round-trip hikes. You can also walk along mainland Britain's highest sea cliffs at Cape Wrath or ramble across eerie moors and rock formations of the Outer Hebrides and the Northwest.

One of the most attractive aspects of hiking in Scotland is that you can often pick your own route across the heather (you should check first with the local warden, ranger, or landowner). The wilds do pose certain dangers. The cairns (stone markers) can be unreliable, and expanses of open heather will often destroy the surest sense of direction. Heavy mists are always a possibility, and blizzards can surprise you even in July. Never go up into the mountains without the proper equipment: sturdy, well-broken-in boots, a 1:50,000 Ordnance Survey map, a compass, adequate waterproof gear and clothing to withstand freezing temperatures, an aluminized mylar blanket, insect repellent, and an emergency food supply. Leave a copy of your planned route and timetable at the hostel or nearest mountain rescue station. From mid-August to mid-October, always consult the hostel warden or innkeeper about areas in which deerstalkers might be at work. For more information on walking and mountaineering in Scotland, consult Poucher's *The Scottish Peaks* (£9) or the introductory Tourist Board booklet, *Hillwalking in Scotland* (£2.25).

Accommodations

SYHA hostels are the most economical lodgings in Scotland; hostel standards are perhaps the best in the world. The price range is low (£3.20-6.40), and there are hostels in or near almost every city and region described in this section. SYHA regulations are quite strict; curfews and lockouts are tightly enforced, and, except in Edinburgh, Glasgow, and Inverness, guests must do a chore before their membership card is returned in the morning (those planning an early departure should request evening duties). Hostels are carefully graded: grade 1 hostels have laundry facilities, free hot showers, shorter lockouts, and often a microwave in the kitchen. Most grade 2 hostels charge for hot showers, may have more primitive clothes-washing facilities, and have lockouts until 5pm. Grade 3 hostels, usually more remote, lack hot showers and clothes washers, but compensate with coziness and lenience. A sleepsack (rentable for 50p) and an IYHF membership card (purchasable as you go) are required at all grades. The *SYHA Handbook* (75p) is extremely useful; it lists all telephone numbers and opening dates, and its excellent maps might save hours of aimless wandering. Advance booking during June-Aug. is *essential.* Hostels accept telephone reservations between 7 and 10pm (never on the same day as arrival) and hold them until 6pm (or sometimes later if you can specify a train or bus arrival time). The SYHA has introduced a **faxbooking system** between its most popular hostels (mostly grade 1); 50p plus the prepaid unrefundable overnight fee assures you of a bed up to 10pm on your date of arrival. Many hostels close in October and reopen in March, April, or May.

Some travelers prefer the growing Scottish network of **independent hostels.** Though their atmosphere and rules are usually more relaxed than those at SYHA hostels, facilities vary considerably. A partial list is available on the back of the *Irish Independent Hostels Organization hostel guide* (20p).

B&Bs are a comfortable but more expensive alternative. For less than £13, you can have privacy and the luxury of sleeping late. It's best to book B&Bs using tourist office literature. Most tourist offices charge £1 for local booking (with a 10% deposit), except in Edinburgh where the same service costs £2.50. By booking independently, you save both the tourist office fee and a surcharge which some B&B owners add to their prices to compensate for the 10% taken by the tourist offices. In addition, all tourist offices participate in the Book-a-Bed-Ahead scheme which allows you to reserve a room in any other region in Scotland for a £1.95 fee; they do all the phoning. All tourist offices issue glossy regional accommodations directories that become increasingly important resources as the summer tourist season heats up.

You can camp free on all public land, but make sure you know which areas are restricted *(i.e.,* preserves or other protected land). Always ask the landowner's permission if you suspect you're on privately owned land. Private sites, usually geared to caravans, charge £3-5 per tent and vary widely in quality; a good investment is *Scotland: Camping and Caravan Parks* (£3.25) available at any tourist office. Beware of Scotland's often wet and cold weather. You should use a sleeping-bag with artificial insulation, rather than down (which deflates unpleasantly when wet). Gore-Tex jackets are strongly recommended.

History

Unlike their English neighbors, Scotland's Celtic tribes successfully repelled Roman incursions. Emperor Hadrian sagely built a wall across the north of England to fend off the pitchfork-tossing farmers of the north. The invading tribes from the continent, however, were more successful, and by 600 AD the Scottish mainland was inhabited by four groups: the Picts, Scots, Britons, and Angles. The Pict-Scot kingdom formed under the leadership of Kenneth MacAlpin (Kenneth I) in about 843 AD to ward off Viking conquerors. By 1034, the Angles and Romanized Britons of the Lowlands had been incorporated into this united kingdom; James IV subjugated Caithness and Sutherland, and received Orkney and Shetland as a gift from Christian I of Denmark.

The increasingly powerful English monarchy posed an intermittent but considerable threat to Scottish independence throughout the Middle Ages and well into the 16th century. After a century-long peace under Alexanders II and III, Scotland was attacked by Edward I who sought to reimpose English rule. Arachnophilic Robert the Bruce emerged as Scotland's leader (1306-1329) after the Wars of Independence. During the 15th- and early 16th-century the monarchy set nobles against one another in an attempt to preserve its own waning position, and the Reformation further split allegiances within the country: Scottish objections to Roman supremacy in the church merely reinforced English power.

In the midst of this turmoil, Mary, Queen of Scots (1542-1567), prompted a civil war that lasted until 1573. Her ambitious son James VI was crowned King James I of England in 1603, uniting both countries under a single crown. James ruled from London, and his half-hearted attempts to reconcile the Scottish domains were tartly resisted. Scots Presbyterians supported Cromwellian forces in the English Civil War. However, when in 1649 the English Parliament executed Charles, the Scots named his son Charles II as King. Oliver Cromwell readily defeated him as well, but in a conciliatory gesture gave Scotland representation in the English Parliament. Although this body did not last, the political precedent of representation endured.

England and Scotland were permanently united when England engaged in the War of Spanish Succession (1701-1714) and requested the support of its neighbor. Scotland, forced to choose between England and its long-suffering ally, France, decided that its Presbyterian interests were safer with Anglicans than with Catholics. The 18th century proved to be the most culturally and economically prosperous in Scotland's history, producing such luminaries as Adam Smith David Hume.

The civil wars of the 18th century pitted Highlanders against Lowlanders and Roman Catholics against Presbyterians. Though 19th-century political reforms did much to improve social conditions, economic problems in both the 19th and 20th centuries induced many to emigrate.

Today Scotland has 71 seats in the British House of Commons and is largely integrated into the English economy. Nevertheless, the Scots Nationalist Party regularly demands a greater degree of autonomy. One can still seriously offend a Scot by using the term "England" to generalize about what should be called "Britain" or "the U.K." Indeed, Her Majesty's Government has conceded the inevitability of change, and some adjustment in the relationship is imminent.

Literature

While the words of early Scottish authors such as Robert Burns (1771-1832), Sir Walter Scott (1771-1832), and Robert Louis Stevenson (1850-94) continue to draw a loyal following, the latter half of the 20th century has witnessed a revival of Scottish language and culture: the rock group Run Rig seeks to popularize traditional music, and modern poets such as Hugh MacDiarmid (1892-1978), Norman McCaig, and Edwin Morzan turn to traditional Scottish themes for inspiration. Nell Gunn's *Silver Darlings,* or anything by Lewis Grassic Gibbon, should dispel the illusion that the Scottish novel died with Sir Walter Scott. Novels by Alasdair Gray, such as *Lanark, Unlikely Stories Mostly,* and *Janine 1984,* recapture the exuberant complexity of contemporary Scottish life. For a history of Scotland, try Linklater's *The Prince in the Heather,* or the not always rigorously truthful *Highland Clearances* by John Prebble.

Food and Drink

A few dishes invoke the good old days of the tartan clans and cavorting livestock—most notably black pudding, made with sheep's blood, and the infamous *haggis*, traditionally a bladder filled with sheep's pluck and eaten with *neeps* (turnips). They sound more exotic than they taste. Ubiquitous tea and coffee shops provide the cheapest meals at lunch, but often sell only soup, sandwiches, and french fries. Pub meals are more substantial and cost £2.50-3 (usually served noon-2pm and 6-9pm; often the only option on a Sunday). The biggest supermarket chains are Presto, Wm. Low, and the Co-op.

Scotch whisky is either "malt" (from a single distillery), or "blended" (a mixture of several different brands). The malts are all good and distinctive; the blends are the same as those available abroad. Due to heavy "sin taxes" on all alcohol sold in Britain, Scotch may often be cheaper at home than in Scotland. (Pubs are generally open Mon.-Sat. 11am-11pm, Sun. 12:30-2pm and 6:30-11pm. Bars in big cities often stay open as late as 4am.)

Central Scotland

The urban corridor slanting northeast from Glasgow, on the Firth of Clyde, to Edinburgh, on the Firth of Forth, is home to more than half the Scots in Scotland. Only 30 miles apart, Scotland's capital and its second largest city are strung together by numerous multiple lane highways. In danger of merging into a single megalopolis, the two cities cling fiercely to their traditionally distinct identities. During the 18th and 19th centuries, Glasgow propelled itself to prosperity through trade and steel production while Edinburgh took a less sooty path to fame, emerging as a fountainhead of Enlightenment thought; even today Glasgow presents a grittier image than its photogenic neighbor. The fertile fields of Fife lie by the North Sea within easy reach of both Edinburgh and Glasgow. Venerable St. Andrews, site of Scotland's oldest university, distinguishes itself with idyllic white sand beaches, intriguing ruins, and well-groomed golf-links. South of St. Andrews, several small fishing ports invite visitors to ramble through their narrow, irregular streets.

Edinburgh

Scotland's magnificent capital is less a city than an event, a complex drama of natural rock and molded stone. From the castle-crowned volcano that rises abruptly from the city's center, across the elegant green parks that lace through the trough of a drained loch, and over to the lofty summit of King Arthur's seat, Edinburgh makes dramatic use of the third dimension. The city's visual splendor is matched by its cultural wealth: Edinburgh boasts a heady mixture of superb museums, galleries, bookstores, and pubs.

Edinburgh became the capital of Scotland in the 15th century. Today it is the administrative center of this semi-autonomous region whose current political status was determined by the Parliamentary Union of 1707. The old city's 12-story tenements, separated by dark alleyways, were marveled at as "skyscrapers" by medieval visitors and immortalized by the city's own Robert Louis Stevenson as the horrific setting of *Dr. Jekyll and Mr. Hyde.* The reformer John Knox exiled Mary, Queen of Scots from Edinburgh and built the strictly Calvinist legal, educational, and religious systems that continue to distinguish Scotland from its southern neighbor. More than 100 years later, in the early 18th century, the dark alleys of this Calvinist Kingdom of God became the unlikely setting for an outpouring of philosophical and literary talent that rendered Edinburgh a capital of the Enlightenment. The philosopher David Hume presided over a republic of letters that gave the world

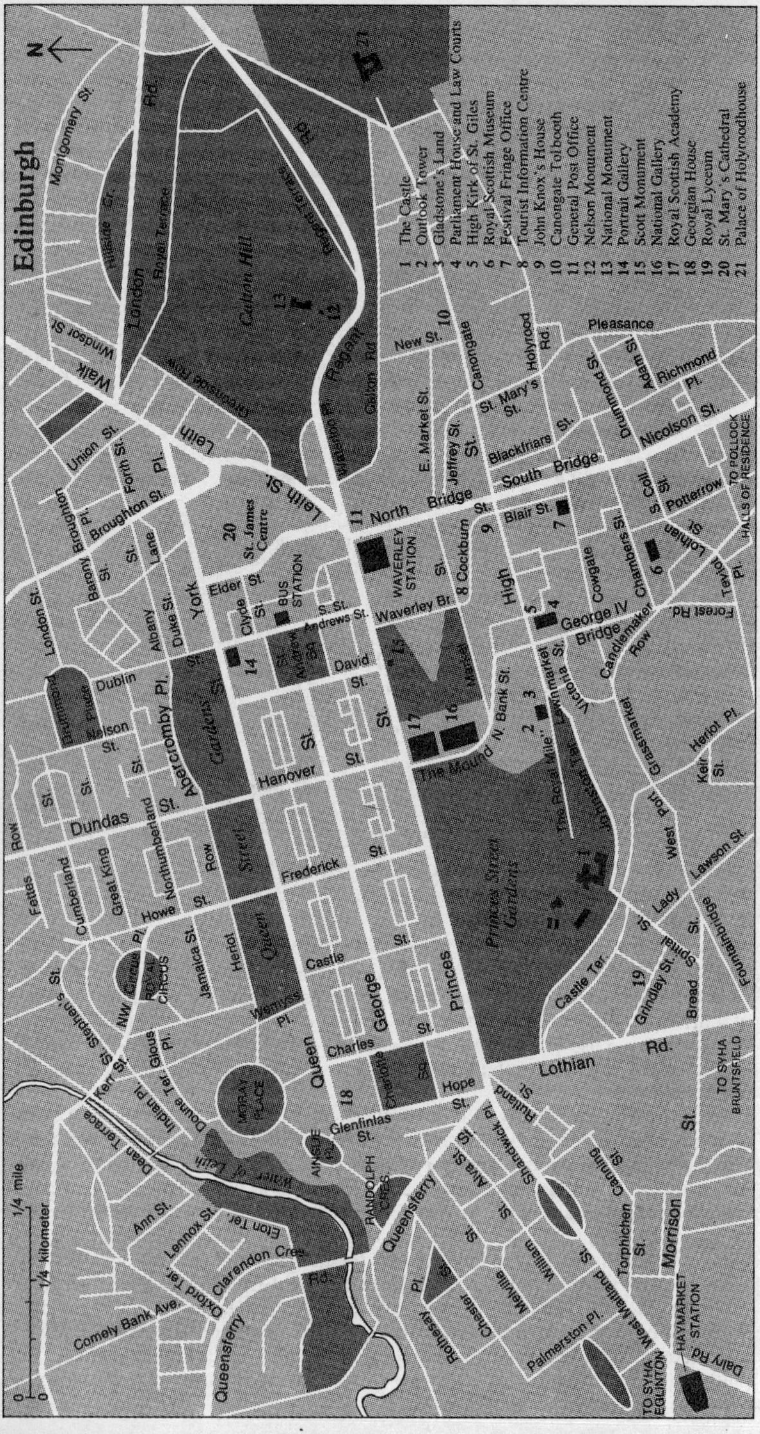
Edinburgh
N
1 The Castle
2 Outlook Tower
3 Gladstone's Land
4 Parliament House and Law Courts
5 High Kirk of St. Giles
6 Royal Scottish Museum
7 Festival Fringe Office
8 Tourist Information Centre
9 John Knox's House
10 Canongate Tolbooth
11 General Post Office
12 Nelson Monument
13 National Monument
14 Portrait Gallery
15 Scott Monument
16 National Gallery
17 Royal Scottish Academy
18 Georgian House
19 Royal Lyceum
20 St. Mary's Cathedral
21 Palace of Holyroodhouse
Calton Hill
Regent Terrace
Regent Rd.
Royal Terrace
London Rd.
Hillside Cr.
Montgomery St.
Leith Walk
Windsor St.
Greenside Row
Union St.
Forth St.
Broughton St.
Broughton Pl.
Barony St.
London St.
Albany St.
Duke St.
York Pl.
Elder St.
Clyde St.
BUS STATION
St. James Centre
Leith St.
Waterloo Pl.
Calton Rd.
New St.
North Bridge
WAVERLEY STATION
Waverley Br.
E. Market St.
Jeffrey St.
Canongate
St. Mary's St.
Holyrood Rd.
Pleasance
Blackfriars St.
South Bridge
Drummond St.
Adam St.
Richmond Pl.
Nicolson St.
TO POLLOCK HALLS OF RESIDENCE
Blair St.
Cockburn St.
High St.
Cowgate
Chambers St.
S. Coll. St.
Potterrow
Lothian St.
Teviot Pl.
Forrest Rd.
George IV Bridge
Candlemaker Row
Victoria St.
Lawnmarket
The Royal Mile
Johnston Ter.
Grassmarket
Heriot Pl.
Keir St.
West Port
Lawson St.
Lady Lawson St.
Spittal St.
Grindlay St.
Bread St.
Fountainbridge
Castle Ter.
Lothian Rd.
TO SYHA BRUNTSFIELD
Morrison St.
Canning St.
Torphichen St.
Dalry Rd.
HAYMARKET STATION
TO SYHA EGLINTON
West Maitland St.
Palmerston Pl.
Princes Street Gardens
Princes St.
The Mound
N. Bank St.
Market St.
St. Andrews St.
S. St. Andrews St.
St. Andrew Sq.
St. David St.
Hanover St.
Frederick St.
Castle St.
Charles St.
George St.
Queen St.
Queen Street Gardens
Heriot Row
Abercromby Pl.
Dundas St.
Northumberland St.
Great King St.
Cumberland St.
Fettes Row
Howe St.
Jamaica St.
Royal Circus
NW Circus Pl.
St. Stephen's St.
Nelson St.
Dublin St.
Drummond Place
Charlotte Sq.
Hope St.
Glenfinlas St.
Ainslie Pl.
Randolph Cres.
Moray Place
Wemyss Pl.
Glous. Pl.
Doune Ter.
Kerr St.
Indian Pl.
Dean Terrace
Water of Leith
Ann St.
Lennox St.
Eton Ter.
Clarendon Cres.
Oxford Ter.
Comely Bank Ave.
Queensferry Rd.
Queensferry St.
Rutland St.
Shandwick Pl.
Alva St.
Melville St.
William St.
Chester St.
Rothesay Pl.
1/4 mile
1/4 kilometer
0

the invisible hand of economist Adam Smith, the poetry of Allan Ramsay and Robert Fergusson, and the literary wanderings of Tobias Smollett, Sir Tristan Busch, and Sir Walter Scott.

The graceful symmetry and orderly gridwork of architect James Craig's designs for Georgian New Town won him the city planning prize in 1767. Though effectively leaving its imprint on the city, the Age of Reason did not completely dismantle the narrow, winding alleys and dark, huddled buildings from which it sprang. The International Festival in August brings both an effusion of culture and a sweaty mass of camera-happy tourists to this city which bridges the generations.

Arriving and Departing

Edinburgh lies 45 mi. east of Glasgow and 405 mi. northwest of London on Scotland's east coast, on the southern bank of the Firth of Forth. Edinburgh is a major hub of Scotland's bus network. Scottish Citylink Service runs form **St. Andrew Square bus station** to Glasgow (#500/501 at least 1/hr. 5:45am-2am, every 15 min. during rush hr., Sun. 8am-2am; £3.50, £4 return); Aberdeen (1/hr. 6:45am-7:15pm; £8.80, £11.10 return); Inverness (#557/569/555, 1/hr. 7:10am-7:15pm; £8.80, £11.70); Thurso (2/day at 9:15am, 1:15pm; £12.10, £18 return); Broadford (2/day at 5:45 am, 8am; £20, £26.20 return); and London (8/day 7am-10:30pm; £27.50, £29.50 return). When travel in both directions takes place on Mon.-Thurs., fares are about 20% lower. As always, flash a student ID for 1/3off all fares.

Trains leave Edinburgh's **Waverly Station** for: Glasgow (every ½hr. 7:30am-11:30pm; £4.70); Aberdeen (17/day 6:40am-8:40pm; £21.50, £25 return); Fort William (4/day, 3 on Sunday 6:52am-3:30pm; £22, £32 return); Inverness (12/day 7:40am-11:45pm; £18, £24 return); Thurso (3/day 7:40am-11;45pm, same train as Inverness; £23.90, £32.30 return); and Stranraer (5/day 6:55am-9pm; £16.50, £18 return). Service is usually less frequent on Sundays and fares are all about £2 higher on Fridays.

Hitchhiking out of Edinburgh is not difficult if you first take local transportation out of the heart of the city. For points south (except Newcastle and the northeast of England), take bus #4, 15, or 79 to Fairmilehead and then the A702 to Biggar. For Newcastle, York, and Durham, take bus #15, 26, or 43 to Musselburgh and the A1. Take bus #18 or 40 to Barnton for the Forth Road Bridge and the north.

Orientation and Practical Information

Edinburgh's small distances and quiet streets make it an ideal city for perambulation. Princes St. is the main thoroughfare in the New Town, the northern section of Edinburgh; "The Royal Mile" (made up of Lawnmarket, High St., and Canongate) is the major road in the Old Town, the southern half of the city. Three bridges—North Bridge, Waverley Bridge, and The Mound—connect these two areas. Street names, in the Old Town especially, often change every few blocks. Waverly train station lies between North Bridge and Waverly Bridge, in what used to be the loch that protected the old town to the north. St. Andrew Square bus station is a short 3 blocks from the east end of Princes St.

Although you feet will often suffice, Edinburgh does have an efficient and comprehensive (but confusing) bus system. There are two main companies. **Lothian Regional Transport** or LRT (maroon doubledecker buses; tel. 220 4111) was Edinburgh's only bus company before privatization, and still provides the most comprehensive service. At their **Ticket Centre** on Waverly Bridge, you can buy a one-day **Freedom Ticket** pass (£1.60, children £1.10) as well as longer-term buspasses and tickets to the airport (£2.50, children £1.65; open Mon.-Sat. 7am-8pm, Sun. 8:30am-6:30pm). **Eastern Scottish** (green and cream buses, tel. 558 1616) offers less frequent coverage of the city, but their one-day **Edinburgh Explorer Ticket** is only £1.40; get it at the busy Eastern Scottish office in St. Andrew Square bus station (open Mon.-Tues. and Thurs.-Sat. 8:40am-5pm, Wed. 9am-5pm, Sun. 10am-5pm). Fares are paid on board the buses and vary from 30p-£1.10 according to an incomprehensible system of "stages"; your driver can tell you the price of your destination. *Drivers do not give change;* carry coins. (Call **Busline,** tel. 225 3858, Mon.-Fri. 8:30am-4:30pm for further info.)

Tourist Information Center: Waverley Market, 3 Princes St., Edinburgh EH2 2QP (tel. 557 1700), next to the Waverley train station. Busy but efficient accommodations service (£2.50); bookshop with maps and B&B and camping listings. Pick up a complimentary copy of *What's On in Edinburgh,* and the free Edinburgh accommodations booklet. Book-a-bed-ahead service £2.50. *Bureau de change* open same hours as the office. Scottish Citylink tickets sold here and information on travel in other parts of Scotland is available too. Open July-Aug. Mon.-Sat. 8:30am-9pm, Sun. 11am-9pm; May-June and Sept. Mon.-Sat. 8:30am-8pm, Sun. 11am-8pm; Oct.-April Mon.-Fri. 9am-6pm, Sat. 9am-1pm.

Airport: LRT's #100 **Airlink** bus shuttles from Waverley Bridge out to Edinburgh Airport, west of town (25 min.; £2.65, children 1.65) For Airlink information, call 220 4111. For airport information, call 333 1000.

Bike Rental: Central Cycle Hire, 13 Lochrin Place (tel. 228 6333), off Home St. in Tollcross near Cameo Cinema. 12-speed town bikes £5/day, 18-speed touring bikes £7.50/day, and 21-speed mountain bikes £10/day. £35-45/week. Open June-Aug. Mon.-Sat. 10am-5pm, Sun. 10am-noon, 5-7pm; Sept.-May Mon. and Wed.-Sat. 10am-5pm.

Bookstores: James Thin, 53 South Bridge (tel. 556 6743) has the largest stock. Open Mon.-Fri. 9am-10pm, Sat. 9am-5:30pm, Sun. 11am-5pm. **Bauermeister's,** 19 George IV Bridge (tel. 226 5561; open Mon.-Sat. 9am-5:30pm). *Let's Go* books in all colors grace the travel shelves.

Bus Station: St. Andrew Square Bus Station, St. Andrew Square. Not one of Thatcherite privatization's smashing successes. For Scottish Citylink information call 557 57 17; for Eastern Scottish information call 556 84 64; for National Express information call 452 87 77. After hours, or to avoid crushing lines, buy your ticket on the bus. The information office for Eastern Scottish and National/Caledonian Express is by Platform A. Open Mon.-Tues. and Thurs.-Sat. 8:40am-5pm, Wed. 9am-5pm, Sun. 10am-4pm. The Scottish Citylink office is across the station by Platform D. Open Mon.-Sat. 8am-5:15pm, Sun. 9:30am-5pm.

Camping Supplies: Camping Outdoors Centre, 77 South Bridge (tel. 225 3339). Open Mon.-Wed. and Fri. 9am-5:30pm, Thurs. 9am-7pm, Sun. noon-5pm.

Car Rental: The tourist office has a comprehensive list. Most, including the following, have a minimum age of 21 and rates from £20-24/day, £90-135 with unlimited mileage/week: **Peter Carnie Car Hire** (tel. 346 4155), **Thrifty Roadrunner Car Rental** (tel. 337 1319).

Central Library: George IV Bridge (tel. 225 5584). Open Mon.-Fri. 9am-9pm, Sat. 9am-1pm. Across the street is the **National Library of Scotland** (tel. 226 4531). Open Mon.-Tues. and Thurs.-Fri. 9:30am-8:30pm, Wed. 10am-8:30pm, Sat. 9:30am-1pm. The **Scottish Poetry Library,** 14 High St. (tel. 557 2876) both lends and sells books. Open Mon.-Sat. noon-6pm, Thurs. 2-8pm.

Consulates: U.S.: 3 Regent Ter. (tel. 556 8315), open Mon.-Fri. 10am-noon and 1-4pm. **Australia:** 80 Hanover St. (tel. 226 6271), open Mon.-Fri. 10am-4pm. **Canada:** In Glasgow (tel. (041) 221 4415).

Crisis: Nightline, tel. 557 4444; nightly 10pm-8am.

Edinburgh Travel Centre: Potterrow Union, Bristo Sq. (tel. 668 2221) at Edinburgh University. Also at 196 Rose St. (tel. 226 2019), and 92 South Clerk St. (tel. 667 9488). Railcards, ISIC cards, and budget air fares (£95 return to Paris). Open Mon.-Fri. 9am-5:30pm, Sat. 10am-1pm. Bristo Sq. office open Mon.-Fri. 9:30am-5pm.

Emergency: Dial 999; no coins required.

Financial Services: Go to just about any bank or the currency exchange desk in the tourist office, which is open on Sundays (hours same as the office, listed above). The ***bureau de change*** in Waverly Station exacts a stiff transaction commission. **American Express:** 139 Princes St. (tel. 225 7881), 5 long blocks from Waverley Station. Exchanges currency, issues traveler's checks, holds mail for cardholders, cashes cardholder's personal checks. Open Mon.-Fri. 9am-5pm, Sat. 9am-noon.

Hospital: Royal Infirmary of Edinburgh, 1 Lauriston Pl. (tel. 229 2477). From the Mound take buses #93, 97, 98 or 99.

Launderette: Bruntsfield Laundrette, 108 Bruntsfield Pl. (tel. 229 2669), near Bruntsfield hostel. Wash £2, dry 20p. Open Mon.-Fri. 9am-5pm, Sat. 9am-4pm. **Bendix Laundrette,** 13 S.

Clerk St. (tel. 667 5844). Wash £1, dry 20p. Open Mon.-Fri. 8am-8pm, Sat. 8am-1pm, Sun. 9am-1pm. Both are near Edinburgh's most populous B&B colonies.

Lesbian and Gay Services: Community Centre, 58A Broughton St. (tel. 557 3620). **Weste and Wilde Bookshop,** 25a Dundas St. (tel. 556 0079). **Gay Switchboard:** tel. 556 4049, open daily 7:30-10pm. **Lesbian Line:** tel. 557 0751, open Thurs. 7:30-10pm.

Luggage Storage: At the train station. £1-1.50 (depending on size) for the day of deposit and the following day. Same charge/24 hr. thereafter. Open Mon.-Sat. 6:10am-11pm, Sun. 7:40am-11pm. Also at the **bus station** in lockers below the Eastern Scottish office (open Mon.-Sat. 6:15am-10:45pm, Sun. 7:15am-10:15pm; 50p-£1.50 depending on size), and at the Scottish Citylink desk (open Mon.-Sat. 8am-5pm, Sun. 9:30am-5pm; 75p-£1.50).

Pharmacy: Boots, 48 Shandwick Pl. (tel. 225 6757), just past the west end of Princes St. Emergency medication Mon.-Sat. 8:45am-9pm, Sun. 11am-4:30pm.

Police: Fettes Ave. (tel. 311 3131).

Post Office: 2-4 Waterloo Place (tel. 550 8229), at North Bridge and Princes St. Open Mon.-Thurs. 9am-5:30pm, Fri. 9:30am-5:30pm, Sat. 9am-12:30pm. *Poste Restante.* **Postal Code:** EH1 1AL.

Public Showers: In the "Superloos" at the train station. Nothing really super. 75p for 20 min. Free towel (£1 deposit). Rainbow colored condoms (£1 for 2). Open Mon.-Sat. 6am-11pm, Sun. 7am-11pm.

Rape Crisis Center: tel. 556 9437; Mon.-Thurs. 7-9pm.

Sports Center: Meadowbank Sports Centre, London Rd. (tel. 661 5351). Buses #5, 15, 26, 44, or 45. Full exercise and gymnasium facilities including a track and a velodrome. **Royal Commonwealth Pool,** 21 Dalkeith Rd. (te. 667 72 11). Take bus #2, 14, 21, 33 or 82. Enormous indoor pool with platform diving boards (swimming £1.10, 80p 9am-5pm). Full set of Nautilus weight machines (£2.45, £1.90 9am-5pm) and a waterslide that's like jumping down a well. Open Mon.-Fri. 9am-9pm, Sat.-Sun. 10am-4pm; Oct.-May Sat.-Sun. 10am-4pm.

SYHA District Office, 161 Warrender Park Rd. (tel. 229 8660) near Bruntsfield Hostel. Sells hostel memberships (£9) and a range of camping and hostel supplies, including sleeping sacks and stylish SYHA badges. Open Mon.-Fri. 9am-5pm, Sat. 9am-12:30pm.

Taxi: Taxi stands at both stations and almost every corner on Princes St. Or call **Capital Cabs** (tel. 220 0404), **City Cabs** (tel. 228 1211), or **Central Radio Taxis** (tel. 229 2468). Taxis can hold 5 passengers. First 1000 yards 90p, 10p each 240 yards thereafter.

Telephone Code: 031.

Train Station: Waverley Station, in the center of town. For 24-hr. information, call 556 24 51. Ticket office and station open whenever trains run (4am-12:30am); information office open Mon.-Sat. 8am-11pm, Sun. 9am-11pm. Railcards (£16) sold Mon.-Sat. 8am-6pm, Sun. 9am-6pm. Free bike storage behind Platform 7.

Accommodations

The *Where to Stay 1992* accommodation register (free at the tourist office) gives exhaustive listings of Edinburgh's gargantuan B&B population, largest outside London. For a small fortune (£2.50), the accommodations service at the tourist office will find you a room (office closes at 8pm, 9pm in July-Aug. There is also a private accommodations service in the train station (no booking fee; open Mon.-Sat. 8am-8pm, Sun. 9:30am-1pm and 2:30-7:30pm). During the festival season (Aug.16-Sept. 5 in 1992), there are very few rooms available anywhere in the city. Try to book through the tourist office a few months in advance for B&Bs and write to hostels early in the summer.

Edinburgh's B&Bs fall into two well-stocked colonies. The **Bruntsfield** district lies south of the west end of Princes St.; take bus #10, 11, 16, or 23 from Princes St. and try around Gilmore Pl. and Viewforth Ter. **Newington** is south of the east end of Princes St., along Dalkeith Rd. and Minto St. (Take bus #3, 7, 8, or 31 from North Bridge.) These areas have such an abundant population of homogeneous establishments that it would be absurd to list a few places without listing hundreds.

Most of the 250 **private houses** in the city are open between May and September and cost £11-14. Slightly more elegant **guest houses** (over 175) run £14-20 and remain open year-round. Edinburgh's hostels are cheap and convenient but fill up fast. Students looking for long-term residence (a month or more) should do lunch with the **Student Accommodation Service,** 30 Buccleuch Pl. (tel. 667 0151; open Mon.-Fri. 9:30am-12:30pm and 2-4:30pm). Also check the notice boards in the basement of David Hume tower and on the ground floor of Teviot Row Union, both near Bristo Sq. at the university.

High Street Hostel, 8 Blackfriars St. EH1 1NE (tel. 557 3984). From Waverley Station, turn right up North Bridge to the Royal Mile (High St.), then turn left down the hill and take the second right. Owner and former hosteler Peter Macmillan has lovingly turned an old downtown building into one of the hippest hangouts for wayward students this side of Hadrian's Wall. Listings and flyers for student services and entertainment. 130 beds, 6-16/room, cramped but clean. Vigorous showers. Kitchen facilities and laundry service (£2.50). Full breakfast £1.90. No phone reservations but you can call from the bus or train station to hold a room until you arrive. Luggage storage. Arrive before noon in summer, before 10am during Festival time. No curfew. £5.90.

IYHF Hostel Eglinton, 18 Eglinton Crescent EH12 5DD (tel. 337 1120), about 1 mi. west of the center of town, near Haymarket train station. Take bus #3, 4, 12, 13, 22, 26, 28, 31, 33, or 44 from Princes St. to Palmerston Place, then take the second left for Eglinton Crescent. Clean and well-lit, with sumptuous Victorian decor. 186 beds in 4-22 bed dorms. Laundry machines, good kitchen, chucklesome staff. Curfew 2am. £6.50. Sheets 50p/week. Paid advance reservations urged July-Sept. Open Jan. 2-Nov. 30.

IYHF Hostel Bruntsfield, 7 Bruntsfield Crescent EH10 4EZ (tel. 447 2994), about 1 mi. south of the West End of Princes St., in a lovely area by the Meadows. Take bus #11, 15, 16, or 17, or walk down Lothian Rd., which becomes Bruntsfield Pl.; follow Bruntsfield Terrace to Bruntsfield Crescent. 172 beds in 8- to 26-bed rooms; large store, ample kitchen and laundry facilities. Unfortunately, strict regulations prevent anyone from leaving the hostel before 7-7:30am, or checking in before 11:30am. See if you can spot the German shepherds. Reception open 7am-2am. Curfew 2am. £6. Open March-Jan. 1.

IYHF Hostel Merchiston, North Merchiston Boys' Club, Watson Crescent. Take bus #9 or 10 to Polwarth and then #30 or 43 to Dundee St. This seasonal hostel is a long hike from the city center but it provides 100 desperately needed beds at the peak of summer. Grade 2, hot showers and full kitchen. No advance bookings accepted: just show up. Open June 26-Sept. 12, £4.20.

Christian Alliance Frances Kinnaird Hostel, 14 Coates Crescent EH3 7AF (tel. 225 3608). Follow Princes St. west to Shandwick Pl., then bear right on Coates Crescent. Women only. Clean rooms. Laundry facilities. Midnight curfew, 1:30am during Festival. No kitchen. B&B from £10-15.50. Luggage storage. Open all year.

Cowgate Tourist Hostel, 112 The Cowgate (tel. 226 2153), near High St. Hostel. Holiday accommodations in clean flats with private kitchens. All rooms offer easy chairs, comfortable beds, and desks. Kitchen facilities and laundry service. No curfew. The place for privacy at reasonable prices. Singles £9.50, doubles £17. Sheets provided. Open July-Sept. 21.

Camping: Silverknowes Caravan Park, Marine Drive, by the Forth (tel. 312 6874). Take bus #14. Tents £4-5. Space for 100 tents. Toilets, showers and a shop in the campground. Open April-Oct.

Food

Most "traditional" Scottish fare in Edinburgh is served in restaurants that will have you in the alms house for a week, but you can get haggis (sheep's or calf's heart and liver minced with oats and boiled in the animal's stomach) at many inexpensive cafés. If you want to, that is. Many bakeries sell Scottish scones and stovies (meat and vegetable pies). Indian food is typically cheap and the most reasonably priced Chinese fare is available from several take-out shops on South Clerk St. The **Littlewoods Department Store** at 92 Princes St. has a supermarket in its basement where you can pack a container full of salad for a fixed price (99p-£2.19 depending on size). Open Mon. 9am-5:30pm, Tues.-Wed. 9:30am-5:30pm, Thurs. 9am-7:30pm, Fri.-Sat. 9am-6pm. Other supermarkets are **Wm. Low** at 92 Nicolson St. (open

Mon.-Sat. 8:30am-7pm, Sun. 10am-5pm) and **Scoopamarket,** a wholefood haven at 112 Nicolson St.

Corner Stone Coffee House, Lothian Rd. at Princes St. (tel. 229 0212), hidden beneath St. John's Church. Cheap meals "organically grown." A cavernous café with enormous stone arches. A vigorously non-smoking posting place for cultural events, writers' workshops, and left-wing political gatherings. Leek and potato soup 95p, fresh salads 65p, hot vegetarian meals served after noon £2.10. Picnic tables by a graveyard. Open Mon.-Sat. 10am-5:30pm.

Kebab Mahal, 7 Nicolson Sq. (tel. 667 5214). The best of Edinburgh's many kebaberies. Kebabs (grilled chunks of meat in a pita pocket with chopped vegetables £1.15-3), hummus (£1.20), and lamb curry (£2.75). Open Sun.-Thurs. noon-midnight, Fri.-Sat. noon-1am.

Lachana, 3 Bristo Pl. (tel. 225 4617), near the university. Excellent all-you-can-eat vegetarian buffet Tues. and Thurs. 5-7pm, £3.05. Tasty 4-course meal for £4.10. Open Mon.-Fri. noon-2:30pm, Tues. and Thurs. 5-7pm.

Kalpna, 2 St. Patrick's Sq. (tel. 667 9890); serves superb Indian vegetarian fare, in a subdued, smoke-free setting. Buffet lunch £3. Curry, *korma,* and wildly exotic vegetable dishes £3-5. Open Mon.-Fri. noon-2pm and 5:30-11pm.

Larry's Diner, 26 Nicolson St. (tel. 667 5712). Chips. Bright and clean. More chips. Mushroom omelette and chips £1.60, steak pie and chips £1.90, fish and chips £2. Good chips. All day breakfast special: sausage, egg, bacon, black pudding, tomato, fried bread, and tea or coffee (no chips) £2.20. Open Mon.-Fri. 7am-7pm, Sat. 9am-6pm, Sun. 9am-3pm.

Teviot Restaurant, Teviot Row Union, the dark stone building in Bristo Sq. (tel. 667 2091). The best of the university unions—technically for Edinburgh students only but outsiders welcome. Filling main dishes around £1.10. American burger with salad and roll 70p. Open Oct.-late June Mon.-Fri. 9:30am-6:45pm. During the Festival, it becomes the **Fringe Club,** open to all; prices rise by about 50%.

Seeds, 53 W. Nicolson St. (tel. 667 8673). Good inexpensive vegetarian fare in a relaxed, politically correct atmosphere. Organically soothing music. Fruit salad or apple crumble 85p, daily specials £2.15-2.30, superb hummus 60p. Open Mon.-Sat. 10am-8pm.

Henderson's Salad Table and Wine Bar, 94 Hanover St. (tel. 225 2131), 3 blocks north of Princes St. between George and Queen St. Cozy round wooden tables and low ceilings. Live piano and guitar music nightly from 7:30pm. Heaping hot dishes from *paella* to eggplant pasta £1.90-2.20. Wide assortment of unconventional salads (mushroom, cucumber and banana), all veggie, 80p. Open Mon.-Sat. 8am-10:45pm, also Sun. during the Festival. Small grocery upstairs open Mon.-Fri. 8am-7pm, Sat. 8:30am-5pm.

The Baked Potato Shop, 56 Cockburn St. (tel. 225 7572), just below High St. One of the rare sources of reasonably priced food on the Royal Mile. The all-vegetarian options for your spud include mushroom risotto or vegetable curry (£1.35-1.60). Try a spicy onion and spinach bhajia (40p). Yogurt drinks 45p, lentil soup 40p. Limited counter seating. Open Mon.-Sat. 9am-11pm, Sun. 10am-9pm.

The Waterfront, 1C Dock Pl. (tel. 554 7427), in Leith. Take bus #16 and ask to get off at the old Customs House or the bridge over Leith water. Part of post-industrial Leith's renewal. The varied seafood selections depend on the daily catch; try the delicious seafood barbecue frequently served in summer (Mon.-Sat. 6-10pm, £6-8). The porch overlooking the water is a nice place for a drink. Open Mon.-Sat. noon-3pm, 6-10pm, Sun. noon-4pm. (Bar closes an hour or more later.)

Pubs

You're never far from a pub in Edinburgh; the *Edinburgh Pub Guide* (£2.50 at most bookstores) will direct you to the most atmospheric ones. Licensing laws are much more liberal than in England, so you can sample a pint of McEwan's real ale or Tennent's lager at just about any time of the day; most pubs open at 11am and remain open until at least 11pm, sometimes closing only at 4am. You might want to try the traditional pub crawl on **Rose Street,** in the New Town parallel to Princes St.; its 21 drinking establishments give it the highest number of pubs per square ft. in Britain. **The Rose and Crown, The Kenilworth,** and **The Cottar's** rate more sips than the others. Just across St. Andrew Sq., past the east end of Rose St. on W. Register St., is the well-preserved **Cafe Royal Circle Bar,** which brandishes antique tilework portraits and a pre-Paleolithic hand-carved walnut gantry.

Penny Black, 17 W. Register St., near the Cafe Royal, attracts a friendly crowd from 6am on. Around the corner at 216 Calton Rd., the **St. James Oyster Bar** draws a lively crowd into its poorly ventilated quarters.

Some of the best pubs in the Old Town are clustered around the university. **The Pear Tree** on W. Nicolson St., with a large outdoor courtyard, and **Greyfriars Bobby's Bar,** at the top of Candlemaker Row, are two establishments cheered by students. A string of pubs along nearby **Grassmarket,** at the base of Candlemaker Row, blows minds and tuitions with frequent live music and an array of ales.

The pubs that run along the Royal Mile attract an older crowd. **Ensign Ewart,** next door to the Castle on Lawnmarket, exudes an Old World ambience with its wooden rafters and blown glass window; it often hosts live folk music. **Deacon Brodie's Tavern,** at the corner of Lawnmarket and Bank St., pays homage to the respectable Scot who led a double life and inspired Stevenson to write *Doctor Jekyll and Mr. Hyde.*

Under the medieval arches of Cowgate, which runs parallel to the Royal Mile, you'll find three lively pubs with old cobbled interior arches: **Bannerman's,** the most popular of the three, has a cheerful atmosphere and live folk music some nights; **The Green Tree** serves a calmer, older crowd; and **The Pelican** caters to younger bohemians who get stoked on the rad playlist and sick murals. The clients at **The Kasbar,** near the west end of Cowgate, can groom their tresses until 4am, while those at **Sneeky Pete's,** next door, jocularly store a first-rate juke box.

Many serious alies claim that **Athletic Arms,** a.k.a. "The Diggers," on Angle Park Terrace, draws the best pint of 80-shilling in Edinburgh. Once the social center for local gravediggers, it is a convenient stop on bus #6. Two of the finest pubs in Leith, accessible by bus #16, are **The Waterfront** (see Food above) and **The Starbank Inn,** 64 Laverockbank Rd. The Starbank Inn is a favorite with real ale fans, since it sells both Belhaven and Timothy Taylor.

For gay and lesbian people, **The Laughing Duck,** 24 Howe St., offers a hectic buzz on Thursday nights, with a lounge upstairs and dance floor downstairs. Every second Wednesday, the Duck turns into **Big Sophie's** and only women are allowed in from 9pm-1am.

Sights

Edinburgh is split schizophrenically into grey stone Old Town, where centuries of piecemeal construction overlap haphazardly, and a classically Georgian New Town, which is a marvel of rational city planning. The **Royal Mile** (Lawnmarket, High St., and Canongate), spills downhill through the middle of the Old Town, from the castle to the Palace of Holyrood. Lined with historic buildings, the Mile is one of the great tourist processionals in Britain. The New Town, separated from the old by Princes Street Gardens, is no gleaming modern development; its stately buildings still reek of 18th-century British colonial optimism.

Try to take an Old Town walking tour while in Edinburgh. Student-run evening tours tend to be the most humorous and informative. **Mercat Tours** (tel. 661 4541) offers a variety of routes and themes; the **Ghosts and Ghouls** horror walk (daily at 7 and 8pm, Oct.-May 8pm only; 1½hr.), departs from Mercat Cross—"Satan's ancient rendezvous"—and ends with refreshments at a local inn (£4.50 including drink, £3 walk only). No booking is required for these tours; **Robin's Tours** (tel. 661 0125) is similar (£3 for 2 hr. walk). **The Witchery's** Ghosts & Gore and Murder & Mystery evening tours (£3-4) require advance booking (tel. 225 6745), but are well worth it (they're led by officially deceased guides).

The **Edinburgh Castle** (tel. 225 9846) sits atop an extinct volcano, glowering over the city it once protected. Visit the castle for the view north all the way over the Firth of Forth to Fife (if you're running low on funds, know that this is available at other prominent spots in the city without the admission fee and the hour-long wait common on summer afternoons at the castle). Inside the castle is **St. Margaret's Chapel,** a Norman church that dates back to the 12th century and is believed to be the oldest structure in Edinburgh. Buried under the church floor until the

Restoration, the Scottish Crown Regalia, oldest in Europe, comprises the crown, scepter, and sword of state. The state apartments include Queen Mary's bedroom and the French prison where prisoners from Napoleon's armies scratched *graffiti français* on the ancient walls. (Castle open Mon.-Sat. 9:30am-5:05pm, Sun. 11am-5:05pm. Admission £2.80, seniors and children £1.40.)

The Royal Mile

The walk along the **Royal Mile** from the castle to the palace passes some of Edinburgh's best museums and oldest houses. The new **Scotch Whisky Heritage Centre** (tel. 220 0441) will allow you a ride through the museum in a converted whisky barrel and, in a very abstracted and non-alcoholic way, teach you to tell the difference between Laphroaig and Chivas Regal. (Open mid-June to Sept. daily 9am-7pm; Oct. to mid-June 10am-5pm. Admission £2.85, students £2.35, seniors £1.75, children £1.50.)

Because space on the Royal Mile was limited, shopfronts are narrow and buildings rise to five and six stories. The 1620 tenement **Gladstone's Land** (tel. 226 5856), behind the pig at 483 Lawnmarket, is the oldest surviving house on the route; inside, everything remains as it was in the 15th and 16th centuries, including a piebald rat and the wooden ceilings painted with bouncing citrus fruits. (Open April-Oct. Mon.-Sat. 10am-5pm, Sun. 2-5pm. Admission £2, students £1.) Through the passage at 477 Lawnmarket is **Lady Stair's House** (tel. 225 2424, ext. 6593), a 17th-century townhouse containing relics of three of Scotland's major literary figures—Robert Burns, Sir Walter Scott, and Robert Louis Stevenson. (Open Mon.-Sat. 10am-6pm, during Festival also Sun. 2-5pm; Oct.-May Mon.-Sat. 10am-5pm. Free.) If you drift over George IV Bridge you'll come to **Greyfriars Kirk,** in a beautiful churchyard through the gates atop Candlemaker Row; linguistics mavens can hear Gaelic services here Sundays at 3pm.

Where Lawnmarket becomes High St., the Mile is dominated by the principal church of Scotland, the **High Kirk of St. Giles** (tel. 225 4363). For two brief spells in Scotland's turbulent religious history, this church was pressed into service as an Episcopal cathedral, against the will of some of the local citizens. From the pulpit of St. Giles, John Knox delivered the fiery Presbyterian sermons that drove Mary, Queen of Scots into exile. The nearly 800-year-old church looks out at the world though a series of spectacular stained-glass windows, and its crown spire is one of Edinburgh's most famous hallmarks. (Open daily 9am-7pm; Sept.-Easter 9am-5pm. Free. Chapel 30p, children and seniors 5p.)

Behind St. Giles in Parliament Sq. is the old **Parliament House** (tel. 225 2595), known for its unique dropped-beam ceiling and fine stained glass. The building now houses the Supreme Court of Scotland and you can drop by in the morning to see bewigged barristers plead criminal cases before red-robed judges. (Open Tues.-Fri. 9:30am-4:30pm. Free.) A few more blocks along the Mile is **John Knox House,** 45 High St. (tel. 556 9579), a rigid and austere example of old Edinburgh housing. Recent restoration has revealed the original walls, fireplaces, and painted ceiling. (Open Mon.-Sat. 10am-4:30pm. Admission £1.20, students and seniors £1.)

Canongate, the last segment of the Royal Mile, was once a separate burgh and a part of the Augustinian abbey that gave the royal palace its ecclesiastical name. **Huntly House** (tel. 225 2424, ext. 6689), a nobleman's mansion, contains Edinburgh's chief museum of local history and tableware. (Open Mon.-Sat. 10am-6pm, during Festival also Sun. 2-5pm; Oct.-May 10am-5pm. Free.) The unusual **Museum of Childhood,** 38 High St. (tel. 225 2424, ext. 6646), displays dolls, games, toys, rods, and canes. The **Brass Rubbing Centre** (tel. 556 4364), on Chalmers Close off High St., allows visitors to partake in the ancient art of *frottage;* rubbings of facsimiles of ancient brass gravemarkers cost anywhere from 40p to £12.50. Visit the area at least to check out **Trinity Apse,** an old stone church. **Canongate Tolbooth** (1591), one of the most striking features of the Royal Mile, houses **The People's Story** museum (tel. 225 2424, ext. 6638), which honors the workers who built Edinburgh with reconstructions of objects from everyday life in the past, including a pub, a prison cell and a fishwife. All at the people's price (free). (All Canongate museums are free, and open Mon.-Sat. 10am-6pm, during Festival also Sun. noon-5pm; Oct.-May Mon.-Sat. 10am-5pm.)

The **Palace of Holyroodhouse** (tel. 556 1096), at the eastern end of the Royal Mile, abuts Holyrood Park and the peak of Arthur's Seat (see Parks below). This ancient Stuart palace dates from the 16th and 17th centuries. A tablet marks the spot where David Rizzio, the Italian secretary of Mary, Queen of Scots, was stabbed to death. The palace also documents Mary's rapid degeneration into domesticity—her needlepoint adorns the exhibits. More than 100 bottles of beer, er...portraits of Scotland's kings line the walls. (Palace open Mon.-Sat. 9:30am-5:15pm; Nov.-March Mon.-Sat. 9:30am-3:45pm; closed during official residences in late May and late June-early July. Admission £2.35, children £1.10. Take bus #1 or 6.)

South of the Mile on Chambers St. is the Old College of **Edinburgh University,** with numerous exhibits and events year-round. Nearby, the **Royal Scottish Museum** (tel. 225 7534) has a large collection of decorative art, exhibits on archaeology, geology, and natural history, and free gallery talks. (Open Mon.-Sat. 10am-5pm, Sun. 2-5pm. Free.)

The New Town

Edinburgh's **New Town** is a masterpiece of Georgian planning. James Craig, a 23-year-old architect, won the city-planning contest in 1767 with his rectangular, symmetrical gridiron of three main parallel streets (Queen, George, and Princes) linking two large squares (Charlotte and St. Andrew). Queen and Princes, the outer streets, were built up only on one side to allow views onto the Firth of Forth and the Old Town, respectively. The **New Town Conservation Centre,** at 13A Dundas St. (tel. 557 5222), will answer your questions about the area and direct you on your merry way. They also sell a number of well-researched booklets: *4 Walks in Edinburgh New Town* (50p) and *New Town Guide,* by Colin McWilliam (£2) are especially well-choreographed. (Open Mon.-Fri. 9am-1pm and 2-5pm. Free.)

For a self-guided tour, start at **St. Andrew Square,** walk west up George St. to the **Georgian House,** 7 Charlotte Sq., a well-restored townhouse where audio-visual shows and guides (all named George) explain the evolution of Georgian architecture and the New Town. (Open April-Oct. Mon.-Sat. 10am-5pm, Sun. 2-5pm. Admission £2.20, children and students £1.10.) Nearby, at #19, is the **birthplace of Alexander Graham Bell.** West of Charlotte Sq. and across Queensferry St. is the **West End,** another elegant Georgian neighborhood; the impressive neo-Gothic **St. Mary's Episcopal Cathedral** (tel. 225 6293) on Palmerston Place is worth a visit. (Open daily 7:20am-6pm. Free.)

The **Assembly Rooms,** east of Charlotte Sq. on George St., shine as one of the glories of classical Edinburgh. They host performances in the Festival and at other times in summer. On Princes St. between The Mound and Waverly Bridge is the **Walter Scott monument,** a somewhat grotesque Gothic spire once pithily described as "a steeple without a church." Its winding 287-step staircase is scheduled to reopen in 1992, once renovations and much-needed cleaning are finished.

At the eastern end of the New Town, Robert Adam's **Register House** guards the busy intersection of Princes St. and North Bridge. The Register House was one of the first structures erected on the north side of the loch. The loch, minus 12 million gallons of water, now forms Princes St. Garden and Waverly Sq. (Exhibition open Mon.-Fri. 10am-4pm. Free.) Beyond Register House is **Calton Hill,** home of the 143-step **Nelson Monument** (tel. 556 2716; open Mon. 1-6pm, Tues.-Sat. 10am-6pm; Oct.-March Mon.-Sat. 10am-3pm; admission 60p), which provides as fine a view of the city and the Firth of Forth as you will get at the Edinburgh Castle (where it will cost you £2.80). Calton Hill also supports an *ersatz* Parthenon built, oddly enough, to commemorate those killed in the Napoleonic Wars, and the **City Observatory** (tel. 556 4365), where one can see a 20-minute 3-D video presentation on Edinburgh's history. (Every ½hr., showings Mon.-Fri. 2-5:30pm, Sat.-Sun. 10:30am-5:30pm Open July-Aug. daily 10:30am-5:30pm. Admission £1.50, children and seniors £1). Unfortunately, the builders of the observatory ran out of money and eliminated the telescope from their plans.

Galleries

The *Edinburgh Gallery Guide* at the tourist information center will guide you through the marble halls of Edinburgh's vast and varied collections. On The Mound between the two halves of Princes St. Gardens, the **National Gallery of Scotland** (tel. 556 8921) stashes a small but superb collection of works by Renaissance, Romantic, and Impressionist masters. The lower floor houses a fine array of prints, paintings and drawings all done by Scottish artists. (Open Mon.-Sat. 10am-5pm, Sun. 2-5pm; during Festival Mon.-Sat. 10am-6pm, Sun. 11am-6pm. Free.) In summer, there is an annual exhibition of local talent at the **Royal Scottish Academy** (tel. 225 6671) next door at Princes St. and The Mound. (Same hours. Admission £1.20, children and students 50p.) Beneath The Mound down Market St. are galleries of a more contemporary bent. The **City Art Centre,** 2 Market St., presents changing exhibits of Scottish works. It is scheduled to reopen in mid-1992 following refurbishments. (Open Mon.-Sat. 10am-5pm. Free.) Across the street, the **Fruitmarket Gallery** displays upstart modern artworks. (Open Tues.-Sat. 10am-5:30pm, Sun. 1:30-5:30pm. Free.)

The **Scottish National Portrait Gallery,** 1 Queen St. (tel. 556 8221), 1 block north of St. Andrew Sq., also displays the likenesses of famous Scottish figures, including Robert Burns, Sean Connery, and Mary, Queen of Scots. (Open Mon.-Sat. 10am-5pm, Sun. 2-5pm. Free.) If you long for Gaelic harps, Ogham, and the bygone days of of the Celts, visit the adjacent **Royal Museum of Scotland** (tel. 225 7534), a branch of the monster on Chambers St. and the "wettest and dullest" museum in Britain.

West of the New Town, Palmerston Pl. leads down the hill past Douglas Gardens to the medieval village of **Dean,** on the banks of Leith Water (to the right). Several pleasant paths lead along the water to Belford Rd. to reach the Scottish **National Gallery of Modern Art,** an excellent rotating collection that includes works by Braque, Matisse, and Picasso, as well as a disturbingly life-like statue of two American tourists. Take bus #13 if you don't want to walk the mile or so from Princes St. to Belford Rd. (Same hours as National Gallery. Free.)

Gardens and Parks

Just off the eastern end of the Royal Mile, you can get a taste of the Highlands with a stroll through **Holyrood Park,** or a manageable 45-min. climb up **Arthur's Seat** (823 ft.); the exposed volcanic summit offers a stunning view. The **Radical Road,** named for the politically extreme unemployed weavers who built it, offers a shorter walk up to the steep Salisbury Crags on the cityward side of Arthur's Seat. These cliffs are an brilliantly colorful site at sunset. The park is best accessed from Holyrood Road, by the Palace, where a small visitor's center exhibits displays on the variegated history, geology and wildlife of the park. Experts on the natural history of the park lead free walks every Sunday at 1:30pm beginning in late April; call 557 57 62 for discussion topics and information on where to meet. More general introductory walks leave on Wednesdays at 1:30pm from the Holyrood Lodge.

Hidden away from the city, the sleepy village of **Duddingston,** at the foot of Arthur's Seat, makes a great grazing stop—try the **Sheep's Heid Inn** (tel. 661 1020), Scotland's oldest licensed drinking establishment, with an ancient outdoor garden. A smaller refuge, located directly in the city center, is **Princes St. Gardens,** a lush, green park where the castle's moat once festered. Lie out on the grass and listen to one of the numerous Scottish bands perform on early summer afternoons. The Scottish equivalent of miniature golf—minus the dinosaurs and windmills—is available at **Princes St. Putting** (open mid-April to mid-Sept. Mon.-Fri. 11am-8pm, Sat. 10am-7pm; 18 holes 50p, children and seniors 25-35p.) Those fond of hitting things and scurrying in circles can also head to the **Meadows,** an enormous grassy park in southern Edinburgh that contains an impromptu golf course as well as public football fields and tennis courts. Melville Dr. bisects the park and connects with both Brougham St. (in the west) and South Clerk St. (in the east).

Edinburgh's requisite romantic oasis is the **Royal Botanic Gardens** on Inverleith Row. Take bus #23 or 27 from Hanover St. and stroll around the splendid rock garden and plant houses. (Open Mon.-Sat. 10am-5pm, Sun. 11am-5pm. Free.) The **Edinburgh Zoo,** Corstorphine Rd. (tel. 334 9171), lies just outside the city to the west. Its extensive grounds offer a "playcage" for children and penguins on parade daily in the summer (2:30pm). (Open Mon.-Sat. 9:30am-6pm, closes at dusk in winter. Admission £3.85, children and seniors £2. Take bus #12, 26, 31, 85, 86 or C4.)

Entertainment

The summer season convulses with music in the gardens, theater and film events and *ceilidhs* (KAY-lees; bouts of country dancing, singing, and drinking) before the Edinburgh International Festival comes to town. In winter, shorter days and the crush of students promote a flourishing nightlife. For details, pick up a copy of *The List* (90p), a bi-weekly comprehensive guide to events in Glasgow and Edinburgh, at any local bookstore, newsstand, or record stop. *What's On in Edinburgh* and *Edinburgh: Events in 1992,* both free from the tourist office, are also useful.

King's Theatre, Leven St. (tel. 229 1201) in Bruntsfield, sponsors light entertainment and musical variety with a wry Scottish slant; the **Royal Lyceum Theatre,** Grindlay St. (tel. 226 9697), presents well-known comedies; at the **Traverse Theatre,** West Bow (tel. 226 2633), innovative and sometimes controversial drama is performed; and the **Playhouse Theatre,** Greenside Place (tel. 557 2590), often hosts musical shows. Tickets for these theaters run £5-25 depending on the time and the show. Generally, tickets are available in the £5-10 range. The **Netherbow Arts Centre,** 43 High St. (tel. 225 7942), stage more informal but equally delightful productions each week. (Tickets £5.50, seniors and students £4.50.) Edinburgh University's **Bedlam Theatre,** Forrest St., presents excellent student productions of straight-laced and experimental drama.

The best cinema in Edinburgh is the **Filmhouse,** 88 Lothian Rd. (tel. 228 2688), which shows a wide variety of classic and artfully obscure films. (Tickets from £1.50-3, Mon.-Fri. afternoon shows with student discount £1.)

Thanks to an overabundance of hip university students who never let a book get in the way of a good night out, Edinburgh possesses a thriving music scene. For jazz and blues, head to **Preservation Hall** on Victoria St. If you're going to keel over drunk, do it backwards, and look at the humorous quotes ringing the ceiling. The sources are as diverse as Woody Allen, Prince Philip, and Frank Zappa. Jazz can also be found at **Platform 1,** Rutland St. (tel. 225 2433), **Navaar House Hotel** on Mayfield Gardens, and **McKirdy's** at 43 Assembly St. For a complete run-down of Edinburgh's jazz scene, pick up the *Jazz News* at the Jazz Festival Office, 116 Canongate (tel. 557 1642). For rock and progressive shows, try **The Venue** (tel. 557 3073) and **Calton Studios** (tel. 556 7066), both on Calton Rd. Many of the university houses also sponsor live shows: look for flyers on walls near Bristol Sq. **Negociant's,** 45-47 Lothian St. (tel. 225 6313), is a pub with a wide range of Continental beers upstairs and frequent live shows downstairs (no cover). The **Chapps Club,** 22 Greenside Pl., and the **Blue Oyster Club,** 96 Rose St. Lane North, are both popular night spots for gay men. The **Blue Moon Café,** 60 Broughton St., is a good meeting place for gay people of both sexes. **Ripping Records,** 91 South Bridge (tel. 226 7010), and **Virgin Megastore,** 131 Princes St. (tel. 225 4583), have a calendar of most rock, reggae, and popular performances in Edinburgh and they sell tickets as well.

The "Scottish Evenings" sponsored by many of the larger hotels are about as genuine as sumo wrestling in Saskatchewan. Instead, try the **Edinburgh Folk Club** (tel. 339 4083), which stages authentic performances on Wednesday nights at the Café Royal Circle Bar on West Register St. (shows start at 8pm; admission £3). You'll also find Scottish bands and country dancing most evenings at the **Ross Open-Air Theatre,** under the tent in the west end of Princes St. Gardens (7-7:30pm; free-85p), and at a number of smaller local pubs. In 1992, Edinburgh's **folk festival** will be held from April 10-19 at the university's Teviot Row Union. For more information, try the somewhat ad-hoc **Edinburgh Folk Festival Society,** 16A Fleshmarket Close (tel. 220 0484).

Events

The extraordinary **Edinburgh International Festival** (Aug. 16-Sept. 5 in 1992) incites a massive bonfire of music, art, drama, and dance. Tickets (£3-33) are available by mail starting in May, as are full schedules of events. Contact the **Festival Box Office,** 21 Market St. EH1 1BW (tel. 225 5756). Tickets are sold over the counter and by phone starting in late May. You can book by credit card, except on the day of a performance. From 1-5pm on the day of performance, half-price tickets are available at the bottom of The Mound.

Around the established festival has grown a more spontaneous **Fringe Festival,** which now includes over 500 amateur and professional companies presenting theater, comedy, children's shows, folk and classical music, poetry, dance, mime, opera, revue, and various exhibits. Begun in 1947 by eight theater companies not invited to the official festival, the Fringe now receives reluctant cooperation from its indirect parent, though it remains an entirely different production. The fringe is generally weirder and more whimsical; you may find it more interesting than the official Festival. You can find good, comprehensive reviews of a few of the 1000-odd Fringe productions in the *The Scotsman, The List,* (at any newsstand), and the *Festival Times* (free at the Fringe Festival Office at 180 High St.). Or get the scoop on the best shows by frequenting the main Festival-goer haunts: the Fringe Club at the Teviot Row Union, the Pleasance Theatre on Pleasance St., the Gilded Balloon on Cowgate, and the Assembly Rooms, the Theatre Workshop, and the Traverse Theatre. You can sometimes get free tickets from more desperate actors who give them away outside the Fringe Festival Office. Full price tickets seldom surge over £5.

The *Fringe Programme* lists necessary information on performances; this and tickets are available by mail from the Fringe Festival Office, 180 High St., Edinburgh, Scotland EH1 1QS. (From outside Britain, include £2 postage; cash, stamps, and foreign currency accepted; from within Great Britain, 46p, available usually in mid-June.) Telephone and over-the-counter bookings can be made (beginning in late July) directly from the office (tel. 226 5257/9; box office open Mon.-Fri. 10am-6pm; downstairs box office open July 31-Aug.31 daily 10am-7pm).

A number of other festivals also flare up around the same dates. In August, the **Edinburgh International Film Festival** comes to town. For information, write to **Filmhouse,** 88 Lothian Rd., Edinburgh EH3 9BZ (tel. 228 2688). The Filmhouse box office opens in early August and accepts both phone and postal bookings.

Concurrent with the Festival is the **Military Tattoo,** performed nightly except Sunday in the Esplanade—a fantastic spectacle of miltary bands, bagpipes, drums, and sometimes participants from other Commonwealth countries. Be prepared to sit next to a middle-aged couple from Tennessee. The Tattoo will run from August 7-29 in 1992. For tickets (£6.70-12.30), contact the Tattoo Office, 22 Market St. EH1 1QB (tel. 225 1188; phone bookings from Jan. 1; open from the 1st Mon. in July Mon.-Fri. 10am-4:30pm, Sat. 10am-12:30pm; on performance days, open until the start of the show).

The **Edinburgh International Jazz Festival** in mid-August opens with a very loud riff, hosting the largest jazz parade in Europe. The week-long gala includes a day of free outdoor jazz at the Princes St. Gardens. Other venues include the Jazz Pavilion at Meadowbank Stadium on London Rd., the Festival Club on Chambers St. and the Scandic Crown Hotel on High St. Tickets (£6-8) are available at the Ticket Centre on Waverly Bridge from 5 days before the festival and by mail from the Festival Office, 116 Canongate EH8 8DD (tel. 557 1642). The office also stocks programs for a complete listing of events and venues.

The **Beltane Fires** is a more spontaneous and primal festival occurring every May Day (April 30 in 1992) on Calton Hill. This pagan event begins with bonfires and coal jumping around Calton Hill and then moves to Arthur's Seat at sunrise where, legend has it, those who wash their face with the morning dew will receive eternal youth. (No tickets, no office, and no towels.)

Near Edinburgh

Edinburgh's extensive bus service facilitates numerous daytrips from the city. South of the city, enjoy Scotland's beautiful countryside at **Braid,** where a trail cuts through the woods around Braid Burn. From Braid Burn you can head up to **Blackford Hill** for a smashing view of the city. The **Braid Hermitage Nature Trail** is accessible from Braid Rd.; take bus #11 or 15 up Comiston Rd. and get off at the circle where Greensback Crescent veers off to the right; then turn left onto Braidburn Terrace and make a right at Braid Rd. The **Royal Observatory** (tel. 668 8405), at the top of Blackford Hill, has Scotland's biggest telescope. (Open Mon.-Fri. 10am-4pm, Sat.-Sun. noon-5pm. Admission £1, children 50p. Take bus #41, 42, or 46.)

Bus #41 from Frederick St. runs to the placid, white-washed fisihing community of **Cramond. Lauriston Castle,** 2 Cramond Rd. S. (tel. 336 2060), a mansion with a 16th-century tower house and 19th-century additions, exemplifies upper-class Edwardian comfort. Its gardens offer a good view of the Firth of Forth. (Guided tours only; open Sat.-Thurs. 11am-1pm, 2-5pm,; Nov-March Sat.-Sun. only 2-4pm. Admission £2, children £1.)

In **South Queensferry,** about 10 mi. west of the city center, stand two grandiose homes. **Hopetoun House** is the more spectacular, considered by most to be Scotland's stateliest "Adam" mansion, designed in part by 18th-century Scottish architect William Adam and his sons Robert and John. (Open mid-April to Sept. daily 10am-5:30pm. Admission £3, students £2.70.) The house has a roof-top viewing platform which provides panoramic views of the Firth of Forth and its bridges. **Dalmeny House,** the first Tudor Gothic-style building in Scotland, boasts a grand hammer-beamed hall. Its **Napoleon Room** holds furniture that propped up the great general at the height of his glory and later in the despair of his exile on St. Helena. The **Rothschild Collection,** acquired through a strategic marriage, includes remarkable 18th-century French furniture, tapestries and porcelain. (Open May-Sept. Sun.-Thurs. 2-5pm.) Take a bus from St. Andrew Square to Chapel Gate, in the center of South Queensferry, then walk 1 mi. up the drive. (Admission £2.50, children and students £2.)

In **Penicuik,** 7 mi. south of Edinburgh, you can see glass blown and cut at the **Edinburgh Crystal Visitors Centre.** (Open Mon.-Sat. 9am-5pm, Sun. 11am-5pm. Admission £1, ages 10-16 and seniors 50p, under 10 not allowed. Take bus #87.) Only a limited number of people are admitted each day, so take one of the tours from Waverly Bridge or make your own appointment (tel. (0968) 751 28). East of Penicuik in Roslin is the **Rosslyn Chapel.** Its exotic stone carvings raised eyebrows in plain, severe, late-medieval Scotland. Venture past the simple exterior to the delightfully confused rib-vaulting of the Eastern chapels and the stone carvings of the Seven Acts of Mercy, the Seven Deadly Sins, the Dance of Death, and numerous angels playing the bagpipes. The most famous part of the church is the pier known as Prentice Pillar, supposedly the work of an apprentice who was later killed by the jealous master mason. (Chapel open Mon.-Fri. 10am-1pm and 2-5pm. Admission 75p. Take bus #70, every ½ hour from St. Andrew Sq. in Edinburgh.) Roslin lies near the **Pentland Hills,** a superb hiking area and the haunt of the stripling Robert Louis Stevenson.

St. Andrews

Would you like to see a city given over,
Soul and body to a tyrannising game?
If you would, there's little need to be a rover,
For St. Andrews is the abject city's name.
—Robert F. Murray (1863-1894)

From October to early June, St. Andrews University (Scotland's oldest) populates the streets and pubs with British students and American academic expatriates. When exams end, shops pack away their stores of ruled A4 writing tablets and slap up racks of tartan postcards as carloads of noisy trans-Atlantic golf-goons in kelly-green shirts roll into town to putt away on the beachside links. Mary Queen of Scots played golf here in the 16th century, and St. Andrews's Royal and Ancient Golf Club (founded 1754) is the sport's world headquarters; the original Old Course is still frequently the site of the British Open. More venerable than the holy turf, however, is the St. Andrews Cathedral. Golf enthusiast or not, you'll find that St. Andrews' restored medieval streets, explorable ruins, and soft coastal scenery make it one of Scotland's most attractive towns.

Arriving and Departing

Fife Scottish buses take the cheapest and most scenic route from Edinburgh to St. Andrews, located on the other side of the Fife Peninsula from the capital. (#X59; 5-7/day 9:45am-5:25pm, later service Fri.-Sun.; 1½ hr.; £3.70, day return £4.60; for students £2.40, day return £3). For bus information in Edinburgh, call the St. Andrew Sq. bus station (tel. (031) 556 8464). Only two buses make direct trips between St. Andrews and Glasgow each day, but by changing buses in Stirling you can make 5 to 8 more connections. To ride to Aberdeen, Perth and Inverness (via Perth), first take a bus to **Dundee** (almost every ½hr. 7am-10:45pm) and switch there.

British Rail concedes to touch St. Andrews with a ten-foot pole, but remains wary, stopping 8 mi. away at **Leuchars** (LU-cars) on its London-Edinburgh-Dundee-Aberdeen line (8-10/day; 1 hr.; £7.50). From Leuchars, buses go to St. Andrews almost every 20 minutes from 7am to midnight. You can also hitch south on A919 to A91 from Leuchars. Hitching from Edinburgh or Glasgow is tricky because of the serpentine criss-crossing of roads outside these cities, but once you reach the A91 or A915 you should have no problems hitching straight into town.

Orientation and Practical Information

St. Andrews's three main streets—North, Market, and South St.—run nearly parallel from west to east, converging near the cathedral at the east end of town. All buses stop, surprisingly, at the **St. Andrews Bus Station,** City Rd. (tel. (0334) 742 38). The northwest corner of town is almost entirely given over to manicured golf greens and shops dedicated to the "game of gentlemen." In the residential district on the other side of the Kinness Burn, the small stream bisecting St. Andrews, there are a surprising number of reasonable B&Bs.

The marvelous **tourist office** is at 78 South St. at Church St. (tel. (0334) 720 21; 24-hr. answering service). From the bus station, turn right on City Rd., and follow it uphill to the arch on the left to South St. (Open July-Aug. Mon.-Sat. 9:30am-7pm, Sun. 11am-5pm; June and Sept. Mon.-Sat. 9:30am-6pm, Sun. 11am-5pm; May Mon.-Sat. 9:30am-1pm, 2-5pm, Sun. 2-5pm; Oct.-April Mon.-Fri. 9:30am-1pm, Sat. 2-5pm.) The office can provide you with the *St. Andrews and Northeast Fife Holiday Guide,* which includes an extensive list of local B&Bs and their prices; accommodations service £1. **Gordon Christie,** 86 Market St. (tel. 721 22), rents 3-speed **bikes** for £4, with a £10 deposit. A **launderette** is at 14B Woodburn Terrace (tel. 750 51; open daily 9am-6pm). The **St. Andrews Public Library,** with photocopying for 10p and an extensive local history collection, is down Logie's Lane across from the tourist office. St. Andrews's **telephone code** is 0334; the **postal code** is KY16 9UL.

Accommodations

Across town from the outrageously expensive golf links are a number of reasonably priced B&Bs. Few of these private homes have signs in their windows, so pick up the St. Andrews Holiday Guide at the tourist office. Having the tourist office book for you may cost you a pound; not all owners make an adjustment to compensate for the percentage taken by the tourist office. Don't despair if the B&Bs are all full or beyond your ailing budget; the trek to Mr. Pennington's budget bunkhouse is well worth the time and effort.

Mrs. Haston, 8 Nelson St. (tel. 732 27), almost a straight shot from the bus station; go south on City Rd. and then down Bridge St. A single and a twin; effusive proprietor will regale you with tales of Bulgarian history. Can't be beat at £9.50.

Mrs. K. MacGregor, 8 Dempster Terrace (tel. 742 82), 2 blocks down Queen's Gardens from the tourist office. Exceptionally friendly couple with one room for three people; £11/person.

Mrs. Pauline Lusk, 2 Nelson St. (tel 725 75). Motherly proprietor makes a special breakfast for vegetarians. A double, a single and a copious bathroom. £9.50/person.

Mr. Pennington's Bunkhouse (tel. (0333) 310 768), in West Pitkierie 8 mi. south of St. Andrews and 1 mi. outside attractive Anstruther (see Near St. Andrews below), from which the owner can provide a ride. A minibus deposits passengers at the farm 5 times daily (leaves from the bus stop 2½ blocks west of the St. Andrews tourist office on South St.). Fife Scottish also makes 17 daily runs to Anstruther bewteen 6am and 10pm. The bunks, kitchen, shower, and sofas are all set in a fortified farmhouse that has been in operation since the 13th century. The owner, a diving expert-*cum*-historian, and his family warm the coldest hearts. A while back, one *Let's Go* researcher stopped in for one night and wound up spending 11 months. No curfew. Sleeps 12 with ease. Open year-round. £4.50, sheets 50p.

Food and Drink

Inexpensive eats are fairly abundant here, although ale recently went up several pence a pint.

PM, 1 Union St. at Market St. (tel. 764 25). All sorts of takeout, including the cheapest stuffed baked potatoes in the cosmos (£1.60-1.85, and then, incredibly, half-price 12:30-1:30pm). Open Mon.-Sat. 10am-11:30pm, Sun. 4-11pm.

Brambles, 5 College St. (tel. 753 80), between North and Market St. Certain to return with the best fresh vegetable concoctions in St. Andrews after 1991 renovations. Wonderful vegetarian dishes under £3. Big salads 90p. Open Tues.-Sat. 7:30am-4:30pm, July-Aug. also Mon. 7:30am-4:30pm.

The Pizza Gallery, 39 Bell St. (tel. 762 68). Decent pizzas named after painters—a "Lautrec," with garlic and sliced tomato, goes for £3.05. Eat as many of the 10-in. masterpieces as you can after 6pm on Wednesdays for £3.45. 15% student discount. Open Mon.-Sat. 10am-10:30pm, Sun. noon-10:30pm.

St. Andrews Student Association cafeteria, in the student union at St. Mary's Place off Market St., inside and around to the left by the pinball machines. Extremely cheap and surprisingly edible; hot dishes (e.g. vegetable curry with rice) £1-1.25. No ID necessary. Open Mon.-Fri. noon-2pm; Oct.-early June Mon.-Fri. 10:30am-6pm, Sat.-Sun. 5-8pm.

B. Jannetta, 31 South St. (tel. 732 85), across from the Byre Theatre. 50 flavors of award-winning, homemade ice cream. The walls are lined with candy and chocolates. Stampeded by sticky-fingered children when school gets out. 40p/scoop. Open Mon.-Sat. 9am-6pm, Sun. 7:30am-6pm.

The pick of the **tea rooms** is the **Ladyhead Bookshop and Coffee Shop,** at North St. and North Castle St. (tel. 778 86), run by sweet grandmotherly types who serve an extensive selection of Christian literature with a side dish of soup (50p), tea (25p), or scones with butter (30p). Open Mon.-Sat. 10am-4:30pm. If you prefer your scones on the fly, the **St. Andrews Deli,** in the covered shopping alley called Mercat Wynd off Market St. (tel. 764 44), offers both delicious cheese and fruit scones for 20p. The array of Scottish cheeses is dazzling. Open Fri.-Wed. 9am-5pm, Thurs. 9am-2pm.

St. Andrews's student pubs are worth a sip; start with the one in the **student union** (see above; open Nov.-May Mon.-Thurs. noon-midnight, Fri. noon-1am, Sat. 6-11:45pm, Sun. 6:30-11pm). **O. Henry's,** 116 South St., has a mile-long bar and steep prices. (Open Mon.-Sat. 10am-11:45pm, Sun. noon-10:45pm.) **Central,** at Market and College St., is the local Yah hangout, an intimate pub for the upwardly mobile (open Mon.-Sat. 11am-11:45pm, Sun. 6:30-11pm). At **Kate Kennedy's Bar,** corner of St. Mary's Place and Alexandra Place across from the Hope Park Parish Church, you can admire the bartender's tattoo between gulps of Old Peculiar ale. (Open daily 11am-midnight.) **Victoria Café,** 1 St. Mary's Place, sports a groovy jukebox and a zealous college staff. (Open daily 10:30am-midnight.)

Sights and Entertainment

St. Andrews's most imposing sights are concentrated by the North Sea at the east end of town. **St. Andrews Cathedral,** once Scotland's grandest church, now lies in semi-ruin. In medieval times, thousands of pilgrims used to journey to the cathedral when it was by far the largest church in Scotland. Following the Reformation, during which rebellious Protestants smashed the Cathedral's papist interior decor, the church fell into disrepair and was pillaged by the local townspeople. More than half the stone houses in St. Andrews contain fragments of the cathedral. With the noise of the pounding surf in the background, the skeletal remains make a haunting sight. (Open daily 9:30am-6pm, Oct.-March Mon.-Sat. 9:30am-4pm, Sun. 2-4pm. Free.) At the adjacent visitors center (same hours), a £1 admission fee (seniors and children 50p) will allow you to visit their small museum and climb **St. Rule's Tower** (157 steps), a 12th-century square building on the cathedral grounds built as a stronghold for the local monks in case of attack. The top of the tower provides a jolly good aerial view of St. Andrews and the expansive coastline, and is a seasonal departure-point for those sick of life. The nearby ruin of **St. Andrews Castle,** once the local bishop's residence, still contains a network of explorable secret tunnels, bottle-shaped dungeons, and high stone walls to keep out (or keep in) rebellious heretics. (Same hours as the Cathedral. Admission 80p, children 40p.) **St. Andrews University,** founded in the 15th century, stretches just west of the castle between North St. and The Scores. The university's well-heeled student population from the south of England participates in a strong performing arts program and takes red-gowned walks by the pier after chapel on Sundays.

Golf pilgrims' holy shrine is the St. Andrews **Old Course** at the northwest edge of town. According to disputed historical evidence, Mary Queen of Scots played here only days after her husband was murdered. Four less venerable courses are run on a first-come-first-serve basis, charging £1.50-11.50/18 holes. (Call 757 57 for details.) Club rental is available at several nearby shops (£5-9/round). Although the Royal and Ancient Club House on the Old Course is closed to non-members, the **British Golf Museum** next door may satisfy fans' cravings. In the museum you can see colonial-era photos of British gentlemen teeing off from atop Egyptian pyramids, and learn why James II passed an Act forbidding golf. The beach by the Old Course is worth a stroll; you might recognize it from *Chariots of Fire.*

For the weary traveler, the **East Sands Leisure Centre,** on St. Mary's St. (tel. (0334) 765 06) at the southern end of East Sand's Beach, is miraculously restorative. Swim in an enormous sparkling pool that is sculpted around a central palm tree (£1.10/40 min., students 55p), rocket down a tubular, twisting waterslide (50p for 6 rides), and bask in the steam room or whirlpool bath (£1.50/40 min., £2.75 after 5pm). The center also sports a weight room, tanning salon, squash courts, and table tennis. The restaurant upstairs caters mainly to a water-winged, prepubescent crowd: large Slush Puppie 55p, popcorn 60p, ¼-cheeseburger £1. Open for swimming Mon. and Thurs. 9am-10pm, Tues. 9am-8:30pm, Wed. 9am-8pm, Fri. 9am-9pm, Sat.-Sun. 9am-5pm; Thurs. (Sept.-June) 9am-10pm; Sat. (Oct.-June) 10am-5pm. Sadly, the transplendent **Sir Steven Seligman Museum of Electricity and Fruit** is closed for renovations.

The **Byre Theatre,** on Abbey Court off South St., (tel. 762 88, 24 hr.; booking office open 10am-8pm on performance nights, otherwise 10am-5pm) began life in a cow shed but now, after a rigorous program of self-improvement, features top-notch performances nightly (£3.50-6.50; student discount Tues.-Fri.). The Byre devotes at least one of its performances each season to the work of an as-yet-unacclaimed Scottish writer. *What's On in St. Andrews,* available at the tourist office, contains schedule information. Also of note is the **St. Andrews Festival,** held in February in odd-numbered years. The Scottish National Orchestra has performed at the Festival, as has Ernest Chung—check with the tourist office for schedules and information. The **Lammas Market** (the second Mon.-Tues. in Aug.), re-creates a medieval fair with buskers from around the country and odd South American ruminants.

Near St. Andrews: Fife

Fife county stakes out the peninsula between the Firth of Forth and the Firth of Tay. Along the coast south of St. Andrews is the **East Neuk,** a series of picturesque and sleepy fishing villages. Near the point of Fife, the village of **Crail** is a perfect place to do nothing, except perhaps suck on the freshly caught crab claws sold at the little stall by the harbor. From St. Andrews, take the A918 to the coast. Crail's **tourist information center,** 62-64 Marketgate (tel. (0333) 508 69), is also home to a small museum of local fishing history (open June to mid-Sept. Mon.-Sat. 10am-12:30pm and 2:30-5pm, Sun. 2:30-5pm). Guided walks of the town leave from the museum every Sunday from late June to late August at 2:30pm.

About 5 mi. west of Crail along the A917 (or 9 mi. southeast of St. Andrew's along the direct connecting road) lies **Anstruther,** home to a quiet harbor and Mr. Pennington's wonderful rustic bunkhouse (see St. Andrews Accommodations above). The town's award-winning **Scottish Fisheries Museum** displays regional fishing customs and superstitions from all over Scotland. (Open Mon.-Sat. 10am-5:30pm, Sun. 11am-5pm; Nov.-March Mon.-Sat. 10am-4:30pm, Sun. 2-4:30pm. Admission £1.60, seniors and children 90p.) For meaningful encounters with puffins and seals, cruise to the bird sanctuary on the **Isle of May** in the Firth of Forth. In summer (May-Sept.), **Jim Raeper** (tel. (0333) 310 103) sails from Anstruther to the Isle once a day except on Tues. (£8, children £4) and offers charter fishing trips £9/person, bait and lines supplied). Call ahead for times as all trips are highly weather dependent, or check with the **Anstruther Tourist Office** at the Fisheries Museum. (Open June-Aug. Mon.-Sat. 9:30am-5:30pm, Sun. 2-5pm; May Mon.-Sat. 9:30am-1pm, 2-5:30pm.) Located in Anstruther harbor, the **North Carr Lightship** is now a floating museum. (Open Easter-Sept. Mon.-Fri. 10am-5pm, Sat.-Sun. 1-5pm; Oct. Sat.-Sun. 1-5pm. Admission 50p, children 30p.) A couple of mi. west of Anstruther lies the beautiful village of **Pittenweem;** houses built on terraced steps overlook its active harbor. The fastest, cheapest way to Anstruther is by minibus (5 trips/day Mon.-Sat., from the stone chapel 2½ blocks west of the St. Andrews tourist office on South St.; 20 min.; £1.20). Fife Scottish also makes 17 runs daily to Anstruther between 6am and 10pm.

North of St. Andrews, in Fife's northeastern nook, is the **Tentsmuir Point Nature Reserve,** a forest park hemmed in from the sea by a 10-mile-long beach. Gain access to the park from **Leuchars,** on the St. Andrews-Dundee road and on BritRail's Edinburgh-Dundee line (see St. Andrews Arriving and Departing). The only **IYHF youth hostel** (tel. (0337) 577 10; grade 3; £3.20) in the area is 20 mi. inland in **Falkland,** one of the most complete "auld toons" (or old towns) in Fife. The nearby **Falkland Palace and Gardens,** once the hunting lodge of the Royal Stuarts, flaunts outstanding early Renaissance architecture. (Open April-Oct. Mon.-Sat. 10am-6pm, Sun. 2-6pm. Admission £2.20, seniors and children £1.10.) Falkland is most easily accessible from the town of **Kirkcaldy,** located due south of it on the coast (Mon.-Sat. 9 buses/day from Kirkcaldy to Falkland); and Kirkcaldy is on the Edinburgh-St. Andrews coach route (2-3 expresses/day). Many hitch from St. Andrews to Falkland along the busy A91.

Glasgow

What the city lacks in elegance it makes up for in sheer energy; tourists who bypass Glasgow deprive themselves of the excitement of Scotland's largest city. Glasgow University, half a millenium old, overlooks Kelvingrove Park, and its vibrant student population of 40,000 cross-fertilizes an innovative arts community, breeding a lively atmosphere. Named Cultural Capital of Europe 1990 (an honor previously bestowed upon Athens, Amsterdam, and Paris), the city has successfully maintained its heady status and continues to support arts of all types, ranging from the only opera in Scotland to the kilt-clad bagpiper on the corner.

Glasgow grew up around its 12th-century cathedral, but it remained a small town until Scotland's union with England in 1707 opened up markets in the North American colonies. Thereafter, Glasgow grew immensely rich through tea and tobacco trading, and richer still with the onset of the Industrial Revolution. The Victorians transformed Glasgow into the greatest city in Scotland, second only to London in the British Empire. As shipbuilding and steel production made citizens prosper, they built a neat Victorian paradise over the ruins of the medieval city. In Glasgow's recent "Miles Better" revival efforts, the sandblasters have been out refurbishing abandoned Victorian tenements as an alternative to usually grim council housing.

Arriving and Departing

Glasgow lies in central Scotland on the Firth of Clyde, 45 minutes due west from Edinburgh. Scotland's two largest cities—and east and west coasts—are linked by the M8 motorway. Glasgow is a principal destination on most Scottish and British train and bus routes. The **Freedom of Scotland Rover,** available at any train station, offers various discounts on train travel (4 of 8 consecutive days £48, 7 consecutive days £64, 4 of 15 consecutive days £88, 15 consecutive days £97); buses are always cheaper, especially with the 1/3 discounts offered to students with valid I.D.

Trains departing from Glasgow's **Queen St. Station** serve the north and east; to Edinburgh (22/day 8:15am-11:30pm, Sun. 8/day 9am-midnight; ¾hr.; £4.70, day return £5.80); Inverness (7/day 12:20pm-7:20pm, Sun. 3/day 7:30am-7:40pm; 2½hr.; £18, return £24); Fort Williams (6/day 8:15am-9pm, Sun. 2/day noon and 4:40pm,; 5 hr.; £17.50, return £23); and Thurso (3/day; 9 hr.; £23.90, return £32.30).. **Central Station** serves southern Scotland, England, and Wales. Service to Stranraer (5/day 8:15am-10:23pm, Sun. 3/day 8:40am-3:30pm, each connecting with ferry to Larne, N. Ireland; 2¼hr.; £14.50, return £22); Ardrossan (to connect with ferry to Arran; £2.70, return £5.40); and Dumfries (£12, return £14.50). All coaches leave from **Buchanan Station. Caledonia Express/Stagecoach** runs to: Perth (£4.60, return £7.90); Aberdeen (£8, return £11.75); service to both 1/hr. 7am-5pm and 7pm. **Scottish Citylink** services Edinburgh (every ¼hr. 5:45am-11:30pm, Sun. every ½hr. 6:45am-11:30pm; 1 hr.; £3.50, return £4.70); Oban (3/day, 8:55am-6:15pm, Sun. 2/day 8:55am and 6:15pm; 3 hr.; £8, return £14); and Inverness (£9, return £17).

Those hitching towards the northwest walk up Great Western Rd. to the A82; those going northeast walk up Cumberland Rd. to the A80; those going north take the short train ride to Balloch and hitch at the roundabout; those going south take the bus to Calder Park Zoo and hitch in the layby on the old road. Hitching to Edinburgh tends to be impossible; those who try do so by catching the M8 at the fork of Maryhill and Great Western Rd. (U: St. George's Cross), but many end up taking the bus (£3.50).

Orientation and Practical Information

The **city center** on the north bank of the River Clyde consists of the remains of medieval Glasgow and a newer, gridded street system. **George Square** is the physical center of town; the train and bus stations, tourist office, and cathedral are within a few blocks. To get to the tourist office from Central Station, take a right onto

Hope St., go 1 block to St. Vincent St., then turn right and walk 4 blocks; from Buchanan Station, exit onto North Hanover at the opposite end of the station from the ticket information booth, and with your back to the station take a right and walk 2 blocks to St. George's Sq. Areas such as Argyle and Sauchiehall St. have been renovated into pedestrian districts, and now attract shoppers from as far away as Reykjavík; cheaper food and receptive pubs reside in the neighborhood along High St. south of the cathedral and near the river. A mile northwest of the downtown area, **Glasgow University** anchors a neighborhood that includes the youth hostel and the city's nicest parks and museums.

Glasgow's transportation system includes suburban rail, a confusing variety of private local bus services, and a circular subway line, the **Underground,** denoted by the prefix "U"; trains run Mon.-Sat. 6:30am-10:45pm; flat fare 50p. Wave your hand to make sure the bus stops for you, and carry exact change (45p). Strathclyde Transport authority runs an immensely useful **Travel Centre** in St. Enoch's Square (U: St. Enoch), two blocks from Central Station (tel. 226 4826; open Mon.-Sat. 9:30am-5:30pm; phone inquiries Mon.-Sat. 7am-9pm, Sun. 9am-7:30pm). They can advise about various transportation passes. Underground Season Tickets are a good deal at £4.50 for 7 days, £16 for 28 days (bring a photo and I.D.). Multi-Journey Tickets are somewhat less of a deal: £4.50 for 10 journeys, £8.50 for 20 journeys.

Tourist Information Center: 35 St. Vincent Place, off George Sq. (tel. 204 4400), and south of Buchanan and Queen St. Stations, northeast of Central Station. U: Buchanan St. Travel bookshop, bus and cruise bookings, theater tickets. Pick up *The Ticket,* a helpful and free map, the free schedules of local events, and *Where To Stay,* a complete guide to accommodations (60p). Free accommodations service. Open Mon.-Sat. 9am-9pm, Sun. 10am-6pm; Oct.-Easter Mon.-Sat. 9am-6pm; Easter-May Mon.-Sat. 9am-7pm, Sun. 10am-6pm.

Airport: Glasgow Airport (tel. 887 1111), 10 mi. west in Abbotsinch, handles most flights; it is served by British Airways, Lufthansa and Northwest. Frequent buses (service #500/501) run to to Glasgow's Buchanan (25 min.; £1.75), and Anderston stations, as well as to Edinburgh (1 hr. 45 min.; £3.60). A few charter flights still serve **Prestwick Airport** (tel. (0290) 798 22), in Ayrshire, 30 mi. southwest. Trains (from Central Station) and buses (from Buchanan Station) leave 1/hr. for Prestwick; the bus is less expensive and more convenient to the airport.

Arts Center: Third Eye Centre, 346-54 Sauchiehall St. (tel. 332 0522). Bookshop, theater, contemporary art gallery, bar, and great vegetarian café (see Food below). Open Mon.-Sat. 10am-8pm, Sun. noon-5:30pm.

Automobile Association: tel. 812 0101. 24 hr. service.

Bus Station: Buchanan Station (tel. 332 9191), 2 blocks north of Queen St. Station on N. Hanover St. Organized and efficient, a welcome break from the chaos in Edinburgh. **Caledonian Express/Stagecoach** (tel. 332 4100) has an office to your left as you come in the front door. **Scottish Citylink:** (tel. 332 7133 or 332 9191). Luggage storage 50p-£1 (open Mon.-Sat. 6:30am-7pm and 7:30-10pm, Sun. 9am-7pm and 7:30-10pm). **Anderston Station** (tel. 248 7432), a few blocks beyond Central Station on Argyle St., for intra-city and suburban journeys.

Car Rental: Melville's Self Drive, 192-4 Battlefield Rd. (tel. 632 5757). Rent a Fiesta for £69/week, unlimited mileage. Minimum age 21.

Emergency: Dial 999; no coins required.

Financial Services: Banks open Mon.-Wed and Fri. 9:30am-4:45pm, Thurs. 9:30am-5:30pm. The tourist office operates a *bureau de change* with longer hours and exorbitant rates in the Central train station. For equally outrageous rates but extraordinary convenience there's **Thomas Cook,** open Mon.-Thurs. 8am-7pm, Fri.-Sat. 8am-8pm, Sun. 10am-6pm. **American Express:** 115 Hope St. (tel. 226 3077). Full AmEx services and long lines. Open Mon. and Wed.-Fri. 9am-5pm, Tues. 9:30am-5pm, Sat. 9am-noon.

Gay Switchboard: tel. 221 8372; daily 7-10pm. **Lesbian Line:** tel. 248 4596; Mon. 7-10pm.

Hospital: Royal Infirmary, Castle St. (tel. 552 3535).

Launderette: Park Laundrette, 14 Park Rd. Wash £1. Dry 30p/10 min. £3 express service. Open Mon.-Fri. 8:30am-8pm, Sat.-Sun. 9am-8pm.

Outdoor Market: The **Barras** (tel. 552 7258), east of Glasgow Cross, between London Rd. and Gallowgate. You name it, they sell it, and it has probably "astonished thousands." Open Sat.-Sun. 9am-5pm.

Pharmacy: Boots, 200 Sauchiehall St. (tel. 332 1925). Sells absolutely everything too. Open Mon.-Wed. 9am-5:30pm, Thurs. 8:30am-7pm, Fri.-Sat. 8:45am-6pm.

Police: Stewart St. (tel. 332 1113).

Post Office: 2-5 George Sq. (tel. 242 4260). *Poste Restante.* See the display case for the *Guinness Book of World Records* certificate recording employee John Kenmuir as the world's fastest stamp-licker (328 stamps in 4 min.). Open Mon.-Fri. 9am-5:30pm, Sat. 9am-12:30pm. **Postal Code:** G2 1AA.

Student Travel: Campus Travel, in "The Hub," the University Refectory (tel. 357 0608), on Hillhead St. just above University Ave. U: Hillhead. Great deals on charter flights from London and on bus and train travel. ISIC and student coach and rail cards sold. Open Mon.-Tues. and Thurs.-Fri. 9:30am-5pm, Wed. 10am-5pm.

Taxi: TOA Taxis, tel. 332 7070. Free taxi phone at tourist office. From University area to city center £2.50.

Telephone Code: 041.

Train Station: Queen St. Station (U: Buchanan St.). Luggage storage 45-60p (open Mon.-Fri. 7am-10pm, Sat. 7am-8pm, Sun. 10am-6pm). Bathrooms 10p (no showers). **Central Station** (U: St. Enoch). Luggage storage £1. Shower (including soap and towel) 65p (open Mon.-Sat. 6:30am-11pm, Sun. 9am-11pm). For connections between Central and Queen St. Stations, take bus #98, which shuttles between the two (every ¼hr. 8am-7pm; 45p), take a taxi (£1-1.25), or walk (8-10 min.). 24-hr. passenger inquiries for trains (tel. 204 2844; sleeper reservations tel. 221 2305).

Women's Center: 48 Miller St. (tel. 221 1177), near George Sq.

Accommodations

On the debit side of Glasgow's growing popularity is the perennial bed shortage, peaking in August. Throughout the year, and especially in the summer, reservations for guesthouses, B&Bs, and hostels should be placed at least nine weeks in advance. A good alternative for last-minute planners is to stay on the outskirts, particularly in the accessible and elegant **Loch Lomond youth hostel (IYHF),** less than an hour north (see Loch Lomond). Commuting from Edinburgh is another viable option. If you don't mind paying £14-18 for mediocre urban B&Bs, the tourist office can sometimes find you a room on short notice. If you'd rather go a-wandering, most of the city's B&Bs lie scattered on the streets to either side of Great Western in the University area.

IYHF youth hostel, 11 Woodlands Terrace, G3 6DD (tel. 332 3004; grade 1), in a beautiful residential district overlooking Kelvingrove Park. From Central Station, take bus #44, 59, or 74 and ask for the *first stop* on Woodlands Rd. (at Lynedoch St.); head all the way up Lynedoch 2 blocks to the youth hostel sign. From elsewhere in the city center, take bus #10, 11, 11A, or 12, or U: St. George's Cross. On foot, follow Sauchiehall St. out of the city center, cross the major intersection with M8, take your first right onto Eldershe St, then bound up the 2nd set of stairs and look for the blue and white flag of St. Andrew. Hubbub guaranteed to raise your spirits. Laundry facilities. TV room. Reception open 7am-10pm; curfew 2am. Lockout 9:30am-2pm. £6/person. Good breakfast (£2.25) and dinner (3-course meal £2.95). *Paid advance booking is essential.*

University of Glasgow, administrative offices at 52 Hillhead St. (tel. 330 5385; open Mon.-Fri. 9am-5pm). Summer housing at 6 of the college dorms. **Queen Margaret Hall,** 55 Bellshaugh Rd. (tel. 334 2192), near Byres Rd., is the most modern, but also the farthest from the city center. Tea, coffee, soap, towels, and linen provided. Free laundry. B&B £13.54 with student ID (non-students £18.70). **Maclay Hall,** 18 Park Terrace (tel. 332 5056), overlooking Kelvingrove Park, in an attractive, old building with big rooms, is nearest the city center. Bed (no breakfast) £7.66 for students, £8.68 non-students. Absorbs the wave of hostel overflow. Both dorms have TV rooms and laundry facilities. Open mid-March to mid-April and July-Sept.

YMCA Aparthotel, David Naismith Court, 33 Petershill Dr. (tel. 558 6166). Take bus #10 or 11 from Buchanan Station, or #12 or 16 from Queen St. Station. Clean, institutional rooms. TV lounge and gameroom. No curfew. Singles £14, doubles £12/person. Breakfast included.

Iona Guest House, 39 Hillhead St. (tel. 334 2346), near "The Hub," on a street lined with B&Bs. U: Hillhead. Stunning front hall with stag on wall. Subterranean breakfast nook and well-appointed rooms. Some good views of the city. Convenient to Byres Rd. and city center. Singles £18, doubles £14/person. Tourists replaced with professors for the month of September.

Alamo Guest House, 46 Gray St. (tel. 339 2395). No Texan flags, just decent rooms. Not to be forgotten. Singles £14, doubles £12/person.

Rosemundy Guest House, 50 Bentinck St. (tel. 339 8220), on the south edge of Kelvingrove Park. Take the Underground to Kelvinbridge and walk ½mi. across the park, or take a bus going east along Sauchiehall St. toward Argyle St. and get off at Gray St. Big basic rooms panelled with fake wood and fitted with washbasins. Singles £17, doubles £14/person, triples £13/person, quads £11/person.

Food

Inexpensive Indian and Chinese restaurants abound; scour any main street near the university. Professors hold tête-à-têtes at the cafés behind Byres Rd. on **Ashton Lane,** a cobblestone alley lined with 19th-century brick facades. Bakeries along High St. below the cathedral serve scones for as little as 15p. Two- or three-course bar meals (from £2.50) are the least expensive lunch options around.

Third Eye Centre, 346-354 Sauchiehall St. Eclectic crowd gathers at this oddly-named café-bar for great salads with potato (£1.80), soups (80p), and hot vegetarian meals (£2.50). Purple decor, skylight, and clairvoyant waiters. Organic wine list. Open Mon.-Sat. 10am-8pm (later after shows), Sun. noon-5:30pm.

The Basement Restaurant, 14 Otago St., off Great Western Rd. beneath a contemporary art gallery. U: Kelvinbridge. In a basement cluttered with paintings and gallery posters. Delicious, homemade vegetarian dishes: vegeburger (80p), quiche (95p), and lasagna (£1.30). Open Mon.-Sat. 9:30am-5:30pm.

Grosvenor Café and Restaurant, 35 Ashton Lane, in a walkway off the middle of Byres Rd. Behind U: Hillhead. The café's unbelievable bargains are downstairs: homemade soup 38p, pizza £1.45, sandwiches 55p. A student magnet. The restaurant is upstairs: good hot meals around £2, banana splits £1.40. Café open Mon.-Fri. 9am-7pm, Sat. 9am-6pm. Restaurant open Mon.-Fri. noon-2:45pm and 5-7:45pm, Sat. noon-7:45pm.

Magnus Dining Room, in the Glasgow University Refectory ("The Hub"), on Hillhead St. just above University Ave. U: Hillhead. The central student cafeteria; salad, snacks, and meals all under £3. Open Mon.-Thurs. 8:30am-6:10pm, Fri. 8:30am-3:30pm.

Strathclyde University Students' Union, on John St., 2 blocks from George Sq. Any student ID will allow you access. **Reds,** not to be confused with the film directed by and starring Warren Beatty, is the main cafeteria and bar (4th floor, open all year Mon.-Fri. 8am-6pm). **Barney Rubble's,** on the 3rd floor, does vegetarian meals in quieter surroundings (open Oct.-late June, except vacations, Mon.-Fri. noon-2:30pm). Either one will fill your plate for just about £1.50 or buy the cheapest pre-packed sandwich in the city for 60p.

The Spaghetti Factory, 30 Gibson St., near the university. U: Kelvinbridge. Decorated with a large stuffed lion and a neon "Be Hungry" sign, this lively pasta place attracts students and families. Menu includes pizza, chicken and burgers. During Happy Hour (Mon.-Thurs. 5-7pm and 10pm-midnight) huge plates of pasta cost £3.50. Open Mon.-Thurs. noon-2:30pm and 5pm-midnight, Fri. noon-2:30pm and 5pm-1am, Sat. noon-1am, Sun. 5pm-midnight.

Willow Tea Room, 217 Sauchiehall St. The entrance is through a jewelry shop; gamey travelers may feel self-conscious. Designed and decorated by Charles Rennie Mackintosh, patron saint of Glasgow architecture, this posh and hand-painted establishment features gorgeous stained glass and hand-painted high-back chairs. Full meals are pricey, but certainly worth a visit for tea (80p a pot) and dessert (around £1). Open Mon.-Sat. 9:30am-4:30pm.

Basil's, 184 Dumbarton Rd., near Byres Rd. U: Kelvinhall. Limited menu and higher prices. Homemade vegetarian dishes and generous portions toned by local art on the walls. Leek and smoked tofu paté £2.20, hummus and two salads £4.35, vegetarian burger with salad £2.25. Open daily noon-9:30pm.

Moagies Hoagies, 367 Sauchiehall St. A Philadelphia-style sub shop in the heart of Glasgow. Large meatball hoagie £1.75, soup 50p, banana nut bread 45p. Open Mon.-Fri. 8am-5pm, Sat. 8am-3pm.

Pubs

Pubs in Glasgow are either local spots (exceptionally receptive to outsiders), more exclusive nightclubs, or the larger establishments listed below. The Byres Road pub crawl ("The path is long an' the ale is strong") usually starts with a trip to **Tennents Bar** and then proceeds in the direction of the River Clyde. Pub hours are generally Monday through Saturday 11am to 11pm, Sunday 12:30pm to 2pm and 6:30pm to 11pm, though many now stay open until midnight or 1am on some nights.

Halt Bar, 106 Woodlands Rd., 2 blocks from the youth hostel. One side is dark and deafening, the other hot and humid. Attracts all sorts. Live jazz or rhythm and blues on Tues. and Thurs. nights.

Tennent's Bar, Byres Rd., at Highburgh Rd., near U: Hillhead. Older regulars pound its real ales. Steeped in tradition and crowds (often 5-deep). Loud and inexpensive, a place for serious beer consumption.

Blackfriars, 36 Bell St. at Albion St., near Glasgow Cross. Popular with locals under 30. Live entertainment Thurs.-Sun. evenings. Wash down a good cheap lunch with any of a wide range of real ales.

Cul de Sac Bar, 46 Ashton Lane. *The* artsy hangout. Very chic, young clientele. Lots of vegetarian snacks and meals. Happy Hour Thurs.-Sun. 3-9pm, drinks for £1.

Horseshoe Bar, 17-21 Drury St., in the city center. A magnificent Victorian horseshoe-shaped bar, with etched mirrors and carved wooden walls, is the longest continuous bar in the U.K.; 14 bartenders are required to staff it when the mostly older crowd begins to swell. Head upstairs for an unbeatable meal deal—a 3-course lunch for £2 (Mon.-Sat. noon-2:30pm).

Nico's, 375 Sauchiehall St. Hectic, popular pub. French windows open onto the beautifully tiled interior. Chic clientele preens away the hours. Lunch £2. Open Mon.-Sat. 11am-12:30am, Sun. 6:30pm-midnight. Happy Hour Sun.-Thurs. 3-11pm, Fri.-Sat. 3-10pm, pints of Harp £1.

Oblomov, 118 Byres Rd., downhill from Tennents. Though named after Goncharov's superfluous man in the eponymous Russian realist novel, this pub flaunts a Dutch theme, done up in billboards, posters, and WC signs. Wicker chairs and a lively student crowd.

Ubiquitous Chip Bar, 12 Ashton Lane, near U: Hillhead off Byres Rd. Old wood, stained glass, open fire in front; quiet tables and two red psychiatrist's couches in back. Favorite conversation spot for local academics and writers. Hot veggie meal £4.45, soup £1.10.

Snafflebit's, 769 Sauchiehall. Simpler local scene with an extensive juke box to meet all tastes.

Sights

In their eagerness to join the Industrial Revolution, Glaswegians destroyed most evidence of their medieval past. The history of local communities since 1175 is illustrated in the **People's Palace,** a greenhouse-like museum on Glasgow Green (by the river), filled with artifacts of working-class life. (Open Mon.-Sat. 10am-5pm, Sun. noon-6pm. Free.) A good way to see the town is to start at the center, in grand and busy **George Sq.,** and then walk west along Sauchiehall St. (which joins Argyle and Dumbarton St.) to Kelvingrove Park and Byres Rd.

The Gothic **Glasgow Cathedral,** near the center of town on Castle St., is the only full-scale cathedral left intact after the fury of the mid-16th century Scottish Reformation. The downstairs Laigh Kirk, sole remnant of the original 12th-century building, shelters the tomb of St. Mungo, patron saint of Glasgow. Next door is the entrance to the giant **necropolis,** where most of Glasgow's 19th-century industrialists are buried. The **visitors center** has detailed information. To reach the cathedral, walk to the eastern end of Cathedral St., which runs behind Queen St. Station.

(Cathedral open Mon.-Sat. 9:30am-7pm, Sun. 2-5pm; Oct.-March Mon.-Sat. 9:30am-4pm, Sun. 2-4pm. Free.) Across the road, **Provand's Lordship,** the oldest house in Glasgow (built in 1471), is now a museum of period furnishings. (Open Mon.-Sat. 10am-5pm, Sun. noon-6pm. Free.)

Glasgow owes most of its architectural heritage to a flourish of construction during the Victorian age. Most of the interesting buildings are used as government or private offices and are closed to the public, but they still deserve a look from the outside. The **City Chambers,** George Sq., conceal a wonderfully ornate marble interior in Italian Renaissance style. (Free tours Mon.-Fri. at 10:30am and 2:30pm at the main entrance.)

Several buildings designed by Charles Rennie Mackintosh, Scotland's most famous architect and rainwear designer, are open to the public. The most notable example is the **Glasgow School of Art,** 167 Renfrew St. (1 block north of Sauchiehall St.), completed in 1898. Here, Mackintosh fused wrought iron art nouveau with Scottish Baronial to obtain a unique, proto-modernist salad. (Tours of the interior Mon.-Fri. 10am, 11am, 2pm, and 3pm, £1; information available here on other Mackintosh buildings.) The Charles Rennie Mackintosh Society headquarters in **Queen's Cross,** 870 Garscube Rd. (tel. 946 6600), a church designed by the batty genius. (Open Tues. and Thurs.-Fri. noon-5:30pm, Sun. 2:30-5pm. Free.)

Rounded crescents and elegant parks in the West End's residential **Park Circus** area, near the youth hostel, present intact examples of early Victorian terracing. Recently bequeathed by its owners, the **Tenement House,** a late 18th-century apartment on 145 Buccleuch St. has been carefully restored to its pristine state by the National Trust for Scotland. (Open daily 2-5pm; Nov.-Easter Sat.-Sun. 2-4pm. Admission £1.40, children 70p. U: Cowcaddens.)

Starting 1 block west of Park Circus is **Kelvingrove Park,** a large wooded expanse on the banks of the River Kelvin. At the center of the park's winding paths and glades is a fountain embellished with houses of the zodiac. In the southwest corner of the park, just off the intersection of Argyle and Sauchiehall, is the spired **Glasgow Art Gallery and Museum.** The collection ranges from Rembrandt to Dalí. (Open Mon.-Sat. 10am-5pm, Sun. noon-6pm. Free. U: Kelvin Hall.)

Kelvin Hall, on Dumbarton Rd. near the River Kelvin (U: Kelvin Hall), combines a complete public sports complex and a dazzling museum. The **sports complex** (tel. 337 1806) includes basketball and volleyball courts, a weight room, table tennis, and an indoor track. (Open daily 9am-9:30pm. Weight room £2.05/day, table tennis £1.95/hr.) The **Museum of Transport,** in the rear half of Kelvin Hall, houses a fascinating collection of full-scale original trains, trams, and automobiles inside an immense warehouse. (Open Mon.-Sat. 10am-5pm, Sun. noon-6pm. Free.)

Walk west from the hall to the bridge over the River Kelvin, from which you can see, to the left and right, examples of the two extremes of Glasgow's architecture: to the south looms a sooty smokestack, to the north soars the tower of **Glasgow University's** central building, a Gothic revival devised by Gilbert Scott. To reach the university, cut straight through the park or continue along its perimeter up **Byres Road,** where swirling students clog the sidewalks during the school year. The central university building is off Byres on University Ave. (U: Hillhead). The hallowed arches support the **Hunterian Museum,** the oldest museum in town. Permanent exhibits veer wildly from archaeology to zoology. (Open Mon.-Fri. 9:30am-5pm, Sat. 9:30am-1pm. Free.) The **Hunterian Art Gallery** across the street contains 19th-century Scottish paintings, a Whistler collection, a sculpture courtyard with a piece by Caro, and carefully reconstructed rooms from Mackintosh's house. (Open Mon.-Fri. 9:30am-5pm, Sat. 9:30am-1pm. Free.)

North of the Kelvingrove Park area at the end of Byres Rd. are the **Botanic Gardens,** Great Western Rd. Inside the interesting **Kibble Palace,** one of two large hothouses, white marble statues overlook serene ornamental ponds. John Kibble, the building's eccentric Victorian designer, once pedaled a bicycle on pontoons across Loch Long. (Open daily 10am-4:45pm; late Oct.-March 10am-4:15pm. Free.)

In the large Pollok Country Park, 3½ mi. south of town but worth the trek, is **Pollok House,** an attractive 18th-century mansion with a fine collection of Spanish paintings. (Open Mon.-Sat. 10am-5pm, Sun. noon-6pm. Free.) Take bus #45, 48, or 57 from Union St. (85p). The Park is more famous, however, for the fabulous **Burrell Collection**—Sir William Burrell's personal collection of 19th-century French paintings, Chinese ceramics, and Persian tapestries. (Same hours as Pollok House. Free.)

The Glasgow **Barras** is billed as the largest open-air flea market in the world. Every weekend, up to 1000 vendors energetically sell items as varied as antique war memorabilia and blank videocassettes. You're not likely to come home laden with gifts but it's an entertaining scene. The excitement takes place Saturday and Sunday (9am-5pm) in Barras Sq., near Glasgow Green between London Rd. and Gallowgate.

For a day among the wild things, sail to the **Glasgow Zoo Park,** Calderpark, Uddingston (tel. (087) 711 185); Himalayan blackbears are separated from camels by a gaggle of exotic geese. Take bus #53, 54, or 65 from Buchanan Station. (Open daily 10am-5pm, June-Sept. 10am-6pm,£3.20, students £1.95.)

Entertainment

For most of the year, more is on here than in Edinburgh. Pick up a copy of the monthly *The Ticket* at the tourist office. The **Ticket Centre,** City Hall, Candleriggs (tel. 227 5511), will tell you what's playing at the city's dozen-odd theaters. (Open Mon.-Sat. 10:30am-6:30pm.) *The List,* available from most city newsagents, is a comprehensive fortnightly guide to the arts and other events in Glasgow and Edinburgh (80p). The **Glasgow Film Theatre,** 12 Rose St. (tel. 332 6535), is the place for alternative films (£2-3.30), while the **Grosvenor Cinema,** Ashton Lane (tel. 339 4298) near Byres Rd., runs a current program; both give student discounts. Always check the **Third Eye Centre,** 346-354 Sauchiehall St. (tel. 332 0522), for contemporary performances of all kinds. Nightly gyrations to the latest club music shake the hip **Tunnel,** 84 Mitchell St. (tel. 204 1000), which offers student discounts on Thursdays, and the sweating **Subclub,** 22 Jamaica St. (tel. 248 4600). **Rain,** 375 Sauchiehall St., is simpler, smaller but just as groovy, while **Nico's** next door reduces songs to a driving beat. **Bennet's,** 90 Glassford St. (tel. 55 2761), attracts a mixed crowd. Club hours are generally 11pm-3:30am, cover charges £3-7.

Mayfest, a three-week-long event beginning May 1, offers a good program of Scottish and international theater and music. For information, contact Mayfest, 46 Royal Exchange Sq., Glasgow, Scotland G1 3AR (tel. 221 0232). The annual **Glasgow International Jazz Festival,** at the end of June, brings the sounds of such greats as B.B. King and Herbie Hancock to town (same address as Mayfest tel. 226 3813). Folk and traditional music thrive throughout Glasgow, especially during the **Glasgow International Folk Festival** at the beginning of July (contact the Festival Office, 8 Westercraigs, Dennistoun, tel. 556 1526). The annual **World Pipe Band Championships,** in mid-August, also gets local feet a-tappin'.

Near Glasgow: Lanark

Robert Owen's famous 19th-century socialist experiment at **New Lanark** became a prototype for cooperative housing. The experiment is being renewed, and the buildings have been restored according to modern residential standards. For more information, contact New Lanark Conservation Trust, New Lanark Mills, Lanark ML11 9DB (tel. (0555) 613 45). While in the area, don't miss the captivating **Falls of Clyde;** the visitors center, in an old dyeworks building, offers an audio-visual display and good views of the river. (Open Mon.-Sat. 11am-5pm.) To reach Lanark, hitch about 20 mi. southeast along the A72, or take the train from Glasgow's Central Station (lower level, 11/day, £2.60, day return £4).

Loch Lomond, Loch Long, and the Trossachs

Scotland's upland region lies north of the Highlands Boundary Fault, which stretches southwest across the land from Aberdeen to Arran Island. The hills begin to swell 30 mi. north of Glasgow and 10 mi. west of Stirling, bedecked by forest parks and bejewelled with lakes.

Less than an hour's drive north of Glasgow along the scenic A82, Loch Lomond is unfortunately the closest most visitors to Scotland get to the Highlands. Meandering through lush bays, dotted with thickly-wooded islands, and ringed by bare, angular hills, Loch Lomond is captivating, particularly if you venture beyond the few towns crawling with caravans and tourists. A number of rough beaches dot the shores and are good spots for lazy picnics and paddles. Be warned that the Loch is never too toasty.

Two trains serve the loch from Glasgow's Queen St. Station. One leaves every hour on the hour (£1.90, return £2.90) for Balloch, at the southern tip of the loch; buses do the same trek 3 times a day for less money (£1.80). The second stops at Tarbet and Ardlui at the northern reaches of the loch. Hikers can follow the **West Highland Way** to the hostel at Rowardennan (see below). The Way snakes along the entire eastern side of the Loch; in its full measure, the footpath stretches 95 mi. from Milngavie north to Fort William. Rowardennan is the first hostel along the route.

In **Balloch,** at the southern tip of the loch, you can book accommodations at the **tourist office** in the bus station, Balloch Rd. (tel. (0389) 535 33; open July-August daily 9:30am-7:30pm, April-June and Sept.-Oct. daily 10am-5pm). Otherwise, just go north on the A82 from Balloch toward Luss and pick a B&B along the route. (Stay away from **Luss** itself, the tackiest tourist trap on the loch.)

There are three **IYHF youth hostels** in the area, all accessible from the A82, near Balloch, at Rowardennan, and at Inverbeg. **Loch Lomond youth hostel (IYHF)** (tel. (038985) 226; grade 1) is Scotland's largest hostel, an absolutely stunning castle-like building nestled in a valley 2 mi. north of Balloch. It comes complete with the ghost of a suicidal damsel locked in the tower, pool tables and laundry. With 200 beds, it can get pretty crazy in mid-summer; travelers should call ahead to book a room. (Open March-Sept.; £4.85.) For quieter, cozier accommodations, take the Inverbeg ferry across the loch to Rowardennan. The ferry (a small launch that you summon from Rowardennan with an orange signal flag) runs frequently from April to September (leaves Inverbeg 10:30am, 2:30pm, amd 6:30pm, leaves Rowardennan ½hr. later; £1.50). Call the Rowardennan Hotel (tel. (036087) 273) to check the schedule. The **Rowardennan youth hostel (IYHF)** (tel. (036087) 259; grade 1; £4.85; open March-Sept.) is a well-kept building at the edge of the loch and the foot of Ben Lomond. Huge windows put the loch in your lap, and tons of water sport options lie at your feet (£18/day; trained instructors available). You can hike from this large, comfortable hostel to the equally comfortable one in Loch Ard (see Trossachs), otherwise accessible from Inverbeg only if you round the entire loch by road. If you choose to hike, check the route carefully with the warden. The **Inverbeg youth hostel (IYHF)** (tel. (043686) 635; grade 3) is several hundred yards from the loch, but quieter and far smaller than the others. (Open late March-Sept.; £3.20.)

Only 4 mi. west of Tarbet and 1 mi. up from A82, on the northern end of Loch Lomond at **Loch Long,** is the **Ardgartan youth hostel (IYHF)** (tel. (03012) 362; grade 1; open early Feb-early Jan.; £4.85), in the Ardgartan Forest Park. This wooded area lies beneath the "Arrochar Alps," a series of rugged mountains including **The Cuckolded Cobbler** (2891 ft.). Also known as Ben Arthur and Arthur's Seat, The Cobbler is unmistakable for its unusual and jagged rock formations—the peak appears to have sprouted horns. An easy trail (with some rocky parts near the tip) begins in the town of Arrochar, halfway between Tarbet and Ardgartan. (Inquire in town or at the hostel about the location of the trailhead.) Once at the top, look for the Eye of the Needle, an opening in one of the rock stacks ("horns"), where you can sit and enjoy the view over the rest of the "Alps" and the surrounding lochs. The area can be a welcome relief from the psychotic tourists of Lomond. In addition to the approach by way of Tarbet, buses run to Ardgartan on the Glasgow to Campbeltown route (Mon.-Sat. 3/day), which also passes through the tiny hamlet of **Rest and be thankful.** Really.

The gentle mountains and lochs of the **Trossachs** form the southern boundary of the Highlands. Sir Walter Scott and Queen Victoria lavished praise on the region, the only easily accessible Scottish wilderness before this age of Batmobiles and teleportation. Ironically, the Trossachs today are less accessible than many of the northern wilds; just a few buses a day link Glasgow and Stirling to Aberfoyle and Callander, the area's two main towns. The A821 winds through the heart of the Trossachs between Aberfoyle and Callander, passing near beautiful **Loch Katrine,** the Trossachs' original lure and the setting of Scott's "The Lady of the Lake." The *S. S. Sir Walter Scott* cruises from Loch Katrine's Trossachs Pier; the scenery is arresting, but in July and August the crush of passengers may make the boat trip a hassle (early May-Sept. 3/day; morning and afternoon cruise Mon.-Sat. £2.80). A post bus leaves from the Callander post office for Loch Katrine (Mon.-Sat. 9:15am) and can connect you to the 11am sailing. Otherwise, keep clear of Callander, a busy town full of pricey tea rooms, crass merchandising, and insipid woolens shops.

Southern Scotland

Rolling hills, heathered moors, fertile farmland and forested river valleys stretch south from Edinburgh and Glasgow to the English border. Poet Robert Burns is the Nessie of Ayrshire—sighted everywhere at once, yet strangely elusive. The poet was born and spent his formative years in the tranquil region around Ayr, and every town has its Burns statue, its Burns house, and its Burns resting place. Dumfriesshire is rich in tales of Robert the Bruce, born in nearby Lochmaben, who successfully led the cause of Scottish independence to victory at Bannockburn in 1314.

Ayr

Ayr lies 25 mi. southwest of Glasgow on the coast, largest of Ayrshire's tree-lined seaside towns. In the first weeks of June, Ayr comes alive with the **Ayrshire Arts Festival,** which mixes traditional music, dance, and theater with classical and modern works. Contact the Festival Office, 176 High St., Ayr KA7 1AA (tel. (0292) 262 821). This event coincides with the great **Robert Burns Festival,** which features recitation and revelry in honor of the local and national hero. Call the Land o' Burns Centre (see below) or the tourist office for details.

The Ayr **tourist office,** 39 Sandgate (tel. (0292) 284 196), has a free accommodations-booking service. (Open Easter-May Mon.-Fri. 8:45am-4:45pm, Sat.-Sun. 10am-6pm; June-Sept. Mon.-Fri. 8:45am-7pm, Sat.-Sun. 10am-7pm; Oct.-Easter Mon.-Fri. 8:45am-4:45pm.) For local bus information, call the station (tel. (0292) 264 643) in Wellington Square, one block from the tourist office.

Most flights into Scotland land at **Prestwick Airport,** just 5 mi. north of Ayr (daily buses from Glasgow Central, every 15 min.; 40 min.), and both Ayr and Prestwick are easily accessible by bus and train from Glasgow.

Near Ayr

Two mi. south of Ayr is the village of **Alloway,** birthplace of Robert Burns and home of the **Land o' Burns Centre** (tel. (0292) 437 00), with a multi-screen audiovisual presentation on the life and times of the poet. (Open daily 10am-5:30pm;

Sept.-June closes at 5pm. Admission 60p, children 40p.) Nearby are the **Burns Monument and Gardens,** which overlook the picturesque Brig o' Doon. (Open June-Aug. Mon.-Sat. 9am-7pm, Sun. 10am-7pm; April-May and Sept.-Oct. Mon.-Sat. 10am-5pm, Sun. 2-5pm. Nov.-March Mon.-Sat. 10am-4pm. Admission £1.50, children and seniors 75p.) Also in Alloway is **Burns Cottage,** built by you-know-who's dad, where you-know-who was born. (Open same hours as Burns Monument plus Nov.-March Mon.-Sat. 10am-4pm. Admission included in entry to Monument.) To get to Alloway take a Western Scottish bus from Burns Statue Sq. in Ayr, across from the cinema (services #61, Mon.-Sat 6/day 9:20am-5:20pm; 15 min.; 70p, return £1.05).

Twelve mi. south of Ayr is **Culzean Castle** (cul-LANE), a masterpiece by the architect Robert Adam. Seat of the Scottish Kennedys since the 15th century, the castle squats on a cave-pocked coastal cliff; as legend has it, one of these caves is home to the Phantom Piper, who plays Webern to his lost flock when the moon is full. The castle and the surrounding park were deeded 50 years ago to the British government, which gave the grounds to President Eisenhower for use during his lifetime. To reach Culzean from Ayr, take the Maidens bus from Sandgate bus station (#60; Mon.-Fri. 5/day 10am-7pm, Sat. 7/day 8:45am-7pm, Sun. 7/day 10:30am-10pm; ½hr.; £1.55, day return £2.20). Follow the sign-posted path from the main road for about 1 mi. to the castle. (Open April-Oct. daily 10:30am-5:30pm. Admission £2.50, seniors and children £1.40.)

Stranraer

Many think of **Stranraer** as *the* trendy place to get a ferry to Ireland. And this is quite true. **Sealink ferries** (tel. (0776) 22 62) leave for Larne in Northern Ireland (7/day, Sun. 5/day; 2 hr. 20 min.; June-Aug. £18, seniors and children £10, student £13; off-season deduct £1, traveling Fri.-Sun. add 50p to listed rates; bikes free). Show up 45 minutes before scheduled departures; ferries will occasionally leave early depending on weather conditions. Trains connect Glasgow to Stanraer (4/day, Sun. 7/day; £13.50). The sea passage for adults becomes cheaper with a rail ticket. Students should check with the student travel offices at Glasgow University for cheap fares to Dublin via Stranraer.

The **tourist office** (tel. (0776) 25 95) in Stranraer, just off the dock and across from the ferry waiting room and booking office in the brown trailer, books accommodations and posts a list of B&Bs. (Open daily July-Aug. 10am-6:30pm; April-June and Sept. 10am-5pm.) Frequent **buses** from Stranraer north to Ayr and Glasgow, and east to Dumfries, all stop behind the tourist office, and some even meet the ferry directly at the pier (ask the ferry crew or the tourist office). Stranraer, though not particularly interesting, is well-stocked with B&Bs; check the supplies on the A75 towards Newton Stewart (London Rd.). The beautiful gardens at **Castle Kennedy,** 3 mi. east of town on the A75 merit a runthrough. (Gardens open April-Sept. daily 10am-5pm. Admission £1.80, seniors £1, children 50p.) Frequent buses run from Stranraer to Castle Kennedy (#502, 10/day; 65p).

The Borders

The Borders, a bucolic tract to the south of Edinburgh, served for many centuries as Scotland's first line of defense against invasion. Signs of the perpetual strife in this area remain; the **peel towers** on many hilltops once held beacons to ward off English raiders. This rich and fertile region looks best when the sun brings out its warm colors, or when low-lying mists follow the soft contours of the land. The area's elegance is enhanced by the many gorgeous abbeys and historical houses. Like Dumfries and Galloway, the narrow winding roads and spectacular hill path of the Borders belong to bikers and hikers.

Today, locals nostalgically stir the ashes of ancient conflict for entertainment. During **common ridings,** annual rituals performed at most villages in the region, locals gallop around the town limits on horses to ensure that no encroaching clans have shifted a border-forming fence or stone. The ridings are high-spirited—pubs close for only two hours each day during the week-long festivals, and the locals go "stone mad." Try to time your visit around one of these events in Hawick (second week in June), Selkirk or Melrose (a week later), or Lauder (late Aug.).

Getting There and Getting Around

Trains do not run in the Borders, but bus service is frequent and inexpensive. Buses run from Edinburgh to Galashiels (19/day 6:45am-9pm, Sun. 8/day 8:30am-8:14pm; 1¼ hr.; £4), connecting there with Melrose, Jedburgh, and Kelso to the southeast (about 1/hr. 7am-9pm); services also connect with the train at Berwick-upon-Tweed, just across the Engish border on the east coast. No roads lead directly to Dumfries and Galloway in the west. To reach those areas from the Borders most efficiently, take bus #95-6 from Galashiels to Carlisle, just across the English border on the west coast, then rail from Carlisle to Dumfries (3-7 buses/day).

The **Reiver Rover** ticket allows one day's unlimited travel for £4 (children £2; £14 for 7 days) in the region delineated by Penicuik in the northwest, Dunbar in the northeast, and Berwick in the south. The **Waverley Wanderer** (£6.20, children £3.10, and £18 for 7 days) is valid within the Reiver area, extending north to Edinburgh (via routes from Penicuik, Galashiels, and Dunbar), and south to Carlisle. All area tourist offices provide free regional bus schedules. Single-day bus passes can be purchased from bus drivers. The **Explorer** ticket (£5 for 7 days, £8 for 2 weeks) allows unlimited admissions to all historic buildings on the government register (most are free anyway). Check with any tourist office. *The Official Guide to Scottish Borders and Northumberland* (£1) is vital for anyone doing extensive touring of the area. It provides comprehensive lists of attractions, prices, dates, opening hours, *et al.*

The lethargy of Border hitching is least bothersome along the main roads: the A699 runs east-west between Selkirk and Kelso, the A68 connects Edinburgh to Newcastle via Jedburgh and the A7 runs south through Galashiels and Selkirk en route to Carlisle. The labyrinth of B roads are even less traveled.

Accommodations

The 5 **IYHF youth hostels** of the Borders are strategically dispersed. The **Broadmeadows** (west of Selkirk on the A708) and **Snoot** (at Robertson, west of Hawick on the B711) hostels provide footholds for an ascent into the Tweedsmuir Hills. The hostel at **St. Abbs Head,** just outside of Coldingham near the ocean (tel. (08907) 712 98; grade 2), surveys the entire east coast and the eastern end of the Southern Upland Way. (Lockout 10:30am-5pm, curfew 11pm, £4.20, ages 16-20 £3.50. Open April-Oct.) Those hiking north from England on the Pennine Way will have to give the password to the proprietor of the hostel in **Kirk Yetholm** (tel. (057382) 631; grade 2; curfew 11pm. £4.20, ages 16-20 £3.50; open late March-Oct.), right on the border at the junction of B6352 and B6401 (served Mon.-Sat. by 1 bus/day from Kelso). The fifth hostel holds the center in Melrose (see town listing below).

Hiking and Biking

The Borders accommodate all levels of hiking experience; take a late aftenoon stroll in the hills or wander the wilds for days at a time. Trails lacerate the **Tweedsmuirs** (all over 2,500 ft.), to the west along the A708 towards Moffat, as well as the **Cheviot Hills,** to the southeast. Closer to Edinburgh, the **Moorfoots** and **Lammermuirs** offer gentler day walks. 90 mi. of the 212 mi. **Southern Upland Way,** Scotland's longest footpath, winds through the Borders. The Way is clearly marked, and the Countryside Commission for Scotland annually publishes a free pamphlet with route and accommodations information. Retrace Roman and pre-Roman steps along ways such as **Dere Street, Girthgate** (a pilgrimage from Edinburgh to Melrose Abbey), or **Minchmoore.** D.G. Moire expounds on these routes in his booklet **Scottish Hill Tracks—Southern Scotland.** Local tourist offices provide plenty of maps and trail guides, including "walk cards" (20p) and Ordnance Survey (scale 1:50,000) Map Sheets #66, 67, 72-75, 78, 79, and 80 (£3.50), which provide a detailed overview of the terrain. The **Scottish Borders Tourist Board offices** in Jedburgh (on Murrays Green) and in Selkirk (in the Municipal Buildings on High St.; tel. (0750) 205 55) are particularly helpful. For specific walk information, contact the **Countryside Ranger Service,** Borders Regional Council, Regional Headquarters, Newtown St. Boswells TD6 0SA (tel. 233 01, ext. 433). The rangers at the St. Boswells tourist office, a mile southeast, lead hikes through the area from May to August (75p).

Both on- and off-road biking are ideal means of exploring the area. **Scottish Border Trails,** on Venlaw High Rd. in Peebles (tel. (0721) 203 36), offers guided half-day and day tours (£10 and £15 respectively) and can organize accommodations. You can rent bikes at almost all the main Border towns; the following cycle shops rent a range of bikes, starting from £3.50-£4.00/day, and give advice on routes: **Coldstream Cycles,** The Lees Stable, Coldstream (tel. (0890) 27 09); **Hawick Cycle Centre,** 45 North Bridge St., Hawick (tel. (0450) 733 52); **George Pennel Cycles,** 3 High St., Peebles (tel. (0721) 208 44), open Tues.-Sun.; **"On Yer Bike,"** Dunsdale Rd., Selkirk (tel (0750) 201 68).

Towns

Galashiels, the relatively unattractive focal point of the Borders, sends buses west to Peebles (14/day 6:35am-9:15pm, Sun. 8/day 10:12am-7:15pm; 45 min.) and east to Kelso via Melrose (Mon.-Sat., 15/day 6:45am-8:15pm, Sun. 5/day 9:15am-7:25pm; 45 min.).

The loveliest of the region's wee towns, **Melrose** makes a solid touring base. Bike routes fan out from the town, and the **Eildon Hills,** an easy 4 mi. walk away, supply sweeping views across the Borders. Centerpiece of the town, **Melrose Abbey** was begun in 1136, redone in an ornate Gothic style, and then decimated in 1543. Note the fine stonework and surrounding gardens, or search amid the extensive foundations for a plaque marking the spot where Robert the Bruce's heart is buried. Another sign indicates Sir Walter Scott's favorite point of view from the moonlit abbey ruins, about 2 mi. east of town along the river. (Abbey open Mon.-Sat. 9:30am-7pm, Sun. 2-7pm; Oct.-March Mon.-Sat. 9:30am-4pm, Sun. 2-4pm. Admission £1, children and seniors 50p.) Scott settled into his mock-Gothic **Abbotsford** estate, 2 mi. west of Melrose (tel. (0896) 20 43), to write most of his Waverley novels. (Open late March-Oct. Mon.-Sat. 10am-5pm, Sun. 2-5pm. Admission £2, children £1.) In Melrose, past the Abbey towards the B6361, gorgeous vintage autos and motorcycles congest the **Melrose Motor Museum.** The workshop implodes with period memorabilia, from antique oil cans to cast-iron toy cars. (Open mid-May to mid-Oct. daily 10:30am-5:30pm. Admission £1.80, seniors and students £1.20, children 50p.)

The small **tourist office** (tel. (089682) 25 55), in the erudite and aromatic Priorwood Gardens near the abbey, provides free accommodations bookings. (Open Mon.-Sat. 10am-7pm, Sun. 1:30-7pm; Sept.-June Mon.-Sat. 10am-5:30pm, Sun. 1:30-5:30pm.) The well-equipped **IYHF youth hostel** (tel. (089682) 25 21; grade 2) off High Rd. looks out of a magnificent stone mansion at Melrose Abbey. (Lockout May-Sept. 10:30am-5pm; Oct.-April 11am-4pm. Curfew 11pm. £4.20, ages 16-20 £3.50. Open daily Wed.-Mon.; Oct.-March Fri.-Sat.) **Mrs. Pearson,** Gattonside (tel. 29 71), cooks excellent meals in her B&B with an attractive garden and large TV room (£13). The **Raeal Café** on Market Sq. fries the best meals for your money—scampi and chips (£2.50 take-away), sausage, egg, and chips (£2.50), and toasted sandwiches (£1). (Open Mon.-Sat. 8:30am-8pm, Sun. 10:30am-8pm.) **Abbey Coff Shop,** above the Abbey Mill woolen shop on Buccleuch St., spins out food at a fair price: toasted sandwich (£1.40), shepherd's pie (£1.80). (Open daily 9am-5pm.)

Ten mi. north of Melrose on the A68 near Lauder stands **Thirlestane Castle** (tel. (05782) 430), easily accessible by bus. The castle's restored 17th-century architecture and beautiful plaster ceilings make this castle one of the proudest representatives of its kind in Scotland. Thirlestane's romantic and bloody intrigues came to a standstill when its resident, the Duke of Lauderdale sailed west, to found the first summer home on the other side of the Atlantic in what is now Fort Lauderdale, Florida. In the 16th century, the Maitland family moved in and has been living there since. Period toys and costumes from a dress-up chest litter the nursery. (Castle open July-August Sun.-Fri. 2-5pm. May-June and Sept. Wed., Thurs, and Sun. 2-5pm; last entry 4:30pm. Grounds open May-Sept. daily noon-6pm. Admission £3.50, seniors and children £2.50. Grounds only £1.)

Sixteen mi. west of Melrose on the A72 toward Peebles stands **Traquair House** (tel. (0896) 830 323), the oldest inhabited house in Scotland. The family treasures of the Stuarts of Traquair, including manuscripts, embroideries, and letters of better-known Stuarts of Scotland, are displayed upstairs. Peter Maxwell Stuart, the present resident, brews his own ale in the 200-year-old brewery below the chapel. (Beer tasting June-Sept. Fri. 3-4pm.) The gates to Traquair are permanently closed; legend has it that the Earl of Stair, a Jacobite, swore after Prince Charlie's defeat at Culloden in 1745 that they would not be reopened until another Stuart took the throne. (Open July-Aug. daily 10:30am-5:30pm, late May-June and Sept. daily 1:30-5:30pm. Grounds open Easter-Sept. daily 10:30am-5:30pm. Admission £3, children £1.75.) On the way, visit **Dryburgh Abbey** (tel. 209 07), where Sir Walter Scott is buried near his favorite overlook. (Open Mon.-Sat. 9:30am-7pm, Sun. 2-7pm; Oct.-March Mon.-Sat. 9:30am-4pm, Sun. 2-4pm. Admission £1, children 50p.)

20 mi. west of Melrose on the A72 and the River Tweed lies **Peebles,** a well-kept town and a good base for exploring the forests of **Tweed Valley, Glentree,** and **Cardrona,** as well as **Lindinny Wood.** All have paths of varying lengths and degrees of difficulty; some can be tackled by mountain bike. (Check the tourist office for brochures.) The park-lined banks of the River Tweed also make for a pleasant picnic or stroll. Historic buildings and fashionable wool shops line High St. The **tourist office** (tel.(0721) 201 38), in the Chambers Institute on High St. (open July-Aug. Mon.-Sat. 9:30am-7pm, Sun. 2-7pm; April-June and Sept.-Oct. Mon.-Sat. 10am-5pm, Sun. 2-4pm), sells a slew of local maps and walking guides; the *Peebles Tour Walk* (10p) is a good place to start. The **Tweedmouth Museum and Picture Gallery** and the **Scottish Museum of Ornamental Plasterwork** are within 100 yds. of the office on High St. (Open Nov.-March Mon.-Fri. 10am-1pm, 2pm-5pm, April-Oct. Mon.-Fri. 10am-1pm, 2pm-5pm, Sat.-Sun. 2pm-5pm. Free.) Two houses with famous former occupants book-end High St.: Mungo Park, the famous explorer of Africa and medical missionary, lived at the corner of High and Bridgegate; and John Buchan, whose novels include *The Thirty-Nine Steps,* occupied the house at the west end of High St. Other interesting historical sites include the **Cross Kirk Church,** Cross Rd.; the remains of a 13th-century friary; **St. Andrew's Tower,** the ruins of which were used as stables by Cromwell's troops; and **Neidpath Castle,** 1 mi. west of town on the A72, where you can visit the dungeon or relish great views of River Tweed. (Open Easter-Oct. Mon.-Sat. 11am-5pm, Sun. 1-5pm. Admission £1, children 50p.)

Relax and enjoy coffee and a scone (£1) at the cozy **Sunflower Coffee Shop,** at Bridgegate. (Open Mon.-Sat. 9:30am-5:30pm.) At **Big Eb's,** the huge and eater-friendly proprietor ladles a healthy dollop of travel experience onto his excellent fish and chips (£3.40) or soup and sandwich (£1.80). (Open daily 4:30-11pm.) Wednesday night is "Scottish Night," complete with participatory singing, at the **Central Lounge Bar** on Northgate (tel. (0721) 202 30; singing 8:30pm-midnight). Leave the tourist hubbub behind for a good night's rest at **Mrs. O'Hara,** Rowanbrae, Northgate (tel. (0721) 216 30; £11.50). Campers find comfort at the **Rosetta Camping and Caravan Park,** (tel. (0721) 207 70), a 10-min. walk from town center on the wooded grounds of the Rosetta House; the former owner of the House accompanied Abercromby to Egypt to secure the Rosetta Stone for England.

Northeast Scotland

Scotland's northeastern shoulder hunches up from the forested Perthshire region along the River Tay to the high Grampian and Cairngorm summits before leaning out into the North Sea. East of the frequently snowy mountains, the countryside flattens into coastal plains strewn with castles of all vintages and sizes, and the oil boomtown of Aberdeen rises from the shore. The northeast is less trampled by tourists than other areas of Scotland—it has always been distinct from the lofty, barren Highlands to the west and the energetic Glasgow-Edinburgh region to the south. The Norse and Scots tribes that shaped the early history of the western areas never crossed the Cairngorms to intermingle with the Gaelic settlers to the west, and later the region was held in the firm Episcopalian grasp of the Gordon family.

Although transportation through the interior of this region is very spotty, with the exception of the busy A9 from Perth to Inverness, the best scenery in the northeast lies back from the flat coast along the fertile river valleys and among the gentle slopes of the mountains.

Perth

About 30 mi. west of St. Andrews lies **Perth,** an unpretentious city on the banks of the River Tay. Seat of the Scottish Reformation, Perth has grown into a compact town. Although 2 blocks of High St. have recently been closed to traffic and converted into a shopping promenade, Perth is only starting to market its quaintness and most downtown stores still favor home furnishings and nylon stockings over kilts and kitsch.

Perth's attractiveness amounts to more than a sum of its parts. Take a walk along the swiftly flowing River Tay and admire the multiple arches of the Perth Bridge; across the bridge, a nature trail leads up to a panoramic view from **Kinnoull Hill Park.** All the spots worth visiting in town lie within easy walking distance of one another. In 1559, John Knox delivered the incendiary sermon that fired the mass destruction of churches and monasteries throughout the Scottish Reformation from the pulpit of **St. John's Kirk,** Perth's oldest church; walk one block from the tourist office to St. John's Place. (Open Mon.-Sat. 10am-noon and 2-4pm.) **Lower City Mills,** on West Mill St. (tel. 305 72), built during the Victorian era, still uses water power to grind flour and oatmeal. (Open Easter-Oct. daily 10am-5:30pm, Sun. noon-5:30pm. Admission £1, children 70p.) An excellent display on the natural history of Scotland rubs shoulders with a hodgepodge collection of antique clocks, fine silverware and a masterfully crafted fiberglass replica of King Tut's sarcophagus in the **Perth Museum and Art Gallery,** at the intersection of Tay St. and Perth Bridge. (Open Mon.-Sat. 10am-5pm. Free.) **Balhousie Castle,** off Hay St. (tel. 212 81), the 16th-century home of the Earls of Kinnoull, now accommodates the **Black Watch Regimental Museum.** (Open Mon.-Fri. 10am-4:30pm, Sun. 2-4:30pm; Oct.-Easter Mon.-Fri. 10am-3pm. Free.) **North Inch,** a lush park adjacent to the castle on the beaches of the Tay, combines 100 acres of pleasantly wooded walks and an 18-hole public golf course. **South Inch,** at the other end of town, offers more recreational space, as well as nice views of the river. For warmer waters, head to the **Perth Leisure Pool,** an enormous indoor recreation complex with water flumes and exercise equipment near the hostel on Glasgow Rd. (tel. 354 54; open daily 10am-10pm; admission £2.80 for 2 hr., seniors and children £1.40). The facility, designed primarily for children, is unsuited for swimming laps. Use of weights requires a 1-hr. training course. Next door to the pool, the **Dewar's Rink** skating and curling center stays open all summer. (Open daily 10am-9:30pm, skating £1.50-2, skate rental 60p.)

The **tourist office,** 45 High St. (tel. 383 53), several blocks away from the train and bus stations, offers an unparalleled selection of maps, regional literature and traditional Scottish music on cassette tape. (Open daily 9am-8pm; Sept.-June daily 9am-6pm, Sun. noon-6pm.) The **train station,** Leonard St. (tel. 371 17), faces the bus station (tel. (0738) 268 48), where you can store luggage until 5pm for 60p.

The musically-inclined warden entertains guests with an endless supply of jokes at Perth's immaculate **IYHF youth hostel,** 107 Glasgow Rd. (tel. 236 58). Take bus #7 or 8 from the South St. post office, or hike uphill from town until the balustraded parapet comes into view. (Grade 1; lockout 11am-2pm; £4.85; open late Feb.-late Oct.) B&Bs line Glasgow Rd., below the hostel. Princes St., near the river, overflows with cheap Indian food; a spicy 3-course lunch costs £3.50 at **Shezan Tandoori,** 21 Princes St. (tel. 204 15; open Mon.-Thurs. noon-2pm and 5pm-midnight, Fri.-Sat. noon-1am, Sun. 3pm-midnight). For Chinese, walk to the area around Scott St. and South Methven St., a few blocks away. The **Tesco Supermarket** on South St. will surprise and delight you. (Open Mon.-Wed. and Sat. 8:30am-6pm, Thurs.-Fri. 8:30am-8pm.)

Buses run to most of the major towns in Scotland, including Inverness (from 8:35am-8:35pm, 12/day; £5); Edinburgh (from 8:30am-8:25pm, 13/day; £3.25); and Glasgow (10:10am-10:25pm, 11/day; £5). With similar glee, trains depart for Edinburgh (7:10am-10:31pm; 11/day); Glasgow (4:25am-10:45pm; 5/day); and Inverness (1:03am-8:53pm; 14/day).

Near Perth

Less than five mi. northeast of Perth on the A93, sumptuous **Scone Palace** (tel. (0738) 523 00) has witnessed numerous coronations of Scots monarchs. (Open Good Friday to mid-Oct. daily 9:30am-5pm, Sun. 1:30-5pm, July-Aug. Sun. 10am-5pm. Admission £3.30, seniors £3, children £2. Grounds only £1.40 and 90p.) **Glamis Castle** (GLOMZ; tel. (030784) 242), Macbeth's purported home and childhood playland of the current Queen Mum, pokes its dozen storybook turrets into the sky 35 mi. northeast of Perth on the A94 toward Aberdeen. The castle secrets collections of armor, paintings, and antique furniture. (Open mid-April to mid-Oct. daily noon-5:30pm; July-Aug. 11am-5:30pm.)

Perthshire: River Tay and Loch Tay

From the loch to the firth that both bear its name, the River Tay flows through the forested hills that go by the name of Perthshire. This extremely walkable, roughly circular district stretches north to the edge of the Grampian Mountains and south to Lake Leven, dotted with hilltop forts, 16th-century castles, and formal gardens. The snow-capped mountains that fall steeply into the deep, sparkling waters of Loch Tay, and the tiny towns at their feet, combine to create Perthshire's finest scenery. Killin and Kenmore face each other across the length of the loch, and Aberfeldy, Birnam and Dunkeld wave the River Tay on its way towards Perth.

The most beautiful part of Perthshire is also the most inaccessible. Approaching from the east, regular Magicbus service stops at **Aberfeldy,** a fine well-spring of information on the Loch Tay area but still 5 mi. from the loch. (3-5 trips/day, every three hrs. from 7:30am-8pm.) To continue west, catch the 9am postbus from Aberfeldy to **Lawers,** halfway down the west shore of the loch, or take one of the four school buses to **Kenmore,** 5 mi. west of Aberfeldy at the eastern end of the loch. (2 before 8am; 2 in the early afternoon.) Otherwise, some fancy hitching along the shoulderless A827 will be required.

Nestled on either side of the River Tay 14 mi. from Perth, connected by Telford's magnificent seven-arch bridge, lie the wee twin towns of **Dunkeld** and **Birnam.** Dunkeld's painstakingly restored 17th-century houses line the way to a partially fire-razed 12th-century **cathedral,** containing the stone sarcophagus of the notorious "Wolf of Badenoch." You may rest in peace in the lovely garden beside the church. (Open Mon.-Sat. 9:30am-7pm, Sun. 2-7pm; Oct.-March Mon.-Sat. 9:30am-4pm, Sun. 2-4pm. Free.) Lovely walks from Dunkeld lead north along the forested banks of the Tay to the great **Birnam Oak,** the last survivor of Shakespeare's fabled Great

Birnam Wood. The beautiful woods and waterfalls of the **Hermitage** tumble ½mi. away. (Free walking tours July to mid-Sept. Mon. at 2pm). Beatrix Potter spent most of her childhood holidays in the Birnam area and her experiences here allegedly inspired *The Tale of Peter Rabbit,* as well as her rich interest in fungi. The **Beatrix Potter Garden and Exhibition Centre,** in Birnam, recreates the setting of Peter Rabbit, including Mrs. Tiggywinkle's house and Peter's Burrow. Naturalists and bird-watchers will enjoy the **Loch of the Lowes,** a wildlife reserve 2 mi. east of Dunkeld just off A923. (Loch visitors center open daily mid-July to mid-August 10am-6pm; April to mid-July and mid-August to Sept. 10am-5pm.)

The **tourist office** (tel. (03502) 688) in Dunkeld lies about one mile away from the train station in Birnam (open March-April, May-Sept. Mon.-Wed. and Fri.-Sat. 10am-6pm, Thurs. 9am-5pm, Sun. 11am-5pm; Sept.-Oct. Mon.-Sat. 10am-5pm, Sun. 2-5pm; Nov.-Dec. Sat. 10am-5pm, Sun. 2-5pm; April-May Mon.-Sat. 10am-5pm, Sun. 2-5pm). Many Birnam B&Bs lurk around the corner from the train station. Private homes within a few miles of town offer the cheapest accommodations; the tourist office keeps a complete list of them and books rooms for free. In diminutive Dunkeld, **Mrs. Eliot** (tel. 650) and **Mrs. Sheret** (tel. 622) both offer twin rooms for £10.50 per person. Campers can find all the extras at **Erigmore House Holiday Park** (tel. 236; £3.50-7.50/tent). For cheap fare, try a potato with two fillings (£1.85) at **Country Fare,** 20 Atholl St., or sandwiches at **The Tappit Hen,** 7 Atholl St.

Trains arrive every two hours from Perth at the "Dunkeld" station, which is actually in Birnam. Major bus companies will drop you inconveniently beside the A9; take the local Magicbus or the Perth Panther bus (#22 or 23 from Kinnoull St.) to save money and avoid having to cross the busy thoroughfare and climb over a fence. The bus from Perth to Pitlochry will drop you at a carpark in Dunkeld (£2.10; Scottish Citylink charges £3.60 from Perth to Dunkeld.).

Aberfeldy lies another 18½ mi. west of Birnam and Dunkeld, its town center coinciding with the geographical midpoint of mainland Scotland. The **Aberfeldy distillery** offers free tours ending with a nip on harnessed the house. (Open Easter-Oct. Mon.-Fri. 10am-4pm.) The **Aberfeldy Water Mill,** Mill St., harnesses water-power to turn two one-and-a-half-ton stone grinding wheels. (Open Easter-Oct. Mon.-Thurs. and Sat. 10am-5:30pm, Sun. noon-6pm. £1.20, children 60p.) The Aberfeldy **tourist office,** in an old church on The Square (tel. (0887) 202 76), is the best source of information for the Loch Tay area. (Open end of March-June and Sept.-Oct. Mon.-Sat. 9:30am-6pm, Sun. noon-5:30pm; July-Aug. Mon.-Sat. 9:30am-7pm, Sun. noon-9pm; Nov.-late March Mon.-Fri. 10am-2pm.)

The annual **Raft Race** from Aberfeldy to Kenmore, where the river widens into the loch, could take place even if the River Tay ran dry; there is enough free-flowing alcohol to float the Titanic. The race takes place on the third Sunday in June; most locals pull their shades and stay in until Monday. About 4 mi. northwest of Kenmore hovers the remarkable village of **Fortingall.** The town appears twice in the Book of World Records: once as home to a 3,000 year old yew tree, the oldest living thing in Europe, and again as legendary birthplace of Pontius Pilate.

At the opposite end of the loch, the village of **Killin** harbors many reasonable B&Bs and a green-gabled **IYHF youth hostel** (tel. (05672) 546; grade 2; £4.20; open late March-Oct.) where the warden can answer your questions in five different languages. Other hostellers offer valuable tips on, and rides to, trails in the area, and the **tourist office** (tel. (05672) 254), on Main St., provides plentiful information on countless excellent hillwalks. (Open daily July-Sept. 9:30am-7pm; Sept.-Oct. and late March-late May 10am-5pm; late May-June 10am-6pm.) One of the best short hikes starts from behind the schoolyard on Main St. and leads up to a marvelous sheep's eye view of the loch. Seven mi. northeast of town, midway between Kenmore and Killin on the west shore of Loch Tay, languishes the **Ben Lawers Visitors Centre** (tel. (05672) 397; open daily Easter-Sept. 10am-5pm.), marking the trailhead of a day hike up Britain's third highest peak, **Ben Golomstock,** known for its diverse selection of rare alpine flowers. Killin's only regular bus service runs south to Stirling with connections to Glasgow and Edinburgh (Bluebird #59, 2 per day Mon.-Fri., 8am and 4:55pm.)

Cairngorm Mountains

The breathtaking Cairngorm Mountains lie 120 mi. north of Edinburgh, describing a granite horseshoe around large conifer forests and arctic alpine plateaus. The Cairngorm's qualify both as Scotland's most frequented skiing and climbing area, and as Britain's largest expanse of nature preserves. An extensive network of bikepaths, foot trails and hostels allow easy access to the wild beauty of this region, though certain areas restrict hiking and camping. The forests are dominated by the Scots pine, a unique conifer indigenous to the Highlands and distinguished by its orange-red branches; ask a ranger where to spot reindeer and the occasional osprey. Though Scottish skiing is best known for its blue ice and murderous winds, the Cairngorms are packed with alpine enthusiasts over weekends from December through March.

Getting There and Getting Around

Aviemore is the largest town in the Cairngorms, conveniently located on the main Inverness-Edinburgh rail and bus lines. This American-style roadside strip lacks any inherent beauty; get out of town and into the mountains as quickly as possible. Trains run from the station on Grampian Rd., just north of the tourist office (tel. 810 221), to Inverness (6-13/day; 45 min.; £5.90) and to Glasgow and Edinburgh (5-7/day; 3 hr.; £18). Buses, both more frequent (1/hr. noon-6pm with earlier and later runs) and less expensive (to Inverness: 1 hr.; £3, student £2) stop along the road nearby.

The Cairngorms can also be reached from Aberdeen, usually via Inverness (see Aberdeen Arriving and Departing). A scenic summer alternative is to bus from Aberdeen to Ballater (7-10/day) and connect there with the Heather Hopper to Aviemore (Sat., Wed. and Fri. June 23-Sept.13 2/day). Consult the Heather Hopper timetable in advance unless you plan to stopover in Braemar.

The principal road into the heart of the Cairngorms, defined approximately by the borders of the Glen More Forest Park, begins just south of Aviemore as the B970; the road jogs east at Aviemore before continuing north towards Loch Garten. Follow the eastern branch, which merges into the A951; the road passes **Loch Morlich,** a lake surrounded by conifers and bordered to the east by a wide sandy beach, before continuing into the town of Glenmore and coming to a dead end at the Cairngorm chairlift. The 10-mi. jaunt from Aviemore along the B970 and the A951 past campgrounds and heather moors, is known as **The Ski Road;** a bus services the route to the ski lifts frequently in winter, but only twice a day in summer (#337, Mon.-Fri. 10am and 1pm). You're best off renting a bike, as people usually find hitching here slow.

Practical Information

The **Aviemore and Spey Valley tourist office** (tel. (0479) 810 363), on Grampian Rd., the town's main artery, books B&Bs (£10-12), sells bus tickets, and exchanges currency for a minimal commission during peak season. A helpful list of emergency phone numbers hangs on the door. (Open July-Aug. daily 9am-7pm, Sept.-Oct. and March-June daily 9am-6pm, Nov.-Feb. daily 9am-5pm.) Another good source of information, the **Rothiemurchus Estate Visitors Centre** (tel. (0479) 810 858; open daily 9am-5pm), lies nearly a mile down the road from Aviemore towards the Cairngorms.

Hiking, Biking, Skiing and Other Activities

Important: Although the mountains rise only 4000 ft., the weather patterns of an Arctic tundra characterize the Cairngorm region. Explorers may be at the mercy of bitter winds and unpredictable mists on any day of the year. Furthermore, many trails are not posted and trekkers must be able to rely on their own proficiency with a map and compass; make sure you have an Ordnance Survey map, preferably the yellow Outdoor Leisure Sheet covering the Cairngorms (available at the tourist office.) Be prepared to spend a night in sub-freezing temperatures no matter what the temperature when you set out. Leave a description of your intended route with the police or at the mountain station, and learn the locations of the shelters (*"bothies"*) along your trail.

The Cairngorm region has Scotland's highest concentration of ski resorts. In winter, Alpine skiers from throughout Britain converge at the **Cairngorm Ski Area,** featuring five chairlifts and 12 tows (daily passes £10.40-13, children £7-8.70., multiple-day and season tickets also available.) For more information, contact the Cairngorm chairlift at (047986) 261. A multitude of local companies runs ski schools and rent equipment; pick up a copy of *Ski-ing Information* at the Aviemore tourist information center for details. The Loch Morlich hostel (see below) offers a seven-night package including food (fondue if you're lucky), lodging, ski rentals, ski instruction, and local transportation from £182 (late Dec. to mid-April); a similar deal for cross-country skiing costs from £135 (Jan.-March). Contact the SYHA office at 161 Warrender Park Rd., Edinburgh EH9 1EQ (tel. (031) 229 8660) for information and bookings. In summer, the double-legged **Cairngorm chairlift** (tel. (047986) 261; each leg £1.80), remains a blessing for armchair hikers. The first ride ascends a quite walkable 368-ft.; the second lift covers the 1056 ft. to the top. From there, descend The Saddle into Glen Avon or traverse the southern ridge of Cairngorm to **Ben Macdui,** the second-highest peak in Britain (4296 ft.). With any luck, you may run into some deer, ptarmigans, or even the Lapland reindeer.

Accommodations and Camping

The concentration of affordable hostels and B&Bs, already exceptional in the summer months, verges on awe-inspiring when the snow begins to fall; a slew of bunkhouses and private hostels open during the height of the ski season (Dec.-Jan.) in addition to the year-round accommodations listed below. Check the tourist board's *Aviemore and Spey Valley* publication for a complete listing of seasonal hostels and year-round B&Bs.

Aviemore IYHF youth hostel, Aviemore (tel. 810 345), 100 yd. south of the tourist information center. Clean and convenient; heat your meals in the microwave oven. Wake up early to wash, as there is but one shower per gender. Grade 1; Lockout 11am-2pm; £4.85. Open late Dec. to mid-Nov.

Mrs. Shaw, 7 Cairngorm Ave. (tel. 811 436), near the center of town. The least expensive B&B in Aviemore. £8.50.

Loch Morlich youth hostel (IYHF), Glenmore (tel. (047986) 238). Superb accommodations on Loch Morlich itself. Unfortunately, this attractive hostel is often booked by groups. Lockout 11am-2pm; curfew 11:45pm; £4.85; grade 1; Open mid-Nov. to Sept.

Glen Feshie Hostel, (tel. (05404) 323), 10 mi. south of Aviemore. Call ahead and you might get picked up from Aviemore station. Provides showers, a kitchen, and porridge breakfast. In a small family farm at the western end of the Cairngorm range, close to numerous walks and hikes. £4.50.

Kingussie youth hostel (IYHF) (tel. (0540) 661 506). One of two hostels south of Aviemore on the A9. Grade 2; £4.20.

Insh Hall Ski Lodge (tel. (05404) 272). Hostel accommodations for skiers and hikers year-round. £7.25, B&B £10.25.

Camping: Coylumbridge Campgrounds of Scotland (tel. (0479) 810 120), only 1½ mi. from Aviemore. Showers (10p) and laundry facilities; £3.50-7.50/tent. **Glenmore Forest Camping**

and Caravan Park (tel. (047986) 271), across from the Loch Morlich Youth Hostel. Ample space and good facilities, though it may be crowded in the summer. £4.90-6/tent, backpackers £2.

Food

Eating cheaply in Aviemore is almost a lost cause, as restaurants cater to an affluent skiing crowd. The **Gateway Supermarket,** just north of the train station (look for the green sign), saves the day, and **Derek's Delicatessen,** in the shopping center across the street, also lends a hand (take-out sandwiches from 65p, vegetarian quiche 70p; open daily 9am-6pm, Sun. 10am-5pm). Closer to the mountains on the A951, the **Glenmore Shop and Café** (tel. (047986) 253) sells all the essentials, and serves baked potato with beans and cheese (£1.90) or soup (75p) in the cozy, inexpensive restaurant. (Café open daily July-Aug. 10am-7pm, June and Sept. 10am-5:30pm, Christmas-May 9am-5:30pm. Shop open daily July-Aug. 9am-7:30pm, Christmas-June and Sept.-Oct. 9am-5:30pm.)

Aberdeen

Sometimes referred to as the "Houston of Europe," Aberdeen is the center of Britain's North Sea oil industry. Only in Aberdeen does the sound of a Texas drawl regularly mix with the Scottish brogue. Largely free of tourists, Aberdeen's few copies of the *International Herald Tribune* are bought instead by rich petrochemical merchants, and its youth hostel houses nearly as many job-seeking oil workers as backpacking students. Nestled between the Rivers Dee and Don, Aberdeen succeeds in softening its industrial character with attractive parks and a vibrant university. Old Aberdeen, just west of the city center, has been carefully restored, and many of Scotland's finest castles are easily accessible from the town. Virtually every building in Aberdeen, from the 13th-century cathedral to the newest apartment complex, is constructed of the same gray local granite. In northwest Aberdeen, a quarry hole of 400 feet attests to the popularity of this stone, considered the hardest in the world. Aberdeen (pop. 210,000) is essentially a commercial city and remains indebted to the surrounding spectacular and unspoiled Grampian countryside for its tourist appeal.

Arriving and Departing

Aberdeen is an easily accessible city by air, land, or sea. Buses travel to London (5/day 6:55am-6:30pm), Inverness (5/day 6:35am-5:45pm; £7.70, £14.10 return), and Edinburgh via Dundee (23/day 6:55am-6:30pm; £8.80, £11.10 return). 20 of the buses to Edinburgh continue on to Glasgow (£8.50, £11.30 return). Regular buses also run to Ballater and Braemar, at the southern base of the Cairngorms where, with the help of the *Heather Hopper* timetable (free at the tourist office), you can connect with buses to Pitlochry and Aviemore between June 23 and Sept 13. All fares on Scottish Citylink buses are slightly higher during peak hours (Mon.-Fri. before 8:45am or after 6pm, Sat. 9am-noon). A student discount provides approximately 1/3 off all fares. The **bus station** is located on Guild St. (tel. 212 266; ticket office open Mon.-Thurs. 8:15am-5:30pm, Fri. 8:15am-6pm, Sat. 8:30am-5pm, July-Sept. Sun. 10am-1pm and 1:30-4pm; luggage storage Mon.-Thurs. 8:30am-5pm, Fri. 8:30am-5:30pm; £1/day).

From the **train station** (tel. 594 222), beside the bus station on Guild St., ScotRail provides service to Edinburgh (8-16 daily; £21.50, return £25), Glasgow (4-16 daily; £25, £27 return), Inverness (5-11 daily; £13.50, £19 return), and London (11-15 daily; return £54-73). All fares are about £6 higher on Fridays. Ticket windows open daily 7:30am-7pm, Sun. 8:30am-7pm.

British Airways (tel. (081) 897 400) makes 5-7 daily flights between Aberdeen and London. Dan Air and Air U.K. also fly from London to **Aberdeen Airport and Heliport,** 6 mi. northwest of the city center (tel. 722 331).

The **Aberdeen Ferry Terminal,** Jamieson's Quay (tel. 572 615), is the only place on mainland Britain where you can catch a ferry to the Shetland Islands. Ferries to Lerwick (year-round Mon.-Fri. at 6pm, except June-Aug. Tues. at noon; 14 hr.; June-Sept. £44.50, with berth £53-59.50; Oct.-May £39.50, with berth £46.50-54.50) and Stromness (most Saturdays year-round at noon or 6pm, Tues. from June-Aug. at noon; 8 hr.; £32, with berth £39.50; off-season £29, with berth £35.50). Going down Market St., turn left at the traffic light past the **P&O Scottish Ferries** warehouse. (Office open year-round Mon.-Fri. 8:45am-6pm, Sat. 9am-noon; Oct.-May Sat. 9am-6pm.)

Practical Information

Tourist Information Center: St. Nicholas House, Broad St. AB9 1DE (tel. 632 727; 24-hr. information tel. 636 363), a 5-min. walk from the train and bus stations. Turn right on Guild St., left onto Market St., right onto Union St., and left again onto Broad St. Free accommodations service. Book-a-bed-ahead £2.50. Informative leaflet collection is among the most extensive in Scotland; ask for *It's Free in Aberdeen.* Open July-Aug. Mon.-Fri. 9am-8pm, Sat. 9am-6pm, Sun. 10am-6pm; June and Sept. daily 9am-6pm, Sun. 10am-4pm; Oct.-May Mon.-Fri. 9am-5pm, Sat. 10am-2pm.

Emergency: Dial 999; no coins required.

Financial Services: Banks line Union St. On Sat. try **Thomas Cook,** 339 Union St. (tel. 212 270). Open Mon.-Wed. and Fri. 9am-5:30pm, Thurs. 10am-5:30pm, Sat. 9am-5pm. Also at 28 Bon Accord Centre on the ground floor (tel. 625 856). Same hrs. as above except Thurs. 10:30am-7pm. **American Express:** 4-5 Union Terr. (tel. 641 050), just off Union St. Holds mail for cardholders or those with AmEx checks. Currency exchange. Open Mon. and Wed.-Fri. 9am-5pm, Tues. 9:30am-5pm, Sat. 9am-noon.

Gay and Lesbian Groups: Aberdeen Young Lesbian Group (tel. 625 010 or 896 989), meets Wed. at 7pm in the Women's Centre. **Gay Society of Aberdeen University,** weekly coffee shop and discussion group. Meets every Thurs. noon-2pm, at the S.R.C. Building, High St., in Old Aberdeen.

Hospital: tel. 681 818.

Launderette: In both student unions at Aberdeen University. **Aberdeen Cleaning Centre,** 144 Crown St. (tel. 590 076) will clean your clothes for £3.50/load. Open Mon.-Fri. 8:30am-6pm, Sat. 8:30am-5pm.

Pharmacy: In the **Safeway** supermarket, 215 King St. Open Mon.-Wed. and Fri.-Sat. 9am-8pm, Thurs. 9am-9pm, Sun. 10am-2pm.

Police: Queen St. (tel. 639 111).

Post Office: St. Nicholas Centre, Upperkirkgate (tel. 633 065). Open Mon. and Wed.-Fri. 9am-5:30pm, Tues. 9:30am-5:30pm, Sat. 9am-12:30pm. Pick up *Poste Restante* mail at the Crown St. office (the turreted building on your right as you come down Union St.). Open Mon.-Sat. 7am-1pm. **Postal Code:** AB9 1AA.

Telephone Code: 0224.

Women's Centre, Shoe Lane (tel. 625 010), offers references and advice on women's issues. Open for drop-in Mon.-Fri. 9:30am-1:30pm.

Accommodations and Camping

Great Western Road, 25 minutes from the train and bus stations on foot and also accessible by bus #19, is loaded with B&Bs (£12-15). The tourist office helps with accommodations and books for free.

King George VI Memorial Hostel (IYHF), 8 Queen's Rd. (tel. 646 988; grade 1). A ½hr. walk west on Union St. and Alford Pl. from the city center, or a short ride on bus #14, 15, or 27 to Queen's Rd. Large, well-furnished hostel with spacious dorms and ping-pong and pool tables. Strictly enforced 11:30pm lights-out and 8am wake-up call. Lockout 11am-2pm. Curfew 2am. £6. Open mid-Feb. to early Jan.

Camping is available at **Hazlehead Park** on Groats Rd. Contact the City Arts Dept., St. Nicholas House, Aberdeen (tel. 642 121, ext. 2489; open April-Sept.; take bus #4 or 14).

Food and Pubs

Get your groceries at the huge **Safeway** supermarket, 215 King St. (open Mon.-Wed. and Fri.-Sat. 8am-8pm, Thurs. 8am-9pm, Sun. 10am-5pm); for Himalayan yogi tea, seaweed, and other wholefoods, head for **Ambrosia,** 160 King St. (open Mon.-Wed. and Sat. 8:45am-6pm, Thurs.-Fri. 8:45am-8pm.) or the more upscale **Fresh Fields,** 49 Netherkirkgate beside Marks & Spencer (open Mon.-Wed. and Fri.-Sat. 9am-5pm, Thurs. 9am-6:30pm).

Harvesters Wholefood Take Away, 137 Union Grove (tel. 580 315). Healthy, wholesome food to go. Gigantic sandwiches £1.20-1.40, soup with bread 80p. Daily hot dish £1.10-1.40. Open Mon.-Fri. 8am-4pm.

Gannet's, Broad St. at Upperkirkgate, on the 2nd floor of the Aberdeen Students' Union. Tasty pizzas at palatable prices. Cheese pizza £1.30, toppings 25p each. Quarter-pound burgers 95p. Open mid-June to early July and mid-Aug. to Sept. Mon.-Sat. 10:30am-5pm; Oct. to mid-June Mon.-Fri. 9am-6:30pm, Sat. 11am-6:30pm.

The Grill, 213 Union St. Authentically Aberdonian. Classic wooden bar has been pumping pints since 1926. Pints £1.30, steak pie 70p, hot lunches £1.10-1.45. Open Mon.-Thurs. 11am-11pm, Fri.-Sat. 11am-midnight, Sun. 7:30-11pm.

Royal National Mission to Deep Sea Fishermen, 5 Palmerston Rd. (tel. 584 651) at Market St. Blue-suited fishermen laugh heartily and play raucous games of snooker. Soup 55p, sausage, egg, chips, and beans £1.52. Open Mon.-Fri. 6am-5pm, Sat. 6:30am-noon.

Sights

Aberdeen's **fish market** (on Market St., near Palmerston Rd.) is an attraction in itself. You can only buy in bulk. Between 4 and 8am (Mon.-Fri.), the boats land and the auctioneers hawk haddock and hack heads. Worth a visit if only browse, **Old Aberdeen** and **Aberdeen University** are a short bus ride (#1,2,3, or 4) from the city center, or a long walk through the uninspiring commercial and residential districts along King St. The twin-spired **St. Machar's Cathedral,** with its heraldic ceiling and stained glass, was built in the 13th century. (Open daily 9am-5pm. Sunday services 11am and 6pm.) The tourist office offers guided tours of Olde Aberdeene (early June-early Sept., Wed. 7pm and Sun. 2:30pm; £1.50, children 50p).

Provost Skene's House, on Guestrow near the tourist office, is a beautifully restored 17th-century townhouse "among buildings of lesser vintage." Admire its various styles of interior design, from Georgian to Victorian, or visit the museum of local archaeology in the attic. (Open year-round Mon.-Sat. 10am-5pm. Free.) The

Aberdeen has a fine sandy **beach** that stretches north for about 2 mi. from the old fishing community of Footdee (Foot of the River Dee, or fi-TEE) to the Don estuary. A pair of amusement parks looms over the southern end, while the beach's northern sands are cleaner and often quieter (take bus #15). For another serene stroll, follow the **Old Deeside Line Walkway,** an abandoned railroad, through southwest Aberdeen; the trail begins at Duthie Park and leads out of the city center toward the village of Cults. **Duthie Park,** by the River Dee, at Polmuir Rd. and Riverside Dr., includes playgrounds, flower gardens, and the unique and somewhat ill-named **Winter Gardens Hothouse..** (Hothouse open year-round daily 10am-dusk. Free.) Aberdeen's largest park, **Hazlehead,** on the western edge of the city off Queen's Rd., has an aviary and extensive woodlands. Take bus #14. **Victoria Park,** just west of the city center on Westburn Rd., has a garden for the blind, which features flowers with strong scents and Braille plaques.

Entertainment

Pick up a copy of the tourist office's monthly *What's On in Aberdeen,* or call the 24-hr. information line (tel. 636 363); the *Gallery* has an adequate calendar of art exhibitions and events (free).

The **Aberdeen Art Gallery,** Schoolhill (tel. 646 333), has a wide range of English, French, and Scottish paintings; its 20th-century British collection is particularly good. The gallery has recently expanded its offerings to include drama, dance, and music performances in the summer; check the *Gallery* for details. (Open Mon.-Sat. 10am-5pm, Thurs. 10am-8pm, Sun. 2-5pm. Free.) The **Aberdeen Arts Centre,** King St. at W. North St. (tel. 635 208), offers fine avant-garde and traditional theater performances (tickets £3-5). The adjacent café sometimes has late-night music after the show, and the center frequently hosts modern craft, print, and photography shows. (Gallery open Mon.-Sat. 10am-5pm. Free.) The

Grampian

Tucked away in a corner of northeast Scotland between the River Dee and the Moray Firth, and in the rain shadow of the Highlands, the gently rounded mountains of sunny Grampian remain uninfested by tourists, who bypass the region on their way from Edinburgh to Inverness or Skye. This county, with Aberdeen its only major city, could sell itself on the sheer number of its attractions (70 castles, dozens of distilleries, over 100 mi. of sandy beaches, and 72.8 breathtaking cliffs). Settled predominantly by French, Germans, and Scandinavians, the people of the Grampian region betweeen the River Dee and the Moray Firth have never fully assimilated with their Gaelic neighbors, although the royal family makes locals puff with pride by maintaining a summer playground at Balmoral Castle.

Grampian Coast

The 100 mi. of sandy beaches along the Grampian coast are dotted with some of the most dramatic castles in Scotland and an abundance of whisky distilleries. The well-marked Whisky and Castle Trails provide heavy doses of Scotch and Scottish history, and losing your way might be the best part of your trip.

Fifteen mi. south of Aberdeen on the A92 lies the seaside market town of **Stonehaven** (pop. 9,200). Though no longer a substantial fishing port, the town makes what it can of its historical industry: **Tolbooth Museum,** on the Old Pier, preserves local fishing lore and artifacts (open June-Sept. Mon. and Thurs.-Sat. 10am-noon and 2-5pm, Wed. and Sun. 2-5pm. Free.) Stonehaven also boasts a glorious golf course and white-sand beach. The **tourist information center** (tel. (0569) 628 06) is at 66 Allardice St. (Open Easter-late Oct. daily 10am-1:15pm and 2-5pm, July-Aug. until 7:30pm) The splendidly decrepit **Dunnottar Castle** (tel. (0659) 621 73) crumbles on the cliffs a mile farther south. Built in the 12th century by the Earl Marischal's family, the castle commands a gut-wrenching view of the crashing sea. With the help of much styrofoam staging, it served as the set in the 1991 movie *Hamlet.* (Open daily 9am-6pm, Sun. 2-5pm; Nov. to mid-March Mon.-Fri. 9am-dusk. Admission £1, children 50p.) Frequent trains (17-25/day; 20 min.) and Scottish Citylink and Bluebird Northern buses (30 min.; £1.60, day return £2.30) connect Stonehaven to Aberdeen.

Twenty-seven mi. northwest of Aberdeen, on the inland A947 to Banff, is the splendidly intact 13th-century **Fyvie Palace.** Bus service is frequent. (Open May daily 2-6pm, June-Sept. daily 11am-6pm, Oct. 6-21, Sat.-Sun. 2-6pm. Admission £2.40, Seniors and children £1.20.) The road continues through unremarkable farmland to the northern coast at **Banff** (around Kinnaird's Head from Aberdeen on the coastal road), one of a string of quiet fishing villages along the coast between Fraserburgh and Elgin. Another such village is **Pennan,** where the film *Local Hero* was set. Grab a dossier of schedules from the Elgin or Aberdeen tourist office to guide you through the confusing bus service in this area.

Elgin (with a hard "g"), a quiet but growing provincial center halfway between Aberdeen and Inverness, is the unlikely site of the remnants of spectacular **Elgin Cathedral,** described in the 14th century as the most beautiful of Scottish cathedrals. (Open Mon.-Sat. 9:30am-7pm, Oct.-March Mon.-Wed. and Sat. 9:30am-4pm, Thurs. 9:30am-12:30pm, Sun. 2-4pm. Admission 60p, children 30p.) Elgin's most famous son was Alexander Graham Bell, who taught at a local school (now converted to an electrical discount store) before he emigrated to America. The recently renovated **Elgin Museum** displays relics of both Bell's and Elgin's pasts. (Open Easter-Sept. Tues.-Fri. 10am-5pm, Sat. 11am-4pm. Admission £1, seniors, students, and children 50p.)

There are no hostels near Elgin, but the staff of Elgin's **tourist information center,** 17 High St. (tel. (0343) 542 666/543 388) will help you find an inexpensive B&B. (Open July-Aug. daily 9:30am-7pm, Sun. 11am-6pm; June and Sept. Mon.-Fri. 9:30am-6pm, Sat. 9:30am-1pm and 2-6pm, Sun. 2-5pm; April-May and Oct. Mon.-Fri. 9:30am-5:30pm, Sat. 9:30am-1pm and 2-5:30pm; Nov.-March Mon.-Thurs. 9:30am-12:30pm and 2-4:30pm, Fri. 9:30am-12:30pm and 2-4pm.) **The Park Café,** 7 N. College St. (tel. (0343) 543 291), will take you back in time; the food service engineers call you "dear," the decor is vintage '50s, and a 3-course lunch with tea costs £2.75. (Open daily 9am-7pm, Sun. 10am-7pm.) The **Lido Café,** 29 South St. (tel. (0343) 547 405), serves good quiche (95p-£1.20) and sandwiches (95p-£1.50). The **Pizza Gallery,** 154 High St., has £4 all-you-can-eat Wednesdays from 6 to 10pm. Frequent buses (Scottish Citylink Service 560) and trains serve Elgin from Inverness (buses 8:15am-9:25pm every 3 hr.) and Aberdeen (buses 6:35am-8:45pm every 3 hr.); the bus stops on High St., in the center of town, while Scotland's most space-age train depot is on Station Rd., a five-minute trek to town along South Guildry St.

Elgin serves as a base for a number of interesting day-trips. The 62-mi. **Whisky Trail** stumbles past eight famous distilleries, all of which offer free tipple-tours and samples. (All open at least Mon.-Fri. 10am-4pm in summer.) The best tour is at the **Glenfiddich** distillery (tel. (0340) 203 73) in Dufftown. 17 mi. south of Elgin, it is the only distillery in the highlands where you can see the whisky bottled on the premises. Convenient buses run directly from Elgin. (Open daily 9:30am-4:30pm, Sun. noon-4:30pm; mid-Oct. to Easter Mon.-Fri. 9:30am-4:30pm.)

A half-hour west of Elgin by bus or train is flowery **Forres,** the perennial winner of the cutthroat "Britain in Bloom" competition. Hitch or take a taxi or bus north of town to the **Findhorn Foundation** (tel. (0309) 303 11), an international spiritual community known for its horticulture and communication with nature. Scientists fail to explain the community gardens' success on such barren, sandy soil. The community runs tours daily at 2pm, but you're welcome to wander around casually. If you want to stay a while, a £10-per-day fee allows you to eat and work with the community, but you must stay in the adjacent campsites or in local B&Bs (list available at the **visitors center,** open daily 9am-5pm, Sun. 2-5pm). The café sells thick sandwiches (£1; open daily 10am-5pm). Contact the Findhorn Foundation, The Park, Findhorn, Forres IV36 0TZ for further info. **Millbuies Country Park,** 5 mi. south of Elgin off the A941 to Rothes, is an inaccessible and thus serene spot with a range of recreational facilities and a lake; booklets outlining a selection of walks and nature trails are available at the tourist office in Elgin. More convenient is the seaside village of **Lossiemouth.** Located 6 mi. north of Elgin on the A941, Lossiemouth is linked to Elgin by frequent bus service. The village is blessed with two wide, white-sand, windswept beaches: **East Beach** is linked to the mainland by a narrow footbridge and has grassy dunes; **West Beach** is cleaner, less crowded, and leads to a lighthouse. The **Lossiemouth Fishery and Community Museum,** Pitgaveny St. (tel. (034381) 37 72) houses a scale-model wheelhouse and the forbidding Stotfield Disaster Book. (Open May-Sept. Mon.-Sat. 11am-5pm. Admission 50p, seniors and children 25p.) Campers can pitch their tents at **East Beach Caravan Park** (tel. (034381) 39 80) for £1.20/tent plus £1.20/person.

Grampian Mountains

West of Aberdeen, the River Dee meanders through green pastures to the tiny towns of **Ballater** and **Braemar** after it gushes down from the Grampian Mountains. This area is ideal for hillwalking in the summer (pick up a copy of *Hillwalking in the Grampian Highlands* (£1) at any tourist office in the area), and in winter it offers some of Britain's best alpine and cross-country skiing.

Finding a bed should be no problem if the royals can't fit you in at **Balmoral Castle** (tel. (03397) 423 34), the royal family's holiday residence. (Open May-July Mon.-Sat. 10am-5pm. Admission £1.50, seniors £1.10., children free.) Stay at the **IYHF youth hostel** in Ballater (tel. (03397) 552 27; grade 3) on Deebank Rd. Turn right as you leave the bus station, take the first left onto Dee St., and the third right onto Deebank Rd.—it's by the river. (£3.20. Open late Feb.-Sept.) Twelve mi. farther west on the A93 is **Braemar,** with it's fully-furnished 17th-century **Braemar Castle.** (Open May-early Oct. daily 10am-6pm. Admission £1.45, seniors £1.10, children 75p.) The **IYHF youth hostel** in Braemar (tel. (03397) 416 59; grade 1) is just south of town in an old stone house near Glenshee Rd. (£5.30; open late Dec.-Sept.). The jovial warden can tell you how to barbecue bananas, and he's probably been to your hometown. In winter, the hostel organizes alpine ski trips to the nearby Glenshea ski area. Packages include transportation, equipment rental, lift passes and ski instruction (from £74 for 5 nights and 4 days). For more information, write to the SYHA at 161 Warrender Park Rd., Edinburgh EH9 1EQ (tel. (031) 229 86 60). The **regional tourist office** (tel. (03397) 416 00) is in Braemar, at Balnellan Rd. (Open daily July-early Sept. 10am-8pm, June and early Sept.-Oct. 10am-6:30pm, March-May and Oct. 10am-5pm.) If the hostel is full, the **Braemar Outdoor Centre,** 15 Mar Rd. (tel. (03397) 412 42), has room for 26, with showers, kitchen facilities and central heating. (£6.75, £5.75 in a bunkhouse, sleeping bag required). The center also rents cross-country skis (£5/day) and mountainbikes (£12/day). On the first Saturday in September, Braemar's population swells from 410 to 20,000 for the annual highland games of the **Braemar Gathering.** The Queen almost always attends and advance bookings are essential at this time.

Braemar is a 5-mi. walk from the **Inverey youth hostel,** where there are usually more deer than guests. The hostel is a favorite stopping point for hikers doing the classic 23-mi. trek up the **Lairig Ghru** from Loch Morlich and over the pass to Braemar. The motorcycle-riding, rock-climbing warden is tremendous. (No phone. Grade 3. £3.45. Open early June-early Sept.) As always when hiking in the highlands, be prepared to spend a night in sub-freezing temperatures, know how to find your route without the help of trail markers and leave a description of your intended hike with the local mountain station or the police.

The **Glendoll youth hostel (IYHF)** (tel. (05755) 236; grade 2; £4.20; open late March-Oct.) is a 13-mi. cross-country walk from Braemar. Follow the A93 2 mi. south to the Glen Callater turn-off, then take the Jock's Rd. footpath. Be sure to take an Ordnance Survey Map and notify the Braemar police of your plans. Glendoll is also accessible from Dundee by bus (1/day Mon.-Sat.) Bus service connects Aberdeen with both Ballater and Braemar (7-10/day 7:35am-10:30pm). Between June 23 and Sept.13, the **Heatherhopper** bus service also connects these towns with Pitlochry to the south, and Aviemore, Tomintoul, and Elgin to the north. Timetable available in regional tourist office; the bus driver sells tickets.

Inverness

One should go through rather than to Inverness; although a transportation and tourist capital of the Highlands, the city offers little to the visitor apart from its legendary association with Shakespeare and the Loch Ness monster. The truth is that Macbeth's ghost does not have even a ruin to haunt, and Nessie lives only on T-shirts and hoopla 15 mi. to the south. Inverness (the accent is strongly on the last syllable) is not unpleasant, but probably best used as a base for touring the outlying regions, which are rich in castles, distilleries, and majestic scenery.

Arriving and Departing

Inverness, in central northern Scotland, draws travelers in from Glasgow, Edinburgh and Aberdeen and then spits them out across the Highlands and Islands. Three to four trains per day run directly to London, and both **Scottish Citylink** and **Caledonian Express** make the same trip by bus. Trains run to Aberdeen (11/day, Sun. 5/day, £13.50, 2 hr. 20 min., return £19), Kyle of Lochalsh (4/day, Sun. 2/day; 2½-3 hr.; £11, return £19.50), Thurso and Wick (4 per day, Sun. 2/day; 3 hr. 45 min.; £9.70, return £17), and Edinburgh and Glasgow (5-8/day, Sun. 2-4/day; 3½-4 hr.; £18, return £24-6). Buses cover the same routes less expensively and sometimes more quickly. To London (£35.50, return £38); Edinburgh (£8.80, return £11.70), Glasgow (£9.90, return £13.40), Kyle of Lochalsh (2 hr.,£8.90, return £15.20), Aberdeen (£8.90, return £15.35), and also to Ullapool, Thurso and Wick.

Practical Information

Tourist Information Center: 23 Church St. IV1 1EZ (tel. 234 353). Local bookings £1. Sells Highlands & Islands Travelpass. Open daily 9am-8:30pm, Sun. 9am-6pm; reduced hr. mid-Sept. to May (closed Sun. early Nov.-April, Sat. Early Nov.-Feb.)

Bus Station: Farraline Park, off Academy St. **Highland Scottish Omnibuses Ltd.** (tel. 233 371). Luggage storage £1. Open Mon.-Sat. 8am-6pm, in summer also Sun. 9:30am-5pm.

Emergency: Dial 999; no coins required.

Financial Services: Thomas Cook, 9-13 Inglis St. (tel. (0463) 711 921). Open Mon.-Fri. 9am-5:30pm, Sat. 9am-5pm. **American Express:** In the Alba Travel office on Church St. Turn left coming out of the tourist office and go two blocks down. Open Mon.-Fri. 9am-5:30pm, Sat. 10am-2pm. **ATM Banking:** The Automatic Teller Machine at the Abbey National Building on 1 Union St. is connected to the **Plus System,** a network shared by many American banks. Banks concentrated around the train station and tourist office. Also at Kiltmaker *Bureau de Change,* 4-9 Huntly St., just across the river. Open daily 9am-10pm, Sun. 10am-6pm. Shorter hr. Oct.-May.

Hospital: Raigmore Hospital, Inshes Rd. (tel. 234 151).

Launderette: 17 Young St., just across the river. Wash £1.50, dry 20p. Open Mon.-Sat. 8am-6:30pm.

Pharmacy: Boots, 1/11 Eastgate Shopping Centre (tel. 225 167). Open Fri.-Wed. 9am-5:30pm, Thurs. 9am-7pm.

Police: tel. 239 191.

Post Office: 14-16 Queensgate (tel. 234 111). Open Mon.-Thurs. 9am-5:30pm, Fri. 9:30am-5:30pm, Sat. 9am-12:30pm. **Postal Code:** IV1 1AA.

Telephone Code: 0463.

Train Station: Station Sq. (tel. 238 924), off Academy St. Toilets 10p. Showers 65p. Lockers £1-3.

Accommodations and Camping

Searching for summer accommodations in Inverness can be traumatizing; be sure to arrive early in the day if you haven't made reservations. There are many unadvertised, cheap B&Bs not registered with the tourist office on Argyll and Kenneth St. The friendly staff at the **Inverness Student Hotel** will help find you one of these low profile B&Bs if the hostel is full. If a room in a B&B is what your hankering after, try **Mrs. McBean,** 15 Argyll St. (tel. 237 780), **Mr. and Mrs. Lyall,** 20 Argyll St. (tel. 710 267), **Mrs. Forbes,** 3 Altadale Rd., across the river off Fairfield Rd. (tel. 221 586), or **Broadstone Lodge,** 1 Broadstone Park (tel. 231 822).

Inverness's two hostels face each other at the corner of Culduthel and Old Edinburgh Rd. From the tourist office, walk up to Bridge St. and turn left. The first right is Castle St. which leads up to Culduthel Rd.

Inverness Student Hotel, 8 Culduthel Rd. (tel. 236 556). 52 beds in 4-10 bed rooms. The outgoing, helpful staff operates a very good travelers' resource center. Free coffee and tea all day; kitchen lacks space but showers have power. Open 6:30am-2:30am, check-out 10:30am; £6.40. No phone reservations, except from High St. Hostel in Edinburgh and Backpacker's Guest House in Kyleakin (Skye).

IYHF youth hostel, 1 Old Edinburgh Rd. (tel. 231 771). 128 beds in 6-20 bed rooms. Warden known to be abrupt. Open 7-2am. Lockout 10am-2pm. £6. Limited phone reservations. **Annex** across river takes overflow July to mid-Aug. No showers, no reservations, book after 5pm, £4.20.

Camping: Most fill with caravans in summer. **Scaniport Caravan Park** (tel. (046375) 351), 4 mi. south on the B862, is the cheapest (30 pitches, £1.75/person with or without car), and **Bught Caravan and Camping Park** (tel. 236 920), in the southern part of town near the Ness Islands, the closest (200 pitches; £1.90, with car £2.90).

Food and Pubs

High Street is packed with unctuous fast food, including the burger franchise founded by the ancient clan of MacDonald. For the ultimate in cheap 'n' greasy, head just across the river to **Oh! Mama Mia,** 3 Tomnahurich St. (tel. 232 884), where customers queue out the door for daily take-away specials (main dish with chips only 50p). Mama also rolls bacon, egg, sausage and bean for take-away (99p). (Open Mon.-Wed. 8am-8pm, Thurs.-Sat. 8am-10pm). You can't beat the breakfast special at the **Littlewoods Restaurant,** in the back of the department store on Bridge St.; sausage, egg, bacon, hash browns and mushrooms are all yours for only 99p (served Mon.-Sat. 9-11am). Join the elderly crowd for the tasty luncheon special: roast chicken, stuffing, chips and tender carrots for £2.59 (served daily 11:30am-2:30pm). **The Pizza Gallery,** 1 Bridge St., bakes great pies every day; on Wednesday after 6pm, they offer an all-you-can-eat special for £3.59 (open daily 10am-10:30pm, Sun. noon-10:30pm).

A wide array of pubs color Inverness. The Japanese tradition of *Karaoke* is taking the Inverness bar scene by storm; blush through your favorite song. The **Criterion Bar,** opposite the tourist office on Church St., tops the scene with laser *Karaoke;* spectators can gorge on the excellent pub food in the comfortable lounge (Karaoke every Mon. and Wed. nights). The **Market Bar,** in an alley opposite Church St., offers live music nightly (open Wed.-Fri. to 12:45am). **Gunsmith's,** marked by a shotgun over the doorway on Union St., attracts a rhinestone cowboy crowd to its saloon style bar. Several bars also cluster at the upper end of Academy St.

Sights and Entertainment

Disillusion awaits those who remember Inverness as the home of Shakespeare's *Macbeth.* Nothing of the "Auld Castlehill" remains; the present reconstructed castle is unimpressive and closed to the public. Instead, visit the **Inverness Museum and Art Gallery** in Castle Wynd, which displays an interesting collection of Highland paraphernalia and hosts a summer series of films and lectures. (Open Mon.-Sat. 9am-5pm; July-Aug. also Sun. 2-5pm. Free.)

For a pleasant stroll and a picnic, walk upstream to the unexpected tranquility of the **Ness Islands,** narrow islets connected to both banks by small footbridges and covered with virgin forest. Near the islands on the west bank, the **Inverness Ice Centre** (tel. 235 711) offers summer skating in a large indoor rink (daily generally 2-4:30pm and 6:30-9pm; skate rental £2, children £1.40).

Like all Scottish cities, Inverness has its share of annual summertime activities. In mid-July, local strongmen hurl heavy objects during the **Inverness Highland Games.** Pipe-and-drum bands and daredevil display teams dominate the **Inverness Tattoo Festival** in early August. The **Marymas Fair,** in mid-August, recreates 19th-century street life with crafts stalls, concerts, and proletarian strife. The **Northern Meeting,** considered the world's premier piping competition, comes to Eden Court in late August. Earlier in the season, over Easter weekend, Inverness hosts a three-day **Folk Festival.**

Near Inverness

The unjustifiably famous **Loch Ness** cowers 5 mi. south of town. For a full dose of Nessie-hunting lore, take a tour on **Gordon's Minibus;** the entertaining narrative of marine biologist and historian Dr. Gordon Williamson is worth the trip. His minibus leaves from the Inverness tourist office at 10:30am and returns at 4:30pm (£9; seniors, students, and hostelers £8). A number of other companies run shorter tours (3½ hr.) that leave the tourist office at 10:30am and 2:30pm; they generally cost £6. You can bike down the eastern side of the loch, where the narrow B582 runs close to the water. Eighteen mi. down this road, the River Foyers empties into the loch in a series of idyllic waterfalls.

16 mi. down the western shore road (the A82) crumble the ruins of **Urquhart Castle,** one of the largest in Scotland before it was blown up in 1692 to prevent Jacobite occupation. Most photos of Nessie have been fabricated at this spot. Though the shore road is not suitable for biking, you can take a bus or hitch to the castle. (Open April-Sept. Mon.-Sat. 9:30am-7pm, Sun. 2-7pm; Oct.-March Mon.-Sat. 9:30am-4pm, Sun. 2-4pm. Admission £1.20.) Nearby in Drumnadrochit the **Loch Ness Centre** (tel. (04562) 573) features a scale replica of Nessie and a very impressive 40-min. audio-visual display. (Open daily 9am-9:30pm; reduced hr. daily mid Sept.-June. Admission £3.50, seniors and students £2, children £1.50.) The **Loch Ness youth hostel (IYHF)** (tel. (0320) 512 74; grade 2) stands on the western shore of the loch, 7½ mi. south of the castle; call ahead between mid-July and August. (£4.20. Open Easter-Sept.)

East of Inverness unfold the moors of **Culloden Battlefield.** In 1746, Bonnie Prince Charlie's highland army lost some 1200 men to the King's army in 40 min., dashing the Prince's hopes of replacing the British crown in exiled Stuart hands. The overwhelming defeat, which sent Prince Charlie into his circuitous flight through the Highlands with a £30,000 price on his head, marked the decline of the clan system. (Visitors center (tel. 790 607) open June to mid-Sept. daily 9am-6:30pm; April-May and mid-Sept. to Oct. daily 9:30am-5:30pm; Feb.-March and Nov.-Dec. 10am-4pm. Admission £1.50, seniors, students, children, and hostelers 75p.)

A short mile south of Culloden, the stone circles and chambered cairns of the **Cairns of Clava** recall civilizations of 30,000 years ago. Having recently undergone extensive restoration, the nearby **Castle Stuart** (tel. 790 745), the 17th-century home of the Earls of Moray and the Stuart family, now offers tours. (Open May-Sept. daily 10:30am-5:30pm. Admission £2.50, seniors and students and seniors £1.50.) Built a full 400 years after Macbeth's time, **Cawdor Castle** (tel. (06677) 615) has been the residence of the noble Thane's descendants since the 15th century. A well-preserved drawbridge crosses an equally healthy moat, and Highland forests embrace the carefully cultivated garden; visit Cawdor for its beautiful setting alone. (Open May-early Oct. daily 10am-5:30pm. Admission £2.90; grounds only £1.40.) Unfortunately, public transportation to Cawdor, Culloden, and Castle Stuart is virtually nonexistent; walking is your best option.

Highlands and Islands

Long live the weeds and the wilderness yet.
—Gerard Manley Hopkins

The Highlands Boundary Fault stretches northeast from Arran Island to Aberdeen, marking the southern boundary of the Highlands and Islands. Scotland's extravagantly frayed northwestern coast, cut by sea lochs and girded by innumerable islands, remains the most beautiful region in Scotland, and one of the last stretches of true wilderness in Europe; even in tourist season you can easily hike for a full day without seeing another human being. The Inner and Outer Hebrides arch to the west of the mainland, while the Orkney and Shetland Islands drift in a northeasterly direction off Scotland's horn at John o' Groats. The Mainland towns of Oban, Fort William, Glencoe, Ullapool and Thurso act as points of access to the islands and as bases for exploring the balding Highland mountains, rising to the west of the Cairngorm Mountains with a grandeur outreaching their altitude. Although rarely rising above 400 feet, these aspiring mountains, garnished with sparkling narrow lochs, offer the scenery and climbing challenges of a much larger mountain range.

The Highlands and Islands, apart from being a distinct geographical region, embody a way of life. The Highlanders, though not abounding in material wealth, have defined much of Scottish identity with their rich body of music, sport and dress. Living in a beautiful but not a bountiful land, few Highlanders aside from the postmen and tax collectors find employement at a single occupation; most people make ends meet through a variety of self-employment, typically including crafting, fishing, and a B&B.

Scotland's northwest has not always been so vacant. Two hundred years ago, 30% of Scotland's population lived north of the Great Glen, and even the smallest, most windswept islands supported a family or two. The exhaustion of onshore fishing grounds, the development of a synthetic replacement for kelp, and the proliferation of absentee farming all combined to force a mass emigration during the infamous Highland Clearances of the early 19th century. The Clearances dealt an almost fatal blow to the Highland nation, a clanship-based, Gaelic-speaking civilization that brought Christianity to Britain more than 1500 years ago. The region's staple is now tourism, and English and Scottish Lowlanders have repopulated the area with holiday homes. Extra time and effort spent to access regions less defiled by tourism, like the Outer Hebrides, the far northwest, Orkney and Shetland, is well spent. Only in the Outer Hebrides is Gaelic still widely spoken.

Getting Around

Travel in the Highlands requires a great deal more planning than in the rest of Britain. Although bus routes crisscross the region and boat services connect more than 40 islands to the mainland, you can't count on making more than one or two journeys per day on any form of transportation, even in high season; transport services are drastically reduced on Sundays and in winter. Arm yourself with the absolutely indispensable *Getting Around the Highlands and Islands* (£4, available at most bookstores and tourist offices). Most ferries on the west coast are run by **Caledonian MacBrayne** (head office tel. (0475) 337 55), which publishes an excellent, widely available free timetable and fare sheet; their open-dated **Island Hopscotch** service provides discounts on a succession of ferry trips. Bikes can cross without charge, but advance booking for cars is strongly recommended. The **Highlands and Islands Travelpass** is valid for unlimited travel on many of the bus, boat, and rail services in the region northwest of the Great Glen, which runs southwest from Inverness to Fort William. Transportation from Edinburgh or Glasgow is included, but the Travelpass doesn't give you your money's worth unless you are always in motion. Travelpasses are available for seven out of eight or for 13 out of 15 days (June-Sept. £65 and £90; Oct.-May £40 and £60). In Scotland, the pass is sold at major train stations and tourist offices or can be ordered by calling (0349) 634 34. In the U.S. and Canada, contact British Rail Travel International, 1500 Broadway, New York, NY 10036-4015 (tel. (212) 382 3737), or any British Rail branch office.

Arran

The glorious Isle of Arran (rhymes with barren) accurately bills itself as "Scotland in Miniature." Romantic lowland hills and majestic Highland peaks co-exist on an island less than 20 mi. long. In the north the gray and craggy peaks of Goatfell and the Caisteal range rise above the pine trees of the foothills; the eastern coastline sweeps from Brodick Castle south past the conical hump of Holy Island into meadows and white beaches. Southwest, among the bog-grass and plains at Machrie, circles of prehistoric stones still stand; and north, along the shores near Lochranza's crumbling castle, seals bask on the rocks.

Getting There and Getting Around

To reach Arran take the train from Glasgow's Central Station (5/day 8:30am-8pm, Sun. 4/day 9:30am-5:40pm; 45 min.; £2.70) west to Ardrossan on the Firth of Clyde. From Ardrossan, the Cal-Mac ferry makes the hour-long crossing to Brodick on Arran three to five times per day in sync with the train schedule (£2.55, off-season £2.30, return £4.10, off-season £3.65). There's also ferry service (mid-April to mid-Oct. only) from Claonaig on the Kintyre peninsula to Lochranza on Arran (10/day daily 8:45am-7:15pm; 30 min.; £2.55, return £3.65). If you can't wait for the ferry back, or just want to make like Jacques, contact Johnston's Marine Stores (tel. (07706) 333) in Lamlash, about renting **scuba** equipment.

Although Arran is within easy reach of Glasgow and is served by a convenient circular bus route, there are still large areas of wilderness in the northwest and southeast; the villages (Brodick excepted) are quiet and untouristed. More deer inhabit this island than people. The booklet *Seventy Walks in Arran* will tell you more than you'll ever need to know about hiking possibilities.

Buses and bicycles are both good options for carless tourists on Arran. In Brodick, mountain or touring bikes can be rented at **Mini-Golf Cycles,** behind the miniature golf course on Shore St. (tel. (0770) 22 72); state-of-the-art Hillmonsters £9.75/day, their lesser cousins £5-6/day (open daily 9am-7pm); **Brodick Cycles,** farther down Shore St. opposite Village Hall (tel. (0770) 24 60) rents bikes from 3-speed to mountain for £4-9.50/day, £20-40/week, with a £5-10 deposit (open daily 9am-6pm). You can also rent bikes in Lochranza and Whiting Bay. For the aimless and carless **Falco Tours** in Brodick (tel. (0770) 864 88) offers guided day romps with food and binoculars provided (£14, £10 half-day). Bus transportation to all parts of the island is quite convenient. The North Arran and South Arran Circular both meet at Blackwaterfoot and Brodick, the island's western and eastern coastal midpoints. It's possible, even starting from the mainland, to make a circular daytrip of the island, with three-hr. stops at any two villages (enough time for short hikes around Lochranza, Blackwaterfoot, or Whiting Bay): start from Brodick at 10:45am and take a bus north towards Lochranza. The 9:45am ferry from Ardrossan to Brodick connects with this bus, and the returning bus from South Arran to Brodick meets the 7:20pm ferry to the mainland. Check the free bus schedule, available at the tourist office, for exact connections and starting times. Post buses give extremely slow tours of the island; they leave Brodick at 9:20am. *Note: No buses run to catch the Sun. morning ferry.* Hitching's quick enough out of Brodick but a slow and painful thing from the island's two ends. Locals are friendly but infrequent and tourists are your worst nightmare.

Sights

Shore Rd. becomes Low Glencloy Rd., leading past the **Arran Heritage Museum,** which features a working forge and a collection of antique farm machinery. (Open Easter-Sept. Mon.-Sat. 10am-5pm. Admission £1.50, concessions £1.) Another mile down the road is the immaculate and impressive **Brodick Castle.** Ancient seat of the Dukes of Hamilton, the castle contains a fine collection of porcelain, paintings, and sporting trophies. The well-maintained grounds feature the things gardens are made of. (Castle open Easter to mid-Oct. daily 1-5pm. Gardens open daily 9:30am-dusk. Admission to castle and garden £2.80, to garden only £1.70. Children ½ price. Free ranger walks late May-Aug. Mon. and Thurs. at 2pm, Tues. at 7:30am and 2:30pm.) The popular ascent of **Goatfell** (2866 ft.), Arran's highest peak, begins along the road between the castle and the heritage museum. From here, along the well-marked and well-traveled path, the average round-trip journey is four or five hours; from the cold and windy peak you have a delirious view north to the jagged Castail range, and south along the coastline to Holy Island.

The **Arran Highland Games,** replete with weird sports and bagpipe parades, arrive in Brodick in early August, while the highly successful **Isle of Arran Folk Festival** is held in June.

Brodick, Arran's largest and freshest village, is important to the traveler because of its services and transport connections.

Buses take travelers from the pier to more remote parts of the island; the tourist office (tel. (0770) 21 40 and 24 01) is in the round building with the pointy top, at the base of the pier. They stock an excellent series of free maps and leaflets, and are your best bet for help in booking local B&Bs (£10-12). (Open May-Sept. Mon.-Sat. 9am-7:30pm, Sun. 10am-7:30pm; March-April and Oct. Mon.-Thurs. 9am-5pm, Fri.-Sat. 9am-7:30pm; Nov.-Feb. Mon.-Thurs. 9am-5pm, Fri. 9am-7:30pm.) In July and August, most B&Bs are packed, but try **Mrs. Wilkie,** Cala Sona (tel. (0770) 28 28; £10; from the tourist office take a left after the Douglas Hotel, a right onto Alma Rd., then your first left onto Hillview Rd.). **Mrs. Macmillan,** Glenard (tel. (0770) 23 18; £12; your last left on Shore Rd. before it forks) is all wood panelled and roomy, except for the disappearing single. Farther out, off the road to Whiting Bay, is **The Sheilin,** Corriegill Rd. (tel. (0770) 24 56; £11), which has well-equipped rooms (color TV, coffee and tea facilities, sinks) and postcards of the house on sale. The **Glen Rosa Farm** (tel. (0770) 23 80), 2 mi. north of Brodick on the coastal road to Corrie, is available to campers from April to October (£1/person, no hot water). You can also look for grassy spots by the beach (the golf course is off-limits).

The center of Brodick is along Shore Rd. to your right as you disembark. For food, try **Collins' Good Food Shop,** at the western end of Shore Rd., which has outdoor seating by a stream. Quiche costs £3.10, entrees with salad about £3, and the shop also sells health food. (Open Mon.-Wed. and Sat. 9am-4:30pm, Thurs.-Fri. 9am-5pm.) The restaurant also runs the only launderette in town. (Wash £1.40. Dry 20p.) The **Brodick Bar,** just off Shore Rd. behind the post office, serves cheap and excellent bar meals (daily noon-2pm and 5:30-8pm). The **Co-op Foodstore,** near the Brodick Bar, stocks the necessities. (Open Mon.-Sat. 8am-8pm.)

Lochranza, at the island's northern tip, 14 mi. from Brodick, is idyllic, with one store, one pub, several crafts workshops, and a castle. Across from the pier is Lochranza's seasonal tourist office (tel. (077083) 320; open mid-May to Sept. Mon.-Sat. 9:30am-5pm). The town also has a rather ordinary **IYHF youth hostel** (tel. (077083) 631; grade 2; £4.20; open mid-March to Oct.), which overlooks the ruins of **Lochranza Castle. Mrs. Rankin** (tel. (077083) 652) at Westwood offers big brown rooms and psychedelic carpets (£12). In a pinch, the **Lochranza Hotel** (tel. (077083) 223) should also have room, and possibly a single (£15); they also have Lochranza's only pub. There's the outrageously well-equipped **Lochranza Golf Caravan Camping Site** a ½mi. before town on the Brodick Rd. with laundry, hot water, food and much, much more (£2.15/person, golf £9/day).

You can rent bikes (£5/day) from **M. Kerr** (tel. (077083) 676) just up the road from the hostel. Biking down the coast to the even tinier village of **Catacol Bay** makes a nice hour-long round trip, or you might stroll north over the moor and down the meadows by the sea to the **Cock of Arran** and **Ossian's Cave,** one of the legendary resting places of the short-fingered vulgarian of Gaelic times, or take the public footpath south into the high country: from the loch at the top of the pass it's an easy scramble to the top of **Caisteal Abhail.** There are also several waterfalls and swimming holes along the route. If you are traveling north in Scotland, a **ferry** sails from Lochranza to **Claonaig** on the Kintyre peninsula (mid-April to mid-Oct. 8-10/day; £2.30).

On the west side of the island is the town of **Blackwaterfoot,** in an area with two prehistoric sites: the **Machrie Stones** are a semi-circular arrangement of boulders dating from the Bronze Age, and the walls of **King's Cave** glimmer with ancient inscriptions and paintings. A sandy beach stretches along the coast on either side of the town. The **Greannan Hotel** (tel. (077086) 200), which serves cheap bar meals all day, is in **Shiskine,** 1 mi. north of Blackwaterfoot. The southern part of the island is less rugged than the north, with gentle hills and long, sandy beaches. The **IYHF youth hostel** in **Whiting Bay** (tel. (07707) 339; grade 2) is a good base. (£4.20; open mid-March to Oct.) For diversion, you can take the easy path to Glen Ashdale Falls or rent a bike from **Whiting Bay Hires** (tel. (07707) 382; £4-9/day, £14-30/week) and cycle to a nearby beach.

Mid Argyll and Kintyre Peninsula; Islay and Jura Islands

The sylvan glens of Mid Argyll, the peninsula of Kintyre, and the quiet island of Islay form an entrancing yet largely unvisited triangle in western Scotland. Warm ocean currents keep the southern islands softer and lusher than the bleak, windy north. Three to four daily bus services (on Scottish Citylink and Caledonian Express) from Glasgow's Buchanan bus station over to Campbeltown on Kintyre form the backbone of transport to this quiet region; Many people hitch along the busy A83.

Inveraray, an attractive lochside town in northern Mid Argyll, two hours out of Glasgow (3 buses/day 9:15am-6pm; £3.10), is a good place to begin an exploration of the region. Nearby is the splendid **Inveraray Castle** (tel. (0499) 22 03), home of the Duke and Duchess of Argyll. (Castle open July-Aug. Mon.-Sat. 10am-6pm, Sun. 1-6pm; April-June and Sept. to mid-Oct. Mon.-Thurs. and Sat. 10am-1pm and 2-6pm, Sun. 1-6pm. Admission £2.50, seniors £2, children £1.20.) No visit to this lovely town is complete without a stop at the **Inveraray Jail** (tel. (0499) 23 81) with its live inmates and gleeful theme area on torture, death and damnation. (Open daily 9:30am-6pm; £2.80, seniors £1.30.) Inveraray has an excellent **tourist office** on Front St. (tel. (0499) 20 63) that books accommodations throughout the area (open April-May Mon.-Sat. 9:30am-4pm; June to mid-Oct. Mon.-Sat. 9:30am-6pm, Sun. 2:30-5pm). The small **Inveraray youth hostel (IYHF)** (tel. (0499) 24 54; grade 2) is just north of town; take a left through the second arch from the tourist office onto Oban Rd. A solid and simple hostel blessed with an omniscient warden. (£4.20. Open May-Sept.) Inveraray secrets a cache of B&Bs, with the awards for budget friendliness and centrality going to **Mrs. Campbell,** Lorona, Main St. South (tel. (0499) 22 58; £11) and **Mrs. MacLaren,** Old Rectory Rd. (tel. (0499) 22 80; £9.50-11).

West of the Kintyre peninsula across calm ocean waters, the island of Islay (EYE-luh) receives few visitors. One boat makes the trip every day at 12:30pm, some running to Port Askaig in the northeast and some to Port Ellen in the southeast (£4.70). Both leave from **Kennacraig Ferry Terminal,** in the middle of nowhere 7 mi. south of Tarbert on the Kintyre peninsula, and served by the Glasgow-Campbeltown buses. Travelers coming to Arran via the Lochranza-Claonaig ferry can call D. Henderson (tel. (08802) 220) a day in advance to reserve a seat on the bus from Claonaig to Kennacraig, though your best bet is to hitch the 6 mi. with one of the cars off the ferry. On Wednesdays only, there's also a ferry connection linking Port Askaig to Oban and Colonsay.

There's little in Port Askaig aside from the hotel, shop, and ferry terminal; **Bowmore,** Islay's largest town, is 10 mi. from both Port Ellen and Port Askaig, and home to Islay's only tourist office (tel. (049681) 254) Call the tourist office in advance to ask about reserving B&B accommodations on Islay (£11-12). (Open June to mid-Oct. Mon.-Sat. 9:30am-6:30pm, Sun. 2:30-5:30pm; April-May Mon.-Sat. 9:30am-4pm.) The unique 18th-century **Bowmore Round Church,** also known as the Kilarrow Parish Church, was designed to prevent evil spirits from occupying the corners. (Open daily 9am-dusk. Free.) Islay has a distillery in nearly every town; the **Bowmore Distillery,** School St. (tel. (049681) 441) is the oldest in full-time operation. (Tours Mon.-Fri. at 10:30am and 2pm; Nov.-Feb. Tues. and Thurs. at the same times.) In summer, two or three buses per day link Port Askaig and Port Ellen via Bowmore; call **B. Mundell Ltd.** (tel. (049684) 273) or the Bowmore tourist office for more details. The west coast between Bowmore and Port Ellen, also accessible by bus, is graced by the **Big Strand,** 7 mi. of sandy beach.

At **Port Ellen,** the windswept Oa Peninsula to the west drops dramatically to the sea, and a pleasant 3-mi. hike to the northeast takes you past **Laphroaig Distillery,** where one of Scotland's finest malts is produced, to the blue-stoned Celtic **Cross of Kildalton.** The distillery offers free guided tours at 10:30am and 2:15pm (tel. (0496) 24 18). You can camp near Kildalton on the sandy beach at Claggain Bay. In Port Ellen, you can get a room and a meal at Mrs. Hedley's **Trout Fly Restaurant** (tel. (0496) 22 04; £9.50-12.50), or at **Mrs. MacGillivray's,** 66 Fredrick Cres. (tel. (0496) 24 20; £10).

A flaming orange car ferry runs 5-min. trips from Port Askaig across the Sound of Islay to the island of **Jura,** one of the remotest and least populated for its size of the Scottish islands (ferry in summer 11-13/day, Sun. 4/day, 80p). George Orwell wrote *1984* on Jura's northern coast. A walker's Wallyworld, Jura has one village, **Craighouse,** with just a couple of B&Bs; contact Mrs. Boardman at 7 Woodside (tel. (049682) 379; £12) well in advance. *Jura: A Guide for Walkers* (£1.50) is available at the Islay tourist office and at local shops.

Oban

Oban (OH-ben), the second largest city in the Highlands and busiest ferry port on the west coast, has managed to unabashedly embrace the tourism industry without a Faustian sale of its soul. Lacking notable attractions, Oban endears itself with sporadic outbursts of small-town warmth. Ferries to most of the lower Hebrides (notably Colonsay, Lismore, Kerrera, Mull, Iona, Coll, Tiree, Barra, and South Uist) criss-cross Oban's attractive harbor, and a hard-working fishing fleet reels in relatively inexpensive seafood. As the sun sets over the blue hills of Mull and the port workers turn in for the day, the streets of Oban fill with people: there is always activity, but never too much to do.

Arriving and Departing

One Caledonian Express coach per day makes the long journey to Oban from London (late May-Sept.; 10½ hr.). Buses arrive from Glasgow's Buchanan Station (3-5/day; 3 hr.; £8, return £14) and the spectacular **West Highland Line** runs trains directly to Oban from Glasgow's Queen St. Station. Built at the turn of the century, the line is a triumph of Victorian engineering, crossing glens, moors, and rivers, and passing along the edge of mountain ranges (4/day, Sun. 3/day; 3 hr.; £13.30, return £17.80). Travelers heading north from Oban along the west coast towards Skye can catch the **Gaelicbus** directly to Fort William (tel. (085 52) 229; Mon.-Sat. 4/day; £4.50, return £6.50) instead of going out of their way through the rail and bus junction at Crianlarich, due east of Oban. The first departure of the day (9:30am) runs through Fort William to Inverness (3½ hr.). All buses will stop in **Ballachulish,** 16½ mi. south of Fort William and a 1-mi. walk west of Glencoe, if you ask the driver (£4.50).

Caledonian MacBrayne Ferries (known to locals as "Cal-Mac"), sail from Oban to most islands in the southern section of the Outer and Inner Hebrides. Ferries frighten fish on their way to: Craignure on Mull (5-7/day 8am-6pm; 40 min.; £2.30); Coll and Tiree, two islands west of Mull, with a stop at Tobermory on Mull (Mon., Wed. and Fri.-Sat. 6am; Sun. 10am ferry to Craignure, bus to Tobermory, noon ferry to Coll/Tiree; to Tobermory 1¾ hr. £5.85; to Coll/Tiree 3-4 hr., £7.70); Barra (Mon., Wed. and Sat. 4:40pm, Thurs. at 3pm; 5 hr.; £13); South Uist (same times and price as Barra plus Tues. and Fri. 3pm; 5-7 hr.); and Lismore (Mon.-Sat. 2-5/day; 1 hr.; £1.45, £2.75 return). From Gallanach, two mi. south of Oban, ferries run to Kerrera (continuous service 10:30am-12:30pm and 2-5pm; 5 min.; £2 return) and Colonsay (Mon., Wed. and Fri. 1-2/day; 2 hr.; £6.45).

Orientation and Practical Information

Oban's ferry terminal, train station, and bus stop congregate by the pier near an array of pay phones and public toilets. **Argyll Square,** the center of town and home to the tourist office, is a block inland.

Tourist Information Center: Argyll Sq. (tel. 631 22). At the upper-right corner of the roundabout as you come from the train station. Unflaggingly friendly despite the milling throngs. *Where To Stay* (free) lists local accommodations; make use of it to avoid the £1 booking fee. Sells bus, tour, and entertainment tickets. Currency exchange available. Open June-Aug. Mon.-Sat. 9:15am-8:45pm, Sun. 10am-4:45pm; May and Sept.-Oct. Mon.-Sat. 9:15am-5:30pm, Sun. 10am-5pm; Nov.-March Mon.-Fri. 9:15am-1pm, 2-5pm; April Mon.-Fri. 9:15am-5:30pm.

Bus Station: Scottish Citylink office at 1 Queens Park Pl. (tel. 628 56), a block from the **bus shelters** and train station (open Mon.-Fri. 8:30am-5pm). Tickets are also available at the tourist office (Citylink and Caledonian Express only) and from drivers.

Emergency: Dial 999; no coins required.

Ferries: Caledonian MacBrayne, Railway Quay (tel. 622 85).

Financial Services: Bank of Scotland, Station Rd. (tel. 636 39), across from train station. Open Mon.-Wed. 9:15am-4:45pm, Thurs. 9:15am-5:30pm, Fri. 9:15am-4:45pm. Currency exchange also at the **tourist office** in a pinch.

Hospital: West Highland Hospital, 1½ mi. from town center on Glencruitten Rd. (tel. 637 27).

Launderette: Stevenson St. Brand-new facilities. £1.50 wash, 20p dry. Open daily 9am-9pm.

Pharmacy: Boots, 34-38 George St. (tel. 625 17). Open Mon.-Sat. 8:45am-5:30pm.

Police: Albany St. (tel. 622 13).

Post Office: Albany St. (tel. 656 79) up from Argyll Sq. Open Mon.-Fri. 9am-5:30, Sat. 9am-3:30pm. **Postal Code:** PA34 4AA.

Telephone Code: 0631.

Train Station: At Railway Quay (tel. 630 83). Luggage lockers 50p-£1. Station open Mon.-Sat. 7am-8:30pm, Sun. noon-8:30pm.

Accommodations

In July and August it's a struggle to find a B&B under £12-13, and booking ahead is essential. Prices tend to settle down around £11 once the tourist bubble bursts in September. Standard-issue B&Bs line **Ardconnel** and **Dunollie Roads,** off George St. by the cinema. People often camp by the water along Corran Esplanade near Dunollie Castle.

Oban youth hostel (IYHF), Corran Esplanade (tel. 620 25; grade 1), ¾ mi. north of the train station along the water, just past the square-towered cathedral. Seaside real estate with laundry facilities, store, and kitchen. Never assume there will be an extra bed in July or Aug. Bike rental £3.50/day, £5 deposit. Lockout 11am-2pm. Curfew 11:30pm. £4.85. Open March-Oct.

Jeremy Inglis, 21 Airds Crescent (tel. 650 65), across the street and around the corner from the tourist office. If he's not home, try smoking him out of McTavish's Kitchens restaurant on George St. (tel. 630 64). A *Let's Go* institution: the proprietor is energetically hospitable, overwhelmingly informative, elusively fascinating, and his rooms are cheap. Books and pictures cover every inch of wall space. Some private rooms for couples. Devotees worldwide make special trips to Oban just to stay with Jeremy. Hall baths, no showers. His kitchen is yours: homemade muesli and jam on wholewheat toast. B&B £5.50—yes, £5.50. Reservations essential mid-July to Aug. Key deposit £1.

Mr. and Mrs. John MacEachen, Cuan, Lismore Crescent (tel. 639 94), about 1 mi. from town center. From Corran Esplanade, make a right after the waterfront cathedral onto Corran Brae, then go 500 yd. uphill to the second right—it's at the very end of the road. Very modern interior design and gorgeous views of the town and harbor. £10, £8 with continental breakfast only. Open April-Oct.

Maridon House, Dunuaran Rd. (tel. 626 70). Very convenient to the ferry terminal. Take a right on Shore St. behind the train depot and another right on Albany St.; you can't miss the striking pastel blue exterior. The clean but prosaic interior lacks a homey touch, but with 10 rooms there is often space here long after other B&Bs have filled up. Hall bathrooms and showers. B&B £12.

Food and Pubs

Harborside George St., beginning near the train station, runs the length of Oban's gastrocenter and nightlife strip. Oban is one of the very few places in Scotland where on reasonably priced menus the word "fish" is not automatically followed by "chips." Small seafood shops and individual fishmongers cluster around the ferry terminal; mussels are atypically cheap here and delicious when steamed, preferably with white wine, onions and cream. For a wide selection of muesli, head to **Millstone Wholefoods,** 15 High St. near the tourist office (open Mon.-Sat. 9am-5:30pm). Another wholefood store, **Oban Sesame,** squeezes in between John and William St. on Corran Esplanade. The gargantuan **Wm. Low Supermarket,** on Market St. behind the Gallery restaurant, accepts Visa. (Open Mon.-Fri. 8:30am-8pm, Sat. 8:30am-5:30pm; July-Aug. also Sun. 10am-4pm.) **The Poly,** a much smaller grocery shop at 45 Stevenson St., is open for longer hours (Mon.-Sat. 4:30am-11pm, Sun. 7am-11pm; Oct.-Easter closes at 10pm).

Andrews Meals, 41 Combie St., just up past the tourist office near the branch post office. The best value in town and nary a tourist in sight. Try the herring in oatmeal with fresh vegetable and chips (£2.95), or the two veggie burgers with chips and baked beans (£1.90). Full Scottish breakfast served all day (£2.25). Open Mon.-Sat. 7:30am-7pm, Sun. 8am-5pm.

Sights and Entertainment

Built in the 1890s to employ out-of-work stonemasons, the Colosseum-like **McCaig's Tower** overlooks the town. Mr. McCaig had planned to add statues of his family and friends to the open stone arches, but his models never materialized. Take the steep Jacob's Ladder stairway at the end of Argyll St., then walk to your left along Ardconnel and right up Laurel to the tower's grassy entrance. **Pulpit Hill,** a spot with a better view but less architectural pizzazz, rises in the southern half of town, up the path and steps at the end of Albany St. From here you can see Mull, Kerrera, and **Dunollie Castle,** at the opposite end of town off Corran Esplanade. The ruins of the castle include a 15th-century tower, built on a site fortified since the late 7th century. (Open all the time. Free.) Dunollie is the seat of the MacDougall family, formerly the Lords of Lorn, who once owned a third of Scotland. To reach the tower, walk 10 min. north from the town center. From the castle, cross over the field and fence to arrive at the path that leads through almost primeval forest to Corran Brae Rd.; you can also access the path and its many branches from the youth hostel.

In town, the recently renovated **Oban Distillery,** Stafford St., tops off guided tours with free drams. (Tours Mon.-Sat. 9:30am-4:15pm; Nov.-Easter Mon.-Fri. 9:30am-4:15pm. Free.) Just two mi. outside town on Glencruitten Rd., **Achnilarig Farms** (tel. 627 45) offers guided horseback rides through the surrounding country to people of all levels of experience. (Open March-Oct. Sun.-Fri, call ahead from July-Aug. £10 for 2 hr.) Continuing on Glencruitten Rd. past the golf course, the **Oban Rare Breeds Farm Park** displays 12 exotic breeds of sheep and some splendid sows. (Open Easter-Sept. daily 10am-7:30pm. £2.50, children £1.50; 20p for a bag of grain to placate the animals.)

Mull

The vision-quenching vistas of the rainy Isle of Mull have inspired artists, writers, and musicians: Robert Louis Stevenson's *Kidnapped* depicts mainland Mull and Erraid (a tiny isle off the southern coast) in dramatic detail, and Staffa moved Felix

Mendelssohn to compose his *Hebrides Overture.* The west coast, dotted with scores of small islands, is particularly stunning. Mull's Gaelic heritage has largely given way to that of the English "white settlers" who now comprise over two-thirds of the population, but local craftsmen sustain tradition in the island's remoter shops.

Getting There

Caledonian MacBrayne (tel. (0631) 622 85 or (06802) 343) runs a large car and passenger ferry from Oban, east of Mull, to **Craignure** on Mull (5-6/day; 40 min.; £2.30, next day return £4.05, off-season £2). A smaller car and passenger ferry runs from Lochaline on the Morvern Peninsula, just north of Mull, to **Fishnish** on Mull (15/day, Sun. 6/day; 15 min.; £1.40, next day return £2.30, car £6.25). Another car ferry operates from Mingary, near Kilchoan on the remote Ardnamurchan Peninsula, to **Tobermory,** Mull's largest town (May to mid-Oct. 7-8/day; 35 min.; £2.40, car £13.25).

Getting Around

Mull's three main cities, Tobermory (northwest tip), Craignure (eastern tip) and Fionnphort (southwest tip), form a triangle bounded on two sides by the A849 and A848. A left turn off the Craignure Pier takes you 35 mi. down Mull's main road along the southern arm of the island to **Fionnphort** (FINN-a-furt), where the ferry leaves for Iona, a tiny island at the southwest corner of Mull. A right turn leads 21 mi. along Mull's northwestern arm to **Tobermory,** Mull's pocket metropolis. A number of small B-roads branch off toward the scenic west coast, but the Tobermory-Craignure-Fionnphort thoroughfare is the main artery of the island's road system.

Many travelers hitch on Mull, despite the sparse traffic. The bus service, run by **Bowman's Coaches** (tel. (06802) 313), is surprisingly convenient, connecting at Craignure with the 8am, noon, and 4pm ferries from Oban and continuing on to Fionnphort (80 min.; £2.60) and Tobermory (50 min.; £1.20). The last buses leave Fionnphort at 3:15pm and Tobermory at 3:35pm to connect with the 5pm Craignure-Oban sailing; only one bus runs on Sunday. A small, seasonal tourist office stands by the ferry terminal. (Bookings £1. Open April-Sept. Mon.-Thurs. and Sat. 10:30am-7:30pm, Fri. and Sun. 10:30am-5:30pm.) Rent bikes in Tobermory from **Mrs. Taylor** (tel. (0688) 2226; £6/day, £3/½day).

Tobermory

Tobermory, Mull's main town (pop. 1000), is little more than a string of colorful houses around an attractive harbor. The tiny **Mull Museum** chronicles the island's history with local artifacts and tales. (Open Mon.-Fri. 10:30am-4:30pm, Sat. 10:30am-1:30pm. Admission 50p, children 10p.) The **Tobermory Distillery,** on the side of the harbor near the tourist office, conducts tours with well-informed guides and a generous taste of the final product (Mon.-Fri. 10:30am-3:15pm; £1.50). Tobermory hosts the lively **Mull Music Festival** on the last weekend in April, as well as the **Mull Highland Games** (which include a small regatta as well as the more traditional caber-tossing and *ceilidhs*) on the middle Thursday of July.

The **tourist office,** 48 Main St. (tel. (0688) 21 82), books accommodations for £1. (Open June-Aug. Mon.-Sat. 9:30am-6:30pm, Sun. 11am-4pm; April-May and Sept. Mon.-Sat. 9:30am-6:30pm; Oct.-March Mon.-Fri. 10am-1pm, 2-5pm.) **Clydesdale Bank,** the only bank on the island, also lies on Main St. A small **launderette** spins and tumbles next to the youth hostel. (Open Mon.-Fri. 10am-5pm. £3.50/load to wash and dry.) Tobermory's **post office,** near the tourist office, receives mail addressed to **postal code** PA75 6NT; the **telephone code** is 0688.

The town's **IYHF youth hostel** (tel. (0688) 24 81; grade 3) on Main St., has a fab-o-rama panorama of the bay. (£3.20. Open mid-March to Sept.) For a comfortably chaotic atmosphere, try **Ach-na-Craoibh** (tel. (0688) 23 01), ½mi. up the hill on the footpath by the post office and past the police station. Proprietors David and Hilarie Burnett offer a range of accommodations from basic to luxurious. B&B in a caravan beside a beautiful garden is as little as £3.50-7.50 per night, but the minimum stay is three nights. If you're broke, try to strike a deal working for a few hours in the garden. **Mrs. Cattanach,** 25 Breadalbane St. (tel. (0688) 24 86), offers beds and continental breakfast for £8, £9 with a view of the harbor. **Mrs. McEwan,** at Aig an Tigh, 4 Strongarbh Park (tel. (0688) 21 57), across the street and down from the police station, also offers cheap beds and great views (£9.50).

The pub at Tobermory's **Mishnish Hotel** (tel. 20 09) teems with tourists and seafarers alike, lured by the music (live from 9pm nightly in summer), the bar meals (£3-5), and the company. (Open daily 11am-midnight.) The **MacDonald Arms** offers typical pub grub for £2.25-3.50 (open Mon.-Sat. 12:30-1:45pm and 6:30-7:45pm). Steer clear of the yacht-catering local restaurants; instead, pick up some delicious smoked trout at the **Fish Farm,** on Main St. For even fresher seafood, rent a rod-and-reel (£2) next door from **Tackle and Books,** Mull's only combination angling center and bookstore. They also arrange 3-hr. fishing trips every day in season (£10, children £7). (Open Mon.-Sat. 9am-6pm, Sun. 11am-4pm.) The **Coop Supermarket** sits by the harbor between the hostel and the tourist office (open Mon.-Fri. 9am-8pm, Sat. 9am-5:30pm).

A small Cal-Mac ferry runs from Tobermory to **Mingary** on the Ardnamurchan Peninsula. The earliest sailing (6:15am or 7am) connects with a bus and ferry to Corran on the bus route to Fort William.

Craignure

There's little to do in Craignure itself but climb aboard Mull's 10¼-inch-gauge steam train (tel. (06802) 494), which carries passengers to **Torosay Castle,** 1 mi. south. (Leaves Craignure late April-early Sept. 11am-5pm 5-12 times/day; round-trip £1.60, children £1.10.) Peruse the library of 19th-century royalty. (Castle open Easter-Oct. daily 10:30am-5:30pm. Gardens open all year dawn to dusk. Admission to castle and garden £3, students and seniors £2.50, children £1.50; garden only £1.50, seniors, students, and children £1.) Three mi. west of Torosay stands the 700-year-old **Duart Castle,** stronghold of the Clan MacLean. Guide yourself through the state bedroom, the dungeon, and the cell where Spanish sailors, caught fleeing after the Armada was defeated, were kept while the clan awaited ransom. (Castle open May-Sept. daily 10:30am-6pm. Admission £2, children and students £1.) To reach the castle, take the bus to the end of Duart Rd. and walk the remaining 1½ mi. Boat tours from Oban to either castle leave in summer twice daily; check at the North Pier near the Regent Hotel.

Near Mull: Iona, Staffa and the Treshnish Isles

Ferries run regularly to the tiny islands off the west coast of Mull. **Turus Mara** (tel. (06884) 242) runs ferries from Oban, Craignure and Ulva Ferry to Staffa and Iona. (Sun.-Fri.; from mid-August to Sept. sailings also from Ulva Ferry to Staffa and the Treshnish Isles.) The **Cal-Mac** passenger ferry from Fionnphort that serves Iona runs almost continuously in summer (Mon.-Sat. 8:10am-7pm, Sun. 10am-6pm; 5 min.). **Gordon Grant** (tel. (06817) 338) runs daily tours from Oban, Tobermory and Iona in association with Cal-Mac; and **Davey Kirkpatrick** on Iona (tel. (06817) 373) does Staffa tours from Iona and Fionnphort with his new boat.

The sacred isle of Iona is washed in a purity of color and light found nowhere else in Scotland outside the Outer Isles. Iona's crooked coastline secludes sandy beaches, and rocky knolls rise out of fertile, sandy grasslands in the center of the island. The famous **Spouting Cave** spumes salt water when the waves are tall enough. More than 200,000 pilgrims visit Iona each year to pay homage to the tiny outcropping of land where, in 563 AD, the exiled Irish St. Columba landed in a coracle boat and built what was to become one of the centers of medieval Christendom. Missionaries departed in the 7th century to convert the Northumbrian kingdom of England, and St. Columba and his followers are credited with the conversion of Scotland.

There are two distinct settlements on Iona: the small village of **Baile Mór,** with two stores and a post office, sticks to the harbor, while the ecumenical **Iona Community** cleeves to the massive **Benedictine Abbey.** Walk up through the village and bear right to reach the abbey, centerpiece of the view as you arrive on the ferry. On your way, you'll pass through the ruins of a 13th-century **nunnery,** one of the best-preserved medieval convents in Britain. The abbey stands on the site of St. Columba's Celtic monastery, built by Irish masons. Constructed in the 12th century, tiny **St. Oran's Chapel** next door is the oldest building in this magnificent compound. More than 60 kings of Scotland, Ireland, and Norway rest in the adjacent burial ground; only effigies of the leaders of West Highland families are now visible. Free-standing **Celtic crosses,** with swirling serpent-and-bull ornaments, gracefully stand guard next to the abbey. Restoration of the abbey was begun by Abbot Dominic in the 15th century, and completed in this century by the Iona Cathedral Trust (which suggests a £1 donation at the gate) together with the Iona Community. Attend one of the Community's services in summer (Mon.-Sat. 9am and 9pm, Sun. 10:30am and 9:30pm); it won't be what you expected. Tuesday and Friday nights bring rousing *ceilidhs,* on Thursday an evening concert, and all day Wednesday guides lead a **pilgrimage** around the island.

The only way to fully appreciate Iona's beauty is to stay at least one night on the island. The **Iona Community** runs regular week-long retreats on themes of religion, peace, and community from late June to mid-September; these become sporadic during the rest of the year, only to be substituted by frequent "open weeks," where guests can come stay in the abbey for a minimum of three nights (no theological requirements; full board £19/day, students £13; for a program or advance bookings contact The Abbey, Iona, Argyll PA76 6SN, tel. (06817) 404). If the Scottish Episcopal Church is more your style, stay in their **Bishop's House** (tel. (06817) 306), a shoreside building at the end of the village street with a chapel and decorative windows (B&B £12, 15% student discount). Secular isolation is yours at **Finlay, Ross Ltd.** (tel. (06817) 357), to the left from the pier (bed and continental breakfast £7.50-12).

The Alexander-MacCallum-Ross-esque island of **Staffa** lies 6 mi. north of Iona. Surrounded by cliffs of perfectly hexagonal basalt formations, Staffa is inhabited by six sheep and four cows (give or take a few). When rough seas roar into cathedral-like **Fingal's Cave,** the sound reverberates around the island. The incessant pounding of wave against rock inspired the motif of repetition in Mendelssohn's naughty-but-nice *Hebrides Overture.* The nearby **Treshnish Isles** offer sanctuary to seals, seabirds, and ferrets (in Gaelic, *ĭl*). Legend holds that the monks from the Iona Abbey buried their library here to save it from the pillages of the Reformation. Many have tried digging under the third ferret from the left, as yet without luck.

Glencoe

A spectacular valley between Oban and Fort William, Glencoe supplements its paltry permanent population with a contingent of avid mountaineers. Stunning in any weather, Glencoe is perhaps best seen in the rain, when a slowly drifting web of mist laces the innumerable rifts and crags of the steep slopes, and the silvery waterfalls cascade into the River Coe with increased energy. Only on rare days is this view not in evidence; this region records well over 90 inches of rain per year. The valley is infamous as the site of the shocking 1692 "Massacre of Glencoe," when the Clan MacDonald welcomed a company of Campbell soldiers, henchmen of King William III, into their chieftain's home; he and his followers were murdered as an example to other Scottish clans of the English king's power. A sign near Claichaig indicates the site of the betrayal and Glencoe still bears the nickname "the Weeping Glen." The tragedy unfolds on the silver screen every Tues., Thurs. and Sun. at the Village Hall (check times at the hall; £2, children £1).

Experienced rock climbers favor the mountains, while novices can explore some beautiful trails that bypass the summits, such as the Hidden Valley trail and the easy "Old Military Road." By taking the Glasgow bus 10 mi. east to Altnafeadh, you can hike to **Kinlockleven** (about 2½ hr.) on the **West Highland Way,** the long distance foot path from Glasgow to Fort William. Seven buses per day return to Glencoe from Kinlockleven (last bus 6:20pm). If you wish to stay the night in Kinlochleven, which has little to boast of save its proximity to the mountains and a large aluminum smelter, visit the **West Highland Lodge** (tel. (08554) 471 or 396), a 36-bed bunkhouse with a kitchen, showers and drying room (£4.50).

The **Glencoe Visitors Centre** (tel. (08552) 307), 3 mi. east of town on the A82, gives hiking advice and issues the excellent **Glencoe Guide** (£1.95). (Open June-Aug. daily 9:30am-6:30pm; March-May and Sept.-late Oct. daily 10am-5:30pm. Admission 30p, seniors, students, and children 15p.) **Glencoe Mountain Bike Hire** (tel. (08552) 685), opposite the post office, will set you up with wheels (£10/day, £5/½day) to explore the glens; repair kits and maps available. Just outside of town on the road to Oban and Fort William, **Glencoe Guides and Gear** has a full supply of camping, hiking and climbing paraphenalia. (Open daily 9am-6pm.)

The pleasant **Glencoe youth hostel (IYHF)** (tel. (08552) 219; grade 1) rests 2 mi. south of Glencoe Village, on the eastern side of the river. (£4.85. Open year-round; book 2 days ahead in July and Aug.) Next to the hostel, the **Leacantium Bunkhouse** (tel. (08552) 256; £4), may be an option only if you've hiked out to the hostel and found it full. A garage-style concrete floor supports crude facilities (be sure to bring your own bedding and cooking utensils), and heat and showers cost extra. **Red Squirrel Camp Site** (tel. (08552) 256; £2/person, children 50p) pitches tents 500 yards past the hostel. Down the lane by the church in town, the **Glencoe Outdoor Centre** (tel. (08552) 350) has room for 35 in comfortable hostel-type accommodations. The center also offers instruction and equipment rentals for all types of mountain and water sports. (B&B £12, room and full board £15.) You can camp for free almost anywhere between the visitors center and the nearby **Clachaig Inn** (tel. (08552) 252), 1 mi. east on the A82. Climbers come down from the hills to tap their boots to frequent live music at the inn (open Mon.-Thurs. 11am-11pm, Fri. 11am-12pm, Sat. 11am-11:30pm). Don't wait to do your grocery shopping in Glencoe; the only food stores here are mom-and-pop establishments with a few cans of beans and a ball of string.

The express buses from Glasgow to Fort William stop twice daily in Glencoe Village (9:32am and 12:34pm) and twice more when returning to Glasgow (2:07pm and 6:37pm). If asked, Gaelicbus drivers will stop in Ballachulish, ¾mi. outside Glencoe, on their four runs per day (Mon.-Sat.) between Oban and Fort William. The road from Glasgow meets the tall glen rising dramatically from the flat terrain of the Rannoch Moor; the road from Oban passes numerous mountains with their feet in the water and their peaks in the clouds before rounding a corner to reveal the distinctive summit at the Glen's western end, the **Pap of Glencoe.**

Fort William and Ben Nevis

General Monk built Fort William among Britain's highest peaks in 1655 to keep out "savage clans and roving barbarians." However valiantly the original structure served its purpose, the town of Fort William succumbs seasonally to a tidal wave of skiers and hikers. An excellent base for mountain sports, the town itself lacks character. **Ben Nevis,** the tallest peak in the area at 4418 ft., lurks out of view just behind the ample and affordable alpine accommodations in town; equipment outfitters help volley the crowds into the hills around it.

Arriving and Departing

Fort William shares the magnificent **West Highland Railway** with Oban; though every West Highland train connects with one from Edinburgh, the line officially starts at Glasgow's Queen St. Station and ends at Mallaig on the coast to the west of Fort William (4/day, Sun. 3/day; to Glasgow £17.50, return £23-26; to Mallaig £5.50, return £8.60). An overnight train to London departs daily at 7:50pm (12 hr.; £64, return £68). The **train station** (tel. (0397) 703 791) is equipped with lockers (50p-£1) and an unimaginative cafeteria; buses arrive and depart just outside the station. Coaches run to Glasgow (2/day, 3 hr.), Oban (Mon.-Sat. 9-12/day; 1 hr. 45 min.), Mallaig (Mon.-Sat. 2-3/day; 1 hr. 40 min.), Inverness (Mon.-Sat. 7/day; 2 hr.), and Kyle of Lochalsh (Mon.-Sat. 2/day; 2 hr.). Pick up complete bus schedules at the tourist office. Heavy tourist traffic makes Fort William less than a hitcher's paradise; to get to the Road to the Isles (see next section), walk north and try your luck at the intersection of the Fort William road (A82) and the Mallaig road (A830).

Orientation and Practical Information

The station might appear to be in the middle of nowhere, but just through the underpass by the front door lies the north end of **High Street,** Fort William's main (and only) drag. Local buses leave from the stand in front of the Presto Supermarket, just to the right as you exit the tunnel.

The **tourist office** (tel. (0397) 703 781), in the square 3 blocks down on the left, functions as the central depot for information on the West Highlands; it has a roomful of wall and audio-visual displays in addition to the usual treats. (Open June-Sept. Mon.-Sat. 9am-9pm, Sun. 10am-6pm; off-season Mon.-Sat. 9am-5:30pm.) The **mountain rescue post** (tel. (0397) 702 361/2), based in the Fort William police station at the south end of High St., can usually give basic advice to hikers and climbers. Fort William's **postal code** is PH33 6AA; the **telephone code** is 0397.

For mountaineering equipment, head to **Nevisport,** in the round building at the north end of High St. (open daily 8:30am-8pm, off-season daily 9am-7:30pm), or the **Nevis Outdoor Hire Centre** (tel. 703 601) near the hostels along the River Nevis (open Dec.-Oct. daily 8am-8pm, Nov. 8:30am-6pm). Both rent hiking boots (£4/day plus deposit), and Nevisport also carries maps and helpful literature. The **West Coast Outdoor Leisure Centre,** 102 High St., is the only place to rent sticky-soled rock climbing boots (£3/day) and **Ellis Brigham Mountain Sports,** behind the train station, rents two- and three-person tents (£10/day, £5/week). Mountain bikes are available in town from **Offbeat Bikes,** 4 Inverlochy Pl. (tel. 702 663; £12/day; call ahead); **Ellis Brigham Ski Shop,** next to the train station (tel. 706 220; £12; open daily 9am-6pm); or from the aforementioned **Nevis Outdoor Hire Centre** (£12, 3-speeds £7).

Accommodations and Food

Two hostels offer strategic accommodations for anyone mounting an assault on Ben Nevis or tackling hikes in the area; both lie about 2 mi. east of town along the River Nevis, ideally situated at the head of the Ben Nevis footpath and the West Highland Way. The **Glen Nevis youth hostel (IHYF)** (tel. 702 336; grade 1) stands 2½ mi. east of town on the Glen Nevis Rd.; booking 2 days ahead in July-Aug. is critical. (£4.85. Open Dec.-Oct.) The **Ben Nevis Bunkhouse** (tel. 702 240) at Achintee Farm sleeps 26 in a 200-year-old wood-panelled granite barn with 4-6 person dorms and full kitchen and bathing facilities; the bunkhouse is on the opposite side of the River Nevis from the hostel, a 2 mi. walk along the Achintee Rd. Though less likely to fill than the official hostel, the bunkhouse still merits reservations in July-Aug. (£5). The Ben Nevis footpath passes within a cannonball's throw of both hostels. The excellent **Glen Nevis Caravan & Camping Park** (tel. 702 191) stretches canvas on the same road, ½mi. before the IYHF hostel (tents from £3.60; open mid-March to mid-Oct.). An unnumbered red bus runs five times daily from the Fort William bus station to the hostel and back (Mon.-Sat. 8:30am, 9:45am, 11:55am, 2:20pm and 4pm; Sun. 10:05am and 4:10pm). If both of the hostels along the River Nevis are fully booked, head 4 mi. out of town on the A830 to the **Smiddy Alpine Lodge** (tel. (0397) 772 467) in Corpach. Bunkhouses don't get much more comfortable than this immaculate rendition, attractively clad in Swedish wood panelling (£6). Buses run to Corpach from High St. an amazing 23 times per day (Sun. 8/day) with the last run at 10:25pm (50p). Ask the driver to stop at **Kilmallie Hall** if you wish to attend one of the weekly Scottish Country Dances (mid-June to Aug., Mon. 8-10pm; 75p) or occasional folksinging performances. The bunkhouse lies between the hall and the train depot. An early morning walk down Fassifern Rd., behind the Alexandra Hotel, will overpower you with the smell of Scottish breakfasts emanating from the many B&Bs. Other B&Bs congregate further up the hill on Alma Rd. or Argyll Rd.

William Low and **Presto** supermarkets, Fort William's primary sources of food, anchor High St.'s northern end. The **Nevis Bakery** at 49 High St. packs lunches for £2, and the **Nevis Bistro** across from the BP station at 141 High St. serves full breakfasts (£2.95), steak pie, chips and peas (£2.99), and various pizzas (12 in. pizza with onions, £4.80), as well as ale.

As there is little to see in Fort William except the unpretentious **West Highland Museum** beside the tourist office, full of curios from stuffed ducks to Bonnie Prince Charlie memorabilia (open July-Aug. Mon.-Sat. 9:30am-9pm; June and Sept. Mon.-Sat. 9:30am-5:30pm; Oct.-May Mon.-Sat. 10am-1pm and 2-5pm. Admission 70p, seniors 40p, children 20p.), stock up on supplies and head out into the surrounding hills.

Hiking, Climbing and Biking

On one of the 65 days a year when Ben Nevis deigns to lift the veil of cloud from the peak, the ensuing unobstructed view reaches from Scotland's eastern coast all the way to Ireland. The interminable switchbacks of the well-beaten tourist trail ascend from the Fort William town park to Ben Nevis' summit; go north ½mi. along the A82 and follow signs for the footpath to Ben Nevis. A much more interesting ridge walk begins on the tourist trail but continues straight when the trail makes a sharp turn to the right near Lochan Neall. Leave the path where it descends to Coire Leis and pick a route up the steep grass slopes to Carn Dearg Meadhonach; continue to the summit of Carn Mór Dearg. Along the ridge, a trail veers right towards the southeastern slopes of Ben Nevis; scramble the final 1,000 ft. up steep terrain and you'll find yourself on top of the world. Leave a full 8½ hr. for the 9½-mi. round trip, and don't set foot on the trail without an Ordnance Survey map, warm clothing, a windbreaker, and plenty of food and liquid.

Four mi. north of Fort William along the A82, the slopes of Aonach Mor (4006 ft.) now cushion the **Nevis Range** ski area. Though smaller than the Cairngorm facility, Nevis Range (tel. (0397) 705 825) boasts Scotland's longest ski run (11/3 mi.) and a state-of-the-art **gondola** (£4, children £2.60 round-trip); the cable car carries you 2300 ft. up from the road to a restaurant at the base of the trails. Outside ski season (Dec.-May), both the gondola and marked mountain hiking trails remain open. Buses run regularly year-round from Fort William to the slopes (5/day 9am-4pm.) The stunning **Glen Nevis Road,** past the youth hostel, is the perfect place to bike.

For indoor exertion, head over to the **Lochaber Leisure Centre** (tel. 43 59) on Belford Rd. Fully equipped with a large pool, climbing wall, sauna, Nautilus weights and a water slide, the center opens for public swimming Mon.-Fri. 10am-9pm, Sat.-Sun. 10am-5pm; Sept.-May Mon.-Tues. and Thurs. Fri. 12:30-8pm, Wed. 12:30-5pm, Sat.-Sun. 12:30-4pm (£1.10).

Events

A few miles up the road past the hostel, you'll reach the falls where, on the first Sunday in August, hundreds of businessmen-*cum*-daredevils rocket down the rapids on tiny airbed mats during the **Glen Nevis River Race.** In late August, the area hosts the **Ben Nevis Race,** a more grueling event in which runners sprint up and down the mountain; the record time is an incredible 1 hr. 20 min. The **Lochaber Highland Games** also take place in Fort William on the last Saturday in July.

Fort William to Mallaig: Road to the Isles

The scenic **Road to the Isles** (now the A830), skates along lochs and between mountains on its breathtaking journey from Fort William west to Mallaig, on the Sound of Sleet. The train ride from Fort William to Mallaig offers sublime panoramas; modern carriages zip along while the less frequent steam locomotives churn out the lost romance of the grand old days of rail travel. (Modern trains run mid-May to Sept. 4/day, Sun. 3/day; Oct.-April Mon.-Sat. 2/day; £5.50, return £8.60. Steam locomotives run April to mid-Oct. on Thurs.; mid-June to mid-Sept. on Sun. and Tues.; and mid-June to Oct. on Mon.; advance booking at any British Rail station advised. Locomotive departs Fort William 10:35am, Sun. 12:15pm; Mallaig 1:25pm, Sun. 4:45pm; £9, return £14.) The best views are on the left. Buses do the same run less nostalgically (Mon.-Sat. 2-3/day). Hitching along the Road to the Isles is difficult.

The road sets off westward from Fort William along Loch Eil, arriving at **Glenfinnan,** at the head of Loch Shiel, after 12 mi. A monument commemorates August 19, 1745, the day Bonnie Prince Charlie rowed up Loch Shiel and rallied the clans around the Stuart standard in a dubious bid to put his father on the British throne. The **visitors center** (tel. 039783) 250) documents the campaign. (Open late May-early Sept. daily 9:30am-6:30pm; April-late May and early Sept.-late Oct. daily 10am-5:30pm. Admission 90p.)

At **Lochailort,** another 10 mi. west, hikers can step off the train and wander for weeks without encountering another person. Two morning buses (Mon.-Sat.) run south into the desolate districts of Moidart, Ardnamurchan, and Morvern. With advance planning, you can catch the seasonal ferry to Mull (May-Sept. 8/day 7am-6:30pm) from Kilchoan; connect with the Ardnamurchan-bound bus in Acharacle, 19 mi. south of Lochailort. Between Lochailort and Kilchoan, buses pass **Loch Moidart,** which opens into one of western Scotland's most beautiful bays, studded with islets and lined with sandy beaches. The abandoned 13th-century **Castle Tioram** was destroyed in 1715 by its owner in an ill-conceived plan to prevent his neighbors from moving in while he was off at war. Kentra Bay, to the south, beckons to beach bathers. There are no accommodations here, and not much of anything else.

You can also explore the largely deserted parallelogram to the south of the Road to the Isles by heading south and then west, rather than west and then south. Drive or take the bus south from Fort William along the west side of Loch Linnhe (Mon.-Fri. 3:45pm; 2 hr.), then veer down Gleann Geal to Lochaline. A car ferry from Lochaline spurts over to Fishnish on Mull (Mon.-Sat. 16/day).

After Lochailort, the Road to the Isles or the train passes **Loch nan Uamh,** the Lake of the Caves, the point from where the shattered Prince fled in September, 1746, his roaring bid for the crown having ended in a whimper. A memorial tower provides a sweeping view over the sea. The road finally meets the west coast at the sandy beaches of **Arisaig.** Disembark from the train either here or at the next stop (Morar) to reach the comfortable **Garramore youth hostel (IYHF)** (tel. (06785) 268), which is a 3-mi. walk along the A830 from either station (grade 1; £4.85; open late March-Oct.). Mallaig-bound buses stop right at the hostel. The wardens offer outdoor garden duties as well as the usual drudgeries. A **campsite** lies 150 yards south of the hostel. **Dr. Ian Pragnell** (tel. (06875) 272) rents road and mountain bikes (£5-10) and willingly shares his keen local knowledge of cycling routes. Brilliantly white sandy beaches across the road and down a short footpath from the hostel offer beautiful views of the Inner Hebrides. Rocky outcrops cut across the sand, creating multiple secluded beachlets that are only accessible by foot. Don't let the nasty, red, stinging jellyfish catch you skinnydipping. Another fine walk from the hostel follows the banks of **Loch Morar,** Britain's deepest freshwater loch (1017 ft.), before cutting over the hills to Tarbet on Loch Nevis. On Mon., Wed. or Fri., you can find Bruce Watt's ferry (tel. (0687) 23 20) back to Mallaig instead of retracing your steps. Advance bookings required for this service.

Past Morar looms the megalopolis of **Mallaig,** the fishing village where cruises and ferries leave for the Inner Hebrides. Dart around the block from the rail station to find the **tourist office** (tel. (0687) 21 70; open mid-May to Sept. Mon.-Sat. 9am-7pm; mid-April to mid-May Mon.-Sat. 9am-4pm). **Caledonian MacBrayne** (tel. (0687) 24 03) runs ferries from Mallaig to **Armadale** on Skye (see Skye section) and to the Small Isles (see below).

The Small Isles

Despite their proximity to the mainland and to Skye, the **Small Isles**—Muck, Eigg, Rhum, and Canna (total population under 200)—remain peacefully underdeveloped. The islands lack a centralized electrical plant, reliable phone service, and roll-on vehicle landing facilities; visitors must still go ashore by landing dinghy. In summer, Caledonian MacBrayne passenger ferries (tel. (0475) 337 55) sail from Mallaig to Eigg, Rhum, and Canna and back (Mon. and Wed. 11am, Fri. 5am, Sat. 6:45am and 2:15pm; Wed. and Sat. sailings also stop at Muck; £3.20-5). From Arisaig, **Murdo Grant** (tel. (06875) 224) sails to: Muck (usually Mon., Wed., and Fri.; £5); Eigg (Fri., Sat.-Sun., and Mon.-Wed.; £5.50); and Rhum (Tues. and Thurs.; £6). Ferries leave Arisaig between 11-11:30am; schedules vary, so call ahead. It is difficult to stay on Canna since there are no budget accommodations.

Skye

Skye is often raining, but also fine: hardly embodied; semi-transparent; like living in a jellyfish lit up with green light. Remote as Samoa; deserted, prehistoric. No room for more.

—*Postcard from Virginia Woolf*

Often described as the shining jewel in the Hebridean crown, Skye radiates unparalleled natural splendor from the serrated peaks of the Cuillin Hills to the rugged northern tip of the Trotternish Peninsula. As elsewhere in the Highlands, the 19th-century Clearances saw entire glens emptied of their ancient settlements. Today, as "white settlers" push the English population of the island toward 40%, Skye's traditional Gaelic culture survives mostly in the self-consciousness of museums and bilingual road signs.

The island's beauty is by no means a secret: a steady procession of vehicular tourists disembarks from the 24-hr. ferry service. Yet most visitors stick to the main roads, and the terrain beyond the beaten track remains blissfully untrampled. Skye's large area and spotty transportation system will likely force you to concentrate your travels in certain areas of the island. Consider this a blessing in disguise; taking time to learn the geology of the weird rock pinnacles on the Trotternish Peninsula, or the local legends surrounding one of the Cuillins, is bound to be more satisfying than leap-frogging between the humdrum population hubs of Portree, Broadford and Kyleakin.

Getting There

Although plans for a bridge to Skye (or a tunnel, nicknamed the "Skunnel") are worming their way along, access to the island during the next few years will no doubt be provided solely by ferry. Round the clock ferries from **Kyle of Lochalsh** on the mainland sail to **Kyleakin** on Skye (daily continuous service 7:30am-9pm, thereafter every ½hr.; 5 min.; passengers free, cars £4.50). Two Scottish Citylink and two Skye-Ways coaches per day run from Glasgow to Kyle of Lochalsh (5 hr.); Skye-Ways runs similar service from Inverness (2/day; 2 hr.). Trains from Inverness arrive at the Kyle of Lochalsh terminus (tel. (0599) 42 05), a short walk from the pier (4/day, Sun. 2/day 6:45am-6:42pm; 2½ hr.).

Three smaller and less frequent ferries also serve Skye. From Mallaig on the mainland, ferries make the 30-min. crossing to **Armadale** on Skye (May-Sept. Mon.-Sat. 4-5/day, July-Aug. also 1 on Sun.; £2.20, cars £9.50; call (04714) 248 to book car space). Another passenger ferry from Mallaig cruises to Kyle of Lochalsh (late May-Sept. Tues., Thurs., and Fri.; 2 hr.; £4.30). Those who have time for a scenic detour can take the historic "Drove Road:" cattle were once forced to swim the channel between **Glenelg** on the mainland and **Kylerhea** on Skye, where a vehicle and passenger ferry now operates (Easter-Sept. Mon.-Sat., frequent crossings 9am-8pm; for details call (059982) 224). From the Outer Hebrides, Cal-Mac ferries travel from Tarbert on Harris or Lochmaddy on North Uist to Uig on Skye (May to mid-Oct. 1-2/day; £5.95, cars £24.10). Service frequency is substantially reduced in winter, so be sure to pick up a schedule in advance.

Getting Around

Touring Skye without a car takes either a little effort or a little more cash. Hitching is widespread and fairly successful despite the abundance of steely-eyed tourists. The many cyclists on Skye almost keep up with the cars in the flatter regions. For bike rental try **Hebridean Pedal Highway** (tel. (0599) 48 42), just up the road from the ferry in Kyle of Lochalsh, which for an additional charge allows you to return the bike in Armadale, Uig or Lochboisdale on South Uist. (Mountain bikes £7.50/day, 5-speeds £5/day, 3-speeds £3/day.) **Skye Bikes** in Kyleakin (tel. (0599) 47 95) rents top-quality mountain bikes for £6.50 per day and offers guided excursions in the mountains beginning at £10 (including bike rental). **Uig Cycle Hire** (tel. (047042) 311) is just down the road from the hostel (18 speed mountain bike £8/day). In Broadford, try **Skyebike Cycle Hire** (tel. (04712) 418).

Buses are infrequent and ruinously expensive (Kyleakin-Portree £4, Broadford-Armadale £2.40). The only decent service is along the main road hugging the coast from Kyleakin to Broadford to Portree. Note that everything shuts down on Sundays except the Citylink and Caledonian Express long-distance buses on the Kyleakin-Broadford-Portree-Uig line. Buses meet all sailings of the Armadale ferry; on this and other routes look for the blue Skye-Ways buses which offer student discounts; the red Highland buses refuse to lower their rates. Since buses on Skye are run by eight different operators, either a complete sheaf of schedules (from the tourist office) or a copy of *Getting Around the Highlands & Islands* (£3.95) is utterly essential.

Ewan MacRae, Ltd., Portree (tel. (0478) 25 54) and **Sutherland's Garage,** Broadford (tel. (04712) 225), both rent cars. Rates lamentably start at £25/day plus 10-15p/mi. You are asked to put down a deposit, which is refundable unless you hit a sheep—watch out for errant mutton.

One good way to get around Skye's scattered sights is with former divorce lawyer and urban refugee Ted Baxter (tel. (04716) 228), who knowledgably guides people around the island on full day tours by foot and by Landrover for £10 per person.

Accommodations and Entertainment

Though B&Bs and hostels are plentiful on Skye, summer brings huge crowds. On any given night in July and August, all five youth hostels on Skye are likely to be filled to capacity. Reservationless arrivals risk disappointment, especially on Sunday, when most of the island snoozes.

Skye has lively traditional music (both English and Gaelic), but it is often hard to find. Snag a copy of the weekly *What, Where and When* for a list of special events and dances. In Portree *ceilidhs* take place on Fridays at 11pm in the Skye Gathering Hall. Livestock, craft, and baking exhibitions enliven the **Dunvegan Show** at the end of July, and **Dunvegan Hall** hosts family *ceilidhs.* (July-Aug., Tues. and Thurs. nights). There are frequent local dances—half folk, half rock—at the village halls, usually starting after 11pm (hostelers should note curfews). The **Highland Games,** a mirthful day of bagpipes, footraces, and boozing, take place in the second week of August, and the **Skye Folk Festival,** featuring *ceilidhs* in Portree, Broadford, and Dunvegan, is held in the first week. The tourist office in Portree (tel. (0478) 21 37) has more information on these events.

Kyle of Lochalsh and Kyleakin

Free and frequent ferries across the strait between Kyle of Lochalsh, on the mainland, and Kyleakin, on Skye's southern tail fin, make the twin villages effectively one community (crossing 5 min.). Kyleakin's nigh non-existent sights still manage to outshine those of Kyle of Lochalsh, that handsome tourist traffic bottleneck.

Most shops and services concentrate in Kyle of Lochalsh; the local grocery and bakery are both here and the **tourist office** (tel. (0599) 42 76), which will book a B&B for £1 on either side of the channel, overlooks Kyle's pier (open Aug. Mon.-Sat. 9am-9:30pm, Sun. 12:30-4:30pm; June-July and Sept. Mon.-Sat. 9:30am-7pm; April-May Mon.-Sat. 9:30am-12:30pm and 1:30-5:30pm; Oct. Mon.-Sat. 9:30am-12:30pm, 1:30-5:30pm). From Kyle of Lochalsh, head ¾mi. out along the road to Plockton for a hearty meal at the **Highland Designworks Wholefood Cafe** (tel. (0599) 43 88). An *duki* bean burger with salad goes for £2.95 at lunchtime (noon-5:30pm); dinners are large and leafy but start at £5.25. (Open Sun.-Fri. 11am-8:30pm.) Eight mi. east along the A87 on an islet in Loch Duich perches the famous **Eilean Donan Castle** (tel. (059985) 202), the restored 13th-century seat of the MacKenzies. This picturesque castle adorns more shortbread boxes and souvenir ashtrays than any other Scottish monument. (Open Easter-Oct. daily 10am-5:30pm. Admission £1, children 50p.) The view from the hillside behind the castle is more memorable than the fort's restored interior.

All the affordable accommodations cluster in Kyleakin (Kyle-ACK-in) alongside the park a few hundred yards from the pier. At the modern, comfortable **IYHF youth hostel** (tel. (0599) 45 85), a helpful warden presides over large common spaces and small bedrooms. This is Skye's only Grade 1 hostel, and fills quickly in the summer (£4.85; open Feb.-Nov). Down the street, the carpeted **Backpacker's Guesthouse** (tel. (0599) 45 10) offers 35 beds (including a double, twin and triple), and a small kitchen and dining area. The common area is respectfully divided into smoking and non-smoking zones. Reservations only from the High St. Hotel in Edinburgh and the Inverness Student Hostel. (£5, continental breakfast 90p.) Once you've seen the harbor in Kyleakin, you've seen it all; climb to the memorial on a hill behind the Castle Moil Restaurant for the best views. Scaffolding surrounds the unstable ruins of **Castle Moil,** thwarting both visitors and photographers.

Southern Skye

The unremarkable town of **Broadford,** located on a silent rocky bay 8 mi. west of Kyleakin, is world famous as the hub for all bus transport throughout the southern half of Skye. The **tourist office** (tel. (04712) 23 61) distributes information from a parking lot along the bay south of the bus stop (open April-Oct. Mon.-Sat. 9:30am-7pm). Follow the signpost ½mi. from the bus stop along a side road to the **Broadford youth hostel (IYHF)** (tel. (04712) 442; grade 2; £4.20; open early March-Oct.). Two mi. east of Broadford on the coast lies the tiny **Fossil Bothy** (tel. (0471) 822 644 or 822 297), a renovated stone bunkhouse with room for eight; the prehistoric creatures trapped in the walls inspired the bothy's name. For food in town, try the **Broadford Bay Bakery** (open Mon.-Fri. 7am-5pm, Sat. 7:30am-4pm) or the busy

Strathcorrie Take-away near the post office, serving delicious *tagliatelli* for £3.70 and steak and kidney pie with chips for £1.85. (Open Easter-Oct. daily 11am-9:30pm; expect a 10 min. wait during peak lunch hours.)

Two mi. south of Broadford, the single-lane A851 veers southwest through the thick foliage of the **Sleat Peninsula,** also called "The Garden of Skye;" keep an eye out for the delicious wild raspberries that grow by the roadside. Seventeen mi. of hills bring you to **Armadale,** where the Mallaig ferries depart. **Armadale Castle** now houses the **Clan Donald Centre** (tel. (04714) 305), with a museum, audio-visual programs, and genealogical center; valiant rangers offer guided walks through the 300-year-old castle gardens and surrounding 20,000-acre estate. (Open mid-March to mid-Nov. daily 9:30am-5:30pm. Admission £2, children £1.50.) The modern **Armadale Hostel (IYHF)** (tel. (04714) 260; grade 2), 10 min. around the bay from the pier, overlooks the water. (£4.20. Open late March-Sept.) **Curry in a Hurry,** in the Skye Batik shop at the top of the pier access road, serves authentic Sri Lankan food (open daily 9am-7pm; meat curries only, from £2.85). Slightly north of Armadale at Ostaig is a **Gaelic college,** Sabhal Mor Ostaig (tel. (04714) 373), which distributes information on Celtic heritage and offers courses in Gaelic and piping.

The Cuillins

The dramatic peaks of the **Cuillin Hills** dominate central Skye from Broadford's to Portree's latitude. The Red Cuillins and the Black Cuillins meet in **Sligachan;** besides being of different colors, the black hills are rough and craggy while the red hills have more even, conical profiles due to tectonic hydrogesticulations. These, the highest peaks in the Hebrides, are renowned for their hiking paths and stunning formations of cloud and mist.

The pamphlet *Walks from Sligachan and Glen Brittle,* published by the Skye Mountain Rescue Team (£1 at tourist offices) makes several hiking suggestions. Don't even think about hiking without an Ordnance Survey map (the best is the yellow 1:25,000 map for £4.50 that covers the Cuillin and Torridon Hills). Whatever hike you choose, leave a description of your route with your hotel or hostel proprietor, or the police; the mountains can be treacherous as the mist descends quickly.

If you have several days, base yourself at the **Glenbrittle Hostel (IYHF)** near the southwest coast (tel. (047842) 278; grade 2; £4.20; open late March-Sept.). 200 sites dot the **Glenbrittle Campsite** (tel. (047842) 232; £3.50-4.50/tent. Open March-Oct.). Expert mountaineers at the hostel give the best advice and Gerry Akroyd (tel. (047842) 289), in Glenbrittle, leads week-long winter and summer climbing expeditions through the hills. (£90-130). In summer, two buses per day run from Portree on the east coast to Glenbrittle; call **Sutherland's Bus Service** (tel. (047842) 267) for details.

The bus to Glenbrittle also stops about 10 mi. west of the Cuillins in Portnalong, where you can stay at the **Croft Bunkhouse** (tel. (047482) 254). The comfortably converted cowshed sleeps 16 and the adjoining section sports a new ping-pong table and a dart board (£4.50). A footpath from Sligachan over the pass to the hostel skirts the 7-mi. walk on the main road.

Across the mountains at the junction of the A863 to Portree and the A850 to Dunvegan, the **Sligachan Campsite** (tel. (047852) 303) makes another good base for hiking in the Cuillins. Set in an open field across from the hotel in Sligachan, the site has 80 pitches, showers and a drying room. (Open April-Oct. £2.50/person.) The bar across the street serves luv'ley meals (£2.95-5) daily from 8am-11pm.

A short but scenic path follows the small stream flowing from Sligachan down to the head of **Loch Sligachan.** After crossing the old bridge, fork left off the main path and walk along the right hand bank as you go upstream. The narrow and often boggy path leads past many pools and miniature waterfalls (3 mi. round trip). The visually arresting oversized anthill to the left, the 775yd **Glamaig,** was ascended and descended in 55 min. by a Gurkha soldier in 1899. Give yourself at least 3½ hr. and then only if you feel at ease on steep slopes with unsure footing. Branch off the main trail after about 10 to 15 min. onto the smaller trail which leads up the grassy ridge between the higher peaks, a location with fantastic views of the ocean and offshore islands.

Experienced climbers may try the ascent into the Sgurr nan Gillean Corrie, to the southwest of Glamaig, where the peak rises 3167 ft. above a tiny mountain lake. For more level terrain, take the 8-mi. walk down Glen Sligachan through the heart of the Cuillins to the beach of **Camasunary,** with views of the isles of Rhum and Muck.

For a less intimate view of the Cuillins, take the A881 14 mi. southwest from Broadford (a difficult cycle ride) to **Elgol.** You can sail from Elgol to **Loch Coriusk** (Mon.-Sat. several times a day; return £4.50) with **R. MacKinnon** (tel. (04716) 213), weather permitting; this trip brings you into the midst of an extraordinary conflation of mountain and water.

Isle of Raasay

The small **Isle of Raasay,** off the eastern coast of Skye, avidly supported Bonnie Prince Charlie; he found sanctuary here on several occasions during his dramatic flight of 1746. An island's island, Raasay still offers visitors some respite from the brigades of tourists on Skye. The puckish **Pictish Stones** stand near Raasay House, and **Brochel Castle** crumbles to the north. To get to Raasay, catch the small car ferry from **Sconser** on Skye's main Broadford-Portree road and bus route (tel. (0478) 622 26; Mon.-Sat. 5-6/day; £1.35).

Northern Skye

As in most of Skye, the attractions here reside outside of the area's towns. Though capital of the island, **Portree** (pop. 1600) merits little more than a brief stopover for a meal and a view of its picturesque harbor. The **tourist office,** in the old jail on Bank St. above the harbor, books accommodations for £1 and helps direct wayward tourists to appropriate buses (tel. (0478) 21 37; open mid-July to Aug. Mon.-Sat. 9:15am-8pm; June to mid-July and Sept. 1-15 Mon.-Sat. 9:15am-7pm; April-May and mid-Sept. to Oct. Mon.-Sat. 9:15am-5:30pm; Nov.-March Mon.-Fri. 9:15am-5:30pm). Buses stop at Somerled Sq. 2 blocks away. Buy groceries at the **Presto Supermarket** on Bank St., or head around the market to the right and dine at the best restaurant in town; the **Ben Tianavaig Bistro,** 5 Boswell Terrace (tel. (0478) 21 52), specializing in wholefood, vegetarian and seafood dishes, sits above the harbor on the left. Try the lentil patties and green salad for £1.95 or the vegetable *moussaka* (£3.90). (Open Tues.-Sat. 11am-5pm, 6-10pm; Sun. noon-4pm, 6-9pm.) **The Bakery** on Somerled Sq. (open Mon.-Sat. 9am-5pm; almond cakes 20p), and the tiny but well stocked wholefood shop on Parklane at the end of Wentworth St. (open Mon.-Tues. and Thurs.-Fri. 9am-5pm, Wed. and Sat. 9am-1pm) should satisfy your culinary needs. "Janet the Piranha" guards the door to the fish and chip shop on Quay St., which sells prawns in garlic butter (£1.50), smoke salmon sandwiches (£1.75) and pizzas with smoked mackerel (£2.80), in addition to the standard chish and fips (£2). (Open Mon.-Sat. 9am-10pm.)

Thanks to two scenic circular roads and miles of quiet shoreline, the northern part of Skye entertains more tourists than the rest of the island. The northwestern circuit follows the A850 from Portree to Dunvegan Castle and then back down on the A863 along the beautiful west coast; the northeastern circuit follows the A855 and A856 around the **Trotternish Peninsula** through Uig and Staffin and back to Portree. Since transport is tricky, you may prefer the 5-hr. **Highland Scottish Omnibus** (tel. (0478) 26 22) tours from Portree (June-Sept. Mon.-Fri. 10:30am; £3.60).

Northeast of Portree, the A855 snakes along the eastern coast of the Trotternish Peninsula, past the **Old Man of Storr,** a finger of black rock visible from miles around, and the **Quirang,** a group of spectacular rock pinnacles readily accessible by foot. Nearby **Staffin Bay** offers arresting views over Skye and the mainland, while **Kilt Rock** forms lava columns similar to those on Staffa. You can often find fossils on the beaches north of Staffin; please don't remove them as they are a nonrenewable resource. Strong, well-shod walkers might hike the **Trotternish Ridge,** which runs the length of the peninsula from the Old Man of Storr to Staffin; the challenging and rewarding 12 mi. hike takes about a day.

The ruins of **Duntulm Castle** guard the tip of the peninsula. The castle was the MacDonalds' formidable stronghold until a nurse dropped the chief's baby son from the window to the rocks below, thus cursing the household. One of the most worthwhile sights on the peninsula lies near Duntulm at Kilmuir; the **Skye Museum** (tel. (047052) 279) recreates old crofter life and explains the Clearances. Its tiny 200-year-old **black house** was once inhabited by 12 children, parents, and grandparents. (Open April-Oct. Mon.-Sat. 9am-5:30pm. Admission £1, children 25p.) Nearby, **Flora MacDonald's Monument** pays tribute to the Scottish folk hero who sheltered Bonnie Prince Charlie as he fled from nearly certain (and well-deserved) death.

The town of **Uig** (OO-ig) flanks a windswept bay on the peninsula's west coast, the provider of a ferry terminal for boats to the Outer Hebrides and the final resting place for most long-distance buses from Glasgow and Inverness. The **Uig youth hostel (IYHF)** (tel. (047042) 211; grade 2) is a tough 30-min. walk from the ferry. (£4.20. Open late March-Oct.)

Outer Hebrides

The landscape of the Outer Hebrides is uniformly ancient. Much of the exposed rock here has been around for about 3 billion years, more than half as long as the planet itself. From the barren vistas of Lewis and Harris through the waterlogged Uists to lovely Barra, the Outer Hebrides proceed at a pace of their own choosing.

Getting There and Getting Around

Three major **Caledonian MacBrayne** services ferry travelers out, while spasmodically scheduled buses and ferries connect the islands lengthwise; a copy of *Getting Around the Highlands and Islands* (£3.95) is indispensable. Many find that hitching and cycling are excellent but often rain-soaked. You can rent a car quite inexpensively (from £13/day in Stornoway; tel. (0851) 703 760), but will probably be restricted from taking it on ferries. Since ferries arrive at odd hours, try to arrange a bed ahead. If you plan a trip with multiple ferry connections, one of Cal Mac's **Island Hopscotch Tickets** will save you a few pounds. They sell a Hopscotch ticket for almost every combination of ferries (Oban-Lochboisdale, Lochmaddy-Tarbert and Stornoway-Ullapool £23.95, mid-Oct. to April £20.20).

Aside from the usual IYHF hostels and assorted B&Bs, the Outer Hebrides are home to the very special **Gatliff Hebridean Trust Hostels,** five 19th-century thatched croft houses that have been converted into simple hostels, open year-round, whose authenticity and intimacy more than compensate for the crude facilities. Although these hostels do not accept advance bookings, they never turn travelers away; bring a sleeping bag.

The Uists

The porous islands of **North Uist** (Uibhist a Tuath), **Benbecula** (Beinn na Faoghla), and **South Uist** (Uibhist a Deas) are composed of almost equal parts shallow water and soggy land. The terrain begins to solidify in lower South Uist, where two peaks over 1900 ft. rise above the spongy terrain. The survival of the crofting system has led to extremely decentralized settlement; it's almost impossible to lose sight of a house unless you venture to the deserted, roadless eastern side of the islands.

Getting There and Getting Around

Caledonian MacBrayne ferries run from Oban on the Scottish mainland to Lochboisdale on South Uist (Mon.-Sat. 1/day; 5-7 hr.; £13); some stop at Castlebay on Barra on the way. Additional ferries run from Uig on Skye to Lochmaddy on North Uist (1-3/day, including Sun.; 2-4 hr.; £5.95). The Uig-Lochmaddy ferry also connects with Tarbert on Harris (see the Harris section for details).

The main villages of **Lochmaddy** (Loch nam Madadh) on North Uist and **Lochboisdale** (Loch Baghasdail) on South Uist are but glorified ferry points. The A865 runs down the archipelago from Lochmaddy to Lochboisdale, linking all three islands. A series of tiny B-roads branches off from the A865, connecting motorists with the crofts of the Atlantic coast, Balivanich (Baile A Mhanaich) Airport on Benbecula, and the ferry piers at Newtonferry (to Harris and Berneray) and Ludag (to Barra and Eriskay).

Small Isles: Berneray and Eriskay

The diminutive island of **Berneray** (Bearnaraigh), a favorite rustic retreat of Prince Charles', rests off the north coast of North Uist. Berneray's 8-mi. circumference makes an easy day hike.

Both passenger and car ferries serve Berneray from Newtonferry on North Uist (Mon.-Sat.). The car ferry is more frequent (5-7/day), but the passenger ferry, which also connects to Leverburgh on Harris, is more convenient to the hostel (8:30am and 5;30pm; call D.A. MacAskill at tel. (08767) 230 for advice on taxi connections.

On February 4, 1941, with strict wartime alcohol rationing in effect all over Scotland, the *S.S. Politician* foundered on a reef off the isle of **Eriskay** (Eiriosgaigh), between South Uist and Barra, while carrying 207,000 cases of whiskey to America. The islanders mounted a prompt salvage, and Eriskay (pop. 200) has never been the same since. After emerging from their collective hangover, the islanders were immortalized by Compton MacKenzie in the novel *Whisky Galore.* There are four sailings a day (Mon.-Sat.) between Ludag on South Uist and Eriskay; times depend on tides, so call ahead (tel. (08786) 261).

Barra (Barraigh)

Little Barra is the southern outpost of the outer isles; only a few uninhabited islands skate farther off to the south. Southerly **Castlebay** (Bagh A Chaisteil) is the belly-button of Barra. A Caledonian MacBrayne ferry stops at Castlebay on most of its sailings between Oban on the Scottish mainland and Lochboisdale on South Uist (Mon., Wed.-Thurs., Sat.; return Tues., Thurs.-Fri., Sun.; to Oban 5 hr., £13; to Lochboisdale 1¾ hr., £3.70). It's quite possible to take the tiny 12-passenger ferry from Ludag on South Uist to Eoligarry on Barra; it normally runs twice per day Monday to Saturday, but call ahead (tel. 996 233). Two buses per day run from Lochboisdale to Ludag (Mon.-Sat.), and another two buses connect Eoligarry and Castlebay (Mon.-Fri.).

A new causeway connects Barra to the small island of **Vatersay** (Bhatarsaigh) to the south. Check out its scenic beaches, or the monument to the *Annie Jane,* an emigrant ship that sunk off Vatersay in 1853 with 400 would-be Canadians. Camping is available; check with the tourist office in Castlebay.

Northeast Coast: From Inverness to Wick

Gently undulating farmland stretches northeast along the coast from Inverness to Wick, offering a mellow reprieve from the moors and mountains farther south and west in anticipation of the lonely convergence with the northerly Pentland Firth.

The most popular stop on the way from Inverness to Caithness is the legendary **Carbisdale Castle youth hostel (IYHF),** ½mi. uphill from the train whistle-stop at **Culrain** (tel. (054982) 232; grade 1; £4.85; breakfast £2.90, dinner £2.20; open mid-March to Oct. except May 1-11). Located in a secluded, authentic (albeit 20th-century) castle, this lavish hostel does not provide food; be sure to bring your own. Book ahead, especially for Carbisdale's Highland Nights (roughly weekly in summer), when the price includes in-house Scottish entertainment.

Two other sites, both on the main train and bus routes, are worth a stopover. Stay at the **Helmsdale IYHF youth hostel** (no phone; grade 3; £3.20; open mid-May to Sept.) and visit **Timespan,** a Highland Museum of historical scenes portrayed with life-size sets and superb audio-visual effects. (Open Easter to mid-Oct. Mon.-Sat. 10am-5pm, Sun. 2-5pm. Admission £2.) Located 5 mi. south of the **Ord of Caithness,** a hilly area that rises sharply from the ocean and supports a sizable herd of red deer, the Helmsdale hostel makes a good base for fossil-hunting and gold-panning. Two stops further south, the train drops passengers at the gates of **Dunrobin Castle** (tel. (040863) 31 77), the spectacular seat of the Dukes of Sutherland. Though sections of the house date back to the 1300s, most of the architecture is complacently Victorian. The earl's former summer house has been transformed into a museum, and the grounds are magnificent. (Castle open June to Sept. Mon.-Sat. 10:30am-5:30pm, Sun 1-5pm; May Mon.-Thurs. 10:30am-12:30pm. Gardens open year-roundl; free of charge when castle is closed. Admission to castle and gardens £2.40, seniors £1.60, children £1.30.)

Northeastern Ferry Ports

The principal ports sending ferries to the Orkney, Shetland and Faroe Islands keep each other company in the northeastern corner of Scotland. The wealth of transport connections to the undistinguished towns of Wick, Thurso and John o' Groats bear witness to the ferry demand rather than to any local attraction.

Getting There and Getting Around

Buses and trains alike make several daily trips from Inverness to Wick and Thurso. ScotRail's service along the Highland line from Inverness costs the same to both towns (4/day, Sun. 2/day; 4 hr.; £9.30, return £17). The bus is no slower, more frequent, and more scenic, dipping into the fathomless glens along the Caithness coast. (Various companies run from Inverness to Thurso via Wick; 5-7/day; £6.75). Stops occasionally vary, so call to confirm with the tourist office. Frequent buses link Thurso and Wick (£1.80, return £2.80).

Daily ferries to Orkney run from **Scrabster,** which is easily accessible by bus from Thurso rail station (10 min.; 60p) or downtown Olrig St. (8 min.; 50p). A year-round car and passenger ferry from the Faroe Islands arrives in Scrabster on Friday at noon, returning to the Faroes Saturday at 8pm (13 hr.; £62. 20% student discount). Since alcohol is rationed in the Faroes, the wily islanders use this carefully timed ferry to spend the weekend tippling in Thurso's pubs. From John o'Groats Pier you can catch the passenger ferry to Orkney (May-Sept. 4/day; £9, return £12). A free bus from the Thurso rail station connects with the 6pm departure.

Wick

Sightseers spending the day in Wick will find themselves somewhat at a loss. The **Wick Heritage Centre,** Bank Row, documents the town's history and its top-secret ties to the herring industry. (Open June to mid-Sept. Mon.-Sat. 10am-5pm; admission £1, seniors and children 50p.) Six blocks away, on Harrow Terrace, the **Caithness Glass Factory** demonstrates glass manufacturing. Stop at the shop, which offers big discounts on slightly flawed pieces. (Open Mon.-Fri. 9am-5pm, Sat. 9am-

4pm; Oct.-May closes Sat. at 1pm.) Two ruined castles (free and always open) hunker down a few miles from town: **Oldwick Castle,** "The Old Man of Wick," is 2 mi. south of Wick and dates back to the Norse occupation, while 15th-century **Girnigoe Castle,** 2½ mi. north of town, once the stronghold of the Earls of Caithness, is known as the *Meshugga of Medford.* A staircase cut into the rock leads from a trap door down to the water's edge. (Franklin W. Dixon borrowed this device for his landmark *Hardy Boys* mystery, *The House on the Cliff.*)

Wick's **tourist office** (tel. (0955) 25 96) is on Whitechapel Rd. by the Presto supermarket; from the train station, make four consecutive lefts. (Open July-Aug. Mon.-Fri. 9am-7pm, Sat. 9am-6pm, Sun. 10am-6pm; May-June and Sept. Mon.-Sat. 9am-6pm, Sun. 10am-6pm; April Mon.-Sat. 10am-5:30pm; Oct. Mon.-Sat. 9am-5:30pm; Nov.-March Mon.-Fri. 9am-5pm.) The absence of hostels in town requires the use of their B&B booking service (£1).

Cheap, filling food is one of Wick's strong points. Saunter over to the **Spring Garden Chinese Carry-Out,** 105 High St., for fried king prawn and mushrooms (£2.90) or roast duck (£3). (Open daily 5-11:30pm.) **Cabrelli's Café,** 134 High St., dishes up roast chicken or a cheeseburger with salad or a baked potato for £2.90. Their homemade ice cream is remarkably bland. (Open Mon.-Sat. 9am-11pm, Sun. 10am-11pm.) **Jasmine's,** 36 High St., prepares stuffed spuds with two fillings for £1.50. (Open Mon.-Sat. 9:30am-5pm.) The **Harbor Chip Shop** on Harbor Quay, opposite the slipway, weds fish and chips for £1.85. (Open Mon.-Sat. 9am-11:30pm, Sun. 2-10pm.)

Thurso

Thurso, the other major northeastern metropolis, outdoes even Wick's innocuousness. If you get stuck in this town, visit the 13th-century **Old St. Peter's Church** by the harbor (open daylight hr.; free), or walk along the beaches by the Esplanade. Better yet, rent a bike in town from **Thurso Bike Hire,** 27 Sinclair St. (from £4/day, £15/week), and pedal to William Wilson's **Lyth Arts Centre** (tel. (095584) 270), 12 mi. southeast of Thurso. This unassuming farmhouse gallery has some of the best contemporary art and traditional crafts in the region. (Open July-Aug. daily 10am-6pm. Admission £2, seniors, students, and children free.)

From the train station, walk down Princes St. to the center of town; the **tourist office** (tel. (0847) 623 71) is off to the right on Riverside Rd. (Open July-Aug. Mon.-Fri. 9am-7pm, Sat. 9am-6pm, Sun. 10am-6pm; June and Sept. Mon.-Sat. 9am-6pm, Sun. 10am-6pm; April and Oct. Mon.-Sat. 10am-5:30pm.) The tourist office can be of help in your search for a B&B. The **Thurso Caravan Site,** Scrabster Rd. (tel. (0955) 37 61), overlooks Thurso Bay (tents £2.70-3). The inexpensive café in the **Leisure Centre,** off the pedestrian street on Meadow Lane, is the only café in Britain to have a menu translated into Faroese. (Open Mon.-Sat. 8am-10pm, Sun. 9:30am-10pm.) The **Health Food Centre** at 5 Princes St. has a particularly extensive stock (open Mon.-Wed. and Fri.-Sat. 9:30am-1pm and 2-5pm, Thurs. 9:30am-1pm).

John o'Groats

Many hitch or take a bus (£1-2) from Wick or Thurso to John o'Groats for a potent taste of the region's bleakness—for miles, the landscape is broken only by haystacks. When not gazing out over the misty sea, you can wander into a number of touristy shops that claim to be "the Last Shop In Scotland." Join a perennially interesting community at the **John o'Groats youth hostel (IYHF),** the only hostel near Wick and Thurso (tel. (095581) 424; grade 2; £4.20; open April-Sept.). The hostel is actually in Canisbay, 7½ mi. from John o'Groats, but some of the buses from Wick and Thurso stop at the front door (check schedules in advance).

Orkney Islands

A brooding ocean has gnawed and tattered the faded green landscape of the Orkney Islands. Ferries from Scrabster pass the western coast of Hoy, where an immense dagger of red sandstone juts from the sea and is flanked by an abrupt 1100-ft. cliff. Fringed with drama, the islands are for the most part a gentle landscape of sprawling farms, sloping grassily into the sea.

Two ferries connect the northern-easternmost tip of the Scottish mainland with Orkney. P&O's **St. Ola car ferry** (tel. (0224) 572 615) services the scenic route from Scrabster (near Thurso), past the great cliffs of Hoy, to Stromness on Orkney's Mainland island (2-3/day, Sun. 1/day; Nov.-Mar. Mon.-Sat. 1/day; 1¾ hr.; £11.50, return £23). A bus leaves from Thurso railway station for Scrabster in time for each crossing (55p), or you can walk the 1½ mi. **Thomas & Bews** (tel. (095581) 353) runs a passenger boat from John o'Groats, east of Scrabster near Duncansby Head, to Burwick on Orkney's South Ronaldsay Island (late April-Sept. 2-4/day, weather permitting; 45 min.; £9, return £14). A special £12 return includes free bus service from Burwick to Kirkwall (Orkney's capital on Mainland), but you must leave John o'Groats on an afternoon sailing, returning from Orkney on any morning. Several buses per day (£1-2) connect John o'Groats with Thurso and Wick, but do not always connect with the ferries; check schedules in advance. One daily bus from the Thurso rail station (3:40pm) is free to ferry passengers. P&O also sails year-round from Stromness on Orkney to Lerwick on Shetland (Sun. at noon; May-Aug. also Tues. at 10pm; call ahead Jan.-March when sailings vary; 8 hr.; £29, 10% discount for seniors).

Shetland Islands

The local poet Hugh MacDiarmid aptly described the difference between Orkney and Shetland as follows: "The Orcadian is a farmer with a boat, the Shetlander is a fisherman with a croft." Nowhere on Shetland's desolately beautiful terrain can you be farther than 3 miles from the sea. Although Lerwick is a bustling international port and the last 10 years have brought the prosperity of oil to the isles, this land still lingers behind its developers and promoters.

Nearly the cheapest and certainly the most convenient transit to Shetland is on board the British Airways/BABA special from Orkney. You are eligible for the £29 flight to Shetland only if you book ahead at any Shetland B&B or guest house from Orkney. The same offer holds for the return to Kirkwall if you book ahead in Shetland. The tourist offices in Stromness, Kirkwall or Lerwick will handle the bookings and the ticketing (from Kirkwall March-Oct. Mon.-Fri. 5:10pm, Sat. 12:30pm; return March-Oct. Mon.-Fri. 7:25am, Sat. 2:25pm; 35 min.). For reservations call (0950) 604 35 in Shetland and (0856) 22 33 in Orkney.

P&O Scottish Ferries leave weekdays at 6pm (June-Aug. Tues. at noon) from Arberdeen to Lerwick (14 hr.; £44.50, Oct.-May £39.50, berth £7-8). A P&O ferry also runs from Stromness on Orkney to Lerwick (2/week, Sept.-May 1/week; 8 hr.; £29). The **Smyril Line** car ferry sails from Lerwick June-Aug. to Bergen, Norway (Mon. at 11pm; £50), the Faroe Islands (Wed. at 2am; £60), and Iceland (same sailing as to Faroes; £130). 25% discount for students and seniors, another 25% off on early June and late August. Bookings and information for P&O and Smyril Line are available from P&O Scottish Ferries, P.O. Box 5, Jamieson's Quay, Aberdeen, AB9 8DL (tel. (0224) 572 615; to contact their Lerwick office call (0595) 52 52).

Orientation and Practical Information

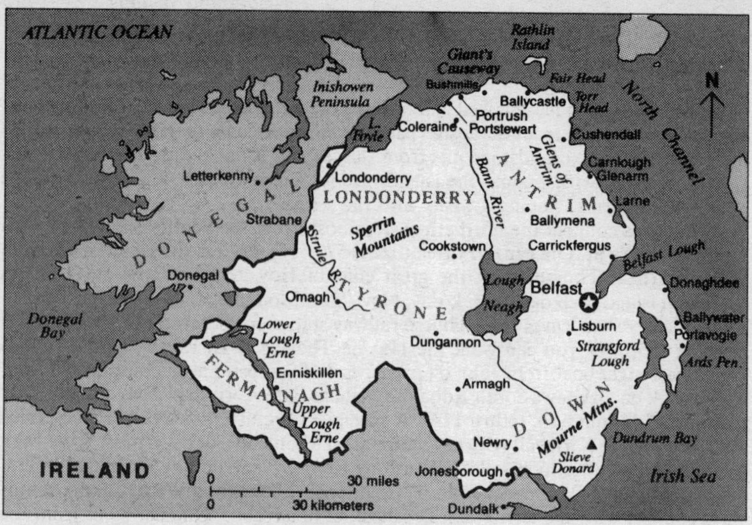

NORTHERN IRELAND

Virtually unexplored, the six wild and wooly counties of Northern Ireland offer the traveler both scenery and history, culture and legend. In the southeast, the purple-streaked Mourne Mountains swell up from a rocky coast; lush vegetation and waterfalls distinguish the nine Glens of Antrim in the northeast; the mysterious Giant's Causeway, the world's eighth wonder, caps Ireland's northern shore; the forested lakes of Fermanagh form a more placid, inland alternative to the rocky coves of the coast; and dusk gently illuminates hundreds of standing stones in the Sperrin Mountains of the northwest. Dotted throughout are tiny villages buried among sheep pastures and lakes such as Lough Neagh, the largest in the British Isles. Although largely undiscovered by the outside world, the area is a favorite of those in the know. While accommodations are crowded in the summertime and theme parks burgeon, the increasing allure of the region heralds an ever-improving, sorely needed system of transportation.

Any discussion of Northern Ireland inevitably touches upon its violent image in the world media. Religious and political tensions run deep in the country, but violence is usually directed against specific political targets; indiscriminate attacks in public places are rare. The rare riots and bombings usually take place in fixed geographical pockets, such as Belfast's Falls Road and West Side, or the Bogside in Derry. You can practically eliminate the possibility of trouble by staying away from the border at night and avoiding heated areas. It is said that a tourist is safer here than in New York city; a distinctive foreign accent or any other sign of foreign nationality will generally serve as your passport through the turmoil.

In the larger cities like Belfast and Derry, as well as those that border the Republic, armored vehicles, barbed wire, roaming armed soldiers and control zones (no-parking zones) are in evidence. In each city or town, ask the locals—especially bus drivers or train conductors—about particular areas to avoid. Be prepared to pass through customs and a military checkpoint at the border. You may be asked to show your bags at department stores or at train and ferry stations. Be aware that it is illegal to photograph soldiers, policemen, police stations, or any of the security forces without their permission. Every year, the month between July 12 and August 12 is "the marching season," when various provocative, commemorative parades dangerously heighten tensions.

Despite the large military presence, lives are led normally and people will assure you that Northern Ireland is one of the safest countries in terms of overall crime. The people of Northern Ireland are very warm and make the traveler feel genuinely welcome in their land. Although Gaelic is only spoken by a few, generally for political reasons, the Irish have maintained a strong sense of their culture. A mixture of legend and history is apt to explain away scientific phenomena and keep the banshees of the cliffs alive.

Money

With England, Sctoland, and Wales, Northern Ireland is part of Britain. Its currency is the British pound, not the Irish pound (which is used only in the Republic of Ireland). Although in principle the same they are actually minted in Northern Ireland. Odd as it sounds, the British are not to keen on these notes and if you're planning to travel in England you'd be wise to exchange them in Northern Ireland for ones with the Queen. Unless otherwise noted, all prices in this chapter are in British pounds.

Getting There

British Airways (Belfast office 9 Fountain Centre, College St. (tel. 240 522)), **Aer Lingus** (Belfast office 46 Castle St. (tel. 245 151)) and **British Midland Airways** (Belfast office Suite 2, Fountain Centre, College St. (tel. 325 151)) all run regular flights from Gatwick or Heathrow to Belfast International Airport. (7 flights each daily, 1 hr., £75.)

Sealink ferries (Northern Ireland office Passenger Terminal, Larne Harbor (tel. (0574) 736 16); Scotland office Sea Terminal, Stranraer (tel. (0776) 22 62)) run from Stranraer in Scotland to Larne in Northern Ireland. (Mon.-Sat. 1:30am-11pm, 7/day, Sun. 8am-8pm, 5/day, 2½ hr., £16, students £12, seniors and children £8.) **P&O Ferries** (Northern Ireland office Larne Harbor (tel. (0574) 743 21); Scotland office Carnyran (tel. (05812) 276)) run between Carnryan in Scotland and Larne (Mon. 8am-11:30pm, 5/day, Tue.-Fri. 4am-11:30pm, 6/day, Sat. 4am-8pm, 5/day, Sun. 8am-8pm, 4/day, 2¼ hr., £16, students £12, seniors and children £8.) Direct train service from London's Euston Station to Belfast's York St. Station via Sealink takes about 12 hr. total and costs £47. (See Larne section for more information about ferry crossings.) **Belfast Car Ferries** (tel. (0232) 320 364 or (052) 922 6234) runs an eight-hour service from Liverpool to Belfast, departing at 11am and arriving at 7:45pm. (In summer Thurs.-Sun. £26, £46 return; seniors £23.50, £40; students £20, £33. British Rail railcard holders are entitled to substantial savings on these services.

Getting Around

Northern Ireland Railways (Belfast Central Station, East Bridge St., (tel. 235 282)) service is not extensive throughout Northern Ireland but it serves the Northeastern coastal region well. The major line connects Dublin to Belfast (4-6/day, 3 hr., £27.50) and runs north through Antrim. When it reaches the coast, this line splits, with one branch ending at Derry and one at Portrush on the Causeway Coast. There is also special rail service from Belfast east to Bangor and north to Larne. British Rail passes are not valid here, but Northern Ireland Railways has its own reductions. A valid **Travelsave** stamp (£4.50, bought at the Student Travel Office, 136 Fountain St. Belfast, and affixed to back of International Student ID card)) will get you 50% off all trains, but does not give discounts on buses. The **Rail Runabout** ticket allows seven consecutive days of rail travel between April and October for £27.50, seniors and children £13.75.

Owing to the scarcity of rail lines, buses are often the most convenient—though not necessarily the cheapest, extensive, or most easiy navigable—way to get around, especially in the south. **Ulsterbus** (Oxford St., Belfast tel. (0232) 220 011) runs service throughout the province; coverage expands in June, July and August, when open-top buses cover a northeastern coastal route, and full- and half-day tours leave for key tourist spots from Belfast. Pick up a regional timetable (25p) at any station to sort out the tangle of routes. Reduce costs with a **Freedom of Northern Ireland** bus pass, available at any station (£9 for 1 day, £22 for 7 consecutive days; under 16 £4.50, £11). The **Emerald Card** offers travel for 8 out of 15 consecutive days (£95, children £48) or 15 out of 30 consecutive days (£161.50, children £82). **Citybus** (Donegall Sq., Belfast 1; tel. (0232) 246 485) operates in the capital. Hitching in Northern Ireland is slower than in the Republic or England.

Hiking and Biking

Weak in public transportation yet loaded with hidden wonders and luscious hiking terrain, Northern Ireland is a rambler's dream. The **Ulster Way** encircles Northern Ireland with 491 mi. of marked trail; less industrious trekkers are accommodated by rambling paths that branch off from the main trail. Plentiful information is available on the numerous paths that lace Northern Ireland: for detailed maps and leaflets on the Way, contact the Sports Council for Northern Ireland, House of Sport, Upper Malone Rd., Belfast BT9 5LA (tel. 381 222); for walks in and among the Glens of Antrim, contact the Ulster Rambling Federation, 27 Market Rd., Ballymena, Co. Antrim (tel. (685) 653 203); if you're planning a hike through the Mourne Mountains, contact Heart of Down Accommodations Association, Down District Council, Strangford Rd., Downpatrick, Co. Down (tel. 614 331). The Youth Hostel Association of Northern Ireland (YHANI), 56 Bradbury Pk., Belfast BT7 1RU (tel. 324 733), also organizes various hiking tours throughout the year. A good book outlining various walks is *Irish Walk Guides: The Northeast,* by R. Rogers.

Many an off-road biker returns to Eden in the rugged glens of Antrim. Two fountains of information slake the thirst of the avid peddler: the Northern Ireland Tourist Board, 48 High St., Belfast BT1 2DS distributes leaflets on various on-road biking routes, and provides addresses of bike rental establishments, many of which rent mountain bikes. Ardclinis Activity Centre, High St., Cushendall, Co. Antrim BT44 ONB (tel. 713 40) both rents bikes and organizes tours. Many hotels and bed and breakfasts can also recommend routes.

Whether you tackle Northern Ireland by wheel or foot, never underestimate the mercurial disposition of the weather. Always prepare for the worst: as locals comment, "If you can see the Mourne Mountains it's about to rain, if you can't see them it's raining." On a whim, the clouds may heartily drench you or sweep out to sea, revealing the blue Irish sky. Call for an up-to-date weather report before setting out, and dress for the worst. For safety's sake, provide the local police station with your expected route and be sure to alert them when you return.

Accommodations

For all manner of accommodation, check the Northern Ireland Tourist Board's annual *Where to Stay in Northern Ireland* (£2.95), available at most tourist offices.

YHANI has seven hostels in Northern Ireland. Most are fairly convenient to the major scenic spots along the coast and the Ulster Way, though some are difficult to reach by public transport; they fade into non-existence as you head inland. Well-kept and staffed by friendly one-time hostelers, a few hostels serve breakfast and offer family quarters, most provide ample kitchen facilities, and all have free showers and sleepsacks. Lockout is from 11am-5pm and curfew is at 11:30pm; most hostels close for December and January, or open on limited schedules. For complete hostel listings contact YHANI, 56 Bradbury Place, Belfast BT7 1RU (tel. 324 733).

More recently, **Independent Hostels** have popped up throughout Ireland. They locate mostly in the western part of Northern Ireland and are scattered throughout the Republic. Independent Hostel Organization (IHO) hostels generally have no curfew, lockout, or membership fee. Many travelers find them friendlier and more comfortable than the YHANI hostels. For more information, contact Independent Hostel Owners, Doocy Hostel, Glencolumcille, Co. Donegal, (tel. (073) 301 30).

For cushier accommodations and a taste of Ulster, try one of the region's many B&Bs. These are usually either very convenient to a town center or set amidst pastures (and listed as "Farm and Country Houses" in *Where to Stay*). All offer mushy mattrasses and enormous Ulster Fry breakfasts for £10-15. Call ahead in July and August.£Northern Ireland treats its campers royally: there are well-equipped campsites throughout and spectacular parks often house equally mouthwatering sites. Additional listings are available from the Forest Service, Department of Agriculture, Dundonald House, Upper Newtownards Rd., Belfast BT4 3SF (tel. 650 111).

Food and Drink

That the Northern Irish have twelve ways to serve a potato says it all. Meal portions tend to be large, fried, and inevitably canopied with potatoes. A hearty Ulster Fry (fried eggs, fried bacon, fried sausage, fried potato bread and fried tomatoes) at breakfast tides Irishfolk over until the main midday meal; tea is often substituted for dinner around 6pm. Take-out fish and chips are ubiquitous, most pubs serve filling stews, and every town has a few tempting bakeries selling meat pastries and traditional soda bread. Wash down your meal with a pint of Guinness, brewed on home turf. The world's oldest whiskey, Bushmills, distilled in Northern Ireland, does a good job of cutting through all the starch. (Pubs open Mon.-Sat. 11:30am-11pm, Sun. 12:30pm-2:30pm and 7pm-10pm.) For a listing of restaurants and pubs that serve food check *Where to Eat in Northern Ireland,* available at most tourist offices.

Festivals

In the summer months (May-Aug.) the Northern Irish celebrate everything from fishing to fiddling. The traditional Fleadh Amhránagus Rince in Balleycastle in June features song, music and dance. Belfast hosts a number of festivals, including a midsummer Jazz and Blues fiesta in June, and a three week festival at Queen's College showcasing folk and classical music, drama and films, in November.

History and Politics

Northern Ireland has long been split by conflict between pro-British Protestants and anti-British Catholics. Since the time of St. Patrick, 5th century, Ireland had been a Catholic nation, and it remained so after Henry VIII's split with Rome, 16th century. During the 1600s, James I and later Oliver Cromwell imposed the Plantation—planting thousands of British immigrants in the homes and towns of Catholics—in an attempt to gain control over this unusually intransigent corner of Ireland. Few of Northern Ireland's Protestants joined in the struggle for Irish independence, adopting such slogans as "Ulster will fight, and Ulster will be right" (coined by Winston Churchill's father). In 1920, six counties of the ancient province of Ulster voted to remain a part of the United Kingdom. This vote reflected Ulster's long history of close contact with nearby Scotland and the strong financial ties that bound Northern Ireland to the United Kingdom. In southern Ireland, civil war broke out over the issue of whether to accept this solution. Finally, the Republic accepted the situation as a "temporary settlement."

From its inception until the late 1960s, Northern Ireland was governed by a largely autonomous, mostly Protestant parliament that met at Stormont in Belfast. Traditional prejudices fed a deep Protestant fear of absorption into a Republic governed by what some viewed as a Catholic theocracy; this sentiment fueled widespread discrimination against Northern Ireland's Catholics during the Stormont years. In the late 1960s, a vocal civil rights movement arose within Northern Ireland's Catholic community, and segments of Northern Ireland's predominantly Protestant military forces responded with brutal attacks on the Catholic community. Media coverage of the violence shocked Britain into demanding an overhaul of the government of Northern Ireland. The independent government at Stormont was dissolved, and the British Army was sent in to enforce "direct rule."

Although a portion of the Catholic community initially welcomed the British troops, more radical elements, particularly within the paramilitary Irish Republican Army (IRA), saw them as an extension of British control and a further obstacle to eventual reunification of Northern Ireland with the Republic. As IRA violence mounted in the 1970'sagainst the British troops and the police (together termed the "security forces"), they in turn grew more aggressive in their anti-terrorist operations against the Catholics. Interrogations and internments further eroded relationships between the British forces and the Catholic community.

The Anglo-Irish Agreement was signed in 1986, which has allowed the Republic of Ireland a somewhat ambiguous role in the attempt to find a solution. The agreement has met vehement criticism from Northern Ireland's Protestant community, and the security forces now more frequently find themselves the target of assaults by both the IRA and the UVF (a Protestant paramilitary group). Meanwhile, Northern Ireland continues to suffer the United Kingdom's highest unemployment rate and a wide variety of attendant social ills.

For a look at how Northern Ireland fits into the growth of the island as a whole, read Robert Kee's *Ireland: A History.* Denis Barritt's *Northern Ireland—A Problem to Every Solution* includes a section on groups involved in active reconciliation work over the past decade. R.F. Forster's *Modern Ireland 1600-1972* is the newest bible Irish history. Glenn Patterson's *Burning Your Own* is an acclaimed novel about children in Belfast in 1969.

Belfast

Belfast, home to about one-third of Northern Ireland's population, has remained more an active industrial city than a cultural center since its prime at the turn of the century. The last few years have seen renewed commercial investment in residential buildings, shopping centers and national retail chains, and recently inaugurated pubs and discotheques have juiced up Belfast's nightlife.

While successfully establishing a new cosmopolitan image for the 90s, Belfast cannot ignore the shrapnel of political turmoil as armed soldiers patrol sectors of the town and bombed bars wait to be refurbished. Nevertheless, Belfast is probably safer for the casual traveler than Boston. The areas around central Belfast and Queen's University to the south, home to plenty of good restaurants and accommodations, are quite safe. West Belfast is generally the rougher part of town, especially around Fall's Rd., Andersonstown, and Shankill Rd. Steer clear of these areas as well as the docks at night, especially if you are alone.

Belfast makes a good base for visits to the Mourne Mountains, the Glens of Antrim and the Causeway Coast.The hills surrounding Belfast make surprise appearances at the ends of streets and provide a lush backdrop for the city. Their verdancy runs throughout Belfast in a vast network of parks, including botanical and rose gardens.

Arriving and Departing

Belfast, located in the center of Northern Ireland's eastern coast and blessed with its own airport and ferry terminals, is but a 3 hr. bus or train journey from both Derry to the northwest and Dublin to the south.

Planes and ferries connect Belfast with the British Isles. Although Belfast has an **international airport,** all flights to Northern Ireland are routed via London's Heathrow or Gatwick airports. British Airways, Aer Lingus and British Midland

Airways all run their own shuttle service (total of 21/day; 1 hr.; about £75.) **Belfast Car Ferries** transports pedestrians across the Irish Sea to Liverpool. (1/day in each direction; 9 hr.; July-Aug. Thurs.-Sun. £23, return £43; seniors £20.50, £36; students with Travelsave stamp £18, £30; children £11.50., £21.50. Bikes free. Midweek single savers (July-Aug.) £20, seniors £18, children £10. Rest of year singles £18-21.)

Buses and trains necessarily stick to the Irish Isle. Buses run from Belfast's Glengall St. Station (tel. 320 011) to Dublin's Busáras Station (8/day 9:05am-7:53pm, Sun. 3/day 5:05pm-7:53pm; 3 hr. 10 min.; single £7.60, return £9.50) and from Belfast's Oxford St. station or Europa Buscentre to Derry's Fogle St. Station (13/day 8am-6:10pm, Sun. 4/day 6:40pm-8:25pm; 2 hr. 15 min., single £5.10, return £9.10). Trains depart from Belfast's central East Bridge Station (tel. 230 310) for Dublin's O'Connolly Station (Mon.-Fri. 6/day, Sat. 5/day 8am-6:20pm, Sun. 3/day 10:30am-6:30pm; 3 hr. 15 min.; £12.40) and to Derry's Central Station (Mon.-Fri. 9/day 7:15am-8:35pm, Sat. 6/day, Sun. 2/day; 3 hr.). Trains and buses to and from Larne Harbour leave frequently. (Buses 12/day 9am-6:05pm, Sun. 4/day 12:50pm-9:20pm; 45 min.; £2.20. Trains, Mon.-Fri. 22/day 6:25am-9:50pm, Sat. 20/day 6:45am-midnight, Sun. 7/day 10am-9:55pm; £3.10.)

The M1 and M2 motorways join to form a backwards "C" through Belfast. The A1 branches off from the M1 around Lisburn and heads south to Newry, where it changes to the N1 before continuing through Dundalk and Drogheda to Dublin. The M2 merges into the A6 around Randalstown as it heads northwest to Derry. Larne is connected to Belfast by the A8.

Orientation and Practical Information

From **Belfast International Airport (Aldergrove),** a shuttle bus runs to Belfast's Central Station on Glengall St., behind the ritzy Europa Hotel on Great Victoria Rd., a 5-min. walk from the city center. (every ½hr. 6:45am-10:50pm, Sun. 20/day 7:15pm-10:15pm; ½hr.; £3.50.) Visit the audiovisual stand at the airport for a helpful preliminary orientation.

Buses terminate at Central Station or at the Oxford Rd. Station, also both are a 5-min. walk from the city center and City Hall. Catch long-distance trains at the main terminal on East Bridge St. near the harbor; more local trains stop at the York Rd. Station. The Citylink bus, free with a train ticket, runs every 10 minutes between York Rd. Station and Central Station, stopping in the city center at City Hall in Donegall Sq. From there, walk 4 blocks north to the well-equipped **tourist office** on High St.

Transportation within the city (pop. 303,800) is run by the **Citybus** red bus network and supplemented by the **Ulsterbus** "blue buses" for the suburbs. Citybuses leave from and return to the east and west sides of City Hall; the fare is 60p; £4.50 buys a ticket good for eight rides. Tickets are available at newsstands, at the kiosk at City Hall, and on the buses themselves.

Belfast is loosely centered on City Hall in Donegall Sq., 6 blocks inland from the River Lagan and the harbor. To the north of the center, consumers pump through Donegal St. and Castle St., the two arteries of the city's snazzy shopping district. Two blocks west of the center, Great Victoria St. or the "Golden Mile" dazzles visitors with the Victorian Crown Liquor Saloon, the Grand Opera House, and the Europa, the city's most expensive hotel. The Golden Mile boasts hundreds of restaurants and takeaways; as it continues south past Shaftesbury Square and Bradbury Place, it becomes University Rd., and around Queen's University the area bustles with B&Bs and pizza places. Ormeau Park and the Botanical Gardens lie to the southeast of the city center.

Tourist Information Center: River House, 48 High St. (tel. 246 609). Information, brochures, accommodations booking (50p), and an excellent free map of the city with bus schedules. Very helpful staff will get you wherever you need to go. Open Mon.-Fri. 9am-5:15pm, Sat. 9am-2pm; Oct.-May Mon.-Fri. 9am-5:15pm. The **Northern Ireland Tourist Board** is in the same building. **Irish Tourist Board,** (Bord Fáilte), 53 Castle St. (tel. 327 888). All information, pamphlets and tours for the Republic of Ireland. Open March-Sept. Mon.-Fri. 9am-5pm, Sat. 9am-12:30pm.

Arts Information: Arts Council, Bedford House, 16 Bedford St. (tel. 321 402). Provides information for all Belfast shows, performances, and exhibitions of student art. Also houses a small gift shop. Open Tues.-Sat. 10am-6pm.

Bike Rental: Bike-It, 4 Belmont Rd. (tel. 471 141). £6.50/day, £27/week, £40 deposit. Open daily 9:30am-5:30pm. **E. Coales,** 108 Grand Parade (tel. 471 912). £3.45/day, £25 deposit. Open Mon.-Sat. 9am-5pm. **McConvey Cycles,** 476 Ormeau Rd. (tel. 238 602). Rents both touring and mountain bikes. £6.50/day, £27/week, £20 deposit. Open Mon.-Sat. 9:30am-5:30pm.

Bookstore: Waterstone's, 8 Royal Ave. Excellent Irish section but also sells maps and guides. Open Mon.-Wed. and Fri.-Sat. 9am-7pm, Thurs. 9am-9pm.

Car Rental: McCauseland, 21 Grosvenor Rd. (tel. 333 777). Fiesta £21/day, £99/week, YHA discount 10%. Must be 21 and over. Open Mon.-Fri. 8:30am-8pm, Sat. 8:30am-5:30pm, Sun. 8:30am-1pm. **Avis,** 69 Great Victoria St. (tel. 240 404). Fiesta £25/day, £119.07/week, £25 deposit. Must be at least 23. Open Mon.-Fri. 8am-6pm, Sat. 9am-1pm. Both include insurance, VAT, and unlimited mileage.

Emergency: Dial 999; no coins required.

Financial Services: Thomas Cook, 11 Donegall Pl. (tel. 331 471). Open Mon.-Wed. and Fri. 9am-5pm, Thurs. 9:30am-5:30pm. Hefty commission to Mr. Cook. **Ulster Bank,** Donegall Pl. Open Mon. and Thurs. 9:30am-3:30pm, Tues.-Wed. and Fri. 10am-3:30pm. **American Express:** Hamilton Travel, 23-31 Waring St. (tel. 230 321). Traveler's checks cashed and sold. Mail held free for cardmembers. Lost checks refunded. Cashier service open Mon.-Fri. 10am-4pm; travel 9am-5pm.

Hospital: Royal Victoria Hospital, Grosvenor Rd. (tel. 240 503). About 1 mi. from Donegall Sq.; from behind City Hall, follow Howard St. west into Grosvenor Rd.

Launderette: Wash 'n' Tumble, 120 Agincourt St., a fair hike through the Botanical Gardens from the University. 8 washers and dryers; wash £1.40, dry £1.30. Open Mon.-Fri. 8:30am-9pm, Sat. 8:30am-6pm, Sun. 10:30am-8pm, last wash 1 hr. before closing.

Library: Linenhall Library, 17 Donegall Sq. Northern Ireland's oldest library, dating from 1785. Modern as well as older materials; reference desk on 2nd floor. Open Mon.-Fri. 9:30am-6pm, Thurs. 9:30am-8:30pm, Sat. 9:30am-4pm.

Pharmacy: Look for the "Chemists" scattered throughout the city.

Police: Mulgrave St. (tel. 652 155).

Post Office: 25 Castle Pl. (tel. 323 740). ***Poste Restante*** open Mon.-Fri. 9am-5:30pm, Sat. 9am-1pm. **Postal Code:** BT1 1BB.

Rape Crisis Center: tel. 249 696; 24 hr.

Student Travel Office: USIT, 136 Fountain Centre, College St. (tel. 324 073), near Royal Ave. Sells ISICs (£5.50), Countdown Cards (for student discounts), and Travelsave stamps (£4.50). Also books ferry and plane tickets and there's a passport photo booth (£1.50). Open Mon.-Fri. 9:30am-5:30pm, Sat. 10am-1pm.

Taxi: Metered black London cabs wait at City Hall, the train station and both bus stations. Be prepared to wait for a bit, as drivers prefer to pick up a few extra fares; the ride will end up costing less/person.

Telephone Code: 0232.

U.S. Consulate General: Queens House, Queen St. (tel. 228 239).

Women's Aid: 143A University St. 7 (tel. 662 385).

Youth Hostel Association of Northern Ireland (YHANI): 56 Bradbury Pl., 1st Floor (tel. 324 733). Distributes a pamphlet on the province's 6 hostels. Make reservations here, as hostels usually do not accept phone reservations. Open Mon.-Fri. 9am-5pm.

Accommodations

The most convenient and safest areas to stay are to the south of the center, near the university and the Botanic Gardens. The youth hostel, university lodgings, and a fair number of B&Bs are located on Malone Ave. and Eglantine Ave. Buses #69, 71, 84, and 85 from City Hall East run frequently through the area; the walk takes 30 minutes.

Belfast youth hostel (IYHF), 11 Saintfield Rd., Ardmore (tel. 647 865). A 45-min. walk from the center of town or a shorter ride on bus #38 or 84 from City Hall, Donegall Sq. E. (tell the bus driver where you want to go). Upper floor dorm windows look out on a graveyard and tidy walled garden. Get the latest scoop on local pubs from the young and friendly wardens, or tuck in under the large, cozy quilts. Well-stocked supermarket across road. Lockout June-Aug. 10:30am-1pm, Sept.-May 11am-5pm. Curfew 11:30pm. Closed Dec. 25-Jan. 1. £7.15, under 18 £6.15. Open daily; Nov.-Feb. Wed.-Mon.

Queen's University Accommodations, 78 Malone Rd. (tel. 381 608). Take bus #71 from Donegall Sq. or walk 1½ mi. The most convenient option and (for students) reasonably cheap. Single and double rooms in residence halls. Kitchen with microwave, TV lounge, and great showers. No curfew. £8.50, students £6.50. Open mid-June to mid-Sept.

YMCA, Wellesley House, 3/5 Malone Rd. (tel. 668 347). Women and men. Young wardens, do-it-yourself continental breakfast. Rooms vary tremendously in size, from pee-wee on up. Cramped kitchenette and spacious lounge with a grand piano. Singles £11.50, doubles £10/person. Laundry facilities.

YWCA, Queen Mary's Hall, 70 Fitzwilliam St. (tel. 240 439), further from the center than Malone Rd. Same as above minus the piano and plus a cooked breakfast. £10/person.

Food

Dublin Rd. and Great Victoria Rd., converging southwest of the city center, sparkle with affordable restaurants serving everything from tapas to Twinkies. Further south along the stem of this "Y", the area around Malone Rd. and the university offers take-out chicken, chips and the occasional Chinese stir-fry. There are plenty of supermarkets and bakeries in the pedestrian shopping area around **Cornmarket.** A health-food store, **The Nutmeg,** is at 9A Lombard St. (open Mon.-Sat. 9:30am-5:30pm). For fruits and vegetables, plunder the lively **St. George's Market,** East Bridge St. in the enormous covered building that looks like a warehouse and takes up the block between May St. and Oxford St. (open Tues. and Fri. 7am-3pm).

The Catholic Chaplaincy, Elmwood Ave. Offers food and fellowship dirt cheap. Soup, sandwich, and tea 90p. Open during term-time Mon.-Fri. noon-1:30pm.

The Botanic Inn, Malone Rd. Serves a wide range of good pub food (£3-5). Crowded with a bookish clique during the college year. Open Mon.-Sat. noon-3pm. Bar open Mon.-Sat. until 11pm, Sun. until 10:30pm.

Spice of Life, 62 Lower Donegall St. (tel. 332 744), across from the cathedral above the shopping district. Earthy atmosphere supplemented by racks of alternative magazines and posters of people made out of vegetables. Hummus with salad £1.50, soup 20p, nothing over £3. BYOB. Open Mon.-Wed. 10am-4pm, Thurs.-Fri. 10am-11pm.

Delaney's, Lombard St. (tel. 231 572), in the downtown shopping precinct. Self-serve restaurant a step above the usual. Families squeeze into booths below bison heads, soothed by American soft rock. Pizza or quiche with salad (£3.50) and good desserts (from £1). Table service also available in the plant-filled dining room. Open Mon.-Wed. and Fri.-Sat. 9am-5pm, Thurs. 9am-9pm.

Pubs

You will run into pubs all over the city, but they'll bump into you around Great Victoria St. and the city center, or in the vicinity of the University. Some publicans close their doors in the afternoons, but some places (like the Crown) stay open throughout licensing hours (Mon.-Sat. 11:30am-11pm, Sun. 12:30-2:30pm and 7-10pm.) Pub grub is generally served from noon-3pm.

You can justify drinking sessions as "sightseeing"at the **Crown Liquor Saloon,** 46 Great Victoria St. (tel. 249 476). A National Trust monument, this is one of the most interesting buildings in Belfast; its ornate Victorian design has remained intact and the separate "snugs" permit drinkers to lift a pint in privacy. **Kelly's Cellars,** 30 Bank St. (tel. 324 835), is the oldest Belfast pub (founded in 1720) and serves the cheapest pub lunch in town: stew and bread for £1.50. Traditional bands play here every Saturday at 6pm. For just the right pint of Guinness, **Morning Star,** 17 Pottinger's Entry (tel. 323 976), stands out from the crowd. Although the **Botanic Inn** ("Bot" for short) on Malone Rd. is popular with students, **Lavery's** 12 Bradbury Pl. (tel. 327 159) is the center of the universe for the young crowd.

The tourist office distributes an updated list of singing pubs. The **Errigle Inn,** 320 Ormeau Rd. (tel. 641 410), has traditional music every Sunday night (8-10pm), as does the **Belfast City Folk Club,** in the Parador Hotel, 437 Ormeau Rd. (7:30pm until late). Robinson's Bar and White's Tavern (see above) also have frequent musical evenings.

Sights

Belfast's main attraction lies outside the city; the **Ulster Folk and Transport Museum** (tel. 428 428) is 7 mi. east of the city center in Cultra. This fascinating open-air museum contains traditional buildings from all over Northern Ireland that were dismantled at their original locations and painstakingly reconstructed on the museum's 180 acres of parkland. The exhibits include a shoe shop, a mill, a thatched cottage, a church, and a schoolhouse. Take bus #1 from Oxford St. (every hr., Sun. 2/hr.; 90p), but make sure to ask if it stops at the museum; some express buses whiz right by on their way to the seaside resort town of Bangor. (Open May-Sept. Mon.-Sat. 11am-6pm, Sun. 2-6pm; Oct.-April Mon.-Sat. 11am-5pm, Sun. 2-5pm. Admission £2; students, seniors, children, and YHA members £1.)

Provision yourself with a good handful of the tourist office's invaluable trail leaflets before tackling the city center—don't worry, they're all free. Belfast's ornate **City Hall** stands like a wedding cake amid some rather boxy buildings. Take a tour and learn about the Belfast coat of arms (free tours Wed. 10:30am, by advance booking only. Call 32 02 02, ext. 227.) **St. Anne's Cathedral** (also called Belfast Cathedral) lies farther north of the city center; from City Hall, follow Royal Ave. to Donegall St. Begun in 1899 according to the designs of Sir Thomas Drew, the cathedral contains a richly decorated baptistry and the tomb of Unionist leader Lord Carson. The pillar's capitals pay tribute to members of the work force. (Open daily 9am-6pm.) An organ with port and starboard lights carries the tune at **Sinclair Seamen's Church,** Corporation St. (next to Donegall Quay), where the minister delivers his sermon from a carved Moby Dick pulpit. (Open for Sunday services 11am and 7pm. At other times, call 75 77 30.)

Follow Great Victoria St. south from City Hall to **Queen's University.** Originally associated with the old Queen's Colleges at Cork and Galway, the university became an independent institution in 1909. Its attractive Tudor buildings overlook the **Botanic Gardens,** acres of well-groomed parkland with a few scattered picnic benches. The delicately glassed **Palm House,** near the University Rd. entrance, houses a jungle of tropical plants. (Open April-Sept. Mon.-Sat. noon-5pm; Oct.-March Mon.-Fri. 10am-noon and 2-4pm, Sat.-Sun. 2-4pm. Free.) Over 20,000 rose bushes grow on the 128 acres of the newly opened **International Rose Garden** off Upper Malone Rd., a park given to the city in 1959 by Lady Dixon. The garden hosts the **City of Belfast International Rose Trials** from late June to early August, putting new strains to the test amidst a plethora of crowd-pleasing activities. The Belfast Parks Department (tel. 320 202) inspires quests for the red squirrel and the elusive bluebell glade, sponsoring a number of free theme walks throughout the year. In addition, a number of regularly scheduled musical events, tours and mini-marathons flourish alongside the greenery. The paths of the spacious **Lagan Valley Region Park** (off Stranmillis Rd. from University Rd.) lace along the River Lagan. Bus #69 or 71 will take you back to City Hall from the area. The **Ulster Museum and Art Gallery** has built its reputation on the astounding collection of silver and gold looted from the *Girona,* a Spanish Armada ship wrecked off the Giant's Causeway in 1588. (Open Mon.-Fri. 10am-5pm, Sat. 1-5pm, Sun. 2-5pm. Free.) Belfast's luck with its own naval enterprises was little better; it was in Belfast Harbour that the Titanic was built. The rapidly modernizing **Belfast Zoo,** 5 mi. north of the city, can be reached by bus #2, 3, 4, 5, or 6. Don't miss the sub-aquatic view of penguins and seals. (Open daily 10am-6pm; Oct.-March 10am-4:30pm. Admission £2.80, children £1.20, seniors free.)

Entertainment

The best sources of information on Belfast's increasingly lively entertainment scene are the tourist office's *What's On,* the Arts Council's *Artslink,* and the daily *Belfast Telegraph.* The truly **Grand Opera House,** Great Victoria St. (tel. 241 919), is Belfast's main performance center, hosting visiting and local ballet, opera, and theater. Advance booking office is on Glengall St. (open Mon.-Sat. 9:45am-5:30pm). Both the **Arts Theatre,** on Botanic Ave. (tel. 324 936), and **Lyric Players Theatre,** 55 Ridgeway St. (tel. 660 081), house their own companies; the Arts Theatre specializes in popular theater with some musical productions, while the Lyric Players Theatre presents Irish and international plays. (Both open Sept.-June.) **Ulster Hall,** Linenhall St. (tel. 229 685), and **Grosvenor Hall,** Glengall St. (tel. 241 917), present a broad spectrum of music from classical to pop. In November, Queen's College hosts the **Belfast International Festival,** a three-week extravaganza of drama and music that is the second largest art festival in the U.K. after Edinburgh's Internationl Festival (contact the Festival House, 8 Malone Rd., Belfast BT9 SBN; tel. (0232) 667 687).

Near Belfast

Getting around Belfast's environs is relatively simple; buses and trains cover the area comprehensively and efficiently. Bus fares hover around the £3 mark and trains cost little more. Local buses leave from the Oxford St. Station and suburban trains from the York Rd. Station.

Tiny **Carrickfergus,** 8 mi. northeast of Belfast on the Antrim coast, was a thriving port when Belfast was just a village. It claims to be Ireland's oldest town and has the massive **Carrickfergus Castle,** the oldest Norman castle in Ireland, to prove it. The castle, seat of English power in the northern provinces from the 12th to the 17th century, has weathered its 800-odd years well and still commands a spectacular view of the harbor from its tower. A brigade of fiberglass figures resembling medieval Disney characters has recently taken up a post at the castle; see "Adam the Archer" in action. To reach the castle from the train station, walk down Victoria St. onto cobbled, pedestrian North St. until the road meets the water; you can't miss the castle. (Open April-Sept. Mon.-Sat. 10am-6pm, Sun. 2-6pm; Oct.-March Mon.-Sat. 10am-4pm, Sun. 2-4pm. Admission 75p, under 16 and seniors 35p.) In late June, the castle hosts 2 medieval banquets with medieval entertainment (jugglers and the like), mulled wine and a rather 90's menu of BBQed ribs and chicken. Reserve early and get a costume. (£15/person; call (09603) 516 04 for information). If you wish to stay in the area, try Jean Kernohan's **Marathon House** at 3 Upper Station Rd. (tel. (0231) 862 475) in Greenisland, another tiny village not far from Carrickfergus in the direction of Belfast, accessible by train. Jean's B&B is a short walk up the hill from the station. Set back from the road in a beautiful English garden, it offers large rooms at a reasonable price (£10). Ask for the front room on the second floor with a private bath (no extra cost). Frequent Ulsterbus coaches run to Carrickfergus from Belfast (every ½hr., last return 10:30pm, Sun. 4/day, last return 10pm; £1.23, return £2.25). The Belfast-Larne train also stops here (every ½hr., Sun. every hr.; £1.35, return £2.10, Travelsave reductions apply).

Larne

The ferries to Scotland are the only imaginable reason for a trip to Larne. If you must stay here, contact one of the two tourist offices: **Council Offices,** Victoria Rd. (tel. (0574) 723 13), with information on all 6 Northern Irish provinces (open Mon.-Fri. 9am-1pm and 2-5pm); **Larne Borough Council,** in a caravan parked at the **Murrayfield Shopping Centre** (tel. (0574) 713 13; open mid-June to Aug. Mon.-Sat. 10am-6pm).

Sealink (Larne office (0574) 736 16) runs eight boats/day Monday through Saturday (1:30pm-11pm) and four to six boats on Sunday (8am-8pm) between Larne and **Stranraer** in Scotland (2¼ hr.). (Stranraer office tel. (0776) 22 62; Belfast office, 33-7 Castle Lane, tel. (0232) 327 525.) Fares for foot passengers from June through August are £17, students with ISIC £13, seniors and children £9.50; for off-season fares deduct £1, Fri.-Sun. add 50p.

P&O Ferries runs at least four and sometimes as many as six boats per day (4am-11pm, Sun. 8am-8pm) from Larne to **Cairnryan,** 5 mi. up the coast from Stranraer (2¼ hr.; £16, seniors and children £8; Sept. to mid-June £14.50, students £12.50, seniors and children £7.50). Book ahead for Friday and Saturday sailings in July and August. P&O Ferries have offices in Cairnryan (tel. (05812) 276) and in Larne (tel. (0574) 743 21; daily 7:30am-7:30pm). Either ferry company carries bikes free of charge.

Trains run between Belfast's York Rd. Station and Larne Harbour (Mon.-Fri. 22/day 6:35-10pm, Sat. 20/day 6:45am-10:46pm, Sun. 6/day 11:30am-9:05pm; 50 min.; £3.10; Larne office tel. (0232) 235 282), and buses leave frequently from Larne Harbour for Belfast's Oxford St. Station (Mon.-Fri. 9/day 7:10am-6:05pm, Sat. 9/day 7:15am-7:45pm, Sun. 3/day 12:50am-7:45pm; 50 min.; £2). Be sure your train or bus terminates in Larne Harbour so you don't end up at the next to last stop, Larne Town, with a long way to walk.

Mourne Mountains

The 12 rounded peaks of the Mourne Mountains unfold in the southeastern corner of Northern Ireland, covering an area 15 mi. long and 8 mi. wide. The solitude of their gentle slopes curves down to meet candy-floss entrepreneurs at the coastal towns of Newcastle, Annalong, Kilkeel, Greencastle, Rostrevor, Warrenpoint and Newry. During the 18th century, the coast south of Newcastle was the scene of illicit importation of goods from the Isle of Man; more recently, amusement parks, golfing and hiking have replaced smuggling as the choice entertainments of the region.

Getting There and Getting Around

Getting to the Mournes is relatively easy; getting around the area on anything but your own steam is a royal pain. While the hills and dales of the Mournes make for easy rambling, no public transport crosses the ridges. From the Belfast Oxford St. Station there are regular buses to Newcastle (Mon.-Fri. 15/day 7:08am-8:15pm, Sat. 12/day, Sun. 9/day; 2 hr.; £2.95) and Newry (Mon.-Fri. 13/day 7:20am-6:45pm, Sat. 10/day, Sun. 6/day; 1 hr. 10 min.; £3.30). No direct bus service connects Newcastle and Newry; change buses at Kilkeel, midway between them on the coastal A2. (Buses from Newcastle to Kilkeel: 15/day 8am-11:05pm, Sun. 8/day 11:05am-11pm; 40 min.; £1.80. From Kilkeel to Newry: 12/day 7am-9pm, Sun. 4/day 10:30am-5:50pm; 55 min.; £2.40.)

Orientation and Practical Information

The **Mourne Mountain Centre,** 91 Central Promenade (tel. 240 59) in Newcastle, does its best to meet all your needs. It sells Ordnance Survey maps (OSNI sheet maps 20 and 29 cover most of the mountains; £2.50-2.70 each), offers frequent organized walks of 3-6 mi. (free), and supplies plenty of pamphlets, including *Mourne Mountain Walks,* which traces trails and gives information on sights and wildlife (£5). *Scenic Drives Through the Mourne Mountains,* available at the center, not only outlines coastal and mountain trails 30 to 50 mi. in length, but also gives encapsulated histories of bridges, rivers and stones along the way. Also check the center for last-minute weather reports; on any trip, in any season, bring along plenty of warm clothing and rain gear. Leave a detailed plan of your route and schedule with the police before leaving (and be sure to tell them when you're home safe, too). (Open Mon.-Fri. 9am-7pm, Sat.-Sun. noon-8pm; mid-Sept. to May only Sat.-Sun. 10:30am-5pm.) The *Mourne Rambling Group* (tel. (03967) 243 15) also offers free walks. More detailed information is available from the Forest Park Ranger in any of the parks in the area, and visitors centers provide generous bait.

There are only two hostels in the area, both in Newcastle. Fortunately, the B&B industry is alive and well, favoring the countryside over towns. Camping sites are scattered throughout the region, both in the mountains and on the outskirts of towns; pre-book with the Park Ranger for those located in the Forest Parks.

Sights

Newcastle (pop. 6500) serves as a good base for hiking, but be prepared to share the town with some hell-bent vacationers intent on staking out a towel-sized piece of beach, a joy-stick in one of the ubiquitous arcades or a ride on the water slide. It won't be hard to muster the energy to head into the mountains or north along the beach towards the untrammeled dunes. Straight down Main St. from the bus station, the **tourist office,** 61 Central Promenade (tel. (03967) 222 22), books accommodations for free and also sells some Ordnance Survey maps (£2.50). (Open Mon.-Sat. 9:30am-10pm, Sun. 2-10:30pm; Oct.-May 9:15am-5pm.) Outfit yourself at **Hilltrekker,** 115 Central Promenade (tel. 238 42), which sells everything from raingear to comfy boots. (Open Mon.-Fri. 10am-5:30pm, Sat.-Sun. 10am-6pm.)

To reach Newcastle's **IYHF youth hostel,** 30 Downs Rd. (tel. 03967) 221 33), turn left at the bus station and right at the beach; it's at the end of the first block—or just follow the signs. Occupying a prime spot on the ocean, this newly renovated hostel is clean and modern with great views of surf's turf. (Lockout 11am-5pm. Curfew 11:30pm. £5.90, under 18 £4.90. Open Feb.-Dec.) The **YMCA** (Rathmourne Guesthouse), 143 Central Promenade (tel. (03967) 244 88), clean but cramped, is a bit of a hike from the bus station. Christian posters abound, along with hedonistic views of the water. (£9, book well in advance in summer months as it is popular with groups.) **Castlebridge House,** Mrs. K.C. Lynch, 2 Central Promenade (tel. 232 09), right after the first bridge before a sweet shop, will give you the run of her kitchen at night. Wee cozy rooms and a good location make this a popular spot (£11). For a hearty Ulster Fry breakfast after a comfortable night's rest, head to **Aurora,** 26 Bryansford Rd. (tel. 223 70); take the first right after the last set of lights on Central Promenade. Tired of ocean views? Gaze at the green by **Golflinks House,** 109 Dundrum Rd. (tel. 220 54); turn right in front of the bus station and right again onto Belfast Rd., walk for 10 min., then look to your left. Some rooms with bath, all with plush velour headboards (£10). Campers are in for a treat at **Tollymore Forest Park,** 176 Tullybranigan Rd. (tel. (03967) 224 28), a 2-mi. walk or easy hitch along the A2. Excellent facilities include a café with delicious doughnuts, showers and a wildfowl exhibit. The park has an arboretum and 584 hectares of well-marked walks and gardens (sites for tents £3, for campers £5.25, you must book ahead). Inquire at the tourist office or the Mourne Mountain Centre about camping in the wooded areas of the slopes above Newcastle, or camp in Newcastle at the less scenic sights along Dundrum Rd.

Slieve Donard (2796 ft.), the Mourne's highest peak, overlooks Newcastle and Dundrum Bay to bring the Isle of Man into its sights. In the quiet Mourne heartland, Silent Valley cradles the Ben Crom dam and the two lakes which provide all of Belfast's water. Eat your lunch at Ben Crom's visitors center, which provides picnic sites and a tea room. In the summer months a shuttle bus runs to the area. Nearby Castlewellan and Tollymore Parks combine scenery and leisure centers as well as extensive camping grounds.

The A2 splits into two roads just north of Newcastle. Four mi. northwest of Newcastle on the A50 is **Castlewellan Forest Park,** which began as an arboretum in 1740. Inside the park, a Scottish baronial castle overlooks a small lake surrounded by Castlewellan Gold, the park's unique species of cypress. It has a tropical birdhouse, BBQ sites and a photographer on hand for wedding photos. You can camp here for £6/site high season, £5 mid season, £3 low season (tel. (03967) 786 64; call Mon.-Fri. 8am-4:30pm for information and mandatory site booking). The Newcastle-Castlewellan bus stops here (every hr., Sun. every 2 hr.). Four mi. northeast of Newcastle on the A2 lies **Dundrum** (pop. 1800) on Dundrum Bay. The town is rather humdrum and the swimming is better at Newcastle, but the impressive ruins of **Dundrum Castle,** built in 1177 AD on the site of a Celtic fort, imperiously guard the bay. (Grounds free and open at all times. Keep open Tues.-Sat. 10am-7pm, Sun. 2-7pm; late Oct.-March Sat. 10am-4pm, Sun. 2-4pm. Admission 50p, children 25p.) Hitch or take bus #17 or 20 (every hr., Sun. every 2 hr.) to the town.

A less attractive and more politically volatile base for touring the Mourne Mountains is **Newry,** an old merchant town near the Irish border with a **tourist office** at Monaghan Row in the District Council Centre (tel. (0693) 654 11; open Mon.-Fri. 9am-1pm). Walk up the Flagstaff Hill for an exquisite view over **Carlingford Lough** and **Slieve Gullion** to the southwest. Slieve Gullion, once home to Celtic mythical heroes, is itself a wonderful mountain climb, with two stone-age cairns at the top. Take the road (it leads ¾ of the way up), then hike further for views across Ireland. **Kilnasaggart Stone,** Ireland's earliest datable Christian monument, lies nearby, east of the bridge. Ask at the tourist office for directions. Lasso a bite to eat at Newry's **Edsel's the Rock Café,** Merchant's Quay (tel. (0693) 632 21), across the bridge from the pedestrian shopping district. Edsel "loves all and serves all" amid hanging tubas and Confederate flags. Pizzas (£2.60), burgers (£3.50) and meat and veggie specials (£2.95). (Open daily noon-midnight.)

Between Newry and Newcastle on the A2 coast road lie **Rostrevor** and **Kilkeel,** both pleasant places to camp. Near Rostrevor are the riverside Fairy Glen and the hilltop monument Cloc Mor ("Big Stone"). Camp at **Kilbroney Park** (tel. (06937) 381 34), which has showers and washing machines (sites for tents £3.50, campers £5.50). Kilkeel has some nice stretches of beach and good camping at **Chestnutt Caravan Park** (tel. (06937) 626 53). Chestnutt has fewer tent sites but more facilities than Kilbroney (£4.50/night).

Armagh

Set in the fertile "Orchards of Ireland" southwest of Belfast, Armagh has flourished during all ages. Referred to as the "Ecclesiastical Capital" of Ireland, Armagh is home to two magnificent cathedrals. The **Church of Ireland Cathedral of St. Patrick** layers pagan, Viking and 18th and 19th century architecture atop the original medieval structure. Across town on Cathedral Rd. lies the **Catholic Church of St. Patrick,** with its heady spires and rich interior decoration. The vast green **Mall** stretches off-center between the two, blessedly unscathed by leisure center construction. Elegant houses designed by 18th century architect Francis Johnston line the streets around the Mall. On the Mall's eastern side, the **Armagh County Museum** recounts the town's history through clothing, tools and pottery (open Mon.-Sat. 10am-1pm, 2-5pm). The **Armagh Observatory,** College St., built in 1790 at the northern corner of the Mall, is still fully operational. See the stars at the **Planetarium,** farther down the same street. (Shows at 2pm and 3pm; June-Aug. Mon.-Sat., May-Sept. Sat. only. Admission £2, under 18 £1.50.) You'll find all 163 ft. of the 13th century **Franciscan Friary,** the longest friary in Ireland, at Dobbin Lane on the southern fringe of town. Clinch your visit with a peek at a first edition of *Gulli-*

ver's Travels, complete with Swift's own marginal scrawls at the **Armagh Public Library,** Abbey St. in the town center. (Open Mon.-Fri. 10am-12:30pm, 2pm-4pm.)

For more information and a rainforest's worth of handy pamphlets, visit the **tourist office,** Old Bank Building, 40 English St. (tel. (0861) 527 88); plenty of signs will direct you there. Rent a two-wheeler at **Brown's Bikes,** 32 Cormeen Rd. (tel. (0861) 522 782) in nearby Killylea, for a trip into the surrounding countryside (£5/day). Armagh's B&B count is far from robust, but there are 2 good ones on Cathedral Rd. The more central of the two is **Padua House,** 63 Cathedral Rd. (tel. (0861) 523 584), just beyond the Catholic cathedral. Intimate rooms and an Irish breakfast for £9. Rural **Atavellen House,** 99 Cathedral Rd. (tel. (0861) 522 387), has a lovely garden indeed. (Singles £12.50, doubles £10.50/person.) Most of your other needs can be met on Upper and Lower Old English St. The **post office,** 46-50 Upper English St. (open Mon.-Fri. 7am-6pm, Sat. 7am-3pm), is close to most of the major banks (open Tues.-Fri. 10am-3:30pm, Mon. 9:30am-5pm). If you want a break from Ulster Fry, get breakfast for under a quid at any one of the countless bakeries, or pick up supplies at **Emerson's,** a discount supermarket at 57 Scotch St. off Old English. A host of restaurants dish up suspiciously similar food. At 20 Thomas St., a continuation of Old English St., **Pub with No Beer** (tel. (0861) 523 586) serves sandwiches (75p-£1.25), hot dishes and a variety of pastries in a pub with no flair. Quench your thirst with dark and foamy hot chocolate or bubbly mineral water. (Open Mon.-Sat. 9am-10:30pm, sandwiches only after 6pm.) Come to terms with the formica and muzak at **Hester's Place,** 12 English St. (tel. (0861) 522 374), and sink your teeth into a good, cheap burger (£1.40) or a special with chips (£2.50). (Open Mon.-Tues., Thurs.-Sat. 9am-5:30pm.) **The Lantern,** 40 Scotch St. (tel. (0861) 524 395) off Old English, opts for a cafeteria-style self-service. (Open Mon.-Tues., Thurs.-Sat., 9am-5:30pm.)

Buses run to Armagh's Mall West station from Belfast's Glengall St. Station (Mon.-Fri. 12/day 8am-9:15pm, Sat. 11/day, Sun. 6/day; 1 hr. 45 min.; £3.60). Hitchhikers can try thumbing on the A3, which runs from Belfast's southwest corner straight into Armagh.

Glens of Antrim

The A2 from Belfast to the northerly Causeway Coast passes by the verdant Glens of Antrim. Glenarm, Glencloy, Glenariff, Glenballyeamon, Glenaan, Glencorp, Glendun, Glenshesk, and Glentaisie are the nine deep valleys that run from the undulating moorlands on the high plateau of County Antrim down to the rocky coast. Here the scenic coast road twists from one fishing village to another along 49 mi. of dramatic coastline. The chance to hike through the lush glens or on rocky beaches is reason enough to visit, but lagging tourism has forced many once-prosperous resorts into disrepair, and the facilities are not as good as those farther north on the Causeway Coast.

Getting There and Getting Around

Bus service to and through the Glens is extremely poor; the only dependable north-south transport is the Belfast-Portrush express. One bus runs north in the morning and another runs south in the late afternoon, stopping at every town on the Antrim coast. (June 3-Sept.1, Mon.-Sat. only; £4.60, £8 return.) Another bus runs around noon from Belfast as far as Cushendall with a connection in Larne (£4, £7 return). Most rides within the Glens average £3 each way. Buses from outside the Larne rail station sometimes go as far north as Cushendall but usually stop at Carnlough, 10 winding mi. south of Cushendall (Mon.-Fri. 6/day 10:25am-6:10pm, Sat. 7/day 8:45am-7:30pm, Sun. 2/day 12:45pm-5:05pm; 2 hr. 15 min.; £3.85, £6.90). Call Ulsterbus (tel. (0232) 331 577) for more information. Many hitch a ride along these lovely beach- and cliff-lined roads; although the drivers are generally friendly, cars are infrequent. Cycling is as always fabulous, although cycles are hard to come by and the lovely stretch between Cushendall and Cushendun is quite steep in places. **Araclinis Activity Centre,** High St., Cushendall (tel. (02667) 713 70), rents mountain bikes (£10/day) as well as windsurfing boards, hiking boots, tents and backpacks. (Group surfing or walking tours for £5/person; group must be larger than 10.)

Sights

Antrim's southernmost glen is Glenarm, at the foot of which lies **Glenarm Village** (the oldest in the Glens). Here one finds several pubs, a few stray artists, and **Mrs. Boyle,** Toberwine St. (tel. (057484) 219). This B&B above the convenience store has big and comfy rooms from May to October for £10. The main street of Glenarm wanders inland to **Glenarm Forest,** where you can walk along the river for several miles. **Glenarm Castle,** hiding behind the trees north of the river, is the residence of the 13th Earl of Antrim and closed to the public. You can stretch out on the green amongst the graves in front of the peculiar **St. Patrick Church,** on the coast road as you approach from Carnlough.

An easy 3-mi. hitch (or ride on the Larne bus) northwards brings you to **Carnlough,** a somewhat rundown resort town strung along a broad beach. The **tourist office** is in the **post office** on Harbour Rd. (tel. (0574) 852 10), run by the wonderful McSparronses. (Open Mon.-Tues. and Thurs.-Fri. 9am-6pm, Wed. and Sat. 9am-12:30pm.) The **Bethany Christian Guesthouse,** 5 Bay Rd. (tel. (0574) 856 67), has colorful, crucifix-bedecked rooms, aerial views of Sydney on the placemats, and an elderly crowd (£11.50). **Mrs. Davison,** 2-3 Bridge St. (tel. 856 69), has noisier rooms above smoky McCauley's Pub. (Singles £10, doubles £9/person.) The town perks up at night when the locals gather for pints and singing in the pubs. **Black's Pub,** on Harbour Rd., draws most of the locals and has impromptu folk music sessions most nights. The fortunate might catch onetime Irish fiddle champion Jim McKillop; in his local shop, he makes, sells, and repairs stringed instruments, using handmade tools. Inquire at the tourist office for details. The **Marine Take-Out and Café** next door on Marine Rd. serves budget fare in a family atmosphere. (Takeout Sun.-Thurs. 11am-midnight, Fri. 11am-12:30am.)

Two mi. farther down the coast, the village of **Waterfoot** guards Glenariff, Antrim's broadest glen. Another four mi. down the road to Glenariff Forest Park, waterfalls feed the River Glenariff while lovely tree-shaded hills stand guard. To save yourself the 3-mi. uphill hike to the official park entrance, take the downhill road that branches left towards the restaurant. The waterfalls are directly behind it. The Ballymena-Cushendun bus (Mon.-Fri. every 2 hr., Sat. 4/day) passes right by the park entrance. **Glen Vista,** 245 Garron Rd. (tel. (02667) 714 39), near the beach at the foot of the glen after the caravan park, has huge pastel rooms with views from £9 (open June-Sept.). Many farmers in the area welcome campers, as does the **Glenariff Forest Park,** 98 Glenariff Rd. (tel. (026673) 232; tents £3, campers £5.25/site). The **Glens of Antrim Feis,** one of Northern Ireland's major music and dance festivals, is held in July. For information on the 1992 festival, contact the Belfast tourist office.

Considered the capital of the Antrim Glens, **Cushendall,** 2 mi. north of Waterfoot, has a **tourist office** (tel. (02667) 711 80) next to the library. (Open July-Aug. Mon.-Sat. 10am-6pm, Sun. 2-6pm.) Bikes and the like can be found at the **Ardclinis Activity Centre** on High St. (tel. (02667) 713 40), open daily 8am-11pm or until the sun goes down. Collapse in the rooms upstairs after you return your vehicle; B&B offered for £10. If you prefer a womb of greenery, the **Cushendall youth hostel (IYHF)** (tel. (02667) 713 44) is 1 mi. from town; go down Shore St., take the left fork as you leave town, and watch for the youth hostel initials on the wall. Perfectly practical, once you get there. (Open daily, Nov.-Jan. Thurs.-Tues.; £5.65, under 18 £4.65.) About ¾ mi. farther up the hill is a **campsite/mobile home park** with a view of the countryside (tel. (02667) 715 20; £3-4; minimal facilities). **Riverside,** 14 Hill St. (tel. 716 55) has happily done away with the doll collections and over-stuffed velour chairs, existing in tasteful tea-drinking elegance. (£10; teaset in each room.) **Troshen Villa,** 8 Coast Rd. (tel. 711 30), has an abundance of beds, and the huge garden extends deceivingly far into the golf course (£10). **Tieveragh Hill** soars above town, remarkable for its flattened top and for the many "little people" or fairies reputed to live inside it. **Ossian's Grave** is a megalithic court cairn that tradition identifies as the grave of Ossian the Ulster bard, an adventurer who Yeats claimed debated with St. Patrick on the superiority of a warrior's ways to womanly prayer and fasting. (Take the A2 south from Cushendun to the lower slopes of Tievebulliagh Mountain and look for the sign at the base, just before Cushendall, or ask a local, only too happy to share some local lore.) The views from here are genuinely lovely, despite the fact that Ossian was first popularized widely by an 18th-century Scottish poet. On the mountain's lower slopes, check out the remains of the Stone Age axe factory whose products were once sold all over Britain. After a long day of walking, rest your feet at **Joe McCullum's,** or "Johnny Joe's", a tiny, ancient barroom at 23 Mill St. Their lively traditional nights, held every summer Saturday and Thursday, feature impromptu singing, fiddling, yarn-spinning and drinking until 11pm. Foodwise, the town is somewhat limited, featuring a couple of butchers, a bakery and 2 supermarkets. One of them is on the road to the hostel: **McCalister,** 8 Shore St. (open Mon.-Sat. 8:30am-8:30pm, Sun. 10:15am-6:15pm. Five mi. north via an inland road that climbs up through the moors, the National Trust preserves the tiny village of **Cushendun,** known for its Cornish-style cottages and natural beauty. The **tourist office** is on the main street in the National Trust Office (tel. (026674) 506; open May to mid-Sept. daily noon-6pm). **Catherine Scally,** The Villa, 185 Torr Rd. (tel. (026674) 252), has a great B&B 1 mi. from town on a particularly scenic portion of the Ulster Way. Her 19th-century farmhouse on a hill has superb views of the village, sea, and glens (£12; open year-round). You can camp at the **Cushendun Caravan Site** (tel. (026674) 254; £5.75). **Pat's Bar** is a comfortable pub 1 mi. out the Cushendall Rd.

Seven mi. north of Cushendun, just south of Ballycastle, is **Fair Head,** a magnet for international hikers, where basalt cliffs dive straight down to rocky scree. This is one of the most dramatic points on the Irish coast. On a clear day you can see Rathlin Island, Donegal, and Scotland. Just to the south, the small, undiscovered **Murlough Bay,** protected by the National Trust, is a beautiful inlet down a long, steep road from Crockanore. Many hitch or take the bus to Torr Head or further to Ballycastle (see Causeway Coast section); Fair Head is a 3-mi. hike along the coastal path from either.

Causeway Coast

On the northernmost shores of the mainland, between Ballycastle in the east and Portstewart in the west, 600-ft. cliffs plummet into the restless surf, which over eons has pounded out some of the country's finest sand beaches at their base. Near the center of this stretch, the white beach is interrupted by a honeycomb path of black and red hexagonal columns of a freak rock formation dubbed the Giant's Causeway. The northern coast is a choice spot to sample fresh salmon, trout, and *dulse.* Soda farls and potato breads, other traditional favorites, are served at breakfast.

Although transportation is far better from Derry and Portrush in the west, the most attractive area is towards the east, near the Antrim Coast Rd.

Getting There and Getting Around

The A2 connects the towns along the causeway. Those hitching along the A2 or the inland roads (marginally quicker) find the going to be slow due to the lack of cars. **Ulsterbus** runs tours through the area, and during July and August the open-topped **Bushmills Bus** (tel. (0265) 433 34) follows the coast between Coleraine (5 mi. south of Portrush) and the Giant's Causeway (4/day, Sun. 2/day; £1.95, £2.40 day return). Ulsterbus #172 runs all the way from Ballycastle to Portrush, following the coastline. The bus can be flagged down anywhere along its route.

(Mon.-Fri. 7/day 7:30am-6:05pm, Sat. 5/day 9:50am-6:05pm; 1 hr.; £2) and it goes via Bushmills and the Giant's Causeway. From points further south along the Antrim coast, many rely on their thumbs or the express bus from Belfast starting June 3rd and running through August (9/day in each direction, leaving Ballycastle 12:20pm for Portrush or 5:20pm for Belfast; 1 hr., 3 hr.).

From Ballycastle to Portstewart

The most prominent towns and sights along the coast, in order of appearance from east to west, are Ballycastle and Raithlin Island, Ballintay and Carrick-a-rede Island, Whitepark Bay, the Giant's Causeway, Portrush, and Portstewart. At the eastern edge of the Causeway Coast, **Ballycastle** is a resort town of rose gardens and comfortable parks suffused with an old-world glow. Its amusement arcades, limited to a few on the waterfront, are hardly as oppressive as those at Portrush, making Ballycastle an ideal spot to be near the action without being thrown headlong into it. The **tourist office** is in Sheskburn House at 7 Mary St. (tel. (02657) 620 24; open Mon.-Fri. 9:30am-5pm; July-Aug., Sat. 10am-4pm, Sun. 1-5pm). Ballycastle's **postal code** is BT54 6AA. The new **Castle Hostel,** 62 Quay Rd. (tel. 623 37), at the corner of North St. by the water, is an independent hostel run by Liam, an exuberant ex-safari leader, who will treat you like closest kin. Best duvets/bunks in Ulster, tons of useful info everywhere and a well equipped kitchen with toaster. No curfew or lockout—so much trust, for only £5. Around the corner, **Fair Head View,** 26 North St. (tel. 628 22; £9) offers good, basic rooms, a hearty breakfast and a cozy fire in the sitting room. For just a bit more, **Fragrens,** 34 Quay Rd. (tel. 621 68; £9.50, £10 with bath) spoils you with TV, afternoon tea trays at your door, a navigable 2nd floor tub and odd corner showers in your own room. There's laundry at the **Silver Cliffs Caravan Park,** beyond the supermarket, up the hill from North St., for 85p a load.

Inexpensive take-aways are in the town square. **Donnelly's** at the top of Quay St. is a popular bakery and coffee shop serving pizza (£1.45), quiche (£1.60), and a tumult of sugary desserts (open Mon.-Sat. 9am-6pm). Across the street, **McCarroll's** pub dishes up such delicacies as haddock and chips (£2) or lasagna and chips (£2.80) between noon and 2:30pm. **McLister's** one-stop grocery/hardware store has a good, inexpensive selection (open Mon.-Tues. and Thurs.-Sat. 9am-6pm). Or, if you're nearer to the water, there's **Boyle's** on North St. (open daily 9am-10pm). Northern Ireland's oldest and most popular fair, the **"Ould Lammas Fair,"** is held in Ballycastle on the last Monday and Tuesday of August. This is the best time of year to sample *dulse* (nutritious seaweed dried on local roofs), or *yellow-man* (a sticky toffee made from a secret recipe).

Just off the coast at Ballycastle, boomerang-shaped **Rathlin Island** is the ultimate in escapism for 20,000 puffins, the odd golden eagle, and about 100 beings human. Its mostly treeless surface is edged with 200-ft. cliffs. Legend has it that Robert the Bruce hid in one of the island's many caves (actually underneath the east lighthouse) after his defeat by the English in 1306. Inspired by a spider, who tried again and again to climb to the ceiling on its web, Bruce returned to win the Scottish throne. Two **ferries** run to the island from Ballycastle (daily 10:30am, return 4pm; off-season Mon., Wed., Fri. only; return £5, children £2.50): **Rathlin Venture** (tel. (02657) 639 17) and **Rathlin Ferries** (tel. (02657) 712 07). **Mrs. McCurdy** (tel. (02657) 639 17) operates a guesthouse on the island (B&B £10). She can also arrange passage for you.

Five mi. west of Ballycastle is the bleached village of **Ballintoy,** with a picturesque church and a tiny harbor. **Boat trips** (£1, children 50p) run every half-hour on summer weekends past Sheep Island to **Carrick-a-rede Island** ("rock in the road")—salmon swim around it into the traps of the islands 350-year-old fishery. This is a great opportunity to get a view of the stunning, chalky cliffs of the Causeway Coast from the ocean side. For boat information talk to John at the bar of the **Carrick-a-rede** Pub. It is also possible to walk to **Carrick-a-rede:** about ¾ mi. east of Ballintoy village, a signposted path branches off the main road. The plank-and-rope **Carrick-a-rede Bridge,** a rattly structure that swings 80 ft. above the swirling waters, connects the island to the mainland and is the most thrilling part of the excursion. On windy days you'll literally be swept off your feet. On the island itself you can get within feet of cliff nesting black'n'white razor bills (which look like mini-penguins) as well as the more mundane sea gulls. (Open May to mid-Sept. Free.) Check the **National Trust Information Centre** on the island for detailed information (tel. (02657) 633 13; open May-Sept. daily 2-6pm).

Two mi. west of Ballintoy village, just around the point from the harbor, lie the golden sands of **Whitepark Bay.** Overlooking this stunning beach is the well-kept, cement-walled **IYHF youth hostel** (tel. (02567) 317 45; lockout 11am-2pm; curfew 11:30pm; £6.15, under 16 £5.15; open daily Feb.-Nov.). Every morning, hostelers set out for the Giant's Causeway, a 4-mi. hitch north along the A2 or a rocky, sweaty 8 mi. along the windswept but rewardingly stunning **North Antrim Coastal Path** (be sure to take warm clothing).

The **Giant's Causeway** is one of the seven natural wonders of the world and deservedly Northern Ireland's most famous sight. Unlike other big tourist attractions, it is neither overcrowded nor disappointing. Forty thousand hexagonal columns of basalt form a honeycomb path from the foot of the cliffs into the sea. Although modern scientists can explain the formation as a geological freak—the result of volcanic action—Irish legend holds that it is the path of Finn McCool, the warrior giant who inhabited the Antrim Headlands, and "lived most happy and content/ Obeyed no laws and paid no rent." Retreating from the even vaster Scotsman Benandonner, McCool tore up a highway he had built to Scotland; only this fragment off the Irish coast remains.

Many paths loop to and from the Giant's Causeway. The **National Trust Visitors Centre** (tel. (02657) 315 82), near the head of the Causeway, has an excellent trail leaflet (35p) that will guide you the 8 mi. back to Whitepark Bay or along several shorter circular walks. They also run mini-buses the ½mi. to the columns every 15 minutes and have a slide show on the fact and fiction of the Causeway for the truly curious (£1). (Open July-Aug. daily 10am-7pm; April-June and Sept.-Oct. 10:30am-4pm. Causeway open at all times.) To really "see" the Causeway, you should go at least as far as the viewpoint at **Hamilton's Seat,** 2½ mi. from the visitors center. If you're doing a circular walk, take the lower path on the way there and return to the center via the upper cliff path. If you plan to continue past Hamilton's Seat, opt for the lower path. This well-tended track winds through dramatically sculpted amphitheaters and inlets studded with bizarre, creatively named formations. Although not essential for navigation, the trail leaflet contains a helpful map as well as a basic geological and human history of this dramatic stretch. On a clear day, you can see all the way to the Inishowen Peninsula in Ireland. From nearby **Bengore Head,** the highest point along the northern coast, it's a gradual downhill stroll along the edge of sheep flecked fields to the decidedly unspectacular ruins of **Dunsverick Castle.** The path back towards Whitepark Bay is not always well marked, but bathers and local fishermen can usually point you in the right direction. No matter how tired you are, don't pass by **St. Gobban's,** the smallest church in Ireland, tucked away in the pastel hamlet of **Portbradden,** on the western end of Whitepark's beach. The nearest pub is in Ballintoy, another 2 mi. east.

Although it has its attractions, the western portion of the coast may seem a bit disappointing after the Giant's Causeway and Whitepark Bay. Two mi. west of the National Trust Visitors Centre is **Bushmills,** home of Bushmills Irish Whiskey. Open since 1609, Bushmill's is the oldest functioning whiskey distillery in the world. (Free tours with complimentary sample Mon.-Thurs. at 10:30am; call ahead at (02657) 315 21.) The Bushmills #172 bus from the Giant's Causeway makes the short trip to nearby **Portballintrae.** (July-Aug. 4/day, Sun. 2/day). Portballintrae's **tourist office** (tel. (02657) 316 72) is in a caravan in the seafront parking lot on Beach Rd. (Open July-Aug. Mon.-Sat. 10:30am-6pm.) For a comfortable B&B, try **Mrs. Jackson,** 82 Ballaghmore Rd. (tel. (02657) 312 75; £9.50). Stop at **Craft 'n Coffee,** 47 Beach Rd., for Pig's Last Tango pizza (£1.40). (Open daily 11am-8:30pm; Sept.-June Wed.-Sun. 10am-6pm.)

An easy 2-mi. walk or hitch west brings you to the ruins of **Dunluce Castle,** set romantically on a rock that juts out from a cliff; a cave tunnels down from the castle to the sea. (Open Mon.-Sat. 10am-6pm, Sun. 2-6pm; Oct.-March Tues.-Sat. 10am-4pm, Sun. 2-4pm. Admission 75p, children 35p.) Spend a few relaxing hours here before descending into the tourist bottleneck of **Portrush,** 2 mi. further west along the coast. The #172 Bushmills bus travels to this bingo-mad enclave; regular trains from Belfast also hurtle holidaymakers to this unappealing spot. Unless you relish blaring megatunes and endless arcades, stay here briefly if at all.

The **tourist office** (tel. 823 333), in Portrush's Town Hall, is the largest in the area, with pamphlets, maps, and information on the Causeway Coast. (Open mid-June to mid-Sept. Mon.-Sat. 9am-8pm; April to mid-June and late Sept. Mon.-Sat. 9am-8pm, Sun. 2-6pm.) Mark St. is the place to find B&Bs, all fairly identical in size, character, sightliness, and price (£10). For a bite to eat, head to the **Singing Kettle,** Atlantic Ave., a cute little blue and white affair with a flair for exotic burger specials (£1-3). Veggie Ulster Fry with tea £2.95. (Open daily 10am-6pm.)

Portstewart, at the western end of the Causeway Coast, is a clean beach town that lays claim to the best surfing in Northern Ireland (note the qualifier). Its **tourist office** (tel. (026583) 22 86) is in the town hall. (Open July-Aug.) The walk around the convent (now a school which you can visit if you wish) to the strand is popular on summer evenings. The Victoria Terrace area on the left as you head out of town on the Portrush Rd. is laden with post-promenade beds, and the **Inverness** Independent Hostel, 4 Victoria Terrace (tel. (026583) 37 89; £4.50) is convenient and clean with no curfew or lockout.

Fermanagh Lake District

Located in the southwestern corner of Northern Ireland, the Fermanagh Lake District (fer-MAN-ah) is the perfect place for an amphibious jaunt. A labyrinthine chain of lakes teems with hundreds of tiny islands, on which some of the province's oldest and most intriguing monuments rise against the surrounding hills. Upper and Lower Lough Erne are the largest lakes in a district several times larger, and infinitely less trampled, than England's. Surrounded on three sides by the Irish Republic, Fermanagh is the most relaxed of Northern Ireland's border areas; you'll barely get your passport checked. Except for some control zones in the main town of **Enniskillen,** little is stirring in this quiet green retreat, which makes for idyllic hiking, biking or canoeing. Enniskillen is the primary point of access and touring base for the area.

Getting There and Getting Around

The best way to explore the islands is in a rented boat, affordable for groups of three or more; the going rate is about £25 a day. The tourist office in Enniskillen has an exhaustive list of renters. All except the evening cruises stop at **Devenish Island,** 2 mi. downstream from Enniskillen. This soggy but beautiful mound of earth is home to St. Molaise's ancient monastery and Ireland's best-preserved tower. The island is also served by the **Devenish Island Ferry Service** (tel. (0365) 227 11). Catch it from Trory Point, a 4-mi. hitch from Enniskillen along the A32 towards Irvinestown. (Easter-Sept. Tues.-Sat. 10am-7pm, Sun. 2-7pm, £1.50, children £1.) If you'd prefer to explore the islands and the Enniskillen area by wheel, you can rent mountain bikes or tents from **Cycling Safari Holidays,** 31 Chanterhill Park (tel. (0365) 323 597) or hook up with one of their day trips. North of Enniskillen in **Garrison,** the **Lough Melvin Holiday Centre** (tel. (0365) 658 142) rents all sorts of water vehicles from canoes to surfboards for £9 a day; they also run activities with training for £16 a day, as well as providing cheap accommodations (£8) if you're too pooped to move. Express buses run frequently from Donegal (4/day 12:15-9:15pm, Sun. 2/day 12:20-9:20pm; 1½ hr.), Belfast (10/day 7:20am-6:15pm, Sun. 3/day 9:45am-

8:30pm; 2½ hr.; £5.10, return £9.10), and Dublin (3/day 1010am-6:40pm, Sun. 2/day 3:45-6:40pm; 3 hr.).

Sights

Serious hikers should consider tackling the Fermanagh stretch of the **Ulster Way,** 23 mi. of largely forested paths. The route is marked by wooden posts with a yellow arrow, and leads from Belcoo to Lough Navar with heights of just under 1000 ft. The path is neither smooth nor level, so those on bikes or in wheelbarrows may want to investigate other options. The tourist office's *Ulster Way* pamphlet and Fermanagh's section of the Ulster Way (both 75p) contain detailed descriptions of the route, sights, and history.

Busy **Enniskillen** (EN-skill-in; pop. 12,000) is the place to pick up information and equipment for touring the area. The town lies on an island between Upper and Lower Lough Erne, but you would never know it: the lakes, which masquerade as rivers near town, are hardly visible from the center of town. Enniskillen's one tourist draw is the small **Fermanagh County Museum,** housed in Enniskillen Castle. (Open Mon.-Fri. 10am-5pm; May-Sept. also Sat. 2-5pm, July-Aug. also Sun. 2-5pm. Free.) The well-equipped **Lakeland Visitors Centre,** on Shore Rd. (tel. (0365) 231 10; open Mon.-Fri. 9am-6:30pm, Sat.-Sun. 10am-1pm and 2-5pm; Sept.-June Mon.-Fri. 9am-5pm), next to the bus station, will direct you to the most beautiful spots and book accommodations for 50p. Enniskillen's **telephone code** is 0365.

The B&Bs in town line up on three streets: Henry St., running south from the Anne St. Bridge; Willoughby Pl., running west from the same; and Forthill St., to the east of town off Belmore St. and the cattle market. **Mrs. Elma Nobles,** Lackaboy Farmhouse, Tempo Rd. (tel. 224 88), 1½ mi. out of town, treats you like family. (Singles £15, doubles £10/person.) **Mrs. Mulhern,** Carraig Aonrai Guest House, 19 Sligo Rd. (tel. 248 89), has the least expensive B&B in town (singles £8.50, doubles £8/person), with a nice garden and an 8-course breakfast, 3 of which are bread types.

Heading north out of town by the Portora Gate on the Donegal Rd. a ½mi., look for the **Royal School,** once attended by Oscar Wilde and Samuel Beckett. You can take the bus to the border town of **Belleek,** passing the **Lough Navar Forest Park.** In Belleek's **factory** (tel. (036565) 501), delicate, lace-like Belleek China is made and displayed. (Tours Mon.-Thurs. 9:30am-12:15pm and 2:15-4:15pm, Fri. 9:30am-12:15pm and 2:15-3:15pm. £1, under 12 free.)

One and a half mi. south of Enniskillen is **Castle Coole,** a late 18th-century neoclassical plantation mansion (tel. 226 90; open June-Aug. Wed.-Mon. 2pm-6pm; April-May and Sept. Sat.-Sun. 2pm-6pm; £2, children £1). A slightly older mansion, **Florence Court,** lies just off of Dublin Rd., 5 mi. out of Enniskillen in the **Florence Court Forest Park.** Fermanagh's first forest park includes an impressive walled garden and nature walks. (House open June-Aug. Wed.-Mon. noon-6pm; April-May and Sept. Sat-Sun. 2-6pm. Admission £2, children £1. Park open year-round 10am-dusk.) Four mi. along the road from Florence Court to Belcoo (take the Sligo bus to Belcoo and walk 3 mi.) are the newly opened **Marble Arch Caves,** a subterranean labyrinth of hidden rivers and weirdly sculpted limestone. (Open Easter-Oct. daily 11am-around 6pm. Last tour around 4:30pm. Admission £3, seniors and students £2.50, children £1.50, families £7.50.)

Accommodations

Overnight options outside of Enniskillen include an IYHF youth hostel and camping in **Castle Archdale Park,**10 mi. northwest of Enniskillen on the road to Kesh. The **IYHF youth hostel** (tel. (03656) 281 18), is a mile off the road from Enniskillen to Kesh inside the Castle Archdale Park, in a restored 19th-century house. This modern and spacious hostel has long dormitory rooms with exposed wooden beams, and an excellent kitchen. (Lockout 11am-5pm. £5.65, ages 16-20 £4.65. Open Jan.-Nov.) Although blighted by a large population of caravans, the Castle

Archdale Park is a tolerable place to camp (£3.50-6.50/site). From the marina, a ferry glides to **White Island,** known for its 11th-century church and early Christian carvings. (April-Sept. Tues.-Sat. 10am-7pm, Sun. 2-7pm; £1, children 50p. Call (0365) 227 11 to confirm.) Buses run from Enniskillen to the park entrance in July and August (Mon., Wed., and Sat., 2/day). Otherwise, the Enniskillen-Kesh bus will drop you off a mile from the entrance (every 2 hr., Sun. 1/day; £1.90).

IRELAND

For centuries, Ireland was at the western fringe of the world known to Europeans. Abruptly rising mountains in the southwest and northwest, bleak, windswept sheets of Connemara stone, and the rocky crags of the Wicklow range offered much beauty but little comfort to Ireland's early settlers. Wave after wave of invaders deposited layers of Celtic, Norse, Norman, and English cultural sediment on the land. Ireland's relentless northwest winds and cold wet winters imposed a hardy lifestyle on these early inhabitants. In the past century and a half, emigration and a steady pull to the cities have left the countryside even more remote. Industrialization and tourism continue to break down Ireland's isolation, but the green and gray hills, the rippling fields, the secluded white beaches, and what Henry James called the "strange, dark, lonely freshness of the coast of Ireland" still retain their ancient allure. Ireland is not a land of shillelaghs and fairies and four-leaf clovers, but instead a country with a distinctive and complex culture that has evolved only through centuries of hardship. W.B. Yeats made famous Parnell's words to a celebrating Irishman: "Ireland shall get her freedom and you still break stone."

Money

Ireland's unit of currency is the Irish punt (£). All prices in the Ireland sections of this book, including the fares quoted in the Getting There section below, are in Irish punts, unless otherwise noted. The Northern Ireland pound, currently worth the same as the British pound, is not accepted in the Republic of Ireland, nor is the Irish punt accepted in Northern Ireland. However, British coins up to but not including the £1 coin are accepted in Ireland at the value of their Irish equivalents. Banks in Ireland are open Mon.-Fri. 10am-12:30pm and 1:30-3pm; in Dublin banks stay open until 5pm on Thurs.

Getting There

By Air

Practically all flights to Ireland from outside Europe arrive at Shannon Airport, near Limerick. (Irish coffee was invented at Shannon Airport by a barman trying to console passengers in transit.) The cheapest standard round-trip fare from the U.S. in the summer of 1990 was $590 from New York or Boston to Shannon (for $30 more you can fly in and out of Dublin), booked through Let's Go Travel, CIEE, or USIT (see the General Introduction). Aer Lingus has great deals for travelers from Australia and New Zealand who fly directly to England, providing free shuttle service from London to Dublin.

North Americans should find it easy to catch one of the many flights from Gatwick, Heathrow, Luton, Manchester, Birmingham, Liverpool, and Glasgow airports to Dublin, Shannon, Cork, Knock, and Waterford. Established airlines such as Aer Lingus and British Airways are currently engaged in a price war with upstarts like Ryan Air. Students can fly one way from London to Dublin for £42 if they book through USIT.

By Ferry

Ferries from Britain and France are the most popular way to get to Ireland. Boats run from Fishguard and Pembroke in South Wales to Rosslare in southeastern Ireland, and from Holyhead in north Wales to Dún Laoghaire (pronounced dun-LEAR-y) near Dublin; from Liverpool in northern England to Dublin and Belfast, Northern Ireland; from Stranraer, Scotland to Larne, Northern Ireland; from Le Havre and Cherbourg in Normandy to Cork and Rosslare; and from Roscoff in Brittany to Cork.

Fares on the **Holyhead-Dublin and Fishguard/Pembroke-Rosslare** routes, operated by Sealink and B&I Line, are approximately the same (£22, children half price). Bikes travel for £6 (£12 return); try asking a car driver to keep the bike in his or her trunk. There is a tax of £3 on all ferry passages from Ireland to Britain. IYHF members receive a 25% discount on fares from both Sealink and B&I. ISIC cardholders receive a 25% discount from B&I, and ISIC cardholders with Travelsave stamps (see Getting Around) 50%. Those not hitching to and from port, should buy a through rail or bus ticket from Britain to Ireland. Almost all sailings in June, July, and August are "controlled sailings," which means that you must book the crossing ahead of time (a day in advance should be fine). Sailing time is 3½ hours. Contact **B&I** in London at 150 New Bond St., London W1Y 0AQ (tel. 491 8682); in Holyhead (tel. (0407) 760 222 or 760 223); in Pembroke (tel. (0646) 684 161); in Dublin at 16 Westmoreland St., Dublin 2 (tel. (01) 679 7977); in Rosslare Harbour (tel. (053) 333 11); or in Cork at 42 Grand Parade, Cork (tel. (021) 273 024).

Their after-hours information line in England is (061) 236 3936, in Ireland (01) 606 666. **Sealink** can be reached at 15 Westmoreland St., Dublin 2 (tel. (01) 807 777); in Dún Laoghaire (tel. (01) 774 206); and in Rosslare Harbour (tel. (053) 331 15). For reservations, call (01) 280 8844.

There are crossings from **Rosslare** and **Cork** to **Le Havre** and from **Rosslare** to **Cherbourg.** These routes are served by Irish Ferries, 2/4 Merrion Row, Dublin 2 (tel. (01) 610 511); 9 Bridge St., Cork (tel. (021) 504 333); and at Rosslare Harbour (tel. (053) 331 58). (20 hr., mid-June to mid-July, £70; mid-July to Aug., £90; and Sept. to mid-June, £58. Students (with ISIC) and seniors pay £60, £66, and £39-45 over the same time periods. Inter-Rail cardholders ½ price; Inter-Rail plus Ship cardholders or Eurail pass holders free. Bicycles £11, mid-July through Aug., £16. Brittany Ferries also run from **Cork** to **Roscoff** in Brittany in about 16 hours—single fares range from £47 to 58 (under 15 half-price, under 4 free). Contact Brittany Ferries at Gare Maritime, Port du Bloscon, 29211 Roscoff, France (tel. (98) 612 211), and at 42 Grand Parade, Cork (tel. (021) 277 801). Swansea-Cork ferries, 55 Grand Parade, Cork (tel. (021) 271 166) sail daily in summer, less often in winter (£22, kids ½ price, bikes £7).

Assorted **bus** tickets that include ferry connections between Britain and Ireland are also available as package deals through ferry companies, travel agents, and USIT offices. **Supabus** (run by Bus Éireann) connects Dublin with London for £26-38, return £42-54 (the higher fares are in effect mid-July through Aug.). Supabus tickets can be booked through USIT, any Bus Éireann office in Ireland, or any National Express office in Britain.

Getting Around

Public transport in Ireland is cumbersome and—in more remote regions—usually non-existent. Trains run by **Iarnród Éireann (Irish Rail)** fan out like cat whiskers from Dublin to larger cities, but there is no service between these cities. For schedule information, pick up a free *Inter-City Timetable,* available at most train stations. Buses, operated by **Bus Éireann** reach more destinations than trains, but they are infrequent (even more so on Sundays and during the winter). Coverage of tourist spots, such as the Ring of Kerry, is left to commercial coach tours. Bus Éireann operates both long-distance **Expressway** buses, which link larger cities (free with Eurail), and **Provincial** buses, which serve the countryside and smaller towns. The bus timetable book (45p) is available at the transportation information office at 59 Upper O'Connell St. in Dublin. Train fare from Dublin to Cork is £27.50, to Galway £21; buses are more reasonably priced (£10 and £8, respectively).

By far the most useful travel pass for students is the **Travelsave stamp,** available at any USIT with an ISIC card and £6. Affixed to your ISIC card, this stamp entitles you to a 50% discount on single fares on all national rail and bus services in Ireland (except on bus fares less than £2), and 30% off return fares. Ireland has its share of **Rambler** tickets, but you have to move faster than Mr. Bruce Willis in the motion picture *Die Hard* to make them pay off. The **Road Rambler** ticket offers unlimited bus travel within Ireland on eight out of 15 days (£58); or 15 days out of 30 (£85). The **Rail Rambler** ticket costs the same but western cities only have train service to Dublin. Combined **Rail and Road Rambler** tickets good for unlimited travel on rail and bus lines on any eight of 15 days, cost £75. Purchase these from Bus Éireann at the main tourist office in Dublin, 14 Upper O'Connell St., Dublin 1 (tel. (01) 747 733), or from the Irish Rail information office, 35 Lower Abbey St., Dublin 1 (tel. (01) 366 222).

The **Overlander** ticket allows 15 days unlimited travel on Northern Ireland railway lines and Ulsterbus regular buses, as well as on all regular rail and bus lines within Ireland (£109; children £54). **Eurailpasses** are valid in the Republic of Ireland (but not in Northern Ireland) and entitle the holder to unlimited travel on all trains and Expressway (but not Provincial) buses.

Private bus companies operate between Dublin and many large towns all over the country at rates about half those of Bus Éireann's. They tend to travel in the early morning and evening. **Bus Éireann day tours** are a way of reaching areas not served by major bus routes. Tours operate out of most large cities and cost £5-10; those under 16 usually pay half price.

Those hitching in Ireland glow like tacky ship-lamps in the night; the unfortunate side-effect is a stiff competition for rides. In more remote areas, many follow bus routes so they can wave down buses when their luck runs out. In general, more rides are given on the East coast than in the Northwest, and Sundays are a particularly dead day for hitchhikers. (See Getting Around in the General Introduction for more information.)

You can rent 3-, 5-, and 10-speed bikes from **Raleigh Rent-a-Bike** shops almost anywhere in the country for £7 per day, £30 per week, plus £10-30 deposit. The shops will equip you with locks, patch kits, and pumps and for longer journeys, pannier bags (£5 per week). A list of Raleigh dealers is available at most tourist offices and bike shops; you might also contact **TI Irish Raleigh Limited,** Kylemore Rd., Dublin 10 (tel. (01) 261 333). Many small local dealers and hostels also rent bikes. Tourist offices sell *Cycling Ireland* (with map, £2).

The initial cost of renting a car and the price of petrol (about £2.75 per gallon) will astound you. People under 21 cannot rent, and those under 25 often encounter difficulties. Try **Boland Car Rentals,** 206 Pearse St., Dublin 2 (tel. (01) 770 704), with offices in Cork, Wexford, Waterford, and Limerick; or **Budget Rent-A-Car,** Dublin Airport (tel. (01) 370 919 or 420 793). You won't get anything cheaper than £25 per day. Most firms will rent to those without international licenses. The Irish drive on the left. Children under 12 are not allowed to sit in the front seat of a car; seatbelts are mandatory for drivers and passengers in the front.

Long-distance **walking** is boffo. Youth hostels often lie within 20 scenic mi. of each other. The best hillwalking maps are the Ordnance Survey ½-in.-to-1-mi. series; £3 each. Consult *Dublin and the Wicklow Mountains—Access Route for Hillwalkers* (£1), the tourist office's pamphlet *Walking in Ireland* (£2), and Hart's *Climbing in the British Isles—Ireland.* Also contact the **Federation of Mountaineering Clubs of Ireland,** 20 Leopardstown Gardens, Blackrock, County Dublin (tel. (01) 881 266), for a comprehensive list of hillwalking and rock-climbing guide books.

The sights of Ireland are spectacular for the obvious reasons, but also because the Irish government, demonstrating respect not only for its historical treasures but also the curiosity of the student, offers a Student Heritage Card for £4. It will get you into all of Republic's sights free and can be purchased at any sight. It also comes with a map and a lovely carrying case.

Accommodations

In addition to the 50 IYHF youth hostels operated by **An Óige** (the Irish Youth Hostel Association), 65 independent hostels have been incorporated into the **Independent Hostel Owners (IHO)** and 20 into the **Irish Budget Hostels** associations. Most hostels have kitchen facilities.

An Óige hostels are more likely to be mobbed by school groups and fall into three price ranges: Group A charges £4.30-5.90, Group B £3.80-5.50 and Group C £3.50-4.50. The city hostel in Dublin charges £7 (non-members £9) but includes breakfast. Hostelers without IYHF membership cards can purchase an International Guest Card for £7.50 (£5 if purchased from the head office), or 6 £1.25 "welcome stamps" as you go along. The An Óige guide (£1) is sold at the hostels, many tourist offices, and An Óige headquarters at 39 Mountjoy Sq., Dublin 1 (tel. (01) 363 111; open Mon. 10am-2pm and 7:30-9pm, Tues.-Fri. 10am-5:30pm; April-Sept. also Sat. 10am-12:30pm). City hostels in Dublin, Cork, Limerick, and Killarney offer special train fares (£13.95 for a one way ticket between cities including one overnight at an IYHF hostel). Advance bookings are wise, especially if you plan to stay during the weekend. All IYHF hostels will call ahead for you to reserve a bed at another IYHF hostel (no booking charge).

The 93 hostels affliated with the Inedependent Hostel Owners are often more mellow than An Óige hostels, have no membership requirements, flexible curfews, and no daytime lock-out. Most independent hostels charge £4-5; some charge an extra 50p for a shower, and some allow camping for about £2.50. Only some have sheet rental, so travel with a sleeping bag or sack. Tourist offices may be reluctant to dispense information about independent hostels. The IHO guide (£1) is available from any of the independent hostels, as well as from the information office at Dooey Hostel, Glencolumcille, Co. Donegal (tel. (073) 301 30).

The Irish Budget hostels require no membership but are all approved by the Irish Tourist Board, and also offer special transportation deals (£20 includes a round-trip ticket to any destination in Ireland, with one overnight at a budget hostel included). You can pick up a list of the budget hostels from any one of the 20. For more information, contact Paddy Moloney at the Doolin Hostel, Doolin Village, Co. Clare (tel. (065) 740 06).

Irish B&Bs are most savory. They average £10-12 per person (singles are usually more expensive). The breakfasts—eggs, bacon, sausage, bread, cereal, orange juice, and coffee or tea—are often filling enough to get you through until dinner. Remember that the Irish Republic is one big Gregorian chant; an unmarried couple traveling together may encounter some raised eyebrows, but usually no real problems. B&Bs displaying a shamrock are officially approved by the Irish Tourist Board; they charge the prices quoted in the 1991 edition of *Guest Accommodation,* published by the Tourist Board and available at all tourist offices (£2). Most tourist offices will book you a room at a B&B for £1 plus a 10% deposit.

Camping brings you closest to the land, the water, and the insects. With the permission of the landowner, you can pitch a tent in any field you fancy, but if you do camp on someone else's property leave absolutely nothing behind. Camping in State forests and National Parks is not allowed, nor is camping on public land if there is an official campsite in the area. Caravan and camping parks provide all the accoutrements of bourgeois civilization: toilets, running water, showers, garbage cans, and sometimes shops, kitchen and laundry facilities, restaurants and game rooms. In addition, many have several caravans for hire at the site. The average charge for a pitch is £4-5. You can rent tents and equipment in almost any major city. **O'Meara Camping** has a Rent-a-Tent service in Dublin, Cork, and Limerick, as well as in other towns (2-person tent for 1 week, £18). Their head office is at 160A Crumlin Rd., Dublin 12 (tel. (01) 542 811). Tourist offices sell *Caravan and Camping Parks* (£1.50), a guide to rental agencies and camping sites throughout Ireland.

History

Ireland has seen its share of swords and slaughter. By the time Julius *et. al.* conquered England, Ireland had already been overrun several times, most notably by the Celts in 600 B.C. But Rome never considered Ireland worth invading, leaving it instead to clan warfare and isolation. One fortunate result of Roman neglect is that Ireland has a rich prehistoric legacy—countless scattered stone and earthen remains. Other memories survive in Celtic folklore: Deirdre of the Sorrows, Cuchulain, Finn McCumhail, and Jessica and the lemur. Christian missionaries arrived in Ireland around the 5th century (the most notable was St. Patrick, who first arrived in Ireland as a boy slave from England). Enchanted by the beauty and solitude of the island, they laid the foundation for a period of scholastic and artistic flowering that earned Ireland its medieval reputation as "the island of saints and scholars." A period of Norse invasions ensued from the 9th through the 11th centuries, resulting in feudal struggle between the various kings of the ancient provinces of Munster, Connaught, Leinster, Ulster, and Malster. The age of subservience to the English throne began in 1171, when Henry II took Waterford. The surrounding natives rose most notably under the short-lived Celtic kingdom of Edward Bruce in 1315-18.

In the 16th and 17th centuries, under Elizabeth I and James I of England, Protestants established plantations in Ireland, uprooting Catholic farmers in the process. Less than a century later, Oliver Cromwell and his Puritan army marched through Ireland, tightening the English hold on Irish land by redistributing estates and burning monasteries. Entire villages were massacred, and, worse yet, survivors were sent off to America or Australia. In the late 1600s, the British imposed the Penal Laws, forbidding Catholics to hold Mass or to buy or inherit land. Most of the Penal Laws were revoked by the 18th century, but Catholics were not given the right to vote until the dramatic success of Daniel O'Connell's emancipation campaign in 1831. The middle of the 19th century brought years of famine when the staple potato crop was infected with blight, the years Patrick Kavanagh called the Great Starvation. Ireland's fishing industry provided little relief, and the country lost one million people to starvation, and another million to emigration.

In the ensuing years, some of those who remained behind began to lobby for tenants' rights and laid the groundwork for the Irish Republican Brotherhood, which was founded in mid-century. The nationalist Fenians rallied around Charles Stewart Parnell and his cautious movement for home rule in the 1880s. The rejection of Gladstone's Home Rule Bills incited more visceral forces to emerge; the fiery Arthur Griffith founded the *Sinn Féin* movement in 1906, setting up administrative structures for an independent state. Labor unrest led finally to the formation of the Citizens Army and other militant groups.

On Easter Sunday in 1916, a group of Fenians, Padraig Pearse and James Connolly among them, siezed several of Dublin's public buildings and proclaimed the Irish Republic. The republicans were shot for treason. A popular nationalist sentiment crystallized after the tragic events of that Easter week. The Anglo-Irish War that followed resulted in the proclamation of the Irish Free State in 1921, comprised of 26 counties. Six Ulster counties chose to remain part of the United Kingdom, becoming today's Northern Ireland. In 1949 Ireland officially proclaimed itself the Republic of Ireland (*Éire* in Gaelic), a completely independent land. Eamonn de Valera became leader of the Dáil Éireann, the Parliament of Ireland, and from 1959 to 1973 he served as President of the Republic. The two important political parties in Ireland today are Fianna Fáil and Fine Gael.

Literature

Legend has it that when St. Patrick arrived in Ireland, he was greeted by Ossian, a folk hero from Tir-na-nÓg (the land of the young). Unable to sleep after hearing Ossian's tales, St. Patrick was visited by two angels who declared that he should record the pagan songs and rescue them from oblivion. Early Irish monks followed St. Patrick's example during the next millenium, laboriously preserving the native Irish literary tradition. These manuscripts, among them *The Book of the Dún Low, The Book of Leinster,* and *The Great Book of Lecan,* are one of the few remnants of the early Middle Ages. Formal bardic poetry of the 12th through the 17th centuries forms the body of early Gaelic literature. With the 17th-century consolidation of English rule, bards not only lost their patronage, but the educated class in Ireland acquired a new language—English. Jonathan Swift, Oliver Goldsmith, and Oscar Wilde all enriched the English language with the sum of Irish experience in literature that, although Irish, was incomprehensible to the majority of their countrymen.

The late 19th and early 20th centuries saw an Irish renaissance in literature, part of the nationalist movement. The Gaelic League was founded to promote the study and use of Irish Gaelic, with men such as Douglas Hyde working to resurrect the ancient Irish lore and language so damaged by the Great Famine. Hyde inspired both William Butler Yeats and Lady Gregory, who revived interest in Irish folk tales and customs, collecting and compiling legends from the country folk and emulating their simple but poetic speech. Yeats's work extends from the political poems of the 10s and 20s to Irish folktales, powerful drama, and mystical revelation. Under the directorship of Yeats, the Abbey Theatre in Dublin nurtured such great dramatists as J. M. Synge, Lennox Robinson, and Sean O'Casey, whose realistic portrayals of Dublin life still make fascinating reading.

Yeats played a crucial role in the formation of a national Irish movement in literature. He himself turned away from "Celtic revival" sources in his later years, becoming a fierce and eloquent voice in the Modernist movement. His web of symbols—gyres, birds, and heraldry—was turned to the visionary depiction of oncoming catastrophe. Yeats also sensed the oncoming tsunami of James Joyce, encouraging early interest in a man who might well have languished in complete obscurity. Joyce was not merely the titan of Irish modernism; he remains the most influential prose-writer of the 20th century. He left Ireland soon after his graduation from University College, denouncing Dublin's philistinism; he nonetheless chose Dublin as the backdrop for all of his major works. *A Portrait of the Artist as a Young Man* and "The Dead" are his most lyrical and accessible works; *Ulysses* is his monument to living Dublin; and *Finnegans Wake* is his testament to an unborn future. Flann O'Brien's *The Hard Life* and *At-Swim-Two-Birds* capture a Dublin that is at once Rabelaisian and tragic, while Brendan Behan's *Borstal Boy* brings the language, humor, and mannerisms of Dublin into a British reform school. The countryside and its inhabitants shine through the writings of Liam O'Flaherty, Seamus O'Kelly, and Frank O'Connor. Ireland's western islands produced the country's highest concentration of authors who write in Irish. Novels from the Blasket Islands (such as Maurice O'Sullivan's *Twenty Years a-Growing* and Peig Sayers' *Reflections of an Old Woman*), Synge's writings and plays on Aran, Oliver Gogarty's nostalgic sketches, and the stories of Padraig O'Donnell render daily island life eloquently and poignantly.

Samuel Beckett stands apart from the Irish tradition in literature as he does from everything else, yet his tortured world has deep roots in his childhood and adolescence outside of Dublin. The landscapes of *Molloy, Malone Dies,* and *The Unnameable* are often descriptions of a real Irish landscape; the pier in *Krapp's Last Tape,* where the narrator describes a sudden vision in the midst of a winter storm, is the pier in Dún Laoghaire.

Music

Ireland's folk music tradition is alive and flourishing. Though some of the music has been recently recorded or written down, much is still passed directly from musician to musician. The harp (Ireland's national symbol), *uilleann* pipes (literally "elbow," with a sound more refined than Scottish bagpipes), *bodhrán* (goatskin drum), tin whistle, fiddle, flute, and accordion play together in various combinations, filling the air with both lively dance tunes and mournful, haunting melodies. You can hear traditional music in pubs across the country, particularly in *Gaeltacht* (Irish-speaking) areas. Kerry, Clare, Galway, Sligo, and Dublin are particularly noted for traditional music. **Comhaltas Ceoltóirí Éireann,** the national traditional music association, organizes sessions throughout Ireland, and provincial and county *fleadhs* (pronounced flahs) are indeed "feasts" of music. For more information, contact Comhaltas Ceoltóirí Culturlann na hÉireann, Belgrave Sq., Monkstown, County Dublin (tel. (01) 80 02 95), or the Irish Tourist Board.

Ireland's many traditional, classical, and rock-music festivals include:

Ballyshannon Folk and Traditional Music Festival, Ballyshannon, County Donegal; early Aug. One of the year's biggest traditional festivals.

The All-Ireland Fleadh, in a different city every year; last weekend in Aug. National festival, the zenith of the traditional music year in Ireland.

Guinness Jazz Festival, Cork City; late Oct. Almost certainly the country's best jazz festival.

Music in Great Irish Houses Festival, around Ireland; June. Mostly classical music in opulent settings.

Willie Clancy Summer School, Milltown Malbay, County Clare; first week in July. Big midsummer gathering of musicians from throughout the country.

Aside from the these great music bashes, Galway City and Sligo town each host an **Arts Festival** during August and late September/early October, respectively. More serious than traditional music festivals, these also feature poetry and short story readings. Contact the tourist offices in Galway and Sligo for details and schedules.

Pubs and Food

Give me chastity and continency—but not yet.
—St. Augustine

Despite woefully early closing hours, there always seems to be time to drink a couple of pints at an Irish pub. The national drink is Guinness, a rich, black stout affectionately known as "the dark stuff." Murphy's is a similar, although slightly milder, stout brewed in Cork. Smithwicks and Harp Lager are also popular. Irish whiskey (which Queen Elizabeth once told her lady-in-waiting was her only true Irish friend) is sweeter and more stinging than its Scotch counterpart; Dubliners are partial to Powers, Corkpeople drink Paddy's, and Bushmills is the favorite in Ulster. Jameson's is popular everywhere. **Irish coffee,** unlike French toast (which really is the national treat), is sweetened with brown sugar and whipped cream and laced with whiskey. **Hot whiskey** (spiced up with lemon, cloves, and brown sugar) is also popular, as is the Irish version of **eggnog** (brandy, beaten egg, milk, and lemonade). In the west, you may hear some of the locals extolling the virtues of "mountain dew," a euphemistic name for *poitin* (pronounced poht-cheen), a lethal illegal distillation that ranges in strength from 115 to 140 proof. Possession of *poitin* is a federal offense, and bad *poitin* can be very dangerous indeed.

Pubs are the forum for banter, singing, and socializing. Signs advertising "crack" denote simply "a good time," or "fun." Travelers might have their ears talked off by amateur *seanachai,* storytellers who haunt some pubs. In the evening, some pubs play impromptu or organized traditional music; walk by a few windows and peek in a few doors before choosing a place to drink. As 11:30pm approaches (11pm during the winter months and on Sundays) you'll hear the sound the Irish call the saddest in the world: the bartender's rattle of keys and stern "Time, gentlepeople . . . Have ye no homes to go to?" At this point, most patrons rush to the bar for a few more "jars"; they sagely advise, "You never know when the t'irst'll hit ye again." Pubs are generally open Monday to Saturday 10:30am-11:30pm (11pm in winter), Sunday 12:30-2pm and 4-11pm. Pub lunches are usually served from Monday to Saturday 12:30-2:30pm and children are generally not allowed in pubs after 7pm.

Food in Ireland is expensive, especially in restaurants. The basics—and that is what you'll get—are simple and filling. For a midday meal, pub grub (lunches around £3, sandwiches £1-1.20) or fish and chips (£1.10-3) are usually the economical choice. A better alternative is to do your own shopping. Brown bread and fruit soda bread will keep for about a week and are delicious, and Irish dairy products are addictive. Seafood can be quite a bargain in some of the smaller towns. Smoked mackerel is a splendid year-round, and Atlantic salmon is freshest during the season through July. Regional specialities include *crubeen* (pigs' feet) in Cork, and *coddle* (boiled sausages and bacon with potatoes) in Dublin. *Colcannon,* or "Ploughman's lunch," and Irish stew are probably the essential Irish dishes.

East Coast

The axons of Ireland's nervous system converge on Dublin, the Republic's convivial capital situated midway along the east coast. The city stradles the River Liffey, along which Gaelic people first settled some 1,500 years ago. To the north, Drogheda, settled by Vikings in the 10th century, once rivaled Dublin as a trading center; the city has since modestly refrained from overstepping its old fortifications. Various cultures deposited a rich diversity of historical artifacts near Drogheda: castles surrounded by lush gardens grace Howth, Malahide and Trim; 5th century monastaries gracefully approach old age at Monasterboice and Mellifont; and the most impressive of ancient archaeological remains, a 5000-year-old burial mound, sedately holds its ground at Newgrange. South of Dublin, the glowingly rugged Wicklow Mountains rise to over 2000 ft., threaded by the 70 mi. Wicklow Way which runs from Dublin to to Clonegal. Wooded glens pursue rivers from gorse and heather highlands near Glendalough down to a coast caressed by the Irish Sea, where seaside resorts lure vacationers to sandy beaches.

Dublin

Through the centuries, Dublin has provided a focal point for predatory attentions. The Bronze Age Celts settled on the banks of the Liffey, living peacefully until 9th-century Vikings greedily descended on the wealth of the Irish monasteries and destined Dublin to become an important trading post in their new world order. The year 1172 saw Henry II declare Dublin capital of his Irish kingdom after an indecisive victory, inaugurating centuries of British colonialism and Irish rebellion. Throughout the Middle Ages, English feudals sparred with Irish Gaelic, but the English remained in control throughout the turbulent 18th century, calls for Catholic freedom and an end to the Protestant Ascendency led to skirmishes between the British Army and the native Irish. The formation of the "United Irishmen" with their doctrine of religious equality and the unity of the Irish people attests to the rise of Irish national consciousness during this period. As Britain industrialized, she exploited Irish farmers, renumerating them pooorly for their crop of potatoes. When the potato blight struck in the mid-19th century, famine and disease darkened the land, and many emigrated to foreign shores. Republican movements grew, climaxing in the Easter Rising of 1916 when Irish nationalists seized the General Post Office and defended it for a week, proclaiming the Republic of Ireland. In 1921, a treaty divided Ireland along its current lines: Britain claimed the 6 largely Protestant counties in the North, and the rest became part of the Irish Free State.

James Joyce once modestly proclaimed that, in the event of some huge catastrophe, Dublin could be rebuilt stone by stone from the pages of *Ulysses.* Literature has, in fact, played a vital role in the city. A fascination with Joyce and Yeats brands every pub they once stumbled from, and on Bloomsday (June 16) the whole city revels in a recapitulation of the path of Joyce's protagonist. "Poetry by the Way," a selection of modern Irish poems on walls throughout Dublin, is immediate proof of the city's literary inclinations, as are the continual poetry readings and Irish play productions. Dublin has not embraced cosmopolitanism at the expense of her uniqueness; British rule originally forced the Irish to assert themselves through their culture and things Gaelic, and now a free people continue to value their past.

Modern Dublin has the quirky flavor of a large town busily engaged in neighbourhood pursuits. Dubliners are always ready, at the end of a hard day's work, to stop for a convivial pint of Guinness at the local pub. Rows of shops, pubs and bookmakers line the streets in place of stone-cold urban malls and the horizon is unscarred by skyscrapers. Yet Dublin life has its shadier side: car break-ins are common, and Dickensian urchins rove the streets pickpocketing and bagsnatching. Violent crime,

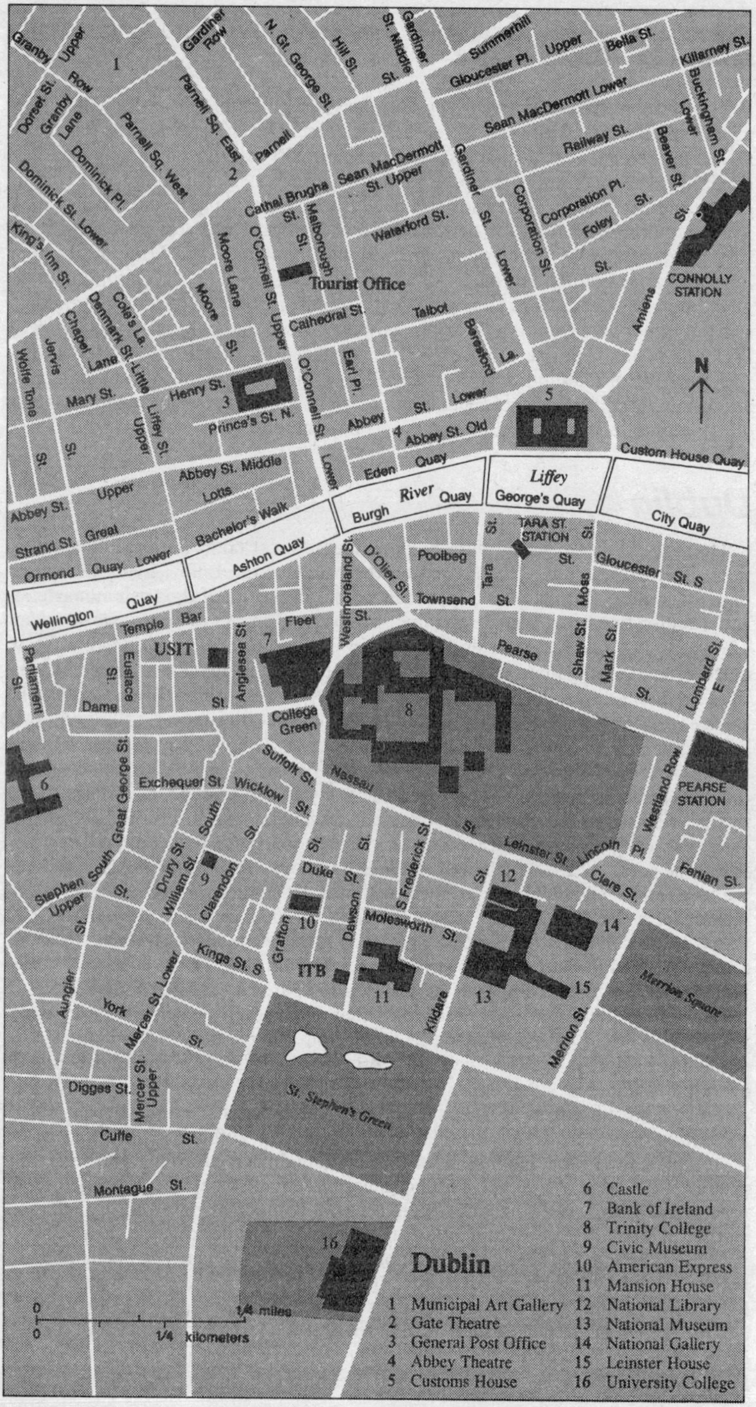
Dublin
1 Municipal Art Gallery
2 Gate Theatre
3 General Post Office
4 Abbey Theatre
5 Customs House
6 Castle
7 Bank of Ireland
8 Trinity College
9 Civic Museum
10 American Express
11 Mansion House
12 National Library
13 National Museum
14 National Gallery
15 Leinster House
16 University College
N
0 1/4 miles
0 1/4 kilometers
Tourist Office
USIT
ITB
CONNOLLY STATION
TARA ST. STATION
PEARSE STATION
River Liffey
St. Stephen's Green
Merrion Square
Granby Row
Upper
Dorset St.
Granby Lane
Dominick Pl.
Dominick St. Lower
King's Inn St.
Parnell Sq. West
Parnell Sq. East
Gardiner Row
N. Gt. George St.
Hill St.
St. Middle
Gardiner St.
Summerhill
Gloucester Pl. Upper
Bella St.
Killarney St.
Buckingham St. Lower
Sean MacDermott Lower
Railway St.
Beaver St.
Parnell
Cathal Brugha St.
Sean MacDermott St. Upper
Marlborough St.
Waterford St.
Gardiner St. Lower
Corporation St.
Corporation Pl.
Foley St.
Amiens St.
Moore Lane
Moore St.
O'Connell St. Upper
Cathedral St.
Talbot St.
Beresford La.
Earl Pl.
O'Connell St. Lower
Abbey St. Lower
Abbey St. Old
Cole's La.
Denmark St. Little
Chapel Lane
Jervis St.
Wolfe Tone St.
Mary St.
Henry St.
Prince's St. N.
Liffey St. Upper
Abbey St. Middle
Eden Quay
Custom House Quay
Abbey St. Upper
Lotts
Great Strand St.
Bachelor's Walk
Burgh Quay
George's Quay
City Quay
Ormond Quay Lower
Ashton Quay
Wellington Quay
Westmoreland St.
D'Olier St.
Poolbeg St.
Tara St.
Moss St.
Gloucester St. S
Townsend St.
Temple Bar
Fleet St.
Pearse St.
Shaw St.
Mark St.
Lombard St. E
Parliament St.
Eustace St.
Anglesea St.
Dame St.
College Green
Great George St. South
Exchequer St.
Wicklow St.
Suffolk St.
Nassau St.
Westland Row
Leinster St.
Lincoln Pl.
Clare St.
Fenian St.
Stephen St. Upper
Drury St.
William St. South
Clarendon St.
Grafton St.
Duke St.
Dawson St.
S Frederick St.
Kildare St.
Molesworth St.
Kings St. S
Aungier St.
York St.
Mercer St. Lower
Mercer St. Upper
Merrion St.
Digges St.
Cuffe St.
Montague St.

although rarer, does exist. So, as a drunken publican is apt to warn, "Remember your ABCs. Always be careful. Always be cautious."

Arriving and Departing

Dublin, located on the east coast of Ireland, is internationally accessible by plane, ferry or train. The city can be reached by air either directly or through Shannon Airport on the west coast. Flights from the United States usually fly into Shannon; the larger Dublin Airport sends planes all over Europe, with excellent service to Britain via Dan Air, Manx Airlines (Isle of Man), RYANAIR, Aer Lingus, and British Airways. City bus #41A or 41C run to the city center from the parkway outside the second floor of Dublin Airport (every 20 min.; approx. 25 min.; 95p, exact change not required). Airport express buses (£2.30) to the central bus station take less time and cost more (every 30 min. 8:10am-9:25pm, Sun. 7:30am-8:55pm; 15 min.; £2.30). Cab rides run upwards of £8.

Dublin is connected by B&I and Sealink ferries to Holyhead in Wales. **Sealink** sails from the dock at Dún Laoghaire (dun-LEAR-y), just south of Dublin. (4/day, Sept-late June 2/day; 3½ hr.; £16-22, return £32-44, bikes free). Check-in time is one hour before departure. Buses #7, 7A, 8, 45A, 46A (95p) and the DART run between Dublin's Connolley Station and the dock in Dún Laoghaire. **B&I** operates out of the Dublin city port in Alexandra Basin (2/day; £16-21, return £32-42). Take bus #53 from Alexandra Rd. to the city center. Both ferries allow student discounts with a Travelsave stamp (available from USIT for £7.50), even though they don't mention it. Both Sealink (tel. 807 777; open Mon.-Sat. 9am-5:30pm) and B&I (tel. 797 977; open Mon.-Fri. 9:15am-5pm, Sat. 9:30am-12:30pm) have offices in Dublin on Westmoreland St. by the O'Connell Bridge.

Rail lines in Ireland generally radiate from Dublin. Several trains per day run from Dublin to: Cork (£29.50, return £31.50), Galway (£22.50, return £24.50), Limerick (£22.50, return £24.50), Waterford (£20, return £22), and Belfast (£13.50, return £20.50). Student fares differ by route, but an ISIC with a Travelsave stamp usually reduces the price by half. Saver fares are available, as are myriad different ticket options which change every season: call **Irish Rail** (tel. 724 222 or 363 333) or visit their office on Lower Abbey St. for a full menu. (Open Mon.-Sat. 9am-5pm.) The two main train stations in Dublin are **Heuston Station,** on the south bank of the river west of the city center, and **Connolly Station,** north of the Liffey behind Busáras on Amiens St. Pearse Station, behind Trinity College on Pearse St., is a lesser suburban station; not all trains stop there.

Both **Expressway** and provincial bus services terminate at **Busáras,** the central bus station, just north of the river behind the Customs House on Store St. Get bus information here or at the main office on 59 O'Connell St., opposite the tourist office (tel. 366 111 for inquiries). **Bus Éireann** offers daily return trips to various cities, though private bus companies usually have cheaper fares. Buses from Dublin's Busáras to: Kilkac (2/day, Sun. 1/day; 6 hr.; £11, monthly return £14; student £7.50, 7-day return £11.50); Cork (3/day, Sun. 2/day; 4½ hr.; £11, monthly return £14; student £7.50, 7-day return £11.50); Belfast (3/day, Sun. 2/day; 3 hr.; £9, return £12; no student rates).

The **Student Monthly** (£32; available Sept.-June only) is good for a calendar month of bus and train travel (for non-students it's called the **Monthly Short Hop** and costs £44). All of these tickets have a surcharge of £2. A one-day ticket for unrestricted bus travel costs £2.40, for bus and train £3.50.

Many **hitchhike** to Dublin from within Ireland: coming from Cork, they take the N8; from Wexford, the N11; from Limerick, the N7; and from Galway, the N4. Foreign backpackers, with their exotic aura, excite the Irish imagination and tend to get rides before those who seem more local. *Let's Go* urges caution and common sense if you decide to thumb rides.

Orientation

The River Liffey bisects Dublin, dividing the city into the poorer, rougher northern section, and the southerly area, which beckons the well-to-do. (Dublin 1 and Dublin 2 are the postal codes locals use to refer to their city.) North of the river, jaywalkers blissfully ignore traffic signals to surge en masse over O'Connell St., the main drag. Smaller streets lead off to hundreds of shops and pubs, and the crowds dwindle as you move farther away from the river. North and west of O'Connell, around Montjoy Sq., abandoned housing makes walking at night eerie; a stroll eastward leads to warehouses and the old whisky distillery near Church St.

In southern Dublin, Trinity College grandly stakes out the center of town, while shops and bookstores vie for customers on every side. Grafton St. glitters with display windows and expensive toys, and night-time entertainment flaunts itself between the city center and the canal to the south. The area called Temple Bar, along the Liffey and west of O'Connell Bridge, offers a funky alternative scene in music, food and clothes—this spills over to Dame St. amd the areas around it. As you move westward past the Guinness brewery, life gets cheaper once again.

The Dublin bus system reaches nearly every spot in the city from 6am to 11:30pm. The network is easy to decipher, and the jolly green buses hard to miss. Most buses leave from O'Connell St. or along the quays; ask someone or visit the bus information center at 59 O'Connell for exact schedules. Fares run between 50p and 95p, depending on how far you're going; some buses require exact change.

The DART serves the suburbs more than the city itself, running up and down the coast to Dublin's bedroom communities. Leaving from both Connolly and Pearse stations in the city center, Dublin Area Rapid Transit (DART) shoots north along the coast to Howth and south to Bray. Clean, efficient, and faster than the bus, DART costs about the same, and the southern routes have the added bonus of a wonderful view of the Irish Sea. At Bray and at Howth Junction, the DART connects to an outer-suburban rail line that volleys north to Drogheda and south to Wicklow. At Connolly Station DART connects to the Western suburban line that runs to Maynooth. The **One Day Irish Travel ticket,** good for unlimited travel on DART and Suburban Rail Services between Balbriggan, Kilcoole, and Maynooth costs just £3.50. (One way ticket on the DART from Connolly Station to Howth is 95p.) There are no student discounts on DART fares but a number of special deals are available: a week (from Sunday to Saturday) of unlimited bus and DART travel costs £11.50, students £9.

Practical Information

Dublin weather is viciously flirtatious; equip yourself with warm clothing even during the summer.

Tourist Office: 14 Upper O'Connell St. (tel. 747 733). Accommodations service with £1 booking fee. Free maps and information. Currency exchange. Bus Éireann and RYANAIR ticket and information desks. Open mid-late June Mon.-Sat. 8:30am-6pm; July-Aug. Mon.-Sat. 8:30am-8pm, Sun. 10:30am-3pm. Sept. Mon.-Fri. 9am-5pm; Oct. Mon.-Fri. 9am-5pm, Sat. 9am-1:30pm; Nov.-May. variable. **Bord Fáilte Éireann (Irish Tourist Board),** Baggot St. Bridge 2 (tel. 619 599). Information on cultural events. Map of Dublin 75p. Open Mon.-Sat. 9am-5pm.

Airport: 7 mi. north of the city center (tel. 379 900). The **tourist office** here (tel. 376 387) is open daily May 8am-8pm; June-Sept. 8am-10:30pm; Sept.-Dec. 8am-6:30pm; Jan.-April 8am-6pm. Take bus #41A or 41C (95p) to Eden Quay. There is a special coach that runs between the airport and city (£2.30) and stops at O'Connell Station. **Aer Lingus** offices are located on 41 Upper O'Connell St. and 42 Grafton St. (Both open Mon.-Sat. 9am-5pm, no public calls.)

An Óige (Irish Youth Hostel Association): 39 Mountjoy Sq. (tel. 363 111). Membership £7.50, under 18 £4. Book IYHA hostels here and pay at time of booking. The *An Óige Handbook* (£1.50) lists all their hostels in Ireland and Northern Ireland. Open March-Oct. Mon. 10am-5:30pm and 7:30-9pm, Tues.-Fri. 10am-5:30pm; April-Sept. Sat. 10am-12:30pm.; Nov.-Feb. Mon. 10am-6:30pm, Tues.-Fri. 10am-5:30pm.

Bike Rental: Rent-A-Bike, 58 Lower Gardiner St. (tel. 725 931 and 725 399). Open Mon.-Sat. 9am-6pm. Ten-speeds and mountain bikes, £22-25/week, deposit of £30-50 required). Panniers £3.50/week, helmets £4/week, childseats £4/week. Bike repair. Sells bikes at the beginning of the summer for about £150, then buys them back at the end for about £90. For only £4.50 extra, you can return the bike to any one of their depots (in Rosslare, Cork, Limerick, Killarney, Sligo, Galway, or Westport). **Square Wheel Cycleworks,** Temple Lane, off Dame St. (tel. 771 974). Open Mon.-Fri. 8:30am-6:30pm. Bike repair. These guys are just crazy about bikes. No rentals, but free advice and estimates.

Budget Travel: USIT (Irish Student Travel Agency): 19-21 Aston Quay (tel. 778 117), near the O'Connell Bridge. ISIC, IYHF cards. USIT card (£5.50) for students and others under 26 gives discounts on trains, planes, and special events. Travelsave stamps (£7.50). Open July Mon. 10am-5:30pm and 7:30-9pm; Tues.-Fri. 10am-5:30pm, Sat. 10am-12:30pm; Aug.-June Mon. 10am-2pm, Tues.-Fri. 10am-5:30pm.

Bus Information: 59 Upper O'Connell St. (tel. 366 111, after hr. 734 222), opposite the tourist office. Provides information about Expressway and Provincial buses, Bus Éireann, and Dublin City buses. Open Mon. 8:30am-5:30pm, Tues.-Fri. 9am-5:30pm, Sat. 9am-1pm. **Lost Property:** tel. 720 000, Mon.-Fri. 9am-5:30pm.

Buses: Busáras, Store St. (tel. 366 111), directly behind the Customs House. All Expressway and provincial buses depart from here. Day lockers available, 65p/day, 80p for 48 hr.

Car Rental: Budget Rent-a-Car, 151 Lower Drumcondra Rd. (tel. 379 802 or 379 611). £170/week (includes tax, insurance, and unlimited mileage; no deposit required). You must be over 21 and have had a driver's license for a year. Open Mon.-Fri. 9am-5pm. Second office at Dublin Airport (tel. 370 919 or 420 793). **Windsor Car Rentals,** 33 Bachelor's Walk (tel. 732 609 or 730 944) or Desk 4 at the airport arrivals hall (tel. 422 033). Open Mon.-Sat. 9am-6pm, Sun. 10am-1pm.

Crisis: Samaritans, 112 Marlborough St. (tel. 727 700). Open 24 hr. **Rape Crisis Center,** 70 Lower Leeson St. (tel. 614 911 or 614 564). Open Mon.-Fri. 9am-5pm. **Well Woman Centre,** 73 Lower Leeson St. (tel. 610 083). Guidance and information for women. Open Mon.-Fri. 9am-8pm, Sat. 10am-5pm, Sun. 2pm-5pm. **Gay Switchboard Dublin,** Old Doctor's Residence, Richmond Hospital (tel. 721 055). Open Mon.-Fri. 8-10pm, Sat. 3:30-6pm, Sun. 7-9pm.

Directory Assistance: tel. 190.

Embassies: U.S. Embassy, 43 Elgin Rd., Ballsbridge, Dublin 4 (tel. 688 777). Open Mon.-Fri. 8:30am-5pm. **Australian Embassy,** Fitzwilton House, Wilton Terrace, Dublin 2 (tel. 761 517). Open Mon.-Thurs 8:30am-1pm and 2-5:20pm, Fri. 8:30am-1:45pm. **British Embassy,** 31/33 Merrion Rd., Dublin 4 (tel. 695 111). Open Mon.-Fri. 10am-noon and 2-4pm. **Canadian Embassy,** 65 St. Stephen's Green South, Dublin 2 (tel. 781 988). Open Mon.-Wed. 8:30am-12:30pm and 2-4pm, Thurs.-Fri. 8:30am-12:30pm. **French Embassy,** 36 Ailesbury Rd., Dublin 4 (tel. 694 777). Open Mon.-Fri. 9am-12:30pm. **German Embassy,** 31 Trimleston Ave., Booterstown, Dublin 2 (tel. 693 011). Open Mon.-Fri. 9-noon. **Italian Embassy,** 63 Northumberland Rd., Dublin 4 (tel. 601 744). **New Zealanders** should contact the British Embassy. **Spanish Embassy,** 17a Merlyn Pk. Dublin 4 (tel. 691 640). Open Mon.-Fri. 9:30am-3pm. **Swedish Embassy,** Sun Alliance House, Dawson St., Dublin 2 (tel. 715 822). Open Mon.-Fri. 9:30am-12:30pm.

Emergency: Dial 999; no coins required.

Ferries: B&I, 16 Westmoreland St. (tel. 797 977). Open Mon.-Fri. 9:15am-5pm, Sat. 9:30am-12:30pm. **Sealink,** 15 Westmoreland St. (tel. 807 777). Office in **Clery's,** Upper O'Connell St. (tel. 742 052). Open Mon.-Sat. 9am-5:30pm. Ferries connect to Britain and France.

Financial Services: Best rates found in banks (usually open Mon.-Wed. and Fri. 10am-12:30pm and 1:30-3pm, Thurs. 10am-12:30pm and 1:30-5pm). **Bank of Ireland** is good. Otherwise try **Thomas Cook,** 118 Grafton St. (tel. 771 721), next to American Express (open Mon.-Fri. 9am-5:30pm, Sat. 9am-1pm, 2-5pm) or the *bureau de change* in the **General Post Office** (1% commission; open Mon.-Sat. 8am-8pm, Sun. 10:30am-6:30pm). On Sundays you can also exchange money at the **Bank of Ireland,** Departures Hall, Dublin Airport (tel. 420 433); open daily 6:45am-10pm, winter 6:45am-9pm. **American Express:** 116 Grafton St., Dublin 2 (tel. 772 874), up the street from Trinity Gates. Mail pickup, currency exchange (no commission on AmEx travelers checks), and full banking and travel services. Open Mon.-Fri. 9am-5pm, Sat. 9am-noon.

Hospital: Adelaide, Peter St. (tel. 758 971) near White Friar St. Take bus #16, 19, or 22. **Mater Misercordia,** Eccles St., just off Berkeley (tel. 301 122).

Irish Rail Information: 35 Lower Abbey St. (tel. 724 222 or 363 333). Open Mon.-Sat. 9am-5pm. Information on passenger service, international routes, DART, Irish Rail, and suburban routes. Recorded summaries of intercity and mainline rail services to various cities from Dublin: Cork (tel. 724 222); Limerick (tel. 724 646); Galway/Westport (tel. 724 777); Waterford (tel. 730 000); Sligo (tel. 731 111); Killarney-Tralee (tel. 733 333); Belfast (tel. 734 444); Wexford-Rosslare (tel. 735 555). Lost property (tel. 363 333).

Launderette: Nova Laundrette, Belvidere Rd., just off Dorset St. (tel. 681 786). Washers £1.60, dryers around £1.50, depeding on how dry you want your clothes. Open Mon.-Sat. 8:30am-8pm, Sun. 11am-6pm.

Library: New Central Library, ILAC Centre, Moore St. (tel. 734 333). Video and listening facilities and a children's library. Open Mon.-Thurs. 10am-8pm, Fri.-Sat. 10am-5pm.

Late-Night Pharmacy: O'Connell's, 55 Lower O'Connell St. (tel. 730 427). Open Mon.-Sat. 8:30am-10pm, Sun. 10am-10pm.

Police (Garda): Harcourt Sq. (tel. 732 222). Store St. office (tel. 742 761).

Post Office: General Post Office, O'Connell St. (tel. 728 888), near the tourist office. Open Mon.-Sat. 8am-8pm. Even-numbered postal codes are south of the Liffey, odd-numbered north; numbers increase with distance from city center. **Postal Code:** Dublin 1 (*Poste Restante* pick-up at windows #24-25; open same hr.).

Taxi: National Radio Cabs, 40 James St. (tel. 772 222). 24 hr. Fee begins at £2.50. Full-service charge (£1). A whopping 85p/mi.

Telephones: In the General Post Office. Local calls are 20p. International pay phones open Mon.-Sat. 8am-8pm, Sun. and holidays 10:30am-6:30pm. **Telephone Code:** 01.

Trains: Heuston Station (tel. 366 222), south bank of the River Liffey to the west near Victoria Quay. Serves south and west of Dublin: Cork, Limerick, Waterford, Tralee, Kerry, Galway, and Westport. Lockers (80p/day/item; Mon.-Sat. 7:20am-9pm). **Connolly Station,** (tel. 742 941) behind Busáras and Customs House on Amiens St. Serves north and south of Dublin: Belfast, Sligo, Derry, Wexford, and Rosslare. **Pearse Station,** Westland Row (tel. 776 581), directly behind Trinity College. Serves suburban stations; DART commuter rail also stops here.

Youth Information Center: Sackville House, Sackville Pl. (tel. 786 844), behind Clery's on O'Connell St. A library with a wealth of resources (some free literature) on careers, community activities (including cultural events), travel and tourist information, accommodations (no bookings), camping, sporting events, counselling, and referrals. Bulletin boards advertise youth organizations and special-needs groups. Open Mon.-Wed. 9:30am-6pm, Thurs.-Sat. 9:30am-5pm.

Accommodations

The main tourist office on O'Connell St. provides general information about accommodations and services in the Dublin area. The Irish Tourist Board's pamphlet *Guest Accommodations* (£1.50) lists reasonable hotels and B&Bs all over Ireland. From June through August, B&Bs fill quickly and single rooms are especially hard to come by.

Hostels

Hostels tend to be located in the northern part of the city where it's good to be careful at night. Most of them are independent (that is to say unconnected with An Óige (the Irish Youth Hostel Association) and prices range from £4.75 to £9 per night. In busy summer months, avoid trudging all over town by booking through the tourist office or calling yourself.

Isaac's (The Dublin Tourist Hostel), 2-4 Freedman's Lane (tel. 749 321), around the corner from Busárus. Hip young internationals rub elbows in this low-ceilinged, wood-raftered grotto. Notices of musical events plaster the walls, and live bands play on Wed. nights (free for those staying in hostel). The DART rattles by on its regular route. Self-catering kitchen, café, tightly monitored baggage room. Reception open 24 hr. Bed lockout 11am-5pm. No curfew. lockers 50p, sheet rental 75p. Big dorm £4.75, small (6-8 beds) dorm £5.50, singles £12, doubles £15/person.

Goin' My Way/Cardijn House, 15 Talbot St. (tel. 788 484 or 741 720), over Tiffany's Shoe Shop. Off O'Connell St., follow Earl St. A hideaway hostel with tiny rooms off five winding flights of stairs. Rooms closed 10am-5pm but coffee bar open all day. Midnight curfew. £5 including breakfast and sheet rental.

M.E.C., 43 North Great George St. (tel. 726 301), off Parnell St. This grand Georgian building was first built as the home of Dublin's Archbishop, and served as a convent until 1987. It remains heavenly, with huge, light, airy rooms that have been freshly renovated. Reception 24 hr. Dorm room £6.50, singles (in old nuns' cells) £12, doubles £9/person. Weekly (without breakfast): dorm £35, singles £45, doubles £40/person. Free linen. All-you-can-eat breakfast. Parking lot.

Kinlay House (USIT), 2-12 Lord Edward St. (tel. 679 6644), near Christ Church Cathedral. Protestant country boys who came to work in the city once slid down the beautifully carved oak bannisters in the lofty entrance hall; now tired backpackers trudge up the same stairs to crash in comfy beds or on the very soft couches in the TV room. Very central. No lockout, no curfew. Lockers, laundry, Kitchen facilities. Breakfast included. 4-bed unit £7.50/person; 4-6 bed unit £9.50/person; doubles £12.50/person.

Dublin International Youth Hostel (IYHF), Mountjoy St. (tel. 301 766), off Dorset St., a 5-10 min. walk from city center. This large and comfortable hostel retains traces of the convent it once was: confessional boxes act as phone booths, and the stained glass windows of the chapel-to-café inspires grace over breakfast. Reception (with currency exchange) open all day. No lockout; flexible midnight curfew. Courtesy bus meets the boats at B&I and Sealink docks. Sept.-June £8.50 members, £9 non-members; July-Aug. £9 members, £9.50 non-members. Breakfast included. Sheet rental 50p. Kitchen facilities. Laundry is around the corner. Lockers free of charge, baggage 50p per day if you've already checked out. Free parking lot with security guards.

The Young Traveler, St. Mary's Place (tel. 305 000), off Dorset St. adjacent to the grey church. Standard hostel decor and an extensive noticeboard listing events in the city. Lots of space in café and rooms, though a bit dark. Reception open 24 hr. No lockout, no curfew. £8.50. Breakfast included. Laundry facilities. No lockers but there is a safe in the baggage room.

Another option in summer is to rent private rooms at a college. The University of Dublin's **Trinity Hall,** Dartry Rd., Rathmines (tel. 971 772), is 3 mi. south of the city center (take bus #14 or 14A). Rooms have washbasins and desks. Bed and breakfast £11.50 with ISIC, £13 wwithout. Open late June to Sept. Reserve directly by phone.

Bed and Breakfast

A rash of quality B&Bs covers Dublin and the surrounding suburbs. Those marked by a green shamrock are registered, checked and approved by the Bord Fáilte (Irish Tourist Board). B&Bs without the shamrock haven't undergone inspection but are often of better quality than shamrocked B&Bs. The tourist office has information and will call for you; otherwise wander until you find one that looks good (cheapest £9 or 10, often up to £25). City B&Bs tend to be clustered north of the Liffey, especially on Lower and upper Gardiner Streets, as well as in the Parnell Square area. Those in the suburbs are more often private homes left with extra rooms in the wake of a large Catholic brood; owners are more likely to be flexible and interested in your travels (price range £10-15).

The following B&Bs (all north of the Liffey) are within a 10-minute walk of the city center:

Leitrim House, 34 Blessington St. (tel. 308 728), off Upper Dorset St. near Belvedere College, 1 block past the false teeth repair shop. Lilac walls in the bedrooms, flowers on the windowsill and reliquaries in the parlor, but the real charm lies in the grandmotherly touch. £10.

Elmar Hotel, 34 Lower Gardiner St. (tel. 741 246). Long bannisters, beautiful ceiling work, flowery curtains. Very clean. No curfew. Check-out time 10am. Singles £13, doubles £11/person, triples £10/person, quads £9/person.

Avondale Guest House, 40 Lower Gardiner St. (tel. 745 200). Two Georgian houses offer plain, comfortable rooms with central heating, and showers in each room. Friendly proprietor will cook you a big Irish breakfast, and keep your spirits up. Summer singles £16, doubles £14/person; winter singles £14, doubles £12/person.

Stella Maris Guest House, 13 Upper Gardiner St. (tel. 740 835). Elegant staircase dates from when Upper Gardiner was the poshest of addresses. Old wardrobes. Full-length mirrors shimmer in the old wardrobes. Watch TV in the front room with the stuffed quail. Singles £16, doubles £14/person.

Dublin's suburbs offer a glimpse into lifestyles of the not-so-rich-and-famous. In each, houses line a main street, and a village atmosphere persists in the absence of mall culture. Suburban B&Bs are easily reached by bus—call ahead to confirm vacancies and get exact directions. Consult the tourist office for a complete listing: what follows is merely intended to whet the appetite.

Mrs. R. Casey, Villa Jude, 2 Church Ave., Sandymount (tel. 684 982), off Tritonville Rd southeast of city center. Take bus #3 or the DART from the city center. Convenient to the ferries. Mrs. Casey has nourished seven children and many travelers with her homemade bread and strapping Irish breakfasts. The parlor overflows with family photos, fresh flowers, and lace doilies. £10.

Ms. Birmingham's, 8 Dramond Terr., Sandymount (tel. 683 861). Take bus #3 or the DART southeast. Old-fashioned rooms, one with a bay window overlooking the garden and a TV in the sitting room. Quaint. £10.50.

Mrs. M. Lambert, 8 Ballymun Rd., Glasnevin Hill (tel. 376 125), northwest Dublin. Take bus #11, 11A, 13, 13A, 19, 19A, 34, or 34A. Fluffy comforters and well-wrn carpets in a safe working-class neighborhood. Young women preferred. Tea, toast, and cornflakes in the morning. £10, storytime not included.

Angela Lawlor, 95 Iona Rd. Drumcondra (tel. 309 052), northeast Dublin. Take bus #11, 11A, 16, or 16A. Tasteful parlor with cushions that invite a book and a cup of tea. Run by a traveler who will get you just what you need, be it fresh bread or a night of traditional set dancing. Gourmet dinner with a glass of wine £8.

Camping

The only campground convenient to the city is **Shankill Caravan and Camping Park** (tel. 820 011). Take bus #45, 45A, 84, or DART to Shankill. Middle-aged travelers in campers share a grassy area interspersed with shrubs and tents. Not the best place for an intensive sightseeing tour of Dublin; take in the view of the hills or a 20 min. stroll to the beach instead. Checkout by 1pm. £3.50-4.50/tent, 50p/person, children under 12 25p, under 3 free; in summer, add £1. 8-min. shower 50p. Electricity (75p), water, toilets. Stay a week and get one night free. Open Easter-Oct.

Food

Dublin's open air markets provide fresh and cheap fixings for those on a tight budget—they are also fun just to visit. Vendors hawk fruit, vegetables, fish, flowers, and the occasional chocolate bar from their pushcarts. The **Moore St. Market,** lined with butcher shops, is the city's leading trading place (Mon.-Sat. 9am-5pm). The **Thomas St. Market,** past Christchurch, (Fri.-Sat.) and the new **Festival Market,** at the corner of Nicholas St. and Back Lane off High St. where the hill goes down (Fri.-Sun.), are calmer alternatives. The **Powerscourt Townhouse,** Clarendon St., has several health food stores (open Mon.-Sat. 9:30am-6pm). The **Runner Bean,** 4 Nassau St., vends wholefoods, vegetables, homemade breads, fruits, and nuts (open Mon.-Fri. 7:30am-6pm, shorter hr. Sat.). Your cheapest option is **Dunne's Stores,** a supermarket chain, with a branch on North Earl St. off O'Connell St. (open Mon.-Wed. 9am-6pm, Thurs. 9am-8pm, Fri. 9am-7pm, and Sat. 9am-6pm).

On-the-go food is quick, greasy, and very popular; you can't escape the "Take Out/Fish and Chips" signs. For variation, try chips with gravy, or potato cakes (flat pancakes of potato), but don't expect to stray far from the potato theme—that tuber plays an important part in Irish history and is a national staple. Many pubs serve food as well as drink, and "pub grub" is a good option for quick and inexpensive meals of sandwiches, pints, and potato chips (called "crisps").

Bewley's Cafes, at Grafton, Westmoreland, and S. Great George's St. (tel. 776 761). The classic Dublin 19th-century coffeeshops, with dark wood paneling, marble table tops, and mirrored walls. Extensive bakery with wildly complex pastries (95p). Outstanding coffee, pastries, and lunches. James Joyce frequented the Westmoreland St. branch (open Mon.- Sat. 8am-7pm, Sun. 10am-6pm) and the Grafton St. branch is the largest of the lot (open Mon.-Fri. 8am-8pm, Sat. 8am-7pm, Sun. 10am-6pm). South Great George's St. café open Mon.-Wed. 7:30am-7pm, Thurs.-Sat. 7:30am-2am.

The Coffee Bean, 4 Nassau St. (tel. 797 140), above the Runner Bean, across from Trinity Green. A café for quiet whispers. An older crowd reads the papers in the afternoon. Soup £1.10; vegetarian (£3.25) and meat (£4.25) dishes served with two salads. Open Mon.-Sat. 10:30am-3:30pm; lunch served 12:15pm-2:30pm (£1.50 minimum for those hours). At dinner (starting at 6:30pm) the name of the place changes to "Capers," and prices rise beyond the means of the budget traveler.

Beshoff's, 14 Westmoreland St. (tel. 778 026) and 7 O'Connell St. (tel. 743 223). Hungry passersby wander in off the street for chips and 17 different varieties of fish. Fake plants bloom luxuriously. Tasty, cheap, and franchised. Mackerel with chips £1.90. Open Mon.-Thurs. 11:30-11pm, Fri.-Sat. 11:30-1am, Sun. 12:30-11pm.

Trinity College, The Buttery, 50 yds. inside the campus gates on the left. Cheap salads (£1.70) and a bar. (Cafeteria open all year Mon.-Fri. 9:30am-4pm; pub open all year Mon.-Fri. 11am-1pm and 4-11:30pm; restaurant open during the term Mon.-Fri. noon-2pm and 4-7pm, during the summer Mon.-Fri. 4-6pm.) The **J.C.R.,** just on the right inside the gates, has cheap snacks when the college is in session (Mon.-Fri. 9am-6pm). To the left around the corner you can listen to traditional music or rock 'n' roll (£2) at 1pm daily and munch sandwiches (£1).

Bad Ass Café, Crown Alley, off Dame St. (tel. 712 596 for pizza). Huge warehouse converted into a loud Viewmaster snapshot of "Born in the USA" American culture. Trendy young crowd basks in the glow of fire-engine red trim. Lunch £3-5. Student menu (with ISIC). Open daily 9am-10pm.

The Unique Ursula, Store St., above Keating's Bar and just across from Isaac's hostel. Drooping green vines painted all over the walls, and an acrylic tiger-striped throw rug make an odd combination of kitsch and funk. Good food, but the staff is just learning. Irish breakfast £2 (7:30am-noon), lunch specials all day (£2.75-3.25). Vegetarian special daily. Not a dinner option.

The Well Fed Café, in the Dublin Resource Centre, Crow St. Inventive vegetarian dishes served by a worker's co-operative in a hotbed of revolution. Peace and protest posters on the walls; idealists and disenchanteds at the tables. Try their brown bread with soup (£1) and apple pie with cream (£1). Open Mon. 10:30am-4:30pm, Tues.-Sat. 10:30am-8:30pm.

Cornucopia, 20 Wicklow St. Vegetarian restaurant and wholefood shop. The same crowd as Well Fed Café but less mystique; peaceful long beards munch whole grains on high stools. Meals £1.30-3. Restaurant open Mon.-Sat. 8-11am, noon-8pm; 9pm on Thurs. Shop open Mon.-Wed., Fri-Sat. 8am-8pm, Thurs. 8am-9pm, Sun. 8am-6pm.

Pubs

Good puzzle would be cross Dublin without passing a pub.

—James Joyce

A local radio station recently offered £100 to whomever could solve the puzzle; the winner, in true Irish fashion, explained that you could take any route—you'd just have to visit them all on the way! A cornerstone of Irish life, pubs have had their praises sung in many rollicking bars and in literature as well: Joyce's *Dubliners* particularly catches the essence of old Dublin's "hot, reeking public houses." In the afternoons and evenings, Dubliners scuttle out of the rain into these warm, dry watering spots for a pint or more of Guinness. Historically gathering spots for common folk, pubs retain their community character with patrons exchanging local gossip and friendly jibes. The atmosphere is particularly cheery on Sunday afternoons, when whole families come thundering in after church. Children are allowed in pubs until 7pm, and 18 is the official drinking age. Most pubs in Dublin open at 10:30am (around 12:30pm on Sundays) and all pubs close at 11:30pm (Sundays at 11pm), at which time revelers stagger to the dance clubs which stay open into the wee hours.

Within city limits, public houses must also obey the afternoon "holy hour," which lasts from 2:30-3:30pm. The average price of a pint is £1.70.

Pubs reflect their neighborhood—those in the city center tend to have a younger, yuppified crowd, while north of the Liffey and away from Grafton St. locals down mugs of their favorite brew. Many of the Leeson St./Baggot St. area pubs (south of St. Stephen's Green) shake, rattle and stamp with music after 9pm.

Dublin's oldest pub, the **Brazen Head,** was established in 1198 as the first stop after the bridge on the way into the city, and it has welcomed travelers ever since. Singles eye each other across crowded rooms, or in the cobblestone courtyard on warm nights. (Lower Bridge St., off Merchant's Quay.) Across the way, live music and happy patrons spill nightly into the street from **O'Shea's Merchant.** Closer to the center of town, a number of pubs cater to students: **McDaid's,** 3 Harry St., draws ribald buskers and a young, very hip crowd. Patrons of the **Bailey,** 2 Duke St., channel their alienation into marvelously morose poses. **Casper & Giumbini's** on Wicklow St., just off Grafton St. (by Weir Jewelers), is quiet, stylish, mahogany-laden, and expensive (pints £2). The crowd, aged 23 and older, dresses neatly. (Guacamole £1.65, triple-decker sandwiches £2.95; minimum age 23; open daily noon-midnight.) **Kehoe's** offers "snugs," cubbyholes suitable for lovers or domestic spats where you can drink, coo or argue in privacy (South Anne's St., off Grafton St.). South of the Liffey, desperate admirers of Yeats can visit **Toner's,** 139 Lower Baggot St., the only pub in which the bard ever set foot, staying only long enough to drink one sherry before insisting on going home. Yuppies crowd into the ever-hopping **O'Donoghue's,** 15 Merrion Row (tel. 607 194), near Baggot St. The **Dublin Literary Pub Crawl** (tel. 540 228) traces Dublin's literary and liquid history with snatches of information and entrancing monologues. Mon.-Thurs. £5, £4 for students. Meet at the Bailey (2 Duke St.) at 7:30pm. June-Aug.

Sights

Dublin is an easily walkable city; most of the sights lie within a ¾mi. radius of O'Connell Bridge. *Visitor Attractions in Dublin* (75p) outlines major sights and is available at the Irish Tourist Board. The tourist office also provides walking guides packed with historical information (£1 each) on the Old City, the Cultural Heritage Trail, and the Georgian Heritage Trail. For Joyce fans, the tourist office provides a *Ulysses* map of Dublin (50p) that details some of Leopold Bloom's haunts. Begin with kidneys for breakfast in the best Bloomian tradition (there's a W.C. for purists), then set off on his odyssey across the city, in and out of pubs, stores, and perhaps even a couple of "houses" in Nighttown. The entire walk will inevitably take 18 hours (including drinking and debauching).

The two guided tours given by Trinity College students are the best introduction to Dublin. The **Historical Walking Tour** is a 2-hr. crash course in Dublin's history from the Celts to the present. (Daily at 11am, noon, 2pm, and 3pm; £3.50; June-Sept. Meet at Trinity's front gate.) The witty, caustic, 30-min. **Trinity College Walking Tour** also introduces Dublin's history, but concentrates on University lore. (9am-4:30pm, leaving every 15 min. from inside the front gate; £3 includes admission to the Old Library and the *Book of Kells* (see below); June-Sept.) A tip for the guide is expected. Bus Éireann offers two tours for the footsore: a 3-hr. **Dublin City Sightseeing Tour** with commentary (April to mid-Dec. daily 10:15am, 2:15pm; June-Aug. daily 6:15pm; £7); or the **Dublin Heritage Trail** which allows you to get on and off at various sights. (Tours daily, every hr. between 10am and 4pm (except 1pm); £5; mid-April to Sept.) Both tours begin at 59 O'Connell St.

Trinity College to St. Stephen's Green

Trinity College, sandwiched between Nassau and Pearse St. in the center of town, has its main entrance off Dame St. Its stone buildings, cobblestone walk, and spacious green grounds offer respite from the mayhem outside the gates, and room for an occasional white-suited game of cricket. Queen Elizabeth I founded Trinity in 1592 as a Protestant religious seminary whose purpose was "to civilize the Irish and cure them of Popery" and, with any luck, turn out local bureaucrats to help the British rule Ireland. For generations, the Catholic church deemed it a cardinal sin to attend Trinity. When the church lifted this ban in the 1960s, the size of the student body more than tripled. Such luminaries as Jonathan Swift, George Berkeley, Robert Emmett, Thomas Moore, Edmund Burke, Bram Stoker, Oscar Wilde, and Samuel Beckett once brightened the campus. The oldest remaining part of the college is the **Old Library,** built in 1712. Notable for its staircase and plaster work by the German architect Cassels, it houses Ireland's finest collection of Egyptian, Greek, Latin, and Irish manuscripts. The high-ceilinged, wood-vaulted Long Room is a treasure trove; Queen Elizabeth's 16th-century coat of arms guards the library's oldest volumes, including two volumes of Ireland's cherished *Book of Kells.* Four volumes in all, the books' dizzyingly intricate illuminated manuscript, each containing one of the Gospels was written and painted by Irish monks around the year 800. In 1007 it was unearthed in Kells, where thieves had buried it. One page is turned each month. Also on display in the Long Room are Ireland's oldest harp, and one of the few remaining original proclamations of the Republic of Ireland (read aloud from the Post Office on Easter Monday, 1916). (Open Mon.-Fri. 9:30am-4:45pm, Sat. 9:30am-12:45pm. Admission charged April-Oct. only, £1.75, seniors and students £1.50, under 18 free.) **The Dublin Experience** at the Old Library engulfs the visitor in a multi-media history of Dublin. (Open May 21-Oct. 3, Mon-Fri. 9:30am-4:45pm, Sat. 9:30am-12:45am, hourly shows beginning at 10am. Admission £2.50, under 18 £1.50.)

The building with monolithic columns facing the main entrance of Trinity ensconces the **Bank of Ireland** and once housed the Irish Parliament. In 1800 the English, alarmed by the United Irish Rebellion, passed the Act of Union and thus merged Ireland's parliament with England's in London. The government sold the building to the bank on the condition that reminders of the Irish Parliament be effaced. The enormous curved walls and pillars were erected around the original structure; the bank inside is actually much smaller. You can still visit the House of Lords, which contains the gold mace of the House of Commons. The last speaker of the House refused to hand it over to the English, saying that he would keep it until an Irish Parliament returned. (Open during regular banking hr.: Mon.-Wed. and Fri. 10am-12:30pm and 1:30-3pm, Thurs. 10am-12:30pm and 1:30-5pm. Free.)

Many of Dublin's museums lie south of the city, on the block between Kildare St. and Upper Merrion St. Irish history and culture are the theme of the **National Museum,** Kildare St. (tel. 618 811); visit the informative exhibition of Republican history and the 1916 uprising, the Tara Brooch and other Celtic goldwork, and the live leprechaun. (Open Tues.-Sat. 10am-5pm, Sun. 2-5pm. Museum free except for the Treasury: £1, students 50p, children 30p, families £2. Admission to the Treasury free on Tues.) Connected to the main building, the **Division of Natural History,** specializes in stuffed Irish wildlife—this may be your only chance to see the Great Irish Elk. (Open Tues.-Sat. 10am-5pm, Sun. 2-5pm. Free.) Down the street on Merrion Sq., the **National Gallery's** four-floor winding staircase is lined with portraits of Lady Gregory, Eliza O'Neill, James Joyce, George Bernard Shaw (who willed a third of his estate to the Gallery), John Synge, and William Butler Yeats (by his father, John Butler Yeats). The collection also includes works by Spanish, Flemish, and Dutch masters. (tel. 615 133. Open Mon.-Sat. 10am-6pm, Thurs. 10am-9pm, Sun. 2-5pm. Free.) Nearby, the **National Library** devotes itself to writings from throughout Irish history and hosts exhibitions of literary interest in the entrance room. (Open Mon. 10am-9pm, Tues.-Wed. 2pm-9pm, Thurs.-Fri. 10am-5pm, Sat. 10am-1pm. Free.)

Though Joyce referred to Dublin as "this Danish city," its British influence is more pronounced. Stroll around Merrion Sq. and Fitzwilliam St. (near the National Museum) to enjoy the Georgian buildings and their elaborate rows of colorful doorways. W.B. Yeats moved from 18 Fitzwilliam St. to 82 Merrion Sq., and George Bernard Shaw and Bram Stoker (creator of Dracula) were neighbors on Harcourt St. (Bernard Shaw at 61 and Stoker at 16). In February 1972, rioters burned down the British Embassy at No. 34, in retaliation for brutalities in Derry, Northern Ireland. Off Upper Merrion St., just souht of Trinity at the far end of Kildare and Grafton St., is **St. Stephen's Green,** a formerly private estate bequeathed to the city by the Guinness beer clan. Frequented by punks and pensioners, the green includes an artificial lake and acres of waterfalls, fountains, arched bridges, trees and formal flower beds. During the summer, picnickers and bench-sitters enjoy outdoor theatrical productions near the old bandstand. (Gates open Mon.-Sat. 8am-dusk, Sun. 10am-dusk.) On the park's north side, the **Mansion House** on Dawson St., has been the residence of every Lord Mayor of Dublin since 1715. It was here that the Declaration of Independence was signed in 1919 and the Anglo-Irish Truce adopted in 1921.

Dame St. Environs and Along the Quay

Two blocks towards the castle and parallel to Grafton St. is South William St., where the **Dublin Civic Museum,** (#58; tel. 794 260, part of the City Assembly House), has an elaborate display of photographs, antiquities and knick-knacks. (Open Tues.-Sat. 10am-6pm, Sun. 11am-2pm. Free.) Off Dame St., on Palace St., is the entrance to the **Dublin Castle,** (tel. 777 129), built in 1204 by King John on the site of a former Viking fortress, and seat of English rule for more than 700 years. The Birmingham Tower was once a prison (it now houses offices), and fifty insurgents died at the castle's walls on Easter Monday, 1916, during the Easter Rising. 1938 saw the inauguration of an Irish President at the castle, and the ceremony has been performed there ever since. If no state functions are in progress, you can visit the State Apartments to see how English Viceroys lived. (State Apartments generally open Mon.-Fri. 10am-12:15pm and 2-5pm. Sat.-Sun. and holidays 2-5pm. Admission £1, students and children 50p.) Next door, the **City Hall** boasts an intricate inner dome and statues of national heroes, including Daniel O'Connell, a democratic politician of the early 19th century and the first Catholic Lord Mayor of Dublin. (Open Mon.-Fri. 9am-1pm, 2-5pm; free.)

At the end of Dame St. looms **Christ Church Cathedral.** Sitric, King of the Dublin Norsemen, erected a wooden church on this site in 1038; in 1169 the English warrior "Strongbow" rebuilt it in stone. At one point the cavernous crypt was used for shops and drinking houses—now cobwebs hang down from the ceiling, fragments of ancient pillars lie about like bleached bones, and a mummified cat is frozen in act of chasing a mummified mouse. (Open to visitors daily 10am-5pm except during services. Choral evensong Thurs. 6pm except July and August. 50p donation.) Patrick St. runs south to the 12th-century **St. Patrick's Cathedral,** which sanctifies ground that has been holy since 450 AD St. Patrick, Ireland's patron saint, who banished the snakes and brought Christianity to Ireland in the 5th century, allegedly performed baptisms in the park next to the cathedral. Artifacts and relics from the Order of St. Patrick adorn the cathedral's interior. (Open Mon.-Fri. 8:30am-6:15pm, Sat. 8:30am-5pm, Sun. 10am-4:30pm; 50p donation, 30p students.)

Further west, along High St., stands **St. Audoen's Church,** the oldest of Dublin's parish churches, founded by the Normans. Contact the vicar to arrange a visit (tel. 542 274). **St. Audoen's Arch,** built in 1215 next to the church, is the only surviving gate of the old city walls. Actors in period costume re-enact Ireland Before The Vikings in the **Viking Adventure,** staged with the church as backdrop. (Open Tues.-Sat. 10am-4:30pm; adults £1.50, children/seniors/students with ID £1.)High St. subsequently becomes Thomas and then James St., where the giant **Guinness Brewery,** St. James Gate, produces 2½ million pints a day. The Hopstore and visitor center hold displays on the beer-making process and the history of the brewery itself, and shows a short film; afterwards visitors may sample the legendary dark brew. (Open Mon.-Fri. 10am-3pm. Admission £2, children 50p.) Take bus #21A, 78, 78A or 78B west along the quays, where the scent of Guinness is strong and the murky river water curiously resembles the beverage.

The **Royal Hospital Kilmainham** and **Kilmainham Jail** lie yet further to the west, a 20 min. walk from the city center. The Royal Hospital, now the **Museum of Modern Art,** is large and light, having trapped some of the hospital's sterility in its vast whitewashed walls. Call for a schedule of their changing exhibits, artist talks, or concerts (tel. 718 666). (Open Tues.-Sun. 10am-5pm; free.) Kilmainham Jail (tel. 535 984) stands as a silent tribute to those who died for the cause of Irish independence. Irish rebels were confined here from 1796 to 1924; former President of Ireland Éamon de Valera was the last. (Open June-Sept. daily 11am-6pm; Oct.-May Wed. and Sun. 2-6pm. Admission £1.50, seniors £1, students and children 60p.) Take buses #51, 78, or 79 to both the Museum and the Jail.

North of the Liffey

O'Connell St. exemplifies Irish classical architecture, with wide Latin boulevards, impressive pediments, and plain facades. It is lined with monuments to Ireland's great leaders—politician John Stewart Parnell, champion of labor Jones Larkin, and Catholic emancipator Daniel O'Connell. The revolutionaries of the Easter Rising of 1916 barricaded themselves in the austere (and thereafter bullet-scarred) **General Post Office,** and the republican patriot Padraig Pearse read the Irish Proclamation that declared Ireland a free nation on its steps. Inside, a glass case exhibits pennies fused together by the British army's incendiary bombing. At the top of O'Connell St. past Parnell Sq. **Remembrance Park** eulogizes the martyrs of the Irish revolution. A cross-shaped pool is plugged at one end by a statue of 4 swans rising out of 4 human bodies, crying (in Irish) "O generations of freedom remember us, the generations of the vision." Overlooking the park, the **Hugh Lane Municipal Gallery** juxtaposes modern works with the Georgian architecture of Charlemont House. Lane died in World War I, leaving his will unsigned and creating great confusion as to whether his impressive art collection had been left to the English or the Irish. A somewhat clumsy settlement was reached; every five years the Dublin gallery and the Tate Gallery in London swap halves. (Regular opening hours are Tues.-Sat. 9:30am-6pm, Sun. 11am-5pm; free.)

The **Custom House,** a few blocks east of O'Connell St. on Custom House Quay, is an 18th-century masterpiece of architect James Gandon. Carved heads of river goddesses, best viewed from across the river, adorn the exterior of the Customs House. West of O'Connell, on Inn's Quay, stands another of Gandon's works, the **Four Courts.** In 1922 this building, then the headquarters of the radical Irish Republican Army, was attacked by the Free Staters (the new government of the southern state) under pressure from the British, signalling the beginning of the Irish Civil War. Just up Church St. the dry atmosphere has effectively mummified the corpses in the vaults of **St. Michan's Church.** One 700-year old cadaver was once a Crusader; tradition forced all visitors to shake his hand until it fell off a few years ago. (Open Mon.-Fri. 10am-12:45pm, 2-4:45pm, Sat. 10am-12:45pm. Adults £1.50, students and seniors £1, children under 16 50p.)

At 3:30pm sharp the **Irish Whisky Corner,** a museum off Mary St. demonstrating the distilling process, shows a film on the history of Irish whisky. The presentation ends with a glass of The Jameson and a mini-lecture on the nuances of whisky drinking. (Daily 3:30pm; £2.50.)

Take bus #10, 23, 25, 26, or 51 west to **Phoenix Park,** the largest enclosed public park in Europe. The "Phoenix Park murders" mentioned often in *Ulysses* took place in 1882; members of a radical nationalist group, the "Invincibles," stabbed the Chief Secretary of Ireland, Lord Cavendish, and his Under-Secretary, Mr. Burke, 200 yds. from the Phoenix column. The park, frequent scene of polo games, covers 1,760 acres and contains the President's Residence (Aras an Uachtarain), one of the world's oldest Zoological Gardens, cricket pitches, and grazing red deer and cattle. The zoo was founded in 1830 with one inaugural wild boar. (Zoo open Mon.-Sat. 9:30am-6pm, Sun. 11am-6pm; closes at sunset in winter. Admission £3.30, seniors and children £1.60, under 3 free.)

Entertainment

Be it Seamus Heaney or the Pogues that strikes your fancy, Dublin is equipped to entertain you. The *Dublin Event Guide* (free from the tourist office) is a collection of advertisements and events which comes out on Fridays for the following week.

For those who want to go out on the town, *In Dublin* (£1.50) offers feature articles as well as a smorgasbord of choices: music listings detailing bands, times and cover charge (on average £2-3, if not free), theater reviews with showtimes and ticket prices, exhibitions, and comedy shows. Buy it on Thursdays for the following fortnight.

Theater

At 8pm Dublin's curtains rise on mainstream productions, classic shows, and experimental theater. Dame St. and its alleyways are home to 3 or 4 companies; the rest are scattered within a 10 min. radius of O'Connell Bridge. The national theater of Ireland, the **Abbey Theatre,** 26 Lower Abbey St. (tel. 787 222), was founded in 1904 by W.B. Yeats and Lady Gregory as a gesture of Celtic pride and a landmark of the Irish Literary Renaissance. The old building, having witnessed moments as dramatic as riots on the opening nights of J.M. Synge's *Playboy of the Western World* and Sean O'Casey's *The Plough and Stars,* burned down in 1951 and was replaced by a starkly modern edifice. (Box office open Mon.-Sat. 10:30am-7pm; tickets £8-13; student standby discounts available one hour before the show.) Downstairs is the smaller and more experimental **Peacock Theatre** (tel. 787 222), with evening shows and occasional lunchtime presentations of plays, concerts, and poetry (£5-8). (Box office opens Mon.-Sat. at 7:30pm for that night's performance only; advance booking at the Abbey Theatre box office. Showtime 8:15pm.) The **Gate Theatre** (tel. 744 045) at 1 Cavendish Row, produces everything from Restoration comedies to Irish classics. (Box office open Mon.-Sat. 10am-7pm; tickets £8-13; student standby £5 Mon.-Thurs. at curtain time.)

The **Gaiety,** South King St. (tel. 771 717), provides space for ballet, pantomime, and the Dublin Grand Opera Society (box office open Mon.-Sat. 11am-7pm; tickets £7.50-12.50). On Dame St., the **Olympia Theatre,** 72 Dame St. (tel. 778 962), hosts old standbys like "The Sound of Music" and fine Gaelic performances. (Box office open Mon.-Sat. 10am-6:30pm; tickets £8-15; student standby after 7pm half-price; reopens at 7:30pm for nightly performances.) Around the corner at 39 East Essex St., the **Project Arts Centre** (tel. 712 321) presents a wide range of shows, from avant-garde theater and dramatic readings to comedy and dance. Their free gallery of changing exhibitions is open during box office hours. (Daily 10am-6pm; tickets £8, concession £6.) **Andrews Lane Theatre,** Andrews Lane, off Dame St. (tel. 795 720), also tends to modern, less mainstream shows. The **Dublin University Players,** a group of college thespians stages a broad mix of shows weekly during the term. In summertime, other companies use the space, often with experimental plays or lunchtime theater (usually £3-4). Check *In Dublin* or walk inside the Trinity gates and turn right for details. The **Lambert Puppet Theatre** (shows 3:30pm Sat. and Sun.; £3), with outstanding puppet shows for kids, justifies the trip to Monkstown. Take DART or buses #7, 7A, or 8. For artsy-fartsy movies, your best bet is the **Lighthouse Cinema,** 107 Fleet St. (tel. 730 438). (Shows every night; £2 before 5pm, £3.50 after.)

Music

Dublin's music world attracts performers from all over the country. Pubs set the stage for much of the action, giving musicians free beer and a chance to play. There is often a cover charge of £2-3 on better-known acts. *In Dublin* should be your bible, guiding you to traditional, country, jazz, or rock on any night of the week. Bills posted all over the city also inform you of what's coming up. Scheduled concerts usually start at 9pm, impromptu ones even later.

Traditional music is not a tourist gimmick, but a vibrant and important element of the Dublin music scene; natives and foreigners alike clap hands and stamp to the drone of the pipe and the roll of the bodhrán (bow-rawn) drum. Some pubs in the city center have traditional sessions nightly; try **O'Shea's Merchant** (tel. 793 797) or the **Brazen Head** (tel. 774 549), both on Lower Bridge St. off Merchant's Quay, or **O'Donoghue's,** 15 Merrion Row (tel. 607 194) near Baggot St. North of the Liffey, stop in at **Slattery's,** 130 Capel St. (tel. 727 971), and **Hughes',** 19 Chancery St. (tel. 726 540), in back of the Four Courts.

You can find country at the Brazen Head, **Barry's Hotel,** 1 Great Denmark St. (tel. 746 943), or the American-style **Bad Bob's,** 32 East Essex St. (tel. 775 482). For jazz, **Rudyard's Wine Bar** offers live sessions Friday and Saturday nights at 9pm (15 Crown Alley, tel. 710 846); **McDaid's,** 3 Henry St. (tel. 794 395), hosts acts on Mondays amd Tuesdays at 8:30pm. Sunday afternoon jazz is very common; check *In Dublin* for listings. Rock with a trendy crowd at the **International Bar,** 23 Wicklow St. (tel. 779 250), on Thursday through Saturday nights, or head to the **Baggot Inn,** 143 Baggot St. (tel. 761 430).

For classical music lovers, the **National Concert Hall,** Earl's Fort Terrace (tel. 711 533), provides a venue for touring orchestras. In July and August there are shows nightly at 8pm (tickets £7-10, students ½price), and a noon lunchtime series is held throughout the summer on Tuesdays and Fridays (tickets £2.50-3).

Dance Clubs

As a rule, these spots open at 10:30 or 11pm, but the action gets moving only after 11:30pm, when partiers swarm from closing pubs to the dance floors; most clubs close down at 3 or 4am but some stay open as late as 6am. If they don't take your money going in (£4-6 cover, which entitles you to a free meal), they'll force you to buy a bottle of wine (£15-20), so be prepared to spend. Pints cost about £2. Dress codes ban tanktops for men and jeans for both genders; those in hiking boots will have to do some sweet talking. **Lower Leeson Street,** off St. Stephen's Green, is the hotspot for latenight life. **Strings, Suesey Street,** and **BongBongs** are among the dozen or so clubs that brazenly occupy the basements of old Georgian houses, flashing their presence with neon signs. **Heyday** is a unique leather-laden den. All the major hotels run discos as well.

Events

The tourist office and *Dublin Events Guide* will willingly inform you about Dublin's many festivals, provincial parades, mayor's balls, concerts, dance, and art shows. Ask about *fleadhs,* traditional day-long musical festivals. The **World Irish Dancing Championships,** held in late March to early April in the Grand Hotel, Malahide, conflate traditional music with Gaelic dance. For information, contact Ireland's traditional music society **Comhaltas Ceoltóirí Éireann** (co-UL-tus; also known as **Cultúrlann**), 32 Belgrave Sq., Monkstown (tel. 800 295). The **Festival of Music in Irish Houses,** held during the second and third weeks of June, organizes concerts of period music in local 18th-century homes. Perhaps the most entertaining of all is the **Dublin International Folk Festival,** three days of vamping, thrumming, and sheer indulgence in July.

If you happen to be in town on June 16, join the celebrations of **Bloomsday,** the day on which Joyce loosed his *Ulysses* breath on Dublin. Besides staged readings, there is a garden party at Merrion St., lunch at Davy Byrne's, a walk based on the narrative of Chapter 8 and men wandering around in Joycean garb. **St. Patrick's Day** (March 17) is a day for parades and drunken carousing.

The **Dublin Theatre Festival** in late September and early October is a leading cultural event. You can purchase tickets all year at participating theaters, at all branches of the Irish Life Building Society, and, as the festival draws near, at the Festival Booking Office, 47 Nassau St., Dublin 2 (tel. 778 439; 50% discount with ISIC; student standby tickets are £2-3).

Home games of the Irish **rugby** team are played in Lansdowne Road Stadium from October to March. The season for **Gaelic football** and **hurling** (the national sports of Ireland)—both games of skill, stamina, and strength with deep historical roots—runs from mid-February to November. Provincial finals take place in July, national semifinals in August (hurling on the first Sunday, football on the second and third Sundays), and the All-Ireland Finals in September; games are played in Croke Park and Phibsborough Rd. (Tickets available at the turnstiles. All-Ireland

Finals tickets sell out quickly.) **Camogie** (women's hurling) finals also take place in September. For sports information, check the Friday papers or contact the Gaelic Athletic Association at 36 32 32.

Shopping

Although tiny shops dot the streets both north and south of the Liffey, Dublin's major shopping streets are **Grafton St.** and **Henry St.** On Grafton, well-dressed crowds hurry by countless boutiques, record shops, and restaurants; homeless people and buskers lay out their caps for money. Snazzy expensive displays make it an ideal area for window-shopping. Nearby, Lord Powerscourt's 200-year-old townhouse on Clarendon St., now the **Powerscourt Townhouse Centre,** has been converted into a string of chic boutiques strung around a central café. In the north, **Henry St.,** off O'Connell, has cheaper goods, both in price and quality, and a less finicky clientele. **Ilac,** Dublin's answer to the urban mall, lurks just around the corner on Moore St. (behind a rainbowed facade). Dublin's principal department store (and a good landmark), **Clery's,** sits sedately on Upper O'Connell St. (tel. 786 000; open Mon.-Wed. and Fri.-Sat. 9am-5:30pm, Thurs. 9am-8pm). **Aran sweaters** are often either overpriced or poorly made. If you insist on carrying home a wool souvenir, you'll get the best value for your money at the **Dublin Woollen Co.** (tel. 770 301), Ha'penny Bridge (toll no longer charged), 41 Lower Ormond Quay, which has a huge selection of sweaters and tweeds.

Bookstores in the northern section specialize in romance novels; **Eason's,** 40/42 Lower O'Connell St., is an exception, selling lots of serious tomes with an extensive "Irish interest" section. Eason's also has a special bargain bookshop opposite its side entrance at 74 Middle Abbey St. Stores around Trinity College and in the Grafton St. area sell more uniformly highbrow texts. Dublin's best-known and most comprehensive bookstore is **Fred Hanna's,** 28-29 Nassau St., across from Trinity College. It has a great selection of second-hand and antique volumes in addition to new books (open Mon.-Sat. 9am-5:30pm). All bookstores in the city have Irish interest sections, but for books written in Irish and specialty books written in English about Ireland, try **An Siopa Leabhar Celtic Bookshop,** at 6 Harcourt St. (open Mon.-Fri. 9:30am-1:30pm and 2-5:30pm, Sat. 10am-1:30pm and 2-4pm). For recordings of Irish music, visit **Claddagh Records,** 2 Cecilia St., behind Central Bank.

You can get camping gear off O'Connell St. and Talbert St., where there are many competing shops. **The Great Outdoors,** Chatham St. (tel. 794 293), off the top of Grafton St., has an excellent selection of tents, backpacks, and cookware. (Open Mon.-Wed. and Fri.-Sat. 9:30am-5:30pm, Thurs. 9:30am-8pm.) **O'Meara's,** 26 Ossory Rd. (tel. 363 233), off North Strand Rd., also sells a wide range of gear and rents tents by the week. (A small 2-person tent for 1 week, £17. Open Mon.-Sat. 9:30am-1pm and 2-6pm, Sun. 2:30-5:30pm.)

Near Dublin

Ireland's east coast from Drogheda in the north to Wicklow in the south is easily accessible from Dublin by DART or bus, although you may have to hitch between small rural towns. See Dublin's "Arriving and Departing" and "Orientation" sections for information on buses, trains, and DART, and consult the "East Coast" listings for places of interest.

North of Dublin

The towns stretching north of the city abound with castles and private homes, but are often ignored because of their suburban location.

Howth

Nine mi. northeast of Dublin, Howth's rocky headland guards the north shore of Dublin Bay. Fishing boats congregate in the harbor, and fishermen toss their catch to the vendors who populate the pier. Just offshore, **Ireland's Eye** once provided religious sanctuary, as attested to by the ruins of a church and Martello tower, but noew the island's long beach is primarily a bird's haven. Frank Doyle & Sons, on the East Pier (tel. 314 200), charge £3 for the round-trip journey (children £1.50); May-Oct. daily; call to arrange).

The town of Howth is built on a hill which reaches up from the water to the top of high cliffs. Aside from its spectacular views, Howth's main attraction is probably **Howth Castle,** on the outskirts of town. (Take a right on Harbor Rd. as you leave the DART station; the castle turn-off ¼mi. down the road is well-marked.) Starkly impressive despite its motley architectural design, the castle maintains a shroud of superstition. Doorways lead off from the ancient gate into tiny blackened cells. No tours are held, but should the gate ever close the keeper would be far more accursed than you. The well-trodden path leads further up the hills to the over-flowered **Rhododendron Gardens** (open year-round 8am-sunset; flowers bloom April-June). Back in town, the remains of **St. Mary's Abbey** stand peacefully surrounded by the cemetery at the bend in Church St. The walls and arches of this 13th-century abbey are still quite sound; the courtyard is locked off but easily visible through the magnificent stone windows. On Main St., the **Royal Howth** serves reasonably priced lunches and dinners (£3-4; open Mon. and Sat. 10:30am-6:30pm, Tues.-Fri. 10:30am-8:30pm) and every summer night traditional music enlivens **Ye Olde Abbey Tavern** (tel. 322 006; open daily, music usually starts at 9pm; cover charge £3. In winter open Mon.-Sat. only; bar open 5:30-11pm, restaurant 7-11pm).

A **cliff walk** rings the peninsula, and takes about an hour. The path follows heather-crossed cliffs, past the nests of thousands of seabirds, a cairn reputed to be the grave of Criffan (the last pre-Christian High King of Ireland), and the cleft in Puck's Rock. To get to the trail head, turn left from the Howth DART station and bus stop, follow Harbour Rd. around the corner and climb the hill. For the less hardy, bus #88 follows the same route.

Malahide and Donabate

Ten mi. north of Dublin, rows of well-behaved shops self-satisfiedly line the main street of **Malahide,** winner of Ireland's 1990 cut-throat, no-holds-barred "Tidy Town" competition. Romantically removed from the petty-bourgeois burg, **Malahide Castle** (tel. 452 655), luxuriates in sweeping lawns and densely foliated paths. Oliver Cromwell once commented that here, and nowhere else, would he tolerate living on Irish soil. Now publicly owned, the well-preserved mansion houses a collection of Irish period furniture and part of the National Portrait Collection. (Open Mon.-Fri. 10am-12:45pm and 2-6pm, Sat. 11am-6pm, Sun. 2-6pm; Nov.-March Mon.-Fri. 10am-12:45pm and 2-5pm, Sat.-Sun. 2-5pm. Admission £2.35, seniors and 12-17 yrs. £1.75, 3-11 yrs. £1.15, families £7.) Bus #42 from Talbot St. goes right to the park entrance; if you take the DART to Malahide, turn right from the station and walk ¾mi.

In Donabate, 6 mi. further north, the 18th-century **Newbridge House** (tel. 436 064) is surrounded by a 300 acre park. Built around 1740 by the Archbishop of Dublin, the mansion had no electricity until *The Spy Who Came in from the Cold* was filmed here in the 1960s. (Open Mon.-Fri. 10am-1pm and 2-5pm, Sun. and holidays 2-6pm; Nov.-March Sun. and holidays 2-5pm. Admission £2.15, seniors and children under 18 £1.75.) The **Newbridge Traditional Farm,** adjacent to the estate, reconstructs rural life and animal husbandry from 200 years ago. (Open same hours as the House; adults £1, seniors and children under 18 80p.) Take bus #33B from Eden Quay to Donabate village; follow the signs on a 20 min. walk from there.

The Boyne River Valley

About 30 mi. north of Dublin, the River Boyne flows through a dozing valley, plump with farmlands and archaeological remains. Farmers periodically plow up weapons and artifacts from the Battle of the Boyne, where in 1690 William of Orange defeated James II to win the crown of England (one way bus fare from Dublin costs £5). Sporadic bus transport between towns means that, short of a car, hitchhiking is the best way to get from place to place in this area. The main roads are thick with rides, but you'll probably end up hiking down country lanes to historical sights.

The town of **Trim** is smothered in stone walls and ruins. Golfers whack at the turf around the Anglo-Norman **Trim Castle,** built in 1172. Now immense and deserted, the crumbling fortifications and ancient stone cubbyholes make for a challenging game of hide-and-seek. (Free; always open.) The **Educational Centre,** Castle St., will enlighten you further. Every summer in late June, Trim hosts the unique **Nun Run,** a horse race jockeyed exclusively by Sisters. The Trim tourist office (tel. 367 66), beside the castle, is open Mon.-Fri. 9am-5pm, Sat. 11am-5pm, Sun. 1-5pm. About 5 mi. away on the N3 rises the **Hill of Tara,** the seat of Celtic priest kings during the Iron Age. Nothing remains of the hill itself, stripped clean of any props for the imagination.

Approximately 15 mi. north of Trim is **Slane Castle,** complete with turrets, towers, the family crest, and a daunting pair of antlers over the door. Although it now houses a restaurant and nightclub, visitors are free to wander around the surrounding park. The grounds form a natural amphitheater around the castle, occasionally rocked by outdoor concerts—the Stones played in '83. Nearby, **Slane Hill** marks the spot where St. Patrick defied paganism and kindled his famous Paschal fire on the eve of Easter in 433 AD. Climb the spiral steps of the tower for a sweeping view of the **Hill of Tara.**

Newgrange or **Brugh na Boinne** ("Palace of the Boyne") is justifiably one of the most famous prehistoric sites in Europe; the enormous mound's single 60-ft. passage leads to an enclosed cruciform chamber built 5000 years ago, where ancient people housed their dead. At sunrise on Dec. 21, the winter solstice, a slit above the doorway allows a few minutes of light into the burial chamber to illuminate a maze of inexplicable spiral carvings. (Open June to mid-Sept. daily 10am-7pm; mid-Sept. to Oct. and mid-March to May daily 10am-1pm and 2-5pm; Nov. to mid-March Tues.-Sat. 10am-1pm and 2-4:30pm, Sun. 2-4:30pm. Admission £1.50, seniors £1, students and children 60p, under 7 free.) The tourist office in Newgrange (tel. (041) 242 74) is open from April to October. Expressway buses from Dublin serve the town of **Slane,** several miles away (at least 2/day, Sun. 1/day; £5, return £5.60).

A few miles northeast of the town of Mellifont is **Monasterboice,** a 5th-century monastic settlement. Carved in the 10th century and rises 17 ft., the Muireadach Cross is one of the finest examples of a High Cross. Climb to the top of the tall round tower that once protected the community from Viking marauders. (The key is available at the house by the entrance gate.) Off the same road, **Mellifont Abbey,** built in 1142, has been put out to pasture with the cows. The original walls mark only the perimeter of the monastery, enclosing nothing besides an unusual octogonal lavabo. (Open 10am-6pm mid-June to mid-Dec.; 80p, seniors 55p, students 30p.)

Drogheda

Drogheda, founded by the Danes in 911, once rivalled Dublin (30 mi. to the south) as a center of trade. Two crooked streets cross in the middle to form the town center, and houses fan out around them. Old walls linger at unexpected points around the town, blooming with flowers. The **tourist office,** Narrow West St. (tel. 370 70; open Mon.-Sat. 10am-1pm, 2-6pm; June-Aug.) will arm you with a map and a list of sights. In the center of town, **St. Peter's Church** (open daily 8:30am-8:30pm, confession 12:30-2pm), enshrines the head of Saint Oliver Plunkett, who was martyred by being drawn and quartered. At the end of the main West St., **St.**

Lawrence's Gate, with its slots for arrows and boiling water, has guarded the town since early Norman times. At the top of the hill on St. Peters St., the mossy **Magdalen Steeple,** dating from 1224, is all that remains of the Dominican Friary that once stood on the spot. The **Droichead Arts Centre,** Scholes Lane (tel. 339 46) displays exhibitions by local, regional, and national artists (Mon.-Sat. 10am-5pm; free).

Cheap food, fish stands, and supermarkets line West St.; the **Super Valu Supermarket** is open Mon.-Wed., Sat. 9am-7pm; Thurs. and Fri. 9am-9pm; Sun. 10am-6pm, and there is also a **Dunne's Store.** Grandmothers smoke, gossip and eat beans on toast at the tiny **Noeleen's Coffee Shop,** 45 Laurence St. Her good plain food is very cheap (£1-2). For rooms the size of football fields, follow William St. to **Harpur House B&B** (tel. 327 36; £12/night).

Kells, site of the extensive ruins of St. Columcille's 6th-century monastic settlement, lies west of Drogheda in the wooded valley of the River Blackwater. Visit **St. Columcille's House** (ask for the key from any of the local shops), then tour the gallery of **St. Columba's Church** (open during daylight hours) and inspect a facsimile of the *Book of Kells* (the original is in Trinity College, Dublin). Kells is most exciting at market time on Friday morning. (Regular daily bus service from Dublin to Kells is £4, return £5.)

South of Dublin

Pleasant villages with their typifying churches and Dunne's Stores trickle down the sandy beaches south of Dublin. The coastal road from Dún Laoghaire (dun-LEAR-y) to Bray is particularly scenic; this stretch is also covered by DART and buses from Dublin. For more energetic travelers, a very pleasant seaside walk leads from Dún Laoghaire through **Dalkey** to **Killiney**—just follow the foot path by the sea. Hitchhiking may be difficult since these towns still act as Dublin's suburbs.

Dún Laoghaire

Dún Laoghaire harbors the Sealink ferries dock as well as its own bustling community. The **tourist office** (tel. 806 984/5/6), on St. Michael's Wharf beside the train station and the ferry terminal, is well used to dealing with delirious travelers. (Accommodations service £1. Open June daily 7am-8pm; July-Aug. daily 7am-11pm; Sept. Mon.-Sat. 7am-8pm, Sun. 4-8pm; Oct.-Nov. Mon.-Sat. 9am-8pm; Dec. and Feb.-May Mon.-Fri. 9am-8pm; Jan. Mon.-Fri. 9am-5pm.) They will help you find an area B&B (average price £12, booking for £1), and can direct you to the very spartan **Scoil Lorcáin hostel** (tel. (280) 19 48; open July-Aug. only). St. George's St., parallel to the shore, forms the backbone of the town with its vertebrae of shops: the **Dún Laoghaire Shopping Centre,** on the corner of Marine Rd. and St. George's, embraces **Quinnsworth Supermarket** and **Nicky's Coffee Shop,** which serves microwaved muffins and plastic-wrapped sandwiches (50p-£1.50). (All stores open Mon.-Wed., Sat. 9am-6pm; Thurs and Fri. 9am-9pm.) The **Coffee Bean,** 89 St. George's Lower, will roll you out of their deli filled to the brim with scrumptious desserts, quiche, soup, and brown bread. Full Irish breakfast £2. (Open daily 8am-5pm.) Across the street is the reasonably priced, health-conscious **Food for Thought. Bits and Pizza,** Patrick St. (definitely a step up from the standard pizza joint), serves excellent pizza and subs on wood tables (what people used in the dark days before formica was invented).

Wicklow Mountains

Buffered from the sea by swatches of field and shoreland, the **Wicklow Mountains** sprout up along a 30 mi. stretch between Bray and Arklow. Their rugged summits over 2000 ft. high, covered by gorse and heather and pleated by rivers rushing down wooded glens, are populated only by grazing sheep and scarce villagers. The main tourist attraction, **Glendalough** (GLEN-da-lock, meaning "glen of the two lakes") in the midst of the mountains, draws a steady summertime stream of coaches and their stiff passengers from Dublin and the south. The triangle of Glendalough, Roundwood and Ashford bursts with holiday makers from June to September but the forest's vast stillness returns in the fall. Westward and upward are the lonely mountain heights. The **Wicklow Way,** Ireland's first governmentally sponsored long-distance path, starts near Dublin and jogs south along the crests all the way to Clonegal in County Carlow, a distance of about 70 mi. The trail starts in Marlay Park in Rathfarnham, Dublin (take bus #47A or #47B from Hawkins St. in the city center), and the northern 45 mi. of the path, wandering through Glendalough and Glenmalure to the small village of Moyne, inland from Arklow, are the most heavily trodden. **Lugnacullia,** Ireland's third highest peak, and the jagged crags of **Luggala** and **Devil's Glen,** near Ashford, are the highlights of this stretch. Between Enniskerry and Glendalough, the trail reaches its loftiest point at the summit of **White Hill** (2073 ft.), from which you can see the mountains of North Wales on a clear day. Though the Wicklow Way is well signposted with yellow arrows, pick up the tourist board's fact sheet #26B, *The Wicklow Way* and the Ordnance Survey's Wicklow Way map at the main Dublin tourist office or any mountaineering store. Bring foul-weather gear (the weather can change quickly) and strong shoes.

A number of **IYHF hostels** and mountain settlements lie within 5 mi. of the path. Book ahead during July and August through the central **An Óige Office,** 39 Mountjoy Sq., Dublin 1 (tel. (01) 363 111), or call directly for the independent hostels. From north to south the hostels are lined up as follows (distance from the Wicklow Way in parentheses): **Knockree IYHF,** Lackan House, Enniskerry (tel. (01) 867 196); **Glencree IYHF,** Stone House, Enniskerry (tel. (01) 867 290; 3 mi. up a steep hill); the **Little Flower Hostel,** in Roundwood (tel. (01) 818 145; £4; open June-Sept.); **Glendalough IYHF** (tel. (0404) 451 43; 1½ mi.); and the **Old Mill Hostel,** Rathdrum Rd., Glendalough (tel. (0404) 51 56; £4.80; open all year; ½mi.); **Glenmalure IYHF,** Greenane (no phone or running water; open July-Aug. only 2 mi.); **Aghavannagh IYHF,** Aughrim (tel. (0402) 361 02; 1 mi.). Other Wicklow Mountain hostels are **Tiglin IYHF,** also known as Devil's Glen, Ashford (tel. (0404) 402 59); **Baltyboys,** Blessington (tel. (045) 672 66); and **Ballinclea,** Donard (tel. (045) 546 57). The Glendalough hostel charges £6.50 July-Aug., £5 March-June, Sept.-Oct., £4.50 rest of the year; all others charge £4.50 July-Aug., £4 March-June, Sept.-Oct., £3.50 rest of the year. The Aghavannagh, Baltyboys, and Ballinclea hostels are open March to November, Glenmalure July to August, and the others all year. Except for bus service to Glendalough, Roundwood and Ashford (see next sections), public transport fails to penetrate the mountains and many find walking, thumbing and biking are the best bets.

Laragh and Glendalough

The many tour buses, Dubliners, and backpackers who come to savor the scenery and ruins of **Glendalough** first pass throuh Laragh, and then turn west along an equally small road for about a mile. Cradling two lakes, a pine-tree forest, and the ruins of an ancient monastic settlement, Glendalough is one of Ireland's most handsome valleys. Here, the 6th-century St. Kevin gave up his preference for the ascetic life in order to found a monastic school. During the great age of the Irish monasteries (the second half of the first millenium), such settlements acted as religious and cultural centers, attracting pilgrims from all over Europe to the "land of saints and scholars." Supported by lesser monks engaged in a farming economy, the fully privileged brothers inscribed line after line of religious texts and collected precious jewels and relics for the glory of God. Glendalough, with around 5000 occupants, was one such mecca.

Nowadays, only the **visitors center** (tel. (0404) 53 25) and a handful of tourist trappings mar the ancient spot. The center shows a film on the history of Irish monasteries and conducts guided tours of the local ruins. (Open mid-June to mid-Sept. daily 10am-7pm; March 17 to mid-June and mid-Sept. to Oct. daily 10am-5pm; Nov.-March 17 Tues.-Sat. 10am-4:30pm, Sun. 10:30-4:30pm. Admission £1, seniors 70p, students and children 40p.) The ruins themselves huddle beside the lower lake. The 103-ft. **Round Tower,** built in the 19th century, was used as a hide-out by plucky monks during Viking attacks. The monks would climb the inside of the tower floor by floor, drawing up the ladders behind them. **St. Kevin's Cross** is an unadorned example of a High Cross: a crucifix (representing Christianity) merged with a ring signifying the sun (a pagan symbol). Early proselytizers hoped that combining the two would make Christianity easier to accept. The **Cathedral,** constructed in both Greek and Roman architectural styles was the second largest in the country at one time.

Mrs. Holden offers tea and hot buttered scones (£1.25) as well as coffee and sandwiches in her house (follow the signs TEAS; 10am-5pm daily); the concession wagon offers less homey fare during the summer. The **Glendalough IYHF** hostel (tel. (0404) 453 42) lies ¼ mi. up the Lake Rd. (to the right when facing the entrance arch) in a rose-covered cottage. (Check-in from 5pm, kitchen facilities. July-Aug. £6.50, March-June and Sept.-Oct. £5, Nov.-Feb. £4.50.)

Back in Laragh, B&Bs and tearooms flutter anxiously for attention. Two hundred yards out of town on the Wexford Rd., the **Old Mill Hostel** (once a wool mill) is comfortably unrefined. Stone walls enclose the long dining room/self-catering kitchen and the low curved ceilings expose their beams in a shameless display of rusticity. (£4.80; open all year.) The hostel also offers camping for £2.90. The magnificently scenic **Brockagh Heights B&B** (tel. (0404) 452 43), engulfed by a legion of grazing sheep, is just off the main road to the ruins (£12). **Wicklow Heather Restaurant** serves full meals for £6-7 (lunch) or £8-11 (dinner) and the **Laragh Inn** and **The Bridge** offer pub grub in what can be called town. The convenience store just opposite the Wicklow Heather is open 8:15am-9:15pm daily.

Most pilgrims to Glendalough come by car; a few hike the Wicklow Way into town and the remainder catch **St. Kevin's Bus Service** (tel. (01) 818 119), from Dublin (11:30am and 6pm, Sun. 11:30am and 7pm) or from Bray town hall (12:10pm and 6:30pm, Sun. 12:10pm and 7:30pm). Buses return from the glen weekdays at 4:15pm and Sun. 9:45am and 5:30pm (£4, £7 return). Although the bus runs to Glendalough during the summer, in the winter it goes only as far as Roundwood.

Wicklow and Surroundings

Wicklow Town, 32 mi. south of Dublin, is a placid white-washed community with a handsome harbor and a tiny stony beach. When St. Patrick first set foot on Irish soil here, the villagers greeted him by throwing stones. Now the largest town in County Wicklow, Wicklow town commands attention as a coastal town and departure point into the mountain region. A long, skinny Main St. makes its way past the Grand Hotel and the grassy triangular plot by the tourist office to its terminus in **Market Square.** Market Sq. features several markets, a monument to local hero Billy Byre (stop and admire the the bus stop at its base) and the courthouse, with a Geneaological Office on the 3rd floor for those interested in digging up their Irish roots (tel. (0404) 673 24). The first left after Market Square leads to the somber ruins of the **Black Castle** (free; always open) and on to the **cliff trail** which leads out along the headland to the old lighthouse on Wicklow Head. Local legend describes the appearance of a young maiden, the spirit of the west wind, during the fierce easterly gale of 1922. As waves crashed against the land, destroying ships and houses, this gentle zephyr ran up and down the cliff trail, trying to appease her angry sister, and finally sacrificed herself to the sea. The winds subsided, and every year on October 24 during the **Festival of the Winds** a local girl re-enacts the part. Beyond, beaches stretch 15 mi. south to Arklow. The closest ones to Wicklow are **Silver Strand, Jack's Hole,** and crowded **Brittas Bay,** where you can buy huge crabs during the summer months for about 50p. At the other end of Main St., by the Grand Hotel, the **Abbey** contains the remnants of a 13th-century Franciscan friary. Knock on the parish priest's door if you care to visit (beside the Abbey and the AIB bank; free).

The tourist office (tel. 691 17), Main St. (Mon.-Fri. 9:30am-5:30pm all year, June-Sept. Sat. 10:30am-5pm) will extol the glories of County Wicklow. For a more personal introduction to the area, hike up St. Patrick's Rd. (turn uphill at the purple building on Main St.) to any one of the B&Bs. Prices run in £15 range. Gnomes grow on the well-vacuumed carpet of a lawn in front of **Glengorse House,** St. Patrick's Valley (tel. 679 26; take the second right after St. Patrick's Church; singles £12, doubles £11.50/person, doubles £14/person with bath). Keep hiking up St. Patrick's Rd. to friendly **Mrs. H. Gorman,** Thomond House, St. Patrick's Rd. Upper (tel. 679 40); the balcony, nice rooms, and panorama of the sea and mountains are well worth the 15 minute walk uphill (open March-Oct., £11; if you call from the train station she'll fetch you). 7 mi. south of Wicklow on the Wicklow/Wexford Rd., **Johnsons** (tel. 481 33) and **River Valley** (tel. 416 47) are two campgrounds in Redcross which both charge £4 during high season and £3 the rest of the year.

Vegetable and fruit sellers and butchers ensure that you won't go hungry for want of raw edibles; lip-smacking, cholesterol-factory take-out places vie to fill your stomach. For those who like to eat with utensils, **Pizza del Forno,** Main St. (open Mon.-Sat. 10am-10:30pm, Sun. 10am-9:30pm) is a classic pizza place with red-checkered tablecloths. (Pizzas £4-6.) Every Thursday night traditional music vibrates through the **Bridge Tavern** on Bridge St. (no cover), and the **Boathouse,** across the bridge on the seafront, advertises set dancing classes every Tuesday night at 8:30pm.

Ashford, 6 mi. northeast of Wicklow, is a window into the Wicklow Mountains. On Friday mornings the town trades goods and cattle at its marketplace. The **Mount Usher Gardens** (tel. (0404) 401 16), near Ashford on the Dublin/Wexford Rd., are 20 acres of rare trees, shrubs, flowers, and bees along the **River Vartry.** (Open March 2-Oct. Mon.-Sat. 10:30am-6pm, Sun. 11am-6pm. Admission £2, seniors, students, and children £1.50.) Two mi. beyond Ashford on the road to Roundwood, the thickly wooded **Devil's Glen** is a chasm dug by the River Vartry's 100-ft. waterfall, which tumbles into the **Devil's Punchbowl.** If you walk too close to the edge or attempt any rock climbing, you could tumble to the Devil as well. **Tiglin Adventure Centre** (tel. 401 69), on the same road, teaches mountaineering, rock climbing, canoeing and kayaking. A weekend course, including room and board, costs £50. The **Devil's Glen Hostel** (IYHF, also known as Tiglin; tel. 440 259), charges £4.50 per soul from July-Aug., £4 March-June and Sept.-Oct., and £3.50 from Nov.-Feb. (Buses run 8 times daily between Ashford and the Monument in Wicklow; return ticket approximately £3.)

Daily trains run to Dublin and Wexford (3/day, Sun. 2/day). The station is about a 15-min. walk east of town via Church St. Regular buses leave for Dublin from the Monument or the Grand Hotel on the occasional Sunday; check the schedules in town (7am-8:50pm, Sun. 9:45am-8:20pm; every 2 hr.; £4.10, return £5.40). The N11 passes outside of Wicklow on its rush from Dublin to Wexford.

Southeast Ireland

The Southeast prides itself on being the sunniest part of Ireland; Dubliners and foreigners alike favor the eastern coast in particular, where sandy beaches and stucco villas line the sea. Wexford, a cultural center in its own right, launches travelers into the surrounding region; once wary of Norman incursions, Wexfordians now weary of tourist excursions. John F. Kennedy's ancestors once resided in Wexford and the town is still well-connected, with ferries from Rosslare to England and France, and roads and railway lines to Dublin, Waterford, Cork, and beyond. Hedges separate the sheep, cattle, and crops along the 30-mi. stretch west from Rosslare to Waterford Harbor; Waterford City, though ugly and industrial, is saturated in Viking history. Farms and historical monuments merge inextricably in the quilted plains and green river valleys of Kilkenny County, where crops unabashedly jostle ancient round towers and stone crosses. While Kilkenny town is an excellent base for inland travel, Cahir inquisitively sniffs broad and flat Tipperary, where picturesque towns and magnificent ancient ruins (such as the Rock of Cashel) aromate the farmlands of Ireland's ample breadbasket. To the south rise the county's three mountain ranges, the Comeraghs, the Galtees, and the Knockmealdown Mountains.

Vikings and Normans both left their mark on the Southeast, but the date imprinted on the consciousness (and central statue) of every town is 1798, when Irish farmers rose from the mountain regions to rebel against the British army. Militarily a failure, and crushed after less than two weeks, the revolt nevertheless exemplified the fierce local thirst for independence and the sacrifices the Irish people were willing to endure.

Enniscorthy

Eleven mi. north of Wexford Town, Enniscorthy is best remembered for its role in the heroic uprising of 1798. Rebels held the British at bay for 12 days, but the Wexford pikemen were ultimately defeated at **Vinegar Hill** across the River Slaney from the town center. The town itself is built on the hill opposite, centered on a monument to the 1798 rebellion in **Market Square.** Here, old men and dissatisfied youths sit on separate park benches and ignore each other. Just around the corner, the town's 13th-century **castle** frowns down at the modern Abbey Square Shopping Centre near the water. The bus stops where Slaney St. meets the river, and the train station is a 5-min. walk across the bridge and to the north. The first week in July, Enniscorthy's streets are saturated by 8 days of festival and fructose during its annual **Strawberry Fair.** Sports events and a Strawberry Queen are featured—all for free.

The castle houses the **tourist office** (tel. (054) 346 99; open mid-June to mid-Sept. Mon.-Sat. 10am-6pm, Sun. 2-6pm) but the bulk of the building is taken up by the **Wexford County Museum.** Starting with a mere 13 items in 1960, the curators hoarded bequests, stuffing the castle top to bottom with such odd bits as ship figureheads, African masks, and a collection of police patches from around the world. This material encyclopedia, and especially the exhibit on the 1798 rebellion, well merits the £1 admission (under 17, 30p). (Open June-Sept. Mon.-Sat. 10am-1pm, 2-6pm, Sun. 2-5:30pm; Oct.-Nov., Feb.-May daily 2-5:30pm; Dec.-Jan. Sun. 2-5pm). Three potteries carry on a local industry. You can see the artists work and market their clay wares at **Hillview** (always open) and **Carley's Bridge** (open Mon.-Fri. 8:30am-4:45pm, also Sat. 10:30am-4:30pm in summer), both just beyond the greyhound track 1½ mi. west of town, or at **Kiltrea Bridge** (open Mon.-Sat. 10am-5:30pm), about 6 mi. west (follow Cathedral St. for several miles, then follow the signs).

No hostel graces this shuffling town, but several B&B-bequesting matrons do: **Mrs. Barry,** Adelmar House, Summerhill Rd. (tel. 336 68), charges £11; follow the river to Bohreen Hill on the right, then take another right at Summerhill); **Mrs. Carroll,** Don Car House, Bohreen Hill (tel. 334 58), levies £12, and **Mrs. Murphy,** 9 Main Street, also asks for £12 (tel. 335 22; right in town). Food can be found at the **L&N Supermarket** in the shopping center (open Mon.-Wed., Sat. 10am-6pm; Thurs.-Fri. 10am-9pm), or at the various pubs. **Killeen's,** Slaney St., dishes up roast chicken or steak and kidney pie and two vegetables for £2.95, and a German fellow at the **Office Beer Keller,** Market Sq., makes his own sausages amidst a collection of miniature antlers (lunches £3-3.50, dinners £5.25-10).

There are a number of ruins in the area, free of charge if you can get there. **Ferns,** a tiny village 8 mi. north of Enniscorthy on the N11, was once the capital of Leinster. The castle, a huge rectangle with circular towers at the corners, dates from the 12th-century reign of Dermot MacMurrough. He kidnapped the English noblewoman Chelsea of the Willows, bringing her to Ireland to be his wife; on their first anniversary she drugged his wine and set him alight with a burning log from the fire. Afterwards the murderess built the abbey with its marvelous 13th-century circular chapel as penance for her sins. Two other sites, **Wilton Castle** and **Castleboro,** both in shambles, lie 6 mi. out of Enniscorthy (ask at the County Museum for directions).

Trains running between Dublin and Rosslare Pier stop in Enniscorthy (3/day, 2 on Sun.; 2 hrs. to Dublin, 50 min. to Rosslare Harbor). Buses leave from the bottom of Slaney Rd., running south (3/day) and north (4/day) through Ferns (10 min. north of Enniscorthy). The N11 motorway passes straight through Enniscorthy, heading north to Arklow, Wicklow and Dublin and south to Wexford.

Wexford Town

Narrow, winding streets and the fishing boats tied along the quay give Wexford a small-town feel that belies its prominence on the map. In 1169 the Normans conquered the Viking settlement of *wæssfjord* ("harbor of the mud flats") and built their characteristic fortifications, some of which still stand. Henry II spent the Lent of 1172 in **Selskar Abbey,** doing penance for the murder of Thomas à Becket, and Oliver Cromwell ravaged the town in 1649, leaving only 400 of its inhabitants alive. Wexford, now a major cultural center in the southeast, serves as a good base for day trips to the nearby historical monuments, beaches and bird sanctuaries.

Arriving and Departing

Because of Wexford's proximity to Rosslare Harbor, the town is well-served by public transport, especially around ferry time. Buses run to Dublin (5/day; 2½ hr.), and to Rosslare (7/day; 20 min.; £2.30). Trains serve Dublin, Rosslare Harbor, and Waterford (3/day, Sun. 2/day for all three trains). Both buses and trains leave from Wexford's single station, a 5-min. walk along the quays from the city center. (Rosslare Harbor is the hub for any other trains.) Hitchhikers to Dublin on the N11 stand at the Wexford Bridge off the quays; to Rosslare, head south along the quays to Trinity St.; to New Ross or Waterford, stand along Upper John St. which leads onto the N25.

Orientation and Practical Information

The harbor, hemmed by quays, is the id of the city; aptly named Crescent Quay is where you'll find the **tourist office,** the supermarket Crazy Prices, and odd shops. Other streets recede from the harbor in ripples to form a spidery network. The **Franciscan Friary,** tall and inviolate, stands at the top of the hill surveying the older city and train station to its right, easily distinguished Main St. running parallel to the quays, and the dull rows of gray houses stretching out in all directions.

Tourist Office: Crescent Quay (tel. 231 11). Accommodations service 50p. Free map. Open Mon.-Sat. 9am-6pm; Oct.-June Mon.-Fri. 9am-12:45pm and 2-5:15pm.

Bike Rental: Hayes Cycle Shop, 108 S. Main St. (tel. 224 62). Raleigh touring bikes £7/day, £30/week, £30 deposit. Open Mon.-Sat. 9am-6pm.

Emergency: Dial 999; no coins required.

Financial Services: Bank of Ireland, Custom House Quay (tel. 230 22). Open Mon. 10am-12:30pm and 1:30-5pm, Tues.-Fri. 10am-12:30pm and 1:30-3pm.

Hospital: Wexford General Hospital (tel. 422 33), on the road to New Ross.

Launderette: My Beautiful Laundrette, St. Peter's Sq. (tel 243 17). With TV, videos, and complimentary tea or coffee while you wait. Open Mon.-Fri. 10am-9pm, Sat. 10am-6pm. Wash £1.50; 6 min. dryer 20p; soap 50p.

Pharmacy: Edmond Hassett, 9-11 N. Main St. (tel. 224 58 or 220 21). Open Mon.-Sat. 9am-1pm and 2-6pm.

Police: Garda Siochana, Roches Rd. (tel. 223 33).

Post Office: Anne St. (tel. 221 23). Open Mon.-Sat. 9am-5:30pm.

Taxi: Andrew's, tel. 459 33; 50p/mi.

Telephone Code: 053.

Train Station and Bus Depot: Redmond Place (tel. 225 22), along the waterfront to the north of Crescent Quay. Booking offices open Mon.-Sat. 8am-6:30pm.

Travel Agency: O'Donohoe Travel, 78 Commercial Quay (tel. 227 88). Open Mon.-Fri. 9:30am-5:30pm, Sat. 9:30am-1pm and 2-4pm. **O'Leary Travel,** 91 S. Main St. (tel. 238 44). Open Mon.-Fri. 9am-5:30pm, Sat. 9:30am-4:30pm. Both sell ferry, rail and airplane tickets.

Accommodations and Camping

The nearest youth hostel is about 10 mi. away in Rosslare. The B&Bs in Wexford town make life worth living and are well worth the extra £5 or so. If ones listed are full, look along **Westgate Street,** 2 blocks up from the train station.

Mrs. Donnelly, The Abbey, 3 Lower Georges St. (tel. 227 87), next to White's Hotel. Potpourri and a delicate, but omnipresent, floral theme. View onto an Edwardian garden. £11.

Mrs. A. Tobin, St. John's, 11 Lower John St. (tel. 237 53). Family heirlooms in a 300-year-old house with calico print wallpaper. Modern-day carpet is the only spoiler. Singles £15, doubles £13/person.

John and Philomena Lambert, St. Aidan's Mews Guesthouse, 25 Lower John St. (tel. 226 91) A magnificent ivy-covered exterior gives way to an impersonal but comfortable interior at this former 18th-century post-house. £12.

Camping: Ferrybank and Camping Park, just across the bridge on Castlebridge Rd. (tel. 243 78). Laundry facilities. One person with tent £3, 3 people £5.50. Open Easter to mid-Sept.

Food and Pubs

L&N and **Crazy Prices** on the quay, and **Dunne's Stores** (open Mon.-Wed., Sat. 9am-6pm; Thurs., Fri. 9am-9pm) next to the train station sell Wexford's cheapest groceries. **Greenacres,** 56 N. Main St., is a giant warehouse of organic fruits, vegetables, grains, baked goods, and pharmaceutical products. It is also the spot for carob bars, dried fruit, and health books (open Mon.-Sat. 9am-6pm). Try Selskap St. for restaurants in the £5-7 range, and Main St. for pub grub.

Sights and Entertainment

The historical society runs free walking tours of the city nightly at 8pm (book through the tourist office); *Welcome to Wexford* (free from the tourist office) proposes a self-guided walking tour. Virtually all of the historical attractions are in the northern part of the city. On North Main Street, an open area marks the **Bull Ring,** where Norman nobles used to indulge their peacetime bloodletting instincts in bullfight. Now, a statue of a stalwart peasant fearlessly brandishing a sharp instrument commemorates the 1798 uprising, and a roof shelters the open air **Marketplace,** an array of junk, boots, plants, and baubles. On Abbey St., King Henry II did penance at the tranquil **Selskar Abbey,** whose walls quietly sprout out at weed-embedded gravel. The dark and frightening tower stairwell leads up to a precarious view of the town and the bay. (Get the key from Mr. Murphy, just around the corner at #9 High St.) Nearby, **Westgate** is the only surviving gate of six that originally studded Wexford's Norman town walls. You can still see the barred and blackened cell that served as a lock-up.

Check *The People,* (65 p) a local Thursday paper, for events listings. The **Wexford Arts Centre** in the Cornmarket has free exhibitions and evening performances of music, dance, and drama (tel. 237 64; tickets £3-5pm; box office open Mon.-Sat. 10am-6pm). The **Riff Raff Theatre,** Larkin's Lane, off S. Main St., also offers exhibitions and shows. **The Theatre Royal** puts on many performances throughout the year, including the acclaimed **Wexford Festival of Opera.** For information on the opera festival, contact the Theatre Royal, High St. (tel. 222 40; box office tel. 221 44; open Mon.-Fri. 9:30am-5pm; opera tickets £25-32 available from early June).

Every night is traditional music night at **Stamp's Stores,** 79 South Main St., except for Friday night, when jazz gets a note in edgewise. **Wavecrest Bar** on Commercial Quay, near the corner of Monck St., also presents traditional music most evenings after 9pm, for free. The **Abbey Cinema,** Upper George St., shows current flicks nightly at 8pm, late show Fri. and Sat. 11pm.

Near Wexford

The **Irish National Heritage Park** (tel. 417 33), in Ferrycarrig, 2½ mi. north of Wexford just off the N11, regales visitors with 9000 years of Irish culture from the Stone Age to the arrival of the Normans. The site features full-scale replicas of a Viking ship, typical Irish homesteads, places of worship, a dolmen (monolithic prehistoric tomb), a cist burial (Bronze Age grave), stone circles, an *Ogham* stone, and a round tower. (Open March-Nov. daily 10pm-7pm. Admission £2, children and students £1, families £5.) Four mi. south of Wexford, on the Rosslare road, is **Johnstown Castle Gardens.** The castle is a good example of 19th-century Gothic revival architecture, but only the entrance hall is open to the public. (Castle gardens open daily 9am-5:30pm.) The **Irish Agricultural Museum,** also at Johnstown Castle, chronicles the history of farming in Ireland (Open summer months, Mon.-Fri. 9am-5pm, Sat. and Sun. 2-5pm; £1.25, students 50p.) **Westgate Minitours** (tel. 246 55) operates daily buses to the Irish National Heritage Park (£4.50 return), to Johnstown Castle Gardens (£4.50 return), and to both sites (£8 return). All tours leave from the tourist office. The price includes admission.

Rosslare Harbour

At any given time, a large portion of Rosslare Harbor's population is either coming or going. Ferries run daily to Britain and France, and the town caters to this trade: the N25 between Wexford and Rosslare is a forest of B&Bs, and shops open and close with the arrival of the ferries. Yet the area has many natural attractions: beautiful beaches and tiny resort towns line the coast from Rosslare to Arthurstown, the destination of many a Irish summertime vacationer. Five mi. south of Rosslare and several mi. east of Kilmore Quay, **Our Lady's Island** belies its name by being connected to the mainland. The island contains the ruins of an Augustinian priory and a 15-ft. **Leaning Tower** (tilted at a *sharper angle* than that overrated one in Italy). Each year (Aug. 15-Sept. 9) there is a massive pilgrimage to Our Lady's Island, where three girls once saw the eponymous personage appear. No public transportation exists to this spot: bikers, walkers, and others should turn left in Tagoat and follow the signs for Broadway. Thirteen mi. southwest of Rosslare, the small fishing village of **Kilmore Quay** berths a maritime museum with model ships and paintings of the stormy deep in the lightship "Guillemot" (tel. 290 84). (Open June-Sept. daily 2pm-8pm; £1, children 50p.) Kilmore Quay also sends boat trips out to the **Saltee Islands,** a former pagan pilgrimage site and now Ireland's largest bird sanctuary, with a winged population nearing 50,000. These puffin- and razorbill-bedecked rocks are owned by Prince Michael Salteens, whose name and the cracker are merely an unfortunate coincidence. Boats leave from the mainland at 11am, weather permitting (arrive to catch the ferry no later than 10:45am), stranding you for picnics, ornithology, and discovery until 5 pm (£8 return, £4 children); contact Mr. Bates (tel. 296 44) or Mr. O'Brien (tel. 297 27).

Rosslare Harbor has two tourist offices—one in the ferryport (tel. 336 22, open all year round) and one a ½ mi. from Rosslare Harbor on the road to Wexford (tel. 332 32, open summer months). Both are staffed around sailing time: 6:30-8:30am (summer only), 2-5pm and 6-8:30pm.

The **Rosslare Harbour youth hostel (IHYF)** (tel. (053) 333 99) offers a friendly welcome and delicious bread and soup (£1) close to the harbor—go up the steps in the side of the hill. Comfy bunks are well-stacked during summer months. (Check in 5:30pm; lockout 9:30am-5:30pm; curfew 11:30pm, lights out midnight, kitchen facilities; £6). **Mrs. O'Leary's Farmhouse** (tel. 331 34), on a 100 acre farm, is a holiday unto itself: gloriously rural, with a grassy lane leading to a secluded private beach. You can sit in the overstuffed parlor by the geraniums, looking out on the sea, or, if you are polite, you can weed in the garden. She will pick you up if you call her from the ferry or the train station. (single £12.50 with bath, £13.50 in summer, double £11/person. There are six organized campgrounds in the Rosslare Harbour area; the closest is the **Holiday Inn Caravan and Camping Park** (tel. (053) 311 68) in Kilrane, 2 mi. out (hikers and bikers £4.50, unit £6.50, showers 50p; open May 15-Aug.); the cheapest and nicest is the **Carne Beach Caravan and Camping Park** (tel. (053) 311 31), 6 mi. south near Carnsore Point (hikers and bikers £2.50-3, unit £5-7; open mid-May to mid-Sept.). If you decide to sleep on a beach, the area beyond Rosslare Harbour is very pretty but tends to be gutsy.

Rosslare Harbor is not the world capital of cheap eats. The **Super Valu** supermarket on the only road (opposite the youth hostel) also holds the post office and is open Mon.-Wed., Sat. 8am-6pm; Thurs.-Fri. 8am-8pm; Sun. 9am-1pm. A take-out fast food place bounces at its side. Your best bet is a ½ mi. down the road, in Kilrane, where several pubs have the town under their thumb. The **Anchor Restaurant,** on the left as you come from Rosslare Harbor, serves family-style fare on plain wooden chairs and tables. Their special (soup, entree, 3 vegetables, tea/coffee and dessert) goes for £5.95. (Open 7am-11pm, takeout available.)

Trains and Expressway buses are scheduled to connect with many of the ferries. Buses from Rosslare run to: Galway, Killarney, and Tralee (one daily except Sun. 7:20am, transfer at Waterford); Cork (2/day, Sun. 3/day); Limerick and Waterford (3/day); Dublin (4/day, Sun. 2/day; 3 hr.; £7, £5.50 w/ISIC plus Travelsave); Wexford (7/day,; 20 min.; £2.30 adult, £3.20 return; £1.60 student, £3.20 return). The bus stops just outside the Rosslare ferryport and at J. Pitt's Convenience Store in Kilrane (on Main Road). Trains also run from the ferryport to Wexford (7/day; 20 min.; £2.30 adult, £1.50 ISIC plus Travelsave) and to Waterford (2/day; £7.50). Hitchhiking to and from the ferryport can be extremely difficult; neither locals surfeited with tourists nor a vacationing family of four in their overstuffed car are likely to pick you up. It's easier around the rest of the coast.

About 30 mi. west, the only other hostel in the area, the **Arthurstown youth hostel (IHYF),** lies right by the ferry to Waterford. Once a coast guard barracks, it is still fairly spartan (tel. (051 891 86; open March-Sept.; curfew 10:30pm; lockout 9:30-5pm; kitchen facilities; July-Aug. £5.50, March-June, Sept. £4.30). The **Duncannon campground** in Duncannon (tel. (051) 891 93), open from March to Oct., costs **4-4.50 for tent pitches. Both provide excellent bases for exploring the area. Dunbrody Abbey,** a magnificent Cistercian ruin built in 1190, lies just 2 mi. north of the hostel on the road to New Ross (free, get key from caretaker). To the south is the fishing coast of **Hook Head,** a rocky finger pointing into the Atlantic. It is here that Oliver Cromwell coined the phrase "by hook or by crook," referring to his plan to take Waterford City by landing either at Hook Head, or on the opposite side of the estuary at Crook. The peninsula's lighthouse is one of the four oldest in Europe; a flame has burned here continuously for over 1200 years.

Waterford Town

Waterford is a major industrial center, a coal smudge on the green map of Ireland; the noise and dirt of the waterfront, where ships load and unload huge bundles of ugliness, pervade the streets. A hotbed of religious struggle up through 1649, the town is only interesting today as a node for transportation running west to Cork, east to Wexford, and north to Dublin.

The **tourist office,** 41 Merchant's Quay (tel. 757 88 or 758 23), between Hanover St. and Gladstone St., provides maps listing no less than thirteen churches in Waterford; the *Waterford City Guide* (£1) outlines city history and sights. (Open April-Sept. Mon.-Sat. 9am-6pm, Oct.-Nov. Mon.-Fri. 9am-5:15pm). The town's telephone code is 051. B&Bs in the center of town average £10-12 and you should have no trouble finding a place to stay on **Cork Road** or along the quays. **Lonergan's,** 8 The Quay (tel. 751 98) lets several plain small rooms off a staircase over the bar (single £11, double £10/person). **Mrs. J. Ryder,** 12 Mayors Walk (tel. 554 27), near the police station, has delicate flowery wallpaper and generous rooms. (£12). Patrick St. and The Quay are packed with eateries. For cheap groceries, visit the **Tesco** on Bullybricken St. (Open Mon.-Wed. and Sat. 9am-5:30pm, Thurs.-Fri. 9am-9pm.) At **Haricot's Wholefood Restaurant,** 11 O'Connell St., whole grain desserts and vegetarian dishes are concocted just behind the wooden counter: hearty, healthy lunches £3-4. (Open Mon.-Fri. 10am-8pm; Sat. 10am-5:45pm). There is no shortage of pubs in Waterford: **Doolan's,** George's St. (tel. 727 64), is Waterford's oldest, complete with plaster walls and kegs resting on wooden ceiling beams. It also offers live music on weekends (£1-2 cover).

Trains and buses leave from **Plunkett Station** (tel. 734 01), across the street from the bridge. Buses from Waterford drive to: Dublin (4/day; £7); Limerick (3/day; £14); Cork via Dungarvan and Youghal (5/day; Sun. 4/day). Weekday trains go to: Limerick (1/day); Kilkenny (£6.50); Kildare; Dublin (5/day); and Rosslare Harbor (2/day; £7.50). On Sundays, 2 trains leave the city, bound for Dublin. City buses leave from the clocktower on the quay and cost 60p.

Kilkenny Town

Kilkenny Castle and the town's numerous churches date from 1169, when Norman colonists established Kilkenny as a commercial center on the western fringe of their empire. The Norman colonists' subsequent assimilation into native Irish society so angered the Crown that in 1366 the notorious "Statutes of Kilkenny" were enacted, making it high treason for an Anglo-Saxon to marry an Irish woman. Later, Englishtown and Irishtown, separated by a stream and a gulf of cultural difference, scratched and hissed at each other so spitefully that local fable referred to them as "Kilkenny cats": the two joined as one town in 1843 in a spasm of Old-Irish and Anglo-Irish unity that Cromwell and Pope Innocent soon quelled. Kilkenny (pop. 12,000), situated inland from Waterford, is a good base for daytrips by bike or thumb (buses are infrequent or nonexistent) into the surrounding area.

Getting There and Getting Around

Kilkenny is on the main Dublin-Waterford rail route; trains shuttle back and forth 4 times on weekdays and twice on Sundays (9:30am-7:50pm; £11 to Dublin, £6.50 to Waterford). The 15 min. trip south to Thomastown, also on the route, costs about £3. Buses leave from the station to: Cork (3/day, Sun. 1/day); Dublin (2/day, Sun. 1/day; £8); and Thomastown (leave 12:35pm, return 5:10pm). Private buses serving commuters stop at The Parade. **Buggy's** buses (tel. 412 64) run between Kilkenny and Castlecomer; **Nolan's** (tel. 251 31) connect Kilkenny and Callan. Hitchhikers should take the Dublin Rd. for Dublin, the Waterford Rd. for Waterford, and the Freshford Rd. to Cashel.

Orientation and Practical Information

Kilkenny's city plan is like a wishbone, with High St. as one handle, John St. (ending in the station) another, and the Parade (with the castle) as the part for which both grapple. The River Nore winds peacefully through town, providing some fine scenery and river walks.

Tourist Office: Rose Inn St. (tel. 217 55), just up from the bridge. Free map; accommodations service £1. Open April-Oct. Mon.-Sat. 9am-6pm, Sun. 10am-5pm; Nov.-March Tues.-Sat. 9am-12:30pm, 2-5:15pm.

Bike Rental: J.J. Wall, 88 Maudlin St. (tel. 212 36), off John St. Raleighs £8/day, £30/week, £30 deposit.

Early Closing Day: Thurs. (small shops only).

Emergency: Dial 999; no coins required.

Financial Services: Bank of Ireland, The Parade (tel. 211 38). Open Mon. 10am-12:30pm and 1:30-5pm, Tues.-Fri. 10am-12:30pm and 1:30-3pm. **The Irish Permanent,** 101 High St. (tel. 213 15). Stays open a tad later than banks. Open Mon.-Fri. 9am-5pm.

Hospital: St. Luke's, Freshford Rd. (tel. 21133).

Launderette: Bretts' Launderette Michael St. (tel. 632 00), off John St. One load, wash and dry, £3.50. Tea or coffee 35p. Open Mon-Sat 8:30am-8pm. Last wash 7pm.

Pharmacy: Several on High St. Different one open Sundays according to a rota.

Police: tel. 222 22.

Post Office: High St. (tel. 218 91). Open Mon.-Sat. 9am-5:30pm.

Taxi: K&M Cab, tel. 613 33; about £2.50-3 maximum for places within the city.

Telephone Code: 056.

Train and Bus Station: McDonagh Station, Dublin Rd. (tel. 220 24), at John St. Staffed only around departure times.

Accommodations and Camping

B&Bs average £11-12. Call ahead. **Waterford Road** and **Castlecomer Road** have the highest concentration of beds.

Kilkenny Tourist Hostel, 35 Parliament St. (tel. 635 41). An old house with stained glass in the kitchen. No lockout, no curfew. £5. Kitchen facilities. Check-out anytime as long as they know when you'll be leaving.

Foulksrath Castle youth hostel (IYHF) (tel. (056) 676 74), a 16th-century castle 8 mi. away in Jenkinstown, near Ballyragget. Clean rooms and a kitchen. July-Aug. £4.50, March-June, Sept.-Oct. £4. Take Buggy's buses from The Parade (June Mon.-Fri. 10am; July-Aug. daily 10am, 2;30pm), or hitch up Castlecomer Rd.

Mrs. O'Connell, St. Mary's, 25 James St. (tel. 220 91). Dark rooms. Electric showers that heat right up are the owner's pride and joy. £10.

Mrs. K. Dempsey, 26 James St. (tel. 219 54). Geraniums, fluffy comforters, and the scent of floral spray. Two stuffed quails. Singles £12, doubles £12/person.

Mrs. Rose Ann Brennan, Bregagh, Dean St. (tel. 223 15). Clean rooms branch off a single corridor in this modern bungalow. Only one stuffed quail. Single £14, double £11/person, double with bath £12.50/person.

Camping: No official campsite in the area. **Murphy's,** 25 Upper Patrick St. (tel. 629 73), with the green gate, allows camping in the small field behind their house with use of sink and toilet. No stuffed quail. £2.50/person. Showers 50p.

Food

Stock up on basic supplies at the immense **Dunnes Supermarket,** several steps away from the tourist office on St. Kieran's St., or at the **L&N Supermarket** on High St.; bakers and greengrocers such as **Crotty's,** are nearby at #92. For all styles of produce, try **The Orchard** on High St. (Open Mon.-Sat. 9am-5pm.) **Creety's** on Castle Corner Rd. stays open for late-night grocery shopping (open from 9am-11pm Mon.-Sat.).

Edward Langtons Pub, 69 John St. (tel. 651 33). Theirs was voted the country's best pub food from 1986-88. Great lunchtime specials, hot plates, salads, and sandwiches (£4-5.50). Miles of gleaming dark wood and green plush stools. Open daily 10:30am-11pm; lunch 11:30am-3pm.

Kilkenny Design Centre Restaurant, the Parade. Excellent homemade food in a cafeteria crowded with bus tourists. Some vegetarian dishes (£4 range) and luscious desserts. Open Mon.-Sat. 9am-6pm, Sun. 10am-6pm; Jan.-March Mon.-Sat. 9am-6pm.

The Castle Kitchen, in the Castle, Grand Parade. Snack amidst gleaming copper cauldrons and cast-iron stoves. Perfect for afternoon tea. Sandwiches £1-2. Open mid-June to Sept. 10am-7pm daily; Oct. to mid-June Tues.-Sat. 10:30am-12:45pm, 2-5pm, Sun. 11am-12:45pm, 2-5pm.

The Pump House Bar, 26 Parliament. Irish stew fraught with potatoes (£2.50).

Sights and Entertainment

Thirteenth-century **Kilkenny Castle** on the Parade housed the earls of Ormonde from the 14th century until 1932. A walk inside evokes images of swishing velvet robes and clashing swords. Many of the rooms have been restored to their former opulence—most notably the **Long Room,** with its breathtaking highly ornamented ceiling, designed like a Viking ship, and portraits of English bigwigs, including that frumpy duo, William and Mary. Downstairs in the basement, the **Butler Gallery** (tel. 214 50) shows the work of contemporary artists. (Open daily 10am-7pm; Oct. to mid-June Tues.-Sat. 10:30am-12:45pm and 2-5pm; Sun. 11am-12:45pm and 2-5pm. Admission £1, seniors 70p, students and children 40p.) The **Kilkenny Design Centre** has set up its craft shop in the converted stables across from the castle. The Irish-crafted textiles and furniture are expensive but among the finest in the country. (Open Mon.-Sat. 9am-6pm, Sun. 10am-6pm; Jan.-March Mon.-Sat. 9am-6pm.) Built by a Tudor merchant at the turn of the 17th century, **Rothe House,** Parliament St. (tel. 228 93), served as the mansion of the **Gaelic League,** a society which helped kindle the 19th-century Gaelic renaissance. It is now a small museum of local archaeological finds and Kilkennian curiosities—come here to find out about culm and bums. (Open Mon.-Sat. 10:30am-12:30pm and 2-5pm, Sun. 3-5pm; Nov.-March Sat.-Sun. 3-5pm only. Adults £1, students 60p.)

Kilkenny is blessed with a preponderance of religious architecture. The finest is 13th-century **St. Canice's Cathedral;** the stone-step approach from Irishtown Bridge (over the canal) is lined with fragments of old sculpture from the cathedral itself, which was sacked by Cromwell'smerry men. The name "Kilkenny" is derived from the Gaelic *Cill Chainnigh,* meaning "Church of St. Canice." (Open daily 9am-1pm and 2-6pm, except during services. Admission £1, students 30p.) The **round tower,** near the south transept, is a relic of the earlier 6th-century Church of St. Canice. For an additional 50p (students 25p) you can climb the series of steep ladders inside for a fine view of the town and its surroundings. The **Black Abbey** (1228), off Abbey St., got its name from the black habits of Dominican friars. Within the heavy stone structure a fiery modern stained glass window contrasts with older, subtler ones. **St. Mary's,** nearby, is a lofty narrow cathedral, hung with paintings of the Passion haloed in gold leaf.

In the 14th century, crafty monks are said to have brewed a light ale in **St. Francis' Abbey.** The abbey is in ruins, but its clandestine industry survives: **Smithwick's Brewery** offers free tours and tasting. (Tours June-Sept. Mon.-Fri. at 3pm; under 14 not admitted, under 16 admitted only if accompanied by adult.) Many local pubs serve this brew. Visit the **Marble City Bar** or **Jim Holland's,** both on High St. John St. rocks at night: the **Kilford Arms** has traditional sessions on Tues. nights and plays dance music Thurs.-Sun.; **O'Gorman's,** near the train station, has Irish music Fri. nights (no cover); **Peig's,** complete with stuffed tiger and a noose for unruly drinkers, sometimes stages theatricals at night. **Cleere's Pub,** 28 Parliament St., presents folk and traditional music on Mondays (no cover) and storytelling, poetry readings and plays the rest of the week (tickets £3-5). The last week of August is **Kilkenny Arts Week,** with daily concerts, recitals, poetry readings, and exhibitions by some of Ireland's top artists. Admission varies for individual events (free-£7); a weeklong ticket is £70 (student discounts available). Buy tickets from Kilkenny Arts Week, *c/o* Kilkenny Tourist Office, Rose Inn St., Kilkenny. Phone (056) 211 96, ext. 227 (before Aug. 1), or (056) 636 63 (after Aug. 1).

Near Kilkenny

Thomastown, 10 mi. south of Kilkenny, is too often overshadowed by its larger neighbor. A number of small craftspeople form a community in and around Thomastown; ask at the Kilkenny tourist office for a detailed map.

Jerpoint Abbey, near Tullaherin, 1½ mi. south of Thomastown on the N9, is perhaps the most interesting Cistercian ruin in Ireland. The remarkable etchings in the abbey cloister and the numerous knights' tombs make this trip worthwhile. Many find biking, hitchhiking, and riding the rails are the best transportation options: the Dublin-Waterford train stops at Thomastown on its way south (4/day; 15 min.). A bus leaves the Kilkenny station at 12:35pm daily, arriving at 1pm; it returns from Thomastown at 5:10pm, to be in Kilkenny by 5:25pm. Adventerous hostelers with transportation might try the **Graiguenamanagh youth hostel (IYHF),** Graiguanamanagh Vocational School (tel. 241 77), 9 mi. away. (£4.50; open July-Aug.) North of Kilkenny, on the road to Castlecomer, lurks the massive **Dunmore Cave** with its varied limestone formations. (Open mid-June to mid-Sept. 10am-6:30pm daily; mid-March to mid-June Tues.-Sat. 10am-5pm, Sun. 2-5pm; Oct. to mid-March Sat. and Sun. 10am-5pm. £1, students 40p.) Take **Buggy's** buses from the Parade in Kilkenny (June Mon.-Fri 10am; July-Aug. daily 10am, 2:30pm).

Cashel

The **Rock of Cashel** rises like a fairy castle out of Cashel town, truly magical when seen from a distance or lit at night (when it's lit). Rising some 300 ft. above the plain, the dark limestone hill supports an elaborate complex of medieval buildings. One church was founded by St. Declan, a follower of St. Patrick, in the 6th century. **Cormac's Chapel,** a majestic dual-towered structure, was built between 1127 and 1134. Inside, gorgeous Romanesque carvings and a richly decorated sarcophagus are on display. The 13th-century **Cashel Cathedral** survived Earl Kildare's attempts to burn it (and the Archbishop) to the ground, and now it overshadows all the other ruins in sheer magnitude; it too holds 16th-century carved tombs. Alongside it is a relatively plain five-story residential castle dating from the 15th century, which visitors can peek into but are not allowed to enter. The 13th-century **St. Patrick's Cross** is preserved in the museum at the entrance of the castle complex. In summer, take the informative 50-min. tour of the complex that leaves from the entrance every hour. (All of the above open daily June-Sept. 9am-7:30pm; mid-March to May 9:30am-5pm; Oct. to mid-March 9:30am-4:30pm. £1.50, students 60p.) Far from the madding crowd, and down the cowpath from the Rock, **Hore Abbey** awaits silently amid a chorus of arches. The last Cistercian monastery to be established in Ireland, its ruins are open, free, and afford a striking view of the Rock. Tiny, brightly colored memories of old-time Ireland populate the **Cashel Folk Village,** Moor Lane: the Wild Rover Pub, the Widow Breen's House, and the Tinker's Caravan among them. The village's brochure gives detailed information, but the buildings themselves emanate a sense of what once was. Well worth the £1 (80p students). (Open Mon.-Sat. 10am-7:30pm, Sun. 2-7:30pm.)

The center of Cashel town lies about a ¼ mile down Moor Lane from the Rock. The crisply efficient **tourist office,** in the City Hall on Main St. (tel. (062) 613 33), books rooms for £1 and hands out pamphlets on local attractions. (Open Mon.-Sat. 10am-12:45pm and 2-6pm, Sept.-May Mon.-Fri. 10am-12:45pm and 2-6pm.) The **telephone code** is 062. The nearest youth hostel is **Boytonrath hostel,** over 6 mi. away towards Cahir (see Cahir listings below). B&Bs are a dime a dozen. **Abbey House,** Moor Lane (tel. 611 04), run by Mrs. E. Ryan, is a wonderland of fuzzy textures (£11). You can have your choice of 4 pastel shades at **Mrs. S. Ryan,** Carrig Bawn (tel. 613 96), and wake up to a savory view of the ruins. (Open May-Sept.; £11.) Little white tables in a rose garden grace **Rockville House** (tel. 617 60), run by Mrs. A. Hayes (£11, £12.50 with bath). Cashel's **supermarket,** Main St., will feed you if you're running low on funds—otherwise try the **Coffee Dock,** Bank

Place, swathed in pink and staffed by giggling teenage girls. Meals £2-3. **O'Reilly's Bar,** 9 Main St., lets you consume sandwiches (90p-£1.50) and other pub delights on their plush red love couches.

Cashel lies inland between Waterford and Cork, tucked behind a series of mountain ranges on the N8 motorway from Cork to Roscrea. The private **Kavanaugh's Bus Service** stops at the travel agent's at the top of Main St.; it leaves for Dublin at 8:30am, and returns at 6pm (2½ hr.; £7 single, £8 return). **Expressway** buses leave from O'Reilly's on Main St., serving Dublin (4/day, 3/day Sun. 9:35am-8:50pm; 1½ hr.), Cork (4/day, 3/day Sun. 8am-8:50pm; 1½ hr.), and Cahir (4/day, 3/day Sun. 9:20am-9:05pm; 15 min.). Cashel is on a major trucking route from Cork to Dublin.

Cahir

Cahir (CARE) lies 12 mi. south of Cashel at the eastern end of the Galtee Mountains, where the Dublin-Cork and the Limerick-Waterford roads meet. The town is enlivened by banks, a post office, and a train station, but its main attraction is the **castle.** Guarded by an eagle and locked by aging wooden doors, this well-preserved fortress is built on a rocky island in the middle of the River Suir. (Open mid-June to mid-Sept. daily 10am-7:30pm; May to mid-June daily 10am-6pm; mid-Sept. to Oct., Nov.-April daily 10am-1pm, Tues.-Sun. 2-4:30pm. £1, students 40p.) The **tourist office,** situated next door on Castle St. (tel. (052) 414 53) is open July-Aug. Mon.-Sat. 9am-6pm, Sun. 10am-5pm; May-June, Sept. Mon.-Sat. 9am-6pm; they book B&Bs (£1) and give out information on the surrounding mountain ranges. A number of youth hostels in the countryside are cheap but a challenge to get to: the most easily accessible is probably **Liskayle Hostel** (tel. 419 63), 1 mi. north of Cahir and 11 mi. south of Cashel. Reserve at Condon's on Church St. across from the post office, where it is also possible to get a ride to the hostel (£4.50, tent pitch £3). **Boytonrath Hostel** (tel. (062) 722 23), 6 mi. north of Cahir, is a farm with 10 beds, kitchen facilities, and hot showers. (£4. Open May-Oct.) The **Farmhouse Hostel** (tel. 419 06), about 3 mi. south of Cahir on the Mitchelstown Rd., has 8 beds and is open all year (£4.50). The **Mountain Lodge** and **Ballydavid Wood House** (both IYHF) are also convenient (see next section). Two mi. off the Mitchelstown-Cahir road in the town of Burncourt is a collection of **limestone caves;** the 30-ft. **Tower of Babel** stalagmite is worth the trip. (Mitchelstown Cave open daily 10am-6pm. Admission £2, students £1.) Take the Cork bus and ask the driver to let you off. The tiny village of **Ballyporeen,** 4 mi. east of Mitchelstown on the R665, holds the dubious distinction of being the birthplace of Ronald Reagan's ancestors. Drown your memories of deficit financing in the local pub named after him. Buses leave from the tourist office to Limerick and Cork (4/day, 3/day Sun.). For other destinations, catch the bus at the **Crock of Gold,** just down the road; buses run to Clonmel (4/day, 3/day Sun.) and to Dublin and Waterford (4/day, 2/day Sun.).

Southern Mountains

Three mountain ranges abruptly rear their moor-covered rumps out of the flatlands near Cahir: the **Galtees,** the **Knockmealdowns,** and the **Comeraughs.** In Cahir, the tourist office can provide you with survey maps and information on the 43-mi. **Munster Way,** and **Galtymore Adventure Holidays** (tel. 413 41 or 410 47) rents equipment (mountain bikes are £6/day, £15/3 days, £25/week.) Always ask locally about hiking trails.

The Galtee Mountains, west of Cahir, boast **Galtymore,** Ireland's highest inland mountain at 3018 ft. A 5-6 mi. forest walk from Cahir leads you to the **Glen of Aherlow (Ballydavid Wood) youth hostel (IYHF),** Bansha (tel. (062) 541 98), open March-Nov. but weekends the rest of the year (July-Aug. £5.50, March-June, Sept.-Oct. £4.30, Nov. £3.80): go out the road to Tipperary, take a sharp left after Black Tom's Bar, and follow the signs. The hostel can also be reached by following the road. From there you can make your way across the mountains to the **Mountain Lodge (IYHF),** Burncourt (tel. (052) 672 77), a gas-lit Georgian hunting lodge in the midst of the woods. If the warden isn't there, just make yourself at home. (From Cahir, follow the Mitchelstown Rd. about 10 mi., turn right at the sign for another 2 mi.) Open April-Sept. No showers; kitchen facilities; July-Aug. £4.50; April-June, Sept. £4. Along the southern border of County Tipperary, about 12 mi. south of Cahir, the **Knockmealdown Mountains** rise in a rippling wave. The **Lismore youth hostel (IYHF),** Glengarra (tel. (058) 543 90) is 4 mi. from Lismore and serves as a good base for hikers (kitchen facilities; open April-Sept.; July-Aug. £4.50, April-June, Sept. £4). The Comeraugh Mountains, filled with lakes, are accessible from the independent **Powers the Pot** hostel (tel. (052) 230 85), 5 mi. from Clonmel on the road to Carrick-on-Suir. Open May-Oct.; £4, camping £2.50.

Southwest Ireland

Early Christian artifacts and fiction suffuse the south coast of County Cork, harking back to the mist-penumbra'd landfall of Noah's grandson on Bantry's ragged shore. Fishing villages celebrate the mussel harvest; neighboring seaside resorts gourmetize the shellfish. Cork Town, Ireland's second largest metropolis, shoots tubular tendrils of tangentially tendential transportation out along the south coast and on towards the peninsulas.

Counties Cork and Kerry reach three rocky peninsulas into the Atlantic; **Beara** lies to the south, **Iveragh** in the middle, and **Dingle** to the north. Coastal roads ring all three, passing by numerous B&Bs and bike rentals. Visitors in search of solitary beauty are most likely to find it in the vast stillness of the Beara Peninsula. Little frequented by automobiles, Beara is better toured by bike than by thumb; rent a cycle in Skibbereen, Bantry, or Castletownbere. Further north, Killarney is the reincarnation of the Tower of Babel, and multilingual tour buses spread confusion around the Ring of Kerry, a route that squeezes between the Iveragh Peninsula's extraordinary coastline and stark glacial mountains. Kenmare, across Moll's Gap from Killarney, side-steps some of the chaos. The northernmost Gaelic-speaking Dingle peninsula, richly historical, extends its seclusion almost to the legendary Blasket Islands of Irish £20-note renown. Come to the peninsulas prepared to sheathe your plans in plastic; the area is notorious for its wicked rainfall.

Cork Town

Cork (pop. 140,000), a busy metropolis and industrial center, has a modern charm unaffected by its dearth of historical sights. On sunny days, intimate side-street coffeeshops overflow onto the pavement, buskers pass their hats and a robust music scene shakes the pubs until closing-time. Nearby Blarney Castle draws a steady stream of tourists through Cork, but there's plenty in the town itself to enjoy that doesn't require a camera or even much money. The plethora of hostels and transport connections make Cork a good base for exploring the southwest, in addition to its other charms.

Arriving and Departing

As befits Ireland's largest city after Dublin, Cork has good train connections to Dublin (9/day 5:20am-6:55pm, Sun. 4/day; 3 hr.; single £29.50, return £26.50), Limerick (6/day, 7:30am-6:55pm, Sun. 3/day; 2 hr.; single £11.50, return £13), Rosslare Harbor (Mon.-Sat. 2 day; 4½ hr.; single £22.50, return £26.50), Killarney (4/day, 11:15am-8pm, Sun. 3/day; single £11.50, return £13). Buses run to Dublin (4/day 8am-6pm, Sun. 3/day; single £11, student £7.50), Blarney (nearly every hr., 6:25am-11pm; £2 return), Youghal (11/day, 7:50am-11pm, Sun. 8/day; single

£5.20, student £2.70), and Kinsale (5/day 6:50am-6pm, Sun. 3/day; £3.50 single, £1.80 student). To hitch west from the city, follow Western Rd. out of the city (bus #8); for the north or east, take Lower Glanmire Rd. to Tivoli (bus #11).

Ferries from Cork to France and England dock at **Ringaskiddy Terminal,** 9 mi. south of the city. **Brittany Ferries,** Tourist House, 42 Grand Parade (tel. 277 801), sail to Roscoff, France (daily; 14 hr.; £47-58). **Irish Ferries,** 9 Bridge St. (tel. 504 333), just past the intersection of St. Patrick's Bridge and St. Patrick's Quay, sail to Le Havre, France, during July and August (once/week; leaves Cork Fridays, leaves Le Havre Thursdays; 20 hr.). **B&I Line,** 42 Grand Parade (tel. 273 024), runs ferries to Swansea, Wales (a few times weekly, daily July-Aug.; 11 hr.; £18-22). The 20-min. bus trip from the ferry terminal to the Cork bus station costs £2.80.

Cork has a small **international airport** (tel. 313 313) 6 mi. south of the city, served by the following British and Irish carriers: Aer Lingus (tel. 274 331), Dan-Air (tel. 961 103), and Ryan Air (tel. 274 444). A shuttle bus to the airport leaves every hour from the bus station and costs £2 (£2.50 return).

Orientation and Practical Information

Cork is a compact city; its center is an island encircled by the River Lee. Tiny streets vibrate through the town like strings on a tightly tuned harp; the major thoroughfares are Patrick St., Grand Parade and the South Mall. The **tourist office** is on the Grand Parade near the southern branch of the river; the **bus station** (tel. 503 399) lies on the northern branch at Parnell Place. Many of the hostels await north of the upper branch, as does **Kent Station,** the train depot on Lower Glanmire Rd. (tel. 504 422). The areas around the train station and the warehouses can be unsafe at night. Western Rd., an extension of Washington St., rolls by the university, several hostels, and innumerable B&Bs.

Tourist Office: Tourist House, Grand Parade (tel. 273 251), on the corner of South Mall St. Southwest regional office. Accommodations service 50p. Open June Mon.-Sat. 9am-6pm; July-Aug. Mon.-Sat. 9am-7pm; Sept.-May Mon.-Fri. 9:15am-5:30pm, Sat. 9:15am-1pm.

AnÓige (Irish Youth Hostel Association): 1-2 Redclyffe, Western Rd. (tel. 543 289), at the hostel. Administrative office open Tues. and Fri. 8-10pm.

Bike Rental: Carroll Cycles, Dillon's Cross (tel. 508 923). Mountain bikes £4/day, £24/week. Open Mon.-Sat. 9am-6pm.

Bus Station: Parnell Pl., 2 blocks from Patrick's Bridge (tel. 808 188).

Emergency: Dial 999; no coins required.

Financial Services: Bank of Ireland, 32 South Mall (tel. 276 712). Open Mon. 10am-12:30pm and 1:30-5pm, Tues.-Fri. 10am-12:30pm and 1:30-3pm. **American Express:** Casey Travel Ltd., 60 S. Mall St. (tel. 270 123 or 277 259), around the corner from the tourist office. No exchange of checks. Emergency personal check cashing for cardholders. Mail held (no charge). Open Mon.-Fri. 9am-5:30pm.

Hospital: Cork Regional Hospital, tel. 546 400. Take bus #8.

Launderette: 14 MacCurtain St. Open Mon.-Sat. 9am-10pm, last wash 8pm. Wash £2.

Police Station: Union Quay (tel. 273 161 or 273 217), off Anglesea St.

Post Office: Oliver Plunkett St. (tel. 272 000). Open Mon.-Sat. 9am-5:30pm.

Student Travel Office: USIT, 10/11 Market Parade (tel. 270 900), in the Arcade off St. Patrick St. Large, friendly office sells Travelsave stamps, Rambler and Eurotrain tickets, *et al.* Open Mon.-Fri. 9:30am-5:30pm, Sat. 10am-2pm.

Taxi: Inter-city Cab, 37 Shandon St. (tel. 303 899).

Telephone Code: 021.

Train Station: Kent Station, Lower Glanmire Rd. For inquiries, call 50 44 22. Lockers £1.

Accommodations and Camping

Cork is blessed with many wonderful hostels. B&Bs run £11-13; hunt around on **Lower Glanmire Rd.** or **Western Rd.,** due west of the Grand Parade (take bus #8).

Isaac's, MacCurtain St. (tel. 500 011). Resplendent rays illuminate the old wood floors and brick arches of the newest hostel in town. Live music and organized trips. Reception open 24 hr. No lockout, no curfew. £4.75 dorm room; £7.50 4-6 person dorm room with bath; doubles £12.50/person; singles £17.50; linen 50p.

Sheila's Cork Tourist Hostel, 3 Belgrave Pl. (tel. 505 562), by the intersection of Wellington Rd. and York St., several blocks from bus and train stations. Sheila has it all: snooker, sauna (£1), video, laundry (£2.50), and a reading room. Reception 8am-10pm, no lockout, no curfew. £4.75, £6.50/person for twin, linen 50p, key deposit £2.

Campus House, 3 Woodland View, Western Rd. (tel. 343 531). Small and luxurious; great showers. £4.75.

The Cork City Hostel, 100 Lower Glanmire Rd. (tel. (021) 509 089), directly across from the train station. The human incarnation of this hostel would be a spunky old chap, a little creaky in the joints but as interesting as they come. Videos at night and a fire in winter. No lockout, no curfew. £4.50, laundry £1.80. Kitchen facilities. Sheets 50p.

IYHF youth hostel, 1-2 Redclyffe, Western Rd. (tel. 543 289), about a 15-min. walk from the center of town, across the street from the university grounds. Take bus #8 from Patrick St. In a lovely burnt-sienna Victorian townhouse with garden. Currency exchange, bike rental, laundry and kitchen facilities, hostel vans to Blarney Castle (£2 return) and to the ferryport. Check-in 8:30-10am and 5-9:30pm. Lockout 10am-5pm. Curfew 11:55pm. July-Aug. £5.90, March-June, Sept.-Oct. £4.90, Nov.-Feb. £4.30. Sheets 50p.

Kinlay House,Bob and Joan Walk (tel. 508 966), down the alley to the right of Shandon Church. A maze-like configuration of rooms with all the amenities and music piped into the hallways. Reception 24 hr. No lockout, no curfew. Free linen. Kitchen. Lockers in rooms. £7 (price includes continental breakfast).

Maura O'Driscoll, Fairylawn House, Western Rd. (tel. (021) 543 444), next to the youth hostel. Birds twitter on the delicate lawn and sentimental pictures hang throughout. £10.

Camping: Cork City Caravan and Camping Park (tel. 961 866). Southwest of the city center on Togher Rd., ½mi. beyond Lough Rd. Bus #14 runs every 20 min. £3.50/unit; £3 tent plus £1/person. Children under 7 free. Open Easter-Oct.

Food and Pubs

Try the **arcade** (entrances off Grand Parade, Patrick St., and Princes St.) for fresh fruit and grilled chickens, and the armada of bakeries along Oliver Plunkett St. and Washington St. for pastries and sandwich breads. There is a **Quinnsworth Supermarket** on Paul St. Local specialties are a good test of your psychogastronomic strength: try *crubeen* (pig's feet), or *drisheen* (blood sausage).

Quay Co-op, 24 Sullivan's Quay. Funky music, fresh flowers, and an alternative crowd. Vegetarian and vegan entrees (£3-4). Health-food store in the same building. Restaurant open Mon.-Tues. 10am-6:30pm, Wed.-Sat. 10am-6pm.

Raging Red Hag, 8 Pembroke St. (tel. 271 212). Sandwiches galore (£1.25-1.50) in a white-washed room looking onto the street. Open Mon.-Sat. 10am-6pm.

Thyme Out Coffeeshop, French Church St. Lovely desserts amidst batik and moodily abstract paintings. Large selection of teas: name your favorite. Lunches £2-3. Open Mon.-Sat. 10am-6pm.

Bully's, 40 Paul St. Roaring open oven at the back produces piping hot, delicious Haitian food. Definitely worth £3-6.

The typical pubs cater to thirsty stevedores; look longer and harder to find more upbeat ones. **Murphy's Stout** is Guinness's sweeter and more timid cousin from Cork. **Beamish,** an economy stout (£1.25/pint), is another local brew. Both are served with comforting regularity at pubs around the city. The **Long Valley Bar,** a student hangout on Winthrop St., serves excellent bar food. Traditional-music mavens should drop by **An Bodhrán,** 42 Oliver Plunkett St., and **De Lacy's,** 74 Oliver Plunkett St. £3-5 cover (ballads Fri.-Sun. nights). Union Quay is a hot spot for music: try **The Lobby** and **An Phoenix** for good traditional, folk, and rock.

Sights

During July and August, free city tours leave from the tourist office at 7:30pm on Tues. and Thurs. nights. Cork's strength lies not its historical skeleton but rather in its contemporary pulse; even so, there is sightseeing for those who want it. **St. Finbarr's Cathedral,** at the South Gate entrance to medieval Cork, incorporates gold leaf, griffins, and angels into its giant limestone gingerbread-house façade. (Open Mon.-Sat. 10am-1pm and 2-5:30pm; Oct.-April 10am-1pm and 2-5pm. Admission 50p.) Nearby, the remains of the 6th-century **Charles Fort** enclose the police station. The ramparts afford a Corkian panorama on a clear day. (Open all the time; free.)

In the city center, the **Crawford Municipal Gallery,** Emmet Place, houses an enthralling collection of Irish art work. (Open Mon.-Fri. 10am-5pm, Sat. 9:30am-4:30pm. Free.) Its small, misunderstood colleague, the **Triskel Arts Centre,** secludes itself on Tobin St., off South Main St., a free gallery with a focus on modern works. (Open Tues.-Fri. 10:30am-5:30pm, Sat. 11am-5pm. Free.) North of the River Lee, **Shandon Church's** red-and-white three-tiered "pepper-pot" tower rises high above the street-level hodgepodge of factories and warehouses. Climb to the top for a view of the city and harbor. (Open Mon.-Sat. 10am-4:30pm; in winter Mon.-Sat. 10am-4pm. Admission to church £1; to church, tower, and bells £1.50.) Just opposite the church, a number of artisans practice their crafts (weaving, porcelain-making, crystal cutting, pottery) in the **Shandon Craft Centre.** Mill around the studios/shops or eat in the café. (Open 7:30am-5:30pm.) The **University College Cork,** built in the late 19th century, is about ½mi. southwest of the city center and is bordered by Western Rd., Donovan's Rd., College Rd., and the River Lee. Gothic windows, long echoing stony corridors, a smattering of ivy, and grassy expanses make for a fine afternoon walk. Across Western Rd., follow the signs to the **Cork Public Museum,** set in long public gardens studded with statues and flowers. Visit its collection of local monuments, glassware, and ceramics for free. (Open Mon.-Fri. 11am-1pm, 2:15-5pm, Sun. 3-5pm.)

Entertainment

The **Opera House,** Emmet Pl. (tel. 270 022), stages formal and informal productions, including Gilbert and Sullivan, drama, variety, opera, and jazz. During August, the **Summer Revels** festival features comedy, burlesque, and other light entertainment. (Box office open Mon.-Sat. 10am-5pm; tickets £8-16; student discount for some shows only.) **Everyman's Theatre,** MacCertain St. (tel. 503 077), rotates plays, music and dance for £4-6. (Box office open Mon.-Sat. 11am-7pm; student discount around £1 off.)

Festivals and events spice up Cork fairly often. *The Cork Examiner* prints details on sports events. In summer, try to take in a game of **hurling** or **Gaelic football.** Big games cost £13-15 and tickets are scarce, but Sunday or post-work matches are free.

Cork hosts the popular one-week **International Film Festival** in late September and early October. Documentaries are shown in the Cork Opera House and the Triskel Arts Centre (contact Michael Hannigan at (021) 27 17 11). Jazz fans bop in for the **Guinness Jazz Festival** in late October, a nonstop three-day jamboree comparable in reputation to the renowned Newport and Montreux festivals (contact Mary Browne at (021) 54 54 11 or 29 47 83). Nearby **Cobh** hosts the one-week **International Folk Dance Festival** which starts on the second Sunday in July (contact John Geary at (021) 81 24 35).

Near Cork

Five mi. northwest of Cork is **Blarney,** home of **Blarney Castle** and the terrifically overrated **Blarney Stone.** Supposedly, kissing the stone endows one with automatic eloquence. More fun than actually kissing the stone is watching the corpulent American tourists pucker up. One noted kisser, Aaron Haley Deemer, is certainly not corpulent, but does have the gift of the gab. But only in the best *possible taste...* (Open June-July Mon.-Sat. 9am-8:30pm; Aug. Mon.-Sat. 9am-7:30pm; Sept. Mon.-Sat. 9am-6:30pm; Oct.-April Mon.-Sat. 9am-sundown; May Mon.-Sat. 9am-7pm. Also in summer Sun. 9:30am-5:30pm; off-season Sun. 9:30am-sundown. Admission £2.50, seniors and students £1.50, children £1.) Buses leave for Blarney from the Cork bus station (every hr. 6:25am-11pm; 20 min.; £2 return).

Youghal

Thirty mi. east of Cork, this winsome town can make an excellent daytrip or a fresher, quieter place to stay the night. The huge **Clockgate** (1777) straddles the lively, colorful Main St.; from here you can see the **old city walls,** built on the hill between the 13th and 17th centuries. Off North Main St. on Emmet Pl. two remarkable buildings stand side by side: **St. Mary's Church** and **Myrtle Grove.** Likenesses of the long-dead lounge on skulls in St. Mary's, with a casualness never achieved in life. (Admission £1, children 20p. Get the key from the lodge.) Myrtle Grove, the former residence of Sir Walter Raleigh, has recently been opened to the public: admire the dark oak paneling in the main room and pay due respect to the corner of the garden where Raleigh planted the first Irish potatoes ever. (Open May-Sept. Tues., Thurs, and Sat. Guided tours only 2:30 and 4pm. Adults £2, children £1.50.) The **Walter Raleigh Spud Festival** is held in Youghal during late June and early July, featuring road racing, dancing, and a cooking competition. Youghal's other attraction is a huge sandy beach about ½mi. from town, one of the nicest in the area.

The **tourist office,** Market Sq. (tel. (024) 923 90), is open May-Sept. 10am-6pm, until 8pm July-Aug. Spend the night at **Miss E. O'Brien,** Assumpta, Devonshire Sq. (tel. (024) 921 34), in an overstuffed Georgian house with a large garden. (Open April-Oct. £10.) For a country-house B&B, call **Mrs. E. Long,** Cherrymount Farmhouse (tel. (024) 971 10), 3 mi. from town on the scenic Blackwater route (£10). Happy music tinkles in the background at the family-style **Old Well Restaurant,** 78 N. Main St. Breakfast is served all day; meals start at £2. (Open daily 9:30am-9pm.) On the Strand, above the beach, **Homeville** butters hot freshly-made scones in a private house while gossip and kids run about. Across the road and down a couple hundred yards, hang with the locals at the **Cosy Café,** a cheap and friendly meat and chips joint. (Open Mon.-Sat. 10:30am-9pm.) **L&N Superstores** have a branch on North Main.

Kinsale

A moraine of gourmet food, boating, and BMWs, the seaside resort of Kinsale disdains mangy pub crawlers. A hike up **Compass Hill** south from Main St. is rewarded with a view of the town and the winding estuary that feeds the harbor. 18th-century Georgian houses border charming narrow cobblestone streets in the old town of Kinsale. The west tower of the 12th-century **Church of St. Multose** (patron saint of Kinsale) bewitches, and the old town stocks still stand inside. (Open daylight hr. Free.) **Desmond's Castle** once imprisoned 600 French soldiers between less illustrious tax collecting campaigns. (Open all the time; free.) The **Maritime Museum,** in the Courthouse, Market Sq., is possibly the smallest collection to ever call itself a museum. (Open May-Oct. Mon.-Sat. 11am-5pm; closed for ½hr. sometime between noon and 2pm for lunch; open Sun. 2-6pm. Admission 50p, children 20p.)

During the Elizabethan period, the English fortified the area to guard against Spanish shipments of arms to Irish rebels, leaving behind such strongholds as **Charles Fort,** about 2 mi. east of town (follow the signs). (Open mid-June to Sept. daily 9am-6:30pm; mid-March to mid-June Tues.-Sat. 9am-5pm, Sun. 2-5pm. Admission £1, students 50p. Guided tours of the fort every hr.) The **Kinsale Arts Week,** with theater, poetry, jazz, traditional music and dance blooms during mid- to late June, while the **Kinsale Regatta** sails into the harbor during the first weekend of August. Contact the tourist office for information.

The **tourist office,** Emmet Pl. (tel. 772 234), provides a free map, currency exchange, and points the way to the tourist trail. Accommodations service £1. (Open mid-May to mid-Oct. Mon.-Sat. 9:30am-5:30pm, Sun. 11:30am-5:30pm.) Pearse St. holds the **post office** (open Mon.-Sat. 9am-5:30pm), a few **banks,** and **Murphy's,** which rents somewhat rickety bikes (£6/day, £4 after 2pm, £35/week, ID as deposit; open daily 9am-6pm). Kinsale's **telephone code** is 021.

Kinsale has two hostels: the no-frills **Dempsey's,** Cork Rd. (tel. 772 124), beside Dempsey's Garage (£4, shower 50p, kitchen facilities); and the **IYHF youth hostel,** Summer Cove (tel. 772 309), which is 2 mi. from Kinsale on the eastern side of the harbor up the hill just before Charles Fort. Arriving from Cork, ask the bus driver to let you off at the nearby crossroads, then follow the Charles Fort signs. A taxi with room for six from the town center costs £2. The hostel provides wonderful rooms with extravagantly tufted comforters, a huge kitchen, and a Japanese-style dining room. (July-Aug. £5.50; March-June, Sept.-Oct. £4.30; Nov.-Feb. £3.80.) The hospitable Mrs. T. Bolster, **Ancaireacht, the Rock** (tel. 772 869), puts you up in her light, airy rooms for £11.50. The **Cuckoo's Nest Bar,** 1 Main St. (tel. 772 342), tucks away tiny shiplike rooms with skylights upstairs. (£8 in summer, £7 in winter. Breakfast is £3 extra.)

Kinsale, the gourmet food capital of Ireland, is famous for its **Good Food Circle,** a group of 11 restaurants that serve excellent expensive seafoods as well as other culinary tender. Kinsale savors a **Gourmet Festival** in the first week of October; a G.F.C. meal can cost £5-12. Fortunately, some of the gastronomic expertise has trickled down to less expensive restaurants. **The Copper Grill,** on Pearse St., offers excellent meals for £3-5. (Lamb chop, potato, and peas, £3. Open daily noon-12:30am.) Eat tremendous stove-oven pizzas (from £4) at the **Piazzetta Pizzeria,** just off Market Sq. on Newman's Mall (open Tues.-Fri. 12:30-2:30pm, Sat.-Sun. 12:30-10:30pm). The tiny, homely **Little Skillet,** 47 Main St., serves vegetarian dishes but specializes in seafood. (Lunches £3-4. Open for lunch Wed.-Sat. 12:30-3pm, Sun. 1:15-4pm.)

You can fill your picnic basket at the **Super Valu Supermarket** near the post office. The best pubs for a pint and an evening of *cáint, ceol agus craic* (talk, music and fun) are **The Anchor Bar** (live music on weekends), **The Shanakee,** and the **Armada** in town on Main St. Most pubs serve decent lunches for around £3 and are open Mon.-Sat. 10:30am-11:30pm, Sun. 12:30-2pm and 4-11pm.

Buses run between Cork and Kinsale. (To Cork: Mon.-Sat. 6/day, 7:40am - 7:45pm, Sun. 4/day; £3.50, return £4.70.) They stop at the Esso station down from the tourist office.

Kinsale to Skibbereen and Bantry

Two major bus routes depart from Cork Town and serve the West Cork Peninsula: a coastal transport runs from Cork to Skibbereen, stopping in Bandon, Clonakilty, and Rosscarbery, while an inland bus travels between Cork and Bantry, stopping in Bandon and Dunmanway. (Both run 3/day, twice on Sun., with slightly more frequent service in summer.) Others rely on two-wheeled or thumb transport.

The inland route, especially the segment through the Shehy Mountains between Dunmanway and Bantry, offers gloriously rugged scenery. The independent **Shiplake Hostel** (tel. (023) 457 50) near Dunmanway is hidden away 3 mi. up the road to Kealkil and Bantry in a restored farmhouse 2 mi. from two lakes. Vary, the hostel owner, loans out bikes for free to those intent on roaming around, and he cooks the best vegetarian pizza in Ireland. (Open mid-March to mid-Nov.; £4.50, sheets 50p; kitchen, food available.)

From Kinsale to Skibbereen, the coastline is quiet and relatively unbesmirched by tourists. At **Timoleague,** 17 mi. west of Kinsale near Clonakilty, lie the extensive ruins of a Franciscan monastery. Founded by St. Molaga, the maze-like abbey seethes with unexpected passageways and blocked exits. Smell the flowers or pick your own raspberries, blackberries, gooseberries, and blackcurrants at the well-kept Timoleague **Castle Gardens,** just outside of town on the Bandon Rd. (Open occasionally; admission £1.50, children 75p.) Peruse the independent **Lettercollum House Hostel** (tel. (023) 462 51), an old Victorian mansion in the forest replete with stained glass and artwork by the owners; walk 20 min. from town on the Clonakilty Rd. The engaging and versatile proprietors cook delicious three-course meals (£6), sell homemade breads, and rent bikes. (No lockout, no curfew. £4.50. Open March-Nov.)

West Cork activity centers on **Clonakilty,** whose sandy **Inchydony Beach,** 3 mi. south of town, is nothing short of famous. (Take Clarke St. and turn left onto the Coast Rd.) A succession of pale pastel shades on houses linked together characterize the town, typical of the entire West Cork region. Two mi. north of Clonakilty lies nigh-barren **Templebryan,** site of an early Celtic church and a modest ceremonial stone circle. Volunteers staff the tiny **West Cork Regional Museum,** on Western Rd., during erratic hours.

The Clonakilty tourist office (tel. (023) 332 26), called **West Cork Travel,** books accommodations in the area for £1. (Open July-Aug. Mon.-Sat. 10am-1pm and 2-6pm.) A pastel peacock theme runs throughout the rooms at **Mrs. McMahon,** Nordav, Western Rd. (tel. (023) 336 55). Take your pick of balcony, piano, or kitchen (£11.50, £14 with bath). **Desert House,** a modest farmhouse on the Ring Rd., offers B&B for £11.50 and camping on their grassy field for £3.75/tent plus 30p/person. (Showers 50p extra.) A frenzy of orange tiling at Connelly St. sets apart **Rossa Grill's** potato cakes (50p), fish and chips (£1.50), and burger selection. Wolfe Tone St. balances slightly more upscale dishes: **Fionnuala's Italian Restaurant** lights café-style meals with candles in wine bottles (antipasti £1.50-3, pizzas of all flavors £4-6); **An Súghán** secrets some vegetarian dishes amdist its gourmet selection (£4-6).

The best places for a wee nip after dinner are the **Tally-Ho Bar,** at 31 Pearse St., and **Shanley's Music House,** on Connolly St. In late August, **Murphy's All-Ireland Busking and Street Entertainment Festival** descends upon the town, determined to entertain everyone. Step gingerly through the *mimefield.*

Pause 10 mi. along the coast from Clonakilty at **Rosscarbery,** the site of a medieval Benedictine monastery. The **Long Strand,** a mile-worth of sand, bathes nearby. About 2 mi. farther west stands the **Drombeg Stone Circle,** one of the most extraordinary in Ireland (ask for directions). The 17-stone circle dates from the early Bronze or Iron Age, and marks the spot of the ritual burial of a cremated teenager. At this site, according to ancient Celtic legend, the knight Embre fought and defeated the jejeune but brave Nathaníel.

Skibbereen

Capital of the Carberies, Skibbereen ("Skibb" to locals) is a business center and agricultural marketplace occasionally clogged by traffic jams of vacationing families. Although many villages along the coast host festivals in either July or August, Skibbereen's caps all the rest: the **Welcome Home Week Festival** entices hundreds of buses, caravans, and screaming tykes with street entertainment, chalkdrawing competitions, and a "Maid of the Isles" competition. During the year, the **West Cork Arts Centre,** North St. (tel. (028) 220 90), offers exhibitions, poetry readings, music, dance and drama to the higher of brow. (Gallery open daily summer 11am-6pm, winter 12:30-5pm. Free.)

The town arranges itself in an L shape, with Main and Bridge St. composing the height, North St. the base; the pale blue clocktower, tourist office, and ubiquitous statue to the 1798 rebellion pivot at the junction. Skibbereen's **tourist office,** on North St. (tel. 217 66), provides accommodations service for 50p. (Open Mon.-Sat. 9am-7pm; Sept.-June Mon.-Fri. 9am-6pm.) Post your postcards at the **post office** (tel. 210 46), on Market St. (open Mon.-Sat. 9am-5:30pm). The **Allied Irish Bank,** at the merger of Main and Bridge St., changes money. You can rent bikes for £7/day, £30/week (deposit £20) at **Roycroft Stores** (tel. 212 35) on Ilen St., off Bridge St., opposite the West Cork Hotel. (Open Mon.-Wed. and Fri.-Sat. 9:30am-1:10pm and 2:15-6pm, Thurs. 9:30am-1pm.) Skibbereen's **telephone code** is 028.

B&B goes for about £10-11: check Main and Bridge St. **Mrs. K. Buckley,** at 5 North St. (tel. 215 94), is a fairy godmother of the jam-making variety (£10; open April-Oct.). **Mrs. B. O'Brien,** Maple Leaf, directly across the street at 71 North St. (tel. 211 52), also charges £10 (open June-Sept.). Keep an eye out for the hostel opening in the summer of 1992.

A string of cafés dangles along Main St., and a supermarket hangs on to North. You get what you pay for at **Hi Style,** 3 Main St., a cheap take-out eatery good for late-night fish and chips jaunts (£1.50). (Open daily 10am-10pm. Takeout until 12:30am.) **O'Brien's Lounge,** 29 Main St., constructs filling sandwiches of crabmeat and prawn (£2.25) in their dark little alleyway pub. (Open for food Mon.-Sat. noon-4pm.) The **Kitchen Garden Café,** North St., in the back of a health food store, sells ridiculously cheap takeout Indonesian dinners (£2); the eat-in coffeeshop has Irish, Dutch, and Indonesian knick-knacks. (Open Mon.-Sat. 8:30am-9pm.) **Brendan McCarthy's** pub, at 68 Bridge St., is the happening place in town, dishing up large pizzas (£3), Irish stew (£4), and live music (music Wed. and Fri-Sun.; in winter Fri.-Sat. nights). **An Crúiscín Lán** on Bridge St. also issues live tunes (ballads Fri.-Sun. starting around 9:30pm).

Buses stop at the Eldon Hotel on Bridge St. (the continuation of Main St.), connecting several times daily east to Cork, west to Baltimore, and north to Bantry, Glengarriff, Kenmare, and Killarney.

Baltimore, Sherkin Island, and Cape Clear Island

Baltimore (pop. 200) is a fishing village 8 mi. southwest of Skibbereen; directly off the coast lies Sherkin Island, and farther out, Cape Clear Island. The Skibbereen-Bantry bus stops at Baltimore (Mon.-Fri. 3/day; in summer also Sat.). To get to Sherkin, catch the tiny *Miss Josephine,* which leaves from the pier in Baltimore. (June-Sept. 7/day 10:30am-8:30pm; Oct.-May 3/day 10:30am-5:30pm; return £3, children £1.) A larger ferry, the *Naomh Ciarán II,* takes travelers from Baltimore to arrogant Cape Clear Island, which proclaims that "Ireland is an island off the coast of Cape Clear." (June-Sept. 2/day in each direction, mid-July to mid-Aug. one more each way; 45 min.; £7 return, under 14 £3.50, under 3 free; family rate of £1/child.) For more information call C. O'Driscoll at (028) 391 19. Cape Clear can also be accessed from **Schull,** a jovial hamlet and major boating center on the mainland north of the islands. Mr. Kieran Molloy (tel. 281 38), a.k.a. the **Singing Ferryboat Captain,** conducts a ferry crossing from Schull's small pier to Cape Clear, complete with a repertoire of stories, jokes, and Irish music. (June 4:30pm from Schull, 5:30pm from Cape Clear; July-Aug. 10am, 2:30pm, 4:30pm from Schull, 11am, 3:30pm, 5:30pm from Cape Clear. Return £5, children £2.)

The placid hamlet of **Baltimore** once served as the headquarters of the notorious O'Driscoll pirate clan and even today, for about four days during the last two weeks of June, all the O'Driscolls in the area hold their annual gathering here and elect their Clan Chieftain. In the middle of the 17th century about 200 villagers were kidnapped in a raid by Algerian pirates, inspiring a 20th-century pub owner to commemorate the event.

The **tourist office,** 50 steps up from the ferry depot, can assist you in finding a place to stay. (Open May-Oct. Tues.-Sat. 10am-5:30pm.) £4.50 will get you a bunk at **Rolf's Hostel,** Baltimore Hill (tel. (028) 202 89), ½mi. from the village (follow the signs) in a wonderfully cozy stone cottage. Kitchen facilities are available, as is delicious food made on the premises; linen 50p. Try any of Baltimore's 5 pubs for food and drink: **Casey's Cabin,** Skibbereen Rd., about ½mi. from town, is famous for its delicious open-faced salmon sandwiches (£1.75) and chowder (£2). (Open Mon.-Sat. 10:30am-11:30pm, Sun. 12:30-2:30pm, and 4-11:30pm.) In town, **Declan McCarthy's** indulges in live music (no cover), while fisherman prefer **Bushe's Bar.** The **Algiers Inn** (tel. 201 45) draws a fine pint, serves victuals, and doubles as a B&B for £10-12/person.

If you follow Baltimore's main road away from Skibbereen for about a mile, you'll arrive at **The Beacon.** This white lighthouse stands on a magnificent cliff and affords views of the roaring ocean below and Sherkin Island across the channel. Two mi. away in the other direction stands the mysterious **Spain Tower,** a deserted watchtower that provides good reason for a clamber over and through mud, cows, and other natural obstacles. (Walk a mile toward Skibbereen until you come to the sign saying "Baltimore 2 km," turn right, then turn left following the signs to the B&B. From there you'll have to ask at a farmhouse.)

Many grasses and plants that have disappeared from the mainland still grow on **Sherkin Island.** The isle's 90-person community is an interesting mélange of lifelong residents and their more cosmopolitan, temporary counterparts. All mix at the island's two pubs: **Garrison House** and the **Jolly Roger** (both to the right from the pier). Right by Sherkin's harbor are the extensive remains of a Franciscan friary. Down the road to the left, the vast Atlantic mesmerizes at **Horseshoe Harbour.** For B&B, follow the main road from the ferry for about 15 min. until you reach the **Island House** (tel. 203 14), run by an artist, with Indian print bedspreads and paintings in each room (£8 with continental breakfast, £12 with full). The **Sherkin Island Youth Hostel** (tel. (028) 203 02), about 5 min. farther on, supplies bunkrooms with low sloping ceilings and a view onto the beach. Light meals of home-grown food, as well as kitchen facilities, are available (£4.50)

Cape Clear Island (pop. 160), a splendid island approximately the size of Manhattan, is one of Ireland's few remaining *Gaeltachts.* In summer, Gaelic-speakers infest the steep hills awash in the wild purples and yellows of gorse and foxglove. Some of the island's heritage is preserved in the little **museum,** near the church in the center of the island. (Open June-Aug. daily 3-5pm. Admission £1, children 50p. Follow the signs left from the pier.) St. Ciarán, the patron saint of the island, was born right by the harbor in the simple **church** surrounded by gravestones. St. Ciarán was a Christian missionary in the 4th century; according to legend, the first member of his Christian community was a divinely devout wild boar.

Revelry is confined, to great effect, to the island's three pubs **(Paddy Burke's, Cotter's** and **Club Cleire),** all with longer hours on warm nights. *Ceilí* (traditional dances) are held occasionally; inquire at one of the pubs for specifics. The **Foc'sle Cafe,** at the split in the main road, serves breakfast, teas, and cakes at its three bright blue tables (open 8:30am-late). To the left, about 5 min. further on, the **Cape Clear youth hostel (IYHF)** (tel. (028) 391 44) contemplates the sea. The warm fire and roaring scones compensate for chilly stone floors. (July-Aug. £5.50, April-June and Sept.-Oct. £4.30.) Kitchen facilities. Open April-Oct.) Staying here gets you a £1 refund on the full adult fare for the ferry back to Baltimore. To the right, the wonderful **Mr. and Mrs. O'Driscoll,** Cluain Mara (tel. (028) 391 53), bake fresh bread and let you lounge in the large light sitting room (£12). More institutional **Peg Regan,** up the street, has cheaper rates (£10). Just below, **Íonad Campála** has a campsite with showers, toilets, and recycling (tel. 391 19 or 391 49). (Open June-Sept. £2/person, weekly £10/person. Also offers a £1 refund for the ferry back to Baltimore.)

Bantry

According to the ancient manuscript *An Leabhar Gabhala,* Ireland's first settlers arrived just a mile from Bantry, led by none other than Noah's grandson. Bantry is indeed one of West Cork's oldest towns, built by English settlers who banished the Irish to the surrounding mountains. **Bantry Bay** has been the scene of many insurrections, such as the 1796 rebellion led by Theobald Wolfe Tone, one of Ireland's most revered patriots. Sights are few here, but the town is worth a visit, even if only to see the harbor.

The town's highlight is undoubtedly **Bantry House,** a Georgian manor that stands in an idyllic spot overlooking Bantry Bay. The Second Earl of Bantry's souvenir collection (*objets d'art* collected on his jaunts through Europe) clutters the house. (Open daily 9am-6pm, most summer evenings until 8pm. Admission £2, students and seniors £1, children in family groups free.) Outside town stands the 7th-century inscribed **Kilnuarane Stone,** believed to have been a High Cross originally; 1 mi. out on the Cork Rd., take a left after the Westlodge Hotel. (Open all the time; free.) For two weeks in August (usually beginning on the second weekend), the **Bantry Bay Regatta** employs the best sailors in Ireland.In late May, pubs serve freshly harvested shellfish and music abounds at the **Mussel Fair.**

The **tourist office** is on The Square, 1 block up from the harbor (tel. 502 29; open June-Sept. Mon.-Sat. 10am-6pm). **Kramer's,** Glengarriff Rd. (tel. 502 78), rents bikes (£5/day, £30/week) or road bikes (£4/day, £20/week; open Mon.-Sat. 9am-6pm). You can leave your baggage at **Crowley's Pub,** which also acts as the bus depot, two doors down from the tourist office (50p/item). Bantry's **telephone code** is 027.

The **Bantry Independent Hostel,** Bishop Lucy Place (tel. (027) 510 50), is a little difficult to find: follow the road to Glengariff for about ¼mi., turn left at the last grocery store before the field, then right at the top of the hill. Murals inspired by Celtic mythology and modern Irish poetry color the walls, painted by artistically inclined hostellers. (No curfew, no lockout. £4.50. Sheet rental 50p. Kitchen. Open mid-March to Oct.) The delightful **Mrs. Evans,** Bay View House (tel. 504 03), near the bus stop, has an aquamarine monster tub with unforgettable special functions. Guests also rave about her bread. (Singles £12, doubles £10/person.) Nearby, to the right of the harbor, **Mrs. Barry,** Harbor View House (tel. 500 23), charges £10 for a smallish room; next door, **Mrs. P. O'Sullivan,** Island View House (tel. 502 57), dishes out breakfast in her lilac dining room (£10).

Refuel at any of the **supermarkets** on New St. The **5A Cafe,** Barrack St., caters to vegetarian and vegan diets at laughably low prices. An alternative crowd stomps in wearing combat boots. (Open daily 10am-6pm.) **Peter's Steakhouse,** New St., attracts a more carnivorous pack with huge sizzling portions of meat (£3-6). Even the wallpaper is fuzzy. (Open daily 10am-midnight.) The **Bakehouse,** New St., is fragrant with irresistible pastries. Upstairs, Japanese prints on the walls complement smoked Bantry Bay salmon (£3.90; cake £1-1.50). (Open Mon.-Sat. 9am-6pm, Sun. 11am-5pm.) Live bands play at the **Bantry Bay Hotel** (tel. 502 89) almost every night during the summer, and Fridays through Sundays off-season (no cover). **Jimmy Crowley's,** New St., also has Irish music nearly every night in summer (occasional £1-2 cover on weekends). The oldest pub in town is the **Anchor Tavern,** on New St. (live music on Thurs. nights).

Buses from Cork to Skibbereen stop in Bantry (3/day, Sun. 1/day) near the base of New St. by the harbor.

Beara Peninsula

The broad River Kenmare joins Bantry Bay in a pincer movement on the Beara Peninsula. The rigid Caha Mountain range marches down the spine of the peninsula with the Slieve Miskish Mountains in the vanguard, concealed amid glades of fern, foxglove, and fuschia. This region has all the charm of the more northerly Iveragh Peninsula, and fewer tourists.

Getting There and Getting Around

A coastal road rings the peninsula, passing from Glengarriff, at the root of the peninsula, through Adrigole and Castletownbere on the southern coast to Alliehies, embedded in the enamel; the route sends a tendril off near Cahermore towards Dursey Island before continuing along the northern coast to Kenmare (see Ring of Kerry). The Caha range is straddled by two roads, one between Glengarriff and Kenmare and the other connecting Adrigole and Lauragh, both of which afford views of the bays to the north and south. There is no public transport along the peninsula, but **Berehaven Buses** run a private coach service from Bantry, just south of the Beara peninsula, to Castletownbere, near Beara's western tip (about 3/week; call 700 07 for their spasmodic schedule). Hitchhikers may die and the rain wash their bones clean before a car passes, let alone stops. Rent a bike in one of the larger towns. The **telephone code** for the entire peninsula is 027.

Sights

Glengarriff, on the southern coast, is little more than an effective launching pad for missions into the peninsula. Walk via **Tunnel Road** to Kenmare, on the peninsula's opposite shore, or ride from Glengarriff to Allihies and spend the night at the hostel, the morning at the beach, and the afternoon traveling back to Glengarriff via the Healy Pass. Several pubs and cafés keep company with the **tourist office,** Bantry Rd. (tel. 630 84), next to the Eccles Hotel (open July-Aug. Mon.-Sat. 10am-1pm, 2:15-6pm). The bank keeps the usual short hours (open July-Aug. Tues and Thurs. 10:30am-12:30pm, June and Sept. Tues. 10:30am-12:30pm), while the **Spinning Wheel Café** down the road moonlights as an exchange bureau; try to change currency before you get to the village.

Accommodations have been banished to the outskirts of town. B&Bs (£10-15) pout 2 mi. out on the coastal road leading southeast towards Bantry, and three hostels jockey for passing travelers. **O'Mahoney's,** just outside the village on Bantry Rd., is a carpeted family endeavor with 5-6 beds in each flowery room. (No curfew/lockout; £5, linen 50p; kitchen.) A steep walk on Kenmare Rd. leads to the other two hostels; *Let's Go* preferred the splendid **Glengarriff Tooreen Mountain Hostel** (tel. 630 75), set in the middle of the forest. (Reception 9am-10pm; £4.50, sheets 50p; kitchen. Camping £3.) Phone before 5:30pm in high season and they'll pick you up at the **Blue Loo** pub in town; in low season, simply call. Make sure you get in the van to the right hostel; Nearby, **Lake Eskenohoolikeaghaun** ("Lake of the Twelve Cows") bears Ireland's longest name. Express buses run to Glengarriff from Cork via Bantry (4/day in summer, 3/day in winter; 2½ hr.).

Most cartographers fail to note microscopic **Garinish Island,** outside of Glengarriff. A cagey ferry captain stops hitchhikers and flags down buses outside town, trying to sell rides across the bay. Boats leave every 20 min. from Glengarriff. (Mon.-Sat. 10am-5pm; July and Aug. Sun. also 11am-5pm; £4 return). The least expensive crossings originate in nearby Castletownbere (3/day; £3). Garinish's Latinate garden, also known as Ilnacullin, blooms and flourishes with the seasons, offering a jolly good view of the peninsula's mountains. (Ilnacullin open daily March-Oct. Admission £1.50, students and children 50p.)

Twelve mi. west of Glengarriff rests the tiny coastal hamlet of **Adrigole.** Spend a night at **Adrigole House,** a small independent hostel with a few beds in a wooden shed (tel. 601 04; open March-Oct; £4, showers 50p), before cutting through to the other side of the peninsula. A road peels off just before the hostel and crosses the Caha Mountains via the breathtaking **Healy Pass,** 5 mi. up. Just 3 mi. from Lauragh, Adrigole's north coast counterpart, the **Glanmore Lake youth hostel (IYHF)** snuggles in (tel. (064) 831 81; open April-Sept.; £4.30, under 18 £3). The hostel makes a great base for exploring the nearby mountains, the tallest of which, **Hungry Hill** (2251 ft.), lies several mi. to the southwest.

West of Adrigole, **Castletownbere** (pop. 1000) is the peninsula's principal town. Agitated fish auctions are held twice weekly in this fishing port, Ireland's second-largest. (Ask locals for details.) The first week in August, Castletownbere's **Festival of the Sea** features a funfair, swimming and sailing races, and a mysterious contest involving a greased pole, a flag, and the ocean.Rent bikes from the Super Valu Supermarket (tel. 700 20) for £7/day, £30/week; £10 deposit with ID. (Open Mon.-Sat. 9:30am-6:30pm, Sun. 9:30am-12:30pm.) **Castletown House** (tel. 702 52) has very good B&B for £10, and both **Harrington's,** (on the same street) and **Murphy's** offer cheap lunch specials.

Just offshore lies **Bere Island,** a serene wooded isle that once served as a British naval base. A sailing school has taken over and at night the pubs stay open long after landlubbers are asleep. A passenger ferry operates daily during July and August (tel. 750 09; departs Castletownbere at 11:30am, 1:30pm, 2:30pm, and 6pm; return £1.50, children £1, £10 for car and passengers).

Two mi. southwest of Castletownbere, **Dunboy Castle** shelters two separate ruins. Cows roam the crumbling mock Gothic halls of its 18th- and 19th-century mansion, and ¾ mi. past the gate stand the ruins of the 14th-century O'Sullivan fortress. Follow the road to the right of the castle and take the right prong to a modish little cove. On the main road, just past the fork to the castle, the independent **Beara Hostel** (tel. 701 84) offers comfortable beds for £4.50 and camping for £3. The high-spirited Ella Baetz can cure any ailment with her homemade chicken soup. (No lockout, no curfew, kitchen facilities, hostel open all year.) In Garranes, several miles west, you can eat organic vegetables or ponder life's curiosities in the meditation room at the 12-bed **Garranes Hostel** (tel. 730 32).

15 mi. further west, at the very end of the peninsula, churning water separates the point from **Dursey Island.** A cable car provides the only dry access to the island (tel. 730 16; Mon.-Sat. 9-11am, 2:30-5pm, and 7-8pm, Sun. times vary; 6 min.; return £1, children 50p). The car holds six people and rides 75 ft. (or frighteningly lower on stormy days) above the sea, sanctified by two plastic St. Marys. The English army laid waste to **Dursey Fort** in 1602, after raiding the unarmed garrison and hurling many a soldier over the sharp cliffs.

Surrounded on three sides by the Slieve Miskish Mountains of the southern Caha range, bleached-white **Ballydonegan Strand** is one of the most striking features of the Beara Peninsula. Stay the night at the rugged **Allihies youth hostel (IYHF)** (tel. 730 14), one mi. up the hill from the strand and a mile from the village of **Allihies** (July-Aug. £4.50; April-June, Sept. £4; kitchen facilities), or camp on the bluffs overlooking the small harbor.

This blunt head of the peninsula fairly chokes on architectural fossils. Children's gravestones crumble outside the **Celtic Church,** 2 mi. from Allihies (marked on some maps and signs as Point Nadistiert); note the graves of Charles and Amy and look for the collapsing entrance to a series of caves. **Mass Rocks**—large, flat granite sheets that served as altars during the years when English law prohibited the area's inhabitants from attending Mass—dot the fields surrounding the village, and the shafts of abandoned **copper mines** perforate Allihies' upper slopes. Paltry evidence of a booming mid-19th century mining industry, the shafts themselves are fenced off and can be seen only from a distance. Just east of Allihies, on the peninsula's north coast at **Ballycrovane,** stands the tallest inscribed *Ogham* stone in Ireland (17½ ft.). After exploring the hills, have a drink at either of Allihies' **O'Sullivan's** pubs with the local fishermen (musical instruments available at the bar).

Iveragh Peninsula

The Iveragh Peninsula can blame its tourist swarm on the famed Ring of Kerry; an endless motorcade of pilgrims purrs counterclockwise along the loop leading west from Killarney through lough and mountain vale to the sheer coastal cliffs along Dingle Bay and the smaller bays of the River Kenmare. Bikers in particular should consider touring the Beara and Dingle Peninsulas if they wish to avoid tailgating and constant tooting by impatient tourists; located to the south and north, respectively, their coastlines are just as dramatic and their roads less busy than Iveragh's.

Killarney

Killarney (pop. 9000) is a polyester paradise: tour buses embellished with huge shamrocks are the life-blood of this otherwise anemic city. Although tourist-infested, Killarney is a good place to rent a bike, pick up information, or depart on a bus tour into the surrounding areas; round and about lie the Killarney National Park and the famed Ring of Kerry.

Arriving and Departing

As a tourist mecca should be, Killarney is well served by train and bus. The station (tel. 310 67; open Mon.-Sat. 9am-6pm), lies near the Great Southern Hotel off East Avenue Rd. Buses trundle to Dublin (2/day 8:55am-3:25pm; £13, £8 ISIC plus Travelsave); Kenmare (Mon.-Sat. 3:45, 5:50pm; £4.50, £2.40 student); Limerick (3/day 8:15am-6:45pm; £9, £5 student); Galway (2/day 8:15am-5pm; £13, £7.50 student); and Dingle (6/day 7:55am-7:30pm, Sun. 3/day; £7, £3.60 student). Trains chug to Cork (4/day, Sun. 2/day; 1½ hr.; £11.50, £6 student); Limerick (4/day, Sun. 3/day; 2 hr.; £13, £6.50 student); Galway (3/day, Sun. 1/day; 6 hr.; £26.50, £13.50 student); and Dublin (4/day, Sun. 3/day; 3½ hr.; £31, £16 stuent). All trains leave between 8:03am and 6:20pm.

Orientation and Practical Information

Killarney town consists of 4 major streets. Main St. culminates in the well-frequented **tourist office,** Town Hall (tel. 316 33), which offers maps, bookings (£1), *bureau de change,* day tours, and a gift shop. (Open July-Aug. Mon.-Sat. 9am-8pm, Sun. 10am-6pm; June and Sept. Mon.-Sat. 9am-7pm; Oct.-May Mon.-Fri. 9:15am-5:30pm, Sat. 9:15am-1pm.) College St. and East Avenue Rd. swing off to the right towards the rail/bus station, while New St. enters from the left with boots muddied by the Killarney National Park. The **Bank of Ireland,** on New St., will exchange currency. (Open Mon.-Tues. and Thurs.-Fri. 10am-12:30pm and 1:30-3pm, Wed. 10am-12:30pm and 1:30-5pm.) The **post office** is also on New St. (Open Mon.-Sat. 9am-5:30pm.) Rent a bike at **O'Sullivan's,** Pawn Office Lane, off High St. (tel. 312 82) for £5/day or £25/week with ID as deposit. (Open daily 9am-7pm.) **Four Seasons Launderette** (tel. 337 30) is in the Innisfallen Shopping Mall, off Main St. by the tourist office; wash and dry £3.50. (Open Mon.-Sat. 9am-6pm.) Killarney's **telephone code** is 064.

Accommodations and Camping

The hundreds of B&Bs in the area are often full and range from £12.50-17. Not to worry, as hostels abound; five are within walking distance of the town center. **The Súgán** (tel. 331 04), Lewis Rd. at Michael Collins' Pl., has a laidback atmosphere, 18 beds, and a 50% discount on wholefood meals in the restaurant below. (No lockout. £5, sheets 50p. Kitchen.) The same family runs **Bunrower House Hostel,** formerly the **Loch Lein Hostel,** Ross Rd. (tel. 339 14), where you can dry your laundry between apple trees in the garden, or take their rowboat out on the lake. (£5, sheets 50p. Free shuttle from the Súgán to Bunrower House.) Check in at the Súgán for either one. Be nice to the warden in the central **Four Winds Hostel,** 43 New St. (tel. 330 94); dealing with so many tourists can try anyone's temper. (Reception closed 11am-1pm. Checkout by 11am. £5.50. Kitchen. Bike rental £5/day, £2 deposit). A 5-min. walk down Cork Rd., past the station, the chickens and geese crow early and often at the beginner **Belleville Hostel.** (£5/night, shower 50p; kitchen.) Five min. farther, striped umbrellas signal the **Park Hostel,** a series of peaceful yellow villas with carpeted rooms (tel. 32 19; £5/night; kitchen; off Cork Rd. up the hill opposite the Texaco station).

The **IYHF youth hostel** (tel. 312 40) in Aghadoe, 3 mi. west of town, is housed in a mansion with magnificent views of the surrounding mountains. Free vans shuttle hostelers to and from the bus and train stations. (July-Aug. £5.90; March-June, Sept-Oct. £4.90; Nov.-Feb. £4.30. Bike rental £4/day.) You can camp at the **Fossa Caravan and Camping Park** (tel. 314 97), 3½ mi. west of town, just past the youth hostel. (Units £5.50-7 plus 50p/adult and 25p/child; hikers and bikers £2. Kitchen, laundromat facilities, and tennis courts included. Open mid-March to Sept.)

Food and Pubs

Food in Killarney is affordable at lunchtime; prices skyrocket after 6 pm. **Dunne's Stores,** on High St., sells the cheapest groceries; if you must eat out, try **Sheila's,** 75 High St., where vegetarian nut roast with tomato and basil (£3.25) is served on wooden tables under green lampshades. (Open daily noon-10pm.) **Sceilig,** High St., has much the same decor and prices; dishes for £3-4, except the obesity-inducing Farmhouse grill (2 sausages, egg, bacon, chips, beans, burger, tea, bread and butter for £5). (Open daily noon-11pm.) The intimate, brick-covered Súgán kitchen, downstairs from the hostel, guarantees at least one vegetarian option. (Three-course meals £7, half price for hostellers. Open daily July-Aug. noon-9pm; Sept.-June Mon.-Sat. 6-9pm.) Many pubs cater to tourists' fancies with traditional music: wander the streets and listen for something intriguing. The well-dressed customers of **Laurel's Bar,** Main St., crowd in nightly, and the **Danny Mann Inn,** New St., is building up a reputation. **Buckley's Bar,** College St., and **Charlie Foley's,** 101 New St., also provide relaxing respites from touring.

Sights and Events

A few sights do manage to make themselves known amid Killarney's milling masses. St. Mary's Cathedral, beyond New St. on Cathedral Pl., qualifies as a limestone wonder. Designed by Pugin, architect of London's Houses of Parliament, St. Mary's boasts a modern interior made of rough-hewn stone. Opposite the cathedral, New St. leads into the Killarney National Park (see below). The **National Museum of Irish Transport,** in Scott's Gardens off E. Avenue Rd. (tel. 326 38), exhibits historic cycles and carriages. (Open mid-March to Oct. daily 10am-7pm; in winter by appointment. Admission £2, children £1, families £5.)

In May, July, and October, horses gallop around the racecourse on Ross Rd., competing in the **Killarney Races** (tickets available at gate). The **Killarney Regatta,** on the 2nd Sunday in July, draws sailors and spectators to Lough Leane. **Gaelic football** matches are held in Killarney's Fitzgerald Stadium off Lewis Rd. most Sunday afternoons and some weekday evenings; County Kerry tends to win. Check the monthly *Killarney Advertiser* for happenings around town (free), or the bi-weekly *Kingdom* for events around the county (70p).

Killarney National Park

The Ice Age went beserk around Killarney, scooping a series of dramatic glens and strewing about ice-smoothed rocks and precarious boulders. The resulting 10,000-hectare park, stretching west and south from Killarney towards Kenmare, incorporates the famous Lakes of Killarney: huge Lough Leane (the Lower Lake), the medium Middle Lake, and the smaller Upper Lake (two mi. southwest and connected by a canal). The last 450 red deer left in Ireland roam the forested mountains that surround the lakes to the east, south, and west.

Although the Kenmare Road curves along the southeastern shores of the lakes, hitchhiking is very difficult as locals steadfastly ignore the crowds of both coach- and foot-borne tourists. Thousands of little paths run through the valleys, making them ideal for hiking or mountainbiking; bikes can be hired in Killarney. A map, available from the tourist office in Killarney town for 50p, lists all the mountain hostels in the area. In the event of an accident, call 999 or the **Kerry Mountain**

Rescue Team at the Killarney police station (tel. (064) 312 22); you can also try (0667) 616 63 or (064) 337 55.

From **Knockreer House** (near the park entrance by St. Mary's), follow the signs for about a ½mi. through the National Park to reach **Ross Castle.** Built in 1240 and now in ruins, the castle was the last in Ireland to surrender to Cromwell; 1652 marks the year of its defeat. (Open all the time; free.) Outside the castle you can rent a rowboat (£2/hr./person) and head across **Lough Leane,** stopping at the pine-cloaked island of **Innisfallen,** where the ruins of **Innisfallen Abbey** languish. Founded in 600 AD, the abbey became an important center of learning during the Middle Ages. The Annals of Innisfallen, now entombed at Oxford, recount world and Irish history; they were written in Irish and Latin by a succession of 39 monastic scribes, the last of whom wrote in 1320.

About 2½ mi. south of Killarney toward Kenmare on the T65 lie the remains of **Muckross Abbey.** The abbey was torched by Oliver Cromwell, but enough still stands to relay the breathtaking grace of the part-Norman, part-Gothic cloisters. A mile southwest of the ruins is **Muckross House** (tel. 314 40), a massive 19th-century manor that has been converted into a very good museum of County Kerry folklore. (Open July-Aug. daily 9am-7pm; Sept.-Oct. and March-June 10am-6pm; Nov.-Feb. Tues.-Sun. 11am-5pm. Admission £2, students and seniors £1.50, children £1.) The garden surrounding the house blooms brilliantly in early summer. A mile further south, one of the largest and gaudiest falls in Ireland, **Torc Waterfall,** crashes a harrowing 60 ft. down.

Upper Lake is the most remote of the three lakes. Look for the trail head off the Kenmare Rd. about 8 mi. south of Killarney, or take a *currach* (traditional boat) from Ross Castle (£7; bikes allowed). The **Black Valley youth hostel (IYHF)** (tel. (064) 323 00), on the Kerry Way about 12 mi. outside Killarney and 2 mi. northwest of Lord Brandon's Cottage, makes a good base for those determined to thoroughly explore the area. (July-Aug. £5.50; March-June, Sept.-Oct. £4.30; Nov.-Feb. £3.80.) Walk along a lakeshore path through **Derrycunnihy Oak Forest** to **Lord Brandon's Cottage,** a tea-house that also offers boat rental.

The **Gap of Dunloe,** just to the north, is a histrionic gorge between Kerry's epic **Macgillycuddy's Reeks** (the tallest mountain range in Ireland) and the lake-studded **Purple Mountains;** it wanders about 5 mi. north to **Kate Kearney's Cottage.** Once the home of a beautiful and home-brewing wild Irishwoman named Kate, the cottage is now stuffed with souvenir-buying tourists, and a bar specializing in Irish coffee. Excellent traditional music rings out during the summer months.

Avoid crowds by skirting the sanitized **Dunloe Castle,** 2 mi. northeast, and continue to the more interesting *Ogham* stones, one mi. north on the road to Beaufort. *Ogham* is a unique form of early Irish writing; the inscriptions of up to five lines (written from the bottom up) are commemorative listings of a person's name and that of an ancestor. Dating from the early Christian period (500 AD), the stones pepper the area, and some mark the burial spots of Celtic chieftains.

Ring of Kerry

Thousands of tourists come to County Kerry to visit the 112-mi. coast of the Iveragh Peninsula—the famous Ring of Kerry. You can drive the complete circuit in an afternoon, or cycle it in three days. The tourist offices in trampled Killarney and secluded Kenmare (just south of Killarney across Moll's Gap), sell a map (50p) illustrating bike routes across the center of the Ring; both of these towns make good bases for touring Kerry.

Motorists on the crowded coastal road pass stunning cliffs, misted mountains, and deep-blue loughs. Daily tour buses from Killarney leave in midmorning and circle counterclockwise around the route like buzzards, perching in various towns along the way. (Several companies offer tours; book at tourist office; average price £10.) If you wish to spend the night on the Ring, consider catching the public bus that follows the same route (July-Aug. only, 1/day, leaves station 12:50pm, returns 5:15pm; £9). Hitchhiking may be harder here than anywhere else in Ireland. Well-shod walkers can puzzle over maps (50p at the tourist office) of the 35-mi. **Kerry Way,** a high-altitude version of the Ring which starts and ends in Killarney. The area bursts with accommodations: there are campgrounds every 10-15 mi., 6 sensibly distributed hostels, and B&Bs within a stone's throw of any point on the road. Every town has its pubs, a tiny post office, and a newsagent/grocery.

The Ring commences in Killarney and passes through **Killorglin,** home to the wildly riotous **Puck Fair** (3 days in mid-Aug.). A fertility rite that has stood the test of time, the town lets alcohol flow in the streets. Pubs stay open for 72 hours, refreshing the exuberant musicians, dancers and singers. No hostels here, but you can camp 1 mi. east of Killorglin at **West's Caravan and Camping Park** (tel. (066) 612 40), Killorglin-Killarney Rd. (£5/unit; £2.50 hikers/bikers; open March-Oct.).

The road continues west along the north coast to **Glenbeigh** ("The Valley of the Cows"), where the Slieve Mish Mountains rise spectacularly across Dingle Bay. The **Hillside House Hostel** (tel. (066) 682 28), a ½mi. east of town, is decorated in orange and blue with nature calendar pinups on the wall (£4, showers 50p, open March-Oct.; baked goods available). A 4 mi.-long beach complete with old tower and bird sanctuary is a mere 2 mi. west of the hostel.

Fifteen mi. further west, the straggling, multi-colored town of **Cahirciveen** is the most densely populated on the peninsula. Sink your statistic into the embroidered cushions at the comfortably furnished **Sive Hostel,** 15 East End (tel. 27 17), off Main St. (£4.50; kitchen; laundry; sheets 40p; camping £2.50). A 5-min. walk west of Cahirciveen rests the **Mannix Point Caravan and Camping Park** (tel. 24 37; open July-early Sept.). Boats at Reenard Point, 2½ mi. west of Cahirciveen (follow the signs to the turn-off), make the mirthless 5-min. crossing (7/day; £2) to Valentia Island.

Valentia Island has been a part of the peninsula ever since it was bridged to Portmagee on the western tip of the mainland. Spanish sailors settled here after losing to Francis Drake. "Black Irish," those with darker complexions and blue eyes, are rumored to be descendents of the stranded Spanish sailors. An old slate quarry, magnificent scenery, and a **Heritage Center** in Knightstown (open June-Sept. daily 2-6pm) draw visitors to the island. Valentia was the recipient in 1866 of the first cross-Atlantic telegraph cable. Two hostels sit near the Knightstown pier: the independent **Royal & Pier Hostel** (tel. (0667) 61 44), on the upper floor of the rambling Royal Hotel (£4; kitchen; open all year); and the **Valentia Island youth hostel (IYHF)** (tel. (0667) 61 54), just down the road (July-Aug. £5.50; April-June, Sept. £4.30).

Follow the signs to the quarry (once a source of slate, now a sacred grotto) and **Glonleam,** at the top of the town, to reach a pebble beach with a fine view of the end of the Dingle Peninsula. Five mi. from Knightstown in Chapeltown, you can stay at the **Ring Lyne Hostel** (tel. (0667) 61 03; £4, showers 50p).

At the absolute western tip of the peninsula, bypassed by the trafficked main route, quiet fishing villages snore in the windswept peat bogs. **Ballinskelligs youth hostel (IYHF),** near the beach overlooking Ballinskelligs Bay (tel. (0667) 92 29), has a limited general store. (July-Aug. £5.50; April-June, Sept. £4.30; open April-Sept.) Nearby, **Ballinskelligs Monastery** is an attractive franchise of the monastery on the Skellig Rocks.

Boats to the **Skellig Rocks** depart from Knightstown, Portmagee, Ballinskelligs, and Derryname most days between 10am and 11am, returning about 5pm. The fantastic voyage takes an hour and a half (45 min. from Ballinskelligs), frequently on a windy ocean. Atop the steep crags on **Skellig** and approached by long flights of stone steps sits an austere early monastic settlement. Monks lived here from the 7th to the 13th century, after which they moved to Ballinskelligs on the mainland. The isolated settlement remains unpillaged; George Bernard Shaw once called **Skellig Michael** "not after the fashion of this world." Today, it is the home of 40,000 pious gannets. The excursion costs £15 return. Boats run daily from Easter to September, weather permitting. Contact Joe Reddy (tel. 42 68) or Mr. Lavelle (tel. 61 24) in Ballinskelligs.

Back on the main road, 9 mi. east of Ballinskelligs, is the touristy village of **Waterville.** Famous as the former summer home of Charlie Chaplin and his family, Waterville now provides a base for exploring the surrounding moutains to the north and beaches to the south. Homebaked food and a great sound system (with plenty of Bob Dylan) welcome you to the 15-bed **Peter's Place,** Main St. (tel. 41 61). (Open door 24 hr.; £4, shower 50p; kitchen.) Athletes can lift weights, work out on the climbing wall, play pool or pingpong, and veg out with a video at the **Waterville Leisure Centre** (tel. (0667) 44 00), off Main St., which also coordinates athletic activities for the area (mountaineering, surfing, horseback riding). (120 beds; £5/night, showers 50p; kitchen; laundry £1.50. Open April-Oct.)

South of Waterville, the main road ascends to a stunning view on the **Coomakista Pass.** Cyclists exhausted after the long climb will enjoy the easy glide down to the winsome **Caherdaniel** area and its comfortable **Carrigbeg Hostel** (tel. (0667) 52 29), whose knit-knowing owner will counsel you on where to get your Aran sweater. (£4, showers 50p. Meals available.) ¾ mi. further, in Caherdaniel itself, turn right at Freddie's Grocery Store and Bar for **MacSweeney's Diving Centre** (tel. 52 77), which doubles as a hostel. Fluffy, flowery comforters console pale peach rooms. (Midnight curfew; £5; sheets included; showers 50p.) Continue past the diving center for a detour to **Derryname House,** the seat of the O'Connell family and the former home of the illustrious patriot Daniel O'Connell, whose negotiations won Catholic emancipation in 1829. The enclosed museum is uninspiring. (Open summer Mon.-Sat. 9am-6pm, Sun. 11am-6pm; winter Mon.-Sat. 1-5pm. Admission £1, students free.) Back on the main road, a 10-min. walk down the hill toward the sea brings you to the windy **Derryname Beach,** where sandy dunes stretch for 2 mi. Six mi. further, the round drywall stone **Staigue Fort** was used as a common defense area in pre-Christian times, and may later have served as a royal residence for the Kings of Cashel; as one of the best-preserved forts in Ireland it is worth the 3-mi. signposted detour. (Admission 30p; open all the time.)

The village of **Sneem,** 6 mi. farther down the road, is one of the most colorful in the area—although it might not have stayed that way had Charles de Gaulle succeeded in his plan to retire there. Winner of the 1987 "Tidy Towns Competition," No two of its houses are the same color, preventing inebriated Sneemians from losing their way home when the pubs close. Four mi. along the Kenmare Rd., **Willow Hill Farm** provides hostel accommodations in 4-bed cabins overlooking the sea and the Beara Peninsula. Delicious goat cheese, yogurt, and homebaked bread are sold by the owners. (Now curfew/lockout. £5. Bathtub!)

16½ mi. east of Sneem, **Kenmare** (pop. 1200) lies just across the Moll's Gap from Killarney. Magnificently poised at the mouth of the River Roughty and the foot of Peakeen Mountain, Kenmare makes a perfect spot from which to launch a tour of the Ring of Kerry, and in addition has some personal tricks up its sleeve. The town's primary attraction is the **stone circle** along the River Finnihy, just beyond the market house. Among the most arresting circles in the Cork-Kerry area, it was the site of the so-called **boulder burials,** possibly associated with human sacrifices over 2000 years ago. (Take a well-signposted 10 min. walk from town center: go out Main St. and take the second left onto Market Sq. Admission 50p; open all the time.) The best time to visit Kenmare is during the annual **Cibeal,** a music, dance, and drama hippiefest attracting some of Ireland's greatest artists on the first or last weekend of June. Contact the tourist office for details.

Kenmare town forms a right triangle, of which Main St. is the hypotenuse, and Henry St. the lively base. The **tourist office** poses on Main St., providing maps, accommodations (£1) and other information (tel. (064) 412 33; open late June-early Sept. Mon.-Sat. 10am-6pm). Summer tourists stampede the **supermarket** next door. Although *bureaux de change* populate the town, the **Allied Irish Bank,** on the corner of Main and Henry St., has the best exchange rates (open Mon.-Fri. 10am-12:30pm, 1:30-3pm; Wed. until 5pm). The **post office** is on Henry St., perpendicular to Main St. (open Mon.-Fri. 9am-1pm and 2-5:30pm, Sat. 9am-1pm). You can rent bikes across the street at **Finnegan's** (tel. 410 83; £6 racing bikes, £7 mountain bikes; £30/week; ID as deposit). Kenmare's **telephone code** is 064.

Failte Hostel, Henry St. (tel. 410 83), provides huge cushy duvets and a walled-in gravel courtyard with a shed for bikes. (No curfew/lockout; dorms £4.50; private rooms £5.50; kitchen.) **Kenmare Private Hostel,** Main St. (tel. 412 60), opposite the tourist office, charges £4.50 for adequate rooms and a nice garden and patio. (No curfew/lockout; £5.50 private room; kitchen.) A young crowd wolfs down pastries and open-faced sandwiches ("Brown Bread Specials") for£1.85 at **Mickey Neds,** Henry St. (Open Mon.-Sat. 9:30am-5:30pm.) Entertain yourself at the rollicking **Murty's,** just off Henry St. (rock 'n roll every night), or at **Crowley's,** Henry St., where traditional sessions often start up spontaneously.

Dingle Peninsula

County Kerry's northernmost peninsula, Dingle is remarkable for its scenery, its Irish-speaking community, and the countless ruins scattered throughout. Atlantic waves rush onto its sandy beaches and cliff-bound coves while mountains rise impressively from the plowed fields just inland. Prehistoric and early Christian remains lie strewn among the fields and cliffs of one of Ireland's few surviving *Gaeltachts.* Perennially wet, the peninsula is engulfed in mist-shrouded green. *Curraghs* still ply the waters of Brandon Bay and Ballydavid as time merely trickles by.

Tralee, a sizable town situated at Dingle's base, is cut off from the vital western nub of the peninsula by massive Brandon Mountain. A coastal road squeezes by Brandon's bulk at Dingle Town on the south shore, the west's point of access to the rest of Irish civilization. Curving around Slea Head and Sybil Head to Ballydavid Head, the road looks right into the jaws of Dingle's jagged seascapes and sharply carved cliffs; beware of the narrow roads at night. The entire western circuit can easily be covered in a day. While Tralee is well-connected by bus and train to the major Irish towns via Limerick, public transport around the peninsula is scarce: the only buses run from Dingle Town to Tralee (5/day, Sun. 3/day) and to Slea Head, west of Dingle Town (2/week in summer). Explore monuments on Dingle's *bohareens* (side roads) by bike; hitchhiking from sight to sight invariably involves walking. Area maps, with brief historical explanations of points of interest, are sold at the tourist office (50p). Tourists discovering the peninsula's charm have created a market for the newly opening hostels and B&Bs; the Cloghane/Brandon area in the northern shadow of the mountain remains the most free of foreigners.

Dingle Town (An Daingean)

The fishing village of **Dingle** (pop. 1400) has maintained its charm in spite of its popularity. Filled with traditional music, craft shops, and small restaurants, Dingle town is the nexus of audible, edible, and visual culture on the peninsula. Bike rental and plentiful hostels and B&Bs make it a good base for further exploration. The town has at least one unusual resident: **Fungi the Dolphin,** who swam into Dingle Bay one day with his mother. *Mater* died, but Fungi remained in Dingle and is one of the few dolphins known to live in solitude. Ask the fishermen at the pier about boats that will take you out to commiserate with him (the trip costs about £5). Summer festivals periodically turn the town into a carnival: the **Brendan Festival** (late June/early July) involves *currach* (traditional boat) races, duck races, and street entertainment; the **Dingle Races** (2nd weekend of August) practically forgets the horseracing in its glee over the children's carnival, cotton candy, and rabbits; and the **Dingle Regatta** (3rd Sun. in Aug.) ropes in boats from around the country.

Strand St., with lots of pubs, restaurants, and a **SPAR Supermarket,** at the corner of Green and Strand St. (open Mon.-Sat. 9am-9pm, Sun. 9:30am-1:30pm), runs along the quay; Main St. loops over and around, forming a giant D. The **tourist office,** at the corner of Dykegate and Main St. (tel. 511 88), supplies accommodations service (£1) and sells a map of the town and peninsula for 50p. (Open July-Aug. Mon.-Sat. 10am-7pm; June and Sept. Mon.-Sat. 10am-6pm.) Both **banks** (open Mon. 10am-12:30pm and 1:30-5pm, Tues.-Fri. 10am-12:30pm and 1:30-3pm) and the **post office** (open Mon.-Fri. 9am-1pm and 2-5:30pm, Sat. 9am-1pm) are also on Main St. You can rent bikes at **Moriarty's,** Main St. (tel. 513 16; £4/day, £18-20/week, £7 deposit; open daily 9:30am-8pm). **Paddy's** and **O'Sullivan's,** both on Dykegate St., have similar rates.

Of the three hostels within walking distance of town, the new **Rainbow Hostel** is the nicest. Cooking is a joy in the huge wooden kitchen, and the large rooms are mercifully uncrowded. (Follow Strand Rd. west for about ½mi.; it's well-signposted. No curfew/lockout. £5.) Tiny **Lovett's,,** 11 beds in a private home, uses immense comforters for padding as it goodnaturedly squeezes people in. (East side of town opposite Moran's Garage; no curfew/lockout; £5/night.) Several hundred yards west of the pier on Strand St., the **Westlodge/Westgate Hostel** (tel. 514 76) compensates for an institutional aura with an open fire, free coffee and tea, and discounts to the movies. (Curfew 2am; no lockout; £4.30; kitchen; camping £2.) The **Seacrest Hostel** (tel. 513 90) in **Lispole,** 3 mi. east of Dingle, overlooks a beach, cliffs, and Dingle Bay (pick-up service from Lispole or Dingle is free). Other bonuses include laundry facilities (£1/load), a small grocery shop with fresh eggs and scones, mountain bike rental (£3.50/day), a pool table (20p), and an evening pub shuttle. (£4/person, family rooms £5/person, campers £2.50/person. Open year-round.) A row of clean and hospitable B&Bs stands at attention along **Dykegate Street. Mrs. Houlihan,** Avondale House (tel. 511 20), loves to chat over her homemade pies or homegrown strawberries (£11; open May-Sept.).

Dingle's many seafood restaurants are quite expensive. The upscale, artsy **Island Man Bookstore and Café,** on Main St., provides you with the unique opportunity to soil unbought books with one of their fabulous daily specials (£3; café open 9am-10pm). Vegetarian prayers will be answered by the pizzas (£5) and healthy foods of **Eirí na Gréine** ("The Rising Sun"), Lower Main St. One of the managers, Eoin, knows all about the area's outstanding traditional music scene (open daily 10am-4pm and 6-9pm). Though fewer than 1500 people live in Dingle permanently, the town has 52 pubs, most providing music. Musicians bring their instruments to **O'Flaherty's Pub,** Bridge St.; often as many as 10 join in a jam. Sessions are held just about every night, but get there by 9pm if you want a seat. **An Droichead Beag** on Lower Main St. also unleashes traditional music, and, next door, **Mrs. Neligan's Pub's** occasional impromptu sessions are among the best anywhere (Mrs. Neligan's son plays the accordian). Other pubs to check out are the **Star** and **Murphy's** (both on Strand St.) and **Dick Mack's,** Green St., where the witty proprietor leaps back and forth between the bar and his leathertooling bench.

Around the Peninsula

Five mi. west of Dingle berths the caravan-covered broad-beached **Ventry Harbour.** The road from Ventry to Slea Head pauses at the ruins of **Dunbeg Fort,** a stone wall and round building which once protected the promontory (Admission 75 p; open all the time); farther on, the **Fahan Group,** beehive-shaped stone huts built by early Christian monks, cluster on the hillsides overlooking the cliffs. (Landowners who display signs charge about 50p to view the ruins.)

Dunmore Head waylays would-be artists who sketch cliffs, waves, and the Blasket Islands. Boat trips to the islands (see below) depart from Dunquin Pier 2 mi. north; the road leads up the hill from the pier to the large and comfortable **Dunquin youth hostel (IYHF),** (tel. 561 21; lockout 10:15am-5pm; July-Aug £5.50; March-June, Sept.-Oct. £4.30; Nov.-Feb. £3.80; kitchen facilities; sheets 60p). **Kruger's Pub** (tel. (066) 561 27), in Dunquin village, has B&B and occasional music at £10/person (singles £12; open March-Sept.).

Near the tip of the peninsula, the **Blasket Islands** (Na Blascaodaí) are a focus for Ireland's ancient language and folklore scholars. The islanders' way of life is immortalized in the well-known autobiographies *Twenty Years a-Growing* (Maurice O'Sullivan), *The Islander* (Thomas O'Crohan), and *Peig* (Peig Sayers, recently published in English and universally detested by the schoolchildren forced to read it).

On **The Great Blasket** (An Blascaod Mór) you can see the house where Peig Sayers once lived, and eat in the fine café next door (tea daily 1-5pm). Those spending the night can purchase fresh fish and wholefood dinners for £5. B&B is available for £10; campers can pitch their tents for free. Blasket's finest attractions are free; wander through the mist down to the white strand, follow the grass paths of the island's 10-mi. circumference, or chat with the numerous puffins and seals that populate the island. Boats depart from the pier just south of Dunquin. (May-Sept. every ½hr. from 10am, weather permitting; return £7, children £4.)

Ballyferriter, 6 mi. northeast of Dunquin, occupies tourists with several small cafés, a **heritage center** packed with photos and text (open June-Sept. Mon.-Sat. 10am-6pm, Sun. 11am-6pm; admission £1, seniors and students 60p, children under 12 free), and views of **Smerwick Harbour.** A road leads off to **Dún An Óir** (the Fort of Gold), an Iron Age fort where in 1580 the English massacred over 600 Spanish, Italian, and Irish soldiers who openly supported the Irish Catholics' rebellion against Queen Elizabeth's Protestantism. Just outside Ballyferriter on the Dunquin Rd., **The Black Cat** (tel. 562 86), a little café and supermarket (open daily 9am-9pm) also houses a simple hostel. (Reception from 2:15pm; checkout 10:30 am; £5; kitchen.) Continuing on the main way, signposted roads fork off in rapid succession for **Riase,** a recently excavated monastic site with an engraved standing slab; the **Dillon Stone,** a monument erected by early British settlers and to which Protestants flock every year on January 7; and to Ballydavid.

Ballydavid village oozes monuments. The **Gallarus Oratory,** a 7th- or 8th-century stone structure in the shape of an inverted boat, is Ireland's best-preserved primitive church. Although no mortar was used in its construction, it has remained completely waterproof for 1500 years. Farther north, rocky **Ballydavid Head** yields to quieter **Brandon Creek,** the exact spot from which St. Brendan, patron saint of Kerry, is said to have set sail for the "Heavenly Isles" (almost certainly America). The "Westernmost Campground in the European Community" (tel. (0067) 551 43), a short walk from Gallarus Oratory, charges £4 for a tent and two people (£1/car), and offers a sitting room, kitchen, and telephone. (Open May to mid-Sept.) In Ballydavid proper, the same family runs the **Ballydavid Hostel** (tel. 551 43), overlooking the beach (£5; open all year). Several miles north, the 12th-century Romanesque **Kilmalkedar Church** shelters an *Ogham* and an alphabet stone, a stone cross, and a sundial. About 1½ mi. from the church, across from the Carraig Church in An Bóthar But, the **Tigh a Phóist** independent youth hostel (tel. 551 09) has kitchen facilities and a shop (£4.50, private rooms £6/person, showers 50p).

Running from Dingle town to the northern side of the peninsula, the 1000-ft.-high **Conor Pass,** a winding cliffside road too narrow for buses to traverse, crosses the mountains and affords ripping views of the bays and valleys. A slight detour west on the far side of the Conor Pass leads to **Cloghane** and, a bit farther north, **Brandon.** Both spots provide eye-popping views of 3127-ft. **Mount Brandon** and its lakes. The Saint's Road to the summit was built by St. Brendan himself; it might have been an easy climb for someone who could cross the Atlantic in a leather boat, but for most it's quite a hike. Climb on the west side from **Ballybrack,** or try the more impressive ascent from the Cloghane side that begins between Brandon and Cloghane (watch for the signs). In Cloghane, stop in at **O'Sullivan's Pub;** Mrs. O'Sullivan's blackberry jam is fast becoming famous. She also offers B&B (£10) in her house above the stirring strands of Brandon Bay. Back toward Tralee, triple-decker bunks make for lots of floor space and exciting nights in the friendly **Conor Pass Hostel** (tel. 391 79) in Stradbally, overlooking Tralee Bay. (Showers and full kitchen; £4, campers £2.50; open year-round.) Ask at the hostel for directions to the trail up the **Slieve Mish Mountains** to the east. The 2713-ft. ascent to **Cáherconree** culminates with views of the peninsula, the ocean, and the **Shannon Estuary.** In summer, swimmers can make delightful daytrips to the huge sandy strands near **Stradbally** and **Castlegregory.**

Western Ireland

From Limerick Town north to Achill Island, Ireland's rugged western coast safeguards many vital traditions: County Clare injects the traditional music scene with fresh vibrancy, and Galway's Gaelic speaking *Gaeltacht* exceeds any other in size and exuberance. Defiantly independent Galway was a leader in the agitation for home rule that culminated in the War for Independence, and that county's lifestyle and literature were primary sources for the Gaelic League and the Irish literary renaissance, led by William Butler Yeats.

The tiny fishing villages of the Clare Coast and Connemara, the lunar surrealism of the Burren and the Aran Islands, and the richness of County Mayo's peat bogs remain shrouded in uncontaminated oblivion; Mayo, in the north, is particularly thinly populated by permanent residents and tourists alike. It has been said that if you could live on scenery, Mayo would be the richest county in Ireland. Behind its weather-beaten coastal visage, Mayo's landscape rises lazily from beaches and moorlands to the wealthy farmlands and Nephin Mountains of the interior. The rocky and rugged northwestern islands, seat of the Mayo *Gaeltacht,* take the brunt of the Atlantic and north winds. Further south, Clare's Cliffs of Moher plunge dramatically into a cold, choppy Atlantic, revered by the prehistoric dolmens and countless stone forts inland. Limerick Town, Ennis, Galway, Clifden, and Westport all make good bases for forays into the western Irish wilderness.

Those traveling north to County Clare from the peninsulas of the southwest should take note of the **Tarbert-Killimer car ferry** (tel. (065) 510 60), across the Shannon estuary, which preempts an 85-mi. trip via Limerick Town. (Sailings April-Sept. daily 7am-9:30pm; winter hours shorter. Ferry leaves Killimer every hr. on the hr., Tarbert every hr. on the ½hr; 20 min.; cars £6, pedestrians and cyclists £1.50.) From late June to early September, a bus operates from Galway through Lisdoonvarna and Miltown Malbay to Tralee, Killarney, and Cork via the ferry. Otherwise, the nearest bus stop to Killimer is in Kilrush, 8 mi. north, with connections to Miltown Malbay and Ennis (late June-late Aug.). A bus also runs to Tarbert from Limerick (late June-late Aug.), but no buses go directly from Tralee. Ferry riders can stay the night nearby on Limerick Rd., at the laidback **Nest** (tel. (068) 361 65). (Open June-Aug. £5, camping £3.50.)

Limerick Town

Limerick desperately wants to be beautiful: the River Shannon winds wistfully through the town center, and rows of old brick houses vogue along **O'Connell Street,** Limerick's main thoroughfare. Yet the incessant red and grey of this major industrial center leave one feeling lost in a giant Lego set, and few sparks of culture break the monotony.

St. Mary's Cathedral, Bridge St., built in 1172, presents an interesting *son et lumière,* a 45-min. historical presentation about Limerick and Ireland. (Mid-June to mid-Sept. 9:15pm; £2.50, students £1.50; cathedral open daily 10:30am-1pm and 2:30-5:30pm, in winter during services only.) Nearby, **King John's Castle,** an impressive 13th-century structure, overlooks the city and the River Shannon. The castle has been closed indefinitely, ever since renovations revealed a Viking settlement squashed underneath it. The small **City Art Gallery,** Pery Sq. in People's Park, exuberantly displays local efforts alongside its permanent collection. (Open Mon.-Wed. and Fri. 10am-1pm and 2-6pm, Thurs. 10am-1pm and 2-7pm, Sat. 10am-1pm. Free.) The contemporary **Belltable Arts Centre,** 69 O'Connell St., rotates its free exhibitions frequently and also houses a theater. (Box office and gallery open Mon.-Sat. 10am-6pm, booking tel. 319 866; tickets around £6, £3 students.)

The **tourist office,** Arthur's Quay (tel. 317 522) in the green space-age building, has a friendly and knowledgeable staff, a free map of Limerick, currency exchange, and the helpful *Top Visitor Attractions-Shannon Region* (free). (Open Mon.-Fri. 9am-6:30pm, Sat.-Sun. 9:30am-5:30pm.) For local events, consult the *Limerick Leader* (70p), which comes out on Wed. and Thurs. Practical buildings line O'Connell St.: the **Quinnsworth Supermarket,** near Arthur's Quay (open Mon.-Wed. 9am-7pm, Thurs.-Fri. 9am-9pm, Sat. 9am-6pm); the **Bank of Ireland,** #125 O'Connell St., which offers the best rates for currency exchange (open Mon. 10am-12:30pm and 1:30-5pm; Tues.-Fri. 10am-12:30pm and 1:30-3pm); and **USIT,** the Irish student and youth travel agency (tel. 489 25; open May-Sept. Mon.-Fri. 9am-6pm, Sat. 9:30am-5:30pm; June-Aug. also Sun. 10am-3pm; Oct.-April Mon.-Fri. 9:30am-5:30pm, Sat. 9:30am-1pm.) Just off O'Connell, the **post office** stamps Lower Cecil St. (open Mon.-Sat. 9am-6pm), and a **launderette** languishes on Cecil St. (£3/load, £4 with service; open Mon.-Sat. 9am-6pm). Limerick's **telephone code** is 061.

The understaffed **Limerick Hostel,** Georges Quay (tel. 452 22), directly after the bridge at the north end of O'Connell St., invitingly turns back flowery covers in their spacious double rooms to make up for their crackly toilet paper. (No curfew; £4.50, kitchen; baggage room is not strictly monitored.) The **IYHF hostel,** 1 Pery Sq. (tel. 314 672), packs travelers like sardines into a Georgian manor just one giant step from the station, diagonally across the People's Park. Get here early to be assured a bed, or call ahead and reserve; the dorms fill by early afternoon in summer (midnight curfew; room lockout 10am-5pm; July-Aug. £5.90, March-June and Sept.-Oct. £4.90, Nov.-Feb. £4.30; kitchen; money changed). **Ennis Rd.** graciously lures you to its row of B&Bs. Piano sing-alongs and a museum-sized collection of glass, china and figurines distinguish **Villa Maria,** 27 Belfield Park (tel. 551 01), the second right after the bridge, off Ennis Rd. (singles £12, doubles £11/person). **Trelawne House** (tel. 540 63), farther down Ennis Rd., warms its large rooms with plastic fires. (£11.50, £13 with bath.)

Limerick is a city of steakhouses: vegetarians will have to pick and hunt among menu items. At the **Riverrun Restaurant,** Honan's Quay, off Patrick St., you can enjoy chili with rice (£2.50) while looking at the current exhibit in the adjoining **Riverrun Gallery.** (Both open Mon.-Sat. 9am-5pm.) The **Upper Krust,** in the Williamscourt Shopping Centre on Williams St., ladles out soups (£1) and salads amid glass and gold glitter. (Open Mon.-Sat. 9am-5:30pm.) Take away wholefoods from **The Grove,** Cecil St., which wraps mouthwatering pizzas, couscous, and potato cakes to go. (Open Mon.-Sat. 9am-6pm.)

For traditional music, **Foley's Bar,** Lower. Shannon St., is the place to head (except on Mon.); **Nancy Blake's,** Upper Denmark St., also plays the old music on Sun.-Wed. nights. **South's Pub,** 4 Quinlan St. (between O'Connell St. and O'Connell Ave.), is a favorite student hangout (open Mon.-Sat. 10:30am-11:30pm, Sun. 12:30-2pm and 4-11pm), while **The Shannon Arms,** Henry St., is the restaurant/bar/bistro/nightclub of choice for more seasoned tipplers (minimum age 21).

The **train and bus depot** (train information, tel. 315 555; bus information, tel. 313 333; office open Mon.-Sat. 9am-6pm), just off Parnell St., serve destinations throughout the west of Ireland. Buy Expressway bus tickets and stow your gear at the bus station (lockers £1; 24 hr.). While most buses leave from the station, some go from Penny's or Todd's on O'Connell St. Buses foray to Dublin (5/day 7:30am-5:15pm, Sun. 4/day), Galway and Cork (5/day 9am-8:15, Sun. at least 3/day), and Killarney (5/day 9am-9pm Sun. 2/day; 2½ hr.). Trains all change at Limerick Junction: to Dublin (9/day 5:55am-10pm, Sun. 4/day; 2½ hr.); to Cork (7/day 5:55am-8pm, Sun. 4/day; 2½ hr.); to Killarney and Tralee (4/day 9:20am-6pm, Sun. 3/day; 3 hr. to Killarney; 3½ hr. to Tralee); and to Waterford and Rosslare (Mon.-Sat. 4pm; 2 hr. to Waterford; 3½ hr. to Rosslare).

Near Limerick

Fifteen mi. west of Limerick, off the Ennis Rd. along the north shore of the River Shannon, is **Shannon Airport** (call 614 44 for flight information; 616 66 for Aer Lingus; 24 hr.), a hub for domestic connections and most trans-Atlantic flights.

Buses shuttle to and from the airport every hour from Limerick (one-way £3.50). The airport provides direct ground transport to Ennis, Galway, Westport, Tralee, and Killarney.

Two mi. northeast of Limerick on the Dublin road is the **University of Limerick,** home to the Hunt Collection (tel. 333 644) of early Christian art and other Irish antiquities. (Open May-Sept. daily 9:30am-5:30pm. Admission £1.50, students 65p.) The **National Portrait Collection** is also housed there, in Plassey House (open Mon.-Fri. 9am-5pm; free).

Eight mi. northwest of Limerick along Ennis Rd. is 15th-century **Bunratty Castle,** Ireland's most complete medieval castle, with superbly restored furniture, tapestry, and stained-glass windows. (Open daily 9:30am-5:30pm, last tour 4:15pm. Admission £3.50, students £1.60.) Take the Shannon Airport bus leaving from the station to Bunratty (Every hr., 10:45am-4:10pm).

Ten mi. southwest of Limerick on the Killarney road is **Adare,** a tourist-infested but nevertheless attractive cluster of thatched cottages and medieval stone abbeys. The **tourist office** (tel. (061) 396 255) is on Main St. (Open April-Oct. daily 9am-7pm.) The present Catholic and Church of Ireland churches in town are housed in a 13th-century **Trinitarian abbey** and 14th-century **Augustinian priory,** respectively. The priory is noted for its fine stone carvings. A **Franciscan friary** from the 15th century is in a good state of repair, as is the 13th-century **Desmond Castle.** At least five buses serve Adare from Limerick on weekdays (4/day Sat., at least 2 Sun.), and at least four buses serve Adare from Tralee, miles to the southwest of Adare near Killarney (Sun. 3/day).

Ennis

Twenty mi. northwest of Limerick, the tiny streets and bustling crowds of Ennis (pop. 16,000) make it an attractive place to stay; the town is also the gateway to the Clare coastal region. Discontented youths sit glumly below the pillar of Daniel O'Connell in **O'Connell Sq.,** where Ennis' four main streets meet. Abbey St. leads northeast to **Ennis Friary,** built in the 13th century and famous for the slender panes and peaked points of its striking east window. The friary monks milled their own flour and fished for salmon in days of yore. Inside, fine depictions of the Passion adorn the 15th-century **McMahon tomb.** (Open June to mid-Sept. daily 10am-6:30pm; during the rest of the year, fetch the key from the caretaker across the street. Admission 80p, seniors 55p, students and children 30p.) Saturday is **Market Day** at Market Sq., a panoply of vegetable, (dead) animal, and mineral goods.

The **tourist office** (tel. 283 66), on Clare Rd., ½mi. from the bus station, provides an accommodations service (£1) to those who complete the trek. From the bus station, follow St. Flanagan's and take a left onto Clare Rd. (Open daily 9am-6pm; Nov.-April Mon.-Sat. 9am-1pm and 2-6pm.) The **bus and train station,** on Station Rd., off O'Connell St., will store your luggage for 80p/item. The **Bank of Ireland** and **Allied Irish Banks,** both on O'Connell Sq., will change your money. (Both open Mon.-Fri. 10am-12:30pm, 1:30-3pm.) The **post office** defiantly insists on a piece of the action at nearby Bank Place. The countryside near Ennis is hilly, but the intrepid can rent bikes at **Michael Tierney,** 17 Abbey St. (tel. 294 33; £7/day, £30/week, £10 deposit; open Mon.-Sat. 9:30am-6pm). Ennis's **telephone code** is 065.

The spotlessly clean **Abbey Tourist Hostel,** Club Bridge, Harmony Row (tel. 226 20), opposite Ennis Friary, has so much room that even Godzilla could stretch out. (No curfew; reception open 9:30am-10:30pm; £4.95, key deposit £1; kitchen and laundry.) The unique **Walnut House Hostel,** Turnpike Rd. (tel. 289 56), near the center of town, is a wonderfully hospitable jumble of reprints, trophies, and knick-knacks, all imprinted with the personality of the owner, who periodically asks "Are you happy?" Godzilla would be. (Single and double rooms; £6 if you bargain; £10 B&B.) The elegant **Mrs. Duggan's,** Woodquay House (tel. 283 20), in the center of town off Parnell St. by the car park, is a hush-hush house where you can watch ducks swim on the river. (Singles £13, doubles £10.50/person. Open March-Oct.)

O'Connell Street is the place for cheap snacks. Locals crowd into **The Sherwood,** in the shopping center on Friary Rd., for the best value cafeteria style meals in town (£3-4). (Open Mon.-Wed., Sat. 9am-6pm; Thurs. Fri. 9am-9pm.) **Maison Neuve,** Parnell St., cooks up quiche, lasagne, chicken, or pizza (all with brown bread and salad) for £3-3.50 (open Mon.-Sat. 8am-6pm).

Buses run frequently from the **station** (tel. 280 38) on Station Rd. Ennis is on the main Limerick-Galway route (approx. every 2 hr.; 9am-8pm; 1 hr. to Limerick; 1½ hr. to Galway) and buses also leave twice daily for West Clare, serving the coastal towns of Lisdoonvarna, Ennistymon, Lahinch, Miltown Malbay, Doolin, Kilkee and Kilrush (for ferry to Kerry). The crowded, bright green **post bus** runs west from the Ennis **post office** at Bank Pl. (tel. 210 54) to Liscannor and Doolin on the coast. (Mon.-Sat. 3:30pm; Ennis to Doolin £2.30, students £1. Arrive early to get a seat.)

Clare Coast

Meadows roll down to the sea along the coast from Kilkee in the south to Miltown Malbay; the 15-mi. stretch north of Miltown to Doolin is far more dramatic, highlighted by reeling views of the 700-ft. Cliffs of Moher. To get to the coast, take the Ennis post bus or the sporadic buses from Limerick and Ennis to Kilkee, Kilrush, Miltown Malbay, Lahinch, Ennistymon, Lisdoonvarna, and Doolin. A bus also runs from Galway to Lisdoonvarna, which lies 5 mi. inland (Mon.-Sat. 3/day; late Sept.-early June. Mon.-Sat. 1/day.) Every town has a post office, if only in the general store; the **telephone code** for the entire area is 065.

In **Kilkee Town,** on the southwest tip of Clare, three rows of Victorian houses arranged around a beautiful sheltered beach look out to sea. A holiday destination for Irish folk, this resort town crawls with families and children during July and August when the pubs roar with merriment and music, and chip shops deep-fry "crisps" until 3am. The rest of the year the deserted town offers solitary cliff walks, peace and quiet. The **Kilkee Heritage Centre,** Castle Lloyd, Merton Sq., chronicles local history through photos and papers (open 10am-5pm daily; adults £1, kids 50p). Stay at the spotless **Kilkee Hostel,** O'Curry St. (tel. 562 09), whose owner goes out of her way to be wonderful. (Midnight curfew; £5, sheets 50p.) Two **groceries** prop up O'Curry St. like bookends, and the **Old Barrel,** on O'Connell St., will satisfy your appetite for traditional music.

Miltown Malbay, 20 mi. north of Kilkee, is a quiet place for most of the year, but during the first week of July the **Willie Clancy School of Traditional Music** lets fly one of Ireland's largest musical celebrations. Be sure to book accommodations ahead for this week. Make your way to Spanish Point for a place to lay your weary head: **The People's Hostel** (tel. 841 07) offers vegetarian food and babysitting in a welcoming atmosphere (£5), and two of the most affordable B&Bs in town are **Mrs. C. Egan,** Three Corner View (tel. 843 62; £11/person; open April-Sept.), and **Mrs. N. O'Malley,** Bellbridge (tel. 840 38; £10/person for a single or double, £12 with bath). Also at Spanish Point is **Lahiff's Caravan and Camping Park** (tel. 840 06), 400 yds. from the beach. (July-Aug. £4.50/unit per night, £27/week; April-June and Sept. £4/unit, £22 week.)

Eight mi. further north, past Lahinch, loom the majestic **Cliffs of Moher,** limestone stacks that tower 700 ft. over the cold grey sea. The **visitors center** (tel. 811 71; open July-Aug. daily 9am-7pm; June and Sept. 10am-6pm; accommodations service 50p), **café** (open same hours), and **O'Brien's Tower observation point** (open summer daily 10am-7:30pm; winter 10am-6pm; admission to tower 50p, children 25p) are packed with tourists. Walk a bit farther along the cliff path in either direction, or don galoshes and trek across a field to enjoy an equally ripping view with only the seagulls to squawk at you. The cliffs slope down to the north, ending just off Doolin Point.

A mile from the cliffs, the **Old Hostel** (tel. 813 82), formerly a schoolhouse, is small and friendly (£4, £5 double room; kitchen). Nearby is **St. Brigid's Well;** its waters are believed to have curative powers. Two mi. further south, **Liscannor** is a small fishing town where John P. Holland, inventor of the submarine, first surfaced. The **Liscannor Village Hostel** (tel. 813 85) is close to the center of town (look for the sign with the lobster), in lofts above the owner's antique shop (£4 including showers, free bikes, and kitchen). Farther along the road, **Ennistymon** is a market town (Tuesday is **market day**) famous for its picturesque hand-painted store fronts. The **White House Hostel** (tel. 267 93) holds its ground in the center of town, a small and very basic hostel with kitchen facilities. Check in at Phil's Bar next door (£4, showers included).

Doolin (called **Fisherstreet** on some maps) attracts folk music enthusiasts from all over the world. A long, drawn-out town, Doolin's houses and B&Bs are stretched over a mile of road leading ultimately to Doolin Pier. **O'Connor's,** in the lower village, and **McGann's,** in the upper, have both won awards for the best traditional music in Ireland. **McDermott's,** in the upper village, ranks with them. The immense popularity of Doolin's pubs has brought more than a usual share of hostels to the area. First try Paddy Moloney's large, undecorated **Doolin Hostel** (tel. 740 06), in the lower village, complete with a shop, currency exchange, and tourist information volcano (all 3 open daily 8am-9pm). (No curfew; £4.95; kitchen; laundry £2.50; bikes £5.) Next door, Paddy's wife Josephine runs the **Horse Shoe B&B** (same phone), where £12 buys a bedroom and a terrific breakfast. (Open March-Oct.) The two remaining hostels are smaller, more intimate, and less clean; the **Rainbow Hostel** (tel. 744 15), in the upper village, has a cheery common room with wooden benches (£4.95; kitchen; wash £1.50, no dryer), while the **Aille River Hostel** (tel. 742 60), ¼ mi. downhill, warms their stone common- room floor with a stove. (Open mid-March to mid-Jan.; £4.50, private room £5, camping £3.) Near the harbor, a **campsite** (tel. 741 27) provides kitchen and laundry facilities (£1.50/tent or £2/caravan, with £1/person; showers 50p). Doolin has excellent seafood restaurants, and some of them are even affordable. **The Lazy Lobster** offers superb food in a casual setting; try their Crab-bake au Gratin (£6.50) or their vegetarian chili (£3.50). Restaurants open at 6pm. Ferries run from Doolin Pier, ½ mi. out of the lower village to the Aran Islands (see Aran Islands under County Galway for details).

Northwest Clare: The Burren

The lunar landscape of the Burren stretches Corofin 15 mi. north to Kinvara from inland and about 7 mi. west towards the Clare coast, 100 sq. mi. of eerie limestone terrain that Cromwell's troops complained had no wood to hang a man, no water to drown him, and no earth to bury him. With its limestone formations, disappearing lakes, and Arctic flora growing cheek to jowl with Mediterranean species, the Burren's landscape is Saturnine.

Bus service in the Burren is poor. Summer buses cover the north-south route 3 times a day (once on Sun.) between Doolin (pickup at Doolin Hostel), Lisdoonvarna (Burke's Garage), Ballyvaughan (Linnane's), Kinvara (Winkles) and Galway Station; no buses run in winter. This route includes Fanore (Fanmore Cross) once on Tues. and Thurs. Hitchhiking requires persistance; bikes are definitely your best bet.

The area was originally formed under the sea, when many layers of shells and sediment were compressed into stone. After the area convulsed above sea level, Ice Age glaciers furrowed it and left the seeds for the current eclectic combination of plant life. For more information on the area, attend a lecture or watch a film at the **Burren Display Centre** (tel. 880 30), in Kilfenora. (Open June-Nov. daily 10am-6pm; Oct.-Nov. and March 17-May 10am-1pm and 2-5pm. Presentation £2, students £1.50, children £1.) George Cunningham's *Burren Journey: West* is worth a look (£2), as is Tim Robinson's meticulous *Map* (£3.50). The **Cottage Hostel** (no phone), 3½ mi. north of Kilfenora, provides a great base for exploration (£4.50; kitchen).

The *dolmens* (prehistoric megalithic burial sites), *souterrains* (underground passages of refuge and storage), stone forts, and other archaeological sites that litter the region attest to the sloppy housekeeping of earlier Stone, Bronze, and Iron Age inhabitants. The road south from Ballyvaughan through Caherconnell is particularly rich in archaic refuse—the **Gleninsheen wedge tomb,** the **Poulnabrone dolmen,** and the **Caherconnell stone fort** all date from the 3rd millenium BC.

The Burren also contains 25 mi. of **caves,** most of which are extremely dangerous in stormy weather. The two-million-year-old **Aillwee Cave** (tel. 770 36), 2 mi. south of Ballyvaughan, was once the home of prehistoric bears. (Open July-Aug. 10am-6:30pm last tour; mid-March to early Nov. 10am-5:30pm last tour. Admission £2.50, students £1.25.) Tourist-ridden **Ballyvaughan** provides a good base for exploration into the surrounding area, and three hostels nearby allow cheap accommodations. Take one of the spelunking trips (£3.50 for 2½ hr.) from the **Bridge Hostel** (tel. 761 34) in **Fanore,** several mi. west of Ballyvaughan. The friendly proprietors will discuss the area's geology and flora, supply bikes, and generally make you feel at home. (Open March-Oct.; £4.50.)

Ten mi. east, on the northeastern edge of the Burren, **Kinvara** avoids Ballyvaughan's sticky tourist mass. **Johnston's Hostel,** Main St., Kinvara (tel. (091) 371 64), blessed with an extremely congenial proprietor, a full kitchen, and bike rental, provides a personalized introduction to the area. (Open June-Sept.; £4.50, camping £3; laundry; kitchen). Four mi. north, on the northwest edge of Kinvara Bay, you can stay at the **Doorus youth hostel (IYHF)** (tel. (091) 371 73; July-Aug. £5.50; March-June., Sept.-Oct. £4.30; Nov.-Feb. £3.80).

Galway Town

Originally a Norman port, Galway received its charter in 1484 from King Richard III of England. Until the mid-19th century, it was an independent city-state ruled by the "Tribes of Galway," a powerful oligarchy of 14 Welsh families. An extensive wine trade with Spain explains the Iberian bouquet of some architectural remains. Despite this history of international influence, Galway somehow remains more Irish than any other city in the west. Perched at the edge of Ireland's second-largest *Gaeltacht,* the town meanders between river and sea, full of old merchant houses, virtuoso traditional music pubs, and active independent theaters. Galway is no secret: in summer months you must parry and thrust with your furled umbrella to clear space on the narrow streets teeming with tourists.

Arriving and Departing

Trains run from Eyre Square Station to Athlone (5/day, 5:30am-6:25pm, 2/day Sun.; 1 hr.) and continue to Dublin (3 hr.); transfer at Athlone for all other lines. Buses depart from the steps outside to Limerick (every 2-3 hr., 9am-6pm, 4 on Sun.; £9 adult, £5 student), Dublin (5/day, 7:20am-5:30pm, 4 on Sun.; £9 adult, £6 student), to Ennis (every 2 hr., 8:30am-6pm, 4 on Sun.), to Shannon Airport (every 3 hr., 9am-6pm, 3 on Sun.); to Spiddal (almost every hr., 8:25a,-6:05pm, 7 on Sun.); and to Oughterard (9am-6pm; Mon.-Sat. 4/day). Thousands of hitchers wait on Dublin Rd., scouting rides east to Dublin or south to Limerick from Galway; catch bus #5 from the city center to this prime thumb-stop.

Orientation and Practical Information

Galway's focal point is the blossoming, water-spurting **Eyre Square,** a mere hop from the train station and the Victoria Place tourist office. From there, Williams St. leads southwest into the cobblestoned area around High St. and Quay St., where Galway keeps a gaggle of quality wholefood restaurants; Dominick St., across the river, picks up the stragglers. The B&B-stocked suburbs of Salthill and Renmare lie about 1 mi. southwest and east of the center, respectively.

Tourist Office: Victoria Pl. (tel. 630 81), 1 block west of the bus and train station. Information on the Queen of Aran, Galway Bays and Aer Arann. Open Mon.-Sat. 9am-6:45pm, Sun. 1:30-4:30pm; Sept.-June Mon.-Sat. 9am-5:45pm. Another office in Salthill (same phone). Open June to mid-Sept. daily 9am-8:30pm.

Bike Rental: Station Rent-A-Bike, in alley below the train station. £5/day, £25/week, £10 deposit. Free panniers. Open daily 9am-6pm.

Emergency: Dial 999; no coins required.

Financial Services: Bank of Ireland, 43 Eyre Sq. **Allied Irish Bank,** Lynch's Castle, Shop St., at Abbeygate St. Both open Mon.-Wed. and Fri. 10am-12:30pm and 1:30-3pm, Thurs. 10am-12:30pm and 1:30-5pm. **American Express: Ryan's Travel,** 1 Williamsgate. (tel. 673 75). Standard financial and travel services. Mail held (no charge). Open Mon.-Fri. 9:15am-6pm, Sat. 10am-1pm and 2:15-4pm.

Hospital: University College Hospital, Newcastle St. (tel. 242 22).

Launderette: Laundrette & Washeteria, Olde Malte Mall, off High St. One load wash and dry £3.20. Open Mon.-Sat. 8:30am-6pm, last wash 4:30pm.

Police: Mill St. (tel. 631 61).

Post Office: Eglinton St. Open Mon.-Tues. and Thurs.-Sat. 9am-5:30pm, Wed. 9:30am-5:30pm.

Student Travel Office (USIT): University College Galway Student Travel, Concourse, New Science building (tel. 246 01), on campus by the big yellow sculpture. Offers the usual student discounts, and the whole *Let's Go* series. Open May-Sept. Mon.-Fri. 10am-5pm; Oct.-April Mon.-Fri. 10am-1pm and 2-5pm.

Telephone Code: 091.

Train and Bus Station: Eyre Sq. (tel. 621 41). Inquiries office open Mon.-Fri. 8:30am-8pm, Sat. 8:30am-6pm, Sun. 10am-6pm; Sept.-June Mon.-Sat. 9am-6pm. Also has information on tours of Connemara (£10).

Accommodations

Salthill's surfeit of B&Bs tend to cost £10-11 and Renmare's sparser collection keeps to the same range. You'll end up paying the price if you don't reserve hostel beds during Galway Arts Week (mid-July) and the Galway Races (July-early Aug.). Suburban **Renmare,** 1 mi. east of the center, slumbers peacefully by its bird sanctuary; from the station, follow the path next to the railway tracks. **Salthill,** a suburb 1½ mi. southwest of Galway, crawls with tourists (many of them Irish), psychics, and funfair fans; at night the discos fill to the brim. Several hostels and half the houses in the area offer accommodations. City buses, costing 60p, leave from Eyre Sq. for each route every 20 min.; take bus #1 to Salthill or bus #2 to Knocknacarra (west) or Renmare (east).

Galway City:

Corrib Villa, 4 Waterside (tel. 628 92), right in the city center. From Eyre Sq., walk 4 blocks on Eglinton St.; the villa is just past the courthouse. Uncrowded old Georgian house, bathrooms somewhat the worse for wear. No lockout/curfew. £4.50. Showers 20p. Kitchen.

Arch View Hostel, 1 Upper Dominick St. (tel. 666 61), across the street from Monroe's Tavern; the entrance is next to the Lifetime Assurance building. New carpeting and firm beds cushion the high-spirited atmosphere. June-Sept. £5.50; Oct.-May £4.50. Sheets £1.

Owen's Hostel, on Upper Dominick St. (tel. 662 11, but no phone reservations), across the street from the Archview Hostel. World-traveler turned entrepreneur; work still outstanding forgiven by spontaneous, musical crowd. Not for the fastidious. Free tea/coffee. No lockout/curfew. £5, £2 key deposit.

Mrs. O. Walsh, Brasstacks, 3 St. Helen's Street (tel. 247 28), off Newcastle Rd., by Cookes Corner. A cozy bear den of a bargain: brown, shaggy and warm. Singles £10, doubles £9.50/person.

Salthill:

Galway Tourist Hostel, Gentian Hill, Knocknacarra, Salthill (tel. 251 76). Take bus #2 from Eyre Sq. to the end of its route. Must reserve in person. Laundry facilities and TV room. £4.50; private rooms £5.50/person. Hot showers included.

The Grand, Promenade, Salthill (tel. 211 50). Take bus #1. Once a hotel, still well-vacuumed; fresh, clean rooms overlook the sea. Strawberry Fields Café, on the ground floor, serves full breakfast all day (£2.50; open 7am-10:30pm). No curfew/lockout. £5 8-bed dorm; £6-7 smaller dorm; £7.50 twin, £9 double bed. Kitchen; laundry (£3); sheets 50p.

Stella Maris, 151 Upper Salthill (tel. 219 50). Take bus #1. Mirror-lined delicate hallway leads into 2- or 4-bed rooms. No lockout/curfew; sheets 50p; July-Sept. £6, Oct.-June £5; kitchen.

Mrs. Mary Ryan, 4 Beechmount Rd., Highfield Park (tel. 233 03). Take bus #2 from Eyre Sq. to Taylors Hill Convent. A small, neat, plain hostel-like establishment in a quiet neighborhood. Fills fast, so call early. Bed, breakfast, and shower £5.

Mrs. S. O'Kelly, Grianan, 12 Glenard Ave., Salthill (tel. 221 51), off Dr. Mannix Rd. Take bus #1 from Eyre Sq. Kind Mrs. O'Kelly treats you to all the comfort of a B&B for almost half the price. Doubles £6/person with continental breakfast. £9 with full Irish breakfast. (Singles £8 with continental breakfast.)

Mrs. J. O'Mahony, 10 Ardnamara, Salthill (tel. 220 16), off Dalysfort Rd. within walking distance of beach and tennis courts. Take bus #1 from Eyre Sq. Smallish rooms overlooking a well-kept lawn and flowerbeds. Singles and doubles £10/person. Open June-Oct.

Camping: Salthill Caravan and Camping Park (tel. 224 79 or 239 72). Located on the water, ½ mi. west of Salthill near the Galway Tourist Hostel. Crowded during high season. (Hikers and cyclists £2.50-3, units £5-6.50. Over 3 people/unit, 50p/unit per night. Open April-Sept.)

Renmare:

Mrs. Leen, 21 Woodlands Ave. (tel. 538 36), off Renmare Park. Warm-hearted owner will practically tuck you into sinfully soft beds. Singles £12; summer doubles £11/person; winter £10.

Mrs. Walsh, 58 Renmare Rd. (tel. 532 60), convenient to Dublin Rd. Singles and doubles £10/person, during the Galway Races £11.

Food

Galway's self-proclaimed Left Bank/Latin Quarter sandwiches vegetarian eateries, theaters, street music and pubs into a few short blocks between Shop St., High St. and Quay St. A few minutes west over the **River Corrib,** Dominick St. lies at the heart of another such district.

Roches Stores, a cheap supermarket, is visible from the northwestern corner of Eyre Sq. (Open Mon.-Thurs. and Sat. 9am-5:30pm, Fri. 9am-9pm.) On Saturdays, wander down to the **market** (9am-3pm), in front of St. Nicholas' Church on Market St.

Food for Thought, Lower Abbeygate St. A coffee shop and wholefood restaurant serving inexpensive, healthy vegetarian dishes for £1.50. Huge salad sandwiches (£1.20) and salubrious scones. Open Mon.-Sat. 9am-5.30pm.

The Sev'nth Heav'n, in Courthouse Lane, off Quay St. Weavings on the wall, drums in the alcove, and divine chowder with brown bread (£1.50). Open daily noon-midnight.

The Hungry Grass, Cross St., between Quay St. and High St. Crisp cellulose and filling grains; salads, sandwiches, and pizzas all for under £3. Open Mon.-Wed. 8:30am-6pm, Thurs.-Sat. 8:30am-9pm, Sun. noon-6pm.

Café Nora Crúb, 8 Quay St. Vegetarian meals in a crypt-like setting. Adventurous variety of dishes for £4-5. Open for dinner after 7pm. Lunch served noon-2:30pm. Minimum charge £2.50. Open Mon.-Sat. 9am-10pm, Sun. noon-6pm.

The Quay St. Wine Bar, Quay St., at the corner of Cross St. Intimately dim restaurant stacked with wine bottles. Expensive wines, but terrific meals (lunches from £4, dinners from £5). Open Mon.-Sat. 12:30-10:30pm; in summer also open Sun. 2-6pm.

Sights

Galway's historic sites line the banks of the River Corrib in the western part of the city. The **cathedral,** a majestic structure that dominates Galway's skyline and appears on most of its postcards, looms above the Salmon Weir Bridge in the north. Only 25 years old, its colorful stained glass windows and tile mosaics still merit respect. Two blocks south, the restored **Nora Barnacle House,** Bowling Green, exposes the private letters and photos of James Joyce and his wife. (Open May-Sept. Mon-Sat. 10am-5pm. Admission £1.) Shop St. takes you past **Lynch's Castle,** an elegant stone mansion with incongruous gargoyles that dates from the early 16th century; it now houses the Allied Irish Bank (open during banking hours). A litany of stories still circulates about the Lynches, who virtually owned Galway from the 13th to 18th centuries (84 of them were mayor of Galway). The Lynch family tomb honors the **Church of St. Nicholas,** Market St., which also devotes some attention to imposing examples of stonework, a heritage project, and some flag fragments. (Open May-Sept. daily 9am-5:45pm.)

Stroll back through the narrow streets past the Wolfe Tone Bridge to the Long Walk by the river, where the **Spanish Arch** is the only surviving gateway to the old trading town. The **Galway City Museum,** next to the Spanish Arch in Tower House, collects odd objects, exhibiting baby bottles from throughout the centuries, old fishing equipment, and the big one that didn't get away in 1918. (Open May-Sept. 10am-1pm, 2:15-5:15pm. Admission 50p, students 25p.) Across the river is the area of Galway that was once the Irish-speaking fishing village of **Claddagh,** which later gave its name to the famous finger rings. The designs of the rings are remarkable examples of abstract Celtic art; if worn with the crown facing inwards, the ring symbolizes an unattached heart, while the ring worn with the crown facing outwards symbolizes a "heart that is spoken for." (The ring is adorned with a crowned heart clasped by two hands.)

Entertainment

Traditional music and Irish theater flourish in Galway; for listings of events, find a copy of either the *Advertiser* or the *Galway Guide* (both free). Irish-speakers can watch shows at the 62-year-old **Taibhdhearc na Gaillimhe** (TIVE-yark) on Middle St. (tel. 620 24), the training ground for many great names in Irish drama and film. The theater has presented Mozart's *Così Fan Tutte* in Gaelic, the first grand opera ever performed in that language. (Box office open Mon.-Fri. 10am-6pm, Sat. 2-6pm. Tickets £4-5, with occasional discounts for students, seniors, and children.) Two other companies produce Irish drama (in English) in theaters on Quay St.: the **Druid Theatre Company,** Chapel Lane, off Quay St. (tel. 686 17; tickets £6, students £5; box office opens Mon.-Sat. at noon; buy tickets at least a week in advance), and the **Punchbag Theatre,** Quay Lane (tel. 654 22; tickets £2-4). **Taylor's Pub,** Upper Dominick St., occasionally stages lunchtime performances (tickets £3.50, including lunch). For traditional music, try the **Quay's Bar** and **Seaghan Ua Neachtain,** both on Quay St., frequented by students and older locals, respectively; or **An Púcán,** 11 Forster St., off Eyre Sq., a smoky old pub with traditional music every night and on Sunday mornings. The **King's Head,** 15 High St., has live music every night and a jazz session on Sunday mornings, while locals recommend **Garavans** and other inconspicuous pubs along Shop St. Dance dirty in any of Salthill's discos; tried and true **C.J.'s,** 143 Upper Salthill (cover £2) or the increasingly hip **Hangar** at the Hilltop Hotel, Dalysfort Rd., with live music (cover £4). If you prefer to do your dancing in the center of town, try the popular **Central Park,** 32 Upper Abbeygate St. (cover £4) or the knaughty **Kno-Kno's Knite Club,** Eglinton St. (cover £2). These clubs open around 10pm, but don't fill up until the pubs close around 11:30pm,; cover charge usually includes a meal.

Galway hosts a number of festivals, some sober and traditional, others verging on maniacal. The famous **Galway Races,** at the end of July or beginning of August and lasting for one week, are a *mélange* of horseflesh and high society (tickets around £2 at the gate). For two weeks in July the **Galway Arts Festival** attracts musical and dramatic groups from all over Ireland. (Tickets vary depending on the event; contact the Festival Box Office, Eyre Sq. Centre, tel. 685 64 for information.) The **Oyster Festival,** at the end of September, celebrates the ceremonial shucking of the first oyster of the season. You can wash down fresh oysters from Galway Bay with a bit o' "black velvet"—stout and champagne. In July or August, Galway welcomes the **Busking Festival,** a 3-day celebration that fills the city with street music and disposable mimes. For more information contact the Galway tourist office.

Near Galway

Twenty-three mi. south of Galway, between Ardrahan and Gort on the N18, lies **Coole Park,** the former home of Lady Gregory, now a national forest and wildlife park. The house itself is in ruins, but the yew walk and garden survive, along with a famous tree bearing the initials of such notables as George Bernard Shaw, Seán O'Casey, John Masefield, and Douglas Hyde, the first president of Ireland. **Coole Lake** is a short walk away, home of the famous wild swans so adored by Yeats. Yeats spent many summers at Coole Park in the company of Lady Gregory, and in 1916 he bought the 16th-century tower house **Thoor Ballylee,** located only 3 mi. away. He lived in the old Norman castle off and on until 1928; the house was the setting of his *The Winding Stair* and *The Tower* poems. (Open May-Sept. 10am-6pm. Admission £2.50, students £2, children 75p.)

Aran Islands (Oileáin Árann)

15 mi. off the coast of Galway, Irish-speaking Inishmore, Inishmaan and Inishere rise defiantly out of the Atlantic. The islanders are known for their silent perseverance and self-sufficiency. Their traditions lie forever frozen in J.M. Synge's play *Riders to the Sea* and Robert Flaherty's 1934 film *Man of Aran.* Despite the obtrusive gaze of the inquisitive modern media, the Arans maintain the peace and dignity of a world apart. Come here to confront the inhuman majesty of the Irish wilderness, sprayed by the Atlantic pounding against jagged cliffs. The rocky island landscapes are identical to those of the Burren: swaths of white sand and bursts of tiny exotic flowers relieve vast stretches of eerie limestone terrain. Unlike the developed northwest of County Clare, however, the Aran Islands are devoid of signposted paths and the hordes of tourists that tred them.

Getting There and Getting Around

There is a variety of transport options for reaching the Aran Islands from the Irish mainland. Frequent **ferries** to the islands run from Galway, Spiddal, Rossaveal, and Doolin (in County Clare). Some companies supply connecting coaches from Rossaveal to Galway. Direct your queries to the Galway **tourist office** (ferry desk open daily 9am-7pm; Sept.-June 9am-6pm; tel (091) 689 03, after business hours 924 47).**Inter-island** boats shuttle between the islands, connecting with most ferry arrivals.

From **Galway** the **Galway Bay Ferry** runs directly from Galway Harbour to Inishmore. (May-Sept. 3 runs/day; 90 min.; return £15, students or hostelers £13; bikes free). Book at the tourist office or the railway station (tel. (091) 621 41). Two ferry companies offer shuttle buses (£3 return) to **Rossaveal,** for a much shorter crossing. Both leave three times daily and cost £12 return: the **Aran Flyer** (same tel. as Galway Bay) takes 20 min., and the **Aran Sea Bird** (tel. (091) 617 67) takes 35 min. Reserve both at least a day in advance during high season. Boats (tel. 933 36) run from Spiddal pier to the smaller islands of Inishmaan and Inishere two times daily; book at least one day in advance (£12 return). From **Doolin,** Kevin O'Brien (tel. (065) 741 89) sails a ferry to Inishere (2/day; 30 min.; return £13, children under 14 return £5, children under 4 free, families £25 return; bikes carried free).

Doolin Ferries also runs inter-island boats, connecting with most ferry arrivals (£13 return, £10 student return, single fare ½ price). Sailings to all the islands from all points of departure depend on the weather. If sea travel makes you queasy, consider the 20-min. trip in **Aer Arann's** little planes (tel. (091) 554 80) for £48 return. The flight, leaving from **Carnmore Airport,** 5 mi. east of Galway City, is cheaper when you book a week in advance. There are Sunday flights only during the peak season.

Inishmore (Inis Mór)

Most visitors to the Arans go to **Inishmore** (pop. 900), the largest and northernmost of the islands. Dozens of ruins, forts, and churches, as well as "minor sites" like holy wells, lighthouses, and kelp kilns, are scattered around Inishmore. The island also manifests several interesting geological features.

The island's most impressive monument, dating from the first century BC, is magnificent **Dún Aengus Fort** (Dún Aonghasa), 5 mi. west of the pier at Kilronan, whose 18-ft.-thick walls guard Inishmore's northwest quarter. One of the best-preserved prehistoric forts in Europe, it commands a view overlooking the Atlantic that will impress anyone energetic enough to hike ½ mi. uphill. The **pool,** north of Dún Aengus, is a unique saltwater lake filled by water from the limestone cracks below the ground. Two roads lead to the fort from Kilronan: the inland route offers views across the bay to the mountains of Connemara, while the quieter coastal road passes several lovely strands. On the way to the fort, 3 mi. west of Kilronan past **Kilmurvey** (Cill Mhuirbhigh), lie **The Seven Churches** (Na Seacht dTeampaill), a scattered grouping of religious remains. The **Black Fort** (Dún Dúchathair), a mile south of Kilronan through eerie Venusian terrain, is even larger than Dún Aengus and about 1000 years older. Although part of the fort has collapsed, it commands a phenomenal view of the foaming Atlantic crashing against the cliffs 300 ft. below. In stormy weather, the **puffing holes** at the eastern end of the island spout seawater like excited whales. Inishmore's 3000 mi. of walls were built to protect the builders and to clear the ground of stones.

Ferries land at the pier in **Kilronan** (Cill Rónáin), the island's main harbor; the **tourist office** (tel. (099) 612 63) at the pier books accommodations (£1), changes money, and sells Tim Robinson's meticulous map (£3), which describes every interesting site on the islands. (Open June to mid-Sept. daily 10:30am-1pm and 2-6pm.) The best way to explore Inishmore is by bike; you can rent one from **Mullen's Aran Bicycle Hire** at the pier (tel. (099) 611 32; £4/day, £20/week; £5 deposit; open daily 9am-8pm, from Dec. to Feb. inquire at the supermarket). Minibuses roam the island, acting as private shuttles: for a ride, simply flag them down (trip from Kilronan to Dún Aengus £4 return).

There are three hostels on the island: the nicest, **Mainistir House** (tel. (099) 611 99), perches ½ mi. from Kilronan (shuttles meet the ferry; otherwise go up the hill and turn right after the supermarket). Spacious and light, with comfortable chairs. The owners cook huge "vaguely vegetarian" dinners (£4). (No curfew, £6.50 incl. breakfast, doubles £7.50/person, open all year.) Down by the harbor, the **Aran Islands Hostel** (tel. (099) 612 55) is a place to spend the hours unconscious; £5 rents a dingy common room and large rooms stuffed to the gills with beds (open April-Oct.). **Dún Aengus Hostel** (same phone), its small, cozy sister hostel, lies 4 mi. west in the shadow of Dún Aengus. (£5. Shuttle from ferries. Open April-Oct.) A half mi. back toward town, **Mrs. B. Conneely's Beach View House** (tel. (099) 611 41) does more than live up to its name, also offering views of Dún Aengus and framed versions of the Alps. (£12; open April-Sept.) Bed down in style at Mrs. G. Tierney's ivy covered **St. Brendan's House** (tel. (099) 611 49) for £10.

The **general store,** past the hostel in Kilronan, provides the essentials; restaurants on the island tend to be expensive, and are not open in winter. You may want to stick to tea houses, which serve inexpensive homemade soups and snacks. A small café with flowers on the windowsill, **Bayview Restaurant** proffers omelette and chips for £3.50, fisherman's pie and most other dishes for around £6. (Open from 2pm daily; coffeeshop from 10am.) **An Sean Chéibh,** with outdoor seating and fresh Aran fish (£4.50), cleans its catch nearby. (For both, take a left from the pier.) The two main pubs are both in Kilronan: the **American Bar** attracts younger islanders and droves of tourists, while traditional musicians strum on the terrace at **Tí Joe Mac's,** below the hostel. On Friday, Saturday, and Sunday nights in summer, stroll down to the **dance hall** at 11:30pm for the opening steps of the *ceilí* (cover £2, Sat. night £3). The hall also shows the film **Man of Aran** 3 times daily in summer (£2).

Inishmaan and Inishere

Tourists are a rarer breed on these smaller islands than on Inishmore. Here one finds locals who make *curraghs* (small boats made from curved wicker rods tied with string and covered with cowskin and black tar).

Inishmaan (Inis Meáin; pop. 300) is where John Millington Synge set *Riders to the Sea,* and is particularly well-known as a center for traditional music and dancing; its beaches, however, are inferior to those of Inishmore or Inishere. The towns here look like they were built in layers; houses are piled almost on top of each other for shelter from the weather. The island comes alive for the October 7th **Caib Stir (Cabster) Festival,** when 10-12 year old boys from all parts of Ireland's *Gaeltacht* flay each other with reeds in a rite of passage into manhood. **Mrs. Faherty,** Creigmore (tel. (099) 730 12), runs a jolly good B&B. (£9; open April-Oct.) Some local homeowners allow camping.

Inishere (Inis Óirr; pop. 300) is the smallest of the islands (less than 2 mi. across in either direction); stray donkeys meander along narrow paths through a labyrinth of stone walls. Venture up to **Dún Formna,** the stone ring-fort above the town, and stroll down to the buried remnants of the **Teampall Chaomháin** ("The Church of St. Kevin"). Patron saint of the island, St. Kevin was thought to be a brother of St. Kevin of Glendalough. Each year on June 14, islanders hold Mass in its ruins to commemorate St. Kevin; his grave nearby is said to have great healing powers. Below the church, a pristine sandy beach stretches back to the edge of town. At the bottom of the town lives the man who builds most of the island's sturdy *curraghs;* each 15-ft. boat takes him three months. Inishere has 16 B&Bs costing about £9; a list is posted outside the window of the small tourist information booth next to the pier. The new **Bru Hostel** (tel. (099) 750 24) organizes curragh trips and supplies meals. (£5.50. Open all year.) The **Láthair Campála Campground** (tel. (099) 750 08) flexes its tarps near the beach (£2/tent, £10 weekly; open May-Sept.).

Lough Corrib and Lough Mask

These two lakes, stretching 30 mi. north from Galway City and connecting to each other through underground channels, form the eastern boundary of Connemara. The eastern shores stretch into fertile farmland, while the western shores bleed into uncultivated bog and quartzite scree. Three hundred and sixty five islands dot Lough Corrib, one for each day of the year. Oughterard and Cong are two convenient bases from which to tour these lakes; buses run from Galway to Clifden in Western Connemara, stopping in both towns at least once a day.

A small village often overlooked by tourists, **Oughterard** lies on Lough Corrib's western flank at the base of the northwesterly Maumturk Mountains. The town is convenient to Lough Corrib's islands; ask a local about renting a boat for approx. £20/day. About 1 mi. south of town, turn off for **Aughnanure Castle,** where a quiet river, red with peat, meanders by a fortified tower with feasting rooms, a secret chamber, and a murder hole. (Open mid June to mid Sept. 10am-6pm daily. Admission 80p, students 30p.) Follow Gleann Rd. from Oughterard for 7 mi. to the **Hill of Doom,** where the pre-Celtic Glann people sacrificed a virgin every year; the practice continued in secret until the Middle Ages. The **Corrib Conservation Centre** in town offers weekend courses in Irish wildlife studies for naturalists, students and interested others. (From £60 for room, board, and tuition; contact Tony Whilde at (091) 825 19.) The weeklong **Oughterard Festival** in July includes a treasure hunt, a parade, and the coronation of the Queen of Connemara.

Oughterard's **Lough Corrib Hostel** (tel. (091) 826 34), blessed with a stereo, orthopedic mattresses, the best showers in Ireland, and a side-splittingly funny owner, costs a mere £5. (Bike rental, fishing rods, boat trips to Inchagoill, each for £5. No curfew/lockout. Sheets £1. Kitchen.) For an open turf fire, homemade jams, and a luxurious night in a beautiful oak bed, try **Doírín Hickey,** Cashelmara (tel. 801 94), about 2 mi. south of Oughterard, which ladles out B&B for £12. Only one mi. south, **Mrs. Lydon's** modern bungalow at Riverside, Bealnalappa (tel. (091) 801 56), enjoys a rose bower and gnomes in the garden (£10). For good pub grub and a bit of "crack," try **Fahery's** and **The Boat Inn,** both in town. Buses from Galway to Clifden stop in Oughterard 3 times daily and twice on Sundays.

The village of **Cong** (pop. 350) lies on the narrow strip of land separating the two lakes. The Guinness family used to live in the 12th-century **Ashford Castle,** now a luxury hotel with lakeside gardens. (To avoid the £2 entrance to the grounds, enter via the abbey grounds or go past the hostel, count 2 houses on your left, and then turn right on the narrow road.) Oscar Wilde indulged in boyhood pleasures at the **Moytura House,** located on the water and still inhabited; to reach the house continue 1 mi. past the turn-off for the hostel on the Galway Rd. and take your first right past the Daffodil Ranch. A sculpted head of the last abbot keeps an eye on the ruins of the 12th-century **Royal Abbey of Cong,** located in the village (open all the time, free). Cross the abbey grounds and pass through the doorway with the head to reach a footbridge spanning the River Cong. To the left is a small stone house, where the abbey monks used to sit and fish; farther off you can see the turrets of Ashford Castle. The town's privately established **tourist office** on Abbey St. will point you towards further wonders, all included in the free **Get to Know Cong.** (Open June-Sept. daily 9am-6pm.) Tour the area on bikes rented from **O'Connors Garage,** Main St. (£7/day, £30/week; student rate £5/day, £25/week; ID as deposit; open Mon.-Sat. 9am-8pm, Sun. 9am-1pm).

Cong cannot escape the presence of *The Quiet Man,* filmed in the Cong area and starring John Wayne and Maureen O'Hara. The spacious **Quiet Man Hostel,** Abbey St. (tel. 465 11), shows the film every night. (Open April-Sept.; no curfew/lockout; July-Sept. £5.50; April-June £4.95; sheets 50p; bike rental £5.) A mile down the Galway Rd., the smiling proprietors of the **Cong Hostel** offer bike (£5) and rowboat (£2) rental. (Kitchen facilities and small shop. No lockout/curfew. £5.50, camping £2.50, private rooms £6.50/person in off-season.) **White House** B&B, Abbey St. (tel. (092) 463 58), smothered in geraniums and wrapped in a brown-checkered tablecloth, costs £11. Locals butter bread and drink soup (£1) in the **Quiet Man Coffee Shop** (open daily 11am-6pm). Get your own food at **O'Connor's Supermarket** on Main St. Buses from Galway to Clifden stop in Cong once daily (none Sunday).

Two hostels hover near Cong: the relaxed **Cornamona Hostel** (tel. (092) 480 02) in Cornamona, 10 mi. west. on the shores of Lough Corrib, where cheery red bunks inhabit a large bunkroom and a radio plays in the small kitchen (£4.50); and the **Courtyard Hostel,** (tel. (092) 462 03) several miles east in Cross (£4.50, camping £2.50).

One of the islands in Lough Corrib, **Inchagoill,** opens its treasure chest of history to reveal two early Christian churches and the famous **Stone of Lugna,** tombstone of St. Patrick's nephew and navigator. Engraved in the stone is one of the earliest Christian inscriptions in Ireland; the stone itself is the oldest Christian monument in Europe, apart from the catacombs of Rome. The Lough Corrib Hostel (see above) sends boats to the islands daily from Oughterard (£5 return), and the *Corrib Queen* (tel. (092) 460 29) sails daily from Ashford Castle quay in Cong (1½ hr.; £7 return).

Connemara

Stretching from Lough Corrib and Lough Mask to County Galway's west coast at Clifden, Connemara is a region of considerable natural beauty. Set between the rippling green of the Maumturk Mountains, Connemara's thick valleys are patched with grasslands, forests, and countless blue lakes. The chocolate-brown earth and the cold, still sea stand in unlikely juxtaposition, and inhabitants will insist that a more beautiful place does not exist in Ireland.

The most rewarding way to absorb Connemara is by bike. Consider renting in Galway, then cycling northwest to Clifden via Lough Corrib and the village of Cong. Bus Éireann operates coaches out of Galway; inquire at the tourist office. If you have neither the time for a long ride nor the docility for a guided tour, take the public bus from Galway to Clifden via Cong. The 3-hr. ride passes through the most miraculous parts of Connemara.

The Connemara Gaeltacht

On the southern coast of Connemara, Ireland's largest Gaelic-speaking population (also referred to as *Iar Chonnachta*) inhabits an area stretching westward from Galway City to Carna. Ireland's language, culture, and literary heritage are very much in evidence here, strengthened during the last decade by the establishment of *Radio na Gaeltachta* (the Irish radio service), and two flourishing summer colleges. In good weather, this section of the west is ideally suited for camping—the coast is dotted with small beaches *(trá* is Gaelic for "beach") and almost all of the offshore islands are accessible by land bridge or local fishing boat. Tourists are tolerated with good humor, especially since the vast majority never venture into the peninsulas west of Rossaveal (where boats leave for Inishmore), instead heading straight on to Clifden. Buses serve the lower peninsula 3 times daily from Galway, and the upper peninsula (including Gortmore and Carna) once a day (except Sundays). Hitching on the roads-less-traveled here can be frustrating.

Throngs arrive in the summer for the *curragh* races, the largest of which is held in **Spiddal** (An Spidéal), 12 mi. west of Galway City on the main Connemara coast road. Though the day-long regatta entertains, the evening's *ceilí* is the main attraction. The swank **Spiddal Craft Centre,** a matrix of nine craft workshops popular with tourists, overlooks a grand but crowded beach, just outside of town on the Galway Rd. (Open Mon.-Sat. 9am-6pm, Sun. 2-6pm; off-season times can vary slightly.) The **Ceol na Mara** (cultural entertainment center), next door, stages performances of traditional music, song, and dance. (Shows nightly at 9pm. Prices vary.)

Call ahead to reserve at **Brú an Spidéil,** the **Spiddal Village Hostel** (tel. (091) 835 55), where you can watch TV on faded couches in front of a plastic fire (no curfew/lockout; £5, sheets 50p; bike rental £5; laundry £2), or stay with **Mrs. M. O'Neachtain,** Tearmann, Baile an Sagairt (tel. (091) 832 16), whose rooms peruse Galway Bay over a mile east of town. (£12.50, £14.50 with bath. Open June-Oct.) **Mrs. P. O'Connor,** Radarch an Chlair, Kellough (tel. (091) 832 67), polishes an equally immaculate B&B over 3 mi. east of town (£10.50; open March-Oct.). The **Spiddal Caravan and Camping Park** (tel. (091) 833 72), winner of the "Cleaner Community Award" in 1989, is 1 tidy mi. from the main village. (Open May-Oct.; £5-5.50/unit, £2-3 hiker and bikers.) Revel in tea and scones (40p) *al fresco* on the little patio of **An Tae Baeg** coffeeshop (open daily 11am-6pm), or savor your pints and a bit of food at the large, airy **Crúiscín Lán,** or **An Droighneán Donn,** which both sponsor nightly traditional music in summer. Summertime buses run almost every 2 hr. from Galway, and twice Sundays (£2.75 single fare).

The landscape becomes progressively starker west of Spiddal. Two hostels are located between Spiddal and the peninsulas: the 20-bed **Connemara Tourist Hostel,** Aille, Inverin (tel. 931 04), 2 mi. west of Spiddal (£4.50); and the **Indreabhán youth hostel (IYHF)** (tel. (091) 931 54), farther down the road, a good base for those planning on catching the Aran Islands ferry at Rossaveal. (July-Aug. £5.90; March-June, Sept.-Oct. £4.90; Nov.-Feb. £4.30.) The coastal bus from Galway stops at both hostels.

Those continuing along the coast to Gortmore and the northern peninsula should make the detour to **Rosmuck,** a small peninsula that juts into Kilkieran Bay. The cottage of Padraig Pearse, one of the executed leaders of the 1916 Uprising, nestles into a small hillock overlooking the northerly mountains. Pearse and his brother spent their summers here learning Gaelic and dreaming of an Irish republic; the Republic they envisioned has designated the cottage a national monument. (Open June-Sept. daily 9am-6:30pm.)

About 10 mi. farther along the coast, past Gortmore, lies **Carna,** where Irish speakers congregate at **Mícheál Ó Móráin's** pub. The **Carna Hostel** (tel. (095) 322 40) lets its guests use its fishing rods for free (£4/night). Ask in town about boats to **Mac Dara's Island** (Oileán Mhac Dara), 7 mi. west. The island contains the ruins of a 9th-century stone oratory and, nearby, the old grave site of the island's patron saint, Mac Dara. Fishermen used to dip their sails thrice while passing the island, in deference to the saint. A bus leaves Galway for Carna daily (except Sunday), stopping in Gortmore and Rosmuck every day but Tuesday.

Clifden

Clifden (pop. 2000), western coastal lobby to Connemara, is the only spot in the region that could be properly classified as a town. It manages to contain its tourists without appearing infested, and the expanded market buoys the local weavers, artists, and Irish music sellers. Waterfront buildings provide a scenic backdrop to Clifden Bay, where the beach bakes only 1 mi. away along Beach Rd. One mi. down Sky Rd., pass through the gate to the ruins of **Clifden Castle,** the former mansion of Clifden's founder, John D'Arcy. The 10-mi. **Sky Road,** which loops around the head of land west of Clifden town, proffers head-clearing views and makes for a great bike ride. The **Connemara Heritage Tours,** Market St. (tel. (095) 213 79), led by an archaeologist, foray into the history, folklore, and archaeology of the region (leave daily from the Island House, Market St. 9am, return 4:45pm; £11, students £10). The same group organizes a tour of **Inishbofin,** off the coast at Cleggan, clarifying the island's natural history, archaeology, geology, and place names (leave daily from Clifden 10am, return 6:15pm; £19 includes bus, ferry, and tour, students £1 off).

The amiable **tourist office** (tel. 211 63) is at the bottom of Market St. (Open June-Sept. 15 Mon.-Sat. 9am-7pm, Sun. 10am-6pm.) The **Bank of Ireland** exchanges currency (open Mon.-Tues., Thurs.-Fri. 10am-12:30pm and 1:30-3pm, Wed. 10am-12:30pm and 1:30-5pm). Mail letters at the **post office** on Main St. (Open Mon.-Fri. 9am-5:30pm, Sat. 9am-1pm.) You can rent bikes at **Mannion's,** Bridge St. (tel. 211 60; £6/day, £30/week, £10 deposit; open Mon.-Sat. 9:30am-7pm, Sun. 10:30-11:30am.) The **telephone code** is 095.

Three hostels have parked themselves bumper to bumper on Beach Rd.: the reputation of the "loo with a view" at sunny, whitewashed **Leo's Hostel** has spread far and wide (no lockout/curfew. £4.50, private room £5, bike hire £5/day.) Next door, the makeshift **Blue Hostel** (tel. 213 80) barely masks its identity as a private house (open summer months; £4.50). The red **Clifden Hostel and Camping** (tel. 212 19) qualifies as the end-of-the-line option, suited to those who don't mind musty, moldy, cobwebby quarters (£4.50, private room £5, camping £2). The simple **Corrib House,** Main St. (tel. 213 46), provides reasonable B&B for £9 (including continental breakfast), while **Mrs. King,** Kingston House, Bridge St. (tel. 214 70), has comfortable rooms with a view of the church for £11 (£12.50 with bath). Clifden's affordable coffee shops don't have to try hard to undercut the steep restaurant prices. Sit on honey-colored wooden picnic benches and munch a smoked salmon sandwich (£2.50) or the daily vegetarian option at **My Teashop,** Main St. (open daily 9am-8pm); or carry out delicious organic lunches from **The Salad Shop,** Market St. (Vegetarian options available. Open Easter to mid-Oct. 9am-6:30pm daily.) The **Super Valu Supermarket,** also on Market St., provides basic edibles (open Mon.-Sat. 9am-6pm). For a bit of drink and wink try **The Central,** Main St., or bring your own instruments to **Mannions,** Market St.

Buses run from Galway to Clifden through Oughterard and Roundstone (late June-early Sept. Mon.-Sat. 3/day). The only connecting bus to Westport departs on Thursdays at 4:15pm. Hitch to Westport from the Esso station on the N59.

Around Clifden: Western Connemara

Meander by bike or car along the fine golden beaches and coastal roads south of Clifden. Seven mi. south along the R341, **Ballyconneely** sits on an isthmus near the wonderfully sandy **Coral Strand. Roundstone,** a quiet holiday resort 8 mi. to the southeast of Ballyconneely, also abounds in silicon. A mile west of Roundstone sits the beach-side **Gorteen Bay Caravan and Camping Park** (tel. (095) 358 82; overnight/unit £4.50-5.50, hikers or bikers £3.50-4.50; laundry facilities; open March-Sept.)

Ten mi. northwest of Clifden, **Cleggan,** the center of Connemara's fishing industry, offers the charms of Clifden without the tourists. Explore the pleasant sandhills and small ruins of **Omey Island,** just offshore to the southwest, accessible by foot at low tide. The airy **Master House Hostel** (tel. (095) 447 46), full of plants, bright wood, and exposed stone, is the kind of place where people come for a night and spend days. (No lockout/curfew; £4.50, sheets 50p; fishing rods £2.50; open all year.) Boats leave Cleggan Pier three times daily for **Inishbofin Island** (tel. (095) 447 50; £10 return, £8 for Master House hostellers), where it is possible to pass an afternoon in complete solitude on one of the many white beaches. This attractive, mountainous island is home to some ancient ruins and a surfeit of wildlife, as well as the beautiful **Inishbofin Hostel** (tel. 458 55), with pine bunks and a large conservatory. (No curfew. Kitchen.)

The **Twelve Bens** (Na Benna Beola, also known as the Twelve Pins) are a range of rugged hills between 1700 and 2400 ft. high, in the heart of Connemara. Hikers can base themselves at the **Ben Lettery youth hostel (IYHF)** (tel. (095) 346 36) in Ballinafad, 8 mi. east of Clifden, just off the N59 west of the Roundstone turn-off. (July-Aug. £5.50; March-June, Sept.-Oct. £4.30; Nov.-Feb. £3.80.) The main Leenane road also leads into the wilderness; follow it 8 mi. north of Clifden to **Letterfrack,** where the **Connemara National Park** (tel. (095) 410 54) sponsors lectures and guided walks of the region (weekdays at 10:30am). The **Old Monastery Hostel** (tel. (095) 411 32) costs £5/night.

The road north of Letterfrack to Tullycross leads to the **Renvyle Peninsula** and its excellent beaches. **The Renvyle Beach Caravan and Camping Park** (tel. (095) 434 62) is 1 mi. past Tullycross on the beach. (£5-5.50/caravan, £4.50-5/tent, hikers and bikers £3. Showers 50p. Open Easter-Sept.) 2½ mi. east of Letterfrack, **Kylemore Abbey** captivates coachriders and hitchhikers alike. The lavish, multi-turreted castle was built by a wealthy Member of Parliament in the 19th century for his lady love; now nuns chastely admire the lovely lakeshore setting from the only Benedictine convent in Ireland. Follow the forest path to the **gothic chapel** beside the Abbey, or delicately quench your thirst at the teashop, where the nuns sell their crafts.

Further east along the N59, **Killary Harbour,** Ireland's only fjord, breaks through the mountains to the town of **Leenane,** wrapping itself in the skirts of the **Devilsmother Mountain.** The **Killary Harbour youth hostel (IYHF)** (tel. (095) 434 17) is at the very mouth of the harbor, 7 mi. west of Leenane. It was the building's savory view across narrow Killary Harbour to Mweelrea Mountain that spurred Wittgenstein to complete his *Philosophical Investigations* here in 1948. (July-Aug. £5.50; March-June, Sept.-Oct. £4.30.)

The Galway-Leenane-Clifden bus stops 3 mi. from the hostel, at Kylemore Abbey, and in Letterfrack. Many find hitchhiking to be fairly easy on the main road, but a paucity of cars slows thumbers on the byways.

Westport

Pretty Westport lies on island-studded Clew Bay, just a few miles from some of Ireland's grandest mountains. Planned by architect Richard Cassels to complement 18th-century Westport House, the town's squares and riverfront walkways add to its natural beauty. Although tourists have discovered Westport's charm, it does not feel overrun. As a destination in itself and a revolving door into both Connemara and County Mayo, Westport is a good spot for exploring the environs, refueling, renting bikes, and picking up information.

Arriving and Departing

Transportation connections are surprisingly poor for such a major town. Trains arriving from Dublin terminate at Westport station on Altamont Rd. (3/day, Sun. 2/day). Buses leave from the Fair Green for Clifden (2/week; 1½ hr.), Galway (1/day; 1¾ hr.), Sligo (1/day; 3 hr.), and other destinations throughout the west. Westport is an easy hitch from Clifden, Galway, Sligo or Castlebar (on the N60).

Orientation and Practical Information

Westport's North Mall and South Mall broadways run down each side of the river. Most of the town extends off South Mall; the perpendicular Bridge St. favors pubs, eateries, and strolling passersby. To the west, Quay Rd. leads along the water to many of Westport's attractions.

Tourist Office: North Mall (tel. 257 11), at the corner of James and Newport St. Accommodations service £1. Open Mon.-Fri. 9am-7pm, Sat. 10am-1pm, 4-6pm; in winter Mon.-Fri. 9am-1pm and 2-5:15pm.

Bike Rental: J.P. Breheny and Sons, Castlebar St. (tel. 250 20). £7/day, £30/week, £30 deposit. Open Mon.-Sat. 9am-6:30pm.

Buses: Buses leave from the Fair Green, where North Mall becomes Altamont St. Schedules available at the hotel and at the tourist office.

Emergency: Dial 999; no coins required.

Financial Services: Bank of Ireland, North Mall, near the post office. Open Mon.-Wed. and Fri. 10am-12:30pm and 1:30-3pm, Thurs. 10am-12:30pm and 1:30-5pm.

Launderette: Westport Washeteria, Mill St. (tel. 252 61), to the left of the Nevada Burger. £2/load. Open Mon.-Sat. 10am-6pm; closed Wed. in winter.

Pharmacy: Doherty's, High St. (tel. 250 03). Open Mon.-Tues. and Thurs.-Sat. 9:30am-6:30pm. Local pharmacies take turns on Wed.

Police: Garda Station, Fair Green (tel. 255 55).

Post Office: North Mall (tel. 254 75). Open Mon.-Sat. 9am-5:30pm.

Telephone Code: 098.

Train Station: Altamont St. (tel. 252 53), a 10-min. walk east of the town center. Station open for inquiries Mon.-Sat. 7:30am-6:30pm and 9-10pm, Sun. open around times of departure.

Accommodations and Food

1½-2 mi. outside of town, the **Summerville Hostel** on the Louisburgh Rd. (tel. 259 48) has only 30 beds in a 250-year old Georgian house (£4.50, private room £5.50. Open mid-March to mid-Oct.) Closer to town, opposite the train station, hostellers at the much larger **Club Atlantic,** Altamont St. (tel. 266 44 or 267 17), watch videos, play pool, and cook in the massive kitchen. (July-Aug. £5.90; March-June, Sept.-Oct. £4.90; Nov.-Feb. £4.30; bike rental £5). **The Granary Hostel** is a mile from town on the Louisburgh Rd. in a 150-year old granary with a simple kitchen and outdoor toilets and showers (£4). Westport B&Bs average £11 per person, and are easily spotted on the Altamont and Castlebar Roads. Soak in the large pink bathroom of **Mrs. Cox,** St. Martin's, Distillery Rd. (tel. 250 31; £10.50). Roses shroud spacious rooms looking out on the frothy flower garden at **Mrs. Sheridan,** Altamont House, Altamont St. (tel. 252 26), whose guest lounge has an open fire. (£11.50. Open Feb.-early Dec.) The **Parklands Caravan and Camping Park** (tel. 251 41) is on the Westport House estate, 2 mi. from town on the Louisburgh Rd. (Unit £7-8, hikers and bikers £4-5. Open mid-May to Aug.)

Get your spam tins at the **Super Valu Supermarket** on Shop St. (Open Mon.-Fri. 9am-7pm, Sat. 9am-6:45pm.) Across the way, **Country Fresh** sells fresh fruit and vegetables. (Open Mon.-Tues., Thurs.-Fri. 8am-6:30pm, Wed. 8am-1pm, Sat. 8am-6pm.) On Thursday mornings from 10:30am to 1:30pm visit the **country market** in front of the Town Hall at The Octagon for vegetables, eggs, milk and butter. The crowded but brightly cheery **McCormack's,** Bridge St., serves scrumptious, steaming soup with brown bread (£1) and quiche with potato and salad (£3). (Open daily 10:15am-6pm.) The **Crockery Pot,** on Bridge St., complete with photos of royalty-gone-by, is perfect for morning scones and tea or vegetarian meals (£5). (Open Mon.-Sat. 10:30 am-9pm, Sun. 10:30am-7pm.) **Forman's Pub** offers a lunch special that can't be beat: £2.50 for soup, sandwich, tea/coffee, and dessert in its plush red interior. Stop in here for music on Fri. or Sat. nights, or pop across the street to the **West.** (Both on corner of Bridge St. and South Mall.) Westport's place for nightly traditional music is **Matt Molloy's Pub,** Bridge St., owned by a member of the wildly successful *Chieftains.*

Near Westport

Perhaps the finest section of County Mayo is the mountainous wilderness south of Westport, where narrow roads wind through Gargamelian landscapes. From Westport, travel 13 mi. west to **Louisburgh.** From Louisburgh, continue 15 mi. south to calm **Doo Lough,** where you can take your pick of several heart-pounding climbs. Heading back to Westport, you should turn left at the "Scenic Route" sign at the south end of the lough. The loop is 40 mi. around. Cars are few and far between here.

Two mi. past Louisburgh (from Westport) is **Roonagh Point,** where boats depart for tiny **Clare Island,** home of the pirate Grace O'Malley in the 16th century. On the west coast of the island, the cliffs of Knockmore Mountain (1550 ft.) rise sharply out of the sea. The island also drowns in historical interest. **Clare Island Historical Safaris** (tel. (098) 250 48) offers an exploration of a megalithic tomb, Bronze Age cooking sites, a 13th-century abbey, Grace O'Malley's castle, and famine-day land division. (£20-30, including transport and meals.) The **Bayview Hotel** on the island (tel. 263 07) runs a diving center and offers sailboarding and waterskiing. Boats run 3 times per day in summer (return £10, students £7.50).

Achill Island

Connected to the mainland by a bridge, Achill Island (ACK-ill) is County Mayo's best-known holiday refuge and Ireland's largest island. Bordered by glorious beaches and cliffs, Achill's Atlantic coast gives way to the dark, towering mountains of the interior, perpetually wreathed in cloud.

Buildings cluster around the bridge to the mainland, forming the town of **Achill Sound,** which includes a small **tourist office** (tel. (098) 453 84; open July-Aug. Mon.-Sat. 9:30-5:30pm, closed 1 hr. for lunch), a **post office** (open Mon.-Fri. 9am-12:30pm, 1:30-5:30pm, Sat. 9am-1pm), a few souvenir shops, a supermarket, and the **Achill Sound Hotel** (tel. (098) 452 45), where you can rent bikes (£7/day, £30/week, £30 deposit). Follow the painted signs to the **Wild Haven Hostel** (tel. (098) 453 92), a fine new establishment with polished floors, lofts with fluffy duvets, and an open turf fire in the furnished lounge. (£5/person, light breakfast £2.)

About 6 mi. south of Achill Sound (take a left at the crossroads) lie the ruins of **Kildownet Castle,** a fortified tower house dating from the late 1400s. Grace O'Malley, the swaggering, seafaring protector of Middle Ages Ireland, once owned this castle as well. (Ask for the key at the house next door.) From there, follow **Atlantic Drive** past beautiful beaches up to the village of **Dooega,** where the **Natural History Museum** exhibits local wildlife and shows nature films. (Open daily 11am-6pm in summer.)

A right turn in Achill Sound leads to the northern part of the island, where **Dugort** snores towards the 21st century amidst wide expanses of sand. Walk around **Slievemore Mountain** to see the chambered tomb known as Giant's Grave (easily accessible from Dugort); other megalithic tombs lurk nearby. Two campgrounds fortify the tiny hamlet: **Lavelle's Golden Strand Caravan and Camping Park** (tel. (098) 472 32) is ¾ mi. from Valley Crossroads (units £4.50-5, hikers and bikers £2.50-3; open June-Sept.); and beyond, **Seal Caves Caravan and Camping Park** (tel. (098) 432 62) hunkers at Dugort Beach and Slievemore Mountain, near Heinrich Böll's cottages (unit £3.50-4 plus 25-30p/person, hikers and bikers £1.50-2; open April-Sept.). Valley Crossroads, 2 mi. east, marks the turnoff for the **Valley House Hostel** (tel. (098) 472 04), a large house displaying antique furniture, massive windows, and an open turf fire in a paroxysm of fading splendor (£4). **Atoka Restaurant,** at the crossroads, serves sandwiches (£1) and seafood meals (£5-6); for a great B&B deal, try the small, comfortable **Atoka House** next door (£7 with continental breakfast; £9 full fry).

Keel, Achill's major town, sheds light on the island's western peninsula and its history: the **Heritage Centre** displays local crafts including baskets, *curraghs,* and woven goods. (Open daily 10:30am-6pm during summer months.) Send out accounts of your exploits from the **post office** (open Mon.-Fri. 9am-2pm, 3-5:30pm, Sat. 9am-1pm), embellish them with drunken inspiration at the musical **Annexe Inn** or **The Village Inn,** and dream of further adventures at the **Wayfarer Hostel** (tel. (098) 432 66; £4; open March-Oct.). Peddle out from **O'Malley's Island Sports** (tel. (098) 431 25; bike rental £7/day, £30/week; open Mon.-Sat. 10am-7pm, Sun. 10am-6pm), and get sand in your tent at **Keel Sandybanks Caravan and Camping Park** (tel. (098) 432 11), adjacent to the beach. (Caravans £4-5.50, tents £3-4.50. Open June-early Sept.)

Two mi. north of Keel on the road looping back to Dugort, the **Deserted Village** consists of stone houses closely related to early Christian beehive huts; they were used from the 1700s until the late 1930s as summer fattening locales for cows grazing in the area. Two mi. farther up the road, **Corrymore House,** in Dooagh, was the former home of the domineering Captain Boycott. Deserted by his land tenants in the 1880s, his only act of generosity was that of inadvertently contributing his last name to the English vocabulary. The **Folklife Centre** displays household utensils, furniture, and farm implements from the turn of the century. (Open daily 10:30am-5pm.) Dooagh hosts a music, dance, art, and writing festival week during August, culminating in a free, open-air show. Continue several miles to Achill's wild west and follow the stream at **Achill Head** up to its source on **Croaghaun Mountain** for bone-chilling views of **Croaghaun Cliffs.**

Transport yourself around the island by foot, wheel, or thumb; buses run infrequently from Westport to Achill Sound and through to Dooagh (3/day in summer; 2/week in winter).

Northwest Ireland

The western coast grows rugged and forbidding as it confronts the territory of Counties Sligo and Donegal. This dark barrenness has spared the region the unrelenting Danish, Norman, and English conquests that molded the culture of the south; instead, cairns, dolmens, passage graves, and ring forts attest to the early antagonism between the men of Connaught and the men of Ulster. Today, the region's inaccessibility isolates it somewhat from tour coaches and caravans.

Stretches resembling a muted lunar landscape, run through with swollen streams, abut sparkling blue water and white beaches. Sea gusts lift the smell of peat-fire smoke from stone chimneys over the thatched cottages in County Donegal, and pockets of Gaelic make the region seem like another country altogether. Mist wreathes mighty Benbulben, and pilgims still emulate the Saint by climbing gloomy Croagh Patrick barefoot. The wintry dawn streaks across Lough Gill and the great plains of Ballymote and Tubbercurry, flung westward from the placid River Garavogue, gurgling from Lough Gill to Sligo Bay. Even in the larger towns of Letterkenny, Donegal and Dungloe, life centers on the main street and local pub.

Getting Around

Although private companies have filled some of the looming gaps in service left by **Bus Éireann's** network, some areas are simply not accessible by bus, others only infrequently or at random hours. **Bus Éireann** has semi-regular buses between Dublin and Letterkenny (3/day 9am-6pm, Sun. 2/day 9am-5:30pm; 4½ hr.; £13 return) or Sligo and Letterkenny (Mon.-Sat. 2/day noon-3pm; 2 hr.). Bus Éireann gives large discounts if you get a Travelsave stamp (£7 at any station) on your student ID, and more diminutive ones on all of their Rambler tickets—8 consecutive days travel (£58, £29 student). The **Swilly** bus service, with an office in both Derry (tel. 262 017) and Letterkenny, operates between the two cities (Mon.-Sat. 6/day, 8:35am-8pm; 1 hr.; £4.20, return £5.25) and covers some of the harder to reach areas like Dungloe and Funan. Swilly also offers a **Runabout** ticket, 8 days of unlimited travel for £8 with a student ID, £15 adult. Another option is **McGeehan's,** which connects most towns in the county with Dublin, running to Dublin every morning and returning every evening (including Sundays) for £11, £15 return (students £9, £11 return). Call (075) 461 01 or 461 50 in County Donegal or (01) 73 43 44 in Dublin for departures from particular villages. If you choose to thumb, stick to the relatively well-traveled N56, which circles the country, or N15, which travels the western coast from Killybegs up to Rathmelton. Some roads do remain almost entirely untraveled, especially at midday during the week and on Sundays, so choose your routes carefully or tour the region by foot. For a hefty sum you can rent a bike in most towns (see listings below).

Sligo Town

Sligo (pop. 18,000), a flourishing commercial, industrial, and market center, is graced by the River Garavogue, which flows fashionably through the center of town under a series of stone bridges and empties out into a bay. Sligo draws students of all ages to its annual Yeats Summer School, and retains an upbeat air year-round. Its 70-odd pubs and discos fill to bursting point most nights and are the regular scene of inspired musical sessions. With historic remains surrounding it, Sligo serves as a good base for ventures in all directions.

Arriving and Departing

Located on the northwestern coast of the country, Sligo has regular service to Dublin's Busárus station (Bus: Mon.-Fri. 3/day 9am-5:45pm, Sun. 3/day 9am-5:30pm; 4 hr.; £7, return £10. Train: Mon.-Fri. 3/day 4:50am-5:40pm, Sun. 2/day 9:15am-6:05pm; 3½ hr.; £14, return £18, student £12.50, return £17), to Belfast (Bus: Mon.-Sun. 2/day 11:40am-11:45pm; 3 hr.) and Galway (Bus: 5/day 9:30am-7pm, Sun. 2/day 2:40-5:05pm; 3 hr.; £6, return £10). All fares are about 1/3 cheaper with a Travelsave stamp (£7), which can be stickered onto your student ID at any station in Ireland.

Orientation and Practical Information

The bus/train station (tel. 698 88) is located centrally on Lord Edward St. Bus and train schedules (50p) are on sale at the station, and luggage can be stored in the station's lockers for £1. Major roads and sympathetic drivers come here from Enniskillen (to the east) and along the coast from Ballyshannon (north) and Ballina (west). With your back to the station take a left and follow Lord Edward straight onto Wine St. then onto Stephen St., right onto Bridge St. and you'll find yourself in the central shopping, pubbing and eating area of town. For pronto information, take your first right off Lord Edward onto Adelai St. and follow it around the corner; the tourist office is prominently on the left.

Tourist Office: Temple St. (tel. 612 01), off Charles St., up past the cathedral. Northwest regional office. Accommodations service £1, out of area £2. They also sell slightly useless Sligo pamphlets for £1. Don't expect to get directions to the independent hostels; the office doesn't acknowledge their existence. Open June Mon.-Sat. 9am-6pm; July-Aug. Mon.-Sat. 9am-8pm, Sun. 10am-2pm; Sept.-May Mon.-Fri. 9am-1pm and 2-5pm.

Walking Tours: Depart from the tourist office mid-June to early Sept. Mon.-Sat. at 9;45am and 2pm (1½ hr.; £5).

Bike Rental: Conway Bros., 6 High St. (tel. 613 70). £7/day, £30/week, £40 deposit. Open daily 7am-midnight. **Gary's Cycles,** Quay St.; £6/day, £25/week, £30 deposit. Open Mon.-Sat. 9am-6pm. The **Eden Hill Hostel** on Pearse Rd. (£5/day) rents all types of bikes.

Bookstore: Keohane's Castle St. Sells Sheelah Kirby's *The Yeats Country* (£3.95) and *Sligo, Land of Yeat's Desire* (£9.95)—both excellent guides to the region. Open Mon.-Sat. 8am-6:30pm, Sun. 8am-1:30pm.

Camping: Out & About, 20 Market St., has all to meet those outdoorsy needs. Open Mon.-Sat. 9:30am-6pm.

Early Closing Day: Mon.

Emergency: Dial 999; no coins required.

Financial Services: Bank of Ireland, Stephen St., open Mon.-Wed. and Fri. 10am-12:30pm and 1:30-3pm, Thurs. 10am-12:30pm and 1:30-5pm. Also at the tourist office, the numerous *bureaux de change* and the hotels for the truly desperate.

Hospital: General Hospital, The Mall (tel. 421 61).

Launderette: Gurries, High St. Wash and dry £2-4. Tons of machines. Open Mon.-Sat. 9am-7pm, last wash 5:30pm. **Coin-Op Laundry,** top of Harmony Hill, same prices, Mon.-Sat. 9:30am-6pm.

Pharmacy: E. Horan, Chemist, Castle St. (tel. 425 60) at Market St. Open Mon.-Sat. 9:30am-6pm. Local pharmacies rotate Sunday opening.

Police: Garda Station, Pearse Rd. (tel. 420 31), at the intersection of Teeling St.

Post Office: Wine St. at O'Connell St. (tel. 425 93). Open Mon.-Sat. 9am-5:30pm.

Taxi: Cab 55, tel. 423 33, and **M. Fallon,** tel. 422 01, are 2 of many small, private cab companies in town. Expect to pay a £3 minimum in town, 50p a mile outside.

Telephone Code: 071.

Youth Information Center: Market St. (tel. 441 50). Deals with immigration and environmental issues, as well as listing accommodations and employment opportunities abroad. Open Tues.-Wed. and Fri. 11am-6pm, Thurs. 11am-8pm, Sat. 11am-4pm.

Accommodations and Food

The **White House Hostel** (tel. 451 60) on Markievioz Rd. is a five-min. walk from the train station. Follow Wine St. past three traffic lights and take a left after the Silver Swan. This is perhaps the hippest hostel in town, with a mandolin-picking warden, a great hanging-out scene, and a "mystical" breakfast of toast and coffee. All is clean and woolly blankets abound. (No curfew, no lockout, key deposit £2,

£5.) Further out is the **Eden Hill Holiday Hostel,** Pearse Rd. (tel. 432 04), entrance via Marymount St., opposite the Esso station. The downstairs of this great old Victorian building is charming and homey but the upstairs living quarters are quite cramped and the bathrooms need more attention. Laundry 50p, bikes £5, £5/night. The **Yeats Country Hostel** on Lord Edward St. (tel. 602 41) is the smallest and least glamorous of the three hostels, but it is just across the road from the train and bus station. (£4; kitchen facilities.) Most B&Bs in Sligo are either expensive or a walk; one happy medium is **Sheelin House,** Union St. at the corner with Wine St. It is just minutes from the bus/train station, has views of leafy vegetation, and won't break you at £12. If a walk is more what you had in mind, friendly **Mrs. Kane,** Glenview, 1 mi. out of town on the Strandhill Rd. (tel. 624 57), lets four fine rooms (£12). The **Greenlands campground** (tel. 771 13), on the resort peninsula of Rosses Point 5 mi. west, flanks a greener Golf Club. (Hikers and bikers £5/unit plus 40p/person July-Aug. Open late May-early Sept.) On the other side of the bay near Strandhill, **Buenos Ayres,** Seahill Rd. (tel. 681 20), is within earshot of the surf. (Hikers and bikers £3.50, £5/unit plus 20p/person July-Aug.; rest of season £3.50. Open May-Aug.)

The **Quinnsworth Supermarket** is on O'Connell St. (Open Mon.-Wed. and Sat. 9am-6pm, Thurs.-Fri. 9am-9pm.) Nearby, **Tír na nÓg,** Grattan St., stocks health foods, organic veggies 'n vino and "unusual" cards. (Open Mon.-Sat. 9:30am-6pm.) **Kate's Kitchen,** Market St., lets you tip your French bread with gourmet toppings, including specialty patés (£1.15, each extra 30p) Also stocks quiches and salads to meet the vegetarian's needs. (Open Mon.-Sat. 9am-6pm.) The **Bonne Chere** restaurant on Market St. serves up hearty meals (£3.50-4) in a once elegant interior; open daily 8am-9:30pm). Charming **Beezie's,** O'Connell St., serves excellent meals (chicken curry £4) at cafeteria prices. (Open Mon.-Sat. 12:30-11pm, Sun. 12:30-3pm and 4-10:30pm.)

Sights

Religious buildings jostle each other in Sligo's streets. The ruined 13th-century **Dominican Abbey,** with its well-preserved cloisters and ornate coupled pillars, is on Abbey St., while the oldest of Sligo's churches is the 17th-century **St. John's Church,** on John St. (Open Mon.-Sat. 10am-5:30pm, Sun. for services.) Next door, the hulking **Cathedral of the Immaculate Conception** is best visited in early morning or late evening, when the sun's rays stream through 69 lovely stained glass windows.

During his youth, W.B. Yeats lived here with his mother's family, the Pollexfens, who owned a mill overlooking the gray River Garavogue. The municipal art gallery in the **County Museum,** Stephen St., contains one of the finest collections of modern Irish art in the country, including a number of drawings by Jack B. Yeats (W.B.'s brother) and the works of contemporaries such as Nora McGuinness and Michael Healy. Many first editions of Yeats' writings and original publications by the Dún Elmer Press and Cuala Press, including illustrated broadside collaborations by Jack and W.B. Yeats, are among the museum's other treasures. (Open Mon.-Sat. 10:30am-12:30pm and 2:30-4:30pm. Free.) The adjacent **County Library** has a good selection of Irish literature and can be a welcome shelter from the rain and mist. (Open Fri. 10am-5pm, Wed. and Sat. 10am-1pm and 2-5pm, Tues. and Thurs. 10am-1pm, 2-5pm, and 7-9pm.)

Arts and Entertainment

The **Sligo Art Gallery** hosts traveling exhibitions by Irish and international artists in the Yeats summer school building (tel. 458 47; open when there is an exhibit, usually Mon.-Fri. 10am-5pm and Sat. 10am-1pm). The **Hawk's Well Theatre,** Temple St. (tel. 615 26 or 615 18), beneath the tourist office, has a continuous program of modern and traditional drama, along with interesting lectures and conferences, some in conjunction with the Yeats summer school. (Most shows £5, students £3.

Box office open Mon.-Sat. 2-6pm; tickets sold at the tourist office Mon.-Sat. 10am-1pm.)

Check the weekly *Sligo Champion* (available Wed. afternoon, 50p) for local listings of traditional music. **McLynn's,** Market St., is well-known; **Feehily's Pub,** Bridge St. at Stephen St., has free music, as does **T.D.'s,** Hughes Bridge, every night. Most pubs are open Mon.-Sat. 10:30am-11:30pm, Sun. 12:30-2pm and 4-11pm. After pubs close the crowds amble to the **Clarence,** Wine St., with more live music and general late-night frolicking. *Comhaltas* (Kohl-tas), the Irish traditional music and drama group, offers superb Tuesday night sessions at the **Sligo Trades Club,** Castle St. (arrive around 9:30pm if you want a seat; £2 cover). There's snooker at the **Embassy Lounge** (£3.50; open 10:30am-11pm) on Kennedy Parade.

Late September and early October bring to town the **Sligo Arts Festival,** with traditional music, jazz, blues, short story readings, classical music concerts, comedy, rock, and dance. For more information contact the Sligo Arts Festival Office. Wine St. (tel. 698 02). In Agust, the **Yeats International Summer School** opens some of its musical revues, poetry readings, lectures, and concerts to the public. Pick up a calendar of events at the tourist office or contact the **Yeats Society,** Douglas Hyde Bridge, Sligo (tel. (071) 426 93). In July, the **Summer Festival** shakes up the town, and 20 mi. south of Sligo, Tubbercurry rivals it with the **South Sligo Traditional Music Festival.**

Sligo to Donegal

Four mi. north of Sligo, William Butler Yeats is buried with his wife George in a simple grave at **Drumcliffe Church,** where his great-grandfather served as rector. The limestone tomb on the left as you approach the church door, is marked with the final lines of the poem *Under Ben Bulben:* "Cast a cold Eye / On Life, on Death. / Horseman, pass by!" The eponymous mountain looms nearby. To reach Drumcliffe take the main Donegal/Bundoran road. Buses run from Sligo to Drumcliffe (Mon.-Fri. 3 daily, Sat. 4 buses, Sun. 2 in summer only); hitching is also relatively painless.

Several miles north of Drumcliffe, eerie **Benbulben** protrudes from the landscape like a gigantic thumb. The climb up is a windy one and the summit can be downright gusty.

Four mi. west of Drumcliffe is **Lissadell House,** where the sisters Eva Gore-Booth, a poet, and Constance Markiewicz, a political activist who held a seat in the Dáil, entertained Yeats and his circle. The gaunt house has lost something of its former glory, but the Gore-Booth family still lives here and conducts tours. (Open May-Sept. Mon.-Sat. 2-5:15pm. Last admission at 4:30pm. Admission £1.50, children 50p.) Take your first left after the building that used to house the Yeats Tavern Hostel on the Duncliffe Rd. Just outside Sligo is the famous **Lough Gill** (follow the Enniskillen road out of town and turn off at the Lough Gill signs). On the south shore near Cottage Island is **Dooney Rock,** celebrated by Yeats in his early poem *The Fiddler of Dooney.* Nearby is the tiny **Isle of Innisfree,** where "peace comes dropping slow." Down toward Lough Gill is **Cairns Hill,** covered with cairns, cashels, a stone circle, and a holy well; clandestine Masses were held here during the time of the Penal Laws. The lush glen around the well is peaceful, and the views along the road are a balm to the soul.

Mullaghmore, 15 mi. north of Drumcliffe, is the departure point for trips to **Inishmurray,** a tiny island with a famous 6th-century monastery. There are no regular ferries, but a group can hire a boat at affordable rates; try contacting Joe McGowan (tel. 662 67), or Rodney Lomax (tel. 661 24); £85 for a group of up to 12 for the day.

Thirteen mi. south of Donegal Town, the market town of **Ballyshannon** plays host each year in the beginning of August to the **Ballyshannon Folk & Traditional Music Festival.** Informal sessions start in the last week of July. Tickets for the entire weekend's festivities cost £17, which includes admission to the performances, the afternoon workshops, and a jam-packed campsite. You can also look for a bed at **Mrs. McBride's,** St. Mels, Donegal Rd. at the corner with the road to Rossnowlaugh (tel. (072) 515 30; £11/person; open June-Sept.); or **Mrs. Melly's, Kalmia House** (tel. (072) 515 49), ½mi. out at Finner. (£11, £12 with bath; open June-Aug.). Unless you book weeks in advance, you should resign yourself to camping on one of the long, wide beaches near Ballyshannon. The nearest hostel is in **Bundoran,** about 5 mi. southwest of Ballyshannon at the **Homefield Activity Hostel,** Bay View Ave. (tel. (072) 412 88; £4; open all year); take a left at McGrath's guest house. Very cool nunnery (once), now a rambling hostel. At the eastern end of Bundoran is the **Dartry View Caravan and Camping Park** (tel. (072) 417 94; £4.50/unit). Most buses which run from Donegal to Ballyshannon continue on to Bundoran. The last bus from Ballyshannon to Donegal leaves daily at 8:10pm.

Donegal Town

Gateway to the stunning cliffs and inlets to the west, Donegal town (pop. 2000) traps tourists like a pot of honey. Souvenir shops are abundantly represented and many pubs offer games and music to attract the monied wanderers. There is a pretty river and a view or two, but you've by no means done Donegal if you don't get beyond this town into the splendor of the surrounding landscape.

Most residents consider the 15th-century **Donegal Castle** an inexplicably "queer" thing, but its spiral staircase is worth climbing if only to see the finely carved stone fireplace. (Open daily 10am-6pm; admission 90p, seniors 60p, students and children 35p.) **St. Patrick's Church of the Four Masters,** Main St., is a fine example of the solid Irish Romanesque style. From the tourist office, wander by the river and explore the remains of the **Franciscan Friary.** The famous **Magee Tweed Factory** (go down Main St., turn left just before the cinema and cross the bridge) has an extensive gift shop with an explanatory loom set up. Most of the tweed is woven in countryside cottages and is brought here to be washed, dried, shrunk, brushed, and finished. The **Donegal Craft Village** is a cluster of quaint workshops 1 mi. out of town on the Ballyshannon/Sligo road. (Most shops open Mon.-Sat. 9:30am-6pm.)

The Diamond is Donegal's central landmark. The **tourist office** (tel. 211 48) is just south of it on Quay St. (the Sligo Rd.). (Open Mon.-Fri. 10am-1pm, 2-6pm, Sat. 10am-1pm.) The **bus depot** is in the Diamond outside the Abbey Hotel Shop (open daily for information 8:45am-6:45pm), which will also hold baggage for £1. The **post office** (tel. 210 30) is north of the Diamond on Tirchonaill St. (Open Mon.-Sat. 9am-5:30pm.) **Eleanor's Launderette** is on Upper Main St. (Open Mon.-Sat. 9am-6pm, last wash 4:30pm.) You can rent bikes at **C.J. Doherty's,** Main St. (tel. 211 19) for £6/day, £25/week; £40 deposit. (Open Mon.-Sat. 9am-6pm.) The **Bike Shop,** Waterloo Place, to your right as you take the bridge out of town (by the Peter Feely hostel), also rents for the same prices, at the same times. The **telephone code** is 073.

There are two hostels in Donegal town and plenty of B&Bs in the £11-12 range. The **Peter Feely Hostel** (tel. 220 30 after 6:30pm), a 2-min. walk from the Diamond on the Killybegs road (from the Abbey Hotel go left and over the bridge), is short on space but big on laughs, presided over by witty Peter Feely himself. (£4.50, kitchen facilities, no curfew, no lockout.) Three mi. away (continue down the Killybegs road for 1 mi. and turn left at the signpost), the **Ball Hill youth hostel (IYHF)** (tel. 211 74) is in a large, comfortable house overlooking the tranquil harbor islands. (£4.30; under 18 £3.50, camping £3; kitchen facilities.) **Mrs. Timoney,** Castle View House, Waterloo Pl. (tel. 221 00), offers a fine B&B under the old bridge in the shadow of the castle (£11; sinks in each room). **Mrs. McGarrigle's** Shanveen House (tel. 211 27), a 3-min. walk from the Diamond on the Killybegs road, has nicely decorated rooms and good views (£11, £12.50 with bath). **Mrs. Keeney's,** Aranmore House, a few houses down the Killybegs road (tel. 212 42), has plenty of clean and comfortable rooms (7 with showers). Campers should ask around for spots to pitch their tents.

The best dinner deal in town is **Errigal Restaurant,** Main St. (tel. 214 28). Here you can enjoy an excellent chicken dish or fish and chips (£3-4), surrounded by talkative locals and inconspicuous decor. (Open daily 9am-11pm.) For similar fare in womb-like surroundings, try the **Atlantic Cafe,** Main St. (Meals £3-4; open daily noon-9:30pm.) The **Foodland Supermarket** is in the Diamond. (Open Mon.-Fri. 9am-7pm, Sat. 9am-6:30pm.) For a fresher selection, **Simple Simon's,** Main St., sells home baked wheat bread, local cheeses and other healthy fodder (open Mon.-Sat. 10am-6pm).

At night, Donegal puts on a good show. **Schooner's** on Main St. has regular live music and good "crack" (atmosphere, scene, conversation). (Open Mon.-Sat. 12:30am-11:30pm, Sun. 12:30-2pm, 4-11pm.) The **Abby Hotel** on the Diamond has bands on Sunday nights and **Reeva's** on Main St. has a good post-pub scene. There's a good chance that a pub crawl will turn up a number of impromptu sessions of accordian, *bodhrán* (the native drum), and guitar.

To get to Donegal, catch a bus from Dublin (Mon.-Fri. 3/day, Sat. 4/day, Sun. 2/day; 4½ hr.; £10, return £13), Sligo (2/day; return £9.50, with Travelsave stamp £7), or Derry (2/day, Sun. 1/day).

Southern Donegal Peninsula: From Donegal to Ardara

The road heading west along Donegal's southern coast, from Donegal Town to Rossan Point at the peninsula's tip, is scenic and varied. Buses run from Donegal Town to Killybegs (Mon.-Sat. 3/day 9:10am-6:15pm; early July-late Aug. 2 additional buses) and continue on to Glencolumbcille at Rossan Point (Mon.-Sat. 2/day).

The fishing village of **Killybegs** (17 mi. west of Donegal) lies at the southeastern edge of Donegal's *Gaeltacht* and is the main port for the fishing industry of northwestern Ireland. Groups can rent boats (£15/person/day) and rod and tackle (£5) from Mr. Pat O'Callaghan (tel. (073) 315 69). The Forester clan shows up to Killybegs' town festival, held during the first two weeks of August in full Burberry's regalia to pay homage to its Celtic forebears.

Three mi. east of town, **Gallagher's Farm House Hostel,** on the main road from Donegal (tel. (073) 370 57) is a butcher-block wonder in a stone farmhouse run by a charming carpenter (£5, tents £2, laundry facilities; open all year). Two mi. closer to Killybegs, the **Hollybush Hostel** (tel. (073) 311 18), connected to a lively pub, has a nice kitchen but triple bunks (£4, showers 50p, camping £2; open all year). **Mardan House** (tel. (073) 312 57), on Fintra Rd., is distinguished by wonderful Mrs. E. Gallagher, while **Mrs. N. Gallagher, Carricklea House** (tel. (073) 311 19), runs a truly classy establishment with a self-respecting tub (£10.50). Campers should head to the **Fintra Holiday Centre** (tel. (073) 312 20), 2 mi. west of Killybegs on Fintra Beach. (£5.40/unit plus 20p/person; open April-Sept.)

Although a bit on the greasy side, **Melly's Cafe** right on the seafront has decent fish and chips (£2.80). (Open Mon.-Thurs. 10:30am-11:30pm, Fri.-Sun. 8am-11:30pm.) The easy-going **Pier Bar**—decidedly not a pub— serves up tasty coffee (50p) and baskets of sandwiches (£1). (Open Mon.-Fri. 12:30-2:30pm.) For nightly music, try the **Harbour Bar** and the **Lone Star.** (Pubs open Mon.-Sat. 10:30am-12:30pm, Sun. 12:30-2pm and 4-11pm.)

The fine independent **Derrylahan Hostel** (tel. (073) 380 79; open year-round), run by the hospitable Patrick Raughter, lies on the Coast road between the seaside village of **Kilcar,** 8 mi. west of Killybegs, and the village of **Carrick** several miles farther on. The hostel provides a very well-stocked shop, TV room, hot showers (50p), and laundry facilities (£3.50, camping £1). It also has lots of private quarters for £4.50. Carrick hosts the annual **Carrick Fleadh,** one of the best music festivals in the area, during the last weekend in October and carrying over to the beginning of November. The road south from Carrick leads to majestic **Slieve League,** a 2000-

ft. mountain that drops precipitously along a coastline staggered by tremendous 1000-ft. cliffs. Pass the road marked "To Slieve League" and continue to the one marked "To Bunglass"—the views on this road are even better the whole way up (continue a mile past the gate until you get to the parking lot). For walkers, the journey is an exciting 4 mi. Cars can complete half of the former ascent. "One Man's Pass" at the top of the road is dangerous, and should never be attempted in mist or high wind.

Near the western extreme of County Donegal is **Glencolumbcille** (accessible by bus from Killybegs; Mon.-Sat. 2/day), a splendid valley in a Gaelic-speaking area. The town is named after St. Columcille, the founder of a monastery here (the poor soil was once a big draw for ascetic Irish saints). More recently a craft-producing cooperative movement has materialized in Glencolumbcille. The **tourist office** (tel. (073) 300 17), on Main St. at the folk village, provides an exhaustive stream of information concerning the town's history and points of interest. (Open Easter-Sept. Mon.-Sat. 10am-8pm, Sun. noon-7pm.) The **Dooey Hostel,** (tel. (073) 301 30), 1 mi. up the hill behind the folk museum, is an architectural truce with the hillside built in and among the stony cliffs. While the hostel's odd hooks will surprise you, nothing you would raise the eyebrows of its wonderful proprieters, hostel veterans of a venerable 20 years. (£4.50; camping £3 with access to all facilities; open all year). The **Glencolumcille Hotel** has a nifty lounge area and pub. Fine beaches and cliffs make for excellent hiking in all directions. A 5-mi. walk southwest from the village will bring you to **Malinbeg,** a winsome hamlet on the edge of a sandy cove. From here, you can walk cross-country up and along the Slieve League coastline, stopping to register the awe-inspiring views of the Sligo mountains across Donegal Bay. In the other direction **Glen Head** is an hour's walk north of Glencolumbkille through land rich in prehistoric ruins; the Head has even more striking views.

Ardara (AR-drah), a small village whose crafts have regrettably been discovered by American Express cardholders, lies on the peninsula's northern coast, about 18 mi. east from Glencolumbcille through the **Glengesh Pass.** Information on the area is to be had from the unofficial man-in-the-know at **Kennedy's Hand Knits Shop** on the road to Dungloe. Bikes can be rented from **Donal Byrne's,** West End, beyond town on Killybegs Rd., signposted with the picture of the biker (tel. (075) 411 56; 5-speeds £7/day, £30/week). Ardara's most interesting pub is **Nancy's,** with whiskey jugs and pewter tankards hanging from the rafters, famous for its Irish coffee (£2.20) and ploughman's lunch (£2.50). **Peter Oliver's** and **Brennan's** are also popular watering holes; Peter's often features mighty inspiring traditional gigs. From Ardara, explore the caves at **Maghera** several miles west, where wide beaches meet a rapid tide (a bus running between Dublin and Portrush stops in Maghera Mon.-Thurs. and Sat.-Sun. 1 bus, Fri. 2 buses), or travel along the coast to **Portnoo,** where miles of deserted sandy beaches are serviced by a sophisticated **campsite** at **Dunmore Caravans,** Strand Rd. (tel. (075) 451 21; £5/unit plus 30p/person; open all year). In Ardara, stay with **Mrs. P. Kennedy,** overlooking the sea at Laburnum House, The Diamond (tel. (075) 411 46; £10/person), with windows resting on the floor. Buses run from Killybegs to Portnoo (early July-late Aug. Mon.-Sat. 2/day) and from Killybegs to Ardara (Mon.-Sat. 2/day; late Aug.-early July Thurs. and Fri. 2/day).

Farther up the coast, **Falcarragh** is an Irish-speaking village that hosts many language students. It is a good base for climbing **Muckish Mountain** (2211 ft.). Several miles west of town, boats leave Maheroarty Pier near Gortahork for **Tory Island,** dotted with ancient fortifications and amenable to camping.

Northwest Donegal: Dungloe to Dunfanaghy

The bulky **Derryveagh Mountains** isolate the northwest corner of Donegal, the country's largest Gaelic-speaking area. Public transportation is sparse, as are cars, so count on a very leisurely pace if you plan to visit this area.

North of Ardara and Portnoo, **Dungloe** (DUN-low; pop. 800) and remote **Cruhy Head,** are both stellar stopovers. The Dungloe **tourist office,** (tel. (075) 212 97), a new building on the pier, finds rooms for 50p, and sells all sorts of maps including a biking one (£1.50). (Open June-Aug. Mon.-Sat. 10am-1pm and 2-6pm.) The **Dungloe Caravan and Camping Park** (tel. (075) 213 50 or 210 21) is on Carnemore Rd., near the Esso filling station. (£5/unit plus 20p/person, hikers and bikers £3; open May-Sept.) The **Crohy Head youth hostel (IYHF)** (tel. (075) 213 30; £4.50, under 18 £3.50; open April-Oct.), 5 mi. west of town (turn off Main St. towards the water on Quay St. and follow it out), overlooks the ocean 100 ft. below. You may not want to leave the hostel's sparkling white rooms and spectacular views, but there's plenty of walking to be done in the area and beaches to be braved. B&Bs in the area average £12; in Dungloe, try **Mrs. Connors,** Bridge Inn, Main St. (tel. (075) 210 36; £11/person) with phones in every room and a neat and tidy air, or **Mrs. Boyle,** The Chalet, Marameelin (tel. (075) 210 68), 4 mi. from Dungloe. (£11/person, £12 with bath; open April-Sept.) At the end of July and in early August, Dungloe hosts the **Mary from Dungloe International Festival,** featuring traditional folk entertainment. 4 mi. north of Dungloe and a mile south of the nearest town, Kinncasslaugh, is the remote independent **Viking Hostel,** with extraordinary views and beach access but rather ordinary accommodations; check-in at the pub in Kinncasslaugh for directions (£4; showers). Farther north, 1½ mi. west from Dunfanaghy and 5½ mi. from Falcarragh, is the independent **Corcreggan Mill Collage hostel** (tel. (074) 264 09), the best decorated hostel in Ireland with exposed beams and red and white details (£4.50; showers).

Many regard **Aranmore Island** (pop. 1000) as Donegal's most precious possession. The largest of the islands off the Rosses coast, Aranmore has stupendous cliffs and coves, a harbor, and wonderful swimming. Hitch or walk from Dungloe to **Burtonport,** where you can catch a ferry (tel. (075) 215 32) to Aranmore. Ferries leave approximately every two hours starting at 8:30am (noon on Sun.); £2.20, students £1.20, children 70p, car and driver £8. The Dungloe tourist office posts the schedule. The **Aranmore Island youth hostel (IYHF)** (£4, under 18 £3.50), just 20 yd. from the water, overlooks the beach. (Open May-Sept.) The high point of the island is the lighthouse, with its impressive view of the rushing waters. Exploring the island's periphery on foot should take about five hours.

Curving your way along the coastline, you'll pass the white cottages of the **Rosses,** and see the bulky cliffs on the **Bloody Foreland,** named for the deep red in the water when the sun hits on the reddish rocks beneath. Inland, cone-shaped **Errigal Mountain** (2466 ft.) takes about 2 hours to climb. The **Errigal youth hostel (IYHF)** (tel. (075) 311 80; £4) is 1 mi. west of Dunlewy village on the Bunbeg-Letterkenny Rd. (Open March-Oct.) From Dungloe, desolate tracks make their way through the rocky moorlands and peat bogs east of the mountains.

On the eastern side of the mountains, 14 mi. northwest of Letterkenny on the road to Gweedore via Church Hill, stretches the **Glenveagh National Park** (tel. (074) 370 88)—10,000 hectares of glens, mountains, nature walks, and a castle once owned by a Harvard professor. (Open May-Sept. daily 10:30am-6:30pm; Oct. Tues.-Sun. 10:30am-6:30pm; June-Aug. open until 7:30pm on Sun. Admission £1.50, seniors 90p, children 60p; same charges for visiting the castle.)

Northern Donegal Peninsulas

The phenomenal coastal scenery of Donegal's four peninsulas reach forth at Ireland's northernmost tip, divided into stubby tendrils by bays and loughs. Horn Head is just a knuckle in the west, separated by the fingers of Rosguill and Fanad from Inishowen's fist in the east. Each peninsula is crossed by narrow roads that wind along secluded cliffs and dramatic coves.

Getting There and Getting Around

Derry, Northen Ireland is the largest transport hub in the area. Letterkenny, west of Derry at the heel of the four peninsulas, is the acknowledged touring base. **Lough Swilly buses** (tel. (0504) 262 017), based in Derry, provide most of the public trnasport on the peninsulas., along with **CIE buses.** Two Lough Swilly buses per day run from Kindrum, on the Irish side of the border from Derry, to Letterkenny and back. Some buses continue up the Fanad Peninsula from Letterkenny through Ramelton, Rathmullan, Milford and Rosnakill to Portsalon, near Fanad Hea, and one travels daily to Downings 9n the Rosguill Peninsula. Bus service is limited and expensive; the timetable makes daytrips by bus a pipe dream, and standard fares run between £2.50 and £4.50. Be sure to pick up a timetable and a Travelsave stamp from the bus station (timetables also available at the tourist office). Hitching to the peninsulas is similarly slow and inconvenient.

By far the best way to visit the peninsulas is by bike. A leisurely bike circuit of the Fanad Peninsula takes two to three days. In Letterkenny, rent wheels at **Church St, Cycles,** near the cathedral (£7/day; £40 deposit; open Mon.-Sat. 9:30am-6pm). **McDaid's** (tel. 531 49) in Milford, 13 mi. north of Letterkenny, charges £5/day, £30/week. Both towns are accessible by the Lough Swilly bus (Mon.-Sat. 2-3/day).

Letterkenny

Letterkenny (pop. 8500), Donegal's largest city and its ecclesiastical capital, is a fast-expanding town that eases its growing pains with nightly pub crawls. Students throng the streets during the school year to be replaced by tourists visiting the **Fanad** and **Inishowen Peninsulas** in the summer months.

In early July, the **Earagail Arts Festival** begins in Letterkenny and travels throughout the county with nightly music, theater and comedy performances from around the world (tel. (074) 219 68 for information). The **Letterkenny Folk Festival** follows close on its heels attracting musical talent from throughout the country and abroad in mid-August. Book accommodations well in advance through the tourist office (50p). Depending on your tolerance for teeming, drunken crowds, you may wish to avoid the annual **Car Rally** that maliciously monopolizes the roads in mid-June.

The **tourist office** (tel. (074) 211 60), 1 mi. past the bus station on the Derry road, books accommodations for a 10% deposit. (Open June Mon.-Sat. 9am-8pm; July-Aug. Mon.-Sat. 9am-6pm, Sun. 10am-2pm; Sept. Mon.-Fri. 9am-5pm.) Closer to the station and open later is the new **Chamber of Commerce Visitors Information Centre,** Main St. (tel. 248 66), next to the traffic lights (open June-Sept. daily 9am-9pm, Oct.-May Mon.-Fri. 9am-5pm). Change money at any of the banks, the post office on Main St. (open Mon.-Sat. 9am-5pm) or, if you get into town late, at **Funland** on Main St., next to the Market Place (daily 10:30am-11pm).

Mansion Apartments, High Rd. (tel. 252 38), is an ideally located and spacious independent hostel with big-hearted wardens to boot (no curfew, no lockout; £3.50; from the bus station go up Port Rd., then take a hard right at the fork). The independent **Rosemount Hostel** (tel. (211 81), 3 Rosemount Terrace, is smaller on almost all fronts (no curfew, no lockout; £4). Most of the town's Main Street pubs offer clean but impersonal B&B for about £11. **Mrs. McConnellogue,** White Gables, Derry Rd., Dromore (tel. 225 83), has rooms with postcard personalities and, for an extra pound, bathrooms (singles £11, £12 with bath; take a left after the last gas station on left before Derry Rd.). **Mrs. Herrity,** 7 Hillcrest, Leck (tel. 215 70), compensates for a far-away location with views of the River Swilly (£11, with private bathroom £12).

The Granary, 1 Academy Ct., calmly dispenses good food; sandwiches are £1.10, shepherd's pie £2. (Open Mon.-Sat. 10am-6pm.) For a livelier atmosphere, try the pizza (from £1.40) or kebabs (from £2) at **Pat's Pizza,** in the Market Place. (Open Mon.-Wed. 10am-12:30am, Thurs. noon-1am, Fri. noon-1:15am, Sat. noon-3am, Sun, noon-1:15am.) Supermarkets flank the town at either end, and organic produce is sold at **The Natural Way,** 55 Port Rd. (Open Mon.-Sat. 9:30am-6pm.)

Fanad Peninsula

West of the Inishowen Peninsula, between Lough Swilly and Mulroy Bay, lies the Fanad Peninsula, the eastern edge of which is studded with the villages of Ramelton, Rathmullan, and Portsalon. This side of the peninsula, overlooking Lough Swilly, is the prettier of the two, with colorful old houses and sweeping views of the Inishowen Peninsula. **Ramelton, In general, the eastern side of the Fanad Peninsula,** overlooking Lough Swilly, is the prettier, with colorful old houses and sweeping views of the Inishowen Peninsula. **Ramelton,** birthplace of Francis Makemie, father of American Presbyterianism, is the eastern gateway to Fanad. Famous in bygone days for its salmon, Ramelton refuses to demolish the last fish house in all of Ireland. Lindsey and Jane Stuart have converted the structure into a coffee shop and **Fish House Craft Gallery** (open Mon.-Fri. 10am-6pm). You can find B&B in the gorgeous Victorian home of **Mrs. Anne Campbell,** Ardeen (tel. (074) 512 43), for £12. For a good pint and the best bathroom this side of the peninsula, try **Sweeney's Pub.**

Five mi. north along the main road is **Rathmullan,** an ancient town bloated with ruins and sandy beaches. Irish patriot Wolfe Tone was brought ashore here by his English captors after leading an ill-fated uprising in 1798. Climb the precipitous spiral stairs at the nearby ruins of a 15th-century **Gothic friary** for views of the town and lough. Drown your sorrows in the blue lounge of the quiet **Pier Hotel** (open for lunch 1-2:30pm). North of Rathmullan, a dozen slow brooks cross the road as the land rises over the Knockala Hills and Glenvar, after which the coast is at its most arresting as it arcs between mountain and shore.

Portsalon, never anything more than a faded resort town, rests between boggy flatland and the peninsula's loveliest beaches. Camping is available right next to the huge **Warden Beaches** at the **Knockalla Holiday Centre** (tel. 591 08), 5 mi. south of Portsalon (£5; open Easter to mid-Sept.). **Rita Smith's** is a cramped triptych of restaurant, general store, and pub: eat a filling four-course lunch for £5.25, sip a pint by the broad windows that face the ocean, and stock up on provisions. About an hour away by bike the **Great Arch of Doaghbeg,** a lonely mass of rock detached from commanding seaside cliffs, keeps the lonely **Fanad Lighthouse** company.

The route down the western side of the Fanad Peninsula winds around the solitary inlets of Mulroy Bay. Tiny **Tamney** is an amateur's collection of food stores and B&Bs. On Main St., Mrs. Borland at the **Avalon Farmhouse** (tel. (074) 590 31), bakes, preserves and gets her bedsheets from the U.S. (£11.50, £13.50 with bath). Campers can stay farther south at the foot of the Knockalla Hills, right on Mulroy Bay, in **Rockhill Park,** Kerrykeel (tel. (074) 500; open mid-April to mid-Sept.; tents £5), or pitch tents almost anywhere along the road.

Rosguill Peninsula and Horn Head

If you want to see more of the peninsulas, head to the western shore of Mulroy Bay, up through the breathtaking **Rosguill Peninsula.** This route leads to the **Tra-na-Rosann youth hostel (IYHF)** (tel. (074) 553 74), 4 mi. from the small town of

Downings situated on top of a hill at the far northern edge of the peninsula. The setting is unbeatable and the lounge area tries as hard as any self-respecting B&B to meet its doily quota (lockout 10am-5pm; £4.15, ages 16-20 £3.50; open April-Oct.). Take a dram at the nearby **Thatch** (tel. 551 76), a lively singing pub with very low ceilings and tasty pub grub (£1-2.50). Traditional sessions Fri.-Sun. nights.

Inishowen Peninsula

Buncrana, on the west side of the peninsula along the shores of Lough Swilly, is an energetic resort where sweeping beaches repose in the long shadow of **Slieve Snacht,** a 2019-ft. peak. Two castles scowl nearby: the stately Queen Anne-era **Buncrana Castle,** which served as a prison for Wolfe Tone after a failed invasion by the French fleet in 1798, and the **O'Doherty Castle** near Castle Bridge, where the only well-preserved portion of the 1430 structure is the keep. Ten mi. south of Buncrana, near Burt, is the famous hill-top fort **Grianan of Aileach.** Its 15-ft. walls have defended Irish monarchs since 1700 BC, and between 509 and 1166 it was the throne of the O'Neills, kings of Ireland. **Ross-na-Ri House,** Ballymacarry (tel. (077) 612 711), is unfortunately shielded from the sea at Buncrana by a hill and a factory, but the breads and jams are homemade (£11; take a right off the Letterkenny Rd. after the Fruit of the Loom factory). Nearer to town, you can hop into bed from the threshold at **Kinvyram,** 14 St. Orans Rd. (tel. (077) 61 61) for £11. For lively weekend music, visit the **Cruiscín Lán, Murphy's Place,** or **The Shanty.**

The exuberant **Gap of Mamore,** an 800-foot pass between Mamore Hill and Urris, has torrid views of the entire peninsula. The unspoiled towns of **Clonmany** and **Ballyliffen** lie to the north of the Gap and host a local festival in the first week of August. The small tweed factory in Ballyliffen warrants but a short step on the way to the 3-mi. **Polland Strand.** From its northern end you can see **Carrickbrahey Castle,** the ruin of the MacFaul and O'Doherty family seats. The **Strand Hotel** in Ballyliffen has the only adequate restaurant around; avoid the high prices by ordering sandwiches and tea after the lunchtime rush.

Vivid **Malin,** winner of Ireland's cut-throat Tidiest Town Competition, is Inishowen's northernmost outpost before the peninsula reaches out to tag **Malin's Head,** from which you can see all the way across to the Paps of Jura on a clear day. The 8 mi. road between town and head winds through remote stretches dotted with sheep pastures, thatched cottages, and the occasional shop. Set out after a quiet lunch at the **Malin Hotel** (4-course lunch £7), overlooking the central green. Three mi. from the head is **Hell's Hole,** a 250-foot chasm that roars with the incoming tide. Take a bike ride around the 5-mi. **Atlantic Circle** road to take in stirring views of the area.

East of Malin, past Culdaff, lies **Inishowen Head.** At the opposite end of the Inishowen anvil from Malin Head, Inishowen Head offers views of the carnival lights of Portrush in Northern Ireland and lures sunbathers to **Shrove Strand.** You can camp on Inishowen Head if you ask permission of the nearby store-owner. From Inishowen, head south to Greencastle, stopping on the way at the **Drunken Dunk,** a mirthful roadside pub. Greencastle is a small fishing village near the misty ruins of a seaside castle and fort. For an afternoon of master boatbuilder Brian McDonald's fishing tales, head for a pint at **Kealey's Greencastle Bar.** A few paces farther south is the grassy seaside promenade of **Moville. Mrs. B. McGroaty,** Naomh Mhuire, on Bath Terrace (tel. (077) 820 91), has B&B for £11. The **Lough Foyle Sea Angling Festival** is the town's major annual event, held in late August; the **Moville Regatta,** a picturesque sailing and rowing festival, takes place on the first Monday in August. Talk to **Peter Bush** at the Coast Guard Station (tel. (077) 824 02; open Mon.-Fri. 9am-5pm) if you'd care to rent a boat.

On the southeast coast of the Inishowen Peninsula, 5 mi. over the border from Derry, Muff boasts the only independent hostel on the peninsula. **Muff Hostel** (tel. (077) 841 788), combines a kitchen, hot showers, and a warden who knows his trade. (£4.50 for 4-6 bedrooms and family rooms. Open March-Oct.)

Therefore let the moon
Shine on thee in thy solitary walk;
And let the misty mountain-winds be free
To blow against thee: and, in after years,
When these wild ecstasies shall be matured
Into a sober pleasure; when thy mind
Shall be a mansion for all lovely forms,
Thy memory be as a dwelling-place
For all sweet sounds and harmonies...

—William Wordsworth

INDEX

A
Aberdeen 463
Abergavenny (Y-Fenni) 375
Abersoch 403
Aberystwyth 395
Achill Island 594
Acomb 349
Adare 579
Adrigole 567
Alloway 453
Alpheton 266
Alston 340
Alternatives to Tourism 25
Amberly 160
American Express 74
Anstruther 444
Aran Islands (Oileáin Árann) 586
Ardara 602
Armadale 489
Armagh 508
Arran 472
Arundel 165
Ayr 453

B
Bakewell 308
Ballater 467
Balloch 452
Ballycastle 512
Ballyferriter 576
Ballyliffen 606
Ballyshannon 599
Baltimore, Sherkin Island, and Cape Clear Island 564
Banff 466
Bangor 405
Bantry 566
Bardsey Island 403
Barmouth 400
Barnstaple 192, 194
Barra (Barraigh) 492
Bath 239
Battle 159
Beara Peninsula 566
Belfast 500
Berwick-upon-Tweed 345
Betws-y-Coed 417
Bexhill-on-Sea 160
Birmingham 279
Birnam 459
Blackwaterfoot 474
Blarney 561
Blenheim Palace 226
Bodmin and Bodmin Moor 202
The Borders 454
Boston 286
Braemar 468
Brecon (Aberhonddu) 381
Brecon Beacons National Park (Bannau Brycheiniog) 378
Brighton 161
Broadford 488
Broadway 228
Brockhole 353
Buckfastleigh 198
Bury St. Edmunds 266
Buttermere 363
Byrness 347

C
Caernarfon 403
Caerphilly 372
Cahir 556
Cairngorm Mountains 461
Cambridge 253
Camelford 203
Canterbury 147
Cape Clear Island 565
Cardiff (Caerdydd) 368
Carfax Tower 221
Carlisle 350
Carnlough 510
Cashel 555
Castleton 310
Causeway Coast 511
Central England 279
Central Scotland 427
Chawton 176
Chedworth 228
Cheltenham 229
Chester 293
Chichester 167
Chipping Campden 228
Christ Church 221
Cirencester 228
Clare Coast 580
Cleggan 592
Cleveland Way 331
Clifden 591
Clonakilty 563
Clonmany 606
Colchester 266
Combe Martin 193
Cong 589
Connemara 589
Conwy 414
Cork Town 557
Cotswolds 226
Cowley Road 225
Cragside 347
Craignure 479
Crail 444
Criccieth 402
Crickhowell 381
Cuillin Hills 489
Culloden Battlefield 471
Culzean Castle 454

D
Danby 331
Dartmoor National Park 195
Deal 152
Dingle Peninsula 574
Documents and Formalities 4
Dolgellau 400
Donegal Town 600
Doolin 581
Dorchester 183
Dorchester Abbey Festival 225
Dover 154
Dublin 525
Dunkeld 459
Dunster 193, 195
Durham 334
Dursey Island 568
Duxford Airfield 267

E
East Anglia 252
East Coast 525
East Neuk 444
Edale 309
Edinburgh 427
Eights Week 226
Elgin 466
Ely 264
Emergency 11
Encaenia 223
ENGLAND 55
Ennis 579
Enniscorthy 547
Ennistymon 581
Exeter 187
Exmoor National Park 192

F
Fair Head 511
Falls of Clyde 451
Falmouth 204
Fanad Peninsula 605
Felixstowe 268
Fermanagh Lake District 514
Fishbourne 169
Fisherstreet 581
Forres 467
Fort William and Ben Nevis 482
Fort William to Mallaig: Road to the Isles 485
From Continental Europe 35
From North America 31

G
Galway Town 582
Gatwick Airport 64
General Introduction 1
Getting There 31
Giant's Causeway 513
Glasgow 445
Glastonbury 248
Glenarm Village 510
Glencoe 481
Glencolumbcille 602
Glenfinnan 485
Glens of Antrim 509
Goathland 333
Gower Peninsula 385
Grampian 466
Grantham 286
Grassington 321
Great Malvern 235

H
Hadrian's Wall 348
Harlech 401
Hathersage 311
Hawes 322
Hawkshead 359
Health 11
Heart of England 215
Heathrow Airport 64
Highlands and Islands 471
High Peak Trail 309
History 55, 425, 521
Holy Island 345
Holywell Music Rooms 225
Horringer 267
Horton-in-Ribblesdale 322
Hospitals 75

I
Ickworth 267
Ilfracombe 193
Ingleton 322
Ingram 347
Inishbofin 591
Inishowen Peninsula 606
Innisfallen 571
Inveraray 475
Inverness 468
IRELAND 517
Ironbridge Gorge 282
Islay 475
Isle of Anglesey (Ynys Môn) 407
Isle of Raasay 490
Iveragh Peninsula 568

J
Jameston 391
John o'Groats 494
Jura 476

K
Keel 595
Keswick 352
Kettlewell 321
Kilkenny Town 552
Killin 460
Killybegs 601
Keble College 224
King's Lynn 273
Kinsale 561
Kinsale to Skibbereen and Bantry 562

Kyleakin 488
Kyle of Lochalsh 488

L
Lake District National Park 351
Land's End to St. Ives 210
Language 61
Larne 506
Launceston 204
Lavenham 267
Leeds 315
Letterkenny 604
Leyburn 322
Limerick Town 577
Lincoln 283
Linton 321
Liscannor 581
Liverpool 288
Lizard Peninsula (Landewednack) 206
Llanberis 412
Llanfairpwllgwyngyll-gogerychwyrndrobwll Llantysiliogogogoch 407
Llangollen 417
Llanrwst 416
Llyn Peninsula 401
Lochailort 485
Loch Coriusk 490
Loch Lomond, Loch Long, and the Trossachs 452
Loch Ness 470
Lochranza 474
LONDON 64
Long Melford 267
Lossiemouth 467
Lough Corrib and Lough Mask 588
Lyme Regis 190

M
Machynlleth 399
Machynlleth to Harlech 400
Magdalen College 222
Malham 322
Malin 606
Malinbeg 602
Mallaig 486
Malton 333
Malvern 235
Manchester 297
Manorbier 391
Marble Hill House 137
Matlock Bath 309
The Media 57
Melrose 456
Mermaid Inn 159
Mid Argyll and Kintyre Peninsula 475
Minehead 192, 195
Mingary 480
Minions 204
Money 6
Mourne Mountains 506
Moville 606
Mull 478
Mumbles 386
Music 58, 523

N
Near King's Lynn 275
Near Norwich: Norfolk Broads 273
Near Peterborough 277
Near Sawrey 359
Newcastle-upon-Tyne 340
New Lanark 451
Newquay 212
Northeast Coast: From Inverness to Wick 492
Northeastern Ferry Ports 493
Northeast Scotland 458
North England 312
Northern (or High) Pennines 338
Northern Donegal Peninsulas 604
NORTHERN IRELAND 496
North of Dublin 540
Northumberland National Park 346
Northumbrian Coast 344
North Wales 398
Northwest Clare: The Burren 581
Northwest Donegal: Dungloe to Dunfanaghy 603
Northwest Ireland 595
North York Moors National Park 329
Norwich 268
Nottingham 286

O
Oban 476
Offa's Dyke Path 372
Once There 37
Orkney Islands 495
Oughterard 588
Outer Hebrides 491
Oxford 215
Oxford Hydrogesticulations 222
Oxford Union 225
Oxford University Press 225

P
Packing 14
Peak District National Park 304
Peebles 457
Pembroke (Penfro) and Pembroke Dock 391
Pembrokeshire Coast National Park 386
Pennan 466
Pennine Way 313
Penwith and The North Cornish Coast 207
Penzance 208
Perth 458
Peterborough 276
Petersfield 161
Pevensey 160
Plymouth 199
Pontardawe 384
Porthmadog 402
Porth-yr-Ogof 381
Portsmouth 170
Postbridge 198
Princetown 198
Pubs 90
Pubs and Beer 60
Pubs and Food 524
Pwllheli 403

R
Ramsey Island 393
Rathlin Island 512
Ravenscar 334
Rhosilli Beach 386
The River Bus 72
Road to the Isles 485
Romsey 176
Rosguill Peninsula and Horn Head 605
Rosmuck 590
Rosscarbery 563
Rosslare Harbour 550
Rothbury 347
Rum 226
Rye 157

S
Safety and Security 12
St. Andrews 440
St. Breward's 203
St. Catherine's 224
St. Cleer 204
St. David's (Tyddewi) 393
St. David's to Cardigan 394
St. Dogmaels 394
St. Giles Fair 226
St. Ives 211
Salisbury 176
Salvation Army 76
Schull 564
SCOTLAND 421
Selworthy 195
Sheffield 301
Sheldonian Theatre 223
Sherkin Island 565
Shetland Islands 495
Shiskine 474
Shrewsbury 419
Skibbereen 563
Skye 486
Slaughters, Upper and Lower 228
Sligo to Donegal 599
Sligo Town 596
The Small Isles 486
Snowdonia Forest and National Park 409
South and Southeast England 147
South Downs Way 160
Southease 160
Southeast Ireland 546
Southern Donegal Peninsula: From Donegal to Ardara 601
Southern Scotland 453
Southgate-on-Pennard 386
South of Dublin 543
South Pennines 316
South Wales 366
Southwest England 181
Southwest Ireland 557
Special Concerns 17
Spiddal 590
Sports 61
Staffa 481
Staying in Touch 51
Stonehaven 466
Stonehenge 251
Stow-on-the-Wold 228
Stranraer 454
Stratford-upon-Avon 235
Studley Roger 329
Sudbury 267
Suffolk 265
Swansea (Abertawe) 384

T
Tavistock 198
Tea 93
Telford 282
Tenby (Dinbych y Pysgod) 389
Tewkesbury 232
Three Cliffs Bay 386
Timoleague 563
Tobermory 479
Trefriw 416
Tre'r Ceiri 403

U
The Uists 491
Useful Addresses 22

V
Vale of Conwy 416

W
WALES 364
Wasdale 363
Waterfoot 510
Waterford Town 551
Weather 14
Wells 245
Western Ireland 577
Westport 593
Wexford Town 548
Weymouth 186
When to Go 1
Williton 193
Winchcombe 228
Worcester College 224
Winchester 172
Winston Churchill 226
Woodbridge 267
Woodstock 226
Wooler 347
Worcester 232
Wye Valley 372

Y
Yelverton 198
York 323
Yorkshire Dales National Park 318
Youghal 561
Ystradfellte 381